Nineteenth-Century Literature Criticism

Guide to Gale Literary Criticism Series

For criticism on	Consult these Gale series
Authors now living or who died after December 31, 1999	*CONTEMPORARY LITERARY CRITICISM (CLC)*
Authors who died between 1900 and 1999	*TWENTIETH-CENTURY LITERARY CRITICISM (TCLC)*
Authors who died between 1800 and 1899	*NINETEENTH-CENTURY LITERATURE CRITICISM (NCLC)*
Authors who died between 1400 and 1799	*LITERATURE CRITICISM FROM 1400 TO 1800 (LC)* *SHAKESPEAREAN CRITICISM (SC)*
Authors who died before 1400	*CLASSICAL AND MEDIEVAL LITERATURE CRITICISM (CMLC)*
Authors of books for children and young adults	*CHILDREN'S LITERATURE REVIEW (CLR)*
Dramatists	*DRAMA CRITICISM (DC)*
Poets	*POETRY CRITICISM (PC)*
Short story writers	*SHORT STORY CRITICISM (SSC)*
Literary topics and movements	*HARLEM RENAISSANCE: A GALE CRITICAL COMPANION (HR)* *THE BEAT GENERATION: A GALE CRITICAL COMPANION (BG)* *FEMINISM IN LITERATURE: A GALE CRITICAL COMPANION (FL)* *GOTHIC LITERATURE: A GALE CRITICAL COMPANION (GL)*
Asian American writers of the last two hundred years	*ASIAN AMERICAN LITERATURE (AAL)*
Black writers of the past two hundred years	*BLACK LITERATURE CRITICISM (BLC)* *BLACK LITERATURE CRITICISM SUPPLEMENT (BLCS)* *BLACK LITERATURE CRITICISM: CLASSIC AND EMERGING AUTHORS SINCE 1950 (BLC-2)*
Hispanic writers of the late nineteenth and twentieth centuries	*HISPANIC LITERATURE CRITICISM (HLC)* *HISPANIC LITERATURE CRITICISM SUPPLEMENT (HLCS)*
Native North American writers and orators of the eighteenth, nineteenth, and twentieth centuries	*NATIVE NORTH AMERICAN LITERATURE (NNAL)*
Major authors from the Renaissance to the present	*WORLD LITERATURE CRITICISM, 1500 TO THE PRESENT (WLC)* *WORLD LITERATURE CRITICISM SUPPLEMENT (WLCS)*

ISSN: 0732-1864

Volume 316

Nineteenth-Century Literature Criticism

Criticism of the Works of Novelists, Philosophers, and Other Creative Writers Who Died between 1800 and 1899, from the First Published Critical Appraisals to Current Evaluations

Lawrence J. Trudeau
Editor

Produced in association with
Layman Poupard Publishing

GALE
CENGAGE Learning®

Farmington Hills, Mich • San Francisco • New York • Waterville, Maine
Meriden, Conn • Mason, Ohio • Chicago

GALE
CENGAGE Learning

Nineteenth-Century Literature Criticism, Vol. 316

Layman Poupard Publishing, LLC

Editorial Directors: Richard Layman, Dennis Poupard

Editorial Production Manager: Janet Hill

Permissions Manager: Kourtnay King

Quality Assurance Manager: Katherine Macedon

Production Technology Manager: Natalie Fulkerson

Content Conversion, Data Coding, Composition: Apex CoVantage, LLC

Advisors to LPP:
Ward W. Briggs
Robert C. Evans
James Hardin
Joel Myerson
Andrew S. Rabin

Volume Advisors:
Tenille Nowak, University of Wisconsin-Stevens Point (for "Jane Austen")
Richard M. Vernon, University of North Carolina at Chapel Hill (for "Almeida Garrett")
Melissa Fegan, University of Chester (for "James Clarence Mangan")

Gale
27500 Drake Rd.
Farmington Hills, MI, 48331-3535

LIBRARY OF CONGRESS CATALOG CARD NUMBER 84-643008

ISBN-13: 978-1-4103-1384-3

ISSN: 0732-1864

Printed in Mexico
1 2 3 4 5 6 7 19 18 17 16 15

Contents

Preface vii

Acknowledgments xi

Jane Austen 1775-1817 1
Entry devoted to the novel Mansfield Park *(1814)*

Almeida Garrett 1799-1854 163
Portuguese poet, playwright, biographer, critic, essayist, novelist, and short-story writer

James Clarence Mangan 1803-1849 195
Irish poet, translator, essayist, and short-story writer

Literary Criticism Series Cumulative Author Index 325

Literary Criticism Series Cumulative Topic Index 447

NCLC Cumulative Nationality Index 471

NCLC 316 Title Index 475

Preface

Since its inception in 1981, *Nineteenth-Century Literature Criticism* (*NCLC*) has been a valuable resource for students and librarians seeking critical commentary on writers of this transitional period in world history. Designated an "Outstanding Reference Source" by the American Library Association with the publication of its first volume, *NCLC* has since been purchased by over 6,000 school, public, and university libraries. The series has covered more than 600 authors representing 38 nationalities and over 38,000 titles. No other reference source has surveyed the critical reaction to nineteenth-century authors and literature as thoroughly as *NCLC*.

Scope of the Series

NCLC is designed to introduce students and advanced readers to the authors of the nineteenth century and to the most significant interpretations of these authors' works. The great poets, novelists, short-story writers, playwrights, and philosophers of this period are frequently studied in high school and college literature courses. By organizing and reprinting commentary written on these authors, *NCLC* helps students develop valuable insight into literary history, promotes a better understanding of the texts, and sparks ideas for papers and assignments. Each entry in *NCLC* presents a comprehensive survey of an author's career, an individual work of literature, or a literary topic, and provides the user with a multiplicity of interpretations and assessments. Such variety allows students to pursue their own interests; furthermore, it fosters an awareness that literature is dynamic and responsive to many different opinions.

Volumes 1 through 19 of *NCLC* feature author entries arranged alphabetically by author. Beginning with Volume 20, every fourth volume of the series is devoted to literary topics. These topics widen the focus of the series from the individual authors to such broader subjects as literary movements, prominent themes in nineteenth-century literature, literary reaction to political and historical events, significant eras in literary history, prominent literary anniversaries, and the literatures of cultures that are often overlooked by English-speaking readers. With *NCLC,* Volume 243, the series returned to a standard author approach, with some entries devoted to a single important work of world literature and others devoted to literary topics.

NCLC is part of the survey of criticism and world literature that is contained in Gale's *Contemporary Literary Criticism* (*CLC*), *Twentieth-Century Literary Criticism* (*TCLC*), *Literature Criticism from 1400 to 1800* (*LC*), *Shakespearean Criticism* (*SC*), and *Classical and Medieval Literature Criticism* (*CMLC*).

Organization of the Book

An *NCLC* entry consists of the following elements:

- The **Author Heading** cites the name under which the author most commonly wrote, followed by birth and death dates. If the author wrote consistently under a pseudonym, the pseudonym will be listed in the author heading and the author's actual name given in parentheses on the first line of the biographical and critical introduction. Also located here are any name variations under which an author wrote, including transliterated forms for authors whose native languages use nonroman alphabets. Uncertain birth or death dates are indicated by question marks. Single-work entries are preceded by a heading that consists of the most common form of the title in English translation (if applicable) and the author's name (if applicable).

- The **Introduction** contains background information that introduces the reader to the author, work, or topic that is the subject of the entry.

- The list of **Principal Works** is ordered chronologically by date of first publication and lists the most important works by the author. The genre and publication information of each work is given. In the case of works not published in English, a translation of the title is provided as an aid to the reader; the translation is a published translated title or a free translation provided by the compiler of the entry. As a further aid to the reader, a list of **Principal English Translations** is provided for authors who did not publish in English; the list focuses primarily on twentieth-century translations, selecting those works most commonly considered the best by critics. Unless otherwise indicated, plays are dated by first performance, not first publication, and the location of the first performance is given, if known. Lists of **Representative Works** discussed in the entry appear with topic entries.

- Reprinted **Criticism** is arranged chronologically in each entry to provide a useful perspective on changes in critical evaluation over time. The critic's name and the date of composition or publication of the critical work are given at the beginning of each piece of criticism. Unsigned criticism is preceded by the title of the source in which it appeared. All titles by the author featured in the text are printed in boldface type. Footnotes are reprinted at the end of each essay or excerpt. In the case of excerpted criticism, only those footnotes that pertain to the excerpted texts are included. Criticism in topic entries is arranged chronologically under a variety of subheadings to facilitate the study of different aspects of the topic.

- A complete **Bibliographical Citation** of the original essay or book precedes each piece of criticism. Citations conform to recommendations set forth in the Modern Language Association of America's *MLA Handbook for Writers of Research Papers,* 7th ed. (2009).

- Critical essays are prefaced by brief **Annotations** describing each piece.

- An annotated bibliography of **Further Reading** appears at the end of each entry and suggests resources for additional study. In some cases, significant essays for which the editors could not obtain reprint rights are included here. Boxed material following the list provides references to other biographical and critical sources on the author in series published by Gale.

Indexes

A **Cumulative Author Index** lists all of the authors who have appeared in a wide variety of reference sources published by Gale, including *NCLC.* A complete list of these sources is found facing the first page of the Author Index. The index also includes birth and death dates and cross references between pseudonyms and actual names.

A **Cumulative Topic Index** lists the literary themes and topics treated in the series as well as in *Classical and Medieval Literature Criticism, Literature Criticism from 1400 to 1800, Twentieth-Century Literary Criticism, Contemporary Literary Criticism, Drama Criticism, Poetry Criticism, Short Story Criticism,* and *Children's Literature Review.*

A **Cumulative Nationality Index** lists all authors featured in *NCLC* by nationality, followed by the number of the *NCLC* volume in which their entries appear.

An alphabetical **Title Index** accompanies each volume of *NCLC.* Listings of titles by authors covered in the given volume are followed by the author's name and the corresponding page numbers where the titles are discussed. English translations of titles published in other languages and variations of titles are cross-referenced to the title under which a work was originally published. Titles of novels, plays, nonfiction books, and poetry, short-story, or essay collections are printed in italics, while individual poems, short stories and essays are printed in roman type within quotation marks. All titles reviewed in *NCLC* and in the other Literary Criticism Series can be found online in the *Gale Literary Index.*

Citing *Nineteenth-Century Literature Criticism*

When citing criticism reprinted in the Literary Criticism Series, students should provide complete bibliographic information so that the cited essay can be located in the original print or electronic source. Students who quote directly from reprinted criticism may use any accepted bibliographic format, such as University of Chicago Press style or Modern Language Association (MLA) style. Both the MLA and the University of Chicago formats are acceptable and recognized as being the current standards for citations. It is important, however, to choose one format for all citations; do not mix the two formats within a list of citations.

The examples below follow recommendations for preparing a works cited list set forth in the Modern Language Association of America's *MLA Handbook for Writers of Research Papers,* 7th ed. (New York: MLA, 2009. Print); the first example pertains to material drawn from periodicals, the second to material reprinted from books:

Franklin, J. Jeffrey. "The Victorian Discourse of Gambling: Speculations on *Middlemarch* and *The Duke's Children.*" *ELH* 61.4 (1994): 899-921. Rpt. in *Nineteenth-Century Literature Criticism.* Ed. Jessica Bomarito and Russel Whitaker. Vol. 168. Detroit: Gale, 2006. 39-51. Print.

Frank, Joseph. "*The Gambler*: A Study in Ethnopsychology." *Freedom and Responsibility in Russian Literature: Essays in Honor of Robert Louis Jackson.* Ed. Elizabeth Cheresh Allen and Gary Saul Morson. Evanston: Northwestern UP, 1995. 69-85. Rpt. in *Nineteenth-Century Literature Criticism.* Ed. Jessica Bomarito and Russel Whitaker. Vol. 168. Detroit: Gale, 2006. 75-84. Print.

The examples below follow recommendations for preparing a bibliography set forth in *The Chicago Manual of Style,* 16th ed. (Chicago: The University of Chicago Press, 2010); the first example pertains to material drawn from periodicals, the second to material reprinted from books:

Franklin, J. Jeffrey. "The Victorian Discourse of Gambling: Speculations on *Middlemarch* and *The Duke's Children.*" *ELH* 61, no. 4 (winter 1994): 899-921. Reprinted in *Nineteenth-Century Literature Criticism.* Vol. 168, edited by Jessica Bomarito and Russel Whitaker, 39-51. Detroit: Gale, 2006.

Frank, Joseph. "*The Gambler*: A Study in Ethnopsychology." In *Freedom and Responsibility in Russian Literature: Essays in Honor of Robert Louis Jackson,* edited by Elizabeth Cheresh Allen and Gary Saul Morson, 69-85. Evanston, Ill.: Northwestern University Press, 1995. Reprinted in *Nineteenth-Century Literature Criticism.* Vol. 168, edited by Jessica Bomarito and Russel Whitaker, 75-84. Detroit: Gale, 2006.

Suggestions Are Welcome

Readers who wish to suggest new features, topics, or authors to appear in future volumes, or who have other suggestions or comments, are cordially invited to call, write, or fax the Product Manager:

Product Manager, Literary Criticism Series
Gale
Cengage Learning
27500 Drake Road
Farmington Hills, MI 48331-3535
1-800-347-4253 (GALE)
Fax: 248-699-8884

Acknowledgments

The editors wish to thank the copyright holders of the criticism included in this volume and the permissions managers of many book and magazine publishing companies for assisting us in securing reproduction rights. Following is a list of copyright holders who have granted us permission to reproduce material in this volume of *NCLC*. Every effort has been made to trace copyright, but if omissions have been made, please let us know.

COPYRIGHTED MATERIAL IN *NCLC,* VOLUME 316, WAS REPRODUCED FROM THE FOLLOWING PERIODICALS:

Delaware Notes, v. 29, 1956. Public domain.—***Dispositio,*** v. 7.19-21, 1982. Copyright © 1982 Department of Romance Languages, UMI. Reproduced by permission of *Dispositio*.—***Eighteenth-Century Fiction,*** v. 6.3, 1994. Copyright © 1994 *Eighteenth-Century Fiction*. Reproduced by permission of the publisher.—***Éire-Ireland,*** v. 41.3-4, 2006 for "'Broad Farce and Thrilling Tragedy': Mangan's Fiction and Irish Gothic" by Richard Haslam. Copyright © 2006 Richard Haslam. Reproduced by permission of the author.—***Études irlandaises,*** v. 35.1, 2010. Copyright © 2010 Presses Universitaires de Rennes. Reproduced by permission of the publisher.—***Hispania,*** v. 38.1, 1955. Public domain.—***Irish University Review,*** v. 6.2, 1976; v. 8.2, 1978; v. 14.2, 1984; v. 19.2, 1989. Copyright © 1976, 1978, 1984, 1989 *Irish University Review*. All reproduced by permission of the publisher.—***Joyce Studies Annual,*** 2009. Copyright © 2009 Fordham University Press. Reproduced by permission of the publisher.—***Luso-Brazilian Review,*** v. 21.2, 1984. Copyright © 1984 the Board of Regents of the University of Wisconsin. Reproduced by permission of University of Wisconsin Press.—***Nineteenth-Century Literature,*** v. 52.1, 1997. Copyright © 1997 the Regents of the University of California. Reproduced by permission of University of California Press.—***Quarterly Journal of Ideology,*** v. 10.3, 1986 for "Martyr without a Cause: James Clarence Mangan and the Ideology of Irish Nationalism" by Kevin J. H. Dettmar. Copyright © 1986 Kevin J. H. Dettmar. Reproduced by permission of the author.—***Religion and Literature,*** v. 43.2, 2011. Copyright © 2011 *Religion and Literature*. Reproduced by permission of the publisher.—***Revista canadiense de estudios hispánicos,*** v. 9.2, 1985. Copyright © 1985 *Revista canadiense de estudios hispánicos*. Reproduced by permission of the publisher.—***South Atlantic Bulletin,*** v. 44.2, 1979. Copyright © 1979 South Atlantic Modern Language Association. Reproduced by permission of the publisher.—***Translation and Literature,*** v. 22.2, 2013. Copyright © 2013 Edinburgh University Press. Reproduced by permission of the publisher.—***Wordsworth Circle,*** v. 10.2, 1979. Copyright © 1979 *Wordsworth Circle*; v. 17.2, 1986. Copyright © 1986 Marilyn Gaull. Both reproduced by permission of *Wordsworth Circle.*

COPYRIGHTED MATERIAL IN *NCLC,* VOLUME 316, WAS REPRODUCED FROM THE FOLLOWING BOOKS:

Auerbach, Emily. From ***Searching for Jane Austen.*** University of Wisconsin Press, 2004. Copyright © 2004 the Board of Regents of the University of Wisconsin System. Reproduced by permission of University of Wisconsin Press.—Boyle, Nicholas. From ***Sacred and Secular Scriptures: A Catholic Approach to Literature.*** University of Notre Dame Press, 2005. Copyright © 2005 University of Notre Dame Press. Reproduced by permission of the publisher.—Burgess, Miranda. From ***Recognizing the Romantic Novel: New Histories of British Fiction, 1780-1830.*** Ed. Jillian Heydt-Stevenson and Charlotte Sussman. Liverpool University Press, 2008. Copyright © 2008 Liverpool University Press. Reproduced by permission of the publisher.—Coughlan, Patricia A. For "'Fold over Fold, Inveterately Convolv'd': Some Aspects of Mangan's Intertextuality" in ***Anglo-Irish and Irish Literature: Aspects of Language and Culture; Proceedings of the Ninth International Congress of the International Association for the Study of Anglo-Irish Literature Held at Uppsala University, 4-7 August, 1986.*** Ed. Birgit Bramsbäck and Martin Croghan. Vol. 2. University of Uppsala, 1988. Copyright © 1988 Patricia A. Coughlan. Reproduced by permission of the author.—Cusack, Andrew. From ***Popular Revenants: The German Gothic and Its International Reception, 1800-2000.*** Ed. Cusack and Barry Murnane. Camden House, 2012. Copyright © 2012 the editors and contributors. Reproduced by permission of Camden House.—Dull, Monique W. From ***Restoring the Mystery of the Rainbow: Literature's Refraction of Science.*** Ed. Valeria Tinkler-Villani and C. C. Barfoot. Rodopi, 2011. Copyright © 2011 Editions Rodopi, B.V. Reproduced by permission of Brill Academic Publishers.—Fegan, Melissa. From ***1848: The Year the World Turned?*** Ed. Kay Boardman and Christine Kinealy. Cambridge Scholars, 2007. Copyright © 2007 Kay Boardman, Christine Kinealy, and contributors. Reproduced by permission of Cambridge Scholars Publishing.—Morini, Massimiliano. From ***Jane***

Austen's Narrative Techniques: A Stylistic and Pragmatic Analysis. Ashgate, 2009. Copyright © 2009 Ashgate Publishing, Ltd. Reproduced by permission of the publisher.—Nachumi, Nora. From ***Performing the "Everyday": The Culture of Genre in the Eighteenth Century.*** Ed. Alden Cavanaugh. University of Delaware Press, 2007. Copyright © 2007 Rosemont Publishing and Printing Corporation. Reproduced by permission of Associated University Presses.—O'Donoghue, D. J. From ***The Life and Writings of James Clarence Mangan.*** Geddes, 1897. Public domain.—Parrill, Sue. From ***Jane Austen on Film and Television: A Critical Study of the Adaptations.*** McFarland, 2002. Copyright © 2002 Sue Parrill. Reproduced by permission of McFarland and Company, Inc.—Perry, Ruth. From ***Monstrous Dreams of Reason: Body, Self, and Other in the Enlightenment.*** Ed. Laura J. Rosenthal and Mita Choudhury. Bucknell University Press, 2002. Copyright © 2002 Rosemont Publishing and Printing Corporation. Reproduced by permission of Associated University Presses.—Rita, Annabela. From ***Gardens of Madeira—Gardens of the World: Contemporary Approaches.*** Ed. José Eduardo Franco, Ana Cristina da Costa Gomes, and Beata Elzbieta Cieszynska. Cambridge Scholars, 2010. Copyright © 2010 José Eduardo Franco, Ana Cristina da Costa Gomes, Beata Elzbieta Cieszynska, and contributors. Reproduced by permission of Cambridge Scholars Publishing.—Shanahan, Ann M. From ***Text and Presentation, 2012.*** Ed. Graley Herren. McFarland, 2013. Copyright © 2013 the Executive Board of the Comparative Drama Conference. Reproduced by permission of McFarland and Company, Inc.—Smith, Leroy W. From ***Jane Austen in a Social Context.*** Ed. David Monaghan. Barnes and Noble, 1981. Copyright © 1981 Leroy W. Smith. Reproduced by permission of Rowman and Littlefield Publishers.

Mansfield Park
Jane Austen

English novelist.

The following entry provides criticism of Austen's novel *Mansfield Park* (1814). For additional information about *Mansfield Park,* see *NCLC,* Volume 95; for additional information about Austen, see *NCLC,* Volumes 1 and 119; for additional information about the novel *Pride and Prejudice,* see *NCLC,* Volumes 13, 150, and 207; for additional information about the novel *Emma,* see *NCLC,* Volumes 19 and 210; for additional information about the novel *Persuasion,* see *NCLC,* Volumes 33 and 222; for additional information about the novel *Northanger Abbey,* see *NCLC,* Volumes 51 and 242; for additional information about the novel *Sense and Sensibility,* see *NCLC,* Volumes 81 and 271; for additional information about the novel *Lady Susan,* see *NCLC,* Volume 314.

INTRODUCTION

Jane Austen (1775-1817) wrote *Mansfield Park* between February 1811 and July 1813. By the time the novel was published in May 1814, both of her well-reviewed first two novels, *Sense and Sensibility* (1811) and *Pride and Prejudice* (1813), were in second editions. With her third novel, Austen turned her attention to a heroine whom she judged in an 1813 letter "not half so entertaining" as those in her earlier books. Readers and reviewers were baffled by the shy, passive protagonist, Fanny Price; by the attractiveness of the morally lax Crawfords; and by the moralistic tone of *Mansfield Park.* Modern critics, including Rachel Trickett (1985), have pointed out that no other Austen novel has elicited such consistently divergent reactions.

PLOT AND MAJOR CHARACTERS

Mansfield Park begins with ten-year-old Fanny's journey to the titular estate of her mother's sister Lady Bertram and her husband, Sir Thomas Bertram. The narrator explains that Fanny's mother has eight other children and a military husband no longer fit for service. Because Fanny's mother cannot support her entire family, her sister the widowed Mrs. Norris, who resides near Mansfield Park, suggests that their other sister, Lady Bertram, take in their niece. Sir Thomas and Lady Bertram have four children, Tom, Edmund, Maria, and Julia, who, with the exception of Edmund, ignore their poor, uneducated, shy cousin. As Edmund befriends Fanny, supervises her education, and protects her, she falls in love with him. When Sir Thomas and Tom depart on urgent business to the West Indian island of Antigua, Mrs. Norris dotes on the rest of children but treats Fanny like a servant. In the meantime, Maria accepts a marriage proposal from Mr. Rushworth, a rich but dull-witted neighbor.

The family's life is enlivened by the arrival of the fashionable Henry Crawford and his beautiful, vivacious sister, Mary, who are visiting their half-sister Mrs. Grant, the wife of the local vicar. Henry soon becomes the object of Maria's and Julia's romantic interest, while Mary attracts the attentions of Edmund and Tom, who has just returned from Antigua, leaving his father on the island. The young people go on an excursion to Sotherton Court, the Rushworth estate. At the urging of his friend Mr. John Yates, a visitor to Mansfield Park, Tom decides that the group will stage a version of August von Kotzebue's risqué play *Lovers' Vows* (1791) to entertain themselves. Rehearsals for the production provide the other characters an opportunity to flirt and misbehave, but Fanny declines to join the activities. Sir Thomas's unexpected return from Antigua brings preparations for the play—and the behavior it encouraged—to an abrupt halt. Though she still feels attracted to Henry, Maria marries Mr. Rushworth and moves with her husband and sister, Julia, to London.

Following the departure of the Bertram sisters, the relationships among the remaining characters intensify. Edmund, who desires to be a clergyman, divulges his feelings about Mary to Fanny, who is still attracted to him. Henry falls in love with Fanny and proposes marriage, but she turns him down, suspicious of his flirtatious and flighty nature. Incensed at her perceived ingratitude, Sir Thomas sends Fanny to visit her family in Portsmouth. Expecting a joyous return, Fanny is distressed and disappointed by their lack of interest, as well as by the poverty and slovenliness she finds at her old home. Henry follows her to Portsmouth to press for a reconsideration of his proposal. Although she is touched by his apparent earnestness, Fanny still has doubts about Henry's character. She refuses him again, and he departs.

Mary writes to Fanny while she is at home to describe the current disorder of Mansfield Park, relating the recent events of its inhabitants: Tom has fallen seriously ill after a prolonged bout of drinking, Julia has eloped with Mr. Yates, and the newly married Maria has run off with Henry. Distressed at the news, Fanny returns to the estate to offer some consolation. In the midst of the turmoil, Sir Thomas forgives her for refusing to marry Henry, acknowledging that she was correct in her reservations about his character. In the end, Fanny's arrival helps to restore order at Mansfield Park. Tom recovers and reforms his ways, Maria and Henry quarrel and separate, and Edmund—profoundly disappointed by Mary's desire for Tom to die so that Edmund could be the heir to the Bertram estate—loses his interest in her. Maria and Mrs. Norris leave for Europe and set up an inharmonious household together. *Mansfield Park* ends with Edmund and Fanny professing their love for each other, marrying, and moving into Thornton Lacey, the local vicarage.

MAJOR THEMES

The central theme of *Mansfield Park* is Fanny's development. Unlike many of Austen's heroines, who are garrulous, sociable, and self-confident, Fanny is weak, shy, and reserved. She almost never speaks her mind openly, but Austen emphasizes Fanny's moral rectitude and inward piety throughout the novel. Fanny rarely participates in the turbulent events around her, acting instead as a silent witness. Despite this lack of direct involvement, she proves herself to be a woman capable of independent thought. Her strong principles are evident in her refusal to marry Henry even at the risk of inciting Sir Thomas's anger and disappointment. By virtue of Fanny's insistent ethical stance and steadfast goodness, she comes to occupy the moral center of *Mansfield Park.* As a result of her unassuming influence, the novel's errant characters are either reformed or removed from the core group, and at the conclusion of the novel, Austen hints that Fanny and Edmund will work for the betterment of their community. Because of these qualities, Fanny has sometimes been perceived by readers as dull, prudish, and too unremarkable to be a heroine. Complicating matters further is Austen's portrayal of the sophisticated Henry and Mary, who are in some ways much more appealing and attractive than Fanny. Even though Austen reveals Mary and Maria to be morally deficient, their failed relationships at the end of *Mansfield Park* have struck many readers as more compelling than Fanny's pious union.

Commentators have noted the greater presence of religious ideas and symbols in *Mansfield Park* than in Austen's other novels. Some scholars, including Michael Giffin (2000; see Further Reading), have gone so far as to characterize it as religious allegory, with Fanny playing a Christlike role in a historical period during which England was becoming increasingly secularized. Although she suffers emotional abuse at the hands of all her cousins except Edmund, Fanny remains loyal and vigilant, and in the end, she helps usher in social and spiritual regeneration for the residents of Mansfield Park.

Critics have also viewed *Mansfield Park* as a microcosm of England and its social and political problems in the early nineteenth century. Fanny's family is so destitute that her mother agrees to let her grow up in the household of her wealthy cousins, where she is often demeaned and isolated. Fanny is expected to accept Henry's marriage proposal because it is a chance for upward social and economic mobility. The Bertrams' plantations in Antigua, the basis of their fortune, reflect England's worldwide empire and financial dependence on slave labor. The novel presents a picture of England as rural and leisured, with the estate and the church the heart of the community, but it also shows the need for careful oversight, as the degeneration that occurs in Sir Thomas's absence implies.

CRITICAL RECEPTION

Many critics have considered *Mansfield Park* Austen's most ambitious novel, praising her narrative design and insightful focus on character, family issues, and love. Scholars have also deemed it Austen's most difficult novel, which has continued to polarize readers and reviewers since its publication. Emily Auerbach (2004) suggested that, given Fanny's self-righteous and self-deprecating character, Austen may have intended to present the novel's narrator, who combines the traits of Fanny and the more appealing but compromised Mary, as the ideal. Felicia Bonaparte (2011) discussed Fanny in terms of Austen's narrative and thematic intent in *Mansfield Park.* She described Fanny as "a realistic character but also a figure in a design," who facilitates a sense of order and the spirit of religion in what Austen regarded as an increasingly secular world.

Critics have also focused on the implications of Austen's choice of Kotzebue's *Lovers' Vows* for the home theatrical in *Mansfield Park.* Nicholas Boyle (2002-03) observed that in Austen's novel, "the popularity of the German dramas of Goethe's adversary, Kotzebue . . . have an insidious influence on the society depicted and are at the very least a sign of indolence and irresponsibility." Discussing dramatic elements in the novel, Ann M. Shanahan (2012) showed how facets, including the wealth of dialog and the emphasis on Fanny as audience, testify to Austen's theatrical inclination.

Contemporary scholars have shown an ongoing interest in Austen's depiction of imperialism and slavery in *Mansfield Park.* In his influential essay "Jane Austen and Empire" (1989; see Further Reading), critic Edward W. Said traced imperialist sensibilities at work in the novel. Giffin explored *Mansfield Park* as a social parable, pointing out Austen's "carefully constructed commentary on the state of England in the early modern period."

Jelena Krstovic

PRINCIPAL WORKS

Sense and Sensibility: A Novel. As "A Lady." 3 vols. London: The Author, 1811. Print. (Novel)

Pride and Prejudice: A Novel. As "The Author of *Sense and Sensibility*." 3 vols. London: Egerton, 1813. Print. (Novel)

Mansfield Park: A Novel. 3 vols. London: Egerton, 1814. Print. (Novel)

Emma: A Novel. 3 vols. London: Murray, 1815. Print. (Novel)

Northanger Abbey; and Persuasion. 4 vols. London: Murray, 1817. Print. (Novels)

A Memoir of Jane Austen. By J. E. Austen-Leigh. London: Bentley, 1870. Rev. and enl. ed. *A Memoir of Jane Austen: To Which Is Added* Lady Susan *and Fragments of Two Other Unfinished Tales by Miss Austen.* London: Bentley, 1871. Print. (Memoir, novel, and novel fragments)

Lady Susan, and The Watsons. New York: Munro, 1882. Print. (Novel and unfinished novel)

**Love and Friendship and Other Early Works: Now First Printed from the Original MS.* London: Chatto and Windus, 1922. Print. (Short stories)

The Novels of Jane Austen. 5 vols. Ed. R. W. Chapman. Oxford: Clarendon P, 1923. Print. (Novels)

The Watsons. London: Parsons, 1923. Print. (Unfinished novel)

Fragment of a Novel Written by Jane Austen January-March 1817 [*Sanditon*]. Ed. Chapman. Oxford: Clarendon P, 1925. Print. (Unfinished novel)

Lady Susan. Oxford: Clarendon P, 1925. Print. (Novel)

Plan of a Novel according to Hints from Various Quarters. Ed. Chapman. Oxford: Clarendon P, 1926. Print. (Correspondence and notes)

Two Chapters of Persuasion, Printed from Jane Austen's Autograph. Oxford: Clarendon P, 1926. Print. (Novel fragment)

Volume the First: Now First Printed from the Manuscript in the Bodleian Library. Ed. Chapman. Oxford: Clarendon P, 1933. Print. (Juvenilia)

Volume the Third: Now Printed from the Manuscript. Ed. Chapman. Oxford: Clarendon P, 1951. Print. (Juvenilia)

Jane Austen's Letters to Her Sister Cassandra and Others. 2nd ed. Ed. Chapman. Oxford: Oxford UP, 1959. Print. (Letters)

Volume the Second. Ed. B. C. Southam. Oxford: Clarendon P, 1963. Print. (Juvenilia)

Jane Austen's Manuscript Letters in Facsimile: Reproductions of Every Known Extant Letter, Fragment, and Autograph Copy, with an Annotated List of All Known Letters. Ed. Jo Modert. Carbondale: Southern Illinois UP, 1990. Print. (Letters)

Jane Austen's Letters. Ed. Deirdre Le Faye. 3rd ed. Oxford: Oxford UP, 1995. Print. (Letters)

Persuasion: Authoritative Text, Backgrounds and Contexts, Criticism. Ed. Patricia Meyer Spacks. New York: Norton, 1995. Print. (Novel)

Mansfield Park: Authoritative Text, Contexts, Criticism. Ed. Claudia L. Johnson. New York: Norton, 1998. Print. (Novel)

Pride and Prejudice: An Authoritative Text, Backgrounds and Sources, Criticism. Ed. Donald J. Gray. 3rd ed. New York: Norton, 2001. Print. (Novel)

Sense and Sensibility: Authoritative Text, Contexts, Criticism. Ed. Johnson. New York: Norton, 2002. Print. (Novel)

The Cambridge Edition of the Works of Jane Austen. Ed. Janet Todd et al. 9 vols. Cambridge: Cambridge UP, 2005-08. Print. (Novel fragments, novels, and short stories)

Emma: An Authoritative Text, Contexts, Criticism. Ed. George Justice. 4th ed. New York: Norton, 2011. Print. (Novel)

*This work was originally published with a typographical error as *Love and Freindship.*

CRITICISM

David Cowart (essay date 1979)

SOURCE: Cowart, David. "Wise and Foolish Virgins (and Matrons) in *Mansfield Park.*" *South Atlantic Bulletin* 44.2 (1979): 76-82. Print.

[*In the following essay, Cowart elaborates on Austen's comparison of her own writing to the art of limning, the act of painting miniature portraits on ivory. For Cowart, Austen applies the same level of patience and attention to detail to scenes in* Mansfield Park *as the limner does in portraying an event on a smaller scale.*]

When Jane Austen likened her work, in an oft-quoted remark, to a "little bit (two Inches wide) of Ivory,"[1] she was comparing it to the art of "limning," or the painting on ivory of miniature portraits by artists like Nicholas Hilliard or Hans Holbein the Younger. Nor does her observation exhaust the similarity between miniature portrait and novel, for both belong to the "private" arts, i.e., those not intended for public presentation or display. The miniature, if not actually carried on one's person, graced the lid of some small private box, while the novel, as Ian Watt has shown,[2] gained popularity in an age when domestic architecture began to feature the private rooms, with doors and locks, that made solitude possible and solitary diversions desirable. But Austen's famous remark suggests as well a similarity between her novels and the small ivory bas-reliefs that vied in artistic importance with architecture in Byzantium and with manuscript illumination in the Frankish kingdoms that became the Holy Roman Empire. Commonly adorning prayer books for personal devotion, these, too, provided private aesthetic experience. In fact, the analogy between Austen's work and the medieval ivory is finally the more cogent one since Austen, as novelist, rendered not one portrait, like the limner, but a large scene with several figures, like the carver of the ivory plaque.

Working a bit of ivory scarcely wider than two inches, the Carolingian or Ottonian artist depicted religious scenes—Crucifixions, Assumptions, Adorations of the Magi, Presentations at the Temple—ranging from the rustic to the tragic and from the intimate to the spectacular. Delicacy of workmanship and minuteness of scale need not, in other words, restrict thematic range. Like the medieval artist, Austen knew how to work with extraordinary economy. She learned to treat a subject of great universality and complexity, the relations between the sexes, so profoundly and exhaustively as to preclude her reader's ever desiring a broader focus than the "3 or 4 Families in a Country Village"[3] she allowed herself. Thus if one examines the novel as written by Austen with the same patience and attention required by the ivory miniature, one makes similar discoveries, since the most impressive aspects of both are the harmony of design and the fineness of detail. The critic serves Austen best, then, by tracing the intricacy of her work under his most powerful lenses and by demonstrating the harmony of its details with the design of the whole. Consequently I propose, by examining some of the fine detail in ***Mansfield Park,*** to show in a small way how meticulously Austen's language is keyed to the larger thematic concerns of her fiction.

In an early chapter of this novel Sir Thomas Bertram must attend to pressing business matters in the West Indies, and on the eve of his departure he reconciles himself with difficulty to the idea of leaving home just as his two daughters, Maria and Julia, have reached marriageable age. But to these young women

> his absence was unhappily most welcome. They were relieved by it from all restraint; and without aiming at one gratification that would probably have been forbidden by Sir Thomas, they felt themselves immediately at their own disposal, and to have every indulgence within their reach.[4]

The blamelessness of aiming at no forbidden gratifications seems precariously balanced with the consciousness of the availabilty of "every indulgence." One senses that the blamelessness of the Miss Bertrams' aspirations is at best problematic. "Relieved from all restraint" is a phrase gravid with suggestions of imminent moral vitiation, and the slippage, which leads ultimately to the twin catastrophes of Maria's adultery and Julia's elopement, is discernible quite early in the book—before the scandalous home theatricals, and even before the visit to Sotherton, the estate of Maria's fiancé (where the flirtation between Maria and her future paramour, Henry Crawford, begins to be less and less excusable). The slippage is discernible, in fact, as soon as the father's inhibiting influence disappears. I should like to suggest that the first hint of this deterioration lies in the unseemly *activity* which follows the departure of Sir Thomas with the kind of indecent haste one associates with Gertrude's remarriage on the death of King Hamlet.

Seemingly harmless, seemingly unconnected with the later disasters, this activity generates an atmosphere conducive to those developments which gradually make plain the growing moral threat to Mansfield Park. We shall find, moreover, that the characters who err most seriously at the end of the novel are precisely the ones who take maximum advantage of the absence of Sir Thomas at the beginning—the ones whose thirst for activity leads them to plan balls, to enter into hasty engagements, to organize outings, and even, eventually, to turn Mansfield into a theatre. The activity commences in the short chapter which follows the leave-taking: in ten pages Sir Thomas and his eldest son arrive in Antigua; Maria gets engaged to a fatuous but wealthy neighbor; Fanny Price, the impecunious cousin taken in by the Bertrams, gets a new exercise pony; the exotic newcomers Henry and Mary Crawford arrive; and Mrs. Grant, the local clergyman's wife, plans marriages for both of them. It may be objected that these developments take place over the course of many months, but the narrator clearly means, by accelerating the exposition, to suggest a like acceleration in the events at Mansfield Park. With Sir Thomas gone, Mansfield becomes a very busy place; nearly everybody, it seems, is "relieved from all restraint" in one way or another.

While the culpability of the inhabitants of Mansfield Park may be measured by the extent to which they take advantage of their season of license, the decadence hardly manifests itself in saturnalian revels. It is visible, rather, in the gleeful precipitancy with which the Miss Bertrams, encouraged by their officious aunt, Mrs. Norris, embark on an exploration of "every indulgence." Austen contrasts characters who do things—who *act*—with characters who stand by patiently, quietly maintaining the status quo pending the return of Mansfield's moral arbiter, Sir Thomas. The women of his household should in other words live modestly and watch, like Wise Virgins, for that return. This code of conduct does not lack comic features, since the ridiculously inert Lady Bertram is one of its exemplars.

But though her indolence is a source of humor, her conduct is at least always decorous—as is that of the retiring Fanny, the only character in the book who actually qualifies as a Wise Virgin. Equating quietness with decorum, then, and busy-ness with its opposite, the author depicts the Miss Bertrams as Foolish Virgins, flinging themselves into activities that contrast sharply with their cousin Fanny's modest behavior and punctilious manners.

Even less like Fanny in this regard is Mrs. Norris, described in the novel's first paragraph as imbued with "a spirit of activity" which leads her to write an offensive letter (before Fanny's birth) to the sister who had "married … to disoblige her family" (p. 3), and so to effect the breach between Mansfield Park and the Price household. The busiest person at Mansfield, Mrs. Norris continually engages in a supererogatory pother of scheming which, in its ultimate ramifications, proves so ill-considered as to appear more than a little morally irresponsible. When all of the young people at Mansfield except Fanny and her cousin Edmund begin agitating to produce a play, Mrs. Norris embraces the idea because of the scope it will offer for "hurry, bustle and importance" (p. 129). Thus Fanny and her aunt are the two dominant personalities early in the book—Fanny because she is, however passive, the heroine, and Mrs. Norris because she is masterminding much of the action. The reader perceives them as two poles, one of unassertive meekness, the other of domineering activity. This contrast is reflected stylistically in the verbs associated with the two characters. Nonvivid verbs in simple past tense describe Fanny's minimal activity: she "talked," "listened," "read," "loved to hear," "walked," "thought." Mrs. Norris, on the other hand, bears down on one in a spate of present participles, as she engages in "assisting," "displaying," "looking about," "mixing," "seeking," "indulging," "walking," "superintending," and, repeatedly, "promoting." The participles also figure in the narrator's merciless rendering of the busy-minded locutions—"Mrs. Norris could not help thinking," "she could not help feeling"—that make her such an eminently recognizable type.

The Miss Bertrams, meanwhile, though active, are drawn not with verbs but with nouns. One paragraph, devoted to an ironic appraisal of the Bertram debutants, contains a revealing progression of nouns: "belles," "beauty," "acquirements," "manner," "civility," "obligingness," "favour," "admiration," "vanity," "airs," "praises," "behaviour," "faults." The interstitial words are almost as unnecessary as the vowels in Hebrew orthography, for the marshalling of nouns is to a large extent the source of the narrator's irony. But here is the latter part of the paragraph, fleshed out:

> Their vanity was in such good order, that they seemed to be quite free from it, and gave themselves no airs; while the praises attending such behaviour, secured, and brought round by their aunt, served to strengthen them in believing they had no faults.
>
> (p. 35)

As the particular protégée of Mrs. Norris, Maria Bertram is the more spoiled of the two sisters. Her motivations in getting engaged to the wealthy neighbor, Mr. Rushworth, can be summed up as (1) cupidity, and (2) the desire to outshine her family socially:

> Maria Bertram was beginning to think matrimony a duty; and as a marriage with Mr. Rushworth would give her the enjoyment of a larger income than her father's, as well as ensure her the house in town, which was now a prime object, it became, by the same rule of moral obligation, her evident duty to marry Mr. Rushworth if she could.
>
> (pp. 38-39)

Her suitor is also motivated by a superficial (if less mean-spirited) consideration: he "was from the first struck with the beauty of Miss Bertram …" (p. 38). Their preliminary courtship and engagement, which might furnish a more digressive novelist with a great deal of material, fills not even one sentence: "After dancing with each other at a proper number of balls … an engagement … was entered into … (p. 39).

Maria's materialism, the fact that "her happiness should center in a large income" (p. 40), distresses her brother Edmund, the younger son of Sir Thomas. He fails, however, to recognize the impropriety of that predilection for activity which she shares with her sister and aunt. His impercipience on this point stems from his own involvement in the activity—an innocent enough involvement in view of his being entitled, as a man, to wider freedom of action. But on one occasion Edmund's altruism nearly seduces him into action that could be construed as improper: he replaces Fanny's exercise pony over the irritating yet cogent objections of his aunt. Mrs. Norris "was sure … that to be making such a purchase in [Sir Thomas'] absence, and adding to the great expenses of his stable at a time when a large part of his income was unsettled, seemed to her very unjustifiable" (p. 36). The reader knows that this objection is not just another example of his aunt's pettiness because Lady Bertram seconds it. His action, when it comes, is excusable precisely because, in making the expense strictly his own, he takes the absent father into account; moreover, by providing Fanny with another horse he preserves the status quo. His action, then, is positive and blameless in that it does not contribute to the gradually pervasive disregard of those values which Sir Thomas would preserve were he at home.

Although a genuine consideration for his father's best interests guides Edmund, the same cannot be said for Maria. The reader is told that her engagement is entered into "with a due reference to the absent Sir Thomas" (p. 39), but the due reference is merely *pro forma,* for Sir Thomas is to hear nothing of the match "but the perfectly good and agreeable" (p. 40). The fact of the matter is that Sir Thomas and all he stands for have been merrily forgotten by Maria, and by all of those who abet or encourage her irresponsible trifling with the state of marriage. Yet however great her present folly, and however great her later fall from virtue, Miss Bertram is not really the book's most instructive example of the Foolish Virgin. If literature is not to falsify life and its moral ambiguities, the face of error must not be too easily recognizable. Thus the author gains added depth in her portrayal of youthful license and its consequences by "doubling" Maria with a less transparently wicked character, one who appears as winsome on first acquaintance as any deceptively attractive incarnation of error in Spenser.

Miss Bertram's attitudes in the absence of her father prefigure those of the similarly-named Mary Crawford, who arrives on the scene in the company of her brother at the end of the chapter following Sir Thomas' departure. Herself recently freed from parental restraint, Mary could easily be more susceptible to error than Maria, because she has been longer independent of anything like Sir Thomas' moral supervision, and her temporary home with her uncle, Admiral Crawford, was hardly the place to learn right thinking. The scope and intensity of Mary's "activity" has been much greater than Maria's, for she has for some time resided in London. Maria, with her desire for "the house in town," aspires to a life of similar freedom. Like Maria, Mary would like to get married: "Matrimony was her object, provided she could marry well . . ." (p. 42). Both characters think of marriage in the same way, but because Maria's thoughts are ironically summarized by the narrator—

> A marriage with Mr. Rushworth would give her the enjoyment of a larger income than her father's . . .

—the reader tends to assume that they are more reprehensible than Mary's, which are expressed in her own words without being undercut by the narrator's irony: "I would have everybody marry if they can do it properly . . . everybody should marry as soon as they can do it to advantage" (p. 43). The reader may not notice that her outlook is essentially the same as Maria's, if a little less petty. Although Mary is hardly the shallow schemer that Maria is, one should not fail to observe that the two share similarities of attitude and situation, similarities that should inspire a wariness of the charming newcomer. The most important similarity, at least to my thesis, is the fact that they are both, in a sense, "relieved from all restraint." With the introduction of Mary Crawford, the underlying moral preoccupation of the chapter—the problem of activity versus inactivity on the part of young women with "every indulgence within their reach"—is broadened and made less parochial.

In this early chapter the impropriety of "activity" at Mansfield Park in the absence of Sir Thomas adumbrates the more flagrant impropriety of "acting" there, as that absence is prolonged, in the home-theatricals sequence of later chapters. The author comes closest to making plain the metaphoric significance of these key words when she speaks of the "itch for acting so strong among young people" (p. 121), for both the activity and the acting anticipate the calamitous "act" of passion on the part of Maria and her lover, Henry Crawford. The words "activity," "acting," and "act"—all partly derived from the Latin *agere,* 'to drive, do'—constitute an axis of meaning in the book, and the etymological link between "act" and "drive" encourages one to think of "activity" early in ***Mansfield Park*** as nothing less than a highly refined metaphor for those passional drives which Freud says must be sublimated not only to make civilization, but to preserve it. In Austen's novel civilization is represented by the house that gives the book its title. The surrender of Maria Rushworth and Henry Crawford to their "lower nature," as it was called in Austen's day, poses a threat to Mansfield Park, for by definition a "park" exists only where "nature" is subdued and made orderly. As Sir Thomas begins to realize at the end of the book, his home and the order it exemplifies depend for their preservation on discipline and unflagging moral vigilance.

Notes

1. Jane Austen, "To J. Edward Austen," 16 December 1816, Letter 134, *Jane Austen's Letters to Her Sister Cassandra and Others,* ed. R. W. Chapman, 2nd ed. (London: Oxford University Press, 1952), p. 469.
2. *The Rise of the Novel* (Berkeley: University of California Press, 1957), p. 188.
3. Jane Austen, "To Anna Austen," 9 September 1814, Letter 100, *Jane Austen's Letters,* p. 401.
4. Jane Austen, *Mansfield Park,* Vol. III of *The Novels of Jane Austern,* ed. R. W. Chapman, 3rd ed. (London: Oxford University Press, 1934), p. 32. Subsequent references are to this edition.

Gene W. Ruoff (essay date 1979)

SOURCE: Ruoff, Gene W. "The Sense of a Beginning: *Mansfield Park* and Romantic Narrative." *Wordsworth Circle* 10.2 (1979): 174-86. Print.

[*In the following essay, Ruoff observes that in* Mansfield Park, *Austen employs narrative strategies that differ considerably from those used in her earlier novels, including* Pride and Prejudice. *In contrast to the limited and compressed narrative of* Pride and Prejudice, *Ruoff finds that in* Mansfield Park, *Austen "stretches out the story itself, giving Fanny more space for growth than any other of her heroines and—a crucial formal change—over twice as many separate appearances as Elizabeth."*]

I

> Hard task to analyse a soul in which
> Not only general habits and desires

> But each most obvious and particular thought,
> Not in a mystical and idle sense
> But in the words of reason deeply weighed,
> Hath no beginning.
>
> (*Prelude* (1798-99), II, 262-67[1])

This extraordinary passage from Wordsworth's first sustained attempt at his autobiographical poem is heavy with implications for narrative art. That it occurs early in the poem, while *The Prelude* is still predominantly linear in form, an overgrown but underdeveloped "Tintern Abbey," is especially instructive. Wordsworth has reached a point in his story where he must make the most ordinary kind of transition. Around his fourteenth year Nature, "intervenient till this time / And secondary" (II, 240-41), and loved with feelings "humble though intense, / To patriotic and domestic love / Analogous" (II, 228-30), is "now at length" to be "sought / For her own sake" (II, 241-42). Nothing should be easier than recording such a change, because centuries of developmental narrative have prepared the way for it. His language suggests the concept of a ladder of love, as he works within narrative conventions normally devoted to tracing the stages of a romantic involvement. The turn is from loving habitually and unconsciously to falling in love.

And indeed the turn is made effortlessly, too effortlessly as it seems, because the poem immediately turns against its own narrative formula, denying its adequacy to experience. "But who," the poet asks,

> shall parcel out
> His intellect by geometric rules,
> Split like a province into round and square;
> Who knows the individual hour in which
> His habits were first sown, even as a seed;
> Who that shall point as with a wand and say,
> This portion of the river of my mind
> Came from yon fountain?
>
> (II, 242-49)

As the passage develops, its harshest words are reserved for the abuses of the new epistemology that has dominated the last century. A wry skepticism pervades Wordsworth's mock deference to those who have been so "aptly skilled … to class the cabinet / Of their sensations" (II, 257-59) and to "Run through the history and birth of each / As of a single independent thing" (II, 260-61). At the same time, however, the passage is an indirect celebration of the triumph of the school of Locke. However dismally associationism may have failed in its increasingly grandiose attempts to anatomize the mind, it has made it impossible to think of experience in the old ways. By insisting on the formative role of the past in any present sensation, empirical thought has jeopardized any number of presuppositions about mimetic narrative. Among the endangered species are any firm belief in the finiteness of an event, any security in determining a causal chain, and—to turn one of our favorite phrases on its head—the sense of a beginning. After stating that "each most obvious and particular thought … / Hath no beginning," Wordsworth literally begins his poem anew: "Bless'd the infant babe," he says, and retreats even more radically into past experience to trace conjecturally "the progress of our being" (II, 267-69).

The passage I have been considering is an anxious one, but the poet suffers from a narrational rather than epistemological anxiety. Wordsworth habitually assumes and affirms, even exults in his knowledge that experience is composed of intertwisted elements of obscure origin and inscrutable destination. The new understanding of the soul is a better understanding. His artistic problem lies in the assumptions of the narrative forms he has inherited: that life is a journey, that its progress may be conceptualized in terms of straight and narrow paths, crossroads, and dangerous byways. *The Prelude* is filled with vestiges of this tradition. Up to the turn I have been discussing, the 1798-99 version of the poem has been largely a recollected compilation of little journeys. The motif even touches his telling of the story when the poet remarks that he will "hasten on" to speak of the change in his life. But Wordsworth does not understand his growth as a journey along a road. He persistently likens it to a flowing stream, a growing river in which at any moment the waters of many sources are indescribably intermixed.[2] At no point in any version of the poem does Wordsworth arrest the flow, stop to attempt a total cross-section of a particular stage of his development. His understanding of his growth has gone beyond the inescapable sequentiality of his narrative medium. From the productive collision of two givens—the impossibility of capturing the truth of human experience in sequential narrative forms and the incapacity of language to try to do anything else—many of the shifts and stratagems of Romantic art are born.

Although *The Prelude* admirably illustrates some of the essential problems faced by Romantic narrative, it is a bad example for their characteristic solutions. It is too good. The dominant fictive time of the work will ultimately become the time of its telling: it begins when its first word is spontaneously uttered, moves from this utterance to a search for a poetic beginning, discovers its subject in the poet's own beginnings, and ends when its telling is over. A magnificent evasion, I think, which is probably not equaled until Conrad's *Lord Jim.* A more common answer to narrative problems is a much simpler evasion: the refusal to tell a story at all. The triumphant contribution of Romantic poetry to poetic form is the work quite long enough to tell a story which declines to move at all, or at least insists on standing still at the same time. I am thinking, of course, of the greater Romantic lyric, which M. H. Abrams has so lucidly described (in *From Sensibility to Romanticism,* ed. Frederick W. Hilles and Harold Bloom [1965], pp. 527-60). The tendency of this form to stress the temporal continuity of the moment by tracing the persistence of past experience in present sensation, as well as shaping speculations about the future from these emerging patterns, makes it answer almost completely the dilemmas posed by Wordsworth's passage from *The Prelude.* Indeed, the form becomes a basic compositional unit of that poem.

In the end, though, stories must be told, and Romantic narrative tells them in strange ways. Some of the devices seem to be efforts toward the end that Wordsworth said was characteristic of his contributions to *Lyrical Ballads*: "one other circumstance ... distinguishes these poems from the popular poetry of the day ... that the feeling therein developed gives importance to the action and situation, and not the action and situation to the feeling" (1800 Preface, *Prose Works,* ed. W. J. B. Owen and J. W. Smyser [1974], I, 128). The most obvious ways of de-emphasizing action are by muting it ("Simon Lee," "Michael," ***Persuasion***) or by spoofing it ("The Idiot Boy," *Peter Bell,* ***Northanger Abbey,*** *Don Juan*). I would not wish to argue at length the similarities of "Michael" and *Don Juan,* but the narrative voices of both poems are idiosyncratic. Each poem depends for its effect on the reader's sensing a profound distance between the story as story—the tale of the wayward youth as it could and would ordinarily be told—and the story as it is being told.

Romantic narrative is prolific with eccentric narrators: Wordsworth's retired sea captain in "The Thorn," Coleridge's ancient mariner, Scott's ubiquitous Peter Pattieson, Keats's dreamer of "The Fall of Hyperion," Mary Shelley's Victor Frankenstein, and the Wordsworthian narrator of Shelley's "Alastor." While debate seems endless about how seriously intended and fully created these narrative voices actually are, we might remember that Wordsworth's comments on "The Thorn" provide our earliest formal description of the dramatic monologue. And one of the best kept secrets in literary history may be that Maria Edgeworth's Preface to *Castle Rackrent,* which appears in the same year as the first Preface to *Lyrical Ballads* and bears astonishing similarities to that more famous document, is the comparable manifesto for inadequate narration in the novel. Such persistent efforts toward impersonal narration entail a price, and the burden of the cost falls primarily on narrative plot. Accentuating a narrator's eccentricities diverts a reader's attention from story and action. Attention is a finite commodity.

Where narrative beginnings are concerned, a characteristic Romantic device is that heightened mode of formal reflexiveness we call parody. "Peter Bell" begins with a prologue spoofing the matter of popular romance before entering the story itself with a parody of conventional epic beginnings. Byron toys with the same epic convention in *Don Juan*: "Most epic poets plunge 'in *medias res*' / ... That is the usual method, but not mine— / My way is to begin with the beginning" (I, 41-50)—and we are already fifty lines into the poem with no beginning in sight. Jane Austen starts ***Northanger Abbey*** with an account of her heroine's origins that inverts the obligatory formulae of sentimental fiction. In *Waverley,* Scott begins with a mock solemn account of the profound deliberations that have underlain the author's selection of a title. Other works such as Maria Edgeworth's *Castle Rackrent* and Hogg's *Confessions of a Justified Sinner* evade the problem of conventional fictive beginnings altogether by posing as works of nonfiction. Both parody and narrative imposture offer handles on a story, a way of getting started. That they should so generally be felt necessary in the Romantic period is evidence of the acute narrational self-consciousness of the age.[3] The matching years of our own century may offer the strongest parallel to such extensive narrative experimentalism. It is not coincidental that the innovations of classic Modernism come in the wake of the writings of Bergson, Freud, and others who posed again the technical problem originally laid bare by empiricist epistemology: how to reflect in narrative the interpenetration of past and present. The last associationist is the father of Virginia Woolf.

II

> Elizabeth's spirits soon rising to playfulness again, she wanted Mr. Darcy to account for his ever having fallen in love with her. 'How could you begin?' said she. 'I can comprehend your going on charmingly, when you had once made a beginning; but what could set you off in the first place?'
>
> 'I cannot fix on the hour, or the spot, or the look, or the words, which laid the foundation. It is too long ago. I was in the middle before I knew that I had begun.'
>
> ***Pride and Prejudice,*** Vol. III, Ch. 18[4]

Of all the major narratives of the Romantic period, ***Pride and Prejudice*** might seem most certain of its beginnings. It moves from a wry "truth" directly into an initiatory action: a conversation between Mr. and Mrs. Bennet provides necessary exposition, establishes the thematic center of the novel, reveals their respective characters, and anticipates the substantial action that will set the plot in motion, the movement of Bingley and his entourage to Netherfield Park. That action is only the first of what is to become a system of actions in the opening volume of the novel, as a small and unproductively static country neighborhood is subjected to a series of incursions—by the family and friends of Bingley, the wondrous Mr. Collins, and Wickham and a regiment of redcoats. Volume II follows this pattern of predominantly male incursions by a balancing system of female excursions: Jane to London, Lydia to Brighton, Elizabeth first to Rosings and then virtually to the gates of Pemberley. Volume III begins with Elizabeth's arrival at her true home before breaking down into a frantic series of departures and returns: Elizabeth back to comfort her family as Lydia and Wickham are off to God knows where, Mr. Bennet off to join Mr. Gardiner in the search, Darcy's whereabouts unknown in the central portion of the volume, and finally Mr. Bennet back, Lydia and Wickham home in simpering triumph, a surprise visit by Lady Catherine, and initially puzzling reappearances by Darcy and Bingley. The dizzying motion ends at last with a satisfying definitive resettlement, characters in their places with appropriately ordered motion established among them.

Aristotle would have been pleased by the formal unity of the work. Elizabeth's recognition scene is simultaneous with the reversal of her intentions, and her recognition arises directly from the action itself. The way in which the simple plot involving Jane and Bingley subtly highlights the complex plot involving Elizabeth and Darcy might even have changed his mind about double plots. Principally, though, Aristotle would have delighted in Jane Austen's skill in imitating a complete action rather than chronicling a life. More formalist studies of classic stature have been generated by ***Pride and Prejudice*** than by any other of her novels. In addition to the valuable commentaries of Mary Lascelles, Dorothy Van Ghent, and Reuben A. Brower, Karl Kroeber has recently pointed out how thoroughly self-sustaining the novel is, considered solely as a verbal structure.[5] As little new remains to be said about the unity of the work, I offer only a few observations on its temporal self-containment and some of its aesthetic consequences, justified by the rather obvious fact that the formal triumph of ***Pride and Prejudice*** is one that Jane Austen did not choose to repeat.

Our sense of the classical tautness of ***Pride and Prejudice*** is enhanced, perhaps even distorted, by our knowledge of what came before and after it. ***Northanger Abbey*** and ***Sense and Sensibility*** had begun in exposition, the one exploring the deficiencies of Catherine Morland as a sentimental heroine, the other establishing in its first two chapters the economic degradation of the family of the late Henry Dashwood, which engenders the removal of Mrs. Dashwood and her daughters from Norland to Barton Cottage. ***Pride and Prejudice*** could easily have followed either narrative pattern, beginning with the prehistories of either Elizabeth or the Bennet family. Instead, Jane Austen chose to begin with an action, which I have discussed already, filtering in necessary exposition as her story progressed. Surprisingly little exposition is necessary, much of that devoted simply to clarifying the positions of the various families in the social hierarchy. The only significant events that antedate the central action of the novel revolve around the relationship of Wickham to the Darcy family, and the bulk even of this exposition is dramatized, either through Wickham's skewed oral history or through Darcy's letter to Elizabeth. This complication and clarification is simplicity itself compared with the untangling necessary to unearth the buried secrets that explain the convoluted actions and characters of Edward Ferrars, Colonel Brandon, and Willoughby.

Most importantly, no past action by Elizabeth, our center of interest in ***Pride and Prejudice,*** materially affects the plot of the novel. Indeed, Elizabeth seems in some peculiar fashion to have been born yesterday. We are led to believe, for example, that an intimate friendship has prevailed between Elizabeth and Charlotte Lucas, young ladies of twenty and twenty-seven, who live in a society that is obsessed by matrimony. Yet the scene in which Elizabeth and Charlotte weigh the prospects of a match between Jane and Bingley is barren of any suggestion that they have ever before shared their perspectives on marriage (pp. 13-15). Ideas and attitudes are dramatized—the prevailing tendency throughout the novel—but credibility is risked. After Charlotte has accepted the proposal of Mr. Collins, Jane Austen covers some of her tracks. Elizabeth reflects, "She had always felt that Charlotte's opinion of matrimony was not exactly like her own, but she could not have supposed it possible that when called into action, she would have sacrificed every better feeling to worldly advantage" (p. 88). That *always* is asked to do a lot of work. Striving for full dramatization in ***Pride and Prejudice,*** Jane Austen takes on the aesthetic problems that afflict a playwright. We all know those wooden speeches in which a friend has to explain to a friend that they are indeed friends, that they both have parents, that they haven't seen one another in over a year, and so forth. And we are only too familiar with the excesses that proceed from the textbookish demand that fiction be dramatized, such as the timeless (and mindless) scene in which, in order that a character's appearance may be described, he must gaze deeply in the mirror, contemplating the brilliant blue depths of his eyes, his pectoral development, and—increasingly of late—salient details of his lower anatomy. Even though Jane Austen is happily incapable of such atrocities, her narrative displays some of the tensions that inevitably result when fiction invokes the dramatic model.

The aesthetic dilemma that underlies ***Pride and Prejudice*** is best revealed in the scenes that are the turning point of the narrative, Darcy's first proposal and Elizabeth's reading of his letter of the following day. The proposal itself gives us Jane Austen the dramatist, who thrives on conflict. After Darcy has burst forth with his declaration of love, we watch as his subsequent expression of his misgivings about the alliance polarizes Elizabeth's feelings until, having controlled herself "to answer him with patience" (p. 131), she delivers her chillingly analytical rejection. The fun of the scene increases with the polarization, until the verbal battle that ensues threatens to render unthinkable any further communication, to say nothing of understanding. Such a scene, so readily transferable to the stage, illustrates Jane Austen's dramatic dimension, noted by A. C. Bradley and underlined recently in Donald Greene's gorgeous debunking of the myth of limitation.[6]

This vigorous action is followed by a movement to meditation that is simply impossible dramatically. Darcy writes a letter; the act has meaning because we have, with Miss Bingley's assistance, watched him write one before. We know it as a considered action—painstaking, reflective, precise. The scene in which Elizabeth reads and rereads this letter is at the center of the principle of change within the novel, and change occurs not through action but through reflection. The scene is one of the great triumphs of English fiction because in it we visibly watch a character grow. Elizabeth is forced to rehearse the action of the novel to this point, weighing and pondering it, reconsidering her evaluations of others and, as importantly, her means of evaluation. All along she has not been just the narrational center of the novel: she has been acting consciously as a story-teller—assessing character, studying interconnections among characters, imagining underlying realities from observable actions. And the plot she has created has been wrong. As she is forced to remember the story to date, the gulf between actions as remembered and actions as observed becomes mortifying. Wickham's gross inconsistencies are patently obvious in retrospect. Like Wordsworth in *The Prelude* she has had to begin her story again: the turning point of the action is a new beginning, which is made possible by a period of extended reflection.

Such a formal disjunction between contiguous scenes—one in which a lot goes on but nothing significant happens, the other in which nothing observable happens but everything permanently important does—surely illustrates priorities of a work, and the priorities of this novel are not finally dramatic. Action separates while reflection unites. ***Pride and Prejudice*** is very nearly two works interleaved: a novel of action in which the causal chain, if occasionally obscure, is unbroken, and a novel of feeling in which changes of attitude and personal growth are often inversely related to the action. Darcy's major growth occurs offstage in the wake of Lydia's elopement, when he is both lost to the reader's view and, so far as she can tell, irreversibly lost to Elizabeth. Consequently, when we reach the conversation between Elizabeth and Darcy with which I prefaced this section, the question is perfectly real. Even after all the clarifications have been made, Elizabeth still does not know the beginning of Darcy's love for her, and he cannot tell her. He was in the middle before he knew he had begun. A little earlier, in answering Jane's identical question, Elizabeth had playfully spoofed the idea of a beginning of her own love: "'It has been coming on so gradually, that I hardly know when it began. But I believe I must date it from my first seeing his beautiful grounds at Pemberley'" (p. 258). A novel about love, formed on the strictest dramatic principles and employing a beautifully articulated causal plot, cannot tell us when its hero and heroine fell in love. It is a strange hybrid, using and perfecting traditional narrative forms while it heartily distrusts them. The author's ability to have it both ways is a grand achievement. But again, Jane Austen did not repeat it.

III

> If any one faculty of our nature may be called *more* wonderful than the rest, I do think it is memory. There seems something more speakingly incomprehensible in the powers, the failures, the inequalities of memory, than in any other of our intelligences. The memory is sometimes so retentive, so serviceable, so obedient—at others so bewildered and so weak—and at others so tyrannic, so beyond controul!—We are to be sure a miracle in every way—but our powers of recollecting and forgetting, do seem peculiarly past finding out.
>
> ***Mansfield Park,*** Vol. II, chap. 4[7]

The road from Pemberley to Mansfield Park offers one of the most interesting journeys in Romantic narrative, but it is seldom taken. Comparisons of the two novels have been so preoccupied with thematics and the superficies of character analysis that they have successfully obscured any firm understanding of Jane Austen's development as a writer of fiction. Seen from the vantage point of the Aristotelian precision of ***Pride and Prejudice*** (or the Jamesian precision, for there is really very little difference), ***Mansfield Park*** must initially seem a retrograde step. Its fictive time greatly extended, it becomes more nearly a chronicle of a life than an imitation of an action. Its beginning provides a useful index to its difference from the preceding novel: four chapters of summary narration, interspersed with brief scenes and snatches of dialogue, relate the histories of the Misses Ward of Huntingdon, their marriage and progeny, successes and disappointments, the background of the Mansfield family itself, how Fanny Price came at the age of ten to become a dependent of the Sir Thomas Bertrams, and how she passed her first eight years on the estate. In this section even the scenes and dialogue are largely expository in purpose, establishing character and theme rather than advancing the plot of the narrative. After ***Pride and Prejudice*** the form of ***Mansfield Park*** must seem lax, as though Jane Austen, having perfected the curricle-hung gig, that racy conveyance so dear to John Thorpe, had dutifully set about inventing the sledge.

The very different narrative strategies of ***Mansfield Park*** must in some way have proceeded from a limitation sensed in those employed in ***Pride and Prejudice.*** As Jane Austen told Cassandra on January 29, 1813, she had certainly "lop't and crop't" that work successfully (***Letters*** [***Jane Austen's Letters***] ed. R. W. Chapman, [1952], p. 298), but she clearly avoids such compression in the following novel. Instead she stretches out the story itself, giving Fanny more space for growth than any other of her heroines and—a crucial formal change—over twice as many separate appearances as Elizabeth.[8] The more scenes dramatized, the lighter the burden any one has to carry, and that disjunction I noted between action and reflection in ***Pride and Prejudice*** is repeated many times over in ***Mansfield Park,*** as Fanny scurries from one fray or another to her haven in the East Room.[9] But more than anything else, the multiplication of scenes calls attention to the continuity within the growth of Fanny's character, creating a field of memory far more extensive than that of Elizabeth Bennet, whose recollections are equally central to her development but are severely foreshortened by being limited to her reflections on the fictive time-span of the narrative. Fanny is even allowed memories which extend beyond the more expansive bounds of this narrative—in her early nostalgia for her brothers and sisters at Portsmouth and, more importantly, in those childhood experiences she relives with her brother William during his visit at Mansfield. With William "all the evil and good of their earliest years could be gone over again, and every former united pleasure and pain retracted with the fondest recollection. An advantage this, a strengthener of love, in which even the conjugal tie is beneath the fraternal. Children of the same family, with the same first associations and habits, have some means of enjoyment in their power, which no subsequent connections can supply" (pp. 234-35). This passage parallels that in which Darcy and Elizabeth attempt joyously to retrace the beginning of their love, but as it strikes so much earlier in the experience of William and Fanny, it points to greater depths of character. I'm not suggesting for a moment that Fanny is a "deeper" character than Elizabeth; if I thought that sort of impressionism meant anything, I'd probably disagree with it. But by the virtue of Jane Austen's narrative choices in ***Mansfield Park,*** Fanny's character is *presented* more deeply.

Stuart Tave has discussed brilliantly the thematic role of memory in ***Mansfield Park*** (*Some Words of Jane Austen* [1973], pp. 194-204). Assuming his point that strength of memory is an index to ethical consistency in the novel, I will try to develop one of the major narrative consequences of this theme, the radical change in the concept of plot which underlies ***Mansfield Park.*** I suspect that in her reconsiderations of ***Pride and Prejudice*** Jane Austen began to feel about its brilliantly realized balance, formal unity, and enclosure something of the same way that Virginia Woolf—perhaps Jane Austen's best early critic as well as the finest critic of fiction generally in the first half of this century—felt about the finely tuned novels of some of her own contemporaries:

> The writer seems constrained, not by his own free will but by some powerful and unscrupulous tyrant who has him in thrall to provide a plot, provide comedy, tragedy, love interest, and an air of probability embalming the whole so impeccable that if all his figures were to come to life they would find themselves dressed to the last button of their coats in the fashion of the hour. The tyrant is obeyed, the novel is done to a turn. But sometimes, more and more often as time goes by, we suspect a momentary doubt, a spasm of rebellion, as the pages fill themselves in the customary way. Is life like this? Must novels be like this?
>
> (*The Common Reader, First Series* [1925], pp. 153-54)

I have already suggested that in ***Pride and Prejudice*** Jane Austen managed to satisfy both the tyrant and herself. But such achievements have their price. Part may be found in the loss of a certain degree of authenticity: could a character capable of growing as Elizabeth does during the reading of Darcy's letter actually have been so devoid of prior experience as to have been taken in by Wickham in the first place? I think not—but not, I notice, while I am reading the scene. Another part of the price may be that extorted by any formal triumph that is at bottom a tour de force, a thoroughgoing enactment of received forms without an equally thorough belief in their fidelity to experience.

In any event, ***Mansfield Park*** answers that life is not like that, and that novels need not be either. Life is continuous, without sharply demarcated beginnings and endings; revelations are not sudden, and genuine turning points are not dramatically vivid. This is the ultimate narrative message of ***Pride and Prejudice,*** but there it is encoded against the grain of a hostile plot. In ***Mansfield Park*** it overtly structures the fable, as dramatic action explicitly belongs to melodrama, the world of *Lovers' Vows.* The narrative has melodramatic emotions and actions, to be sure, but they are part of the experience of those characters who make melodrama of their lives—Henry and Mary Crawford, Mr. Yates, Mrs. Norris, Tom, Julia, and Maria Bertram, and even Sir Thomas when he rouses himself to step into the role of wicked stepfather. Dramatic actions and actors impinge upon the lives of others. They destroy Rushworth, endanger Edmund, and discomfort Fanny; but continuous selves are not finally determined by them. A slight overstatement might help to frame the issue: in ***Pride and Prejudice*** the plot functions to bring two strangers together; in ***Mansfield Park*** it functions to keep two intimate friends, already lovers in the general sense of the word, apart long enough for there to be a story.

Pride and Prejudice, after all, is a stellar example of the conventions of exogamous romance, enshrined in the works of Shakespeare as well as those of virtually every sentimental writer Jane Austen could have laid her hands on. Prospective husbands are by definition handsome outsiders from distant places. Courtship is a form of aggression the end of which is conquest. England conquers France, after which its dashing young king takes a slight breather to win the heart of fair France as well. Now Jane Austen has been criticizing the excesses of this convention as long as she has been writing, and she knows that predators come in both sexes. Although the parodic inversions of ***Love and Friendship, Lady Susan,*** and ***Northanger Abbey*** could easily be called into evidence, ***Sense and Sensibility*** provides the writer's clearest and most interesting critique of the tradition. For Marianne Dashwood, inveterate foe of second attachments, love is literally something else, removed from such common modes of feeling as liking and esteem. Uncertain that she will ever feel the touch of this exalted emotion, she finds it stimulated by Willoughby, the young and handsome outsider who arrives on melodramatic cue to preserve her body and win her heart. Everything the conventional suitor of sensibility should be, he is unfortunately also everything the successful rake should be. In his confrontation scene with Elinor, Willoughby admits to having entered his flirtation with Marianne thinking of her as a conquest, akin to the unfortunate Eliza Williams. Slowly and insensibly, he says, he became genuinely attached to Marianne. The fascinating thing about this is that the closest study of his early relationship with Marianne cannot locate any change in his emotions, because until his sudden departure his behavior never changes. The forms of exogamous courtship and seduction are identical: a feather will turn the scale, and without it Marianne could easily become a Miss Williams, as the clandestine visit to the home of Mrs. Smith—a kind of shadow elopement—clearly suggests. The real danger to Marianne lies in her emotional paradigm, which ironically she shares with Willoughby. The severity of the critique is intensified by Marianne's being bracketed with Lucy Steele, the only character who can vie with her in protestations of the intensity of her feelings (if not in the purity of her diction).

Pride and Prejudice sharply denotes its marital and sexual marauders. Mr. Collins is our living embodiment of the marital conquistador, our hearty, thriving wooer. Wickham is our charming seducer, punished as thoroughly by his success as ever man has been. Still, Darcy is an attenuated aggressor figure, whose ritual battles with Elizabeth inevitably recall those of Shakespeare's comedies. The forms are satisfied. In ***Mansfield Park,*** though, Jane Austen abandons the exogamous marital convention itself, which is damned in the work by its adherents. Its staunchest spokesman, Mrs. Norris, declares a marriage between Fanny and either of the two cousins with whom she will be raised "'morally impossible. I never knew of an instance of it'" (p. 6). Sir Thomas later ships Fanny back to Portsmouth to educate her into the convention, as it is represented by the advantageous connection with Henry Crawford. Of the four eligible outsiders who invade Mansfield, Henry and Mary Crawford are charming but corrupted sexual adventurers reminiscent of Willoughby, Yates is a decadent aristocrat, and Rushworth is a fool. The first marriage formed on the exogamous model, uniting the estates of Mansfield and Sotherton, ends as a shambles; the second, between Julia and Yates, bids only to be a "less desperate business" (p. 462) than it initially appeared. The exogamous principle of conquest is reduced to its most melodramatic embodiment in a catastrophic dual seduction and elopement, while of the two older exponents of this romantic model, Mrs. Norris is exiled and Sir Thomas cured.

Expunging exogamy is one thing. Finding a narrative form to replace its patterns is something else again. In place of a mode of romance that had enhanced dramatic occurrences—first meetings, flirtations, misapprehensions, quarrels, and conquests—we must substitute one that exemplifies continuity of feeling, a growth of emotion so slow that its very stages are virtually undetectable, one that in its very pattern of presentation will reflect Darcy's statement that he was in the middle before he knew he had begun. The pattern Jane Austen chooses, as we all know whether we admit it or not, is the love of brother and sister. To glance back at a passage I have already cited, the conjugal tie must become as much like the fraternal as possible. The lover must be one who has grown with the beloved and who consequently shares many of those "first associations and habits" (p. 235). Edmund does Darcy one better: his love is almost full-grown before he knows it has begun. Within thirty pages of addressing Fanny as "my only sister—my only comfort now" (p. 444), Edmund is moving into the Mansfield parsonage with Fanny and their unborn child. Only the dullest of elves could fail to imagine the work of time that has caused them "to begin to want an increase of income, and feel their distance from the paternal abode an inconvenience" (p. 473).

It should be a truth universally acknowledged, of course, that every solution to narrative problems creates new ones. We owe a great debt to R. F. Brissenden for having breathed the dread word *incest* in relation to the marriage of Fanny and Edmund. As he points out, Mrs. Norris raises the issue early in the novel, Fanny becomes Edmund's youngest sister in their early relationship, Fanny's ardent love for her brother William ignites Henry Crawford's passion, Henry works on Fanny's emotions by serving William, and Fanny becomes both the true daughter of Sir Thomas's heart and Edmund's "only sister" shortly before she becomes his wife ("*Mansfield Park*: Freedom and the Family," in Halperin, pp. 156-71). I think it not altogether wise, though, to see Jane Austen either playing with the incest taboo, adding a touch of spice to an otherwise dull romance, or consciously or unconsciously satisfying her own or her readers' repressed fantasies. Like many of her contemporaries, she is experimenting with ways of presenting new and rather unsettling understandings of human relationships. These understandings, like the very basic alterations in our conceptions of how we apprehend reality, are part of the heritage of empirical thought, which had delighted in tracing analogies among conventionally disparate modes of feeling.

The sort of endogamous union celebrated in ***Mansfield Park*** calls feeling in aid of feeling, blending fraternal love into romantic love into a broader familial love and finally into an enhanced and indivisible love of tradition and continuity. This attempt is a thoroughly Romantic enterprise. We see Wordsworth blurring the boundaries of maternal and sexual love in "The Mad Mother"; we occasionally have to chase down his nouns in *The Prelude* to find out whether he is addressing Coleridge, Dorothy, or Nature; we remember that the passionate lamentations of "Dejection" were at one time or another addressed to almost everyone Coleridge had loved; we may wince when we hear Shelley salute Teresa Viviani as "Spouse! Sister! Angel! Pilot of the fate / Whose course has been so starless" ("Epipsychidion," ll. 130-31), and go on to propose a living arrangement that, if not altogether novel, is at least intriguing; and we recall that Elizabeth Lavenza, the cousin and betrothed of Victor Frankenstein, had grown in his household from playfellow to friend to beloved. Although any or all these examples could be viewed as evidence of individual or cultural psychopathology, and Romanticism could offer even more flagrant specimens, it is more productive to see them as attempts at creating an emotional counterpart to the perceptual device we know as synaesthesia. Because of their interest in presenting the complex and often unlikely unity of experience, Romantic writers were nervous about compartmentalizing either sensation or emotion—recall Wordsworth on the tyranny of the eye. The exogamous convention of romantic feeling had isolated this mode of love from other kinds of affection, leaving it at one extreme analogous to warfare or theft, and at the other extreme elevating it above all merely human passions. As ***Sense and Sensibility*** so beautifully demonstrates, these extremes are reverse sides of one coin. The endogamous plot of ***Mansfield Park*** is of a piece with other contemporary attempts to adapt existing narrative forms to meet the challenge of presenting an integrated rather than a fragmented self.

After Stuart Tave has coupled Jane Austen with Wordsworth as "singers of prothalamia," he goes on to underline the incompatibilities that separate them ("Jane Austen and One of Her Contemporaries," in Halperin, p. 72). Their ultimate ends seem so distant that even Emma might have declined to forward the match. On the basic processes of union, though, the means of marriage, they are tantalizingly close. *The Prelude* tells the story that leads to the "consummation of a Poet's mind" ([1850], XIV, 304), its marriage to Nature, as ***Mansfield Park*** tells of Edmund's marriage to Fanny. But what is the relationship of each story to its consummation? In neither case is *finding* a mate important; like Fanny, Nature has been there—and been loved—all along. On this point ***Mansfield Park*** differs from Jane Austen's earlier novels. It takes a complex chain of actions to bring together Catherine and Henry, Elinor and Edward, and Elizabeth and Darcy. The plot of ***Mansfield Park*** only delays the union of Fanny and Edmund. The major obstacle of the story, Edmund's infatuation with Mary Crawford, is almost the precise narrative equivalent of Wordsworth's flirtation with France. Like Nature (with Dorothy's help), Fanny is the sustaining force who brings Edmund through his disappointment. Wordsworth's comments on his "beloved Sister" are apposite:

> like a brook
> That did but *cross* a lonely road, and now
> Is seen, heard, felt, and caught at every turn,
> Companion never lost through many a league—
> Maintained for me a saving intercourse
> With my true self.
>
> ([1850] XI, 337-42)

All either Wordsworth or Edmund ever really has to do is to come home. Jane Austen's earlier novels had ended with the sense of wonder that such things could come to be. The sense of wonder underlying the conclusions of ***Mansfield Park, Emma,*** and ***Persuasion*** is that such things could almost not come to be.

We are accustomed to noting that the end of *The Prelude* is its beginning. The same is true of ***Mansfield Park.*** In conventional terms Edmund begins to love Fanny three pages from the end of the story—so much, the novel tells us, for those conventional terms. The way Jane Austen puts it is in perfect keeping with Wordsworth's hesitancy at singling out those individual hours in which our habits first were sown:

> I purposely abstain from dates on this occasion, that every one may be at liberty to fix their own, aware that the cure of unconquerable passions, and the transfer of unchanging attachments, must vary much as to time in different people.—I only intreat every body to believe that exactly at the time when it was quite natural that it should be so, and not a week earlier, Edmund did cease to care about Miss Crawford, and become as anxious to marry Fanny, as Fanny herself could desire.
>
> (p. 470)

This is all that survives in ***Mansfield Park*** of the glorious recognition and reversal scene on which ***Pride and Prejudice*** turns, here cunningly delayed and subversively understated. It is part of the narrative audacity of the novel that this brief paragraph is, in large part, the whole story of the novel that came before it. This passage, with its long-delayed beginning, does strange things to the plot of ***Mansfield Park***: it converts all the operatic emotions and melodramatic actions that have preceded it to the status of a prelude, causally related to the ultimate resolution of the novel only through some dark, inscrutable workmanship:

> How strange that all
> The terrors, pains, and early miseries,
> Regrets, vexations, lassitudes interfused
> Within my mind, should e'er have borne a part,
> And that a needful part, in making up
> The calm existence that is mine when I
> Am worthy of myself!
>
> (*Prelude* [1850] I, 344-50)

But then, for Romantics as well as Romanticists, preludes have a certain fascination.

Notes

1. Citations from *The Prelude* follow the reading text of *The Prelude, 1798-99,* ed. Stephen Parrish (1977).
2. The journey motifs of the poem receive extensive commentary from Herbert Lindenberger, *On*

Wordsworth's Prelude (1963), and Geoffrey Hartman, *Wordsworth's Poetry, 1787-1814* (1964).

3. For an overview of self-conscious and unreliable narration, see Wayne Booth's bibliography to *The Rhetoric of Fiction* (1961).

4. For convenience in citing commentary on the novel, all references are to the edition of Donald J. Gray (1966). The quotation is from p. 262.

5. The earlier essays are reprinted by Gray. Kroeber's "*Pride and Prejudice*: Fiction's Lasting Novelty" is in *Jane Austen: Bicentenary Essays,* ed. John Halperin (1975), pp. 144-55.

6. Relevant portions of Bradley's study are reprinted by Gray. Donald Greene's "The Myth of Limitation" is in *Jane Austen Today,* ed. Joel Weinsheimer (1975), pp. 142-75.

7. Citations from *Mansfield Park* follow the text of *The Novels of Jane Austen,* ed. R. W. Chapman, 3d ed. (1934). The quotation is from pp. 208-9.

8. The count is from the tabulations of Karl Kroeber, *Styles in Fictional Structure* (1971), p. 231.

9. On the importance of Fanny's retreats, see Barbara Hardy, *A Reading of Jane Austen* (1976), pp. 28-30.

Leroy W. Smith (essay date 1981)

SOURCE: Smith, Leroy W. "*Mansfield Park*: The Revolt of the 'Feminine' Woman." *Jane Austen in a Social Context.* Ed. David Monaghan. Totowa: Barnes and Noble, 1981. 143-58. Print.

[*In the following essay, Smith addresses the tension between personal freedom and social mobility in* Mansfield Park *by identifying the influence of patriarchal society on Fanny. By defending her freedom to choose within a constrictive environment, Smith argues that Fanny challenges conventional beliefs about femininity.*]

No other novel of Jane Austen's has stimulated such diverse interpretations as ***Mansfield Park,*** her deepest probe into family relations, and no other heroine such divergent responses as Fanny Price. Recently, however, critics have tended to develop one or the other of two emphases—the novel is about the threat to an existing order and its reform or vindication,[1] or it is about a heroine of principle[2]—and they have been led, in Joseph Wiesenfarth's apt summary, to ask the following question: 'Does or does not ***Mansfield Park*** show that a meaningful personal freedom and integrity are viable within a traditional pattern of morals and manners?'[3]

Professor Wiesenfarth answers the question affirmatively. The central issue of ***Mansfield Park,*** he says, is 'the threat to the integrity of the self that comes from an easy life lived without principle.' The central conflict thus is within the self rather than between the self and a threatening family or society. Fanny 'refuses not to be free within the bonds of duty, and duty does not direct her to sacrifice herself either to the consequence or to the convenience of others.'[4] However, a number of other critics who admire the heroism of Fanny Price regard it as demanded of her in a battle with her family and social environment.[5] In this view Fanny embodies the self's desire to preserve its independence, and the family and society seek to subject her to their authority.[6]

At issue also among the admirers of Fanny is Jane Austen's purpose in writing ***Mansfield Park.*** In Clyde L. de Ryal's opinion, she wished to examine 'what it means to have formed a central core of self' in a 'modern *Zeitgeist* ... destructive of individual integrity and wholeness of being.'[7] At the other extreme, Robert Donovan suggests that Jane Austen wished to set herself 'the most difficult artistic challenge': could she 'deprive her heroine of all the outward graces and ... command our admiration for strength of character alone?.'[8]

How should one view Fanny Price? Is the main concern of the novel the welfare of the social order or the welfare of the heroine? What moved Jane Austen to write ***Mansfield Park***?

To answer these questions one must first define the relationship between Fanny Price and the society of Mansfield Park. The essential fact is that in this novel, as in all Jane Austen's novels, the society is patriarchal in character. Ownership of property is vested in the male and transferred from father to son. More emphasis is placed on property rights than on human rights. In the family patriarchalism encourages the deification of the parents, a high evaluation of the father's role, suppression of the child's aggressive and sexual impulses, and the fostering of dependency in children. It is supported by the artificial polarisation of human qualities into sexual stereotypes. The masculine stereotype derives from the image of the person in authority: the male is hyper-rational, objective, aggressive, and possesses dominating and manipulative attitudes toward other persons and his environment. The feminine stereotype is the opposite: the 'feminine' woman is tender, genteel, intuitive rather than rational, patient, unaggressive, readily given to submission. Her essential characteristic is passivity.

The women of Jane Austen's novels live in a male-dominated society in which they are inferior and dependent. This standing is imposed upon them by education and social tradition. From infancy a girl is taught to revere the male; in adolescence she discovers the economic and social foundations of male superiority. She is brought up to be subordinate, praised for being 'feminine,' and offered 'advantages' for acquiescing. Playing the 'feminine' role, she finds herself in a vicious circle: the less she exercises her freedom to understand, the fewer resources she discovers in herself and the less she dares to affirm herself as a subject. Marriage is her chief means of support and the chief justification of her existence. As a result, getting a husband is her most important undertaking, and the disposition she makes of herself in marriage is the most critical event in her life.

What Jane Austen found in the parlour was the drama of woman's subjugation and depersonalisation. But whereas in ***Pride and Prejudice*** the emphasis is on the problem of making a desirable marriage in a patriarchal society, in ***Mansfield Park*** it falls on the broader problem of how the patriarchal system affects the personality and destiny of its members, presented, specifically, in terms of how it works to stifle the potential for selfhood of Fanny Price. This emphasis is manifested by several features of its plot: ***Mansfield Park*** is the only one of Jane Austen's novels to follow the heroine's history over a period of years; it gives as much attention to the relations of parents and children as to the relations of the sexes; it shows more interest in the making of wrong marriages than of right ones; and it dares, as a proof of its honesty, to feature a heroine whose most celebrated trait is her passivity.

Mansfield Park, home of the Bertram family, is a model of the patriarchal order. Sir Thomas is master at the Park and the principal patriarchal figure: grave, Olympian, seeing only what he wants to see. His eldest son Tom enjoys a favoured place among his children. Although Sir Thomas reminds the reader of General Tilney of ***Northanger Abbey,*** he is more broadly and positively conceived. His acts proceed, we are told, from a concern for himself and society and a wish to do right. He first appears as the guardian of what is good and proper, but soon reveals defects: a narrowly conceived plan of education, a moral blindness and vulgarity, and a smug authoritarianism.

The females at the park are subordinate figures whose fates are decided by the marriages they make. Lady Bertram is an extreme example of the reduction of the female to virtual non-being by the patriarchal system. Having achieved a fortunate marriage, she has no further sense of purpose in life. She is helpless without masculine support, totally selfish and self-centred, too indolent even to enjoy her daughters' social success. She thinks more of her dog than of her children and misses her husband only when his return reminds her that he has been gone.

Maria and Julia Bertram are the female offspring of patriarchalism: 'remarkably fine' in appearance and in cultivation of drawing-room graces; raised in idleness and without purpose except to marry well; selfish, vain and insensitive. Although both girls outwardly comply with the process of their dehumanisation, they strive to escape the boredom and the constricted life of their society. Marriage seems to offer attraction for them as a means to gain freedom from parental control as well as to achieve status and economic security, but they find that it is an exchange of one confinement for another. A girl such as Maria Bertram, in Simone de Beauvoir's eyes, is fated for adultery: as a married female, the 'sole concrete form her liberty can assume'[9] is infidelity. Maria's final disgrace exhibits both society's double standard (468) and the greater danger to the female in a sexist society of succumbing to sexual temptation (a point made more fully in ***Sense and Sensibility***).

In ***Mansfield Park*** the abuses of the patriarchal system, not the transgressions of individuals, are Jane Austen's main subject. All the characters, with the possible exception of Mrs Norris, possess the potentiality for suitable behaviour were they to live in a different setting. Even the system's champion, Sir Thomas, is no villain. His intentions are good, and at the conclusion he not only acknowledges his errors but modifies his behaviour. Faulty upbringing—the inculcation of faulty values and selfish attitudes—accounts for the behaviour of both parents and children. The emphasis on wealth and position has a debilitating effect on the personality of both those who possess them and those who do not. No one is as independent or assertive as Elizabeth Bennet or possesses as strong a sense of self.

Jane Austen stresses four principal faults of the patriarchal system: the failure of female education; the absence of love and understanding between parents and children; the cultivation of shallow goals and inadequate moral standards; and the perversion of courtship and marriage.

Whether or not one accepts Professor Wiesenfarth's statement that the education of Fanny Price is the subject of ***Mansfield Park,*** the failure of female education in a patriarchal society is an important issue. In Denis Donoghue's view, 'the sins of Julia and Maria have been prefigured, from the beginning of the novel, by instances of their defective education';[10] and the faulty upbringing of the Crawfords is cited as the source of their failures in principle and judgement.[11] Patriarchal education prepares young women only to carry out their limited function, which is to add lustre to a family while a part of it and to add to its greatness when they leave it by marriage. Sir Thomas saw his daughters 'becoming in person, manner, and accomplishments every thing that could satisfy his anxiety' (20).

But for all their promising talents and early acquired information the Bertram sisters (and their brother Tom and the Crawfords as well) are deficient in self-knowledge, generosity and humility. At issue is the difference between an education that emphasises 'accomplishments' and that models behaviour on social example or other-directedness and one that emphasises the interiorisation of values. Although Fanny escapes her cousins' formal schooling, she does not escape the broader educating effects, the social conditioning, of being brought up as a dependent female in a patriarchal society. She receives as little preparation as her cousins and Mary Crawford to act as a free and responsible individual.

A second fault of the patriarchal society—the absence of love and understanding between parents and children—is a principal cause of the misbehaviour of the Bertram children. Sir Thomas' view is that members of a patriarchal family exist for the sake of its advancement. He is not outwardly affectionate, and his reserve represses the flow of his children's spirits toward him (19). Having placed them under the care of a governess, with proper masters, he believes that they could need nothing more. As a result 'their father was no object of love to them, he had never seemed the friend of their pleasures, and his absence was unhappily most welcome. They were relieved by it from all restraint' (32).

Jane Austen's third criticism is that patriarchalism cultivates shallow goals and inadequate moral perception. All the prominent adults are self-centred and guided by materialism. The society encourages self-gratification in young males with little concern for consequences, since they are protected by their favoured position; and it turns young females away from any substantial activity in favour of an interest in appearance, manners, accomplishments and admiration.

The fourth principal fault—patriarchalism's corruption of courtship and marriage relationships—is as important an issue as the failure in education. One observers the same materialistic attitude toward the making of marriages as in ***Pride and Prejudice.*** Since Maria Bertram regards her happiness as assured by Mr Rushworth's large fortune, she regards it as her duty to marry him if she can (38-9). Marriage is also Mary Crawford's object, provided she can marry well. Sir Thomas expects his daughters' marriages to produce alliances advantageous to the family, and Lady Bertram is stirred for almost the only time in the prospect of Fanny's marrying a man of such good estate as Henry Crawford. Mary Crawford sums up the view of marriage in her society: it is the transaction in which people expect the most from others and are themselves the least honest; one should marry as soon as it can be done to advantage. From observation she can see that it is a 'manoeuvring business' (46).

The plot of ***Mansfield Park*** turns on two events: an abortive revolt against the restraints of patriarchalism by its favoured offspring and a successful revolt against its constraints by Fanny Price. In the first revolt the 'corrupted' children of patriarchy seek independence in order to indulge their whims, but their rebellion tends toward moral chaos. In the second revolt, however, Fanny Price, seeking to preserve her moral integrity and selfhood from the depersonalising demands of the patriarchal order, rehabilitates the moral order.

The cause of the first revolt is the upbringing of the Bertram children (and of the Crawfords and Mr Yates). They put personal pleasure and gratification of vanity above all else. The occasion is Sir Thomas' absence. The means is a private theatrical performance. In the opinion of Edmund and Fanny, to stage it in their father's house while he is absent and in some danger would show 'great want of feeling' (125). They also believe that he would regard it as unfit for home representation (140) and a danger to the privacy and propriety of the house (158). Edmund at first stands firm with Fanny as an upholder of the authority of Sir Thomas and a defender of decorum. When he enters into the activity, however, Fanny is left alone as the defender of the patriarchal order, wretched in her personal predicament. The first revolt collapses with Sir Thomas' unexpected return. It was shallowly conceived and lacked substance; the 'corrupted' children could only offer behaviour that would destroy both the system and what remained of their own selfhood. However, with Sir Thomas reinstated as master, nothing changes and nothing is learned.

In the second revolt the morally mature, responsive and sensitive Fanny Price seeks to protect her freedom to choose a husband in accord with personally defined criteria. Forced upon her and fully provoked, her revolt is the ultimate response of a morally mature person to a concerted and uncompromising attack by the parents and children of patriarchy on her integrity and selfhood.

Fanny Price first appears to be the model of a passive and submissive female, formed for and created by a patriarchal society. She is gentle, affectionate, desirous of doing right, and possessing great sensibility. Her disposition and lowly circumstances encourage timidity and very low self-esteem. Unlike her cousins she does not place personal pleasure above other considerations (131), values 'fond treatment' (365), and is concerned to please and do her duty. In the eyes of the representatives of the system, Fanny perfectly fits the stereotype of female and wife (276, 294).

Jane Austen gives special attention to Fanny's relationship with Sir Thomas. The two figures appear to carry to an extreme the types of the dominant patriarchal father and the submissive patriarchal daughter. Fanny's awe and fear of Sir Thomas' opinion and her desire to please him are emphasised (321). She regarded him as 'so discerning, so honourable, so good' (318). His advice is that of an 'absolute power' (280). She is afraid that she will not appear properly submissive.

Thus, prior to her revolt, Fanny's behaviour exhibits much of the 'false' humility, the psychological paralysis, and the emotional dependence rooted in low self-esteem that Mary Daly describes as the by-product of the internalisation of masculine opinion brought about in the female in an androcentric society through social conditioning.[12] She appears to be a partner in what Elizabeth Janeway describes as the collusion of weakness and power to preserve subordination by the withdrawal of the weak from the possibilities of action.[13] Fanny's case seems almost a perfect illustration of Simone de Beauvoir's representation of the formation of the 'feminine' woman.[14]

However, Fanny's personality is more complex than those around her perceive. Her taste is strong (337), she is responsive to natural environment and to anything that warms her imagination with scenes of the past (85-6), and she is clever and has a 'quick apprehension' as well as 'good sense' (22). She is perceptive and reactive to those around her, as is shown particularly by her disgust at what she believes to be Henry Crawford's want of feeling (329). She is not to be won by gallantry and wit or without the assistance of sentiment and feeling and seriousness on serious subjects. But Fanny can feel temptation, can unconsciously adapt her attitude to circumstances, and can, at least momentarily, temper moral considerations with personal concern. She has all the heroism of principle and determination to do her duty, but she also has many of the feelings of youth and nature.

During the first revolt Fanny has the fineness of feeling to recognise her debt to the patriarchal society, to appreciate its values, to be loyal, to be cautious about self-assertion, and to keep her poise between the claims of judgement and the heart. She has, in fact, come to embody the order's potential virtues more satisfactorily than its more favoured members. Edmund tells his father that only Fanny had judged rightly throughout, and she is embraced by the latter as his sole faithful and upright child.

Subsequently, Sir Thomas treats Fanny with a new kindness. Her health and beauty markedly improve, as she seems to have earned a place in the patriarchal order. But the happy outcome is only temporary. The aborted theatricals were only a dress rehearsal for the later, more reprehensible breakaway of the Bertram sisters and the Crawfords. Furthermore, Fanny's recognition and promotion only follow upon her appearing to fill, as Sir Thomas' natural daughters did not, the role of a model patriarchal child. In fact, as Fanny's worth is recognised, the patriarchal order moves to appropriate her will and exploit her gifts. In the remainder of the novel her integrity and selfhood come under attack by three males whose goal is her submission. The response is Fanny's revolt.

Henry Crawford authors the first attack on Fanny's integrity and selfhood. Attracted by her new spirit and improved appearance, he decides to amuse himself by making her fall in love with him. As his thoughts turn from flirtation to marriage, two themes emerge: the increase of his interest as he perceives how well Fanny fits the patriarchal idea of a model wife; and the inconceivability to all that Fanny can refuse his offer. Henry ticks off her qualifications: strong affections, a dependable temper, a quick and clear understanding, manners that 'were the mirror of her own modest and elegant mind,' and strong principles, gentleness and modesty. He especially praises 'that sweetness which makes so essential a part of every woman's worth in the judgment of man, that though he sometimes loves where it is not, he can never believe it absent' (294). Mary Crawford assures him that Fanny 'is the very one to make you happy' (295). Crawford, of course, cannot believe that he can ask Fanny in vain. When he is understood, he must succeed. Mary Crawford seconds him with the arguments of convention: Fanny's upbringing must influence her to accept, and her gentle and grateful disposition would assure her consent even if he were less pleasing (293). To these constraints upon Fanny are added her gratitude to Crawford for William's promotion and her sense of the improvement in his own behaviour (328).

But Fanny's objection to Henry Crawford is deeply rooted. She refuses him because she perceives an absolute incompatibility of personality and attitudes. She has often been oppressed by his spirits. Still more does she object to his character. She has seen him behaving 'very improperly and unfeelingly' (349). Her most serious charge: 'And, alas! how always known no principle to supply as a duty what the heart was deficient in' (329).

The attack from Sir Thomas is even more serious and oppressive because it brings the patriarchal father and daughter into direct conflict. The encouragement Fanny has received from Sir Thomas and her own increased affection for him only add to the pressure upon her. She appears doubly ungrateful because she has received a genteel upbringing beyond her expectations. Upon her refusal of Crawford, Fanny is thrust back into her former fearful relationship, augmented by an increase in guilt. She feels almost ashamed for not liking Henry Crawford (316).

The scenes between the two illustrate how the patriarchal system demands the female's submission and self-effacement. For all his merits Sir Thomas represents the parent as tyrant. In accord with his notions of marriage and the relations of parents and children, he believes that after his sanction nothing remains but Fanny's acquiescence. Consequently, he is dumbfounded by her assertion that she cannot return Crawford's 'good opinion.' Three times Sir Thomas asks if she refuses Crawford, uncomprehending. His displeasure mounts as he finds no explanation for her behaviour (318). Finally, he addresses her with the cold accents of the patriarchal father whose authority and wishes have been defied (the accents of Richardson's Mr Harlowe); his words reflect the assumptions that support the patriarchal family structure:

> It is of no use, I perceive, to talk to you. We had better put an end to this most mortifying conference. Mr. Crawford must not be kept longer waiting. I will, therefore, only add, as thinking it my duty to mark my opinion of your conduct—that you have disappointed every expectation I had formed, and proved yourself of a character the very reverse of what I had supposed. … I had thought you peculiarly free from wilfulness of temper, self-conceit, and every tendency to that independence of spirit, which prevails so much in modern days, even in young women,

> and which in young women is offensive and disgusting beyond all common offence. But you have now shewn me that you can be wilful and perverse, that you can and will decide for yourself, without any consideration or deference for those who have surely some right to guide you—without even asking their advice. … The advantage or disadvantage of your family—of your parents—your brothers and sisters—never seems to have had a moment's share in your thoughts on this occasion. How *they* might be benefited, how *they* must rejoice in such an establishment for you—is nothing to *you*. You think only of yourself; and because you do not feel for Mr. Crawford exactly what a young, heated fancy imagines to be necessary for happiness, you resolve to refuse him at once, without wishing even for a little time to consider of it … , and for really examining your own inclinations—and are, in a wild fit of folly, throwing away from you such an opportunity of being settled in life … as will, probably, never occur to you again.
>
> (318-19)

Understanding the import of Sir Thomas' speech is crucial to understanding the basic relationship between Fanny Price and the society of Mansfield Park. The words are those of the dominant patriarchal male parent. Sir Thomas expresses the system's intolerance of any independence of spirit and identifies as wilful and ungrateful any concern for self that opposes the parents' wishes. He places the interests of the family above those of its individual members. He places material values and a concern for status and security in the society above personal aspirations and emotional happiness. He finds any deviation from its standards more reprehensible in the female than in the male. Fanny is a subverter of the patriarchal order, to a worse degree even than the 'corrupted' children.

Sir Thomas decides that kindness may be the best way of working with such a gentle-tempered girl. But his retreat from a dogmatic and demanding position is only tactical. He still intends to manipulate her, and he hopes for a resolution in accord with his wishes. In encouraging Crawford's departure, he hopes that Crawford will be missed and that the loss of consequence will cause regret in Fanny's mind (366). And his prime motive for sending Fanny to Portsmouth is the hope that abstinence from elegance and luxury will induce a juster estimate of the value of Crawford's offer (369).

Fanny too hopes that time will favour her. She

> trusted … that she had done right, that her judgment had not misled her; for the purity of her intentions she could answer; and she was willing to hope … that her uncle's displeasure was abating, and would abate farther as he considered the matter with more impartiality, and felt, as a good man must feel, how wretched, and how unpardonable, how hopeless and how wicked it was, to marry without affection.
>
> (324)

Fanny here identifies the basic concern prompting her revolt: her right to make a marriage choice in accord with her own view of what would constitute her happiness or welfare. At issue is the question of location of authority over the self. The individual who seeks self-fulfilment is in conflict with the patriarchal order that would subordinate the individual to the group. As in all of Jane Austen's novels, the clash occurs in most striking form in the choice of a spouse, where the pressure of the patriarchal society to conform is most severe and potentially traumatic.

The attack from Edmund Bertram is the most dangerous of the three. It occurs when Crawford's behaviour is attracting favourable response from Fanny and when Sir Thomas has substituted siege for assault. Edmund is Fanny's first and principal friend, toward whom she has a respectful, grateful, confiding, tender feeling (39). Since he casts himself in the role of a kind of mediator and seeks to provide a rationale for surrender, his attack comes in insidious form.

Although at the outset Edmund is the protector and mentor of Fanny, as the story develops one observes an ironic reversal of roles: the pupil becomes the teacher. Edmund reveals two deficiencies in moral development: his powers of moral discrimination are not as fine as Fanny's and his adherence to what he believes is right is less firm. As a result he lapses twice in behaviour: he joins in the revolt of the 'corrupted' children and in the attempt to coerce Fanny into a bad marriage. Despite his attractive qualities, his kindness to Fanny, and the affinity of feeling and principles that they possess, Edmund is susceptible to the same impulse for self-indulgence and the pursuit of selfish goals that guides the others.

Edmund too is a scion of patriarchalism. His sexism is not as aggressive or overt as Crawford's or Sir Thomas', but well engrained. For example, his use of stereotyping is implicit in his criticism of Mary Crawford: 'No reluctance, no horror, no feminine—shall I say? no modest loathings!' (455). His attitudes concerning marriage are also in perfect accord with those of his patriarchal society. He is entirely on Sir Thomas' side and hopes for a match (335).

At first Fanny is reluctant to talk to Edmund because she assumes that they think too differently, but when he professes his objection to marriage without love, especially where her happiness is at stake, he appears to be wholly on her side (347). However, in Edmund's words, 'the matter does not end here.' Since Crawford's is no common attachment, he perseveres with the hope of creating that regard which has been lacking. His gentle admonition is as firmly patriarchal as Sir Thomas' bluster: 'let him succeed at last, Fanny, let him succeed at last. You have proved yourself upright and disinterested, prove yourself grateful and tender-hearted; and then you will be the perfect model of a woman, which I have always believed you born for' (347). Briefly he tries to explain away the problem of their different tempers. Finally, he summons up the traditional arguments for woman's submission. There are, first of all, his assumptions about the difference between marriage roles. Henry Crawford will be 'a most fortunate man … to attach himself to such a creature—to a woman, who firm as a rock in her own principles, has a gentleness of character so well adapted to recommend them. He has chosen his partner, indeed, with rare felicity. He will make you happy, Fanny, I know he will make you happy; but you will make him every thing' (351). Then there are his assumptions about her obligations of duty and gratitude and her need to be rational (meaning practical or prudent): 'I cannot suppose that you have not the *wish* to love him—the natural wish of gratitude' (348). Finally, because he cannot shake himself free from traditional assumptions about woman's nature, he assumes that her resistance must be due to the force of her attachment to the Park (347-8). If she can get used to the idea of Crawford's being in love with her, a return of her affection should follow (356). Edmund has completely missed the point of Fanny's objection.

Fanny's devotion to principle and sense of duty to self is as unyielding to Edmund's attack as it was to Sir Thomas.' Her anguish is even greater: 'Oh! never, never, never; he never will succeed with me' (347). Her justification is the same: one should not marry without love; she cannot love where she does not admire (349). To his suggestion that when Crawford's love becomes familiar to her it will become agreeable, and to the charge, conveyed by Crawford's sisters, that a woman who would refuse such an offer must be out of her senses, Fanny makes the fullest and most forthright defence of the independence and power of woman's feeling and of woman's right to choose for herself and the most direct attack on sex-role stereotyping to be found in Jane Austen's novels. In context Fanny's sense of self, honesty, and directness are remarkable:

> I *should* have thought … that every woman must have felt the possibility of a man's not being approved, not being loved by some one of her sex, at least, let him be ever so generally agreeable. Let him have all the perfections in the world, I think it ought not to be set down as certain, that a man must be acceptable to every woman he may happen to like himself. … In my situation, it would have been the extreme of vanity to be forming expectations on Mr. Crawford. … How was I to have an attachment at his service, as soon as it was asked for? His sisters should consider me as well as him …—we think very differently of the nature of women, if they can imagine a woman so very soon capable of returning an affection as this seems to imply.
>
> (353)

Fortuitously, all ends well for Fanny. The Crawfords' misbehaviour frees her from Henry's suit and opens Edmund's eyes to Mary's unsuitability. Sir Thomas discovers his own errors of belief and judgement. Edmund is loved by Fanny, and reasonably soon after his disappointment he discovers where his true interest lies.

From close examination of the contention between Fanny Price and the patriarchal social order of Mansfield Park, one answers the questions cited at the outset with confidence: Fanny Price is a 'heroine of principle'; the main concern of the novel is her welfare; the patriarchal society at the Park is the 'enemy'; the contention springs from the latter's attempt to dictate Fanny's marriage choice; and Fanny's ordeal and triumph provide the dramatic centre of the novel. One also perceives that Fanny is originally a victim of the social order, never its foe; that the society is on trial; that any advantage she receives from it is accidental; that she becomes its preserver; and that the threat to the social order results from its own shortcomings. To the question identified by Professor Wiesenfarth—is a meaningful personal freedom and integrity viable within a traditional pattern of morals and manners?—the answer would appear to be a cautious 'yes.' The needs of the self and of the society are not incompatible. But an equilibrium is reached only after a very painful ordeal for the heroine and a difficult lesson painfully learned by the leaders of the established order.

One question remains: what was Jane Austen's purpose in writing ***Mansfield Park***? At the heart of the matter Jane Austen is concerned about the threat to selfhood of a social order that subordinates the needs of the individual to those of the society; specifically, in ***Mansfield Park*** she depicts what for her would be the most pressing and disturbing form of this danger—the victimisation of the female in a male-dominated society.

Jane Austen's treatment of Mary Crawford confirms the point. In the eyes of many readers the charming and gifted Mary far outshines the presumably dull heroine. Yet Fanny enjoys a final 'triumph' and Mary a 'defeat.' The most common explanation is that Jane Austen's didactic intention inhibited or deflected her personal preference and artistic judgement.

Unquestionably the presentation of Mary Crawford serves the author's intellectual and moralising purpose. But to assume that these purposes are adequately served by the trite association of charm with moral obtuseness and dullness with moral discernment discounts Jane Austen's artistic capability and possibly her intelligence. What is important to recognise is that Fanny and Mary are both raised in a patriarchal society and thus are both potentially 'victims' of the society. The divergence in their fates is a result of the differences in their relationships to that society. Their personality differences accentuate the irony of the contrast in their fortunes. Despite her apparent subjugation, Fanny's position as 'outsider' both helps her to develop the capability to take a moral stand (a moral education in reverse) and it shields a natural capacity for moral judgement from corruption, whereas Mary's favourable position, along with the pressure of positive reinforcement, both subverts an inborn moral capacity and encourages only pragmatic, materialistic and cynical attitudes, hallmarks of the 'privileged' female and the 'corrupted' child in the patriarchal society.

Mary Crawford is an actual victim of the patriarchal order, just as Fanny is a potential victim. She is rich, beautiful, gifted with wit, good humour and musical skill, and courageous. Nevertheless, the faults of her upbringing display themselves quickly. These defects, we are repeatedly told, are the product of her exposure to a selfish, materialistic and sexist society. The point is made most forcefully by Edmund, following his breaking off from Mary:

> This is what the world does. For where, Fanny, shall we find a woman whom nature had so rightly endowed?—Spoilt, spoilt!—. . . No, her's is not a cruel nature. I do not consider her as meaning to wound my feelings. The evil lies yet deeper; in her total ignorance, unsuspiciousness of there being such feelings, in a perversion of mind which made it natural to her to treat the subject as she did. She was speaking only, as she had been used to hear others speak, as she imagined every body else would speak. Her's are not faults of temper. She would not voluntarily give unnecessary pain to any one. . . . Her's are faults of principle, Fanny, of blunted delicacy and a corrupted, vitiated mind.
>
> (455-6)

(He had spoken earlier of her mind being 'tainted' [269].) In corroboration, the narrator says that Miss Crawford had 'shewn a mind led astray and bewildered, and without any suspicion of being so; darkened, yet fancying itself light' (367). For Mary the victim, as for Louisa Gradgrind of *Hard Times,* there is no happy ending. Though discontented with her life, she cannot free herself from the warping of her nature by her environment (469). It is a bitter ending for Mary Crawford, caught between two worlds and essentially undeserving of her fate.

An understanding of the relationship between Fanny Price and the environment at Mansfield Park discourages the view that the novel is cautious and conservative or nostalgic and fearful of the future, in favour of the view that it challenges convention and the *status quo* and looks toward the future. It favours those interpretations that see the novel as examining selfhood,[15] condemning a decaying environment that relegates women to a state of subjection,[16] and expressing the importance and difficulty of being free[17] and the need to preserve order by partisan commitment to action[18] over those interpretations that see it as exposing the dangers of individuality or counselling a retreat to a life of art, ritual and imposed form.[19] Finally, this perception supports the belief that there is a 'feminist' element in Jane Austen's fiction. Jane Austen presents Fanny Price as representative of an oppressed sex. Unaware of the conflict between herself and the family structures that have provided a crippling security, she is forced by necessity to speak from the self. But in defending her integrity and her personal freedom to choose, an effort that is more moving in that she makes a stand, alone and weak, against the patriarchal family and the world, Fanny Price defends the birthright of everyone.

Notes

1. Douglas Bush, *Jane Austen* (New York: Macmillan, 1975), p. 109; W. A. Craik, *Jane Austen: The Six Novels* (London: Methuen, 1966), p. 92; Joseph M. Duffy, Jr, 'Moral Integrity and Moral Anarchy in *Mansfield Park,*' *ELH,* 23 (1956), 73-9; Alistair M. Duckworth, *The Improvement of the Estate: A Study of Jane Austen's Novels* (Baltimore, Md.: The Johns Hopkins Press, 1971), p. 31; David Lodge, 'The Vocabulary of *Mansfield Park,*' *Language of Fiction* (London: Routledge and Kegan Paul, 1966), p. 97; Avrom Fleishman, '*Mansfield Park* in Its Time,' *Nineteenth-Century Fiction,* 22 (1967), 1-18; Joseph Wiesenfarth; *The Errand of Form* (New York: Fordham University Press, 1976), pp. 86-108.

2. See Robert Alan Donovan, '*Mansfield Park* and Jane Austen's Moral Universe,' *The Shaping Vision* (Ithaca, NY: Cornell University Press, 1966), p. 150; Lionel Trilling, '*Mansfield Park,*' *The Opposing Self* (New York: Viking, 1955), pp. 221, 230; Joseph W. Donohue, Jr, 'Ordination and the Divided House at Mansfield Park,' *ELH,* 32 (1965), 171, 178.

3. Wiesenfarth, p. 86.

4. Wiesenfarth, pp. 107, 90.

5. See Donovan, pp. 153, 171; Trilling, pp. 225-30; Donohue, pp. 171, 178.

6. See Janet Burroway, 'The Irony of the Insufferable Prig: *Mansfield Park,*' *Critical Quarterly,* 9 (1967), 135-8. Stuart M. Tave describes Fanny as redeeming her society by her insistence on personal integrity in making a marriage choice ('Jane Austen and One of Her Contemporaries,' *Jane Austen: Bicentenary Essays,* ed. John Halperin [Cambridge: Cambridge University Press, 1975], p. 73); D. D. Devlin says that by not submitting Fanny threatens the society and proves that she alone is free ('*Mansfield Park,*' *Ariel,* 2 [1971], 35).

7. 'Being and Doing in *Mansfield Park,*' *Archiv,* 206 (1970), 346, 359.

8. Donovan, p. 150.

9. *The Second Sex,* trans. and ed. by J. M. Parshley (New York: Bantam 1970), p. 176.

10. 'A View of *Mansfield Park,*' *Critical Essays on Jane Austen,* ed. B. C. Southam (London: Routledge and Kegan Paul, 1968), p. 50; see also Kenneth Moler, *Jane Austen's Art of Allusion* (Lincoln, Nebraska: University of Nebraska Press, 1968), pp. 111-45.

11. Norman Sherry, *Jane Austen* (London: Evans, 1966), p. 98.

12. *Beyond God the Father: Toward a Philosophy of Women's Liberation* (Boston, Mass.: Beacon, 1973), pp. 50-4.

13. *Man's World, Woman's Place* (New York: Morrow, 1971), pp. 107-9.

14. de Beauvoir, pp. 261-2, 267-9, 337.

15. Ryals, *op. cit.*

16. Madeline Hummel, 'Emblematic Charades and the Observant Woman in *Mansfield Park,' Texas Studies in Language and Literature,* 15 (1973), 251-65.

17. Devlin, *op. cit.*

18. Burroway, *op. cit.*

19. D. W. Harding, 'Regulated Hatred: An Aspect of the Work of Jane Austen,' *Scrutiny,* 8 (1940), 346-62; Duckworth, *op. cit.*; Duffy, *op. cit.*

Rachel Trickett (essay date 1985)

SOURCE: Trickett, Rachel. "*Mansfield Park.*" Spec. issue of *Wordsworth Circle* 17.2 (1986): 87-95. Print.

[In the following essay, originally presented at a conference in 1985, Trickett considers the "peculiar position" of Mansfield Park *in relation to Austen's other novels. Though she contends that* Mansfield Park *is not as "perfectly constructed" as her next novel,* Emma *(1815), Trickett argues that Austen's earlier work "remains essentially fascinating" because of its "purely imaginative quality."]*

I want to talk about ***Mansfield Park*** in relation to Jane Austen's other novels and because of its peculiar position in relation to them. In 1813, two days after receiving a copy in print of ***Pride and Prejudice,*** which had just been published, Jane Austen wrote to her sister Cassandra "now I will try to write about something else, and it shall be a complete change of subject—ordination." Well, indeed, a complete change of subject, but not perhaps so complete in its implications about the role of the hero. Jane Austen had already written two novels in which the hero either was, or was about to be, ordained, ***Northanger Abbey*** and ***Sense and Sensibility.*** And although there are long and important discussions on the nature of the priesthood and the duties of the clergy between Mary Crawford and Edmund Bertram in ***Mansfield Park,*** it can scarcely be said that we finish the book with the feeling that this is the theme of the work. No doubt, however, her confession to Cassandra suggests that the tone of the book, the inspiration behind it, was of a very different nature from that which had animated her favourite novel, ***Pride and Prejudice.*** She had already confessed to a private fondness for the more spirited work, though she was later teasingly to say that having heard it read aloud by her mother to the family she saw that it needed more shade. That is probably just as much a comment on Mrs. Austen's way of reading aloud as on the nature of ***Pride and Prejudice.*** And her next novel, ***Mansfield Park*** would have this sense of perspective, of light and shade, for the implication in the letter is that what she's looking for is a less certain, less brightly-lit work. Yet it's a fact that after she had finished ***Mansfield Park*** she returned to the devices of high comedy in ***Emma,*** which is the most perfectly constructed of all her books. ***Mansfield Park,*** however, remained Cassandra's favourite among all her novels and it has retained, I think, a peculiar place especially with contemporary and academic readers.

If it is not the most perfect, it is perhaps the most interesting of Jane Austen's novels. Critics have happily lost themselves in speculation over what Jane Austen *really* felt about amateur theatricals. Indeed, in a very brilliant essay the distinguished critic Lionel Trilling erected a whole ingenious theory of role-playing and its dangers from Sir Thomas's disapproval of the production at Mansfield, when in fact every member of his family, from high to low, understands exactly why he will disapprove so strongly of them. Interestingly enough, however, there are other aspects of ***Mansfield Park*** which arouse our curiosity, historical and critical. One example is the fact that there are more allusions to contemporary literature in ***Mansfield Park*** than in any other of her novels, even ***Persuasion,*** and critics have speculated about the range of Jane Austen's interests and appreciation from these, and also about a new romanticism that appears in her descriptions of place and climate and season and time of the day.

She's also more concerned with alluding to contemporary affairs in ***Mansfield Park.*** It is here that the whole action of the novel is set against wartime, and we know for instance that between the first and the second edition of the book she revised the nautical terminology in the description of the *Thrush* leaving Portsmouth under the advice of one of her two naval brothers, Charles. You remember that two of Jane Austen's brothers eventually were made admirals, and of course Fanny's passion for William and William's profession is very much an autobiographical touch. Then there are the references Tom Bertram makes to Dr. Grant at the dance at Mansfield to "that strange business in America." Critics have had a field day on that and have not yet decided what precisely it alludes to. Fanny also turns to Sir Thomas on his return from Antigua to ask him about the slave trade. And, most of all, critics have been interested in the possibility that in ***Mansfield Park*** Jane Austen had come under evangelical influence which accounts for the special tone of seriousness in the work.

I referred earlier to a new kind of hero and heroine, Edmund and Fanny. They are, of course, not pictures of perfection. Jane Austen herself said in a letter to her niece Fanny Knight "patterns of perfection make me sick and wicked," two years after having written ***Mansfield Park***—so she clearly did not intend Fanny to be a pattern of perfection, though one sometimes wishes that might be a little more evident in her tone towards her in the book. Though imperfect, Fanny at least is undeceived unlike Edmund, and morally impeccable, and set at a great distance in this regard from any other character in the book except Sir Thomas himself, though Sir Thomas has his failings—too unbending a gravity, too strong a sense of the importance of the role of *paterfamilias.* The sheep are separated from the goats in no uncertain way in ***Mansfield Park,*** and the goats for once are in the majority. Now if this is possibly true in life, it is certainly not so in Jane Austen's earlier novels. From ***Sense and Sensibility, Northanger Abbey*** to ***Pride and Prejudice*** the admirable and the amiable characters are more evenly balanced against the disagreeable and the disgraceful, and either side is presented in the vein of comedy. Mrs. Jennings and her well-meaning ministrations to Marianne in ***Sense and Sensibility*** may be absurd, but they are essentially affectionate. The Thorpes and the Steeles of the earlier works are selfish vulgarians, but they are not monsters like Mrs. Norris. Mrs. Bennet's stupidity and the odious nature of Lady Catherine's snobbery are equally funny in ***Pride and Prejudice.*** And Mr. Bennet's witty and culpable indifference is infinitely more entertaining than Sir Thomas Bertram's humourless *gravitas.* In fact, the extraordinary thing about ***Mansfield Park,*** to my mind, is that none of the characters is wholly amiable with the intended exception of the hero and heroine, and some of us find them too profoundly priggish to touch the affections.

I ought to admit at once that Fanny Price is my least favourite Jane Austen heroine. Her imperfections are so unselfconscious, so much a matter of her status and her innate timidity on the one hand, and so connected with her moral sensibility which far too often expresses itself as censoriousness on the other, that the uneasy reader begins to see these as a flaw in the novel rather than as they should be, a strength. Now I know that to relate the success of the work with any one character may seem hopelessly naive, especially to today's critics, as a starting point. But I would maintain that it is as inevitable in Jane Austen's novels as it is in Shakespeare's comedies, for her books are all technically comedies, conditioned by the move towards a happy ending, and their mood or tone depends to an unusual degree in each case on the nature or temperament of the main protagonist, which is the heroine, as it is indeed in Shakespeare's comedies. Three of Jane Austen's books, ***Northanger Abbey, Pride and Prejudice*** and ***Emma*** are endowed with high-spirited, impulsive, witty or active heroines and all three of them are comedies in the highest sense. They are conducted at a level of narrative management, contrivance of dialogue and episode which is entirely in the tradition of the theatre, and in their perfection of construction they moved Archbishop Whately, the early nineteenth century rhetorician, to wonder whether it could be possible that Jane Austen had read Aristotle. The three whose heroines are passive: ***Sense and Sensibility, Mansfield Park,*** and ***Persuasion*** are, on the other hand, complicated by the interposition of moral questions which are not wholly resolved through the action. The interposition in ***Mansfield Park*** of considerable pain and suffering, gives a darker cast to the pictures of selfishness, and indifference, and self indulgence which Jane Austen sees as the basic faults of human nature.

It would I think be wrong to suggest that there is any lack of feeling in ***Northanger Abbey, Pride and Prejudice,*** or ***Emma.*** Catherine Morland, Elizabeth Bennet and Emma Woodhouse are all capable of impulsive, generous and spontaneous warm-heartedness. The last two are more sophisticated and self-conscious, but equally open to the most genuine feelings. Their problems are genuine too, but they are never intrinsically insoluble. They are never presented with a situation which cannot be rationally solved. Henry Tilney, Darcy, and Mr. Knightley do not have to struggle with any divided romantic feelings about the women they love. And this I suppose is most brilliantly shown in ***Emma*** when Emma at last begins to suspect from poor Harriet's self-deception that Harriet has supplanted her in Mr. Knightley's heart. She sits watching the sad sight of the wind despoiling the shrubbery for a whole evening to suit her melancholy reflections, yet she is really secure in that comic certainty which the famous sentence of self enlightenment summarises perfectly for us: "it shot through her with the speed of an arrow that Mr. Knightley must marry no one but herself."

But Marianne in ***Sense and Sensibility,*** on the other hand, has to endure the pain of Willoughby's desertion. When she reads the appalling letter he sends her under the instructions of his new fiancée, she almost screams in agony. When she meets him at the reception she has to submit to the mortification of rushing up to him and saying "Will you not even shake hands with me?" Fanny in ***Mansfield Park*** has to see Edmund genuinely fall in love with Mary Crawford, and Anne Elliot in ***Persuasion*** believes with an appearance of justification that Captain Wentworth no longer feels anything for her, and cannot blame him for this. The painfulness of these emotions is never minimised by Jane Austen. The novelist L. P. Hartley said that a friend of his whose literary opinion he valued greatly had re-read ***Sense and Sensibility*** and said to him in surprise, "I found myself crying at the pain and misery in that book." Charlotte Brontë was wrong in suggesting that Jane Austen had no acquaintance with what she calls "that stormy sisterhood," the passions. Jane Austen may claim as she does in ***Mansfield Park*** that she will let other pens dwell on guilt and misery, but guilt and misery are essential ingredients in the texture of that novel. "That great black word miserable" haunts Fanny, as she cries at Sir Thomas's reproaches of ingratitude. Let me remind you of that passage which is full of the most genuine confused and conflicting emotion—

> Another burst of tears; but in spite of that burst, and in spite of that great black word 'miserable,' which served to

> introduce it, Sir Thomas began to think a little of relenting. Her mind was all disorder. The past, present, future, everything was terrible. But her uncle's anger gave her the severest pain of all. Selfish and ungrateful! to have appeared so to him! She was miserable for ever. She had no one to take her part, to counsel or speak for her. Her only friend was absent. He might have softened his father; but all, perhaps all, would think her selfish and ungrateful. She might have to endure the reproach again and again; she might hear it, or see it, or know it to exist for ever in every connection about her. She could not but feel some resentment against Mr. Crawford; yet, if he really loved her, and were unhappy too!—it was all wretchedness together.

"Her mind was all disorder," Jane Austen says in that paragraph. The possibility of tragic disaster is there. The supposition which she even concedes in this moment is that perhaps even Henry Crawford is to be pitied, "if he really loved her and were unhappy too. It was all wretchedness together."

The shadow of a tragic disaster, then, looms over this little domestic love tale, and in one sense it is not inappropriate that all the characters of the Bertram and Crawford families except Fanny should eventually be involved in a melodramatic catastrophe. Such a concatenation of circumstances as the last chapters of ***Mansfield Park*** are, Tom's illness, Maria and Henry's adultery, Julia's elopement, Edmunds' disillusion with Mary, all these suggest the most rigid system or formula of poetic justice—poetic justice, at least, for those involved in the original performance of *Lovers' Vows*. The vows are worthless indeed, and if not broken deliberately in the course of the book, they are wrecked by reality. It is not so much the assumption of role-playing which is brought to our mind by the brilliant use of amateur theatricals in ***Mansfield Park*** but rather that aspect of the drama which has always fascinated novelists, from Fielding who frequently refers to and introduces plays in his novels, to the marvellous passages in Dickens about theatrical performances. What fascinates the novelist is the interplay of illusion and reality in a stage performance. It is interesting in ***Mansfield Park*** that Jane Austen never lets the performance take place. She is only concerned with the rehearsal. We never actually get that moment of illusion when the thing takes off and the play is happening, as we do in the performances of Hamlet in *Tom Jones* or in *Great Expectations*. And I do think that, whether deliberate or not, the imagination of this great novelist was well aware of what she was doing in that context. Fanny, you remember, is fascinated by the drama. Lady Bertram is very indulgent and says—now don't scold her she's not been to a play before and its very nice for her to see this, she's delighted by it—to the annoyance of Mrs. Norris who tells Fanny to bustle about and do things. Against her will she is caught up in it, watching particularly the performance of Henry Crawford, but Jane Austen is aware of the nature of the illusion and it is compounded by the fact that the actors are not even professionals—they are amateurs. Edmund's objection to the acting in the first place is that it can't be serious acting "not good hardened acting," that is, professional, not amateur playing. But to Fanny there is a little razor-edge moment when she is almost moved out of her condemnatory attitude by the fascination of the illusion. But it is broken, and broken perfectly, by the sudden interruption of Julia saying "my father has arrived," and the whole of the intended illusion collapses.

If it were not for the extraordinary artistic skill with which Jane Austen has constructed the novel, the melodramatic dénouement I mentioned in which all those taking part in *Lovers' Vows* are punished, would seem almost crudely and moralistically contrived. But what happens in the last chapters of the novel doesn't seem, as we are reading it, either crude or improbable.

I want now to look not only at the theatrical performance, or lack of performance, in ***Mansfield Park,*** but also at certain other devices Jane Austen uses which show how aware she was of the danger of any appearance of crudity in the poetic justice of the conclusion. Nowhere else but in ***Mansfield Park*** does she allow herself quite so much freedom of moral commentary in her own voice. Nowhere else is she so anxious to point out in advance the shortcomings of which her characters themselves are unaware. Nowhere else does she allow her heroine such certainty of moral response and such a correspondence with the author's own attitude. At the same time as we are aware of Henry Crawford's charm, of his first steps towards conversion, of the possibility of his being changed by his love for Fanny, Jane Austen is warning us that it won't happen. While she is forestalling our astonished grasp that there might be a different ending to the story, an alternative happy ending, she is denying us the satisfaction of gambling on it. And the device she uses to do this is by insisting on Fanny's being in love already. This is the real stumbling block to her loving Henry, this and his basic unseriousness. Given Jane Austen's own determination to develop to the full the theme of the appalling moral dangers of frivolity, selfishness and the effects of bad education on Mary and Henry, she must prohibit the movement towards change by whatever device she can exploit, whether it be authorial comment, or an almost too selfconsciously artificial introduction of speeches that reveal Mary's deep vulgarity. Even for instance in the touching last scene of Mary's goodbye to Fanny and to Mansfield.

This is an unusual episode because it shows both Fanny and Mary in a good light, and yet at the same time it shows the complete separation between their attitudes. What joins them together is their genuine love for Edmund. Mary comes into the east room—Fanny's little room—and recalls the occasion earlier, before the abortive performance of *Lovers' Vows,* when Fanny heard her and Edmund repeat their parts, acting as prompter and audience.

> 'Hah!' [Mary] cried with instant animation, 'am I here again? The east room. Once only was I in this room before,' and after stopping to look about her, and seemingly

to retrace all that had then passed, she added, 'once only before. Do you remember it? I came to rehearse. Your cousin came too; and we had a rehearsal. You were our audience and prompter. A delightful rehearsal. I shall never forget it. Here we were, just in this part of the room; here was your cousin, here was I, here were the chairs. Oh, why will such things ever pass away?'

Happily for her companion she wanted no answer. She was entirely self-engrossed. She was in a reverie of sweet remembrances.

'The scene we were rehearsing was so very remarkable, the subject so very—very—what shall I say? He was to be describing and recommending matrimony to me. I think I see him now, trying to be as demure and composed as Anhalt ought, through the two long speeches. "When two sympathetic hearts meet in the marriage state, matrimony may be called a happy life." I suppose no time can ever wear out the impression I have of his looks and voice, as he said those words. It was curious, very curious, that we should have such a scene to play! If I had the power of recalling any one week of my existence it should be that week, that acting week. Say what you would, Fanny, it should be *that*; for I never knew such exquisite happiness in any other. His sturdy spirit to bend as it did! Oh, it was sweet beyond expression. But alas, that very evening destroyed it all. That very evening brought your most unwelcome uncle. Poor Sir Thomas, who was glad to see you? Yet, Fanny, do not imagine I would now speak disrespectfully of Sir Thomas, though I certainly did hate him for many a week. No, I do him justice now. He is just what the head of such a family should be. Nay, in sober sadness, I believe I now love you all.' And having said so, with a degree of tenderness and consciousness which Fanny had never seen in her before, and now thought only too becoming, she turned away for a moment to recover herself. 'I have had a little fit since I came into this room, as you may perceive,' said she presently, with a playful smile, 'but it is over now; so let us sit down and be comfortable; for as to scolding you Fanny, which I came fully intending to do, I have not the heart for it when it comes to the point.' And embracing her very affectionately, 'Good gentle Fanny! when I think of this being the last time of seeing you for I do not know how long, I feel it quite impossible to do anything but love you.'

Fanny was affected. She had not foreseen anything of this, and her feelings could seldom withstand the melancholy influence of the word 'last.' She cried as if she had loved Miss Crawford more than she possibly could; and Miss Crawford, yet further softened by the sight of such emotion, hung about her with fondness, and said, 'I hate to leave you. I shall see no one half so amiable where I am going. Who says we shall not be sisters? I know we shall. I feel that we are born to be connected; and those tears convince me that you feel it too, dear Fanny.'

Fanny roused herself, and replying only in part, said, 'But you are only going from one set of friends to another. You are going to a very particular friend.'

'Yes, very true. Mrs. Fraser has been my intimate friend for years. But I have not the least inclination to go near her. I can think only of the friends I am leaving; my excellent sister, yourself, and the Bertrams in general. You have all so much more *heart* among you than one finds in the world at large. You all give me the feeling of being able to trust and confide in you; which, in common intercourse, one knows nothing of. I wish I had settled with Mrs. Fraser not to go to her till after Easter, a much better time for the visit—but now I cannot put her off. And when I have done with her, I must go to her sister, Lady Stornaway, because *she* was rather my most particular friend of the two; but I have not cared much for *her* these three years.'

There is indeed a further and much longer development two pages later of Mary's essential vulgarity of attitude towards her old friends, and combined with the extraordinary emotional charm which is conveyed here, this is an excellent example of Jane Austen's use of the delicate balance between condemnation and understanding.

But why is this particular scene so very powerful? Because the room and the circumstances in which Mary is talking and Fanny is very tersely replying are suffused with sincere feeling from earlier in the novel. There *is* sincere feeling underlying the parting between the two girls; even Fanny's reluctance to feel any is very sincere. Both girls are genuinely in love with Edmund, but the room in which they are sitting is the room where Fanny felt the grief of recognising Mary and Edmund's love, and it is the most important room in the house to Fanny because it is her room and her retreat. It is the room which Jane Austen, unusually, describes in great detail, the room in which Fanny had found her solace in childhood.

The description of it is most unusual in Jane Austen. She is not a woman who describes interiors with great elaboration. Readers forget that, because we supply in our own imaginations the furniture and the rooms and the details, but in comparison with George Eliot, for instance, there is very little detail apart from the odd sofa or the pianoforte or the window in Jane Austen, except here.

> The aspect was so favourable, that even without a fire it was habitable in many an early spring and late autumn morning, to such a willing mind as Fanny's; and while there was a gleam of sunshine she hoped not to be driven from it entirely, even when winter came. The comfort of it in her hours of leisure was extreme. She could go there after anything unpleasant below, and find immediate consolation in some pursuit, or some train of thought at hand. Her plants, her books—of which she had been a collector, from the first hour of her commanding a shilling—her writing desk, and her works of charity and ingenuity, were all within her reach; or if indisposed for employment, if nothing but musing woud do, she could scarcely see an object in that room which had not an interesting remembrance connected with it. Everything was a friend, or bore her thoughts to a friend; and though there had been sometimes much of suffering to her,—though her motives had been often misunderstood, her feelings disregarded, and her comprehension undervalued,—though she had known the pains of tyranny, of ridicule, and neglect,—yet almost every recurrence of either had led to something consolatory; her aunt Bertram had spoken for her, or Miss Lee had been encouraging, or what was yet more frequent or more dear—Edmund had been her champion and her friend;—he had supported her cause, or explained her

> meaning, he had told her not to cry, or had given her some proof of affection which made her tears delightful,—and the whole was now so blended together, so harmonised by distance, that every former affliction had its charm. The room was most dear to her, and she would not have changed its furniture for the handsomest in the house, though what had been originally plain had suffered all the ill-usage of children; and its greatest elegancies and ornaments were a faded footstool of Julia's work, too ill done for the drawing-room, three transparencies, made in a rage for transparencies, for the three lower panes of one window, where Tintern Abbey held its station between a cave in Italy and a moonlight lake in Cumberland, a collection of family profiles, though unworthy of being anywhere else, over the mantelpiece, and by their side, and pinned against the wall, a small sketch of a ship sent four years ago from the Mediterranean by William, with *H. M. S. Antwerp* at the bottom, in letters as tall as the mainmast.

This is the room in which that crucial meeting between Fanny and Mary takes place; here their differences of nature are exposed, but gently, and with a sympathetic understanding of the feelings of both on the part of the author; here Jane Austen binds together the peculiar status of the heroine in ***Mansfield Park*** and the circumstances that surround her.

Let us think about Fanny's position for a moment, because it is very important with regard to the moral structure of the work as Jane Austen sees it. In ***Sense and Sensibility*** she divided the two qualities of the title between two sisters. In ***Mansfield Park*** she unites them in one character. Fanny is an unusual character in this sense, however, because from the beginning of the book her status is paradoxical. She is at once the victim, the outcast, the rejected and at the same time she is Cinderella, the recipient of generosity, the child meant to be brought in from the cold to be involved with a new family, a new set of circumstances, and a new life. So that the idea of gratitude, is particularly, peculiarly, intensely felt by the child at the beginning and by the young woman at the end of the novel. The opening scene I don't need to quote to you; it is one of the most brilliant in fiction, like so many scenes to do with children. But it is worth noticing how skilfully Jane Austen manages its pathos, with Edmund coming across the little girl sobbing on the attic steps. It is not much written in direct speech; most of it is indirect narration; the passive voice is used a great deal. Only when Edmund actually comes forward and performs acts of kindness for little Fanny does the whole scene spring to life. He rules the lines on her writing paper for her so that she can write to William. It is a perfect opening scene because it epitomises the nature of the relationship between them and the quality of their feelings.

Fanny's own feelings are of excessive sensibility. One of the unusual things about Fanny as an Austen heroine is that she is very much a romantic. She is not only deeply moved by poetry, but also by landscape. She exclaims in the Grant's garden, "The evergreen, how beautiful the evergreen!" though her idiom of enthusiasm is a little comically stiff. Even more imbued with sensibility are the early scenes, the child's vulnerability and her realization of loneliness, of being rejected, of being removed from her true family, is ministered to not only by his practical help, but by the kindness and affection of Edmund. So this early scene is immensely important, as indeed is the description of her room later, for the parting between her and Mary at the end of the second volume of the novel. We can begin to see here the way in which these scenes and episodes interrelate in Jane Austen's imagination, ringing the changes on the themes of separation and connection, and on the sense of isolation combined with the feeling of sympathy.

It is very important to notice that again and again Fanny's isolation is underlined, particularly in the first volume. Her timidity and genuine fear of rejection are repeated in many scenes. For instance, she sees Edmund and Mary coming back from riding; Mary is much better than she is on horseback. Fanny stands there and has to hear the groom say how much more lively Mary is on horseback than she, after which through the window she sees them coming in happily together. Then comes her headache when they arrive after Edmund has allowed Mary to use the pony for two weeks or more and Fanny has not had any exercise at all. There follows the great climax of the Sotherton expedition where Fanny is left alone, literally dumped on a seat while everyone else gets on their own affairs, and this is underlined by Julia's coming up and saying "What Fanny all alone? How could they have left you like this?" Yet again her isolation, her sense of rejection, is underlined. Particularly brilliant is the scene where Edmund and she remember how they used to star-gaze together. It is at the end of the Sotherton expedition and they are back home. Edmund is already evidently falling in love with Mary, and, as he watches her leave the two of them, he says:

> 'There goes good humour, I am sure … There goes a temper which would never give pain! How well she walks! and how readily she falls in with the inclination of others! joining them the moment she is asked. What a pity,' he added, after an instant's reflection, 'that she should have been in such hands!'
>
> Fanny agreed to it, and had the pleasure of seeing him continue at the window with her, in spite of the expected glee, and of having his eyes soon turned, like hers, towards the scene without, where all that was solemn, and soothing, and lovely appeared in the brilliancy of an unclouded night, and the contrast of the deep shade of the woods. Fanny spoke her feelings. 'Here's harmony!' said she; 'Here's repose! Here's what may leave all painting and all music behind, and what poetry only can attempt to describe! Here's what may tranquillise every care, and lift the heart to rapture! When I look out on such a night as this, I feel as if there could be neither wickedness or sorrow in the world; and there certainly would be less of both if the sublimity of nature were attended to, and people were carried more out of themselves by contemplating such a scene.'

This is Jane Austen's romanticism—the idea that contemplating such a scene carries you out of yourself.

'I like to hear your enthusiasm, Fanny. It is a lovely night, and they are much to be pitied who have not been taught to feel in some degree as you do—who have not at least been given a taste for nature in early life. They lose a great deal.'

'*You* taught me to think and feel on the subject, cousin.'

'I had a very apt scholar. There's Arcturus looking very bright.'

'Yes, and the Bear. I wish I could see Cassiopeia.'

'We must go out on the lawn for that. Should you be afraid?'

'Not in the least. It is a great while since we have had any star-gazing.'

'Yes, I do not know how it has happened.' The glee began. 'We will stay till this is finished, Fanny,' said he, turning his back to the window; and as it advanced, she had the mortification of seeing him advance too, moving forward by gentle degrees towards the instrument, and when it ceased, he was close by the singers, among the most urgent in requesting to hear the glee again.

A perfect and touching example of social tragi-comedy, in a very intimate and simple form, but again it repeats the rejection and separation motif that we have recognized so strongly in the first section of the book. Perhaps more deeply, and more sympathetically even than here (though this is an exquisite moment I think in the book), is the expansion of Fanny's sympathies and sensibilities in the *Lovers' Vows* section. Here she recognizes somebody else's isolation and rejection in Julia, the sister Henry Crawford has rejected in favour of Maria.

Julia *did* suffer, however, though Mrs. Grant discerned it not and though it escaped the notice of many of her own family likewise. She had loved, she did love still, and she had all the suffering which a warm temper and a high spirit were likely to endure under the disappointment of a dear, though irrational hope, with a strong sense of ill-usage. Her heart was sore and angry, and she was capable only of angry consolations. The sister with whom she was used to be on easy terms was now become her greatest enemy: they were alienated from each other; and Julia was not superior to the hope of some distressing end to the attentions which were still carrying on there, some punishment to Maria for conduct so shameful towards herself as well as towards Mr. Rushworth …

Fanny saw and pitied much of this in Julia; but there was no outward fellowship between them. Julia made no communication, and Fanny took no liberties. They were two solitary sufferers, only connected by Fanny's consciousness.

This is very frequently the case in ***Mansfield Park.*** It is true even of Mary and Fanny in that scene we began with, that they are essentially solitary, only connected by Fanny's consciousness. Fanny's consciousness, whether we like her or not, is the centre of the novel. Again and again, Jane Austen reminds us that her consciousness is superior to Mary's liveliness and wit. There is the moment, for instance, when Fanny is sitting with her at the Parsonage at Mansfield and talking about the shrubbery:

'This is pretty, very pretty,' said Fanny, looking around her as they were thus sitting together one day; 'every time I come into this shrubbery I am more struck with its growth and beauty. Three years ago, this was nothing but a rough hedgerow along the upper side of the field, never thought of as anything, or capable of becoming anything; and now it is converted into a walk, and it would be difficult to say whether most valuable as a convenience or an ornament; and, perhaps, in another three years we may be forgetting—almost forgetting what it was before. How wonderful, how very wonderful the operations of time, and the changes of the human mind!' And following the latter train of thought, she soon afterwards added: 'If any one faculty of our nature may be called *more* wonderful than the rest, I do think it is memory. There seems something more speakingly incomprehensible in the powers, the failure, the inequalities of memory, than in any other of our intelligences. The memory is sometimes so retentive, so serviceable, so obedient; at others, so bewildered and so weak; and at others again, so tyrannic, so beyond control! We are, to be sure, a miracle every way—but our powers of recollecting and of forgetting do seem peculiarly past finding out.'

Miss Crawford, untouched and inattentive, had nothing to say; and Fanny perceiving it, brought back her own mind to what she thought must interest.

'It may seem impertinent in *me* to praise, but I must admire the taste Mrs. Grant has shown in all this. There is such a quiet simplicity in the plan of the walk!—not too much attempted.'

'Yes,' replied Miss Crawford carelessly, 'it does very well for a place of this sort. One does not think of extent *here,* and, between ourselves, till I came to Mansfield, I had not imagined a country parson ever aspired to a shrubbery or anything of the kind.'

'I am so glad to see the evergreens thrive!' said Fanny, in reply. 'My uncle's gardener always says the soil here is better than his own, and so it appears from the growth of the laurels and evergreens in general.'

Fanny is that perpetually attractive English female character, the gardener. She instinctively knows about the soil:

'The evergreen! How beautiful, how welcome, how wonderful the evergreen! When one thinks of it, how astonishing a variety of nature! … You will think me rhapsodising; but when I am out of doors, especially when I am sitting out of doors, I am very apt to get into this sort of wondering strain. One cannot fix one's eyes on the commonest natural production without finding food for a rambling fancy.'

'To say the truth,' replied Miss Crawford, 'I am something like the famous Doge at the Court of Louis XIV; and may declare that I see no wonder in this shrubbery equal to seeing myself in it.'

Before we are too sure that Jane Austen was entirely on Fanny's side perhaps it's worthwhile remembering that Dr.

Johnson would have agreed with Mary Crawford: "one blade of grass is like another blade of grass, let us discourse upon the admirable diversity of human nature." Nevertheless, there is no doubt that Jane Austen's depiction of Fanny in these circumstances and her brilliantly funny account of Mary's complete insensitivity to Fanny's rather subtle discourse on memory, is meant to indicate the difference between a lively, sympathetic open mind, like Fanny's, and a mind that appears to be witty, social, bright, amusing but is quintessentially closed because it is entirely self-centred. And this is an attitude which we can only infer from the book by genuinely close reading and not by allowing our own instinctive prejudices for or against Fanny's character to interfere.

In the second part of the novel the theme of isolation and rejection is reversed and Fanny becomes the pursued, not the rejected. But again, paradoxically, her position is no better; in fact it is far worse because she is pursued by the man she doesn't want. So she has to attempt to escape. In any other novel of Jane Austen it would seem to me that the quintessential comedy of this situation would have been underlined. But here precisely the opposite is done, and it is a sense of the potential tragedy which is allowed to dominate the more static mood of the book.

Lionel Trilling in his article talks of a moral stasis in the work. The refusal of change, which as I pointed out earlier, Jane Austen is exercising when she keeps telling us that though Henry Crawford might have won Fanny he is not going to, creates a moral stasis. What interests me particularly is that there is a sense of temporal stasis in the book, too. It seems to be the longest of Jane Austen's novels, but in fact it's not. It is not as long as ***Emma.*** Yet very little happens in it really, apart from the amateur theatricals, the early dance before that (where Tom, very comically, drags Fanny off at the last minute, because he wants to avoid playing whist with his mother), and the Sotherton expedition, the ball at Mansfield, one or two dinner parties at the Parsonage, and then finally the Portsmouth expedition. All these events take only from July of one year to May of the next, and the chronology and the seasons are very carefully marked. The events do not take even a full year, yet time seems to stretch out interminably, particularly in the middle section. Jane Austen effects this partly by repetition, continuous repetition of the idea of isolation and of frustration, Fanny always being in the same position even when the roles are apparently reversed. The things that break that stasis are the contrived melodramatic conclusion I discussed earlier, but even more, the famous Portsmouth sequence.

The episode of Fanny's return home is a deeply important imaginative moment where this child who has been trying to locate herself in the new home goes back to the old. It has been a source of endless dispute as to whether Jane Austen was essentially a snob because she shows Fanny as appalled by the noise, the din, and the general disorder of Portsmouth. The fact is she is equally rigorous in her condemnation of selfishness whether at Mansfield Park or at Portsmouth and this is one of the main themes of the novel—not money, or lack of it, or class, but consideration for other people. The open mind or the closed mind are the choices. What Fanny finds when she goes home is that she is treated with complete indifference: nobody cares. The children rush past her. The *Thrush* is suddenly leaving which is all they are interested in. This sister, who has come back so elevated, and her grand relations are completely ignored. It is a comic *peripeteia,* but at the same time Mrs. Price is not exonerated, nor is Fanny's father for their total indifference to their child. It is contrasted with Fanny's practical consideration (like Edmund's for her as a child), about solving the family quarrel between Susan and Betsy over the knife. She has the very sensible notion of going out and buying another knife, and Betsy is much better pleased by it than by the sentimental memento of the dying sister who had left it to Susan. Here again Fanny's extreme sensibility and clarity are shown by the way in which she knows exactly what to do. Jane Austen speculates how those other two sisters—Lady Bertram and Mrs. Norris—would have made out on Mrs. Price's income with ten children, and objectively affirms that Mrs. Norris would have been far more successful at it. She would indeed have made a very respectable wife in these circumstances, and the acknowledgment of this makes us trust the truth of Fanny's response to her home.

It is in the sequence at Portsmouth that a vivacious, impressionistic, immediate descriptive technique is assumed by Jane Austen. This is quite unlike the retrospective, related narrative description of the earlier part. Suddenly everything is vivid. It is April weather though it is only March. The effect of the sun on the water is vividly and dazzlingly conveyed. And there is almost again, in that immediacy of the spring light, a touch of the idea of illusion and reflection and refraction. This is the moment at which Henry Crawford almost changes and moves into the ranks of the sheep as opposed to the goats. So that it is essential at this stage of the denouement, and of the book's pattern, that Fanny should be re-integrated into Mansfield Park and that it should become to us, as it does to her, a sort of paradise, where the good and the considerate are rewarded, and the indifferent punished. (Admittedly it is hard to know into which category Lady Bertram comes—neither good nor bad, and she is certainly not punished. She is one of those archetypal figures of comedy whom the author can allow to stray out of the work's moral categories.)

The question we are left with is, do we actually believe, having been told of the possibility of Henry Crawford's conversion, in his elopement with Maria? To some readers it seems the perfect conclusion, showing exactly what Jane Austen has been trying to say throughout, that there is something ineradicable in genuine triviality, or genuine self-centredness, as there is in stupidity like Lady Bertram's. No amount of education, or influence, not even love itself, can transform it. But there *is* uncertainty in the conclusion of ***Mansfield Park,*** and it is one of the reasons I think that we find it such an exceptionally interesting book.

I have had no time now to say anything about some of the elements I would like you to notice in it, particularly the literary allusions, but I would like to draw your attention to the interesting discussion between Edmund and Henry Crawford about Shakespeare, which is one of the several literary critical passages in ***Mansfield Park.*** They are talking about the peculiarity of Shakespearean influence on English thought, and then go on to discuss the liturgy. I am bound to say that it seems to me that Henry Crawford might, not perhaps surprisingly, in our own day have been one of those who would support the alternative services. He finds the ancient liturgy, though it has its beauties, somewhat repetitive.

I would have thought that it is partly because of the open-endedness of so many questions that the book remains essentially fascinating, whether we like Fanny or whether we find her always a little too fagged and under the weather or alternatively a little too censorious. It is hard for me to reconcile my heart to the final scene where she and Edmund coolly dissect the characters of the Crawfords, who anyway have lost—and one would have thought that that in itself was sufficient punishment. But what I hope I have had the chance to convey to you, however clumsily, is something of the purely imaginative quality of the book, in particular the use of scene, of certain emotional situations related to the paraphernalia of comedy, social comedy, but which come out as poignant, and touching and romantic. This reminds me of a remark, perhaps a rather tart remark, of Henry James's which I would like to conclude with. In an essay on the life of Balzac, he is talking about the way in which novelists affect him, the impression they leave on his mind—"the life that overflows in Dickens seems always to go on in the morning or in the very earliest hours of the afternoon. In George Eliot the sun sinks forever to the west, and the shadows are long and the afternoon wanes. Why is it that in Charlotte Brontë we move through an endless autumn? Why is it that in Jane Austen we sit quite resigned in an arrested spring?" Of all her novels ***Mansfield Park*** comes closest to the implications of that brilliant phrase.

Mary Waldron (essay date 1994)

SOURCE: Waldron, Mary. "The Frailties of Fanny: *Mansfield Park* and the Evangelical Movement." *Eighteenth-Century Fiction* 6.3 (1994): 259-82. Print.

[*In the following essay, Waldron comments on the controversial reception of* Mansfield Park, *noting that "the charm of the 'bad' characters" in the novel frustrated initial readers and has continued to make scholars question her "odd" characterization. While previous critics have argued that* Mansfield Park *features an "ideal woman" as its protagonist because Austen wished "to atone for the flawed heroines of the three earlier novels," Waldron finds that the novel "actually questions, in a new and much more challenging way, the validity of some favourite contemporary moral and social assumptions."*]

"She is never, ever, wrong." This estimate of Fanny Price, made by Tony Tanner in 1966 in his Introduction to the Penguin edition, is often taken for granted by critics writing about ***Mansfield Park*** and is frequently assumed as the basis for her present-day position as Austen's most unpopular heroine. Not all, it is true, take up exactly the same unequivocal position. For instance, in 1967 Robert A. Colby found some faults in Fanny—she is occasionally jealous and uncharitable. Avrom Fleishman, in the same year, suggested that "Fanny is presented not as a paragon of virtue, but as a weak woman with self-defensive and self-aggrandizing impulses." Kenneth Moler in 1968 said "Jane Austen did not intend Fanny to be . . . the moral paragon that many readers take her to be." At least one other more recent critic has seen imperfections in Fanny but has considered them unintended fallout from the author's struggles with her material: Bernard Paris (1978) says "It is difficult to feel as positively about Fanny's goodness as Jane Austen wants us to . . . it is rigid, desperate, compulsive. Fanny is not actively loving or benevolent." Nina Auerbach, in a very unusual view of Fanny, relates her to most of the predatory villains of literature from Grendel to Dracula.[1] Alongside such as these, however, a more traditional view of Fanny persists: in 1975 Marilyn Butler called her "an exemplary heroine" and bases her radical criticism of the novel's structure upon this assessment, which is not modified in the reissue of her book in 1987. In that year Park Honan still regarded Fanny as "a potent, deeply effective redeemer of Mansfield." Sometimes critics see faults but excuse them. In 1988 Claudia L. Johnson saw that in Fanny Austen criticizes too great a reliance on the patriarchal system of family organization—she blinds herself to the inadequacy of the men in her life, but is not to blame for the outcome. Oliver MacDonagh (1991) asserts that "Fanny is no saint or ranter . . . within limits . . . her principles can be overborne, though it is also made clear that her inner citadel is inviolable." For MacDonagh, Fanny's principles remain superior to those of others in the novel despite the assaults made on them. Recently Roger Gard has noted "Fanny's half-misleading reputation for moral rigour"[2] but, having pointed out incidents in which Fanny behaves less than perfectly, he attributes them to a vulnerability built into the plot to emphasize the moral dilemmas which she finally resolves. These references must necessarily be selective; in the great mass of comment on this essentially puzzling novel there are many shades in the assessment of the character of Fanny, but the great majority of critics finally see her as guiltless in a venal world. Even Claudia Johnson, who otherwise seriously questions the more common estimates of the novel, sees Fanny as ultimately triumphing over the errors of the deluded males, remaining innocent herself. I believe this represents an inadequate reading of a prismatic and complex work. This essay will examine these conflicting views in more detail and with closer reference to the action, and will offer, in the light of this novel's probable genesis and its interaction with some aspects of contemporary ethical and religious thought, a less confused and more justifiable assessment of the character of its heroine.

From the time of its first appearance in 1814, ***Mansfield Park*** has attracted controversy and criticism. Some contemporary readers objected to the charm of the "bad" characters; and although we do not now find this charm morally reprehensible, we often find it odd: whose side are we supposed to be on? Fanny Price exasperates because she appears to conform to a contemporary womanly ideal which certainly does not satisfy the modern reader, and which Austen had seemed to reject, or at least vigorously modify, in her three earlier novels; Mary Crawford at first seems to have more in common with Elizabeth Bennet than the declared heroine of ***Mansfield Park***; and the reader is puzzled by the apparent primness of the authorial presence—what Isobel Armstrong, in her very interesting essay of 1988, calls the "difficult gravitas of the text."[3] A link with contemporary popular conduct-books such as James Fordyce's *Sermons to Young Women* (1776), Dr John Gregory's *A Father's Legacy to His Daughters* (1774), and Thomas Gisborne's *An Enquiry into the Duties of the Female Sex* (1794) cannot well be avoided in a consideration of Fanny Price. From poking fun at Fordyce in ***Pride and Prejudice,*** Austen seems almost to have joined forces with him. Elizabeth Bennet, Marianne Dashwood, and Catherine Morland are delightfully misguided, they have spirit and energy; Fordyce, Gregory, and Gisborne are unlikely to have approved of *them*—at least until their trials have taught them compromise. Even Elinor Dashwood wavers in her perfect response to the received code of social morality. Fanny, in contrast, is passive and submissive, fond of silence and anonymity—everything the conduct-books recommend. These qualities appear to triumph unchanged at the end of the novel, thus defeating our expectations of an Austen heroine, who typically has to modify her natural, but unacceptable, reactions to reach an accommodation which eventually brings her happiness. So far, in the first three novels, the interest has lain in the difficulties of the compromise, and also in the attractiveness of the non-conformity, which is never entirely abandoned. After ***Mansfield Park,*** Austen appears to return to this model in ***Emma. Persuasion*** is rather different; Anne Elliot is also a "good" heroine, but she has already discovered, at the beginning of the novel, that submission is not an adequate response to life. This does not seem, on the surface at least, ever to be the case for Fanny Price. Many critics attribute the differences in ***Mansfield Park*** to a change of heart on the part of the author about true womanly excellence, and a wish to make the central figure an ideal woman, on the lines of the conduct-books, to atone for the flawed heroines of the three earlier novels. This change has often been seen as part of a shift by Austen towards a conservative and paternalistic ideology which was gaining ground at the turn of the century as a reaction against radical, democratic ideas associated with the French Revolution. This view might be acceptable if the three earlier novels could be described as in any way democratic or radical. But this is not so; in all the novels, including ***Mansfield Park,*** the heroines operate within a social structure which they accept. Nor, evidently, was it the wish of the author to depart from her habit and present a woman without flaw in a novel: she later, in 1817, tells her niece Fanny that "pictures of perfection" made her "sick and wicked"; and in 1814, the year in which ***Mansfield Park*** was published, she criticizes her other niece Anna's own novel-character, Cecilia, for being "too solemn and good."[4] Is it credible, then, that she should at that precise time produce just such a heroine?

I should like to show that ***Mansfield Park*** actually questions, in a new and much more challenging way, the validity of some favourite contemporary moral and social assumptions. In the first three novels the heroines make silly but ultimately harmless mistakes; authority figures such as parents are shown to be in error, but good sense finally comes to the rescue. Fanny, on the contrary, is caught up in a dangerous and damaging ethical system from which there is no real escape at all. This essay will explore the reasons for Austen's apparent break with her custom here, on the basis of her own acknowledgment, especially in her letters, of concern about popular notions of social morality and her remarks about the books that people were reading when she was considering the plot of ***Mansfield Park.***

* * *

One of the strongest and most obvious features of the reaction to political radicalism in the nineties was the Evangelical movement (that movement within the Anglican church which included the "Clapham Sect"), which clearly both repelled and attracted Austen. It was dedicated to the revival of "serious" and "active" Christianity, partly as a defensive reaction to Methodism, which, with its outdoor meetings, public conversions, and extempore prayer, was regarded as politically subversive, especially after the outbreak of war in 1793, and partly to galvanize a decadent clergy into carrying out its proper duties. It was in the main bourgeois-led and aimed at social control through paternalism; it was to that extent a political movement. At its centre was the doctrine that individual submission to duty would, by example, act as a corrective to what was seen as contemporary moral corruption.[5] It produced in the early 1800s a spate of didactic works. In 1809, in a letter to her sister Cassandra, Austen states categorically, apropos of one of these, Hannah More's *Cœlebs in Search of a Wife,*[6] just published and very much in demand, that Evangelicalism did not appeal to her. The novel was an imperfectly fictionalized conduct-book by the chief literary proponent of the movement; it was a compendium of Evangelical ideas touching all ranks and generations, setting out their duties and responsibilities—particularly those of young women. Austen was reluctant to read it. Her comments are typically oblique and sardonic, but leave one in little doubt as to the reasons for her reluctance:

> You have by no means raised my curiosity after Caleb [*sic*];—My disinclination for it before was affected, but now it is real; I do not like the Evangelicals.—Of course I shall be delighted, when I read it, like other people, but till I do I dislike it.
>
> (***Letters*** [***Jane Austen's Letters***], p. 256)

The implication is that the appeal of *Cœlebs* was popular, superficial and therefore, to Austen, suspect. She was wearying, perhaps, of this genre. Clearly she would not react "like other people." In her correspondence with her niece Fanny Knight in 1814, however, we find a different view in her recommendation of a modest and unassuming young man as a suitor. Fanny seems to be in some doubt about him, chiefly on the grounds of his "goodness," which she thinks might lean towards Evangelicalism (Fanny appears to assume that her aunt will agree that this is altogether undesirable). Austen replies:

> And as to there being any objection from his *Goodness,* from the danger of his becoming even Evangelical, I cannot admit *that.* I am by no means convinced that we ought not all to be Evangelicals, and am at least persuaded that they who are so from Reason and Feeling, must be happiest and safest.
>
> (***Letters,*** p. 410)

Later in the correspondence, presumably in answer to Fanny's protest about this, she says:

> I cannot suppose we differ in our ideas of the Christian Religion. You have given an excellent description of it. We only affix a different meaning to the Word *Evangelical.*
>
> (***Letters,*** p. 420)

This change in Austen's way of referring to Evangelicalism needs some consideration, for her approval may not be as wholehearted as it at first appears. During the period 1809 to 1814, she seems to have reached an accommodation with the movement, but only by dint of modifying her definition of it to suit her own rational and intellectual tastes. She does not appear to have accepted the whole package. She may have approved of its political thrust—no doubt agreeing that social control of this sort was necessary to a healthy society. But there is a suggestion of compromise about the words "happiest and safest"; the implication is that she liked the cosy personal relationship with the creator which the movement offered, but set aside the "enthusiasm," the reforming zeal. In its missionary aspect she must have seen clearly a deep contradiction which is evident in most of the didactic works of the time—they enjoin quietism and submission to duty in the rank to which you had been called together with firmness in the face of error and a steady opposition to sin. This would, they aver, finally call others from their evil ways. But in real life it is difficult, not to say impossible, thus to combine subjection and assertiveness.[7] Populist Evangelical propaganda paid little attention to actualities. Hannah More's *Cheap Repository Tracts* certainly show a fine disregard for them. They offer Evangelicalism packaged in primary colours for the masses. They set up a totally unreal model for the lowly and weak to follow, which promises unfailing reward for "right" action—obey the rules and you will get modest reward on earth as well as lay up treasure in heaven.[8] The heavenly treasure may or may not have been sure, but the reward on earth, as More must have been aware, was at the mercy of economics. The tracts are intrinsically dishonest, for, while apparently recommending social progress, they aim at stasis. *Cœlebs,* to which Austen seems to object in 1809, brings together the whole range of Evangelical maxims designed to keep people operating in the stations to which they had been called, and is particularly insistent about the duty of young girls. Cœlebs, an extremely eligible young man, goes in search of the perfect life-partner. He visits several families with nubile daughters, only to find them frivolous, superficially religious, and educationally deficient. At last, in a family which exemplifies the Evangelical domestic ideal of duty happily accepted by all, he meets Lucilla Stanley, who presents an altogether improbable combination of right female submission with a lively capacity to speak her mind on subjects concerning religion and propriety—but only when asked to do so. For most of the novel she remains decorously silent. Lucilla is the living embodiment of More's *Strictures on the Present System of Female Education* (1799), in which, in chapter 1, "The Effects of Influence," she deplores the propensity of women to "defend the cause of religion … in a faint tone, a studied ambiguity of phrase" but at the same time insists on proper deference and silence—girls should not be argumentative. The *Strictures* makes heavy demands on the reader's willingness to reconcile contradictions. The novel also advocates the cultivation of mutually exclusive virtues, a mixture of prudential caution and large-minded generosity. A properly educated young man will want a sensible, morally upright wife with Evangelical principles, who is not interested in fashion and frippery, who is innocent and deferential and silent, but confident enough to engage in abstruse moral discussions when required and to speak up for her beliefs when they are attacked. This is so patently a caricature of real life that it is a wonder that anyone listened to it; but *Cœlebs* was spectacularly popular, going into many editions. All the same its failure to take into account so much about human relationships would have worried Austen; she criticizes Mary Brunton's *Self-Control* (1810)—another attempt at fictionalizing the ideals of Evangelicalism—for being "excellently-meant … without anything of Nature or Probability in it" (***Letters,*** p. 344). Austen's correspondence with her sister and nieces during the gestation of her novel has led twentieth-century critics to see the Austen of ***Mansfield Park*** as writing under the "shadow" of Evangelicalism. In 1943 Sheila Kaye-Smith proposed this reading in *Talking of Jane Austen*; Q. D. Leavis's Introduction in 1957 agreed that ***Mansfield Park*** has imperfections which are due to the influence of Evangelicalism.[9] Through the 1960s and 1970s there was a reaction: more critics—notably Fleishman and David Monaghan—saw the novel as critical of the movement. Colby, however, in 1967, regarded Austen as "sharing Miss More's ethical views."[10] In 1986 Marilyn Butler directly challenged Fleishman on this topic, and Oliver MacDonagh in 1991 also saw Austen as mainly approving of the movement.[11] It seems more likely that her initial reservations remained, that she never really became comfortable with all the aims of Evangelicalism, and that ***Mansfield Park*** is an exploration of her dissatisfaction in a story which deals with the application of some of its ideals in everyday life. Stanley Grove, the abode of Lucilla, is safe in its moral complacencies. In Austen's novel, duty and submission fail to prevent a series of calamities involving the near destruction of a whole family.

* * *

What is not often remarked upon in discussion of ***Mansfield Park*** is the almost unmitigated disaster of the ending. Claudia Johnson refers to it as "unsettling" and later explains this by noting how "conservative ideologues" are "obliged to discredit themselves with their own voices"; though Gene Koppel says that the conclusion "almost shatters the novel," he also sees it as offering alternatives—"the reader must choose" whether to see the ending as destructive or as the initiation of a "positive vision."[12] Fleishman seems at one point aware of the destructiveness and of the ending as a deadly compromise—"a feeling of peace after loss of vitality"—but reverts to the more usual view, referring to Fanny as "the child who inherits the future and justifies the sufferings of the past."[13] Johnson comes closest to my view of the ending as calamitous. All three critics see the conclusion as essentially ambiguous. There is undoubtedly ambiguity in the language, but it is ironic ambiguity, for the choice is not really open. Though Fanny is rescued and Edmund at least patched up, nothing much else is saved from the wreck. It is customary to attribute the chastisement meted out to a kind of chill and brutal retribution on the part of the author towards the characters she disapproves of, and to make it evidence of a change in moral attitude, for she has not previously handed down harsh punishments even to the most culpable (consider, for instance, the fate of Maria in contrast to that of Lydia Bennet or Willoughby). But the tragedy for the parents and their disappointment in their potentially fine family is not given much critical prominence, though it is unquestionably present in the text. Sir Thomas cannot credibly be satisified with the substitution of the Price children for his own, however much he may finally blame himself for the outcome. The triumphal language of the conclusion conceals another message—Fanny will have to live with the knowledge that though *she* is to be rewarded, almost everyone around her is suffering and will continue to suffer. It is difficult to imagine that her comfort will be unalloyed. Either, as Koppel suggests, Austen is caught up in the "contingency" of the realism of the novel and nearly "shatters" it in her efforts to end it, or the language of the conclusion is ironically seeking to direct the reader to the real state of affairs. Claudia Johnson puts this well—the surface meaning "will not bear the scrutiny Austen's own style is always inviting."[14] I would go further: the message is that the brand of "goodness" embodied in Fanny, Edmund, and, to some extent, Sir Thomas has not prevailed. It exists, but has been impotent. The power of example, as proffered in the work of Hannah More, has, in this realist novel, failed, because it has largely rescued those who were never really in danger. In *Cœlebs,* a dissolute neighbour of Lucilla's father, Mr Carlton, is turned from his evil ways by the visible piety of his wife (2:258-63). ***Mansfield Park*** deliberately rejects this stereotype; good example fails to avert a shipwreck; and a reading which is unbiased by assumptions about Austen's accommodationism to contemporary ethics must reveal not only that the subscription to Evangelical notions in Edmund and Sir Thomas is hollow and powerless, but that Fanny, the chief representative of the Evangelical ideal, is responsible for the shipwreck, because her kind of goodness is by definition cautious and passive. Its quietism can rarely be combined with active intervention in the cause of moral reform; on the contrary, it leads to a loss of energy, negativism, failure of generosity, and ultimately a concentration on self. She is the reality—Lucilla Stanley a phantasm. Austen may be tender to "my Fanny," but this does not mean that she is presenting her as having done much to avert the moral chaos at Mansfield—indeed, she herself is part of it.

These aspects of Fanny's character are clearly present in the text of the novel, but become more obvious if we have Hannah More's novel in mind.[15] A number of crucial incidents show Fanny, not as a perfectly good Lucilla-type, but as entangled in her Evangelical piety to the extent that she falls spectacularly from grace, and not only fails to exert any moral influence upon anyone except her sister, Susan, but herself becomes a destructive force.

Sir Thomas Bertram's regime at Mansfield is typical of the way in which Christianity operated among the rich and powerful. Attention to the virtues of kindliness, good manners, obedience to authority, and religious observance went alongside the more or less unrestricted enjoyment of the good things of life if you happened to have access to them. Sir Thomas has imbibed some Evangelical ideas—he believes in residence for the clergy, for instance, submissive behaviour in young women, and the exclusion of "noisy pleasures" from the domestic scene, but it is clear from the start that these ideas have had minimal effect on most of his children. Unlike Mr Stanley in *Cœlebs* he has not managed to govern his household so that all the inhabitants consciously and dutifully adapt their behaviour to a pious ideal. Moreover, it is made clear from the start that Sir Thomas is quite unaware of his failure. Self-denial has very little place in the real education of the young Bertrams, whatever may have happened in the schoolroom. Horse-racing and debt are the natural propensities of a young heir; balls and the marriage-market the proper duties of the daughters. Edmund, the younger son, destined without real choice for the church, turns out differently; he finds out early that his father's somewhat selective adherence to Evangelical principles has some relevance for him. He decides to be a proper parson, with all that it entails in moral concern for his flock and consciousness of reponsibility for the moral health (that is, stasis) of society as a whole. Fanny, from childhood dependent upon Edmund, also builds her life on the Evangelical ideal of active duty. The sociable joys of Maria and Julia and Tom are replaced in Fanny and Edmund by the satisfactions of conscious virtue. From the start they have a problem, for their ideals necessarily imply criticism of what they observe around them; and yet the very code by which they mean to live excludes the possibility of its expression, especially to their elders.

A telling example is Edmund's advice to Fanny when she thinks she may have to go and live with Aunt Norris—both know very well how mean and selfish she is, but their principles will not allow them to rebel, and they make the best of it; Edmund mouths some pious untruths about Mrs Norris's upright nature which, he says, is only cloaked by an unfortunate manner, and Fanny escapes from actually criticizing her aunt by blaming herself for "foolishness and awkwardness."[16] Already we are shown piety, obedience, and respect for elders leading to a distortion of the truth and a deliberate dilution of any realities which conflict with their code. There is no authorial comment—no blame is assigned, only a signal given of the contradictions inherent in the system within which Edmund and Fanny are trying to operate.

But neither experiences any real strain until the arrival of the Crawfords, who are completely oblivious to Evangelical principles in religion or anything else. Their extreme insouciance is highly attractive to all the young people living under a comfortable but rather dull social order. The older members see nothing in them to object to; Sir Thomas is absent, in any case, in Antigua. It is usual to regard the Crawfords as representatives of the outer, more wicked, world which is about to attack the moral stronghold of Mansfield. But it should be remembered that there is in fact nothing much to attack. No one at Mansfield is in possession of an unassailable set of principles. Fanny is not strong in her principles—she only thinks she is, because she has learned a set of rules which she supposes will guide her in any crisis. Edmund is much the same. The difference between the Crawfords and the Bertrams lies not so much in their respective moral standards as in the fact that the Crawfords are accustomed to a much more sophisticated and complex metropolitan version of the sexual game than the young Bertrams have any notion of; their ignorance in this respect adds spice to the Crawfords' usual round of shallow flirtation. Austen proceeds from this point to demonstrate how *all* the inhabitants of Mansfield, in different ways, fall victim to the unfamiliar game-strategy of the Crawfords—except perhaps Tom, who is in any case part of their world and clearly quite skilled himself. Maria, already engaged to the booby Rushworth, and Julia are fascinated by Henry, who deliberately sets out to entrap them. Both Fanny and Edmund are precipitated into a situation for which their "active Christianity" has given them no guidelines—Edmund begins to fall in love, and Fanny, who is, without quite realizing it, in love already, to experience jealousy. Significantly, Edmund does just what More's Cœlebs does *not* do; he falls for a girl who is the complete opposite of the conduct-book model. The whole episode subverts More in a most interesting way. Cœlebs is extremely cautious in his assessment of Lucilla, making sure that he does not fall in love until he has satisfied himself that her virtues accord with his (and his dead mother's) ideals, and that Lucilla is perfectly "consistent" in them. Then:

> I could not persuade myself that either prudence or duty demanded that I should guard my heart against such a combination of aimiable virtues and gentle graces … [she presented] a fabric of felicity that my heart, not my fancy had erected, and that my taste, judgement, and my principles equally approved, and delighted to contemplate.
>
> (*Cœlebs,* 1:232-33)

Edmund's heart is by no means guarded, and he falls into dreadful error, delighting to contemplate what he can only approve by distorting his principles. The exchange between Edmund and Fanny at this juncture is very significant. This is a sort of Socratic dialogue, in which Miss Crawford's character takes a beating, but Edmund makes specious excuses for her and is satisfied; Fanny does *not* see it all as he does, and does not say so. Edmund draws her into a discussion of Mary's character and encourages criticism:

> "But was there nothing in her conversation that struck you Fanny, as not quite right?"
>
> "Oh! yes, she ought not to have spoken of her uncle as she did. I was quite astonished. An uncle with whom she has been living so many years, and who, whatever his faults may be, is so very fond of her brother, treating him, they say, quite like a son. I could not have believed it!"
>
> "I thought you would be struck. It was very wrong—very indecorous."
>
> (3:63)

But Fanny wants to go farther than this, and charges Mary with ingratitude, one of the blacker eighteenth-century vices. Edmund will not have this, and begins to equivocate by claiming that it is *excess* of gratitude to her aunt which gives her a difficult choice; he does not want to go beyond "impropriety" in his charges. But, says Fanny, perhaps the aunt is not all that she should be not to have taught Mary better; Edmund leaps on this to hope that she may now be in better hands, and proceeds to admire her affection for her brother; Fanny rather righteously objects to Mary's teasing remarks about the letter-writing habits of brothers. Edmund's reply shows how his growing thraldom is causing him to dwell only on the appearance, not the substance, of female excellence:

> "And what right had she to suppose, that *you* would not write long letters when you were absent?"
>
> "The right of a lively mind, Fanny, seizing whatever may contribute to its own amusement or that of others; perfectly allowable, when untinctured by ill humour or roughness; and there is not the shadow of either in the countenance or manner of Miss Crawford, nothing sharp, or loud, or coarse. She is perfectly feminine, except in the instances we have been speaking of. *There* she cannot be justified. I am glad you saw it all as I did."
>
> (3:64)

To the reader it is obvious that Fanny disagrees completely and is suddenly beset by a number of painful conflicts: she must approve of Edmund, but can see that he is bending the rules. Far from having an ideal woman here, we have suddenly a very human girl with a problem.

The situation deepens and intensifies as time passes. While Julia and Maria, differently but just as defectively educated, are allowing that unacknowledged force, sexual passion, to disturb their lives, Fanny and Edmund are essentially doing the same. Throughout the novel there are parallels, particularly between Fanny and Julia, which make clear that Sir Thomas's system has served none of them well.

While Tom is simply getting conventionally into debt, the others are laying up all kinds of trouble for themselves. Mary and Henry are not exempt; they have more experience of sexual tension, but *their* education has left them unprepared for love. Ultimately, not one of the young people knows how to cope with real life. But Fanny has the the most serious problem. Almost every spontaneous feeling that she has conflicts with some duty which is part of her code. She gradually has to acknowledge to herself that she is in love with Edmund, which as a cousin and a dependant she has no right to be. (This idea does not actually surface until later: "Why did such an idea occur to her even enough to be reprobated and forbidden? It ought not to have touched on the confines of her imagination," 3:264-65.) Disgust with Maria and Julia, disappointment in Edmund, jealousy of Mary all lead her into very reprehensible emotions which she tries hard to disguise, or rather to defuse. A small but significant incident exemplifies this. While waiting rather impatiently for Mary to finish her riding lesson, she pretends to herself that she is sorry for the horse: "if she were forgotten the poor mare should be remembered" (3:68).[17] Then, unable to throw off her "discontent and envy" she lapses into headache and languor on the sofa, does not deny it when asked by Edmund, and stands by mute while her aunts are arguing about whose fault it is (3:74). It is Edmund's fault, and she "had been feeling neglected . . . struggling against discontent and envy." The struggle is admirable, but ineffective. Her code allows her to be silent; she does not need to reassure anyone. Lucilla Stanley would not have used her silence to cloak resentment, for she never experiences any. In Fanny, the feminine meekness of demeanour described in the conduct-books only serves to conceal from onlookers (but not from the reader) a mind in very human turmoil. Not for the last time we see Fanny using approved feminine silence to avoid positive generosity; here we have "Nature and Probability," not a moralistic fiction.

As the novel advances there are several episodes which superficially present Fanny as superior to Maria and Julia—particularly Julia—but at another level as very similar. At Sotherton, while Henry is playing one sister off against the other, Julia is described as suffering under the necessity of hiding her feelings of jealousy; when Henry detaches Maria from the party on the terrace and leaves Julia with Mrs Norris and Mrs Rushworth, she, too, has a struggle:

> The politeness which she had been brought up to practise as a duty, made it impossible for her to escape; while the want of that higher species of self-command, that just consideration of others, that knowledge of her own heart, that principle of right which had not formed any essential part of her education, made her miserable under it.
>
> (3:91)

But she does manage to conceal her perturbation, just as, shortly afterwards, we find Fanny doing the same; although her manner is different, and she feels more guilt, she suffers "disappointment and depression" for much the same reason, and finds these feelings difficult to control. Fanny may use approved Evangelical self-examination but she still feels unacceptable resentment. The episode also emphasizes, in a symbolic way, the inability of Fanny's moral principles to do anything to help others out of their confusion and moral dilemmas; her habits of submission, respect and obedience make this impossible. Edmund is more culpably ineffective; we cannot avoid remembering that he has just been discoursing piously upon the duty of the clergyman to guide the conduct of others (3:93), and is now oblivious to the dangerous game being played out under his nose, dazzled by the company of a pretty girl. The dynamics of the episode make it impossible to believe that Fanny is not sorrowfully conscious of his backsliding. She tries, ineffectually, and from a sitting position, to prevent Maria from going into the park with Henry and to defuse Julia's jealousy. This is symbolic irony: active religion, or Evangelicalism—in this case, Fanny—from its internal contradictions can do little to reform anyone; it can protest weakly while real people blunder on in their own disastrous courses. The easy solutions of *Cœlebs* are mere chimeras. More crucially, the system which Fanny has sought to guide her conduct can make its proponents adept at judging people but useless at saving them. Fanny, for all her "goodness," is here quite useless. Her moral standards are ineffective even to herself, because they are too simple to deal with real-life crisis—just as Edmund's are.[18] Austen now shows Fanny almost replicating Julia's behaviour. While attracting sympathy from the reader for her plight, Fanny goes on a parallel pursuit of Edmund and Mary, which results in unspoken, but real, resentment. Fanny has been wanting to see the avenue all morning; now she finds that Edmund and Mary have reached it together and she has been forgotten:

> Fanny's best consolation was in being assured that Edmund had wished for her very much . . . but this was not quite sufficient to do away the pain of having been left a whole hour.
>
> (3:103)

Fanny may exercise more control over the expression of her feelings than Julia does (though even Julia only says what she really thinks about the situation to Fanny herself—someone she is not bound to respect) but the emotional residue is the same.

* * *

The episode of the play emphasizes Fanny's moral impotence—she can do nothing to prevent what she sees, rightly in terms of the novel, as an iniquitous proceeding. It also repeats, several times, the Fanny/Julia motif: Fanny feels sorry for her—"could not think of her as under the agitations of *jealousy,* without great pity" (3:136); Fanny recognizes their similar feelings, but judges Julia—"Julia was a sufferer too, but not quite so blamelessly" (3:160); she is conscious of Julia's unhappiness, and the breach between her and her sister, but "there was no outward fellowship between them. Julia made no communication, and Fanny took no liberties. They were two solitary sufferers" (3:163). Fanny may be "blameless" in one sense, but the episode's chief impact on the reader is the way in which the system under which they all live excludes any possibility of Fanny's "active principle" doing anything to help Julia. And is Fanny really blameless? At Sir Thomas's unexpected arrival Julia actually voices what Fanny has been trying for throughout the episode: "*I* need not be afraid of appearing before him" (3:175). The clash of their manners only points up the parallel of their situations and blurs the fact that Fanny has fallen short in several ways. She has condoned a moral lapse in Edmund, and she has somehow sufficiently cleared away her earlier conviction that the play *Lovers' Vows* was "improper" and the language "unfit to be expressed by any woman of modesty" (3:137) to learn most of it by heart; by 3:165 she believes she derives "as much innocent enjoyment from the play as any of them"; and she is only saved from finally agreeing to take the part (temporarily) of the Cottager's Wife by the arrival of Sir Thomas. Bernard Paris points out that she deceives herself about her involvement in the play when she helps to make Mr Rushworth's cloak: "It is difficult to understand the difference between acting and sewing."[19] Her principles have not stayed firm. The narrative centres on her consciousness of what *ought* to happen; but she is no more able to cause it to do so than Edmund, the only other person who recognizes that anything is amiss.

The play episode also produces a new trial for Fanny. Mary, so far the *bête noire,* the wicked interloper, suddenly shows herself to have spontaneously warm and human feelings which anyone of Fanny's professed Christian beliefs ought to be able to appreciate. Mrs Norris tries to shame Fanny into doing what Tom and the others want, by a crude reference to her inferior status—"I shall think her a very obstinate, ungrateful girl . . . very ungrateful indeed, considering who and what she is" (3:147). Mary is "astonished," and does everything she can to comfort Fanny after this brutal and vulgar attack. The authorial voice intrudes here to assert that Miss Crawford is "almost purely governed" by "really good feelings." When the next day Edmund announces to Fanny that he is going to rescue Mary from the necessity of having to act with a stranger, Fanny cannot bring herself to acknowledge Mary's "really good feelings"; she tries for "greater warmth of manner" and cannot complete her "generous effusion" (3:155-56). Is she governed by her concern for the doubtful morality of the whole proceeding? Or does she really want Edmund to leave Mary to her fate, thus obeying the rules they both believe in and staying on her side? The final sentences of the chapter answer this question. Fanny is not concerned about generalized right and wrong; it is Mary who is the enemy—"Alas! it was all Miss Crawford's doing." The final words of her internal monologue are: "Things should take their course; she cared not how it ended. . . . It was all misery *now.*" Although she is presented as telling herself that his moral consistency is her chief concern, the words convey the fact that it is mainly Edmund's relation to herself that she cares about. What is being demonstrated here is the ease with which unacceptable human feelings can be camouflaged in a system like Evangelicalism—a useful set of moral imperatives can be used to transform and make laudable such things as jealousy and cold-heartedness. When the system fails, an individual is left with an uncomfortable amalgam of self-righteousness and despair. Moreover, in this case, Fanny, for all her "goodness," has no means of helping Edmund to deal honestly with his problems, for her own desires are too much involved.

The play episode takes its course and reaches its conclusion; Maria is disillusioned about Crawford and marries Rushworth. Julia goes away with them and Fanny moves to centre stage. Given every encouragement by Sir Thomas, Edmund, Mary, and later by William and Henry, Fanny reaches a position in which she should be able to bring her principles more definitely into play. Mary's sophistication has already been modified by her feeling for Edmund. In a crucial episode she appeals to Fanny for help; she shows herself to be moving slowly towards an acceptance of the life which Edmund could provide for her and asks for Fanny's agreement. She describes a somewhat modified version of the life she might expect, and the possible enjoyment of country pleasures which she has before derided, saying "One need not envy the new Mrs. Rushworth with such a home as *that*" (3:210).

Fanny is unable to make any relevant response to this. We all recognize this situation. When we do not want to discuss the real subject introduced by our interlocutor, our best escape is to repeat the last remark, however irrelevant. This is what Fanny does—"Envy Mrs. Rushworth!" Her reply is meaningless in context—a refusal to discuss the matter. A chance to influence Mary, to turn her from her corrupt city ways to rural innocence—a dominant theme in *Cœlebs*—is missed. Of course it is. Fanny does not *want* Mary to reconcile herself to the life of the wife of a country parson, and therefore the conversation takes a totally different course, and one more acceptable to Fanny. By the end of the exchange Mary has shifted back to the contemplation of more magnificent enjoyments at Maria's grand establishment in London. The irony of this passage is clear—again silence, the approved female virtue, is used for unworthy motives. Fanny treats Henry's efforts at improvement in the same way. At Mrs Grant's dinner (3:246) Sir Thomas perceives her behaviour as "so proper and modest, so calm and uninviting"; but for the reader it is a rigid determination to do nothing to encourage Henry to find a home near Mansfield or to change in any other respect.

For all her piety she cannot give either Mary or Henry the benefit of any doubt, or credit for changing feeling. Once polluted, always polluted. The kind of religion that Edmund and Fanny have tried to practise serves no moral purpose—it produces at best confusion (Edmund) and at worst a chill intolerance aggravated by intellectual dishonesty (Fanny). Her "proper" behaviour simply cloaks a quite understandable and human desire, but not one that would be at home in an Evangelical novel—to get rid of the Crawfords and have Edmund all to herself again.

During the run-up to the ball, we are shown Fanny's grip on her moral code slipping even further; she is dominated by one thing only—her feeling for Edmund—and all tolerance and charity go out of the window. Her reaction to the gift of the necklace is wary and suspicious (3:260), and when she receives the chain from Edmund, in her haste to exclude the Crawfords from her relationship with both William and Edmund, she falls into real insensitivity to other people's feelings. She wishes to return the necklace because it is "not wanted." She tries to soften her response by suggesting that, since it was originally a gift from her brother, Mary would clearly prefer to keep it. Her suggestion shows the extent of her moral muddle; Edmund himself is shocked and immediately straightens her out; it almost seems as if he has kept a greater hold on charity and loving-kindness than Fanny for the very reason that his Evangelical principles are weaker: "She must not suppose it not wanted, not acceptable at least; and its having been originally her brother's gift makes no difference, for as she was not prevented from offering, nor you from taking it on that account, it ought not to affect your keeping it" (3:263).

After this episode, in which Edmund clearly shows the strength of his feeling for Mary, Fanny is described as trying hard to "regulate" her feelings by recourse to duty and prayer, in the kind of self-examination so central to the Evangelical system. This she signally fails to do, and the episode is described with all the charm of "Nature and Probability":

> She would endeavour to be rational, and to deserve the right of judging of Miss Crawford's character and the privilege of true solicitude for him by a sound intellect and an honest heart.
>
> She had all the heroism of principle, and was determined to do her duty; but having also many of the feelings of youth and nature, let her not be much wondered at if, after making all these good resolutions on the side of self-government, she seized the scrap of paper on which Edmund had begun writing to her, as a treasure beyond all her hopes.
>
> (3:265)

In fact, Fanny succeeds only temporarily in accepting what seems to be the inevitable; as the time of the ball approaches and she knows that Edmund is at the Parsonage talking to Mary, she relapses into depression, only managing to cheer up when poor Edmund comes dispiritedly back after a tiff with Mary about his approaching ordination which seems to have ended all his hopes. Fanny is positively glad—"She had felt nothing like it for hours" (3:270). Though understandable in the circumstances, this is hardly the reaction of the exemplary heroine. Tony Tanner says: "We are used to seeing heroes and heroines confused, fallible, error-prone. But Fanny always thinks, feels, speaks, and behaves exactly as she ought."[20] Fanny, however, behaving as she does in accordance with nature rather than principle, is very "error-prone." She forgets all about sharing Edmund's pain and disappointment, and is caught up in her own joy at the likelihood of Miss Crawford's final banishment—"Now, every thing was smiling" (3:270).[21] Does this look like "that higher species of self-command, that just consideration of others" which we have been told earlier that *Julia* lacks? Fanny has all of the faults denied by Tanner, and frequently falls into ordinary human error; but unless the reader can stand back from her point of view here, the moral subtleties implied in the sequence of events and conversations, and in Fanny's internal discourse, may be missed.

The ball over, and the three young men temporarily absent, Mary again tries to engage Fanny's sympathetic attention.

She is sorry for her behaviour to Edmund about his ordination—"She wished such words unsaid with all her heart" (3:286); she misses him sorely and is worried about his protracted absence and jealous of the daughters of the family with which he is staying. Again we see her softened and ready for a radical change of attitude. Here is a soul to be saved, but Fanny once more fails to overcome her own desires and take the opportunity, confining herself to the shortest possible answers. As Mary tries to prise some reaction, Fanny is forced into an acknowledgment that she does not think him likely to marry one of the "Miss Owens"—or, she hopes, anybody. She is clearly preoccupied with this new danger. Her response is guarded and unsatisfactory (3:287-89). She will do nothing to encourage Mary, nor—more important—will she help in any way to make her more fit, in her terms, to be Edmund's wife. Quite naturally and humanly she would prefer Mary to remain hardened in her materialism and therefore unacceptable to Edmund. The kind of selfless love which would enable her to devote herself to Mary's improvement for Edmund's sake—surely more in line with the ideals of *Cœlebs*—is quite alien to Fanny. Moreover, she is alarmed enough at Mary's suggestion to question Edmund about the Miss Owens on his return (3:355).

* * *

Henry's decision to marry Fanny provides a slightly different demonstration of Mary's change of heart. Here the reader, not Fanny, is supposed to approve the material disinterestedness of Mary's response; a girl who only a short time ago would not have anyone "throw themselves away" is observed supporting Henry's determination to do exactly that. It may be that she is influenced by a feeling that it will now be easier for her to do what *she* really wants—to marry Edmund—but that, too, betokens a changing attitude. At this point she has clearly decided against materialism.

Austen continually reminds us that it is Fanny's love for Edmund which is the main motive for her determined rejection of Crawford and her dislike and fear of Mary. She can hardly tell Edmund this; in her conversation with him about it, "avoiding a direct answer," she uses Crawford's behaviour at the time of the play to explain her rejection (3:348-49). She does the same with Mary; she will neither love Mary nor tolerate Henry because, she convinces herself, they are irredeemably *corrupt*; this makes it possible for her to believe that her feelings are independent of her strong wish to banish the Crawfords and have Edmund once again all to herself. But they are not, and her internal discourse betrays how unsubtle—even crude—is her real state of mind—"If Mr. Crawford would but go away! … go and take his sister with him" (3:311). We have the support of the narrator that Fanny is wrong both about herself and about the Crawfords; Edmund has returned, and his hopes have revived; he has been able to rid himself—"nobody could tell how"—of "the doubts and hesitations of her ambition." Fanny believes that Mary will now accept his offer. She muses: "and yet, there were bad feelings still remaining which made the prospect of it most sorrowful to her, independently—she believed independently of self" (3:367). The interpolation of "she believed" here must indicate a doubt, even in her own mind. The next sentences of Fanny's internal discourse accuse Mary of something which is at this juncture also applicable to herself: "In their very last conversation, Miss Crawford, in spite of some amiable sensations, and much personal kindness, had still been Miss Crawford, still shewn a mind led astray and bewildered, and without any suspicion of being so; darkened, yet fancying itself light" (3:367). There is an ironical dimension to this, and to emphasize its message the narrator's voice interrupts, addressing "older sages" who might at this point justly impugn the total enlightenment of Fanny's own mind:

> Experience might have hoped more for any young people, so circumstanced, and impartiality would not have denied to Miss Crawford's nature, that participation of the general nature of women, which would lead her to adopt the opinions of the man she loved and respected, as her own.—But as such were Fanny's persuasions, she suffered very much from them, and could never speak of Miss Crawford without pain.
>
> (3:367)

This authorial comment strongly enjoins a view of Fanny as biased in her estimate of Mary by her own interest, and the Crawfords as redeemable.

But Fanny is to be tested again—can she become the ideal female, who can set aside her own desires for the good of others, who can be really fair and just in her judgments, or will she continue to be "astray"? She goes to Portsmouth and is there taught a bitter lesson. While she is accusing Mary in her mind of having "learnt to think nothing of consequence but money," she herself is having to learn how dependent upon ease, refinement, and money is the kind of morality she wants to practise. She has great difficulty in maintaining the proper respect for her parents under conditions of privation to which she is not accustomed. And one aspect of her visit shows her mind to be as "astray" as Mary's—her project to save Susan, her sister. In their different ways both Susan and Mary may be regarded as victims of a defective moral and social education, but Fanny sees Mary's mind as "polluted," and therefore unchangeable, while Susan is simply "far from amiable" and a proper subject for reform. Again her attitude is a disguise for her real wishes. She has no vested interest in keeping Susan in her present unamiable state. When Susan asks for advice, she gives it without stint (3:397). How different from her attitude to Mary! Partly as a result of Fanny's refusal to build on Mary's incipient change of heart, Mary has lapsed into materialism and triviality in London. Henry's efforts are also rejected; on his visit to Portsmouth he tries to interest Fanny in his management of his estate, actually asking for her advice.

She refuses to give it, with as chill a reply as it is possible to imagine:

> "I advise!—you know very well what is right."
>
> "Yes. When you give me your opinion, I always know what is right. Your judgment is my rule of right."
>
> "Oh, no!—do not say so. We have all a better guide in ourselves, if we would attend to it, than any other person can be. Good bye; I wish you a pleasant journey to-morrow."
>
> (3:412)

At the end of the novel Henry's failure to go to Everingham is presented as the result of weakness and vanity; but we can if we choose remember that Fanny had the chance to encourage him and did not do so. Fanny is not altogether innocent; though "without guile" she is not harmless, representing as she does an inflexible system which has little room for generosity and which gives her every opportunity for self-deception. An enthusiastic response to Henry's plans might have given him the final incentive to do the right thing. Instead, he goes to Richmond. The stage is set for the catastrophe.

The well-known first sentence of the last chapter of ***Mansfield Park*** is apt to distract our attention from the second, which is this: "I quit such odious subjects as soon as I can, impatient to restore every body, not greatly in fault themselves, to tolerable comfort, and to have done with all the rest." It should be noted that the words are "not greatly in fault," *not* "completely innocent," and these people are to be restored not to great happiness but to "tolerable comfort." That is all that anybody enjoys in the end, and this comfort is built on the wreck of most of Sir Thomas and Lady Bertram's hope in their fine family. The language of the dénouement conveys a sense of picking up the pieces: nobody has got quite what he or she wanted—except Fanny, and even she must always remember that she is Edmund's second choice, and that he would have married Mary, faults and all, if events had fallen out differently. We are reminded of the ideal, alternative ending in the last pages:

> Would he [Henry] have deserved more, there can be no doubt that more would have been obtained; especially when that marriage had taken place, which would have given him the assistance of her conscience in subduing her first inclination, and brought them very often together. Would he have persevered, and uprightly, Fanny must have been his reward—and a reward very voluntarily bestowed—within a reasonable period from Edmund's marrying Mary.
>
> (3:467)

This is a vision of redemption for everyone, which was not to be fulfilled. Who, then, is to blame? On the face of it, it is Henry, but Fanny bears much of the responsibility—for her rejection of Crawford's last appeal is the pivot upon which the novel finally turns towards its calamitous conclusion. And yet, any expectation that she could single-handedly push events in a different direction is unreal. This is why, in spite of everything, she does not come across as a monster of selfishness. Her principles, though rigid, are not strong; her code of good conduct will not bear the pressure of circumstances; but none of this is her fault; she is a victim, not a villain. The fact that Austen chose not to cast Fanny as redeemer shows that her aim was to give the lie to Evangelical certainties, which would have allowed a conventionally happy ending, involving selfless renunciation on the part of Fanny and varying degrees of reformation in all the others. Such things do not happen.

Mansfield Park does not, then, accommodate itself to early nineteenth-century moral and political reaction but can be seen as a serious challenge to its increasing reliance on a system—Anglican Evangelicalism—which made moral and social responsibility a simple matter of duty, quietism, and example, taking far too little account of the complexity of human affairs. The fact that this challenge is presented so obliquely allows it to be overlooked if the reader dwells only on the novel's surface structure. As Sir Thomas contemplates the wreck of most of his hopes, he takes responsibility for it and creates a mood of optimism as the novel closes; but the reader is conscious of the fact that he has no solution to the question of the moral education of those who are *not* "born to struggle and endure," but to enjoy unlimited ease and luxury; or indeed to any of the other intractable problems of human motive and desire the novel has identified and from which no one—certainly not Fanny—has been able to escape. No single answer is offered, but the attentive reader is left in no doubt, in terms of the story, as to the ultimate inadequacy of the "practical piety" of William Wilberforce and Hannah More.

Notes

1. Tony Tanner, ed., *Mansfield Park* (London: Penguin Books, 1966), Introduction, p. 8; Robert A. Colby, "*Mansfield Park*: Fanny Price and the Christian Heroine" in *Fiction with a Purpose: Major and Minor Nineteenth-Century Novels* (Bloomington: University of Indiana Press, 1967), pp. 66-104; Avrom Fleishman, *A Reading of "Mansfield Park": An Essay in Critical Synthesis* (Baltimore and London: Johns Hopkins University Press, 1967), p. 46; Kenneth Moler, *Jane Austen's Art of Allusion* (Lincoln: University of Nebraska Press, 1968; reprinted, Landmark, 1977), p. 146; Bernard Paris, *Character and Conflict in Jane Austen's Novels: A Psychological Approach* (Brighton: Harvester Press, 1978) p. 49; Nina Auerbach, "Jane Austen's Dangerous Charm—Feeling as One Ought about Fanny Price" in Janet Todd, ed., *Jane Austen: New Perspectives* (New York and London: Holmes and Meier, 1983) pp. 208-23.

2. Marilyn Butler, *Jane Austen and the War of Ideas* (Oxford: Clarendon Press, 1975; reprinted, with new

Introduction, 1987), pp. 248-49; Park Honan, *Jane Austen: Her Life* (London: Weidenfeld and Nicholson, 1987), p. 339; Claudia L. Johnson, *Jane Austen: Women, Politics and the Novel* (Chicago: University of Chicago Press, 1988), pp. 94-120; Oliver MacDonagh, *Jane Austen: Real and Imagined Worlds* (New Haven and London: Yale University Press, 1991), p. 12; Roger Gard, *Jane Austen's Novels: The Art of Clarity* (New Haven and London: Yale University Press, 1992), p. 136.

3. Isobel Armstrong, *Jane Austen: "Mansfield Park"* (London: Penguin Books, 1988), p. 99. In section 3 of this critical study, Armstrong surveys the balance of views on Jane Austen's conservatism (pp. 95-104).

4. R. W. Chapman, ed., *Jane Austen's Letters* (Oxford: Oxford University Press, 1964), pp. 486-87, 402. References are to this edition.

5. See Peter Garside and Elizabeth McDonald, "Evangelicalism and *Mansfield Park*," *Trivium* 10 (1975) 34-50. This summarizes the seminal text of Evangelicalism, William Wilberforce's *Practical View of the Religious System of Professed Christians in the Higher and Middle Classes in this Country Contrasted with Real Christianity* (London: Cadell and Davies, 1797). See also Leonore Davidoff and Catherine Hall, *Family Fortunes* (London: Hutchinson, 1987), pp. 81-95 and Oliver MacDonagh, chap. 1, passim, for accounts of Anglican Evangelicalism. Marilyn Butler sees the movement as partly supported by the aristocracy ("History, Politics, and Religion" in *The Jane Austen Handbook with a Dictionary of Jane Austen's Life and Works,* ed. J. David Grey [London: Athlone Press, 1986], p. 104), but most of its leaders, though rich, were rather short on ancestry and much involved in respectable trade. Hannah More, for instance, was very much a self-made woman; see my essay "Ann Yearsley and the Clifton Records," *Age of Johnson* 3 (1990), 311.

6. Hannah More, *Cœlebs in Search of a Wife, Comprehending Observations on Domestic Habits and Manners, Religion and Morals* (London: T. Cadell and W. Davies, 1808). References are to this edition.

7. Davidoff and Hall point out the contradiction I refer to in their discussion of More's message in *Cœlebs*: "On the one hand she confined women to the sphere of the private and domestic, on the other she argued for the central importance of women's influence in nurturing morality in an amoral world" (p. 171).

8. See especially *The History of Tom White the Postilion*: "He soon found out that there was some meaning in that text which says, that *Godliness hath the promise of the life that now is, as well as of that which is to come*: for the same principles which make a man sober and honest, have also a natural tendency to make him healthy and rich."

9. Sheila Kaye-Smith and G. B. Sterne, *Talking of Jane Austen* (London: Cassell, 1943), p. 108; Q. D. Leavis, ed., *Mansfield Park* (London: Macdonald, 1957), p. xii.

10. Fleishman, p. 22; David Monaghan, "*Mansfield Park* and Evangelicalism: A Reassessment," *Nineteenth-Century Fiction* 3 (1978), 215-30. This essay surveys the critical work on *Mansfield Park* from 1943 to 1978, noting the disagreements and fine distinctions among treatments of Austen's attitude to Evangelicalism; Colby, p. 85.

11. Butler, "History, Politics, and Religion," pp. 190-208, esp. p. 206: "Fleishman argues that Austen cannot be considered an Evangelical because the details of Edmund's ordination do not fit current Evangelical precept. This is to miss the underlying goal of the movement. ... The novel unmistakably refers to a range of issues that the contemporary reader would identify as Evangelical . . . nonresidence; family worship; private self-examination; slavery . . . and amateur acting"; MacDonagh, chap. 1.

12. Johnson, p. 120; Gene Koppel, "The Role of Contingency in *Mansfield Park*: The Necessity of an Ambiguous Conclusion," *Southern Review* 15 (1982), 306-13.

13. Fleishman, pp. 68-69.

14. Koppel, p. 310; Johnson, p. 119.

15. Austen must have overcome her repugnance and read *Cœlebs*; there are more oblique allusions than can be attributed to coincidence.

16. *The Novels of Jane Austen,* ed. R. W. Chapman, 5 vols (London: Oxford University Press, 1960), 3:25-26. References are to this edition.

17. See Butler, *Austen and the War of Ideas,* p. 223n2. Butler sees this as "genuinely objective concern for the horse"; another reading suggests that, on the contrary, Fanny does not really know herself at this time.

18. See Garside and McDonald, where attention is drawn to Fanny's impotence during this episode (p. 229).

19. Paris, p. 53. Paris cites a number of incidents which reveal Fanny as anything but perfect; but he regards these as almost accidental on the part of the author. He suggests that "the combination of mimetic characterization, comic action and moral theme poses artistic problems which may be insoluble" (p. 19). The implication is that Austen made Fanny more complex than she intended.

20. Tanner, p. 8.
21. Paris notes this inappropriate euphoria also occurring at the end of the novel, when Fanny returns to Mansfield from Portsmouth (p. 60).

Douglas Murray (essay date 1997)

SOURCE: Murray, Douglas. "Spectatorship in *Mansfield Park*: Looking and Overlooking." *Nineteenth-Century Literature* 52.1 (1997): 1-26. Print.

[*In the following essay, Murray uses the Claude glass, a type of mirror whose tinted lenses could obscure some colors of a landscape and enhance others, as a way of understanding the characters of* Mansfield Park. *According to Murray, Austen's characters seek pleasurable experiences by selectively choosing their frame of reference and excluding others, which he calls "selective spectatorship." Though Fanny's scope widens through the course of the novel, Murray contends that she ultimately regresses to selectiveness.*]

One of the strangest—but most revealing—items of paraphernalia carried by the fashionable tourist in search of the picturesque was the Claude glass.[1] This device came in two forms. Sometimes, Claude glasses were sets of colored lenses—gray, blue, yellow—through which travelers could view landscape. Countryside thus mediated would immediately recall a painting by Claude Lorrain, with its characteristic "harmony and tenderness of tints."[2] Perhaps more frequently, the Claude glass was a mirror such as Thomas Gray used in his travels: "a Plano-convex Mirror of about four inches diameter on a black foil, and bound up like a pocket-book."[3] The device immediately rendered countryside into "pictures": into images seen from a single point of view, with a frame—either rectangular or oval—determined by the shape of the glass or mirror, and with a single tonality of color contributed by the mirror or filter.

It is easy to grant such a device the low aesthetic status of the Polaroid camera, and no doubt better effects were produced—though more slowly and painstakingly—by pen or pencil sketches or watercolors. But the oddity and simplicity of the Claude glass should not obscure that it functioned much as the more exalted picturesque drawing, sketch, or watercolor. All these media render scenes aesthetic through arrangement, selectivity, and exclusion. The camera or glass focuses toward and on certain features—and disregards and ignores others. And the resulting images assist the traveler in controlling and possessing—at least momentarily—the countryside. The beauties of nature are appropriated and taken away, at least in the mind's eye.

It might seem odd to begin a discussion of Jane Austen's ***Mansfield Park*** (1814) with a description of Claude glasses, for no one in the novel mentions them, and we have no evidence that Austen traveled with a set. Nonetheless, the Claude glass provides a pertinent, useful introduction to Austen's most troublesome novel, for most characters in the novel are perennially engaged in a process that recalls the device: they are on the prowl for pleasing visual experiences, and they tend to achieve these experiences by framing and exclusion. Fanny Price is as guilty of selective spectatorship as anyone: she carefully cuts and frames her experiences and memories. She begins to see more fully—and to be more fully seen—when she enters the public places of Portsmouth, but by the end of the novel she can become a heroine only by not seeing the distresses of others; she retreats (Austen regretfully reports) to old habits.

Readers of ***Mansfield Park*** have long recognized the importance of aesthetic issues in the novel. Its "improvers" of property have long been the subject of critical scrutiny and, generally, displeasure,[4] and every reader agrees that the visit to Sotherton Court announces many of the novel's preoccupations. It is now a critical commonplace that every reader must beware of those in the novel who go through the Northamptonshire and Norfolk countryside uprooting trees and replacing buildings—or at least dreaming of doing so.

The usual charge made against the "improvers" is that they do not show proper respect for the traditions embodied in preexistent buildings and landscape. It is argued that they do not recognize that a country seat, like the library at Pemberley, is the work of many generations. They, like the Whigs in Dryden's *Absalom and Achitophel* (1681), want to tinker with the kingdom, "To change Foundations, cast the Frame anew."[5] According to many readers of the novel, Austen disapproves of such changes; it is assumed that they remind her of the worst excesses of the French Revolution.

Such wholesale condemnations of the "improvers," however, cannot be sustained. First, Jane Austen was an "improver" herself, writing approvingly to her sister Cassandra of the changes being made at the Steventon Rectory in a letter of 27 October 1800: "Our Improvements have advanced very well;—the Bank along the *Elm Walk* is sloped down for the reception of Thorns & Lilacs; & it is settled that the other side of the path is to continue turf'd & be planted with Beech, Ash, & Larch."[6] The Austen women's move in 1807 to the Castle Square house in Southampton was accompanied by "alterations & improvements" in the house and garden (***Letters*** [***Jane Austen's Letters***], p. 119; 8-9 February 1807); some of the projects—such as clearing away borders "to receive Currants & Gooseberry Bushes" (p. 119)—are quite complex.

Second, Austen does not condemn all improvement in ***Mansfield Park*** but rather distinguishes between desirable and undesirable alterations.[7] For example, attentive readers might applaud Henry Crawford's plans to reorient Edmund's Rectory at Thornton Lacey. Its "entrance and principal rooms"[8] currently face the north, ensuring that they would receive no sun for six months of the year and that every opening of the door would admit both guests and the north wind. But Henry advocates a new orientation to the east, where the sun is better and "where," as he says, "the view is really very pretty" (p. 218). Henry continues with excellent horticultural advice, suggesting a "new garden . . . sloping to the south-east"—"which will be giving it the best aspect in the world"—and a new hedge on the north, thus protecting the Rectory from the harshest of the winter blasts. It is true that Henry's sound advice derives from mixed motives: he desires not only the comfort of the inhabitants of the house but also an announcement of their status. But his advice is generally excellent nonetheless, since he follows the advice of Pope in the "Epistle to Burlington" (1730-31): "To build, to plant, whatever you intend . . . / In all, let Nature never be forgot. . . . / Consult the Genius of the Place in all."[9]

Edmund quickly repulses most of these improvements, and we can safely conclude that Fanny, as usual, agrees with her mentor (pp. 219-20), but we have no reason to believe that Jane Austen endorses their inertia. Austen, in contrast, is able to distinguish between good and bad "improvements," and it is easy to determine the principles on which her judgments are based. In ***Mansfield Park*** those "improvements" that she questions and satirizes are those that shield and occlude, that—like a Claude glass—screen characters from realities that the author would prefer them to confront. For example, in "improving" the Rectory at Mansfield, the late Revd. Mr. Norris and his lady planned that they "should have carried on the garden wall, and made the plantation to shut out the churchyard" (p. 48). This change has been put in place by the present incumbent, Dr. and Mrs. Grant. The suggestion that anyone, most particularly a clergyman, should wish to exclude views of the church and churchyard—salutory reminders of morality and mortality—arouses our most intense suspicions. Similarly, the most significant—and disturbing—changes that have been made at Sotherton Court are exclusions. The chapel itself has almost completely been occluded. Once a place of daily family prayers, now it is viewed only on the infrequent tours of the house: note that Mrs. Rushworth barely knows her lines.

The suspicious alterations that Henry Crawford suggests at Thornton Lacey are exclusions as well. He wishes to exclude images of farmwork and the lower social classes: he recommends "the removal of the farm-yard," which he labels a "terrible nuisance" (p. 219). And, he says, "the farm-yard must be cleared away entirely, and planted up to shut out the blacksmith's shop" (p. 218). Note that these suspect "improvements" are the very ones that Edmund endorses: as he says, "the farmyard must be moved" (p. 218). Thus Edmund is as implicated in cutting and framing as Henry Crawford is. The theme of "improvements" undoubtedly commands importance in ***Mansfield Park***; but instead of providing a simple method of dividing characters into the bad "improvers" and the good conservatives, as has often been assumed, this motif indicts everyone in the novel; all characters in ***Mansfield Park*** live by evasion.

Austen's characters associate "improvement" with Humphry Repton (1752-1818; see ***Mansfield Park,*** p. 47 and passim), and they—and Austen—might have learned about the exclusionary nature of picturesque aesthetics from Repton's work itself.[10] Often Repton, like Henry Crawford and Edmund Bartram, recommended hiding reminders that great country seats had originally been working farms. His before-and-after designs for Harleston Hall, sometimes considered the model for Mansfield Park,[11] demonstrate that Repton recommended the removal of old farm buildings (here replacing them with Palladian stables). As Repton wrote in his commentary on these images, "the House . . . formerly . . . was encumbered by stables and farm yards."[12] At Harleston, Repton also planted a large lawn over the old approaches to the house (thus making much longer the distance by road from the foreground prospect point to the house), and he eradicated the practical wooden stile (which controlled the wanderings of wild and farm animals).[13]

The best-known pair of images from Repton's pen, included as a summation and advertisement of his aesthetic in his *Fragments on the Theory and Practice of Landscape Gardening* (1816), are the two versions of the "View from my own cottage, in Essex." These drawings illustrate Repton's aesthetics with particular clarity. Here Repton's proposed high hedge and extension of the foreground are devices intended to shield. By a profusion of roses, he hides the local butcher's shop. Thus the viewer is insulated from the sight of workers or any unpleasant reminders of the true nature of food production. Repton hides or—worse—sends away the lame, half-blind beggar, undoubtedly a soldier injured in Britain's defense during the recent wars with France. Has this veteran, now unemployed in the postwar economic depression, been hidden in the local poorhouse or merely sent to beg in another parish? Repton allows the view of distant carriages—no doubt as patriotic reminders of England's superior post and transportation systems and no doubt to draw the eye down the road attractively, invitingly winding in the distance. But he excludes the view of nearby carriages: presumably the aesthete walking on Repton's exclusive lawn has no desire to see distinctly the sort of coach passenger who can only afford to travel atop the vehicle. Note that, in the "improvement," Repton has annexed a portion of the public roadway. As he wrote in *Fragments,* the house "stood originally within five yards of a broad part of the high road; this area was often covered with droves of cattle, of pigs, or geese. I obtained leave to remove the paling twenty yards farther from the windows; and by this Appropriation of twenty-five yards of Garden, I have obtained a frame to my Landscape" (p. 235). Repton, of course, is unconcerned that his frame is secured by appropriating ground formerly held in common.[14]

Similar modes of overlooking characterize spectatorship in ***Mansfield Park.*** Characters typically love to overlook while looking, both in their aesthetic experiences and in their moral and social lives as well. The Bertram family habitually wears Claude glasses when, for example, looking toward the issue of slavery. Jane Austen herself undoubtedly knew that the wealth of many great houses such as Mansfield Park derived from the work of slaves. Several Austen relatives owned plantations, one of her brothers saw service in the Caribbean, two of her brothers married into the planter class, her father tutored heirs of plantations, and she had friends among the ruling families of Antigua and Jamaica.[15] She must have realized that it was only through vagueness and evasion that such sources of wealth can be discussed at all. For example, Sir Thomas travels to Antigua, as the narrator tells us, "for the better arrangement of his *affairs*" (p. 28; emphasis added); "*Unfavourable circumstances* had suddenly arisen," causing "*very great uncertainty*" (p. 33; emphasis added). To many readers, such deliberately, ostentatiously vague language has suggested Austen's lack of interest in business and public affairs. Instead, such deliberate occlusion is radically intentional and transcribes the dominant verbal—and moral—evasiveness at Mansfield Park. Life in the English country house can only be possible if inhabitants do not see slaves laboring in the fields or hear their sad complaints.

Fanny, of course, is the one character in the novel who mentions slavery, and for doing so she deserves our praise, though she does so in a remarkably ineffectual and tentative manner. We should not conclude too quickly, however, that on all subjects she sees life clearly and sees it whole, for she wears Claude glasses as often as anyone in the novel. She aestheticizes places by cutting and framing. On the way to Portsmouth she forgets her inattentive mother and father and paints a pretty picture of herself in Portsmouth "in the centre of such a circle, loved by so many, and more loved by all than she had ever been before" (p. 336). Austen probably excuses Fanny here, for Mansfield Park has not treated her well by insisting that she marry Henry Crawford against her will. Within a dozen pages, however, Fanny has busily retouched her memories of Mansfield itself: with amazing swiftness she recalls that "in her uncle's house there would have been … an attention towards every body which there was not here [in Portsmouth]" (p. 348)—though, of course, the most recent attention she had been receiving had been unstinting advice to marry against her better judgment. All during the Portsmouth visit Fanny "could think of nothing but Mansfield, its beloved inmates" (p. 357)—including, presumably, the inattentive Bertram sisters and the publicly cruel Mrs. Norris.

Readers of ***Mansfield Park*** can cite other passages where Fanny renders scenes or characters beautiful by omission or denial. She claims to "have great pleasure in looking at" Mary Crawford (p. 56), but she can do so only by momentarily silencing her moral objections and by refusing to acknowledge her jealousy. It is also arguable that Fanny aestheticizes in the famous scene in which she overlooks Edmund teaching Mary how to ride: Fanny tries to enjoy the scene as something akin to a painted conversation piece in a rural setting. The scene, after all, would produce a fine painting: in its background is "a view of the parsonage and all its demesnes, gently rising beyond the village road"; in its foreground is the "happy party" in the meadow (p. 60). But, once again, Fanny can pretend to enjoy only by refusing to acknowledge her feelings of loneliness, desertion, and jealousy (pp. 60-61).

Fanny most cunningly—perhaps most selfishly—reviews and avoids in the famous beginning of the last chapter of the novel. Austen prepares us for Fanny's final acts of omission by mentioning herself for the first time in the text; she performs her own acts of exclusion: "Let other pens dwell on guilt and misery. I quit such odious subjects as soon as I can" (p. 420). These lines have been cited approvingly as evidence of Austen's irrepressible good—or frivolous—spirits, or as evidence of haste, as if she could not bear to finish so unpleasant a story as this ironic endorsement of conservative values.[16] Coming as this statement does after analogous acts of exclusion, I see in it Austen's announcement that closure to her complex novel requires multiple acts of evasion; she herself must put on Claude glasses to wrest a happy ending out of such unpromising material.

Austen continues in one of the most remarkable passages in the novel:

> My Fanny indeed at this very time, I have the satisfaction of knowing, must have been happy in spite of every thing. She must have been a happy creature in spite of all that she felt or thought she felt, for the distress of those around her. She had sources of delight that must force their way. She was returned to Mansfield Park, she was useful, she was beloved; she was safe from Mr. Crawford, and when Sir Thomas came back she had every proof that could be given in his then melancholy state of spirits, of his perfect approbation and increased regard; and happy as all this must make her, she would still have been happy without any of it, for Edmund was no longer the dupe of Miss Crawford.
>
> (p. 420)

Note that Fanny's happiness depends on ignoring the unhappiness, the "distress," the "melancholy" of others; she is happy, as the narrator apprehensively puts it, "in spite of every thing." The insistent reiteration of the pronoun "she"—it appears nine times in the paragraph—indicates that Fanny's triumph can be considered such only from a single perspective, her own: "*She* had sources of delight that must force their way. *She* was returned to Mansfield Park, *she* was useful, *she* was beloved; *she* was safe from Mr. Crawford" (emphasis added). Austen further discredits her heroine by following this paragraph about Fanny's happiness[17] with a paragraph about Edmund: "It is true," the new paragraph begins, "that Edmund was very far from happy himself" (p. 420). And if Edmund is unhappy, what of the defeated, exiled characters—Mrs. Rushworth or Mrs. Norris? Even those remaining at Mansfield Park have little to celebrate: the "poor" and "melancholy" Sir Thomas (p. 420), now feeling "bitterly" (p. 422) and "wretchedly" (p. 423); the disgraced Lady Bertram; and the diminished Tom, now safe because he—like Mr. Rochester in *Jane Eyre*—has been disempowered through illness.

Austen does not lead us to hope that, in the future, inhabitants of Mansfield Park will rise to wider vision or sympathy. As Fanny's sister Susan travels to her new residence, toward a house of sickness and disgrace, accompanied by her cousin Edmund, who was "evidently suffering under violent emotions," she is surprisingly *happy*: as the party leaves Portsmouth, "Susan's face wore its broadest smiles. . . . Sitting forwards, however, and screened by her bonnet, those smiles were unseen" (p. 406). Susan is not an anomaly in ***Mansfield Park.*** She reenacts its principal mode of spectatorship: she makes up and inhabits a private heaven despite the misery of others. And her close bonnet[18]—allowing, even encouraging both blinkered vision and solitary enjoyment—symbolizes the novel's dominant modes of looking and overlooking.[19]

* * *

Though Fanny Price is one of literature's most habitual spectators, she does not relish the gaze of others turned upon her. Through most of the novel she is so nearly invisible that Margaret Anne Doody has playfully suggested that she died as a child and that it is her ghost, rather than a living girl, who haunts the novel.[20] When we first see her she is "shrinking from notice" (p. 9), the verb suggesting both physical withdrawal and gradual diminishing. At family discussions she turns "into the window" (p. 101), almost disappearng into curtains and window recesses. For much of the book, she, as at Sotherton Court, "was left, . . . watched . . . and listened" (p. 87), catching telling fragments of conversation. In addition to being nearly invisible, she is inaudible: at first she "could scarcely speak to be heard" (p. 10).[21] The great house does nothing to draw her out: as Edmund tells her, "*here,* there are too many, whom you can hide behind" (p. 23). Austen suggests that Fanny fears visibility more than cruelty. When Mrs. Norris calls Fanny "a very obstinate, ungrateful girl . . . considering who and what she is" (p. 133), Fanny does not react to this statement as cruel and unfair: what affects her is "to be called into *notice* in such a manner" (p. 135; emphasis added). Like Anne Eliot in ***Persuasion,*** Fanny feels that she "can never be important to any one" (***Mansfield Park,*** p. 22).[22] Also like Anne, she gradually takes on increased visibility with praise. When Edmund tells her that "there is no reason in the world why you should not be important where you are known," she "*colour*[*s*] at such praise" (p. 22; emphasis added). Austen here employs, to be sure, the worn cliché of the modest female blushing, but she also suggests increased visibility with increased attention: the ghost takes on flesh.

Unfortunately for Fanny, taking on flesh, moving into adulthood, and "coming out" are rituals that require being seen. She most fears the male sexual gaze turned upon her, "the very aweful ceremony of walking into the drawing-room," of having men such as Henry Crawford there "to observe her" (p. 201). When Edmund relays his father's observations on Fanny's "figure" (p. 178)—or is this *his* recognition of her sexual power transferred to his father?—she turns away, indicating the threat that that embodiment holds for her.

Fanny's much-discussed horror of appearing on the stage must be considered a manifestation of this fear of visibility. Since the time of Lionel Trilling, Fanny's firm "no, indeed, I cannot act" (p. 131) has been read as her highest moment of moral fortitude. To many readers Fanny becomes the noble Platonist rejecting the illusions of the stage,[23] perhaps even Jesus Christ rejecting the kingdoms of this world. Fanny is indeed a principled character, but we must acknowledge that part of her hesitancy derives from a simpler motive: from her desire not to be seen. When the pressure of the young Bertrams and the Crawfords is upon her, when she begins "to feel that almost every *eye* was upon her" (p. 132; emphasis added), her cry "I really cannot act" is as much a desire for invisibility as an indicator of moral fortitude.

Fanny is perpetually in hiding, and it is surely significant that her most rhapsodic utterances are spoken in praise of places of concealment and darkness. The chapel that she so fervently recalls from Walter Scott's *Lay of the Last Minstrel* is " 'blown by the *night* wind of Heaven' " (***Mansfield Park,*** p. 77; emphasis added). The avenue at Sotherton Court for whose fate she expresses such fear would of course provide shade from the sun and prying eyes (p. 50). Her favorite garden features seem to be shrubberies, as in her unexpected paean at the Grants' Rectory: "The evergreen!—How beautiful, how welcome, how wonderful the evergreen!" (p. 188). At Mansfield Park she rhapsodizes over night and "the deep shade of the woods": "Here's what may leave all painting and all music behind, and what poetry only can attempt to describe" (p. 102). It is also significant that being "in a hot sun" (p. 65) gives Fanny a headache, for the sun—all-seeing, all-illuminating—makes possible the visibility that she finds so painful.

* * *

Despite its heroine in love with concealment, ***Mansfield Park*** is in fact one of the most plein air of Jane Austen's fictions, demonstrating its author's knowledge of the "public spheres" of the Enlightenment: that is, those places and media that made possible and encouraged the free circulation of people, information, and ideas during the early modern period.[24] The novel interests itself in up-to-date communication, belying Austen's reputation—still prevalent in some quarters—as a shy, retiring spinster unaware of the world around her.

News sometimes travels in the novel by old-fashioned means, such as by word of mouth: Mary Crawford's harp "was seen by some farmer, and he told the miller, and the miller told the butcher, and the butcher's son-in-law left word at the shop" (pp. 51-52). But newer methods of commercially distributed information figure prominently as well. Newspapers are particularly important. Henry Crawford has been in the habit "for many years" (p. 209) of subscribing to the newspaper "esteemed to have the earliest naval intelligence" (p. 210), and this journal publishes news of William Price's promotion. Late in the novel another newspaper brings to Portsmouth communication of Henry's elopement with Maria Rushworth (pp. 400-01). "Gossip" columns, with their coy but easily penetrable inclusion of initials, ensure that "private" scandals quickly become public information; as the paper itself says, it announces its news "to the world" (p. 401). These columns serve a disciplinary function by urging readers to "cut" public offenders—those who have violated marriage, society's chief arrangement for its continuity and for the orderly transfer of property. Such columns function efficiently in the novel, much as disciplinary stocks and branding had functioned in past eras.[25] If news travels efficiently in ***Mansfield Park,*** physical travel is sometimes still a problem—but not an insurmountable one. At the very beginning of the novel we learn that England has an efficient mechanism to transport an unaccompanied ten-year-old the considerable distance from Portsmouth, on the south coast of England, to Mansfield Park in Northamptonshire (pp. 5-6).

Though Fanny gathers with delight any public information about her brother, she avoids public places through much of the novel. As we have seen, balls distress her, largely because of the possiblity of sexual gazes being directed at her. Though she speaks well, she does not cultivate the alert exchanges that characterized the enlightenment public sphere of the coffeehouse or salon; she is no Elizabeth Bennet. Her conversation, as Pam Perkins says, is "stilted, exclamatory."[26] In fact, the only public place in which Fanny flourishes is the church, and it is no accident that she wishes to become the wife of a clergyman. But note that Fanny's allegiance is to the *rural* church, attended by a stable, familiar, homogenous population. Edmund and Fanny have nothing kind to say about urban congregations, which attract "crowds" (pp. 83-84). Fanny finds "chapel" services bearable in Portsmouth because it is customary there for men and women to sit apart (p. 372).[27]

During her sojourn in Portsmouth, however, Fanny finds herself often in public, away from the protective shrubberies of Mansfield Park. She—surprisingly—walks "on the ramparts" (p. 372) in broad daylight. Fanny's sojourn in Portsmouth offers experiences consonant with the name of the town: Portsmouth is, of course, a "port"—simultaneously a temporary home and a place from which one launches explorations. It is also a "mouth," locus of speech and taste, of exchange between inner and outer, public and private. As a port, the meeting place of water and land, it is a place of margins, of possible transformations, for both Fanny and Henry Crawford.

Readers of the novel have too often painted Portsmouth as defective, dirty, and noisy, in contrast to the calm of Mansfield Park.[28] Purveyors of such critical commonplaces do not sufficiently discriminate between the Price household and Portsmouth itself. Most of these critical commonplaces derive from Fanny herself, a source of doubtful reliability. When she most misses Mansfield, she remembers—with dubious accuracy, as we have seen—"its beloved inmates, its happy ways. … At Mansfield, no sounds of contention, no raised voice, no abrupt bursts, no tread of violence was ever heard; all proceeded in a regular course of cheerful orderliness; every body had their due importance; every body's feelings were consulted" (p. 357). In Portsmouth, Fanny looks back with sorrow at her "present exile from [the] good society" of Mansfield (p. 358)—though that society included the dull Dr. Grant and Mr. Rushworth, the licentious Bertram sisters (quarreling like Goneril and Regan over Henry Crawford), and the dangerous Crawfords themselves.

In point of fact Portsmouth is by no means completely bad for Fanny. It serves to remind us that she had not always been so passive. William recalls her childhood energy there: "We used to jump about together many a time, did not we? when the hand-organ was in the street? I am a pretty good dancer in my way, but I dare say you are a better" (p. 226). These lines suggest that the vibrant young Fanny could indeed have become another Elizabeth Bennet. On the trip to Portsmouth, Fanny's demure demeanor warms: "Of pleasent talk between the brother and sister, there was no end" (p. 341).

It is true that, in Portsmouth, Fanny's parents do not seem to merit her respect (p. 354), and she finds herself barely noticed by her father upon her return (pp. 344-45):

> With an acknowledgement that he had quite forgot her, Mr. Price now received his daughter; and, having given her a cordial hug, and observed tht she was grown into a woman, and he supposed would be wanting a husband soon, seemed very much inclined to forget her again.
>
> (p. 346)

This meeting is quite rightly held against Mr. Price. But we should note that his ignorance of Fanny does not much differ from that of Sir Thomas. That Sir Thomas does not know that Fanny sits in the cold schoolroom surely indicates that he had not visited it for years, not since the time his own daughters left off receiving instruction. Mr. Price's comment about Fanny's marriageability finds a parallel in

Sir Thomas's attention to Fanny's "figure" (p. 178). Since Sir Thomas's supposedly avuncular comment on Fanny's physical development shades into erotic connoisseurship, perhaps Mr. Price's inattentive matter-of-factness is preferable after all.

Once Fanny is settled in Portsmouth she makes decisions, takes control. Within the disorderly Price household she chooses to befriend and cultivate Susan. She settles quarrels between younger siblings. She organizes space to create a room for independent activities: "By degrees the girls [Fanny and Susan] came to spend the chief of the morning up stairs" (p. 363). And more significant, Fanny ventures, with considerable success, outside of the Price's small house. She subscribes to a circulating library: "She became a subscriber—amazed at being any thing *in propria persona,* amazed at her own doings in every way; to be a renter, a chuser of books! And to be having any one's improvement in view in her choice! But so it was. Susan had read nothing, and Fanny longed to give her a share in her own first pleasures" (p. 363). Fanny takes part in the circulation of knowledge: she receives, she sends forth to her sister. By spending her money, she circulates currency as well as ideas. She supports booksellers and authors through the entrepreneurial middleman of the circulating library. She takes on a legal identity, renting *in propria persona.*

The climax of Fanny's participation in public life in Portsmouth is her Sunday-afternoon walk on the ramparts of the town (pp. 372-73), ramparts that, according to Samuel Lewis's *Topographical Dictionary of England* (1844), "afford extensive views."[29] This walk is introduced as Mrs. Price's "public place; there she met her acquaintance, heard a little news, talked over the badness of the Portsmouth servants, and wound up her spirits for the six days ensuing" (***Mansfield Park,*** p. 372). The key phrase here is "public place": this is no darkened chapel, no landscaped park of arching trees and dense shrubbery, no rural parish church, not even a quiet circulating library. At Portsmouth Point one encounters the full tide of human existence:

> . . . there were enjoyments in the day and in the view which would be felt.
>
> The day was uncommonly lovely. It was really March; but it was April in its mild air, brisk soft wind, and bright sun, occasionally clouded for a minute; and every thing looked so beautiful under the influence of such a sky, the effects of the shadows pursuing each other, on the ships at Spithead and the island beyond, with the ever-varying hues of the sea now at high water, dancing in its glee and dashing against the ramparts with so fine a sound, produced altogether such a combination of charms for Fanny, as made her gradually almost careless of the circumstances under which she felt them.
>
> (pp. 372-73)

Despite the attentions of Henry Crawford (who is walking between the two Miss Prices "with an arm of each under his" [p. 372]), Fanny does not feel his gaze—or the pressure of his arm—to be uncomfortable. She does not fear the gaze of other promenaders. For the first time, in fact, Fanny participates without pain, without self-consciousness, in the system of public gazes that characterizes the Enlightenment. Her pleasure does not derive from excluding part of the scene: all is spectacle, and she herself is happy to be a part of it. Here is no evergreen shrubbery behind which one can hide. The bright sun—her enemy in the Mansfield garden—becomes a source of beauty, varying the "hues of the sea" (p. 373). This is the first time Fanny has waxed enthusiastic over a daytime scene. Beauty here is not motionless, like the fallen trees in Cowper's poem *The Task* or the distant stars in the cold night sky, but all is "dancing" and "dashing." The sea in the distance is wild and sublime—note the sounds of the waves—but alive with human spirit and activity in the form of ships, for Portsmouth was a very busy harbor, "the general rendezvous where all ships either homeward or outward bound take convoy, and frequently 700 merchantmen have sailed at one time from Spithead" (*Topographical Dictionary,* III, 580). Austen's evocation of the harbor looks as if the Portsmouth chapters were written in praise of Britain's naval and mercantile endeavors, as if she—or even Fanny Price herself—has put away her Scott and Cowper and taken Dryden's *Annus Mirabilis* or Pope's "Windsor Forest" off the shelves of the circulating library.

The phrase "combination of charms" suggests the vigorous bombardment of Fanny's senses, and the phrase "almost careless of the circumstances" suggests that this most hesitant of heroines could act impulsively. The experience draws her psychologically, romantically close to someone unlike her:

> The loveliness of the day, and of the view, he [Henry Crawford] felt like herself. They often stopt with the *same* sentiment and taste, leaning against the wall [in physical contact with the scene], some minutes, to look and admire; and considering he was not Edmund, Fanny could not but allow that he was sufficiently open to the charms of nature, and very well able to express his admiration.
>
> (p. 373; emphasis added)

The use of the phrase "charms of nature" is Austen's sly trick. Of course, this is *not* a natural scene, with the ships, crowds, and the human-ordered communication and trade with distant places. Austen uses free indirect discourse here:[30] she transcribes Fanny's thoughts, and the telling word "nature" is Fanny's. For the first time Fanny feels that the public sphere—this constructed, human world of gazing and being gazed upon—is as comfortable and natural as Cowper's glen or Mansfield's shrubbery.

At this moment it also seems natural for Fanny to be attracted to someone very unlike her. Previously Fanny, dangerously narcissistic, has looked with favor only on other versions of herself.[31] She repeatedly acknowledges that her closest bond is with her brother William, and Austen represents her reunions with him as restorations of childhood unity (see pp. 210, 213, 225). Fanny can imagine no better future than restoring this past unity and living in a nonerotic parody of marriage, in a "comfortable" "little cottage" with her brother (p. 341). Her more overtly erotic relationship is with a first cousin and, even more important, someone who has long been a substitute for William. When Fanny, at the command of the patriarchs of her family,[32] leaves Portsmouth at the age of ten (p. 9). she finds distress in the new adult world, in "rooms [that] were too large for her to move in with ease," in which "she crept about in constant terror of something or other" (p. 12). The one person at Mansfield Park who is kind to her is Edmund, and it is clear that, from the moment when he finds her "crying on the attic stairs" (p. 12), she fixes her familiar affection for William onto her cousin. By means of a psychological transference, Edmund begins, as Austen tells us, to fill the role of "William, the eldest, a year older than herself, her constant companion and friend" (p. 13). Loving Edmund provides Fanny a socially acceptable mode of loving her brother.[33] Edmund's relationship to Fanny extends further, for he is not only brother-substitute but also the sympathetic, attentive father-teacher,[34] molding her young mind, attending to the young child as her own father had not: "he recommended the books which charmed her leisure hours, he encouraged her taste, and corrected her judgment; he made reading useful by talking to her of what she read, and heightened its attraction by judicious praise. In return for such services she loved him better than any body in the world except William; her heart was divided between the two" (p. 19). With so much shared by Fanny and Edmund, it is hardly surprising when Mary Crawford tells Fanny, "you *have* a look of *his* sometimes" (p. 151).

At Portsmouth, however, Fanny for the first time finds herself comfortable with someone unlike Edmund. Such loss of self-consciousness, such loss of the inhibiting fear of the gaze, recalls one of the key images found in the work of Jean-Jacques Rousseau: the concept of liberation brought by communal spectacle and public festivity.[35] According to Saint-Preux in *La Nouvelle Héloïse* (1761), the grape-harvest festivals (the "heureuses vendanges") in the village of Clarens combine enjoyment and utility ("l'agréable à l'utile").[36] The "fête" brings the villagers together in a sweet equality: "Tout ... dans la plus grande familiarité" (p. 607), in "la douce egalité" (p. 608). Events are unscripted, improvised, avoiding the confinement and precision of ritual. Perhaps most important for Rousseau and for Austen's Fanny Price, every participant in the "fête" is simultaneously actor and spectator ("donnez les Spectateurs en Spectacle").[37] As a result, debilitating self-consciousness disperses, and hearts and minds open, symbolized by Rousseau's frequent use of sun imagery: at the beginning of Saint-Preux's description of the "vendange" the sun lifts the fog as a curtain rises to reveal a stage ("le voile de brouillard que le soleil éleve au matin comme une toile de théatre" [p. 604]), revealing a public sphere in which citizens are not afraid to see and be seen. Here and in the Portsmouth section of ***Mansfield Park,*** Rousseau and Austen share a belief (or a desire) that places should (or do) exist where visibility is not dangerous, where looking is not painful, where the complex system of illumination and gazing that was the Enlightenment could bring citizens together.

* * *

Jane Austen, like every other citizen of the Enlightenment, felt the eye of public surveillance upon her. The pressure—to substitute imagery of weight for that of sight—of being in the public eye was especially great for the young women of Austen's social class. Their persons and behavior were subject to the perpetual scrutiny of relatives and neighbors. From their early teens they were scrutinized by potential marriage partners as well. It is possible that the most penetrating, the most discriminating gazes of the Enlightenment were aimed at young women in Bath, a city Austen visited in the 1790s and later inhabited with considerable reluctance and unhappiness. The Bath years left their scars on Austen, for her creativity slowed, and a career that had begun so promisingly, with many short works and with drafts of three fine novels, appeared to come to an abrupt conclusion. Austen wrote shockingly little during the first decade of the nineteenth century.

For Austen, the gazes directed upon her by her society were intensified by her vocation as writer of fiction. From the time of ***Volume the First*** and before, her works had been subject to examination and comment by family and friends. As her work reached a larger public with the appearance of ***Sense and Sensibility*** in 1811 and ***Pride and Prejudice*** in 1813, her fiction became subject to more fearsome scrutiny by a distant, impersonal "reading public" and by professional book reviewers. It should hardly surprise us that in ***Mansfield Park*** Austen provides a nuanced, complex picture of the pain of being seen. Fanny Price, like most heroes and heroines of fiction, is a partial self-portrait of the author.

Self-portraits, of course, are not always flattering. Sir Joshua Reynolds, as Austen undoubtedly knew, painted himself with the spectacles made necessary by his near-sightedness.[38] Austen would not have wanted to present an idealized image anyway: as she memorably wrote to her niece, Fanny Knight, in March 1817, "pictures of perfection" made her "sick & wicked" (***Letters,*** p. 335). Fanny Price is a part of Austen that she herself did not like. Fortunately, Jane Austen contained more selves than Fanny. After the move to Chawton in 1809 Austen was able to rebuild her career and her confidence; she introduced her novels into the public sphere. They were successes, and we can still see in Austen's letters her deep pleasure at hearing them discussed. This pleasure—this blossoming under the gaze of the public—continued in her careful attention to her relatives' and neighbors' **"Opinions of *Mansfield Park*"** transcribed in 1814 and 1815, and later of ***Emma,*** transcribed in 1816.[39] For Austen these years must have been happy and, indeed, heady, not least because in ***Mansfield Park*** she had tried to lay a ghost to rest, a ghost of one of her past selves. In Fanny Price, Austen summons and dismisses the girl with the Claude glasses—the figure who fears to be fully seen and to see fully, the girl who thrives on invisibility and on partial vision.

Notes

1. A full description of Claude glasses—or Gray glasses, as they were sometimes called, after the poet Thomas Gray—is to be found in Malcolm Andrews, *The Search for the Picturesque: Landscape Aesthetics and Tourism in Britain, 1760-1800* (Stanford: Stanford Univ. Press, 1989), pp. 67-73. See also John Dixon Hunt, "Picturesque Mirrors and the Ruins of the Past," *Art History,* 4 (1981), 257-58.

2. Thomas Martyn, *The English Connoisseur; Containing an Account of Whatever Is Curious in Painting . . . ,* 2 vols. (London: L. Davis and C. Reymers, 1766), I, 4.

3. William Mason, *Memoirs of the Life and Writings of Mr. Gray* (1775); quoted in Thomas Gray, *Correspondence of Thomas Gray,* ed. Paget Toynbee and Leonard Whibley, 3 vols. (Oxford: Clarendon Press, 1935), III, 1,076n.

4. See Alistair M. Duckworth, *The Improvement of the Estate: A Study of Jane Austen's Novels* (Baltimore: Johns Hopkins Univ. Press, 1971): "In [Austen's] view, radical improvements of the kind Repton made were not improvements at all but 'innovations' or 'alterations' of a destructive nature" (p. 47).

5. John Dryden, *Absalom and Achitophel,* in *Poems, 1681-1684,* ed. H. T. Swedenberg, Jr., and Vinton A. Dearing, vol. 2 of *The Works of John Dryden* (Berkeley and Los Angeles: Univ. of California Press, 1972), p. 29, l. 805.

6. *Jane Austen's Letters,* ed. Deirdre Le Faye, 3d ed. (New York: Oxford Univ. Press, 1995), p. 51. Further references to this work appear in the text as *Letters.*

7. Duckworth, in *The Improvement of the Estate,* fails to distinguish between desirable and undesirable improvements: "Given Jane Austen's symbolic mode, . . . Crawford's suggestions are insidious enough. His plans to 'clear away,' 'plant up,' and 'shut out' features of the landscape are to be read as a rejection of a traditional shape of reality, while his wish to re-orient the front of the house suggests a desire for complete cultural re-orientation" (p. 52).

8. Jane Austen, *Mansfield Park,* ed. James Kinsley and John Lucas (New York: Oxford Univ. Press, 1980), p. 218. Further references to *Mansfield Park* are to this edition and appear in the text.

9. *Moral Essays: Epistle IV: To Richard Boyle, Earl of Burlington,* in *The Poems of Alexander Pope: A One-Volume Edition of the Twickenham Text,* ed. John Butt (New Haven: Yale Univ. Press, 1963), p. 590, ll. 47, 50, 57.

10. Austen was almost certainly familiar with Repton's Red Books—paired before-and-after images that he prepared for potential clients, generally in the form of ingenious drawings with moveable flaps. Austen's cousin, the Revd. Thomas Leigh of Adlestrop, called in Repton to work on his estate of Stoneleigh Abbey, and Repton, as usual, prepared one of his Red Books to illustrate his proposals (see Mavis Batey, "Jane Austen at Stoneleigh Abbey," *Country Life,* 30 December 1976, pp. 1,974-75).

11. Ellinor W. Hughes argued that Harleston House, Northamptonshire (now demolished; formerly Harleston Park) was the prototype of Mansfield Park ("The Last of 'Mansfield Park,'" *Times Literary Supplement,* 9 November 1940, p. 572), a view repeated by F. Alan Walbank in *The English Scene in the Works of Prose-Writers since 1700,* ed. Walbank, 2d ed. (London: Batsford, 1946), p. 8; by Dorothy Stroud in *Humphry Repton* (London: Country Life, 1962), p. 147; and by Edward Hyams in *Capability Brown and Humphry Repton* (New York: Scribner, 1971), illustrations 33-34. Duckworth writes that Harleston is "the house most frequently considered the model of Mansfield Park" (p. 51), though he suggests that Repton's set of plans for Harleston most resemble Henry Crawford's before-and-after descriptions of Thornton Lacey (p. 52). However, R. W. Chapman seems to accept Sir Frank MacKinnon's suggestion that Cottesbrooke was Austen's model (see *Jane Austen: Facts and Problems* [Oxford: Clarendon Press, 1948], p. 84).

12. Humphry Repton, *Fragments on the Theory and Practice of Landscape Gardening* (1816); quoted in "Notes on the Illustrations," in *Mansfield Park,* ed. R. W. Chapman, vol. 3 of *The Novels of Jane Austen,* 3d ed. (New York: Oxford Univ. Press, 1934, 1988), p. 552.

13. Repton's published works, which contain accounts of his projects, similarly advocate tearing down barns, stables, laundries, and even "a few miserable cottages" (*Sketches and Hints on Landscape Gardening* [London: W. Bulmer, 1794], pp. 10, 53; and Plate 4); he replaces working fields and grazing land with lakes for the enjoyment of gentlemen boaters; he drains non-picturesque ponds that merely refreshed thirsty cattle (see *Observations on the Theory and*

Practice of Landscape Gardening [London: T. Bensley, 1803], pp. 40, 208, and 179). Such improvements ensure that from a few points of view—from the landowner's drives, walks, windows, and terraces—no jarring elements intrude.

14. Awareness of the partial perspectives inherent in the picturesque has recently become a concern of readers of Wordsworth's "Tintern Abbey" (1800). Marjorie Levinson and Kenneth R. Johnston have established that this classic of Romanticism and the picturesque deliberately occludes certain social and physical realities: the presence of homeless vagrants in the woods above Tintern Abbey, who are "the casualties of England's tottering economy and of wartime displacement"; the presence of poor beggars in the Abbey itself; the crowded and noisy town and iron works active within a half-mile of the ruins; and the pollution caused by these foundries (Marjorie Levinson, "Insight and Oversight: Reading 'Tintern Abbey,'" in *Wordsworth's Great Period Poems: Four Essays* [Cambridge: Cambridge Univ. Press, 1986], pp. 29-30). See also Kenneth R. Johnston, "The Politics of 'Tintern Abbey,'" *The Wordsworth Circle,* 14 (1983), 6-14; reprinted in *Romantic Poetry: Recent Revisionary Criticism,* ed. Karl Kroeber and Gene W. Ruoff (New Brunswick, N.J.: Rutgers Univ. Press, 1993), pp. 123-38. As Levinson writes, "when one reconstructs the picture of the *place* . . . and of the poet's *particular* (state of) mind . . . , one learns that the narrator achieves his penetrating vision through the exercise of a selective blindness. By narrowing and skewing his field of vision, Wordsworth manages to 'see into the life of things.' At the same time and quite casually, so it seems, he excludes from his field certain conflictual sights and meanings—roughly, the *life* of things" (pp. 24-25). The poem's "primary poetic action is the suppression of the social. 'Tintern Abbey' achieves its fiercely private vision by directing a continuous energy toward the nonrepresentation of objects and points of view expressive of a public . . . dimension" (pp. 37-38). It is possible—and tempting—to argue that Austen, anticipating Levinson and Johnson, noted Wordsworth's omissions. Fanny Price, of course, endorses Wordsworth's "romantic" view of Tintern Abbey, as evidenced by a transparency of the structure and its surrounding scenery that "held its station" in the window of Fanny's sanctum, the East Room at Mansfield Park (*Mansfield Park,* p. 137). Meanwhile, Austen herself had encountered evidence of the "realistic" state of the Tintern region: the truth is to be found in William Gilpin's *Observations on the River Wye* (1782), a work Austen consulted in preparing her description of the Vale of Usk in *Love and Friendship* (see Austen, *Catharine and Other Writings,* ed. Margaret Anne Doody and Douglas Murray [New York: Oxford Univ. Press, 1993], pp. 76 and 314n). Gilpin's book is also one of the chief works on which Levinson and Johnson rely in researching the unpicturesque realities surrounding Tintern Abbey.

15. For helpful considerations of Austen and slavery, see Edward W. Said, "Jane Austen and Empire," in *Raymond Williams: Critical Perspectives,* ed. Terry Eagleton (Cambridge: Polity Press, 1989), pp. 150-64; Moira Ferguson, "*Mansfield Park*: Slavery, Colonialism and Gender," *The Oxford Literary Review,* 13 (1991), 118-39; Ruth Perry, "Austen and Empire: A Thinking Woman's Guide to British Imperialism," *Persuasions,* 16 (1994), 95-106. The heiress Elizabeth Newman (née Hall) to whom the "Rice Portrait" was given (or lent) in about 1817, and who presumably was a friend of the novelist, derived her fortune from plantations in Jamaica. See Margaret Anne Doody and Douglas Murray, "A Portrait of Jane Austen" (London: Privately Printed, 1995), pp. 5-6, 9-10.

16. Claudia L. Johnson commments on this passage in "Gender, Theory, and Jane Austen Culture," in Nigel Wood, ed., *Mansfield Park* (Buckingham: Open Univ. Press, 1993), p. 116: "The conclusion of *Mansfield Park* averts the guilt and misery towards which the rest of the novel has been heading."

17. Nina Auerbach, writing perceptively of Fanny's "predator's comedy," notes "Austen's pitiless repetition of 'happy'" ("Jane Austen's Dangerous Charm: Feeling as One Ought about Fanny Price," in *Jane Austen: New Perspectives,* ed. Janet Todd [London: Holmes and Meier, 1983], p. 215).

18. Susan no doubt wears the sort of "close bonnet" identified by Mary Crawford (p. 43) as appropriate for girls not yet out. Such bonnets contained extensions on each side of three to four inches, allowing smiles such as Susan's to remain unperceived.

19. My view of Susan's translation to Mansfield Park contrasts with Tony Tanner's optimism: Tanner sees Mansfield as typically taking in "fresh potential" and "raw material," then refining it (*Jane Austen* [Cambridge, Mass.: Harvard Univ. Press, 1986], p. 148). Malcolm Kelsall argues similarly (see *The Great Good Place: The Country House and English Literature* [New York: Columbia Univ. Press, 1993], p. 113).

20. See "A Regency Walking Dress and Other Disguises: Jane Austen and the Big Novel," *Persuasions,* 16 (1994), 83-84.

21. Fanny is invisible, too, when she visits Portsmouth (see pp. 343, 344, 345, 346, 348). We learn that Fanny's mother had never much valued her daughters: "Her daughters never had been much to her" (p. 355).

22. See my discussion of *Persuasion* in "Gazing and Avoiding the Gaze," in *Jane Austen's Business: Her World and Her Profession,* ed. Juliet McMaster and Bruce Stovel (Basingstoke: Macmillan, 1996), pp. 42-53.

23. See Trilling, *The Opposing Self: Nine Essays in Criticism* (New York: Viking Press, 1955), pp. 218-20; and Tanner, *Jane Austen,* pp. 162-63.

24. My discussion of the public sphere, like many current discussions of the Enlightenment, is indebted to Jürgen Habermas's *The Structural Transformation of the Public Sphere: An Inquiry into a Category of Bourgeois Society* (*Strukturwandel der Öffentlicheit* [1962]), trans. Thomas Burger with Frederick Lawrence (Cambridge, Mass.: MIT Press, 1989).

25. Mr. Price's violent response to the article—"I'd give her the rope's end as long as I could stand over her" (p. 401)—is merely a strong version of the response to adultery that his society expects and finds "proper."

26. "A Subdued Gaiety: The Comedy of *Mansfield Park,*" *Nineteenth-Century Literature,* 48 (1993), 6. Perkins interestingly argues that Fanny embodies sentimental comedy, which does not encourage wit and sparkle.

27. Presumably the Prices attend the garrison chapel, which "once appertaining to the monastery of *Domus Dei,* [had] been thoroughly repaired, for the use of the officers and soldiers of the garrison" (Samuel Lewis, *A Topographical Dictionary of England . . . ,* 4 vols. [London: S. Lewis, 1844], III, 580).

28. The demonization of Portsmouth is a commonplace of Austen criticism. For Lionel Trilling in *The Opposing Self* Portsmouth is "what we mean by vulgarity" (p. 225). To Alistair Duckworth in *The Improvement of the Estate,* it is "a Hobbesian state of incivility" (p. 77). Malcolm Kelsall in *The Great Good Place* calls Portsmouth "vulgar, common, uncultured" (p. 113). See also Tony Tanner, *Jane Austen,* pp. 145-48. My discussion of Portsmouth below differs greatly from theirs, for they find in the novel a celebration, as Trilling would have it, of "security, . . . fixity and enclosure, a refuge from the dangers of openness and chance" (p. 210). The public sphere in the Enlightenment, and Portsmouth in *Mansfield Park,* do not exemplify the qualities that Trilling praises. In my view, Austen's favorable depiction of Portsmouth, the site of the Royal Naval Academy, anticipates rather than contradicts her later praise of the Navy in *Persuasion.*

29. According to Lewis, "the view of the town from Portsdown Hill, combining an infinite variety of objects of the deepest interest, is strikingly magnificent. The fortifications, which are the most complete in Europe, combine beauty with strength. . . . The harbour, which is unrivalled for capaciousness and security, is about 250 yards broad at the mouth, and, expanding into a broad open lake, extends for several miles to the north, affording shelter to ships of the largest burthen" (*Topographical Dictionary,* III, 579-80).

30. In free indirect discourse, a technique used frequently by Austen, the author transcribes a character's thoughts without direct commentary. In *Mansfield Park* this technique is exemplified in the passage early in the novel when Fanny observes Edmund and Mary Crawford riding her horse (pp. 60-61).

31. For psychological accounts of the relation between Edmund and Fanny, see Glenda A. Hudson, *Sibling Love and Incest in Jane Austen's Fiction* (New York: St. Martin's Press, 1992), pp. 35-50; and Barbara Rasmussen, "Discovering 'A New Way of Reading': Shoshana Felman, Psychoanalysis and *Mansfield Park,*" in Wood, ed., *Mansfield Park,* pp. 121-55; and Misty G. Anderson, "'The Different Sorts of Friendship': Desire in *Mansfield Park,*" in *Jane Austen and the Discourses of Feminism,* ed. Devoney Looser (New York: St. Martin's Press, 1995), pp. 170-71.

32. As Rasmussen suggests (p. 143), Austen here anticipates Jacques Lacan's theory that the "nom de pere" wrenches the child from the unity of childhood experience into an uneasy recognition of selfhood.

33. See Claudia L. Johnson, *Jane Austen: Women, Politics, and the Novel* (Chicago: Univ. of Chicago Press, 1988), pp. 116-18, for a discussion of Austen's treatment of incest in the novel.

34. Enlightenment fiction provides many examples of eroticized teacher-pupil relationships. See the relationships between Harriet Byron and the title character in Richardson's *Sir Charles Grandison* (1753-54), between Julie and Saint-Preux in Rousseau's *La Nouvelle Héloïse* (1761), and between Miss Milner and Dorriforth in Elizabeth Inchbald's *A Simple Story* (1791).

35. The importance of public festivals in Rousseau received important attention in Jean Starobinski, *Jean-Jacques Rousseau: La transparence et l'obstacle* (Paris: Gallimard, 1971), pp. 110-21. Starobinski calls the "fête idéale l'une des images-clés de l'œuvre de Rousseau" (p. 117). Jacques Derrida also considers this theme in *Of Grammatology* (*De la Grammatologie* [1967]), trans. Gayatri Chakravorty Spivak (Baltimore: Johns Hopkins Univ. Press, 1974, 1976), pp. 302-9. Of course, in *Mansfield Park* Fanny generally avoids public spectacles, not only amateur theatricals

but also Christmas observances: "Fanny had no share in the festivities of the season" (p. 30).

36. *Julie, ou la Nouvelle Héloïse,* in vol. 2 of *Œuvres Complètes de Jean-Jacques Rousseau* (Paris: Gallimard, 1961), p. 604.

37. *Lettre à M. D'Alembert,* in vol. 5 of *Œuvres Complètes* (Paris: Gallimard, 1995), p. 115.

38. See *Reynolds,* ed. Nicholas Penny (New York: Harry Abrams, 1986), pp. 320-22.

39. Brian C. Southam provides these dates in Austen, *Minor Works,* ed. R. W. Chapman, vol. 6 of *The Works of Jane Austen* (New York: Oxford Univ. Press, 1954, 1988), p. 431.

Sue Parrill (essay date 2002)

SOURCE: Parrill, Sue. "*Mansfield Park.*" *Jane Austen on Film and Television: A Critical Study of the Adaptations.* Jefferson: McFarland, 2002. 80-106. Print.

[*In the following essay, Parrill surveys the major television and film adaptations of* Mansfield Park, *pointing out the most effective and ineffective aspects of each rendition.*]

Following the popular ***Pride and Prejudice,*** Jane Austen published ***Mansfield Park*** (1814). Critic and recent editor of the novel Claudia Johnson calls it "Austen's most controversial novel" (Introduction xii). Certainly it is different from the more "light and sparkling" ***Pride and Prejudice,*** but Austen was confident that it would be well received and unhappy when it was not. One of the problems with the novel for the modern reader is its protagonist. Fanny Price is modest, retiring, decorous, and prudish. Moreover, she is said to be physically unattractive and weak. Except for her stubborn resistance to Sir Thomas Bertram's insistence that she marry Henry Crawford, she is essentially passive. She waits patiently for the man she loves to realize that he loves her. ***Mansfield Park*** is also the least witty and satiric of Austen's novels. Fanny herself is without humor, and Mary Crawford, the only character who is full of wit and clever repartee, is unsympathetic.

Until recent years, modern critics (Trilling 136, Duffy, Mudrick 157) characterized Sir Thomas Bertram as an honorable man—one who has high principles and good intentions. Although he made mistakes in the raising of his children and in his harshness with Fanny, he has been called the only really admirable father in Austen's novels. During the 1980s and 1990s, critics (Johnson, *Jane Austen* 107; Fleishman 7-8; Lew 283; Kirkham 117; Said 87; Stewart 113) pointed out that Sir Thomas is a slave-owner and that the prosperity of Mansfield Park depends on the labor of slaves on his Antiguan plantation. They found his values warped by his connection with slavery and found even his mistreatment of Fanny connected to his ownership of slaves.

The protagonist of the novel is Fanny Price, the impoverished niece of Sir Thomas's wife, who is sent to Mansfield Park to enjoy the advantages of being associated with this prominent, wealthy family. As usual in Austen's novels, ***Mansfield Park*** is about money and social status. Although Fanny's mother, Mrs. Norris, and Lady Bertram are sisters, they represent three different social levels, defined chiefly by money. Lady Bertram is the wife of a baronet and mistress of a grand estate and large income. Fanny's mother married a common Lieutenant of Marines and has an income of only 400 pounds with which to sustain a large family. Mrs. Norris became the wife of a clergyman with the living at Mansfield Park worth 1000 pounds. After her husband's death, she is much at Mansfield Park. Although all contact between Lady Bertram and Mrs. Price has ceased, Mrs. Norris convinces Sir Thomas to bring ten-year-old Fanny Price to live at Mansfield Park. Although Mrs. Norris declines the financial responsibility for Fanny, she willingly undertakes to keep Fanny in a position subordinate to the Bertram sons and daughters. Among the Bertram children, only Edmund, the younger son, is sympathetic and helpful to Fanny. She comes to love him more than anyone, except perhaps her favorite brother, William.

In Chapter Three, Sir Thomas sails for Antigua, with his elder son, Tom, to look after affairs in his holdings there, leaving Edmund and Mrs. Norris in charge. When he finds that he cannot return by the end of a year, he sends Tom back to England. By the summer of the following year, Fanny is eighteen. In July, Mary and Henry Crawford come to pay a visit to their sister, Mrs. Grant. Dr. Grant had taken over the living at Mansfield Park after the death of Mr. Norris. Thus, two attractive and eligible young people enter the limited society of Mansfield Park. Maria Bertram, the elder daughter of the house, has recently become engaged to Mr. Rushworth, who has a fine estate and 12,000 pounds a year. However, when Henry Crawford comes on the scene, both Maria and Julia are attracted to him. Mary comes to Mansfield Park intending to make a marital play for Tom Bertram, but when Tom shows more interest in his horses than in her, she finds herself attracted to Edmund. Through much of the narration up to this point Fanny has little part. Edmund arranges for her to have a horse to ride, and although she is left out of the dances and parties which the others attend, she is present at Mansfield Park when the Crawfords visit and is included in an outing to Sotherton, Mr. Rushworth's estate. She is in the background, observing and listening, but too humble to feel slighted at her neglect. She watches as Edmund and Mary grow more attracted to each other, and as Henry Crawford flirts with both sisters.

When Tom convinces the others that they should put on a play, Fanny and Edmund speak against the enterprise. After Edmund defects to the other side, Fanny alone resists the pressure to take part in the play. She thinks that Sir Thomas would not approve of these theatricals and she sees that Henry Crawford, for whom the play provides opportunities for flirting with Maria, is coming between Maria and her fiancé. Meanwhile, Julia feels jealous and rebuffed. Lady Bertram and Mrs. Norris are oblivious to these emotional currents, the former too indolent to take notice and Mrs. Norris wholly concerned with economy and management.

At this point, Sir Thomas returns home. He sets out to banish all signs of the theatricals and to restore his house to its original state. When Henry Crawford announces that he is going to Bath, Maria realizes that he is not really interested in her. She urges her father to allow her to marry Rushworth within a few weeks. After the newlyweds and Julia leave Mansfield Park, Fanny begins to receive more of Sir Thomas's attention. He had commented on the day that he returned that she had improved in looks. Mary Crawford also turns to Fanny for companionship. When Henry Crawford returns to the parsonage, he decides to amuse himself by making Fanny fall in love with him.

When Fanny's brother William returns to England from sea duty, Sir Thomas invites him to Mansfield Park. Noticing Henry Crawford's interest in Fanny and wishing to compliment Fanny and William, Sir Thomas decides to give a ball in their honor. Edmund, meanwhile, is conflicted because Mary Crawford does not see herself as the wife of a practicing clergyman. Fanny sees with distress that Edmund would like to marry Mary Crawford. Henry, having perceived that his best way to Fanny's favor is by getting preferment for her brother, manages to acquire a second lieutenancy for William. With this news in hand, he proposes to Fanny, who is delighted at William's promotion, but astonished and displeased at the proposal.

The next day, Henry tells Sir Thomas of his desire to marry Fanny. Pleased with this news, Sir Thomas goes to Fanny's room to give his permission to the match. He is amazed and angry when Fanny refuses to marry Henry. Mindful that Henry has already helped William and is wealthy enough to assist others in her family, he accuses her of selfishness and ingratitude. This match is far above what she might be expected to make. Even Edmund urges Fanny to accept Henry. She tells him that she objects to Henry's character and mentions his careless behavior toward Maria. Edmund decides that Henry has been too precipitous in his suit but feels that if he persists he will succeed. He convinces his father to give her time. Sir Thomas agrees, but he sends Fanny home to Portsmouth with William, thinking that she will soon tire of the privations of her home and better appreciate what Henry has to offer.

Once Fanny is home she finds herself little valued in her parents' home, a place where confusion and noise reign. Her mother is much like Lady Bertram in her inability to manage anything, except having children. She does not discipline her children or control her servants. Fanny's father makes coarse jokes at Fanny's expense or ignores her. Fanny sorely misses the order and decorum of Mansfield Park.

About four weeks after Fanny has come to Portsmouth, Henry Crawford appears at the family's dwelling. After a visit of two days, Fanny begins to see him in a more favorable light than before. He is kind and considerate to her family and seems to have reformed his morals as well. He also has the advantage of reminding her of the world of Mansfield Park, which she misses.

Fanny now expects to be sent for around Easter, but letters from Mansfield Park report that Tom has been brought home very ill and that Edmund is tending him. Mary, apparently not desolate at the possibility of Tom's death, writes to assure Fanny that Henry is faithful to her. Then Mary sends a letter warning Fanny not to believe any rumors she may hear about Henry. She hears no more until her father reads from a newspaper that Mrs. Rushworth has run off with Henry Crawford. She is shocked and horrified, but not surprised that Mary would prefer that the affair be hushed up. Fanny worries about the impact on Sir Thomas and Edmund. Then she receives a letter from Edmund telling that Julia has eloped with Mr. Yates. Edmund plans to come after Fanny immediately and invites her sister, Susan, to come to Mansfield Park, as well.

At Mansfield Park, Fanny learns the whole story of Maria's affair and the elopement with Henry Crawford. Edmund, meanwhile, realizes that Mary Crawford's morals are defective. He tells Fanny that Mary looks upon the affair as merely an indiscretion and that the detection of the affair is what she laments. She thinks that if Henry can be convinced to marry Maria, all may yet be smoothed over.

The novel concludes with Tom's recovery and reformation, Julia's contrition and reconciliation with her father, Sir Thomas's realization of his errors in raising his daughters, Mrs. Rushworth's going into seclusion with only Mrs. Norris as her companion, and finally Edmund's realizing that he has loved Fanny all the time. Sir Thomas gladly consents to their marriage, realizing that Fanny is the daughter that he had wanted. After Mr. Grant's death, Edmund and Fanny end up at the parsonage at Mansfield Park.

The first adaptation of the novel, based on a screenplay by Ken Taylor, was produced by ITV for BBC television in 1983. It was directed by David Giles, who has made several mini-series based on adaptations of literary classics for the BBC, including *Sense and Sensibility* (1971). In November 1999, another adaptation was released by Miramax, first to theatres in the United States, and in April 2000, to theatres in Great Britain. This film was written and directed by Canadian director Patricia Rozema. In spite of some rather sensational subject matter, the film was a financial failure and received mixed critical reviews. Most Janeites were horrified at the very thought of this most moral of novels being made into a film which exhibited nudity and emphasized slavery, drug use, and madness.

Sylvestra Le Touzel plays Fanny Price in the 1983 BBC adaptation. Le Touzel continues to perform on British television, as in the BBC's *Vanity Fair* (1998). Reading about this physically unattractive heroine in the novel is not painful for the reader, who forgets about her unattractiveness and focuses on her thoughts and actions. But to have to watch a really plain actress portray a character whose primary virtues express themselves in resistance rather than action verges on torture. This is the case with Le Touzel. She is small, she is plain, and she has no physical grace. She even affects some small nervous mannerisms. Amanda Root, who plays Anne Elliot in the 1995 *Persuasion,* is not a beautiful actress, but she has charisma, and even projects a kind of beauty toward the end of the film. Le Touzel acquires some curls toward the end, but these are not enough to compensate for a crooked nose and a square chin. Let's face it. Television and film are visual media. The choice of Sylvestra Le Touzel for the role of Fanny was fatal to the success of this adaptation. Ironically, the child who played Fanny as a ten year old (Katy Durham-Matthews) was pretty, and it is unlikely that she would have grown up to look like Le Touzel.

The other characters are generally well-cast, but with no really outstanding performances. Nicholas Farrell plays Edmund Bertam with a kind of strong-jawed resoluteness. Farrell has had a lengthy and respectable acting career. He was in *Chariots of Fire* (1981), performed in several BBC productions of Shakespeare's plays (e.g., played Horatio in the 1996 *Hamlet*), and appeared in 2001 in the big Hollywood production *Pearl Harbor.* His character is actually more appealing on film than it is in the novel. Robert Burbage plays Henry Crawford appropriately as a Regency dandy. At one point he wears a pink top hat and a pink waistcoat under a pale gray suit. He is affected in manner and does a lot of posing. Anna Massey is convincingly obnoxious as Fanny's Aunt Norris. Bernard Hepton plays a rather young looking Sir Thomas Bertram. (Hepton may be recalled as playing Emma's hypochondriac father in the BBC's 1995 *Emma.*) The witty Mary Crawford is well portrayed by Jackie Smith-Wood, who is far easier to look at than Le Touzel. Maria Bertram is played by another actress familiar in Austen adaptations—Samantha Bond—who plays Miss Taylor, Emma's former governess, in the 1996 A&E *Emma.*

In dramatizing ***Mansfield Park,*** Ken Taylor followed the story-line of the novel closely. For many Janeites, this faithfulness to the novel makes up for other deficiencies. The liberties which Patricia Rozema, as director and writer, took with the novel have incurred the wrath of this coterie. One must bear in mind, of course, that Rozema's film, at about 112 minutes, is much shorter than the television mini-series, which ran serially for about 261 minutes, but the omission of much of the content of the novel is by no means their chief complaint. Rozema has, to use her own term, "reinterpreted" the novel (DVD Commentary). In this reinterpretation she has been much influenced by recent critics, such as Claudia Johnson, who have emphasized the importance in the novel of the issues of slavery and the oppression of women, particularly as they relate to the character of Sir Thomas Bertram and his treatment of Fanny Price. Rozema sets the film clearly in the context of a specific social and political milieu—the chief events of the story-line occurring in 1805 and 1806.[1] She said that she is just pointing out social and political realities which would have been obvious to contemporary readers (DVD Commentary). The BBC mini-series, on the other hand, focuses mainly on the costumes and manners of the times. A comparison of the two versions is revealing about two entirely opposite approaches to adaptation and to filmmaking.

Rozema's *Mansfield Park* opens with young Fanny (Hannah Taylor-Gordon) about to leave her home in Portsmouth to go to Mansfield Park. We see her pregnant mother (Lindsay Duncan) with a child in her arms (Rozema's infant) and five other young children around her telling Fanny goodbye. Young Fanny is poorly dressed and her hair disheveled. She asks her mother to write to tell her when she is to come home, but her mother turns away, not answering.[2] This child-actress, with her big dark eyes, conveys well Fanny's uncertainty and unhappiness as she realizes that she has been given away. However, in keeping with Rozema's recreation of Fanny's character, we see even in young Fanny a bright intelligence. Indeed, the film begins with Fanny telling her sister Susan a story of her own invention. In contrast, in the BBC mini-series, young Fanny is well-dressed, in a red cloak and a hat, and too shy to speak unless spoken to.

Mansfield Park's house and grounds are also presented differently in the two adaptations. Rozema used Kirby Hall in Northhamptonshire for both the exterior and some of the interior scenes of the Bertrams' great house. This mansion dates from the Elizabethan period and thus is not the "modern" house mentioned in the novel. The house is imposing, but its disrepair enabled Rozema to suggest that the Bertram family fortunes are on the wane. She said that she wanted to show something "grand and majestic, but worn and faded" (DVD Commentary). The set design for the interior of the house also gives the impression of coldness and age. Furnishings are minimal, and the floors and walls are mostly bare. When Fanny takes her first tour of the house, she walks up bare stone stairs and down bare halls, finally ending up in what looks like an attic storage room, full of castoff furniture and toys. The BBC adaptation, on the other hand, presents a beautifully furnished and decorated interior. This style is much more in the "heritage" tradition, with careful attention given to period decor. The exterior of the house is of the "Adam"[3] style, which would corroborate the novel's statement that the house was "modern." Unlike most of the other BBC adaptations, many scenes are filmed out of doors. Obviously, more money has been spent on the production of this mini-series than the BBC spent on mini-series in the 1970s, yet the outdoor scenes are filmed with little design rather than to permit opportunity for characters to walk and to converse in a variety of settings.

The Miramax film exploits the outdoors for both beauty and symbolism. In one particularly evocative scene, as Fanny and Edmund come back to the house when Tom Bertram is desperately ill, Mansfield Park appears with the early morning fog enveloping it like a shroud. It is a scene of beauty, yet of foreboding. Another scene of spectacular beauty is an aerial shot showing the chalk cliffs near Durdle Door, with a tall ship just off shore.

In the Miramax version, Fanny arrives at Mansfield Park at 5:00 a.m. and waits in the darkness until Mrs. Norris (Sheila Gish) comes to take her inside. Tom Bertram, who was drinking on a balcony when Fanny arrived, had told the coachman to leave her there. Sir Thomas Bertram (Harold Pinter) welcomes Fanny, and when Mrs. Norris reveals that she has no intention of taking Fanny into the parsonage, Sir Thomas reconciles himself to keeping Fanny at Mansfield. Mrs. Norris gladly accepts his charge that she never let Fanny forget her second-class status at Mansfield Park. In both versions, he states that Fanny is inferior to his own children and he wants her to be aware that she is not their equal. In the BBC version, he expresses this opinion out of Fanny's hearing, but in the Miramax version she hears him say this while she stands in the hall outside the room where Sir Thomas is talking to Mrs. Norris, his wife, and daughters. Thus, it is established that Fanny understands her status from the beginning. In both versions, Mrs. Norris assures Sir Thomas that there is no danger that his sons will see Fanny as other than a sister.

An important difference between the two versions is that Rozema has made Fanny a budding writer, a young Jane Austen. Claudia Johnson asserts that Rozema's film "[. . .] gives us what many of us love about Austen in the first place, what other movies never deliver: Austen's presence as a narrator" (*TLS* 16). Often, as Fanny reads to Edmund or speaks in voiceover what she has written, we hear passages taken from Jane Austen's juvenilia. For example, when the film opens, young Fanny is reading to her sister from a story she has written. The story comes from Austen's ***Love and Freindship*** (sic), but Rozema has combined parts of sentences and omitted passages. In Austen's story, in **"Letter the 13th,"** Sophia is "majestically removing" (that is, stealing) a bank note from Macdonald's desk drawer when Macdonald catches her in the act. Sophia chides him for interrupting her and denies that she was stealing anything (*MW* [*Minor Works*] 96). Her friend Laura (not Eliza) is not present at this time. In the film, Fanny reads:

> . . . and just as Eliza was majestically removing a fifty pound note from the Drawer to her own purse, we were suddenly, most impertinently interrupted by old Macdonald himself. We called up all the winning dignity of our sex to do what must be done: Sophia shrieked and fainted and I screamed and instantly ran mad. For an Hour and a quarter did we continue in this unfortunate situation—Sophia fainting every moment and I running Mad as often.

Rozema has drawn some of this material from a passage occurring later in Letter 13, in which Laura and Sophia see their husbands lying dead in the road. This passage reads in part:

> Sophia shreiked (sic) and fainted on the Ground—I screamed and instantly ran mad.—.We remained thus mutually deprived of our Senses some minutes, & on regaining them were deprived of them again—. For an Hour and a Quarter did we continue in this unfortunate Situation—Sophia fainting every moment and I running Mad as often.
>
> [*MW* 99]

It is apparent from Rozema's film that Fanny is a precocious child with a head full of romance novels and an eye for the absurd. Jane Austen was apparently fifteen when she wrote ***Love and Friendship*** (***MW*** 1). Much later in the film, just before Sir Thomas informs her of Henry Crawford's marriage proposal, the mature Fanny reads aloud to herself from what she has written: "From this period, the intimacy between them daily increased till at length it grew to such a pitch, that they did not scruple to kick one another out of the window on the lightest provocation." This passage, which substitutes "they" for "the families of Fitzroy, Drummond, and Falknor," comes from Austen's ***Frederic and Elfrida: A Novel*** (***MW*** 6), which Austen wrote when she was between twelve and fifteen (***MW*** 1). Ironically, the lines which Fanny was supposed to have written at eleven and the lines which Fanny was supposed to have written at twenty-one were both written by Jane Austen as a teenager.

Rozema shows young Fanny becoming older Fanny as she reads from Austen's juvenile work ***The History of England.*** First she looks at the camera and reads: "It was in this reign that Joan of Arc lived and made such a row among the English. They should not have burnt her but they did. . . ." Following a dissolve, Fanny continues to read: "Henry the 7th. His majesty died, and was succeeded by his son Henry whose only merit was his not being quite so bad as his daughter Elizabeth." (The Fanny in this scene is seen only indistinctly, but she is older than the first speaker.) After another dissolve, Fanny (Frances O'Connor) looks at the camera and reads: "And then that disgrace to humanity, that pest of society, Elizabeth, who, Murderess and Wicked Queen that she was, confined her cousin, the lovely Mary Queen of Scots for 19 YEARS and then brought her to an untimely, unmerited, and scandalous

Death. Much to eternal shame of the Monarchy and the entire Kingdom." At this point, we also see the older (about 26) Edmund (Jonny Lee Miller[4]) for the first time. He has been Fanny's audience for her reading from her history of England.

This Fanny is also more assertive and much more physically active than the Fanny of the novel. After the child Fanny turns into a young woman, she can be seen chasing Edmund as they run downstairs toward the stables. Later, she actually rides her horse, Mrs. Shakespeare, at night in a rainstorm. There is never any mention of her feeling ill or weak. She is reminiscent of Elizabeth Bennet in the 1995 *Pride and Prejudice*—obviously in robust health and something of a tomboy. Fanny, however, is on a more familiar footing with a male friend than any of the other Austen film characters, except perhaps Cher in *Clueless.* At one point we see Fanny lying on her stomach on her bed, kicking her feet in the air, while Edmund listens to her read aloud. This scene, like many others, presents Fanny as having a twentieth century girl's ease with the opposite sex.

An important omission from the Miramax adaptation is Fanny's brother William. William is Fanny's correspondent and the dearest member of her family. He is particularly important because Henry Crawford's successful efforts to get him a commission complicate Fanny's reaction to Henry's proposal. In addition, the BBC film often has Fanny in voiceover reading the letters she writes to him, and thereby reporting events at Mansfield Park. In the Miramax version, Fanny's letters to her sister are read in voiceover to convey information to the viewer. William is also important as a reason for the ball's being given, since Sir Thomas wishes to honor both William and Fanny. In the Miramax film it is given solely for Fanny's benefit, to show her off to prospective suitors.

The issue of slavery enters the Miramax film early and pervades it. As Fanny is on her way from Portsmouth to Northhamptonshire, the coach pauses on the road overlooking a bay where a tall ship lies at anchor. She hears a plaintive song coming from the ship. The coachman says, "Black cargo" and he explains that perhaps a captain or ship's doctor is bringing some "darkies" home for his wife. This song will be heard again when Fanny is on her way back to Portsmouth and again during the credits. Rozema explains in her commentary on the DVD that the lyrics of the song, "Djongna" (slavery), tell how a young African has been taken from his home. He sees a bird and asks it to take a message telling of his plight first to his mother, then to his father and then to the elders of his village. When this song is first heard it can easily be associated with Fanny, who, like the slaves on board the ship, is being taken far from home.

In the novel slavery is mentioned only one time—Fanny tells Edmund that when she brought up the subject of slavery in the presence of the family, nobody said anything. In the BBC film, the topic is not mentioned. In the Miramax film, slavery is mentioned again when, after Sir Thomas has chided Fanny for her boisterous behavior, she tells Edmund that Sir Thomas is sorry that he ever took her in. Edmund tells her that he speaks harshly because he is troubled over "problems with the plantation." He adds, "The abolitionists are making inroads." Fanny responds, "That's a good thing, isn't it?" Edmund points out that they all live off the profits from slavery, even Fanny.[5] Edmund appears to be justifying his father's manner and even his role as a slave-owner, but in a later scene he rebukes his father for his mistaken ideas about mulattos. Rozema commented that she had intended to show Sir Thomas reading a ledger which listed the slaves who had died on the plantation, but in the final cut the viewer cannot see what he is reading (DVD Commentary).

The handling of the character of Tom Bertram (James Purefoy) in the Miramax film is also significantly different from both that in the novel and that in the BBC version. In both the novel and the BBC adaptation, Sir Thomas takes Tom into his study and chastises him for his reckless expenditures, which have caused Sir Thomas to have to sell a benefice meant for Edmund. Tom is penitent and says that he hopes to have better fortune. However, he does not intend to give up gaming and horse racing. He just hopes for better luck. In the Miramax film, Tom is not just the indulged elder son. He is also a deeply troubled young man. We have earlier seen him drinking as a teenager. On the day that Fanny arrived at Mansfield Park, Mrs. Norris points out to her one of Tom's paintings—a self-portrait showing himself holding a canvas in one hand, with his other hand palm outward to the viewer, and the figure of Death with its hand on his shoulder. When we next see Tom, he and his father are raging at each other. Sir Thomas says to him, "You will do as I say." Tom says, "And do as you do? Even I have principles, Father." As will become clear by the end of the film, Sir Thomas is to blame for his son's self-destructive and rebellious behavior. It is interesting that Tom, who has only a minor role in the novel, takes on the role of his father's conscience in this film. Edmund, who is so right-thinking in the novel and in the BBC adaptation, seems untouched by the family's ownership of slaves. The ambiguity of Edmund's attitude toward his family's ownership of slaves is problematic in the film, and makes the viewer unsure that a person so indecisive and complacent really deserves to win Fanny.

When Sir Thomas goes to Antigua to attempt to improve his income from his plantation, he takes Tom along. The BBC adaptation devotes considerable time to showing how Mrs. Norris manages to get Maria engaged to Mr. Rushworth while Sir Thomas is gone. We also see the introduction of Mary and Henry Crawford to the family, and the important episode in which Fanny, Mrs. Norris, Henry, Mary, Maria, and Julia visit Sotherton. On this outing, we see the jealous maneuvering of the two sisters to win Henry

Crawford's affection, and we hear Maria say to Henry that, although engaged to Rushworth, she anticipates feeling restrained in her marriage. She compares herself to the starling in Laurence Sterne's *A Sentimental Journey,* who laments, "I can't get out." Henry suggests that, just as they may go around the gate, to which Rushworth has the key, so may she evade the confinement of marriage.

The Miramax film omits the visit to Sotherton. However, Rozema effectively stages the introduction of the Crawfords to the bored inhabitants of Mansfield Park. When the butler announces the pair, we first see only their backs as they face the family. Then, in slow motion, at thirty frames a second instead of the usual twenty-four, Rozema shoots the reactions of Maria (Victoria Hamilton), who drops her cards, Rushworth (Hugh Bonneville), who gapes, Julia (Justine Waddell) and Lady Bertram (Lindsay Duncan), who smile widely, and Fanny, who has a quizzical look on her face. Then she shoots the Crawfords from the front. The camera tilts up to show Mary Crawford (Embeth Davidtz) from feet to head; then the camera starts at the boots of Henry Crawford (Alessandro Nivola) and tilts up his body to his face. The family is so stunned by the appearance of this elegant pair that Henry sarcastically calls them a "dreary lot." Recovering their wits, Maria and Julia both vie for Henry's attention. As the Crawfords walk back to the parsonage they discuss their visit. Henry says that he prefers an engaged woman because she is more "safe" than an unmarried girl. Mary laments that Tom, the elder son and heir to Mansfield Park, is away from home.

The film makes clear the fascination the Crawfords have for the Bertrams. The Crawfords are like aliens visiting from another world, their world being the fashionable society of Regency London. In the novel and the BBC adaptation we are told that they have imbibed in their uncle's home and from their fashionable friends a laissez-faire morality. Some critics have said that the novel is about the conflict between the town and country, and that Sir Thomas represents country virtues (Mudrick 173; Trilling 136). Edmund blames Mary's uncle for her occasional lapses of decorum. When asked about whether she knows William's captain, Mary indicates that she meets only the higher level naval officers. When she puns that she is familiar with "rears" and "vices," Edmund and Fanny are shocked. In the film, she is even more indiscreet. She plays billiards with the men, and she takes a drag from Henry's cigarillo. In the novel, she asks the question, "Who is to be Anhalt? What gentleman among you am I to have the pleasure of making love to?" (***MP*** [***Mansfield Park***] 143). The BBC adaptation places no particular emphasis on this speech, but in the Miramax version, it is a show stopper. Here Mary leans back against the billiard table and addresses this speech to the men. They react with astonishment. Rozema obviously expects the viewer to interpret "making love" as the carnal act, its twentieth-century meaning, rather than as wooing, its nineteenth-century meaning.

The costumes which the women wear in the two adaptations reflect the directors' different approaches to filming the novel. In the BBC version, Fanny's clothing is plain and unadorned, in white or pastel colors. Mary also wears mostly pastel colors, but her clothes are more elegant and more tailored. On several occasions she wears a crimson velvet spencer over her dress. Her bonnets are far more elaborate than Fanny's. We are told that the white dress that Fanny wears to visit the parsonage and that she wears to the ball is the one which she was given to wear to Maria's wedding. Neither Fanny, Mary, nor the Bertram girls, shows much décolletage. In the Miramax version, Fanny wears dark nondescript jumpers of a heavy material over long-sleeved blouses as her everyday clothing. Troost and Greenfield, citing a press release, state that Andrea Gale, the costume designer, in her choice of clothing for Fanny, "went for simplicity of dress coupled with strength" ("Mouse" 191). Fanny's clothing is in keeping with the wardrobe of a girl who is not concerned about how she looks, and her dresses are loose and full enough that she can ride her horse without changing into a riding habit. However, the dress she wears to the ball is white with embroidered flowers on it, a frock suitable for Cinderella. Indeed, the contrast between her previous clothing and this dress make her seem to be a Cinderella. It is in the empire style, with a shaped bodice and décolletage. In the scenes following the ball, Fanny continues to wear dark loose dresses, but she now shows a great deal of bosom. (Perhaps this is what is meant by "coming out," a term much discussed in the novel.) Fanny wears a form-fitting red coat and no hat when she travels to Portsmouth. Apparently, Rozema felt that hats were not appropriate for Fanny, even for traveling. Given the obsession with hats manifested by the women of the period, Fanny's hatlessness represents a significant disregard for period fashion on the part of the director.

The most striking apparel is that worn by Mary Crawford. In her first appearance at Mansfield Park she wears a mannish hat, a dark skirt, a blouse with a high white ruff, and a form-fitting long-sleeved jacket. In her two most shocking scenes (the scene in the billiard room and the scene in which the family hears of Maria's disgrace) she wears the same flowing black velvet dress—with décolletage and long perforated sleeves. She never wears pastels. Mary's apparel is darker than one would expect for 1806, when young unmarried women wore mostly light colors. The clothing of the Bertram girls is more typical of period clothing. Mary exudes sophistication and, perhaps, decadence. The women's costumes are just one more area where Rozema modernized the look of the film and attempted to suggest qualities of character through costume. She generally operated on the principle that visual impact is more important than authenticity.

In the treatment of the play we also see entirely different sensibilities and purposes at work. As usual the BBC version follows the novel closely. Tom and his friend Yates

(Charles Edwards) are the prime instigators, but Henry is also eager to act. When Henry urges Julia not to play the role of Agatha, she sees clearly that he favors Maria. Julia declares that she will not play any role. When Tom calls on Fanny to play the cottager's wife, she vehemently refuses, saying that she cannot act. Mrs. Norris chides her for not being willing to assist her cousins. Fanny has two reasons for refusing. For one thing, she does not want to exhibit herself. It is also clear in the novel and the BBC version that she agrees with Edmund that the play, Mrs. Inchbald's *Lovers' Vows,* is not suitable for them to present, especially given Maria's situation as an engaged woman. Mrs. Norris, instead of seeing the unsuitability of the play, concentrates her efforts on saving money on the green cloth that must be bought for a curtain. Lady Bertram is, as usual, swayed by whoever talks to her last. The outcome is that Edmund is too much tempted by the thought of playing a key role opposite Mary Crawford to sustain his resistance to the scheme. Fanny is uncomfortable when both Mary and Edmund come to her to rehearse their lines, forcing her to become a reluctant observer of their courtship.

Reviewers were agog over what they interpreted as lesbian overtones in the Miramax film, particularly in the scene in which Mary rehearses her lines with Fanny. In this adaptation, Fanny does not refuse to play a role in the play. Rather, when Henry asks her opinion of the project, Aunt Norris embarrasses Fanny by telling her to go about her work. She apparently fears that Fanny is being looked upon as the equal to the privileged young people. Fanny sheds tears of frustration as she stands outside the room and hears Henry discussing with the others whether Fanny is "out" in society. When the plans go forward for the play, Edmund comes to Fanny's room to complain that an outsider is to be brought in to take part. Then, Mary, wishing to rehearse with Fanny, comes into her room. Edmund decides to play Anhalt only after he watches Mary reading her part with Fanny. This scene is profoundly suggestive. The camera circles Mary and Fanny as Mary stands close to Fanny and puts her hands around Fanny's waist. Using one of her favorite camera techniques, Rozema enables the viewer to look beyond the girls in the foreground to Edmund, who is watching them.

In this scene, Mary is obviously doing more than practicing her role. She is also flirting with Edmund, and perhaps even with Fanny. Fanny is quite passive at this time, as she is when Mary later removes her wet clothing after finding Fanny outside the parsonage in the rain. Rozema says of the latter scene that Mary's chief interest is in finding out from Fanny what Edmund says about Mary. She calls Mary "Machiavellian" (DVD Commentary). Some reviewers have suggested that Fanny willingly participates in Mary's lesbian advances (Serpico, Kantrowitz). They might legitimately suspect Rozema had included scenes with suggestions of lesbianism, since her earlier films (*When Night Is Falling,* 1995, and *I've Heard the Mermaids Singing,* 1987) include lesbian characters, but the director, in her comments about the making of the film, says only that Fanny is fascinated by Mary (DVD Commentary).

In the Miramax version, Sir Thomas arrives home to find his house in turmoil: Julia is drinking, Rushworth is preening before a mirror, and Maria, her make-up and clothing awry, is standing close to Henry Crawford. The BBC adaptation does not include such unseemly discoveries, but emphasizes Sir Thomas's displeasure with Yates, whom he finds declaiming in his billiard room, and with Aunt Norris for her cooperation in the play-acting scheme. In both versions, after the dust has settled, Maria realizes that Henry Crawford is not in love with her and asks her father to allow her to marry Rushworth as soon as possible.

The Miramax adaptation includes an effective scene in which Maria watches through a half-open door as Henry Crawford reads to Fanny from Laurence Sterne's *A Sentimental Journey.* Maria realizes that Henry is wooing Fanny. The camera circles Henry and Fanny as he reads about a captive starling. The narrator has heard the bird say, "I can't get out," and he tries to open the cage but cannot. The circling camera and the different views we get of Fanny's apprehensive expression indicate that Crawford is trying to ensnare Fanny and that Fanny is at least vaguely aware of the fact. Rozema introduces the image of the caged starling in order to apply it to both Maria and Fanny, and to the various kinds of captivity which they experience. Rozema points out, however, that the image does not simply suggest that women are locked into cages by men. Maria chooses her cage—marriage with Rushworth (DVD Commentary).

In a telling scene in which Sir Thomas talks freely to his assembled family, he speaks about his slaves. He praises the beauty of mulattos. He says, "The mulattos are in general well-shaped and the women especially well-featured. I have one so easy and graceful in her movements as well." The enthusiasm with which he praises the beauty of his female slave is disturbing to the viewer. He goes on to say that mulattos are like mules, in that two mulattos are unable to produce children. Edmund exchanges a look with Fanny and then chides his father for speaking nonsense. Sir Thomas advises Edmund to read Edward Long's *History of Jamaica* to learn the truth. He says that he is thinking of bringing a slave back to England to work as a servant. At this point Fanny chimes in, saying that if he did so, the slave might have to be freed. She says that she has been reading Thomas Clarkson. No part of this scene appears in the novel. However, in one of Jane Austen's letters she professed admiration for Thomas Clarkson (***Letters** [**Jane Austen's Letters**]* 198). He was a key figure, along with William Wilberforce and Granville Sharp, in the fight which resulted in the abolition of slave trading in the British colonies in 1807. On the other hand, Edward Long, a Jamaican plantation owner, defended the use of African slaves on the sugar plantations in the West Indies and compared mulattos to mules (Long II 335-336). Rozema's addition of these details fits neatly into the time period of the film. Regarding the novel, Avrom Fleishman has pointed out that Jane Austen's contemporaries would have been well aware of the novel's historical context—the economic situation in Antigua resulting from the French embargo which impeded the marketing of the produce of the British-owned sugar plantations and of the abolitionist efforts which led to the Abolition Act (7-8). Since neither the modern reader nor the film viewer would have such awareness, perhaps we can see some justification for Rozema's foregrounding the subject of slavery.

It is surprising, given Sir. Thomas's irascible nature, that he does not take offense at Fanny's comment about slaves. Instead, he reiterates his praise of her improved appearance and speaks of the beauty of her complexion and figure. In the novel, he also notices improvement in Fanny's appearance, but in the Miramax film, Rozema has associated his praise of Fanny with his praise of the beauty of his mulatto slave. When Edmund attempts to focus his father's attention on Fanny's intelligence and upon her writing style, Sir Thomas ignores his remarks. He proposes that he give a ball in Fanny's honor and says, "Surely some young man of good standing will sit up and take notice." Overwhelmed by this unwelcome attention, Fanny leaves the room hastily. When Edmund follows her, she tells him angrily, "I'll not be sold off like one of your father's slaves." She has understood that Sir Thomas perceives that her improved beauty makes her a more marketable product.

Since dances are so much a part of most adaptations of the other Austen novels, it is interesting to contrast their use in these two. In the BBC version, Fanny is horrified when Sir Thomas tells her to lead off the first dance. Fanny looks as attractive as this actress can look, with her hair in curls and wearing her white dress and the cross that William brought her. We see Fanny dancing first with Henry, then with William, and next with Edmund, in a variety of period dances. Her dance with Henry is slow and stately; with her brother she dances a lively jig. When she dances with Edmund, the dance is elaborate and formal, but the dancers hold hands and move close together. Fanny obviously enjoys this dance more than any other. As in the novel, Sir Thomas is the benevolent despot who is pleased with his benevolence toward his poor relations and who finally orders Fanny to bed for her own good. In the Miramax adaptation, the dances are period dances which, according to Rozema, have been adapted to make them more intimate (DVD Commentary). Rather than the overall patterns or movements, Rozema shows close-ups of hands clasping, hands on waists, laughing faces. She shoots part of the dancing in double time (48 frames per second). When Crawford rejoices that Fanny has complimented his dancing, Fanny says to him, "Keep your wig on." After recovering from shock at this most outrageous modernizing, I was pleased at both Rozema's and Fanny's audacity. The viewer's general impression of the ball is of Fanny's delight in the dancing and of Henry's and Edmund's appreciation of Fanny. Fanny leaves the dance of her own accord, wine glass in hand, to go to her room.

A strong subtext in the Miramax film is the similarity of the situation of women in that time to the captivity of slaves. Women moved from their parents' control to their husbands' control. Those who were not able to find a husband found themselves enslaved by poverty or by the whims of relatives. Jane Austen experienced, if not poverty, living with only a small income and sometimes was embarrassed because she was unable even to tip the servants appropriately at her brother's mansion when she stayed there (Myer 120). Marriage could bring a woman a measure of independence and security, but marriage was a terminal state. As Maria Bertram discovers after she has married Rushworth, she is like a bird in a cage. She can't get out. Only death or disgrace will deliver her from her marriage. Fanny feels bound by gratitude and material obligations to Sir Thomas, who has been her surrogate father. After all, he has supported her and educated her for ten years. Sir Thomas is more dictatorial to Fanny, his wife's niece, than to his daughters. He tells Maria that she does not have to marry Rushworth if she does not love him. After Henry proposes to Fanny, Sir Thomas insists that Fanny marry him, even when she says that she does not love him.

In the BBC version, as in the novel, Sir Thomas is not so ferocious to Fanny as he is in the Miramax version. He does not understand her reluctance to marry a man who has helped her brother and could help her family. He thinks it extraordinary good luck for this penniless girl to have made such a good catch. Even Edmund thinks that in time Fanny will accept Henry, and he encourages his father in this belief. After Sir Thomas gets over his outrage, he calms down and speaks kindly to her. He invites Crawford to frequent the house so that he may further his suit. Finally, however, Sir Thomas decides to send Fanny with William back to Portsmouth, thinking that being deprived of the luxuries of Mansfield Park might make her more ready to accept Henry.

Harold Pinter as Sir Thomas shows great severity in his manner to Fanny. His language is essentially that of the novel, but presented as if in a harangue delivered over the space of several days in different places in the house. We get close-ups of Pinter's dark, frowning countenance as he accuses Fanny of ingratitude to him, selfishness, and "wilfulness of temper, self-conceit, and every tendency to that independence of spirit which prevails so much in modern days. [. . .]" Although this accusation is taken directly from the novel (***MP*** 318), in the context of the film, it associates Fanny with the perverse voices of the times which were calling for freedom for all enslaved peoples.

The portrayals of Fanny's home in Portsmouth mainly differ in that Rozema emphasizes the extreme poverty of Fanny's home. The BBC portrayal, and that of the novel, emphasize the lack of order and quiet. These are the qualities of Mansfield Park which Fanny chiefly misses. It is made clear that nobody appears to care whether Fanny is there or not. Her mother, father, and brothers are much more interested in William than in Fanny. Fanny is an outsider in her own home. Rozema says that she tried to make the poverty of Fanny's home "visceral" (DVD Commentary). She conveys vividly the smallness, the congestion, and the darkness of the rooms. She shows dirty dishes and maggots on the table. When Crawford visits, he surreptitiously wipes off a fork and reluctantly takes a bite of what Rozema describes in the published screenplay as "a glob of grisly meat in a vomitlike sauce" (112). Fanny is also shown cutting up vegetables and tending the fire. In the bed which she shares with two sisters, Fanny scratches in her sleep, obviously fending off a bed-bug or other insect.

Some reviewers of the Miramax film objected to having Fanny accept Crawford's proposal and then reject him. They find this vacillation out of keeping with Fanny as Austen portrayed her. Rozema justifies this deviation from the novel by saying that she based the incident on Jane Austen's own acceptance and next-day rejection of Harris Bigg-Wither (DVD Commentary). It is also possible to justify it from the novel itself, since we are told that had Henry not dallied with Maria, then Edmund would have married Mary, and Fanny would probably have married Crawford. A particular reason for Rozema to have Fanny accept Crawford at Portsmouth is that it shows Fanny, after she thinks that Edmund is going to marry Mary Crawford, yielding to the temptation to escape the poverty which appears to be her only other choice. Henry Crawford is very attentive. He offers to assist her parents. He realizes that Fanny loves Edmund, and he comforts her when Edmund's letter tells her that he can see himself marrying no one except Mary Crawford. The present which he has delivered to the door one morning is symbolic. A boy delivers a crate of white pigeons on a cart. As another boy plays an hand organ, the first boy lights fireworks and releases the pigeons. They soar into the air and thus express the freedom which Fanny desires—a freedom from poverty which Henry Crawford can supply.

This film makes Henry Crawford a more sympathetic figure than that in the BBC film. Whereas in the novel and the BBC adaptation Henry Crawford sets out to amuse himself by making Fanny fall in love with him, in the Miramax film he appears really to fall in love with her. We come to empathize with Crawford as he tries to win Fanny, and to feel sorry for him when she tells him that she has changed her mind. He comes into the kitchen the morning after she accepted him, bearing a bouquet of daisies, sneaks up on Fanny who is facing the fire, and sings out, "Good morning, Miss Price." When she turns and rebuffs him, we cringe in empathetic embarrassment.

Mrs. Norris in the BBC adaptation is presented as an officious busybody, parsimonious and very much a toady when it comes to ingratiating herself with Sir Thomas. Anna Massey is effective in this interpretation of the character. She has a pinched, narrow face and rushes about talking incessantly. Rozema states, however, that she sees Mrs. Norris as one who thought that she should have been the mistress of Mansfield Park, instead of her indolent, beautiful sister (DVD Commentary). Thus Rozema chose a different type of actress, one who still has the vestiges of good looks. Sheila Gish as Mrs. Norris is a sour and envious woman who cannot endure seeing Fanny the recipient of the kind of marriage offer that she would like to have had. We glimpse her personal vanity when, like Maria and Julia, she primps in front of a mirror in preparation for the arrival of the Crawfords.

In another daring characterization, Rozema presents Lady Bertram as a laudanum addict. In both the novel and the BBC film, Lady Bertram (Angela Pleasence) is an indolent and slow-witted couch potato, who cares more about her pug dog than about her children. In the Miramax film, she is indolent and oblivious. We see her dozing in the background of several scenes. When Sir Thomas returns from Antigua, she greets him happily, but gives the impression that whether he had been gone a year or a day would have been all the same to her. Ironically, she is the only one really happy to see him. Lindsay Duncan, who plays this role, also plays Mrs. Price, Lady Bertram's sister. Having the same actress play both roles suggests to the viewer that Lady Bertram in a hovel would have been as slatternly and as poor a housekeeper as Mrs. Price.

Rozema has remarked on the novel's ambiguous sexuality. On the DVD, she comments on the brother/sister relationship of Fanny and Edmund, and the film shows them struggling to deal with their growing sexual love for each other. In particular one recalls the scene where Edmund's head falls over on Fanny's bosom as they ride in the carriage toward Mansfield Park. Later, when Edmund is attempting to comfort Fanny after she has found Maria and Crawford together, they nearly kiss each other on the mouth. The marriage of first cousins was much more common and acceptable in Jane Austen's time than it is today. Sir Thomas in the novel was apprehensive about the possibility of one of his son's being interested in Fanny mainly because he considered his sons worthy of a better match. Rozema's treatment of this romance suggests something of a modern disapproval of it. Her suggestion that a father may have a sexual interest in his daughter is, however, even more typical of modern attitudes. Rozema shows Fanny's father (Hilton McRae) as overly enthusiastic about his daughter's appearance as he greets her upon her homecoming and embraces her, while shots of her mother's and Susan's reactions suggest an uneasiness perhaps deriving from their own experience. Even the scene in which Sir Thomas dwells on Fanny's improved beauty makes the viewer squirm with discomfort.

In the novel and in the BBC film Fanny learns about Henry and Maria's flight while in Portsmouth. She also learns of

Tom's illness and yearns to be summoned back to Mansfield Park. Edmund comes to take both Fanny and Susan back to Mansfield. In the BBC adaptation, the family, including the invalid Tom, greets them. Sir Thomas is in London. Later, as Edmund and Fanny sit alone together, with rain falling outside the window, Edmund tells Fanny about his last meeting with Mary in London. A close-up of Edmund's face fades to show in a flashback Mary receiving Edmund in the library. She condemns Henry and Maria, not for the sin of adultery, but for their lack of discretion. She says that Fanny is to blame for the affair, because she did not return Henry's affection. In her opinion, had Fanny married Henry, the relationship between Henry and Maria would have ended in a kind of "regular standing flirtation." She says that they must urge Henry to marry Maria and it may yet all turn out well. They can invite the couple to dinners and gradually reintroduce them to good society. She says that fortunately there is "more liberality" about such things nowadays. While she is speaking, Edmund looks shocked. He finally says to her, "To be detected in a folly is the greatest crime you know." He says that he is appalled at her indifference to morality and to feeling. He realizes that the woman he has loved is a creature of his imagination. She retorts that he is preaching to her. He excuses himself and leaves. As he goes out into the hall, she follows him and calls to him, but he resists the temptation to go back to her. Following the flashback, he tells Fanny that, even though he regrets his loss, he knows he did the right thing. We see Fanny in profile, as she listens to him call her his "dearest Fanny" and as he takes her hand. He says, "What shall I do if you ever go away?" She says, "I shall never."

The Miramax film picks up considerable speed following Fanny's return to Mansfield Park. Four big scenes fall like thunderbolts on the viewer. In the first one Fanny finds Tom's sketchbook, full of drawings of slaves being abused. Although the viewer may feel that such explicitness is unnecessary to make the point that Sir Thomas's wealth derives from the blood of slaves, Rozema said that this scene is the reason that she made the film (DVD Commentary). She said that she wanted "to show the disregard for human dignity that must have been the case" (DVD Commentary). Thus, we see in one sketch Sir Thomas whipping a slave and in another a female slave kneeling in front of Sir Thomas, perhaps to perform a sexual act. One drawing, done by William Blake, a contemporary of Jane Austen, shows a slave bound with ropes and hanging on a hook. In another, a woman is being gang raped by several young men; this sketch is ironically titled "Our Neighbors." While Fanny is looking at these images, and while the sound of groans and screams merge with the music in the background, Sir Thomas comes into the room, grabs the sketchbook, and begins to feed the pages into the fire. He says, "My son is mad." Indeed, the viewer does not know whether the sketches showing Sir Thomas represent reality or Tom's fevered imagination. The viewer wonders how Sir Thomas could have any redeeming qualities if he is as bad as Tom thinks him.

The second shocker occurs later that evening. Earlier that day, Maria and Julia have come home, and later Henry Crawford calls at Mansfield Park. We see Crawford with Maria in the library. She says that she wishes that he could feel about her as he does about Fanny. That night we see a shadowy figure approaching Mansfield Park. Fanny, hearing noises, gets out of bed to go to Tom's room. Her candle having gone out, Fanny goes into Maria's room rather than Tom's. She finds Henry Crawford in bed with Maria. She staggers out into the hall and into Tom's room, where Edmund asks her what is wrong. Sobbing, she can only point down the hall. Edmund goes in that direction and finds Henry Crawford, now with his pants on, and Maria in bed with a sheet pulled up to cover her nakedness. Henry doesn't speak, but Maria attempts to justify herself by saying, "I can't get out," reiterating the refrain of Sterne's caged bird. Edmund goes back to Fanny to comfort her.

After this, a comic interlude provides some relief. Maria's husband arrives with a newspaper reporter in tow. He has already been to the parsonage looking for Henry and has not found him. Now he is looking for Maria to brag about how the newspaper will carry an article about the improvements to his estate. The reporter is obviously much interested to find that Mrs. Rushworth, as well as Henry Crawford, has disappeared.

The third big scene shows the family gathered in a salon, with Mary Crawford also present. Sir Thomas asks Fanny to read an item in the newspaper reporting that Mrs. Rushworth has run away with Henry Crawford. When Fanny finishes reading, Mary tells the family that they must make the best of Henry and Maria's indiscretion. They must do nothing, but hope that Henry will marry Maria. Then, if the Bertrams receive the couple, all may be well. She says that she and Edmund will give good dinners and large parties and enable Henry and Maria to reenter society. Wearing her slinky black dress, she walks back and forth in front of her mostly silent audience. Fanny asks her how she and Edmund will be able to afford these dinners and parties. Mary shocks everyone, even the befogged Lady Bertram, by saying that she expects Tom to die, thereby making Edmund the heir. She says to Fanny that "it could all be construed as your fault" for not marrying Henry. Mary says that if Fanny had accepted Henry, he would not have run off with Maria. They could merely have had a "regular standing flirtation" when they met in society. When she has finished her monologue, Edmund stands up and says, "You are a stranger to me." He tells her that he does not know her, and that he does not want to know her. She leaves the room. This scene is much more dramatic than either the novel's presentation of Edmund's conversation with Mary or the BBC's. It includes the whole family, except Tom, and contrives to show both Mary's amorality and her callous and mercenary hope that Tom will die.

The final scene before the epilogue is set in Tom's bedroom, where Sir Thomas, holding the hand of his sleeping son, hears the doctor say, "Time can do anything." Sir Thomas says that he knows Tom will recover. He reminisces that as a boy Tom liked to pretend that he was Tom the Knight. He would ask his father to give him a noble mission. The implication is that as Tom grew up he realized that Sir Thomas was no King Arthur, but a slave-owner. Sir Thomas accepts responsibility for the psychological problems which have led Tom so near the death that he had anticipated as a youth. He says to Tom, "I'm sorry, Tom. So sorry." In the novel Sir Thomas experiences awareness of his failings, mainly regarding the education of his daughters. In this film, his sins of omission and commission are much greater. They are perhaps too great to justify as happy an ending as Rozema provides.

The BBC film ties up the loose ends by having Fanny read in voiceover her letter to William. Here we learn that Mr. Rushworth gets his divorce. Mrs. Norris, who has left Mansfield Park to set up a home for Maria, is seen traveling in a carriage. Julia and Yates, who had eloped shortly after Maria had run off with Crawford, are married and come home to make peace with Sir Thomas. Then we see Fanny's mother, children, and father in church. Fanny in voiceover tells William that today she is to be married to Edmund, and we see Edmund and Fanny standing before a clergyman in the church. Fanny also tells William that since Dr. Grant is leaving, she and Edmund will live in the parsonage, "within the view and patronage of Mansfield Park." The final shot is of Fanny and Edmund sitting on a bench on the parsonage lawn, with Pug (or an offspring of Pug) in front of them.

In the Miramax film, Fanny in ironic voiceover tells the viewer that things might have turned out differently, but they didn't. Swooping flocks of computer-generated starlings and a soaring camera separate the episodes of the epilogue. As the narrator tells us that Henry Crawford did not marry Maria, we see Mrs. Norris and Maria in a cottage by the sea, both looking regretful. Next, a soaring camera shot shows Henry and Mary Crawford with a pair of stylish young people taking tea on a lawn. There's a freeze-frame shot of Henry and Mary looking off in opposite directions, while their companions look slyly at each other. Apparently the Crawfords have found kindred spirits with whom to pass the time. More swooping starlings, and the camera soars again to come to rest at Mansfield Park, where Edmund and Fanny sit by a pond. Edmund declares his love to Fanny. He says that he has loved her all of his life—"as a man loves a woman. As a hero loves a heroine." They embrace and Fanny smiles confidingly at the viewer over Edmund's shoulder. Behind them Sir Thomas and Lady Bertram may be seen strolling on the lawn, she making a witticism about Fanny and Edmund—"It looks as if they're finally getting someplace." The narrator says that Susan (Sophia Myles) has come to live at Mansfield Park. We see her reciting a history lesson to Julia, who is much interested in a letter which she has received from Mr. Yates.[6] We also see Tom seated in a chair on the lawn, sketchbook in hand.

The voiceover tells us that Sir Thomas gave up his interests in Antigua and decided to pursue "opportunities in tobacco." In the published screenplay this voiceover statement is present, but in the earlier, unpublished screenplay the voiceover states that he chose some "exciting new opportunities in India" (165). Apparently Rozema was uncertain about how Sir Thomas could give up being a slave owner yet support Mansfield Park. If Sir Thomas divested himself of his plantations in Antigua, he probably sold the land and slaves to someone else. If Sir Thomas invested the money gained from the sale of his slaves, he would still be living off money earned by slave labor, and to invest in tobacco doubles the likelihood that the labor of slaves would be generating the interest on his investment. Had Sir Thomas been truly sorry for his exploitation of slaves, he might have liberated his slaves and have paid them wages to operate his plantations. Susan Morgan states that after 1802 it was frequently argued in Parliament that planters could actually improve their profits by turning to wage labor. She cites Henry Brougham's pamphlet "Inquiry into the Colonial Policy of the European Powers" (1803), which supported the abolition of slavery partly on this basis (90). If, as Alistair Duckworth asserts, Rozema's purpose is "to depict the moral ruin of Mansfield Park's inhabitants" (565), she backs away from any real penance for Sir Thomas. If Sir Thomas were as bad a man as he is portrayed in the film, a greater sacrifice, and not only of money, would have been necessary to redeem him—perhaps the death of his elder son.

Finally, as we see Fanny and Edmund walking toward the parsonage, he tells her that a publisher is interested in her writing. The conclusion is vaguely nostalgic and whimsical, as the narrator reiterates that it might have turned out differently, but it didn't. Claudia Johnson points out that this refrain, which accompanies the vignettes of the epilogue, reminds the viewer of the "benign yet unblinking intervention" of Fanny's art (Rozema *Final Shooting Script,* Introduction 9).

The cover of the videotape, of the DVD and of the published screenplay of the Miramax *Mansfield Park* shows a smug-looking Frances O'Connor looking directly at the viewer. She holds a large key close to her bosom. At the bottom of the picture is a great house in the Adam style. The implication appears to be that Fanny has the key—spiritually and physically—to Mansfield Park. With her intelligence, her keen sense of morality, and her persistence, she has emerged triumphant over those who have sought to corrupt Mansfield Park and, by reforming even the master of the house, has established herself as the true daughter of the house. This is indeed very much the point of the novel and of the BBC mini-series. However, Rozema has stated that Fanny has escaped from the "decay" and "rot" at the heart of Mansfield Park. "Fanny Price finally escapes with, yes, her true love to another place: a parsonage!" ("Place" 3). Troost and Greenfield, in another twist, which makes even better sense than Rozema's interpretation, argue that Fanny's writing constitutes her key to freedom, a freedom not dependent on Mansfield Park or her marriage to Edmund ("Mouse" 201). I feel that in some ways the conclusion to the Miramax *Mansfield Park* exemplifies the problems implicit in Rozema's radical reinterpretation of the novel—the problem of Sir Thomas's penance, the problem of Edmund's acceptance of the family's dependence on slaves, the problem of Fanny's love for Mansfield Park. Perhaps the reinterpretation was not radical enough.

Notes

1. Critics disagree on the dates of the chronology in the novel. See <http://mason.gmu.edu/~emoody/mp.calendar.html> for a summary of the discussion.

2. The published screenplay includes a short scene in which Mrs. Price, in her kitchen after parting with Fanny, bursts into tears (14). In the film she shows no emotion at losing Fanny, nor any when Fanny returns. The novel says only that Mrs. Price was surprised that one of her fine boys was not the one sent for (*MP* 11). When Fanny returns with William, her mother meets her with "looks of true kindness," but she immediately turns her attention to William (*MP* 377-378).

3. Named for Robert Adam (1728-1792), architect and exponent of architecture based on Greek, Roman and Renaissance Italian models. It was characterized by free use of ornamentation, delicate colors, Venetian windows, and smooth or scored stucco fronts (Watkins 65).

4. An interesting bit of trivia: When Jonny Lee Miller was ten, he played the role of Charles Price, Fanny's brother, in the 1983 adaptation of *Mansfield Park.*

5. Omitted from the film but present in the published screenplay are Edmund's comments about a load of slaves from Loanga, West Africa, which Sir Thomas had bought. Edmund says that these slaves are unhappy, and Fanny observes that the slaves must miss their families. Edmund reminds her that Mansfield Park "is entirely dependent on the profits of that operation . . . It's not, it's not . . . clear" (33).

6. There's no sight or mention of Julia in this scene in the published screenplay.

Bibliography

Austen, Jane. *Jane Austen's Letters.* Ed. Deidre LeFaye. 3rd ed. London: Oxford UP, 1995.

———. *Emma.* Ed. R. W. Chapman. 3rd ed. London: Oxford UP, 1933. Cited as *E.*

———. *Mansfield Park.* Ed. R. W. Chapman. 3rd ed. London: Oxford UP, 1933. Cited as *MP.*

———. *Minor Works.* Ed. R. W. Chapman. 3rd ed. London: Oxford UP, 1933. The spelling and punctuation of this edition have not been standardized. Cited as *MW.*

Clueless. Dir., Screenplay by Amy Heckerling. Paramount, 1995. Laserdisc.

Duffy, Joseph M., Jr. "Moral Integrity and Moral Anarchy in *Mansfield Park.*" *ELH* 23 (1956): 71-91.

Emma. Dir., Screenplay by Douglas McGrath. Columbia/Miramax, 1996. Laserdisc.

Emma. Dir. John Glenister. Screenplay by Denis Constanduros. BBC TV, 1972. Videotape.

Fleishman, Avrom. *A Reading of Mansfield Park: An Essay in Critical Synthesis.* Minneapolis: Minnesota UP, 1967.

Johnson, Claudia L. *Jane Austen: Women, Politics and the Novel.* Chicago UP, 1988.

Kirkham, Margaret. *Jane Austen, Feminism and Fiction.* Totowa, NJ: Barnes and Noble, 1983.

Lew, Joseph. "'That Abominable Traffic': *Mansfield Park* and the Dynamics of Slavery." *History, Gender and Eighteenth Century Literature.* Ed. Beth F. Tobin. Athens, GA: U of Georgia P, 1994. 271-300.

Long, Edward. *The History of Jamaica or General Survey of the Antient* (sic) *and Modern State of That Island.* Ed. George Metcalf. 2 vols. Frank Cass, 1774.

Mansfield Park. Dir., Screenplay by Patricia Rozema. BBC/Miramax. 2000. DVD. Commentary by Patricia Rozema.

Mudrick, Marvin. *Jane Austen: Irony as Defense and Discovery.* Princeton UP, 1952.

Myer, Valerie G. *Jane Austen: Obstinate Heart.* New York: Arcade, 1997.

Persuasion. Dir. Roger Michell. Screenplay by Nick Dear. BBC/Sony Pictures Classics, 1995. Laserdisc.

Rozema, Patricia. *Mansfield Park: The Final Shooting Script.* Introduction by Claudia Johnson. New York: Talk Miramax Books, 2000.

———. "A Place in the Sun." *Montage* (Spring 2000) 29 Mar. 2001 <http://www.patriciarozema.com/a_place_in_the_ sun.htm>.

Said, Edward. *Culture and Imperialism.* New York: Knopf, 1993.

Sense and Sensibility. Dir. Ang Lee. Columbia/Mirage, 1995. Laserdisc.

Sense and Sensibility. Dir. Rodney Bennett. BBC, 1980. Videotape.

Sense and Sensibility. Original Motion Picture Soundtrack. (Notes on CD package) Sony, 1995.

Stewart, Maaja A. *Domestic Realities and Imperial Fictions: Jane Austen's Novels in Eighteenth-Century Contexts.* Athens, GA: U of Georgia P, 1993.

Trilling, Lionel. "*Mansfield Park.*" *Jane Austen: A Collection of Critical Essays.* Ed. Ian Watt. Prentice Hall, 1963. From *The Opposing Self.* New York: Viking, 1955.

Troost, Linda, and Sayre Greenfield. "The Mouse That Roared: Patricia Rozema's *Mansfield Park.*" Ed. Linda Troost and Sayre Greenfield. *Jane Austen in Hollywood.* 2nd Ed. Kentucky UP, 2000. 188-204.

Watkins, Susan. *Jane Austen in Style.* London: Thames and Hudson, 1990.

Ruth Perry (essay date 2002)

SOURCE: Perry, Ruth. "Jane Austen and British Imperialism." *Monstrous Dreams of Reason: Body, Self, and Other in the Enlightenment.* Ed. Laura J. Rosenthal and Mita Choudhury. Lewisburg: Bucknell UP, 2002. 231-54. Print.

[*In the following essay, Perry discusses Austen's connections to British colonialism and the impact that colonial expansion had upon her fiction. Perry emphasizes the role of slavery in* Mansfield Park, *focusing on Fanny's servant status and her desire to question that position.*]

Ever since Edward Said published his essay, "Jane Austen and Empire,"[1] declaring that Jane Austen's novels helped to naturalize the relations of colonialism, scholars have been debating the meaning of her colonial references. The contradictory impulses of the Enlightenment itself come into play on both sides of the argument, with its eighteenth-century mixtures of reason and superstition, nationalism and imperialism, revolution and colonialism—contradictions apparent in the conjunction of the widely circulating accounts of Captain Cook's voyages of explorations with his racialized sense of European superiority and his experiments with antiscorbutics or the military conquest of India and Canada on the one hand versus the celebration of revolutions in America, France, and Haiti on the other. It is the aim of this essay to spell out some of the ambiguous cultural contexts in which Austen wrote her novels with their references to British colonialism, contexts both familial and international.

In what follows, I will sketch in the changing fortunes of England and of the Austens in relation to British colonial expansion, for Jane Austen's attitudes were affected by the tidal wave of nationalism that swept her country during the struggle with Napoleon, and her judgments about British exploration and expansion changed with the changing vicissitudes of her country. By the end of her life she was ready to glorify the British navy in which her brothers made their fortunes and to believe them brave and noble sailors all, although she had imaged the military men of her earlier novels as shallow, flashy, or opportunistic. There are references to the English slave trade and to the English colonial presence abroad in the last three novels, but only in ***Persuasion*** does she endorse this imperial reach rather than question it. By the time she drafted that novel, Napoleon had been defeated at Waterloo and the pleasure and relief of the English in their unconquerableness overwhelmed all other scruples.

One could start with 1797, the year the fiancé of Jane Austen's beloved sister Cassandra, Reverend Thomas Fowle, died of yellow fever off Santo Domingo and was buried at sea, to the "great Affliction" of all those at Steventon. Eliza de Feuillade wrote to her cousin Philadelphia Walter: "He was expected home this Month, from St. Domingo where he had accompanied Lord Craven, but Alas instead of his arrival news were received of his Death. … Jane says that her Sister behaves with a degree of resolution & Propriety which no common mind could evince in so trying a situation."[2] Like Edward Ferrars, who disappeared from Elinor Dashwood's life in ***Sense and Sensibility,*** offering an opportunity to demonstrate heroic strength of character in suffering—or Bingley, who provides the same exquisite opportunity to Jane Bennet in ***Pride and Prejudice***—the ghost of Thomas Fowle peers through Jane Austen's novels, the original of all the disappearing suitors. Cassandra's uncommon "resolution & Propriety," just what one would expect from the exemplary eldest daughter, likewise presages several Austen heroines.

Thomas Fowle was accompanying Lord Craven on a military mission to the West Indies as his personal chaplain when he contracted yellow fever, a "minister of the Prince of Peace serving in the host of the God of War," as Melville described these posts.[3] Lord Craven is said to have repented of his choice after the fact, because yellow fever was epidemic among British troops in the Caribbean and he would not knowingly have exposed an engaged man to this danger. Yellow fever killed three times more Europeans than muskets or cutlasses in the colonial wars in the Caribbean theater at the turn of the century. By the time Thomas Fowle died, some 80,000 British soldiers had perished in three-and-a-half years of war with France. In October of 1796 "it was said in Parliament that every person in the country had lost an acquaintance in the Caribbean campaigns"; "the obituary columns of the *Gentleman's Magazine* were strewn with the names of the officers who had died of yellow fever."[4] The war became as scandalously unpopular in England as the Vietnam war was in the U.S. in the early 1970s. The degree to which the West Indian theater of operations sapped England's strength in her contest with France, the extraordinary casualties from tropical disease, and the growing opposition of the English public to the slave trade upon which the colonial economy depended—these led to a cease-fire and the withdrawing of troops from Santo Domingo the year after Thomas Fowle died.

If Tom Fowle had returned and Cassandra had married him and nurtured and attended to him instead of her sister, who knows what Jane Austen would have written? England's colonial war in the Caribbean was momentous for Jane and Cassandra Austen and, as it turns out, for posterity, because Tom Fowle's death and Cassandra's subsequent spinsterhood undoubtedly contributed to Austen's decision to remain single and to write.[5] It is also worth noting that the cause for which Thomas Fowle gave his life had a different relation to colonial slavery from the later contest in which Captain Frederick Wentworth played such a heroic role in Austen's last novel, ***Persuasion.*** Thomas Fowle died defending slavery, whereas Captain Wentworth proved himself protecting English supremacy at the battle of Santo Domingo and resisting Napoleon's attempt to re-enslave that island. The changing meaning of the English presence in the West Indies during the last decade of the eighteenth century and the first decade of the nineteenth century needs clarification because England's official stance toward slavery in its colonies changed as its contest with France went through various stages. Austen's successive novels map these ideological permutations.

By 1788, France was winning the colonial competition with England over Caribbean sugar production. France had double the land mass of the British colonial holdings in the West Indies and French colonies were individually more productive due to diversification of crops (the French pioneered coffee production in the West Indies), irrigation, smaller holdings, and less absenteeism. The wealth pouring into France from her colonies far exceeded what England was able to extract from hers.[6] Four-fifths of Britain's entire overseas investment income came from her West Indian colonies; but the French colony of Santo Domingo alone—occupying the western one-third of the island of Hispaniola—produced more sugar than all the British colonies put together.[7] Ironically, the brisk British slave trade that supplied slave labor to the plantations in Santo Domingo nearly doubled French sugar production between 1783 and 1789.[8] The English government, in the person of William Pitt, motivated by the desire to slow down this spectacular production competing with English sugar on the European market, pressed abolitionist William Wilberforce into service to champion the cause of an abolition bill in Parliament. At the same time, Pitt encouraged experiments with sugar agriculture in India.[9]

Meanwhile, the English abolition movement was gathering momentum. The Society for Effecting the Abolition of the Slave Trade was founded in 1787, chaired by Granville Sharp, following the publication of Thomas Clarkson's powerful *An Essay on the Slavery and Commerce of the Human Species* in 1786.[10] Two former slaves, Ottobah Cugoano and Olaudah Equiano, both of whom had endured the "middle passage," published their first person accounts in 1787 and 1789 respectively, adding real voices to an antislavery discourse that otherwise spoke for objectified captives.[11] A wave of abolitionist feeling swept England, finding direct political expression in tens of thousands of signatures on one hundred two abolitionist petitions presented to Parliament in 1788.[12] In 1788 Clarkson published *An Essay on the Impolicy of the African Slave Trade,* building on his earlier work by pointing out the commercial advantage of trading in African hardwoods, gums, spice, cotton, rice, and peppers rather than "the human species." Pitt's ministry encouraged this public discussion, interested in abolishing the trade that supplied French Santo Domingo with forty thousand slaves a year, thus enabling her phenomenal prosperity.[13]

Jane Austen was just beginning to write her juvenilia during this phase of popular abolitionism—none of which, except for ***Catharine, or The Bower,*** engages colonialism. Her brother Charles was enrolled in the Royal Naval Academy at Portsmouth and her brother Francis had just shipped out to the East Indies as a midshipman in His Majesty's ship *Perseverance.*[14] When the French Revolution erupted across the channel, Austen's cousin Eliza de Feuillade was visiting in Hampshire, although her pseudo-aristocratic husband was still in France. English abolitionists, heartened by the example of the French revolutionaries' belief in the perfectability of human arrangements, collected money to send Clarkson to France to distribute antislavery literature and to funnel financial assistance to the newly formed French "Friends of the Negros."

In 1791, as Jane Austen turned sixteen, the shocking news reached London that over one hundred thousand slaves were in revolt in the French colony of Santo Domingo, killing whites and burning down plantations. The price of sugar skyrocketed; not coincidentally, abolitionists exhorted the public to boycott West Indian sugar if they wanted to aid the cause and prevent further mistreatment of captive Africans. Stories circulated of dismembered body parts boiled up in West Indian sugar, metaphors of a society feeding on its poor, not unlike the horror stories told about meat packing plants memorably recorded in Upton Sinclair's *The Jungle.*[15] By 1792, Clarkson boasted that three hundred thousand English consumers had given up sugar.[16]

In 1793, war broke out again between France and England. The official British stance toward liberté, fraternité, and abolition turned sour, reinforced by a popular backlash against the French Revolution and its bloody deeds. French Domingan planters, who had taken refuge in England during the late disturbances on the island, agitated for English intervention in Santo Domingo—now that France and England were at war again—and circulated stories of the brutality of the newly free slaves. Reminding English officials of the potential productivity of this valuable colony, they offered their allegiance if England would invade the newly liberated island and reestablish their racial hegemony.[17] In September, 1794, the English, aided by some of these French planters, launched a preliminary expedition against the French West Indies. Martinique, Santa Lucia, and Guadeloupe fell, but the losses from yellow fever were enormous. Santo Domingo, by now guided by the able military and diplomatic leadership of Toussaint L'Ouverture and receiving aid from the revolutionary government in France, proved impossible to capture.

This was the phase during which Thomas Fowle died, along with eighty thousand other Englishmen (the estimates vary by twenty thousand more or less), during England's five-year-long attempt to re-enslave the finest colony in the Caribbean.[18] The revolutions in France and in Santo Domingo, with their spectacular violence, had seriously dampened British enthusiasm for liberty and equality. Moreover, the English ministry's earlier interest in ending the slave trade was compromised by the new possibility of its owning Santo Domingo itself. If England proved successful in this venture, Santo Domingo could provide a lucrative home market for the English slave trade as well as fabulously wealthy sugar plantations. During these years the cause of abolition languished in Parliament, at odds with the national interest and the prosecution of the war with France.

By 1798 English troops gave over the struggle for Santo Domingo. Defeated, they withdrew from the island and, making a virtue of necessity, concluded a commercial and nonaggression pact with Toussaint L'Ouverture that they trumpeted widely. As C. L. R. James puts it: "The British, after having been driven out of the island in September, were posing in December as the authors of 'the happy revolution,' and rejoicing at the freedom of a people, to enslave whom they had just lost 100,000 men."[19]

In the brief peace that followed English withdrawal, Toussaint L'Ouverture consolidated his authority over the entire island of Hispaniola, which he declared to have "dominion status" under the French revolutionary government, and set about to restore the war-torn island to its former prosperity. But before long he was compelled to defend the island again, this time from the French. Assured of British noninterference by the 1802 Peace of Amiens, Napolean (whose wife Josephine owned property in Santo Domingo and Martinique), sent his brother-in-law, LeClerc, with twenty-five thousand soldiers to re-enslave Santo Domingo.[20] The British, officially neutral, nevertheless sympathized with the European invaders. Mme LeClerc, wife of the French commander (and Napoleon's sister), sent Lady Nugent, the wife of the British lieutenant governor of Jamaica, a "pink and silver dress" and a "cargo of Parisian fashions."[21] Lady Nugent in turn expressed much sympathy for the exhausted French troops—fourteen thousand of whom had died of yellow fever in a few months—and sent Mme LeClerc some English cut glass and a "hobbyhorse, with silver appointments for her son."[22]

When hostilities between France and England resumed again in 1803, the remaining Domingan planters appealed to England to again intervene and reconquer the island. Lady Nugent's diary reports that an embassy of "planters and remaining inhabitants" from Santo Domingo approached her husband "to give the colony up to the English—they have been so ill treated by the French troops, and suffered so much from their rapacity and injustice, that they say it is impossible to look to them for any security. ... It is, upon the whole, a most embarrassing situation for my dear N."[23] The embarrassment for "my dear N." of course, was being caught between conflicting loyalties to race and nation. Which claims were stronger: the Eurocentric claims of shared skin privilege with the French or the appeal of national pride and English colonial power?

Meanwhile, LeClerc tricked Toussaint L'Ouverture into believing he would respect the freedom of former slaves and negotiate a peace with them. He seized Toussaint L'Ouverture and arrested and deported him to France where he died in a dungeon in Joux Fortress in the Jura Mountains.[24] His fellow revolutionaries—Dessalines, Christophe, Clerveau, and Petion—tore the white band from the *tricolore* and fought the French under a new flag. In 1804 they renamed the new republic with a word taken from the Carib Indians: Hayti. England's subsequent skirmishes with the French in those waters had the effect of protecting Hayti's right to self-determination while retaining dominion over its own plantations in the West Indies.

Jane Austen's Colonial Connections

It is probable that Jane Austen's family followed these developments in the West Indies, for they had many connections in the planter class. Her father's older half-brother, William-Hampson Walter, had two sons (William and George) who settled in the West Indies. A letter from Jane's mother, Cassandra Austen senior, to her niece Philadelphia Walter at Christmastime 1786, wishing she were with them and describing the happy family circle at Steventon, declared "You might as well be in Jamaica keeping your Brother's House, for anything that we see of you or are like to see."[25] Mrs. Austen's own brother, James Leigh-Perrot, married Jane Cholmeley, heiress to an estate in Barbados.[26] James Langford Nibbs, Esq., an Antiguan planter whom Jane's father probably tutored at St. John's College, Oxford, was godfather to the Austen's oldest son James and a close enough family friend so that his portrait hung at Steventon. In his marriage articles, James Langford Nibbs designated George Austen as the trustee responsible for arranging a jointure of £500 per annum to be paid to his wife from his Antiguan property should he predecease her. Had Mr. Nibbs died early, Jane Austen's father would have been expected to manage the plantation in Antigua to fulfill this legal obligation![27] The first wife of James Austen—Anne Mathew—was the daughter of General Mathew, commander in chief of the Windward and Leeward Islands and governor of Grenada. And Jane's younger brother Charles married Fanny Palmer, daughter of the former attorney general of Bermuda, whom he met on duty there.

The Austens also had colonialist connections in the East Indies. George Austen's sister Philadelphia Austen had gone to India to find a husband in 1752 where she succeeded in meeting and marrying Mr. Hancock, twenty years her senior, a surgeon for the East India Company. Jane Austen recorded this family fact in her early fragment ***Catharine, or The Bower,*** in which the elder Miss Wynne goes to India to make her fortune. There she marries a wealthy man "double her own age, whose disposition was not amiable, and whose Manners were unpleasing, though his Character was respectable."[28] Mr. Hancock, whom there is no reason to think unamiable or unmannerly, was a friend of Warren Hastings, who stood godfather to the Hancocks' daughter Elizabeth, born in Calcutta.[29] This was the cousin Eliza who was visiting the Austens in Hampshire when the French Revolution broke out. Her first husband, M. de Feuillade, was subsequently guillotined by the revolutionaries in 1794 and she afterwards married Jane's brother Henry in 1797.

Although family connections are easy to trace, attitudes of Jane Austen's class toward slavery and abolition at this time are less obvious. To begin with, what was at issue was never manumission, but only the abolition of the "commerce of the human species" as Thomas Clarkson put it. After the English were expelled from Santo Domingo, it was in the interests of the English planters to abolish the slave trade, for they already had three times as many slaves as the French colonies or Spanish Cuba, and Santo Domingo was irretrievably lost as a slave market.[30] Moreover, during the brief Peace of Amiens in 1802-3, when the French colonies were returned to France, British planters found it against their interest to have to compete with the formerly (and now again) enemy colonies flooding the market with tropical produce and driving down prices on their own home market, protected by British trade agreements.[31] In short, the West Indian lobby saw that there were few advantages to either a continued slave trade or the annexation of enemy colonies.

As landless gentry or lesser gentry,[32] the Austens could be said to come from what William Cobbett called "Britain's 'negro-pampering' upper class," whom he criticized when he called upon laboring people to look out for their own interests and not to worry about Africans or West Indians.[33] Jane Austen's brother Francis opposed slavery, having seen the system firsthand on a number of West Indian islands, including Antigua. Comparing the treatment of West Indian slaves to that on the East India Company's island of St. Helena in his journal, he noted that slaves on St. Helena were not "treated with that harshness and despotism which has been so justly attributed to the conduct of the land-holders or their managers in the West India Islands." The laws of St. Helena gave masters the right only to their slaves' labor—enforceable solely with civil and not private power. "This is a wholesome regulation as far as it goes," wrote Francis Austen, "but slavery however it may be modified is still slavery, and it is much to be regretted that any trace of it should be found to exist in countries dependent on England, or colonised by her subjects."[34] These sentiments were penned by Francis Austen in 1807, the period represented by his author sister as that in which her fictional hero, Captain Wentworth, shipped out to the British West Indies after his broken engagement with Anne Elliot, patrolling the waters in consequence of the passage in both houses of Parliament of the 1806 bill for abolition of the slave trade.

Francis Austen's experiences with West Indian slavery occured when he was captain of His Majesty's ship *Canopus.* Shortly after the Battle of Trafalgar—which he missed, to his great disappointment—he was posted to the Caribbean, where, as everyone knows, Admiral Croft was also stationed after Trafalgar in ***Persuasion.*** There, in 1805, Jane Austen's brother had his hour of glory at the battle of Santo Domingo in a squadron under the command of Admiral Duckworth. As he described it to his fiancé, Mary Gibson:

> The action commenced at half-past ten, and was finally over by half-past twelve, when three of the enemy's ships were in our possession, and the other two dismasted and on the rocks. The frigates escaped. Had we been two miles farther off the land we should have got the whole. We must, however, be truly thankful for the mercies which have been showed us in effecting such a victory with a comparatively inconsiderable loss. The Admiral is sending the prizes, and such of our own ships as have suffered most, to Jamaica . . . I am in hopes this action will be the means of our speedy quitting this country, and perhaps to return to Old England. Oh, how my heart throbs at the idea![35]

Frank Austen's share of the spoils of war, as captain of the *Canopus,* made him rich enough to return to England in the summer of 1806 to marry Mary Gibson. Several West Indian governments and trading associations added their gratitude and remuneration to the general applause, and Parliament voted its thanks to the Admirals and officers engaged at Santo Domingo in its next session.[36]

These events, significant in Austen's family, find fictional expression in the adventures of Frederick Wentworth, "who being made commander in consequence of the action off St. Domingo . . . came into Somersetshire in the summer of 1806" where he fell in love with the nineteen-year-old Anne Elliot for a short period of "exquisite felicity." The narrator tells us that he subsequently patrolled the waters around the West Indies for two years in an old sloop denominated *The Asp,* where he took "privateers enough to be very entertaining" and pursued a French frigate. The storm that followed this encounter, at which the Miss Musgroves shudder so deliciously in retrospect, is reminiscent of Frank's secondhand description to Mary Gibson of the storm following the Battle of Trafalgar. Captain Wentworth, like Francis Austen, was defending England's colonial possessions in the Caribbean, and the naval successes that enriched him, like those that enriched Captain Austen, made it possible for him to marry.

Colonialism in Jane Austen's Fiction

Austen refers to the slave trade and England's colonial wars in all three of her late novels with some significant shifts in attitude and emphasis. A number of critics have compellingly argued that ***Mansfield Park*** is predominantly *about* slavery. Both Moira Ferguson and Joseph Lew have pointed out that its title is associated with a landmark legal decision of 1772, in which Lord Mansfield declared that all persons of whatsoever race or personal history were free so long as they were on English soil, and could not be compelled to return to servitude in the slave-holding colonies.[37] In ***Mansfield Park,*** famously, Sir Thomas Bertram, baronet and member of Parliament, part of the West Indian planter interest, arranges to have Fanny Price brought from Portsmouth to live as a second-class citizen within his household and to serve his wife. Ignorant of the symbolism of global location when she first comes to Mansfield Park, Fanny "cannot put the map of Europe together." Her cousins mock her for referring to the Isle of Wight as "*the Island,* as if there were no other island in the world." She learns about her uncle's plantation in Antigua as she learns about her own place in the scheme of things, subject to the tyrannies of Mrs. Norris, whose name, as Moira Ferguson has pointed out, was the name of a particularly duplicitous proslavery advocate described in Clarkson's *History of Abolition,* which Austen read.[38]

That Norris, a slave captain responsible for transporting boatloads of captives (as, in a domestic register, Mrs. Norris is responsible for transporting Fanny to her new servitude in Mansfield Park), represented himself to Clarkson at first as a humane opponent of the slave trade, interested in its amendment and even its abolition. But he evaded Clarkson's efforts to bring him before the king's privy council in March 1788 to report corruptions and brutalities in the slave trade and appeared unexpectedly instead as a "Liverpool delegate in support of the Slave-trade." He argued that the Africans were so barbaric, cruel, and murderous to one another that bringing them away and introducing them to European culture was actually a blessing.[39] Moreover, he said that many slaves were prisoners of war and would have been put to death had they remained in Africa, "whereas now they were saved" (481). This astonishing testimony carried the day, according to Clarkson, who then "had the mortification to hear of nothing but the Liverpool evidence." The convinced privy council returned the verdict that "the major part of the complaints against this Trade are ill-founded" (482-83).

Refracting Mrs. Norris's treatment of Fanny through Clarkson's anecdote is chilling, particularly her self-justifying explanations, her duplicity, and the extent to which she exploits Fanny all the while exclaiming on Fanny's luck in enjoying the advantages of Mansfield Park. Clarkson's stories about the slave captain Norris give a sinister shadow to Mrs. Norris's unreflecting selfishness. But whether the translation from slave captain to managerial aunt serves to demonize the aunt or to naturalize the slave captain remains a question. Readers who do not believe that the daily exploitation of dependent women should be used as a political figuration of racialized slavery—because these evils are incommensurate—will see in Austen's appropriation of Clarkson's materials the alchemy of a mind transforming the genuinely political into the merely personal. On the other hand, readers who see continuities between tyranny in the home and tyranny in the political colonies will find this superimposition of the duplicitous slave-captain on Aunt Norris's self-aggrandizement a powerful commentary on all exploitative human relations.

Antigua was known to Austen, both from her father's connection to James Langford Nibbs and from her brother's firsthand report from his *Canopus* days.[40] The "Antiguan negro code," more humane than laws on other islands, included the right of slaves to trial by jury and placed no restrictions on manumission. But Moira Ferguson quotes a remarkable bit of social history in which Lord Lavington, governor of the island and commander in chief of the Leeward Islands, used a pair of tongs to receive letters or parcels from the "fingers of a black or coloured man . . . to guard against such *horrible* defilement,"[41] corroborating Frank Austen's judgment about the "harshness and despotism" of the "land-holders or their managers in the West India Islands."

Like other English colonies in the Caribbean at the time of Sir Thomas Bertram's visit, Antigua suffered from falling prices for sugar and war-inflated rising costs for everything else. Britain's recapture of sugar-producing colonies from France and Holland had flooded the home market and was driving prices down.[42] By December 1806, 1,464,102 hundred weight of sugar was sitting in warehouses or onboard ships in English ports.[43] In Jamaica, between 1799 and 1807, sixty-five plantations were abandoned outright, thirty-two were sold up to meet bankruptcy claims, and suits were pending in one hundred fifteen others. Three parliamentary commissions were established between 1807 and 1808 to study planter distress.[44] Antigua was particularly hard hit during the period in which

Austen sends Sir Thomas to see to his affairs there, for in addition to the falling price for sugar, an unusual drought had withered the crop to a third of its usual size.[45] Mrs. Norris observes merely that "Sir Thomas' means will be rather straitened, if the Antigua estate is to make such poor returns"; but planters on the island were, in fact, unable to meet their taxes. Governor Lavington wrote from Antigua in the summer of 1805: "Bankruptcy is universal, and is not confin'd to the Public Treasury, but extends to the Generality of Individuals resident in the Colony."[46]

Sir Thomas's business in Antigua between 1805 and 1807, of course, had to do with more than the financial problems of plantation owners during a sugar glut—it had to do with the nature of slavery itself. The bill to abolish the slave trade had been ratified in both houses in 1806 and passed into law in 1807, from which date all slave traffic to the Caribbean ceased. When Fanny Price asks Sir Thomas Bertram about the slave trade on his return, she is inquiring about the consequences of this fact. The "dead silence" that follows her query indicates her cousins' lack of interest in or opposition to the measure, quite as much as a breach of decorum through which one can glimpse the ugly exploitative relations that undergird the social position and material luxury of Mansfield Park.[47]

In addition to ending the trade in slaves, the Abolition Bill also presaged new, milder treatment for existing slaves in the West Indies. If there were to be no new slaves brought into the islands from Africa, the human property already in the colonies would have to be treated better. It could not be abused or worked to death but would have to be handled so as to encourage its health and reproduction. Fanny's question thus also figures a change in her own status at Mansfield Park insofar as she is a creature of the Bertrams. Despite Mrs. Norris's indignation at these new considerations, she is to have a fire in the east room and use of the carriage when she is invited out to dine. Fanny's seemingly innocent question about the slave trade is also a prelude to her passive rebellion against Henry Crawford's suit and Sir Thomas's masterful pressure. She will not mate and breed as they direct her.

Gender and Class

When Edward Said accused Austen of unconsciously accepting slavery and British colonialism, exemplifying how "humanistic ideas coexisted so comfortably with imperialism," he repeated Raymond Williams's famous comparison between the class consciousness of William Cobbett and Jane Austen.[48] He claimed that Cobbett was aware of class stratification in his society, whereas Austen's social vision was restricted to the moral discriminations and social details of a single class. Her obliviousness to the privileges of class was evident, he said, in her "uninflected, unreflective citations of Antigua (or the Mediterranean, or India, which is where Lady Bertram in a fit of distracted impatience, requires that William should go "'that I may have a shawl . . .')."[49] It was precisely because Austen—among others—took for granted that English colonies must support the Sir Thomas Bertrams of the world, and that these Bertrams had to take long and dangerous voyages from time to time to supervise and regulate their overseas property, according to Said, that created the "broad expanse of domestic imperialist culture without which the subsequent acquisition of territory would not have been possible."[50] In other words, Said accused Austen of referring to Antigua and to the slave trade casually, merely by way of adding decor to her story of domestic rearrangements in the upper classes, thus contributing to the naturalizing of those unnatural elements, slavery and colonialism.

But, of course, nothing in Jane Austen's novels is ever "uninflected" or "unreflective," and I think Said is wrong to imagine the references to the slave trade in ***Mansfield Park*** as morally neutral—any more than references to colonialism or war in ***Persuasion*** (although from the other side of the political fence) are morally neutral. Because Said was unable to imagine the dependent status of women despite his use of the terms "gender" and "feminism" in his introduction, he did not notice that colonialism in all the late novels is associated with women. Not only is Fanny torn from her family, transported to Mansfield Park, and put at the disposal of Lady Bertram and Mrs. Norris—all for the price of her maintenance—but she is treated like recalcitrant property when she refuses to marry as Sir Thomas commands. That it was she, rather than her entitled cousins, who wanted to know about the slave trade is hardly "uninflected." And when she raised the question with her master in the context of its recent abolition and is met with "dead silence," while her cousins sat "without speaking a word, or seeming at all interested in the subject," that too means something.

In ***Emma,*** it is the dependent Jane Fairfax, about to hire out as a governess, who speaks of "offices for the sale—not quite of human flesh—but of human intellect." Officious Augusta from Bristol, England's premier slave trading port, who has just bought Mr. Elton for "so many thousands as would always be called ten," understands the reference but not the domestic context or personal implication.[51] "You quite shock me," she retorts, "if you mean a fling at the slave-trade, I assure you Mr. Suckling was always rather a friend to the abolition."[52] This exchange, with its two levels of meaning and consciousness, is calculated to call attention to the economics of the marriage market and to women's uncertain and dependent status. As Mary Astell summarized the problem a century earlier: "If *all Men are born free,* how is it that all Women are born Slaves?"[53]

One has to read Austen's fictional references to slavery and colonialism structurally—where and how these references are used—because context and position speak eloquently about oppressive and unequal relations closer to home whenever these references are introduced. In ***Mansfield***

Park, Fanny's question about the slave trade is juxtaposed to Sir Thomas Bertram's reassertion of control over his property—human as well as horticultural—reinforcing the reader's sense of Fanny's subordination. In ***Emma,*** these remarks about the slave trade bubble up at the point of crisis in Jane Fairfax's dealings with her secret fiancé, Frank Churchill, underscoring her utter dependence on a "good" marriage to save her from a worse servitude. Slavery in these novels figures the dependent status of women without money of their own. The "slave trade" is a trope for the marriage market and for the tyranny of marriage, a displacement of the subject status of captive Africans onto women.

In ***Persuasion,*** too, colonial possessions are associated with the weakest and most dependent woman in the novel, Mrs. Smith, Anne Elliot's old schoolfellow who rents a few rooms in the unfashionable Westgate buildings in Bath. Left penniless by the death of her husband, unable to collect the money owed him by the duplicitous and vicious gentleman, Mr. Elliot, she cannot claim her inherited property in the West Indies without a male agent. This alienated property in the West Indies, presumably a sugar plantation operating on slave labor, represents at once a literary convention—a standard eighteenth-century novelist's plot device for restoring lost fortunes—and a simultaneous reminder that without a man, a woman's authority over even her own plantations was null and void. Without a man, a woman cannot cash in on colonial possessions. Located in the aftermath of the extended struggle with France over colonial territory, ***Persuasion*** romanticizes both the long contest and the objects of imperial contention as a proving ground for British manhood. Emphasizing Mrs. Smith's helplessness as a woman, dependent on a man's intervention to claim her property, the episode also calls attention to Captain Wentworth's manly capability in this as in all else.[54] Thus the fruits of colonialism in the form of Mrs. Smith's West Indian property become a kind of benevolent attention that Captain Wentworth gallantly bestows upon the impoverished and invalided woman.

Austen was still working on these issues—the gendered terms of colonialism—in her last unfinished novel fragment. However she intended to work out the plot of ***Sanditon,*** she fused the issues of gender and race in the character of Miss Lambe, an overprotected and privileged half-mulatto West Indian heiress, whom Austen seems to have set up as a target both for money-making schemes and for seduction. The town leaders, commercially minded Mr. Parker and the shrewd, eccentric matriarch Lady Denham, have joined forces to turn their sleepy little town into a tourist attraction, a resort for taking wholesome waters, a new Bath. Among their earliest longed-for customers are the headmistress of a finishing school with three of her charges.

> Of these three, & indeed of all, Miss Lambe was beyond comparison the most important & precious, as she paid in proportion to her fortune.—She was about 17, half Mulatto, chilly & tender, had a maid of her own, was to have the best room in the Lodgings, & was always of the first consequence in every plan of Mrs. G.
>
> (6:421)

Old Lady Denham sees in Miss Lambe the very type of a seaside invalid for their new resort town: rich and sickly, a steady customer for her medicinal milch asses' milk, and an heiress for her nephew by marriage, Sir Edward, to marry. Sir Edward, for his part, aspires to be a rake, handsome and dangerous, a nouveau Lovelace, and this wealthy innocent appears heaven-sent to be his sacrificial lamb. Thus the West Indian heiress, because she is a woman, is cast as the victim of colonialism as well as its beneficiary. I imagine that in the exact moral and spiritual calibrations of this "chilly & tender" character, one of whose grandparents was brought to the island in chains, Austen was planning to chart the interrelations between the traffic in women and the slave trade with their corresponding moral corruptions.

Jane Austen's sense of class, like her gender and her patriotic sense of Englishness, was affected by the wars with France and by British imperialism. But Raymond Williams and Edward Said are mistaken; it was *because* of her class—which was lesser gentry without unearned income—that she revised her estimation of English militarism and imperialism in the last years of her life. Because she watched the wars of colonialism over territory enable her brothers' upward mobility, she became something of a British chauvinist in the end—a change of heart recorded in ***Persuasion.*** That last novel reveals a new attitude about England's global destiny, informed by nationalistic pride over the triumphal defeat of Napoleon and her brothers' successful careers within the naval establishment. The years that Austen replays in ***Persuasion,*** the years between 1806 and 1808—the very years that Sir Thomas Bertram is absent from his English plantations in ***Mansfield Park***—become in this last novel not a period of moral anarchy but of idealized personal history for the new self-made man and his mate. Admirable though Anne Elliot is, sociologically speaking Austen created her as a rootless woman, severed from her family, tender and nurturing, ready to follow her man and to support him in his new "profession which is, if possible, more distinguished in its domestic virtues than in its national importance."

Persuasion is a tribute to class mobility, meritocracy, and professionalism. England needed more professional leaders than its upper classes could supply, and good men were beginning to make their fortunes serving the state. Where once the family of origin determined class status, national service was beginning to offer an alternative route to class mobility for men of the middling classes. Without family or connections, with "nothing but himself to recommend him," Wentworth rises "as high in his profession as merit and activity could place him" and takes so many ships for his country as to secure £25,000 for himself. The navy, as Sir Walter Elliot complains at the beginning of ***Persuasion,*** had become "the means of bringing persons of obscure birth into undue distinction, and raising men to honors which their fathers and grandfathers never dreamt of."[55] Just as Frank Austen's part in the action off Santo Domingo enabled him to marry Mary Gibson, so England's wars of imperialism permit Wentworth to make enough of a fortune to marry a baronet's daughter.

Austen links this possibility for class mobility in her last novel with the creation of new kinds of families, families with greater potential for happiness than old-style families such as the Elliots or the Musgroves.[56] Louisa Musgrove speaks from the heart of the novel when she declares herself "convinced of sailors having more worth and warmth than any other set of men in England; that they only knew how to live, and they only deserved to be respected and loved." The emphasis is there in the very last sentence of ***Persuasion,*** which couples domestic virtue with national importance and in which service to the nation is rewarded by the love of a good woman. Throughout the novel, the navy enables better domestic arrangements. "Nothing can exceed the accommodation of a man of war," confides Mrs. Croft cheerfully, although a frigate is "more confined." Harville's carvings and curiosities from around the world deck-out his cosy little house—the fruits of colonial contact enriching the English hearth. The navy becomes a true brotherhood, a better source of hospitality and neighborliness than relatives. The nation-state supplies the deficiencies of family and community alike.

As a woman of the lesser gentry, benefitting through her brothers from these new rewards for colonial service, Austen saw the analogies between the subjugation of women and the subjugation of captive peoples (***Mansfield Park*** and ***Emma***) more clearly than she recognized the collusion of women of her own class in colonialist exploitation (***Persuasion***). She did not see—or did not mind—that the colonialist solution to class inequality was made possible by displacing class subordination onto the people of another culture. Precisely *because* of her class location, Austen found the class mobility enabled by colonialism to be very appealing. In ***Persuasion,*** for instance, the class context always determines the valence of her colonial references. One is never encouraged to feel that Wentworth's success is at the expense of the labor and property of colonized peoples even though the national project in which he proves his worth and makes his fortune depends on extracting wealth from the natural resources of colonized territories and the labor of captive peoples. Nor has Austen any qualms about imagining Mrs. Smith enriched by property and slaves in another part of the world insofar as she casts Mrs. Smith's story as a story of class triumph, where class has been imposed by gender and is reinforced by class antagonism in the person of the heartless baronet-to-be, William Elliot. Mrs. Smith has been victimized by a vicious gentleman and is helped to her rightful West Indian property by a self-made man.

There is evidence in Austen's letters as well as her novels that her sensibility was increasingly shaped by the rising tide of nationalism in England, intensified by its struggles with France. As she moved into the period in which she wrote ***Persuasion,*** she is drawn to the ringing, patriotic diction that she would have mocked in her youth. It was a higher grade of redcoat mania than Lydia Bennet suffered from—motivated, one could even argue, by family feeling—but it was undeniably the same disease. She wrote to Cassandra in 1813 about a book that she was enjoying contrary to her expectations:

> *I* am reading a Society octavo, an Essay on the Military Polic[y] and Institutions of The British Empire by Capt Pasley of the Engineers, a book which I protested against at first but which upon trial I find delightfully written and highly entertaining. I am as much in love with the author as ever I was with Clarkson or Buchanan, or even the two Mr. Smiths of the city—the first soldier I ever sighed for—but he does write with extraordinary force and spirit.[57]

The "two Mr. Smiths of the city" were a pair of brothers, a solicitor and a stockbroker, who had put together an hilarious collection of spoofs of contemporary authors in 1812. A spurious set of "Rejected Addresses" solicited from the public at large on the occasion of the opening of the rebuilt Drury Lane theater, all but one of these literary parodies in the manner of Wordsworth, Southey, Cobbett, M. G. Lewis, Coleridge, Crabbe, Dr. Johnson, Scott, had been composed by the Smiths. It is not surprising that Jane Austen would have listed them here among the authors she "was in love with," for their satiric vein is like her own. What is surprising is that these literary figures should be named in the same sentence with Clarkson, Buchanan, and Pasley—whose writerly claims come not from a playful sense of literary parody but from a polemical sense of urgency about England's role in international relations.[58]

Pasley's book is an exhortation to all right-minded Englishmen to support building a stronger military establishment to defend England. Written in 1808 (although not published until 1810), Pasley's opening sentence warns his countrymen that they live in perilous times:

> In times when the British nation is placed in a situation of danger, to which its past history affords no parallel, menaced with destruction by a much superior force, which is directed by the energy of one of the greatest warriors that has appeared; every man in this country must think with anxiety upon the result; every man must feel, that nothing but the greatest unanimity and firmness on the part of the nation, nothing but the wisest measures on the part of the government, can save us, and with us the rest of the civilized world, from swelling the triumph of the haughty conqueror.

Pasley reads like one of the new-style manly Englishmen about whom Claudia Johnson has written,[59] whose type begins to turn up as the hero of late-eighteenth-century fiction. Both practical and courageous, a cross between Captain James Cook, the intrepid explorer, and Josiah Wedgewood, the enlightened entrepreneur—natural, vigorous, strong, plainspeaking, rational, informed, strictly adhering to principle, not Frenchified or feminized—this new kind of hero constructs his own pedigree out of intelligent competence and force of character. Written with "extraordinary force and spirit," Pasley's *Essay on the Military Policy of the British Empire* is a book that privileges and celebrates masculinity—"the first soldier I ever sighed for," remarks Austen, mocking her own attraction for male heroics in this unabashed document of British imperialism. Pasley could be one of the brave navy men in ***Persuasion,*** calling for firmness and wisdom on the part of the nation, the sort of Austen hero that Louisa Musgrove goes into raptures over.

Austen's lighthearted letter to Cassandra goes on to compare the tastes of the Chawton book club to those of Steventon or Manydown.

> The Miss Sibleys want to establish a Book Society in their side of the country, like ours. What can be stronger proof of that superiority in ours over Steventon & Manydown society, which I have always forseen & felt? . . . what are their Biglands & their Barrows, their Macartneys & Mackenzies to Capt Pasley's Essay on the Military Polic [y] of the British Empire. . . . ?

The Biglands and Barrows, Macartneys and Mackenzies, the best that the Steventon and Manydown book society had to offer, were Bigland's *History of Spain* (1810), Barrow's *Account of Travels into the Interior of South Africa* (1801), Macartney's *Travels to China* (1810), and Mackenzie's *Travels in Iceland* (1811), all travel books that reflect the expanding English preoccupation with the rest of the world.[60] Macartney's *Travels to China* describes the 1792 British embassy to the Peking court, an unsuccessful attempt to open trade with China under the guise of cultural exchange, sponsored by the East India Company.[61] Fanny Price is reading this book in ***Mansfield Park*** when Edmund interrupts her to tell her of his decision to play Anhalt in *Lovers' Vows,* to save Mary Crawford from having to play a love scene with a stranger. Fanny's reading thus figures Mary Crawford's unsuccessful attempt to negotiate a more permanent "treaty" with Edmund under the pretense of a harmless cultural exchange. Austen's comparison of Pasley to the Biglands and Barrows, the Macartneys and Mackenzies, implicitly connects all these books to each other—as if she were aware at some level of the continuities between the accounts of British travelers, observing other cultures with Eurocentric eyes, and the nationalistic prose of Captain Pasley, rousing Englishmen to maintain their overseas dominions. Moreover, her account of the two provincial book societies shows the interest of the English reading public in accounts of travel and exploration. Whether facing the elements, trading with "natives," fighting off wild animals, parlaying with painted chiefs, or simply taking possession of an island or a territory in the name of the king of Great Britain, all of these books demonstrate English mastery of the world—physically, psychologically, and morally.

In 1806 Austen gave her eight-year-old nephew, James-Edward (James's child with Mary Lloyd), *The British Navigator, or A Collection of Voyages made in Different Parts of the World,* a typical adventure book of the day.[62] Packed with stories of ships becalmed or ships overwhelmed by tempestuous seas, *The British Navigator* took its readers from the North Pole to the South Seas. One reads of choked pumps, leaks in the hold, a ship filling up with water and gradually sinking while a small boat is launched on the open seas with a few courageous men and provisions enough for only a few days. The expeditions land at uncharted or mischarted shores with names like those in a morality play—Port Desire, Port Famine, Cape Virgin Mary, Deceitful Bay. The brave and enlightened captains, responsible to posterity as Englishmen must be, record the strange birds and animals they find with a naturalists' care. They note what edible produce of land or sea sustain them for those who may come after. Eight-year-old James-Edward would have read of the intrepid and amiable Commodore Byron encountering a magnificent Indian, the very embodiment of the noble savage with his animal skin thrown over his shoulders.

> The person who advanced appeared to be a chief, and was very near seven feet in height. Round one of his eyes was a circle of black paint and a white circle round the other; the the rest of his face was painted in streaks of various colours. He had the skin of a beast, with the hair inwards, thrown over his shoulders. The commodore and the Indian having complimented each other, in language equally unintelligible to either, they walked together towards the main body of the Indians.[63]

Clarkson, Buchanan, and Pasley were also adventurers in this spirit of the English Enlightenment, traveling to meet "the other," exchanging diplomatic compliments, and trying to change behaviors in other parts of the world. Clarkson was a fierce abolitionist who wrote and lectured about Africa and captive Africans; Buchanan was an English missionary in India, agitating for a branch of the Anglican church there and translating the Bible into indigenous languages; and Pasley, a captain in the corps of royal engineers, was an frank advocate of armed imperialism, arguing for the need to maintain British hegemony in the world with a standing army. All three men represented engagement with a new international world order, although with our late-twentieth-century sensitivity to colonial exploitation, their values seem incompatible to us. The contradictions that are so apparent to us among their positions were contradictions inherent in the Enlightenment itself. But in their day, these three men shared a new way of thinking about peoples (and markets) in the rest of the world in relation to England—whether to convert, to protect, or to conquer them.

Buchanan was a professor of classics, an educator, responsible for commissioning the translation of the gospels into Hindustan, Persian, Chinese, Maylay, Orissa, Mahratta, and Bengalese. He understood his mission as part and parcel of colonial territorial expansion and believed that his enlightened version of Christianity was superior to Hinduism, whose sanguinary practices he reported with horror (the annual ritual suicides beneath the wheels of the Juggernaut; the immolation of females; the sacrifice of children).[64] Although he failed in his pet project to establish the Church of England in India, Buchanan probably achieved a more profound cultural colonization of Asia with the dissemination of the translated, printed gospels than either Clarkson with his rhetoric or Pasley with his sword.

These three figures—Clarkson, Buchanan, and Pasley—all believed in their responsibility to impose English morality on the conduct of human affairs elsewhere in the world. All were visionaries, looking to the future, imagining the implications of the global economy for their particular concerns, whether slavery and its abolition, a worldwide Christian church, or England's military strength. They believed in progress, the European enlightenment, expanded horizons, rational action, operations on an international scale—the full consequences of which we are still reaping in our own day with GATT, NAFTA, and the World Trade Organization, the political leverage of religious leaders, and international military aid and interventions. Austen's grouping of these men—she says she is "in love" with them all—suggests a more profound understanding of the changes wrought in her society by commerce and militarism than she is often given credit for.

Austen's relation to colonialism and slavery was thus conditioned by her gender and her class and the history of England in her lifetime. Opposed to enslaving anyone, she used the discourse of abolition to comment on the dependent position of women without means in her society. She seems to have been refining those perceptions about the commodification of persons—and the gendering of that commodification—in ***Sanditon.*** At the same time, because of her own class location, she knew that the navy provided upward mobility for men without fortune, family, or connections. Her last novel, written after Waterloo, has an appreciative sense of the national destiny that made this mobility possible. Thus she registered the democratizing of power across class for men, oblivious that it entailed colonial domination elsewhere, and at the same time recorded her sense of the personal limitations facing women.

Her comparison of Pasley's book on armies and empire to Clarkson's *History of Abolition* (1808) and Buchanan's *Christian Researches in Asia* (1811) shows a sensitivity to the politics of internationalism that is before her time. Nor should her awareness of this socioeconomic phenomenon surprise anyone who grants her extraordinary grasp of other complex socioeconomic phenomena of her day. Her late novels highlight the contradictions of Eurocentric humanism because they are written from the point-of-view of a woman of the lesser gentry—rather than from the point-of-view of a man of any class or a woman of another class. She understood the implicit remasculinization of Englishmen in the imperial project and responded to it even as she gently mocked it ("I am as much in love with [Pasley] as ever I was with Clarkson or Buchanan"). She represented the hypocrisy of the enterprising Bristol slave traders in Augusta Elton and Mrs. Norris and the responsible authoritarianism of the West Indian plantocracy in Sir Thomas Bertram. In the equivocal lineaments of her characters, Austen traced the lived meanings of British imperialism in all their ironies. Cheerful Mrs. Smith in ***Persuasion,*** confined to her room while nevertheless eking out a charitable mite for the poorer families in town by selling homemade thread cases and pincushions, owns a plantation halfway around the world. Neither "unreflective" nor "uninflected," Austen's references to British colonialism are complicated and refracted through the controversies of her day. The slavery that Jane Fairfax refers to is not just a literary metaphor but was a reality witnessed by members of her family. Men of her generation went to India to retrieve their fortunes while women went there to find husbands. Living in an expanding imperialist society, Austen represented its ideological pressures even as she was susceptible to them. Rather than demonstrating her obliviousness to the privileges of class and global location, Austen's colonial references reveal rather the deep contradictions of Enlightenment thought, the problems implicit in exporting humanism, capitalism, and technology to the rest of the world.

Notes

1. First published in 1989, the essay was reprinted in *Culture and Imperialism* (New York: Knopf, 1993), 80-97.

2. Deirdre, Le Faye, *Jane Austen: A Family Record,* (originally written by William Austen-Leigh and Richard Arthur Austen-Leigh) (Boston: G. K. Hall & Co., 1989), 94.

3. Herman Melville, *Billy Budd, Sailor: An Inside Narrative,* ed. Milton R. Stern (Indianapolis: Bobbs-Merrill Educational Publishing, 1975), 121.

4. David Geggus, "British Opinion and the Emergence of Haiti, 1791-1804," in *Slavery and British Society, 1776-1846,* ed. James Walvin (Baton Rouge: Louisisana State University Press, 1982), 123-49, esp. 128.

5. Ruth Perry, "Home at Last: Biographical Background to *Pride and Prejudice*" in *Approaches to Teaching Austen's* Pride and Prejudice, ed. Marcia McClintock Folsom (New York: Modern Language Association, 1993), 46-56, esp. 47.

6. Robin Blackburn, *The Overthrow of Colonial Slavery, 1776-1848* (London: Verso, 1988), 163.

7. Paul Kennedy, *The Rise and Fall of British Naval Mastery* (London: Ashfield Press, 1976), 129. See also Lowell Joseph Ragatz, *The Rise and Fall of the Planter Class in the British Caribbean, 1763-1833* (1928; reprint, New York: Octagon Books, 1963), 127.

8. C. L. R. James, *The Black Jacobins: Toussaint L'Ouverture and the San Domingo Revolution* (1938; reprint, New York: Random House, 1963), 55.

9. Ibid., 52-3. Eric Williams, *Capitalism and Slavery* (London: Andre Deutsch, 1964), 146-48.

10. Ragatz, *Fall of the Planter Class,* 250.

11. Clarkson's essay was originally written in Latin as a dissertation for Cambridge University, where it was accorded first prize in 1785. For Cugoana and Equiano, see *Three Black Writers in Eighteenth Century England,* ed. and introduced by Francis D. Adams and Barry Sanders (Belmont, Calif.: Wadsworth Publishing Company, Inc., 1971), and more recently, *Unchained Voices: An Anthology of Black Authors in the English-Speaking World of the Eighteenth Century,* ed. Vincent Caretta (Lexington: University of Kentucky Press, 1996). The full narrative of Olaudah Equiano is now available in a Penguin edition edited by Vincent Caretta (1995), and the first edition of *Thoughts and Sentiments on the Evil of Slavery* by Ottobah Cugoano was reprinted with an introduction by Paul Edwards (London: Dawsons, 1969).

12. Blackburn, *Overthrow of Slavery,* 144.

13. Williams, *Capitalism and Slavery,* 147.

14. J. H. and Edith C. Hubback, *Jane Austen's Sailor Brothers* (London: John Lane, 1906), 15-16.

15. Ragatz, *Fall of the Planter Class,* 260-63.

16. Thomas Clarkson, *The History of the Rise, Progress, and Accomplishment of the Abolition of the African Slave-Trade by the British Parliament,* 2 vols. (London, 1808), 2:349-50.

17. Geggus, "Emergence of Haiti," 125-26; Ragatz, *Fall of the Planter Class,* 217.

18. Geggus, "Emergence of Haiti," 127-28.

19. James, *Black Jacobins,* 227.

20. Blackburn, *Overthrow of Slavery,* 245.

21. Lady Nugent, *Lady Nugent's Journal,* ed. Frank Cundall, published for the Institute of Jamaica by the West India Committee (London, 1934), 142, 149.

22. Ibid., 156-57.

23. Ibid., 222.

24. Blackburn, *Overthrow of Slavery,* 250.

25. Le Faye, *Family Record,* 54.

26. Ibid., 9.

27. Frank Gibbon, "The Antiguan Connection," *Cambridge Quarterly* 11 (1982): 298-305, esp. 300.

28. Jane Austen, "Catharine, or The Bower," in *Minor Works,* ed. R. W. Chapman, vol. 6 of *Collected Works* (London: Oxford University Press, 1954), 6:194.

29. Deirdre Le Faye, "Jane Austen and Her Hancock Relatives," *Review of English Studies* n.s. 30 (1979): 12-27.

30. One sign of complicated planter attitudes are the entries in Lady Nugent's Jamaican diary of 1801-02 recording that she was devoting a good deal of her time to reading Wilberforce (Nugent 57, 72).

31. Ragatz, *Fall of the Planter Class,* 292.

32. Jan Fergus discusses the appropriateness of Terry Lovell's term, "lesser gentry," or David Spring's "pseudo-gentry," when describing the Austens' class status in "Jane Austen: Tensions between Security and Marginality," in *History, Gender and Eighteenth-Century Literature,* ed. Beth Fowkes Tobin (Athens and London: University of Georgia Press, 1994), 258-59.

33. *Cobbett's Political Register,* 4:933-37, quoted in Geggus, "Emergence of Haiti," 141.

34. Ibid., *Austen's Sailor Brothers,* 192.

35. Ibid., 175.

36. Ibid., 179; Thomas Southey, *Chronological History of the West Indies* (London: Longman, Rees, Orme, Brown, and Green, 1827), 344-55.

37. Margaret Kirkham observed this association between Lord Mansfield's decision and the title of Austen's novel in *Jane Austen: Feminism and Fiction* (New York: Methuen, 1986), 117-18.

38. Frank Gibbon first suggested the association of Aunt Norris with Clarkson's slave captain Norris in "The Antiguan Connection," *Cambridge Quarterly* 11, 2

(1982): 298-305, but Moira Ferguson elaborates the connection in her fine article.

39. Clarkson, *History of Abolition,* 1:378 ff. and 477 ff.

40. Historians of the West Indies report Antigua as exceptional among the British colonies in several respects. It was the only British colony where the white planters showed any interest in agricultural improvements, possibly because it had a greater number of permanent residents among the landowners (Ragatz, *Fall of the Planter Class,* 66).

41. Ferguson, "Slavery, Colonialism, and Gender," 120.

42. St. Lucia and Tobago from the French, Essequibo, Demerara and Berbice from the Dutch.

43. Ragatz, *Fall of the Planter Class,* 306.

44. Williams, *Capitalism and Slavery,* 149.

45. Ragatz, *Fall of the Planter Class,* 306.

46. Ibid., 306.

47. *Mansfield Park,* ed. Tony Tanner (1814; reprint, London: Penguin, 1966), 213. Brian Southam disputes this interpretation by fixing Sir Thomas Bertram's return from Antigua in October 1812 rather than 1807 on the strength of the publication of Crabbe's *Tales* in 1812, which is one of the books on Fanny's table in the east room when Edmund goes to speak to her there. The other books, *The Idler* and *Macartney's Travels,* were published by 1807. See the *Times Literary Supplement,* 17 February 1995, 13-14. It is worth noting that although Crabbe's *Tales* were not published until 1812, a number of his works had been published earlier, including "The Village" in 1783 and a collected volume of *Poems* published in 1807 that included a number of narrative poems such as appeared in *Tales.*

48. Said, "Jane Austen and Empire," 82.

49. Ibid., 93.

50. Ibid., 163.

51. As Clarkson rode into Bristol to gather information about the slave trade, he "anticipated much persecution … and I questioned whether I should even get out of it alive." *History of Abolition,* 1:293-94. He escaped without violence in Bristol but was set upon by assassins in Liverpool.

52. Chapter 35.

53. Mary Astell, *Some Reflections upon Marriage* (London, 1700), 11.

54. Claudia Johnson's afterword to *Equivocal Beings,* "'Not at all what a man should be!': Remaking English Manhood in *Emma,*" [*Equivocal Beings: Politics, Gender, and Sentimentality in the 1790s* (Chicago: University of Chicago Press, 1995), 191-203)] argues that *Emma* is preeminently about the refashioning of English masculinity in the aftermath of a wave of male sentimentality brought on by the crisis in gender identity caused by the French Revolution. I am suggesting here that in *Persuasion,* Austen continues that trajectory by creating an ideal type of "the new man" in Captain Wentworth: professional, self-made, helpful, reliable, capable.

55. Traditionally, the English navy was a more democratic institution than the English army; Horatio Nelson was the son of a rector whereas Arthur Wellesley, the duke of Wellington, was the son of Garrett Wesley, second baron and first earl of Mornington. These class associations are reversed in the U.S. armed services, where the navy is associated with the educated class and the army with the working class.

56. The idealization of Wentworth's domestic virtues and the concommitant and symmetrical satire on Sir Walter's selfishness is elaborated brilliantly in Maaja Stewart's important study of class and colonialism in Austen's fiction, *Domestic Realities and Imperial Fictions* (Athens and London: University of Georgia Press, 1993), 91.

57. The letter is dated Sunday, 24 January 1813. *Jane Austen's Letters to Her Sister Cassandra and Others,* ed. R. W. Chapman, 2 vols. (Oxford: Clarendon Press, 1932).

58. For a thorough history of *Rejected Addresses* with an introduction, notes, and a bibiliography, see the edition edited by Andrew Boyle (London: Constable & Company Ltd., 1929).

59. See note 53 above.

60. "Barrow" might also refer to Sir John Barrow's *Selection from the Unpublished Writings of the Earl of Macartney* (1807), drawn from Macartney's journal.

61. The sketches and drawings of people, scenes, implements, houses, etc. made by William Alexander, a junior draughtsman employed by Macartney, are a vivid pictorial record of this embassy and are preserved in the British Library's Oriental and India Office Collection. For more information about the Macartney expedition, see Aubrey Singer, *Lion and Dragon* (London: Barrie and Jenkins, 1992) and Helen H. Robbins, *Our First Ambassador to China* (London: John Murray, 1908).

62. Le Faye, *Family Record,* 135.

63. This is taken from an account of Commodore Byron's voyage around the world 1764-66 in *The British Navigator; Containing An Account of Voyages round the World, Performed by Commodore Byron, Begun in the Year 1764, and finished in 1766. By Captain Wallis, Begun in 1766, and finished in 1769. To which is prefixed, An Account of the Loss of His Majesty's Ship the Centaur, Commanded by Captain Inglesfield, and of the Miraculous Escape of the Captain and Part of his Crew* (London, 1783); it describes an encounter with Amerindians in what is now Argentina.

64. These are the particular practices mentioned in *Christian Researches in Asia: With notices of the translation of the scriptures into the Oriental Languages* (Boston: Samuel Armstrong, 1811).

Nicholas Boyle (lecture date 2002-03)

SOURCE: Boyle, Nicholas. "Faces (2): *Mansfield Park.*" *Sacred and Secular Scriptures: A Catholic Approach to Literature.* Notre Dame: U of Notre Dame P, 2005. 205-20. Print.

[*In the following lecture, delivered in 2002-03, Boyle considers the indirectly secular nature of* Mansfield Park, *noting that Fanny's main concern is her principles. Though the narrative never portrays a sermon or service of worship, Boyle observes, the Catholic Church operates in the text as an institution of principle.*]

Unlike *Moby-Dick*, ***Mansfield Park*** (begun in 1811 and first published in 1814)[1] is not an obviously Faustian work. It is probably the least popular of Jane Austen's novels, no doubt because of the rather prim character of its heroine who has the misfortune—as far as readers are concerned—of being always right. That there are nonetheless points of contact with Goethe's world of reflection is shown by some remarkable parallels with his novel *Elective Affinities,* written just after he had completed *Faust: Part One* and published in 1809.[2] The parallels would deserve a study of their own, for which there is no space here, but it is worth mentioning some of them as an indication that the unusual character of this novel in Jane Austen's oeuvre is due to a deep understanding of the needs of the age rather than to a regrettable lapse into moralizing. Both novels concern the trial of virtue in a country house setting, both largely observe a unity of place, and both have heroines who come from penurious backgrounds and are from the beginning in a state of uncomfortable dependency on their benefactors. In both novels contemporary intellectual fashions—a vogue for landscape gardening and the aesthetic "improvement" of estates, for example, and in ***Mansfield Park*** the popularity of the German dramas of Goethe's adversary, Kotzebue—have an insidious influence on the society depicted and are at the very least a sign of indolence and irresponsibility. In both cases too, though more elaborately and extensively in *Elective Affinities,* the artificially altered landscape takes on a symbolic role, representing in space the moral transgressions of the characters. Above all, both novels are so structured as to present a steadily growing threat to the increasingly isolated heroine, who seems beset by ever subtler threats of corruption and ever more left to her own resources. This gradually intensifying structure is in both cases composed of two parts, the second presenting the problematic of the first in a yet more intractable form, so that an insistent theological undertone becomes apparent in both works, though the theology is very different.

In the case of ***Mansfield Park*** the first part, consisting of the first of the original three volumes and the first chapters of the second, introduces us to Fanny Price, daughter of an overprolific Lieutenant of Marines, to her four wealthy cousins, and to the establishment at Mansfield Park, the seat of Sir Thomas Bertram. It also introduces us to the beginnings of Fanny's affection for the younger son of the family, Edmund, an affection admitted to no one and scarcely even to herself, since the inequality of their worldly positions rules out any question of marriage—as Sir Thomas notes when first consenting to Fanny's being brought up in his house. The stern authority of Sir Thomas, a benevolent man but unable to make any outward show of affection, is felt in these early pages as an oppressive presence reinforcing Fanny's subordination to her aunts and her lack of confidence in her own worth. His departure for a year and more to attend to his plantations in the Caribbean, taking his elder son, Tom, with him, leaves the house without a guiding hand—much to the relief of his two daughters. The elder, Maria, is soon engaged to a harmless dolt, Mr. Rushworth, who is summed up in Edmund's judgment, thought, not spoken: "If this man had not twelve thousand a year, he would be a very stupid fellow" (***MP*** [***Mansfield Park***] 30). Also as soon as Sir Thomas has left, another and more seriously disturbing element arrives at Mansfield Park with Henry and Mary Crawford, the brother escorting his sister who has come to live with her relatives at the parsonage. Vivacious but crucially lacking in refined moral perception, the Crawfords are also culturally alien: although Henry has a country property he pays it little attention except in the shooting season, and like Mary he prefers to spend his time in London. Money talks to both of them far louder than nature. Mansfield Park is an old-fashioned agricultural estate. Mary shows no understanding of it and is struck with incredulity when money cannot hire her a horse and carriage during the harvest,[3] while Henry's interest in "improvement" (see ***MP*** 166-67) is aesthetic and theoretical rather than economic and practical. Although he professes to have a great eye for the "capabilities" (***MP*** 64) of a place, he worked out his scheme for his own property not on the ground but while he was at school and university (Cambridge, incidentally, then notorious for its hunting fraternity, not the learned

Oxford, attended by Edmund). His use of the term "capabilities" shows of course his pretension to emulate Lancelot Brown, employed to modernize the parklands of many of the great English families, most notably perhaps the Temples at Stowe in Buckinghamshire—but the Temples were Whigs, and it is more than clear that the Bertrams are Tories. The presence of the Crawfords subjects Fanny to a series of trials that are increasingly demanding: Mary Crawford at once begins to make advances to Edmund and usurps the pony on which Fanny, thanks to Edmund, has been learning to enjoy outdoor exercise. This is a purely private sorrow for Fanny, though it causes her to "struggle" for some days, we are told, "against discontent and envy" (***MP*** 54), but she soon faces a more complex social dilemma. On a visit to the Rushworth estate Henry Crawford flirts outrageously with both the Bertram sisters, to the point that Mr. Rushworth is left deserted by his fiancée and at risk of a public humiliation which even he is capable of perceiving, and Mary Crawford renews her assault on Edmund. Suppressing her own disappointments, Fanny stays alone at her post while the party scatters around the park, and she is able to manage Rushworth's perplexed vanity so as to prevent a disaster. The third trial is more elaborate still. It forms the novel's famous centerpiece and for the first time shows the strong conscience that we have come to recognize in Fanny under deliberate attack from others. Young Tom returns from the West Indies ahead of his father and brings another new element into the company, an enthusiast for amateur theatricals. The idea for a private production of a drama of Kotzebue's is born and is enthusiastically supported by the Crawfords. Despite her curiosity about the theater, which she has never experienced, Fanny watches with alarm the development of a scheme which she is sure would not be approved by Sir Thomas. She has rightly sensed, moreover, not just that the plan is undignified but that the project is arousing and gratifying wrongful emotions: Henry Crawford and Maria Bertram spend an excessive amount of time rehearsing together, Rushworth is made to play an asinine count, and even Edmund is drawn in to play a pastor married off at the end to Mary Crawford. The persuasion of Edmund to take part is a special triumph for Mary Crawford: nonplussed when she first learned that he intends to become a clergyman, she has since been doing her best to belittle that profession without alienating him altogether. Not content with persuading Edmund to travesty his future vocation, the would-be players turn on Fanny: she too is needed, if only for a minor part, and although she stands firm for a while, she is inveigled into assisting with a private rehearsal, is surprised by a last-minute request just to read some lines, and is on the point of being entrapped when Sir Thomas's unexpected return puts an end to the whole project.

With the restoration of external authority, the first part of Fanny's testing is concluded. Order returns to Mansfield Park; Maria and Rushworth are married and leave; Edmund announces his intention to seek ordination in the near future. But this interval of calm is only preparing for Fanny the more serious trial which occupies the second half of the book. An underemployed Henry Crawford turns his attention to Fanny and out of sheer mischief forms the purpose of making her love him. Up to this point in the story we have been able to see Sir Thomas Bertram as the embodiment of moral authority: his return as a deus ex machina seems to have confirmed that role, and the terror he inspired in Fanny as a child could easily be interpreted as the source of her sense of right and wrong, as well as of her timorousness. Her pronounced moral sense would then be little more than submission to established social power. But in the second phase of the narrative Sir Thomas himself, his judgment and authority, is called into question, and he becomes Fanny's adversary and tempter. For to Sir Thomas Henry Crawford seems a most desirable match for his niece, who is fortunate to have the attentions of a man of such means, and he lends his support to the suitor. And to do him justice, Henry Crawford is soon the victim of his own stratagem and starts genuinely to pursue Fanny, and with a serious intent of marriage. Or at least he thinks his pursuit is genuine and his intent serious. In order to resist him Fanny has to believe not only that she knows better than Sir Thomas, but that she knows Henry Crawford better than he knows himself. She knows from what she has seen of him before Sir Thomas's return that he is a man of no "permanence" (***MP*** 31) and that his behavior during the theatrical venture, and his recollection of that episode as the happiest time of his life, prove him to have "a corrupted mind" (***MP*** 155).

But Jane Austen knows Fanny, and human nature, well enough to tell us that she would have been unable to resist the intensive courtship of "such a man as Crawford, in spite of there being some previous ill-opinion of him to be overcome, had not her affection been engaged elsewhere" (***MP*** 159). Her unrequited love for the kindly Edmund, undeclared as it must be to anyone, sustains her throughout her confrontation with Sir Thomas—as Crawford makes himself ever more genuinely agreeable, uses his influence to be of service to her beloved brother, and finally declares himself in form. Her love sustains her even through the hardest trial of all, her effective banishment from Mansfield Park to her parents' home in Portsmouth, where Sir Thomas hopes that an intensive course in the reality of poverty will bring her to her senses. All Fanny's supports are stripped away. The man whose voice was law has become her persecutor, she has to tell him "that he was wrong" and conceal her love from his suspicions (***MP*** 213, 215); she has been expelled from the place that had brought order and a measure of consolation to her vulnerable existence; and when Edmund goes to London to join the Crawfords' circle for a while, she has to live in terror of the letter from him that will tell her of the engagement that will withdraw the last prop supporting her resolution "never, never, never" (***MP*** 236) to say yes to the corrupted Mr. Crawford. Denuded of everything that has protected her, she is exposed to the final assault: Henry Crawford seeks her out in her exile in Portsmouth and in the guise of a reformed character—unrepulsed by her restricted surroundings, civil and genial to her nautical father, who smells of spirits, showing now, since months of absence have elapsed, a real persistence in a single course, showing too a change of heart towards his Norfolk estates to which he intends to return in order to save an honest tenant from being done out of his due by his manager (***MP*** 280). When he leaves, Fanny reflects that he is "astonishingly more gentle and regardful of others than formerly" (***MP*** 281). The dénouement, however, is swift. Henry Crawford does not return to a life of good works in Norfolk but stays in London and enters on an adulterous liaison with Maria Bertram, now Mrs. Rushworth, with whom he elopes. While he commits this act of social suicide, an illness of Edmund's brother Tom causes Mary Crawford to think that Edmund may soon be the heir to Mansfield Park and that she can perhaps overcome the rooted objections she has so far felt to being anything as dull as a parson's wife. Fanny reads her accurately at once: "she had . . . learnt to think nothing of consequence but money" (***MP*** 296). But Edmund is horrified at the levity with which Mary Crawford treats her brother's transgression and breaks off his suit at the moment when she thinks she might yield to him. Mansfield Park is in mourning, but there are now no obstacles to the recognition of the manifest destiny of Edmund and Fanny. "Let other pens dwell on guilt and misery," Miss Austen breaks in (***MP*** 312)—and in the final chapter she briskly distributes rewards and punishments all around and unites her lovers as the first worthy occupants of the parsonage that her story has seen.

The structure of ***Mansfield Park,*** then, is a relentless, single-minded—if two-stage—tightening of the focus on one point only: Fanny's resistance to the temptation represented by the intrusion of the Crawfords into Mansfield Park. The temptation, the testing, penetrates ever more layers of distraction and protection and comes ever closer to the core of her being. She has to overcome the temptation in the form, first, of pain to her comfort and self-esteem when the Crawfords first arrive; then as a challenge to show fortitude and self-denial in keeping a society together when the party visits Mr. Rushworth's estate; then as an unvarnished suggestion that she should do wrong during the theatrical episode. Then it speaks with the insinuating tones of impersonated love; then with the borrowed voice of social authority itself; then as the more than merely external pressure of the reduced circumstances of life in Portsmouth—for the spiritual deprivation of her family is even more oppressive. And finally it speaks as a direct appeal to her sense of morality and the possibility of reform. Two related questions arise about this structure: what is the nature of the temptation? and what is the nature, the core, of Fanny's resistance?

As to the first question, we are clearly dealing with a struggle for power—a struggle which the book enables us to identify as, no doubt among other things, a struggle between social and economic "interests" (as Sir Thomas calls them) (***MP*** 30) for the future of England (represented here by the future, bodily and spiritual, of Fanny Price). In the simplest contemporary terms it is a struggle between Whig interests and Tory—between trade and finance, on the one hand, the "money" that alone is of consequence to Mary Crawford, and land, on the other. On the one hand, there is the busy, cruel, fashionable world of London where nothing lasts, certainly not marriages, and for which the country is simply a place to which one retires occasionally for entertainment or to "improve" the "beauty" and "ornament" (***MP*** 166) of one's properties. On the other hand, there is Mansfield Park, ordered and slow-moving, a place of serious husbandry, where Nature is acknowledged as a power in her own right: Edmund and Fanny even share an interest in the stars (***MP*** 81), in a Nature beyond all human "improvement," while Mary Crawford sees "nature, inanimate nature, with little observation" (***MP*** 58; cp. 142). On the one hand, there are tasteless modern German plays, which when the novel was being written had for over ten years been condemned by the English press as socially subversive and no better than French Jacobin tracts.[4] On the other hand, there are the inexhaustible riches of Shakespeare, eloquently declaimed by Mr. Crawford (though he admits he never read him much before) when he is seeking to impersonate the cause of virtue.

However, we have only to put the issue in terms of these simple oppositions to realize that they are inadequate. For Mansfield Park itself is compromised by its accommodations with the other party: how otherwise could it be so susceptible to the lure of the Crawfords? It is Sir Thomas's absence while seeing to his Caribbean ventures that permits them to establish their hold on his family. He allows the consideration of Rushworth's enormous wealth to override his judgment that the man is a dunce and his certain knowledge that his daughter does not love him (***MP*** 138). It is an inability to give value to human feeling, as pronounced in its own way as the insensitivity of the Crawfords, added to that overvaluation of material advantage, that makes him try to impose his will on his niece. In their confrontation it becomes clear that the true resistance to the corrupting interests represented by the Crawfords lies, not in some countervailing political or economic or social party, but in Fanny. Her consistent integrity will in the end rescue even Sir Thomas from his compromises—the man who at one point seemed the embodiment of solidity and authority.

But what is it in Fanny that resists? Gradually the story strips away the contingent and secondary elements to reveal what is primary and essential to her opposition to the Crawfords. It is not just personal pique, for she rises above that in the pony episode. It is not just the timorous and diffident personality, for which Sir Thomas upbraids her, for her opposition to the theatricals is public and isolating. It is not mere passivity, for sensitive intervention is required to hold the party together during the visit to the Rushworth estates. It is not, obviously, the blind submission to Sir Thomas of Fanny's aunts. It is not even the fear of losing Mansfield Park, for that is taken from her when she is sent to Portsmouth. We can perhaps identify it negatively by the Crawfords' lack of it, a lack which leads them both to be characterized, at different points, as "evil" (***MP*** 206, 309). When Edmund has seen through Mary Crawford, after hearing her blame her brother not for his adultery but for his making it so public through elopement, he tells Fanny, "[H]er's is not a cruel nature. I do not consider her as meaning to wound my feelings. The evil lies yet deeper; in her total ignorance, unsuspiciousness of there being such feelings. … Her's are faults of principle, Fanny" (***MP*** 309-10). When Fanny is trying to understand the repugnance she feels at Crawford's renewed assault once his good services to her brother have put her at a disadvantage, she discerns "a gross want of feeling and humanity where his own pleasure was concerned. And, alas! … no principle to supply as a duty what the heart was deficient in" (***MP*** 223; cp. 215). When Sir Thomas has learnt his lesson, has rid his household of all association with the Crawfords and set his hopes on Edmund and Fanny, he is said to be "sick of ambitious and mercenary connections" and "prizing more and more the sterling good of principle and temper" (***MP*** 320). "Principle" is what distinguishes Fanny from the Crawfords: principle, the first beginning of the moral life, so primary that Lévinas would call it beginningless, that is what the analytic structure of ***Mansfield Park*** finally isolates as the core of Fanny's resistance. That, in her own words to Henry Crawford, is "a better guide in ourselves, if we would attend to it, than any other person can be" (***MP*** 280). It is principle that keeps her alone firm when everyone around her falls victim to delusion or compromise.

Or is it? One other element is not stripped away from Fanny in her experience of purgation and suffering, though she is in mortal terror that it may be: her love and hope for Edmund. That is the secret that she keeps from the searching gaze of Sir Thomas and the even more penetrating insight of her rival, Mary Crawford. That he has a "pre-engaged heart to attack" Henry Crawford has "no suspicion" (***MP*** 221). Fanny's love is almost as private to her, almost as central to what she is, as her principle. Almost—but not quite. The presence of this hidden motive in Fanny's heart casts a slight air of ambiguity, a hint of calculation over her words and thoughts at times, which perhaps explains why some readers find her a prig and a hypocrite. It is all a matter of an "almost." The recital of his last interview with Mary Crawford leaves Edmund "so much affected, that Fanny, watching him with silent, but most tender concern, was almost sorry that the subject had been entered on at all" (***MP*** 310). Is she "almost" sorry—rather than just "sorry"—because her compassion for Edmund is modified by principle, by the recognition that he has been saved from disaster and that articulating his feelings, painful though it may be to do so, will help to secure him against regret? Or is she "almost" sorry because her compassion is modified by her hidden motive, by the surely joyful thought that Mary Crawford's rivalry is at an end. We are, after all, told at the start of the conversation that Fanny listens "with … curiosity and concern … , … pain and … delight" (***MP*** 308). How do we assess her decision to "add … to [Edmund's] knowledge of [Mary Crawford's] real character, by some hint of what share his brother's state of health [i.e., the likelihood that Tom might die and Edmund become the heir] might be supposed to have in her wish for a complete reconciliation" (***MP*** 312)? Can we be sure that the interests of "reason" are here unalloyed by any other consideration? Fanny, we are told, felt "more than justified" in telling Edmund the truth—"more than" is another "almost." Was she *fully* justified, because she was acting on principle? Or was she justified—and something more as well? Gratified, perhaps? It is the last turn in the narrative before the author enters in her own person in the final chapter, and the question in our minds is left unresolved, just as the relationship between Edmund and Fanny is left by the last words of the chapter in a state of promise rather than finality: "Fanny's friendship was all that he had to cling to" (***MP*** 312).

It seems that even a narrative as circumstantial and purposeful as ***Mansfield Park*** cannot disengage principle from the tangle of human motives and exhibit it in its pure state. If ever there was a novel that exerted itself to discern and formulate the primal command in human life, the original ethical modification of our being, this surely is it. And the conclusion is that it cannot be done. The limit cannot be transgressed that separates secular from sacred writing, though only the attempt to reach it, through that progressive tightening of the focus, produces the circumstantiality and the purposeful analysis. The final chapter, in which the author makes her bow to the audience and defines her work as "entertainment" (***MP*** 320), contains a surprise as extraordinary in its way as the conclusion to Goethe's *Faust,* a sign of deference towards what cannot be uttered, achieved by the same device of the alternative ending. Jane Austen, in her distribution of summary justice to all her characters, includes in her account of Henry Crawford's fate a vision of what might have been, a vision of what might have happened had that last element of support been stripped away from Fanny and had she been obliged to renounce her love for Edmund. The course Henry Crawford had engaged in when visiting Fanny at Portsmouth was the "way of happiness." He had only to hold to it. The impersonation of reform might have become reform itself. "Would he have deserved more, there can be no doubt that more would have been obtained. … Would he have persevered, and uprightly, Fanny must have been his reward—and a reward very voluntarily bestowed—within a reasonable period from Edmund's marrying Mary." The view back from this rewriting of the story's end is quite dizzying. Were all those scenes and sufferings, was all that fearful firmness of purpose in the confrontation with Sir Thomas, the certainty of the corruption of Crawford's principles and the gross inhumanity of his feelings (***MP*** 215, 223), the absolute assurance that she could never, never, never marry him only so much disguising—by Fanny, from Fanny—of one overriding motive: to leave herself free for Edmund? Was that all her principle amounted to? I think not. But I do think that Austen elaborates her alternative ending in order that we should ask these questions. What they amount to, I believe, is the final stage in that ever more focused questioning which gives the book its structure—and the question being asked, from the start of the book is, what is principle? We already know that it is not, for example, fear of authority or need for security. Now we discover that it is not a psychological factor, or a state of mind, and not a trait of character either, not "temper" as it is called, from which the book more than once distinguishes it. Principle is not a motive at all, in the sense in which love for Edmund is a motive. Principle is the awareness that, whatever one's motives or circumstances, life is to be lived as a duty, as subject to the Law, and not as a possession, to be either risked or consumed. The mental experiment shows that in the absence of that last supporting motive, the love for Edmund, the story of Fanny's principled life could, subject to two conditions, become a very different story, though her life would not for that be any less principled: it would become the story of how a girl of strong ethical sense but immature judgment learned to redirect her affections and reassess a man who, under her influence, was genuinely capable of reformation. The two conditions would be that Mary Crawford's distaste for a clerical marriage should be overcome; and that Henry should have done his duty by his deserving tenant and gone to Norfolk rather than stayed in London. The conditions have nothing to do with the purity of Fanny's principle: the events we have seen in the plot so far could be part of that different story, and yet we would not have to reinterpret them as evidence of her hypocrisy. The conditions depend on the behavior of people other than Fanny, and if they were fulfilled we would certainly have to reassess Fanny's judgment but not her moral integrity. But we only have to utter those words "if they were fulfilled" to see the fallacy in the mental experiment. For how could those conditions be fulfilled? Austen seems to be presenting them playfully as within the power of her authorial caprice, as if those changes could be brought about by a little more of the brisk tidying up that goes on in the rest of this final chapter. Thereby—deliberately, of course—she provokes us to object that the whole of her story so far has shown these conditions to be impossible. Fanny's judgment is right, as are her principles. She has judged, almost for as long as she has known them, that Henry is the sort of man who would neglect an important duty for the sake of his own pleasure and that Mary is the sort of person who has, as Edmund put it, "a total ignorance, an unsuspiciousness of there being such feelings" as those which lead him to wish to be a clergyman. We have believed that judgment to be right and not just to be determined by psychological motives, not just to proceed, for example, from Fanny's love for Edmund and consequent feelings of rivalry, as if, were that love to be thought away in a mental experiment, we should have to think away her assessment of the Crawfords as well. We know Fanny's assessment of the Crawfords' lack of ethical principle is right because we have evidence of it, evidence as direct as any secular narrative can provide, within the limitation that no secular narrative can directly represent the ethical imperative itself. Our objective evidence—as we might call it—of the rightness of Fanny's judgment of the Crawfords is their behavior in church.

The church is the central theme of ***Mansfield Park***—not one theme among others, nor a quaint excrescence that gives the book a distinctive (or possibly more disagreeable) profile. The church is necessarily central because "principle" is central, and the church is principle made visible, principle given a name and a face, embodied in a particular time and place and social context. Let us cast our minds back to Part 1, in which I considered the relation of the Jewish Law to the original obligation of responsibility for the neighbor. Christ was the embodiment of the Law, its fulfillment in the flesh, and Christ's mystical, spiritual body was the church. And that means even the church of Jane Austen's early-nineteenth-century England, a prey to rationalism and neglect, to worldliness and indolence and all the maladies of establishment, that are shown with satirical ferocity in the progression of the Mansfield pastor Dr. Grant, brother-in-law of the Crawfords, from dinner to dinner, from a goose to a canonry to an apoplectic fit. The church may be in this novel like the chapel in the Rushworths' family seat—"left to the silence and stillness which reigned in it with few interruptions throughout the year" (***MP*** 64)—but its stillness is that of the still center. It is tacitly present with us throughout in the issue that divides Edmund from Mary Crawford and unites him with Fanny: his resolve to become a clergyman.

It may be something of a canard that Austen claimed the subject of ***Mansfield Park*** was ordination,[5] but the idea gained currency only because it reflected a truth about the book. To be ordained is, in the most general sense, to accept a historically and institutionally defined station in life as a means of responding to the original ethical imperative, and Edmund makes it clear to Mary, as soon as she knows of his intention, that this is how he understands it. To her, who judges by London standards, by the standards of the world of money and ever-changing fashion, "[a] clergyman is nothing" (***MP*** 66), and to want to be one is to be devoid of any comprehensible ambition. Edmund replies:

> I cannot call that situation nothing, which has the charge of all that is of the first importance to mankind, individually or collectively considered, temporally and eternally—which has the guardianship of religion and morals, and consequently of the manners which result from their influence. . . . The *manners* I speak of, might rather be

> called *conduct,* perhaps, the result of good principles; the effect, in short, of those doctrines which it is [the clergy's] duty to teach and recommend.
>
> (***MP*** 66)

To Edmund as to Fanny the "manners" to which this novel could seem to be devoted are the result of "principles," and thus are the visible practice of religion, with the guardianship of which the clergy are charged at ordination. When Sir Thomas, at the end of the story, reflects ruefully on the errors in his upbringing of his daughters, he makes the same equation of principle and religion:

> He feared that principle, active principle, had been wanting, . . . that sense of duty which can alone suffice. They had been instructed theoretically in their religion, but never required to bring it into daily practice.
>
> (***MP*** 314)

Edmund, by contrast, envisages his life as a clergyman as precisely a daily obligation (***MP*** 170), not just delivering a sermon on Sundays, but living among his parishioners and giving them his "constant attention"—as, we are told, it is not possible to do in the large London parishes from which the Crawfords take their conception of the clerical state (***MP*** 66). The Crawfords, however, see life not as a matter of a station to which one is ordained, a call that is heard, and which imposes a daily obligation of responsibility: the Crawfords, in their London way, see life as a game.

The conversation in which Edmund rejects Henry's plans for the "improvement" of his parsonage as incompatible with the duties of his state is interleaved with the progress of a game of cards in which Henry shows himself "preeminent in all the lively turns, quick resources, and playful impudence" that the game requires and that are characteristic of his way of living (***MP*** 165). Tony Tanner has noticed the symbolic significance of Mary Crawford's play.[6] She stakes too much for the return that is on offer, just as in life she pays too much in the currency that really counts for the sake of victory in inessentials: "The game was her's, and only did not pay her for what she had given to secure it" (***MP*** 166). But it is important also to notice the structural contrast with the surrounding conversation.[7] There is an alternative to the modern way of life, and it is represented by the church. Similarly there is a structural contrast throughout the book between acting and ordination, the actor who plays all roles and the clergyman who accepts the call to one. Edmund defends throughout the seriousness of the call to ordination, and it is, as Tanner also remarks,[8] the low point in his development when he briefly accepts the part of stage clergyman in Kotzebue's play. Henry Crawford sets out to make Fanny love him, as a game, and in the same spirit in which he plays cards. He sets out to act the part of the lover of a serious woman (and is then trumped and overtrumped by the seriousness of life: in the course of his playacting he discovers the real attraction of Fanny, and then loses her for real too). The summit of his deception—and it is self-deception also, for he is not devilish and is no Iago—is to reverse Edmund's transgression and play the part of clergyman in real life. He engages in serious discussion with Edmund about "liturgy" (***MP*** 231)—the false note struck by that fashionably intellectual word warns us of his true intent—and about the qualities of a good sermon, even offering to preach himself, if only from time to time and before a London audience, all as part of his assault on Fanny's affections (***MP*** 231). Fanny sees through him, as he realizes, when he condemns himself out of his own mouth, admitting that he could not play such a part "of a constancy." Constancy is of course the decisive distinction between acting and ordination, for roles cease but ordination goes on: constancy demonstrates principle.

Henry Crawford's final stratagem—with which, when his story ends, he is perhaps on the point of convincing himself as well as Fanny—is to play the part of the constant lover. The last scene in which we see him in this role, the last scene in which he is directly represented to us at all, shows him in Portsmouth accompanying the Price family to church. Whatever its defects, however slatternly the housekeeping and however poverty-stricken their accommodation, Fanny's family has two great merits that between them make it plausible that so powerful a sense of duty as hers could have been born there: first, Fanny's father, though overfond of the bottle, stays faithful to his wife; and, second, the whole family goes to church, regularly, and together. The Crawfords would seem to have lacked both these supports in their childhood. Henry Crawford, by joining the Prices for Sunday morning service, comes to the very heart and origin of Fanny's moral experience, and it is only at this point that she begins to waver. But we know that even here, even by entering the house of God, Henry Crawford cannot show himself to be a man of principle, without a break with his past more decisive than anything he hints at to Fanny. For we inevitably recall his first appearance in a place of worship, at the start of his relations with the Bertrams, the only other occasion when the narrative takes us inside a sacred building. In the Rushworth family chapel Mary Crawford made Fanny, we are told, "too angry for speech" (***MP*** 62) when she painted a satirical picture of the agonies of tedium suffered in that place by previous generations of Rushworths and their servants, until the practice of morning and evening prayer conducted by a domestic chaplain was discontinued by the present Mr. Rushworth's father. "Every generation has its improvements," was Mary Crawford's comment (***MP*** 62), as if we had not already learned to be suspicious of that word *improvement.* These improprieties in Mary's words, however, only pave the way for Henry's far greater impropriety in action. With Maria Bertram and Mr. Rushworth standing side by side, looking at the chapel's east end, it is suggested that if Edmund were ordained the marriage ceremony could be performed then and there. Henry Crawford chooses this moment, which is figuratively, therefore, or at least in travesty, a wedding, to "whisper . . . gallantries" to Rushworth's fiancée. He does not like to see her so close to the altar, he says, and if called on to give her away would do so with great reluctance (***MP*** 63). The chapel is thus made a place not of marriage but of adultery, and this act of desecration both prefigures the development that is to come and inaugurates it. It is the beginning of the playacting that will end in real wrongdoing. When Henry Crawford enters the church in Portsmouth is he concluding that development with another act of desecration? The events that follow suggest that he is. The alternative ending allows that even then there was perhaps still hope for him.

In Fanny's world and circumstances the established Church of England is the socially and institutionally visible and audible presence of the call to principle, the call of the Law. The Crawfords' disrespect for the church, in word and deed, is not merely an offense against Fanny or Edmund's sense of propriety, as if it were a matter personal to them and the moral quality of what the Crawfords do or say were determined by Fanny or Edmund's motives for feeling or ignoring the offense. Rather the Crawfords' attitude, and the London world and way of life from which they have derived it, is shown by that disrespect for the church to be both socially and institutionally subversive. It is not after all true to say that the only opposition to the Crawfords shown in the novel lies in Fanny's principles. The opposition to the Crawfords is shown to lie in the church, for the Crawford way of life subverts the operation of a Law in whose nature it is to have such a social and institutional face. That face is turned to us in the novel's representation of the Church of England, in the profanation of it by the Crawfords but also in the acceptance of its order by Edmund and Fanny. Jane Austen thus resolves the fundamental problem posed for her by her desire to write a novel about the operation of "principle"—the problem, namely, that principle, the first origin and source of the ethical life, is unrepresentable by secular writing. For on the one hand she shows us the different responses of the Crawfords, Edmund, and Fanny to the appeal of principle, that speaks through the features of its social and institutional face, the church. And on the other hand she pointedly refrains from even attempting to communicate to us the appeal itself, to speak with its words or in its name. We are never introduced into a church in order to hear the words of a sermon or a service, for all the discussion of both that takes place between Edmund and Henry; we are never made privy to any prayers or devotions of Fanny, though her trials furnish ample occasion for both; nor are her thoughts, or indeed those of the Crawfords, stylized into struggles of conscience between virtue and vice, between the words of Scripture and the words of some tempter, for all the insistence throughout the novel on the need to turn religion into a matter of daily practice. Instead there is a conflict between two English social institutions, London and the Church, presented to us as a conflict between two evaluations of Edmund's decision to be ordained: Mary Crawford's—that it is an empty gesture, a nothing, which nonetheless stands in the way of a desirable and possibly profitable union—and Fanny Price's—that it is confirmation of a shared responsiveness to the unnameable Law which, if it cannot unite her to Edmund, must at least distance her from Henry Crawford, so long as he does not share it too. The church, and ordination to it, is therefore central to the novel, for it is what enables Jane Austen to present the social fabric of England, and its continuation in the "manners" and "conduct" of her characters, as mattering, as the battleground of "principle."

By the same token, the church is also the element in the novel's structure which enables Jane Austen to present it, and herself, its author, as the voice of a particular time and place, as accessible to the historical hermeneutic that applies to secular rather than sacred literature, to what is spoken rather than to what is written. The Church which is here the historically specific face of unrepresentable "principle" is the early-nineteenth-century church of rural England.[9] It is a modest affair, depicted unsparingly but without polemic, a church of unsung and largely unnoticed constancy in prayer and in its "attention" to its duties. Its character is suggested to us in the description of the Rushworth family chapel—"nothing awful[,] . . . nothing melancholy, nothing grand . . . no aisles, no arches, no inscriptions, no banners," just mahogany pews and crimson velvet cushions installed, we are told, in the time of James II (***MP*** 61-62). There may, in other words, have been some overlavish expenditure, as was to be expected of that era, but there was clearly no compromise with that monarch's Catholicism; the Anglicanism of ***Mansfield Park*** is unshaken by Gothic revivalism, the Catholic resurgence of the period after 1800, or indeed by Methodism. It may seem a dry and sober affair—it certainly did to Mary Crawford—but it was, the novel tells us, true to the essential. We should also remember that this was the church that later in the nineteenth century first nurtured England's finest Catholic poet since Pope, for Gerard Manley Hopkins was as an Anglican a disciple not only of Pusey but also of George Herbert. The last stage of my investigation of the relation between sacred and secular literature requires us to consider in more detail some literary and cultural reflections of the relation between the Law of God and the church in England.

Notes

1. Jane Austen, *Mansfield Park* (Norton Critical Edition), ed. Claudia L. Johnson (New York: Norton, 1998); henceforth *MP.*

2. Goethe, *Die Wahlverwandtschaften,* in *Goethes Werke,* ed. Erich Trunz, 6 (see note 2 to ch. 11 above).

3. Tony Tanner, *Jane Austen* (London: Macmillan, 1986), p. 150.

4. Marilyn Butler, *Jane Austen and the War of Ideas* (Oxford: Clarendon, 1987), pp. 92-93, 114-17, 232-34; the campaign against German drama may be dated from the first publication of *The Anti-Jacobin* in 1797: Catherine Waltraud Proescholdt-Obermann, *Goethe and His British Critics: The Reception of Goethe's Works in British Periodicals, 1779-1855* (Frankfurt am Main: Lang, 1992), pp. 96-104.
5. Butler, *Jane Austen,* 236n. The punctuation of Austen's letter to her sister Cassandra of 29 January [1813] is, however, best left unamended, for its ambiguity surely reflects the associative flow of the writer's consciousness. She might not wish to reduce the subject of her new book to a single word, but getting the details of ordination procedures right has a high priority for her.
6. Tanner, *Jane Austen,* p. 158.
7. Throughout the scene there is a contrast between the details of the game and the topic of the conversation, which culminates in Mary Crawford's reflection, "It was time to have done with cards if sermons prevailed" (*MP* 170-71).
8. Tanner, *Jane Austen,* p. 164.
9. Austen's religious position is identified as "Georgian Anglicanism" and "the *via media* of mainstream Anglicanism" in Michael Giffin, *Jane Austen and Religion: Salvation and Society in Georgian England* (London: Palgrave Macmillan, 2002), pp. 24-25, but Giffin does not refer to the Rushworths' chapel or to Henry Crawford's behavior in it.

Emily Auerbach (essay date 2004)

SOURCE: Auerbach, Emily. "All the Heroism of Principle: *Mansfield Park.*" *Searching for Jane Austen.* Madison: U of Wisconsin P, 2004. 166-200. Print.

[*In the following essay, Auerbach questions why Austen chose to write about such an unappealing, self-righteous heroine as Fanny. She speculates that the novel contrasts Fanny's personality with that of Mary and that Austen's intention was to present her readers with a possible synthesis of the two characters, embodied in the novel's narrator, who "combines Mary's wit with Fanny's conscience."*]

> Be strong and of good courage; be not afraid, neither be thou dismayed; for the LORD thy God is with thee wherever thou goest.
>
> Joshua 1:9

> No coward soul is mine,
> No trembler in the world's storm-troubled sphere:
> I see Heaven's glories shine,
> And faith shines equal arming me from fear.
>
> Emily Brontë, *Last Lines*

> Fanny ... was nearly fainting: all her former habitual dread of her uncle was returning. ... Too soon did she find herself at the drawing-room door; and after pausing a moment for what she knew would not come, for a courage which the outside of no door had ever supplied to her, she turned the lock in desperation. ... She had all the heroism of principle, and was determined to do her duty.
>
> ***Mansfield Park***

With the successful publication of ***Sense and Sensibility*** (1811) and ***Pride and Prejudice*** (1813), both revisions of novels begun in the 1790s, Jane Austen could have chosen to publish as her third novel a new tale of a lively, laughing heroine like Elizabeth Bennet or an eager, impassioned young woman like Marianne Dashwood. Instead, she seems deliberately to have chosen something new and challenging to her powers, acknowledging in a letter that this novel about a shy, pious heroine and clergyman-hero would be "not half so entertaining" as her previous work (6 July 1813). ***Mansfield Park*** (1815) is the only Austen novel permeated with religious imagery and terminology such as altars, crosses, clergy, morals, principles, ordination, chapel, church, religion, sermon, prayer, piety, and pulpit. Perhaps the death of her father, a clergyman and tutor, in 1805 and the rising careers of two clergymen brothers gave her reason in this novel to pay homage to a religious life and to consider questions of piety, loyalty, and conscience. Morality forms the basis for heroism in ***Mansfield Park.***

As narrator, Austen leaves little doubt that she approves of her moral heroine (Fanny Price) and serious hero (Edmund Bertram). At the same time, she refuses to join this grave couple in abandoning wit, humor, and clever game playing. From the very first paragraph of ***Mansfield Park,*** the narrator adopts a brightly ironic voice, as when she observes, "there certainly are not so many men of large fortune in the world as there are pretty women to deserve them" or refers to Mr. and Mrs. Norris's "career of conjugal felicity" while demonstrating the opposite (3). Wit and learning, Austen suggests in ***Mansfield Park,*** can be gateways to wisdom, not necessarily distractions from it. If the novel asks readers to value the humorless but virtuous Fanny Price more than the sparkling but tainted Mary Crawford, the narrative voice simultaneously reassures us that we can have *both* morality and wit. Through clever allusions and hints, Austen invites perceptive readers to play a game of detection with her. Searching for Jane Austen between the lines of ***Mansfield Park*** leads to a veritable pot of gold.

No other Austen creation has provoked more widely divergent responses than the one and only Fanny Price. In an essay called "What Became of Jane Austen?" novelist and critic Kingsley Amis wondered why the creator of Catherine Morland, Marianne and Elinor Dashwood, and Elizabeth Bennet invented such an unappealing weakling as the heroine of ***Mansfield Park.*** Kingsley Amis calls Fanny "a monster of complacency and pride" operating "under a cloak of cringing self-abasement."[1] Although some early readers praised Fanny's quiet, modest, moral nature, others were disappointed with her passivity. "Insipid Fanny Price," Jane Austen's own mother remarked, and Austen's lively niece Anna similarly "could not bear Fanny" (**"Opinions of *Mansfield Park* and *Emma*," *MW* [*Minor Works*]**, 432). Many later readers have agreed with Mrs. Austen and have found the heroine insufferably self-righteous and unendurably timid: Fanny has been called a bore, "the most terrible incarnation we have of the female prig-pharisee," an "unyieldingly charmless heroine," and "the prig in your first-grade class who never, ever misbehaved and who told the teacher when enyone else did."[2] Lionel Trilling concludes that readers of ***Mansfield Park*** cannot help but be "repelled by its heroine."[3]

For the first and only time in Austen, we meet a "supine" heroine who cries frequently, tires easily, and acts "exceedingly timid and shy, and shrinking from notice" (395, 12). Austen uses phrase after phrase to portray Fanny as the *opposite* of courage, self-confidence, importance, and energy. She is described as *afraid of everybody, trembling, trembling about everything, trembling and fearing to be sent for, so low and wan and trembling, forlorn, fearful, disheartened, awed, overcome, mortified, abashed, so shy and reluctant, most shy and uncomfortable, nearly fainting, fearful of notice, too much frightened to have any enjoyment, dependent, helpless, friendless, neglected, forgotten, very timid, and exceedingly nervous, always so gentle and retiring, all agitation and flutter, almost stunned, delicate and nervous, on the point of fainting away, timid, anxious, doubting, finding something to fear in every person and place.* As Lydia Bennet might exclaim, Good Lord!

No athletic tomboy rolling down green slopes or jumping over fences, Fanny Price gets a headache after walking half a mile or being out in the sun to cut roses, for "every sort of exercise fatigues her so soon" (95). Unlike Jane Austen, who observed in a letter, "There were twenty Dances & I danced them all, & without any fatigue" (24 December 1798), Fanny Price gets "breathless," "knocked up," and "tired so soon" at a dance and feels "fatigued and fatigued again" throughout this novel (279, 387). We long to give her iron supplements.

Fanny also could use public speaking classes. If she utters anything at all, it is in a *faltering voice,* a *low voice,* a *shrinking accent,* a *self-denying tone,* or a *quiet way.* Excluded from most of the dialogue, Fanny relishes her wallflower role and shrinks from notice: "She was not often invited to join in the conversation of the others, nor did she desire it" (80). When Fanny does speak up at one point, this "creepmouse" is "shocked to find herself at that moment the only speaker in the room" (145-46). At another instance when she says *two sentences* in opposition to Henry Crawford's cavalier attitude about Sir Thomas, she trembles and blushes at the thought of having spoken "so much at once" (225).

We know from the juvenilia that Austen could create heroines who were outspoken and fearless. For example, Eliza in **"Henry and Eliza"** sails on a man-of-war, raises an army, climbs out of a dungeon, and walks thirty miles without stopping. Sukey in **"Jack and Alice"** heaves rivals out the window. Why might Austen choose in ***Mansfield Park*** to present such a physically weak, self-deprecatory, and cowering heroine?

In ***Mansfield Park*** Austen seems interested in examining the causes of timidity. Readers meet Fanny at a younger age than other Austen heroines: she is ten when she comes to Mansfield Park in a state of homesickness, mortification, and delicate puniness. Austen emphasizes Fanny's small size by having others refer to her as the *little girl,* the *little visitor, poor little thing,* and *the dear little cousin* with the *little heart* and *little soul.* The naturally sensitive daughter of an alcoholic father and a slatternly mother who neglects her, Fanny Price arrives at the formidable mansion of her relatives primed to feel insignificant. "I can never be important to any one," Fanny laments (26). Thinking "too lowly of her own claims" and "too lowly of her own situation," Fanny becomes "much too humble" (20, 35, 176). She accepts Aunt Norris's admonition, "Remember, wherever you are, you must be the lowest and last" and ends up "as usual, believing [her]self unequal to anything!" (221, 351).

Certainly Fanny seems unequal to humor. Readers may discover Fanny giving an occasional smile ("Fanny could not avoid a faint smile") or feeling "not unamused" by her observations of others, but even those faintly amused moments are rare (363, 131). In the nearly five hundred pages of Chapman's edition of ***Mansfield Park,*** Fanny only gets close to laughing one time. When Tom Bertram must rapidly shift subjects, Austen writes ambiguously, "Fanny, in spite of every thing, *could hardly help laughing*" (119; my italics). Readers have to guess as to whether Fanny actually emitted an audible laugh. Fanny has only two other close encounters with near-mirth: at one point we see Fanny "*almost* laugh," and in another scene we are told she "*tried* to laugh"—but cannot (64, 411). As she admits of herself, "I suppose I am graver than other people" (197).

Why did the brilliantly comic Austen choose as her heroine someone that even Mary Bennet and Mr. Collins might find too gravely serious? Why create such a distance between her own fiercely ironic narrative voice ("Mrs. Norris . . . consoled herself for the loss of her husband by considering that she could do very well without him") and the low-pitched, pious, unjoking, private utterances ("Heaven defend me from being ungrateful!") of the painfully shy Fanny Price (23, 323)?

Perhaps the audacious, self-confident Elizabeth Bennet of ***Pride and Prejudice*** made success seem too easy. Elizabeth, we suspect, *enjoys* standing up to Lady Catherine, arguing with Mr. Darcy, or opposing her mother. In contrast, Fanny Price recoils against such self-assertion. By choosing a bashful heroine unable to use humor as a defense, Austen presented herself with a fictional "problem case" in ***Mansfield Park*** unlike anything else she had written.

In previous novels Austen had touched only briefly on the topic of shyness (the awkward Edward Ferrars in ***Sense and Sensibility*** and bashful Georgiana Darcy in ***Pride and Prejudice***), but in ***Mansfield Park*** shyness takes center stage. One senses in the vivid descriptions of Fanny's timidity and sense of isolation that Jane Austen knew shyness well. Perhaps she drew on memories of her emotions as a young girl sent off from home to attend school. Biographer Park Honan calls the young Jane Austen "a shy country girl" and draws from family accounts a portrait of a Fanny Price-like mouse: "[Jane] seemed an agreeable mouse. Then, and for years later, Jane was shy, mute and uncertain with her peers. . . . At nine and ten she was a timid, imitative observer hovering near a circle of slangy, half-sophisticated girls who talked over her head and laughed at everything. . . . Jane Austen, however mousy and inconsequential she seemed, did not play false to herself, and her shyness was in some ways an advantage."[4] Such a portrait cannot be documented, but it is true that even later in life Austen continued to shun the limelight. Biographical accounts of Austen give the impression that she could resemble *either* Elizabeth Bennet *or* Fanny Price, depending on how comfortable she felt with her visitors.[5]

Rather than viewing Fanny Price as an aberration and asking, "What became of Jane Austen?" Kingsley Amis might have noted the close link between Fanny Price's personality and some of Jane Austen's less well-known letters and prayers. Austen could at times be devout—like Fanny. Readers used to Austen's comic bite may wait in some serious letters for a joke that never comes. For example, Austen writes to condole an acquaintance, "The loss of so kind and affectionate a Parent, must be a very severe affliction to all his Children . . . the Goodness which made him valuable on Earth, will make him Blessed in Heaven" (8 April 1798). To her brother Frank, Austen writes tenderly and reverently:

> My dearest Frank,
>
> I have melancholy news to relate, and sincerely feel for your feelings under the shock of it. . . . Our dear Father has closed his virtuous & happy life, in a death almost as free from suffering as his Children could have wished. . . . Heavy as is the blow, we can already feel that a thousand comforts remain to us to soften it . . . the consciousness of his worth and constant preparation for another world.
>
> (21 and 22 January 1805)

Though savagely funny at times, Austen could also write sober, heartfelt words confessing her sense of sin and doubt; her worries about her conscience; her awareness of the ephemeral nature of human concerns. Fanny Price could have uttered the same prayers that Austen wrote herself:

> Give us grace almighty father. . . . Teach us to understand the sinfulness of our own hearts, and bring to our knowledge every fault of temper and every evil habit in which we have indulged to the discomfort of our fellow-creatures, and the danger of our own souls. May we now, and on each return of night, consider how the past day has been spent by us, what have been our prevailing thoughts, words and actions during it, and how far we can acquit ourselves of evil. Have we thought irreverently of thee, have we disobeyed thy commandments, have we neglected any known duty, or willingly given pain to any human being? Incline us to ask our hearts these questions oh! God, and save us from deceiving ourselves by pride and vanity.
>
> (***MW***, 453-54)

Austen's three surviving prayers contain reminders to herself to be thankful for blessings, to avoid "discontent or indifference," to resist temptations, to make better use of each hour of the day, to rise each morning "with every serious and religious feeling," and to "endeavour after a truly christian spirit to seek to attain that temper of forbearance and patience." Undoubtedly thinking of her brothers in the navy, she offers special prayers for the safety of loved ones who travel by land or sea. I believe that this Austen voice—the one striving to conquer irreverence and rise above discontent in order to be a better soul—comes out most directly in Fanny Price. This is not to suggest that Austen *was* Fanny, nor that she wanted to be like her serious heroine, but only that she understood aspects of her character. Austen adds an autobiographical touch by having William Price give Fanny a cross, just as she and Cassandra had received topaz crosses from Charles Austen.

Austen seems deliberately to present Fanny Price as a blend of all the characteristics her era found desirable in women: modesty, delicacy, piety, and submissiveness. Fanny possesses "looks and voice so truly feminine," "unpretending gentleness," "ineffable sweetness and patience," "gentleness, modesty, and sweetness," and "that sweetness which makes so essential a part of every woman's work in the judgment of man" (169, 296, 294). She perfectly fits conduct-book descriptions of women such as this one in *Wisdom in Miniature* (1795): "The utmost of a woman's character is contained in domestic life; first, her piety towards God; and next in the duties of a daughter, a wife, a mother, and a sister."[6] Austen shows us Fanny's reverence for the church and her loyal behavior as a surrogate daughter to Sir Thomas and Lady Bertram, her faithfulness toward Edmund, her motherly kindness toward her younger sisters, and her ardent love for her brother William. Fanny also satisfies the requirements of Chase Amos's *On Female Excellence* (1792), which praised "mildness, moderation, and kindness towards all" in women and opined that "delicacy of manners and purity of speech are so much expected from an amiable, modest female."[7] The Reverend Fordyce would have approved of Fanny Price, as he calls in his frequently reprinted *Sermons for Young Women,* 1761, for "meekness and modesty . . . soft attraction and virtuous love," as well as the capacity to be "agreeable and useful."[8]

Austen read not only Fordyce (which made Lydia Bennet gape in ***Pride and Prejudice***) but also Dr. Gregory's *A Father's Legacy to His Daughters,* which praises a girl's blushing as "the most powerful charm of her beauty."[9] Indeed Fanny "colours" more than any other Austen heroine. In direct contrast to the imperviously disgraceful Lydia Bennet of ***Pride and Prejudice,*** who shows "no variation of colour" in her cheeks when returning home from her Wickham escapades, the virginal Fanny Price blushes her way through ***Mansfield Park*** (***PP*** [***Pride and Prejudice***], 316). Henry extols Fanny's "colour beautifully heightened" and her "soft skin . . . so *frequently* tinged with a blush" (296, 229; my italics). Austen makes sure we know that Fanny offers not just any old tinge but "so deep a blush" and "the deepest blushes" growing "deeper and deeper" on a "face . . . like scarlet" (362, 259, 313, 316).

Sir Thomas Bertram emphasizes the value of Fanny Price's deeply blushing feminine modesty and gentle submissiveness when he orders Fanny off to bed in front of her would-be husband, Henry Crawford, as a way of demonstrating her obedience: "It might occur to him, that Mr. Crawford had been sitting by her long enough, or he might mean to recommend her as a wife by shewing her persuadableness" (281). Henry indeed seems attracted to Fanny as a sort of angelically gentle, docile woman. He pictures her as a kind of worshipping doll-slave: "I will not do her any harm, dear little soul! only want her to look kindly on me, to give me smiles as well as blushes, to keep a chair for me by herself wherever we are, and be all animation when I take it and talk to her; to think as I think, be interested in all my possessions and pleasures, try to keep me longer at Mansfield, and feel when I go away that she shall be never happy again" (231). As his sister concludes when Henry declares his intention of making the "innocent and quiet" Fanny marry him, "You will have a sweet little wife; all gratitude and devotion" (292).

Fanny may be sweet and little, but her gratitude and devotion are offered only to those *she* chooses. For an angel in the house, Fanny has surprisingly independent thoughts, solid integrity, and hidden power: "Her manner was incurably gentle, and she was not aware how much it concealed the sternness of her purpose" (327). Austen presents Fanny as a paradoxical combination of steely determination and feminine manners, "a woman, who firm as a rock in her principles, has a gentleness of character so well adapted to recommend them" (351).

Although our first impression of Fanny may be of a conduct-book weakling who does nothing but tremble in a corner or yield supinely to others, she in some ways has the most strength of any Austen heroine. She stays loyal to Sir Thomas in his absence, repulses Henry Crawford's advances, refuses either to reveal or to abandon her unrequited love for Edmund, and remains unswayed by the persuasions of her social superiors. Despite her obliging temperament, she resolutely asserts her right to her own feelings. When Sir Thomas Bertram displays his wrath at her refusal of the wealthy Henry Crawford, Fanny feels miserable but does not back down. She speaks politely (using "Sir" in every sentence) but firmly: "I—I cannot like him, Sir, well enough to marry him" (315). Fanny's voice may waver, but not her will. Although Sir Thomas calls Fanny "wilful and perverse" and insists that "independence of spirit . . . in young women is offensive and disgusting beyond all common offense," we treasure Fanny's resoluteness, particularly because we have waited so long for it and because we recognize that it is harder for the innately timid Fanny Price to stand up to Sir Thomas than for the feistier Elizabeth Bennet to hold her ground against her mother or Lady Catherine (318).

Austen demonstrates in ***Mansfield Park*** that even a shy, traditionally feminine, economically dependent, and yielding young woman can summon from within herself the necessary strength to refuse to compromise her beliefs. When Fanny waits at the door trying to muster up enough courage to speak to Sir Thomas, we are told that this is a familiar situation: "pausing for a moment for what she knew would not come, for a courage which the outside of no door had ever supplied her" (177). The "courage which she knew would not come" finally *does* come. Even shrinking violets and wallflowers can blossom. To make even small changes in one's self can require tremendous inner courage, Austen suggests. For Fanny to act and speak in her own person—*in propria persona,* as Austen notes near the end of the novel—requires far greater growth than for a heroine already endowed with self-assurance.

Despite her heartache, Fanny Price has enough inner resources to take pleasure in topics other than Edmund. Excluded from conversation, "Her own thoughts and reflections were habitually her best companions" (80). As Mary Crawford observes, "Why, Fanny, you are absolutely in a reverie!" (360). Frequently deep in thought or musing, engaged in soliloquies, or finding solace in meditation, Fanny contemplates nature, humanity, religion, politics, literature, architecture, and friendship. Austen makes sure that we acknowledge Fanny's fullness of mind by telling us that when Fanny thinks about male and female styles of letter writing, she had "such thoughts as these *among ten hundred others*" (376). Fanny is "clever," with "a quick apprehension as well as good sense, and a fondness for reading" (22). Unlike the chattering majority of men and women who make idle small talk, Fanny speaks infrequently but deliberately. She seems to be the only person in this novel who wants to know where British wealth comes from: "The evenings do not appear long to me. I love to hear my uncle talk of the West Indies. . . . Did not you hear me ask him about the slave trade last night? . . . there was such a dead silence!" (197-98). The shy Fanny asks a politically charged question. Her cousins do not join in the discussion, nor does her uncle give her an answer. Lady Bertram expresses interest in the East or West Indies only as the source of luxury items: "I wish that he may go the East Indies, that I may have my shawl," she says of her son, seemingly indifferent to the danger of such a voyage or the slave labor required for the production (305). The wealthy plantation-owning Bertrams (and, by implication, British society) maintain "dead silence" about the slave trade.

Austen adds irony to scenes like this one by showing that Sir Thomas and Edmund Bertram respond inappropriately to Fanny's seriousness. Right after Fanny talks of the West Indies, Edmund changes the subject and reduces her to a beauty pageant contestant: "Your uncle thinks you very pretty, dear Fanny—and that is the long and the short of the matter. Anybody but myself would have made something more of it, and any body but you would resent that you had not been thought very pretty before; but the truth is, that your uncle never did admire you until now—and now he does. Your complexion is so improved!—... and your figure—Nay, Fanny, do not turn away about it—... You must really begin to harden yourself to the idea of being worth looking at.—You must try not to mind growing up into a pretty woman" (198). As a plain girl Fanny was ignored; as a pretty woman Fanny is noticed only for her appearance. She blushes and squirms with vexation, not pleasure. As Edmund notes, "Ask your uncle what he thinks, and you will hear compliments enough; and though they may be chiefly on your person, you must put up with it, and trust to his seeing as much beauty of mind in time" (197).

Austen makes Fanny's "beauty of mind" clear any time she contemplates the wonder and miracle of creation. Her quietly spoken words are uttered like a philosopher, as in these remarks about memory: "If any one faculty of our nature may be called MORE wonderful than the rest, I do think it is memory. There seems something more speakingly incomprehensible in the powers, the failures, the inequalities of memory, than in any other of our intelligences. The memory is sometimes so retentive, so serviceable, so obedient—at others, so bewildered and so weak—and at others again, so tyrannic, so beyond controul!—We are to be sure a miracle every way—but our powers of recollecting and of forgetting, do seem peculiarly past finding out" (208-9). Such mature discourse is lost on her only listener, the "untouched and inattentive" Mary Crawford. Readers, however, may be startled by Fanny's level of insight and the fact that she is thinking this way at all. Rather than talking of new hair ribbons or smartly dressed officers, like Lydia Bennet, or wallowing in her lovesickness, like Marianne Dashwood, Fanny vividly describes the mysterious, uncontrolled workings of the human brain. Indeed, Fanny articulates the baffling way our minds torment us with memories we do not want yet deny us access to information we need to retrieve.

Often in ***Mansfield Park*** Austen reminds readers that Fanny is following a "train of thought" or that the "tender ejaculation" she utters results from reflection and meditation (151, 208). The sight of evergreens, for instance, leads her to consider ecological diversity and differences among countries: "I am so glad to see the evergreens thrive! ... The evergreen!—How beautiful, how welcome, how wonderful the evergreen!—When one thinks of it, how astonishing a variety of nature!—In some countries we know the tree that sheds its leaf is the variety, but that does not make it less amazing, that the same soil and the same sun should nurture plants differing in the first rule and law of their existence" (209). Though equally filled with exclamation marks, this is a very different kind of response than Marianne's melancholy and solipsistic ode to dead leaves in ***Sense and Sensibility.*** Fanny's thoughts take her out of herself and lead to heightened pleasure and reverence. As she explains to Mary, "You will think me rhapsodizing; but when I am out of doors. ... I am very apt to get into this sort of wondering strain" (209). This is the only time in her novels Austen uses the idea of rhapsody. Contemplating the stars enables Fanny to appreciate the sublimity of Nature: "When I look out on such a night as this, I feel as if there could be neither wickedness nor sorrow in the world; and there certainly would be less of both if the sublimity of Nature were more attended to, and people were carried more out of themselves by contemplating such a scene" (113). Although Fanny assumes that everyone could respond this way to the sky or to evergreens ("One cannot fix one's eyes on the commonest natural production without finding food for a rambling fancy"), she seems to be the only "one" in this novel to do so. While Fanny rhapsodizes about trees and stars, Mary Crawford thinks of herself and Edmund thinks of Mary Crawford.

Fanny's remarks seem to echo Wordsworth's notion of Nature as a nurse and gateway to the divine, the "guide, the guardian of my heart, and soul / Of all my moral being."[10] As if Austen wants to call attention to this poem, transparencies of Tintern Abbey decorate Fanny's room. Throughout ***Mansfield Park*** Fanny applies her poetic fancy to the natural scenes she encounters: "the trees, though not fully clothed, were in that delightful state, when farther beauty is known to be at hand, and when, while much is actually given to the sight, more yet remains for the imagination" (446-47). To destroy an avenue or grove of trees is to eliminate a source of imaginative pleasure and spiritual health. "Cut down an avenue! What a pity! Does not it make you think of Cowper? 'Ye fallen avenues, once more I mourn your fate unmerited'" (56). Like Marianne Dashwood, Fanny cites romantic nature writers Austen liked such as William Cowper and Sir Walter Scott.

Fanny's romanticism also shows in her warmth of heart and acute feelings. Fanny helps to smooth over disputes between her younger sisters, writes to her sailor-brother, worries about leaving her incompetent Aunt Bertram alone, cares about Sir Thomas's feelings, helps the clueless

Mr. Rushworth study his dramatic part, listens kindly to Edmund and Mary, and soothes the spirits of her vexed cousins, Maria and Julia. Fanny's frequent tears throughout the novel result both from her loving, empathetic nature and from her timidity and sensitivity.

Unlike Marianne Dashwood of ***Sense and Sensibility*** feeding her sorrow and openly exhibiting her grief, Fanny Price can hide her feelings. She suffers real pain (Austen repeats the word "stab") but immediately strives to conquer her emotions by praying for strength and consulting her reason: "It was a stab. ... He would marry Miss Crawford. It was a stab. ... Till she had shed many tears ... Fanny could not subdue her agitation; and the dejection which followed could only be relieved by the influence of fervent prayers for his happiness. It was her intention, as she felt it to be her duty, to try to overcome all that was excessive, all that bordered on selfishness in her affection for Edmund. ... She would endeavour to be rational. ... She had all the heroism of principle, and was determined to do her duty" (264-65). Fanny has Marianne Dashwood's excessive feelings but is determined to govern them. Yet Fanny refuses to go as far as the self-controlled Elinor does in dissembling and lying for the sake of social acceptability. Artless Fanny cannot ever play a role: "I could not act any thing. ... No, indeed, I cannot act. ... I really cannot act," she insists truthfully—and redundantly (145-46).

Fanny can stand up to her peers and to her elders if she feels a request will violate her principles. Even the tainted Henry Crawford knows that Fanny is the one truly spiritual person he has met: "Henry Crawford had too much sense not to feel the worth of good principles in a wife ... when he talked of her having such a steadiness and regularity of conduct, such a high notion of honour, and such an observance of decorum as might warrant any man in the fullest dependence on her faith and integrity, he expressed what was inspired by the knowledge of her being well principled and religious" (294). Like Edmund acknowledging Fanny's goodness and "mental superiority," Henry grants her "touches of the angel" and admits to her, "You are infinitely my superior in merit. ... You have qualities which I had not before supposed to exist in such a degree in any human creature" (471, 344, 343).

Did an author who claimed in a letter not to like literary pictures of perfection decide in ***Mansfield Park*** to create a flawless, angelic heroine? As Edmund tells his father, "Fanny is the only one who has judged rightly throughout" (187). Fanny seems a mixture of thinking and feeling, sense and sensibility, displaying both a literate mind and an affectionate heart. So does Austen present Fanny as the model of womanhood? Is anything *wrong* with Fanny Price?

Austen implies that Fanny's chief fault is a tendency to be too overwhelmed by circumstances. Fanny not only must learn to find her voice—to speak up no matter how shy and intimidated she feels inside—but also to "buck up" rather than give up. Fanny's sensitivity is so great that she feels guilty when she does not mourn her stern uncle's absence: Fanny "really grieved because she could not grieve" (33). She flagellates herself for her own emotions, as when for her rival she experiences "feelings so near akin to envy, as made her hate herself for having them" (413). Austen notes that Fanny feels so embarrassed by her unrequited love of Edmund that "she would rather die than own the truth" and feels melodramatically convinced that "she was miserable for ever" (317, 321).

Austen gently mocks Fanny for being too devastated even by the misbehavior of others. Like Jane Bennet, loath to admit humanity's capacity for evil, Fanny seems too thunderstruck by all-too-common moral frailty. For example, when Fanny learns of her married cousin's disgraceful adultery, she indulges in "shudderings of horror" because this "horrible evil" is "too horrible a confusion of guilt, too gross a complication of evil, for human nature, not in a state of utter barbarism, to be capable of!" (440-41). How healthy and helpful is it when Fanny contemplates a sort of mass suicide for the whole Bertram-Rushworth-Crawford family? Fanny thinks "it scarcely possible for them to support life and reason under such disgrace; and it appeared to her, that as far as this world alone was concerned, the greatest blessing to every one of kindred with Mrs. Rushworth would be instant annihilation" (442). Through this hyperbolic language, Austen demonstrates that Fanny needs a thicker skin to withstand the world, whether her parents' noisy, squalid home or the teeming, corrupted metropolis of London. Otherwise she will display a virtue so cloistered that it represents an escape from life rather than an embrace of its true reality.

Much as she gently mocked seventeen-year-old Marianne Dashwood's arrogance of youth in ***Sense and Sensibility*** ("At my time of life opinions are tolerably fixed," [***SS*** [***Sense and Sensibility***], 93]), so Austen smiles at Fanny's realization that maybe at age eighteen she has not yet experienced all life might offer: "She began to feel that she had not yet gone through all the changes of opinion and sentiment, which the progress of time and variation of circumstances occasion in this world of changes. The vicissitudes of the human mind had not yet been exhausted by her" (374). Fanny may be sweet and angelic, but she is a *young,* inexperienced woman who still has a long way to go, Austen suggests. She needs to see more of the world without being "instantly annihilated" by the experience or, like Mary Crawford, corrupted by the encounter.

Although Austen presents Fanny Price as the indisputable heroine of this novel, she goes to great lengths to make Mary Crawford seem a more appealing character in many ways—and one whose voice at times sounds remarkably like Austen's. A mixture of attractive features and unfortunate deficiencies, the witty, energetic, self-assured Mary can draw readers' attention away from Fanny Price as easily as she does Edmund Bertram's. After reading ***Mansfield Park,*** one of Austen's own nephews was "interested by nobody but Mary Crawford" (***MW,*** 431).

While Fanny trembles to hear even *talk* of horses, Mary proves herself a bold horsewoman: "Miss Crawford's enjoyment of riding was such, that she did not know how to leave off. Active and fearless, and, though rather small, strongly made, she seemed formed for a horsewoman" (66). Boasting "I am very strong," Mary has "the conviction of very much surpassing her sex in general by her early progress" in horsemanship (68, 67). By making Mary small, like Fanny, Austen removes the chance that size can be used as any excuse for Fanny's timidity and fragility. Described as "gifted by nature with strength and courage," Mary claims to be a "woman of spirit" who was "not born to sit still and do nothing" (69, 243). Mary would excel in a marathon while Fanny would quit with a headache after a quarter of a mile.

Mary shines indoors as well as outdoors. Instead of wanting to let others beat her at cards, Mary boasts, "I will stake my last" and promptly wins the game (243). She enlivens any drawing room because she possesses genuine artistic accomplishments (like Marianne Dashwood) and a flair for witty conversation (like Elizabeth Bennet). Like Elizabeth Bennet believing that Wickham is virtuous because he appears to be so charming, Edmund feels for Mary "an ecstasy of admiration of all her many virtues, from her obliging manners down to her light and graceful tread" (112).

Like Austen, Mary is well read and loves word play. Joking about the poor morals of the rear admirals and vice admirals she has met, Mary quips, "Of Rears and Vices, I saw enough. Now, do not be suspecting me of a pun, I entreat" (60). She is the only Austen character to *announce* that she is constructing a parody of a parody:

> "Sir Thomas is to achieve mighty things when he comes home," said Mary, after a pause. "Do you remember Hawkins Browne's 'Address to Tobacco,' in imitation of Pope?—
>
> 'Blest leaf! whose aromatic gales dispense
> To Templars modesty, to Parsons sense.'
>
> I will parody them:
>
> 'Blest Knight! whose dictatorial looks dispense
> To Children affluence, to Rushworth sense.'
>
> Will not that do . . .?"
>
> (161-62)

Mary's choice of Isaac Hawkins Browne's parody of Alexander Pope is significant: Browne was a minor poet known for wit, repartee, frivolity, and a squandered talent; a man who admitted that wealth, "the downy couch of ease," and associations with "the vulgar herd" had kept him from contemplation and loftier thoughts.[11] In a novel mentioning the slave trade and Sir Thomas's sugar plantations, perhaps Austen also includes the reference to tobacco as a reminder of another crop in which extensive slave labor in the East Indies and in America was used to provide a luxury for England. Like Browne, Mary Crawford seems to waste her wit on idle, irreverent doggerel.

Austen gives Mary Crawford the breezy tone and sharp bite of her own letters. In private letters, Austen shows her fondness for puns and alliteration, quipping that Alexander Pope is the "one infallible Pope" (26 October 1813) and describing a life of "Candour & Comfort & Coffee & Cribbage" (9 February 1813). Which of the following is an Austen letter and which is a remark by Mary Crawford?

> What a difference a vowel makes! If his rents were but equal to his rants!
>
> It is a Vile World, we are all for Self & I expected no better from any of us. But though *Better* is not to be expected, *Butter* may, at least from Mrs Clement's Cow.

Both Mary and Austen laugh at themselves. Again, which is which?

> Expect a most agreeable letter; for not being overburdened with subject—(having nothing at all to say)—I shall have no check to my Genius from beginning to end.
>
> It is impossible to put an hundredth part of my great mind on paper.

(Answer: first and fourth are Mary [394, 415]; second and third are Austen's letters of 23 January 1817 and 21 January 1801.) Some of Mary Crawford's remarks also sound like those attributed to Austen's flamboyant, Frenchified cousin, Eliza de Feuillide, who used private theatricals to flirt with Austen's brothers and remarked, "I always find that the most effectual mode of getting rid of temptation is to give way to it."[12]

Austen has Mary Crawford drop into conversation phrases such as *menus plaisir, esprit de corps, adieu, bon vivant,* and *lines passionées.* In contrast, the plain-speaking, very English Edmund insists that he cannot produce a *bon mot,* rejecting the sparkling but empty repartee of Parisian wits. Yet Austen herself dots her fiction and her letters with French phrases, as when she notes with greater spirit than accuracy, "What a Contretems!—in the Language of France" (9 February 1807). At the same time, Austen links the witty Mary Crawford to the decadence and selfishness of French culture by having Mary compare herself to the narcissistic Doge in the court of Louis XIV. In addition, Mary's insistence that her brother's adulterous relationship with Maria is just a moment's *étourderie* suggests a thoughtlessness consistent with this character who is "careless as a woman and a friend" (437, 260). Mary's casual, affected language shows that she deems her brother's real act of wrongdoing a trifling matter.

Even when playing the harp Mary seems more bent on uttering clever remarks than on responding genuinely to the music. Like the apocryphal story of Marie Antoinette suggesting that the poor eat cake, Mary Crawford has no compunction against demanding a cart for transporting her harp even if farmers need it for the harvest. She is surprised to find that her selfish arrogance "offended all the farmers, all the labourers, all the hay in the parish" (58). As she tells Fanny at another point, "Selfishness must always be forgiven you know, because there is no hope for a cure" (68). Austen links Mary to the corruption of the city by having her cite "the true London maxim, that every thing is to be got with money" (58).

Mary's cynicism extends to all aspects of society, including the church. Just as Mrs. Ferrars and Fanny Dashwood in ***Sense and Sensibility*** reject the church as not "smart" enough a profession for Edward Ferrars, Mary Crawford totally opposes Edmund's choice of entering the clergy and advises him to go into the law. Mary also has little faith in those who attend church. In the same chapel where Fanny expects awe and magnificence and praises the value of families assembled together for prayer, Mary thinks of the many parishioners who would prefer to sleep late or whose minds are somewhere else entirely.

Austen certainly shared Mary Crawford's irreverence toward those merely pretending to be godly and had already included in her novels young women in church thinking about their clothes rather than the message. In ***Mansfield Park*** she validates Mary's views by portraying Dr. Grant as a clergyman more interested in his dinners than his duties. Like Mary, Austen saw through many instances of "seeming piety" (87). But Mary shows no sign of allegiance to any higher purpose, sense of duty or conscience, or inner spiritual guide. As Edmund concludes, Mary's faults are "faults of principle—blunted delicacy and a corrupted, vitiated mind" (456).

Mary Crawford is nonetheless one of the most discerning and self-aware characters in Austen's fictional universe. She does not sleep through the novel, like the childish Lady Bertram; sponge off others while boasting of generosity, like the mean-spirited Aunt Norris; or join Maria and Julia Bertram in thinking that rattling off the names of kings, cruel emperors, and heathen gods constitutes an education. Mary looks both in the mirror and out the window and knows something is profoundly wanting. An orphan raised by a debauched admiral and his embittered wife in a metropolis teeming with corrupted people, Mary has been robbed of faith. "A tinge of wrong" mars her behavior and taints her mind (269). Frequently restless and discontented, Mary sometimes forces laughter, but her gaiety seems empty: Austen describes her as "trying to appear gay and unconcerned" or trying "to speak carelessly; but she was not so careless as she wanted to appear" (288, 458). A lively, charming, accomplished young woman, Mary Crawford *could* have been truly admirable had she been given a moral education to counter the inescapable corruption of the world around her.

The narrator of ***Mansfield Park*** combines Mary's wit with Fanny's conscience. Like Mary, Austen delights in irreverence and parodies classical syntax. "Much was said, and much was ate, and all went well," the narrator observes, much as Austen in a letter had noted, "They came & they sat & they went" (6 November 1813). But like Fanny, the narrator demonstrates genuine appreciation of nature and an uncompromising moral integrity. By the end of ***Mansfield Park,*** neither Mary Crawford nor Fanny Price has changed much in essentials. Instead, the narrative voice offers readers an alternative combining the best of both women.

In this novel Austen reserves the language of character transformation and moral journey for three male characters: Sir Thomas Bertram and his two sons, Tom and Edmund. This is the only novel to portray a blind father who sees the light, a dissolute elder son who finds goodness, and a serious younger son who has to *learn* to love the heroine.

No other Austen father grows as much as Sir Thomas Bertram does. Mr. Morland stays in the background of ***Northanger Abbey,*** Mr. Dashwood dies in the opening chapter of ***Sense and Sensibility,*** Mr. Bennet lapses back into cynicism by the end of ***Pride and Prejudice,*** Mr. Woodhouse remains a childhood hypochondriac throughout ***Emma,*** and Sir Walter Elliot continues his vanity and snobbery from start to finish of ***Persuasion.*** It is far more difficult to label Sir Thomas of ***Mansfield Park.*** A complex figure, Sir Thomas illustrates the danger of imperialism and patriarchy but also the redeeming power of humility, morality, charity, and love.

From the start, Sir Thomas has good intentions. Austen's phrase "well-meant condescensions" captures her ambivalent view of this slave-holding aristocrat and imperious father (13). Sir Thomas scares Fanny with his harsh, severe demeanor, but his charity in welcoming his sister-in-law's puny daughter into his household suggests his sense of honor and generosity. Proud to be "master at Mansfield Park," he is a serious, dignified, undemonstrative man characterized by "steady sobriety and orderly silence" and a strict sense of decorum (370, 240). His offspring not surprisingly respond by craving laughter and a release from restraint.

A political and social product of his time, Sir Thomas does his duty in Parliament and strives to make his plantations in Antigua profitable. Sir Thomas seems a no-nonsense, unimaginative man who believes "there should be moderation in everything" (313). At home, he composedly accepts a wife as a sleepy ornament, prides himself on having given his children everything they need, and views Fanny Price as socially inferior in rank and rights. In "leaving his daughters to the direction of others at their present most interesting time of life" when he travels to Antigua, he errs in thinking his sister-in-law, Mrs. Norris, would make a good director (32). He also errs in agreeing to a marriage between his eldest daughter and the stupid but wealthy Mr. Rushworth. Devoid of "romantic delicacy," Sir Thomas egotistically views the alliance as beneficial: He is "happy to secure a marriage which would bring *him* such an addition of respectability and influence" (331, 201; my italics). Sir Thomas sees nothing wrong with his children's education, nor does he detect Aunt Norris's lack of judgment, morals, and compassion until everything falls apart. He becomes wrathful when thwarted, as when he subjects a disobedient Fanny to an abusive harangue or dismisses her to her squalid home as a "medicinal project" designed to teach her a lesson (369).

Yet Sir Thomas absolutely should not be viewed as a Simon Legree. Even in the early sections of ***Mansfield Park*** Sir Thomas has a keener sense of honor than many around him. Certainly he shines next to Fanny's drunken, callous, vulgar father, Lieutenant Price, who ignores his daughters and indulges his rowdy sons. A moral man, Sir Thomas encourages Edmund to be the sort of clergyman who lives in his parish and takes his duties seriously. Sir Thomas sadly recognizes that his eldest son lacks Edmund's integrity and sense of responsibility. "I blush for you, Tom," Sir Thomas says as he learns that the future Sir Thomas's extravagant, hedonistic ways have caused debts that will hurt Edmund's opportunities (23). Sir Thomas may be angry with Fanny for refusing to marry Henry Crawford, but he also is appalled to discover that Aunt Norris has never allowed a fire in Fanny's room. As master of the house, he immediately orders a fire to be lit even when he is angry with her.

Most remarkable is Sir Thomas's capacity to admit his errors, feel the sting of self-reproach, and change his ways. Although Austen wraps up ***Mansfield Park*** with a breezy tone ("Let other pens dwell on guilt and misery") promising readers their expected happy ending for hero and heroine, she makes sure that we know that Sir Thomas has suffered longest: "Sir Thomas, poor Sir Thomas, a parent, and conscious of errors in his own conduct as a parent, was the longest to suffer. He felt that he ought not to have allowed the marriage, that his daughter's sentiments had been sufficiently known to him to render him culpable in authorising it, that in so doing he had sacrificed the right to the expedient, and been governed by motives of selfishness and worldly wisdom" (461). Austen spends several pages dwelling on Sir Thomas's guilt and misery, reminding us that although his sense of loss deadens and he finds new sources of comfort, the pain always remains: "the anguish arising from the conviction of his own errors in the education of his daughters was never to be entirely done away with" (463). Had Mr. Bennet or Mr. Price felt their own errors so deeply, they would be on the road to becoming not only far better fathers but also far better men.

Sir Thomas knows that his repression of his children has led them to rebel (could this be a swipe at King George III's approach to that "strange business … in America" mentioned earlier in the novel?), and he admits that delegating authority to Aunt Norris has been "grievous mismanagement" (119, 463). Most importantly, Sir Thomas recognizes that his concept of education has been sorely deficient: "Something must have been wanting *within*. … He feared that principle, active principle, had been wanting, that they had never been properly taught to govern their inclinations and tempers, by that sense of duty which can alone suffice. They had been instructed theoretically in their religion, but never required to bring it into daily practice. To be distinguished for elegance and accomplishments … could have had … no moral effect on the mind" (463). Sir Thomas bitterly, wretchedly confesses that he has meant well but done ill, spent much but accomplished little. His reference to fancy balls in Antigua suggests that, like many British colonialists, he has himself led a life of luxury too far removed from hard work and self-denial. Tom, Maria, and Julia are idly rich yet morally impoverished. Knowing now that he has spoiled his children, Sir Thomas can "acknowledge the advantages of early hardship and discipline, and the consciousness of being born to struggle and endure," recognize the selfish, bossy Aunt Norris as an evil "part of himself," and feel "sick of ambitious and mercenary connections" (465-66, 471). Austen uses strong, repetitive language in the final page of ***Mansfield Park*** ("Sir Thomas saw repeated, and for ever repeated, reason to rejoice in what he had done for them all") to show that Sir Thomas reaps rewards for his early charity in bringing Fanny into his house (473).

Again Austen keeps the spotlight on the distance Sir Thomas has traveled, literally and figuratively. He has faced disorder in Antigua, thousands of miles away, as well as disaster at home. In the concluding chapter of ***Mansfield Park,*** Austen spends far more time on Sir Thomas than on her supposed hero and heroine. She reminds us that Sir Thomas now finds felicity in a union he had originally shuddered to contemplate: "The high sense of having realised a great acquisition in the promise of Fanny for a daughter, formed just such a contrast with his early opinion on the subject when the poor little girl's coming had been first agitated, as time is for ever producing between the plans and decisions of mortals, for their own instruction, and their neighbours' entertainment" (472). Growth occurs not just in youthful, romantic heroes and heroines but also in fathers. Not all drama happens on the way to the altar. Austen's sentence widens its focus from Sir Thomas to "mortals" in general, suggesting that all of us possess the potential over time to become wiser and better human beings. By referring to the "instruction" and "entertainment" produced by contemplating such character changes, Austen reminds readers of her own dual mission as a moral but comic novelist.

Austen suggests that a gentleman is made, not born—and made only through a painful process of self-reflection and discovery. Along with their father, Tom and Edmund

Bertram also are significantly transformed by the novel's end, Tom in his behavior and Edmund in his perception.

As eldest son and the future Sir Thomas, Tom Bertram has been raised to do little but pursue his own pleasures, spend money, and view life as an extended holiday. Unlike his grave younger brother, Tom is full of liveliness, "cheerful selfishness," and the gift of gab, with "easy manners, excellent spirits … and a great deal to say" (24, 47). He has bad friends, a penchant for drink, and an aversion to work. Because he has never had to strive, Tom seems restless, "having so much leisure as to make almost any novelty a certain good" (123). For Tom, as for Marianne Dashwood in ***Sense and Sensibility,*** illness brings change. As his brother nurses him back to health, Tom begins recovering from both a physical and moral sickness, shedding his "thoughtlessness and selfishness" and becoming "what he ought to be, useful to his father, steady and quiet, and not living merely for himself." (462)

Edmund does not need to reproach himself for gambling and drinking as does his brother, but he knows that his infatuation with the dazzling Mary Crawford has blinded him and led him to compromise his own standards. As Fanny notes when Edmund agrees to act in love scenes with Mary in theatricals that he knows his absent father would oppose, "the scruples of his integrity, seemed all done away" (367). Like Marianne finding the handsome Willoughby perfect, Edmund gives Mary Crawford "merits which she had not" and labels her "sweet and faultless" (264, 269). A serious man with "not the least wit" in his nature, Edmund avoids gallant flattery and vapid small talk, but he nevertheless seems drawn to the witty Mary Crawford like a moth to a flame (94).

Edmund possesses all the necessary ingredients for a gentleman ("strong good sense and uprightness of mind," "his sincerity, his steadiness, his integrity") but lacks backbone and discernment (21, 65). He seems to have absorbed some of his father's paternalism, commenting in patronizing tones about how he has shaped, formed, and directed Fanny's mind. Just as Sir Thomas fails to understand Fanny's feelings but likes to advise her, so Edmund trivializes Fanny's emotions when he assumes that it can make no difference to her whether or not she stays at Mansfield Park, or when he speaks of a possible marriage to Henry Crawford as a coup for her. A superior listener and perceiver, Fanny knows Edmund far better than Edmund knows Fanny—or himself.

Like Catherine Morland's awakening, Marianne Dashwood's transformation, and Elizabeth Bennet's enlightenment, Edmund Bertram undergoes a metamorphosis. By the novel's end, he confesses of his infatuation for Mary Crawford, "My eyes are opened. … How have I been deceived!" (456, 459). Edmund now can return to the role suggested by the meaning of his name: Edmund signifies "a gentleman who prospers by helping others." Just as he acted as a true gentleman by serving as kind guardian of the young Fanny from the time she arrives at Mansfield Park, so he now can flourish by nursing his brother Tom, loving the worthy Fanny, helping his afflicted parents, and comforting and guiding his parishioners.

Cassandra Austen faulted her sister for marrying Fanny to the staid Edmund Bertram rather than to the more charming Henry Crawford. As niece Louisa Knight observed, "Cassandra tried to persuade Miss Austen to alter ***Mansfield Park*** and let Mr. Crawford marry Fanny Price … but Miss Austen stood firm and would not allow a change."[13] Fanny stands firm as well, proclaiming her right to say no: "I should have thought … that every woman must have felt the possibility of a man's not being approved, not being loved by some one of her sex, at least, let him be ever so generally agreeable. Let him have all the perfections in the world, I think it ought not to be set down as certain, that a man must be acceptable to every woman he may happen to like himself" (353). Elinor Dashwood in ***Sense and Sensibility*** said wryly of planned marriages, "The lady, I suppose, has no choice in the affair" (***SS,*** 296). Never wry, Fanny Price straightforwardly defends a woman's right to select her own partner in life.

Just as it takes the shy Fanny greater courage to speak up to Sir Thomas than for Elizabeth to bandy words with Lady Catherine, so Fanny faces a greater challenge in rejecting Henry Crawford than any other Austen heroine will face from a suitor. Marianne and Elinor Dashwood receive no extra marriage proposals, and it is easy for Catherine Morland to reject the boorish John Thorpe or for Elizabeth Bennet to disappoint the pompous Mr. Collins. In ***Mansfield Park,*** however, the devil-as-suitor is more cleverly disguised; the temptation to accept him thus is greater. Fanny's powers of discernment allow her to acknowledge that Henry surpasses other men in some respects ("he had more confidence than Edmund, more judgment than Thomas, more talent and taste than Mr. Yates"), but she remains convinced that this "best actor of all" is wrong for her—and tinged with wrong himself (165).

Henry Crawford's flirtation with other women and his adultery with Maria stem from his vanity, selfishness, restlessness, and immorality. Deeming it his "right" to gain Fanny, Henry arrogantly assumes he can *make* Fanny like him and relishes the glory of forcing her to love him. Henry changes for the better in the process of pursuing Fanny, but even when he speaks of his kindly intentions, his ego cannot be suppressed: "My Fanny … my happiness … I am the doer … I am the person to give the consequence. … What can Sir Thomas and Edmund together do … to what I *shall* do?" Henry exclaims, delighting like a competitor in the fact that he can do more for her than others (297). Ego also drives Henry's adulterous relationship with Maria Bertram. Mortified by her rejection of their former intimacy, Henry's vanity is pricked and "he began the attack," determined "to subdue" Maria and make her "wholly at his command" (468).

What makes Henry a harder figure to relegate to the villain heap is that he, like his sister, has an excuse. Orphaned, they have been raised by guardians who have exposed them to corruption and cynicism. Austen seems determined in this novel to call readers' attention to the importance of upbringing. "The admiral's lessons have quite spoiled him," Mary admits of her brother (43). Also like Mary, Henry sees himself in the mirror and finds himself wanting. Nowhere is that more evident than in his envy for Fanny's sailor-brother, the "frank, unstudied, but feeling and respectful" William Price (233).

Unlike Henry, William has faced hardship, whether struggles to transcend a disordered home or adversity at sea for seven years. An open, unsophisticated, loving young man with both skills and scruples, William inspires Henry Crawford's envy: "Henry Crawford ... longed to have been at sea, and seen and done and suffered as much. His heart was warmed, his fancy fired, and he felt the highest respect for a lad who, before he was twenty, had gone through such bodily hardships, and given such proofs of mind. The glory of heroism, of usefulness, of exertion, of endurance, made his own habits of selfish indulgence appear in shameful contrast; and he wished he had been a William Price, distinguishing himself and working his way to fortune and consequence with so much self-respect and happy ardour, instead of what he was!" (236). Like many a New Year's resolution, however, Henry's desire for self-improvement lasts but a moment: "The wish was rather eager than lasting. He was roused from the reverie of retrospection and regret produced by it, by some inquiry ... as to his plans for the next day's hunting; and he found it was as well to be a man of fortune at once with horses and grooms at his command" (236-37). Henry Crawford remains a man of fortune at the end of ***Mansfield Park,*** punished only by whatever momentary regrets he may feel. Like Willoughby in ***Sense and Sensibility,*** Henry will continue to shine in society's drawing rooms by using charm and elocution to mask inner discord. As a woman, Maria will be left disgraced and in exile; as a man, Henry (like Willoughby) can go on with his life. In a bitingly feminist narrative voice, Austen observes, "That punishment, the public punishment of disgrace, should in a just measure attend *his* share of the offence, is, we know, not one of the barriers, which society gives to virtue" (468).

Austen adds an unusual sentence after her description of the unpunished Henry Crawford: "*In this world,* the penalty is less equal than could be wished; but without presuming to look forward to *a juster appointment hereafter,* we may fairly consider a man of sense like Henry Crawford, to be providing for himself no small portion of vexation and regret" (468; my italics). This is the only passage I have found in which Jane Austen invites readers (albeit indirectly, "without presuming") to consider the eternal punishment waiting for scoundrels who blithely walk away scot-free from the wreckage they cause. Of all Austen's novels, ***Mansfield Park*** reminds us most that even if we obtain checkered "happiness à la mortal" or a marriage "as secure as earthly happiness can be," this does not begin to address immortality or the soul.

Another way Austen shows an interest in immortality in ***Mansfield Park*** is by spending far more time exploring the value of a clerical life. In ***Pride and Prejudice*** readers can hardly take the Reverend Mr. Collins seriously when he boasts, "I consider the clerical office as equal in point of dignity with the highest rank in the kingdom" (***PP,*** 97). In Collins's case, this is hardly true, as he is a man of limited intellect, little heart, and less spirituality who cringes before anyone of rank. In ***Mansfield Park,*** however, Jane Austen shows the truth of Mr. Collins's statement. As a clergyman, Edmund Bertram *does* rank as high—or higher—in moral principle as any other man in the novel. Mary Crawford is wrong to label the profession nothing and to assume that it would be stooping for her to ally herself with Edmund if he adopts such a career. As Edmund responds, a clergyman who honors his work can be of "first importance to mankind" because he serves as the guardian "of religion and morals" and affects individuals and groups of people "both temporally and eternally" (92).

If Edmund is correct that "as the clergy are, or are not what they ought to be, so are the rest of the nation," then the nation is a mixture (93). Austen gives us both Dr. Grant, a selfish, claret-drinking clergyman who dies of "three great institutionary dinners in one week," and the upright, conscientious Edmund. As if to underscore the religious focus of this novel, Austen ends ***Mansfield Park*** not with a conversation between the happily married Fanny and Edmund but with a reference to the parsonage. Edmund's replacement of the Reverend Mr. Norris and the Reverend Dr. Grant offers evidence that "the Nation" may be moving in the right direction—at least in the isolated rural world "within the view" of Mansfield Park (473).

Mansfield Park emphasizes not only spiritual life but also "a more fraternal"—brotherly love—rather than the romantic love invariably described in popular fiction. When William Price and Henry Crawford depart from Mansfield Park, Sir Thomas mistakenly assumes that Fanny's heart will be saddened as much by the absence of her handsome suitor as by her sailor brother. The narrator tells us otherwise: "She sat and cried *con amore* as her uncle intended, but it was con amore fraternal and no other" (282). Much as ***Sense and Sensibility*** concludes with the image of close sisters and brothers living in harmony and equality, so ***Mansfield Park*** celebrates fraternity as the soundest basis for human relationships.

Those lacking in fraternal love are morally bankrupt. Lady Bertram and Aunt Norris have cast off their less fortunate sister, Mrs. Price, and the "absolute breach between the sisters" points to their shortage of sensibility and humanity (4). When Tom Bertram becomes dangerously ill, Mrs. Price feels as little for his mother as Lady Bertram would feel for her in a similar predicament: "So long divided, and so differently situated, the ties of blood were little more than nothing. . . . Mrs. Price did quite as much for Lady Bertram, as Lady Bertram would have done for Mrs. Price. Three or four Prices might have been swept away, any or all, except Fanny or William, and Lady Bertram would have thought little about it; or perhaps might have caught from Mrs. Norris's lips the cant of its being a very happy thing, and a great blessing to their poor dear sister Price to have them so well provided for" (428). Like Jonathan Swift but without his irony, Aunt Norris could have written a modest proposal suggesting that killing some of the Price children would help solve her sister's economic distress.

These three sisters' uncaring relationship contrasts sharply with the warm love between William and Fanny Price. Some have found the scenes between William and Fanny nearly incestuous, including William's plan near the end of the novel for a little cottage "in which he and Fanny were to pass all their middle and latter life together" (375).[14] I disagree. Just as Jane and Cassandra Austen lived together happily, forming a warm family life and living primarily off income provided by generous brothers, so William and Fanny Price imagine an alternative domestic oasis, should neither one find a suitable mate. Knowing that life together with William is a possibility, Fanny need not marry for the wrong reasons: she does not have to escape her parents (like Maria and Julia), gain an income (like Mary's ambitious, mercenary friend Mrs. Fraser), or find a moral mentor (like Henry and Mary Crawford). Perhaps their youthful picture of adult life together in a cottage is a bit naive and puerile, overly virginal, but it does offer an alternative form of love should romance be denied them.

Watching Fanny with her brother leads not to prurient discomfort but to admiration in "all who had hearts to value any thing good" (235). Some of Fanny's purest and happiest moments occur when she is with her brother. In a novel laced with political overtones, it is interesting that Austen describes Fanny's felicitous relationship with her brother as lacking in restraint, hierarchy, and repression: it is "unchecked, equal, fearless" (234).

Austen interrupts the tale of her fictional siblings reminiscing about their shared childhood to insert a general paragraph about the superiority of fraternal to conjugal ties: "An advantage this, a strengthener of love, in which even the conjugal tie is beneath the fraternal. Children of the same family, the same blood, with the same first associations and habits, have some means of enjoyment in their power, which no subsequent connections can supply; and it must be by a long and unnatural estrangement, by a divorce which no subsequent connection can justify, if such precious remains of the earliest attachments are ever entirely outlived. Too often, alas! it is so.—Fraternal love, sometimes almost every thing, is at others worse than nothing" (234-35). Just as ***Pride and Prejudice*** overturned romantic notions of love at first sight and celebrated gradually developed esteem, so this description of the long-lasting ties of fraternal love posits a new model for any love: love based on shared memories, mutual enjoyment, and unbroken connections.

To reinforce that idea, Austen shows the relationship between Edmund and Fanny as fraternal affection transformed into conjugal love. Is this another instance of incest? Aunt Norris certainly thinks so, as when she declares to Sir Thomas that it is "morally impossible" for those raised as brother and sister to fall in love (6). Edmund initially looks to Fanny with "the kind smile of an affectionate brother" and refers to her even near the end as "my Fanny—my only sister" (222, 444). Yet ultimately Edmund comes to realize (as Fanny has for hundreds of pages) that "her warm and sisterly regard for him would be foundation enough for wedded love" (470). Implied in that comment is the radical concept of "unchecked, equal, fearless" intercourse between husband and wife.

As narrator, Austen clearly approves of Fanny and Edmund's morality and their felicitous, slow growing "wedded love." At the same time, she ends the novel with vagueness about the details of their courtship ("I purposely abstain from dates"), part of a general pattern in this novel of avoiding the sound of full omnipotence (470). After all, Austen's very first word in ***Mansfield Park*** is a guess ("*About* thirty years ago, Miss Maria Ward") places her at a distance from her material. She speculates ("I have no inclination to believe") rather than announces that Fanny would not be as unconquerable as the "young ladies of seventeen one reads about" (231). She remains vague on how long Fanny expects Henry's affections to last ("It would not be fair to enquire") as well as on how long it takes for Edmund to switch his affections from Mary to Fanny (331). When Mrs. Norris is bundled off with the disgraced Maria to a remote, private establishment in another country, Austen does not follow them there but merely concludes, "it may be reasonably supposed that their tempers became their mutual punishment" (465).

Why this narrative vagueness? Why never give us a conversation between Fanny and Edmund once they have moved beyond fraternal to conjugal affections? John Halperin assumes another "botched ending" resulting from Jane Austen's inability to render romantic scenes.[15] This, however, would fail to explain why she also backs away from the specific fates of her villainous characters ("Let other pens dwell on guilt and misery") and acts as if she does not fully know any of her characters. In a novel about inner lives—the thoughts, reflections, and contemplations of people in solitude—Austen perhaps wishes to remind readers that none of us can really enter into the private recesses of another human mind.

At the same time, she invites us to become mental travelers following her clues. The mind seems a major topic in this novel, whether it is Fanny's struggle to have her "beauty of mind" recognized rather than her pretty figure or the narrator's demonstration of her own wise and witty thoughts. Take, for instance, Fanny's reference to little more than a line of William Cowper's "The Task": "Ye fallen avenues! once more I mourn / Your fate unmerited." This is all we are given on the surface. But what happens if we track down the allusion? The line comes from "The Sofa," book 1 of Cowper's six-book poem. Like Austen describing Lady Bertram lounging on the sofa rather than tending to more important duties, Cowper warns in "The Sofa" that society's move from no furniture to simple stools to elegant sofas may be a loss, not a gain; our increasingly refined, idle rich have obtained an unhappy leisure rather than an active usefulness. Cowper's phrasing ("languid eye," "vapid soul," "tedious card parties") parallels Austen's, as does his attack on cities filled with vice, schools without discipline, and pulpits without honor.[16]

I speculate that Austen hoped her readers would take her quotation of one line from "The Task" as an invitation to dig more deeply into Cowper's poem. It simply seems too coincidental that the poem also includes a ringing indictment of clerical abuses, an attack on the immorality of slavery, and a celebration of the divine power of nature.

In strong poetic language, Cowper calls on his fellow clergymen not to seek applause, perform theatrics, follow fashion, or cultivate empty figures of speech. "Avaunt all attitude and stare, / And start theatric, practised at the glass," Cowper insists. Good preachers can reform their listeners by plainly speaking the truth from their hearts: "I seek divine simplicity in him / Who handles things divine." Austen's creation of Edmund Bertram gives fictional life to the very sort of clergyman Cowper imagines. Edmund's avoidance of bon mots and oratorical flourishes makes him a better conduit for religious truths. Cowper makes it clear that clergymen should reject "lightness of speech," beware the seduction of "popular applause" and avoid jests, grins, "foppish airs and histrionic mummery" that "let down / The pulpit to the level of the stage." If religion relaxes its hold on "the roving and untutored heart," the result is that "the laity run wild."

Those who fault Austen for not going further in her attack on colonialism might revise their thinking if they follow her Cowper allusions. Austen's readers would have known Cowper in a way few of us do today. An ardent abolitionist, Cowper launches an eloquent tirade against "the wrong and outrage" of slavery in the very next book of "The Task," denouncing it as an offense against human brotherhood. Those with "a skin not coloured" the same become "lawful prey" of cruel masters, who chain them, work them to exhaustion, and lash their bodies "with stripes that Mercy, with a bleeding heart, / Weeps when she sees inflicted on a beast." Cowper's words are strong:

> Then what is man? And what man seeing this,
> And having human feelings, does not blush
> And hang his head, to think himself a man?
> I would not have a slave to till my ground,
> To carry me, to fan me while I sleep,
> And tremble when I wake, for all the wealth
> That sinews bought and sold have ever earned.

Cowper concludes, "We have no slaves at home.—Then why abroad?" a question which goes as unanswered in the poem as it does when Fanny raises the topic at Mansfield Park. Perhaps had Maria and Julia Bertram read this lengthy poem they might have joined their reflective cousin in questioning the source of their wealth.

As if she were writing in invisible ink, I believe Jane Austen uses the allusion to Cowper's "The Task" to bring his stirring words into readers' minds. She can thus attack the inhumanity of slavery without turning ***Mansfield Park*** into an abolitionist tract. Her brother Frank had already spoken out against the "harshness and despotism" of "land-holders or their managers in the West India Islands," observing, "Slavery however it is modified is still slavery."[17] Jane Austen knew that her father served as trustee of a profitable slave-tended estate in Antigua. I find it no accident that Austen gives Fanny Price quotations from an abolitionist poet. Had Virginia Woolf caught such indirect references, perhaps she would not have called Austen "too little of the rebel," a woman who "accepted life too calmly as she found it."[18]

Austen's father read Cowper aloud to the family, and Austen even asked her gardener to plant certain flowers in response to floral references in Cowper's verse (see letters of 18 December 1798 and 8 February 1807). By having Fanny and Edmund cite or echo Cowper, Austen links her heroine and hero to her own poetic tastes, spiritual values, and love of rural beauty.

Austen uses another Cowper allusion to describe Fanny's desire to return to Mansfield Park: "Her eagerness, her impatience, her longings to be with them, were such as to bring a line or two of Cowper's Tirocinium for ever before her. 'With what intense desire she wants her home,' was continually on her tongue, as the truest description of a yearning which she could not suppose any schoolboy's bosom to feel more keenly" (431). No longer content just to quote Cowper verbatim, Fanny now has enlarged Cowper's vision to include women. Cowper's "Tirocinium; or a Review of Schools" refers exclusively to a school*boy's* homesickness, his experiences at school, and his bond to his father. Austen has Fanny substitute "she" and "her" in Cowper's original line, "With what intense desire *he* wants *his* home," and she claims her right to yearn as keenly as any schoolboy. Although Cowper's poem encourages fathers to lead their sons to some "philosophic height" for their "wondering eyes," in ***Mansfield Park*** the only philosophizing, wondering being is Fanny. The only time Cowper mentions women in "Tirocinium" is for the sake of a disparaging analogy:

Boys, once on fire with that contentious zeal,
Feel all the rage that female rivals feel:
The prize of beauty in a woman's eyes
Not brighter than in theirs the scholar's prize.[19]

Refuting this suggestion that boys strive for learning while girls value looks, Austen offers in Fanny a thinking, reading, meditating woman eager to gain "information for information's sake," not a female preening herself (418).

As in "The Task," Cowper's "Tirocinium" indicts clergymen who are "Christian in name, and infidel in heart," so interested in playing a fashionable part that they are "mere church furniture at best." The poem attacks poorly disciplined schools that do not prepare boys to become men of conscience and integrity. But why, Austen must have wondered, should a poem stressing the need "to cultivate and keep the morals clean" be aimed exclusively at fathers and sons? Why are only school*boys* thought to feel deeply and crave learning? ***Mansfield Park*** answers and extends "Tirocinium" by demonstrating that (to use Charlotte Brontë's later words), "Women feel just as men do, and they need exercise for their faculties as much as their brothers."[20]

Given the depth of Cowper's poetry, it is not surprising that Fanny has transcended the petty men and women around her, gained empathy, and learned to draw pleasure from her environs. Knowing that lyrics can elevate, Fanny wants to buy books of poetry to share with her younger sister. Austen describes Fanny playing the very role with Susan that Cowper envisioned fathers playing with their sons: that of warm mentor encouraging "clean morals" and "philosophic heights."

Austen also asks her readers to consider why Fanny quotes Sir Walter Scott's "Lay of the Last Minstrel": Fanny laments that the chapel at Sotherton has no banners blown by "the night wind of Heaven" and no signs that a "Scottish monarch sleeps below" (85-86). Fanny has obviously read canto 2 of Scott's long poem, as she takes her first quotation from book 10 and the second from book 12 of this second canto. Between the two lines she chooses, Scott describes a hero who "trampled the Apostate's pride" (book 11). Scott's poem celebrates pastoral values and suggests that some are so busy pursuing worldly gains that they have no time for prayer. Scott's description of human beings enamored with "titles, power, and pelf" and "concentred all in self" applies to many of the worldly, selfish men and women of Mansfield Park.[21]

Although Fanny quotes only Cowper and Scott, she has other books in her room, including Crabbe's *Tales.* As Park Honan notes, "Readers might grasp or miss the joke of Fanny Price's having the poet Crabbe's Tales among her books since the joke depends on our knowing that Fanny Price is the name of Crabbe's own 'meekly firm' heroine in The Parish Register."[22] The name appears at the end of part 2 (called "Marriages") in Crabbe's long poem in verse called "Parish Register":

Last on my List appears a Match of Love,
And one of Virtue;—happy may it prove!—
. . . .
For *Fanny Price* was lovely and was chaste.

An "amorous Knight" tries to seduce Fanny by offering to lift her into a life of luxury, wealth, and fashion. Soft carpets and tall mirrors will fill her room, and she will be an admired and adored object "by the Hands of Wealth and Fashion drest / By Slaves attended and by Friends carest."[23] Just as Henry Crawford's flattery and bribery cannot move Fanny Price to accept his marriage proposals, so Crabbe's "meekly firm" Fanny Price fixes her mind on heavenly comforts, the power of virtue, and her own faithfulness. Like Cowper, Crabbe was both an ordained minister and a writer, perhaps suggesting to Austen the ability to be both literary and religious. Austen joked that she would like to become Mrs. Crabbe.[24] Did Austen take Fanny Price's name from Crabbe's principled heroine just to play a joke or to link her own themes to those Crabbe explored in his extensive theological writings?

Austen also adds extra layers to ***Mansfield Park*** by including references to a prose work: Dr. Johnson's *Rasselas.* Again, although the actual allusion goes by quickly and unobtrusively, the quotation in its broader context yields rich dividends. The reference comes as Fanny compares the disagreeableness of her Portsmouth home to the elegance of Mansfield Park: "In a review of the two houses . . . Fanny was tempted to apply to them Dr. Johnson's celebrated judgment as to matrimony and celibacy, and say, that though Mansfield Park might have some pains, Portsmouth could have no pleasures" (392). When Dr. Johnson's Rasselas says it is better not to marry because discord exists within so many marriages and families, his sister responds that unmarried people become peevish and malevolent "outlaws of human nature."[25] Right before the sentence Austen quotes from *Rasselas,* we find a perfect description of someone like Aunt Norris: "To live without feeling or exciting sympathy, to be fortunate without adding to the felicity of others, or afflicted without tasting the balm of pity, is a state more gloomy than solitude; it is not retreat but exclusion from mankind. Marriage has many pains, but celibacy has no pleasures." Exiled to a remote country at the end of ***Mansfield Park,*** the callous, greedy, resentful Aunt Norris cannot elicit even Fanny's pity: "Mrs. Norris's removal from Mansfield Park was the great supplementary comfort of Sir Thomas's life. . . . To be relieved from her . . . was so great a felicity. . . . She was regretted by no one at Mansfield. She had never been able to attach even those she loved best. . . . Not even Fanny had tears for aunt Norris—not even when she was gone for ever" (465-66). Aunt Norris never truly marries, as she feels nothing when her husband dies, and she appears in the exact state Dr. Johnson's princess describes: a hell worse than solitude in which one is incapable of feeling or stimulating love.

Mansfield Park has been called Austen's least humorous novel, but sometimes as I follow the allusions I can sense her smiling as she writes. I would argue that one such moment might be the discussion in ***Mansfield Park*** of how important Shakespeare is to *men.* Shakespeare is "a part of an Englishman's constitution," Edmund Bertram and Henry Crawford agree, and they also lament the neglect of reading aloud in *boys'* schools (338). But Austen demonstrates in this novel (as well as in her other novels) that Shakespeare is also part of *her* constitution. Austen helps to characterize Henry Crawford by having him read the part of Cardinal Wolsey, a vain, ambitious, "fair-spoken, and persuading" churchman who proves "ever double both in his words and meaning" (*Henry VIII,* 4.2.52, 38-39). Henry's claim that he could play any character from Richard III to Shylock links him to two greedy, power-hungry, merciless men. Henry can quote *Paradise Lost* and read Shakespeare, much as Richard III can cloak his hollow interior with pleasing words:

> And thus I clothe my naked villainy
> With odd old ends stol'n forth of holy writ,
> And seem a saint when most I play the devil.
>
> (*Richard III,* 1.3.335-37)

Austen also includes echoes of King Lear: Sir Thomas's inability to see Fanny's superiority to her two spiteful "sisters," Maria and Julia, resembles Lear's dismissal of the virtuous Cordelia, only to find himself unloved by the selfish Regan and Goneril.

Like Shakespeare providing illuminating plays within the plays in *Hamlet* and *Midsummer Night's Dream,* so Austen weaves the play *Lovers' Vows* into ***Mansfield Park.*** Although many chapters are filled with discussions of the play and descriptions of rehearsals, readers only hear one quoted line from Mrs. Inchbald's 1798 play. Austen evidently trusted readers to know or seek out the play (based on an earlier German drama called *The Love Child*), particularly its warning that the English were confusing wealth with virtue. When Amelia calls the clergyman Anhalt "a very good man," the dissolute Count Cassel defines the term by nationality:

COUNT:

> "A good man." In Italy, that means a religious man; in France, it means a cheerful man; in Spain, it means a wise man; and it England, it means a rich man.—Which good man of all these is Mr. Anhalt?

AMELIA:

> A good man in every country, except England.
>
> (Appendix, ***MP*** [***Mansfield Park***], 498)

The *only* line from the play that Austen includes in ***Mansfield Park*** is "When two sympathetic hearts meet in the marriage state, matrimony may be called a happy life," a line that Mary as the heiress Amelia rehearses with Edmund as the clergyman Anhalt (358). Readers who go in search of more can find that as that line continues in *Lovers' Vows,* Anhalt offers a brilliant description of the joyful and horrifying possibilities of marriage:

> When two sympathetic hearts meet in the marriage state, matrimony may be called a happy life. When such a wedded pair find thorns in their path, each will be eager, for the sake of the other, to tear them from the root. ... Patience and love will accompany them in their journey, while melancholy and discord they leave far behind.—Hand in hand they pass on from morning till evening, through their summer's day, till the night of age draws on, and the sleep of death overtakes the one. ... This picture is pleasing; but I must beg you not to forget that there is another on the same subject.—When convenience, and fair appearance joined to folly and ill-humour, forge the fetters of matrimony, they gall with their weight the married pair. Discontented with each other—at variance in opinions—their mutual aversion increases with the years they live together.
>
> (Appendix, ***MP,*** 504-5)

Just one of many scenes from *Lovers' Vows* relevant to ***Mansfield Park,*** this speech presents marriage as the best of times or the worst of times, a happy life or enslavement.

Anhalt's reference to a wedded couple journeying "hand in hand" suggests Adam and Eve—and Milton's portrayal of them ("They hand in hand ... took their solitary way"). When Austen has Henry Crawford twist part of a line from *Paradise Lost,* readers recall the fuller passage. Henry defends his right to remain single and a horrible flirt by adding emphasis to a line from book 5 of *Paradise Lost*: "I am of a cautious temper, and unwilling to risk my happiness in a hurry. Nobody can think more highly of the matrimonial state than myself. I consider the blessing of a wife as most justly described in those discreet lines of the poet, 'Heaven's *last* best gift' " (43). As his sister notes, a smiling Henry dwells only on the word "last." In Milton, the line is spoken by an innocent, unfallen Adam as he sees his beautiful wife Eve sleeping beside him:

> Awake
> My fairest, my espous'd, my latest found,
> Heaven's last best gift, my ever new delight.
>
> (*Paradise Lost,* book 5, 17-19)

Adam wakes Eve to rejoice with him in nature's beauty, but Eve is troubled by her dream of giving into temptation. Henry's jocular, distorted use of just four words from this passage suggests his inability to value the genuine "ever new delight" of marriage. His quip may seem witty at the time, but when he later throws away any chance of earthly paradise with Fanny by indulging in a moment's temptation with the forbidden Maria Rushworth, his carelessly spoken words seem empty. Henry seems to have taken as his text Andrew Marvell's "To his Coy Mistress": Austen shows Henry helping Maria escape with him through an iron gate, much as the seducer in Marvell's poem pushes through "the iron gates of life" to enjoy momentary pleasures with his mistress.[26] Austen uses patently moralistic terms (temptation, sacrifice, right) when she writes of Henry's seize-the-day approach to passion: "The temptation of immediate pleasure was too strong for a mind unused to make any sacrifice to right" (467).

Whether digging for Austen's references to Marvell, Milton, Shakespeare, Johnson, Crabbe, Scott, or Cowper, one never comes up empty. The same seems true of names. As Park Honan notes, Mansfield was "a name famous for high, honorable courage. As Lord Chief Justice the first Earl of Mansfield had struck at the roots of the African slave trade."[27] Joseph Wiesenfarth adds that the name Mansfield may link this novel to Richardson's *Sir Charles Grandison,* which includes references to a Mansfield House and an estate-owning Sir Thomas Mansfield.[28] Readers of Richardson's lengthy novel (one of Austen's favorites) might remember that the angelic heroine resists numerous suitors and argues for her right to marry only for affection: "Fortune without merit will never do with me, were the man a prince. … I must love the man to whom I would give my hand, well enough to be able … to *wish* to be his wife."[29] Austen's choice of the name "Norris" may echo the name of "the most villainous figure" in a book by Clarkson on African slavery.[30] Scratch the seemingly opaque surface of Austen's prose and one finds intricate designs hiding underneath. How ***Mansfield Park*** must have confounded the early reviewer who had called ***Pride and Prejudice*** "too clever to have been written by a woman"![31]

As I mentioned in chapter 3, Austen insisted in a letter to her sister that she designed her own novels for insightful readers: "I do not write for such dull Elves / As have not a great deal of Ingenuity themselves" (29 January 1813). Perhaps she should have added that her ingenious Elves also need access to an entire reference library. Virginia Woolf noted, "Austen is mistress of far deeper emotion than appears on the surface."[32] In ***Mansfield Park*** Austen brilliantly demonstrates that women can be mistresses of far deeper emotion *and thought* than centuries of men have believed them capable of possessing.

Abbreviations

All references to Jane Austen's writings are taken from R. W. Chapman's standard Oxford University Press edition of *The Novels of Jane Austen* (vols. 1-5, 3rd edition, 1933) and *Minor Works* (vol. 6, 1954). Page numbers are inserted directly into the text, with the following abbreviations used if needed for clarity:

Sense and Sensibility	*(SS)*
Pride and Prejudice	*(PP)*
Mansfield Park	*(MP)*
Minor Works	*(MW)*

Those readers with other editions of Austen's novels who wish to locate a quotation by volume and chapter number may do so easily through one of the many electronic searching methods, such as http://www.pemberley.com/janeinfo/novlsrch.html.

References to Jane Austen's letters are indicated parenthetically by date and, unless otherwise indicated, are taken from Deirdre Le Faye's edition of *Jane Austen's Letters* (Oxford: Oxford University Press, 1995).

Notes

1. Kingsley Amis, "What Became of Jane Austen?" (1957), in *What Became of Jane Austen? And Other Questions* (New York: Harcourt Brace Jovanovich, 1970), 16.
2. Reginald Farrar, "Jane Austen, ob. July 18, 1817," *Quarterly Review* (July 1917), in Southam, *Critical Heritage,* 2: 264; Nina Auerbach, "Jane Austen's Dangerous Charm: Feeling as One Ought about Fanny Price," *Persuasions* 2 (16 December 1980): 9; Karen Joy Fowler, *The Jane Austen Book Club* (New York: Putnam's, 2004), 83.
3. Lionel Trilling, introduction to *Emma* (Boston: Houghton Mifflin, 1957), viii.
4. Honan, *Jane Austen,* 34.
5. Ibid., 354.
6. *Wisdom in Miniature; or the Young Gentleman and Lady's Pleasing Instructor,* 126.
7. Chase Amos, *On Female Excellence, or, A discourse: In which good character in women is described* (Litchfield: Collier & Buel, 1792), 11.
8. Fordyce, *Sermons to Young Women,* 2: 10-11.
9. Dr. Gregory, *A Father's Legacy to His Daughters,* 24.
10. Wordsworth, "Lines Composed a Few Miles above Tintern Abbey," *Selected Poems and Prefaces,* ed. Jack Stillinger (New York: Riverside, 1965), 110.
11. Isaac Hawkins Browne, *A Pipe of Tobacco: In Imitation of Six Several Authors,* ed. H. F. B. Brett-Smith (Oxford: Blackwell, 1923), 2.
12. Honan, *Jane Austen,* 56.
13. Ibid., 340.
14. See for instance Glenda Hudson, *Sibling Love and Incest in Jane Austen's Fiction* (New York: St. Martin's Press, 1999).
15. Halperin, *Life of Jane Austen,* 249.
16. *The Poetical Works of William Cowper* (London: Macmillan, 1924), 183. See also "The Negro's Complaint" and "Pity for Poor Africans," 361-63.
17. Cited in Honan, *Jane Austen,* 3.
18. Virginia Woolf, *Times Literary Supplement,* 8 May 1913, in Southam, *Critical Heritage,* 2: 241.

19. *Poetical Works of William Cowper,* 297.
20. Charlotte Brontë, *Jane Eyre* (Middlesex: Penguin, 1966), 141.
21. *Poetical Works of Sir Walter Scott* (London: Macmillan, 1890), 11-49.
22. Honan, *Jane Austen,* 337.
23. George Crabbe, "The Parish Register II," in *The Complete Poetical Works,* ed. Norma Dalrymple-Champneys and Arthur Pollard (Oxford: Clarendon Press, 1988), 1: 251-52.
24. Le Faye, *Jane Austen,* 158.
25. Samuel Johnson, *Rasselas,* ed. George Birkbeck (Oxford: Clarendon Press, 1927), 99.
26. Joseph Wiesenfarth, *Errand of Form,* 95. The reference is to Marvell's "To his Coy Mistress," lines 41-46.
27. Honan, *Jane Austen,* 333.
28. Wiesenfarth, *Errand of Form,* 90.
29. Harriet Byron in *Sir Charles Grandison,* 9: 24, 131, cited in Wiesenfarth, *Errand of Form,* 87-88.
30. Honan, *Jane Austen,* 334.
31. Le Faye, *Jane Austen,* 175.
32. Woolf, "Jane Austen," in *Common Reader,* ed. McNeillie, 130.

Selected Bibliography

Fordyce, James. *Sermons to Young Women.* 1766; reprint, London: T. Cadell, 1792.

Gregory, Dr. John. *A Father's Legacy to His Daughters.* 1774; reprint, Boston: James Dow, 1834.

Halperin, John. *The Life of Jane Austen.* Baltimore: Johns Hopkins University Press, 1984.

Honan, Park. *Jane Austen: Her Life.* New York: St. Martin's Press, 1987.

Le Faye, Deirdre, ed., *Jane Austen: A Family Record.* London: British Library, 1989.

Southam, B. C., ed. *Jane Austen: The Critical Heritage.* 2 vols. London: Routledge & Kegan Paul, 1968.

Wiesenfarth, Joseph. *The Errand of Form: An Assay of Jane Austen's Art.* New York: Fordham University Press, 1967.

Nora Nachumi (essay date 2007)

SOURCE: Nachumi, Nora. "A Spy in the House of Austen: Literary Critics, Lay Readers, and the Reception of Patricia Rozema's *Mansfield Park.*" *Performing the "Everyday": The Culture of Genre in the Eighteenth Century.* Ed. Alden Cavanaugh. Newark: U of Delaware P, 2007. 130-37. Print.

[*In the following essay, Nachumi utilizes criticism of Rozema's 1999 film adaptation of* Mansfield Park *to show that nuanced readings of the narrative do not necessarily have to come from academic circles.*]

Upon its release in November of 1999, Patricia Rozema's adaptation of ***Mansfield Park*** for Miramax films was attacked and defended in a variety of forums. In addition to comments in scholarly journals and classroom discussions, opinions about the movie were tendered both online and off by nonacademic readers of Jane Austen. The archives of *Austen-L,* the discussion list maintained by Dr. Jacqueline Reid-Walsh of McGill University, are full of comments about Rozema's film. Opinions about the movie also pepper the archives of less academically oriented Web sites like *Janeites* at Yahoo.com and *The Republic of Pemberley,* a self-described "haven" for fans obsessed with Jane Austen.

This diversity, both of opinions and venues, is part of a phenomenon that has created something of a crisis for literary critics who work on Jane Austen. Over the past several years, a number of factors, including the plethora of Austen sites on the internet, the popularity of films based on her novels and the academy's vexed relationship to both popular culture and cultural studies have generated some troubling questions: is popular interest in Austen "good for business," we wonder? Does it invalidate what we do? How does it affect our sense of ourselves as professional scholars? The anxieties fueling such questions may help to explain our contradictory treatment of Austen's fans, people whose love for Austen forms a significant part of their everyday lives. Despite an increase in scholarship that treats Austen's relationship to popular culture with respect, we continue to foster negative stereotypes about these readers, labeling them "Janeites," and describing them as closed-minded amateurs who read Austen merely for the dresses and the romance.

This essay evaluates these stereotypes by comparing scholarly discourse about Rozema's film to discussions about the movie that have occurred in nonacademic arenas (both online and off). Although they differ, both in style and in orientation, these discussions demonstrate that scholars and other denizens of high culture are not the only readers capable of critical acuity in regards to ***Mansfield Park*** (both the novel and the film). In fact, many of the comments posted at nonacademic sites reveal an awareness of the novel's primary concerns and, perhaps more importantly, reflect a critical diversity that belies the stereotypes accorded those who discuss Austen outside the ivory tower (a group which, by the way, includes a sizeable number of academics). Considered as a whole, the readers who participate in these conversations demonstrate that interpreting Austen can be a democratic endeavor, one that does not depend exclusively upon those with professional training (in this sense, the participants resemble the audience for whom Austen wrote). Ultimately, an examination of these discussions suggests that a neat division between different categories of readers may no longer be possible in the age of cyberspace. Whether or not one picks up a pen or turns on a computer, to write about Austen already is to participate in this larger community.

In many respects, the reception accorded the film in academic and nonacademic circles has been a study in contrasts. On the whole, academic discourse about the movie has been characterized by a propensity to evaluate the film as an independent work of art and, subsequently, by a reluctance to condemn it for its departures from the novel. Instead, literary scholars tend to discuss *how* the movie alters or elucidates themes within the book. Thus, in their analysis of the film, Linda Troost and Sayre Greenfield acknowledge differences between the two ***Mansfield Park***s, without measuring one against the other.[1] So too does Alastair Duckworth, who points out that Rozema's transformation of Austen's shy, self-denying heroine into a woman who takes on the world with energy, confidence and a satiric perspective, is merely the clearest of many indications that "we are not being invited to evaluate this adaptation as a transcription of the novel."[2] Besides, he adds, "nothing is less edifying—or begs more questions—than a criticism that faults a film for not being 'true' to the novel."[3]

Claudia Johnson contends that the movie is faithful to the essence, if not the letter of the book because it "foregrounds the unseemliness present in the novel."[4] In what is easily the most favorable review of the film by an academic, Johnson praises Rozema's decision to emphasize the Bertrams' involvement in the slave trade and defends her depiction of sex and sexual tension. Many readers, she declares, read Austen to avoid politics. Moreover, she notes, many "readers and viewers who are usually intelligent become stupid and priggish, as if it is indecent—indecent mind you—to discover sexuality in Austen's novels."[5] Yet ***Mansfield Park,*** she points out, is not only a political novel, but a novel "suffused with frustrated, illicit, wayward, or polymorphous sexuality."[6] Johnson also approves Rozema's transformation of Fanny, a move that gives us "a version of the Austenian narrator we love."[7] Overall, she concludes, Rozema's film is successful both as a representation of Austen's vision and as an original work of art.

Johnson does a brilliant job of describing the ways the film elucidates themes in the novel; however, what intrigues me most about her essay is the dichotomy she sets up between people like Rozema and herself and those who can't see the forest for the trees. To be more specific, Johnson defines those who object to Rozema's film as "Janeites," and the term is far from complimentary. As Deidre Lynch defines it, "Janeites" is the label that "Austen's audiences have learned to press into service whenever they need to designate the Other Reader in his or her multiple guises, or rather, and more precisely, whenever they need to personify and distance themselves from particular ways of reading, ones they might indulge in themselves."[8] Coined by Rudyard Kipling in a short story of the same name, the word sometimes refers to "the reader as hobbyist—someone at once overzealous and undersophisticated, who cannot be trusted to discriminate between the true excellence of ***Emma*** and the ersatz pleasures of *Bridget Jones* or Barbara Pym or a regency romance."[9] The term has also been used to designate a "cohort of cultural purists who, likewise transgressing against common sense … manage to find in the novels' portrait of patrician society an endorsement of their own anachronistic reverence for cultural hierarchies, and of their equally anachronistic, obsequious Anglophilia."[10] Johnson's Janeites are poor readers of Austen. Johnson labels Janeites "the grumpiest of fans" and, by diminishing their authority, dismisses their "umbrage at Rozema's deviations."[11]

Other academics are even less charitable. In the August 17, 2001 issue of the *Chronicle of Higher Education,* Peter Monaghan blames these "enraged, self-appointed guardians of Austen-as-exemplar-of-propriety" for hindering scholarship that reads Austen as subversive.[12] He cites several examples to support his position, including the brouhaha that erupted over Terry Castle's claim that Austen's relationship with her sister, Cassandra, might have contained homoerotic elements. "Horrified readers," he declares, "not only misinterpreted Castle's subtle analysis, but "denounced [her], often ridiculing in the bargain all cultural studies, gender studies, and psychoanalytic glosses of literary icons."[13] Stupid and closed-minded, Monaghan's Janeites are actively hostile to any person or idea that threatens to alter their views of the novels. While Monaghan contends that the climate for reading Austen as subversive has become more favorable in academic circles, he is careful to differentiate academics and lay readers who appreciate "Austen's brilliantly modulated depictions of characters … courtship rituals, and outings" from Janeites.[14] This later group apparently includes the membership of the Jane Austen Society of North America, or JASNA (which, Monaghan admits, contains a sizeable minority of academics), who read Austen to "parse the various kinds and statuses of carriage in nineteenth-century Britain, or learn how to behave at mock Regency dances. The charm," he sneers, "the tranquility."[15]

Comments like these underscore an irony worthy of Austen: as an institution, the academy is more closed-minded about Janeites, than those whom they accuse. In a letter responding to Monaghan's piece, Joan Ray, the current president of JASNA, readily admits that some members are among those "prim Janeites, determined to keep the Austen oeuvre pure."[16] However, she adds, other members appreciate academic approaches to the author. In fact, she points out, "major speakers at JASNA's annual conferences have included many of the university faculty Monaghan quotes in his article."[17] Ray also defends the nonacademic activities Monaghan cites: "Given that for the class of persons about whom Austen wrote … dances were the primary, if not the only, arena for courtship in regency England, it makes sense for Austen readers to know the mores of the ballroom"; Sandy Lerner's talk on carriages, "supplemented the information on carriages that the great Austen editor, R. W. Chapman offered in his hitherto definitive edition (1923) of Austen's works."[18] Such pursuits, she asserts, do not betoken an idealization of the past, but illuminate the novels. Ray's response, which ran two full pages in the *JASNA News,* was severely edited before it appeared in the *Chronicle.* The edited version accords a preeminence to "prim Janeites" that does not appear in the longer version. Although it mentions the diversity of JASNA's membership, it omits comments that support Ray's assertions. Nor does it contain her justification for the activities that Monaghan ridicules. Given the *Chronicle*'s status as a forum for issues that concern academics, its treatment of Ray's letter dramatizes academia's responsibility in proliferating negative stereotypes associated with nonacademic fans of Jane Austen.

It also helps clarify the reluctance of literary scholars (including myself) to criticize Rozema's film. Overall, our primary concern is to differentiate ourselves from such misguided individuals. Instead, we loudly resist the efforts of Austen's narrative style, which, as Johnson explains, "makes us feel so uniquely privileged in our closeness to her that we readily believe that no one could possibly understand or visualize a character as perfectly as we can and in all decency … should not even try."[19] We also assume that Janeites succumb. Indeed, if all adaptations of Austen's novels are greeted with an "obsessive measuring of their devotion—either to the literal 'facts' of the written work, to the historical details of Regency England, or to an ideal that is 'Austen'" then the fault, we suggest, lies with the Janeites.[20]

Do Austen's everyday readers deserve such condemnation? Are they all closed-minded conservatives who tend to froth at the mouth in defense of their Austen? Does their obsession with detail (both textual and historical) make them poor readers, incapable of seeing the forest for the trees? Upon the movie's release, did these cultural purists sit around their Regency tea sets bemoaning Rozema's interpretation of "our dear Jane"? A search of the archives belonging to *Austen-L* and to *Janeites,* and several visits to *The Republic of Pemberley,* suggest such a view is limited at best.[21]

Considered together, the postings at these sites indicate the diversity of Jane Austen pages and fans on the internet. *Austen-L* is one of the most scholarly Internet-based forums focusing on Austen; a substantial number of academics post to the list. At the opposite end of the spectrum stylistically is *The Republic of Pemberley* which began as a site for members of *Austen-L* who wanted to "gush" about the A&E adaptation of ***Pride and Prejudice.*** According to the "Frequently Asked Questions" area of the site, members of *Pemberley* "still honor [their] gushing roots, and the Austen-for-the-masses feel that a demonstrative love of the adaptations brings to the site."[22] The content and tone at *Janeites* fall in between those at *Austen-L* and *The Republic of Pemberley.* Despite their differences, each of these sites accommodates a community of readers whose views about Austen are as varied, and as variously valuable, as those espoused in academic forums.

At each website, comments revealed diverse attitudes about the value of literary criticism. Some members are hostile to scholarship, such as the member of *Austen-L* who complains that most "critics praise Jane's words in involved, complex sentences reife [*sic*] with academic mumbo-jumbo."[23] Others note that "Literary Theory … become[s] 'dated' very quickly."[24] At *The Republic of Pemberley,* a reader of *Janeites* (the book, not the Web site) finds some articles "very interesting" and others "simply dreadful. They are so sociological that … I began to hate scholars and their researches."[25]

Others members disagree. At each site, many participate in critical discussion groups. As one member remarks, "what is most interesting about the study of literature is that … [it] can raise political issues that are very interesting to delve into in a way that no other discipline can."[26] Besides, she adds, "one does not have to be an academic to have [an agenda]."[27] Others agree, like the member who admits: "[o]ne of the problems I have always had in discussing 19th century (or earlier) literature with non-academics (like myself, I'm sorry to say) or even many academics is the very natural tendency we all have to overlay our own morals and customs on the characters of the novels."[28]

Participants at each site also differ about the label "Janeites." One member thinks it "a lovely term"; "I can't help but think of myself as a Janeite in the same way someone might call themselves Catholic or Eskimo. … It is part of my identity."[29] Another agrees with Eve Sedgwick's description of Janeites as "normalizers" who "want to fit Austen into the norm of everything they think is good and right.[30] A third, wonders whether American members of JASNA could possibly identify with one critic's definition of Janeites since "the whole point of being one is to identify with a certain image of Englishness—superior, stoical, witty, ironic, knowing, low-key, self-possessed, and vaguely upper class."[31] A fourth, an academic who belongs to two Austen lists notes that she "can't recall anyone fainting over the idea of Austen contemplating sex"; "[t]he media," she complains, "(and academia it seems) has painted a picture of Janeites as old ladies in black frocks crocheting doilies and shushing the populace for even mentioning the word S-E-X … THAT is what they think of us."[32]

As befits such variety, opinions about the film were hardly unanimous. Some fans were clearly close-minded, like the member who admitted that she probably wouldn't like the film because "it would be so different from my own inner image of MP that it would constantly annoy me."[33] Others focused on anachronisms within the film: "What really annoyed me was the lack of knowledge … regarding the customs of the day" one member writes.[34] A few proved themselves victims of Austen's narrative style, so closely did they identify their own view of the novel with that of the author. Indeed, one outraged member of *Janeites* declared that if "I were Jane Austen and living now, I would run to the nearest lawyer and demand that my name and the name of ***Mansfield Park*** be taken off the credits."[35]

Other comments collapsed differences between the two groups. Like academics, Janeites are a literate bunch. At each site, members examined Rozema's rejection of Austen's restraint; many regarded her sympathies as more akin to the Brontes.' "In this film," one person writes, "Mansfield Park meets Haworth Parsonage, and our tour guide is Edward Said."[36] Another speculates that "this is what Jane Austen would look like if they sent her work to Charlotte Bronte for rewrites."[37] At *The Republic of Pemberley* "Wuthering Park" was voted best new title for Rozema's film.

A sizeable group approached the film as an independent work of art, like the person who resolved to "try to think of [*Mansfield Park*] the way I think of *Pride and Prejudice*—as a story that just happens to share a basic outline and many character names with an Austen novel, rather than an adaptation of that novel. It may prove to be an okay movie on its own."[38] Several shared Johnson's opinion that the film was "true to the spirit of the original book."[39] Another echoed Duckworth's observation that an "equally powerful movie" probably could not have been made with "the novel's Fanny as heroine."[40] One member, revealed a tolerance for anachronism that betokens an ability to see both forest *and* trees: "[I]t's far more fascinating and thought-provoking than watching yet another faithful or failed-to-be-faithful … British t.v. masterpiece" she writes.[41]

Comments that found fault with the film also challenged the presumption that an obsession with detail makes one a poor reader. Instead, they demonstrate that much of what makes Austen Austen is in the details—not in the bonnets or houses, but in the arrangement of a scene or the presentation of a character's behavior and thoughts. Considered together, these comments argue that Rozema's film may be "true" to the novel in the sense it calls attention to the corruption at the heart of Mansfield Park, but its infidelity to the specifics of the novel—and its insensitivity to the importance of those specifics—compromise its ability to dramatize the "essence" of the book.

For many readers, this essence may best be described as a recognition of the difficulty involved in making and living with one's moral decisions.[42] As several comments point out, Rozema's decision to alter Fanny's character affects this aspect of the story significantly. In the novel, Fanny's initial relationship to her cousin, Edmund, is that of student to teacher. Thus Edmund's decision to act in the amateur production of *Lovers' Vows* opposite Mary Crawford devastates Fanny in two different ways: first, it makes her jealous and, second, it forces her to choose between her own convictions and her faith in Edmund. The choice is painful; having habitually subordinated her own opinions to Edmund's, Fanny now realizes that he is deceiving himself. This is the moment that Fanny begins her transformation into someone who relies on her own sense of right and wrong.

Rozema completely omits this first trial by fire. Instead, she establishes Fanny's moral authority by transforming her into an abolitionist. As several members of *Janeites* note, this simplifies the moral choices mapped out in the book and compromises the sense that Fanny loves and respects her uncle. For example, it lessens the impact of a later scene in which Fanny refuses her uncle's demand that she accept Henry Crawford's proposal of marriage. As one member of *Austen-L* observes: "it is precisely because [Fanny] is so naturally timid … that her refusal to marry Henry [Crawford] … is so heroic. There is no joy in defiance for Fanny," which makes it "all the more thrilling that when it comes to big decisions, she makes them alone, and sticks by them."[43] The comparative ease with which Rozema's Fanny stands up to Sir Thomas means that, in this scene at least, Rozema fails to dramatize the cost of resisting patriarchal authority adequately. As another member explains: Austen's "Fanny is so obedient that we expect her to bow her head and cry … over Edmund. Her refusing is startling because of what we have seen of her already."[44] Moreover it undermines Rozema's attempt to create a parallel between slavery and the oppression of women; Rozema's Fanny may be oppressed, but she has far more agency (and more chutzpah) than do the slaves on Sir Thomas's plantation.

Another non-academic objection to the film is Fanny's behavior at Portsmouth, where she is banished after refusing Henry's proposal. In the novel, Portsmouth is Fanny's hardest test; having returned to her family, she experiences the poverty she risks by rejecting Henry's offer. Edmund (whom she loves) is on the verge of proposing to Mary, and Henry appears sincerely committed to reforming his ways. Continued resistance is difficult and Austen makes sure her readers know it by making Henry seem more attractive than at any other time in the novel. Nevertheless, Fanny continues to withstand his entreaties; her judgment is validated when he runs off with her cousin, Maria.

In the film, Portsmouth is different. As one member of *Austen-L* describes it,

> Fanny not only flirts with Henry but discusses her hopeless love for Edmund with him. In an episode borrowed from Jane's life, she agrees to marry him—then … withdraws her acceptance the next morning. "This" Henry does not run off with Maria while still swearing undying love for Fanny. No, "this" Henry screws Maria IN HER FATHER'S HOUSE! WHILE HER BROTHER IS DYING!—because he's heartbroken, poor lad, over Fanny's toying with his affections. And "this" Fanny confesses to Edmund that she does not know her own mind, that she is wracked with ambivalence.[45]

As this posting suggests, Rozema's film makes Fanny (not to mention her judgment) seem less than reliable. In the calmer words of another member of *Janeites*: "a Fanny who accepts Henry is not the same one who refuses him on principle."[46]

While the language of such comments is often subjective, they often resonate with critical readings of the novel. Such is the case with many of the online objections to the end of the movie. In the film, the evil that has tainted the heart of ***Mansfield Park*** is largely eradicated when the Crawfords depart and Sir Thomas—in what is not entirely a positive move—abandons his interests in Antigua and pursues opportunities in tobacco instead. Moreover, as Johnson observes, Rozema's Fanny gets out at last: "'[i]t could have turned out differently, I suppose' Fanny narrates repeatedly in superb scenes that freeze the action and break the illusion of realism to call attention to the intervention of her art."[47] The ending of the book is much darker. Writing of the novel, Johnson observes that Austen's Fanny "has never been lucid enough to recognize what is problematic about [the] authority" of those appointed to govern Mansfield Park; "even as she sees them err, even as she is obliged inwardly and outwardly to resist them" she continues to idolize Sir Thomas and Edmund.[48] As a result, the "failures of conservative ideology fall . . . most heavily . . . on the only member of the household to believe in and act by it fully to the very end."[49] Our vision, Johnson remarks, is more clear: *Mansfield Park* indicts the society that Fanny embraces. As on member of *Austen-L* writes, "the evil in the film is the source of Mansfield's wealth—the abuses of slavery. I think Jane Austen had [a] much more complex and interesting sense of evil lodging in the human heart and altogether mixed up with the good."[50] Such acuity demonstrates that a penchant for minutiae does not render one an inept reader of Austen. As one member of *Janeites* points out, "just because JA had never heard of Marxism, Feminism or romanticism, that does not mean that an analysis of her works from one of those points of view might not say interesting things about JA's world view"; however, he adds, "the standard to hold critics and interpreters to is, does the criticism/interpretation provide an insight regarding the original? If it does . . . it is useful."[51]

This willingness to question the authority of "experts" may explain why some academics dwell on differences between themselves and Austen's nonacademic fans. Despite the aims of individual scholars who work on Austen, our status as professional critics still depends on our difference from amateurs who read Austen for fun. Peter Goodall blames this phenomenon on modernism, a term he associates with an elitist attitude toward mass culture that extends into the 1990s.[52] For modernists, he argues, culture is "a minority phenomenon, a small area of brightness and interest . . . surrounded by a sea of blandness and indifference."[53] Postmodernism, in contrast, generally embraces objects of mass production and, in doing so, "abdicat[es] art's traditional responsibility to differentiate between levels of culture."[54] Within the academy, he argues, the result has been an oppositional relationship between cultural studies—a discipline that "celebrates the culture of the people"—and English, with its investment in "high cultural traditions."[55]

To describe English thus is, of course, to make a huge and somewhat inaccurate generalization. As books like *Janeites* and *Jane Austen in Hollywood* demonstrate, many of us who focus on Austen accord a great deal of respect to her popular appeal. Many of us also support the aims of cultural studies per se. Nevertheless, as literary scholars who write on Austen for an audience of our peers, we make distinctions between high and popular cultures. To publish in refereed journals or through an academic press, for example, is to participate in a system that presumes we can read and discuss literature, films, and popular culture in ways that are different and on some level more authoritative than those practiced outside the ivory tower. The extra authority comes from the referees themselves, from the fact that we hold ourselves to a higher level of responsibility than we do readers who can write purely out of love for their subject (of course the same point can be made about many scholars who write highly theoretical texts under the auspices of cultural studies, but that is another essay entirely).

At present, however, Austen's popularity among everyday readers is calling our authority as "experts" into question. Online and at various meetings of JASNA, nonacademic readers have proven themselves eminently capable of engaging in scholarly discourse. At the same time, many of those same readers refuse to privilege professional literary criticism as the best way to appreciate Austen. In fact, academia's tendency to stereotype Austen's nonacademic readers ultimately may have less to do with their ability to apprehend the novels than with profound differences between the ways each group approaches the texts. As Herbert J. Gans explains, high culture is "creator-oriented" while popular arts are "user-oriented, and exist to satisfy audience values and wishes."[56] Like others who identify themselves with high culture, academics who write about Austen tend to focus on the author, her creations and the sociohistorical context thereof. While many nonacademic readers do so as well, they tend to privilege their own responses to the texts. At JASNA conferences, for instance, there is no "right" way to engage with the novels; members participate in a variety of activities (including lectures, balls, teas, and dances) which, when considered together, challenge the authority of those reading practices that dominate novel studies in the academy today.

The user-orientation of Austen's everyday readers is even more apparent online. At *Austen.com* and *The Republic of Pemberley,* members publish sequels and "lost scenes" to the novels. These sites and others also offer reading subgroups in which participants read and post comments on the novels—or on relevant criticism—according to a predetermined schedule. In each case, the format—which requires members to offer their own opinions and respond to others—renders reading Austen both a communal and a highly subjective experience.

This is not to say that the Internet completely collapses distinctions between high and popular cultures, but that it makes those differences less absolute. Hyper-texts, for example, anchor literary works in their historical and cultural contexts, and make available material that had previously been confined to a single library.[57] While such innovations enable new opportunities for serious scholarship, they also render information available to anyone with a computer. Hypertexts, moreover, are "[r]econstituted in the act of reading, rendering the reader an author and disrupting the stability of experts or 'authorities,'"[58] The mutable nature of identity on the Internet can also disrupt this stability. At each Austen site, academics may choose to conceal their profession; online they can be Janeites without risking the censure of their institutions. Alternatively, they may choose to make their specific type of expertise available to nonacademics as well as their peers.

The Internet, of course, is not a community free of division. Many of those who run websites focusing on Austen warn scholars not to alienate nonacademics through theory and jargon. Meanwhile, "economics, and perhaps the tenure system, have kept academic discourse rather aloof from the universal access of the internet."[59] Certainly, the perception exists among scholars that online journals are less competitive and lower in quality than journals published in the traditional fashion. The superabundance of material on the Web, and the difficulty of ordering that material in a hierarchical fashion also contribute to this perception. So does the sense that material published on the internet is, if not exactly ephemeral, less tangible than material published on paper, perhaps because it challenges the (perhaps preconceived) belief that good scholars make concrete, permanent contributions to the understanding of literature.

Nevertheless, academics may need to reconsider the benefits of discussing Austen online and in other nonacademic forums. One reason for doing so is that the reading/viewing practices of many of Austen's fans resonate with those of Austen's contemporaries. Writing of the opinions Austen collected about ***Mansfield Park*** from her family and friends, Laura Brodie points out that they "constitute the opening chapter in what has become an enduring popular tradition of Austen criticism, a tradition preserved among today's Janeites."[60] Like Austen's early readers, many nonacademic fans experience the texts as written (or filmed) for popular consumption. Likewise, many evaluate the material using "a simple vocabulary of likes and dislikes."[61] Like Austen's contemporaries, however, most lay readers (at least the nonacademic ones) read at an "advanced, albeit unacknowledged level of sophistication."[62] Their predilection for details—and their refusal to organize them within a hierarchical agenda—resonates with that of Austen's contemporaries, for whom everyday detail often countered the regulatory function of the virtue rewarded plot.[63] Other nonacademic reading practices—like the tendency to read the novels as romantic fantasy—resemble those that were denigrated by the Romantics in their attempt to make authorship an elite profession.[64] The opinions of such readers were also devalued by Austen's nephew, James Edward Austen-Leigh, who—Brodie insists—distorted his aunt's project by distinguishing between the comments of "eminent and ordinary readers."[65] Indeed, the process by which Austen became an "elite" writer depended less on her novels than on the aspirations of those who seized the authority to determine how they should be read.

As should be apparent by now, nonacademic reading practices complicate distinctions between high and popular cultures. By demonstrating that what is "high art to one section of the audience may be popular art to another," Austen's lay readers provide evidence that the two are not inevitably and essentially different.[66] Moreover, the fact that a number of fans (especially the younger ones) seem to have read the novels after viewing filmed adaptations of Austen's work supports Harriet Hawkins's claim that often the experience of reading or viewing the texts of popular culture "provides the foundations—intellectual, moral, spiritual, and aesthetic—for reading the texts of high culture."[67] Finally, the sophistication with which many readers engage in literary discussion resonates with recent work on the way people actually read popular texts. Such work, Goodall explains, "has made us aware of the complexity of responses these texts produce. As Tony Bennett and Janet Woollacott have demonstrated, "most phenomena of popular culture ... can generate ways of reading which are not only either popular or sophisticated, but, as in the case of fan obsessions, both."[68]

Austen herself valued the opinions of ordinary readers. In addition to **"Opinions of *Mansfield Park*,"** she collected and transcribed **"Opinions of *Emma*"** upon the publication of that novel in 1816. Perhaps, Brodie speculates, these collections compensated Austen for the "relative dearth of critical interest in her work."[69] Certainly they provided her with an "alternative to a masculine literary culture scarcely amenable to the novel genre."[70] Austen's own words bear this out when, in an oft-quoted passage from ***Northanger Abbey,*** she remarks:

> Let us leave it to reviewers to ... talk in threadbare strains of the trash with which the press now groans ... while the abilities of the nine-hundredth abridger of the History of England, or of the man who collects and publishes in a volume some dozen lines of Milton, Pope, and Prior, with a paper from The Spectator, and a chapter from Sterne, are eulogized by a thousand pens—there seems almost a general wish of decrying the capacity and undervaluing the labour of the novelist, and in slighting the performances which have only genius, wit, and taste to recommend them. "I am no novel reader—I seldom look into novels—do not imagine that I often read novels—it is really very well for a novel." Such is the common cant. "And what are you reading Miss ——?" "Oh! It is only a novel!" replies the young lady, while she lays down her book

> with affected indifference, or momentary shame. . . . [It is], in short, only some work in which the greatest powers of the mind are displayed, in which the most thorough knowledge of human nature, the happiest delineation of its varieties, the liveliest effusions of wit and humour, are conveyed to the world in the best chosen language.[71]

The poor reader for Austen is not the nonprofessional reader, but the (male) literary critic whose investment in "high literature" deprives him of the ability to discern the quality of the novels he decries. Her other target is the young lady—and other ordinary readers—whose ability to appreciate novels is compromised by her susceptibility to those "experts" who dictate what ought to be read. As this passage points out, nonprofessional readers of Austen thus represent an important constituency, reminding those of us who are critics that she wrote her novels with a popular audience in mind.

Our work on Austen only can benefit from this recognition. In *Reading the Romance,* Janice Radway describes an analytic tension between scholars, whose text-based analysis insists that popular romance reinscribes patriarchal authority, and readers who see the act of reading as a form of resistance against patriarchal oppression.[72] By juxtaposing both viewpoints, Radway achieves a richer analysis than what would have resulted from privileging a single approach to her topic.[73] The same may be true for those of us who study Austen. We may discover that valuing the opinions of lay readers enriches our own understanding of the texts. Those of us who peer out the door of the ivory tower also may find that some of these same lay readers are adept at literary analysis and are aware of our work. Indeed, to assert a neat division between different categories of readers may no longer be possible or even desirable. Regardless of the anxiety such a discovery generates, we may already belong to this larger, more democratic community of readers.

Notes

1. Linda Troost and Sayre Greenfield, "The Mouse That Roared: Patricia Rozema's *Mansfield Park,*" *Jane Austen in Hollywood* (Lexington: University of Kentucky Press, 2001), 188-204.

2. Alastair Duckworth, Film Review of *Mansfield Park, Eighteenth-Century Fiction* 12, no. 4 (July 2000): 568.

3. Duckworth, 571.

4. Claudia Johnson, "Run mad, but do not faint: The authentic audacity of Rozema's *Mansfield Park,*" *TLS,* Dec. 31, 1999, http://www.patriciarozema.com/mad.htm (Aug. 8, 2005).

5. Ibid.

6. Ibid.

7. Ibid.

8. Deirdre Lynch. "Introduction: Sharing with Our Neighbors," *Janeites: Austen's Disciples and Devotees* (Princeton, NJ: Princeton University Press, 2000), 12.

9. Lynch, 12.

10. Ibid., 13.

11. Johnson, "Run Mad."

12. Peter Monaghan, "With Sex and Sensibility, Scholars Redefine Jane Austen," *Chronicle of Higher Education,* Aug. 17, 2001, Lexis-Nexis (June 19, 2002).

13. Ibid.

14. Ibid.

15. Ibid.

16. Joan Klingel Ray, "Deflating the JASNA Myth," *JASNA News* 17, no. 3 (Winter 2001): 3.

17. Ibid., 4.

18. Ibid., 4.

19. Johnson, "Run Mad."

20. Mary A. Favret, "Being True to Jane Austen," *The Victorian Afterlife: Postmodern Culture Rewrites the Nineteenth Century* (Minneapolis: University of Minnesota Press, 2000), 64.

21. Archives of *Austen-L,* http://lists.mcgill.ca/archives/austen-l.html; *Janeites* http://groups.yahoo.com/group/Janeites; *Republic of Pemberley,* www.pemberley.com. Although material from these sites is in the public domain, it was not written with publication in mind. Consequently, the authors of these posts are identified by their initials.

22. "Frequently Asked Questions," *Republic of Pemberley,* March 7, 2004, http://www.pemberley.com/faq.html (Aug. 8, 2004).

23. N. M., "Critics," Aug. 28, 1998, http://lists.mcgill.ca/archives/austen-l.html (Aug. 8, 2005). Subsequent citations for posts on this site will use "*Austen-L*" in place of this URL.

24. J. L., "Literary Theory," Sept. 23, 1999, *Austen-L* (June 3, 2003).

25. S. B., "I Second That! (nfm)," Feb. 28, 2002, http://www.pemberley.com/bin/archives/aoaarc.pl?read=14414, (June 3, 2003).

26. S., "Literature, Politics and Agendas," Mar. 25, 1999, *Austen-L* (June 3, 2003).

27. Ibid.

28. K. R., "Re-reading, decency (side issues)," Jan. 30, 2001, *Austen-L* (Aug. 8, 2005).

29. A. W., "Janeites," Oct. 27, 2000, http://groups.yahoo.com/group/Janeites/message/7157 (Sept. 15, 2001). Each message posted to *Janeites* is assigned a reference number that appears at the end of the URL (in this instance, 7157). Subsequent references to messages posted to this site will omit the URL except for this number.

30. E. M., "The Watsons: The "Normalizers" and Lady Osborne," Mar. 3, 1998, *Austen-L* (Aug. 8, 2005).

31. J. S., "Janeites and Englishness," July 15, 1999, *Austen-L* (June 3, 2003).

32. J. L., "[Janeites] online discussion on new research on Jane Austen," Aug. 13, 2001, 9853 (July 10, 2002).

33. D. L., "Patricia Rozema's *Mansfield Park*?," July 15, 2000, *Austen-L* (Mar. 14, 2001).

34. R. G., "M.P.2 Movie," May 5, 2000, 5496 (Mar. 27, 2001).

35. R. G., "Mansfield Park," Feb. 21, 2000, 4313 (Mar. 27, 2001).

36. E. B., "Mansfield Park: The film!!!" Nov. 28, 1999, *Austen-L* (July 10, 2002).

37. C. F., "Controversy Indeed," Jan. 27, 2000, *Austen-L* (Mar. 23, 2001).

38. J. A. Y., "MP2 Preview," Sept. 16, 1999, 2333 (Mar. 27, 2001).

39. N. M., "The 1999 MP: A Must See for Janeites," Dec. 11, 1999, 3321 (Mar. 27, 2001).

40. Duckworth, 570.

41. D. B., "A Fascinating and Daring *Mansfield Park*," Oct. 22, 1999, *Austen-L* (Mar. 29, 2001).

42. See, for example, E. M., "The 1999 _MP_ (_MP2_)," May 5, 2000, 5490 (Mar. 6, 2005); Richard Whatley, Review of *Mansfield Park*, *Quarterly Review*, January 1821, reprinted in *Mansfield Park* (New York: Broadview Press, 2001), 505; Lionel Trilling, "Mansfield Park," *Jane Austen: A Collection of Critical Essays*, ed. Ian Watt (Englewood Cliffs: Prentice Hall, 1963), 123-40.

43. D. L., "Filmmakers again—and long (skip if You're bored with the Rozema thing)," Jul. 21, 2000, *Austen-L* (June 18, 2002).

44. N. M. "Mansfield Park no picnic for Austen Purists," Nov. 24, 1999, *Austen-L* (July 10, 2002).

45. E. B., "Mansfield Park: The film!!!" Nov. 28, 1999, *Austen-L* (July 10, 2002).

46. N. M., "The 1999 MP: A Must See for Janeites," Dec. 11, 1999, 3321 *Austen-L* (Mar. 27, 2001).

47. Johnson, "Run Mad."

48. Claudia Johnson, *Jane Austen: Women, Politics, and the Novel* (Chicago: University of Chicago Press, 1988), 115.

49. Johnson, *Jane Austen,* 116.

50. E. B., "*Mansfield Park*: The film!!!" Nov. 28, 1999, *Austen-L* (July 10, 2002).

51. T. A., "[Janeites] criticism," June 20, 2003, 15241 (Aug. 12, 2005).

52. Peter Goodall, *High Culture, Popular Culture: The Long Debate* (St. Leonards, Australia: Allen & Unwin, 1995), 54-55.

53. Ibid., 55.

54. Ibid., 59.

55. Ibid., 147, 153.

56. Herbert J. Gans, *Popular Culture and High Culture: An Anaylsis and Evaluation of Taste,* rev. ed. (New York: Basic Books, 1999), 62.

57. Rebecca Stephens Duncan, "Sense and Sensibility: A Convergence of Readers/Viewers/Browsers," *A Companion to Jane Austen Studies* (London: Greenwood Press, 2000), 15.

58. Mark Poster, "Cyberdemocracy: Internet and the Public Sphere." *Internet Culture,* ed. David Porter, (New York: Routledge, 1996), 214.

59. Duncan, 14. Claims regarding universal access overlook the fact that many lack the material means or skills to access the Internet.

60. Laura Fairchild Brodie, "Jane Austen and the Common Reader: 'Opinions of Mansfield Park,' 'Opinions of Emma,' and the Janeite Phenomenon," *Texas Studies in Language and Literature* 37, no. 1 (1995): 56.

61. Ibid., 63.

62. Judy Simmons, "Classics and Trash: Reading Austen in the 1990s," *Women's Writing* 5 no. 1 (1998),

Internet http//www.triangle.co.uk/wow/05-01/js.pdf (July, 10, 2002).

63. See William Galperin, "Austen's Earliest Readers and the Rise of the Janeites," *Janeites: Austen's Disciples and Devotees,* 106.

64. Benedict, Barbara. "Sensibility by the Numbers: Austen's Work as Regency Popular Fiction," *Janeites: Austen's Disciples and Devotees,* 64.

65. Ibid., 67.

66. Goodall, 48. Also see Benedict, 68.

67. Qtd. Goodall, 42.

68. Ibid., 49.

69. Brodie, 64.

70. Ibid., 56.

71. Jane Austen, *Northanger Abbey,* 1818 (London: Penguin Classics, 1985), 58.

72. Janice Radway, *Reading the Romance: Women, Patriarchy, and Popular Culture* (Chapel Hill: University of North Carolina Press, 1991), 210.

73. See Mizuko Ito on this passage from Radway in "Virtually Embodied: The Reality of Fantasy in a Multi-User Dungeon" (87-109).

Miranda Burgess (essay date 2008)

SOURCE: Burgess, Miranda. "Fanny Price's British Museum: Empire, Genre, and Memory in *Mansfield Park.*" *Recognizing the Romantic Novel: New Histories of British Fiction, 1780-1830.* Ed. Jillian Heydt-Stevenson and Charlotte Sussman. Liverpool: Liverpool UP, 2008. 208-36. Print.

[*In the following essay, Burgess examines the influence that imperialism has upon Fanny in* Mansfield Park. *According to Burgess,* Mansfield Park *"allows its readers to propose anew the ties between mind, letters, and history—not as an evasion of Britain's troubled political past but precisely as an encounter with it."*]

This essay seeks to answer two questions: how does Fanny Price, the heroine of Jane Austen's 1814 novel ***Mansfield Park,*** experience imperialism, and what might Fanny's experience, and the novel's ways of representing it, tell readers about the novel's, Austen's, or Britain's relation to empire itself? In making the question of experience and its representation the focus of this essay and the novel it discusses, I depart from the recent critical orthodoxy that has made it difficult to read ***Mansfield Park*** other than as a synecdoche for contemporary imperial history.[1] In so doing, however, I aim not so much to reclaim the novel from postcolonial approaches as to propose methods for investigating imperial questions that take into renewed account this novel's specifically Romantic character.

Edward Said's most significant contribution to the study of ***Mansfield Park*** was the respatialization of a novel that had, as Said put it, been read as 'constituted mainly by temporality,' and his insistence on the dynamic interconnectedness of transatlantic space.[2] Yet in establishing Sir Thomas Bertram's Mansfield Park estate in the geographic context of colonialism and plantation slavery, Said represented his approach as supplementary, even prosthetic, in character, a matter of giving voice to what Austen's novel, like nineteenth-century Britain in general, had forgotten or failed to say about its imperial dependency. As a result of this essentially corrective stance, a number of influential readers have responded by defending Austen against Said's charges of inattention or complacency, most often by treating her domestic narrative as an extended metaphor for imperial injustice or suggesting that her characters' forgetfulness of empire is an ironic rebuke to the Britain whose landed interests they represent.[3]

Like Saree Makdisi, whose essay in this volume proposes a similar turn to the 'psycho-affective' dimension of Austen's novel, I want to redirect these debates away from Austen's own geopolitical consciousness—the question of what she knew about empire, and when she knew it—towards the emotion and cognition of the heroine, Fanny Price. Indeed, before the 1990s ***Mansfield Park*** was most often read in a way that emphasized the protagonist's subjectivity, and the atypically Romantic breadth of detail with which her psyche is represented in Austen's novel.[4] Unlike Makdisi, however, I will not suggest that a focus on the heroine's affective experience is intrinsically at odds with a reading focused on what he calls 'geoaesthetic questions.' Rather, the visible workings of the heroine's understanding are what demarcate the place of empire in ***Mansfield Park,*** and they are represented, precisely, in terms that are simultaneously spatial and textual: geographical and literary-aesthetic. The novel's detailed mapping of the movements of a consciousness as it mediates representations of empire and feels its own place in relation to them points to an arena within Romantic fiction more broadly where the representation of empire can be fruitfully observed and investigated.

Said's questions of memory remain central to this discussion. The novel's, or Austen's, marginalization of imperial questions is, as Said suggests, a consequence of forgetting or deliberate erasure, but the forgetfulness in question is Fanny Price's and not Austen's. Moreover, and this is my primary focus here, it is not completely successful. The relation of ***Mansfield Park*** to empire can be charted by revisiting Fanny's processes of remembering and by tracing the novel's detailed anatomy of her memory's failures and successes. That Fanny is weak of memory, and that retentive recollection is the chief index of intelligence and learning at Mansfield Park, are claims made very early in the novel by members of the Bertram family. Before long, however, Fanny trades forgetfulness and a head apparently empty of rote information for a mind that seems, however hard it tries, to be unable to forget.[5] Once unable to recall the accumulated details of the schoolroom, Fanny now finds herself haunted by the recollection of the *process* by which she comes to learn them: by her passage from an impecunious Portsmouth childhood to Mansfield Park and the education that prepares the landed class for participation—imaginative as much as economic—in Britain's imperial enterprise.

If, as I am suggesting, Fanny's aristocratic achievements are troubled by her memories of class subordination that persist despite all efforts to suppress them, then it is worth investigating the ways in which Fanny's history enables her collection of, and sympathy with, the historical remainders, the costs and consequences of imperial triumph. At the same time, it is the proposition of this essay that Austen's rendering of Fanny's cognitive and affective processes, her experience, memory, and sympathy, not only testifies to the reliance of empire abroad on class distinctions at home but actually serves as a record of the processes of reading, thinking, feeling and forgetting that make imperialism possible.

In their essay in this volume, Jill Heydt-Stevenson and Charlotte Sussman characterize the Romantic novel as a form of writing whose 'heterogeneity [. . .] of approaches to the real,' and the genre mixing that serves as its textual register, provoke its readers 'to understand different kinds of communal imagining.' In keeping with this observation, this essay examines the intersections between textual form and human cognition in Austen's portrait of Fanny and her education. It argues that print culture, and the mixing of genres that would later give way to separate disciplines of geography, imperial history and travel writing, provide Fanny's memory with the content that Austen's novel will anatomize.

First, I propose that an apt memory for the political organization of space, the proper object of schoolroom geographic learning, is a key index of imperial competence in the novel, a competence that is both a register and a product of socioeconomic privilege. Second, I trace Austen's mapping of memory through metaphors of space that lay bare the historical content of spatial description and spatial experience. When Fanny looks at the Mansfield Park estate, she sees a museum where memories of her past are stored and an arena within which memory can be transcended by means of a picturesque imagination. The perspectival tension the novel establishes between these two ways of seeing defines Fanny's memory as at once a crucial part and a characteristic, class-marked failure of imperial imagining. Third, I demonstrate that memory and imagination, like imperial space itself, are shown in ***Mansfield Park*** to be thoroughly mediated. Shaped and imprinted by print culture, Fanny's cognition is marked, in particular, by the picturesque pamphlets that serve as the canonical texts of genteel geographical learning and by peripheral nationalist antiquarian texts that unsettle the orthodoxies of the British imperial landscape. The narrative of Fanny's growth, and the representation of her memory, is haunted by the competing genres of imperial and anti-imperial nationalist geography, and by the even more troubling, conflicted historiography produced by the encounter between them.

It is in the representation of Fanny's mind as a locus of empire and a product of print culture that a distinctively Romantic and distinctly critical account of British imperialism emerges in ***Mansfield Park***: a process unfolding in national and personal experience, in imagination and affect as well as in history, and in the memories that alternately feed and haunt the heroine's imaginings.

Education

Mansfield Park begins with an act of importation caught in a web of imperial connections and perceptions. Born to a family with more children than money, the ten-year-old Fanny Price is taken or sent—some readers say torn—from her Portsmouth home to make the 'long journey' to Mansfield Park.[6] Moira Ferguson and Said have compared Fanny's transportation to the contemporary traffic in slaves, Ferguson because of the lack of agency Fanny experiences at Mansfield and Said because she is 'brought in [. . .] and set to work.'[7] In the eyes of her well-married aunt Lady Bertram and her plantation-owning husband, however, Fanny's family, like the Bertrams' Antigua plantations, is a provider of raw materials. The goal of her labours is what Lionel Trilling termed a 'hygiene of the self,' for Fanny herself, as Makdisi also emphasizes, is the stuff on which the young Fanny works.[8] She as closely resembles the imported produce as she does the labourer who processes and transforms it. And she is as much a local product as a source of imported labour, for it is both her kinship to the Bertram family and her distance and difference from them that motivates her importation.[9] Her trajectory within England reproduces the completed circuit of Mansfield Park's, and Britain's, colonial trade: she is brought in to work and be worked on and readied to be sent out again. When Fanny is read metaphorically as an indentured colonial subject, she must also be read within a complex context that requires her to be simultaneously domestic and unfamiliar, at once alien and at home.

Fanny's education at Mansfield Park confirms her ambiguous imperial status. Brought in by a scheme of her mother's family, she becomes subject, alongside the Bertram daughters, to the discipline of the governess Miss Lee. The lessons are structured around the history of empires, Roman as well as British, and the systematic comprehension of space and the systems that order it, from the table of the elements to the geography of Europe.[10] The self-discipline Fanny and her cousins are encouraged to cultivate belongs to an imperial self. At the same time, however, Fanny receives lessons that sustain her difference from her cousins and equate it with inferiority. In planning for her arrival, Sir Thomas Bertram balances his desire to integrate her fully into the household with his need 'to make her remember that she is not a *Miss Bertram.*'[11] The object of both educations is Fanny's memory; their shared tool is her memory's instruction. As an essential part of her adoption into her uncle's family and into the imperial economy in which the Bertrams participate, Fanny's memory training produces a consciousness in line with Homi Bhabha's account of colonized subjectivity: 'a difference that is almost the same, but not quite.'[12]

The novel frames Fanny's growth to maturity between two contrasting scenes, which introduce and recapitulate the imperial investments of ***Mansfield Park.*** The assessment of her inadequate geographical knowledge by Sir Thomas's daughters begins the first volume and her informed discussion of the West Indian slave trade with her uncle introduces the second. The treatment of geography in these scenes, and in the representation of Fanny's memory and its training throughout the rest of the novel, reveals suggestive parallels with contemporary discussions within and about the emerging discipline of geography, which were taking place in the periodical and pamphlet press, as well as in public lectures and scientific institutions, throughout the early nineteenth century.

As Felix Driver has shown in his history of the discipline, geography was in the process of diverging from the polite literature of tourism and travel. Practitioners in these fields of inquiry were negotiating the relations and bounds between them through two intersecting debates: on the necessity and propriety of expertise in each, the appropriate genres for geographical and tourist writing, and whether or not these genres should appeal to leisured but unlearned reading audiences, especially upper-class women; and on the relation of geography, its genres, and their newly defined groups of readers to the formation and development of empire.[13] Austen's investigation of the effects of geographical reading and instruction on Fanny's memory offers a broader comment on the role of a geographical education conducted through polite letters in maintaining the conventions of upper-class femininity and the relation of these conventions to the maintenance of British national and imperial competence. The inconsistencies evident within Fanny's experience of geography, as within the contemporary field of geography itself, enact the complexity of Fanny's imperial relations.

Space and its mastery, its techniques, and their genres are at issue from the moment of Fanny's arrival at Mansfield Park. Her cousins waste no time in taking her measure as uncharted terrain, beginning with 'a full survey of her face and her frock' and 'reflections on her size' before assessing her potential as the designated colonizer of her own still-uncivilized self.[14] Their investigations document, and convey to Austen's readers, a child remarkable only for an 'awkward' demeanour and a total ignorance of geography:

> Fanny could read, work, and write, but she had been taught nothing more; and as her cousins found her ignorant of many things with which they had been long familiar, they thought her prodigiously stupid, and for the first two or three weeks were continually bringing some fresh report of it into the drawing-room. 'Dear Mamma, only think, my cousin cannot put the map of Europe together—or my cousin cannot tell the principal Rivers in Russia—or she never heard of Asia Minor—or she does not know the difference between water-colours and crayons!—How strange! [. . .] Do you know, we asked her last night, which way she would go to get to Ireland; and she said, she should cross to the Isle of Wight. She thinks of nothing but the Isle of Wight, and she calls it the Island, as if there were no other island in the world.'[15]

The apparent randomness of the areas of competency in which Fanny is examined and found wanting belies the systematic character of the education Maria and Julia Bertram expect, and which they themselves receive. Contemporary conduct writers such as James Fordyce include geographical learning—'VOYAGES and TRAVELS' as well as 'GEOGRAPHY,' for these categories have not yet become fully detached from each other—among the 'pleasing' arts such as drawing that, as part of feminine education, 'prevent many a folly, and many a sin which proceed from idleness' and are 'useful in conversation.'[16] Such views of education come under ironic scrutiny in Austen's ***Pride and Prejudice,*** in which Mr Collins, wielding Fordyce's *Sermons,* is no more able than anyone else to prevent Lydia Bennet's elopement.[17]

Although Julia and Maria Bertram both repeat the 'folly' of elopement in ***Mansfield Park,*** however, something more than Fordyce's assumption that the ornamental guarantees the ethical is called into question by Austen's ironic exit survey of the Bertram 'plan of education.'[18] While the testing of Fanny displays an overriding concern with accomplishments as indices of upper-class feminine learning, the list of tests makes clear that a sense of place and of global position are paramount among them. To be unable to tell Ireland from the Isle of Wight, or to discern the relations that unite Northampton to both within the map of Europe, is a climactic defect of knowledge far worse then a confusion among painting implements. Fanny's cousin Edmund, in particular, works to remedy the deficit, recommending the latest narratives by official and imperial travellers and explorers, such as John Barrow's edition of George, Earl of Macartney's voyages in Russia, Ireland and China.[19] Geography is an acquirement of the landed class, to be learned and practised by young ladies in the schoolroom, making the propertied British woman a creature of imperial scope.

That this educational theory participates in a larger context of British thought about the relations between geography and imperial process is emphasized by Austen's narration.

The novel draws the reader's attention to the Bertram sisters' equation of Fanny's educational differences from themselves with an inborn incapacity to learn. Moreover, the narrative emphasizes that in equating ignorance with stupidity, and in taking themselves as the standard against which ignorance and knowledge must be measured, Maria and Julia share the perspective of the adults who oversee their education as well as of the moralists who recommend its plan. To the sisters' complaints about Fanny, their Aunt Norris responds that they 'are blessed with wonderful memories,' while their 'poor cousin has probably none at all. There is a vast deal of difference in memories, as well as in every thing else, and therefore you must make allowance for your cousin, and pity her deficiency.'[20] Like Enlightenment stadial historians, or like Enlightenment travellers looking at the New World or Ireland or the Highlands of Scotland, a class of writers and writings with whom genteel education must have familiarized them, the Bertrams assume that all human intelligence and knowledge exists on a single, developmental scale.[21] Learning is not measured according to any contingent body of knowledge but held up to an ideal of comprehensiveness, which issues in a judgement of perfection or imperfection, primitiveness or maturity that alone accounts for individual variation. A unified grasp of the world and its systems is the endpoint of this uniform intellectual history. In the hands of the Bertrams, educational assessments founded on these principles are both an expression of imperial participation and a scale for its measurement. Where empire as well as education is concerned, Fanny's empty memory places her at the beginning of the developmental scale.

The novel's initial emphasis on Fanny's limited knowledge of the world beyond her Portsmouth home contrasts markedly with the later scene, the capstone of her education, in which she asks her uncle an informed question about his Antigua estates and 'the slave trade' that demonstrates the 'curiosity and pleasure' with which she receives colonial 'information.'[22] Taken together, the two moments establish a parallel, noted by Katie Trumpener and Clara Tuite in particular, between the heroine's growth into maturity and the growth of her imperial awareness.[23] World-making in this novel—'putting the map together'—is an instrument of self-making that must take place in order for the obverse, self-making in the service of empire-building, to occur. The class dimension of these intersecting processes, in which geopolitical space and the selves that inhabit it are manufactured, has gone relatively undiscussed.[24] Yet the 'hygiene of the self' through which Fanny transforms herself demands much in terms of 'carrying,' 'fetching,' 'pains,' and other class-marked forms of labour not demanded of her cousins.[25] The transformations of subjectivity that result are integrally linked to Fanny's visible rise in class position. As a result, any continuing failures of geographical learning can be seen as evidence of imperfect social mobility—in the heroine and her memory—even as the failures themselves carry an imperial significance.

By documenting Fanny's origins in the milieu of her father, a 'Lieutenant of Marines, without education, fortune, or connections' who elopes with her mother, a small-town lawyer's niece, ***Mansfield Park*** demonstrates that its heroine's imperial grasp develops only as a result of her movement to her uncle's landed estate.[26] From the house Lieutenant Price rents at Portsmouth, the Isle of Wight looms large across the harbour, screening in Fanny's view of the world and establishing an outer limit for any aspiration his daughter might have to travel: wherever she might choose to go, 'she should cross to the Isle of Wight' first.[27] At Mansfield, however, Fanny's education eventually gives her the credentials to take her place as 'the only young woman in the drawing-room, the only occupier of that interesting division of a family in which she had hitherto held so humble a third.'[28] With her passage into the heart of the estate, coinciding with her maturation and with the integration of imperial knowledge that defines it, 'not only at home did her value increase,' but in society as well.[29] An eye that takes in Britain's place in its empire and the world, in this novel, is contingent not only on a memory for geographic knowledge, but also on the privileged class position of which such an imperial eye is an expression.

Yet despite the apparent competence Fanny achieves and the novel's affirmation of her value, her rise in position is never fully realized. Although education closes the gap that exists in childhood between her geographical ignorance and the expansive knowledge of her Bertram cousins, a new and jarring fracture opens in adulthood between her eager expressions of concern for colonial matters and her cousins' jaded disinclination for geographical discussion. While Julia and Maria preserve what Fanny calls a 'dead silence' about the history of Caribbean slavery, 'sitting by without speaking a word, or seeming at all interested in the subject,' Fanny asks her uncle a question that declares a lively interest in human conditions in the Caribbean and in the economic dependencies that yoke Mansfield Park to Sir Thomas's plantations.[30]

The difference between Fanny and her cousins can be understood in two ways. First, unlike Bertram's daughters, Fanny cannot wear her learning lightly. To be perceived as a gentlewoman, especially by her uncle, who has engineered and cannot fail of remembering the whole history of her adoption from the indigent household of his wife's sister, she must remind her relations of her geographic understanding. She does so even as she recognizes that she may give the impression of wishing 'to set myself off at their expense' by speaking when they are silent.[31] Second, because she carries with her the lingering memory of her childhood inability to 'put the map of Europe together' and the class distinction exposed by her failure, the adult Fanny emerges not only with the requisite understanding of the physical and political geography of the British empire, but also with an active interest in the human history that has produced it.

Perhaps, like Austen herself, Fanny has been reading Thomas Clarkson's *History of the Rise, Progress and Accomplishment of the Abolition of the African Slave Trade by the British Parliament* (1808).[32] What conditions Fanny's interest, however, is what she remembers: the special position, with regard to empire, of the low end of the urban lower-middle class, to which she by birth belongs. Fanny's father belongs to 'a subordinate and inferior branch of the Navy' that acts as an oceangoing bodyguard to protect ships' officers from mutiny and from onshore attack, not least on imperial adventures.[33] His 'profession' is unlike the church and the law, and equally unlike the army or navy, in being, as the narrator puts it, 'such as no interest could reach.'[34] Fanny's mother, meanwhile, has a continually increasing, imperfectly documented, and uncountable number of offspring, a 'superfluity of children' particularly ill-suited to her 'want of almost everything else,' financial or educational. Her sister Mrs Norris, who attempts to keep up with the Prices' birthrate, 'now and then' tells the Bertrams 'in an angry voice, that Fanny had got another child.'[35] Though the Prices are above the reach of charitable institutions, they are equally far beyond the pale of the Mansfield social circles. They produce children who seem to the Bertrams likely to suffer, at the very least, from 'gross ignorance' and 'vulgarity,' if not a 'really bad' disposition, and who require to be 'introduced into the society of this country,' as Mrs Norris puts it, through what the Prices view, in their turn, as a 'foreign education.'[36] Although three of the Price children eventually learn the polite geographies that initiate them into this society, the family continues to share much with the Bertrams' perception of the colonized peoples that are among geographers' chief subjects.

Yet although they are analogous in the Bertrams' minds to the natives of colonized places, the Price family, like other members of the contemporary lower-middle class, do the daily work of empire, participating in the colonizing of lands they will not own and from which they earn no more than wages.[37] As a naval midshipman, Fanny's older brother William takes tours of duty to the West Indies; a younger brother, 'midshipman on board an Indiaman,' has joined the merchant marine.[38] Having placed William and Fanny decisively among the transactors and beneficiaries of imperialism, Mrs Price's ambitions for her remaining children include the hope of one son's becoming 'useful to Sir Thomas in the concerns of his West Indian property'—'No situation would be beneath him'—and another's being 'sent out to the East,' and it is likely that their father has also laboured at imperial work.[39] Like Fanny herself, they are simultaneously positioned as quasi-colonial raw materials and as eager participants in empire. Their involvement in imperial exploration and commerce is of a sort equally different from the landed stake held by Sir Thomas Bertram and from the consumption of polite tourist literature by his daughters and by Fanny.

To the imperious gaze of Mansfield Park, the Price household is at once domestic and beyond the pale, as peripheral and mysterious as a tract of uncharted ground yet as familiar as those who are sent out to cultivate it. In their relationship to empire, the closest resemblance of the Prices, as the Bertrams' condemnation of their feckless fecundity suggests and as their own desperate willingness to take part in colonial projects equally implies, is to the migrant Irish poor who preoccupied the moralists, political arithmeticians, and political economists of the eighteenth and early nineteenth centuries.[40] As the longstanding subject of British geographical investigation and colonial intervention, Ireland had come, in the wake of the Union in 1801, to confront the United Kingdom with a domestic and increasingly urban set of problems.[41] That Austen's heroine feels some such connection is underlined by the ten-year-old Fanny's striking sense of Ireland's closeness and accessibility: to the Price children, only the Isle of Wight seems to stand between Ireland and their Portsmouth home. Fanny is mistaken, of course, so far as the map is concerned, but in the context of the novel's representation of her own imperial experience, she may not be far wrong in her imaginings, however hard she tries later on to forget.

The novel's paradoxical representation of the Price family as at once the soldiers and objects of empire emphasizes that theirs is work carried out by those who must first, in a practical sense, be colonized. ***Mansfield Park*** ends with Sir Thomas's affirmation of the sameness and the difference of the Prices and Bertrams and his own contribution to each. Conducting a final survey of Fanny, William, and Susan, he believes he has 'reason to rejoice in what he had done for them all, and acknowledge the advantages of early hardship and discipline, and the consciousness of being born to struggle and endure.'[42] To be useful to Mansfield and Britain, the Prices' stationary daughters and seafaring sons must be taught a sense of themselves and their world that is 'almost the same, but not quite' as the imperial eye of the landed classes that employ them. Yet in producing difference, Sir Thomas also emphasizes existing differences, in this case the history of class difference and class subordination that divides the Bertram family from the Prices.

There remains something awkward about Fanny in particular, something poorly adapted to her situation at Mansfield Park, which troubles the landed estate and its imperial investments. The fate of the differences between Fanny and the Bertrams charts the history of class within the novel. Not least, it highlights the effects of domestic class relations on Austen's representation of Britain's imperial interests. This is not to suggest that empire is a vehicle for the exploration of class in this novel, which, as I have been arguing, presents the process of making Britain's empire as both analogous to and reliant on class subordination. Rather, the relation between empire and class as it is represented in ***Mansfield Park*** provides a context for the narrative of the heroine's incomplete class rise as it is played out in her recollections. Faulty at first and then inescapably stubborn, it is, above all, Fanny's memory that registers the presence in Austen's novel of empire's troubling history, in Britain and abroad.

Perspective

In outlining a context in imperial history for the way in which Fanny Price's memory is portrayed in ***Mansfield Park,*** I have come some way from the account of her geographical learning and thinking with which I began. But the journey has been shorter than it first appears, for I want now to propose that Fanny's memory is itself a colonial terrain. To make this argument, let me turn to Austen's representation of her heroine's processes of remembering through metaphors of space, or, to put it another way, to Austen's depiction of geographies as historic sites and devices for the storage of memory. In the two key scenes in the novel in which Fanny reflects on her own history, her change of homes, her education, and her consequent rise in class position, she finds her memory of past events figured in the landscape. Under Fanny's gaze, Mansfield Park and its environs register the contrast between the territory of the past, recalled in its uncultivated natural state, and the tamed and polished landscape of the present, even as Fanny tries and fails to efface the distinction from remembrance. Like Fanny herself, the terrain this novel charts is haunted by historical process.

To turn to these scenes is also to return, in a double sense, to the question of ***Mansfield Park***'s Romanticism: its mixing and quotation of contemporary genres, especially poetry, and its relevance to later debates about the significance of these genres. In depicting Fanny's perception of the spaces around her and her attempts at comprehending them, the novel takes up the problem of relations between history and imagination that is the subtext, as New Historicist scholarship especially emphasized, of much Romantic poetry. It is not my intention to rehearse the debates about history and transcendence that dominated the field of British Romantic studies in the 1980s and early 1990s, but rather to consider the question of Austen's intervention in the contemporary conversations that were their object. In ***Mansfield Park,*** Fanny Price tries and fails to imitate the Romantic approaches to thinking about space that were provided by contemporary locodescriptive poetry and by manuals of picturesque description—genres that outlined many of the assumptions and techniques with which, as William Galperin has shown, Romantic writers approached the depiction of history.[43] When Fanny engages in explicit quotation, and imitation, of William Wordsworth's 'Lines composed a few miles above Tintern Abbey' and William Gilpin's *Observations Relative Chiefly to Picturesque Beauty,* it is precisely in order to grapple with the problem of historical experience. Repeatedly demonstrating Fanny's inability to surmount her past in an imaginative relation to landscape, the novel advances and rejects the idea that nineteenth-century Britons can fully achieve, through imagination, any transcendence of a context that necessarily includes imperial history.

This rejection of the possibility of forgetfulness in ***Mansfield Park*** raises questions for Said's account of the novel's blind-spots about history—an imperviousness or forgetfulness, he suggests, that it shares with Romantic novels more broadly. At the same time, however, Fanny's failed imitation of the cognitive processes she borrows from canonical Romantic genres establishes Austen's novel in a relation of critical distance to these contemporary forms. It is in these scenes that Austen most concretely and insistently raises the question of mediation: the shaping of memory and imagination by print culture and, in particular, by the competing genres of geographical writing—poetic, tourist, scientific—that mark the early-nineteenth-century scene of the discipline's emergence.

The first of Austen's paired scenes takes place between Fanny and Mary Crawford on the grounds of the Parsonage at Mansfield. As the two young women sit in the garden of Mary's sister Mrs Grant, Fanny expresses her admiration of its arrangement:

> Every time I come into this shrubbery I am more struck with its growth and beauty. Three years ago, this was nothing but a rough hedgerow along the upper side of the field, never thought of as any thing, or capable of becoming any thing; and now it is converted into a walk, and it would be difficult to say whether most valuable as a convenience or an ornament; and perhaps in another three years we may be forgetting—almost forgetting what it was before. How wonderful, how very wonderful the operations of time, and the changes of the human mind! [. . .] If any one faculty of our nature may be called more wonderful than the rest, I do think it is memory. There seems something more speakingly incomprehensible in the powers, the failures, the inequalities of memory, than in any other of our intelligences. The memory is sometimes so retentive, so serviceable, so obedient—at others, so bewildered and so weak—and at others again, so tyrannic, so beyond controul!—We are to be sure a miracle every way—but our powers of recollecting and of forgetting, do seem peculiarly past finding out.[44]

Fanny's denization at Mansfield is evident in her reflections on this scene, for although she has travelled no farther than across the park, she borrows the language of the picturesque tour to describe her surroundings. Fanny's rhetorical borrowing from a genre that remains the linchpin of her and her cousins' imperial education points toward what I will argue is the heart of this garden scene: the metaphoric relation between the development of the garden and Fanny's memory training.

Fanny assesses the shrubbery in the terms of Gilpin's *Observations,* drawing her evaluative vocabulary from his strictures on the design of gardens belonging to houses. Because 'a house is an *artificial* object,' Gilpin writes,

> the scenery around it, *must,* in some degree, partake of *art.* Propriety requires it: convenience demands it. But if it partake of *art,* it should also partake of *nature,* as belonging to the country. It has therefore two characters to support; and may be considered as the connecting thread

> between the regularity of the house, and the freedom of the natural scene [. . .]. [The] business of the embellished scene, is to [. . .] remove offensive objects, and to add a pleasing foreground to the distance.[45]

For Gilpin, two processes are crucial in producing such picturesque scenes: the creation of 'distance' and the removal of 'offensive objects' that have become, over time, a part of the garden site. Through these two methods, the gardener enables the viewer to rise, as it were, above the two existing, conflicting characters of the garden, perceiving a new and harmonious beauty in the scene. In advocating such a distanciated perspective on landscape, Gilpin prefigures New Historicist readings of poems such as 'Tintern Abbey,' which emphasizes the speaker's self-positioning above the prospect he describes and his pleasure in the way the elements of his scene, including evidence of pollution and poverty, 'lose themselves' among the harmonious picture of the landscape.[46] Elsewhere in *Observations,* Gilpin writes that although the 'regular intermixture' of domestic, industrial, and natural elements in landscape

> produces often deformity on the nearer grounds; [. . .] when all these regular forms are softened by distance—when hedge-row trees begin to unite, and lengthen into streaks along the horizon—when farm-houses, and ordinary buildings lose all their vulgarity of shape, and are scattered about, in formless spots, through the several parts of a distance, it is inconceivable what richness, and beauty, this mass of deformity, when melted together, adds to landscape.[47]

In *Observations,* Gilpin provides a manual, a groundbreaking set of aesthetic instructions, for viewers who wish, through the achievement of what for him remains a physical and spatial kind of transcendence, to distance themselves from the pain and disorder of history and to understand the distance as improvement. In making use of Gilpin's aesthetic practice in her account of Mrs Grant's shrubbery, Fanny makes the implied connection between transcendent landscape and history more explicit. It is only with the passage of time, she suggests, that the 'beauty' and 'convenience' of the garden have become impossible to distinguish from each other. It is a consequence of passing time that the viewer is distanced from the rough history of the scene, which is lost in a pleasing landscape.

In conjoining time and space, memory and landscape, Austen's scene unfolds a metaphoric as well as a physical geography. Its cohesion, when considered from close up, yields irreconcilable elements that form a counterpart to the contradictions within the narrative of Fanny's geographical education that I discussed earlier in this essay. Yet the rhetoric and outcomes of Fanny's reverie about the shrubbery also replicate the narrator's account of Fanny's own development from roughness into 'value' and from domestic 'convenience' to an ornamental role as 'the only young woman in the drawing-room.'[48] The novel's metonymic linkage of the geography of the tour to polite education intersects with its metaphoric treatment of memory as a terrain to be emptied of disregarded content, refilled, and then charted.

Even so, despite its formal sophistication, the correspondence between Fanny and the landscape that emerges in this scene is attributed to the heroine rather than to the narrator. It is Fanny's own recognition of the parallel that prompts her thoughts in the direction of the nature of memory, whence they move in a now-familiar pattern from a mind that is empty of recollection to one that is uncomfortably retentive. Although Fanny begins her reflections by declaring her awe at the human capacity to forget the past, she stumbles—as Gilpin and Wordsworth never stumble—over the chasm between 'forgetting' and 'almost forgetting' and comes to wonder, equally, at memory's insistence. As it is metaphorized in landscape, memory to Fanny is both marvellous and painful, at times forgetting what needs to be remembered (as in her childhood struggles to make a coherent whole of the map of Europe) and at other, more 'tyrannic' times, stubbornly remembering what she wishes to forget (hence the adult Fanny's uncomfortable recollection of her struggles with education, imitation, and difference).

As in the scene of Fanny's earlier display of geographical memory in conversation with Sir Thomas, it is apparently only the heroine, with her lower-middle-class history, whose glance at the successful transformation of the garden fails to forget the difference between present beauty and past roughness. Instead Mary Crawford sees the reflection of her polished, perfected, aristocratic self.[49] While her way of looking replicates Fanny's self-absorption, Mary is, in two senses, a better viewer of the garden than Fanny, for she does not recognize, and cannot remember, the history of its transformation. Mary has, that is, fully internalized both the explicit and the implicit lessons of the picturesque: that viewers should notice only the finished landscape if they wish to take pleasure from it, and that their pleasure derives from their own perspective on the landscapes they perceive. Like Maria and Julia Bertram, moreover, Mary makes light of her polite but tutored knowledge, so that its origins in the contemporary picturesque tour are no longer visible. Fanny, with her remembrance and quotation of Gilpin's teachings, is unable, once again, fully to inhabit her own learning and so to forget the history of class mobility that complicates it.

As with the earlier scenes of geographical memory to which I have been comparing Fanny's landscape experience, I want to underline the national and imperial as well as the class dimensions of Austen's narrative. An incipient nationalism is evident in Gilpin's text in a form that sets the perspective of the native viewer in natural harmony with the national landscape his or her perspective organizes. Even as Gilpin protests that he does not 'wish to speak merely as an Englishman,' he insists that the act of appreciating landscape is peculiarly and locally English, because, he writes, 'this country exceeds most countries in the variety of it's [*sic*] picturesque beauties.'[50] The supremacy exists because the process of harmonizing the disparate marks history leaves on the land—such as the Wordsworthian 'intermixture of wood and cultivation'—is a strength 'found oftener in English landscape than in the landscape of other countries.'[51] In creating smoothness and sameness from the coming together of discordant elements, Britain, it seems, has colonized its own landscape. The sentiment that takes particular pleasure in this achievement matters more than class divisions among the tourists Gilpin addresses.

Tim Fulford has emphasized Gilpin's detachment of his tourist-readers' pleasure in landscape from the necessity of owning or inheriting the land they view.[52] Reading 'Tintern Abbey' in conversation with Gilpin's relatively egalitarian literature of the tour has allowed readers, such as Fulford, who wish to rethink the New Historicist examinations of the poem to argue that Wordsworth seeks not to transcend historical conflicts and sufferings but rather to enact them metaphorically in the new form of landscape aesthetics.[53] Such readings stress that the poem's scene includes the 'houseless' charcoal burners and the evidence of Enclosure Acts in 'hedgerows,' however 'sportive,' and in farms that are 'green to the very door.'[54] More recently, Debbie Lee has re-examined this revisionist reading of Wordsworthian 'aesthetic distance' in the context of contemporary abolitionism, suggesting that an imagination that transcends the merely local and individual becomes, for such writers, an imagination capable of trans-imperial empathy.[55] It is distance, that is, that allows the imaginative viewer to see common ground in particularity, though, as Lee points out, such a perception does not necessarily oppose itself to imperialism.[56]

To achieve such empathy requires a viewer who has access to a judicious spatial and historical distance. In Austen's depiction, however, the process of viewing landscape by Gilpin's rules—learning to take the long view, and to look with explicitly English eyes—remains unperfected by those who do not participate, or who like Fanny must grow into participation, in landed Britain. The gaze of such participants notes the residue of their own class history in the landed English scene they witness. The scene of Fanny's reveries reveals the mistake the Bertram sisters make when they assume that every education, every intellect, and, by extension, every place and people follows an identical trajectory of development with greater or lesser success. In learning to put the map of England together as Fanny literally does in the Parsonage garden, she follows a path that, as Austen demonstrates, is wholly distinct from theirs. I have argued that Fanny's distinctness is framed by Austen's account of her imperial education and that the framing allows Fanny's experience of her memory training to dramatize her own and her family's ambiguous relation to empire. If Austen's garden set-piece demonstrates that Fanny's relations to Britain remain equally distinct, so, I would like to suggest, the picture of Britain's relation to its imperial entanglements that emerges in the novel not only calls Gilpin's achievement of transcendence into doubt but also questions the perspective that makes Wordsworth's discordant elements 'lose themselves' in harmony.

The second of the paired scenes in which Austen maps the colonial terrain of Fanny's memory brings together an act of landscape appreciation that is founded on Gilpin's, and that refers to Wordsworth's, while enumerating the imperial stakes of such figurings of Britain. Left alone in the former schoolroom at Mansfield, Fanny contemplates the collection of objects that have accumulated there.[57] Deliberately acquired or consigned by chance, all are artefacts of the history that has brought her among a landed class that benefits from empire:

> Her plants, her books—of which she had been a collector, from the first hour of her commanding a shilling—her writing desk, and her works of charity and ingenuity, were all within her reach;—or if indisposed for employment, if nothing but musing would do, she could scarcely see an object in that room which had not an interesting remembrance connected with it.—Everything was a friend, or bore her thoughts to a friend; and though there had been sometimes much of suffering to her—though her motives had been often misunderstood, her feelings disregarded, and her comprehension undervalued; though she had known the pains of tyranny, of ridicule, and neglect, yet almost every recurrence of either had led to something consolatory [. . .]—and the whole was now so blended together, so harmonized by distance, that every former affliction had its charm. The room was most dear to her [though] [. . .] its greatest elegancies and ornaments were a faded footstool of Julia's work, too ill done for the drawing-room, three transparencies, made in a rage for transparencies, for the three lower panes of one window, where Tintern Abbey held its station between a cave in Italy, and a moonlight lake in Cumberland; a collection of family profiles thought unworthy of being anywhere else, over the mantle-piece, and by their side and pinned against the wall, a small sketch of a ship sent four years ago from the Mediterranean by William, with H. M. S. Antwerp at the bottom, in letters as tall as the main-mast.[58]

'Harmonized by distance': here again, Fanny, and thus Austen's novel, is talking about time in conventional, spatial terms. Surveying the borrowed demesne of the schoolroom, Fanny echoes Gilpin's account of diversity 'softened by distance,' or, as the first of the transparencies stationed between her eye and her view of the Park seems to suggest, she imitates the Wordsworth of 'Tintern Abbey.'

For Fanny, however, the tyrannic waywardness of memory means that the disparate elements that make up the landscape of the schoolroom are imperfectly 'blended together.' Every object in the room serves as a repository for memories of emotional experience and the history that has produced them. The long perspective lent by the privileged present cannot entirely harmonize, let alone erase or 'lose,' these isolated, painful traces of the past Fanny shares with objects 'thought unworthy of being anywhere else.' And so her 'works of charity,' signs of the social role of a woman of the landed classes, lie side by side with objects marked with her experience of 'tyranny'; with the remnants of an education designed at once to highlight and to remedy an 'under-valued' intellect by alternating 'ridicule and neglect'; and with the artefact most visibly linked to the imperial role of her family and her native class and place: a sketch of the *Antwerp,* the ship on which her older brother serves not just in the Mediterranean but also in the West Indies of the Bertrams' colonial plantations, all the while failing to rise beyond his position at the bottom of the ranks.[59] The schoolroom is Fanny's British museum, where the artefacts of a complex personal and imperial history are stored. But the broken relics of this history never resolve themselves, as the collections of an imperial nation must, into a narrative of upward and outward progress.[60] Instead they persist, each in its irreducible quiddity, bearing the fractured traces of competing histories.

In ***Mansfield Park,*** Austen rewrites the scene of 'Tintern Abbey' with an eye to the details of British landscape, the physical leavings of a domestic history that is also a history of colonial involvement, which refuse to harmonize or vanish. Fanny's schoolroom musings are more in line than Wordsworth's poem with what Fulford and others argue about the persistence of history in the Romantic poetics of landscape. The citation of 'Tintern Abbey' coupled with the reduction of its scene to a transparency—an object to be seen through, remnant of a brief 'rage for transparencies' and only one among the discordant objects that have found their way into Fanny's museum—emphasizes the perspectival differences that distinguish the novel from the poem and its picturesque apparatus. For Austen, the gulf between these perceptions of Britain arises from the distinction between 'forgetting' and 'almost forgetting.' Born of domestic differences in birth and landed power, the distinction has implications for the experience of empire at home and for the character of Britons' imperial participation abroad.

Mediation

The history of readers' responses to 'Tintern Abbey' opens a window on the larger topic of history and transcendence in British Romantic writing. Austen's representation of the tension between 'forgetting' and 'almost forgetting' in ***Mansfield Park*** allows us to open another that is specific to the Romantic novel. From readings of 'Tintern Abbey' for its aesthetic of 'oversight' to assertions that historicist criticism reinscribes Romantic transcendence, scholars have spent much of the past two decades exploring the relation between the Romantic imagination and history.[61] More recently, revisionist readers have revived the topic of imagination as something more than ideology, emphasizing its continuing historical engagement, or argued that the local and the particular persist in Romantic writing as hallmarks of British nationalism.[62] Still others have suggested that not only what post-Romantic readers notice in Romantic texts, but also which texts they continue to notice, is a consequence of the naturalization of British nationhood, and of a developing national literature, in nineteenth-century criticism, and the novel in particular.[63] In order to fulfil the last of the promises with which this essay began, an account of the mediated character of psycho-affective processes such as 'almost forgetting' in ***Mansfield Park,*** I want to bring these approaches together. The scenes of Fanny Price's geographical education and her response to the landscapes of Britain provide the contours of an aesthetic imagination whose historical engagement is founded on inescapable memory. I will conclude by proposing that Austen's depiction of Fanny's memory as an accumulation of historical details is indeed associated with nationalism, but that the lineaments are drawn from the anti-imperial nationalism of the United Kingdom's peripheries, and that the significance inheres in what the heroine remembers: a mix of British picturesque writing and peripheral nationalist print production.

It will be useful to restate what I have been arguing throughout this essay: that the protagonist's memory, as it is represented in ***Mansfield Park,*** is a thoroughly textual one. Both as a consequence of its training at Mansfield and as a result of Austen's techniques for portraying it, Fanny's mind is an aggregate of imperfectly harmonized passages from books. Picturesque tours and Lake School poetry figure especially prominently in her recollected reading. But Fanny also reads beyond the official Bertram syllabus. All kinds of current books accumulate in the schoolroom, in part because Fanny has early become a 'collector' of them but also, perhaps, because those Bertram acquisitions that do not hold the interest of Maria and Julia—from the picturesque manuals and abolition history whose influence is implicit in Fanny's conversations to Macartney's travels and the narrative poems by Walter Scott and William Cowper Fanny quotes in the novel—are likely to wash up there. Moreover, during Fanny's brief return to Portsmouth, she subscribes '*in propria persona*' to a circulating library, becoming, in her state of textual deprivation, 'a renter, a chuser of books.'[64] As Fanny's reading diverges from Maria's and Julia's, so Austen's mapping of her memory comes to hinge on a genre whose conventions Fanny, alone among the occupants of Mansfield and its neighbourhood, appears to recognize and recall.

Along with the English picturesque tourism of Gilpin and his followers, Fanny's perspective on landscape and history bears the markers of a closely related competitor: the antiquarian tour of Britain's peripheries. Now little read, the antiquarian tour is among the genres whose literary-historical 'forgetting' took place through what Clifford Siskin has theorized as a retrospective attribution of ephemerality.[65] Yet notwithstanding the Bertrams' indifference, the peripheral tour was a popular and diverse Romantic literary form with a readership in Britain.[66] Irish examples encompass poetry as well as prose, ranging from esoterica such as those Charles Vallancey published in his *Collectanea de Rebus Hibernicis* (1781-82) to expensive quartos such as Charlotte Brooke's *Reliques of Irish Poetry* (1789), an urbane collection whose subscribers included Charlotte Smith and Anna Seward.[67] In the work of Irish and Scottish writers alike, the genre often takes the form of included set-pieces within novels and narrative poems, among them Sydney Owenson's *Wild Irish Girl* (1806), Maria Edgeworth's *The Absentee* (1812) and Scott's *Lay of the Last Minstrel* (1805) and *Lady of the Lake* (1810), all of which Austen or her characters cite in writing and conversation.[68]

The peripheral antiquarian tour, as Trumpener has shown, responds dialectically to metropolitan tourist writing, including picturesque tours that considered Ireland as a colonized and thus as an increasingly systematized and coherent terrain.[69] Its techniques centre on imitation of British picturesque writing, in the oblique form of parody and pastiche.[70] What differentiates the genre from the metropolitan picturesque tour, despite an identical range of generic markers, then, is its concentration on landscape, in particular that of colonized Ireland, as 'a site simultaneously of historical plenitude and historical loss.'[71] In this genre, as in Fanny Price's memory and Austen's ***Mansfield Park,*** histories are played out across geographic space and landscape observation becomes a source of historical testimony.

Peripheral nationalist tourists read historical details back into a landscape that has been rendered harmonious by what they see as a distanciated and thus as a superficial perspective. So, for example, the picturesque pleasure Owenson's English tourist Horatio M. takes in his travels from London to the far west of Ireland, where castle ruins 'grand even in desolation, and magnificent in decay' crown a 'wildly romantic' peninsula, is tempered by learning that his ancestors have pushed the castle's owners off more arable land.[72] Similarly, when Edgeworth's Lord Colambre journeys to Ireland to view the effects of his father's absenteeism on his Irish estates, a tenant informs him that 'the desolation of the prospect' is a consequence of mismanagement and distance rather than the intrinsically wild or barren character of the land.[73] The historical breakdown of the picturesque in these novels provides a model for Fanny's querying of harmonious distance and forgetting in the schoolroom and in Mrs Grant's garden. In the antiquarian scenes that Owenson and Edgeworth include in their own Romantic novels, territories once viewed as well-composed romantic landscapes are repopulated and re-historicized in being seen up close.

In recovering the history of each landscape that gives aesthetic pleasure to its viewer, these writers defend the significance of material artefacts, not just as objects to be preserved in picturesque scenes but also as essential sources in the writing of history and historical accounts of landscapes. For Owenson, the assertion that 'manuscripts, annals, and records, are not the treasures of a colonized or a conquered country' because 'it is always the policy of the conqueror, (or the invader) to destroy those mementi' amply justifies an obsessive focus on caches of rusting weaponry, the history of musical instruments, and the details of 'ancient Irish' dress that prefigures Fanny's enumeration of the disparate objects in the East Room at Mansfield Park.[74] In substituting antiquities for narrative, Owenson suggests not only that the evidence of the linguistic past is a kind of frozen history but also that artefacts can speak and be heard.[75] Unlike Fanny, who attempts to divorce her privileged state at Mansfield from her remembered past experience, Owenson demonstrates through the recovery and description of antiquarian fragments that the Irish present is a product of Ireland's past, and of its colonial experience in particular. Yet Fanny's enumeration of the relics in her schoolroom museum, and the almost forgotten memories she unwillingly acknowledges amid attempts to find harmony in distance, recapitulate this accounting of the past, its pains, and the costs of progress. In Fanny's memory, despite her best efforts, the fragments of the past persist and speak.

Conventions drawn from the antiquarian tour give shape to Austen's presentation of what Fanny remembers. The inclusion of these genres in ***Mansfield Park*** marks the return of the heroine's early sense of strangeness. Dividing Fanny from the Bertrams by complicating her relation to the English picturesque of Mansfield Park, these generic recollections simultaneously re-establish Fanny's childhood affinity for Ireland. Bhabha has posited a variety of uncanny experience, a 'paradigmatic colonial [. . .] condition,' that reveals itself as a subject moves between a culture and its colonial others. What should feel familiar is estranged by intra-imperial travel, and painful histories that should have been forgotten return to haunt the present.[76] Fanny's memory, I suggest, is the site of such a haunting: a print cultural uncanny.

In his analysis of Irish Romantic texts such as Owenson's novels, Leerssen identifies 'auto-exoticism' as the means by which their writers distinguished Ireland from Britain and, after Union, from the United Kingdom that had absorbed it. He concludes that 'Romantic exoticism' is 'chronological as well as [. . .] geographical': Irish writers looking at the Irish past appropriate this strange history in much the same way as Britain weaves strange countries and their produce into its seamless imperial fabric.[77] In this way Irish antiquarian tourists transform the history of Ireland into 'an undifferentiated pool of diverse mementos and memories,' paradoxically homogeneous in its calculated difference from the modern British present—a kind of historiographic bog that is, of course, the forerunner of

Fanny's schoolroom, equally crowded with mementos.[78] To Leerssen, antiquarian thinking is an essentially reactionary phenomenon, a nationalism that defends itself against the British impulse towards modernizing the colonies by clinging to the traces of a past the colonial present supersedes.

The characteristic fragmentation of antiquarian objects, however, along with the loss of their lived context, provides material for a history that is alternative to nationalist nostalgia as well as to imperialism, as Yoon Sun Lee has pointed out.[79] There are numerous moments in Owenson's writing that exemplify such a history. Praising a Sligo landscape in *Patriotic Sketches of Ireland* (1807), Owenson begins by echoing Gilpin and Wordsworth as well as her own *Wild Irish Girl*: what she sees is a 'scene of romantic variety, which frequently combines the most cultivated and harmonious traits, with the wildest and most abrupt images of scenic beauty'; an 'expansive prospect' that 'dissolve[s] every object into one mild and indistinct hue.'[80] But Owenson's landscape, like the garden at Mansfield Parsonage and like Fanny's similarly 'blended' and 'harmonized' schoolroom memories, turns out to be imperfectly harmonious. Viewed more closely, the rural Irish picturesque discloses the contrast between past and present, juxtaposing 'opulent' towns with 'ruinous and wretched villages' marked alike by the 'violence of the tide' and 'the vicissitudes of civil dissension.' Owenson concludes that the landscape's details are 'an epitome of the fate of all earthly states' and of 'the rise, climacteric, decline, and fall of every empire,' including Britain's.[81]

In describing the process in which Fanny Price reflects on landscape, Austen mirrors the kind of analytic progression that Owenson establishes in *Patriotic Sketches* and *The Wild Irish Girl*. In her reveries on the Parsonage garden and the schoolroom, Fanny wishes to emphasize the evidence of progress she finds in the present scene: her wonder at the shrubbery's 'valuable' present and her pleasure in the 'charm' of objects 'blended together' in a schoolroom prospect 'harmonized by distance.'[82] Yet, like Owenson, she cannot help falling back into the scene from whose history she has raised and distanced herself, recovering and enumerating the traces of 'rough hedgerow' that lurk in the one and of 'the pains of tyranny, of ridicule, and neglect' preserved in the artefacts of the other.

Perhaps most significantly, Fanny, unlike Owenson, never attempts to exoticize the past or seek out history's traces. Rather they haunt her, emerging unwilled in her memory and appearing randomly in her schoolroom at the whim of the Bertrams: even as she strives to develop a grateful pleasure in the harmony of past and present with which her hardscrabble origins blend into her imperial education, the traces of her history trouble her precisely as 'almost forgetting' troubles the prospect of forgetfulness.

Conclusion

In her experience of haunting by her half-forgotten past, Fanny Price is haunted by genre, and by a generic competition for the authority to define the relation between the national present and its imperial history. Pulled between the inescapable remnants of the past and the desperate quest to forget them, the unstable narrative form of Fanny's historical reveries emerges from the clash between imperial picturesque and colonial antiquarianism. Austen's account of Fanny's cognition itself forms a kind of textual museum, preserving the fragmentary traces of the competing genres that surface in their shared, repeated keywords: harmony, blend, and distance; suffering, tyranny, neglect, object. The mind that emerges is an assemblage of shards from contemporary print culture. This textual form—a new, unstable, and internally conflicted genre—of the heroine's memory is also the genre of empire in this novel as it explores the media of what Heydt-Stevenson and Sussman call 'communal imagining.'

The mapping of memory and imagination in Austen's ***Mansfield Park*** offers an exemplary opportunity for investigating the mediation of empire in the novel of British Romanticism. In representing a consciousness thematically as a product of literary form and in enacting this representation generically, Austen's novel allows its readers to propose anew the ties between mind, letters, and history—not as an evasion of Britain's troubled political past but precisely as an encounter with it. At the same time, in demonstrating the mediated character of its heroine's Romantic mind, ***Mansfield Park*** makes a case for literary writing and reading as a historically active process, capable of serving the British nation's geographical ends but equally capable of preserving the memorials that allow a questioning of Britain's imperial history.

Notes

1. One could instance the literalness with which Patricia Rozema's 1999 film addressed Fanny's curiosity about Antigua. But there is also an extended history in the criticism. Although neither Alistair M. Duckworth nor Marilyn Butler addresses the issue of empire in their ground-breaking political readings of Austen's novels, *The Improvement of the Estate: A Study of Jane Austen's Novels* (Baltimore: Johns Hopkins University Press, 1971) and *Jane Austen and the War of Ideas* (Oxford: Clarendon Press, 1975) respectively, later in the decade Julia Prewitt Brown suggests, in *Jane Austen's Novels: Social Change and Literary Form* (Cambridge, MA: Harvard University Press, 1979), pp. 87-88, that Sir Thomas Bertram's journey to Antigua, and Fanny's interest in it, point to an enclosed national and domestic world that is no longer 'self-sufficient' but marked by 'fear of [political] contamination.' See also Margaret Kirkham's argument, in *Jane Austen:*

Feminism and Fiction (Sussex: Harvester, 1983), pp. 116-20, that Fanny's views on gender might comment more largely on the history of slavery indicated by the title's reference to the Mansfield Decision that abolished slavery in Britain, and the related arguments of Claudia Johnson in *Women, Politics, and the Novel* (Chicago: University of Chicago Press, 1988), pp. 107-108, and Moira Ferguson, '*Mansfield Park*: Slavery, Colonialism, and Gender,' *Oxford Literary Review* 13 (1991), pp. 118-39.

2. Edward Said, *Culture and Imperialism* (New York: Vintage, 1993), p. 84.

3. Susan Fraiman, 'Jane Austen and Edward Said: Gender, Culture, and Imperialism,' in Deidre Lynch, ed., *Janeites: Austen's Disciples and Devotees* (Princeton: Princeton University Press, 2000), pp. 206-23; Katie Trumpener, *Bardic Nationalism: The Romantic Novel and the British Empire* (Princeton: Princeton University Press, 1997), pp. 161-92. See also You-me Park and Rajeswari Sunder Rajan, eds., *The Post-Colonial Jane Austen* (London: Routledge, 2000), especially Clara Tuite, 'Domestic Retrenchment and Imperial Expansion: The Property Plots of *Mansfield Park*,' pp. 93-115.

4. See, variously, Marvin Mudrick, *Jane Austen: Irony as Defence and Discovery* (Berkeley: University of California Press, 1968), p. 166; Butler, *War of Ideas*, pp. 221, 230, 249; Laura G. Mooneyham, *Romance, Language and Education in Jane Austen's Novels* (New York: St Martin's Press, 1988), p. 69. The readings of the novel as a feminist document that predominated in the 1980s also emphasized the role of represented thought and affect. See especially Johnson, *Women, Politics, and the Novel*, p. 96.

5. Mary Lascelles, in her pioneering *Jane Austen and Her Art* (Oxford: Oxford University Press, 1939), pp. 189, 194, highlighted the significance of Fanny's consciousness of time both in the development of the character and in what Lascelles saw as Austen's developing 'technique for using the consciousness of her characters as a means of communication with the reader.'

6. Jane Austen, *Mansfield Park*, ed. James Kinsley (Oxford: Oxford University Press, 1980), p. 9.

7. Said, *Culture and Imperialism*, p. 92; Moira Ferguson, *Colonialism and Gender Relations from Mary Wollstonecraft to Jamaica Kincaid: East Caribbean Connections* (New York: Columbia University Press, 1993), pp. 67, 71-74.

8. Lionel Trilling, *The Opposing Self* (New York: Viking, 1955), p. 218.

9. Clara Tuite, *Romantic Austen: Sexual Politics and the Literary Canon* (Cambridge: Cambridge University Press, 2002), p. 104.

10. Austen, *Mansfield Park*, p. 15. As a discipline, contemporary chemistry was newly systematized. David Knight (in 'Chemistry on an Offshore Island: Britain, 1789-1840,' in Knight and Helge Kragh, eds., *The Making of the Chemist: The Social History of Chemistry in Europe, 1789-1914* (Cambridge: Cambridge University Press, 1998), pp. 101-102) suggests that by the turn of the nineteenth century systematic thinking and synthetic analyses within the discipline of chemistry had ceased to be associated only with 'overweening science' and revolutionary French theory. It influenced even popular textbooks for young ladies, such as Jane Marcet's *Conversations on Chemistry* (London: Longman, 9th edn, 1824), which refers to the 'great change chemistry has undergone since it has become a regular science' (p. 7). The Bertram sisters' tabular conception of the 'Metals' and 'Semi-Metals' reflects this new influence. The reading together of Norse, Greek and Roman legend implied in Austen's reference to 'Heathen Mythology' is part of the prehistory of 'Western civilization' as an Anglocentric concept, inculcated in popular children's literature throughout the nineteenth and early twentieth centuries; see Siân Echard, *Printing the Middle Ages* (Philadelphia: University of Pennsylvania Press, forthcoming 2008).

11. Austen, *Mansfield Park*, p. 8.

12. Homi Bhabha, 'Of Mimicry and Man: The Ambivalence of Colonial Discourse,' in *The Location of Culture* (London: Routledge, 1994), p. 86.

13. Felix Driver, *Geography Militant: Cultures of Exploration and Empire* (Oxford: Blackwell, 2001), pp. 8-20, 50-52.

14. Austen, *Mansfield Park*, pp. 10-11.

15. Austen, *Mansfield Park*, p. 15.

16. James Fordyce, *Sermons to Young Women*, 2 vols. (London: Millar, 1794), Vol. 1, pp. 200-201; Vol. 1, p. 215. See also the insistence of Laetitia Matilda Hawkins (*Letters on the Female Mind, its Powers and Pursuits, Addressed to Miss H. M. Williams, with particular reference to her Letters from France*, 2 vols. (London: Hookham, 1793), Vol. 1, pp. 11, 13) that every 'ornamental science or study' is appropriate to women; Hawkins includes 'geography, natural philosophy, natural history, civil history' and music and drawing among these. Thomas Gisborne, in *An Enquiry into the Duties of the Female Sex* (London: Cadell, 1797), pp. 20-21, is more explicit, dividing polite reading from geographical practices, including

'the acquirements subordinate to navigation; the knowledge indispensable in the wide field of commercial enterprise; the arts of defence, and of attack by land and sea.'

17. Jane Austen, *Pride and Prejudice,* ed. James Kinsley (Oxford: Oxford University Press, 1970), p. 60.

18. Austen, *Mansfield Park,* pp. 412, 422.

19. Austen, *Mansfield Park,* p. 140. John Barrow, *Some Account of the Public Life, and a Selection from the unpublished Writings, of the Earl of Macartney, the latter consisting of extracts from an account of the Russian Empire; a sketch of the political history of Ireland; and a journal of an embassy from the King of Great Britain to the Emperor of China* (London: Cadell, 1807).

20. Austen, *Mansfield Park,* p. 16.

21. When Austen's Miss Tilney wishes to cite the important historians she has read, she names the Scottish Enlightenment stalwarts David Hume and William Robertson (*Northanger Abbey,* ed. John Davie (Oxford: Oxford University Press, 1971), p. 85). See also Margaret Anne Doody, 'Jane Austen's Reading,' in *The Jane Austen Companion,* ed. J. David Grey (New York: Macmillan, 1986), pp. 350-54; Christopher Kent, 'Learning History with, and from, Jane Austen,' in *Jane Austen's Beginnings: The Juvenilia and Lady Susan* (Ann Arbor: UMI, 1989), pp. 59-72. On Enlightenment universal/stadial history, see Ronald L. Meek, *Social Science and the Ignoble Savage* (Cambridge: Cambridge University Press, 1976).

22. Austen, *Mansfield Park,* p. 178.

23. Trumpener, *Bardic Nationalism,* p. 180; Tuite, 'Domestic Retrenchment,' p. 111.

24. Examinations of social and economic status in *Mansfield Park* tend to view the novel as an affirmation of or a brief for the bourgeois improvement of the imperially dependent landed aristocracy, or to view the heroine's anomalous class position in isolation from the matter of the nation and its empire. For the former perspective, see for example Ferguson, *Colonialism,* pp. 66-67; for the latter, see Johnson, *Women, Politics, and the Novel,* pp. 107-108.

25. Austen, *Mansfield Park,* p. 17.

26. Austen, *Mansfield Park,* pp. 1-2.

27. Austen, *Mansfield Park,* p. 15.

28. Austen, *Mansfield Park,* p. 184.

29. Austen, *Mansfield Park,* p. 184.

30. Austen, *Mansfield Park,* p. 178.

31. Austen, *Mansfield Park,* p. 178.

32. Jane Austen, Letter to Cassandra Austen, 24 January 1813, in *Letters,* ed. Deirdre Le Faye (Oxford: Oxford University Press, new edn, 1997), p. 198. That Fanny quotes from a contemporary work from the same publisher, Walter Scott's *Lay of the Last Minstrel* (London: Longman, 1805) suggests that she would have had access to Clarkson's text through her uncle's account with the bookseller.

33. Brian Southam, *Jane Austen and the Navy* (London: Hambledon, 2000), p. 202.

34. Austen, *Mansfield Park,* p. 2.

35. Austen, *Mansfield Park,* p. 2. In the first chapter of *Mansfield Park* (p. 3), Mrs Price is 'preparing for her ninth lying-in' a year before Fanny departs to be adopted by the Bertrams, and she is later described (p. 355) as the 'mother of nine children.' But the list of her named children includes William, Fanny, and Susan, as well as Mary (p. 351), who dies young, 'Betsey [. . .] and John, Richard, Sam, Tom, and Charles' (p. 355). That Mary is five years old when Fanny leaves for Mansfield, and that Charles and Betsey have both 'been born since Fanny's going away,' suggests that the total number of Price children has reached at least eleven, with at least one name going unrecorded.

36. Austen, *Mansfield Park,* pp. 4, 8, 356.

37. See Linda Colley, *Britons: Forging the Nation* (London: Vintage, 1996), pp. 69-71; Benedict Anderson, *Imagined Communities: Reflections on the Origins and Spread of Nationalism* (London: Verso, rev. edn, 1991), pp. 93-94.

38. Austen, *Mansfield Park,* pp. 213, 347.

39. Austen, *Mansfield Park,* p. 3.

40. See Ina Ferris, *The Romantic National Tale and the Question of Ireland* (Cambridge: Cambridge University Press, 2002), pp. 26-37; Mary Poovey, *A History of the Modern Fact: Problems of Knowledge in the Sciences of Wealth and Society* (Chicago: University of Chicago Press, 1998), pp. 120-38; Trumpener, *Bardic Nationalism,* pp. 37-66.

41. See especially Ferris, *The Romantic National Tale,* pp. 3-4, 31-32. Ferris's account is a suggestive supplement to debates on Ireland's status as a colony or a subject of domestic imperialism; see Michael Hechter, *Internal Colonialism: The Celtic Fringe as a Subject of British Colonial Development, 1536-1966* (London: Routledge, 1975); S. J. Connolly, 'Eighteenth-Century Ireland: Colony or Ancien Régime?,' in D. George Boyce and Alan O'Day, *The*

Making of Modern Irish History: Revisionism and the Revisionist Controversy (London: Routledge, 1996), pp. 15-33. The ubiquity of the term 'plantation,' an Anglicization of *colonia,* in contemporary Anglo-Irish historiography implies that Ireland's domestic and colonial status continued, however uneasily, to coexist.

42. Austen, *Mansfield Park,* pp. 431-32.

43. William Galperin, *The Historical Austen* (Philadelphia: University of Pennsylvania Press, 2003), pp. 44-81.

44. Austen, *Mansfield Park,* pp. 187-88.

45. William Gilpin, *Observations Relative Chiefly to Picturesque Beauty, Made in the Year 1772, on Several Parts of England; Particularly the Mountains, and Lakes of Cumberland, and Westmoreland,* 2 vols. (London: Blamire, 1788), Vol. 1, p. xiv.

46. William Wordsworth, 'Lines composed a few miles above Tintern Abbey, on revisiting the Banks of the Wye during a Tour. July 13, 1798,' in *Poems,* ed. Thomas Hutchinson (London: Oxford University Press, 1911), Vol. 1, l. 13. See also Marjorie Levinson, *Wordsworth's Great Period Poems* (Cambridge: Cambridge University Press, 1986), pp. 31-32.

47. Gilpin, *Observations,* Vol. 1, pp. 7-8.

48. Austen, *Mansfield Park,* p. 184.

49. Austen, *Mansfield Park,* p. 189. Fanny's obsessive rememberings, and the way they contrast with Mary's lack of interest while mirroring her reading of the scene as a reflection of herself, complicate Tuite's recent argument, in 'Domestic Retrenchment,' that *Mansfield Park* argues for a bourgeois reform, through Fanny, of a landed aristocracy represented by Mary.

50. Gilpin, *Observations,* Vol. 1, p. 5.

51. Gilpin, *Observations,* Vol. 1, p. 7.

52. Tim Fulford, *Landscape, Liberty and Authority: Poetry, Criticism and Politics from Thomson to Wordsworth* (Cambridge: Cambridge University Press, 1996), p. 142.

53. Fulford, *Landscape, Liberty and Authority,* p. 164; see also Elizabeth K. Helsinger, *Rural Scenes and National Representation: Britain, 1815-1850* (Princeton: Princeton University Press, 1997), pp. 177-79.

54. Wordsworth, 'Tintern Abbey,' ll. 15-20.

55. Debbie Lee, *Slavery and the Romantic Imagination* (Philadelphia: University of Pennsylvania Press, 2002), pp. 29-43, 202.

56. Lee, *Slavery and the Romantic Imagination,* p. 22.

57. Sonia Hofkosh, in *Sexual Politics and the Romantic Author* (Cambridge: Cambridge University Press, 1998), p. 123, points out that Fanny's schoolroom is known as 'the East room,' associating it with the geographic East as well as with the class marginality of the governesses who once occupied it.

58. Austen, *Mansfield Park,* p. 137.

59. Austen, *Mansfield Park,* pp. 213, 270; William does not join the *Thrush* until he gains a lieutenancy, which happens only when Henry Crawford uses his connections in the admiralty.

60. See Thomas Richards, *Knowledge and the Fantasy of Empire* (London: Verso, 1993), p. 11; see also Anderson, *Imagined Communities,* p. 181.

61. Levinson, *Wordsworth's Great Period Poems,* pp. 14-57; Alan Liu, 'Local Transcendence: Cultural Criticism, Postmodernism, and the Romanticism of Detail,' *Representations* 32 (1990), p. 76.

62. See, respectively, Lee, *Slavery and the Romantic Imagination,* David Simpson, *Romanticism, Nationalism, and the Revolt against Theory* (Chicago: University of Chicago Press, 1993).

63. See Clifford Siskin, *The Work of Writing: Literature and Social Change in Britain, 1700-1830* (Baltimore: Johns Hopkins University Press, 1998).

64. Austen, *Mansfield Park,* p. 363.

65. Siskin, *The Work of Writing,* p. 218.

66. On British readers, see Ferris, *The Romantic National Tale,* p. 18. Trumpener (*Bardic Nationalism,* pp. 37-66) and Joep Leerssen (*Remembrance and Imagination: Patterns in the Historical and Literary Representation of Ireland in the Nineteenth Century* (Cork: Cork University Press, 1997) and *Mere Irish and Fíor-Ghael: Studies in the Idea of Irish Nationality, Its Development and Literary Expression prior to the Nineteenth Century* (Cork: Cork University Press, 2nd edn, 1997), pp. 329-76) document the large and diverse range of these texts that appeared during the Romantic period.

67. Charlotte Brooke, *Reliques of Irish Poetry: Consisting of Heroic Poems, Odes, Elegies, and Songs, Translated into English Verse* (Dublin, 1789), pp. x-xxiii; Charles Vallancey, *Collectanea de Rebus Hibernicis,* 6 vols. (Dublin: Marchbank).

68. Jane Austen, Letter to C. Austen, 17-18 January 1809, in *Letters,* p. 166; Letter to Anna Austen, 28 September 1814, in *Letters,* p. 278; *Mansfield Park,* p. 77; Letter to C. Austen, 18 June 1811, in *Letters,* p. 194.

69. Trumpener, *Bardic Nationalism,* pp. 37-66.

70. See my 'The National Tale and Allied Genres, 1770s-1840s,' in John Wilson Foster, ed., *The Cambridge Companion to the Irish Novel* (Cambridge: Cambridge University Press, 2006), pp. 49-54.

71. Trumpener, *Bardic Nationalism,* pp. 45-46.

72. Sydney Owenson, *The Wild Irish Girl,* ed. Kathryn Kirkpatrick (Oxford: Oxford University Press, 1999), pp. 42-44.

73. Maria Edgeworth, *The Absentee,* ed. Heidi Thomson and Kim Walker (London: Penguin, 1999), p. 137.

74. Owenson, *The Wild Irish Girl,* p. 174.

75. See also Yoon Sun Lee, 'A Divided Inheritance: Scott's Antiquarian Novel and the British Nation,' *ELH* 64 (1997), pp. 537-67 [p. 563].

76. Homi Bhabha, 'Introduction: Locations of Culture,' in *The Location of Culture,* p. 11.

77. Leerssen, *Remembrance and Imagination,* pp. 37, 49.

78. Leerssen, *Remembrance and Imagination,* p. 50.

79. Yoon Sun Lee, 'A Divided Inheritance.'

80. Sydney Owenson, *Patriotic Sketches, Written in Connaught* (London: Phillips, 1807), pp. 2-3, 5, 6.

81. Owenson, *Patriotic Sketches,* pp. 7-8. Richard C. Sha, in *The Visual and Verbal Sketch in British Romanticism* (Philadelphia: University of Pennsylvania Press, 1998), pp. 132-33, sees Owenson's comments as a revolutionary threat to Britain; I read them as a reminder, heralding Austen's in *Mansfield Park,* that the disparate pieces that make up empires have their own complex, continuing histories.

82. Austen, *Mansfield Park,* pp. 137, 187.

Massimiliano Morini (essay date 2009)

SOURCE: Morini, Massimiliano. "Narrative Opacity in *Mansfield Park.*" *Jane Austen's Narrative Techniques: A Stylistic and Pragmatic Analysis.* Farnham: Ashgate, 2009. 50-60. Print.

[In the following essay, Morini presents a "de-stylized" version of portions of Mansfield Park *to distinguish between Austen's own voice and the voice of the community in which she writes.]*

Evaluation, Style, Choice

Evaluation is the 'slant' given to a story or a piece of information by the teller or the reporter. It is as pervasive as it is elusive, but when evaluative elements can be isolated, they tell us a lot about the speaker's, or writer's, personality and ideology. As Thompson and Hunston write, one of the main uses of evaluation is 'to express the speaker's or writer's opinion, and in doing so to reflect the value system of that person and their community' (Thompson and Hunston 2000: 6). In this sense, evaluation can be equated with what stylistics calls '(ideological) point of view,' or 'style.' According to such stylisticians as Leech, Short, and Fowler, analyzing a style means distinguishing between a noumenal 'world as it is' and the 'stylistic slant' added by the author or narrator—i.e., evaluation. Analyzing Austen's style, of course—especially in such masterpieces of indirection as ***MP*** [***Mansfield Park***] and ***E*** [***Emma***]—means engaging with the author in a game of epistemic hide-and-seek in which no stylistic fly can be disentangled with absolute certainty from the web of 'evaluative opacity.'

In their seminal and influential *Style in Fiction,* first published in 1981, G. N. Leech and M. H. Short drew a distinction between monism and dualism in interpreting style.[1] They were fully conscious of the artificial nature of the distinction, yet they were also convinced it provided critics with two different and useful ways of looking at (different) texts. In a monistic view of style, a literary work is written in the only possible manner in which it could have been written, and if it had been written in a different manner it would be a different text; while in a dualistic view, each work contains a certain matter which could have been set down in another slightly different manner. Artificial as it evidently is, the distinction serves to identify and analyze two different classes of texts. The style of Joyce's *Finnegans Wake* is *sui generis,* and can hardly be modified without undergoing a complete alteration, without becoming something else: in this case the full gist of the novel—or whatever *Finnegans Wake* is—resides in its unique style. The style of Jane Austen's novels, on the other hand, is characteristic, but can be successfully set against other similar styles, and alternatives may be identified which, if chosen, would not have wholly modified the gist, the content, or the 'story'—whatever these are. Prosaically, and approximately, what happens in *Finnegans Wake* cannot be thought in different words, whereas what happens in ***E*** or ***MP*** can. Of course, nothing remains exactly the same when an element is shifted or altered: the 'fictional element,' as Leech and Short call it, 'is only invariant in a special sense; the author is free to order his universe as he wants, but for the purposes of stylistic variation we are only interested in those choices of language which do not involve changes in the fictional universe' (Leech and Short 1981/1983: 37).

It is only in a dualistic epistemic system that the notion of style as choice becomes materially evident. For in such a system, 'what an author *has* written' can be set 'against the background of what he *might have* written, had he failed to apply certain transformations, or chosen to apply others instead' (Leech and Short 1981/1983: 22). Style, therefore, can be calculated and isolated, provided that we are able to deduct what *might have* been written from what *has* been written. This view, and this analytical method, postulate the existence of two different semantic dimensions, one in which the text is actualized as it is, and another in which it is stripped of something identifiable as the author's 'style.' Leech and Short drew a further distinction, as artificial and as useful as the first, between *sense* and *significance,* the latter being the sum of the former plus what they called 'stylistic value':

> Let us use SENSE to refer to the basic logical, conceptual, paraphrasable meaning, and SIGNIFICANCE to refer to the total of what is communicated to the world by a given sentence or text . . . SENSE + STYLISTIC VALUE = (total) SIGNIFICANCE.
>
> (Leech and Short 1981/1983: 23)

If we take an author's 'fictional universe' (i.e., what is described stripped of the attributes of style) as a fixed, given quantity, we can disentangle the *sense* from the *significance* of the author's words. Sense resides in the fictional universe itself, not as it is evaluated but 'as it is'; while significance is that world as perceived by all those who participate in it (narrator, characters). Style, or rather 'stylistic value,' provides a way of looking at a fictional universe, an 'evaluative' point of view, and is to be identified with all the colours and impressions which are added and give shape to that universe-in-itself. Of course, the only way of identifying that 'stylistic value,' and therefore of distinguishing between sense and significance, is accepting that we cannot escape Spitzer's 'philological circle' (Leech and Short 1981/1983: 13): the insights we have are stimulated by (linguistic, stylistic) observation, but observation in turn is guided by our insights as well as by our prejudices.[2]

Even though we are trapped in the philological circle, and even though any distinction between sense and significance is bound to be arbitrary (but not random or accidental), there is no doubt that in any literary work of art, and in certain works more than in others, a number of linguistic expressions and constructions are identifiable through which a neutral, pre-stylistic 'fictional universe' becomes the author's, or the narrator's, world. In literary texts such as Jane Austen's novels, which work by subtle accumulation of details rather than by sweeping the reader along or constantly disappointing his/her expectations, these 'stylistic markers' are perhaps more evident than elsewhere. Though ultimately (i.e., in a monistic system) no narrative brick can be shifted from ***E*** or ***MP*** as well as from Joyce's *Finnegans Wake,* in ***E*** or in ***MP*** it is easier to isolate the carriers of 'stylistic value,' to identify 'consistent structural options [which], agreeing in cutting the presented world to one pattern or another, give rise to an impression of world-view, . . . a "mind-style"' (Fowler 1977: 76). Fowler's concept of 'mind-style' can be applied to single characters, to a narrator, or even to an author-figure stretching across a number of literary works originated by the same person. Living authors like James Joyce create different mind-styles (and therefore different fictional authors) for each work they write, while the mind-style created by the likes of Jane Austen only undergoes small modifications from one novel to another.

Elsewhere, Roger Fowler drew a tripartite distinction between psychological, spatio-temporal, and ideological point of view, and identified 'mind-style' with the latter (Fowler 1986/1990: 127).[3] From this equation, and from Leech and Short's separation of 'sense' from 'significance,' we derive the idea of style as an ideological, evaluative quantity, the colours and impressions superimposed on the neutral 'fictional world' when it is filtered through a character, a narrator, a (fictional, implied) author. In the traditional view of rhetoric, especially after Ramus's revolution, style is seen as an ornamental layer added to the irreplaceable kernel (and in this traditional view, translation is always possible because only this ornamental layer is replaced). In the (dualistic) view of modern stylistics, style is still an added layer, but one which gives the fictional world a coating of impressions and opinions, i.e., an ideological dimension. Of course, 'ideology' is here intended in its broadest possible sense: not as a system of political beliefs, but as the totality of cultural, social, and personal beliefs brought to bear on a fictional universe. In this broad sense, ideology, evaluation, and style are one and the same thing: the angle from which something is seen.

Once ideology, evaluation, and style are conflated, however, a fundamental problem remains: how can evaluative, ideological 'stylistic markers' be identified with any certainty? In *Linguistic Criticism,* Fowler identified two 'fairly distinct ways' in which 'point of view on the ideological plane may be manifested.' On the one hand there are modal expressions, which 'come from a fairly specialized section of the vocabulary, and are easy to spot.' On the other hand there are other parts of language which are harder to locate, and which convey 'world-view' more 'indirectly but nevertheless convincingly':

> Modality . . . is the grammar of explicit comment, the means by which people express their degree of commitment to the truth of the propositions they utter, and their views on the desirability or otherwise of the states of affairs referred to. Respectively, 'Sir Arthur *certainly* lost his fortune at the gaming table' and 'His gambling was *disastrous* for the family' . . . The forms of modal expression include:
>
> modal auxiliaries . . .
>
> *modal adverbs or sentence adverbs*: certainly, probably, surely, perhaps, etc. . . .
>
> *evaluative adjectives and adverbs*: lucky, luckily, fortunate, regrettably, and many others.
>
> *verbs of knowledge, prediction, evaluation*: seem, believe, guess, foresee, approve, dislike, etc.

> *generic sentences*: these are generalized propositions claiming universal truth and usually cast in a syntax reminiscent of proverbs or scientific laws . . .
>
> There is a perhaps even more interesting sense in which language indicates ideology, or, in fiction, the world-views of author or characters. The modal devices just discussed make explicit (though sometimes ironic) *announcements* of beliefs; other parts of language, indirectly but nevertheless convincingly, may be *symptomatic* of world-view: it has traditionally been assumed in stylistics that the different ways people express their thoughts indicate, consciously or unconsciously, their personalities and attitudes.
>
> (Fowler 1986/1990: 131-2)

If modal expressions are more explicit, and therefore easier to spot, isolating other stylistic-evaluative expressions is harder and inevitably more arbitrary (cf. Chapter 1). Here the philological circle becomes a tangible prison, and we run the risk of finding nothing that we did not set out looking for. But our search, however personal, will always be dictated by the text we deal with, which will present us with continuities and discontinuities in order to impress its stylistic fabric on our investigating eye. We will look for significant elisions and repetitions, and we will stop at those points in the narrative when something could have been said in a markedly different manner. In the terms of information theory, we will keep in mind that 'information-content varies inversely with probability' (Lyons 1968: 89): whenever we find an unlikely expression, a choice which evokes a more likely, normal alternative, we will suspect that we are in the presence of a relevant stylistic feature. In our analysis of the initial orientation of ***MP***, we will see that Mrs Bertram is pronounced by the narrator to have 'captivated' Sir Thomas—where 'captivated' is characterized by its improbability in relation with 'married,' and is therefore informationally marked. It is such linguistic wordings, as well as modal expressions, that we will search thoroughly in our quest for style.

Evaluation and Style in the Orientation of *Mansfield Park*

In Jane Austen's novels, it is not easy to isolate all informationally marked expressions, because they can be figuratively represented as small waves disturbing the surface of a calm, oily sea. The fictional world of Austen's country houses is described by her narrators in a quiet voice and in a predictable manner, except when a single unforeseen epithet, a noun or a verb strangely misplaced, jolt the reader's senses awake and warn him/her that something is amiss, that he/she might be in the presence of a crucial stylistic feature. Also, compared with the works written by more rootless, cosmopolitan writers, Jane Austen's novels neatly show the connection between style and ideology, because almost any remarkable stylistic feature in ***E*** or ***MP*** refers us back in a very straightforward manner to the social and cultural beliefs of early nineteenth-century provincial gentry. When we are told that a woman 'captivates' a man, we immediately recognize some of those beliefs, an integral part of that ideology.

There is, however, a problem with these stylistic-evaluative markers in Jane Austen's novels—one which makes them so easy to read on the surface and so difficult to scan in depth: though we can easily recognize many of those markers, it is never clear how much the single characters or, above all, the narrator endorse the beliefs they represent. It is Austen's celebrated 'irony,' or what we have termed the 'evaluative opacity' of her narrative constructions (cf. Chapters 1, 2).

In all of Austen's novels, and more subtly in ***E*** and ***MP***, the narrator by turns endorses, reverses, subverts, ventriloquizes. When the narrator opens ***P&P*** [***Pride and Prejudice***] by stating, deadpan, that 'It is a truth universally acknowledged, that a single man in possession of a good fortune must be in want of a wife,' we may be tempted to take this statement at face value: but the rest of ***P&P*** leaves us in doubt as to whether the narrator speaks with, or distances him/herself from, what we will henceforth call the 'village voice.'

In the *incipit* of ***MP***, the story of a family (the general 'orientation' of the novel) is told in about 800 words which are packed with significant stylistic-evaluative markers. The narrator is apparently telling a very simple story of marriages, family arguments, and reconciliation—three sisters marry: the first marries a rich man, the second marries a man of middling fortunes, the third marries a good-for-nothing Lieutenant of Marines; as a consequence of this disparity of fate and fortune, the three sisters are severed, and then brought together by the practical difficulties of the third—but these markers invest that simple story with a whole consistent world-view. Once this world-view is recognized and made explicit, the problem remains of assessing the evaluative position of the narrator him/herself. And though we can never definitively fix that position, it will add to our understanding of Austen's style to accept and verify that it cannot be fixed.

In order to appreciate Austen's style, an attempt is made in what follows at producing a 'de-stylized' version of the *incipit*, and therefore at separating sense and significance, a neutral fictional universe from the world as seen and evaluated by the narrator. It is of course impossible to re-create such a world, for the very simple reason that it does not exist. Yet, just as creating an artificial language called 'Proto-German' served the purpose of studying the developments of natural languages, creating an artificial fictional universe 'before' the addition of Austen's style can tell us something about that style.

The re-written text is marked as follows: whenever a 'de-stylized' variant is offered, Austen's original text is given in square brackets (e.g. [only]); if the neutral, de-stylized version requires the substitution of textual material, the substitutional words are in italics (e.g. *married* replacing [had the good luck to captivate]). Also, Austen's text is underlined when euphemistic or ironic (e.g. a woman of very tranquil feelings), and written in small capitals when it ventriloquizes the 'village voice' (e.g. IN THE COMMON PHRASE).

The Orientation of Mansfield Park *Rewritten*

> About thirty years ago, Miss Maria Ward of Huntingdon, with [only] seven thousand pounds, [had the good luck to captivate] *married* Sir Thomas Bertram, of Mansfield Park, in the county of Northampton, and [to be thereby raised to] *acquired* the rank of a baronet's lady, with all the comforts and consequences of an handsome house and large income. ALL HUNTINGDON [EXCLAIMED] *COMMENTED* ON THE [GREATNESS OF THE] MATCH, and her uncle, the lawyer, [himself], [allowed] *declared* her to be at least three thousand pounds short of any [equitable] claim to it. She had two sisters [to be benefited] *who could profit* by her [elevation] *marriage*; and such of their acquaintance as thought Miss Ward and Miss Frances quite as handsome as Miss Maria, did not scruple to predict their marrying with almost equal [advantage] *satisfaction.* But there certainly are not so many men of large fortune in the world, as there are pretty women to [deserve] *marry* them. Miss Ward, at the end of half a dozen years, [found herself obliged to be attached to] *formed an attachment with* the Rev. Mr. Norris, a friend of her brother-in-law, with scarcely any private fortune, and Miss Frances [fared yet worse] *found a husband with no fortune at all.* Miss Ward's match, indeed, [when it came to the point,] was [not contemptible] *fairly satisfactory,* Sir Thomas being happily able to give his friend an income in the living of Mansfield, and Mr. and Mrs. Norris began their [career of conjugal felicity] *marriage* with very little less than a thousand a year. But Miss Frances married, IN THE COMMON PHRASE, to [disoblige] *disappoint* her family, and by fixing on a Lieutenant of Marines, without education, fortune, or connections, did it very thoroughly. She could hardly have made a more [untoward] *unhappy* choice. Sir Thomas Bertram had interest, which, [from principle as well as pride,] from a general wish of doing right, and a desire of seeing all that were connected with him in [situations of respectability] *satisfactory situations,* he would have been glad to exert for [the advantage of Lady Bertram's sister] *his sister-in-law*; but her husband's profession was such as no interest could reach; and before he had time to devise any other method of assisting them, an absolute breach between the sisters had taken place. It was the [natural] result of the [conduct] *opinions* of each party, and such as a very [imprudent] *unsatisfactory* marriage almost always produces. To save herself from [useless remonstrance] *criticism,* Mrs. Price never wrote to her family on the subject till actually married. Lady Bertram, who was a woman of very tranquil feelings, and a temper remarkably easy and indolent, would have [contented herself with merely giving up her sister, and thinking no more of the matter] *given up her sister, and thought no more of the matter*: but Mrs. Norris had a spirit of activity, which could not be satisfied till she had written a long and angry letter to Fanny, to point out the [folly] *wrongness* of her conduct, and [threaten her with] *explain to her* all its possible ill consequences. Mrs. Price in her turn was injured and angry; and an answer which comprehended each sister in its bitterness, and bestowed such very disrespectful reflections on the pride of Sir Thomas, as Mrs. Norris could not possibly keep to herself, put an end to all intercourse between them for a considerable period.
>
> Their homes were so distant, and the circles in which they moved so distinct, as almost to preclude the means of ever hearing of each other's existence during the eleven following years, or at least to make it very wonderful to Sir Thomas, that Mrs. Norris should ever have it in her power to tell them, as she now and then did in an angry voice, that Fanny had got another child. By the end of eleven years, however, Mrs. Price could no longer [afford to] cherish pride or resentment, or to lose one [connection] *tie* which might possibly assist her. A large and still increasing family, an husband disabled for active service, but not the less equal to company and good liquor, and a very small income to supply their wants, made her eager to regain the friends she had [so carelessly sacrificed] *lost,* and she addressed Lady Bertram in a letter which spoke so much contrition and despondence, such a [superfluity] *number* of children, and such a want of almost every thing else, as could not but dispose them all to a reconciliation. She was preparing for her ninth lying-in, and after [bewailing] *complaining of* the circumstance, and [imploring] *asking for* their countenance as sponsors to the expected child, she [could not conceal] *wrote* how important she felt they might be to the future maintenance of the eight already in being. Her eldest was a boy of ten years old, a fine spirited fellow who longed to be out in the world; [but what could she do?] *but how*? Was there any chance of his being hereafter useful to Sir Thomas in the concerns of his West Indian property? No situation would be beneath him—or what did Sir Thomas think of Woolwich? or how could a boy be sent out to the East?
>
> The letter was not unproductive. It re-established peace and kindness. Sir Thomas sent friendly advice and professions, Lady Bertram dispatched money and baby-linen, and Mrs. Norris wrote the letters.
>
> (***MP*** 3-5)

Stylistic-Evaluative Enquiry: Marriage and Economics

If Austen's *incipit* is compared with its de-stylized version, a thematic question immediately meets the eye (is foregrounded, in stylistic terms). The main topic of these 800 words is marriage, but marriage is not described in all its aspects, or in the aspects we most readily associate with it (i.e., affection/disaffection, attraction/repulsion, love/hate). Its social and financial causes and consequences are openly stated and anatomized, as if ***MP*** were an essay in cultural materialism rather than a novel.[4] In order to grasp the exceptionality of such analytic precision, we can compare it with the relative reticence of Elizabeth Inchbald's *A Simple Story* (1791), in a passage which contains in brief a similar story of socially unacceptable marriage:

> The child of a once beloved sister, who married a young officer against her brother's consent, was at the age of three years left an orphan, destitute of every support but from his uncle's generosity: but though Dorriforth maintained, he

> would never see him. Miss Milner, whose heart was a receptacle for the unfortunate, no sooner was told the melancholy history of Mr. and Mrs. Rushbrook, the parents of the child, than she longed to behold the innocent inheritor of her guardian's resentment, and took Miss Woodley with her to see the boy . . . determined to take young Rushbrook to town and present him to his uncle.
>
> (Inchbald 1791/1967: 34)

Though in this case confessional differences may also be imputable for the breach (the brother is a Roman Catholic, whereas the husband is probably a Protestant), there is no doubt that Dorriforth's displeasure mainly arises from social and financial questions (as we understand by the fact that he has to provide for the child whose existence he deplores). But these social and financial questions are covered by a sheen of paternalistic sentimentalism which muddles the matter for all those who are unfamiliar with late eighteenth-century social conventions. In ***MP*** the tables are turned: sentiment is momentarily erased in order to introduce the material conditions in which the characters' thoughts, actions and feelings will unfold. Austen's speaker, however, is not a sociologist but a narrator: the dissection of marriage is obtained not through direct description and definition, but by the subtle insertion of modal expressions or other stylistic markers.

Marriage is described as a hunting campaign, which is conducted by women at the expense of men: the narrator does not simply say, as Inchbald's narrator does, that Miss Maria Ward 'married' Sir Thomas Bertram, but that she 'had the good luck to captivate' him. 'Captivate' can be set against 'fascinate,' and other similar verbs ('charm,' 'enchant,' 'bewitch') which share its main semantic content: it is not chosen by chance, or at any rate the choice is significant in a sentence whose theme and grammatical subject is defined by geographical origin ('of Huntingdon') and financial situation ('with only seven thousand pounds'). The choice is significant because 'captivate' makes us think of 'captive,' and what follows is a comparative description of three sisters' failures and successes in hunting for a quarry. What women need in order to catch a big quarry is, apart from money, beauty, though elsewhere (in ***MP*** and other novels) we are reminded that 'accomplishments' may also be of importance. In the same paragraph, Austen's narrator adds that 'there certainly are not so many men of fortune in the world, as there are pretty women to *deserve* them'—where that 'deserve,' as opposed to 'marry' or even 'catch,' implies that prettiness is a sufficient quality to obtain money in the form of a husband (once again, not love or affection).

Living as most of us do in a society which, at least superficially, prizes love over social and financial convenience, we might be tempted to see moral squalor in such a depiction. But these simplistic ethical considerations are outside the interests of Austen's narrator, who only describes things as they are. Husband-hunting is an absolute necessity for all those women who are not themselves in possession of a big fortune (and since money passed from male hand to male hand, such figures were rare): Miss Ward, the second (but eldest) sister, does not merely 'form an attachment' with Mr Norris, but finds herself 'obliged to be attached' to him. Finding herself in the impossibility of catching a quarry as big as Sir Bertram, she hunts around for the second best, and must, is obliged to, content herself; and the polysemous nature of 'obliged' tells us that she must also be thankful, for she might have 'fared worse'—she might have incurred the third sister's fate.

Marriage is, as Austen's narrator tactfully reminds us, a 'career' (Mr and Mrs Norris begin their 'career of conjugal felicity with very little less than a thousand a year'), and there are very few women who can afford not to embark on it. A brilliant career brings social respect and admiration (and envy, of course, behind the curtains), whereas an indifferent career brings a continual struggle against the tide of domestic difficulties, and a bad career record brings financial hardship *and* social censure. While a good match is looked at as the outcome of 'luck' and is 'exclaimed' upon by the neighbours, a bad match is looked down on as 'untoward' and 'imprudent,' sheer 'folly,' an occasion for 'remonstrance' and threats (Mrs Norris writes to her sister to 'threaten her with all its possible ill consequences'). By choosing the wrong husband, a woman positions herself outside the happy circle within which 'situations of respectability' are to be found. In ***MP,*** the centre of that circle is Sir Bertram, the unmoving *primum mobile* of this small genteel world: all the other social and financial positions are evaluated by his standards; and it is not by chance that the sentence which contains 'situations of respectability' (as opposed to a more neutral 'satisfactory situations') has the baronet as its interpersonal and ideational subject.

What makes a marriage a good 'match' is money, though here as elsewhere, we are reminded in passing that money does not always smell the same, for certain social qualities (epitomized in the term 'respectability') tend to give it a somewhat better flavour.[5] The 'greatness' of a match is measured by the social and financial disparity between the parties. Maria Ward/Lady Bertram has made a very good match, for she had '*only* seven thousand pounds' to her name—the modal adverb signalling a disparity between initial and final social position. She has been '*raised* to the rank of a baronet's lady'—an 'elevation' potentially bringing 'advantage' and benefits ('She had two sisters *to be benefited* by her *elevation*') to other members of the family. At the other end of the spectrum, Miss Frances's choice does not bring any social or financial advantages—the most tangible economic outcome being a 'superfluity' of children which does nothing but add to the 'despondence' of her situation.

What is the narrator's position in relation to all this? We cannot tell with absolute certainty, and that is what makes Austen's mature works, in some respects, like so many detective novels. Since the narrator does not give us clear indications as to his/her evaluative position, his/her approval or disapproval of this or that character/behaviour/situation, it is only with the unfolding of the plot that we can infer something about the general ideological (and ethical) framework of the novel. After the first reading, we can go back to the beginning and understand things we had not been told openly in the first place. Though the narrator tends to remain aloof from the facts he/she narrates and the conversational exchanges he/she reports, those facts and those exchanges cast a revealing light on the narrator's aloofness.[6]

That aloofness, however, can never be complete,[7] and a wry smile—whether of mirth, condescension, or disapproval, it is hard to say—shows through the cracks of impassivity. For one thing, the selection of 'stylistic markers' is, of course, far from neutral. By choosing to present marriage as it were on a dissecting table, ready for the reader's inspection, the narrator breaches a social convention which made it distasteful and tactless to speak openly of financial matters. We should remind ourselves that Austen's characters never (or almost never, for some of these characters *are* tactless; cf. Chapter 4) speak as her narrators do: in ***E,*** when the eponymous heroine rejects Mr Elton, who in turn rejects Miss Smith, each of the two rejections is based on the assumption that there is a social and economic disparity which is never openly stated (Cf. Chapter 6). Thus, in ***MP*** as elsewhere, the narrator is breaching a social norm he/she knows very well, in order to show what lies behind the curtain of 'social respectability.'

Also, in this initial orientation there are a couple of passages in which the narrator seems to distance him/herself from the ideological world he/she is presenting to us. When we read that 'All Huntingdon exclaimed on the greatness of the match,' and that 'Miss Frances married, in the common phrase, to disoblige her family,' we hear the village voice, not the narrator's. At two crucial points in the narrative, where the most advantageous and the most disadvantageous matches are described, the narrator prefers not to speak in his/her own voice—which does not tell us what his/her position is, but leaves us groping in the dark for a clear evaluation of what we are told.

Style and Cohesion

A comparison between Austen's *incipit* and its de-stylized version makes the theme of marriage as a social and economic institution stand out in bold relief: but pointing out what is foregrounded is by no means the only way of discovering what a text or a portion of text is about. The theme can also be identified by tracing the lexical nets innervating the text, as actualized by word repetition, by the use of different forms of the same root, or by the accretion of synonyms, near-synonyms, and lexical items belonging to the same semantic area.

All these phenomena belong to the field of 'lexical cohesion,' as defined by Halliday and Hasan in *Cohesion in English.* After noticing how lexical items can function much as grammatical ties in making a text cohesive, Halliday and Hasan grade these cohesive lexical items according to their degree of differentiation from one another, thus creating a scale which displays on one end sheer repetition, and on the other end what the two scholars call 'collocation.' Collocation, in this case, is defined not so much by the syntagmatic company words keep, but by their paradigmatic relations with other words on the semantic level. Halliday and Hasan shrink from classifying 'the various meaning relations that are involved' (Halliday and Hasan 1976: 287); but that 'collocation' here means 'semantic nearness' is made evident both by the word-chains used as examples (mountaineering/Yosemite/summit peaks/climb/ridge) and by the recapitulatory table for lexical cohesion:

Type of lexical cohesion:	Referential relation:
I. Reiteration	
a. same word (repetition)	i. same referent
b. synonym (or near-synonym)	ii. inclusive
c. superordinate	iii. exclusive
d. general word	iv. unrelated
II. Collocation	

(Halliday and Hasan 1976: 288)

In the three paragraphs making up the *incipit* under discussion, the study of lexical cohesion leads us to the same conclusions as the study of 'foregrounded' evaluative stylistic markers. While the word 'marriage' appears only once (and is arguably substituted, on two more occasions, by 'elevation' and above all 'career of conjugal felicity'), there are words or different forms of the same root that are repeated up to three times, and all these words belong to semantic fields which we could define as 'financial matters' and 'social matters.' As far as money is concerned, while the actual word appears only once, there are three occurrences each for 'fortune' and 'income,' two occurrences for 'pounds,' and these are supplemented by the occurrence of 'maintenance,' 'concerns,' and 'property.' In the field of 'social matters,' 'connections' features alongside 'connected' and 'connection,' as well as 'rank,' 'profession,' 'career,' 'respectability,' and 'interest' (the personal relationship that one can exploit in order to further one's or someone else's career). It is to be noted that most of these lexical items are directly connected with the theme of marriage, in the sense that they are used either to denote or to define the pursuit of a husband or the married state. By contrast, in Austen's quasi-sociological style, lexical items related to the semantic field of sentiment ('love,' 'affection,' 'attraction,' etc.) are virtually absent. The only reference to sentiments akin to love is to 'peace and kindness.' It comes at the end of the passage, and is put into perspective by all that has been said so far and by the narrator's catalogue of how the two more fortunate sisters and Sir Bertram materially express that kindness and celebrate that peace:

> The letter was not unproductive. It re-established peace and kindness. Sir Thomas sent friendly advice and professions, Lady Bertram dispatched money and baby-linen, and Mrs. Norris wrote the letters.

Stylistic Symmetry: A Tale of Three Sisters

MP begins like a fairy-tale or a parable, by telling the story of three sisters[8] who start from roughly the same situation (lower-upper-middle class upbringing—as Orwell would say; Orwell 1937/1997: 113)—some money but not a lot, good looks) but find themselves, at the end of their husband-hunting period, with very different game in their bag. It is a perfect tripartite symmetry, reversed and completed at the end of the novel by the marriage of Fanny and Edmund, i.e., of the unfortunate sister's daughter and the privileged sister's son.[9] It is interesting to note how it seems to be this very symmetry—and the different positions held in society by the three sisters—that shapes their individual characters, rather than the reverse. This is the effect of the narrator first giving us a detailed account of material conditions, and then introducing the characters themselves.

This tripartite symmetry is realized in the initial orientation by the insertion of stylistic-evaluative markers which immediately sprawl the three sisters on their respective hierarchical social pins. As a result of her ability to 'captivate' Sir Thomas, Lady Bertram does not simply acquire a title, but is '*raised to the rank* of a baronet's lady.' Her 'good luck' is underlined by the surprised reactions of her uncle and her community, whose comments show that 'elevation' is perceived as a small breach in the fabric of society, to be marvelled at but also justified (her uncle allows her 'to be at least three thousand pounds short of any *equitable* claim to it'). In Austen's world, those who seek to better their position, by marriage or other means, are looked down upon as social climbers. On the other hand, when the climb reaches the summit, the breach mends itself by its own consequences—the panacea of 'rank' applying the plaster of admiration to the wound of envy.

The other two sisters fare worse than Lady Bertram, and differently from one another. The eldest sister finds herself 'obliged to be attached' to the Reverend Mr Norris—a fact and an expression which, as we have seen, tell us a lot about the condition of early nineteenth-century women. By fixing on a relatively poor parson, Mrs Norris is enrolled, or remains, in the middle ranks of society, or in the lower ranks of country gentry, only a step higher than Miss Bates in ***E***: her match is described as 'not contemptible,' a litotes indicating the short distance between her fate and Mrs Price's. The marriage with the passionless Rev. Norris is described as a 'career of conjugal felicity,' where 'career' suggests hard labour, and 'felicity' a more domestic feeling than 'happiness' would perhaps entail. Mrs Norris's mean and self-centred temperament is suited to (or a consequence of) her married and, later, widowed condition: a woman in her position has to struggle if she does not want to be socially relegated, and one needs money and leisure in order to be disinterested and open-minded.

Mrs Norris's liminal social condition is further underlined by a cohesive element of 'comparative reference' (Halliday and Hasan 1976: 39) 'evaluatively' linking her plight with Mrs Price's. The third sister is said to have 'fared yet worse' than Mrs Norris, thus implying that if Mrs Price's marriage is a downfall, Mrs Norris's is not very far from being contemptible. In Mrs Price we can observe the fate awaiting all (gentle) women who make an 'imprudent marriage,' an 'untoward choice,' who marry 'to disoblige [their] family.' 'Disoblige' is once again an element of cohesion with Mrs Norris's story (Mrs Norris has been 'obliged' to marry a man, also in order to 'oblige' those social norms which are embodied in the familial institution). The choice is 'untoward,' i.e., 'unfortunate,' but also 'unforeseen' and 'unseemly.' It breaches the master law of bourgeois behaviour, i.e., prudence. As a consequence of her imprudence and 'folly,' Mrs Price is cast out from the family, or is at least forced, by her relatives as well as by the circumstances, to humiliate herself in order to be included again after having preemptively excluded herself. The terms in which the 'reconciliation' of the three sisters is described leave us in no doubt that it is only financial factors, and not sororal affection, that lead Mrs Price to make the first move: she can 'no longer *afford* to cherish pride or resentment,' because she is saddled with 'a large and still increasing family' and 'an husband disabled for active service, but not the less equal to company and good liquor.' She needs help, but she is in no position to ask for it, and must beg for it ('imploring'). With a masterstroke of ventriloquism, the narrator incorporates into his/her discourse a stretch of a letter from Mrs Price, where a modal verb is used for the sake of understatement, but presented to the reader as an indicator of how desperate the sender must be ('she *could not conceal* how important she felt they might be').

As observed in the previous sections, the narrator's position is not openly stated, and readers must largely rely, to place their sympathies and antipathies, on the juxtaposition of facts. There are, of course, the stylistic-evaluative markers I have bracketed to show us how the dominant social ideology influences characters' actions: and there are some euphemistic expressions (which I have underlined) whose surface meaning is disproved or reversed by their co-text, and whose deep, ironical meaning casts the light of opinion on the darkness of events.

These expressions are apportioned to all three sisters, reflecting their social positions and their temperaments. Lady Bertram is said to be 'a woman of very tranquil feelings, and a temper remarkably easy and indolent'—where the negative connotations of 'indolent' are counterbalanced by the positive aura of 'tranquil' and 'easy.' When we learn, however, that she would have '*contented herself* with *merely* giving up her sister, and *thinking no more of the matter,*' we begin to suspect that her tranquillity, easiness and indolence are not as harmless as they might appear. We are faced with something akin to Wordsworth's 'savage torpor'—a passivity which is actively capable of hurting others. As for Mrs Norris, we are told that she has a spirit of 'activity'—but in the course of a few lines (she writes 'a long and angry letter to Fanny, to point out the *folly* of her conduct, and *threaten* her with all its possible ill consequences'), we understand that it is an alacrity in hurting others, in putting people in their place and reminding them of their mistakes (she will soon act as self-appointed censor for the young Fanny Price). She receives from her fallen sister a letter containing 'such very disrespectful reflections on the pride of Sir Thomas, as Mrs Norris could not possibly keep to herself'—and at this stage, though no open evaluation of her character has been provided by the narrator, we can see her on her way to Mansfield Park, gloating on each passage of a letter she is holding in her hand.

As to Mrs Price, we are euphemistically informed by the narrator of how her financial difficulties compel her to humiliate herself in front of the very people she has every reason to hate. After eleven years she can no longer 'afford to cherish pride or resentment,' and is 'eager to regain the friends she had so carelessly sacrificed.' The letter she addresses to Lady Bertram is full of 'contrition and despondence'—and it is obviously the latter that induces the former, just as it is the fact that she can no longer afford to cherish pride and resentment that makes her eager to regain her 'friends.' Once all these euphemistic expressions are decoded, very few doubts remain about the motives of the 'reconciliation' and the quality of the 'peace' of which Fanny's arrival at Mansfield Park is a sort of tangible symbol.

Conclusion: Slovenliness Exploited

In a famous essay on 'Politics and the English Language' (1946), George Orwell complains that the English of his time is becoming imprecise and slovenly, its speakers (and above all its writers) mostly unable to express their thoughts clearly through its words. In his opinion, 'prose consists less and less of *words* chosen for the sake of their meaning, and more of *phrases* tacked together like the sections of a prefabricated hen-house'; locked in this prefabricated building, the user 'either has a meaning and cannot express it, or he inadvertently says something else, or he is almost indifferent as to whether his words mean anything or not' (Orwell 1984: 356). This stylistic decline must have external causes in everyday affairs, but the state of everyday affairs in turn is not made a jot better by the decline of language:

> Now, it is clear that the decline of a language must ultimately have political and economic causes: it is not due simply to the bad influences of this or that individual writer. But an effect can become a cause, reinforcing the original cause and producing the same effect in an intensified form, and so on indefinitely. A man may take to drink because he feels himself to be a failure, and then fail all the more completely because he drinks. It is rather the same thing that is happening to the English language. It becomes ugly and inaccurate because our thoughts are foolish, but the slovenliness of our language makes it easier for us to have foolish thoughts. The point is that the process is reversible. Modern English, especially written English, is full of bad habits which spread by imitation and which can be avoided if one is willing to take the necessary trouble. If one gets rid of these habits one can think more clearly, and to think clearly is a necessary first step towards political regeneration: so that to fight against bad English is not frivolous and is not the exclusive concern of professional writers.
>
> (Orwell 1984: 354-5)

In Orwell's indignation against sloppy prose we can trace the influence of another commonplace idea: language, for the novelist, is a mirror of thought, and is more or less successful insofar as it expresses thought clearly and distinctly. Though it is of ancient Greek descent, this idea was formulated for English-speaking modernity in the second half of the seventeenth century, by such thinkers as Hobbes, Locke, and the Royal Society affiliates. Thomas Hobbes wrote in *Leviathan* that 'The generall use of Speech, is to transferre our Mentall Discourse, into Verbal; or the Trayne of our Thoughts, into a Trayne of Words' (Hobbes 1651/1997: 20); John Locke spoke (in the *Essay concerning Human Understanding*) of 'the use and force of language as subservient to instruction and knowledge' (Locke 1690/1877: 10); Thomas Sprat, who in 1668 penned a *History of the Royal Society,* praised its members for their attempt to come back 'to the primitive purity, and shortness, when men deliver'd so many *things,* almost in equal number of *words*' (Sprat 1668: 113). For the men of the seventeenth-century epistemic revolution, it was of course prose, more than verse, that had to bear the weight of denotative precision; and the prose genre *par excellence,* the novel, inherited from the beginning an aspiration to describe the world 'as it is.' Jane Austen and George Orwell both belong to this tradition, and try to describe what they see by means of the language they have at their disposal.

Orwell's remedy against the slovenliness of language is a disposition to think clearly through language, and if necessary against the grain of contemporary English, by avoiding all those expressions that either do not convey any precise content or carry the writer astray from what he/she means to write. Austen's strategy is different: the language she has at her disposal is as imprecise and slovenly, in Orwell's sense, as that of Orwell's contemporaries, because it is full of commonplace expressions and of words the meanings of which are not well definable, though their functions can always be inferred on the pragmatic plane. Words like *prudence, sense, sensibility, judgment, reason, respectability,* are imprecise because they reflect the ideology of a classist male-dominated society that aims at maintaining its privileges while never stating them openly. Instead of refusing to use these words, Austen (or, her narrator) continues to do so, but surrounds them with a co-text in which they are both explained and unmasked.

By first detailing the material conditions in which the events take place (and by means of the contrast between words and events), the narrator of ***MP*** alerts us to the real significance of such expressions as 'respectability,' 'untoward,' 'imprudent,' 'career of conjugal felicity'; and by thus exploiting the tesserae his/her social mosaic is made up of, he/she tells us more about the habits and prejudices of early nineteenth-century country gentry than a whole battery of sociological papers ever could. At the same time, by avoiding any kind of open confrontation with the ideology of his/her world (and with the linguistic expressions which convey that ideology), Austen's narrator maintains a web of 'evaluative opacity' which makes it very difficult to identify his/her moral position, and to catch him/her definitely 'approving' or 'disapproving' the state of affairs he/she is describing. The narrator's position in his/her ideological and linguistic world is at one and the same time acquiescent and subversive, parasitic and critical.

All in all, the initial orientation of ***MP*** resembles a report written by a very careful double-dealing spy for his superiors: the text leads its readers to evaluate a situation in a certain manner; yet no single word is traceable that commits the writer to the evaluation which the text unmistakably proposes.

Notes

1. They also discussed a third, pluralist view of style, but that lies beyond the scope of this chapter.

2. It is to be noted that the description of this circle as a potential cage is mine alone: Leech and Short are more neutral, and Spitzer writes that the philological circle 'is not a vicious one; on the contrary, it is the basic operation of the humanities, the *Zirkel im Verstehen* as Dilthey has termed the discovery, made by the Romantic scholar and theologian Schleiermacher, that cognizance in philosophy is reached not only by the gradual progression from one detail to another detail, but by the anticipation or divination of the whole' (Spitzer 1948/1962: 19).

3. It is of course ultimately impossible to distinguish point of view from 'point of view' (Pugliatti 1985: 1-9); but that is one of the 'dualistic' abstractions we must accept in order to be able to isolate 'stylistic value.'

4. For a detailed description of late eighteenth- and early nineteenth-century middle-class economy as related to women's literature, cf. Copeland (1995).

5. Juliet McMaster has written that 'the gentry and professional classes felt somewhat threatened by the large changes that were coming with the Industrial Revolution, and tended to close ranks against the newly powerful and *nouveaux riches.* Trade represents new money, and money, like wine, isn't considered quite respectable until it has aged a little' (McMaster 1997: 123).

6. It is interesting to compare the author's narrative and epistolary styles. Of Austen's letters, Caroline Austen wrote that 'They were very well expressed, and they must have been very interesting to those who received them—but they detailed chiefly home and family events: and she seldom committed herself *even* to an opinion—so that to strangers they could be *no* transcript of her mind—they would not feel that they knew her any the better for having read them' (La Faye 1989: 249).

7. Though certain contemporary prose writers have managed to make their 'negative' narrators as indecipherable as possible. Many of Carver's short stories can be mentioned as narrative creations whose style seems to reside in the absence of style, and where, as a consequence, all the evaluative colouring appears to be delegated to the selection of facts and speeches.

8. Peter W. Graham provides an interesting 'Darwinian' interpretation of this family history (Graham 2008: 71-6).

9. Fanny works her way into the society of *Mansfield Park* by endorsing its values: comparing her to the model woman of her day, Mary Poovey finds her 'outwardly everything a textbook proper lady should be; she is dependent, self-effacing, and apparently free of impermissible desires' (Poovey 1984: 212; cf. also Chapters 4 and 5). In spite of this textbook perfection, however, Fanny's climb does not reach the social peak where Lady Bertram roosts, because Edmund is a younger son, and as such will not inherit his father's estate. As a clergyman's wife, Fanny will belong to that section of society (termed 'pseudo-gentry' by the historian David Spring [Spring 1983]) which is attached to, but not identifiable with, the landed gentry.

Felicia Bonaparte (essay date 2011)

SOURCE: Bonaparte, Felicia. "'Let Other Pens Dwell on Guilt and Misery': The Ordination of the Text and the Subversion of 'Religion' in Jane Austen's *Mansfield Park.*" *Religion and Literature* 43.2 (2011): 45-67. Print.

[*In the following essay, Bonaparte discusses* Mansfield Park *as Austen's "vision of order" in an increasingly secular world. Bonaparte focuses on the character of Fanny, arguing that Austen shapes her as a consecrating figure who incorporates the spirit of religion into everyday life.*]

The final chapter of ***Mansfield Park*** opens with these curious words: "Let other pens dwell on guilt and misery. I quit such odious subjects as soon as I can, impatient to restore every body, not greatly in fault themselves, to tolerable comfort, and to have done with all the rest" (461). If we have, until this moment, so suspended our disbelief as to take its events and characters as though they existed in actual fact, the opening lines of this last chapter tell us we have misapprehended the true nature of this narrative.[1] For here, as she steps into the text not only as a personal pronoun but as the holder of a pen, Austen makes the maker visible, visible and in truth the arbiter of the destiny of events. Whether the characters are restored to that appropriate level of comfort or are brought to guilt and misery is clearly shown, in this last chapter, to depend not on the facts of some putative universe to whose existence we are asked for the duration to subscribe but on the purely arbitrary decision of the maker's pen. The tale is not to be taken, therefore, as representative of reality but, on the contrary, to be recognized as a fictional invention. The fact, indeed, that Austen gives the reasons she does for her conclusion—not that this is how things are, the normal logic of verisimilitude, but that whoever that "I" may be who is the maker of the novel happens to find such "subjects" "odious" and is "impatient" to provide suitable rewards and punishments for the novel's central characters and "have done with all the rest"—declares that the action is meant to be taken not as a mirror of the world but rather of the maker's mind.

Nor is this the only time Austen subverts verisimilitude in relating the facts of this novel. Not infrequently in the narrative, and often in a mocking way, she calls our attention to the fact that she is structuring her story not in imitation of life but in imitation of fiction, of the conventions of the form. Thus, when the characters on an outing turn, on finding the weather sultry, aside into a shady lane, Austen interrupts the action to assure us that "A young party is always provided with a shady lane" (***MP*** [***Mansfield Park***] 70). Not only is the remark gratuitous, adding nothing to the narration, it is clearly meant to highlight the fact that this is not reality, but a literary device. But here at least, the trope is dramatized and a shady lane appears. This is not always the case, however. Sometimes Austen merely reminds us of the fictional requirement without bothering to enact it, as though, it being understood between the reader and herself that the particulars of the story are but the customs of the genre, she need not trouble herself to realize them. Maria and Rushworth are thus reported to have entered on their engagement after dancing with one another "at a proper number of balls" (***MP*** 39). The number, which would be specified in a realistic narrative or represented in a few instances, is left to the reader here to fill in with any figure he thinks fit. And in one extraordinary passage, occurring near the end of the book, Austen not only foregrounds conventions, she concurrently undercuts them. Following the briefest account of the change of heart in Edmund that has brought him from loving Mary to an equal affection for Fanny, Austen, once more in a personal pronoun that brings her as maker to center stage, adds

> I purposely abstain from dates on this occasion, that every one may be at liberty to fix their own, aware that the cure of unconquerable passions, and the transfer of unchanging attachments, must vary much as to time in different people.—I only intreat every body to believe that exactly at the time when it was quite natural that it should be so, and not a week earlier, Edmund did cease to care about Miss Crawford, and became as anxious to marry Fanny, as Fanny herself could desire.
>
> (***MP*** 470)

This, the novel's happy ending, is offered to us not as fact but as a formal requirement only. We are invited to accept it as a conclusion for the narrative, not to believe it as an event in the reality of the tale.

In *Partial Magic,* Robert Alter argues that metafictional writing, although it turns up now and again before the arrival of postmodernism, is entirely in "eclipse" in the nineteenth-century novel, Victorians being so intent on recording what they observe as realistically as possible that it does not occur to them to think reflexively of the role they play in the making of their own fictions (chapter 4). And yet the opposite would seem to be the far more logical case. If it was, as Ian Watt has argued in *The Rise of the Novel,* Locke and Hume who, through empiricism, provided the grounds for the kind of narrative, sister to science, whose purpose it was to testify to observation by relating it realistically, it was Locke and Hume as well who demonstrated that reality as it is perceived empirically must always be subjective and relative. What seems, and is often assumed to be in our definition of realism, an account of what is observed is only an account, in fact, of the mind of the observer. Realism always conceals metafiction as its twin.

Austen clearly understood this. A highly philosophical novelist, as many have argued in recent years (Marilyn Butler, P. J. Scott, I, as well, and several others), she is profoundly concerned with ideas. And, while she has often been criticized for ignoring in her narratives most of the great events of her time, Austen is also a great historian, drawing our attention to history in subtle but highly visible ways, as, for example, by tracking time through the use of "old" and "new," words that turn up repeatedly, the former forty-six times in the narrative (as for heathen heroes, chapels, trees, prayer-books, and dowagers), "new" eighty-five times, and not only as an adjective (as for fashions, buildings, ideas, friends) but, in combinations, for names (Newbury, Newmarket), with a prefix (renew, renewal), and in such markers of the new as "news" itself, used thirty-one times, and even newspapers which are mentioned thirteen times in conversations. As Leonardo in his *Notebooks*—and I follow Merike Tamm in using examples from graphic art to illuminate Austen's purposes—suggests that artists must paint a tempest not by attempting to capture on canvas the movement of the air itself but by painting its "effects" as it blows across land and sea (Da Vinci 196), Austen, rarely mentioning wars or calling movements by their names, writes about great changes in history simply by showing us their impact. And having spent much of ***Pride and Prejudice*** identifying the implications of a Humean epistemology (see my "Conjecturing Possibilities"), she goes on in ***Mansfield Park*** to define the age she lives in as one whose conceptual foundations are in the process of being shattered and to look for a new *mythos* on which to reconstruct the world. This quest for a *mythos* was, of course, to become the typical quest of the nineteenth-century novel, and a nineteenth-century novel is precisely what she creates, as Kathryn Sutherland has observed (413), not only because she anticipates a cluster of Victorian patterns—Barbara Bail Collins points to some and I shall add a good number of others—but because she suddenly sees that a new era is emerging in which the world must be remade and that fiction must remake it. Thomas Carlyle had not yet called for a "new Mythus" to "embody the divine spirit" of "Religion" (194) when Austen started ***Mansfield Park*** but Friedrich Schlegel, the guiding spirit of the early German Romantics, had already elaborated, in the seminal "Talk on Mythology" of his *Dialogue on Poetry* (1800), the rationale of this idea as well as its philosophic grounds, and in only a few more years Percy Shelley was to speak, in his *Defence of Poetry* (1821), of the artist as a poet in the etymological sense, often writing *poiesis* in Greek to remind us that the "poet" is by definition a "maker," one who is called in the modern world to make not only odes and sonnets but, the old one having crumbled, like a deity, a new world.

The novel is, in a sense, prophetic, and it is therefore of a kind that needs to be read not in the conceptual language of the fiction of its day but in the idiom of the thought and the forms it anticipates. It is in those works in which Victorians were to record the ideas of their age that we must look for patterns and parallels that can explain what Austen is doing. And it is in that context too that we must read the extraordinary words Austen wrote to her sister Cassandra in January of 1813: "Now I will try and write something else, and it shall be a complete change of subject—ordination" (***Letters*** [***Jane Austen's Letters***] 298). These words have puzzled many readers. They seem to announce a new idea for a project that we know was at the time already in progress. Further, Edmund's ordination has, to most readers, not appeared important enough to be called a subject. The first of these problems may never be solved, but Edmund's literal ordination is not a mere detail of the plot. Michael Karounos and Joseph W. Donohue are right to urge us, among others, to look for its wider implications, for it is pivotal to the theme, a theme that ultimately encompasses the ordination of the age and of the fictional form that seeks to address its predicament.

This is the point of the heroine's name.[2] Fanny Price has without question been the single greatest problem posed by this novel to current readers. Taking her to have been intended as a mimetic representation, most have been distressed by her nature—lifeless, timid, self-effacing, on the surface at any rate—and have gone a very long way in an effort to explain her, Elizabeth Jenkins concluding, for instance, that Fanny suffers from nervous trauma brought about by her being forced to leave her home at an early age and Margaret Kirkham that she is meant as a negative example to the young women of the day who are exhorted not to be like her. But the very problems that face us if we take her as realistic should convince us that Austen must have had something quite different in mind. The novel itself is not realistic. For reasons that I will hope to make clear, Austen was one of the first to conceive a fictional form that was to become the idiom of Victorian narrative (Bonaparte, "*Middlemarch*"). We might call it symbolic realism. The idea of this form was often discussed by Victorian writers and, in another graphic paradigm, often assumed by Paul Gaugin. In one of his many remarks on this subject, Ruskin thus writes in *Modern Painters* of the "imaginative verity" we can only come to recognize when we learn to tell it apart from, on the one hand, what is false, and, on the other, mere "realism." Ruskin certainly had no quarrel with realistic representation. Quite the opposite, he insisted that art be faithful to the facts. But "mere external fact," he writes, will imprison us in its "fetters" if we do not look beyond it to "the TRUE nature" that lies within (Ruskin, vol. II:378). Realism can only reveal the phenomenal world of perception. Truth lies in the noumenal realm and must be sought beyond the facts. Similarly, in one of his essays on the form of Victorian fiction, Bulwer-Lytton, the most typical practitioner of the genre himself and one of its most astute historians, writes that the characteristic literary form of his century is the novel of the "double plot." Intent on depicting the world as it is as well as on redressing its ills, such a novel must record as accurately as humanly possible what the writer has observed in the world as it truly is but must also find a way to embed in his narrative a "symbolical signification" that envisions what should be (Bulwer-Lytton 319).

Gaugain often encodes these ideas in the very forms of his paintings. In *The Vision after the Sermon: Jacob Wrestling with the Angel,* we find, for example, a somewhat stylized but clearly mimetic representation of a group of parishioners who, having obviously just heard a sermon on Genesis 32:24, envision the subject of the homily enacted on the grassy lawn immediately in front of the church. Everything looks like what it depicts—the women like women, the tree like a tree, Jacob likewise, and even the angel as angels are usually portrayed—everything, except for the grass, which is painted a bright red. The question of how we read that grass determines what we make of this canvas. We have basically two choices: we can insist that Gaugin intended the objects to be verisimilitudinous, and in that case can only conclude he did not know that grass was green, or, accepting the red grass as the focal point of his argument, as it is of the painting itself, assume that verisimilitude is not at all what he had in mind and allow the objects and colors to guide us to what Ruskin calls their "imaginative verity" (vol. II:378).

Fanny Price is a red lawn. In a striking, postmodern way, she is a realistic character but also a figure in a design. The question we must ask of her is not "Is this character realistic?" "Does she resemble actual people?" The questions Austen invites us to ask are of a very different order and, from a fictional point of view, considerably more sophisticated: "What is the meaning of this design?" "What is the place of this figure in it?" The book as a whole has a comment to make, it goes without saying, about the world. Its very metafictionality is part of its statement, as we shall see. But unlike realistic fiction, in which individual elements may be taken to correspond to some aspects of real life, this is the kind of narrative in which the constituent components cannot be asked to make sense in themselves but only in their collective meaning.

Her very name, which makes a sentence, is one that identifies the role Austen assigns her in the novel. Such sentences came to be common ways of making central thematic points in the nineteenth-century novel—through its etymological roots, Rosamond Vincy tells us in *Middlemarch* that the rose of the world, the *rosa mundi,* will always conquer, from Latin *vincere,* a Darwinian point that proves all too true in her marriage to Lydgate—and Austen makes several in her novel. Clearly the "pearl of great price" Jesus compares to the "kingdom of heaven" in Matthew 13:45-46, Fanny is the embodiment of the essential ideals of religion (KJV).[3] But she embodies those ideals in an age that has abandoned them. In one of the best discussions to date of this aspect of ***Mansfield Park,*** Lionel Trilling speaks of Austen as the first to recognize the coming of the secular era (228). It was to be many more decades before Friedrich Nietzsche declared God dead, but Austen many times in this novel anticipates aspects of Nietzsche's views, and, in the manner Leonardo advises painters to show a tempest, tells us so by itemizing the effects of this secularism: chapels, as Fanny observes at Sotherton, are no longer used for prayers, clergymen are no longer in residence, no one feels, in God's very house, the "awful" presence of the deity (***MP*** 85). All of this is encapsulated in the name of the man who stands at the head of Mansfield Park. Always spoken of in language more fitting for a divinity—he seems "awful in his dignity"; Fanny "knelt in spirit to" him; when he returns, one of his daughters announces him as "My father is come" (***MP*** 172), words that echo passages (such as Matthew 18:11) that frequently announce the deity—Sir Thomas is one of the first of those fathers we find in nineteenth-century novels who take the fictional place of God, so that when he leaves for Antigua, God may not be entirely dead, but he is removed from the scene.

In time, Sir Thomas will return but he will never again assume moral supremacy in his house, nor does Austen want him to. Something is wrong with his religion and was wrong before he left. This is not really religion at all. Sir Thomas is the very epitome of the best of the Enlightenment. He is a good man in many ways, not tyrannical, not severe. He is not even patriarchal, given the terms of life in his day. He is a kindly, rational man, keeping his house in moral order but with a benevolent hand. But his rational enlightenment is precisely where he fails, not because of a flaw in him but because there is a flaw in the age he represents. Peter Knox-Shaw is certainly right that Austen appreciates the Enlightenment for its clarity and reason. But reason is not the same as religion, clarity not the same as faith. It is this perhaps that Austen intended to illustrate in two moments that have, understandably, drawn a good deal of attention: the first, the fact that, to remove him for a time from Mansfield Park, Austen disposes of Sir Thomas by sending him suddenly to Antigua to deal with a problem he does not mention (***MP*** 32); the second, that Fanny is met with silence when she tries on his return to speak to him about the slave trade (***MP*** 198), the reason, we now assume, he left. In *Culture and Imperialism,* Edward Said has pointed out that, while we know from other sources that she objected to slavery, Austen seems oddly cavalier in referring to such an event with little sense of its moral import (112, 115), and Brian Southam has rightly protested that in allowing Fanny's questions to be met by Sir Thomas with silence, Austen misses an opportunity to make a comment on the subject (13-14). No one writing today, it is obvious, would throw such a topic into a narrative and expect to be able to leave it as rapidly as Austen does. Still, because she often works minimally, through subtle hints, it is difficult not to assume Austen has something important in mind here. His failure to reply to her questions not only suggests that Joseph Lew, Maggie Malone, Moira Ferguson, and others have been right to argue that Sir Thomas has a very low opinion of women, women of Fanny's station especially, but, far more, and more thematically, that the rational cast of his mind cannot comprehend her questions, grounded in the transcendent truths of the spirit for which she speaks. This is the failure that requires the making of a new religion, and by introducing her point, quick as it is, in just this way, Austen suggests that her abstract argument has implications to the political as well as moral dimensions of history.

To this failure in his vision Sir Thomas's name is designed to attest, a name recalling the doubting Thomas who asked to have empirical evidence of the wounds of the crucifixion before he could believe he was standing before the resurrected Christ. Although by no means neglected earlier, St. Thomas quickly became, for the period that saw the final collapse of religion, the very embodiment of its doubt. Friedrich Overbeck, the leader of the Nazarenes in Rome—a brotherhood, later to become the model for the pre-Raphaelites, that vowed, in the wake of the German Romantics, to restore the ideal and transcendent to what they saw as the tendency of art to become enslaved increasingly to material representation, which is to say to realism—was to paint this very scene (true, for the Church of St. Thomas in Leeds, but the subject was the reason he accepted the commission), and—from Maggie Tulliver's brother Tom in George Eliot's *The Mill on the Floss* who confesses he cannot imagine anything contrary to fact (34-35), to D. H. Lawrence's Tom Brangwen in *The Rainbow* and *Women in Love* who is tied to the material but reaches out for the ideal by proposing to Lydia Lensky—virtually every Victorian Thomas stands for a concept of the world not necessarily bad in itself but limited strictly to fact and reason. In *Hard Times,* a novel that opens with a demand for nothing but "Facts," this is the name Dickens gives to Gradgrind (7). Sir Thomas himself comes to see his failing when his household falls apart. He had taught his children principles, he concludes at the end of the book, but he had taught them "theoretically" (***MP*** 463) and it had simply not been enough. For a time, he had succeeded in keeping "every body in their place" (***MP*** 162). And yet chaos had erupted the moment he had left for Antigua. Something, he understands at last, had been left empty, "wanting *within*" (***MP*** 463). No surprise that once he leaves, his children, "relieved" of external "restraint" (***MP*** 32), prove they are tethered by nothing at all.

"Within" is the obviously critical word. It is, if the movement had to be summarized in one single basic concept, the word that would define Romanticism and distinguish it from the Enlightenment. Much as she attacks its follies and its sentimental excesses, in this novel as in her others, as William Magee has pointed out (45-46), Austen not only welcomes Romanticism, she understands its essential nature, and, in a Hegelian way, its place in the evolution of time. As though moving above and below the rational space of the Enlightenment, Austen sees the need for something more compelling than mere principle, something transcendent, a new religion, a religion not of creeds, but rather of an inner condition that defines not what we believe but what we are in our very essence.[4]

This is the very inwardness of the first half of Fanny's name. Enormously popular through the century, in male and female forms alike—Austen herself had used it before and was later to use it again—it is a name that gains its meaning almost entirely from the legend told of St. Francis of Assisi, a legend repeated by Anna Jameson in *Legends of the Monastic Orders* (published first in 1850 and republished many times both in England and America), which relates the tale of young Francis coming to pray in the church of St. Damian, a structure that had all but crumbled. Kneeling, St. Francis heard God's voice telling him, in Jameson's paraphrase, to "repair my Church, which falleth to ruin" (240). Fortunately, Francis realized the command was not just literal but, more importantly, also figurative, and he therefore set about not only rebuilding the physical church but reconceiving religion itself in the idiom of his time. Without abandoning rites and rituals or the articles of his faith, Francis focused on the love he took as the spirit of God's truth. This is what he came to symbolize. Shakespeare makes it a point to tell us in *Romeo and Juliet* that Friar Lawrence is a Franciscan (e.g., V.2), which is why he is prepared, unlike others, to marry the couple despite the enmity of their families. It is clear that Alessandro Manzoni, using the play as the frame for his novel *I Promessi Sposi* (1827), understood Shakespeare's point very well when he made his Friar a Capuchin, an order derived from the Franciscan. And in *Diana Mallory* (1908), Mary Augusta Arnold Ward takes her characters to Assisi to suggest that a new religion can be made out of dead creeds just as the modern Italian language was born out of Latin when it died (Ward 340-41). For each of these and many others, Francis invariably represents the need to rebuild, as in each epoch the church of the past falls into ruin, the inner essence of religion in the new idiom of the day. In the nineteenth-century novel, Thomas and Francis are often paired as antithetical principles. In Charles Kingsley's *Two Years Ago,* the curate named Frank, thus a man of the spirit, is the opposite of Thomas, a physician whose vocation is part of what identifies him as a man of the physical world.

As it was for Victorian writers, the problem for Austen is not religion. The problem is epistemology. Josephine Singer is typical of contemporary readers when she admits in her final words that she would have been "better pleased" if "Austen had shown morality" could "exist without religion," but Austen is very well aware that if no absolute truths exist, such as must be derived from religion, however we interpret that word—human judgments being subject always to qualifications—moral positions can only be taken, just as Hume did take them in fact, as nothing more than personal preferences, subjective and relative to all others. In his *Discours sur l'esprit positif* (1844), Auguste Comte was soon to speak of "la profonde anarchie intellectuelle et morale qui caractérise surtout la grande crise moderne" (55). This is precisely the state of affairs Austen describes at ***Mansfield Park*** the moment Sir Thomas leaves for Antigua. Fanny had already, at Portsmouth, lived in a world that seemed to recall the universe of the chaos of Genesis, before the earth and the waters had parted, and that is what she still finds there when she later returns to visit: "noise, disorder, and impropriety. Nobody was in their right place, nothing was done as it ought to be" (***MP*** 388-89). Mansfield Park had seemed a haven from that chaotic world of her home. Now it too appears on the edge of giving way to moral anarchy.

Often described as a modern house—for example, "modern-built" (***MP*** 48)—Mansfield Park is conceived in the novel as the site of the modern world, and the Comtean chaos that threatens it encoded in the theatricals that figure the historical space between the Enlightenment of

Sir Thomas and the Romanticism of Fanny. The old external controls have been lifted, but no new ones are yet in place. This is the moment of absolute freedom. In a moment such as this, Nietzsche, in another parallel, proceeded to write *Beyond Good and Evil,* and Austen is herself aware of how exhilarating it is to be free of moral constraints. Doing and being whatever one likes in whatever role one chooses not only fulfills the heart's desire, it is, in the age in which Jeremy Bentham declared all moral principles to be tyrannical impositions, a philosophical ideal. Even Fanny, who surprises us by deciding to take part, is drawn to the liberation it promises. But liberation wholly unchecked very shortly turns to license, as Tony Tanner has rightly argued (162), which quickly comes to encourage selfishness, which engenders suspicion and jealousy and a general ill will that makes everyone unhappy. Austen insists on moral boundaries not because she is puritanical, as some readers have assumed, but because she sees the end to which total freedom leads.

It is Edmund, put in charge by his father when he leaves, who is entrusted with the task of envisioning a new future. In "Jane Austen and Religion: Salvation and Society in Georgian England," Michael Griffin has well reminded us of Austen's high regard for religion and in "Jane Austen: The Parson's Daughter" and "Jane Austen and the Clergy," Irene Collins has made good headway in showing how highly she held the clergy. Satiric portraits like Mr. Collins, the buffoon of ***Pride and Prejudice,*** express not her contempt for clerics but, on the contrary, her dismay at seeing so many fail in their work because they are vain and worldly men. Edmund is her positive portrait, a man who makes a serious effort to do the great work to which he is called and who helps Austen in this novel define what that effort must be in her time. Significantly, his quest is embodied not in the form of the *Bildungsroman* which was becoming all the rage in the wake of *Wilhelm Meister* (1795-6), but of the medieval romance. With a good deal of theory behind it, the form of the medieval romance had been, for a number of decades when Austen started ***Mansfield Park,*** making an aggressive comeback. Created to trace the development of a young man in his sense of himself and his relations with the world, the *Bildungsroman* was a modern form, focusing on modern questions of human existence in secular terms, mostly social and psychological. Austen had no objection to it and was to use it herself very soon in her education of Emma. Yet we should note that the man in *Emma* who has those morals in his keeping to which Emma herself will be brought is a man whose name is Knightley. Like many of her Victorian successors, Austen turns to the Middle Ages to find what Alice Chandler has called the Victorian dream of order (*A Dream*). But she is not the first to do so. The need for values and a logic capable of supporting them had already inspired others at the end of the eighteenth century to return to the romance. This effort to repossess the romance as the Middle Ages conceived it should not be confused with the common use made in eighteenth-century fiction of the forms that had developed from the medieval genre. The two have entirely different histories and produce very different works, as those who wished to revive the genre in its first and pristine form—writers such as Richard Hurd in *Letters on Chivalry and Romance* (1762), Clara Reeve in *The Progress of Romance through Times, Centuries, and Manners* (1785), and Sir Walter Scott in the essays, "Romance" (1824) and "Chivalry" (1818), written for the *Encyclopedia Britannica*—were, it is obvious, well aware. Without benefit of Hegel, they held a Hegelian view of genres, thanks perhaps to such precursors as Thomas Warton in his popular *History of English Poetry from the Close of the Eleventh Century to the Commencement of the Eighteenth* (1774-81), and were convinced that in the wake of the skepticism and materialism already developing out of empiricism, a form was needed that would carry in its very structure and idiom something of a transcendent ideal. Whenever "this spirit" of the romance, "and its enthusiasm," writes Reeve, "become objects of contempt and ridicule, mankind will set up for themselves an idol of a very different kind.—They will then devote themselves to mean or mercenary pursuits and debase and corrupt the mind" (102). This was the concept of the romance inherited by Victorian novelists and used in countless of their novels. When Eliot ends chapter ten of *Middlemarch* with Lydgate turning from Dorothea, whom he considers dull and boring, and begins chapter eleven by commenting on his attraction to Rosamond, she is setting up the structure of a medieval romance in which a character, an everyman, engaged in a typical psychomachia, is asked to choose between two women, one of whom represents the spirit—Dorothea, the "Gift of God," as her name identifies her—the other who represents the flesh—Rosamond, the "Rose of the World." Lydgate chooses the wrong woman, as too late he comes to realize.

Austen is fully conscious here of the form she is embedding, as she later is in ***Emma,*** and makes sure that we are, too. Not only does she refer to the genre when she has Mary speak of Henry as "the hero of an old romance" (***MP*** 360), words that identify Mary's blindness to the meaning of this form, since Henry is precisely the opposite, she has Fanny, who recognizes the true hero of the genre, say there is "nobleness in the name Edmund. It is a name of heroism and renown; of kings, princes, and knights; and seems to breathe the spirit of chivalry" (***MP*** 211). Like Lydgate, Edmund too is an everyman and the women between whom he stands represent the choices before him.

The Crawfords embody the secular tendencies Austen perceives in the modern world. Like many of their Victorian descendents, they arrive in the novel orphaned, cut off from the legacy of the past, cut off from its philosophic traditions, especially from metaphysics, even the benefits of reason, but most importantly, cut off from the spirit of religion. Although these are not enough in themselves for the making of a new creed, all are essential ingredients in it, and the fact that the Crawfords lack them makes it impossible for them to advance historically into the Romantic age. They are forever stuck in chaos. Bunyan, to whom Austen alludes, as Stephen Derry has pointed out (466-67), would have placed them in Vanity Fair. They are children of the world, "worldly" people (***MP*** 306), as Lauber calls them (204), both in amiable ways, never awkward or ill at ease in a social situation, but in sinister ways as well, desiring only worldly things and caring little how they get them. Mary arrives with the intention of marrying the older brother, whatever kind of man he may be, because she covets the land and title that must go to elder sons. It is true she is in time drawn to want to marry the younger, but feels no compunction in anticipating the death of the elder when he is ill so that the younger will inherit. Austen does not cite chapter and verse, but there can certainly be no doubt she is reminding us of the passage, in Matthew 6:24, that we cannot serve God and Mammon. Mary indeed is greatly taken with Mammon's modern representative. As Austen records the early impact of the shift from a rural society to an urban, industrial nation, Mary is sure the "London maxim" that "everything" can be had "with money" must be universally true (***MP*** 58). She aspires to nothing higher than the apex of her class. When she tells Edmund she cannot marry him if he persists in becoming a minister, she explains, referring herself to the only standard she knows, that a "clergyman" cannot be of any "consequence" in "society" (***MP*** 92). Edmund's defense of his chosen calling, that it shapes "religion and morals," is incomprehensible to her. All she can say, completely befuddled, is that it has no impact on "fashion" (***MP*** 92). Mary is trapped in material realities. She lives in the flesh, not in the spirit. Austen emphasizes her flesh, makes her healthy, robust, vigorous, fond of physical activity and extremely skilful at it. But she seems to possess no soul. In its place, there is only ego. It is "everybody's duty," Mary observes as she rewrites the meaning of the very word that lies at the heart of moral awareness, "to do as well for themselves as they can" (***MP*** 289). "Selfishness," she says again, "must be forgiven" for "there is no hope of a cure" (***MP*** 68). Grounded in ego, both brother and sister are subjectivists and so relativists. "A watch is always," Mary insists when Edmund tries to correct her impression of the time that has passed in their stroll, "too fast or too slow. I cannot be dictated to by a watch" (***MP*** 95).

Appropriately, it is the play of the theatricals that offers Mary an outlet for her character. Play is the essence of her nature. Austen suggests it in many forms: Mary has a "lively mind" (***MP*** 64) that shows itself in a "play of feature" (***MP*** 63). One of the reasons she seems perfect to her brother to "play" Amelia is the "playfulness" of the part (***MP*** 135). Play is a delightful quality, but a dangerous one as well. The name of her favorite game of cards, "Speculation," points to a philosophic position that considers all normative principles questions open to speculation, and while it is obvious that Austen herself sees the positive side of such thinking, as in relation to Sir Thomas, whose normative principles need to change, to have no foundation of any kind is to be morally adrift. Life itself is a game to Mary. Longfellow has long been mocked for his lines, in "A Psalm of Life," "Life is real! Life is earnest! / And the grave is not its goal," but, whether good or bad as poetry, they make a very important point (5-6). The second line explains the first. If there is something beyond the grave, every choice in life must have an eternal consequence. Life is not a game, in that case. It is significant that the subject being discussed while the game proceeds, namely the living at Thornton Lacey, the parish on the Bertram estate, and the qualities of the man who might be suited to occupy it, places the card game in just this context. Mary, however, like countless young men in the nineteenth-century novel and even occasionally young women, in Dickens and Hardy especially, having no faith in anything—and Mary's delightfully amusing "Of *Rears,* and *Vices,* I saw enough" (***MP*** 60) testifies to her cynicism—cannot be serious about life. It is a gamble, like a card game, and while she always likes to win, nothing is of such importance that losing matters all that much.

Edmund is sorely tempted by Mary, and the idea of temptation introduces the means through which Austen shows the moral significance of choosing her in the romance. Several times in the novel, in fact, Austen turns to Edenic imagery to equate the modern age with the world after the fall.[5] One occurrence is when Mary and Edmund, wandering off in the woods at Sotherton, choose to abandon "the first great path" and lose their way on a "serpentine" trail (***MP*** 94-95). Another occurs in the theatricals. Knowing his father would not approve, even as Adam knew that God had forbidden his eating the fruit, Edmund objects to the production, and when Mary says she supposes that if a part could "tempt" him to act, it would certainly be Anhalt, Edmund replies that the man who would choose to become a clergyman would be "the last" to play one "on the stage" (***MP*** 144-45). And yet that is just what he does in the end, inspiring two of his siblings to say that he had "descended" from his "moral elevation" (***MP*** 158). The usual word, of course, is "fallen," and later novelists would use it routinely when alluding to the Fall.

What is metaphor in the language becomes drama in the plot when Henry and Maria elope. With her unerring moral instinct, Fanny speaks of it as a "sin" (***MP*** 440-41). Mary, however, speaks of "folly" and regrets not the act itself but the fact that they were caught (***MP*** 452, 454, 455). "This is what the world does," Edmund exclaims as the full scope of Mary's failings dawn on him (***MP*** 455). He means this is "the way of the world," as it was called in the Middle Ages, the way of this world, not of God's, the way of a world in contrast to God's, and therefore of a secular age. Mary is not, he suddenly realizes, a willful soul led astray but redeemable, as she had appeared before. Mary is a new kind of creature, the harbinger of another era. She lives in a world beyond good and evil, not immoral but amoral.

Nietzsche welcomed that new age, but Austen is not prepared to abandon the moral boundaries of civilization.

The distinction between these words, Mary's "folly" and Fanny's "sin," is what accounts for the novel's tone. Folly, Austen's usual medium, however serious in her books, is capable still of being comic, the subject of irony and wit. ***Mansfield Park*** is her only novel that carries the conviction of sin, as Austen herself suggests when Fanny speaks of the "sorrow" and "wickedness" she perceives in the world around her (***MP*** 113). And sin, while it may be mortal or venial, is hardly ever really amusing.

Similarly, the presence of sin is what sends Austen to religion. Folly can be teased, cajoled, corrected by reason and gentle humor. A sinful world needs to be saved, needs something transcendent, a power beyond common sense and human reason. In the language of this novel, a sinful world needs to be ordained. As the daughter of a minister, Austen obviously understands precisely what this word entails and she uses it very carefully, both in her letter to Cassandra and in the ordination of Edmund, in which the point of the letter is dramatized. For it is clear that, by being ordained, Edmund is not just being certified to represent divine authority as a civil servant might in being appointed to act for the state. A civil servant may have powers, but they are functional, external. They are powers not in himself but in the nature of his position. And being functional and external, they are powers that do not transform, either him when he is appointed or others when he puts them to use. But in the act of being ordained, Edmund becomes the "alter Christus," as the Anglican priest is called, the "other Christ," Christ's self on earth, and he does so not because he has been assigned a function, but because his ordination is an act of consecration. He becomes a sacred vessel. He has taken God within.

For Austen in this novel, therefore, ordination is the place where the true spirit of religion as St. Francis reconceived it intersects in historical time with the inwardness of Romanticism. This is the space that Fanny occupies in the structure of the narrative. All through the novel there are hints, as in their peculiar friendship and Fanny's "fascination" with Mary (***MP*** 208), that Fanny and Mary are intended as alter egos of one another. They are two sides of the human coin, tied in some sense but antithetical. If Mary is bounded by the "extrinsic," to use the distinction Martin suggests, Fanny embodies the "intrinsic" (146). Neither, it should perhaps be emphasized, is offered here as ideal in herself. Every charm entails a flaw, every flaw has its attraction. Edmund is given no easy choices. Austen has no intention of telling us that the good is also the beautiful and the evil, distasteful and ugly. Whatever the manner of the narrative, its matter is thoroughly true to life. The choice must be made, but it comes at a price. Fanny has few of the visible charms that make Mary so seductive, but she does have invisible virtues that are essential to moral life.[6] The world is of little interest to her and material possessions less. She is timid in society. But as the pearl herself of great price, she is at home in the realm of the spirit. The fact that she belongs to the spirit accounts, as Trilling has rightly remarked, for her "puny" and "delicate" frame (***MP*** 11). Her strength, unlike Mary's, is not in flesh (Trilling 128-29). This also explains why she is small, the displacement of space in this novel serving, as in the Middle Ages and later in Victorian fiction—Little Dorrit in Dickens, for instance, or Brontë's Paulina Mary Home, a miniscule creature in *Villette* whose name is taken from *paulus,* "small," and is, in addition, a diminutive—as the measure of materiality. And if Fanny seems "graver" than others (***MP*** 197), it is because, in yet another common nineteenth-century image, she lives so fully in the spirit that she seems beyond the grave. Marylea Meyersohn has argued that she is unnaturally silent. She is silent like the grave, for, as Carlyle was to observe, "Speech is of Time, Silence is of Eternity" (219).

Perhaps because she is Mary's antithesis, Fanny has often seemed old-fashioned, and it is certainly true she rejects the modern spirit of the Crawfords. But she does not reject the modern. Rarely, as Claire Lamont has documented, do we find Austen preferring the old. She has no love for the status quo. When Fanny refuses to be bullied into marrying Henry Crawford, Sir Thomas accuses her of exhibiting "that independence of spirit which prevails so much in modern days" (***MP*** 318). And to an extent, he is right. She will not bow to mere authority. She will not accept the idea that wisdom exists only in the past any more than in the present. She is not enslaved to time. As the eternal truths of religion, she is not tied to old or new. She does what she does not because it was done or because it is being done now, but only because it is right to do. This, of course, is one of the qualities that exasperates modern readers. But looking for that fixed foundation on which to build a moral vision, not like Mary's subjective and relative, Austen needs to create for Edmund, as the everyman of the romance, a woman who is morally rooted.

Fanny is not only rooted, she is the very idea of rootedness. Mary, who suffers from what Hardy was to call "the modern vice of unrest" (104), is hardly ever not in motion. "I must move," she says, "resting fatigues me" (***MP*** 96). Fanny, in contrast, is always at rest. But she is not inactive or passive. Austen takes pains to distinguish her from Lady Bertram and Mrs. Price and their "easy," "indolent" ways (***MP*** 4, 13). Fanny is not inert but immobile, the "fixed" center of the novel (***MP*** 20), the still point of the turning world ("Burnt Norton" I, 62), T. S. Eliot would have called her. She does not move because she stands from the start just where she ought to. Those who do move are those who need to and their delinquency can be determined by where they are in relation to her. This, in fact, is the plot of the novel and its paradigmatic design is presented to us at Sotherton when Fanny, walking through the wood, chooses to sit while all the others hurry and scurry hither and yon in pursuit of one another, ending where she has been all along (***MP*** 94-96). At one point—and there are several moments of this kind in the narrative—when Edmund and Mary are brought "before her" by "windings" in their "serpentine" path, Fanny seems the very deity passing judgment on Adam and Eve (***MP*** 103). To Edmund, she becomes St. Peter. Dickens was later to embody this same figure in Esther Summerson when he has Jarndyce, the novel's "Guardian," as he is called to suggest he stands, like Sir Thomas, as God's surrogate, hand her, on her arrival at Bleak House, a chain with all the keys of the house, designating her symbolically as the one who, through her kindness, has the power of St. Peter to open the gates of paradise. Austen does even more with this image, having Edmund say of Fanny that she is "firm as a rock" in her "principles" (***MP*** 350-51), identifying her thus as the rock, the etymology of "Peter," on which Edmund must build his church even as Jesus chose to build his.

The estate called Mansfield Park comes, in fact, to be that church. Fanny's progress in the novel, physically, through the rooms of the house, tracks the logic of the symbolism that turns the house into a church.[7] Grudging and envious, Mrs. Norris, who seems always to be trying, like the Dickensian fiend she is, to usurp Sir Thomas's place, had warned Fanny at one point not to hope to put herself forward, to remember who she is, always the "lowest" and the "last" (***MP*** 221), having obviously no memory, though her husband was a minister, of the biblical assurance that the last shall be the first. This is precisely Fanny's trajectory. From the attic in which she is placed on her arrival at Mansfield Park to the "school-room" she takes over (***MP*** 150) and finally to the "drawing-room" to which Sir Thomas summons her when he returns from his trip to Antigua (***MP*** 177), Fanny slowly makes her way down the stairs to the main floor and into the center of the house. At the end, when she marries Edmund, she goes to live in Thornton Lacey. It is precisely the right home for the pearl of great price and she has been given that home by precisely the right man. As the modern everyman, Edmund has come at last to recognize, despite his infatuation with Mary and the excitement she had promised, that, as the modern world is threatened by the chaos of dissolution, it is Fanny who makes possible that ordination of the soul that constitutes the inner religion appropriate for the modern era. Thus, it is clear, by the last chapter, that Austen has chosen the name of the house with an eye to its root, "manse," a word hardly ever used today but common in the nineteenth century as a name for a pastor's residence. Had Austen given this name to the parsonage, her point would have been a simple one, merely to match the name to the place. But by bestowing it on the whole of the Bertram's house and lands, Austen suggests that Fanny's presence has consecrated Mansfield Park, ordained, in the symbolic language Austen chooses for her book, the entire space in the novel that represents the modern world. She has made a place for religion in the secular modern age. St. Francis had done the same in his day by taking his work as a monk to the world, choosing to go among the people, practicing his faith in the market-place. He had not only, in consequence, remade religion for his time; he had incorporated its spirit into daily human existence. This is what Fanny does at the end and what Austen does in her book. The heavenly Eden to which Christian is led at the end of *Pilgrim's Progress* on reaching the Celestial City is, in the inwardness of Romanticism, turned into a state of mind that occupies an earthly space. Austen's was soon to become the period of Utopian communities—Brook Farm, the Owenites, the Saint-Simonians, and innumerable others, not excepting Karl Marx—efforts to make an earthly Eden as the heavenly slipped away.

It is for this reason that Austen gives the name Thornton Lacey to the parsonage. A major medieval metaphor based on Genesis 3:18 in which Adam and Eve are exiled to live in a world whose very earth is cursed to bring forth "thorns and thistles," the thorn is the image of that sin that is responsible for their fall (KJV). Further, through the crown of thorns, it is generally connected to the sacrifice of Jesus, taken to be the second Adam sent to redeem the sin of the first. And, in yet another link, it is tied to the popular legend told by St. Ambrose who, making it a part of his story of the Virgin, speaks of a rose that grew in Eden that was perfect, without thorns, the rose of the world (and one is reminded of the many fictional characters who are given the name Rosamond because they embody this worldly rose) coming to acquire its thorn only when it was planted on earth. It is of the flawless rose of Eden that Tennyson speaks when he alludes to the "thornless garden" in *Maud* (1855; stanza xviii, 27) and the Virgin Browning recalls when he speaks of "the rose without a thorn" in his poem "Women and Roses" (1855; line 37). This image turns up in many names in the nineteenth-century novel and always to make a substantive point: in the very title character of Thomas Hamilton's *The Youth and Manhood of Cyril Thornton* (1827), in Gaskell's Thornton in *North and South* (1855), the Thornes of Trollope's *Doctor Thorne* (1858), and in Thornfield in *Jane Eyre* (1847). Brontë's conception is close to Austen's. When Jane refuses to marry St. John and go to India with him to preach because she does not feel the "vocation" (392), but quickly answers Rochester's "call" when he summons her to Thornfield (413), Brontë plays on the root of "vocation" to tell us that Jane has rejected God's "call" so that she may answer man's, a very specific man to be sure, but made generic by the fact that he is the master of Thornfield, a place that, referring to the thorn, is shown to be the earthly realm. One of the first to draw on this image, Austen uses it to identify Thornton Lacey as the place in which, following St. Francis, Fanny brings religion to earth.

Even more important, perhaps, is the fact that, in the process, Austen herself has found a means through which fiction may be ordained. This is the ultimate point of her symbolism, as it is of the symbolism later Victorians were to use. That new *mythos* Friedrich Schlegel in particular had called for, which was to be the new foundation for the remaking of the world, was to him a language as well, the idiom that would provide the images of truths intuited though not seen, transcendent truths themselves ineffable, and capable therefore of being expressed only in symbolic form. In his *Bunyan,* James Anthony Froude was to write that so

> long as religion is fully alive, men do not talk about it or make allegories about it. They assume its truth as out of reach of questions, and they simply obey its precepts as they obey the law of the land. It becomes a subject of art and discourse only when men are unconsciously ceasing to believe, and therefore the more vehemently think that they believe, and repudiate with indignation the suggestion that doubt has found its way into them. After this, religion no longer governs their lives. It governs only the language in which they express themselves, and they preserve it eagerly, in the shape of elaborate observances or in the agreeable forms of art and literature.
>
> (150)

As always, and obviously overlooking the great medieval allegories, Froude speaks from his own perspective as a skeptical Victorian, but the essential point he makes, that secular eras often cling to the language of religion when they begin to lose their faith, is one that Austen sets to her purposes. Seeing her age as increasingly secular, she appropriates this language not as a vestige of religion but, in the Romantic spirit of taking the word of God within, as its symbolic representation in the idiom of her text, a text she thereby consecrates, or in her own metaphor, ordains.

It is through this ordination, figured in an actual rite recorded in the final chapter but occurring at the moment in which he sees with moral clarity the true nature of the good, that Edmund ceases to love Mary and falls in love with Fanny instead: "the charm is broken," he declares, "My eyes are opened" (***MP*** 456). Appropriately on the Christian calendar—like many Victorian novelists after her, Austen uses a mythic calendar as part of her religious symbolism (see my, *Triptych* 78-81), placing many events in the novel on appropriate liturgical dates—Edmund is ordained at Christmas, exactly the time for religious (re)birth.

But this is precisely the point at which the symbolism starts to break down and the *poiesis* to unravel. The remaking of the world depends on the total integration of the real and the ideal, on the ability of the ideal to be embodied in the real. Without such concurrence, all we have is an ideal vision of order that has no relation to or influence on reality, which must therefore remain in chaos. Austen wants to provide concurrence and tries to force it in the last chapter. But she declines to make us believe it because she does not believe it herself. Metafiction takes the place of verisimilitudinous narrative.

In fact, she presents us with two endings. Long before Frank Kermode remarked on the difficulty of finding endings in a secular age, Austen declares that she cannot do it, will not do it, cannot pretend that such a thing as an ending exists. She can offer us a cessation but not a suitable resolution. Rather, she lets her narrative split. Asking us to decide for ourselves when Edmund would have ceased to love Mary (***MP*** 470) is as good as assuring us that in fact he never did, that he would have married Mary and allowed Fanny to marry Henry, as we are told she would have done, had Edmund not been available and had Henry persisted in courting her (***MP*** 467).[8] And to be told that the union takes place in a manner that guarantees that nothing of the kind would have happened asks us to accept two endings in a conclusion that forever separates things as they are from things as they ought to be. Coherence has become the property, not of the world of actual fact, but only of the mind of the maker.

And this is what Austen wants us to know. The novel is a vision of order, not a prediction of things to come. But for the grace of the author's pen, everything would turn to chaos. The artist alone can make order now, but only on the fictional page, and only if he is fully prepared to concede this limitation.

Notes

1. Citing discussions by Wayne Booth, Wolfgang Iser, and Kathleen Tillotson, Lorraine M. York takes such remarks to be ways through which Jane Austen wants to make us aware as readers not only of what she is saying but of how we understand her. I would agree but only suggest that this is a secondary purpose to Austen's metafictional ends.

2. Like John Wiltshire, I take the names of this novel to be significant, but, unlike him, I take their significance to be derived not from characters in works Austen had or might have read but from the meanings they acquired, in a variety of ways, in a symbolic vocabulary that began with the Romantics and became the common idiom of the nineteenth-century novel.

3. How, exactly, she means religion is by no means clear in the novel. Jager and Willis may be right that she means it narrowly, the Anglican or Christian religion. But many Victorians used the word to suggest a set of ideals held in sacred reverence, as Carlyle does in the passage above, and Austen seems to me for the most part to think of it mostly in this way. Here and throughout, references and allusions to the Bible are to the Authorized King James Version, the version Austen would have used herself.

4. A number of readers have made good cases for Austen's engagement with evangelicalism (e.g., Mary Waldron and David Monaghan) but, although I would agree that Austen was sympathetic to it, it is not what she is looking for here.

5. Many have commented on this imagery, most recently in negative terms. Markovitz, for example, takes Austen as always placing "happiness" in the future of her characters and, in consequence, as unable to consider Adam's fall in the light of a *felix culpa* (783). But this may not be quite fair to Austen. She often does see present happiness, as in Edmund's delight in Mary. What she envisions for the future is the misery Mary will bring, and that cannot but make her feel that the *culpa* is less than *felix.*

6. It is in this context, I would suggest, that we can best see the complexities Austen creates in these two characters. She does not invite us, quite the contrary, to measure them against actual people. She does not urge us to search in our hearts for explanations for their actions. That is a kind of realism that is obviously not her purpose. But she does allow her characters to expand into the social and psychological dimensions that help explain and elaborate their moral and historical purposes. Thus, as Melissa Burns has argued, Fanny has genuine self-knowledge, a state of mind that has moral significance, but psychological significance as well. She has a self, as we see most clearly when we compare her to Henry Crawford, a man whose lack of identity is what makes him such a good actor, but also such an unreliable and utterly changeable human being. Similarly, as Alice Chandler ("A Pair of Fine Eyes") and Claudia Johnson have suggested, although she seems to some so ethereal that there is nothing physical in her, Fanny is highly sexualized both through the imagery of the novel and through descriptions that subtly turn her from the child she is at first into a fully sexual being.

7. I build here in part on Lucy M. Schneider's and Melissa Edmundson's explorations of the ways in which her movement through the house helps to develop Fanny's relationship to the Bertrams in Mansfield Park and to the progress of the novel.

8. Although he comes to a different conclusion, Gene Koppel makes an interesting point about the problems of this ending when he speaks of it as contingent.

Works Cited

Alter, Robert. *Partial Magic: The Novel as a Self-Conscious Genre.* Berkeley: U of California P, 1978.

Austen, Jane. *Mansfield Park. The Oxford Illustrated Jane Austen.* Vol. 3. 3rd ed. Oxford: Oxford UP, 1934.

———. *Jane Austen's Letters.* Ed. R. W. Chapman. 2nd ed. Oxford: Oxford UP, 1952.

Bonaparte, Felicia. *The Triptych and the Cross: The Central Myths of George Eliot's Poetic Imagination.* New York: New York UP, 1979.

———. "Conjecturing Possibilities: Reading and Misreading Texts in Jane Austen's *Pride and Prejudice.*" *Studies in the Novel* 37.2 (Summer 2005): 141-61.

———. "*Middlemarch*: The Genesis of Myth in the English Novel: The Relationship between Literary Form and the Modern Predicament." *Notre Dame English Journal* 8.3 (Summer 1981): 107-54.

Brontë, Charlotte. *Jane Eyre: Authoritative Text, Backgrounds, Criticism.* Ed. Richard J. Dunn. 2nd ed. New York: W. W. Norton & Co. Inc., 1987.

———. *Villette.* Ed. Margaret Smith. Oxford: Oxford UP, 2008.

Browning, Robert. "Women and Roses." *The Poetical Works of Robert Browning: Complete from 1833 to 1868, and the Shorter Poems Thereafter.* London: Oxford UP, 1953. 242-43.

Bulwer-Lytton, Edward. "On Certain Principles of Art in Works of Imagination." *Caxtoniana: A Series of Essays on Life, Literature, and Manners.* New York: Harper & Brothers, 1864.

Burns, Melissa. "Jane Austen's *Mansfield Park*: Determining Authorial Intention." *Persuasions* 26.1 (Winter 2005): n.p.

Butler, Marilyn. *Jane Austen and the War of Ideas.* Oxford: Oxford UP, 1975.

Carlyle, Thomas. *Sartor Resartus: The Life and Opinions of Herr Teufelsdröckh.* Ed. Charles Frederick Harrold. New York: Odyssey P, 1937.

Chandler, Alice. *A Dream of Order: The Medieval Ideal in Nineteenth-Century Literature.* Lincoln, NB: U of Nebraska P, 1970.

———. " 'A Pair of Fine Eyes': Jane Austen's Treatment of Sex." *Studies in the Novel* 7 (1975): 88-103.

Collins, Barbara Bail. "Jane Austen's Victorian Novel." *Nineteenth-Century Fiction* 4.3 (Dec. 1949): 175-85.

Collins, Irene. *Jane Austen and the Clergy.* London: Hambledon & London, 2002.

———. *Jane Austen: The Parson's Daughter.* London: Hambledon & London, 2007.

Comte, Auguste. *Discours sur L'Esprit Positif.* Eds. Carilian-Goeury and Vor Dalmont. Paris: Fain et Thunot, 1844.

Da Vinci, Leonardo. *Leonardo Da Vinci's Note-Books: Arranged and Rendered into English by Edward McCurdy.* New York: Empire State Book Company, 1923.

Derry, Stephen. "An Allusion to Bunyan in Mansfield Park." *Notes and Queries* 40.4 (Dec. 1993): 466-67.

Dickens, Charles. *Hard Times.* Ed. Paul Schlicke. Oxford: Oxford UP, 2008.

———. *Little Dorrit.* Eds. Stephen Wall and Helen Small. London: Penguin, 1998.

Donohue, Joseph W. "Ordination and the Divided House at Mansfield Park." *ELH* 32.2 (June 1965): 169-78.

Edmundson, Melissa. "A Space for Fanny: The Significance of Her Rooms in *Mansfield Park.*" *Persuasions* 23.1 (Winter 2002): n.p.

Eliot, George. *Middlemarch.* Ed. David Carroll. Oxford: Oxford UP. 1997.

———. *The Mill on the Floss.* Ed. Gordon S. Haight. Oxford: Oxford UP, 2008.

Eliot, T. S. *The Complete Poems and Plays, 1909-1950.* New York: Harcourt Brace and Co., 1950.

Ferguson, Moira. "*Mansfield Park*: Slavery, Colonialism, and Gender." *The Oxford Literary Review* 13.1-2 (1991): 118-39.

Froude, James Anthony. *Bunyan.* New York: Harper & Brothers, 1880.

Gaskell, Elizabeth. *North and South.* Ed. Dorothy Collin. Harmondsworth, U.K.: Penguin Books, 1970.

Griffin, Michael. "Jane Austen and Religion: Salvation and Society in Georgian Society." *Persuasions* 23.1 (Winter 2002): n.p.

Halperin, John. "The Trouble with *Mansfield Park.*" *Studies in the Novel* 7 (1975): 6-23.

Hamilton, Thomas. *The Youth and Manhood of Cyril Thornton.* Ed. Maurice Lindsay. Aberdeen: Association for Scottish Literary Studies, 1990.

Hardy, Thomas. *Jude the Obscure.* London: Macmillan, 1974.

Holy Bible. *King James Version: Standard Text Edition.* Cambridge, U.K.: Cambridge UP, 1995.

Hurd, Richard. *Letters on Chivalry and Romance.* Los Angeles: Augustan Reprint Society, 1963.

Jager, Colin. "*Mansfield Park* and the End of Natural Theology." *Modern Language Quarterly* 63.1 (March 2002): 31-63.

Jameson, Anna. *Legends of the Monastic Orders as Presented in the Fine Arts.* 4th ed. London: Longmans, Green, and Co., 1867.

Jenkins, Elizabeth. "Jane Austen and the Human Condition." *Essays by Diverse Hands* 39 (1977): 57-75.

Johnson, Claudia L. "What Became of Jane Austen? *Mansfield Park.*" *Persuasions: Journal of the Jane Austen Society of North America* 17 (Dec. 1995): 59-70.

Karounos, Michael. "Ordination and Revolution in *Mansfield Park.*" *SEL* 44.4 (Autumn 2004): 715-36.

Kermode, Frank. *The Sense of an Ending: Studies in the Theory of Fiction.* Oxford: Oxford UP, 1967.

Kingsley, Charles. *Two Years Ago.* London: Macmillan and Co., 1900.

Kirkham, Margaret. "Feminist Irony and the Priceless Heroine of *Mansfield Park.*" *Women & Literature* 3 (1983): 231-47.

Knox-Shaw, Peter. *Jane Austen and the Enlightenment.* Cambridge, U.K.: Cambridge UP, 2004.

Koppel, Gene. "The Role of Contingency in *Mansfield Park*: The Necessity of an Ambiguous Conclusion." *Southern Review* 15.3 (Nov. 1982): 306-13.

Lamont, Claire. "Jane Austen and the Old." *Review of English Studies* 54.217 (Nov. 2003): 661-74.

Lauber, John. "Minds Bewildered and Astray: The Crawfords in *Mansfield Park.*" *Studies in the Novel* 2 (1970): 194-210.

Lawrence, D. H. *The Rainbow.* Parts 1 and 2. Ed. Mark Kinkead-Weekes. Cambridge, U.K.: Cambridge UP, 2003.

———. *Women in Love.* Eds. David Farmer, Lindeth Vasey, and John Worthen. Cambridge, U.K.: Cambridge UP, 1987.

Lew, Joseph. "'That Abominable Traffic': *Mansfield Park* and the Dynamics of Slavery." *Gender & Eighteenth-Century Literature.* Ed. Beth Fowkes Tobin. Athens, GA: U of Georgia P, 1994. 271-300.

Longfellow, Henry Wadsworth. *The Complete Poetical Works of Henry Wadsworth Longfellow.* Charleston, SC: Nabu Press, 2010.

Magee, William H. "Romanticism on Trial in *Mansfield Park.*" *Bucknell Review* 14.1 (1966): 44-59.

Malone, Maggie. "Patriarchy and Slavery and the Problem of Fanny in *Mansfield Park.*" *Essays in Poetics* 18.2 (Sept. 1993): 28-41.

Manzoni, Alessandro. *I Promessi Sposi.* Ed. Dante Isella. Milan: Casa del Manzoni, 2006.

Markovitz, Stefanie. "Jane Austen and the Happy Fall." *SEL* 47.4 (2007): 779-97.

Martin, W. R. "'Ordination' in *Mansfield Park.*" *English Studies in Africa* 9 (1966): 146-57.

Meyersohn, Marylea. "What Fanny Knew: A Quiet Auditor of the Whole." *Women & Literature* 3 (1983): 224-30.

Monaghan, David. "*Mansfield Park* and Evangelicalism: A Reassessment." *Nineteenth-Century Fiction* 33.2 (Sept. 1978): 215-30.

Reeve, Clara. "The Progress of Romance through Times, Centuries, and Manners." *The Progress of Romance and The History of Chaeroba, Queen of Aegypt.* New York: The Facsimile Text Society, 1930.

Ruskin, John. *Modern Painters.* New York: John W. Lovell Company, n.d. 5 vols.

Said, Edward. *Culture and Imperialism.* New York: Borzoi Books, 1993.

Schlegel, Friedrich. "Dialogue on Poetry." *Dialogue on Poetry and Literary Aphorisms.* Trans. Ernst Behler and Roman Struc. University Park, PA: Pennsylvania State UP, 1968. 51-117.

Schneider, M. Lucy. "The Little White Attic and the East Room: Their Function in *Mansfield Park.*" *Modern Philology* 63.3 (Feb. 1966): 227-35.

Scott, P. J. M. *Jane Austen: A Reassessment.* London: Barnes & Noble, 1982.

Shakespeare, William. *Romeo and Juliet.* Ed. Jill L. Levenson. Oxford: Oxford UP, 2008.

Scott, Walter. "Chivalry." *Encyclopedia Brittanica.* Supplement to the 1815-24 ed.

———. "Romance." *Encyclopedia Brittanica.* Supplement to the 1815-24 ed.

Shelley, Percy Bysshe. "A Defence of Poetry." *Shelley's Prose: The Trumpet of a Prophecy.* Ed. David Lee Clark. New York: New Amsterdam Books, 1988: 275-97.

Singer, Josephine. "Fanny and the Beatitudes." *Persuasions* 28.1 (Winter 2007): n.p.

Southam, Brian. "The Silence of the Bertrams." *The Times Literary Supplement* 17 (Feb. 1995): 13-4.

Sutherland, Kathryn. "Jane Eyre's Literary History: The Case for *Mansfield Park.*" *ELH*: 59.2 (Summer 1992): 409-40.

Tamm, Merike. "Inter-Art Relations and the Novels of Jane Austen." *Dissertation Abstracts International* 37 (1977): 5149A-50A.

Tanner, Tony. *Jane Austen.* Cambridge, Massachusetts: Harvard UP, 1986.

Tennyson, Alfred. *The Poems and Plays of Alfred Lord Tennyson.* New York: The Modern Library, 1938.

Trilling, Lionel. "*Mansfield Park.*" *Jane Austen: A Collection of Critical Essays.* Ed. Ian Watt. Englewood Cliffs, N.J.: Prentice-Hall, Inc., 1963. 124-40.

Trollope, Anthony. *Doctor Thorne.* London: Penguin Books, 2004.

Waldron, Mary. "The Frailties of Fanny: *Mansfield Park* and the Evangelical Movement." *Eighteenth-Century Fiction* 6.3 (April 1994): 259-82.

Ward, Mary Augusta Arnold. *The Testing of Diana Mallory.* New York: Harper & Brothers Publishers, 1908.

Warton, Thomas. *History of English Poetry from the Close of the Eleventh to the Commencement of the Eighteenth Century.* London: Ward, Lock, and Co., 1870.

Watt, Ian. *The Rise of the Novel: Studies in Defoe, Richardson, and Fielding.* Berkeley: U of California P, 1957.

Willis, Lesley. "Religion in Jane Austen's *Mansfield Park.*" *English Studies in Canada* 13.1 (1987): 65-78.

Wiltshire, John. "The Importance of Being Edmund: On Names in *Mansfield Park.*" *New Windows on a Woman's World: Essays for Jocelyn Harris.* Ed. Colin Gibson and Lisa Marr. Vol. 2. Dunedin, New Zealand: Department of English, University of Otago, 2005. 138-47.

York, Lorraine M. "'The Pen of the Contriver' and the Eye of the Perceiver: *Mansfield Park,* The Implied Author and the Implied Reader." *English Studies in Canada* 13.2 (June 1987): 161-73.

Monique W. Dull (essay date 2011)

SOURCE: Dull, Monique W. "'Little Irritations' in *Mansfield Park.*" *Restoring the Mystery of the Rainbow: Literature's Refraction of Science.* Ed. Valeria Tinkler-Villani and C. C. Barfoot. Amsterdam: Rodopi, 2011. 249-74. Print.

[*In the following essay, Dull utilizes Scottish physician Robert Whytt's "concept of irritability" to examine the sentimental aspects of* Mansfield Park, *commenting on the work's "tropes of contagion and comparative proportion."*]

> Moral as well as Natural Diseases disappear in the progress of time, & new ones take their place—Shyness & the Sweating Sickness have given way to Confidence & Paralytic complaints.[1]

Sensibility is enjoying a vigorous afterlife. It has stimulated discussion of the second half of the eighteenth century and the early nineteenth century, especially since R. F. B. Brissenden's influential *Virtue in Distress* in 1974.[2] Jane Austen critics have asked whether Austen was for or against Marianne Dashwood's sensibility, whether Elinor, or later, Fanny Price, is not sensible to an extent also, and, if so, whether this is good or bad. John Halperin's critical biography spends pages on the ***Juvenilia***'s games with excesses and absences of sensibility. Halperin summarizes

"Evelyn" in the same way he summarizes **"Love and Freindship"** (*sic*): "It continues the attack on sentimental fiction; almost all the characters are motivated exclusively by an oversupply or an undersupply, as the case may be, of sensibility."[3]

We could either take the centrality of sensibility as proof of sensibility's discursive dominance (together with Halperin) or we could take Austen's parody as a pointer to its waning. Even if the young Jane Austen had, by 1790, excavated its psycho-social function, then maybe another layer awaited her analysis. I suggest that this next object of interest, not yet open to her parody because not yet abused by culture, lay within the wider complex of contemporary psycho-physiology now largely forgotten by historians: the revisionary concept of irritability propounded by the Scottish physician Robert Whytt (1704-1766), with its attendant renovations to the structure of character and plot.

Surveying ***Mansfield Park*** within the field laid out by British medical theorists from the mid-eighteenth century to the early nineteenth century, what strikes me is not the supremacy of sensibility, but rather the quiet reversal of its fortunes during this span.[4] I will briefly trace what I see as the medical prehistory to the emphasis in ***Mansfield Park*** on a modern reactive disposition, what I see as the prehistory to its discarding of sensibility as a novelistic touchstone. Then I will analyse ***Mansfield Park*** for its display of 1814 psycho-physiology, and relate this display to the novel's tropes of contagion and comparative proportion.

Sensibility and nervousness may have become equals, even competitors, but their original relation was more complex: sensibility was a part of the whole which was nervousness, which in turn exceeded having nerves. Ann Jessie Van Sant best situates sensibility in its context of mid-eighteenth-century neurology. Like Brissenden, Van Sant discusses Albrecht von Haller (1708-1777), the great Swiss neurologist, and his theory that the physiological qualities of sensibility and irritability were strictly distinct. Van Sant uses Haller's distinction as a basis for her own traditional focus on sensibility, which she takes to be the psychological end of psycho-physiology, and which she juxtaposes with a somatized irritability.[5]

Yet Van Sant's Hallerian history is a traditionally skewed vision particularly of the British neurological theories of the time. Haller's contention that within the reactive animal system, nerves were "sensible," or registered pain and pleasure, while muscles were solely "irritable," or contractile, was sharply contested by Whytt, whose position derived from a still earlier Anglo-Germanic neurological tradition. Anton van Leeuwenhoek's microscopic discovery of the mylar sheath in 1684 began the modern embodiment of the senses; George Cheyne tried to "account for the Frequency of Nervous Distempers of late"[6] by positing a surplus of nerves, and therefore of sensations, as a bodily basis for the nervous psychology. Cheyne's neurology is both psychologized and biologized in its placing of refined souls within the context of nerve counts. In a prescription to be found in ***Mansfield Park,*** Cheyne suggests that "*Bodily Exercise* and Action,"[7] particularly riding, strengthen the otherwise weak—and therefore overly perceptive—nerve fibres.

Haller's mid-century *Dissertation on the Sensible and Irritable Parts of Animals* split Cheyne's symptomatic body from its psyche. Haller divided the sensible ("I call that sensible part of the human body, which upon being touched transmits the impression of it to the soul") from the irritable ("I call that part of the human body irritable, which becomes shorter upon being touched; very irritable if it contracts upon a slight touch, and the contrary if by a violent touch it contracts but little").[8] Haller's duality was absolute: animal response to stimulus was either conscious and sensible, in that a nerve registered pain; or it was unconscious and irritable, in that a muscle such as the heart contracted without the animal's necessary awareness of this motion. His insistent division was the trademark of Hallerian psycho-physiology: "[Irritability] is so different from sensibility, that the most irritable parts are not at all sensible, and *vice versa,* the most sensible are not irritable . . . irritability does not depend upon the nerves, but on the original fabric of the parts which are susceptible of it."[9]

Haller's split made structurally possible sensibility's metonymic dominance as the psycho-physiological shorthand for psychological feeling. He wedged apart involuntary and voluntary actions, and granted all soulful activity to the nerves and their sensibility. Haller used strongly psycho-spiritual language to emphasize that sensibility and irritability, aligned with nerves and muscles, were also aligned with soul and unconscious body. Since the heart muscle contracts without our consciousness, therefore irritability "is independent of the soul and will." At the same time, since we are always conscious of stimulus to a nerve, sensibility is a symptom of soul, for "The soul is a being which is conscious of itself, represents to itself the body to which it belongs, and by means of that body the whole universe."[10]

We have arrived at the standard current understanding of eighteenth-century sensibility. Brissenden centred his useful explication of contemporary neurology on Haller, in part because Haller's 1749 review of Samuel Richardson's *Clarissa* and his few poems (and their 1794 English translation) provided a handy nexus of psycho-physiology and literary sensibility.[11] But to take Haller's distinction as the mid-eighteenth-century view of the body's complex interaction with its surroundings, or even the dominant view, is simply to write from within Hallerian discourse, or from the corner of sentimental culture that took up Haller and briefly applauded him.

The opinions of experimenters were in fact more varied, and their contestation more widely known, than a historian of Haller might think. Whytt's several treatises on muscular and nervous reactions all treated the problem of willed actions and involuntary actions (such as the heart's contraction). Whytt's 1756 *Observations on the Sensibility and Irritability of the Parts of Men and Other Animals; Occasioned by Dr Haller's Late Treatise on These Subjects* explicitly disputed Haller's bifurcation.[12]

Whytt questioned Haller's bifurcation and the consequent psychologization and privilege attached to Hallerian sensibility. Whytt proved that all the body parts Haller had declared without nerves contained nerves. Whytt argued that muscular contraction did imply sensation, although all feeling did not necessarily bring about contraction: "although irritability always infers some degree of sensibility, yet sensibility does not infer irritability, unless the part be . . . muscular."[13] Thus Whytt reconfigured sensibility and irritability as psycho-physiological set and subset rather than as mutually exclusive properties.

With Whytt's more complex organization came a more nuanced distribution of soul. The irritable has feeling either through its hierarchical dependance on nerves, or possibly (Whytt added) through a feeling specific to the irritable: "the word *irritability* seems to imply a kind of life or feeling in the part endowed with it, which renders it capable of being fretted, provoked, or irritated. . . . We will never talk of irritating a stone, a piece of wood, a tree, or indeed any thing that is without feeling." Whytt answers Haller's methodical erasure of psyche from irritability with this psycho-spiritual counter: "it is probable, that the irritability of the muscles of animals is owing to that living sentient principle which animates and enlivens their whole frame."[14] For Whytt, soul is no longer limited to consciousness, but is everywhere in the body. Irritability, attributed by Haller only to muscles, is redefined by Whytt to become a muted attribute of the whole body, while retaining its primary locus in the muscle.

Whytt implicitly predicted that his answer to Haller would bring about changes. In his introductory paragraphs, Whytt claimed his own motive in debating Haller was the threat of clinical consequences resulting from Haller's convictions (such as Hallerian surgeons cutting muscle and denying patient distress) embedded in Haller's preceding treatise.[15] In retrospect, we can see that when Whytt reassigned irritability to a place within sensibility, and when he consequently redistributed psyche from sensibility alone (as in Haller) to sensibility's more complex subset of irritability as well, he wrought at least three subsidiary effects.

First, Whytt's more complex psycho-physiology diffused the intensity of Haller's mind-focused theses. Sensibility, while it still had psychological import and privilege, was no longer alone in carrying the burden, and gift, of feeling. Sensation and soul under Whytt's regime could live in unexpected places, including lowly extremities such as the achilles tendon.

Second, breaking sensibility's monopoly on feeling in turn democratized sensation itself: as well as diminishing sensibility's psychological stature, sensation's reassignment throughout the body also allowed more nuanced sensation—as though the quality were more thinly spread. Whytt held that Haller's dangerous denial of sensation to most of the body came simply from Haller's lack of perception of "a much more obscure degree of feeling."[16]

Third, since sensation was now shared by sensibility and irritability throughout the body, and since irritable motions symptomatized this "much more obscure degree of feeling," therefore vast tracts of the animal body, and previously undiscussed (and undiscussible) motions, were now open to psychological interpretation. Irritability, Whytt argued, invited understanding of "involuntary voluntary action," or the reactive muscular movement that was neither as unconscious as the heart's contraction, nor as willed as the stitching of needlework. Whytt described what we now call the reflex action as a hybrid of sensation and contraction, without will.[17] The diction of Whytt's reflex act centres on the semantic family of "contract," "involuntary," "repel," "shrink," "startle," and "withdraw." Whytt's involuntary voluntary motion, which falls within the realm of irritability, could be seen as an early somatization of an unconscious, or as psycho-somatization in the most literal sense. It will account for much in ***Mansfield Park.***

An Agitation She Could Not Subdue

Like a fibrous network nearly invisible to readers today, vocabulary with long-dead physiological significances stretches through Jane Austen's narrative, activating passive Fanny and dulling Fanny's more obviously feeling competitors. The psycho-physiological diction of ***Mansfield Park*** ("sensible," "irritable," "agitated," "nervous," "excited," "spirits," etc.) records the subtle reversal of sensibility's and irritability's fortunes by 1814. Sensibility fades from her novel's vocabulary. Jane Austen ultimately supplants these devalued terms with the words and plot of irritability. Like the novel, Fanny could be said to grow out of one psycho-physiology and into another.

At the same time, ***Mansfield Park*** offers a surplus of sensibility reminiscent of Austen's parody in her ***Juvenilia.*** Sensibility, recently used to distinguish the sentimental hero and heroine from their surroundings, here belongs to even the most unlikely candidates. Even Mr Price, who "swore and drank, . . . was dirty and gross," can articulate "expressions of an attached father, and a sensible man."[18] Rather than deny sensibility to Mary Crawford in order to shore up ontological credit for Fanny,[19] we might well agree with Edmund when he declares Mary and Fanny equally sensible:

> Good-humoured, unaffected girls, will not do for a man who has been used to sensible women. They are two distinct orders of being. You and Miss Crawford have made me too nice.
>
> (323)

Mary, with her blushes and hesitations, is sensible to the extent that she is educated and literate; which is the same extent to which Edmund and Henry can call "well-informed men" categorically "sensible" in so far as they have by-now standard literary and romantic taste (307-308).

Edmund is not nearly "nice," or discriminating, enough. Where old-fashioned Edmund sees only "two distinct orders of being"—insensible and sensible—Jane Austen sees at least three, splitting as she does the "sensible" into the "sensible" and the "sensible and irritable," and splitting these into constituent parts in turn. Let us examine them. Fanny is the first "sensible" character in the narrative. In Chapter 1, Mrs Norris hopes she will "be sensible of her uncommon good fortune" (8). Young Fanny proves so sensible of her situation as to cry herself to sleep, and in a few pages is "sensible of gratitude" where she felt pain. Thereafter the epithet spreads promiscuously to other, older characters. The attribute of a child's psyche becomes every well-heeled young adult's accoutrement. Fanny may wear Maria's and Julia's hand-me-downs, but Maria and Julia take on the psychic formation that Fanny's character quickly outgrows.

Sensibility becomes a fashionable accessory in the young adulthood of Fanny's generation. Austen bestows "the highest spirits" (73) on Julia en route to Sotherton, and later grants her "all the suffering which a warm temper and a high spirit were likely to endure" (146). Opportunist Maria goes a step further and dramatizes her sensibility, which Henry flatteringly names for her:

> "Naturally, I believe, I am as lively as Julia, but I have more to think of now."
>
> "You have undoubtedly—and there are situations in which high spirits would denote insensibility."

Henry's inverse compliment (that Maria's low spirits are symptoms of her pre-nuptial sensibility) assumes that sensibility is a desirable quality. Maria signals her membership among the sensible with her reference to Sterne's *Sentimental Journey*: "I cannot get out, as the starling said" (89).

Sensibility is overproduced. A quality so cheaply distributed can no longer bring moral or psychological credit. Maria's sensibility follows Haller in its delineation of her conscious self. Recall that Haller used sensibility to mark the edge of an integral self: "The soul is a being which is conscious of itself, represents to itself the body to which it belongs, and by means of that body the whole universe" (28). Maria's selfhood takes shape with her selfish desire for autonomy: "Independance was more needful than ever; the want of it at Mansfield was more sensibly felt" (182). Maria's reaction to constraint signifies her self-consciousness. Likewise Aunt Norris uses sensibility's sub-vocabulary of "low spirits" to argue her transparently selfish economies (25-26). The comedy of Aunt Norris editorializing on her own "low spirits" depends on our understanding that her self-awareness is simply a euphemism for her selfishness. Both Maria Bertram and Aunt Norris, in arguing sensibility to make selfish claims, are doubly aware. Nightmarish versions of Hallerian self-consciousness, they are explicitly aware of their awareness of their selves.

If sensibility becomes "sensibility" once a self articulates consciousness of its feelings—once someone names himself "sensible"—then Fanny's senses *per se* prevent her from becoming "sensible," in so far as her strong sensations overwhelm and preclude articulation, which is the symptom of consciousness in turn. Fanny's somatized sensations save her from Henry on at least one occasion, since Henry's courtship depends on getting Fanny to articulate her sensible affection for him. As it is, she "remain[s] insensible" of Henry due to her overemployed senses when she learns of her brother's promotion:

> [Henry] spoke with such a glow of what his solicitude had been, and used such strong expressions, was so abounding in the *deepest interest,* in *two-fold motives,* in *views and wishes more than could be told,* that Fanny could not have remained insensible of his drift, had she been able to attend; but her heart was so full and her senses still so astonished, that she could listen but imperfectly.
>
> (272)

Unfortunately for Fanny, the same applies to her sensations upon Edward's gift of the gold chain for William's cross (236). An "agitated manner" distorts what she does say.

To remain moral, in the revisionary terms of ***Mansfield Park,*** reaction must be submerged into Whytt's unconscious. Given the exhausted state of sensibility (overused and evacuated of specific meaning), this submersion depends on irritability. Fanny, who begins as the childish locus of sensibility, declares herself "sensible" only once in adulthood, when she uses the word not as a compliment to herself, but rather to denote awareness of something that does not move her—Henry's early attentions (329-30). Fanny's denial of psychologized sensibility comes perhaps from the fact that her typical reactions are not conscious and articulated, but somatized.

It is not surprising that Fanny becomes the site for the resomatization of response, and thus of psyche. Fanny, having outgrown her childhood psychologized sensibility, is increasingly, overwhelmingly, identified by the narrator as "nervous" and "irritable." Fanny's portrait is dominated by irritability's conceptual and dictional complement to overused sensibility. Sir Thomas "knew her to be ... exceedingly nervous" (289). Following Cheyne's prescription, the Bertrams concede that Fanny needs the favourite "Bodily Exercise" (riding) of the nervous patient; they simply do not supply her with it (31). Yeazell insists on Fanny's sensible "delicacy" in Portsmouth,[20] and Halperin anachronistically declares Fanny "neurasthenic" in Portsmouth,[21] but Austen refers to her nervous "frame and temper." The noises and smells of Portsmouth are further specified within three sentences to be "irritations" in Whytt's tradition of external stimuli: "as to [Mansfield Park's] little irritations, sometimes introduced by aunt Norris, they were short, they were trifling, they were as a drop of water to the ocean, compared with the ceaseless tumult of her present abode" (357). Mansfield Park and Portsmouth are a dyad, not of sensibility and irritability, nerve and muscle, psyche and body (as in a Hallerian system), but actually a Whyttian dyad of comparatively smaller and larger irritations, where irritation is a constant.

Mansfield Park is not only sprinkled with "irritate" and its derivations, but especially with irritation's own symptom, "agitation," a word frequently taken by critics to refer to Hallerian sensibility. "Agitation" was linked instead with Whytt's complex notion of the feeling capacity of irritability. "Agitate," from the Latin *agito, agitare* (to set in motion), referred to literal movement, especially in the context of psycho-physiological experimentation.[22] When Haller, Whytt, *et al.*, poked, burned, stabbed, and did much worse to their unfortunate animals, they looked for signs of reaction, one of which was agitation or muscular movement. Thus Fanny is briefly figured as the object of her narrator's cruel experiment, in which Edward gushes over Mary. "It was a stab," the voice announces; and again in the next sentence: "It was a stab, in spite of every longstanding expectation; and she was obliged to repeat again and again that she was one of his two dearest, before the words gave her any sensation" (239). After this "stab," Fanny experiences an "agitation" that she "could not subdue."

Almost everyone in the novel is driven by irritability and agitation, whether they know it or not. Maria, our best parader of sensibility, seems unaware that the narrator has her in a "good deal of agitation" and "delight and agitation" (173) over Henry's advances and introduction to her father. Maria, also a laboratory animal, has "a moment's struggle as she listened, and only a moment's," when her father—notably after "observation"—prods her about her engagement to Rushworth. Maria struggles "as she listen[s]": Sir Thomas' questions are the stimulus. Hence "when her father ceased," she can show "no apparent agitation" to her experimenter's eyes (180).

But that Maria does become agitated and irritated, Austen makes beautifully clear in the very Sotherton scene in which Maria thinks she advertises her sensibility: "to see only [Mr Crawford's] expressive profile as he turned with a smile to Julia, or to catch the laugh of the other, was a perpetual source of irritation, which her own sense of propriety could but just smooth over" (73). Maria's literal sensation—her seeing and hearing—of Henry's flirtation with Julia, provokes a discomfort specifically named "irritation," not, as Maria and Henry will shortly misidentify it, "sensibility."

Let us accept that irritation, which Jane Austen identifies as a purer, since less frequently invoked, mode of response than sensibility, is already received as the newest way of being. If this is so, then our understanding of Fanny should be drastically revised. She is the most responsive and the most modern figure, albeit responsive and modern in her barely visible displays of a "much more obscure degree of feeling."

Fanny's unconscious adult agitations govern her character in the wake of her retreating childhood sensibility. Austen's irritable vocabulary begins to define Fanny in force at the point of her critical moral maturation during the Mansfield theatricals. From the moment of the private theatricals, in which "her nerves [were] agitated" by the "shock" Tom's attack (135)—a metaphoric transferral from muscles—no less than thirty-two agitations compose Fanny's being, and far outnumber the frequent agitations in the world around her. Fanny's agitation is the same kind as the agitation of others. It signifies either pain or pleasure, or both. But even in its shared "more obscure degree," Fanny's agitation exceeds that of others. Fanny's immediate sensation stands outside of moral consciousness. Upon Sir Thomas' return from Antigua, Fanny's "agitation and alarm exceeded all that was endured by the rest, by the right of a disposition which not even innocence could keep from suffering" (158). Austen emphasizes upon Sir Thomas' return that Fanny's agitation arises despite her own innocence: it is a strong reaction that delineates her self, but it is not within range of her consciousness.

For this reason, Fanny's response is not mediable by her volition, either. The reflexive vocabulary hovering over Fanny collapses to leave no room for will's intrusion. During the theatricals, "She was invested, indeed, with the office of judge and critic, and earnestly desired to exercise it and tell them all their faults; but from doing so every feeling within her shrank, she could not, would not, dared not to attempt it; had she been otherwise qualified for criticism, her conscience must have restrained her from venturing at disapprobation" (153). Governed neither by consciousness nor will, her reaction recalls Whytt's proposal of the "involuntary voluntary motion," or reflex act, the mysterious region within irritability that responds to external stimuli without meditated response. From a Hallerian perspective there could be no response without consciousness, and no self without consciousness. Whytt's observation of the involuntary voluntary motion did not so much frame a paradox as dismantle Haller's bifurcation for good.

Fanny's responses clearly follow Whytt. Her agitation in response to the narrator's "stab" noted earlier is a reaction Fanny cannot immediately subdue. Synonyms for retraction (identified by Whytt as the most common reflex action) almost always refer to Fanny's acts. Her eyes are passively "instantly withdrawn" upon meeting Henry's gaze; and in adulthood she "retreats from noise" even at Mansfield (143). The narrator has her "shrinking" from notice (9) and from compliments (138), and she answers "in a shrinking accent" when Edmund exhorts her to make Henry happy (319). Portsmouth offers her the ultimate irritation of her father, from whom "Fanny shrunk back to her seat" (346).

Driving home the distinction between widespread sensibility and the subtleties of irritability, Austen puts Fanny's clearest involuntary voluntary motions in the chapter featuring Edmund and Henry's discussion of "sensible and well-informed men" and their failure at reading well (308). Fanny is forced to listen to Henry's voice and words, and reacts against her will: "Here Fanny, who could not but listen, involuntarily shook her head, and Crawford was instantly by her side again, intreating to know her meaning." The adverb "involuntarily" cues us to the reflex act, as does the narrator's report that Fanny is "vexed with herself for not having been as motionless as she was speechless" (310).

The reflex introduces an explicitly complex self. Fanny's immediately reactive self, which "shook her head," remains an inarticulate mystery to Henry, who persistently asks "to know her meaning" and " 'What did that shake of the head mean?.' " Fanny articulates no "meaning" for her agitation, but becomes "more agitated and displeased" before prodded into yet another involuntary voluntary motion: "In spite of herself, she could not help half a smile, but she said nothing" (311). After this session of sustained, half-expressed, half-repressed, irritations, Fanny wears a "flush of vexation" and considers, like someone betrayed, her "grievous imprisonment of body and mind" (313).

Fanny's "unmeaning" unconscious motions do bear expressive meaning, at least to Henry and Edmund. If Henry agitatingly asks to know her meaning, Edmund thinks he can ventriloquize Fanny's unconscious for her. Just before Fanny's first explicitly "involuntary" shake of the head, Edmund observes Fanny unconsciously reposition herself for Henry's dramatic reading:

> Edmund watched the progress of her attention, and was amused and gratified by seeing how she gradually slackened in her needle-work, which, at the beginning, seemed to occupy her totally; how it fell from her hand while she sat motionless over it—and at last, how the eyes which had appeared so studiously to avoid him throughout the day, were turned and fixed on Crawford, fixed on him for minutes, fixed on him in short till the attraction drew Crawford's upon her, and the book was closed, and the charm was broken. Then, she was shrinking again into herself, and blushing and working as hard as ever; but it had been enough to give Edmund encouragement for his friend, and as he cordially thanked him, he hoped to be expressing Fanny's secret feelings too.
>
> (306)

Two Whyttian reflexes structure this paragraph: Fanny reacts to Henry's voice; then Fanny reacts to Henry's eyes. Edmund takes the first reflex to mean Fanny's desire, thinking that he translates her "secret feelings." But a Whyttian understanding is more complex and more conflicted: both acts are equally involuntary voluntary motions, and both attraction (Fanny's agitation towards Henry) and repulsion (Fanny's contraction from Henry) are Fanny's secret feelings. Edmund chooses to record only the first motion, perhaps because he still uses the older, cruder vocabulary of sensibility.

Let us recall that Jane Austen's portrait of Fanny is of a self whose very disposition invites psycho-physiological confusion. She exemplifies, if anything, the new complexity and variability of the Whyttian psycho-physiological model. The two conflicted, conflicting, involuntary voluntary motions, framed by Edmund and Henry's discussion of "sensibility," enact Fanny's explicitly—and unwittingly—displayed psyche. She is bound to have "secret feelings" and even conflicted secret feelings by nature—or by "disposition," as the narrator told us upon Sir Thomas' return from Antigua. If other characters are also irritable, swayed and propelling plot by a much more obscure degree of feeling than the sensibility which they think guides them, then Fanny is the exemplary instance of this irritability.

Irritability's complexity brought extensive change not only to character (and, as we will see, to plot), but implicitly to the reader's judgement of character as well. The same ***Mansfield Park*** passage which declares Fanny to have an agitated disposition also insists that Fanny's disposition is specifically reflexive: her reactions cannot be mediated either by consciousness or by will. This explains the explicit lapses between Fanny's agitations and her consciousness (let alone articulation) of her irritation. We have seen the delay between Fanny's agitation and her awareness or "sensation": "It was a stab . . . and she was obliged to repeat again and again that she was one of his two dearest, before the words gave her any sensation" (239). Strewn throughout the novel are comments like this, which further alienates Fanny's response from her awareness of it: "It was long before Fanny could recover from the agitating happiness of such an hour as was formed by the last thirty minutes of expectation and the first of fruition; it was some time even before her happiness could be said to make her happy" (211).

Twentieth-century critics have accused Fanny of calculating her virtue and lacking spontaneity. Yet in irritability's terms, the behaviour by which character was judged was not only muted, but it was also more broadly unplanned. Many motions remained voluntary, of course, but others flourished in Whytt's freshly observed interstice of "involuntary voluntary" acts. While the reader could still judge a character's conscious responses (such as Maria's "sensible" posturing to snare a second lover), the interpreter of irritability could also now judge reflexive, unconscious responses.

The Whyttian body was imbued with subtle psychic meaning. Where sensibility was once the novel's moral and physiological touchstone, Austen clearly demoted it to the symptoms of a self-consciousness that was in itself morally vacuous. Irritability's reflexive body located a preconscious self. It became, or rather it allowed, Austen's "new Disease in the progress of Time."

Natural Repulsions

Yet Fanny's more obscure degree of feeling bored some early readers. And it has left readers from the mid-nineteenth century onwards frankly confused. From Jane Austen's own collection of reactions around her, through the school of Trilling and Mudrick, to the most recent critics, descends a lineage of disappointment. Objections to the novel settle more than usually on the central character. "My Mother—... Thought Fanny insipid," Austen noted in her private list of responses. Her two closest and most adult nieces had these teenage feelings toward the heroine: "Fanny Knight.—... [was] wanting more love between [Fanny] and Edmund," while Anna "could not bear Fanny." Mr J. Plumtre, Fanny Knight's then suitor, showed a clear eye to the principle behind the perception of deficiency. He noted "the want of some character more striking & interesting to the generality of Readers, than Fanny [Price] was likely to be."[23]

Jane Austen's contemporaries chastised her for doing precisely what Scott's 1816 review praised her for doing best: writing a novel "which draws the characters and incidents introduced more immediately from the current of ordinary life than was permitted by the former rules of the novel." Fanny was a product of early realism, then called "the natural," and that is why early readers who disliked her, did so. It is also why the early readers who did cotton on to Fanny, did so. A Mrs Bramstone pointed out in particular that Fanny was "so very natural," a note echoed by Lady Gordon, who contrasted the "Ideal People" invented by other writers with the "natural scenes" and characters of "Miss A-s works, & especially in MP you actually *live* with them."[24] Where Elizabeth Bennet charmed with her natural wit, Fanny either bored or pleased with her natural deficiencies. Marilyn Butler's insight that "Ironically, Fanny's feebleness, which modern readers tend particularly to dislike, is probably a device to make her less perfect, more 'human,' and therefore more appealing"[25] is borne out perfectly by the central point of agreement among Fanny's contemporary readers.

The question of modal classification, which Scott explicitly initiated in his review, still guides ***Mansfield Park*** criticism today. Later objections to Fanny, and later consequent support for Fanny, claimed not that she was too ordinary, but that she was not ordinary enough, or that she was extraordinary: extraordinarily good (Butler), extraordinarily bad (Mudrick, Auerbach), extraordinarily tranquil (Butler, Brown), and even extraordinarily clean (Yeazell).[26] Significantly, twentieth-century critics, puzzling over what can only be described as boredom with Fanny, explain the Fanny phenomenon not in terms of her naturalness, or realism, but instead in the reversed terms of romance, as we see in frequent invocations of the "fabular structure" and "mythical underpinning" of the novel.[27] According to all these readings, not much happens to or in Fanny, because Fanny exists in the world of romance. Maria's and Aunt Norris' expulsion from the novel resonates particularly as romance with modern critics. (Contemporary readers did not once mention the banishment.[28]) Julia Prewitt Brown declares, "Fanny and Edmund finally emerge as monsters."[29] Mr J. Plumtre would be shocked. Here we are far from "insipid," and we could barely survive a "more striking" character than a monster.

Jane Austen's readers in 1814 called Fanny too natural. Austen's readers now explain Fanny away as unnatural. The consistency with which the question of ***Mansfield Park***'s mode arises throughout its reception history suggests that mode is itself a topic of the narrative. Yet as we have just seen, the presentation of Austen's heroine consists not in a suppression of the body and time, as critics such as Julia Prewitt Brown and John Wiltshire claim,[30] but rather in a detailed personification of an ascendant physiology. In light of this forgotten, now barely recognizable physiological vocabulary (of which the constituent words now masquerade under new or impoverished meanings), Fanny is far from fabular and backward-looking. We find it hard to see Fanny's realism now, but clearly readers in 1814 could. Her consciousness is the most natural, the most modern, and the most disappointing in the novel.

The "natural" disappoints. It falls short in the terms the novel uses for it, and that is how best to explain the curious critical emphasis on the novel's mode in explanations of what the novel lacks. Its newly irritable character contracts and reacts to the world's stimuli in a more conflicting, more perceptive, and cautious manner than the preceding dominant sensible one. Fanny, whose peak of happiness is "finely chequered, à-la-mortal" (248), has a muted, but long-lived, affection. Some of her first readers wanted what Scott famously called "the big bow-wow"—the grander gesture of romance. But to us, exiled beyond much of Austen's cultural horizon, Fanny's reactivity is invisible, incomprehensible, and therefore mysterious, perhaps classifiable as romance.

Scott pointed out earlier in his review that the sentimental heroine was already much diminished from the romance heroine from whom she descended, yet she still experienced in her plot a set of possible improbabilities that marked romance.[31] The natural mode, then, was constructed critically with an eye to the diminished figure living through a more probable plot. While writing ***Mansfield Park,*** Jane Austen read Mary Brunton's best-seller, *Self-Control* (1811). She equated the natural and the probable in this letter: "my opinion is confirmed of its being an excellently-meant, elegantly-written Work, without anything of Nature or Probability in it."[32]

The early realism of ***Mansfield Park*** was defined consistently as the comparatively smaller end of a set of ratios: ideal and natural; extravagantly sensible and ordinarily reactive; possible and probable. The new mode was comparative in two senses: it existed in the comparatively smaller end of those ratios, and it existed solely, at least at that point, in relation to the other mode, or the other end of the ratio. The "natural," before it was called "realism" later in the century, could just as easily have been dubbed the "comparative."

Butler also sees Fanny's contemporary appeal (such as it was) as natural for the time. Yet Butler also holds that there was no room for Johnsonian moral exemplarity in an embodied (read, "sensible") heroine of the time. Since Fanny is a moral exemplar, therefore she is not a feeling heroine—beyond the outward gloss of "feebleness" Butler notes—thus leaving Fanny free to be a cerebral, anti-Jacobin throwback.[33] Perhaps Butler's terms are outdated for 1814. While sensibility may not always have accommodated moral imperatives, irritability did. ***Mansfield Park*** foregrounds a distinct somatization of *mores,* or behaviour. Irritability subsumes the moral of the earlier exemplary character because irritability requires an unconscious—posited to explain the involuntary voluntary action—in its psycho-physiological structure. The natural, irritable character subsumes conduct's imperative into this unwilled space.

New Diseases and the Progress of Time

Jane Austen hands the medically informed reader a second key to unlock her story. Related to Austen's psycho-physiology is the contemporary understanding of epidemiology. At the turn of the nineteenth century, reactivity overlapped with contagion. One's physiological state predisposed one to certain diseases. Some of these ills were internal symptoms that followed upon contractility: Thomas Trotter[34] laid out several implicated prosaic ailments, including diarrhoea, flatulence, and headaches (Austen, understandably, relied on "the head ach"). Other ailments entailed by specific psycho-physiologies were distinct diseases. Whytt and his lineage listed in passing the febrile contagions: smallpox and measles.

John Brown (1735-1788) renamed reactivity "excitement," which he defined as the product of an internal factor, irritability, and an external factor, the stimulus.[35] (The fire Sir Thomas demands lit for Fanny "was exciting even painful gratitude" [292].) Similarly, contagions, once contracted, affected the body with a reactive "affection."[36] Brown therefore could write of a "general affection follow[ing] the application of contagion" and then equate this "affection" with an "excess ... of excitement." Likewise, he concluded, "the operation of contagions is stimulant." Smallpox in particular—the contagious disease standing metonymically for contagion as such—was a disease "depending on too much stimulus."[37] Whytt established the irritable disposition; Brown linked this disposition with contagion. Trotter pursued the connection in a footnote, berating the government for its lethargy in taking up Edward Jenner's vaccination project to contain smallpox epidemics.[38]

Contagion plays a subdued role in the diminished plot of ***Mansfield Park.*** Several critics have puzzled over fragments of what is, on closer inspection, an extensive contagion metaphor running through the novel.[39] Yet in pointing out a semantic matrix of references to contagion in the novel, we are merely noticing the obvious.[40] Contagion plays a part similar to that of sensibility: almost everyone within the narrative knows about it, has it, and uses it in arguments to justify bad conduct. Tom Bertram explains away the Mansfield theatricals by this naturalizing metaphor:

> "This was in fact the origin of *our* acting," said Tom after a moment's thought. "My friend Yates brought the infection from Ecclesford, and it spread as those things always spread you know, sir—the faster probably from *your* having so often encouraged the sort of thing in us formerly."
>
> (166)

Tom's "you know, sir" includes middle-aged Sir Thomas in the wide circle of epidemiological literacy. Contagion, in behavioural terms a body's contracted conduct, could be conceived as a consequence of example, on the one hand, and mimesis on the other. Aunt Norris flatters herself that the affection she fancies between Rushworth and Maria will act as a "catching" example on Henry and Julia (106-107). Aunt Norris' simpering over "catching" examples exposes the banality of the trope; her cloying pun on affection and infection demonstrates the fatigue of the love-as-disease truism more generally. In having Aunt Norris use the figure so badly, Austen demonstrates that she herself uses the figure ironically, or that she uses it in order to disembarrass the figure of value within the narrative.

Once more, as with sensibility, characters who consciously apply the trope of contagion and infection to themselves are unlikely to be aware of a truer condition proposed by Austen. The disease of affection—even the specifically contagious and infectious disease figured here—is already an exhausted figure. Tom Bertram uses his spreading infection metaphor just as idiomatically as he uses the long-outmoded humoral theory ("'It raises my spleen more than any thing,'" he complains to Fanny [108]). Perhaps contagion, far from being avant-garde, is instead already as *passé* as the humours. What, then, is the truer condition, the modern disease, replacing contagion and guiding the affective plot of ***Mansfield Park***?

Clearly, smallpox dominated epidemiological discussion as the metonymic contagion standing for the whole. The history of smallpox and the popular method used to restrain it unexpectedly shed more light on the physiologies of Jane Austen's restrained characters and plot. Henry, for example, uses a striking trope when he describes to Mary his plan to gain and then abandon Fanny's affections: "'But I cannot be satisfied without Fanny Price, without making a small hole in Fanny Price's heart'" (208). A sexualized reading that takes the "small hole" as something to penetrate misses the mark: the hole is made by Henry and is strictly speaking not Fanny's hole but rather Henry's hole, an impression he plans to create and leave behind. The narrator picks up Henry's mysterious figure of speech a page later:

> I have no inclination … to think that with so much tenderness of disposition, and so much taste as belonged to [Fanny], she could have escaped heart-whole from the courtship (though the courtship of only a fortnight) of such a man as Crawford, in spite of there being some previous ill-opinion of him to be overcome, had not her affection been engaged elsewhere.
>
> (208-209)

"Heart-whole" connects Henry's metaphor with the traditional picture of the heart broken by love. At the same time the narrator renovates the traditional emblem by punning with "heart-whole" on Henry's "hole in the heart," thus agreeing with Henry's specific figure of a lesion.

Henry's trademark "small hole," to be left after he has made his impression, is most like a smallpox scar.[41] Serving as a foil to accidentally contracted smallpox was the inoculation technique introduced to England by Emanuel Timonius in 1713 and made popular by the pocked Lady Mary Wortley Montagu after 1718. The imported lanceting procedure simply formalized and controlled what rural families had done throughout England for centuries, "buying the pox" for their children by exposing them to a mild case nearby. Small risks aside, the procedure's formality controlled smallpox's randomness and fatality. This, combined with the chicness of inoculation, produced a public health epidemic of its own kind.

Jane Austen was no stranger to inoculation's practice and emerging theory. It held the reading public's fancy to the point of discourses on the relative merits of different methods in *The Gentleman's Magazine* and *The Scots Magazine* well into the 1790s. Jenner's method became extremely popular after some years of conservative scepticism, and was adopted as a local cause in pockets of the United States and Britain. Around the turn of the nineteenth century, the Austens' neighbour at Ashe rectory, "Madam" Lefroy, "personally vaccinated all of her husband's parishioners."[42]

In this context, Austen refines Henry's "small hole" metaphor towards inoculation, not random contagion. Henry appoints himself to make the hole: the narrator tells us that in his earlier experiments on Maria and Julia he generously "did not want them to die of love" (39); and he specifies that his work on Fanny would run its course in "a fortnight" (208), just the time commercial inoculators and journalists advertised the inoculation process to take.

Henry meets with limited success. Julia alone provides a textbook case of inoculation from Henry's experimental affections. Unlike Maria, Julia is not engaged, and is therefore "quite ready to be fallen in love with" (39) upon Henry's arrival. By the time Henry has withdrawn his short-lived attentions from Julia in favour of Maria, Julia is "a sufferer" in affection "too," like Fanny in relation to Mary, although with "a jealousy of her sister that ought to have been the cure" (143). Within the abbreviated affective plot governed here by the figure of inoculation, affection's chief symptom, jealousy, heralds not the full-blown disease but instead its foreclosure. Julia's inoculation leaves her heart "sore" (146), but her minor suffering in Volume I precludes its own repetition and magnification within the same chapter (I, Ch. 17) and still later in Volume III (425).

Maria and Fanny, however, are bound together dialectically as textbook examples of failed inoculations by Henry. Maria follows the incorrectly inoculated patient who fatally exposes herself to infection's dangers; Fanny follows the Jennerian story of a patient who has been unwittingly inoculated already. Jane Austen establishes the notion of Maria's safety through engagement as a foolish idea, one held enthusiastically by Maria but few others. Edmund takes Maria's engagement to Rushworth as a sign of her greater rather than her lesser vulnerability. He uses Maria's "delicate situation" (113) as another reason against the Mansfield theatricals.

Maria's danger comes not from one understanding of inoculation (her own) or another (Edmund's), but from Henry's peculiar layering of the two. Henry claims to believe that Maria is a wholly safe amusement precisely due to her engagement: "'An engaged woman is always more agreeable than a disengaged. … All is safe with a lady engaged; no harm can be done'" (40). "Harm," like "delicacy," medicalizes Maria's affective state. Henry claims he will leave no small hole in Maria's heart: his pun on engagement revives the dead metaphor of engaged affections.

Yet malicious Henry knows that her affections are not engaged by Rushworth. They remain excitable beneath the dead metaphor of her engagement to marry. As he will later desire of Fanny, Henry wishes to excite Maria's first affection. Even in marriage Maria is not affected by

Rushworth. Her exposure to the full stimulus of Henry's charm at Richmond results in a fatal affection. Banishment from Mansfield in the final pages is her narrative death. Maria's fatality accords with her reckless exposure to dangerous affection.

She fulfils a standard fear regarding inoculation. Sceptics dreaded a bungling which would fail to produce an effective, yet relatively safe, infection in the patient. Anti-inoculation rhetoric generally cited cases of inoculation hubris, in which patients, mistakenly thought to be inoculated, boldly exposed themselves to the disease with fatal or disfiguring results. Even Jenner's experimental summary brooded disproportionately over such failures, cautioning:

> . . . let it be recollected, that it is only a different mode of receiving the infectious particles that constitutes the difference between Inoculation and the natural smallpox. . . . Query—In what manner is the smallpox communicated in what is call'd the natural way?[43]

Ratio accompanies inoculation as a theme. Neither buying the pox nor inoculation avoided smallpox. Instead, they were both used to exchange the possibility of fatal or disfiguring smallpox for the probability of induced mild smallpox and its proportionately minimal damage. Inoculation relates to random contagion not as nothing relates to an absolute, but as a little of something relates to an absolute.

Jenner queries the ratio of nature to artifice. Lanceting was artificial insofar as it designed the movement of affection. But Jenner's circumlocution—"what is call'd the natural way"—immediately suggests the trope's reversal: perhaps uncontrolled contagion is unnatural while moderate inoculation is natural. Some earlier discussion of smallpox depicted the accidental mode of contagion as a factor of monstrosity, whereas artificial inoculation left in its wake a more natural patient.[44] Accidental affection either caused a superlative, romantic death, or, passing one by altogether, left a superlatively unblemished body; inoculation caused the comparatively moderate, natural affection. Of course Fanny will be affected in the latter mode.

Maria's case typically shadows Fanny's as a medical inverse. Fanny has unwittingly bought the pox through affection for her cousin. The principle of inoculation—control over a body's initial reaction to a contagion—works against the belated inoculator. Fanny's "affection," we are told by the narrator after the close of the Crawfords' plotting scene, "had been engaged elsewhere" (209). Fanny's already affected state is what prevents Henry from fulfilling his desire to "excite [her] first ardours" (212). Henry's Shakespeare reading moves Fanny for the first time in response to theatre, but his attempt to produce and then deliver news of William's promotion fails: "All those fine first feelings, of which he had hoped to be the excitor, were already given" (210).

Maria's case incites fear; Fanny's case produces intense puzzlement. She has bought the pox so quietly that the increasingly flustered Sir Thomas sounds the same stumped note as inoculators reporting on seemingly non-reactive patients. He scientifically seeks an "explanation": "Young as you are, and having scarcely seen any one, it is hardly possible that your affections—" (286). The irony of Fanny's purchase of the pox is that Sir Thomas and Aunt Norris imported her into Mansfield Park during childhood in part so that Tom and Edmund would, through their exposure to their cousin, feel no affection for her in adulthood. Fanny's affection for Edmund proves low-grade and long-lasting, as though her "more obscure degree of feeling" affords it longer life. Her affection takes not a fortnight for its course, but an entire novel, and we are to assume that Fanny and Edmund run a low fever well past the novel's end. We could take Austen's comment on Fanny and Edmund's dances at the ball as an emblem of Fanny's protractedly engaged state: her "indefinite engagement with *him* was in continual perspective" (252). Fanny's affection proves catching in reverse, rubbing off on the would-be inoculator Henry, who unwisely manipulates affection in young women without ever having been smitten himself.

How much Fanny knows of the structure of her own affections is in doubt well into Volume III. Fanny's musing ("Had her own affections been as free—as perhaps they ought to have been—[Henry] could never have engaged them") is followed by the ironic comment, "So thought Fanny in good truth and sober sadness" (297). Her inoculation is beyond her own control and her consciousness, as though she lived before inoculation's fame but within its principles. As with the governing irritability of which Austen's characters seem unaware, the inoculated state of affections is true so long as her characters remain unconscious of it. Fanny's quiet, modern affection aligns with her irritability, the "more obscure degree of feeling" of which her subtle affectivity is a related symptom. Stimulated by the smallest display of warmth from Edmund, Fanny's affection exists as do her reflex actions: unconsciously, nearly invisibly, and, directed by her disposition, most probably.

Jane Austen presents both ways of being. That is the condition of her comparative, natural mode: she sets nature beside romance; irritability beside sensibility; safe inoculation next to fatal infection. But Austen's novel conducts itself in a way that also belies an irritable disposition presenting and enclosing her many comparisons. Fanny embodies the consciousness directing the novel from her early adulthood on. This changing of the guard from impersonal narrator to Fanny's consciousness corresponds to the shift from Fanny's childhood sensibility to her mature irritability and agitation. From this point, the narrative is a product of irritability.

As such, Whytt would say, ***Mansfield Park*** has an unconscious. It betrays itself most at the site where Whytt posited it: the involuntary voluntary motion. Fanny's final reflex act is subsumed in her narrative. The expulsion of Maria and Aunt Norris from the novel's future as well as from the country in the novel's present has often shocked critics, and is one of the points cited as evidence for the novel's romance formulation. Yet the automatic, unpremeditated mode of the expulsion, and the fact that the exiles embody the claims of romance's superlative stimulus, suggest a reflex act of the narrative unconscious, a modally natural reflex act that repels and contracts from the excitement inflicted by romance.

Fittingly, Edmund's affections move from the stimulus of his "dearest" (239) object towards a comparative, "dearer" one (429). The natural physiology of ***Mansfield Park*** repels the superlative stimulus against which its own irritability has been structured. It finally allows to flourish the more obscure degree of feeling plotted for a home of affection.

Notes

1. Jane Austen, letter to Cassandra Austen, 8-9 February 1807, in *Jane Austen's Letters,* ed. Deirdre Le Faye, 3rd edn, Oxford, 1995, 119.

2. R. F. B. Brissenden, *Virtue in Distress: Studies in the Novel of Sentiment from Richardson to Sade,* New York, 1974.

3. John Halperin, *The Life of Jane Austen,* Brighton, 1984, 44.

4. Criticism of mid-Victorian literature focuses on the mid-century governing notions of neurasthenia and nerves. This in turn is a stopping point *en route* to our fascination with late-century hysteria narratives.

5. Ann Jessie Van Sant, *Eighteenth-Century Sensibility and the Novel: The Senses in Social Context,* Cambridge, 1993. Her first citation is from Whytt's *Observations*: "In some the feelings, perceptions, and passions, are naturally dull, slow, and difficult to be roused; in others, they are *very* quick and easily excited, on account of a greater delicacy and sensibility of brain and *nerves*" (1). Van Sant's footnote to this citation immediately breaks Whytt's connection between body and psyche, giving this Hallerian directive: "It is important to note that physical structures are the location of responsiveness, and their delicacy determines the delicacy and immediacy of feelings; but nerves do not cause the emotions, passions, etc."

6. George Cheyne, *The English Malady, or a Treatise of Nervous Diseases of All Kinds, as Spleen, Vapours, Hypochondriacal, and Hysterical Distempers, &c,* London and Dublin, 1733, 39.

7. *Ibid.,* 125.

8. Albrecht von Haller, *A Dissertation on the Sensible and Irritable Parts of Animals,* London, 1755, 9 and 8 (an anonymous English translation).

9. *Ibid.,* 25.

10. *Ibid.,* 28.

11. Brissenden, *Virtue in Distress,* 39-42. Haller's review of *Clarissa* was reprinted from the French in the *Gentleman's Magazine,* XIX (June and August 1749), 245-46 and 345-49.

12. Robert Whytt, *Observations on the Sensibility and Irritability of the Parts of Men and Other Animals; Occasioned by Dr Haller's Late Treatise on These Subjects* (in *The Works of Robert Whytt, Published by His Son,* Edinburgh and London, 1768). All references are to this edition. Whytt's was no obscure tract: *The Literary Magazine* promptly reviewed Whytt over four pages, placed Whytt's treatise in the context of the Haller-Whytt dispute, and cheerily encouraged its general readers "to the perusal of the book itself" (*The Literary Magazine: Or, Universal Review, for the Year MDCCLVI,* London, 1756, I, 89).

13. Whytt, *Observations,* 280.

14. *Ibid.,* 295.

15. *Ibid.,* 257.

16. *Ibid.,* 273. This phrase in the *Observations* concludes Whytt's section "Of Sensibility" and introduces Whytt's section "Of Irritability," in which Whytt establishes the relatively obscure feeling.

17. Whytt, *An Essay on the Vital and Other Involuntary Motions of Animals,* Edinburgh, 1751, 30. Whytt delineates the body's "involuntary" motions (also called "vital," "AUTOMATIC," and "SPONTANEOUS"), and its "voluntary" motions, which are wilfully committed. Then he describes the reflex act (also called the "mix'd motion" and the "involuntary voluntary motion"): "The third [motion] is strong, but suddenly followed by relaxation, seems to be a necessary consequence of the *stimulus* upon the muscle, and cannot be affected, either as to its force or continuance, by the power of the will."

18. Jane Austen, *Mansfield Park,* ed. John Lucas, Oxford, 1970, 354 and 367. All further references to this edition will be given in the text.

19. As Ruth Bernard Yeazell does in "The Boundaries of Mansfield Park," *Representations,* 7 (1984), 133-52.

20. Yeazell, "The Boundaries of Mansfield Park," 144.

21. Halperin, *The Life of Jane Austen,* 227.

22. Whytt, *An Essay,* 26.

23. *Jane Austen: The Critical Heritage,* ed. B. C. Southam, London, 1968, 48-49 and 50.

24. *Ibid.,* 59, 49 and 51.

25. Marilyn Butler, *Jane Austen and the War of Ideas,* Oxford, 1975, 248.

26. *Ibid.,* 221, 231; Marvin Mudrick, "The Triumph of Gentility: *Mansfield Park,*" in *Jane Austen: Irony as Defense and Discovery,* Princeton, 1952, 155-80; Nina Auerbach, "Jane Austen's Dangerous Charm: Feeling as One Ought about Fanny Price," in *Jane Austen: New Perspectives,* ed. Janet Todd, New York, 1983, 208-23; Julia Prewitt Brown, *Jane Austen's Novels: Social Change and Literary Form,* Cambridge: MA and London, 1979, 99; and Yeazell, "The Boundaries of Mansfield Park," 133.

27. Yeazell mentions among others D. W. Harding, "Regulated Hatred: An Aspect of the Work of Jane Austen" (1940), rpt. in *Jane Austen: A Collection of Critical Essays,* ed. Ian Watt, Englewood Cliffs: NJ, 1963, 173-79; and she drew my attention to Avrom Fleishman, *A Reading of* Mansfield Park*: An Essay in Critical Synthesis,* Minneapolis, 1967, 66-68. To this I would add Marilyn Butler's Introduction to *Mansfield Park,* ed. James Kinsley, Oxford, 1990, ix, and, of course, Yeazell's own anthropologically derived reading.

28. Edward Austen (Jane's brother) judged "Mrs Rushworth's Elopement . . . unnatural" (*Jane Austen: The Critical Heritage,* 49), but not her banishment. Like Edmund Bertram, Edward Austen assigns Maria's overlarge romantic act to a category outside Fanny Price's own domestic plot.

29. Julia Prewitt Brown, *Jane Austen's Novels,* 99-100.

30. Julia Prewitt Brown and John Wiltshire (*Jane Austen and the Body: "The Picture of Health,"* Cambridge, 1992, 9) insist upon Austen's demotion of bodily description, and follow a line of argument towards classifying *Mansfield Park* as romance. This line began as early as 1859 with George Lewes' article on Austen in *Blackwood's Edinburgh Magazine,* LXXXVI (July 1859), 99-113: "[Austen] no more thinks of describing the physical appearance of her people than the dramatist does who knows that his persons are to be represented by living actors . . . thereby [the reader] misses many of the subtle connections between physical and mental organization" (quoted in *Jane Austen: The Critical Heritage,* 158). Lewes' ignorance of Fanny's irritability suggests that our era's ignorance of Whyttian psycho-physiology, which renders Fanny's reactivity invisible to us, started as early as the mid-Victorian period.

31. Quoted in *Jane Austen: The Critical Heritage,* 60.

32. Quoted in Halperin, *The Life of Jane Austen,* 225. Later, she would write to the King's librarian, Clarke, "But I could no more write a romance than an epic poem" (quoted in Halperin, 223). The "probable" attribute remained a criterion for the newly natural mode well into the mid-Victorian realist period. Lewes, who was already blind to certain aspects of Austen's physiological realism in Fanny's character, still commended Austen's plots generally: "romance and improbabilities must be banished as rigorously as the grotesque" (*Jane Austen: The Critical Heritage,* 153).

33. Butler, *Jane Austen and the War of Ideas,* 249.

34. Thomas Trotter, *A View of the Nervous Temperament,* London, 1807.

35. Brown's elaboration was implicit in Whytt's posthumous *An Essay on the Vital and Other Involuntary Motions of Animals,* in which Whytt explains elevated febrile pulse ("those violent motions of the heart, in the beginnings of fevers, small-pox, measles, &c.") as a spontaneous somatic irritation in response to the "admixture" in the blood of the contagion (320). For Brown, I used his *Elements of Medicine, or a Translation of the Elementae Medicinae Brunonis,* Philadelphia, 1814, 35-37. It was first published in 1788.

36. "Affection" significantly meant both infection and love, as can be seen from context in the medical texts I cite. The word still carried both meanings late in the century: Charles Creighton, a late Victorian medical scientist who tried to disprove Jenner, used "affection" for "infection" almost consistently in his *Jenner and Vaccination: A Strange Chapter of Medical History,* London, 1889.

37. Brown, *Elements of Medicine,* 35 and 36.

38. Trotter, *A View of the Nervous Temperament,* 154-55.

39. Cf. Thomas R. Edwards, Jr., "The Difficult Beauty of *Mansfield Park,*" *Nineteenth-Century Fiction,* 20 (1965), 51-69; Tony Tanner, Introduction, *Mansfield Park,* Penguin, 1966; Butler, *Jane Austen and the War of Ideas,* 237, and her Introduction to *Mansfield Park*; Julia Prewitt Brown, *Jane Austen's Novels,* 87; Yeazell, "The Boundaries of Mansfield Park," 135, 141, 144; and Joseph Litvak, "The Infection of Acting: Theatricals and Theatricality in *Mansfield Park,*" *ELH,* 53 (1986), 331-55. Edwards, Butler, and Julia Prewitt Brown use contagion as a critical metaphor, rather than interpreting the metaphor as used by Austen. Yeazell's emphasis on "contamination" and "pollution" suggests grounds for contagion, but she does not explicate the medical trope.

40. Litvak begins to look at fragments of the novel's epidemiological diction, especially Tom's blatant use of "infection" to excuse the theatricals. However, Litvak applies to the 1814 narrative a modern lay immunological metaphor, followed by a metaphor of homeopathy. His observation of a "shift from

metaphors of infection and of seduction to metaphors of debt and repayment" (351) is perhaps better explained by the shift from a metaphor of random contagion to one of inoculation.

41. The *OED* records interchanging and overlapping meanings among "hole," "pit," and "pock." "Hole" is given as "I.1. A hollow place or cavity in a solid body." This eighteenth-century definition of the *frontinella* follows: "That Part vulgarly called the Hole of the Neck" (from John Sparrow's 1771 translation, *Le Dran's Observations in Surgery* [1758], 50). "Pit," in turn, is (9, and 9b.) "A hollow or indentation in an animal or plant body" and "A depressed scar, such as those left on the skin after small-pox." This citation of Randle Holme's 1688 *The Academy of Armory, Or a Storehouse of Armory and Blazon* (Volume II) follows: "Of a Tree . . . the Pit or Hole [is] whereat the branches sprout" (ed. I. H. Jeayes, 1905). "Pock," finally, is (4) "a scar, mark, or 'pit' left by a pustule, esp. of small-pox."

42. Quoted from Anna Lefroy's *Carmina Domestica* (London, 1812), in Deirdre Le Faye's *Jane Austen: A Family Record,* London, 1989, 44. Jane and Cassandra visited and corresponded with the Ashe and Steventon households throughout their times in Bath and Chawton. The vaccination of Ashe parish must have occurred between 1798 and 1804, the year of Madam Lefroy's death. Jane Austen was then between twenty-three and twenty-nine years old.

43. Jenner's "Inquiry into the Natural History of a Disease known in Gloucestershire by the Name of the Cow-pox," printed in *Lancet* (1923), refers in two footnotes to this problem (137 n.2 and 138 n.3).

44. J. B. N. Boyer reversed the ratio in 1717, casting unmoderated and immoderate smallpox in a fairytale (quoted in Genevieve Miller, *The Adoption of Inoculation for Smallpox in England and France,* Philadelphia, 1957, 65).

Ann M. Shanahan (essay date 2012)

SOURCE: Shanahan, Ann M. "The Novel as Drama: Staging Theatrical Aspects of the Narrative in Jane Austen's *Mansfield Park.*" *Text and Presentation, 2012.* Ed. Graley Herren. Jefferson: McFarland, 2013. 61-77. Print.

[*In the following essay, originally presented at a conference in 2012, Shanahan notes that* Mansfield Park *demonstrates a theatrical sensibility, citing the preponderance of dialog in the novel. She notes Austen's use of the techniques of free indirect speech, a rhetorical device through which the narrator implies a character's attitude, and verbal scoring, textual guidance about how certain words or phrases should be pronounced. Shanahan also remarks on Austen's establishment of Fanny as "a sort of* audience*" within the novel.*]

While Jane Austen's ***Mansfield Park*** (1814) deals directly with theatrical subjects, it is the least frequently adapted of Austen's novels for the stage. Themes in the novel echo those of the popular late eighteenth century play, *Lovers' Vows* (1798) and the first volume of the novel includes a performance of that play as a "home theatrical," common in the period. The lack of stage adaptation may be explained by a commonly held critical position that the novel is Austen's most "problematic," and that it paints a negative view of theatre, reflecting Austen's personal opinion of the practice (Byrne 2000:148).

In 2011, I completed a workshop staging of my own adaptation of ***Mansfield Park.*** For this I used the method of Chamber Theatre founded by Robert Breen at Northwestern University, a form of literary adaptation that retains the narrative voice by use of an embodied narrator.[1] While I set out merely interested in exploring the metatheatrical potential of the novel's theatre-based scenes on stage, the application of the Chamber Theatre method revealed additional theatrical aspects to the novel, beyond the overt subjects pursued. This method revealed a theatrical dimension to the narrative point of view in relation to the central female character of Fanny Price. Some of these dynamics have been suggested, at least in part, through textual analysis by scholars interested in Austen and theatre. However the Chamber Theatre method, because of the clarity demanded by its physicality, allowed further development of what has been suggested elsewhere. Consideration of these features may ameliorate some concern for of the "problems" in the novel, especially criticism of its central female character, and clarify some of the questions concerning Austen's views on theatre. Certainly this method illuminated a performance-based structure to the progression of the narrative, rendering it remarkably well-suited to theatrical adaptation.

The Novel and the Theatre

I was originally drawn to the project of adapting ***Mansfield Park*** because of its theatrical content.[2] In the story of Fanny Price's adoption by her rich relations, the Bertrams, her cousins and their fashionable new neighbors, Mary and Henry Crawford, undertake a staging of a popular drama to pass the time while the patriarch, Sir Thomas, is off attending dangerous business in Antigua. Austen connects characters, conflicts, and themes in the novel with those of the chosen play, *Lovers' Vows,* an English adaptation by Elizabeth Inchbald of a late eighteenth century German play by August von Kotzebue, *Das Kind der Liebe* (1780), translated alternately as *The Natural Son* or *The Love Child* (Allen 2006).

A substantial portion of the first volume of ***Mansfield Park*** involves the selection of and preparation for the play.

While the actual performance never occurs because of the surprise return of Sir Thomas at a dress rehearsal, Austen relishes in the details of backstage dilemmas and petty jealousies in the preparation process. Themes related to performance and theatre reemerge throughout the remainder of the novel, as the home theatricals are referenced often throughout, and by a recurring reference to acting, particularly around the character of Henry Crawford, who is credited as a talented actor, on stage and off. As an example of the novel's reference to drama and theatre, in the second volume Crawford performs a section of Shakespeare's *Henry VIII,* and then reflects on his ease and naturalness reading portions aloud:

> Shakespeare one gets acquainted with without knowing how. It is a part of an Englishman's constitution. His thoughts and beauties are so spread abroad that one touches them everywhere; one is intimate with him by instinct. No man of any brain can open at a good part of one of his plays without falling into the flow of his meaning immediately.
>
> [391]

In these sorts of direct references to dramatic literature and theatre practice, ***Mansfield Park*** is immersed in a world of performance to a greater degree than any of Austen's novels.

While the theatrical content of the novel first attracted me to the project, in adapting the material I quickly discovered that the vision of theatre presented by the novel is complicated, even negative. The theatricals initiate acts of moral degradation that the novel ultimately condemns. Furthermore, the theatre and the specific play chosen are criticized and resisted on moral grounds by the main characters with which we identify (Fanny Price and her beloved cousin Edmund), and celebrated by those we censure (Fanny's cousins Maria and Tom Bertram and the conniving Crawfords). When Fanny first reads the play to be rehearsed:

> She ran through it with an eagerness which was suspended only by intervals of astonishment, that it could be chosen in the present instance—that it could be proposed and accepted in a private Theatre! Agatha and Amelia appeared to her in their different ways so totally improper for home representation—the situation of one, and the language of the other, so unfit to be expressed by any woman of modesty, that she could hardly suppose her cousins could be aware of what they were engaging in.
>
> [161]

Likewise, Edmund counsels his brother Tom against the plan to produce a play, especially while their father is away in Antigua:

> In a *general* light, private theatricals are open to some objections, but as *we* are circumstanced, I must think it would be highly injudicious, and more than injudicious to attempt anything of the kind. It would show great want of feeling on my father's account, absent as he is, and in some degree of constant danger; and it would be imprudent, I think, with regard to Maria, whose situation is a very delicate one, considering everything, extremely delicate.
>
> [147]

As Edmund and Fanny anticipate, the rehearsals for the play do indeed spur negative results. Prompted by their intimacy in scenes together, Maria Bertram begins an affair with the rake Henry Crawford, though she is betrothed to John Rushworth. Balance and order is returned to Mansfield when the patriarch Sir Thomas returns and puts an end to the chaos of rehearsals. As a result, Fanny's situation improves significantly, along with her overall happiness. When the affair fanned by the theatricals is revealed later in the novel, Fanny is vindicated in her choice not to accept Crawford's hand in marriage, elevated in her position in the family, and ultimately secure in a happy ending with her love, Edmund. Considering its role in the plot, there is no doubt that theatre functions as a destabilizing, negative element: those who do not participate in it benefit from that choice; those who do suffer disease, censure, and even expulsion from society. Thus, my initial rationale for adapting ***Mansfield Park*** based on its theatrical content was at best complicated, at worst contradicted, by the spirit of the novel's treatment of theatre.

Several critics have argued that the novel's perspective reflects Austen's own negative view of theatre. Chief among these was Lionel Trilling in an essay that was to become the introduction the *Pelican Guide to English Literature* (1957). In her influential book, *Jane Austen and the War of Ideas* (1975), Marilyn Butler argues "there could be no doubt in the minds of Jane Austen and most of her readers that the name of Kotzebue is said to be synonymous with political subversion and dangerous … messages about 'freedom in sexual matters and defiance of traditional restraints'" (233-234). According to critic Paula Byrne, author of *Jane Austen and the Theatre,*

> Butler's influential reading of *Lovers' Vows* along with the older but still frequently-cited work of Lionel Trilling on the novelist's rejections of the "histrionic art," has put the seal on the critical orthodoxy that asserts Austen's condemnation of private theatricals. Even though … a plethora of critical ambiguity surrounds the play acting sequence in ***Mansfield Park,*** few have challenged the assumption that Austen was hostile to the drama.
>
> [2000:249]

Byrne and others, notably Penny Gay, have countered this assumption.[3] These scholars read Austen's novels in light of her participation in home theatricals and play attendance noted in her copious correspondence. Austen and her family themselves engaged in home theatricals at the rectory at Steventon (Byrne 3-28), and she regularly attended the theatre in London, Southampton, and Bath, where she lived just before writing the novel (Jordan 1987:140). *Lovers' Vows* was performed in Bath at least fifteen times between the years the Austens lived there

(1801-1806). To contradict the idea that Austen disliked theatre Byrne offers evidence, mainly from the novels themselves, of Austen's detailed familiarity both with Kotzebue's play and with several other popular plays of the English stage. She argues that Austen would not have known so much about something she censured. Austen's careful treatment and unusual insight into rehearsal dynamics and theatrical practices suggest that she had a great deal of interest in, even love of, the craft: "For some critics what is particularly attractive about Austen's choice of play is the opportunity given them to construe ***Mansfield Park*** an attack against the drama. One of the problems with this argument is that Austen enjoyed going to Kotzebue plays. … She clearly knew *Lovers' Vows* extremely well" (150). Likewise, Byrne points out that the novel and Inchbald's play deal with the same themes and characters:

> Elizabeth Inchbald's play raises considerations about the right of women to choose their own husbands, about father's responsibility to his children, and perhaps most radically about the validity of innate merit rather than social position. In ***Mansfield Park*** Austen is deeply engaged with all of these issues. In order to develop her interest in the relationship between role playing and social behavior, she needed a play that could be interlinked with the characters in her novel.
>
> [153]

Byrne concludes that Austen's vision was deeply intertwined with the practice of theatre. She argues that Austen saw social behavior like theatre: "Far from proposing that acting encourages a kind of insincere role playing in life, Austen suggests in her depiction of polite society that an ability to perform socially is often a necessity" (203). Reviewing all her novels, Byrne argues that "Austen's interest in social mobility is inextricably bound up with her knowledge of eighteenth-century theatre, both public and private, where reversals of rank and station were commonplace" (195). She asserts that Austen's innovations in novel writing owe significant debt to her love and knowledge of the theatre, and in specific reference to ***Mansfield Park,*** "that the range of its allusiveness and variety of its quasi-dramatic techniques, [the novel] is much more deeply involved with the theatre than has hitherto been assumed" (177).

In her book of the same title as Byrne's, Penny Gay arrives at similar conclusions. Like Byrne, Gay points to theatrical qualities in Austen's writing as evidence of both her knowledge of and deep identification with theatre practice. She begins the chapter on ***Mansfield Park*** with reference to the conclusion of the first volume of the novel, when, in a highly theatrical moment, Julia Bertram rushes in to announce the surprise return of Sir Thomas: "Thus in this most apparently anti-theatrical of her novels, Jane Austen employs the methods of the drama with brilliant panache" (Gay 2002:98). Gay arrives at conclusions similar to Byrne's that "the novel's recognition that theatricality, like the world, is always with us—and that it cannot be harnessed uncomplicatedly to serve the cause of morality" (98). She argues that what seems ostensibly like criticism of theatre actually demonstrates its power. In the later parts of the novel Austen uses theatrical methods in profound ways that are not immediately obvious. These devices are successful because Austen has "has prepared the reader for the contemplation of the subtle but pervasive power of these structures by alerting us in Volume I to the power of acknowledged theatricality (108).

The Adaptation Process

Gay's and Byrne's observations on Austen's deep interest in theatre and performance are supported by discoveries during the process of the novel's theatrical adaptation. As I moved into the actual practice of adapting—creating the script and especially *staging* the narrative in physical space—profound performative and theatrical aspects of the novel's content, form, and style began to reveal themselves. These elements suggested reasons why the novel might be better fit for theatrical adaptation than previous practice suggests. The physical staging offers insights beyond those discerned from textual analysis, into the relationship of theatre to Austen's writing, especially in the progression of the narrative voice in relation to Fanny Price.[4]

The most immediate feature of Austen's writing to emerge in my process was the amount of the novel written as *dialogue* and placed in quotation marks. In the program notes to his adaptation of ***Sense and Sensibility*** at Northlight Theatre in Skokie, Illinois (2011), director and writer Jon Jory pointed out not only the dominance of dialogue in Austen's novels (roughly 70 percent of the printed on the page) but also of her skill at evoking character through dialogue. The theatre adaptor's job with Austen's work is thus a relatively easy one. In extracting the dialogue from ***Mansfield Park,*** I noticed a consistent structure to the chapters. Most begin with a brief narrative description followed by a long dialogic section. Some conclude with short return to the narrative, others end in the dialogue itself. This structure is similar to scenes in a play with scene descriptions followed by dialogue.[5]

In addition to the heavy use of dialogue in the novel, the narrative prose also often assumes the voices of characters as if they are speaking. Austen is credited for the development and sophistication of this narrative form, known as "free indirect speech." Her narrators often speak in the third person, through the thoughts and vernacular of the characters she is describing. When Fanny learns her love Edmund is about to participate in the theatrical activity she dislikes, the narrator, without quotations for Fanny, alternates between hers and her heroine's voices: "To be acting! After all his objections—objections so just and so public! After all that she had heard him say, and seen him look, and known him to be feeling. Could it be possible? Edmund so inconsistent. Was he not deceiving himself? Was he not wrong? Alas! it was all Miss Crawford's doing" (183-184). Byrne comments on this authorial feature of Austen's narrative: "the author is able to be simultaneously inside and outside the consciousness of the character, to be both fully engaged and ironic" (99).[6] In her book *The Play of Fiction,* Emily Anderson considers Austen's free indirect speech a narrative form of theatricality in and of itself. "Her free indirect discourse, a rhetorical technique that implies the speaker's attitude, makes her narrator, much like Fanny, a speaker who speaks only when spoken 'through'" (2006:136). Quoting an unnamed colleague, Anderson asserts, "in these moments of free indirect discourse . . . the narrator borrows language and thought from her female characters [to] speak both freely and indirectly—likening these to moments of theatre" (136). Even apart from such considerations as these, free indirect speech is a form of narration readily adaptable to dialogue or soliloquy. In addition to the prevalence of dialogue, several textual features render Austen's text easy convertible to scripted form.

In addition to readiness for spoken text in quotes and free indirect speech, Austen also uses punctuation as a kind of vocal scoring—designed to guide a *speaker,* more than a reader. These would impact the delivery of the lines as spoken on the stage. Dashes, semicolons, italics, and exclamation points impact the way the words are meant to be spoken by characters aloud. Examples are copious throughout: "A pretty trick upon my word! I cannot see them anywhere"; "*That* is Miss Maria's concern. I am not obliged to punish myself for *her* sins. The mother I could not avoid . . . but the son I *can* get away from" (118). While editors point out that much of this punctuation, especially the italics, was commonly added by compositors at printers in the early nineteenth century, most editions of ***Mansfield Park*** rely on the second edition printing of 1816, which Austen herself was able to correct from the 1814 printing; thus its features likely reflect authorial intent (Todd 2005:xl-xliii).

Dialogue, free indirect speech, and vocal scoring through non-traditional punctuation join with several features of Austen's writing to reveal a theatrical sensibility governing her work, and render the material a natural fit for dramatic adaptation. Byrne writes,

> Jane Austen was indebted to the theatrical set piece, or scene. . . . [M]any of the most memorable moments in her works may be perceived in terms of their dramatic impact. Austen's novels are "dramatic" in the sense that her scenes were often conceived and conducted in stage terms. The prevalence of character revealing dialogue is the most far reaching theatrical debt. It should be considered alongside the collecting of characters in appropriate groups and the contriving of entrances and exits.
>
> [177]

One such theatrical "set piece" is the scene at Sotherton early in the novel.[7] This precedes the home theatrical section of the novel, but contains all the trappings of a ready-made theatre scene, complete with witty dialogue, stage directions, and farcical entrances and exits. Byrne extracts the following exchange between Henry Crawford and Maria Bertram as evidence of Austen's skill at writing virtually uninterrupted dialogue, with minimal insertion of narration that functions as "stage direction":

> "It is undoubtedly the best thing we can do now, as we are so far from the house already," said Mr. Crawford, when he was gone.
>
> "Yes, there is nothing else to be done. But now, sincerely, do not you find the place altogether worse than you expected?"
>
> "No, indeed, far otherwise. I find it better, grander, more complete in its style, though that style may not be the best. And to tell you the truth," speaking rather lower, "I do not think that *I* shall ever see Sotherton again with so much pleasure as I do now. Another summer will hardly improve it to me."
>
> After a moment's embarrassment the lady replied, "You are too much a man of the world not to see with the eyes of the world. If other people think Sotherton improved, I have no doubt that you will."
>
> "I am afraid I am not quite so much the man of the world as might be good for me in some points. My feelings are not quite so evanescent, nor my memory of the past under such easy dominion as one finds to be the case with men of the world."
>
> This was followed by a short silence. Miss Bertram began again. "You seemed to enjoy your drive here very much this morning. I was glad to see you so well entertained. You and Julia were laughing the whole way."
>
> "Were we? Yes, I believe we were; but I have not the least recollection at what. Oh! I believe I was relating to her some ridiculous stories of an old Irish groom of my uncle's. Your sister loves to laugh."
>
> "You think her more light-hearted than I am."
>
> "More easily amused," he replied; "consequently, you know," smiling, "better company. . . ."
>
> [114-115]

Phrases such as "speaking rather lower," "after a moment's embarrassment," and "this was followed by a short silence" might be stage directions, as they attempt to convey physiological shifts though outward behavior. Indeed, this section of the novel was lifted for the adaptation with almost no alteration. Narrative insertions such as those above were directly enacted, and helped the actors both with interpretations and in the specifics of playing the beat changes.

Based on the combination of these formal and stylistic features, alongside the fact that the much of the novel is concerned with performance of a play, with what we know of Austen's own regular interest in the theatre, one might go so far to speculate that Austen was writing close to the dramatic medium when she wrote the novel. Her process of writing—observation of her own world, imagination of each character, and the recording on the page—is a kind of internal theatrical act on the part of the novelist. Not only might we consider Austen's procedure as similar to playwriting, but the experience of *reading* the novel evokes one similar to watching a play in the imagination of the reader, especially given the dominance of theatrical features identified above. Emily Anderson's work identifies performance in novel writing, particularly by women, in the eighteenth and early nineteenth century. Significantly, she argues that this trend culminates with Austen: "The novel, like the playhouse or the masquerade, could offer its authors yet another theatrical frame; the fictional text, which announces a discrepancy between its author and the statements it conveys, could function as an act of disguise; and authorship could become an act of performance (2). Women in particular (e.g., Eliza Haywood, Frances Burney, Elizabeth Inchbald, and Maria Edgeworth) writing both novels and plays, "experiment with the fictional frame of the novel, which is highlighted with increasing insistence as the century progresses comes to duplicate the frame of the playhouse; it signals that everything contained therein is artifice" (4).

The Theatricality of the Narrative

This idea of an internal dramatic process in the experience of the novelist and the reader is supported by a close analysis of the narrative voice in relation to the central female character, Fanny Price. Such theatricality is identified by scholars such as Byrne, Gay, and Anderson; however, these aspects were made even clearer by application of Robert Breen's method of Chamber Theatre which suggests a means of preserving the narrative voice in the adaptation of literature for the stage. In the introduction to his book *Chamber Theatre,* Breen writes,

> It is the thesis of this text that there is a technique for presenting narrative fiction on the stage in such a way as to take full advantage of all the theatrical devices of the stage without sacrificing the narrative elements of the literature. … Chamber Theatre is dedicated to the proposition that the ideal literary experience is one in which the simultaneity of the drama, representing the illusion of actuality (that is, social and psychological realism), may be profitably combined with the novel's narrative privilege of examining human motivation at the moment of action.
>
> [Breen 1986:4-5]

Since Chamber Theatre seeks to preserve the narrative aspects of drama and Austen uses dramatic elements in her narrative, the use of this method with adapting ***Mansfield Park*** was a fruitful one, particularly in what it revealed about the narrative in relation to the central female character. I followed one of Breen's suggestions to make a character of the narrator so that she interacts with the other character on the stage. My spatial placement of her in relation to the other characters, particularly Fanny, revealed a theatrical relationship at the very center of ***Mansfield Park*** that might not be as clear from textual analysis alone. These considerations may help rescue the novel from some criticism of its "problems" as they help explain the uncharacteristic nature of its heroine. Likewise these considerations help clarify Austen's stance on theatre, as they reveal her deep identification with acts of observation and performance.

Fanny Price is considered the most problematic of Austen's heroines and not everyone likes her. She is opaque, especially in comparison with such figures as Eliza Bennett. She is criticized as passive, quiet, weak, and morally rigid (Byrne 2000:149). Lionel Trilling mused, "Nobody, I believe, has found it possible to like the heroine of ***Mansfield Park***" (qtd. in Todd lxvi). As we blocked the play in space, I began to see that Fanny's passive qualities and relative silence throughout the first parts of the novel render her a sort of *audience* within its structure. Furthermore, Fanny's journey through the novel may be considered a move from audience to actor, or participant. I learned after completing the adaptation that several scholars have similarly examined Fanny's position as spectator and noted that her role changes over the course of the novel. Marilyn Butler argues that Fanny moves from audience to "experiencing subject" (248). Alistair Duckworth characterizes her development in the novel as a move from "periphery to center" (qtd. in Todd lxxi). Penny Gay details Fanny's move from audience to being "looked at" (117-120).

The question of whether Fanny will participate in events is a recurring refrain in the novel. Edmund regularly champions her opportunities for riding, travel, and excursion of any sort. Even when she does go along, the narrator reminds us "her own thoughts were habitually her best companions" (94), and she is not included in the activities of others. This becomes especially clear first in the long scene at Sotherton described above, a group excursion to the home of her cousin's wealthy fiancé, in which she sits still on a bench while characters enter and exit the wooded knoll around her. As observer alone, she witnesses the treachery of her cousin and the Crawfords before any of the other characters are allowed to see it. In the neutrality of her presence, Byrne observes that Fanny is not a substitute for the ironic narrator, but rather a sort of passive audience, a stand in for the objective, witnessing reader:

> Confusingly, Fanny's ubiquitous presence, rather than focusing the ironies of the scene, offers disarming lack of perspective. Through the quasi farcical entrances and exits of the various characters, her thoughts are shaped largely by her jealous concern for Edmund. But though she seems to be little more than a conduit, it is significant that she should witness Henry in action. Her knowledge of his duplicitous conduct prepares her for her rejection of his advances in the third part of the novel.
>
> [Byrne 183]

The motif of "Fanny as audience" is formally established during the preparations of the play where she serves as audience and prompter:

> ... it was a pleasure to *her* to creep into the theatre, and attend the rehearsal of the first act—in spite of the feelings it excited in some speeches for Maria.—Maria, she also thought, acted well—too well;—and after the first rehearsal or two, Fanny began to be their only audience—and sometimes as prompter, sometimes as spectator—was often very useful.—As far as she could judge, Mr. Crawford was considerably the best actor of all: he had more confidence than Edmund, more judgment than Tom, more talent and taste than Mr. Yates.—She did not like him as a man, but she must admit him to be the best actor, and on this point there were not many who differed from her.
>
> [193-194]

Like in the scene at Sotherton, her outside perspective gives her a unique vantage point on what is happening that others don't share:

> Fanny, being always a very courteous listener, and often the only listener at hand, came in for the complaints and the distresses of most of them. *She* knew that Mr. Yates was in general thought to rant dreadfully; that Mr. Yates was disappointed in Henry Crawford; that Tom Bertram spoke so quick he would be unintelligible; that Mrs. Grant spoiled everything by laughing; that Edmund was behindhand with his part, and that it was misery to have anything to do with Mr. Rushworth, who was wanting a prompter through every speech. She knew, also, that poor Mr. Rushworth could seldom get anybody to rehearse with him: *his* complaint came before her as well as the rest; and so decided to her eye was her cousin Maria's avoidance of him, and so needlessly often the rehearsal of the first scene between her and Mr. Crawford, that she had soon all the terror of other complaints from *him.*
>
> [192-193]

The question of whether or not Fanny will take part in the play itself figures large in the theatrical section of the novel. She staunchly resists, to the criticism of her judging Aunt Norris, her cousin Tom's request that she play Cottager's Wife. She pleads, "I could not act anything if you were to give me the world. No indeed I cannot act" (171). Answering Fanny's reluctance, Tom declares, "you may be as creep mouse as you like, but we must have you to *look at*" (171, my emphasis). Fanny is finally forced to participate when Mrs. Grant fails to show up for the final rehearsal.

Significantly, Fanny is onstage at the climax of the scene, the dramatic close to the first volume of the novel, so the events are not filtered through her eyes as above. "They *did* begin; and being too much engaged in their own noise to be struck by an unusual noise in the other part of the house, had proceeded some way when the door of the room was thrown open, and Julia, appearing at it, with a face all aghast, exclaimed, 'My father is come! He is in the hall at this moment'" (137). Byrne points out that Julia directs attentions to the tableau; however, "there is a double focus: the reader watches as the character in the novel watching a character on stage. Furthermore the scene is not filtered through the eyes of Fanny, for she is also on the stage, about to take her part" (208).

Fanny's participation in the play and momentary position "on stage" alters her relation vis-à-vis the narrative voice. The move at this point in the novel is significant. While her actual appearance as a performer is saved by her uncle's surprise return from Antigua, her role in the real life of Mansfield does increase dramatically at this point in the novel. She is quite suddenly more visible to others and included in more events. Her uncle notices her and compliments her beauty for the first time.

> Sir Thomas was at that moment looking round him, and saying, "But where is Fanny? Why do not I see my little Fanny?"—and on perceiving her, came forward with a kindness which astonished and penetrated her, calling her his dear Fanny, kissing her affectionately, and observing with decided pleasure how much she was grown! Fanny knew not how to feel, nor where to look. She was quite oppressed. He had never been so kind, so *very* kind to her in his life. His manner seemed changed, his voice was quick from the agitation of joy; and all that had been awful in his dignity seemed lost in tenderness.
>
> [208]

Notice of Fanny continues and escalates. As Edmund tells Fanny later:

> Your uncle thinks you very pretty, dear Fanny—and that is the long and the short of the matter. Anybody but myself would have made something more of it, and anybody but you would resent that you had not been thought very pretty before; but the truth is, that your uncle never did admire you till now—and now he does. Your complexion is so improved!—and you have gained so much countenance!—and your figure—nay, Fanny, do not turn away about it—it is but an uncle. If you cannot bear an uncle's admiration, what is to become of you? You must really begin to harden yourself to the idea of being worth looking at. You must try not to mind growing up into a pretty woman.
>
> [231]

When the theatrical party disperses, the narrator reports, "Fanny's consequence increased on the departure of her cousins, becoming as she then did the only young woman in the drawing room, the only occupier of that interesting division of a family in which she had hitherto held so humble a third, it was impossible for her not to be more looked at, more thought of and attended to than she ever had before" (239).

Once invited to the Parsonage, Fanny attracts Henry Crawford's attention and marriage proposal. Penny Gay points out that it is by standing up to Crawford, ironically voicing her opinion against the theatricals, that she is noticed by him (118). This notice spurs the idea for Fanny's ball, a "coming out" where Fanny will make her first appearance in society. Gay notes,

> The phrase is identical to that which announces a new actress in the theatre. Austen is clear about what this new staging implies—commoditization the trade of coming out. . . . Fanny does not want to be "looked at" or introduced to the guests, and is envious of William "walk[ing] at his case in the background of the scene"; Austen's natural application of theatre metaphors to this situation is striking.
>
> [119][8]

While she does not literally perform in the play, the theatrical activities lead to a shift in Fanny's "stage presence" in the world at Mansfield and coincide with a shift in her relation to the narrative voice. If Fanny is the audience to the events of the novel, the narrator is the dramatist creating the scene for Fanny to observe. As the novel progresses, Fanny's interaction with the narrator becomes increasingly active and complex.[9] Fanny acquires more of a voice and presence. The sheer number of her "lines" (passages written in quotation) increases, and she interacts more actively with the narrator in free indirect speech. At the beginning of the novel Fanny cannot speak without crying, but in the later chapters in Portsmouth it is Fanny alone who voices (now with quotation marks denoting autonomy from the narrator) her reaction to events and to letters she receives there. When Edmund defends her rival Mary Crawford, Fanny exclaims:

> "'So very fond of me!' 'tis nonsense all. She loves nobody but herself and her brother. Her friends leading her astray for years! She is quite as likely to have led *them* astray. I firmly believe it. It is an attachment to govern his whole life. Accepted or refused, his heart is wedded to her forever. Oh! write, write. Finish it at once. Let there be an end of this suspense. Fix, commit, condemn yourself."
>
> [492]

The narrator gradually recedes, giving more for Fanny to articulate herself. The resolution of the novel's central conflicts concerning the triangle between Edmund, Mary Crawford, and Fanny occurs in a scene when the narrator is all but absent. Edmund assumes the narration as he relates in flashback his final farewell to Mary Crawford while Fanny observes. Below is the scene as it appeared in my adaptation, showing Edmund's assumption of the role as narrator and the receding authorial voice:

NARRATOR:

> They reached Mansfield on Thursday, and it was not till Sunday evening that Edmund began to talk to her on the subject. Sitting with her on Sunday evening—a wet Sunday evening—the very time of all others when, if a friend is at hand, the heart must be opened, and everything told; it was impossible not to speak . . .

EDMUND:

> She met me with a serious—certainly a serious—even an agitated air; but before I had been able to speak one intelligible sentence, she had introduced the subject in a manner which I owned had shocked me.

MARY:

> I heard you were in town, I wanted to see you. Let us talk over this sad business. What can equal the folly of our two relations?

EDMUND:

> I could not answer, but I believe my looks spoke. She felt reproved. Sometimes how quick to feel! With a graver look and voice she then added,

MARY:

> I do not mean to defend Henry at your sister's expense.

EDMUND:

> So she began, but how she went on, Fanny, is not fit, is hardly fit to be repeated to you. I cannot recall all her words. I would not dwell upon them if I could. Their substance was great anger at the *folly* of each. To hear the woman whom—no harsher name than folly given! So voluntarily, so freely, so coolly to canvass it! No reluctance, no horror—It was the detection, in short—oh, Fanny! it was the detection, not the offence, which she reprobated. (*He stops*)

FANNY:

> And what . . .

NARRATOR:

> . . . said Fanny—believing herself required to speak—

FANNY:

> . . . what could you say?

EDMUND:

> Nothing, nothing to be understood. I was like a man stunned. She went on, began to talk of you; yes, then she began to talk of you, regretting, as well she might, the loss of such a—. There she spoke very rationally.

MARY:

> He has thrown away such a woman as he will never see again. She would have fixed him; she would have made him happy forever. Why would not she have him? It is all her fault. Simple girl! I shall never forgive her. Had she accepted him as she ought, they might now have been on the point of marriage, and Henry would have been too happy and too busy to want any other object. He would have taken no pains to be on terms with Mrs. Rushworth again. It would have all ended in a regular standing flirtation.

EDMUND:

> Could you have believed it possible? But the charm is broken. My eyes are opened. Gladly would I submit to all the increased pain of losing her, rather than have to think of her as I do. I told her so.

FANNY:

> Did you?

EDMUND:

Yes; when I left her I told her so.

FANNY:

How long were you together?

EDMUND:

Five-and-twenty minutes. Well, she went on to say that what remained now to be done was to bring about a marriage between them. She spoke of it, Fanny, with a steadier voice than I can.

MARY:

We must persuade Henry to marry her, and properly supported by her own family, people of respectability as they are, she may recover her footing in society to a certain degree. In some circles, we know, she would never be admitted, but with good dinners, and large parties, there will always be those who will be glad of her acquaintance; and there is, undoubtedly, more liberality and candor on those points than formerly. What I advise is that your father be quiet. Persuade him to let things take their course and it may all end well.

EDMUND:

Now, Fanny, I shall soon have done. All this together most grievously convinced me that I had never understood her before, and that, as far as related to mind, it had been the creature of my own imagination, not Miss Crawford, that I had been too apt to dwell on for many months past. She would have laughed if she could. It was a sort of laugh, as she answered . . .

MARY:

A pretty good lecture, upon my word. Was it part of your last sermon?

EDMUND:

She tried to speak carelessly, but she was not so careless as she wanted to appear. I only said in reply, that from my heart I wished her well. and such has been the end of our acquaintance. And what an acquaintance has it been! How have I been deceived! Equally in brother and sister deceived! I thank you for your patience, Fanny. This has been the greatest relief, and now we will have done.

[Shanahan 2011:66]

Aside from obligatory insertions by Fanny, the narrator has retired entirely here, fully redundant to the present moment and the narrative of the characters she has created.

The narrator does take up her voice again immediately following in the last chapter, which ties together all the loose strands of the plot as a whole, including the union of the lovers which is such a hallmark of Austen's work. "Let other pens dwell on guilt and misery. I quit such odious subjects as soon as I can, impatient to restore everybody, not greatly in fault themselves, to tolerable comfort, and to have done with all the rest" (533). But the narrative position here is complicated. First, she is ready to immediately abandon her project and put down her pen. Second, she refers to Fanny as "My Fanny"—directly assuming for herself an identity for the first time separate from the fiction. "My Fanny, indeed, at this very time, I have the satisfaction of knowing, must have been happy in spite of everything. She must have been a happy creature in spite of all that she felt, or thought she felt, for the distress of those around her. She had sources of delight that must force their way" (533). In this repeated refrain "must have been," the narrator gives up her authority, and Fanny is allowed to exist separate from the narrator's omniscient eye. She is her own agent, actor, person—separate from what the narrator can know for certain.

This agency is not only given to Fanny, but to the general readership. In the description of the long-awaited union of the cousins in love, the narrator evades authorship:

> I purposely abstain from dates on this occasion, that every one may be at liberty to fix their own, aware that the cure of unconquerable passions, and the transfer of unchanging attachments, must vary much as to time in different people.—I only entreat everybody to believe that exactly at the time when it was quite natural that it should be so, and not a week earlier, Edmund did cease to care about Miss Crawford, and became as anxious to marry Fanny as Fanny herself could desire.
>
> [544]

The narrator steps out of her authorial role and every reader becomes their own writer and creator. The artifice and control of the process is abandoned for what is "natural."

With the release of narratorial authority, Fanny is set free. She is no longer audience; she is set free as an actor in her own life. After "waiting in the wings" (Byrne 149) we see Fanny take the stage and then naturally live her life. In the last paragraph, she enters the scene she has observed so long: "They removed to Mansfield; and the Parsonage there, which . . . soon grew as dear to her heart, and as thoroughly perfect in her eyes, as everything else within the view and patronage of Mansfield Park had long been" (548).[10]

CONCLUSIONS

It is significant that ***Mansfield Park,*** written in her late thirties, is Austen's first full-length novel of her adult maturity. It was her first novel to be written and published with no delay, following a relatively long "fallow period" from writing (Le Faye 2002:228) and years devoted to the revision and repeated effort at publication of her earlier novels, ***Pride and Prejudice*** and ***Sense and Sensibility,*** conceived in her early twenties. Fanny Price's move to expression may reflect Austen's move from silent observation (and play watching) to fully confident novel writing and importantly, *publication,* where her work was finally welcome in a public arena. Following the long sought publication of ***Sense and Sensibility*** and ***Pride and Prejudice*** in 1811 and 1813 respectively (Le Faye 1998:110-

111), ***Mansfield Park***—complicated, serious, unusual—was the first of Austen's novels written when she knew she would have an audience. Fanny's move to the center of the stage in Mansfield may reflect Austen's own move to the center of her life as an artist, finally secure after years of upheaval surrounding her father's retirement and death. For the first time she was earning money through publication to support herself, her mother, and sister. The layers of theatricality implied in the transition of Fanny from audience to performer, especially in relation to these features of Austen's biography, are perhaps even more significant to evaluating Austen's relation to the theatre than are the theatrical subjects of the novel. They most certainly provide substantive and interesting ground for dramatic adaptation of ***Mansfield Park*** and the staging of it.

Notes

1. Chamber Theatre is a method connected to the Performance Studies Program at Northwestern University. The teaching and practice of Robert Breen have been influential in the adaptation methods of such director/adaptors as Frank Galati, Mary Zimmerman, Paul Edwards, Jessica Thebus, Eric Rosen, and several members of Lookingglass Theatre in Chicago.

2. I thought the project of adapting *Mansfield Park* contained similar potential as staging the play *Our Country's Good* (1988) by Timberlake Wertenbaker, in which characters rehearse George Farquhar's *The Recruiting Officer* (1706). When I directed Wertenbaker's play in 2010, the project had allowed an in-depth workshop on period performance styles of both the Restoration and the late eighteenth century British stage. However, as I started on *Mansfield Park,* I noticed several points of sharp contrast in the attitudes towards the plays by the main characters and of the situation of play-making in the contexts of the stories. Rather than offering a civilizing influence as in *Our Country's Good,* in *Mansfield Park* theatre initiates the acts of moral degradation that the novel ultimately condemns.

3. Several of these theatrical aspects are covered by Byrne in her book, *Jane Austen and the Theatre,* which was recommended to me after I had completed the adaptation. Her textual study provides valuable analysis of what she calls the "quasi-theatrical" elements in Austen's writing. It is significant that several of the same features became clear from physical enactment as from text and biographical analysis. On the other hand, the physical staging offered additional insights into the relationship of theatre to Austen's writing. These are described in the body of the essay.

4. Many of Gay's arguments resonate with those that emerged through my staging process, especially concerning the role of the theatre and performance in a development of Fanny Price. Gay demonstrates how Austen uses theatre as a tool to educate Fanny Price in sexuality and more broadly in confident embodied habitation of the world around her. While I encountered Gay's scholarship well after the process of adaptation, her conclusions support and enrich those discerned through physical staging.

5. Similar to these conclusions regarding the prominence of dialogue, Paula Byrne develops a sophisticated argument for the influence of drama on Austen's style through comedies of manners by Richardson and playwrights turned novelists, Henry Fielding and Elizabeth Inchbald: "Fielding and Inchbald metamorphosed themselves from playwrights into novelists, and in so doing introduced theatrical effects into the novel. Austen correspondingly abandoned the dramatic and epistolary forms because they lacked a controlling narratorial voice. By adapting the best parts of Richardson's comedy of manners and the quasi-theatrical innovations of Fielding and Inchbald, she achieved a synthesis that enabled her to find her own unique novelistic voice" (102).

6. Byrne mourns the lack of characteristic third person perspective in most film and television adaptations of Austen's novels: "It is for this reason that film and television adaptations—brilliantly as they may render the surface of Jane Austen's comic world—can never seriously satisfy the serious reader of the novels themselves. Screenwriters find it almost impossible to render the ironic third person authorial voice that is so important to Austen's narrative method. Important as the drama was to the making of her fictional worlds, Austen was in the end a novelist" (99). Thanks to the use of the Chamber Theatre technique, which strives for "presenting narrative fiction on the stage in such a way as to take full advantage of all the theatrical devices of the stage without sacrificing the narrative elements of the literature" (Breen 1986:4), in my project this feature of the novel remained strong. "Chamber Theatre is not interested in the problems of transforming fiction into drama; it resists the temptation to delete narrative descriptions and rewrite summaries as dialogue. No effort is made in Chamber Theatre to eliminate the narrative point of view which characterizes fiction; indeed, the storytellers angle of vision is emphasized through physical representation on the stage" (Breen 1986:4). It was in fact this aspect of the adaptation that allowed me to see the theatrical features embedded in the narrative point of view and its progression.

7. Byrne argues that "the Sotherton episode alludes to and adapts one of the most popular comedies of the eighteenth century stage, *The Clandestine Marriage* (1766) by George Colman the Elder and David Garrick" (2000:178-186). Similar elements include the

heroine's name "Fanny," a reformed rake, improvements to grounds, a garden setting and serpentine path, and intrusion by brother and sister of another class.

8. In her chapter on *Mansfield Park,* Gay traces the role of theatre in Fanny's "sex education" (107). She offers several observations on theatrical elements in the narrative and aspects of increasing performance for Fanny, all of which were supported by my observations in staging the novel. Chief amongst these are reference to Fanny's role as "the daughter oppressed by a tyrannical father, a staple of Victorian melodramas to come" and the "Dickensian tropes of Victorian Drama" in the Portsmouth scenes (117-122).

9. As with Fanny's role as audience, other critics have noted a relationship between Fanny and the narrative voice. Citing David Marshall, Emily Anderson notes that "critics frequently use Fanny's self effacing manner as a stylistic template for those other invisible figures, the narrator who spends most of the novel behind free indirect discourse and the supervising author who will not speak in *propria persona*" (135). While scholars have identified Fanny's initial role as audience and her transition to visible participation, as well as her relationship to the narrative voice, none have explicitly identified the theatrical tradeoff that happens between the two. Staging with both figures embodied in physical space made this clear.

10. The staging of this relationship between narrator and the character of Fanny was done rather simply. The physical presence of "Fanny as audience" was simply dramatized by her stationary and relatively peripheral placement on stage. This placement shifted as she began to co-author narrative sections and enter her life as a participant. As this transition unfolded, the narrator could become more remote and recede to the periphery in exchange. In the final scene, the narrator receded to the periphery almost entirely as Fanny and Edmund walked upstage center through a wedding arch. The play concluded with a finishing dance, with Fanny and Edmund up center and the narrator joining as any other dancer from the downstage periphery.

References Cited

Allen, Susan Ford, "It Is about *Lovers' Vows*: Kotzebue, Inchbald, and the Players of *Mansfield Park.*" *Persuasions Online: A Publication of the Jane Austen Society of North America.* 27.1 (Winter 2006).

Anderson, E. H. *Eighteenth-Century Authorship and the Play of Fiction: Novels and the Theater, Haywood to Austen.* New York: Routledge, 2006.

Austen, Jane. *Mansfield Park,* edited by Janet Todd. Cambridge: Cambridge University Press, 2005.

———. *Selected Letters,* edited by Vivien Jones. New York: Oxford University Press, 2004.

Breen, Robert. *Chamber Theatre.* Evanston, IL: William Caxton, 1986.

Butler, Marilyn. "Introduction" to *Mansfield Park,* edited by James Kinsley. Oxford: Oxford University Press, 1990.

———. *Jane Austen and the War of Ideas.* Oxford: Clarendon Press, 1975.

Byrne, Paula. *Jane Austen and the Theatre.* London and New York: Hambleton Continuum, 2000.

Gay, Penny. *Jane Austen and the Theatre.* Cambridge: Cambridge University Press, 2002.

Jordan, Elaine. "Pulpit, Stage and Novel: *Mansfield Park* and Mrs. Inchbald's *Lovers' Vows.*" *NOVEL: A Forum on Fiction.* 20.2 (1987):138-48.

Jory, Jon. "Director's Note to *Sense and Sensibility.*" Northlight Theatre. Skokie, IL, 2011.

Kotzebue, August von. "Lovers' Vows: Adapted by Elizabeth Inchbald." Oxford: Woodstock Books, 1990.

Le Faye, Deirdre. *Jane Austen.* New York: Oxford University Press, 1998.

———. *Jane Austen: A Family Record.* Second Edition. Cambridge: Cambridge University Press, 2003.

———. *Jane Austen: The World of Her Novels.* London: Frances Lincoln, 2002.

Shanahan, Ann. *Adaptation of Mansfield Park.* Loyola University. Chicago: 2011.

FURTHER READING

Author Web Site

"Jane Austen." *The Jane Austen Society of North America.* Jane Austen Soc. of North Amer., 16 May 2015. Web. 5 Aug. 2015.

Provides a biography of Austen and a time line of her publications, as well as pictures of the author and maps for her novels.

Bibliographies

Chapman, R. W. *Jane Austen: A Critical Bibliography.* Oxford: Clarendon P, 1969. Print.

Provides briefly annotated entries on the six novels, later editions, translations, minor works, letters, biographies of Austen, and criticism of her work.

Gilson, David. *A Bibliography of Jane Austen.* Oxford: Clarendon P, 1982. Print.

A comprehensive bibliography on Austen, her works, and the criticism of her novels. Gilson expands upon Geoffrey Keynes's earlier bibliography (see below) to include works published after 1968. Gilson arranges criticism by date, with each entry containing a brief annotation.

Keynes, Geoffrey. *Jane Austen: A Bibliography.* New York: Franklin, 1968. Print.

One of the more comprehensive bibliographies on Austen. Keynes provides briefly annotated entries on the original editions of Austen's works, the American editions, the collected editions, letters and miscellaneous writings by Austen, biographies, and criticism of Austen's works.

Biographies

Jenkins, Elizabeth. *Jane Austen: A Biography.* London: Gollancz, 1968. Print.

A well-researched biography that provides in-depth analysis. Jenkins offers a portrait of the author and the circumstances in which she wrote her novels. Her work, though dated, is a valuable counterpart to more recent biographies of Austen.

Reef, Catherine. *Jane Austen: A Life Revealed.* Boston: Clarion, 2011. Print.

Considers Austen's life in the larger cultural and historical context of the time in which she was writing. Reef addresses each of Austen's six major novels, discussing connections between her works and her private life.

Todd, Janet. *Jane Austen: Her Life, Her Times, Her Novels.* London: Deutsch, 2014. Print.

Provides background on Austen's relationships with family and friends. Todd also discusses the contemporary attitudes that shaped Austen and her writing and considers the locations featured in her novels.

Criticism

Boulukos, George E. "The Politics of Silence: *Mansfield Park* and the Amelioration of Slavery." *Novel* 39.3 (2006): 361-83. Print.

Examines aspects of *Mansfield Park* to show that Austen did not necessarily favor abolishing the slave trade. Boulukos proposes instead that Austen believed the treatment of slaves could be improved and that the slave trade in general could be conducted in a more humane manner.

Butler, E. M. "*Mansfield Park* and Kotzebue's *Lovers' Vows.*" *MLR: Modern Language Review* 28.3 (1933): 326-37. Print.

Compares the plot and themes of *Lovers' Vows* with those of *Mansfield Park.* Butler concludes that, although Austen's characters are more realistic and complex than those in August von Kotzebue's play, her moral censure of them is also much more severe.

Cleere, Eileen. "Reinvesting Nieces: *Mansfield Park* and the Economics of Endogomy." *Novel* 28.2 (1995): 113-30. Print.

Examines the primacy of the family and the metaphorical power of economic endogamy, the tendency to transact within rather than across social groups, that account for the rise in power of Fanny in *Mansfield Park.*

Despotopoulou, Anna. "Fanny's Gaze and the Construction of Feminine Space in *Mansfield Park.*" *MLR: Modern Language Review* 99.3 (2004): 569-83. Print.

Considers how reading gives Fanny the opportunity to remove herself from traditional female expectations of shallow accomplishments and instead become an active participant in the discussions that follow her reading of books.

Giffin, Michael. "Jane Austen and the Economy of Salvation: Renewing the Drifting Church in *Mansfield Park.*" *Literature and Theology* 14.1 (2000): 17-33. Print.

Suggests that *Mansfield Park* should be read in the context of Austen's transition from an allegorical to a psychological style, with Sir Thomas Bertram acting as a God figure and Fanny functioning as a Christlike character who brings about spiritual renewal and social reform.

Husbands, H. Winifred. "*Mansfield Park* and *Lovers' Vows*: A Reply." *MLR: Modern Language Review* 29.2 (1934): 176-79. Print.

Responds to E. M. Butler's 1933 argument (see above) that Austen's stance in *Mansfield Park* is moralistic. Husbands asserts that Austen uses Kotzebue's *Lovers' Vows* in her novel to advance her narrative design for *Mansfield Park* rather than to register indignation. Husbands notes that Austen's treatment of fallen characters in her other novels attests to the fact that she was not a "merciless and savage moralist."

Jenkins, Joyce. "The Puzzle of Fanny Price." *Philosophy and Literature* 30.2 (2006): 346-60. Print.

Compares the moral qualities of Fanny in *Mansfield Park* to those of characters in Austen's other novels. Jenkins discusses topics of romantic fidelity, charm, manners, and principles as well as the often-negative critical reception of the character.

Karounos, Michael. "Ordination and Revolution in *Mansfield Park.*" *SEL Studies in English Literature 1500-1900* 44.4 (2004): 715-36. Print.

Offers evidence disproving Austen's remark that *Mansfield Park* is primarily about ordination and instead attempts to demonstrate that the novel is antislavery. Karounos provides various examples of rebellion, from furniture arrangement to movement and social relationships, and contends that Austen's assertion places too much emphasis on an event of little significance.

Knights, Elspeth. " 'The Library, of Course, Afforded Everything': Jane Austen's Representation of Women Readers." *English* 50.196 (2001): 19-38. Print.

Presents an overview of Austen's depiction of female readers, theorizing that discussions of books in Austen's novels always imply intimacy and reveal the interiority of characters. Knights argues that, in *Mansfield Park,* freedom and equality in reading are portrayed as the basis of mature human relationships.

Lionnet, Françoise. "Gender, Empire, and Epistolarity: From Jane Austen's *Mansfield Park* to Marie-Thérèse Humbert's *La Montagne des Signaux.*" *The Literary Channel: The Inter-national Invention of the Novel.* Ed. Margaret Cohen and Carolyn Dever. Princeton: Princeton UP, 2002. 183-93. Print.

Traces the impact of letter writing and other forms of communication in *Mansfield Park* and Humbert's *La Montagne des Signaux* (1994), another novel that references the West Indies. Lionnet postulates that in both novels "the family system becomes a metaphor for larger social and political structures erected in conjunction with the colonial enterprise."

Murrah, Charles. "The Background of *Mansfield Park.*" *From Jane Austen to Joseph Conrad: Essays Collected in the Memory of James T. Hillhouse.* Ed. Robert C. Rathburn and Martin Steinmann, Jr. Minneapolis: U of Minnesota P, 1967. 23-34. Print.

Discusses the thematic and symbolic importance of the settings in *Mansfield Park,* noting the ways in which Austen uses the locales of Portsmouth, Sotherton, and the Mansfield Park estate in the service of the novel's overall narrative plan.

Perkins, Pam. "A Subdued Gaiety: The Comedy of *Mansfield Park.*" *Nineteenth-Century Literature* 48.1 (1993): 1-25. Print.

Argues that *Mansfield Park* is not a humorless morality tale but rather a serious novel characterized by Austen's spirited incorporation of comic conventions. [Reprinted in *NCLC,* Vol. 95.]

Reitzel, William. "*Mansfield Park* and *Lovers' Vows.*" *Review of English Studies* 9.36 (1933): 451-56. Print.

Suggests that Austen chose *Lovers' Vows* for use in *Mansfield Park* with a full awareness of its reputation as a dangerous and immoral play. Reitzel argues that Austen presented the play as a touchstone for portraying the reactions of various social groups in the novel.

Said, Edward W. "Jane Austen and Empire." *Raymond Williams: Critical Perspectives.* Ed. Terry Eagleton. Boston: Northeastern UP, 1989. 150-64. Print.

Offers a postcolonial reading of *Mansfield Park,* demonstrating how humanistic values in the novel exist side by side with a devaluation of colonized cultures. [Reprinted in *NCLC,* Vol. 95.]

Trilling, Lionel. "*Mansfield Park.*" *Partisan Review* 21.5 (1954): 492-511. Print.

Considers the reasons why *Mansfield Park* and its heroine have been found unsatisfactory by modern readers. Trilling identifies a type of judgment at work in the novel based on principle as "the path to the wholeness of the self which is peace" that was new to Austen at the time.

Urda, Kathleen E. "Why the Show Must Not Go On: 'Real Character' and the Absence of Theatrical Performances in *Mansfield Park.*" *Eighteenth-Century Fiction* 26.2 (2013-14): 281-302. Print.

Discusses Austen's refusal to portray theatrical performances within *Mansfield Park,* positing that she was reacting against other novels of the time in which such performances upset the idea of character as a concrete identity. Urda maintains that Austen chose to focus instead on her characters' reactions to the performances, thereby revealing their real natures.

Additional information on Austen's life and works is contained in the following sources published by Gale: *Authors and Artists for Young Adults,* Vol. 19; *Beacham's Guide to Literature for Young Adults,* Vol. 3; *British Writers,* Vol. 4; *British Writers Retrospective Supplement,* Vol. 2; *British Writers: The Classics,* Vol. 1; *Concise Dictionary of British Literary Biography: 1789-1832*; *Dictionary of Literary Biography,* Vols. 116, 363, 365, 366; *DISCovering Authors*; *DISCovering Authors: British Edition*; *DISCovering Authors: Canadian Edition*; *DISCovering Authors Modules: Most-Studied Authors* and *Novelists*; *DISCovering Authors 3.0*; *Exploring Novels*; *Feminism in Literature: A Gale Critical Companion,* Vol. 2; *Gale Contextual Encyclopedia of World Literature,* Vol. 1; *Gothic Literature: A Gale Critical Companion,* Vol. 2; *Literary Movements for Students,* Vol. 1; *Literature and Its Times,* Vol. 2; *Literature and Its Times Supplement,* Vol. 1; *Literature Resource Center*; *Nineteenth-Century Literature Criticism,* Vols. 1, 13, 19, 33, 51, 81, 95, 119, 150, 207, 210, 222, 242, 271, 314; *Novels for Students,* Vols. 1, 14, 18, 20, 21, 28, 29, 33; *Twayne's English Authors*; *World Literature and Its Times,* Vol. 3; *World Literature Criticism,* Vol. 1; and *Writers for Young Adults Supplement.*

Almeida Garrett
1799-1854

(Born João Leitão da Silva; also known as João Baptista da Silva Leitão and João Baptista da Silva Leitão de Almeida Garrett, Viscount de Almeida Garrett) Portuguese poet, playwright, biographer, critic, essayist, novelist, and short-story writer.

INTRODUCTION

Almeida Garrett is remembered for combining classical styles with Romantic themes to initiate new forms of expression in nineteenth-century Portuguese literature. He wrote in a variety of genres and produced studies on politics, international relations, and education. Seeking to revive his country's theatrical tradition, Garrett authored plays based on characters and events from Portuguese history—the best-known of these is *Frei Luís de Sousa* (1843; published as *Brother Luiz de Sousa*)—and helped to create a national dramatic conservatory. Garrett also served in parliament and held government office. As a statesman, he was celebrated for his oratory and his advocacy of constitutional monarchy and liberal reform. Critics have often studied Garrett in the contexts of Portuguese history and European Romanticism.

BIOGRAPHICAL INFORMATION

João Leitão da Silva was born in Porto, Portugal, on 4 February 1799 to António Bernardo da Silva Garrett, a nobleman and customs official, and Ana Augusta Almeida Leitão. After Napoleon Bonaparte's forces invaded Portugal in late 1807, initiating the Peninsular War, the family fled to property they held in the Azores. While there, the young Garrett studied Latin, Greek, French, Italian, arithmetic and geometry, as well as receiving instruction in classical literature and modern philosophy from his uncle, Bishop Alexandre José da Silva. Garrett's family intended for him to follow in his uncle's footsteps and join the clergy, but instead he enrolled in law school in 1816 at the University of Coimbra. During this period, he became interested in theater and playwriting in the classical tradition. The first performances of Garrett's work occurred in 1819, when a professional company in Coimbra produced *Xerxes,* the text of which has been lost, and the tragedy *Lucrécia.*

Garrett responded with enthusiasm to the liberal revolution of 1820 and its aim of imposing constitutional limits on King João VI, who had reigned from the Portuguese colony of Brazil since the French invasion. Garrett's next play, *Catão* (1821; may be translated as *Cato*), was based on the life of the Roman orator Cato the Younger, who opposed the autocratic ambitions of Julius Caesar. When *Cato* premiered in Lisbon in 1821, its relevance to Portugal's political crisis was clear. That year, Garrett also published the essay *O dia vintequatro d'agosto* (may be translated as *The Twenty-Fourth Day of August*), a critique of absolute monarchical rule, and the narrative poem *O retrato de Vénus* (may be translated as *The Portrait of Venus*), which describes the goddess's beauty in such frank terms that Garrett was forced to defend himself in court against accusations of obscenity. He received a law degree in 1821 and married Luísa Midosi in 1822.

Garrett served briefly as a government official, but he fled Portugal in June 1823 after the king suspended the constitution. He spent the majority of the next decade in exile, mostly in England and France. During these years he worked at a bank; read Romantic poetry and other British, French, and German literature; wrote poetry prolifically; and followed political affairs in Portugal. After King João died in 1826, the struggle between liberals and absolutists developed into a battle for succession between the king's two sons, Pedro—the liberal legitimate successor, at that time serving as emperor of Brazil—and the absolutist Miguel. The civil conflict is variously called the Liberal Wars and the Miguelite Wars. Garrett returned home in 1826 and began writing for political newspapers but retreated into exile again in 1828, after Miguel assumed the throne and invalidated the Constitutional Charter. In 1832 Garrett joined other militant liberals in backing Pedro, who had abdicated the Brazilian throne and returned to Europe with the goal of unseating the Miguelites. Pedro's expeditionary force landed at Porto, where it was besieged for months before ultimately capturing Lisbon.

After helping to draft founding laws for a new liberal government, Garrett was appointed consul general to Brussels in 1834. In 1836 he returned to Portugal and created the position of public inspector of theaters for himself, leading the effort to establish a conservatory for the dramatic arts. He trained actors and dramaturges and helped establish Portugal's first laws on literary and intellectual property. Garrett entered parliament in 1837 and two years later was named Portugal's official chronicler. Having legally separated from his wife in 1835, he fathered several children with his lover, Adelaide Pastor, who died in 1841 giving birth to the only one of their children to survive to adulthood, Maria Adelaide. In 1843 Garrett traveled to the

Santarém Valley, Portugal, and wrote an account based on the journey that was serialized in a Lisbon magazine and later expanded into the novel *Viagens na minha terra* (1846; published as *Travels in My Homeland*). In the late 1840s he had an affair with Rosa Montúfar, an aristocrat and the wife of an army commander. He opened the Teatro Nacional D. Maria II in Lisbon in 1846. Garrett was made a viscount in 1851 and briefly served in the cabinet position of minister of foreign affairs. He died of complications from tuberculosis on 9 December 1854.

MAJOR WORKS

Garrett's abiding thematic interests were love and the glorification of Portuguese history and culture. These concerns are apparent in his early play *Cato* as well as in his efforts to create a stock of historically minded plays to serve as the basis for a national repertory. The first of these works, *Um auto de Gil Vicente* (1838; may be translated as *A Play by Gil Vicente*), pays tribute to the sixteenth-century troubadour of its title, who is generally regarded as Portugal's most important theatrical figure. Vicente himself appears as a character in the play, which includes scenes from one of Vicente's works as a play within the play. Borrowing structural elements from Roman comedies, *A Play by Gil Vicente* was intended to inaugurate a new era in Portuguese theater, a vision Garrett articulated in an introductory essay published with the work in 1841.

Though Garrett's best-known play, *Brother Luiz de Sousa,* was influenced by Greek tragedy, he refused to call it a tragedy because it was not written in verse. The choice of prose was guided by the fact that the historical Luís de Sousa, also known as Manuel de Sousa, was an accomplished prose writer. The play portrays de Sousa's marriage to Dona Madalena, a noblewoman whose former husband, Dom João, is believed to have died alongside the legendary King Sebastião I in the battle of Alcácer Quibir. One day, an itinerant monk arrives and proclaims himself to be Madalena's long-absent husband. The disgraced de Sousa and the guilt-stricken Madalena bid each other farewell and take refuge in cloisters, while their daughter, the consumptive Maria, now revealed to be illegitimate, dies of grief.

Garrett's poetry illustrates his aspiration to revive Portugal's literary culture by reinterpreting material from its folk heritage. The most important of his early poems are the narrative epics *Camões* (1825), which honors the sixteenth-century Portuguese bard Luís de Camões, and *Dona Branca* (1826; may be translated as *Mrs. Branca*). Garrett helped collect and publish traditional Portuguese ballads and lyrics in the 1843 anthology *Romanceiro e cancioneiro geral* (1843; may be translated as *Romances and Popular Songs*), which was expanded to three volumes in 1851. Two other noteworthy verse collections are *Flores sem fructo* (1845; may be translated as *Fruitless Flowers*) and *Folhas caídas* (1853; may be translated as *Fallen Leaves*). Garrett anonymously published the latter volume, consisting mainly of love poetry, probably because of its erotic content and the strain on his public reputation caused by his affair with Montúfar. Scholars believe that she inspired many poems in the collection, including the famous lyric "Cascais."

Travels in My Homeland is the most renowned of Garrett's prose-fiction works. The early chapters of the novel consist of reflections on the author's travels in the Santarém Valley, and the second part depicts the complex love story of Carlos and Joaninha. The work incorporates innovations in narrative fiction developed by such eighteenth-century British novelists as Henry Fielding and Laurence Sterne. Critics have argued that his technique of interspersing the narrator's travelog with the romantic plot yields unexpected reverberations of sentiment and irony.

CRITICAL RECEPTION

Scholars credit Garrett with revitalizing Portugal's literary traditions and burnishing the reputations of such earlier Portuguese authors as Vicente and Camões. Jack Horace Parker (1954) argued that Garrett identified closely with Camões and portrayed his predecessor as a Romantic hero of Portugal. Annabela Rita (2010) contended that Garrett's nationalism informed the romantic subplot of *Travels in My Homeland,* analyzing the magical Santarém Valley and the character Joaninha as metaphorical representations of a mythologized Portugal. Rita referred to Carlos and Joaninha as "a national pair." Phillip Rothwell (2007; see Further Reading) interpreted *Travels in My Homeland* and *Brother Luiz de Sousa* as fictionalized meditations on national mythology, particularly the legacy of King Sebastião I, whom the critic characterized as Portugal's "empty father."

Much scholarship on Garrett addresses his fusion of classical forms and elements associated with Romanticism and other contemporary European trends. J. J. Macklin (1985) agreed with Garrett's estimation that *Brother Luiz de Sousa* is not a tragedy in the Greek sense, noting that the play offers a Christian model of redemption. Garrett's poetry resembles works from the Romantic Movement in its emphasis on emotional expression, particularly with regard to sensual and erotic matters. Kimberley S. Roberts (1956) undertook a quantitative investigation of Garrett's poetic imagery, concluding that he was more interested in human beings than in either the natural world or abstract ideas. Citing the stylized, self-reflexive narrative voice of *Travels in My Homeland,* Linda Ledford-Miller (1984) argued that Garrett's formal experimentation makes him a transitional figure between Romanticism and modernism.

Roger K. Smith

PRINCIPAL WORKS

Lucrécia. Teatro dos grilos, Coimbra. Feb. 1819. Performance. (Play)

Xerxes. Teatro dos grilos, Coimbra. Feb. 1819. Performance. (Play)

**Catão; o corcunda por amor* [may be translated as *Cato; Hunchback for Love's Sake*]. Teatro do Bairro Alto, Lisbon. 29 Sept. 1821. Performance. Pub. as *Catão* [may be translated as *Cato*]. Lisbon: Imprensa liberal, 1822. Print. (Play)

O dia vintequatro d'agosto [may be translated as *The Twenty-Fourth Day of August*]. Lisbon: Rollandiana, 1821. Print. (Essay)

O retrato de Vénus [may be translated as *The Portrait of Venus*]. Coimbra: Imprensa da universidade, 1821. Print. (Poetry)

Os namorados extravagantes [may be translated as *The Extravagant Lovers*]. Sintra. 26 May 1822. Performance. (Play)

Camões. Paris: Livraria nacional e estrangeira, 1825. Print. (Poetry)

Carta de guia para leitores [may be translated as *Guide for Voters*]. Lisbon: Leão, 1826. Print. (Essay)

Dona Branca ou A conquista do Algarve [may be translated as *Mrs. Branca; or, The Conquest of Algarve*]. Paris: Aillaud, 1826. Print. (Poetry)

Parnaso lusitano ou Poesias selectas dos autores portugueses antigos e modernos [may be translated as *Lusitanian Parnassus; or, Select Poetry of Portuguese Authors Both Past and Present*]. Ed. Almeida Garrett. 6 vols. Paris: Aillaud, 1826-34. Print. (Poetry)

Adozinda. London: Boosey/Salva, 1828. Print. (Poetry)

Da educação [may be translated as *On Education*]. London: Sustenance and Stretch, 1829. Print. (Treatise)

Lírica de João Mínimo [may be translated as *João Mínimo's Lyric*]. London: Sustenance and Stretch, 1829. Print. (Poetry)

Elogio fúnebre de Carlos Infante de Lacerda, Barão de Sabrosa [may be translated as *Eulogy for Carlos Infante de Lacerda, Baron of Sabrosa*]. London: Greenlaw, 1830. Print. (Speech)

Portugal na balança da Europa [may be translated as *Portugal in the European Balance*]. London: Sustenance and Stretch, 1830. Print. (Essays)

Um auto de Gil Vicente [may be translated as *A Play by Gil Vicente*]. Teatro da rua dos condes, Lisbon. 15 Aug. 1838. Performance. (Play)

Filipa de Vilhena. Teatro do Saltre, Lisbon. 30 May 1840. Performance. Lisbon: Imprensa nacional, 1846. Print. (Play)

Mérope/Gil Vicente. Lisbon: Morando, 1841. Print. (Plays)

†*O alfageme de Santarém ou A espada do Condestável* [may be translated as *The Armorer of Santarém; or, The Sword of the Constable*]. Lisbon: Imprensa nacional, 1842. Print. (Play)

Frei Luís de Sousa [published as *Brother Luiz de Sousa*]. Teatro da Quinta do Pinheiro, Sete Rios. 4 July 1843. Performance. Lisbon: Imprensa nacional, 1844. Print. (Play)

Memória histórica do Conselheiro A. M. L. Vieira de Castro [may be translated as *Historic Memoir of Councillor A. M. L. Vieira de Castro*]. Lisbon: Morando, 1843. Print. (Biography)

Romanceiro e cancioneiro geral [may be translated as *Romances and Popular Songs*]. Lisbon: Soc. propagadora dos conhecimentos uteis, 1843. Expanded ed. *Romanceiro* [may be translated as *Romances*]. 3 vols. Lisbon: Imprensa nacional, 1851. Print. (Ballads and songs)

Flores sem fructo [may be translated as *Fruitless Flowers*]. Lisbon: Imprensa nacional, 1845. Print. (Poetry)

O arco de Sant'Ana [may be translated as *The Arch of Sant'Ana*]. 2 vols. Lisbon: Imprensa nacional, 1845-50. Print. (Novel)

Viagens na minha terra [published as *Travels in My Homeland*]. 2 vols. Lisbon: Gazeta dos tribunais, 1846. Print. (Novel)

A sobrinha do marquês [may be translated as *The Marquis's Niece*]. Teatro Maria II, Lisbon. 4 Apr. 1848. Performance. Lisbon: Imprensa nacional, 1848. Print. (Play)

Memória histórica da excellentissima Duqueza de Palmella, D. Eugénia Francisca Xavier Telles da Gama [may be translated as *Historic Memoir of the Most Excellent Duchess of Palmella, D. Eugénia Francisca Xavier Telles da Gama*]. Lisbon: Imprensa nacional, 1848. Print. (Biography)

As profecias do Bandarra [may be translated as *The Prophecies of Bandarra*]. Lisbon: Imprensa nacional, 1848. Print. (Play)

Memória histórica de José Xavier Mouzinho da Silveira [may be translated as *Historic Memoir of José Xavier Mouzinho da Silveira*]. Lisbon: Imprensa da epocha, 1849. Print. (Biography)

‡*Folhas caídas* [may be translated as *Fallen Leaves*]. As Anonymous. Lisbon: Casa viúva Bertrand and Filhos, 1853. Print. (Poetry)

Um noivado no Dafundo ou Cada terra com seu uso cada roca com seu fuso [may be translated as *The Wedding Feast in Dafundo; or, To Each Land Its Own Customs*]. Lisbon: Viúva Marques e Filha, 1857. Print. (Play)

Discursos parlamentares e memórias biográficas [may be translated as *Parliamentary Speeches and Biographical Memoirs*]. Lisbon: Imprensa nacional, 1871. Print. (Biographies and speeches)

Helena: Fragmento de um romance inedito [may be translated as *Helena: Fragment of an Unpublished Novel*]. Lisbon: Imprensa nacional, 1871. Print. (Essays, letters, and novel fragment)

O bastardo do fidalgo [may be translated as *The Nobleman's Bastard*]. Porto: Typografia commércio e indústria, 1877. Print. (Poetry)

Obras completas de Almeida Garrett [may be translated as *The Complete Works of Almeida Garrett*]. Ed. Teófilo Braga. 2 vols. Lisbon: Empreza da história de Portugal, 1904. Print. (Biographies, essays, novels, plays, poetry, and short stories)

Cartas de amor à Viscondessa da Luz [may be translated as *Love Letters to the Viscountess da Luz*]. Ed. José Bruno Carreiro. Lisbon: Empresa nacional de publicidade, 1955. Print. (Letters)

Obras completas [may be translated as *Complete Works*]. 2 vols. Porto: Lello e Irmão, 1963. Print. (Biographies, essays, novels, plays, poetry, and short stories)

O roubo das sabinas: Poemas libertinos I [may be translated as *The Theft of the Sabines: Seductive Poems I*]. Ed. Augusto da Costa Dias. Lisbon: Portugália, 1968. Print. (Poetry)

Narrativas e lendas [may be translated as *Stories and Legends*]. Ed. Augusto da Costa Dias. Lisbon: Editorial estampa, 1979. Print. (Short stories)

Escritos do Vintismo, 1820-23 [may be translated as *Writings of Vintismo*]. Ed. Augusto da Costa Dias, Maria Helena da Costa Dias, and Luis Augusto Costa Dias. Lisbon: Estampa, 1985. Print. (Essays)

Doutrinação liberal [may be translated as *Liberal Indoctrination*]. Ed. António Reis. Lisbon: Alfa, 1990. Print. (Essay)

Correspondência inédita do Arquivo do Conservatório 1836-1841 [may be translated as *Unpublished Correspondence of the Conservatory Archive 1836-1841*]. Ed. Duarte Ivo Cruz. Lisbon: Imprensa nacional/ Moeda, 1995. Print. (Letters)

Relações de Garrett com os Bertrand: Cartas inéditas, 1834-1853 [may be translated as *Garrett's Relationship with the Bertrands: Unpublished Letters, 1834-1853*]. Ed. Manuela D. Domingos. Lisbon: Biblioteca nacional, 1999. Print. (Letters)

Cartas a Garrett [may be translated as *Letters to Garrett*]. Ed. Eduardo Honório Pinto da Costa. Maia: Câmara municipal, 2000. Print. (Letters)

Principal English Translations

The "Brother Luiz de Sousa" of Viscount de Almeida Garrett. Trans. Edgar Prestage. London: Mathews, 1909. Print. Trans. of *Frei Luís de Sousa.*

Travels in My Homeland. Trans. John M. Parker. London: Owen, 1987. Print. Trans. of *Viagens na minha terra.*

**Hunchback for Love's Sake* was cowritten with Paulo Midosi.

†Performed as *O alfageme de Santarém* [may be translated as *The Armorer of Santarém*]. Terreiro do Paço, Lisbon. 11 July 1846.

‡Includes the poem "Cascais."

CRITICISM

Jack Horace Parker (essay date 1954)

SOURCE: Parker, Jack Horace. "Almeida Garrett and Camões." *Hispania* 38.1 (1955): 18-22. Print.

[*In the following essay, originally presented at a conference in 1954, Parker offers a brief biographical sketch of Garrett and discusses his epic poem* Camões. *Parker suggests that Garrett identified with the historical Luís de Camões and portrayed him as a Romantic hero of Portugal.*]

One hundred years and a few days ago, on December 9, 1854, there died in Lisbon one of Portugal's most fascinating figures of the nineteenth century.

João Baptista da Silva Leitão was born in Oporto on February 4, 1799, although in his ***Autobiografia*** of 1843 for personal reasons he set back his age to give us 1802. The names under which he is best known, Almeida Garrett, came from his mother, who was an Almeida Leitão, and from an ancestor on his father's side, Garrett, presumably of the Irish nobility. These names were not adopted until his late teens. An interesting note in the *Revista de Portugal* of this past spring states how he pronounced his *apelido inglês*: "O facto, porém, é que o próprio Poeta sempre pronunciou o seu apelido como se em português se escrevesse *garréte,* com *a* surdo na primeira sílaba, o acento tónico na 2.ª, e o *t* perfeitamente proferido."[1]

Almeida Garrett's experiences read like a story book. Aubrey Bell is quite correct in declaring that "his life is the whole history of the time."[2] We remember that in his youth

Garrett suffered exile with his family in the Azores as they fled to their island estate from the Napoleonic invasion. Later on, in 1832, it was from those same islands that, as a private soldier, he played a part in the expedition led by Dom Pedro of Brazilian fame to defeat the Miguelistas and put Maria da Glória on the Portuguese throne. Previously, he had been a lively student at Coimbra and had begun his literary activity, brilliantly defending his ***Retrato de Vénus*** against charges of impiety. Not long after taking government office in 1822 in the Ministério do Reino, he was the victim of autocratic reactions and was forced to emigrate to England. He returned after a few months' exile, but had to leave again in the late summer of 1823 for a longer period abroad.

It is of this brief period of Garrett's life and literary career that I wish to speak today. In exile, separated from his native land and the liberal causes he held dear, his mind turned to Portugal's history and traditions. Influenced by the romantic movement which he was meeting around him, and identifying it with patriotism and looking upon it as literary nationalism, he saw in one of the greatest figures of his country's past, Luis de Camões, a personage who had gone through similar disillusioning experiences. And with his literary ability already proven in earlier works, Garrett proceeded to forge an epic poem. Having moved to France to make his living by working for the banking firm Laffitte, he tells us how he wrote ***Camões***: "[durante as] engelhadas noites de janeiro e fevereiro, que n'uma agua-furtada da rua Coq-Saint-Honoré, passávamos com os pés cozidos no fogo, eu e meu velho amigo o sr. J. V. Barreto-Feio, elle trabalhando no seu *Sallustio,* e eu lidando no meu ***Camões,*** ambos proscriptos, ambos pobres, mas ambos resignados ao presente, sem remorso do passado, e com esperanças largas no futuro."[3]

The poem, in ten cantos, in blank verse, which the author entitled simply ***Camões,*** was published in Paris by the "Imprimerie de J. MacCarthy" in the early months of 1825 and was dedicated to his friend António Joaquim Freire Marréco, who was aiding him in his exile. The poem deals with Camões' last years only, from the time of his arrival back from the East with the manuscript of *Os Lusíadas* until his death, referring, however, to some earlier events. It embodies many of the anecdotal circumstances connected with Camões' life and is not to be taken as an historical document. Indeed in his preface to the first edition, Garrett speaks of the imagined elements, those situations which Theóphilo Braga charges he preferred to invent "phantásticamente."[4] And it is true that the poem often appears "tenue e descolorido," failing to make good epic use of the sufficient historical reality, but on the whole there is an "intensidade lyrica," and an evocation of the great master, which was, one might say, a "call to arms" to the Portuguese people to remember better days in the glorious past and to hope for happier years to come.

The invocation is not to a Muse, nor to a divinity, pagan or christian, but to that mood, sentiment, or state of mind, with which Garrett was filled and which he imagined Camões himself so well expressed:

> Saudade! Gôsto amargo de infelizes,
> Delicioso pungir de acerbo espinho,
> Que me estás repassando o íntimo peito
> Com dor que os seios d'alma dilacera;
> Mas dor que tem prazeres—Saudade!

(***Obras completas*** [***Obras completas de Almeida Garrett***], IV, **Canto I**, p. 11)

The opening scene of the epic is a moving one, to say the least, when, amid the sailors' joyful shouts of "Terra, terra!" and "Terra, e terra da pátria!" (**I**, 13), the ship arrives at the mouth of the Tagus, and we see a figure standing aloof:

> Um só no meio de alegrias tantas
> Quasi insensivel jaz: callado e quêdo,
> Encostado à amurada, os olhos fitos
> Tem n'este ponto que negreja ao longe
> Lá pela prôa, e cresce a pouco e pouco.
> . . . .
> No gesto senhoril, mas annuveado
> De sombras melanchólicas, impresso
> Tem o caracter da cordura ousada
> Que os filhos ennobrece da victoria . . .

(I,14)

This is our introduction to the protagonist. The "gentil guerreiro" with the "feições nobres" has been transformed by the poet into a romantic hero. In his *melancholia* he stands alone; he is the "guerreiro pensativo" who returns home to become immediately involved in a "romantic" situation; for on entering the nearby monastery to which he has been invited by a fellow-traveler, the Spanish missionary, he hears the "ruim agouro" of funereal bells, and he sees in an open coffin a familiar face. Crying out "Natercia," he beholds his Catharina de Athaide (historically in her grave for some time), whom he had loved and lost in the "única ventura" of his life. After the ensuing fainting spell and his regaining consciousness, Camões is led to explain to the missionary his background: his impossible love affair and his fair one's suggestion that he go abroad to do great deeds and return for her. In the East, while reflecting in exile in a grotto in Macau, where he had been sent on account of his protests against evils in the colonies, a message came: "Uma voz cá do íntimo do peito / Cuidei ouvir que assim me respondia: / —Póde mais do que a espada, a voz e a penna" (**IV**, 59).

So he wrote *Os Lusíadas,* "um trabalho de annos," inspired by love and patriotism. Now back in Lisbon, he has been abandoned by love, "neste valle de amargura." His only wish can be: "Oh! Leva-me comtigo à campa fria" (**V**, 64); unless the *pátria* can soothe his wounded heart. And dramatically a ray of hope does appear: the monarch, hearing of his poem, has asked to see him in Sintra. Sintra, the beautiful, the wild and majestic, which inspires Garrett, if not Camões, to break forth in romantic, lyrical verse, in a digression[5] in appreciation of the hospitality which he had enjoyed in rural Britain:

Eu vi sobre as cumiadas das montanhas
De Albion soberba as torres elevadas
Inda feudaes memorias recordando
Dos Britões semi-bárbaros. Errante
Pela terra estrangeira, peregrino
Nas solidões do exilio, fui sentar-me
Na barbacan ruinosa dos castellos,
A conversar co'as pedras solitarias,
E a perguntar às obras da mão do homem
Pelo homem que as ergueu. A alma enlevada
Nos românticos sonhos, procurava
aureas ficções realizar dos bardos . . .

(VII,77)

As in memory he sits among the feudal ruins, speaks to the echoes in the tongue of the minstrels, and invokes "os genios mysteriosos" and "as aéreas vagas formas," it is difficult to say who is being presented to us as the romantic hero, Camões or Garrett himself. And if we are in doubt about the presence of romanticism in the poem, ***Camões,*** and are inclined to take Garrett's protestations too literally,[6] we are soon assured of it by the inspiration drawn from the ruined Moorish castle on the top of Sintra's hill. This time it is a spot presumably visited by Camões in response to a mysterious message received the previous day:

Alli, no mais solemne das ruinas
E no mais alto, alli num canto ainda
Sólido da muralha fabricara
Solitario habitante d'esses ermos
Mansão tranquilla e só. Musgosas plantas
Crescem nas fisgas do cimento antigo,
Tapeçaria de heras verdejantes
Fórra a cortina da parede bronca,
E em cahidos festões se balancea
Sobre a entrada do lôbrego retiro.

(IX,102)

Here, tradition has it, Bernardim Ribeiro, of the sixteenth century, "saudoso e namorado," lamented his Beatriz and carved her name on stones. Here, as "Alfim no oceano se mergulha a lâmpada / Do firmamento máxima. Descia / Como um véo, a nebrina sobre a serra . . ." (IX, 103) a voice speaks out of the fog. It is Camões' deadly enemy and rival for Natercia's hand, who, at her dying request, has brought him her portrait. Moved yet again to show his noble nature, Camões' reply is: "Guardae-o vós, senhor, guardae-o; é vosso: / A um inimigo tal amor o cede" (IX, 106). And the generous character of the two is summed up in the following lines:

Suspensos, mudos ambos se entr'olhavam
Os dois rivais briosos, que alta próva
Assim do nobre peito heroica davam
Em magnânimo duello de virtude.

(IX,106)

Os Lusíadas is published, the King's praise is helpful, but gradually enemies and oblivion rise up to darken Camões' days. He even loses the aid of his old friend, "o virtuoso Aleixo," and King Sebastian's mind is on other things. This king is the young idealist, filled with religious and patriotic zeal, who had thought on hearing Camões' recital of the epic poem: "Um dia offuscarei toda essa gloria, / E a mais altas canções darei assumpto" (VIII, 89). What a succinct characterization of the martyr monarch is contained in those two lines!

So Luis is left alone, to lament:

O número está cheio
De meus dias, contados por desgraças,
Marcados, um por um, na pedra negra
De fado negro e mau."

(X,112)

The Javanese slave, the faithful *Jáo,* who had accompanied him from the East, is forced to find lodging for him and to beg for him in the streets of Lisbon. This popular legend, now discarded, and so many others—the loss of an eye as a youth in saving his father in a battle in Africa, the preservation of the manuscript of *Os Lusíadas* by holding it above the waves and swimming with one arm—all are used by Garrett to good purpose.

Finally the great Camões' thought turns to death: "Terra da minha patria! Abre-me o seio / Na morte ao menos" (X, 115), he cries; and at the same time he has forbodings and a vision of Portugal's tragedy at Alcacer-Kebir and the invasion of the "tyranos" from Spain who will pass "as aguas do Guadiana" (X, 116). And the sad news does come, in a letter to Camões from the missionary, now a prisoner in Fez: King Sebastian, with the flower of Portuguese manhood, has fallen, fighting for the Faith and the Homeland in North Africa.

It is a dramatic final scene, this one in which the fateful letter falls from Camões' hands, his voice becomes weak and his head inclines upon his breast. Closing his eyes, he turns his face to Heaven, murmuring "no arranco extremo": 'Patria, ao menos / Junto morremos. . . .' E expirou co'a patria" (X,118).

The poem ought to have ended there, for the following, final eighteen lines break the dramatic unity and intensity of the denouement. But ***Camões*** is a poem with a purpose, and that purpose may have been more important in Garrett's mind than the artistic creation. Throughout the epic we remember that Camões has been pictured as disappointed, unfortunate, unjustly treated, an outcast, too noble, as it were, for the society in which he lived. So too, perhaps Garrett felt himself to be, as from exile he chided his compatriots for one specific last neglect: Camões' ashes do not even have a marked resting place!

Nem isso! Nem um túmulo, uma pedra
Uma lettra singela!

Ergo-me a delatar tamanho crime.
. . . .
Nem o humilde logar onde repoisam
As cinzas de Camões, conhece o Luso.

(x,118)

In this case, Garrett's words did seem to have some effect. Efforts were made to establish Camões' place of burial, and his supposed remains,[7] at any rate, and those of Almeida Garrett himself, rest today in the National Pantheon of the Jerónimos. And Garrett did not cease, with his poem of 1825, to plead for the rehabilitation of the reputation of Portugal's great epic poet. Nor had he been alone in his initiation of interest in Camões. Certain steps in that direction, chiefly abroad, had preceded him by several years, and several contemporary works in art and letters had served to strengthen his position. Throughout his career as dramatist, journalist, diplomat, politician, theatrical director, orator, folklorist, liberal reformer, renovator of Portuguese literature, and indeed as a great lover, Garrett continued to "believe in" Camões, as he put it in his ***Viagens na minha terra*** of 1845.[8] Just as Lord Byron, musing on the Marathon scene, was led to exclaim: "I dreamed that Greece might still be free" (*Don Juan,* Canto III), so Garrett, reading the beautiful lines, "E já no pôrto da ínclyta Ulyssea . . . ," from Canto IV of *Os Lusíadas,* was extremely moved: "Pouco a pouco amotinou-se-me o sangue, senti baterem-me as arterias da fronte. . . . As lettras fugiam-me do livro, levantei os olhos, dei com elles na pobre náo Vasco da Gama que ahi está em monumento-caricatura da nossa glória naval. . . . E eu não vi nada disso, vi o Tejo, vi a bandeira portuguesa fluctuando com a brisa da manhan, a torre de Belem ao longe . . . e sonhei, sonhei que era portuguez, que Portugal era outra vez Portugal. . . ."[9] This was the effect produced upon Almeida Garrett by what he called "a maior obra de engenho que ainda appareceu no mundo desde a *Divina Comedia* até ao *Fausto*" (***Viagens* [*Viagens na minha terra*]**, I, 37), written by "o nosso Camões, creador da epopéa, e depois do Dante, da poesia moderna" (***Viagens,*** I, 40).

It is fitting that in this "Ano garret-teano"[10] of 1954 we should remember and pay homage to the great Almeida Garrett by re-reading his works,[11] and by pondering the significance of his career. It is a happy circumstance that *his* mind should have dwelt with such appreciation on his country's most glorious literary son. For in honoring Garrett, we thus also pay our due respects to Luis de Camões. The two men of letters did have much in common, and are credited with similar "missions" during their respective periods. These final words, by Theóphilo Braga, written fifty years ago, will suffice to emphasize the point: "Pode-se dizer com verdade, assim como Camões manteve com os *Lusíadas* o fogo sagrado da independencia de Portugal sob a dominação castelhana,[12] a obra de Garrett é uma energia que impede a decomposição da nacionalidade portugueza sob o regimen político que a degrada. Uma mesma missão irmana os dois genios, como representantes e palladios de um povo."[13]

Notes

A paper read at the 36th Annual Meeting of the AATSP, New York, December 29-30, 1954.

1. *Revista de Portugal,* Série A, Língua Portuguesa, Lisboa, XIX, cxxiii (March, 1954), 100.
2. *Portuguese Literature* (Oxford, 1922), p. 288.
3. "Nota da segunda edição." "Camões," *Obras completas de Almeida Garrett,* Edição revista, coordinada e dirigida pelo Dr. Theóphilo Braga (Lisboa, 1904), IV, 122. This edition will be referred to throughout this article.
4. *História da litteratura portugueza* (Porto, 1903), XXIV, 349. The volume has a subtitle: "Garrett e o romantismo."
5. The critics point out that the tendency to digress is one of Garrett's failings. And he himself confesses in the preface to *Lyrica de João Minimo*: "As digressões matam-me." See A. F. G. Bell, *Studies in Portuguese Literature* (Oxford, 1914), p. 169.
6. Well-known and oft-quoted is his statement in the preface to the 1st edition: "Não sou clássico nem romântico, de mim digo que não tenho seita nem partido em poesia" (*Obras completas,* IV, 5). It is necessary to recognize the many influences which had been weighing upon him and the fact that his mode of expression was not static. Georges Le Gentil, in *Almeida Garrett: Un grand romantique portugais* (Paris, 1927), classifying Garrett as "La figure la plus représentative du premier romantisme," which he calls "un romantisme prudent" (p. 3), notes that although "il n'est pas devenu romantique en un jour et il ne le sera jamais entièrement" (p. 16), at the time of writing *Camões* he was certainly "imprégné du mal du siècle" (p. 20). Garrett's own words bear this out: "Referindo-se ao poema *Camões,* em uma nota ao primeiro canto da *D. Branca,* diz Garrett que o escrevera em França quando estava 'todo namorado das melancholias do romantismo'" (quotation from T. Braga, *Hist. da lit. port,* XXIV, 358).
7. See Georges Le Gentil, *Camoëns: L'oeuvre épique et lyrique* (Paris, 1954), pp. 26-27: "Les ossements transférés en 1880 au Panthéon national des Hiéronymites de Belem ne représentent sa dépouille mortelle que par une confusion volontaire."
8. "Viagens na minha terra, I," *Obras completas,* ed. T. Braga (Lisboa, 1904), XVIII, 37: "Eu, apezar dos críticos, ainda creio no nosso Camões, sempre cri."
9. "Viagens na minha terra, II," *Obras completas,* ed. T. Braga (Lisboa, 1904), XIX, 173.

10. See Rodrigues Cavalheiro, *Ocidente,* Lisboa, XLVI, cxciv (June, 1954), 300.

11. See Mário Gonçalves Viana, *Almeida Garrett* (Porto, 1937), p. 131: "Almeida Garrett merece ser lido e estudado, servindo de exemplo e de incentivo a todos quantos pretendam, através da literatura, honrar e engrandecer Portugal. E essa a melhor maneira de homenagear aquêle de quem disse Pinheiro Chagas ter sido 'depois de Camões o poeta mais português que teve Portugal."

12. Garrett states this also, in general terms, in a letter of November 12, 1841: "Muitas vezes tenho pensado, e creio que os *Lusíadas* têm sido melhor cidadella para defender a independencia d'este nosso reininho, do que o forte da Graça e a Torre de San Julião." See T. Braga, *Historia da litteratura portugueza* (Porto, 1905), xxv, 29. The sub-title of this volume is "Garrett e os dramas românticos."

13. "Garrett e a sua obra," *Obras completas de Almeida Garrett* (Lisboa, 1905), XXVIII, 109-110.

Kimberley S. Roberts (essay date 1956)

SOURCE: Roberts, Kimberley S. "Images in the Lyric Poetry of Almeida Garrett." *Delaware Notes* 29 (1956): 87-102. Print.

[*In the following essay, Roberts summarizes a detailed inquiry he conducted into the imagery that appears in Garrett's poetry. The frequent use of conventional images from nature to describe human beings—especially the women in Garrett's love lyrics—leads Roberts to conclude that people, rather than nature, constitute the poet's primary subject.*]

The study of the imagery of the Portuguese poets has received comparatively little attention from students of Portuguese literature, either in Portugal or elsewhere. This omission is all the more surprising when one considers the richness and variety of Lusitanian poetry and the hold which it has had on the Portuguese creative imagination from the time of the medieval court-poets and minstrels down to the present-day Coimbra or Lisbon student who may be studying mathematics or medicine but who writes verses in his free time and discusses poetry with his friends as naturally as a young American would talk about sports. The Portuguese scholar Manuel de Paiva Boléo, in listing important subjects for study in Portuguese literature, suggests that the study of the metaphors of a poet would be an attractive one, but his bibliography of this subject contains no work on a Portuguese poet, although studies have been made on the imagery of Victor Hugo, Corneille, Mallarmé and others. A complete survey of the imagery in Portuguese poetry would, of course, have to be the task of many researchers. The purpose of the present article is to make a contribution to this work by a study of the images in the lyric poetry of one who is probably the outstanding Portuguese writer of the first half of the nineteenth century: João Baptista da Silva Leitão Almeida Garrett (1799-1854).

Although Garrett took an active part in Portuguese political life and worked at nearly every conceivable literary *genre*—novel, drama, autobiography, epic and patriotic poetry, political writings, a travel journal—he never abandoned the lyric and kept on turning out lyric poems from his boyhood almost until his death. These lyrics are contained in four collections:[1]

1. ***Lyrica de João Minimo* ("Lyrics of John the Least")**, written between 1815 and 1824; published in 1829.

2. ***Sonetos* ("Sonnets")**, written between 1814 and 1828; published in 1853.

3. ***Flores sem Fructo* ("Flowers without Fruit")**, published in 1845. Many of the poems in this collection were written in the 1820's and 1830's, while others were written in the early 1840's.

4. ***Folhas Cahidas* ("Fallen Leaves")**, written between 1846 and 1851; published in 1853.

For this study, 140 poems were examined, 52 in ***LJM*** [***Lírica de João Mínimo***], 12 in ***S*** [***Sonetos***], 34 in ***FSF*** [***Flores sem fructo***], and 42 in ***FC*** [***Folhas caídas***]. Several mere imitations of Anacreon, Horace and other classical poets, as well as some translations and imitations of more modern verse, were omitted. A classification of these 140 poems according to subject reveals that 67 poems, almost half the total, are love-poems. Twenty are patriotic in their inspiration, thirteen philosophical, nine deal with nature, six are religious. Four poems are addressed to men, two to women. There are four satirical poems, two *in memoriam,* and thirteen that fit into no special classification. If we eliminate the minor categories, we find that the greater part of Garrett's lyrical production treats of love, the poet's native land, philosophical ideas (generally dealing with the poet's own problems) and nature. It is interesting to note that the proportion of love-poems increases as the poet matures, while the patriotic poetry decreases. In ***LJM,*** there are 15 love-poems out of a total of 52 examined, in ***FSF,*** 14 out of 34, and in ***FC,*** 31 out of 42. Twelve of the 52 poems in ***LJM*** are patriotic; in ***FSF*** one finds four patriotic poems out of 34, and in ***FC*** only two out of 42.

In studying Garrett's imagery, the most effective method, and the one which gave the greatest promise of revealing the direction of the poet's thoughts, was to classify the images according to the subject with which they are connected. In Garrett's lyrics, as we have seen, the most popular subjects are Woman and Love, Portugal, God and Nature. Throughout all the poems, Garrett makes very frequent use of apostrophe and personification, endowing supernatural and non-human entities with human attributes to the greatest possible degree. Whether he is dealing with a manifestation of nature, the pangs of love, a philosophical problem or his country's woes, Garrett feels impelled to endow his creations with human form. Garrett's concern with the feminine attributes of his poetic concepts is strikingly revealed by his frequent use of the word "seio," "breast." The poet's rural retreat is a "seio de paz," "breast of peace." The Portuguese recline on the "seio" of their country. A kiss goes from breast to breast of Cupid's victims. The rose is born in the white breast of Venus. Garrett invites his lady to join him in the "seio da alegria," "breast of happiness." A tempest is stirred up in the breast of the sea. During a storm, the breasts of the clouds are torn apart. One remembers love among the breasts of the flowers, while perfume arises from the breast of the rose. Spring in April is described as scarcely revealing her virginal breast.

Turning now to Woman and Love, Garrett's favorite lyrical inspiration, the poet's frequent comparison of women and flowers, especially roses, makes it impossible at times to put images of women and nature-images into separate categories. The image of the rose occurs in many forms. In the beautiful poem ***A côr da rosa* ("The Color of the Rose"; *LJM*** I, 19) the white rose turns red when Cupid is wounded by a thorn and his blood drops on the flower; the poet, addressing lovers who seek the roses in the gardens of pleasure, tells them that the pain from the thorns is converted into pleasure by love. In ***Consolações a um namorado* ("Consolation to a Lover"; *LJM*** II 9), Garrett compares the many beautiful women in the world to a field full of flowers. In ***A Rosa* ("The Rose"; *LJM*** III 6), dedicated to Délia, one of Garrett's lady-loves, the poet, although praising the rose which is consecrated to the fair sex, says that his Délia is even more beautiful than the flower. ***A minha Rosa* ("My Rose"; *FSF*** II 9) compares the coloring of the lady's face to the unfolding of the petals of a rose, whom the other flowers envy. ***Pallida* ("Pale One"; *FC*** I 13) describes a rose who has lost her color after she has loved. The poet consoles her, assuring her that she is as beautiful as ever and that he loves her all the more now that he has made her turn pale. ***Perfume da Rosa* ("The Perfume of the Rose"; *FC*** I 11) describes a rose whose every action betrays the fact that, despite her denials, she is in love. ***Rosa sem Espinhos* ("Rose without Thorns"; *FC*** I 12) tells of a rose who shows affection to all and cruelty to none. No butterfly or bee is turned away. ***Rosa e Lirio* ("Rose and Lily"; *FC*** I 17) tells of the rose and lily, both flowers of love. ***Coquette dos Prados* ("Flirt of the Fields"; *FC*** I 18) describes a rose who does not feel love but who inspires it in others. The lady described in ***Não és tu* ("It is not you"; *FC*** I 22) smells of pure, fine, white roses. ***A Délia* ("To Délia"; *FC*** II 11) tells of the rose whose ardent lover, the sun, devours her with kisses. In ***Lucinda*** (the name of one of Garrett's loves; ***FC*** II 7) the lady is, for a change, not a rose but a lily, while the graceful woman in ***Bella d'Amor* ("The Belle of Love"; *FC*** I 15) is compared to an unspecified flower that sways on her stalk in the springtime. In ***A Morte* ("Death"; *LJM*** I 9) the dead Isabel Maria van Zeller,[2] to whose memory the poem is dedicated, is called a "plant of blessings and virtue."

It is this same Isabel who is referred to as an "Anjo consolador, alma celeste" ("Consoling angel, heavenly soul"). The symbol of the angel, though less frequent than that of the rose, appears several times. In ***Nunca Mais* ("Nevermore"; *FSF*** II 8), in which Garrett grieves because his love has turned away from him, the lady is referred to an "anjo do céu" ("angel from heaven"). ***Adeus* ("Farewell"; *FC*** I 2) describes another unhappy love-affair, in which Garrett blames himself for enjoying the lady's favors without really loving her. He calls himself base and cowardly, in contrast with the angel which she was. ***O Anjo Cahido* ("The Fallen Angel"; *FC*** I 5) employs a somewhat different metaphor; the woman who has loved unwisely is a fallen angel. In ***Anjo és* ("You are an Angel"; *FC*** I 24) Garrett is not sure whether his angel comes from God or from the Devil, but he is completely in her power, captivated by her fatal, strange being. ***Preito* ("Oath of Fealty"; *FC*** II 16) tells of the poet-vassal[3] submitting, not to a temporal lady-ruler, but to an angelic one.

Woman occasionally is compared to a star; sometimes, she is a queen. In ***A minha Rosa* (*FSF*** II 9) Garrett says that whoever sees his lady's face sees there his star and the queen of his love. ***A Estrella* ("The Star"; *FC*** II 12) describes a star which only the poet can see and whose light is not like that of the other stars. The poet will not even tell in what part of the heavens she may be found. Stars are not always favorable, however. In ***Não te amo* ("I do not love"; *FC*** I 21) Garrett describes a girl who is indeed beautiful, but whom he does not love, since she is the unlucky star that shines at the hour of one's destruction. The queen and vassal theme occurs again in ***A Corôa* ("The Crown"; *FC*** II 2). Vassals, says the poet, are in these days likely to revolt and to give laws to their rulers. The only remedy for the beautiful queen is to have only one vassal: Garrett.

Images of women other than that of the rose, queen and star scarcely exist in Garrett's lyrics. In ***O Exilio* ("Exile"; *LJM*** III 13)[4] the woman who will comfort the poet's exile provides a homeland for Garrett in her arms. In her smile, he will find home and friends. ***As Férias* ("The Holidays"; *LJM*** I 16) is the only poem studied in which Garrett is satirical at the expense of women. Here, he attacks the Portuguese girls who affect English manners as "desairosas bonecas," "awkward dolls."[5]

The cruelty and tyranny of love are referred to a number of times. In ***A Infancia* ("Childhood"; *LJM*** I 10) love is a cruel despot, a monster, who can however by the influence of virtue be turned into something delightful. ***A Julia* ("To Julia"; *LJM*** I 18) presents love in the familiar disguise of the blind god who rules the world. It was love who, together with nature, formed the woman who tormented the poet in ***A Saudade* ("Longing"; *LJM*** II 6). In ***Porfia de Amor***

(**"Love's Quarrel"**; ***S*** **1**) Garrett, although scorned by his lady, continues to give himself over to the torment of love. The sonnet ***Suffoque as iras, cale e sinta e gema*** (**"Stifle your anger, be still and suffer and groan"**; ***S*** **4**) describes the poet as a fettered martyr. While listening to the nightingale in ***O Rouxinol*** (**"The Nightingale"**; ***LJM*** III 9), the poet undergoes the torments of love. In ***Nunca Mais*** (***FSF*** II 8), love proved for the poet worse than death, since it drove him mad, and inflicted hours of torture on him after he was abandoned by his lady. ***As minhas Azas*** (**"My Wings"**; ***FSF*** II 19) tells of the fatal quality of the light shed by bewitched love. ***Adeus*** (***FC*** I 2) describes the fatal fire of love, as black and ugly as the fires of Hell. The same theme is developed in ***Este Inferno de Amar*** (**"This Hell of Loving"**: ***FC*** I 8), where the flame of love destroys life. The fire of love can be delightful, but, as Garrett warns in ***Ai Helena*** (**"Ah, Helen"**; ***FC*** II 4), love deceives and lies and will end up by killing its victim, for whom the angels of Hell lie in wait. In ***Vibora*** (**"Viper"**; ***FC*** I 25) love is compared to a poisonous snake.

At times, the images of love are pleasant rather than sinister. Love in ***A Délia*** (***LJM*** II 16) is a tender infant, who grew bolder as the poet's intimacy with his lady increased. It is love who, in ***A Rosa*** (***LJM*** III 6), removes thorns from roses. ***Faz hoje um Anno*** (**"A Year ago Today"**; ***LJM*** III 7) portrays love, which once was bitter, as a delicious honeycomb. It is again a honeycomb in ***O Mar*** (**"The Sea"**; ***FSF*** I 3). In a more unusual image, love in ***O Pharol e o Baixel*** (**"The Lighthouse and the Vessel"**; ***FSF*** II 14) is a lighthouse of salvation. ***Ella*** (**"She"**; ***FSF*** II 23) presents one of Garrett's favorite images; the loves of the poet's youth are described as having been as sweet and gentle as flowers. ***Adeus*** (***FC*** I 2), which tells of an unhappy affair, calls love an enchanted golden dream, undoubtedly to stress its illusory quality. ***Nunca Mais*** (***FSF*** II 8) compares love to a dream from which Garrett awoke. In comparing the figures used to describe women and those which deal with love, one is struck by the preponderance of the sinister, fatal images used to describe the more or less abstract quality of love, in contrast with the charming portrayal of women in the pleasant disguises of flowers, stars and angels.

Garrett's patriotic poems are largely the products of his earlier years, when Portugal was going through political turmoil and when Garrett was forced into exile in England. Portugal, usually referred to as "Lysia" or "Elysia," is a feminine figure. ***Sonho Prophetico*** (**"Prophetic Dream"**; ***LJM*** I 11) portrays her as a woman in fetters, prostrate at the feet of the armored giant Despotism. ***A Patria*** (**"The Homeland"**; ***LJM*** II 2) again shows her in chains. She is referred to as "pobre, malfadada" ("poor, ill-fated") in ***O Anno Novo*** (**"The New Year"**; ***LJM*** III 17), while in ***A Domingo Sequeira*** (**"To Domingo Sequeira"**; ***FSF*** I 16)[6] she is a "terra maldita" ("cursed land") where Liberty is crucified by a people of ungrateful slaves. In ***A Caverna de Viriatho*** (**"The Cavern of Viriathus"**; ***FSF*** I 17)[7] the Portuguese people no longer have a homeland, but are a nation of slaves and jailers, who have nothing but fetters and prisons. Both ***Ao Rei*** (**"To the King"**; ***LJM*** III 5) and ***A Liberdade da Imprensa*** (**"The Freedom of the Press"**; ***LJM*** II 11) describe the Portuguese people as wretched. The very Tagus river in ***A Lyra do Proscripto*** (**"The Lyre of the Exile"**; ***LJM*** III 14) is "desditoso" ("unfortunate"), its waters full of blood and tears, while Lisbon is a ruin and the nation is dead. The golden bed of the Tagus has turned to iron. The poem ***Filinto*** (***LJM*** I 14), in memory of Filinto Elysio, a well-known poet who died in exile in Paris, calls Portugal ungrateful, since she was a "desamorada mãe" ("unloving mother") to Filinto. ***Ao Corpo Academico*** (**"To the Members of the Academy"**; ***LJM*** II 4) shows Garrett in a less severe attitude toward his countrymen. Here, not all the Portuguese are slaves; only those who support despotism are vile, and these are no longer to be considered Portuguese. In a more optimistic mood, Garrett in ***Filinto*** (***LJM*** I 14) recalls the days of Portugal's glory, when her conquering hand raised the Portuguese banner over distant lands. In ***Anniversario da Revolução de 24 de Agosto*** (**"Anniversary of the Revolution of August 24th"**; ***LJM*** III 4) the river Douro breaks its chains and Portugal, mistress of the trident, regains her sway over the waves and will give laws to the world of the seas. The preponderance of unfavorable images of Portugal and the Portuguese is no doubt due to a sensitive youth's reactions to exile and to the lamentable political situation of his native land.

In spite of the comparatively small number of Garrett's religious poems, anthropomorphic images of God appear throughout his lyrical poetry. ***A Primavera*** (**"Spring"**; ***LJM*** I 1), one of Garrett's earliest creations, mentions the voice of God, which thunders. In ***A Morte*** (***LJM*** I 9) the voice of God again is heard amid the thunder and lightning, while in ***A Victoria na Praia*** (**"Victory on the Beach"**; ***FSF*** II 1) it was God's voice that stopped the Biblical flood. In ***Ella*** (***FSF*** II 23) it was from the mouth of the Lord that came the word which gave to the poet his soul and his being. ***Flor de Ventura*** (**"Flower of Good Luck"**; ***FC*** I 14) describes the divine seed of love, which germinates in the soul only when God breathes upon it. ***A Morte*** (***LJM*** I 9) describes the breath and the hand of God. Other allusions to the hand of God occur in ***Consolações a um Namorado*** (***LJM*** II 9), in ***O Juramento*** (**"The Oath"**; ***FSF*** II 2), in ***Sina*** (**"Destiny"**; ***FC*** II 3) and in ***No Lumiar*** (**"On the Threshold"**; ***FC*** II 17). In ***A Caverna de Viriatho*** (***FSF*** I 17), God extends his right arm to restore freedom and reason to mankind, while in ***O Juramento*** (***FSF*** II 2) Garrett asks God to disarm traitors with His eternal arm.

Garrett never loses sight of God's characteristic role as ruler, father, judge and creator. In ***Filinto*** He is the Being who rules over Beings. ***Ao Corpo Academico*** (***LJM*** II 7) represents Him as the "Being of Beings" and the "Judge of the Worlds." In ***Ao Rei*** (***LJM*** III 5) He is the First Being, in ***O Mar*** (***FSF*** I 3) He is the Father of the Universe. ***Adeus Mãe*** (**"Farewell, mother"**; ***FC*** II 13) calls Him the "Mild

Judge." He is the "Father of the Heavens" in ***Ave, Maria*** (*FC* II 14) and the "Creator of all" in ***A Patria*** (*LJM* II 2). ***A Caverna de Viriatho*** (*FSF* I 17) characterizes Him as a "God of truth, immense majesty" whose justice will punish traitors to Portugal. In ***A Morte de Riego*** (**"The Death of Riego"**; *LJM* III 15)[8] God's punishment will deal with the reactionaries who had the Spanish patriot executed. In only a couple of images does Garrett stress the idea of a God of love rather than a powerful ruler. ***O Amor Paternal*** (**"Fatherly Love"**; *LJM* III 3) speaks of the love that burns in God's heart for the benefit of the human race. And in attacking religious hypocrisy, Garrett in ***O Campo de Sant'Anna*** (**"Saint Anne's Field"**; ***S* 7**) states that a God of love, our merciful God, hates the horrible deeds that hypocrites have done. God imposes reasonable laws, as the poet points out in ***Ao Corpo Academico*** (*LJM* II 7); the worship of God consists of virtue, and the divine laws are those of nature.

Although the images used in connection with the idea of God seem to give proof of Garrett's orthodox religious thinking, there is very little mention in his poetry of Christ, the Virgin Mary and the saints. Two poems, ***O Natal de Christo*** (**"The Birth of Christ"**; *FSF* II 25) and ***O Redemptor*** (**"The Redeemer"**; *FSF* II 26) deal with the birth and crucifixion of Christ, who is referred to in completely conventional and orthodox fashion as the "Son of God" and as the "true God." In ***Ave, Maria*** (*FC* II 14) a father prays to the Virgin for the recovery of his sick daughter. Here, the Virgin is described as the "mãe dos desvallidos" ("mother of the forsaken") and as the "mãe de piedade" ("mother of pity"). These three poems are not merely the only lyrics which have as their subject Christ and the Virgin, but are the only poems in which they are mentioned at all. No saint is invoked by name, while the clergy and nuns are dealt with satirically in the two poems in which they are mentioned. ***As Férias*** (*LJM* I 15) speaks of "frades ignorantes" ("ignorant monks") and Garrett expresses his desire to see his country rid of convents, while ***O Anno Velho*** (**"The Old Year"**; *FSF* I 18) refers to the unlamented old year as "Inutil como un cónego" ("as useless as a canon").

In connection with religion, it is interesting to note that allusions to Graeco-Roman mythology, very frequent in the earlier poems of Garrett, are rare in the later lyrics. In ***LJM,*** 31 out of 52 poems have at least one reference to the Greek and Roman divinities. In ***FSF,*** five poems out of 34 mention these gods and goddesses, while in ***FC*** they occur in only three out of 42.

The question of nature images presents a curious situation. Figures of speech involving some manifestation of nature occur in 98 out of the 140 poems examined, yet only nine of these poems can be considered as being primarily devoted to nature. It is hard to escape the conclusion that Garrett, although fond of bringing nature into his poems and using it as a setting for his love-lyrics or even for his patriotic verse, was not really in deep communion with nature as were Romantic poets such as Wordsworth or Lamartine. Garrett likes to personify nature, to turn her into Mother Nature—more Mother, one cannot help feeling, than Nature. In ***A Primavera*** (*LJM* I 1) Garrett invites his friends to come to the "seio da risonha natureza" ("breast of smiling nature"). He enjoys hours of pleasure in "seio da paz" ("breast of peace") of solitude, which here as elsewhere is often equal to nature, in ***Despedidas do Campo*** (**"Farewell to the Country"**; *LJM* I 2). In ***A Soledade*** (**"Solitude"**; *LJM* I 3) he rests in the lap of "cara Soledade" ("dear Solitude"), whose role is to protect unhappy ones and from whose breast arises a sweet melancholy sadness. In ***O Mar*** (*FSF* I 3) he who has a pure, simple heart may rest on nature's breast. Nature in ***A Morte*** (*LJM* I 9) is described as living and growing; in ***Madrugada*** (**"Dawn"**; *LJM* II 10) she is represented as a creator, who made man great. It was nature in ***O Amor Paternal*** (*LJM* III 3) who distributed appropriate gifts to men and women. She gives a pleasant laugh to a lover in ***Sapho*** (**"Sappho"**; *LJM* III 8) and smiles in ***Melancholia*** (**"Melancholy"**; *LJM* III 11) when she beholds Garrett's lady-love. The poet in the sonnet ***Nas froixas, debeis azas da saudade*** (**"On the feeble wings of longing"**; ***S* 6**) asks his lady to listen to the voice of nature, while the hand of nature is mentioned in the sonnet ***Virtude sem prazer não é virtude*** (**"Virtue without Pleasure is not Virtue"**; ***S* 8**), in ***O Mar*** (*FSF* I 3) and in ***Nunca Mais*** (*FSF* II 8). In ***No Lumiar*** (*FC* II 17) she is all fire and light, constantly pouring forth her love, but in ***Ramo Secco*** (**"Bare Branch"**; *FSF* II 7), with its northern winter setting, she is slow and old.

Although it is difficult in Garrett's lyrics to disentangle the women from the flowers, flower images unconnected with women do appear. In ***A Infancia*** (*LJM* I 10), both childhood and life are compared to flowers. ***O Brasil Liberto*** (**"Brazil Freed"**; *LJM* II 8) introduces the flower of liberty, while the lilies in ***Madrugada*** (*LJM* II 10) play a more erotic role, smiling at the breeze that brings the pledge of love. ***No Album de um Amigo*** (**"In a Friend's Album"**; *FSF* II 3) tells of the simple flowers picked in the valley of exile which have sharp thorns of grief. ***Flor Singela*** (**"Simple Flower"**; *FSF* II 6) describes the simple flower which the bee prefers to the more elaborate varieties, just as love seeks a simple heart. In ***Nunca Mais*** (*FSF* II 8) the flowers represent the poet's hopes. These sad flowers, lashed by the hail, perish. In ***Livro da Vida*** (**"Book of Life"**; *FSF* II 18), flowers are the poet's memories. ***Saudades*** (**"Longings"**; *FC* I 7) describes a branch of "saudades portuguesas" ("longings for Portugal"). The flower on this branch will not lose its freshness even if uprooted, but if planted in the heart will cause every other flower there to die. In ***Sapho*** (*LJM* III 8) inconstancy is guilty of poisoning the flower of the pleasures of love. The sonnet ***E dos olhos gentis da minha amada*** (**"From my lady's gentle eyes"**; ***S* 5**) mentions the snowy flowers of innocence, the gift of virtue. In ***Solidão*** (**"Solitude"**; *FSF* I 21) Garrett compares himself to a plant watered by tears, whose flowers did not bloom, since they were damaged by the hail. ***Ramo Secco*** (***FSF*** II 7) mentions the bare branch of longing, without flowers and leaves, all its beauty spoiled by the winter in the poet's soul. ***A Victoria na Praia*** (***FSF*** II 1) speaks of the flower of happiness which will appear on the olive-branch which the dove will bring to the Ark. ***A um Amigo*** (**"To a Friend"**; ***FC*** II 18) expresses the wish that the wind of disappointment will never blow on the flowers of the years of Garrett's friend. Only in ***O Anno Novo*** (***LJM*** III 17) is vegetation symbolic of something undesirable. The old year, complains the poet, produced only a harvest of trouble, weeds sowed among the wheat by treacherous hands. The fall of leaves as a symbol of sorrow, a figure so familiar to northern poets, appears only once in Garrett's lyrics. In ***O Exilio*** (***LJM*** III 13), written in England in November 1823, Garrett complains that the land of exile is as sad as the sands of the desert, sad as the falling of leaves in faded autumn.

Garrett does not use trees in his images as frequently as he does flowers. ***A Morte*** (***LJM*** I 9) compares Maria Isabel van Zeller to a tree that shed its pleasant shade protectively over its adopted home. The ash-tree in ***A Sesta*** (**"The Nap"**; ***LJM*** I 4) is personified and is represented as being proud of the shade that it provides. The palm-tree in ***Madrugada*** (***LJM*** II 10) proudly lifts her head over the other plants. She is the tall, noble queen of the vegetable kingdom, but she is sad, since she is far from home and in need of a companion for her love. In ***O Ananaz*** (**"The Pineapple Tree"**; ***LJM*** II 14), one of the few poems devoted exclusively to a work of nature, the pineapple tree is "rei dos filhos de Pomôna" ("king of the children of Pomona")—one of the rare masculine personifications found in Garrett's poetry. ***A Guerra Civil*** (**"The Civil War"**; ***LJM*** III 10) introduces the tree of liberty, along with the laurel and cypress, conventional symbols of glory and of mourning, which turn up in various other poems as well. In ***Tronco Despido*** (**"Bare Trunk"**; ***FSF*** I 20), Garrett compares himself to a bare tree-trunk, leafless and flowerless, battered by the winds and tormented by the heat and the cold. The pine-tree, so common in Portugal and often found in the medieval lyrics, gets very little attention from Garrett. He mentions in ***Cascaes*** (***FC*** I 19)[9] and in ***Estes Sitios*** (**"These Places"**; ***FC*** I 20) the "triste pinheiro" ("sad pine-tree"), but these are rare cases. Images involving fruit are scarce. One finds in ***Sapho*** (***LJM*** III 8) the bitter fruit caused by the poison of inconstancy, and in ***Já não sou poeta*** (**"I am no longer a poet"**; ***FSF*** II 17) Garrett tastes the bitter fruit of knowledge. ***Os Cinco Sentidos*** (**"The Five Senses"**; ***FC*** I 16) describes the poet as hungry and thirsty, not for delicious fruit, but for his lady's kisses.

Birds and animals, especially the latter, are rare and furnish no particularly striking images. ***A Sesta*** (***LJM*** I 3) introduces some conventional doves who are making love at the feet of a sleeping shepherdess. In three early poems, ***A Primavera*** (***LJM*** I 1), ***A Sesta*** (***LJM*** I 3) and ***A Morte*** (***LJM*** I 9) the bird is described as a "cantor plumoso" or "plumoso cantor" ("feathered songster"). Poets in ***Filinto*** (***LJM*** I 14) are "cysnes" ("swans"), while in ***Os Meus Desejos*** (**"My Desires"**; ***LJM*** II 5) Petrarch is the "sysne de Vauclusa." ***O Rouxinol*** (***LJM*** III 9) is the only poem addressed to a bird. He is the "fiel companheiro" ("faithful companion") whose song, the lovesick poet hopes, will relieve his torments. Even here the bird, who seems to sing "Délia" and "amor," seems almost more a human companion than a real nightingale. The poet in ***A uma Viajante*** (**"To a Traveler"**; ***FSF*** II 22) compares himself to a nightingale, who sings without knowing what he is doing. The lady's voice in ***Os Cinco Sentidos*** (***FC*** I 16) keeps the poet from hearing the nightingale's beautiful song, while in ***Coquette dos Prados*** (***FC*** I 18) the nightingale sighs for the rose. The crow appears twice. In ***Solidão*** (***FSF*** I 21) he is the bearer of ill-tidings, while in ***A Victoria na Praia*** (***FSF*** II 1) he is the symbol of war. The same poem introduces the dove as the symbol of hope. Bustling city-dwellers are described in ***A Primavera*** (***LJM*** I 1) as a crowd of stupid peacocks.

Tigers appear several times. In ***Filinto*** (***LJM*** I 4) they represent the enemies of the poet Filinto and also hypocrites and fanatics. In ***A Morte de Riego*** (***LJM*** III 15) the tiger is a despot responsible for the Spanish patriot's death. In ***O Campo de Sant'Anna*** (***S*** 7) the tigers are bloodthirsty judges. The only lion image occurs in ***A Victoria na Praia*** (***FSF*** II 1), where the leaders of the army of the tyrant King Miguel are compared to wounded lions as they attack the forces of Dona Maria.[10] Garrett uses in ***Adeus*** (***FC*** I 2) the Biblical figure of casting pearls (his lady's forgiveness) before swine (Garrett himself). The old Duke of Palmela,[11] central figure of ***No Lumiar*** (***FC*** II 17), is called a noble war-horse. People in ***O Natal de Christo*** (***FSF*** II 25) are lined up like cattle to be counted by the Roman authorities. In ***O Redemptor*** (***FSF*** II 26) the familiar figure of the innocent lamb is used to represent Christ. Jealousy, personified in ***Sapho*** (***LJM*** III 8), has hair made of snakes. ***Adeus*** (***FC*** I 2) introduces a viper, generated in the poison of Garrett's wounded heart. A similar viper is the subject of the poem ***Vibora*** (***FC*** I 25). Bees and butterflies occasionally appear in the company of the flowers, as in ***Rosa sem Espinhos*** (***FC*** I 12). In ***No Lumiar*** (***FC*** II 17) the voices of guests at a party are compared to the buzzing of bees. Hope in ***Solidão*** (***FSF*** I 21) is described as thinner than the thread of a spider.

Of the heavenly bodies, the stars get the greatest attention from Garrett's poetic imagination. There are some allusions to the sun, but the moon, the inspiration of so many poets, gets strangely enough very little attention. ***O Monumento*** (**"The Monument"**; ***LJM*** I 8) places the soul of Dr. Fortuna, to whose memory the poem was dedicated, in the "estellifera morada" ("starry dwelling"), from which one can see the rotation of millions of worlds. In ***A Infancia*** (***LJM*** I 10), passion is described as an "astro sem orbita, / Tumultario planeta" ("star without an orbit, / disordered planet"). In ***Longa Viagem de Mar*** (**"Long Sea-Voyage"**;

LJM II 12), the poet asks the stars to witness the suffering in his heart. In ***A Caverna de Viriatho*** (***FSF*** I 17) the fading light of the morning star is compared to the closing of the eyes of a girl in her lover's arms. A lover sees his star when he gazes into his lady's face in ***A minha Rosa*** (***FSF*** II 9), while in the beautiful little poem ***A Estrella*** (***FSF*** II 12) Garrett's lady-love is the star that only he can see. The poet in ***As minhas Azas*** (***FSF*** II 19) contemplates the stars and wishes to fly toward them, the symbols of his ambitions, but he turns his eyes away from the sky and stars and sees a more beautiful light on earth: love. In ***Ella*** (***FSF*** II 23) the poet wandering in the desert of life finds no star to guide him. In the same poem, he tries to find the stars in order to question them about his fate and sees a great light, symbolic of beauty, that fills his soul. ***Adeus*** (***FC*** I 2) characterizes the lady's love which Garrett is about to lose as a star whose brightness is to disappear forever from his eyes. ***Aquella Noite*** (**"That Night"**; ***FC*** I 4) tells of the poet's visit to a ball. On the way, he is unable to see the star which he was always accustomed to see in the sky. Here the star may be his lady, or perhaps one of his ideals. ***Barca Bella*** (**"Beautiful Boat"**; ***FC*** II 11) shows the poet warning a fisherman of an impending storm; the last star in the sky (symbol of pure love) is now concealed.

The sun is personified in ***A Noiva*** (**"The Bride"**; ***LJM*** I 7), where he awakens the grasses and flowers. In ***A Guerra Civil*** (***LJM*** III 10) the sun represents freedom, whose light is cut off by the dark wings of the night of deceit. ***A Julia*** (***FSF*** I 2) shows the sun in his characteristic occupation of darting rays of fire. In ***O Mar*** (***FSF*** I 3) the sun is addressed by Garrett as the Image of the Eternal, the Eye of the World, who gives life to the universe. In ***Longa Viagem de Mar*** (***LJM*** II 12) the sun is again personified, this time as the Father of Light. The moon appears in Garrett's lyrics only five times. ***A Morte*** (***LJM*** I 9) tells of the "luz tremente da froixa lua" ("trembling light of the feeble moon"), while ***O Emprazado*** (**"The Summoned One"**; ***FSF*** II 10) has another mere description of the moon quietly gliding through the sky. In ***Nunca Mais*** (***FSF*** II 8) the passing of six months is expressed by six "lentos giros" ("slow turns") which the moon has made through the heavens. ***Ella*** (***FSF*** II 23) speaks of the "morte luz da lua" ("dead light of the moon") which the poet in his depressed mood compares to a shroud. In ***Lucinda*** (***FC*** II 7) the rising moon is the "astro do delirio" ("star of madness"), a phrase suggestive of the moon's magic characteristics.

The dawn, that faithful companion of lyric poets, is not neglected by Garrett, who likes to consider her in her mythological aspects. She sheds the leaves of her roses and unfolds her cloak of mist in ***A Noiva*** (***LJM*** I 7). In ***Sonho Prophetico*** (***LJM*** I 11) she is the messenger of the new day and mounts onto the balconies of the east, where she lets her golden hair fly in the wind. In ***Anniversario da Revolução de 24 de Agosto*** (***LJM*** III 4) Garrett addresses her as "linda aurora" ("lovely dawn") who unfolds her rosy cloak over the sky and ushers in the new day. In ***O Mar*** (***FSF*** I 3) she is the familiar rosy-fingered maiden who scatters the flowers sprinkled with dew. She combs her hair in ***A Caverna de Viriatho*** (***FSF*** I 17) and the winds blow gently through the flowers which night had picked to adorn her tresses. The same poem alludes to the dawn of liberty, which is soon to appear over the mountains of Portugal. In ***Nunca Mais*** (***FSF*** II 8) Garrett sees the dawn on his lady's face, a dawn which promises many delights to the lover.

Allusions to the sea are not infrequent, yet one might expect a greater number of sea-images, and more original ones, from a poet who spent a large part of his youth on an island in the Azores and who made several sea-voyages. ***A um Joven Poeta*** (**"To a Young Poet"**; ***LJM*** I 6) describes the sea as "vitreo" ("glassy"). In ***Longa Viagem de Mar*** (***LJM*** II 12) the sea is an "insondavel abysmo" ("unfathomable abyss") and a "soledade infinda" ("endless solitude"). The world in ***Melancholia*** (***LJM*** III 11) revolves in the uneasy turbulence of a bottomless sea. In ***O Carcere*** (**"The Prison"**; ***LJM*** III 12) the poet compares himself to one who wanders aimlessly over the seas in the voyage of life. ***O Mar*** (***FSF*** I 3), in spite of its title, is not really a sea-poem. Like most of Garrett's longer lyrics, it does not confine itself to one subject, but touches upon such varied topics as Hope, the river Mondego, the dawn, the earth, the sun, God and love. In this poem the sea is the image of the infinite, a series of vast plains. Once again the reader is left with the impression that Garrett has made use of nature not as a subject for lyrical description alone, but as a background for philosophizing. He even manages to introduce Hobbes into this poem. In ***A Caverna de Viriatho*** (***FSF*** I 17) the rather familiar figures of the sea of blood and the sea of evils as punishments for the wicked appear. ***A Tempestade*** (**"The Storm"**; ***FSF*** I 19), which paints a storm at sea, compares this tempest with the violent agitation in a lover's heart. One smile, one ray of hope from the lady will calm the storm-tossed heart as the sun will drive the clouds away. ***A Victoria na Praia*** (***FSF*** II 1) introduces a more original figure: the tide which withdraws from and returns to the beach is compared to a lover unable to say goodbye to his sweetheart. ***O Pharol e o Baixel*** (***FSF*** II 14) features a dialogue between the sturdy old lighthouse and the pretty little ship that is anxious to venture on the sea of life. In ***Aquella Noite*** (***FC*** I 4) the voices of guests at a ball are compared to the sound of the sea striking the beach.

Winds are generally personified as Zephyrs, who pick flowers in ***O Mar*** (***FSF*** I 3) or steal kisses from the rose in ***A Rosa*** (***LJM*** III 6). In ***Madrugada*** (***LJM*** II 10) Garrett asks the destructive winds to stay away from the flowers and calls on Zephyr to help fertilize them. The gentle Zephyr is so timid and respectful that he does not dare disturb the sleeping shepherdess in ***A Sesta*** (***LJM*** I 4).

Figures involving food and drink are seldom found. The honey of delight turns up in ***O Beijo*** (**"The Kiss"**; ***LJM*** II 15) and in ***Faz hoje um Anno*** (***LJM*** III 7), while in

Melancholia (***LJM*** III 11) Garrett expresses the desire to enjoy nature while others drink from the gold cup of pleasure. In ***Cascaes*** (***FC*** I 19) the cup of pleasure again is mentioned.

In reading Garrett's lyrics and in observing his figures of speech, two aspects of his imagery stand out as most characteristic: 1. Garrett provides many instances of apostrophe and personification, which at times give a dramatic quality to his poems and which leave the reader with the impression that the poet was interested in people rather than in scenery or in abstract ideas. 2. Garrett makes frequent use of images involving nature, often conventional in character, and generally associated with people. The rose is practically never a flower; she is one of the Délias or Julias to whom the poems are addressed. Flowers, indeed, provide Garrett with his favorite nature-images; he also likes to make use of the stars. The sea, sun and moon, trees, birds and animals play a comparatively minor role. Other less important characteristics of Garrett's figures of speech are an almost excessive number of allusions in his earlier poems to Classical mythology, few images taken from any profession or trade, very little humor or irony, very few symbols of Christianity.

To what extent Garrett's concern with people, together with a relative lack of feeling for nature *per se,* is a characteristic of Portuguese poetry in general, is a fascinating subject which would require thorough investigation. The medieval poets of Portugal's great school of court- and minstrel-poetry indeed make frequent use of apostrophe and dialogue and seldom mention nature, except when a girl in love asks the waves of the sea, the deer of the hills, or the flowers of the pine-tree for news of her lover. Is this tendency toward personification and toward a comparative neglect of nature as typical of other Portuguese poets as it is of Garrett? This question could be the starting point for many interesting studies that would help gain a better understanding of the Portuguese poetic temperament.

Notes

1. The following abbreviations for the collections of Garrett's verse are used: *LJM, Lyrica de João Minimo*; *S, Sonetos*; *FSF, Flores sem Fructo*; *FC, Folhas Cahidas.* Roman numerals refer to sections in *LJM, FSF* and *FC*; Arabic numerals refer to individual poems.

2. A beautiful English girl much admired by the distinguished Portuguese circle in which she lived, and who died young.

3. The theme of the poet as his lady's vassal is not new in Portuguese poetry. Many of the medieval court-poets developed this idea.

4. Garrett twice was driven into exile in England because of his liberal political views.

5. The influence of England, always considerable in Portugal, was extremely strong in the early nineteenth century.

6. Domingos Sequeira (1768-1837), one of the outstanding Portuguese painters, is best known for his religious and historical scenes.

7. Viriathus led an insurrection of Celtiberian tribes against Roman rule in 149 B.C. Garrett uses him as a symbol of those elements in Portugal who were struggling against despotism.

8. Rafael del Riego Nuñez (1784-1823), Spanish liberal leader and army officer, executed by royalists during a civil war.

9. Cascaes, or Cascais, a town near Lisbon.

10. Dom Miguel in 1828 usurped the throne of Portugal which belonged by right to his niece, Dona Maria. A revolt against Dom Miguel in 1832 restored Dona Maria to her throne.

11. Portuguese statesman and diplomat.

Linda Ledford-Miller (essay date 1984)

SOURCE: Ledford-Miller, Linda. "Voyage to the Land of the Novel: Narrative Voices in *Viagens na minha terra.*" *Luso-Brazilian Review* 21.2 (1984): 1-8. Print.

[*In the following essay, Ledford-Miller analyzes the narrative and stylistic innovations in* Travels in My Homeland. *She argues that Garrett's use of parody and digressive, self-conscious narration, make the novel a bridge between literary Romanticism and modernism.*]

Almeida Garrett's novel ***Viagens na Minha Terra*** (1846) has been variously received by the critics. According to Helder Macedo, it is "talvez a obra mais importante do Romantismo português."[1] Alberto Ferreira, on the other hand, declares it "o documento mais notável da prosa portuguesa moderna."[2] For João Gaspar Simões, "seria impróprio considerar romance as ***Viagens na Minha Terra,*** quando é certo que, neste livro digressivo e como que improvisado sobre o joelho, o que há é uma história, tão digressivo como o resto, e que de romance quase nada tem."[3] For Simões, "***Viagens*** são uma espécie de viagem ao país do romance, ... um pseudoromance romântico."[4] This divergence of opinion seems to reinforce the author's own declaration that ***Viagens*** is a "despropositado e inclassificável livro," but, he continues, "não é que se quebre, mas enreda-se o fio das histórias e das observações por tal modo, que, bem o vejo e o sinto, só com muita paciência se pode deslindar e seguir em tão embaraçada meada."[5]

As much as they seem to disagree, all of these apparently conflicting critical responses are to some degree correct: the prose of ***Viagens na Minha Terra*** is as romantic as it is modern.[6] It is the book's ability to direct itself both ways, that is, toward Romanticism and at the same time toward modern literature, that makes it a masterpiece of nineteenth-century Portuguese fiction.

The novel begins, like a conventional travel narrative, with a first person narrator determined to travel and relate the story of his journey. This would seem to exemplify what Mikhail Bakhtin calls monologic speech.

> The author's speech ... is handled stylistically as speech aimed at its direct referential denotation: it must be adequate to its object (of whatever nature, discursive, poetic, or other); it must be expressive, forceful, pithy, elegant, and so on, from the point of view of its direct referential mission—to denote, express, convey or depict something; and its stylistic treatment is concurrently oriented toward the comprehension of the referent.[7]

Though this is true of some parts of the novel (the descriptions of the architecture of Santarém in particular), even the first paragraphs of what appears to be direct authorial discourse show symptoms of being dialogic discourse in the Bakhtinian sense.

> Should the author's speech be so treated as to display the individual or typical features of a particular person, or of a particular social status, or of a particular literary manner, then what we are dealing with is already stylization, either the usual kind of literary stylization or that of a stylized *skaz*. ... Thus, within a single utterance there may occur two intentions, two voices. Such is the nature of parody, stylization, and stylized *skaz*.[8]

The essential words here are "to display," that is, to make manifest or to lay bare. The travel narrative of ***Viagens na Minha Terra*** both imitates its literary tradition ("literary manner") and enters into a dialogue with it. ***Viagens*** comments on the whole body of travel literature extant at that time, not just on Xavier de Maistre's *Voyage au tour de ma chambre* to which the text refers.[9] The very exaggeration of this commentary draws attention to itself and, therefore, to the tradition it imitates.

> Que viaje à roda do seu quarto quem está a beira dos Alpes, de Inverno, em Turim, que é quase tão frio como Sam Petersburg—entende-se. Mas com este clima, com este ar que Deus nos deu, onde a laranjeira cresce na horta, e o mato é de murta, o próprio Xavier de Maistre, que aqui escrevesse, ao menos ia até o quintal.
>
> Eu muito vezes ... viajo até a minha janela para ver uma nesguita de Tejo que está no fim da rua. ... E nunca escrevi estas minhas viagens nem as suas impressões: pois tinham muito que ver! Foi sempre ambiciosa a minha pena: pobre e soberba, quer assunto mais largo. Pois hei-de dar-lho. Vou nada menos que a Santarém. ...
>
> (pp. 7-8)

In contrast to St. Hilaire's *voyages* in Brazil, Garrett's trip to Santarém and back to Lisboa will cover less than one hundred miles of Portuguese soil, yet he treats it as a great journey. "What we have here," to quote Tynyanov, "is stylization; it is not a question of following a style but rather of playing with it."[10] Examples of such play abound. In Chapter II, for example, Garrett's ***Viagens*** "declaram-se típicas, simbólicas e míticas." Referring to travel books, he claims a special place among them for his work.

> Estas minhas interessantes viagens hão-de ser uma obra-prima, erudita, brilhante de pensamentos novos, uma coisa digna do século. Preciso de o dizer ao leitor, para que esteja prevenido; não cuide que são quais quer dessas rabiscaduras da moda que, com o título de *Impressões de Viagem*, ou outro que tal, fatigam as imprensas da Europa sem nenhum proveito da ciência e do adiantamento da espécie
>
> (pp. 16-17)

Garrett implicitly suggests here that, contrary to "these scribblings" of others, his travelogue will benefit science and the "advancement of the species." He soon states this more explicitly.

> Já, agora, rasgo o véu e declaro abertamente ao benévolo leitor que a profunda idéia que está oculta debaixo desta ligeira aparência de uma viagenzita que parece feita a brincar, e no fim de contas é uma coisa séria, grave. ...
>
> (p. 17)
>
> Ora nesta minha viagem Tejo-arriba está simbolizada a marcha do nosso progress social. ...
>
> (p. 19)

If we are to take him at his word, we can only assume that "social progress," like his journey, doesn't go far and is frequently postponed.

In passages such as the ones cited above, with their direct address to the reader and open declarations of intent, Garrett calls the reader's attention to the tradition of travel literature, reemphasizes the author's presence as mediator between reader and text, and exposes the text in the process of its creation, all of which combines to question the literary convention within which he is writing. The simple travelogue expected initially has already become something else; it has been transformed from a literary style (or "manner") to a literary stylization, an exposé of itself. The situation becomes further complicated by the introduction of other narrative planes. The plane of the travel narrative has its own subdivision in the numerous digressions which present the author-traveler's thoughts and opinions on politics, religion, and literature (mainly), and any number of other side issues.[11] Enclosed within the text (and later within the context) of the travel narrative is the story of Joaninha, "a menina dos rouxinóis." As Simões notes, Garrett "não resiste à tentação de intercalar no texto das ***Viagens*** um típico romance da época."[12] Superficially, "A Menina dos Rouxinóis" seems to be a romantic novel as typical today as it was in the romantic period—stories of frustrated love and its tragic consequences are still common. This admittedly traditional romance is simultaneously modern, however, and speaks, to return to Bakhtin and

Tynyanov, with "two intentions, two voices," while "playing" with its tradition.

The tale is ostensibly told to our traveling narrator by a traveling companion who knew Joaninha. After several exchanges between the I-narrator and an unidentified second party, the narrator says, "Já se vê que este diálogo se passava entre mim e outro dos nossos companheiros de viagem" (p. 78). Nevertheless, by the end of the chapter the narrator has completely eclipsed the voice of his companion.

> O que eu vou contar não tem aventuras enredadas, peripécias, situações e incidentes raros; é um [*sic*] história simples e singela, sinceramente contada e sem pretensão. Acabemos aqui o capítulo em forma de prólogo; e a matéria do meu conto para o seguinte.
>
> (p. 79)

When he does begin the story several pages later, it has become "minha história." We never hear the companion's voice narrating any part of the story, which proves to be nearly the opposite of "simples e singela."[13] The "romancinho" of Joaninha is, as António José Saraiva asserts, "flagrante na sua estrutura teatral,"[14] and the narrator makes this theatricality obvious from time to time: "Vamos a Santarém, que lá se passa o segundo acto," he says at the end of Chapter XXVI (p. 189). An even clearer example is in Chapter XX: "O oficial . . .—Mas certo que as amáveis leitoras querem saber com quem tratam, e exigem, pelo menos, uma esquissa rápida, e a largos traços, do novo actor que lhes vou apresentar em cena" (pp. 143-44). Aside from making reference to the theater in such words as "actor" and "cena," the narrator "tears through the veil" yet again to make the writing process evident to the reader. The narrator is both inside and outside of his narrative as he creates it while questioning it and questions it while creating it. As Berardinelli comments, "todo esse questionamento do contexto literário em que a obra está forçosamente inserta, ainda que o negando, conserva no leitor a consciência da opacidade do texto."[15] The narrator is a part of and apart from his narrative; he speaks with the double voice of a discourse in jeopardy. Though this "double-voiced discourse" (as Bakhtin calls it) usually exists in ***Viagens*** as a kind of literary stylization, there are some instances of true parody. Although the two are similar in their dislocation of the text, the parodic sections break more violently from it.

According to Tynyanov,

> Stylization is close to parody. Both live a double life: behind the apparent structure of a work, its first level, lies a second level, that of the work it stylizes or parodies. But in parody it is obligatory to have a disjunction of both levels, a dislocation of intent: the parody of a tragedy will be a comedy (it matters little whether this is done through an exaggeration of the tragic intent or through a corresponding substitution of comic elements), and a parody of a comedy could be a tragedy. In stylization there is no such disjunction. There is, on the contrary, a correspondence of the two levels—the stylizing level and the stylized level showing through it—one to another. Nevertheless, it is but a single step from stylization to parody; stylization that is comically motivated or emphasized becomes parody.[16]

Perhaps the clearest instance of parody is in Chapter XXIII. Carlos is anxiously awaiting his evening meeting with his cousin Joaninha, and to pass the time he thinks poetic thoughts. "Porque não hei-de eu dizer a verdade?," says the narrator.—"O desgraçado era poeta" (p. 163). A "fragment of his [Carlos's] poetic aspirations" follows the narrator's explanation to his "amáveis leitoras que não tem metro, nem rima—nem razão . . . Mas, enfim, versos não são" (p. 164). The "fragment" includes two pages of text about the eye color of three of the women for whom Carlos has had tender feelings. After reading these romantic ramblings, the reader is informed that this extant fragment was obtained under very special conditions.

> Infelizmente, não se formulavam em palavras estes pensamentos poéticos tão sublimes. Por um processo milagroso de fotografia mental, apenas se pôde obter o fragmento que deixo transcrito.
>
> Que honra e glória para a escola romântica se pudéssemos ter a colecção completa!
>
> Fazia-se-lhe um prefácio incisivo, palpitante, britante . . .
>
> Punha-se-lhe um título vaporoso, fosforescente . . . por exemplo:—*Ecos surdos do coração*. . . .
>
> (p. 166)

The narrator frames the fragment with his own remarks, setting it like a bas-relief against his introduction and response to it. The image of a "miraculous process of mental photography" is so humorously impossible that the impact of the poetic fragment dissolves from romantic to comical. Any semblance of narrative flow is destroyed; the narrator's voice is in direct opposition to that of his character. This is Bakhtin's "speech [as] a battlefield for opposing intentions," and romanticism lies prostrate, the victim of an inside attack.[17] As an insider, familiar with romantic literature, "the author employs the speech of another, but in contradistinction to stylization, he introduces into that other speech an intention which is directly opposed to the original one."[18] This is overt parody, as is the poem in Chapter III, which the author himself calls "uma espécie de paródia dos famosos fragmentos de Alceu" (Nota D, p. 25). Alceu's line, "eu coroarei de mirto a minha espada," becomes, in Garrett's hands, "Eu coroarei de trevo a minha espada, / De cenoiras, luzerna e beterrava" (p. 25). In the same chapter, the description of the inn is a quasi-parody in dialogue with literary tradition.

> Vamos à descricão da estalagem; e acabemos com tanta digressão. Não pode ser clássica, está visto, a tal descrição.

—Seja romântica.—Também não pode ser. Porque não? . . . e aí fica . . . uma estalagem . . . elegante. É como eu devia fazer a descrição: bem o sei. Mas há um impedimento fátal, invencível. . . . É que nada disso lá havia. . . . verdade e mais verdade. Na estalagem de Azambuja o que havia era uma . . . velha suja e maltrapida que estava a porta daquela asquerosa casa . . . com a sua moça mais moça, mas não menos nojenta de ver que ela, e um velho meio paralítico, meio demente. . . .

(pp. 28-30)

This description is the opposite of romantic because the author feels compelled to tell the (supposed) truth. Truth and fiction collide and Romanticism is wounded again. And yet, despite the narrator's parodic moments which undermine the romantic style, his attack confirms that style by consistently directing the reader's attention toward it. Furthermore, though much of his style may deviate from its romantic model, he is using a romantic form in the story of Joaninha, with its typical romantic characters and plot.

The distinction between truth and fiction, a preoccupation noted early in the book, becomes even more problematic in the context of "A Menina dos Rouxinóis." The author, as traveler narrating his journey, comes to the valley of Santarém and enters the story as a character, ignorant of the comings and goings of the very characters he has created. "Involuntáriamente, parei defronte da janela. . . . No mesmo sítio, do mesmo modo, com os mesmos trajos e na mesma atitude em que a descrevi nos primeiros capítulos desta história, estava a nossa velha irmã Francisca . . . (p. 286). Seeing Frei Dinis, he asks him what happened to Joaninha ("Joaninha está no ceu.") and Carlos. Dinis gives him Carlos's letter to read. Carlos's voice takes over the narrative, and a third narrational plane intersects with those of the I-narrator's travel narrative and the (mostly) omniscient narrator of the story of the valley. Through the letter, we discover that Carlos is an ultra-romantic character. Not content with one love, he has loved three sisters in succession (Laura, Julia, and Georgina) and been involved to some extent with a nun (Soledade) before being stricken with love for Joana. Unfortunately, he falls in love with Joaninha while still in love with, and pledged to, Georgina. He escapes into an exile of sorts by becoming a baron (a social position much maligned in the novel by the first narrator).

Carlos is a romantic type, the young distressed lover, but he is a character whose attributes have been extrapolated to such a degree that he is nearly a parody of himself. Not exaggerated to the point of parody, the character of Carlos is a stylization of its romantic counterpart. The same is true of Frei Dinis, so evil of aspect and almost infinitely mean and mysterious, and of Francisca, the old woman who cries herself blind, and, to a lesser extent, of Joaninha, innocence personified, who dies of frustrated, unrequited love.

Only one short chapter follows Carlos's letter. In it our traveling author, after revealing that he was Carlos's former comrade, learns the final particulars about his characters from the voice of Frei Dinis. History, truth, and fiction all converge in the narrator who invades his own text and "transforma-seassim . . . na mais importante e mais fascinante personagem da narrativa," as Ofélia Paiva Monteiro remarks.[19] The book and the voyage, despite all the digressions, become one: "Assim terminou a nossa viagem a Santarém e assim termina este livro" (p. 320).

Almeida Garrett's *obra-prima* speaks with the many voices of intersecting narrational planes and intermingling literary styles as he uses the romantic style as a vehicle in which to travel, stylizing and parodying his way toward the modern novel. ***Viagens na Minha Terra*** is both a tribute and a challenge to Romanticism. But, perhaps more importantly, ***Viagens*** is a precursor of the modern self-conscious novel with its self-conscious narrators and its emphasis on the process of literary creation.

Notes

1. Helder Macedo, "A Menina dos Rouxinóis," *Colóquio: Letras* 51 (1979), p. 15.

2. Alberto Ferreira, *Perspectiva do Romantismo Português* (Lisboa: Textos de Cultura Portuguesa, 1971), p. 87. Unfortunately, neither Macedo nor Ferreira elaborates on his comment.

3. João Gaspar Simões, *Almeida Garrett* (Lisboa: Editorial Presença, 1964), p. 115.

4. Simões, *História do Romance Português,* Vol. I (Lisboa: Estúdios Cor, 1967), p. 20.

5. João Baptists da Silva Leitão de Almeida Garrett, *Viagens na Minha Terra* (Lisboa: Livraria Sá de Costa, 1954), p. 217. All quotations are taken from this edition.

6. Though Romanticism came late to Portugal and never achieved a strength equal to that of Romanticism in Germany, France, and England, Garrett was familiar with it because of his travels as well as his readings in foreign literatures. As various critics have pointed out (Simões among them), *Viagens* was influenced by Laurence Sterne's novels, *Tristam Shandy* and *A Sentimental Journey,* and by Xavier de Maistre's *Voyage au tour de ma chambre.*

7. Mikhail Bakhtin, "Discourse Typology in Prose," in *Readings in Russian Poetics* (Ann Arbor, Michigan: Michigan Slavic Publications, 1978), p. 178.

8. Bakhtin, pp. 178 and 180. *Skaz* is defined as "in its strict sense, the oral narration of a narrator" (p. 176).

9. *Le Voyage en Orient* (1806-07) and *L'Itinéraire de Paris à Jerusalem* (1811) by Chateaubriand; and the various *Voyages* in Brazil of St. Hilaire, for example.

10. Yuri Tynyanov, "Dostoevsky and Gogol: Towards a Theory of Parody: Part One, Stylization and Parody," in *Dostoevsky and Gogol* (Ann Arbor, Michigan: Ardis, 1979), p. 103.

11. Cleonice Berardinelli, in her excellent article, "Garrett e Camilo: Românticos Hererodoxos?," discusses the three stories alternately presented in the narrative. "A narrativa, inovadora na literatura portuguêsa, apresenta alternadamente três estórias duas das quais não chegam bem a sê-lo, pois uma consiste sobretudo em digressões ou divagações do autor e a outra na descrição da viagem de Lisboa a Santarém. Estória propriamente dita é a de Joaninha, a menina dos Rouxinóis ... (p. 65)." Berardinelli's analysis does not, however, account for such things as the change of voice in Joaninha's story (Carlos's letter assumes the narrative voice). The concept of estória/story implying, as it does, plot and closure, does not seem adequate to this novel. We have chosen to deal instead with the more open concepts of narrational planes and narrational voices.

12. Simões, *Almeida Garrett,* p. 128.

13. Ofélia Paiva Monteiro also points this out: "Nas *Viagens,* a história da Casa do Vale é contada ao narrador por um companheiro que conhecera a Menina dos Rouxinóis, sem que o leitor, todavia, ouça nunca a sua voz." "Algumas reflexões sobre a novelística de Garrett," *Colóquio: Letras,* 30 (1976), p. 20.

14. António José Saraiva, *História da Literatura Portuguêsa,* 3rd ed. (Porto: Porto Editora and Empresa L. Fluminese, n.d.), p. 674. R. A. Lawton discusses the theatrical aspects of the novella as well: "Si l'on examiné la nouvelle de la *Jeune Fille aux Rossignols* ... sa construction réele apparaît ainsi: um premier groupe de chapitres que s'étend de l'apparition de Joaninha (XII) à la fin du 'premier acte' du roman. ... Le second 'acte' que se passe a Santarém, est formé des chapitres XXXII à XXXVI. ... Le second 'acte' se termine par la fuite de Carlos. ... La lettre explicative de Carlos [est l'] épilogue de la nouvells. ... Le roman de la *Jeune Fille aux Rossignols* se compose donc de deux actes et un épilogue. ..." *Almeida Garrett, L'intime contrainte* (Paris: Didier, 1966), pp. 168-69.

15. Berardinelli, p. 69.

16. Tynyanov, p. 104.

17. Bakhtin, p. 185.

18. Bakhtin, p. 185.

19. Paiva Monteiro, p. 15.

J. J. Macklin (essay date 1985)

SOURCE: Macklin, J. J. "Passion and Perception: The Possibilities of Tragedy in Almeida Garrett's *Frei Lúis de Sousa.*" *Revista canadiense de estudios hispánicos* 9.2 (1985): 165-80. Print.

[*In the following essay, Macklin considers Garrett's claim that his play* Brother Luiz de Sousa *is not a true tragedy. According to Macklin, the work departs from the classical model of tragedy in that it embraces a Christian notion of divine redemption.*]

The relative critical neglect which Almeida Garrett's ***Frei Luís de Sousa*** has suffered stands in curious contrast to the unrestrained praise which seems to accompany its mere mention. For José Augusto França, "***Frei Luís de Sousa*** é a obra-prima do teatro português do século XIX,"[1] and for João Gaspar Simões, "é bem o mais alto documento do teatro nacional."[2] Either lost in general surveys of Portuguese Romanticism or subordinated to a more general consideration of its author's life and works, the play has not received the detailed critical attention it would seem to deserve. Yet any critical appraisal of ***Frei Luís de Sousa*** is not without its problems. Unmistakably Romantic in tone and inspiration, the play has undoubted claims to be considered an authentic tragedy, but critics, following the lead of the author himself, have shown a marked reluctance to accord it genuine tragic status. João Gaspar Simões must surely be voicing the feelings of many when he asserts that "Há uma gravidade que não é de tragédia, mas de melodrama, na admirável concepção do ***Frei Luís de Sousa.***"[3] The matter is put slightly differently, and more positively, by J. Almeida Lucas, for whom ***Frei Luís de Sousa*** is "uma peça romántica que, sendo embora um drama, tem muito de tragédia antiga."[4] In this article I wish to examine the causes of this critical hesitation and ambivalence through an evaluation of the tragic elements embedded within the fabric of the play itself.

The critical ambivalence to which I have just alluded was anticipated, and perhaps even created, by Garrett himself in his ***Memória ao Conservatório Real,*** read on the 6th of May, 1843. In this, Garrett states that the basic story underlying the play attracted him by virtue of its simplicity, a quality it shares with many of the outstanding episodes of Portuguese tradition, of which the tragic fate of Inês de Castro is a prime example. In the story of Manuel de Sousa, he says, "há toda a simplicidade de uma fábula trágica antiga."[5] Garrett here seems to be suggesting something akin to the intensity and concentration which is derived from the principle of unity of action, and therefore implies that his subject is serious and fit for tragic drama. In fact, so simple is the situation that Garrett states his awareness of the difficulties inherent in developing its tragic potential in order to determine "se era possível excitar fortemente o terror e a piedade" (1083), in other words, to write a modern tragedy. This is unexceptionable, but the first major difficulty arises when he singles out the Christian element as the quintessential ingredient in the tragedy, for it possesses "aquela unção e delicada sensibilidade que o espírito do Cristianismo derrama por toda ela, molhando de lágrimas contritas o que seriam desesperadas ânsias num pagão, acendendo até nas últimas trevas da morte, a vela da esperança que se não apaga com a vida" (1082). In the first place, the whole idea of a tragedy with hope is a controversial one and, secondly, the very idea of a Christian tragedy seems a contradiction in terms. One recalls the remarks of I. A. Richards: "Tragedy is only possible to a mind which is for the moment agnostic or Manichean. The least touch of any theology which has a compensating Heaven to offer the tragic hero is fatal."[6] In ***Frei Luís de Sousa,*** the tragic death of the two spouses is not physical death, but death to each other and to the world, and their Christian religion, which is in part the cause of their tragedy, is also the instrument of its resolution. Garrett never seemed to sense that there is a profund incompatibility between the tragic and the Christian, and his refusal to call his play a tragedy is on altogether different grounds. Although ***Frei Luís de Sousa*** in essence "é uma verdadeira tragédia," he does not, he says, categorise it as such out of respect for the great works which are so defined, and also because it is not written in verse, as indeed his own youthful works, ***Lucrécia, Mérope, Catão,*** had been. To the modern mind, these formal qualms seem insignificant when compared to the greater question of the internal consistency of Garrett's tragic vision. And yet, although he designates his work as a "drama," Garrett does not wish ***Frei Luís de Sousa*** to be judged by the standards of contemporary Romantic drama: "se na forma desmerece da categoria, pela índole há-de ficar pertenecendo sempre ao antigo género trágico" (1083). In likening his play to the ancient Greek tragedies, Garrett can only be referring to a kinship in theme: man's subjection to the gods, the tragic consequences of human action and, above all, suffering and recognition, which are for many the two indispensable elements of any tragic work.

Of course there is and has been a great deal of theoretical debate about what constitutes true tragedy and what criteria might be applied in its definition. This debate has been enriched and made increasingly complex in our own time. To attempt to define ***Frei Luís de Sousa*** as tragedy inevitably raises questions about the validity of the definition itself and there is a frustrating circularity in theories which use "tragedies" to define tragedy. Aristotle raised more problems than he solved and it seems prudent that any approach to the question should be as undogmatic as possible. One might wish to distinguish between a "tragic vision" and the aesthetic form which embodies it, "tragedy," but in what follows I have assumed the existence of both a particular vision of the world and certain dramatic features which, to a broad consensus of critical opinion, seem to inform any concept of the tragic. But rather than search for some pure, distilled form of the genre, I have preferred to talk of the possibilities of tragedy in ***Frei Luís de Sousa,*** recognising that certain of these may remain approximate or undeveloped.[7]

Of course, ***Frei Luís de Sousa***'s claim to be a tragedy has to be considered in the context of the climate of Romanticism which prevailed at the time in which it was written. When João Gasper Simões, in the observation cited above, alludes to melodrama, there is no pejorative intent here, simply an indication of the play's Romantic overlay. He is not, for example, employing the term in the full sense of the Oxford English Dictionary definition, namely "a dramatic piece characterised by sensational incident and violent appeals to the emotions, but with a happy ending." The critic Frank Rahill writes of melodrama as being "conventionally moral and humanitarian in point of view and sentimental and optimistic in temper, concluding its fable happily with virtue rewarded after many trials and vice punished. Characteristically it offers elaborate scenic accessories and miscellaneous divertissements and introduces music freely, typically to underscore dramatic effect."[8] If such definitions were accepted, ***Frei Luís de Sousa*** could scarcely qualify as melodrama, but although melodramatic works tend to portray in simplistic terms the ultimate triumph of good over evil, this is not necessarily always the case. In the ***Memória*** [**"Memória ao Conservatório Real"**], indeed, Garrett points to the fact that evil is totally absent from ***Frei Luís de Sousa,*** that the characters are good and exist "sem um mau para contraste, sem um tirano que se mate ou que mate alguém" (1083). However, what does characterise melodrama is the particular kind of difficulty the protagonist is called upon to face, for it is invariably a question of difficulties from without rather than from within. The hero is in conflict with forces outside himself which conspire to thwart him. Whereas the tragic hero is perforce torn between two conflicting impulses, one of which can only be sacrificed to the other, the melodramatic hero is at one with himself. The conflict may end in either victory or defeat, but the hero himself is never divided in his purpose or resolve. This means that ultimately he can never attain that state of recognition, the growth of self-knowledge, which accompanies tragic experience. The authentic *anagnorisis* of tragedy is denied him, for he is "whole" throughout.

Before considering in more detail this question, it is perhaps appropriate to indicate in the play those "scenic accessories" to which Rahill refers, for it is they above all which impart the unmistakable stamp of Romantic literature upon it. The importance of plot and action is evident, as are the specific devices which pertain to them: the presence of spectacular action on stage (the setting fire to the house, the death of Maria), the symbolic use of stage settings (the portraits, the proximity of the church, the religious ceremony), the use of disguise and discoveries of identity (Manuel, the Romeiro), elementary stratagems for maintaining suspense and also a sense of foreboding. The love interest itself, which is essentially Romantic, is reinforced by allusions to literary antecedents (Camões, Bernardim Ribeiro, the story of Inês de Castro), and is overtly sentimental and idealised. The raw material of the play is largely historical, with modifications (the couple had no child), and is related to Portuguese tradition most particularly through the myth of Sebastianism. All these elements therefore combine to make ***Frei Luís de Sousa*** a rich and varied work in which the tragic elements are subsumed into a largely Romantic framework. In the following pages, these Romantic features will be taken for granted, alluded to, but not analysed in isolation from the other elements in the work. Rather the emphasis will be on those aspects which are central to an evaluation of the play's tragic vision of man: the tragic hero, guilt, fate, reversal, suffering and recognition.

It is not easy to isolate a main protagonist in ***Frei Luís de Sousa*** and accord to him or her the status of tragic hero. In a sense, it could be said that the focus of attention constantly shifts and the tragic burden is shared. The title of the play appears to give primacy to Manuel de Sousa himself, although he is on stage for only part of the action. Garrett, in the ***Memória,*** seems to have conceived of Manuel de Sousa as an exemplary figure, and the play as portraying the "esquisitos tormentos de coração e de espírito que aqui padece o cavalheiro pundonoroso, o amante delicado, o pai estremecido, o cristão sincero e temente do seu Deus" (1082). He makes his first appearance towards the end of Act I, but some insight into his character is given earlier through the observations of other characters. As early as Act I, Scene ii, Telmo calls him an "acabado escolar" and a "fidalgo de tanto primor e de tão bom linhagem como os que se têm por melhores neste reino," while Madalena refers to his "carácter inflexível," the trait that will subsequently motivate his most important actions in the play. When Manuel himself appears in Scene vii, he comes across as determined and imperious, giving firm orders to each of his servants. His greeting to his daughter is noticeably warmer than that to his wife. His speech is characterised by a degree of erudition and formality, as of one who is conscious of his position, even when explaining his plight to his wife and daughter. Manuel de Sousa reveals a certain inflexibility of attitude already, indicating that his individual actions are motivated to a large extent by a set of socially conditioned norms. This is the episode of most political significance in the play—the threat to occupy the house by members of the government and the insight it gives into Castilian domination in Portugal at the time—and it is presumably because of its relevance as a motive force in the subsequent development of the plot that some critics have used it to give the play as a whole a political interpretation. Eduardo Lourenço, for example, writes: "Garrett escreveu com consciente determinação uma obra *política* ... A consciência dos personagens não está centrada na sua individualidade própria, mas refracta sob ângulos diversos uma relação objectiva: a de cada um com o destino histórico da Pátria, ou melhor, com o seu ser."[9] Although this judgement distorts the main emphasis of the play, it is nontheless true that political, or more properly social, concerns precipitate the tragedy. It could be argued that political structures embody outmoded values, which the Romeiro could be said to represent. However, the tragedy is enacted at a personal, not a public level. What happens is that public and private values collide, not within one character, but within the family relationship. The episode of the governors has two purposes. Firstly, on the level of plot, it provides the justification for the transfer to the house of D. João, which is an important means of increasing the dramatic tension and contributing to the sense of inevitability and doom which is made to pervade the play throughout. Secondly, it provides further insight into the character of Manuel de Sousa himself. He is unable to accept this affront to his personal honour.[10] Indeed, his sense of public dishonour overrides his family feelings. Honour therefore establishes itself as a prominent motive force in the ensuing tragedy. This can be observed clearly in scene viii, where Madalena pleads with her husband to reconsider his decision, but Manuel shows himself to be indeed inflexible. His duty as a "português" exceeds his feelings as a husband, and on this there is a fundamental barrier between himself and his wife. Whereas Madalena is instinctive and emotional, Manuel is apparently rational. He rejects any notion of the continuing influence of D. João over their lives: "Eu não tenho ciúmes de um passado que me não pertencia. E o presente, esse é meu, meu só ..." (I, viii). However, such rationality may be more apparent than real, for Maria earlier gives a contrasting picture of his reaction at the mere mention of the possibility that D. Sebastião might not be dead: "põe-se logo outro, muda de semblante, fica pensativo e carrancudo; parece que o vinha afrontar, se voltasse, o pobre do rei" (I, iii). Instinct is being stifled by reason. Manuel's actions are of course also motivated by certain Christian principles to which he adheres: "Não há senão um temor justo, Madalena, é o temor de Deus; não há espectros que nos possam aparecer senão os das más acções que fazemos" (I, viii). Implied here is the Christian idea of sin and guilt in which atonement is achieved through suffering. If in Greek tragedy, crime and guilt invoked the chastisement of the gods, in the Christian scheme suffering can be viewed positively as preparation for reward in an afterlife. More simply, it can take the form of torments of conscience and remorse, themselves manifestations of the fear of divine retribution. Manuel's words pinpoint, unwittingly, the source of Madalena's anxiety, her guilt at having remarried. For the present, though, he is entirely preoccupied with himself, his public image, his need to be seen as "um homem de honra" (I, xi).

In Act II Manuel plays only a minor role. His political difficulties are resolved and he leaves for Lisbon with Maria. Their departure is a further device within the plot, designed to ensure that Madalena is alone in the house when the Romeiro arrives. Nothing new is added to his character: he continues to show resolution and espouses Christian beliefs: "Deus entregou tudo à nossa razão, menos os segredos da sua natureza inefável, os de seu amor e de sua justiça e misericórdia para connosco" (II, iii). There are two notions here: belief in the power of reason and the rational basis of human action, and an acceptance of the superior and inscrutable wisdom of God. Taken together, they constitute the basic elements which seem to underlie Manuel's ultimate decision. But there is surely an ironic contrast between Manuel's self-confidence, his belief in the power of reason to control human destiny, and his faith in the goodness of God, and the fate which eventually befalls him. The anxieties and intuitions of his wife, which he ignores, are ultimately shown to have more validity than Manuel's reason, which leads him into error.

By the third act, the truth of the situation is known and Manuel's main thought is for his daughter. Again his concern for honour is paramount here, on this occasion her loss of honour and her loss of name, and Manuel for the first time casts himself in the role of the tragic hero: "É o castigo terrível do meu erro . . . se foi erro . . . crime sei que não foi" (III, i). This is the revenge of the gods for the fatal flaw, the fatal error of judgement. This error of judgement cannot simply be the fact of his marriage, but must surely be a kind of arrogance, an excessive self-assurance and egocentricity. Manuel, whose every action is designed to enhance his public reputation, his honour, finds himself in a situation of complete dishonour: "posto de alvo à irrisão e ao discurso do vulgo" (III, i). The dialectic of guilt and innocence is worked out through Maria, but Manuel's suffering is entirely bound up with his public reputation: this is his "paixão," but is it purposeful in terms of personal growth, and is it truly tragic? Jorge attempts to turn it to Christian ends, as atonement on the road to salvation, and the play as a whole becomes increasingly imbued with the ethos of the Christian religion. But it could be argued that Manuel's turning away from the world is really devoid of transcendence. Having met, in his own eyes, the opprobrium of the world, he finds it easy to reject it, to become dead to it. The habit he dons does become an existential shroud and in his self-pity he justifies his departure from his family, and particularly from his daughter, by arguing that Maria "não era deste mundo." In all of Act III Manuel continues to be unshakable in his resolve, and the entreaties of his wife are to no avail. His only vacillations are on whether he wishes his daughter alive or dead, for death would save her "antes de que o mundo, este mundo infame e sem comiseração, lhe cuspisse na cara com a desgraça do seu nascimento" (III, i). So Manuel both despises and fears the world, and his sense of personal honour has a decisive role in shaping the tragedy, but he himself shows none of that sense of being divided which is the hallmark of the authentic tragic hero.

Despite this, it is easy to see how Garrett discovered tragic resonances in his story. Aristotle urged the use of traditional stories in tragedy, stories concerned with heroes or kings. Manuel has some of the eminence of a public figure, and his fall is thereby more dramatic. His fall, moreover, is a public fall. His character has a trueness to life but also an intensity that we expect from a tragic figure: his emotions, motives, principles, ideals, exist in a pure, distilled form, and he acts through the full realization of all of them. It is no ordinary mortal who foresakes wife, daughter, and life itself in pursuit of a concept of honour, and the spectacle of his doing so can only inspire awe. There are other factors too. In Manuel's "fall," if that is what it is, we uncover that tragic interaction of character and circumstance which is essential to the genre, the idea that man contributes in some measure to his own undoing. It is often difficult to isolate a single major cause for the hero's downfall in tragedy, but it must involve in some way the interaction of fate and freedom. The tragic hero exercises choice but the very act of choice is perforce a closing of options. Every choice is thus both positive and negative. It is when the hero has made his most fateful decision and experienced its consequences that the play ends.

To some extent complicity in one's own downfall could more readily be attributed to Madalena with whom the play opens. As the curtain rises, Madalena occupies the stage alone. This is surely significant for she is characterised above all by solitude. Her solitude is her anguish which she strives to contain within herself. She is a prey to "contínuos terrores," and for her, "amor," "felicidade" and "desgraça" are all intertwined. Her opening words sum up her situation: she does not enjoy even that illusion of happiness which can last for a time before being swept away. Madalena enjoys no inner tranquillity and the threat of disaster is with her from the outset. From the moment we first encounter the character the sense of the catastrophe to come is already present. Madalena's happiness has never been complete and, for her, love and suffering are equated. Moreover, she endeavours to hide this anguish from her husband and from others: her intimate passion is hers alone. The second scene draws out the implications of these early insights as Madalena's dialogue with Telmo provides the exposition of the play. For both main participants, Maria occupies a central role. The offspring of Madalena's second marriage, she becomes the focal point of the conflict, highlighting the tragedy because of the possibility of her illegitimacy. She epitomises Madalena's sense of guilt at having eventually succumbed to her passion ("poder maior do que as minhas forças"), and the child's very frailty seems somehow both a consequence and a reminder of her doubtful status. Madalena's conflict between love (and Telmo indicates that she never loved D. João) and her duty is actualised in her altercation with Telmo, who assumes the voice of her first husband. It is Telmo who undermines her dream of innocence with his insinuations of guilt. All the action in this opening scene is psychological. Madalena uses Maria as a defence against Telmo, and Telmo uses Maria constantly to keep alive the past. The interaction of the two characters is crucial to the forward movement of the play. Just as Madalena is torn between love and guilt, Telmo is divided between his loyalty to D. João and his affection for Maria, whom he had originally rejected as a symbol of Madalena's betrayal. Telmo's fidelity to his master and belief in his eventual return feeds Madalena's fears, and his frequent premonitions ("agouros e profecias") underline the mood of imminent catastrophe. In psychological terms, Telmo's actions are construed by Madalena as a form of pleasure on his part, for the sustaining of the myth of D. João's survival is a means of causing unhappiness and thereby exacting a kind of revenge on behalf of his master. Madalena refuses to be led by Telmo either into the past or into the future, for these are the worlds which he inhabits ("Deixemo-nos de futuros ... E de passados também"). Both these worlds threaten Madalena who finds only the present, to a degree, secure. The most striking example of Madalena's fear of the past is her terror at the prospect of returning to D. João's house at the request of her husband Manuel: "Mas tu não sabes a violência, o constrangimento de alma, o terror com que eu penso em ter de entrar naquela casa" (I, viii). Madalena's fear of the house is none other than her pangs of conscience, the fear that she will be punished for her act of treachery. All of Madalena's fears and premonitions relate, directly or indirectly, to her guilt.

Act II is the most significant act from Madalena's point of view. In the opening scenes she does not appear, but her illness, fears and apprehensions are constantly alluded to, and an atmosphere of approaching calamity is thereby created. Madalena's febrile state, her mental instability, are revealed in her exaggerated reactions to bad and good news, her oscillation between relative degrees of security and insecurity. Her psychological need for a stable, human relationship is paramount and so her greatest fear is her isolation. She needs her husband in a way that he does not need her, for in her case human needs and emotions take precedence over abstract principles. The possible loss of her husband haunts her: "eu não tenho cuidados. Tenho este medo, este horror de ficar só ... de vir achar-me só no mundo" (II, viii). Naturally this fear of seclusion and isolation, the need for human contact in this life, condition Madalena's attitude to conventional religious attitudes, and provide another perspective on the Christian dimension of the play. The whole of ***Frei Luís de Sousa*** is imbued with the spirit of the Christian religion. It is exemplified in the person of Frei Jorge and, as we have seen, shapes the attitude and conduct of Manuel. All of the characters invoke the name of God, usually for protection or forgiveness, and the Bible and familiar religious expressions are frequently quoted. The move of Manuel and Madalena to the house of D. João, with its proximity to the Dominican monastery, links the source of the catastrophe with its potential solution in religion. This is most obviously prefigured in the example of Joana de Castro, who took vows and entered a convent while her husband was still alive. For Manuel, her action is an exercise in Christian perfection: "É perfeição verdadeira, é a do Evangelho: 'Deixa tudo e segue-me'" (II, viii). But for Madalena it is a living death, the cell is a "cova," the habit a "mortalha." Characteristically, she emphasises the fact that they are "sós." At all the critical points in the play, Madalena is alone: at the beginning, in D. João's house, when the Romeiro arrives, at the end. The more Madalena is alone, the more she has time for introspection, for brooding on her own supposed guilt. Telmo's accusation in Act I that she never loved D. João is shown to have been justified for, in Scene X of Act II, presumbably under pressure because of the coincidence of anniversaries on the "dia fatal," she confesses to Jorge that "Este amor ... começou com um crime, porque eu amei-o assim que o vi ... O pecado estava-me no coração." Interestingly, Madalena uses the theological concepts of sin and temptation. The view of Christianity presented in ***Frei Luís de Sousa*** is not therefore an entirely simple one. In Madalena's case the strength of her own emotions conflicts with the weight of established tradition, of social and religious codes of accepted behaviour which interpose themselves between her and the full attainment of her own happiness. Her explanation is that as her love was illicit, she could never achieve fulfilment in it. D João's return is a representation of that awareness.

By choosing to marry D. Manuel, Madalena is the cause of her own tragedy. Her passion and the workings of fate (the battle of Alcacer-Quivir and João's presumed death) combine to provide the mainspring of the tragedy. On the role played by Fate in the working out of ***Frei Luís de Sousa,*** J. Almeida Pavão has written: "No caso de ***Frei Luís de Sousa,*** dir-se-ia que o fatum não é um acidente estranho à psicologia dos figurantes, mas está adequado à expressão temperamental de cada um destes."[11] Fate appears to work through Madalena's superstitious character, through Maria's powers of perception, through Telmo's expectations, so that even Frei Jorge is affected: "a todos parece que o coração lhes adivinha desgraça. E eu quase que também já se me pega o mal" (II, ix). The weight of fatality seems to hang most heavily over Madalena. After her initial "crime," committed before the start of the play, she is almost entirely a passive character, living in dread of forces that might act upon her. The moment of crisis for her is, naturally, the arrival of the Romeiro.

In the scene of the arrival of the Romeiro, suspense is gradually built up as Madalena resists, and then finally recognises, the truth. It is for this reason that J. Almeida Pavão designates this a recognition scene and states that it recalls "o processo similar do *Rei Edipo,* no diálogo com Jocasta, até à persuasão do mesmo sentimento da culpa involuntária, ao identificar-se como assassino do pai e, como consequentemente, como motor da tragédia."[12] In fact, this is a recognition only in the sense that Madalena is now aware that D. João is not dead and that her daughter is illegitimate. Madalena has always recognised her role as the potential cause of the tragedy. When she comments, on hearing of the Romeiro's abandonment by his family, "Haverá tão má gente ... e tão vil, que tal faça?" (II, xiv), she is, ironically, making a simple moral judgement upon herself. From this point onwards, Madalena barely appears in the action. In Act III she emotionally pleads the human case, attempts to seek a way out by not submitting to the inevitable, but she is relegated to a totally passive role, made to accept the decision already taken by others. Madalena is a victim of her past, of her husband's resolve, and of the Christian ethic with its attendant social codes. Madalena is not motivated by an abstract set of values, but by human emotion, but her tragedy is that she is unable to inspire the same intensity of feeling in her spouse. Love and human relationships are her necessary defence against isolation and her values are an indispensable part of her psychological make-up.

When Madalena knows the full extent of the catastrophe, her reaction is strikingly similar to that of her husband: "Minha filha, minha filha, minha filha! Estou . . . estás . . . perdidas, desonradas" (ɪɪ, xiv), for in the opening of Act ɪɪɪ, Manuel is at once afflicted by thoughts of his daughter's disgrace. Maria again emerges as the means whereby the tragedy most clearly manifests itself. An exceptional child, sensitive, imaginative, curious, introspective, she is aware of her parents' constant preoccupation with her. Because of the insecurity of her home environment, Maria is unsure of herself, she is beset with a crisis of identity, conscious that her life and her temperament are somehow incompatible: "O que eu sou . . . só eu sei, minha mãe . . . E não sei, não, não sei nada, senão que o que devia ser não sou" (ɪ, iv). Moreover, she is characterised by a spirit of revolt, unable and unwilling to accept things as they are. For example, to Jorge's "o mundo é doutro modo," she retorts, "Emendá-lo" (ɪ, v). This attitude prepares the way for her rejection of that scale of values which involves the disintegration of her family. To an extent, Maria is engaged in a quest to discover the truth and at the same time to find herself. This need to be oneself is reflected in her words to her father when in difficulty: "Mostrai-lhes quem sois" (ɪ, vii). Her symptoms of feverishness, excitement seeking, restlessness are all related to this basic need. Although always present in the minds and decisions of those around her, Maria plays no positive role in the action from which she is absent, from her departure to Lisbon with her father until the penultimate act of the play which is, in essence, her recognition scene. Although she has sensed that the reality of her life was in some way connected with the battle of Alcacer-Quivir and the myth of Sebastianism, when confronted with it, she seeks to deny or discard it. She rejects the claims of the past in favour of the new imperatives of the present, and repudiates a God who would acquiesce in and even demand the destruction of a family: "Que ceremonias são estas? Que Deus é esse que está nesse altar, e quer roubar o pai e a mãe a sua filha?" (ɪɪɪ, xi). Unable to acquire the identity which is hers, Maria dies. Her death is perhaps the most tragic element in the play, the defeat of optimism, the crushing of life by abstract and, it is implied, outmoded values. Her final outburst is a rejection of these very values and acts as a counterweight to the words of Frei Jorge in the last moments of the final act.

The character who perhaps is the most pathetic and innocent victim in ***Frei Luís de Sousa,*** although for a large part of it he exists merely as an abstract entity, a mere hypothesis, is D. João himself. Throughout the play, however, he is a dominating presence, associated with the past and with fate. He lives primarily in the minds of others, in Madalena's fears of his return, in Telmo's hopes for his return, in Maria's faith in Sebastianism, and even in the intuitions of Frei Jorge and Manuel de Sousa. Up until Scenes xiv and xv of Act ɪɪ, João is mainly a catalyst, exacerbating the characters' anxieties and, ironically, he is more of a reality while he remains a mere threat. Once he appears in the play, once he is proved to exist, he lacks existence himself. The other characters embark on courses of action which change their lives but which also release them from the threat of his return. João, from being the "outro," that otherness by which the others defined their existence, becomes "Ninguém." In this sense, the Romeiro undergoes the most profound recognition in the play. His identity is founded upon his former relationships and, once these relationships are superseded, he ceases to have any real identity. He himself appears to recognise from an early stage that he is dead to his family: "contaram com a minha morte, fizeram a sua felicidade com ela; hão-de jurar que me não conhecem" (ɪɪ, xiv). Nowhere is this more strikingly revealed than in his relationship with Telmo. In the first act, as we have seen, Telmo stands as the custodian of his master's memory, feeling the jealousy that he himself might have felt. This loyalty is subsequently put to the test by new bonds of affection so that no value can be seen to be absolute. Telmo's relationship with Maria complicates his relationship with D. João and he senses that ultimately the two cannot co-exist, but that the one will have to be sacrificed to the other. By scene iv of Act ɪɪɪ, Telmo can say: "não sou já o mesmo homem." In the case of Telmo there is a complete reversal of the world he had constructed for himself. The very event which he had anticipated and hoped for provokes, when it finally comes, a wholly negative response on his part. Telmo's love transformed his world. This is the final recongition for João, who says: "D. João de Portugal morreu no dia em que sua mulher disse que morrera" (ɪɪɪ, v). Despite a momentary hesitation in the following scene when he misreads Madalena's words, he accepts his loss of identity. This too is a kind of death, the death of his former self.

Although we may isolate characters in a play for the purposes of analysis, character itself, though important for creating in the audience a sense of involvement in what is taking place, is not of the essence of drama. Aristotle himself talked of "an imitation not of persons but of action and life, of happiness and misery. All human happiness and misery take the form of action."[13] In Aristotle's view, then, action, which is embodied in plot, is paramount. Characters exist for the sake of the action. They are agents, but they are also victims, for their actions, designed to bring them happiness, inevitably lead to situations in which their happiness is in some way frustrated. Tragedy implies a view of human existence where the threat of suffering is always present, and this suffering is neither willed not totally unmotivated. This paradoxical quality is central to the tragic vision, which is founded on tensions and ambiguities. Characters are forced to make decisions or choices upon which their future happiness depends, but these choices involve of necessity either sacrifice or conflict with the desires of other people. Such situations are the seed-bed of tragedy. All of this can be said to apply to ***Frei Luís de Sousa,*** but because of the ending of the play, which underlines a strand that had consistently run through it, the force of the tragedy is attenuated by the all-embracing Christian vision in the context of which the whole action is set. Before attempting to pinpoint the tragic core of ***Frei Luís de Sousa,*** it is essential to consider the implications of this Christian vision.

To the extent that tragedy has, to some measure, to do with man and the gods, if only in the form of Fate or Fortune, it is easy to accept a close correlation between tragedy and religion. Insofar as tragedy sees man in relation to the universe, it transcends the limits of the here-and-now. The fact that tragedy began, in W. Macneile Dixon's words, as "an affair with the gods,"[14] and owes its sense of mystery to this, suggests its religious dimension. Tragedy explores the inscrutable ways of the gods, particularly the source of human suffering, and its most poignant manifestation, death. But when Frei Jorge, in ***Frei Luís de Sousa,*** closes the play with words which direct our attention away from present conflict to a world beyond this one, he is suggesting an altogether different kind of religious dimension from the one outlined here: "Meus irmãos, Deus aflige neste mundo aqueles que ama. A coroa de glória não se dá senão no Céu" (III, xii). These words do not alter the anguish felt at God's visitation of suffering upon human beings, but they do direct suffering towards a defined spiritual purpose. This is not Aeschylus's "Wisdom comes alone through suffering." Rather it is an exhortation towards humility, an acceptance of the order of the world, the very opposite of tragic revolt. Nevertheless, such an outlook embodies a profound and in many respects convincing explanation of the tragedy of human existence. For the Christian, man lives in both time and eternity, and this duality is the source of his tragic conflict. What is necessary to exist in one sphere is denied by existence in the other. Subordinated to the dictates of the eternal, man's life can be only fear, anxiety and tragedy. ***Frei Luís de Sousa*** does explore human life as predicament. The theological substratum of the play means that guilt is inevitably construed as sin. As a Christian, however, Manuel de Sousa is clear in his vision and undergoes no real inner conflict. He suffers, but his suffering involves no growth in knowledge, simply a confirmation of existing faith. The view which ultimately prevails is that Heaven will compensate for suffering in this life, which is as nothing when compared to the joy of the afterlife. There is, as we have seen, no dilemma for Manuel, who cannot be both a Christian and a tragic hero. If we are to discover the germ of tragedy in ***Frei Luís de Sousa*** we must look elsewhere, in the interaction of the characters and their conflicts which constitute the true action of the play.

José Augusto França perhaps comes closest to pinpointing the real tragedy of ***Frei Luís de Sousa*** when he defines Madalena as the "centro trágico de peça," and writes of her: "Com a consciência dividida, igualmente vive a drama da unidade, da coerência do eu. Ama o marido; mas, tendo provavelmente esquecido o Outro, quando este aparece sente-se comprometida numa espécie de dupla fidelidade, irremediável neste baixo mundo."[15] We may of course dispute the contention that she has forgotten D. João, for he is constantly in her thoughts, thereby illustrating the central notion of the importance of the past in the shaping of the present. But Madalena's conflict is accurately depicted by Augusto-França as one of "dupla fidelidade," for dualities and contradictions will always inform the tragic experience. We have seen that Christian man lives in two spheres which demand incompatible values. On a more strictly emotional level, Madalena cannot integrate the opposing facets of her present situation. Madalena suffers because she is unusually sensitive to the contradictions inherent in her own state, crystallised in the existence of her daughter. From the very opening lines of the play, she insists on the vast opposites which characterise the universe and the life of man. The antithesis "felicidade-desgraça" is only her way of articulating this fundamental duality which is expressed in a whole series of opposites: love and duty, desire and fulfilment, what is and what ought to be. The source of her tragic suffering is her awareness of the existence and force of these opposites which struggle to co-exist. The character itself is beset by inner contradictions which manifest themselves in alternate states of anxiety and calm. However, the duality which makes her most truly tragic in the final analysis is the fact that she is simultaneously guilty and innocent. Indeed, without this paradoxical duality, there could be no genuine tragic emotion. If Madalena were simply evil, guilty and punished, there could be no pity; if she were a totally innocent victim, only pity. Rather she exhibits that curious ambivalence of culpability which makes her both tragic and representative of humanity. Her guilt is of course her passion and her decision to marry. Her innocence is the purity of her love. It is made clear that Madalena made every effort to verify the death of her husband and by the standards of common sense and justice she could not be held to have guilt. But her guilt resides within herself, in her own awareness of the possibility of his being alive, and in her readiness to accept the coincidence of chance and her own passion. Once D. João returns, the tragedy focusses on the opposing tendencies of the two spouses or, put in more abstract terms, the conflict between reason and passion. It is hardly surprising that Madalena resists the idea of separation, for the arrival of the Romeiro is merely the actualisation of a dilemma which has existed in her mind all along and on which she had already decided. Thus Madalena illustrates the awesome nature of the fall into guilt, becoming guilty by doing the apparently guiltless thing.

This is one way of construing ***Frei Luís de Sousa*** as tragedy. But in a wider sense too it can be said to embody a vision that is profoundly tragic, and one that is not necessarily incompatible with its obvious Christian inspiration. Suffering is not tragic in itself and in order to be so it must be accompanied by some form of significant recognition. The tragic hero comes out of the other side of his experience in some way transformed, having moved on to a higher level of insight. It is possible of course for this recognition to be transferred to the audience or spectator. In ***Frei Luís de Sousa,*** the idea that the tragic hero in some way leaves the world a better person for his suffering takes the explicit form of the essentially Christian notion of regeneration. This is the Christian tragedy's particular *anagnorisis,* that recognition of ultimate meaning, that glimpse of pattern, purpose and order in the midst of a bewilderingly incoherent and often painful world. This is the perception that is born of passion. Through the tragic experience man sees his situation as whole and paradoxically perceives the happiness that comes from suffering. Experience is given shape and significance as man seems to relate to something beyond himself, to God and to the universe. The religious dimension is as important in tragedy as the social dimension, and both are necessary. The sense of the inscrutability of the Gods adds a peculiar force and power to the story; the moral relations of men with one another in society keep it firmly in the human realm. The connections and dissonances between the two realms underpin the tragic experience, and the recognition that accompanies it may be seen as a kind of conversion. In ***Frei Luís de Sousa,*** this indeed takes the form of being born again and is symbolised in the final putting on of the monastic habit. With the death of Maria and the virtual removal of the two spouses from the social and earthly domain, order is restored. Despair in the face of the world's chaos and incomprehensibility gives way to an acceptance of a wider purpose and design. Nevertheless, if this seems to be the play's final insight, and perhaps none other is possible for a man in Almeida Garrett's time and situation, the articulation of it is not left entirely unqualified. Both spouses are not equally reconciled to their fate, and Maria gives eloquent expression to the belief that not only humans, but the gods too, are fools. This ambivalence, the pity aroused by the vision of apparently undeserved suffering, the terror felt before its ultimately unknowable cause and, in human terms, tragic consequences, all endow human experience with a sense of awe-inspiring mystery in which tensions and contradictions are never fully resolved. It is not the fall of any single tragic figure, but a more universal vision of human existence which traces paradoxical patterns of death in life through the interaction of persons, their circumstances and the unknowable reality beyond, that creates, in a compelling and convincing manner, the possibilities of tragedy in ***Frei Luís de Sousa.***

Notes

1. José Augusto-França, *O Romantismo em Portugal,* Vol. I (Lisbon, 1974), 260.
2. João Gaspar Simões, *Almeida Garrett* (Lisbon, 1964), 114.
3. Gaspar Simões, 114.
4. J. Almeida Lucas, Introduction to his edition of *Frei Luís de Sousa* (Lisbon, 1946), xxxviii.
5. Almeida Garrett, *Obras,* II (Oporto, 1963), 1082. All references are to this edition and are incorporated into the text of the article.
6. I. A. Richards, *Principles of Literary Criticism* (London, 1924), 246.
7. Of the many books and articles that have shaped my thinking on tragedy and which are not acknowledged directly, the following have been particularly valuable: Clifford Leach, *Tragedy* (London, 1969), T. R. Henn, *The Harvest of Tragedy* (London, 1956), Raymond Williams, *Modern Tragedy* (London, 1966), Herbert Weisinger, *Tragedy and the Paradox of the Fortunate Fall* (Michigan, 1953), and the essays in *Tragedy: Modern Essays in Criticism,* edited by Laurence Michel and Richard B. Sewall (Englewood Cliffs, 1963).
8. Frank Rahill, *The World of Melodrama* (Pennsylvania, 1967), xiv.
9. Eduardo Lourenço, *Estética do Romantismo em Portugal* (Lisbon, 1974), 109.
10. Manuel himself talks of "esta afronta" (I, vii). Maria had already used this word twice in connection with her father (I, iii and vi).
11. J. Almeida Pavão, "*Frei Luís de Sousa*: O trágico e uma intromissão do cómico," *Arquipélago* (1980), 183.
12. Almeida Pavão, 196.
13. Aristotle, *On the Art of Poetry,* translated by Ingram Bywater (Oxford, 1967), 37.
14. W. Macneile Dixon, *Tragedy* (London, 1924), 68.
15. José Augusto-França, 261.

Annabela Rita (essay date 2010)

SOURCE: Rita, Annabela. "Two Models of Gardens in the Portuguese Literature and Culture." *Gardens of Madeira—Gardens of the World: Contemporary Approaches.* Ed. José Eduardo Franco, Ana Cristina da Costa Gomes, and Beata Elzbieta Cieszynska. Newcastle upon Tyne: Cambridge Scholars, 2010. 128-37. Print.

[*In the following essay, Rita analyzes Garrett's depiction of Joaninha's garden in the Valley of Santarém in* Travels in My Homeland. *Rita maintains that the Edenic landscape symbolizes an ideal version of Portugal, where national history blends with mythology.*]

We could travel along some routes through the territory of literature and point out some of the more outstanding gardens presences. Since Antiquity (with Pliny the Younger, Ovid, Hesiod, Homer, Virgil or Sappho) passing by Chrétien of Troyes, Guillaume de Lorris and Jean de Meun, Dante, Boccaccio, Rabelais, Boileau, La Fontaine, Saint-Simon, Voltaire, Bernardin de Saint-Pierre, Alphonse de Lamartine, Rousseau, Gustav Flaubert . . . , to our contemporaneity. It would be a long journey, a crossing with many absences and excessively long for the occasion. We choose a briefer option with an itinerary in which we consecrate two different but complementary models, which allow us to point out an aesthetic, imaginary, social and political journey in the way of that universality for which we yearn so much.

The referred two models are to be picked out from known narratives: the interior garden and the one that lies on the edge of the sea. One from the 19th century, of Garrettian memory; the other, from the 20th century, Sophia's. From one to the other, we can symbolise a trajectory of history and literature, national and European: from the interior to the sea, from the most restricted nationality to a desired universality.

So, we start with the geographically interior garden, valley or forest, whose location delimits it.

And we choose Santarem's Valley of ***Viagens na Minha Terra*** (1846),[1] a work that belongs to a long and metamorphic literary lineage that proposes and elaborates a new model: the narrative of journeys. In the text, we get to Santarem's Valley via a bridge, Asseca's bridge, a threshold and symbolic transition between two fictions. It is an exceptional place that begins by being described in a way that identifies it with the mythical Eden:

> Santarem's Valley is one of those places privileged by nature, a mild and charming place in which the plants, the air and the situation are in a very gentle and perfect harmony: There is nothing grandiose nor sublime, but there is a kind of symmetry of colours, tones, of disposition in everything that is seen and felt, so that it seems that peace, health, peace of mind and the quietness of the heart should live there, to live a reign of love and benevolence. Bad passions, mean thoughts, grief and the vilenesses of life must run away. We can imagine here the Eden that the first man inhabited with his innocence and with the virginity of his heart.
>
> To the left of the valley, and protected on the north side by the mountain that sheers down, there is a grass plot, beautifully luxuriant and varied. The beech tree, the ash and the poplar interlace their friendly branches, the honeysuckle and the musk-rose hang their garlands and wreaths of flowers; the congossa, the foetuses and the hollyhock of the valley dress and carpet the ground.
>
> To enhance the beauty of the picture, through the trees can be seen the open window of an old house, but not in ruins—with a certain air of rude comfort and with a colour faded by time and the southern high winds to which it is exposed. The window is wide and low; it seems more ornamented and older than the rest of the building that, nevertheless, can be barely seen . . . That window interested me.
>
> (Chapter X)

Included and delimited, geographically and in the image that the text provides, Santarem's Valley appears as a closed garden, like its mythical archetype, framed by four rivers, which suggests other identifications, one of them being the identification with Portugal, which represents the original Eden.

And, inside the imaginary frame of that closed garden that superposes the national and the mythical, another frame is included: the window of Joaninha, an empty sign to be filled out by the narrative speech. A window that aestheticises definitively the stories felt and seen through it, because it is textually included, as a mechanism of the articulation of the stories, the most emblematic image of the theory of perspective and representation: the Renaissance window of Alberti.[2] Promoting the articulation between two stories that had Santarem's Valley as privileged sceneries, it also insinuates the principle of specularity and identity between exterior and interior, that is to say, between Portugal and Joaninha, both represented in and through the valley.

But let us still consider the character Joaninha in whom Portugal and its literature are reflected and symbolised.

The character's construction outlines a trajectory that begins in Chapter X, different from the European civilisational feminine models (the French, the English and the German) and then, similar to nature (comparing fragments of both) to the point of blending with it, offering us an unforgettable framed portrait whose composition is a point of multiple aesthetic and imaginary confluence.

That "portrait," framed by the denotative signs of the description, opens Chapter XX of ***Viagens na Minha Terra***:[3] Joaninha asleep.

I have already had the opportunity of commenting, in a brief decalogue, on the aesthetic confluence in which this composition was generated, demonstrating that Garrettian writing is filled with traditions and references, named or subtly referenced,[4] and for that reason I will not dwell upon the enumeration of the different lineages, but only in what motivates this evocation: the symbolisation of the eternal feminine.

I call your attention to the portrait included in another landscape before described as 'one' of the most beautiful and delicious places on earth: Santarem's Valley, homeland of nightingales and honeysuckles, strip of beautiful beech trees and of green fresh laurels (Chapter IX):

> On a kind of rustic bench of vegetation covered with grasses and wild camomile, Joaninha, half leaned and half lying, was in a deep sleep. The dim light of the sundown, still filtered by the branches of the trees, delicately illuminated the damsel's expressive features; and the graceful form of her body was softly and sensually drawn in the steamy and vague background of earth's exhalations, with an uncertainty and indecision of outlines that increases the charm of the portrait, and allows the exalted imagination to travel the whole scale of harmony of feminine grace.
>
> She was an ideal of *demi-jour* of Parisian *coquette*: without art or study, nature had prepared it in its *boudoir* of foliage, perfumed by the breeze that came from the meadows.
>
> As in those poetic and popular legends of one of the most poetic books ever written, *Flos Sanctorum,* in which the dear and predestined bird always accompanies the kind saint of its affection—Joaninha was not there without her melodious companion. From the thick foliage, which composed the canopy of that bed of grass, could be heard a torrent of melodies, vague and waving as a jungle in the wind; strong, brave, and amazing in its irregularity and invention like the barbarian songs of a wild poet of the mountains . . . It was a nightingale, one of the dear nightingales of the valley, that was watching and keeping its protectoress company, close to the little girl who was named after the birds.
>
> With the approach of the soldiers, and the whispering of the short dialogue referred to at the end of the last chapter, the delicious song of the little bird had ceased for a while; but when the officer, after posting the sentries, returned on tiptoe and passed cautiously under the trees, the nightingale had already started to sing and did not stop again; he amplified it with trills and chirps, and from the top of its very acute voice he lowered it progressively emitting such painful and deeply felt signs that showed nothing but the prelude of the most tender and soft love scene the valley had ever seen.
>
> (Chapter XX)

The way it blends with nature bestows it the statute of image, double, reflection, emanation, which was already signalised, in the green of fascinating eyes that, besides being the reflection of Santarem's Valley and, through it, of Portugal, also evoked a European tradition rich in a mythical dimension (Venus, heroines of the kingdom of elves, and of love stories, sleeping beauties and others). In its turn, the nightingale associates her with an erudite literary line (where it appears as a representative of the poet and as a companion of young predecessors of dramatic love as is the case with *Menina Moça* de Bernardim) and with a religious lineage of that calendar of martyrs that is *Flos Sanctorum.*

So due to successive implications and symbolic registrations, Joaninha, "ideal and very spiritual," reconciles in herself a plural identitary representation: configures the eternal feminine and associates it with the matricial and telluric nature and with Portugal, usually considered in the political and masculine version of its heroes. And it clouds with apprehension and drama the charm and future of them all: hers, as a protagonist of a love story that is foreseen and that has several precedents, the one of Portugal threatened by the winds of alterity; and the one of nature, mankind is living a nostalgic but hopeless divorce.

Asymmetrically to the old popular story, Sleeping Beauty will wake up to the drama of love that only death appeases.

In this new Eden that Garrett places in Santarem's Valley, a new drama will occur, played by a national pair: Joaninha and Carlos.

Myth(s) and history overlap in fiction, reinforcing certain meanings: exactly the ones that are imported from a hermeneutics of national history. 'Guarding' it, instead of cherubim and flaming swords,[5] the traveller is confronted by two figures of postponed dead: Grandmother Francisca and Frei Dinis, receivers of the tragic Word (Carlo's letter). And the old myth(s) continue(s), therefore, to work as an explanatory outline of reality, giving the authors that update them the aura of an enigmatic Sphinx and giving their narratives an unexpected parabolic dimension.

Now I will move forward towards the sea. And on its shore I search for the example and for a more Universalist representation: "A Casa do Mar,"[6] by Sophia de Mello Breyner Andresen. House—"garden that moves forward through the dune blending with the beach."[7]

"The house is built on the dune and away from the other houses. That isolation creates in it a unity, a world." Thus begins the story by Sophia of Mello Breyner Andresen, retrieving so many other 'whelk-houses' that, in poetry, lie along the sea with gardens of sand, dunes and sea air. And she continues, the description of the place:

> The garden stretches towards the dune and blends with the beach (. . .). From there we can see, southwards, in the end of distance, (. . .) a city that stretches to the seashore. Between the house and the distant city there are so many dunes that it resembles a large deserted garden, uncultivated and transparent, where the wind (. . .) bends the high, dry and fine droughts and fine weeds (. . .).[8]

Framed by a "halo of solitude" and by its isolation in the dune,[9] as well as by textual cyclicality, that place also constitutes a portrait that is offered for our observation as a new and different version of the mythical Eden:

"And everything seems intact and total as if that was the place that preserves in itself the nude force of the first created day."[10]

And it offers itself, influencing our reading through a founding statement of our interpretative gesture: in it, everything is "as if (. . .) it was something else."[11] The text later clarifies this statement, distinguishing two knowledge thresholds and choosing one of them:

> Who looks outside through the hall's windows and sees the granite wall, the distant trees and the roofs to the west, what is seen appears to be any place on earth, like an accident, an occasional place among the chance of things. But whoever moves towards the balcony of the main room sees, ahead, the beach, the sky, the sand, the light and the air, recognises that nothing there is chance but cause, that this is a place of exaltation and wonder where reality emerges and shows its face and its evidence.[12]

Such textual encoding gives the place, that house, the "garden that moves towards the dune and blends with the beach,"[13] the palimpsest dimension, in which the reader should look for alterity.

The reading of the story makes me follow an itinerary in which I will highlight, at least, four interpretative possibilities articulated by progressive aestheticising and by the polysemy and conjugation of certain motives (earth/air/sea/house/whelk/mirror/frame/portrait/window/door/balcony/garden/beach/etc.).

Thus being, in a more literal perspective, we consider ourselves before a description of a house-garden on the beach. A house-garden that the speech makes us observe from the outside and, then, from the inside, on a tour guided by a disguised instance that makes us watch the sea. As we will verify, it is an iniciatic itinerary induced by a sacerdotal presence-absence that will make us see what is described and recognise what is suggested, which I will now point out.

Then, the similarity relation between fiction and existential circumstances, temporal and spatial indefinition and universalising motives make us recognise, increasingly, the house as a symbol of a knowledge of the universe and the paths that lead to it. It is already the full domain of the symbolism where everything is "as if (. . .) it was something else,"[14] a relation woven by the metonymy that draws everything nearer (house-sea-universe).

However, this will not yet be a tranquillising reading: the systematic recognition of motives and images of other texts by Sophia suggests the *story* and the *house-garden* as a kind of *aesthetic synthesis* where authorial insignia are inserted in a kind of identitary museology. The intimate memory of the poet's work is subsumed in him and shapes him: house, sea, gardens at the seashore, elemental images, shells, whelks, etc.), metonymical images (I smell the sea air, etc.), aesthetic and symbolic images (thresholds: door, windows, balcony, beach, mirrors, portraits, etc.) transform the house and the speech that represents it into a kind of house of mirrors that reflects the whole work of the author. Therefore, each object acquires "ambiguous transparency," transformed into a meeting place (. . .) where the "apparition"[15] emerges from the visible: of Sophia and her poetry in superimpositions.

And "A Casa do Mar" appears, for that reason, overflowing with evocations that cipher it and in which it is aesthetically legitimated like a "lagoon where are mirrored narcissistic rose palaces."[16]

After arriving at this point, however, I still confront myself with other recognitions: themes and motives of Western art.

Continuing the journey through the house, I record a multiplicity of mirrors, frames and windows, signs of an art of representation whose geometrisation was encoded by the Renaissance and that art always explored and complexified.

Multiplicity creates an imbricated architecture, complex, reflexive, of shadows, transparencies and reflexes that seem to compose a story of metamorphosis. In this way, the house assumes a sort of museology of Western art, of its ghosts, framing them and hanging them on the wall for us to see.

One of those images, which is central, is the inhabitant of the house. But it appears progressively, staging the story of its own 'revelation.' First, it is a felt presence, its existence and action announced by signals. "(. . .) the cigarette on the ashtray burns (. . .)"[17]

"In the air is the scent of the perfume that rises from a bottle of golden and black glass that someone left open."[18]

Then appear fragments of images, synecdoches of a body of unbearable lightness, of spiritualised woman, ethereal being or reflections-mirages that surprise me or that are surprised by me:

"There the air, in front of the mirrors, oscillates and seems to burn as if the hands (. . .) smoothed and twisted long locks of hair thick as harvest fields and light as fire."[19]

A figure caressed by the wind that

> makes the blond of the hair flutter in front of the eyes,[20] semi-hidden 'by the twilight and the light' in the snapshot of a picture, the polite hand (. . .) that gently rests on the table, the calm and clear profile with the hair shining over the dark dress, the (. . .) delicate neck,[21] emerging from the shadow ('the face emerges white from the shadow') or reflected in the mirror (that 'shows the other side of the profile'). A figure that lets herself be imagined in the room with 'something glaucous and golden':
>
> A woman with green eyes and blond hair, light and long, of a shiny and shady blond, and whose perfume is the scent of sandalwood. The beauty of her forehead is as sober as the beauty of the architrave of a temple. Her wrists are as fragile as stems. In her hands, through the thinness of the skin, the thought emerges (. . .), showing or hiding the endless brightness of the magnetic, green, grey, blue eyes and immense as seas (. . .) [The] hands, soft as magnolia petals (. . .) long locks of hair as thick as harvest fields and light as fire.[22]

A figure, whose classic perfection seems to emerge, finally, identified in all her splendour in the final climax of the story where the incense rises in the air. First, trimmed by it (image advanced by the trimming of the cigarette smoke and the perfume of the open bottle):

> "(. . .) a jar of blue curdled glass full of carnations whose perfume stands out, clear and delimited, in the saline perfume of the air."[23] Then, the incense expands in triumph, in the celebration of beauty's epiphany: "(. . .) and, along the shining sands, sea smells and mists of incense rise as a celebration."[24] It is Venus who, finally, imposes on us, who makes herself be pursued by the "announcement to the final revelation."

And, in that diffuse figure that is finally revealed, Venus, the aesthetic icon, the text and the universe are represented, presenting themselves in triumph, epiphanically:

> Through the gesture of bending the neck and of shaking the manes, the four rows of waves, sweeping the beach, seem like white rows of horses that in the continuous progress count and measure their inner gasp of storm. The breaking of the waves populates the space of triumph and uproar. In the ascent and descent of the waves, the universe ordains its turbulence and its smile and, along the shining sands, sea smells and mists arise as a celebration incense.[25]

The story celebrates, thus, the act of reinstauration, by the Word, of the archetypal Eden. The writing and the reading unite in that creative and iniciatic process. And the garden by the sea imposes its universal dimension.

* * *

In short, the garden, cosmogonic place par excellence, encodes, in a certain way, the identitarian projections of those who lie at its origin, those who actually or imaginably build them.

Many of those gardeners-aesthetes, like Garrett, have the tendency to confine its identification to the place they occupy, to the homeland or motherland that generated them, promoting them to symbols of an identity, simultaneously, individual and national.

Others, like Sophia, drag those gardens to the threshold between that place and the one beyond:

> I saw a garden that spread
> Along a hillside suspended
> Miraculously above the sea
> That from the distance against it rode
> Unknown and immense.
> . . . .
> Garden where the wind fights
> And that the hand of the sea sculpts and carves.
> Nude, rough, devastated,
> In a continuous exaltation,
> Broken garden
> Of immensity.
> Small cup
> Overflowing with annunciation
> That sometimes passes in things.[26]

They see the universe turned into a garden or gardens that welcome them and us:

> In all gardens I shall bloom,
> In all I will drink the full moon,
> When finally in my end I possess
> All the beaches where the sea waves.
>
> One day I will be the sea and the sand,
> To whatever exists I will unite,
> And my blood drags in each vein
> That hug that one day will open.
>
> Then I will receive in my desire
> Every fire that inhabits the forest
> Known by me as a kiss.
>
> Then I will be the rhythm of landscapes,
> The secret abundance of that party
> That I saw promised in the images.[27]

And, with this, they consecrate their integration in the limitless universe where the music of the spheres is heard, to whose rhythm Kepler conceived his *Mysterium Cosmographicum* (1596) and, long before (Pythagoras and others) and long after him, so many wanted to hear . . . projecting themselves in the universe, 'AND through all the presences / walking towards the only unity,'[28] getting lost in it:

> The voice goes up the last steps
> I hear the impersonal winged word
> That I recognise for not being mine.[29]

For this and much more, the garden is one of the most meaningful images of the human imaginary, outstanding in all cultures and times, truly universal and fascinating.

Notes

1. The first six chapters of this work were initially published in *Revista Universal Lisbonense* in 1843; the complete book then appeared in 1845-46 in two volumes (Lisbon: Tipografia Gazeta dos Tribunais).

2. Traditionally, the window imposed itself as an image of the quotation. First, in the quotation of reality: in *Da Pintura (1435-36),* Leon Alberti assumed it to be a cutting or frame surrounding the world, favouring its representative "transportation" to canvas, and Albrecht Dürer, in his reflection on the subject (*Underweysung der Messung,* 1527) presented several instruments through which the artist could "scientifically" paint reality. Others assumed it to be a metaphor of *perspective,* a "cognitive metaphor." It is the case of Claudio Guillen in *Literature as System* (*On the Concept and Metaphor of Perspective* (Princeton: Princeton University Press, 1971) [1st edition 1966], 283-371), Erwin Panofsky, *La Perspective comme Forme Symbolique* (Paris: Minuit, 1975) and so on.

3. I have already spoken about this Garrettian work in "Almeida Garrett: *Viagens*—entre o enigmatismo e a

curiosidade," in *No Fundo dos Espelhos. Incursões na cena Literária* (Porto: Edições Caixotim, 2003), 11-33, see edition with new text fixation published by Edições Caixotim in 2004.

4. See Joaninha Adormecida, "Um 'quadro' habitado de memórias," in *Emergências Estéticas* (Lisbon: Roma Editora, 2006), 13-28.
5. Gen 3, 23-24.
6. Story included in the volume by Sophia de Mello Breyner entitled *Histórias da Terra e do Mar* (Lisbon: Texto Editora, 1994), 57-72.
7. *Ibidem,* 61.
8. *Ibidem,* 61.
9. *Ibidem,* 71.
10. *Ibidem,* 72.
11. *Ibidem,* 65.
12. *Ibidem,* 71.
13. *Ibidem,* 61.
14. *Ibidem,* 65.
15. The quotations are from the edition of *Obra Poética* by the author (used editions: Lisbon: Editorial Caminho, I-II of 1996 and III of 1998). For the sake of convenience, I will make the references using the initials and numbers of the volumes. Here, respectively, *OP* III, 121 and 341.
16. Sophia de Mello Breyner Andresen. *Musa* (Lisbon, Caminho, 1994), 34.
17. Sophia de Mello Breyner Andresen, *Histórias da Terra e de Mar, op cit,* 64.
18. *Ibidem,* 67.
19. *Ibidem,* 68.
20. *Ibidem,* 61.
21. *Ibidem,* 65.
22. *Ibidem,* 68.
23. *Ibidem,* 70.
24. *Ibidem,* 72.
25. *Ibidem,* 72.
26. *OP* I, 82-83.
27. *OP* I, 58.
28. *OP* I, 46.
29. *OP* III, 349-350.

FURTHER READING

Bibliographies

Carvalho, Alberto. "Bibliografia." *Sentido e unidade das* Viagens na minha terra *de Almeida Garrett.* Lisbon: Comunicação, 1981. 71-9. Print.

A bibliography of Garrett's published works and criticism on *Travels in My Homeland,* Portuguese Romanticism, and related contextual sources. Not available in English.

Lima, Henrique de Campos Ferreira. *Inventário do espólio literário de Garrett.* Coimbra: Biblioteca Geral da U, 1948. Print.

A complete bibliography of Garrett's work. Lima includes unpublished manuscripts and correspondence, as well as a list of known holdings of Garrett's personal library. Not available in English.

Biographies

Coelho, Latino. "O visconde de Almeida Garrett." *Garrett e Castilho: Estudos biográficos.* Lisbon: Santos e Vieira, 1917. 91-222. Print.

A detailed biography by one of Garrett's contemporaries. Not available in English.

Gomes de Amorim, Francisco. *Garrett: Memórias biográphicas.* 3 vols. Lisbon: Nacional, 1881-84. Print.

Written by the friend in whose arms the author is said to have died, Gomes de Amorim's account is considered among the best known of Garrett's biographies. Not available in English.

Magalhães, José Calvet de. *Garrett, a vida ardente de um romântico.* Venda Nova: Bertrand, 1996. Print.

Provides information of Garrett's life within the context of Romanticism. Not available in English.

Sousa, José Baptista de. *Almeida Garrett (1799-1854), Founder of Portuguese Romanticism: A Study in Anglo-Portuguese Cultural Interaction.* Lewiston: Mellen, 2011. Print.

Considers Garrett's time in Britain and his correspondence with British figures. Sousa reveals the complicated influence of the British and British Romantic literature on the founder of Portuguese Romanticism.

Criticism

Barbas, Helena. *Almeida Garrett, o Trovador moderno.* Lisbon: Salamandra, 1994. Print.

Collects three lengthy studies on Garrett. In the first, Barbas examines Garrett's 1843 version of *Romances and Popular Songs* and compares the author's nationalist project with similar ideologies among the British Romantics and Renaissance authors. In the second, she analyzes Garrett's efforts to reestablish a national Portuguese theater and revive techniques from Portuguese Renaissance drama in *A Play by*

Gil Vicente. In the final section, Barbas discusses Garrett's 1848 work *As profecias do Bandarra* (may be translated as *The Prophecies of Bandarra*) and his Sebastianism. Not available in English.

Bishop-Sanchez, Kathryn. *Utopias desmascaradas: O mito do bom selvagem e a procura do homem natural na obra de Almeida Garrett.* Lisbon: Casa da Moeda, 2008. Print.

Details the influence of Jean-Jacques Rousseau's concept of the noble savage on Garrett's work. Bishop-Sanchez traces the circulation of Rousseau's writing in Portugal, where it was largely prohibited. Not available in English.

Buescu, Helena. "The *Polis,* Romantic Tragedy, and Untimeliness in *Frei Luís de Sousa.*" *Transforming Tragedy, Identity and Community.* Spec. issue of *European Romantic Review* 20.5 (2009): 603-11. Print.

Examines the contrast between the private and public spheres in *Brother Luiz de Sousa.* Buescu elucidates Garrett's attempt to establish a national drama that exposes the disharmony between the civic duty and emotional turmoil of Portuguese citizens.

Carvalho, Alberto. *Sentido e unidade das* Viagens na minha terra *de Almeida Garrett.* Lisbon: Comunicação, 1981. Print.

Discusses *Travels in My Homeland* in the contexts of Garrett's life, early nineteenth-century Portuguese politics and history, and the nationalistic tensions in Europe during the same period. Carvalho includes an analysis of the novel's structure and bibliographies of Garrett's work. Not available in English.

D'Alge, Carlos Neves. *As relações brasileiras de Almeida Garrett.* Rio de Janeiro: Instituto nacional do Livro, 1980. Print.

Utilizes archival documents to reveal Garrett's interest in Brazil—especially the events surrounding the country's struggle for independence. D'Alge also explores Garrett's influence on Brazilian Romanticism. Not available in English.

Delgado, Isabel Lopes. *Para uma leitura de* Frei Luís de Sousa *de Almeida Garrett.* Lisbon: Presença, 1998. Print.

Investigates Garrett's historical sources for *Brother Luiz de Sousa* and its intertextual relationship with canonical Portuguese texts, other writings by the author, and the Bible. Delgado also examines the play's characters in the context of the gender ideals of the early nineteenth century. Not available in English.

Macedo, Helder. "As *Viagens na minha terra* e a Menina dos Rouxinóis." *Colóquio letras* 51 (1979): 15-24. Print.

Provides an analysis of Garrett's *Travels in My Homeland.* Macedo, who is among the most respected scholars of Portuguese literature, focuses specifically on the episode titled "Menina dos rouxinóis" (may be translated as "Maiden of the Nightingales"). Not available in English.

Mendes, Victor K., and Valéria M. Souza, eds. *Garrett's Travels Revisited.* North Dartmouth: Tagus P at UMass Dartmouth, 2012. Print.

A collection of essays covering Garrett's life, work, and characteristic themes by several of the most respected scholars in the field of Lusophone literature.

Morão, Paula. Flores sem fruto *e* Folhas caídas *de Almeida Garrett.* Lisbon: Comunicação, 1988. Print.

Analyzes several poems from Garrett's *Fruitless Flowers* and *Fallen Leaves.* Morão also provides a biography of Garrett and a bibliography of studies on the author. Not available in English.

Reis, Carlos. "Intertextualidade e ideologia: Uma imagem de Camões." *Homenaje a Camoens: Estudios y ensayos hispano-portugueses.* Ed. Nicolás Extremera Tapia and Manuel Correia Fernández. Granada: U de Granada, 1980. 329-44. Print.

Examines the Romantic ideologies present in Garrett's *Camões,* which many scholars consider to be the first Romantic work in Portuguese. Reis also reviews the relationship between Garrett's poem and the work of the Portuguese Renaissance poet on whom it is based. Not available in English.

Reis, Fernando Egídio, Maria Manuela Ventura Santos, and Maria Neves Leal Gonçalves. Viagens na minha terra *de Almeida Garrett: Análise de obra.* Lisbon: Texto, 1998. Print.

Examines *Travels in My Homeland* in relation to its social, political, and historical contexts. Not available in English.

Rothwell, Phillip. "Ethics, the Thing, and the Father: Almeida Garrett's Contribution to Empty Paternity." *A Canon of Empty Fathers: Paternity in Portuguese Narrative.* Lewisburg: Bucknell UP, 2007. 45-64. Print.

Employs the theories of French psychoanalyst Jacques Lacan to address what Rothwell describes as the theme of the empty or absent father—representing a lacuna or void in the social order—in Garrett's *Brother Luiz de Sousa* and *Travels in My Homeland.*

Additional information on Garrett's life and works is contained in the following sources published by Gale: *Dictionary of Literary Biography,* Vol. 287; and *Literature Resource Center.*

James Clarence Mangan
1803-1849

(Born James Mangan; also known as Clarence Mangan; also wrote under the pseudonyms P. V. McGuffin, Johann Theodor Drechsler, An Idler, Selber, M. E., E. W., The Man in the Cloak, An Out and Outer, and Peter Puff, Secundus) Irish poet, translator, essayist, and short-story writer.

The following entry provides criticism of Mangan's life and works. For additional information about Mangan, see *NCLC,* Volume 27.

INTRODUCTION

James Clarence Mangan was an Irish poet who was most renowned as a translator of German and Gaelic poetry. His translations of medieval Gaelic literature led some to call him the last Irish bard. He lived and published exclusively in Ireland, never placing his work with a London publisher as many of his contemporaries did, which limited his exposure and income. While Mangan was generally reticent about his political affiliations, he is remembered as a nationalist who called for Irish independence, and he has been seen as a precursor of the Irish literary renaissance. He is also recognized as one of the forces behind the introduction of German literature and German literary modes, particularly the Gothic, to Ireland. A brief resurgence of interest in Mangan's work occurred in the early twentieth century, led by James Joyce and William Butler Yeats, and literary scholars continue to study his works.

BIOGRAPHICAL INFORMATION

Many of the details of Mangan's life are unknown. The second son of James Mangan, a grocer, and his wife, Catherine, he was born in Dublin on 1 May 1803. His education included the study of several languages—French, Spanish, Italian, Latin, and possibly German. At the age of fifteen, he had to abandon his schooling to help support his family. He first worked as a copyist in a scrivener's office and then as a legal clerk, jobs he reportedly loathed. It was probably during this time that Mangan began drinking, and alcohol abuse plagued him for the rest of his life. His poverty and addictions later contributed to his reputation as Ireland's foremost *poète maudit,* or "accursed poet," and prompted comparisons to his American contemporary Edgar Allan Poe. Mangan never married, and apart from the mention of a rejected proposal in his unfinished autobiography—an event that many scholars question—there is no evidence that he ever became seriously romantically involved.

By 1832, Mangan was publishing poems in the *Dublin Penny Journal,* and had made a patron and friend of antiquarian and editor George Petrie. He also became friends with Gaelic scholar John O'Donovan who, in 1837, hired Mangan to prepare the printer's copy of his translation from Gaelic of *Annals of the Four Masters.* In 1838, he took a position as a copyist in the historical department of the Ordnance Survey. During the four years Mangan worked for the Ordnance Survey, he studied Irish literary and cultural traditions, and this experience strongly influenced his subsequent works. When the staff at the Ordnance Survey was reduced in late 1841, Mangan lost his position. Petrie secured him a job as a cataloging assistant at Trinity College, where he worked until 1846.

As a writer in mid-nineteenth-century Ireland, Mangan was particularly influenced by several developments: a burgeoning Irish independence movement, the Great Famine (1845-49), the failure of the Young Irelanders Rebellion in 1848, and a cholera outbreak in Dublin in 1849. The first two developments helped propel Mangan and his poetry to fame. Along with his alcoholism, the failure of the rebellion and the spread of cholera contributed to his demise. In 1849, Mangan was discovered near death in a Dublin house and taken to a nearby hospital, where he died of symptoms related to cholera a few days later on 20 June.

MAJOR WORKS

Irish nationalism and independence are two of the themes most commonly associated with Mangan's work, despite an ideological ambivalence that is demonstrated by his publication in periodicals ranging from the Unionist *Dublin University Magazine* to the radical *Nation* and the pro-independence *United Irishman.* Although he published poems frequently in journals under a variety of pseudonyms, Mangan produced only one book during his lifetime, *Anthologia Germanica = German Anthology* (1845), a two-volume collection of translated, and often transformed, popular German poems. A collection featuring his translations of Irish poetry, *The Poets and Poetry of Munster,* was published posthumously in 1849.

In addition to his translations of German works, Mangan wrote original prose shaped by German literary traditions, particularly the Gothic tale. His Gothic-influenced stories include "An Extraordinary Adventure in the Shades," "The Thirty Flasks," and "The Man in the Cloak." "The Thirty Flasks" is perhaps Mangan's best-known prose piece. In this tale, which combines comic and Gothic elements, the impoverished Basil Von Rosenwald begins to trade inches of his stature to a wizened, diabolical magician for gold. Rosenwald's height and fortune are both salvaged in the end by Rubadubb Snooksnacker Slickwitz, who exposes the intentions of the diabolical magician to capture Rosenwald's soul. In "The Man in the Cloak," a reworking of Charles Robert Maturin's *Melmoth the Wanderer* (1820), the protagonist, a bank cashier guilty of embezzlement, falls prey to a mysterious cloaked figure who offers to save him from punishment if he will accept a strange talisman. The cashier takes the talisman, which brings him great wealth but leaves him isolated and miserable. In the end, he passes the talisman to someone else, confesses his sins, and is reconciled to God.

Mangan published many poems translated from Gaelic in periodicals. His best-known poem, "Dark Rosaleen," is a nationalist, allegorical address to Ireland. A translation of Owen Roe MacWard's seventeenth-century "Roisin Dubh," Mangan's poem is likely based on two other versions of MacWard's work by James Hardiman and Thomas Furlong, Mangan's contemporaries. "Dark Rosaleen" and a similar poem, "Kathaleen Ny-Houlahan," are both aislings, or vision poems, in which Ireland appears as a woman. Mangan was not proficient in Gaelic and critics note that he often mastered the spirit of poems, not the actual words. The true extent of Mangan's independent translation of Gaelic works has been the focus of scholarly debate. Many of his renderings of Gaelic poems are likely based on others' translations. Some of them are, nevertheless, among his best-known and most widely discussed works, and some have found his versions to be superior to the originals.

Mangan also created original works that he credited to other sources, such as "An Ode of Hafiz," which he falsely attributed to the fourteenth-century Persian poet, Hafiz of Shiraz. These poems "purporting to be Translations from the Oriental Languages" tend to be discussed separately by critics. In addition, Mangan published original poetry that he attributed to a fictitious German poet named Selber. Although he knew German well, Mangan was not proficient in any of the Eastern languages he claimed to translate. Some scholars have argued that Mangan delighted in publishing hoaxes and have linked his "Translations from the Oriental Languages" to this tendency. Others have maintained that Mangan enjoyed the creative freedom that the false translations afforded and that he used them to veil critiques of such political developments as colonialism and revolution. Still others, including Mangan, have suggested that the impecunious poet found that translations, real or faked, paid better than the publication of original poetry.

CRITICAL RECEPTION

Because of the variety and uneven quality of his work as both a writer and translator, Mangan has represented many things to many scholars. Jean Andrews (1989) described him as "a calculated and enigmatic blend of reality and fiction," an author who "perennially escapes definition." She found him to be a failure as a Romantic writer who attempted to emulate British Romantics such as Lord Byron and Percy Bysshe Shelley, though he never fully understood their works because of his orthodox religious beliefs, celibacy, and social alienation. As a result of his limited experience of life, Mangan could not grasp the passions underlying Romantic and Gothic literature, according to Andrews, and "was therefore forced, in a manner of speaking, to cast a cloak of humour over his inadequacies, with varying degrees of success." Kevin J. H. Dettmar (1986), on the other hand, heralded Mangan as "Ireland's greatest Romantic poet."

The origins of Mangan's translations from Gaelic have been disputed. Mangan published a few dozen poems that he may have either translated directly into English from Gaelic or merely versified from extant prose versions. Jacques Chuto (1976) claimed that although Mangan may have relied upon other sources for some of his early translations of Irish poetry, he probably eventually learned enough Gaelic to badly translate *The Tribes of Ireland* (1852), a satire written in the early seventeenth century by Aenghus O'Daly. Peter MacMahon (1978) disagreed with Chuto, maintaining that John O'Daly, the publisher of the 1852 edition, likely provided a prose rendering that Mangan "versified, piecemeal and hurriedly."

Mangan's debated ability to translate from Gaelic originals has often been linked to his politics. His fame rests in part on his connection to Irish nationalism, but some scholars have asserted that Mangan was less than firm in his political beliefs. Dettmar judged that he was "a man deeply divided, a man who with his right hand wrote poems of rousing nationalism while his left subverted their logic," because "his mind seems to have been tainted by the propaganda of the English usurpers he wished to banish." David C. Lloyd (1984) suggested that Mangan's seeming inconsistencies stemmed from a deeply-rooted sense of anomie, remarking that the "clash of rhetorics in his nationalist poems stands as symbolic of a more general refusal on Mangan's part to integrate and identify with the greater whole." But it was this very alienation, Andrews claimed, that allowed Mangan to capture the depths of human suffering in some of his poetry, including "Siberia," written near the beginning of the Great Famine.

Melissa Fegan (2005) asserted that the Great Famine was central to Mangan's view of contemporary Ireland and catalyzed his political poetry. "A Vision: A.D. 1848," Fegan argued, "is one of the most striking of Mangan's apocalyptic Famine poems." In it, she observed, Mangan reads recent events "as predestined and necessary for Ireland's eventual freedom" and invests "his meagre political capital in the prospect of a violent uprising." Fegan contended that Mangan drew parallels between the Great Famine and political oppression in many poems, juxtaposing, for example, the difficulties Ireland was facing in the mid-nineteenth century under Queen Victoria with the prosperity the island had enjoyed under the twelfth-century rule of Cathal Crobhdearg Ua Conchobair.

Mangan's place in Irish literary history, however, rests on more than his politics. Scholars such as Dettmar have credited him with the revitalization of traditional Irish poetic forms, including the ballad and the aisling. Andrew Cusack (2012) cited Mangan as an important contributor to the "cultural transfer" of the German Gothic to Ireland—and to Great Britain as a whole—because of his translations and his application of Gothic conventions in his original works.

Katherine E. Bishop

PRINCIPAL WORKS

Anthologia Germanica = German Anthology: A Series of Translations from the Most Popular of the German Poets. Trans. James Clarence Mangan. 2 vols. Dublin: Curry, 1845. Print. (Poetry)

The Poets and Poetry of Munster: A Selection of Irish Songs by the Poets of the Last Century. Trans. Mangan. Dublin: O'Daly, 1849. Print. (Poetry)

The Tribes of Ireland: A Satire. With Poetical Translation by the Late James Clarence Mangan; together with an Historical Account of the Family of O'Daly; and an Introduction to the History of Satire in Ireland by John O'Donovan. By Aenghus O'Daly. Trans. Mangan. Dublin: O'Daly, 1852. Print. (Satire)

**Poems.* Ed. John Mitchel. New York: Haverty, 1859. Print. (Poetry)

†*James Clarence Mangan: His Selected Poems.* Ed. Louise Imogen Guiney. London: Lane, 1897. Print. (Poetry)

‡*Poems of James Clarence Mangan (Many Hitherto Uncollected).* Ed. D. J. O'Donoghue. Dublin: O'Donoghue, 1903. Print. (Poetry)

§*The Prose Writings of James Clarence Mangan.* Ed. O'Donoghue. Dublin: O'Donoghue, 1904. Print. (Essays and short stories)

Autobiography. Ed. James Kilroy. Dublin: Dolmen, 1968. Print. (Autobiography)

Selected Poems of James Clarence Mangan. Ed. Michael Smith. Dublin: Gallery, 1973. Print. (Poetry)

||*The Collected Works of James Clarence Mangan: Poems.* Ed. Jacques Chuto et al. 4 vols. Dublin: Irish Academic P, 1996-99. Print. (Poetry)

The Collected Works of James Clarence Mangan: Prose. Ed. Chuto et al. 2 vols. Dublin: Irish Academic P, 2002. Print. (Essays and short stories)

Poems. Ed. David Wheatley. Oldcastle: Gallery, 2003. Print. (Poetry)

Selected Poems of James Clarence Mangan. Ed. Chuto et al. Dublin: Irish Academic P, 2003. Print. (Poetry)

James Clarence Mangan: Selected Writings. Ed. Sean Ryder. Dublin: U Coll. Dublin P, 2004. Print. (Autobiography, essays, letters, poetry, and short stories)

*Includes the poems "Dark Rosaleen," a translation of the Irish folk song "Roisin Dubh," first published in the *Nation* on 30 May 1846; "Kathaleen Ny-Houlahan," first published in the *Irish Penny Journal* on 16 January 1841; "The Warning Voice"; "Lament over the Ruins of the Abbey of Teach Molaga"; "Twenty Golden Years Ago"; "The Nameless One"; and "Siberia," first published in the *Nation* on 18 April 1846.

†Includes a selection of poems "purporting to be Translations from the Oriental Languages."

‡Includes the poem "Lamentation of Mac Liag for Kincora," first published in the *Irish Penny Journal* on 9 January 1841.

§Includes the short stories "An Extraordinary Adventure in the Shades," first published in the *Comet* in January 1833; "The Thirty Flasks," first published in the *Dublin University Magazine* in two parts in October and December 1838; and "The Man in the Cloak (A Very German Story)," first published in the *Dublin University Magazine* in November 1838.

||Includes the poems "Relic of Servi," first published as "An Ode of Hafiz" in the *Dublin University Magazine* in November 1848; "A Vision: A.D. 1848," first published in the *United Irishman* on 26 February 1848; and "The Vision of Egan O'Reilly," first published in the *Irishman* on 27 January 1849.

CRITICISM

D. J. O'Donoghue (essay date 1897)

SOURCE: O'Donoghue, D. J. "Chapter XII" and "Chapter XIV." *The Life and Writings of James Clarence Mangan.* Edinburgh: Geddes, 1897. 129-42; 157-70. Print.

[*In the following essays, O'Donoghue first discusses Mangan's contributions to the journal* Nation, *his political views, and his composition of* German Anthology. *O'Donoghue then comments on* The Poets and Poetry of Munster *and presents general biographical information.*]

Ask him who hath suffered woes untold
From some volcanic strife
Of passionate years if he remember,
Tombed in the grave of Life's December,
Its cancelled golden June.

Mangan

On October 15th, 1842, the first number of the *Nation* was published at the office in D'Olier Street. Charles Gavan Duffy, who had given up the *Belfast Vindicator,* was the only practical journalist among the three founders, and naturally became editor of the new venture. A fairly efficient *corps* of contributors had been organised, but some of these proved of little use, and were dropped when better men came to the front. Mangan's name appears on the prospectus of the new journal as a contributor, and he opened his connection with some effective verses in the first issue, entitled, **"The *Nation*'s First Number."** In these he acts as the herald of the new movement, and announces the attractions in store for the readers of the paper. Naturally, the verses are not of a very high order of merit, but as Mangan had seen some periodicals of great promise disappear very quietly soon after their advent, he could not have been very loftily impressed or earnestly inspired by his theme. Doggerel, but of a superior order, and certainly not unconscious, **"The *Nation*'s First Number"** may be called, but even in this poem—dashed off, doubtless, at Mangan's characteristic lightning speed—there are some tolerable lines. The aims of the paper, he declares, will be—

> To give Genius its due, to do battle with Wrong,
> And achieve things undreamt of as yet save in song.
>
> . . . .
>
> Be it ours to stand forth and contend in the van
> Of Truth's legions for Freedom, the birthright of Man.
>
> . . . .
>
> We announce a new era—be this our first news,
> When the self-grinding landlords shall shake in their
> shoes;
> While the Ark of a bloodless yet mighty reform
> Shall emerge from the Flood of the Popular Storm!

Of the staff of the paper he tells his readers that—

> Critics keener than sabres, wits brighter than stars,
> And reasoners as cool as the coolest cucumber,
> Form the host that shine out in the *Nation*'s First Number!

It is strange that for two or three subsequent years Mangan wrote next to nothing for the *Nation* of a serious character, only epigrams and squibs of his being discoverable, under several different signatures, such as "M.," "Vacuus," "Terræ Filius," and "Hi-Hum." In printing one of his skits,[1] a quasi-political one, the editor refers to the author as—

> one whose name will some day be illustrious in literature. It must not be written here, with a mere bagatelle thrown off in a moment of relaxation; but it will write itself on marble.

A little later[2] the editor prints an anonymous bit of curious rhyming by Mangan (which was, though the editor does not seem to have known it, a reprint from the *Comet* of July, 1833), and prefaces it with a very useful hint to the poet:—

> He ought not, we think, to have thrown away his fine genius upon such a task. From some of his past contributions we know he is capable of the finest verses, grave or gay.

Those "past contributions," however, were not written for the *Nation*. In reprinting subsequently (1844) his eccentric essay, **"My Bugle and How I Blow It,"** the editor makes a remark which proves that Mangan's relations with the *Nation* were so far of the slightest:—

> This pleasant extravaganza, a quiz upon the German school, by a popular writer, was given some years ago to the editor of the *Nation* for a publication of a literary character. It is thought necessary to mention this, as we have not an opportunity of communicating with the author, and he may not choose to be identified with the particular politics of the *Nation*.

As the skit is not political in any way, and some of his squibs written directly for the *Nation* were, this editorial comment is somewhat mysterious. But it may have been suggested simply by an absence, longer than usual for Mangan, from the *Nation* office. His politics were certainly not well-defined at this time. He had, in fact, until the last two or three years of his life, no fixed opinions upon the political questions then agitating the public mind. His writings, however, attest that he had undoubted national feeling, and he certainly became in the end strongly national, allying himself with the more advanced section of Irish nationalists.[3]

He was rarely to be met in the *Nation* office. Duffy says:—

> He could not be induced to attend the weekly suppers, and knew many of his fellow-labourers only by name. He stole into the editor's room once a week to talk over literary projects, but if any of my friends appeared he took flight on the instant. The animal spirits and hopefulness of vigorous young men oppressed him, and he fled from the admiration or sympathy of a stranger as others do from reproach and insult.

It was not till 1846 that he began to contribute largely to the *Nation*. Meanwhile he continued his **"Anthologia Germanica"** [***Anthologia Germanica = German Anthology***] in the *University Magazine*, alternating those papers with occasional articles on Spanish poetry, and the **"Literæ Orientales."** During 1842 some of his best versions from Rückert appeared, including that interesting poem entitled, **"Gone in the Wind,"** to which the following verses belong:—

> Solomon! where is thy throne? It is gone in the wind.
> Babylon! where is thy might? It is gone in the wind.
> Like the swift shadows of Noon, like the dreams of the
> Blind,
> Vanish the glories and pomps of the earth in the wind.
>
> . . . .
>
> Say, what is pleasure? A phantom, a mask undefined.
> Science? An almond, whereof we can pierce but the rind.
> Honour and Affluence? Firmans that Fortune hath signed,
> Only to glitter and pass on the wings of the wind.
>
> Solomon! where is thy throne? It is gone in the wind.
> Babylon! where is thy might? It is gone in the wind.
> Who is the Fortunate? He who in anguish hath pined—
> He shall rejoice when his relics are dust in the wind!

Mortal! be careful wherewith thy best hopes are entwined;
Woe to the miners for Truth—where the Lampless have mined!
Woe to the seekers on Earth for what none ever find!
They and their trust shall be scattered like leaves on the wind.

Solomon! where is thy throne? It is gone in the wind.
Babylon! where is thy might? It is gone in the wind.
Happy in death are they only whose hearts have consigned
All Earth's affections, and longings, and cares to the wind.

The **"Nameless One"** seems to have been written in the year 1842, if Mangan's statement in the poem that he was thirty-nine be reliable, but as I can discover no trace of it in the periodicals of that period it must have been, if written, held over by Mangan till the time when he could no longer conceal the depth of his despair and misery. His muse in 1842 was in anything but a despairing or doleful mood. One of his happiest contributions to the *University Magazine* belongs to that year. It is a very amusing essay on the art of borrowing, and of evading one's creditors, with various translations from Casti, the Italian burlesque poet. It is entitled **"The Three[4] Half-Crowns,"** and Mangan prefaces his actual tackling of the subject proper by a few observations of the nature of the following:—

> The real secret of the happiness poets enjoy is to be sought in their imagination. This is the faculty to which they owe the possession of almost everything they have, and the absence of almost everything they ought not to have. It is this that elevates them, balloon like, sky-high above the petty wants and cares that shorten the days of prosers. ...... It makes more than a monarch of the poet. It is his clue through the labyrinth of life—his tower of strength in peril—his guide, mentor, monitor, oracle, shield, cloak, truncheon, tabernacle, and house of refuge. It is, in a word, the mysterious curtain-cloud that interposes between him and all matters mundane, and prevents him from being affected by anything, except, perhaps, the occasional vision of a dish or decanter. Such is imagination as monopolised by the poet. We have said that he owes almost everything to it. By so saying we have left it to be understood that he now and then owes a little in other quarters. This, unfortunately, is the fact.

The poet proceeds, in a kind of sonnet sequence, to tell how he once borrowed three half-crowns, and of the endless worrying of his creditor to recover the amount. The prose and verse alike are in an inimitable style, full of humour, the rhymes reminding one very much of Byron in his "Don Juan." The ingenuity of the shifts to which the debtor resorts, the amusing fancies about creditors, and the comparisons between them and other persecutors of poets are all highly creditable to the poet's imagination. He doubts, in the sketch, whether a creditor is not worse than an Algerian pirate, and thinks he is, for while the latter only robs you of what you have, the former tries to rob you of what you have not, and never can have, namely—Three Half-Crowns. He goes on to say that various alarming portents having appeared of late, foretelling the imminent end of the world, he is surprised that under the circumstances his creditor does not find something more serious to do than harassing him for three paltry half-crowns. He discovers himself replying to every question, no matter by whom put or upon what subject, "I really haven't got them"; and when he is quite alone, and hears himself asked for them, he finds it is the echo of his own voice which, from force of custom, is asking for "those three half-crowns." He is astonished that wherever he goes he meets his creditor, and muses on the phenomenon in this wise:—

Let Doctors dissertate about Attraction,
And preach long lectures upon Gravitation,
Indulging thereanent in speculation,
For which no human being cares one fraction.
'Tis all mere twaddle—talk and iteration;
Of those mysterious modes of Nature's action
There never yet was any explanation
To anybody's perfect satisfaction.

However, this I stubbornly believe,
And for the proof thereof see no great need
To take down Isaac Newton from the shelf—
That, move where'er I will—morn noon, or eve,
I manage to attract with awful speed
My Three Half-Crowns' Tormentor tow'rds myself!

He says that if he were an astrologer who had found the philosopher's stone, he would rest satisfied, after his great discovery, with coining merely three half-crowns:—

Those old alchymic dreamers!—rest their bones,
And be their souls eternally assoiled—
The Lillys, Arnolds, Gabors, who so toiled
To turn base metals into precious ones!
Sleepless and worn, amid retorts and cones,
And crucibles, they fused and blew and boiled—
Alas! in vain—their sulphurs, salts and stones
Exhaled in smoke—and *they* died, fagged, and foiled.

Yet, after all, why might not Art and Labour
Achieve the project? I don't know. Man's lore
Is vast, and Science day by day increases;
But this I know, that if, by following Gabor,
I could coin Three Half-crowns, I'd ask no more,
But break my pots and furnaces to pieces!

The wit is admirably kept up to the last. Mangan was fond of expatiating upon loans and the inconvenience of not meeting one's creditor's demands. In this connection an absurd story, originating with D'Arcy M'Gee, may be definitely disposed of. M'Gee remarks (in a sketch which he wrote for the *Nation* during the poet's lifetime, but which was declined by that paper, though it afterwards reprinted it from M'Gee's own journal subsequent to Mangan's death),

> I have heard it said of him that being often reduced to extreme want, he was never known to borrow at a time more than one and six-pence, and if more were offered to him, he would neither accept it, nor repeat his request in that direction.

It is a quaint notion, and not improbably emanated from Mangan himself, but it is very far from the actual truth.[5] Mangan was constantly obliged to borrow from his friends, and though in some cases he paid them back in contributions of which they made profitable use, the fact remains, and is one of the points naturally best remembered by his contemporaries, that the need of a small loan was a not at all uncommon reason of a visit from Mangan. *Apropos,* Mr. Martin M'Dermott has favoured me with the following reminiscence of his only meeting with Mangan:—

> During one of my occasional visits to Ireland I happened to be breakfasting with my old friend and school-fellow, Thomas Devin Reilly, when the servant came in, and in a low voice gave him the name of a visitor. He said, 'Ask him to come in,' and turning to me he whispered, 'Clarence Mangan.' I was of course all eyes when the poet entered in the quaint, shabby attire described by Father Meehan, and with a shy, faltering step, seeing the stranger in the room, approached the table. The introduction gone through, my host asked Mangan to join us at our meal, but he declined, still in the same shy, hesitating manner, and asked Reilly if he could have a word with him outside. When the two reached the hall I heard the chink of coin, and my friend came back with one of the silk purses used then—looking very flaccid—in his hand, saying with a sigh, 'Poor Mangan!'

The subject of money naturally crops up in many of Mangan's letters—in too many of them, unfortunately—and some are extremely painful reading on that account. Others, however, are jocular in tone, and in one of these, addressed to the editor of the *Nation,* he says—

> You wish to know why I have not acknowledged the receipt of the letter of credit you sent me. I beg in reply to observe that any acknowledgment of the kind forms no part of my system. Any *given* amount of money, in gold, silver, or paper, I take, put up, and say nothing about. If it be gold, I introduce it into a steel purse; if silver, I drop it into a silk one; if paper, I stow it away in a pocket-book; but I never jingle or display any of them before the eyes of others.

In another characteristic letter to the same friend, Mangan writes in the same vein—

> I look on odes as ode-ious compositions—adulatory stuff, flattery of the flattest sort, worthy to be paid for, not in the glorious renown which all honest, honourable, high-souled and high-heeled men seek, but out of the purse—one pound one a line—not a *camac* less! Now you know I spit upon this sort of thing—I never take money for what I write. It is always given me. pressed on me, sent to me, flung in my phiz—and I, for the sake of a quiet life, pocket the affront!

Sometimes he would ask for a loan with assumed gaiety, but not infrequently (especially, of course, in his last years) when his need was desperate, his appeals for help were as painful ordeals to his friends as to himself—

> "Whether," says Mitchel, "the beautiful and luxuriant world of dreams wherein he built his palaces, and laid up his treasures, and tasted the ambrosia of the gods, was indeed a sufficient compensation for all the squalid misery in the body is a question upon which there is no occasion to pronounce. One may hope that it was, and much more than a compensation, for God is just."

And he adds—

> Some 'poets' there are who desire to own a dream-world and at the same time to own stock in banks and railroads.

Mangan was not one of these, but he was well aware of the value of money, and he so frequently makes it a peg upon which to hang a few rhymes or a few sentences, that perhaps a little space is not altogether wasted in dwelling upon it. He has written a poem on "the way the money goes," which, though based upon Von Gaudy's "Wo bleibt mein geld," is very characteristic and peculiar to himself. It is well worth quoting as a creditable specimen of his witty verse. It is entitled **"Where's My Money?"**—

> Ay, where's my money? That's a puzzling query.
> It vanishes. Yet neither in my purse
> Nor pocket are there any holes. 'Tis very
> Incomprehensible. I don't disburse
> For superfluities. I wear plain clothes.
> I seldom buy jam tarts, preserves or honey,
> And no one overlooks what debts he owes
> More steadily than I. Where *is* my money?
>
> I never tipple. Folks don't see me staggering,
> *Sans* cane and castor, in the public street.
> I sport no ornaments—not even a *bague* (ring).
> I have a notion that my own two feet
> Are much superior to a horse's four,
> So never call a jarvey. It is funny.
> The longer I investigate the more
> Astoundedly I ask, *Where* is my money?
>
> *My* money, mind you. Other people's dollars
> Cohere together nobly. Only mine
> Cut one another. There's that pink of scholars,
> Von Doppeldronk; he spends as much on wine
> As I on—everything. Yet *he* seems rich.
> He laughs, and waxes plumper than a bunny,
> While I grow slim as a divining-switch,
> And search for gold as vainly. Where's my money?
>
> I can't complain that editors don't pay me;
> I get for every sheet one pound sixteen,
> And well I may! My articles are flamy
> Enough to blow up *any* magazine.
> What's queerest in the affair though is, that at
> The same time I miss nothing but the *one.* He
> That watches me will find I don't lose hat,
> Gloves, fogle, stick, or cloak. 'Tis always money!
>
> Were I a rake I'd say so. When one roysters
> Beyond the rules, of course, his cash must go.
> 'Tis true I regularly sup on oysters,
> Cheese, brandy, and all that. But even so?
> What signifies a ducat of a night?
> "The barmaids," you may fancy. No. The sunny
> Loadstar that draws *my* tin is not the light
> From *their* eyes anyhow. Where then's my money?
>
> However, *apropos* of eyes and maidens,
> I own I do make presents to the sex—
> Books, watches, trinkets, music too (not Haydn's),

Combs, shawls, veils, bonnets—things that might
perplex
A man to count. But still I gain by what
I lose in this way. 'Tis experience won—eh?
I think so. My acquaintances think *not.*
No matter. I grow tedious. Where's my money?

There is another poem of his, written at this time, also attributed to an undoubted German source—Schubart—and called by Mangan **"Pathetic Hypathetics,"** which looks very unlike anything in the literature of the Fatherland. A verse may be quoted in support of the suggestion that no German wrote it. There is clearly more of Mangan than Schubart in it. He soliloquises to this effect in the last verse:—

Were Wine all a quiz,
I should wear a long phiz
As I mounted each night to my ninth storey garret.
Though Friendship, the traitress, deceives me,
Though Hope may have long ceased to flatter,
Though Music, sweet infidel, leaves me.
Though Love is my torment—what matter—
I've still such a thing as a rummer of claret!

Mangan, of course, heard a good deal of Father Mathew's crusade against intemperance, and in one of his temperate intervals at this period he formally abjured—in verse—his excessive indulgence in stimulants. The abjuration, which is called **"The Coming Event,"** is as excellent as it is unknown. Here it is:—

Curtain the lamp and bury the bowl,
The ban is on drinking.
Reason shall reign the queen of the soul
When the spirits are sinking.
Chained is the demon that smote with blight
Men's morals and laurels.
Then hail to health and a long good night,
To old wine and new quarrels!

Nights shall descend and no taverns ring
To the roar of our revels;
Mornings shall dawn, but none of them bring
White lips and *blue* devils.
Riot and frenzy sleep with remorse
In the obsolete potion,
And mind grows calm as a ship on her course
O'er the level of ocean.

So should it be! for man's world of romance
Is fast disappearing,
And shadows of changes are seen in advance,
Whose epochs are nearing.
And the days are at hand when the best shall require
All means of salvation;
And the souls of men shall be tried in the fire
Of the final probation!

And the witling no longer or sneers or smiles—
And the worldling dissembles,
And the black-hearted sceptic feels anxious at whiles
And marvels and trembles.
And fear and defiance are blent in the jest
Of the blind self-deceiver;
But hope bounds high in the joyous breast
Of the child-like believer.

Darken the lamp, then, and shatter the bowl,
Ye faithfullest-hearted!
And as your swift years travel on to the goal
Whither worlds have departed,
Spend labour, life, soul, in your zeal to atone
For the past and its errors;
So best shall ye bear to encounter alone
The EVENT and its terrors!

A month or so later in the same year (1844) Mangan contributed a fresh instalment of Ottoman poetry to the magazine, and introduced therein two of the most familiar of his poems—namely, **"The Caramanian Exile"** and **"The Wail and Warning of the Three Khalendeers,"** the last of which will be better remembered, perhaps, by quoting the opening verse—

Here we meet, we three, at length,
Amrah, Osman, Perizad,
Shorn of all our grace and strength,
Poor and old and very sad!
We have lived, but live no more,
Life has lost its gloss for us
Since the days we spent of yore
Boating down the Bosphorus.

In another poem in the same article he exhorts his readers to live nobly, to be patient, meek, docile, and courageous, and to abhor vice—

Woe unto those who but banish one vice for another;
Far from thy thoughts be such damning delusion, O
brother!
. . . .
Donning new raiment is nobler than patching and
piecing—
Such are the tone and the tune of the ditty that *we* sing!
. . . .
Cast away Pride as the bane of the soul; the Disdainful
Swallow much mire in their day, and find everything
painful.
. . . .
Like the bright moon before Midnight is blended with
morrow,
Shines the pure pearl of the soul in the Chalice of Sorrow!

With all his own wretchedness, Mangan never faltered once in his belief in the future of others. He had given up all hope of conquering his one vice, and those who knew of it might have replied to his exhortations, "Physician, heal thyself." But his friends trusted in a final reformation, and they did not, therefore, in spite of its apparent uselessness, cease their entreaties to him to "live his poetry, to act his rhyme." He never resented their earnest expostulations, and often told them with tears in his eyes that it was too late—he could not give up his evil habit. One of them, James Price, tells us of his constant endeavours to bring the poet to a deeper sense of his growing degradation:—

> "His unhappy transgressions," he says, "were more widely known than his genius; *they* were apparent to many, *it* was appreciated only by the few."

And he continues:—

> Many a time have we pleaded with Mangan against the deadly enemy that was slowly, but steadily, destroying him. We have held the glass to his face, and bade him behold the ravages made, and not by Time. 'Yes,' he said, 'I see a skinless skull there, an empty socket where intelligence once beamed; but oh, I look within myself, and behold a sadder vision—the vision of a wasted life!'

About this time, through the kindness of Dr. Todd, he obtained a post as assistant cataloguer in Trinity College Library, a place in which he had often studied, but the salary was very small, and towards the end of 1844 his circumstances became so desperate that his friends conceived the idea of getting some of his writings published in volume form by a London publisher, in order to relieve his necessities; and Thomas Davis wrote to Daniel Owen Maddyn, the author of *Revelations of Ireland* and other books, who was then residing in London, to interest him in them:—

> I think you were a reader of the *University Magazine.* If so, you must have noticed the **'Anthologia Germanica,' 'Leaflets from the German Oak,' 'Oriental Nights,'** and other translations and apparent translations of Clarence Mangan. He has some small salary in the College Library, and has to support himself and his brother. His health is wretched. Charles Duffy is most anxious to have the papers I have described printed in London, for which they are better suited than for Dublin. Now, you will greatly oblige me by asking Mr. Newby if he will publish them, giving Mangan £50 for the edition. If he refuse you can say that Charles Duffy will repay him half the £50 should the work be a failure. Should he still declare against it, pray let me know soon what would be the best way of getting some payment and publication for Mangan's papers. Many of the ballads are Mangan's own, and are first-rate. Were they on Irish subjects he would be paid for them here. They ought to succeed in London nigh as well as the 'Prout Papers.'

Maddyn did not succeed in obtaining a London publisher for Mangan, and the project had to be abandoned. In thanking him for his efforts, Davis wrote:—

> The care you took about Mangan was very kind. He, poor fellow, is so nervous that it is hard to get him to do anything businesslike; but he is too good and too able to be allowed to go wrong.

Maddyn then suggested that a literary pension should be asked for the poet, adding:—

> I entreat that there may be no democratic or high republican squeamishness shown in this matter. So long as we are living under a monarchy, let us at least have the advantages of it. And the Repealers do not profess to be anti-monarchical—neither are they, I am sure. Therefore, let Mr. Mangan's friends not scruple to do for him what Leigh Hunt's did three or four years since, when they sought to interest Queen Victoria for the Radical poet. In short, this point is really of consequence, and if Mangan could be well launched, his future voyages would be easier and more agreeable.

The pension was heard of no more, however, and the German translations were only published in Dublin by M'Glashan when Gavan Duffy, who has said of Mangan that—

> his poems will live as long as Tennyson or Browning's,

and of the poet himself that—

> he was as truly born to sing deathless songs as Keats or Shelley

guaranteed £50 for one hundred copies. M'Glashan, though well enough disposed towards Mangan, was unwilling to risk any money in the venture.

> "I calculate," he wrote, "that the printing, binding, and advertising of Mangan's ***Anthology*** [***Anthologia Germanica = German Anthology***] will cost us nearly £100. Our view was to publish the book, sell as many as possible, and give Mangan an equal share of the profits, and in this manner I conceive he would be more benefited than by any definite sum we could afford to give him. However, as our wish is, as much as yours can be, to serve Mangan, without incurring any unnecessary risk, suppose you pay Mangan £25 in the meantime, and remainder to us until the expenses of the book have been covered. Could I be sure the volumes would sell equal to their merits, there would be little difficulty about an arrangement very profitable to Mangan, but I cannot forget they are verse, and the public took ten years to buy one small edition of Anster's *Faust* a book which all at once occupied a very high position in the literary world."

The following letter from Mangan refers to these transactions with M'Glashan:[6]—

> Thursday, Noon.
>
> My Dear Duffy,—I have just received your exceedingly kind note. You are the soul of goodness and generosity. Will you be at leisure on Saturday, Sunday, or Monday evening? If you can I will be most happy to call out (and out) on you. I say out-and-out, as I conceive that as yet I have made you only a series of half (*and* half—that's paying you back, eh?) drop-in Paul-Pryish visits, or visitations. I have made out the inventory for the sale (excluding, as you advised, pots and pans) and put it into the hands of M'Glashan.
>
> Yours ever faithfully,
> J. C. Mangan.

Another letter to Duffy may be quoted in this connection:—

> Friday, 3 o'clock.
>
> My Dear Duffy,—I am harassed, goaded, made mad! I have but a few days wherein to make up an Anthology for M'Glashan, and my health is failing, though I am now living very regularly, at least very abstemiously. But I would rather fail anywhere than in my duty towards you. Within the last hour I have written what I send you. I hope you will not dislike it, and if you do not, I hope it will be in time. As soon as I have finished the

Anthology I will call on you with more poetry. God bless you.

Ever yours faithfully,
J. C. Mangan.

It had been intended to include a volume of ***Echoes of Foreign Song*** by Mangan in the Library of Ireland series projected by the *Nation,* but the idea was given up, and in June, 1845, or thereabouts, the ***German Anthology*** [***Anthologia Germanica = German Anthology***],[7] comprising a selection of nearly 150 pieces, was brought out in two volumes by M'Glashan. It sold very well, and was warmly praised in many quarters. Mangan's preface to the work is the only professedly direct personal communication to the public from the poet, and as such is worth transferring to these pages:—

> The translations comprised in these volumes have (with a single exception) been selected from a series which have appeared at irregular intervals within the last ten years in the pages of the *Dublin University Magazine.* They are now published in their present form at the instance of some valued friends of mine, admirers, like myself, of German literature, and, as I am happy to believe, even more solicitous than I am to extend the knowledge of that literature throughout these kingdoms.
>
> It will be seen that the great majority of the writers from whom they are taken are poets who have flourished within the current century. In confining myself generally to these I have acted less from choice than from necessity. Little or none of that description of material which a translator can mould to his purpose is to be found in the lyrical or ballad compositions of the earlier eras of the German muse, and the elaborate didactical poems of the seventeenth or eighteenth centuries would not, I apprehend, be likely to suit the highly-cultivated tastes of the readers of the present day. My design, I need scarcely remark, has been to furnish not miscellaneous samples of all kinds of German poetry, but select samples of some particular kinds; and if I have succeeded in this design I have achieved all that my readers would, under any circumstances, thank me for accomplishing.
>
> Of the translations themselves it is not for me to say more than that they are, as I would humbly hope, faithful to the spirit, if not always to the letter, of their originals. As a mere matter of duty, however, I am exceedingly anxious to express—and I do here, once for all, express—my most grateful acknowledgment of the very favourable reception they have experienced from the various periodical publications of the day, and more especially from the newspaper Press. Though I may at times be induced to think that the language of my reviewers has been too flattering, I, nevertheless, gladly accept it as evidence of a generous goodwill on their part towards me, which, while it does them honour, should excite me to such endeavours as might in some degree qualify me to deserve it.
>
> J. C. Mangan.

. . . . .

To stamp dishonour on thy brow
  Was not within the power of earth;
And art thou agonised when now
  The hour that lost thee all thy worth
And turned thee to the thing thou art,
Rushes upon thy bleeding heart?

Mangan

The *Nation,* believing, with Horace Walpole, that only a man of genius can trifle agreeably, gladly printed all the squibs and skits that Mangan sent to it, but its editor did not fail to observe that the poet might have been better employed. In printing a whimsical set of verses on "The Blackwater"—a compound for which Mangan found several rhymes—the editor remarks:—

> Here we have the truest poet this country has produced in our days—to the few we need not name him, to the many it is still premature—writing versicles very much akin to the nonsense verses with which Swift and his friends made war against the spleen and blue devils.

Nevertheless, Mangan proceeded on his way, scattering epigrams and *jeux d'esprit* on the one hand, and reserving his serious work, so far, for the *University Magazine.* There are a couple of articles in that periodical for 1845 which I have no hesitation in attributing to Mangan. They are respectively entitled **"Nightmares"** [**"Of the Nightmare"**] and **"Mares' Nests,"** and are unsigned, but certain passages strongly suggest the author of the polyglot anthologies. With the exception of a rare joke, the articles are in the very serious vein. In the first-named article he says, among other things, that Blake the artist was fortunate in being able to transmit his nightmares to canvas:—

> Happy was Blake, who lived in good understanding with the artist within him, and whose ready pencil transferred the unearthly creations of this latter to insensible canvas, instead of receiving them on his own sensitive skin. The pencil was the conductor which carried off innocuous the destructive-creative force, the lightning that would have smitten and fused his own corporeality into new, anomalous, fantastic forms. . . . Had Blake not been able to paint his nightmares, and his daymares too, they would have painted themselves in wizard marks upon his own body.

The madman, according to Mangan in this article, is he whose power of transmitting his imagination is arrested, and whose own soul receives all its effects. The whole article is marvellously acute, and, did space allow, might be largely quoted with advantage. In the article on **"Mares' Nests"** there are also some interesting and characteristic passages, as, for instance, this:—

> Children are the greatest artists, creative, genial. What a dramatist, what a romancer, what a magician, is the child in his play! That is a lingering after-sheen of the glory of his infancy. And the true artist is a child all his life. Only in so far as he is a child is he a creator; ceases he to be childlike, he is thenceforth no more an artist, but a mechanic: a cobbler, not a genius. He is, in Fichte's phrase, a hodman; useful when building is going on, yet not to be called a builder. He is a picture-wright, or a play-wright, or a tale-wright: a versifier or a prosifier—anything but a poet.[8]

At this same time Mangan was continuing his versions and perversions from the German, and in the number which contains the article on **"Nightmares"** there are some characteristically whimsical pieces from the German of Selber (himself). Even in these, however, we get an occasional line or two of a serious or half-serious character, as where he gives us, in a poem of which the refrain is—

> Hark! again the rueful winds are blowing,
>   And alas! I dwell alone![9]

a verse like the following:—

> O, ye rosy ghosts of buried hours,
>   Haunters of a head which they made hoary,
> How you mock one when Disaster lours,
>   With your shameless Tantalusian glory!
> Memory draws upon her ill-got wealth
>   All the more as Fancy waxes thrifty.
> I want neither! Give me Hope and Health,
>   Give me life, O, Eighteen Hundred Fifty!
> Give me back, not Youth's imaginings,
> But its feelings, which are truer things.

One of his critics truly says that into his rhymes,

> however fantastic or difficult, his language flows with all its unimpaired vitality and grace, like fused metal into a mould.

And the *Nation,* after his death, said of his poetical work with equal truth:—

> He has faults, which he who runs may read, mannerism, grotesque, and an indomitable love of jingling; he often sins against simplicity, but the inexpiable sin of commonplace no man can lay to his charge.

Even his rebuses and acrostics have an air of distinction about them. But the time was nearing when Mangan's thoughts were, of necessity, more often raised above the trivialities of life, when a larger and freer utterance and nobler aspirations took the place of the smaller and, as it were, constrained movements of his earlier career. From the opening of the year 1846, when the fearful shadow of an impending famine was cast over the country, Mangan, though he did not change his own habits or mode of life, almost entirely forgot his mannerism, and assumed the character of an almost inspired prophet. In impressive odes like **"The Warning Voice"** and **"The Peal of Another Trumpet,"** he pointed to the future, and bade his countrymen hold up their hearts, imploring them to act with dignity, moderation, and courage, and not to allow the terrible outlook to overwhelm them with despair. More than anyone of his time, he predicted the misery of the forthcoming years. He urged, above all things, the stern necessity of preparation for whatever the future might bring, the supreme importance of firmness, the danger of weakness and irresolution. Hitherto he had been contented with the name of "poet"; he now appeared as the great national poet of Ireland—the most splendidly endowed with imagination and keenness of vision of any Irishman of his time. And thus in **"The Peal of Another Trumpet,"** he addressed his suffering fellow-countrymen:—

> Revolution's red abyss
>   Burns beneath us all but bared—
> And on high the fire-charged cloud
>   Blackens in the firmament,
> And afar we list the loud
>   Sea voice of the unknown event.
>   Youths of Ireland, stand prepared!
> For all woes the meek have dreed,
>   For all risks the brave have dared,
> As for suffering, so for deed,
>   Stand prepared!
> For the pestilence that striketh
> Where it listeth, whom it liketh,
> For the blight whose deadly might
> Desolateth day and night—
> For a sword that never spared
>   Stand prepared!
> Though that gory sword be bared,
>   Be not scared!
> Do not blench and dare not falter!
> For the axe and for the halter,
>   Stand prepared!

It was to the *Nation* that Mangan contributed his finest National poems, beginning with **"The Warning Voice,"**[10] to which he prefixes the following sentences from Balzac's "Livre Mystique":—

> Il me semble que nous sommes à la veille d'une grande bataille humaine. Les forces sont là; mais je n'y vois pas de général.

In the following week's issue the editor characterises it as "the most impressive poem, perhaps, we ever published," and quotes these words of "a dear correspondent":—

> M.'s poem sounded to me like the deep voice of a dying man, making his last appeal to the good in men's hearts, or a voice from the sky, so far was it above all the littleness of party prejudice or party motives.

From the opening lines—

> Ye Faithful!—Ye Noble!
>   A day is at hand
> Of trial and trouble
>   And woe in the land,

to the *finale,* this fine poem soars high beyond the sometimes petty plaints of the poets of the day:—

> Now, therefore, ye True,
> Gird your loins up anew!
> By the good you have wrought,
> By all you have thought
>   And suffered and done!
>   By your souls, I implore you,
>   Be leal to your mission—
> Remembering that one
>   Of the two paths before you
>   Slopes down to Perdition.
>
> To you have been given
>   Not granaries and gold,

But the Love that lives long
And waxes not cold;
And the zeal that hath striven
'Gainst Error and Wrong,
And in fragments hath riven
The chains of the Strong.

Your true faith and worth
Will be history soon,
And their stature stand forth
In the unsparing noon!

Nearly all his writings in the *Nation* of this year are serious, and indeed lofty in tone. Among them are his most superb poems, like **"Dark Rosaleen," "The Dream of John McDonnell," "Siberia," "Shane Bwee," "A Cry for Ireland," "A Vision of Connaught in the Thirteenth Century," "A Lament for Sir Maurice Fitzgerald,"** and others of lesser note, but he did not give up altogether his mere rhyming exercises. No further examples of his powers in that direction are, perhaps, necessary; but as **"The Rye Mill,"** which appeared in the *Nation* a week after **"The Warning Voice,"** has interesting associations, a couple of verses or so may be given here—

The drab-coloured river rushed on at full speed—
The Rye, that noblest of trout streams—
The coppices around looked very dun indeed,
As dim as the dimmest of Doubt's dreams.
To the north rose a hill o'er a field—or a fen;
But albeit I felt able to climb hill
And cliff like a goat, I didn't see it then—
I saw but the picturesque Rye Mill!
And winged, as with light, were the weeks of my stay
In its neighbourhood! We all know how slips
The long day away with a boy while at play,
With a girl while gathering cowslips:
But mine was but a moment from morn unto eve,
Though in truth I was part of the time ill
With a cold in my throat, which I caught, I believe,
Through a hole in the wall of the Rye Mill.

. . . .

What's the Chancellor himself?[11] A mummy in a wig.
What's his office? At best a sublime ill.
Take the woolsack, O Brougham! but let me sit and swig
Adam's ale[12] on a meal sack in Rye Mill!

This mill, on the Rye, near Leixlip, had a peculiar fascination for Mangan, who had seen it in earlier years, when it had taken a strong hold on his imagination. Not long after the appearance of the poem just quoted, and in the same year, Mangan returns to the subject in the *Nation,* but this time he calls it a saw mill. In sending **"The Saw Mill"** to Duffy, he says:—

The lines I enclose are something *apropos de rien* of a mill that I remember having seen in my boyish days in Rye Valley, Leixlip. If they suit you I shall be glad, and if they do not, why somebody else will be, of course—for spaces must be filled up in newspapers as well as in society.

The poem is so peculiar, so strange, that perhaps readers who do not know it will like to see it. Here it is:—

My path lay towards the Mourne agen,
But I stopped to rest at the hill-side
That glanced adown o'er the sunken glen,
Which the Saw-and-Water-mills hide,
Which now, as then,
The Saw-and-Water-mills hide.

And there as I lay reclined on the hill,
Like a man made by sudden qualm ill,
I heard the water in the Water-mill
And saw the saw in the Saw-mill!
As I thus lay still,
I saw the saw in the Saw-mill!

The saw, the breeze, and the humming bees,
Lulled me into a dreamy reverie,
Till the objects round me, hills, mills, trees,
Seemed grown alive, all and every,
By slow degrees
Took life, as it were, each and every!

Anon the sound of the waters grew
To a dreary, mournful ditty,
And the sound of the tree that the saw sawed through
Disturbed my spirit with pity,
Began to subdue
My spirit with tenderest pity!

Oh, wanderer! the hour that brings thee back
Is of all meet hours the meetest.
Thou now, in sooth, art on the track,
Art nigher to home than thou weetest!
Thou hast thought Time slack,
But his flight has been of the fleetest!

For thee it is that I dree such pain
As, when wounded, even a plank will;
My bosom is pierced, is rent in twain,
That thine may ever bide tranquil,
May ever remain
Henceforward untroubled and tranquil.

In a few days more, most Lonely One!
Shall I, as a narrow ark, veil
Thine eyes from the glare of the world and run
'Mong the urns in yonder dark vale,
In the cold and dun
Recesses of yonder dark vale!

For this grieve not! Thou knowest what thanks
The weary-souled and meek owe
To Death! I awoke, and heard four planks
Fall down with a saddening echo,
I heard four planks
Fall down with a saddening echo!

Whether Mangan, who was, as he himself tells us, "a being of incredible sensibility," actually heard in his boyish visit to the Rye the falling of planks, or whether he merely dreamt of the incident, the poem is highly characteristic. The reference to death reminds one that he had for years looked forward to it as to a release from trials too hard to bear. He did not conceal from his friends—nor even from his readers—that it would be welcome; he mentions somewhere, indeed, that he had serious notions of emulating Cato, and of compassing what he so much longed for.

Although he was now writing almost constantly for the *Nation* and *University Magazine,* his friends were rarely able to meet him. Father Meehan saw most of him during these last years, being prepared to seek him out in the most noisome alleys and courts in the city—places where others would not go. Mangan would not and could not reform to oblige his friends; it is almost certain that, with the loss of a power of restraint, he had also lost the wish or will to restrain himself. James Price says of this period:—

> At last friends could do nothing for him. The ever-gnawing craving for excitement *would* be satisfied, though self-respect and man's esteem were sacrificed. Pity him, weep for him, but censure him not! His own self reproaches were abundant punishment for his fault. The horror of his waking reaction was a terrible expiation to pay for human infirmity.

He would promise earnestly to change his habits, and really made heroic efforts to carry out his promises, but all without avail. In one of his lighter effusions he admits that no amount of teaching can effect a change if the will is not present. A line or two will suffice:—

> Philosophy, thou preachest
> Vainly unto all who take to tippling or the tea-chest;
> Wonder-worker truly wert thou couldst thou but achieve a
> Change in our Teetotalites, who sit and count their siller,
> Or in our Teetotumites who reel from post to pillar.

Yet he would voluntarily abstain, sometimes for weeks, from drink, though it was evident to all who knew him that he suffered agonies in the effort.

Even before he began to drink at all, as has already been stated, his nerves were practically destroyed, and his nervous condition in moments of extreme distress was pitiable to witness. The present writer has heard from the lips of some of those who knew Mangan descriptions which are too painful to write. Only a faint glimpse of him here and there can be attempted. A certain distinguished Dublin physician informs me that he saw him one bitterly cold night, insufficiently clad, steal into the *Nation* office, and hand into Mr. Fullam, the manager, a few pages of manuscript, begging at the same time that some money should be given to him on account. The manager told him that he was prohibited from doing so; he had received peremptory orders not to advance money to any contributor. Mangan implored so earnestly that at last he was given a small sum, and my informant tells me that one would have imagined from his manner in receiving it that he had just been reprieved from a sentence of immediate death. The sequel is pathetic. The manuscript handed in was the **"Warning Voice,"** which appeared in the next issue of the paper. The same scene was often repeated in M'Glashan's office. M'Glashan declined to pay Mangan except in small amounts, knowing full well that the unfortunate poet would have been speedily relieved of the whole sum, if he had got it, by his brother and other hangers-on, though Mangan would solemnly assure him, and often with truth, that he urgently wanted the whole amount for necessary purchases, or to pay off a specially pressing debt for rent. But the publisher was well aware that any artful knave or cajoler among those with whom he chose to associate could easily frustrate any such intention as Mangan expressed. One of the letters already given has some bearing upon this point, and in the following note Mangan explains to M'Glashan what he had done with money which had been given him—money which was not a gift, but due for work worth ten times such remuneration:—

> My Dear Sir—With what you so kindly and off-handedly gave me on Tuesday I was enabled to procure several articles of dress (shirts, stockings, etc). I was, in truth, very much in need of them. If you will say £2 for the enclosed contribution I shall be quite satisfied. This will enable me not only to settle with my worthy hostess, and, I am sorry to say, unworthy laundress, but, my dear sir, it will provide me with the means of procuring some books of Danish and Swedish poetry. I know where these are to be had, and very cheap, and I confess I would prefer the possession of one book purchased with my own earnings to that of a hundred presented to me by others. Alas! if it were not so should I not have a large (foreign) library today? For what munificence could surpass yours towards me in that same article of books?

In another letter he mentions that he has been offered the post of French and German correspondent in a Liverpool house (Wilmington and Pratt's), in which situation, he says, the hours of work will kill him. He asks M'Glashan to save him from this alternative to literature.

> In the name of heaven, advance me something with the generosity which has always characterised your dealings with me. If you will not, let me know the worst. . . . If you decide against doing so—and if you do, I must acknowledge you will decide justly—I shall not complain. My circumstances have rendered me quite reckless.

Then a little later he writes:—

> On reflection I think it better to adhere to my promise, and to ask no more money in advance. I cannot always continue, even for the sake of others, to submit to the forfeiture of self-respect. It would and could only end in destroying the last particle of spirit within me, and would render me alike a reproach to myself and a burthen to others.

One other letter to M'Glashan during this period will suffice just now:—

> I have always, my dear sir, found you very kind and off-hand in your pecuniary transactions; indeed, in this respect I know nobody like you. I make you now a fresh proposal, and I pledge myself to work for you with all the powers of my mind and intellect. I pledge myself to rise early, to labour hard, not to spare myself, to endeavour to cultivate my intellectual powers to their highest point, and, in fine, to redeem the last and past years of my life as far as may be possible. In fact, I pledge myself to become a new man in soul, body, mind, character, and conduct. But my fate now, I say it solemnly, is in your hands. You have been hitherto the kindest of friends to me, and I trust

> in heaven you will not now, in the darkest hour of my life, abandon me.

Another friend of Mangan was John O'Daly, the second-hand bookseller, of Anglesea Street, in whose shop the poet was frequently to be found. He made rough metrical versions of Munster poems for O'Daly, who gave him from time to time very small sums for them. Anglesea Street had several other booksellers of note at this period. One, Patrick Kennedy, was a literary man of no mean order. His collections of folk tales and his Wexford and Carlow sketches have earned a deserved popularity. Another, M. W. Rooney, is remembered as the publisher of many useful school classics, and as the fortunate finder of a very early edition of *Hamlet,* concerning which he has published a pamphlet. O'Daly was chiefly known as a publisher and editor of Gaelic books, but he brought out other works of a creditable character. Finally Bryan Geraghty, another Anglesea Street bibliopole, issued Connellan's *Annals of the Four Masters,* the cost of which ruined him. It did not meet with sufficient support, and, naturally, O'Donovan's far greater and more complete edition injured to a very considerable extent its chances of success. Connellan's imperfect edition has its particular interest here, for it was Mangan who "Englished" it, Connellan not being particularly well acquainted with that language. O'Donovan thus refers to it in one of his letters to Davis:—

> The translation of the *Annals of the Four Masters,* published by Mr. Geraghty, though put into readable English by Mangan, is full of errors, and you will find it very unsafe to trust it.

But it was John O'Daly, among the booksellers, with whom Mangan was mostly connected. He would be found occasionally in Rooney's, where he frequently obtained the loan of books; but he did a considerable amount of work for O'Daly of a more or less crude kind. His translations from the Irish, which form the well-known volume, ***The Poets and Poetry of Munster*** (published after his death), are rarely of high poetical merit. Many of them are decidedly inferior to the previous versions by Edward Walsh, Ferguson, and Callanan. Of the fifty-six poems in the book, not much more than a dozen are worthy of Mangan's gifts. It is very doubtful whether he would have allowed them to appear in their present more or less prosaic form.

The only two pieces which are really well-known are **"The Fair Hills of Erin,"** and **"The Dame of the Slender Wattle,"** though they are not the best poems in the volume. A number of these pieces were written for O'Daly in the little shop, quickly, and almost without consideration, and it is more than probable that Mangan, had he been alive at the time of publication, would have given them, as he often did with his earlier poems, an additional polish, or other necessary revision. That some injury is done to his fame by the popular impression that this is a very important work of his, is clear from the fact that one or two English writers have spoken slightingly of his Irish poems simply from a study of this volume. For example, Mr. John H. Ingram, both in his well-meant but hopelessly innacurate account of Mangan in the *Dublin University Magazine* for December, 1877, and in his somewhat less inadequate criticism of the poet in Miles's *Poets and Poetry of the Century,* characterises his Irish translations as "spiritless" and poor. If he had said that those in ***The Poets and Poetry of Munster*** were generally so, he would have been, even then, rather unduly severe; but the implication that all Mangan's Irish translations (that is, of course, those he is acquainted with) are in the same category, is preposterous. His truly magnificent Irish poems do not belong to ***The Poets and Poetry of Munster,*** and, indeed, were not written for O'Daly at all. The poems translated for O'Daly, are, in fact, mostly mere drafts for future consideration, made from the bookseller's own prose translations, and the volume only contains pieces which were unpublished at his death. In the pieces like **"Dark Rosaleen,"** and **"A Cry for Ireland,"** he followed not his originals but his phantasy, and deviated widely from the former whenever he chose to do so—which was pretty often. They are rather voluntaries upon Irish themes than translations.

Mangan had only the merest smattering of Irish so far, but he began to learn it in earnest, so far as I can make out, some time in this year of 1846, to which we have arrived. O'Daly's shop was one of his known haunts. Its proprietor was a curious man, not specially loved by certain of his countrymen on account of his coquetting with the "soupers," in whose ranks he had enrolled himself somewhat earlier. When the little boys in Kilkenny began to run after him, calling out "souper," he thought it time to give up his new friends, and used to mollify the urchins by saying, "Aisy, boys, amn't I goin' to lave thim?" John Keegan, the poet, has left us in one of his unpublished letters a sketch of O'Daly, which may be worth quoting here:—

> "John O'Daly," he says, "the publisher of the *Jacobite Relics,*[13] is another intimate friend of mine. He and I corresponded every week. He is a County Waterford man. I first met him in Kilkenny in 1833, when he kept the school there for teaching Irish to the Wesleyans of that city. He, I am sorry to say, renounced the Catholic creed, and was then a furious Biblical. He subsequently came back, and is now living in Dublin, secretary to the 'Celtic Athenæum,' and keeps a bookseller's shop in Anglesea Street. He is one of the best Irish scholars in Ireland. He is about fifty-five years of age, low-sized, merry countenance, fine black eyes, vulgar in appearance and manner, and has the most magnificent Munster brogue on his tongue that I ever had the luck to hear."

Before closing this chapter it may be worth while to quote an anonymous squib of Mangan's from the *Nation* of April 4th, 1846. It had then its special significance for Irishmen:—

THE DOMICILIARY VISIT

(*A Scene in the Faubourg St. Antoine, Paris.,*
Dramatis Personæ—
An Officer of the Gendarmerie and a Citizen.)

OFF.:

De par le Roi. You are Pierre Coulisse?

CIT.:

I am.

OFF.:

I thought so. Scan date,
Address, and signature of this!
(*Gives him a paper.*)

CIT.:

(*reads*) "Arrest—by Royal mandate . . ."
Why, what's my crime? *J'ignore*——

OFF.:

Poh! Poh!
Of course, young man, you ignore it—
Your name is in the Black Book, though,
With two red marks before it!
Whence came you by those four cane-swords?

CIT.:

Cane-swords? Which?

OFF.:

Yonder sham-rods!

CIT.:

They are mere tobacco-pipes.

OFF.:

No words!—
(*Writes*—"Two poniards and two ramrods"!)

CIT.:

Heavens! You don't mean——

OFF.:

A Frenchman means
The thing he does. Your press-keys!
(*Opens a drawer.*)
What make you with those tools?

CIT.:

Machines.

OFF.:

Ay, such machines as Fieschi's![14]
Pray, what's that carbine-like affair
Behind the window-shutter?

CIT.:

A walking-stick. (*Il en a l'air.*)

OFF.:

Speak up, sir! What d'ye mutter?

CIT.:

A stick.

OFF.:

Don't shout! A lie's no truth
Because 'tis bellowed louder.
A gun, you mean. A stick, forsooth!
Why, one can smell the powder!
(*Takes up a book.*)
Ha! "Treatise on the Poles"!

CIT.:

The South
And North Poles only.

OFF.:

Rebel!
How dare you ope your *gamin* mouth?
Your explanations treble
Your guilt. South Pole and North? To what
Owes Earth its *revolutions*
If not to these, you leveller-flat
Of thrones and institutions?
Give up that letter! Ha! what's here? (*Reads*)
"Dear Claude, I could not borrow
One hour to-day; but never fear,
I'll do the job to-morrow."
So-ho! The job? Oh, yes!—we hit
The meaning of such letters—
You'll do *the King's* job—eh? That's it!
Come, Jean, put on his fetters!"

Notes

1. March 15th, 1843.

2. May 13th of the same year.

3. A little earlier, when Duffy had asked him to write political articles, he had declined, sending instead some epigrams—"Do not ask me for political essays just now—I have no experience in that *genre d'ecrire,* and I should infallibly blunder. I send you six pages . . . 'Jokeriana,' 'Jokerisms,' 'Flim-flam,' 'Whim-whams,' or anything else you like to call them. . . . They might do for your fourth page—pray Heaven you don't imagine they'd do for your paper altogether."

4. Mangan was fond of the number three; witness his "Three Tormentors," "The Threefold Prediction," etc.

5. "In addition to paying Mangan liberally," says Sir C. G. Duffy, in a letter to the present writer, "for whatever he wrote, I have memoranda in his own handwriting acknowledging about £100, in sums of £5, £10, and £15."

6. See *Irish Monthly,* 1883, p. 381.

7. It is now published in two small shilling volumes by James Duffy.

8. In Macaulay's Diary is a reflection to practically the same effect—that children are the truest poets, by the strength of their imagination.
9. The last refrain of all is—

> Hark! again the rueful winds are blowing,
> And alas! I want a loan!

10. It appeared on February 21st, 1846. Mitchel erroneously attributes it to 1847, when, of course, it would have been practically a prophecy "after the event."
11. Lord Brougham.
12. Water.
13. By Edward Walsh.
14. "I need not remind the reader that Fieschi is regarded as the inventor of the most terrific 'infernal machines' of modern times." (Mangan's note).

Jacques Chuto (essay date 1976)

SOURCE: Chuto, Jacques. "Mangan, Petrie, O'Donovan, and a Few Others: The Poet and the Scholars." *Irish University Review* 6.2 (1976): 169-87. Print.

[*In the following essay, Chuto suggests that errors in Mangan's translation of Aenghus O'Daly's* The Tribes of Ireland *were too obvious to be attributed to Mangan's collaborators John O'Daly, who published the edition in which the translation appeared, and John O'Donovan, who introduced the volume, and thus were probably Mangan's own. Chuto regards the mistakes as evidence that Mangan translated the work by himself.*]

A popular image of James Clarence Mangan represents him as a gaunt, cloak-wrapped figure who walked the shady streets of Dublin, hugging the walls on his way, as John Mitchel puts it, to "the lowest and obscurest taverns," there to consort "with the offal of the human species."[1] Stripped of its romantic sensationalism, the picture may have some relevance to the poet's last years, but is quite misleading when applied to the rest of his life. The *poète maudit* never was a society man, of course, but before turning himself into a social outcast he had known most of the talented people in Dublin.

The present article focuses on the relationship between Mangan and those scholars who were instrumental in the development of Gaelic studies in the first half of the nineteenth century. Mangan's acquaintance with these people had a definite influence on his poetical career since they enabled him to widen the scope of his own work by guiding him into the field of Irish literature.

* * *

Foremost among the scholars were George Petrie and John O'Donovan. Mangan's collaboration with them began in the columns of the *Dublin Penny Journal.* This periodical was started by Petrie and Caesar Otway with the chief purpose of making the Irish public better acquainted with the antiquities of their country. The first number came out on 30 June 1832, and Mangan's first contribution appeared on 15 September.[2] Characteristically enough, it took the form of a hoax. Under the heading "Irish Literature" a translation from the Italian was introduced as follows:

> An Italian gentleman residing in Liverpool who has politely informed us that he is a constant reader of our Journal, after a few very handsome postpaid compliments, has challenged us to produce in all Irish poetry a match to the following *Aria* from Metastasio:
>
> *Timid Love*
>
> Ah! gentle zephyr, ah! if e'er
> Thou find the mistress of my heart,
> Tell her thou art a sigh sincere,
> But never say whose sigh thou art!
>
> Ah! limpid rivulet, if e'er
> Thy murmuring waters near her glide,
> Say thou art swelled by many a tear,
> But not whose eyes those tears supplied.[3]

This rather weak piece was followed by an aggressively sarcastic commentary:

> Very pretty, Signor, and worthy of the land of comfits and confections, of gilt-edged looking-glasses and sugared plums. Why, man alive, an Irish girl would knock the blubbering blockhead down who would sneak after her with zephyrs and sighs, limpid rivulets, and eyes red and swollen, like a child whipt for not taking its physic. . . . Pretty, no doubt it is; but we doubt much if it is not more the language of refined and courtly affectation than that of nature. . . .
>
> Our friend's challenge will have this effect: instead of setting us a hunting after prettily turned conceits, expressed in mellifluous syllabics, it will only stimulate our previously-formed intention of entering the MINE of ancient Irish literature, and bring out from the obscurity of oblivion those treasures of intellect and genius and antiquarian curiosity which are there to be found . . .

And after a scholarly dissertation on Celtic dialects, the writer of the article presents his readers with "the first translation which has ever appeared" of *King Aldfred's Poem*:

> I found in the fair Innisfail,
> In Ireland while in exile
> Many women, no silly crowd,
> Many laics, many clerics . . .

The translation, loaded with learned footnotes, is signed J. O'D.

On 7 August 1832, John O'Donovan had written to George Petrie:

> I made a translation of the poem ascribed to Aldfred, King of the Northumbrian Britons. I intend to get a poetical friend to versify it with a view to getting it published in some periodical.[4]

Did he have Mangan in mind? There does not seem to be any proof of their having met at that time.[5] The translation published in the *Dublin Penny Journal* was not versified, and Mangan's rhymed version of it did not appear until 1846, when it was included in H. R. Montgomery's *Specimens of the Early Native Poetry of Ireland.* Still, it is tempting to conjecture that Mangan and O'Donovan worked hand in hand for that issue of 15 September. Masquerading as a provocative Italian gentleman living in England, the former enabled the latter to assert his "Irishness" all the more stoutly. The cloying sweetness of **"Timid Love"** was meant to be set against the stark vigour of "Aldfred's Poem." Even if the hypothesis is completely fanciful, it cannot have been long before the two men were brought together, because the 'polemic' did not stop there.

The issue of the *Dublin Penny Journal* for 13 October contained the following letter:

> ITALIAN LITERATURE
>
> To the Editor of the Dublin Penny Journal
>
> My dear Sir,—The Editor of the *Liverpool Mercury* has very handsomely noticed your "Weekly Penny Journal" and has made an extract, including the Aria of which he speaks very warmly. I forgive your remarks, which were made, no doubt, in that spirit which is so peculiar to your country, rash and intemperate. The following Arias are from that great dramatist, whose language you say is that "of affectation," and "more adapted to the opera house" than to what?—"the simplicity of the common feelings of humanity"!! Let the reader judge.

There followed two translations which were hardly better than **"Timid Love."** The letter ended with a further paragraph of banter, and it was signed "A Constant Reader."

This letter was allowed to pass unchallenged in the *Dublin Penny Journal* itself. But the following week, the quarrel was taken up in another quarter. On 21 October, *The Comet,* the anti-tithe weekly to which Mangan had been contributing for nearly five months, had an article on Irish literature which denounced

> … a recent attempt through the medium of the *Dublin Penny Journal* to set the lyrical effusions of Italy above those of Ireland. The comparison is as invidious as it is unjust; for the thoughts, feelings, and sympathies of the Irish bards are totally dissimilar to those of the Italian minstrels. In the former we are pleased with continual strains of natural sentiment, and in the latter we are sickened with the constant recurrence of polished rhymes, of art and affectation.

Apparently undeterred by the opposition, Mangan repeated the offence. On 10 November and 1 December, two more Italian translations appeared in the *Dublin Penny Journal.* Both poems were given without comment either from Mangan or from the editor. The signature was a mere 'C,' to which was appended, however, the alleged address of the sender: Clarence Street, Liverpool.[6]

Then, on 22 December, Petrie's *Journal* published a translation in blank verse, **"The Dream of Mac Donnell Claragh"**:

> 'Twas night and buried in deep sleep I lay,
> Strange visions rose before me, and my thoughts
> Played wildly through the chambers of my brain …

It was Mangan's first Irish attempt. The poem was unsigned, but a draft in the poet's hand exists in the National Library of Ireland.[7] This Jacobite relic was preceded by a brief notice on John Mac Donnell, probably written by O'Donovan, who in all likelihood had made the literal translation on which Mangan worked.

There is proof that the poet and the Irish scholar knew each other by this time. On 5 January 1833, Mangan published his first original poem in the *Journal,* **"The Dying Enthusiast to His Friend."** O'Donovan must have been referring to this poem when he wrote to Petrie on 23 December 1832: "I enclose a poem of the original composition of Mr Mangan. I should be glad, if you think it fit for the Journal, that you would insert it."[8] Since O'Donovan was not the editor of the *Journal,* it is unlikely that Mangan would have sent his poem to him unless they were personally acquainted.

By then Mangan had become a regular contributor to Petrie's periodical. In 1833, besides **"The Dying Enthusiast to His Friend,"** he sent the *Journal* two more original poems as well as translations from the Italian and the German. Most of these were signed "Clarence." But on 20 April our old friend the Italian "Constant Reader" from Clarence Street, Liverpool, wrote another letter to the editor. Its main argument is that Irish is difficult to learn because Irish grammars "differ so much in their pronunciation." We may take it therefore that, even at that early date, Mangan had begun to study Irish. The rest of the letter shows a scholarly bent in his ambition:

> I intend, Mr Editor, (Deo volente) in a few years hence, to travel into Denmark, Sweden, Norway, where I might chance to pick up some valuable Irish manuscripts.
>
> I saw, it is two years since, two interlineal translations of St John's Gospel announced in the *Dublin Evening Post*; would your able correspondent O'Donovan inform me which is the better for acquiring a facility in translation?

This sounds most promising. Unfortunately, the *Dublin Penny Journal* failed to be a financial success and was sold. On 3 August 1833, the new owner/editor shamelessly proclaimed his policy:

> The editor will merely say that it is his intention to give his readers good value for their money—that the Dublin Penny Journal shall not be a mere "catch-penny," depending upon

> the number and excellence of its woodcuts for extensive circulation, but containing, as he considers a publication of the kind should do, such a variety of interesting and useful matter as shall render it really valuable.[9]

Small wonder that all former contributors brought their connection with the *Journal* to an end.

* * *

No longer under the immediate influence of O'Donovan and Petrie, Mangan did not turn his hand to Irish translation again for a number of years. That he did not lose all interest in the language, however, can be inferred from the following passage, jocular as it is, of **"A Dialogue in the Shades,"**[10] a prose article published in the *Weekly Dublin Satirist* more than a year after the last letter sent by the "Italian Constant Reader" to the *Dublin Penny Journal*:

> The bibber was too strong in Brutus. We find him haranguing a batch of ragamuffins with the words—
>
> "Friends, *rum'uns,* countryfolks and lubbers." O'Hoolaghan, however, a poet of the Firbolgs, accuses him of shying the genuine poteen, and says of him—
>
> "Trom-ól se munloch ó mhaidin go n-oídche."
>
> That is—"He muddles with hog-wash from daylight till dark."[11]

Mangan and the two Irish scholars were not brought together again, professionally at least, until the poet obtained employment as a copyist in the office of the historical branch of the Ordnance Survey. The head of the department was George Petrie and the office was at his residence, 21 Great Charles Street. The staff fell into two categories. There were those who could be sent to work in the country, and those who always stayed in Dublin on home duty. John O'Donovan (together with Eugene O'Curry and W. F. Wakeman) belonged to the first group, Mangan to the second. The poet's connection with the Ordnance Survey lasted almost four years, from the early months of 1838[12] to 31 December 1841, when the staff was drastically reduced. Although his part in the great work undertaken by Petrie and his team was inevitably modest, it brought him into daily contact with people whose main interests were Irish and antiquarian.

One result, however perverse, of this renewed intimacy may perhaps be found in an article published in the *Dublin University Magazine* for April 1839. Entitled **"A Polyglott Anthology,"** it takes the form of a dialogue between "the Herr Hoppandgoön von Baugtrauter, a celebrated traveller" and "the Herr Poppandgoöf von Tutschemupp, a distinguished critic," and contains "translations" from various languages such as Arabic, Chinese, Chippewawian, Hindustani, *and* Irish. The Irish pieces are five in number, each prefixed with the first line of the alleged original. For instance, **"Tim Sullivan's Plea"**—

> You say 'twas a cowardly spacies o' thievin,'
> Shtrippin' your panthry bare, lady;
> But that's what myself can't be afther believin,'
> For faint heart niver won fare, lady!

—is supposed to be a rendering of an Irish poem beginning with the line: 'Deir-tu gur gadaidhe meata me." The proverb, "Nicontrárdhacht gul don n-gáire" (that is, "Crying is not contradictory to laughter," or in Mangan's rendering, "Though Laughter seems, it never is, the antithesis to Tears") is presented as the opening line of the third canto of a "metaphysical poem"!

But the most interesting Irish item in the article is a fourteen-stanza poem entitled **"Lines on the Death of ***,"** supposedly a translation from a poem by a certain O'Reilly, beginning: "Bhi mo chroidhe trom; sheasas a bhfad o'n ait," that is: "My heart was heavy; I stood a long way from the place." Mangan's first stanza reads:

> I stood aloof: I dared not to behold
> Thy relics covered over with the mould—
> I shed no tear—I uttered not a groan—
> But oh! I felt heartbroken and alone!

Considering Mangan's well-known off-handedness with his originals, the connection between this and the above Irish quotation is close enough for the unsuspecting reader to accept the whole poem as a *bona fide* translation. However, the *Dublin University Magazine* poem was actually the second version of a piece published in *The Comet* six years earlier as an original composition, **"Elegiac Verses on the Early Death of a Beloved Friend."**[13] This friend was Catherine Hayes, a young girl to whom Mangan had been giving private tuition in German. Now, although Mangan was always reluctant to speak in his own voice and often chose to hide his melancholy or his despair behind the *persona* of some foreign poet, it is unlikely that these **"Elegiac Verses,"** which directly relate to an actual tragic event in his life, could have been merely borrowed from the Irish or from any other language. Moreover, the *Comet* version was nineteen stanzas long. For publication in the *Dublin University Magazine,* Mangan left out six stanzas and added this entirely new one:

> So may bright lilies and each odorous flower
> Grow o'er thy grave and form a beauteous bower,
> Exhaust their sweetness on the gales around,
> And drop, for grief, their honey on the ground.

Whereupon Baugtrauter remarks:

> This last stanza is so musical in the original that I must repeat it for you—
> Nois fasadh an lile 's gach fion-sgoth is blath mine,
> Os cionn na leaptha na bh-fuilir mo ghradh sinte,
> A's bidir go milis ad cuideacht a náit daoineadh,
> Ag silead a g-cuid meala air a d-talainh ad gnath cháoineadh.[14]

Mellifluous?

If the poem had really been a translation from the Irish, it is hard to see why Mangan should have excluded from its first version a stanza which he professedly thought so beautiful. It seems more reasonable to assume that these four lines, wherever they came from, were inserted in the second version not merely for their intrinsic value, but as further proof of the Irish authenticity of the whole poem.

"But, pray," Tutschemupp asks at one point in the dialogue, "who supplied you with the Irish? You never kissed the Blarney stone, I believe." Baugtrauter's answer is that he got it from a certain Felix O'Gallagher, a Corkonian poet who died of the yellow fever in the United States! Who this F. O'G. actually was is an open question. The character of Petrie, O'Donovan, or even O'Curry, makes it hardly likely that any of them, knowingly at least, could have lent Mangan a hand in playing such tricks on the readers of the *Dublin University Magazine.*

A more serious collaboration was soon made possible between Mangan and his learned friends and colleagues of the Ordnance Survey. On 4 July 1840 Petrie launched a new magazine, the *Irish Penny Journal,* which was "as like the old one as two peas."[15] Mangan contributed to it from the start, and his increased interest in Irish literature manifested itself in the fact that, out of the seventeen pieces he wrote for the *Irish Penny Journal,* five were translations from the Gaelic. The first of these was **"The Woman of Three Cows"**:

> O Woman of Three Cows, agragh! don't let your tongue thus rattle!
> O, don't be saucy, don't be stiff, because you may have cattle.
> I have seen—and, here's my hand to you, I only say what's true—
> A many a one with twice your stock not half so proud as you.

It appeared on 29 August 1840 under the heading "Ancient Irish Literature, Number I," and was prefixed with a short introduction written by Petrie himself:

> We propose to ourselves, as a pleasing task, to make our literature more familiar, not only to the Irish scholar, but to our readers generally who do not possess this species of knowledge, by presenting them from time to time with such short poems or prose articles, accompanied with translations, as from their brevity, or the nature of their subjects, will render them suitable to our limited and necessarily varied pages—our selections being made without regard to chronological order . . . but rather with a view to give a general idea of the several kinds of literature in which our ancestors of various classes found entertainment.

"The Woman of Three Cows" was followed by **"An Elegy on the Tyronian and Tyrconnellian Princes, Buried at Rome"** (17 October), **"Bodach an Chota-Lachtna, or the Clown with the Grey Coat"** (a prose tale, 24 October), **"Lamentation of Mac Liag for Kincora"** (9 January 1841), and lastly **"Kathaleen Ny-Houlahan"** (16 January). The latter was supposed to begin a new series, "The Jacobite Relics of Ireland," which unfortunately never went any further.

Although his having written these pieces shows that Mangan's interest in Irish literature had kept growing since the days of the *Dublin Penny Journal,* he still seems to have been unable to translate from the Irish single-handed. When Charles Gavan Duffy published his *Ballad Poetry of Ireland* in 1845, he included the first, second and fourth of Mangan's translations for the *Irish Penny Journal.* The praise he gave them in his introduction prompted Eugene O'Curry to send the following letter to Thomas Davis:

> I find Mr Mangan put forth as the best of all translators from the Irish. Now it so happens that Mr Mangan has no knowledge of the Irish language, nor do I think he regrets that either . . . It was I that translated those poems (the three of them) from the originals—that is, I turned the Irish words into English, and Mr Mangan put those English words, beautifully and faithfully, as well as I can judge, into English rhyme. If I have not made a faithful translation, then the versification is not correct, for it contains nothing but what is found in the translation, nor does it contain a single idea that is not found, and as well expressed, in the original.[16]

The tone of this letter is rather strange. It seems to smack of professional jealousy, as though O'Curry resented Mangan's getting all the glory for poems in the production of which the scholar thought he had taken at least as great a share as the poet. To support his claim, it is clear that O'Curry overstated Mangan's faithfulness to the literal translations with which he had provided him. Mangan's rendering of **"Kathaleen Ny-Houlahan"** was prefixed in the *Irish Penny Journal* with a foreword which stated that the translations published by James Hardiman in his *Irish Minstrelsy* in 1831 were "too free to enable the English reader to form any very accurate idea of the Irish originals." He went on to say, "We are therefore tempted to present a series of these relics to our readers with translations of a more literal and faithful description." While it cannot be denied that Mangan's translation of this particular poem sounds more Irish than anything to be found in Hardiman's volumes, his 'adaptation' of the last two lines of the second stanza suffices to contradict O'Curry's assertion. A literal rendering of these should have been: "It's long again 'till she'd be a nursing mother and her brood would be large / If the King's son had Kathleen Ny Houlahan."[17] Mangan glossed over the sexual implications of this, and his translation reads: "Young she is and fair she is and would be crowned a queen, / Were the King's son at home with Kathaleen Ny-Houlahan."

John O'Donovan himself seems to have had his doubts whether Mangan adhered as closely to his originals as he was supposed to do. In a letter to Davis, which was probably written at about the same time as O'Curry's, he says:

> I know English about six times better than I know Irish, but I have no notion of becoming a forger like MacPherson. The translations from the Irish by Mangan, mentioned by

> Mr Duffy, are very good; but how near are they to the literal translations furnished to Mangan by Mr Curry? Are they the shadows of a shade?[18]

Note how the accusation of forgery aimed at MacPherson is implicitly extended to Mangan himself. Is there a hint of professional jealousy here as well?

"Kathaleen Ny-Houlahan" was the last poem Mangan wrote for the *Irish Penny Journal.*[19] The fifth (and last) instalment of "Ancient Irish Literature" consisted of an anonymous version of "The County of Mayo."[20]

* * *

The reason for Mangan's disappearance from the pages of the *Journal* is not known.[21] The magazine did not live much longer anyway. Due to lack of popular support in Ireland itself,[22] it was discontinued at the end of June 1841. However, Mangan's interest in the native literature of his country did not die with it. Although it lay dormant for a few years, as had happened after the breaking up of the original team of the *Dublin Penny Journal,* it came vividly to life again when Mangan joined the Young Ireland movement, and literary curiosity was transfigured by national enthusiasm.

Significantly, the first production of this new epoch in Mangan's life was a rhymed version of the first Irish translation he ever published, **"The Dream of John Mac Donnell"**:

> I lay in unrest—old thoughts of pain,
> That I struggled in vain to smother,
> Like midnight spectres haunted my brain—
> Dark fantasies chased each other.

This appeared in *The Nation,* the organ of the Young Irelanders, on 16 May 1846 and was followed, two weeks later, by Mangan's best-known poem, **"Dark Rosaleen."** From then on the poet's love for Irish literature never abated. He translated poems from the Irish for a number of periodicals including *The Nation,* the *Dublin University Magazine,* the *Irish Catholic Magazine,* and *The Irishman.* Most of his Irish translations for the *Dublin University Magazine* were included in a series of articles entitled **"Anthologia Hibernica,"** in his introduction to which Mangan declared:

> We copy no man. We follow in the track of none. Our labours—inferior as we cheerfully admit them to be—are altogether peculiar to ourself and our own tastes. At the same time we will not deny that the great and general impulse given to the Irish mind of late has exercised its legitimate influence over us. Slender as our talents are, we have become exceedingly desirous to dedicate them henceforward exclusively to the service of our country.[23]

This profession of faith was published in February 1847. The sly "Italian gentleman" of the *Dublin Penny Journal* had certainly come a long way, but what had become of the ambition to learn Irish which he had expressed in April 1833? Was Mangan ever able to translate from the Irish without any sort of scholarly help from outside? It is a much debated point. In a letter to James M'Glashan, the publisher-cum-editor of the *Dublin University Magazine,* also written in 1847, Mangan says: "I have got two or three pupils whom I am instructing in German and Irish and hope to obtain more."[24] It seems hazardous, however, just to take his word for it; nor does it help to compare his translations with their Irish counterparts in order to ascertain whether they are faithful or not. Mangan knew German very well, but this did not prevent him from making free with his originals whenever he chose to do so, which was often. Similarly, even if he knew Irish, it is unlikely that he would always feel bound to be more scrupulous with Irish than with German literature. And although he often draws his readers' attention to the faithfulness of his Irish renderings, on one occasion he adds a most revealing remark:

> Of our own versions we shall say nothing, except that we believe they will be found, upon comparison with the originals, to possess the merit of fidelity—a merit, we admit, occasionally of a very questionable kind in translations.[25]

Like all the Irish poems Mangan had written for the *Irish Penny Journal,* some of his later translations from that language were based on literal translations which were brought to him by a scholarly friend or which he found here and there in books and magazines. It is well-known, for instance, that **"Dark Rosaleen"** and **"O'Hussey's Ode to the Maguire"** were based on the versions he found in Samuel Ferguson's review of Hardiman's *Irish Minstrelsy,* published in the *Dublin University Magazine* in 1834. In the same way, George Petrie's "Address to the Ruins of Donegal Castle," which appeared on 12 December 1840 in the *Irish Penny Journal,* helped Mangan to write his **"Ruins of Donegal Castle"** a few years later.[26] And the third article of the **"Anthologia Hibernica"** consists of two historical poems, "for literal translations of which," says Mangan, "we are indebted to the celebrated Irish scholar, Mr Eugene Curry."[27]

It is clear that Mangan had no need to know Irish to produce these poems. But what is to be made of the footnote he added to his poem **"The Three Plagues,"** published in the *Dublin University Magazine* for January 1848? Mangan here declared:

> For the original of this song, as well as for that of "The Gaels" in the last number of this magazine, I am indebted to the kindness of the distinguished Irish scholar, Eugene Curry, Esq., of the Royal Irish Academy.

Since O'Curry seems to have insisted on his help being acknowledged, as the reference to an earlier debt implies, it is difficult not to believe Mangan when he asserts that in the two instances mentioned he has only been given the *original texts,* not a literal translation of them. One could, therefore, confidently state that by this time Mangan knew enough Irish to be able to translate from it on his own, except of course that he might well have asked someone else to provide a literal translation of O'Curry's text. Such a person was available in John O'Daly, bookseller and publisher, undoubtedly a lesser scholar than Petrie, O'Donovan, or O'Curry, but one who did much for the popularisation of Gaelic studies.

Yet, every time Mangan acknowledges O'Daly's help—and this happens in the case of four poems, three of which appeared in *The Nation* in 1846, and the fourth one in *The Irishman* in 1849[28]—he only states that he is indebted to him for the originals. No mention is made of a literal translation. That Mangan was not simply sinning by omission may be inferred from a letter he wrote to Charles Gavan Duffy, the editor of *The Nation*:

> My dear Duffy, I have been for the last hour translating and transcribing (at the same moment) a poem from the Irish . . . I am exceedingly anxious that it should appear to-morrow—for Daly, of Anglesea St, who gave it to me thinks I am trifling with him, as I have promised any time these three weeks that it should appear in the Nation . . . If you can't print it by tomorrow, pray give me a line to the effect, that I may show it to Daly, for his suspicions have caused me much pain.[29]

This appears to mean that O'Daly was at least as anxious as O'Curry that he should be given his due. He wanted his name to appear in *The Nation,* and if he had provided Mangan with literal translations as well as with Irish originals, it is most likely that he would have wanted the full debt to be acknowledged.

O'Daly seems to have played a less modest part in the making of ***The Poets and Poetry of Munster,*** a volume he published a few months after Mangan's death in 1849, and which included some fifty translations by our poet. According to O'Donoghue, most of these were "mere drafts for future consideration, made from the bookseller's own prose translations."[30] This statement, however, needs to be qualified. There seems to have been a good deal more to it than the mere versifying of a prose rendering in a fair number of these poems. Consider Andrew MacGrath's "An bhláth-bhruingioll," translated by Mangan as **"The Flower of All Maidens."** In his *Love Songs of Connacht,* Douglas Hyde gives the fourth verse of this piece together with his own translation of it.[31] Here are Hyde's and Mangan's versions.

> Hyde: Oh, love of my love, do not *hate me,*
> For love, I am *aching* for thee;
> And my love for my love I'll *forsake* not,
> O love, till I *fade* like a tree.
> Since I gave thee my love I am *failing,*
> My love, wilt thou *aid* me to flee?
> And my love, O my love, if thou *take not*
> —No love for a *maiden* from me.[32]

> Mangan: Oh! loveliest! do not desert me!
> My earliest love was for you—
> And if thousands of woes should begirt me,
> To you would I prove myself true!
> Through my life you have been my consoler,
> My comforter—never in vain,—
> Had you failed to extinguish my dolor,
> I should never have languished in pain!

Hyde's rendering is undoubtedly better than Mangan's from which, among other things, the incantatory changes rung on the word *cumann* (affection) in the original have disappeared (except in the first two lines, where one catches a faint echo of them). Yet two things should be noted. First, the syllabic count is identical in both versions; secondly, although Mangan, unlike Hyde, fails to reproduce the original's play on one vowel-sound throughout the stanza, one can find in his translation what may have looked to him like approximations to interlinear rhyming: desert—earliest—begirt; you—you—prove—true; vain—failed—pain. The result may be thought unconvincing, but the effort was made.

Now, it seems unlikely that a mere literal rendering could have made Mangan aware of the vocalic subtlety of the original (Hyde's own literal translation of the stanza certainly gives no idea of it). Even with a rendering by O'Daly before him, therefore, Mangan must also have taken a close look at the Irish text.[33]

A final element in support of the theory that towards the end of his life Mangan earnestly tried to fulfil his early ambition to learn Irish is, ironically enough, that the undertaking never seems to have been a complete success. Mangan made mistakes. His translation of **"The Tribes of Ireland,"** by the Elizabethan satirist Aengus O'Daly, is a case in point. It appeared in 1852, three years after Mangan's death, as a kind of appendix to John O'Donovan's scholarly edition of that work, and was headed as follows:

> A VERSIFIED PARAPHRASE, or imitation, of AENGHUS O'DALY'S SATIRES, by JAMES CLARENCE MANGAN, arranged to agree with the stanzas as they now stand in the original Irish—with the *ranns* omitted by J. C. M. pointed out in footnotes, by J. O'D.

Since John O'Daly was the publisher of the volume, it is hard to say whether the initials refer to him or to O'Donovan. The point, however, is not very important. More interesting is the fact that the footnotes are not actually restricted to the pointing out of Mangan's omissions. They also comment here and there upon the quality of his rendering, with such remarks as: "The poet Mangan is not very happy in his translation here," or "The translator goes too far here," or again "Mangan totally mistook the meaning of this quatrain."

In none of these instances, however, is it absolutely clear whether Mangan really misunderstood the original or whether, as he so often did when translating from other languages, he deliberately diverged from it to produce something more congenial to himself. But, in at least one instance, the misconstruction is obvious. The third stanza of the section dealing with the tribes of Ulster reads in Mangan's translation:

> My curse on Drumsnaghta, that beggarly hole,
> Without meat-stall or fish-shop,—priest, vicar, or bishop!
> I saw in their temple, and Oh! my sick soul!
> A profound Irish feeling of shame stirs
> Thy depths at the thought, playing hookey, two gamesters.

To which J. O'D. appends the following note:

> *Gamesters.* This is incorrect. Aenghus merely complains that the church of Drumsnat had no Herenach, and that there were only two *cáirnigh* or priests (not *cearbhaigh* or gamesters) at the church. He expected a regular parish establishment; and every parish of any wealth had an Herenach, and three priests at the least.[34]

This note clearly contradicts O'Donoghue's assertion that while translating **"The Tribes of Ireland"** Mangan had "a version by John O'Donovan before him."[35] And since it is unlikely that John O'Daly could have made such a mistake either, it can be safely concluded that Mangan translated this work on his own.

* * *

With the publication of ***The Tribes of Ireland,*** the fecund relationship between Mangan and the Irish scholars was brought to a posthumous close. It is tempting, after all, to assume that it was John O'Donovan who was responsible for the footnotes to Mangan's translation. The rigid scholar can then be pictured, venting in those curt comments his irritation at what must have appeared to him as carelessness or offhandedness on the part of the poet, and looking very much as though he were marking a paper by a former pupil of his who had not turned out as nicely as expected. O'Donovan and his learned colleagues certainly failed to recognise the poet's right to do whatever he wanted with the material they brought him; but this failure does not detract in the least from their merit as men who enabled Mangan to discover Irish poetry and to write a passionate chapter in the history of Anglo-Irish literature.

Notes

1. John Mitchel (ed.), *Poems by James Clarence Mangan* (New York: P. M. Haverty, 1859), p. 18.

2. Not in November, as D. J. O'Donoghue wrongly states in his *Life and Writings of J. C. Mangan* (Dublin:———, 1897), p. 34.

3. The original is given with the translation.

4. National Library of Ireland, MS. 792. In another letter O'Donovan wrote: "I have made a translation of a poem ascribed to Alfred, King of the Northumbrian Britons ... I have given this translation with some notes and observations to the editor of the Dublin Penny Journal, a little publication which appears to me very respectable and which has a very wide circulation" (letter to Myles J. O'Reilly, dated 10 September 1832, Royal Irish Academy, MS. 12 N II).

5. "I was rather a young man when I first met with Mr O'Donovan, who was still younger than I." This is all Mangan tells us in his article on John O'Donovan (*The Irishman,* 14 July 1849). Mangan was born in 1803, O'Donovan in 1809.

6. This is the first appearance of Mangan's well-known *nom de plume,* 'Clarence,' although he had for several months been using the signature 'J. C. M.,' where the middle initial corresponds to nothing in his baptismal name.

7. National Library of Ireland, MS. 138.

8. Royal Irish Academy, MS. 12 N5. The poem was not actually original in the strictest sense, for it had already appeared in *The Comet.* Hence the somewhat peevish remark in that paper on 13 January 1833: "In the Dublin Penny Journal of last Saturday there appeared a poem 'The Dying Enthusiast, to His Friend' headed 'written for the Dublin Penny Journal'; the poem appeared in The Comet of 4th August last. We have inquired into this circumstance and find that this poem through a mistake was given to the Editor of the Dublin Penny Journal as an original." Mangan may well have 'helped' O'Donovan to make that mistake ...

9. Quoted in "The *Dublin Penny Journal,*" an article by Samuel Ferguson published in the *Dublin University Magazine* for January 1840.

10. "The Shades" was the name of a tavern in College Green.

11. *Weekly Dublin Satirist,* 21 June 1834.

12. The first reference to Mangan in the Larcom Papers (Captain Larcom was the general head of the Ordnance Survey) occurs in a letter from Larcom to Petrie dated 3 April 1838: "Mr Mangin [*sic*] should understand the hours of attendance at your office are from 9 to 4"! National Library of Ireland, MS. 7565.

13. *The Comet,* 10 February 1833.

14. "Now may the lily and every white flower and sweet flower grow / Over the bed in which you my love are stretched, / And they will be sweet in your company instead of people; / Shedding their honey on the ground for ever keening you." For this and the preceding literal translations, as well as for advice and information concerning several other points in this article, I am indebted to Robert Welch of the University of Leeds.

15. James Hayes, "Old Popular Pennyworths," *The Irish Book Lover,* May 1911.

16. Quoted by O'Donoghue, op. cit., pp. 120-21. It may be safely inferred from this that it was also O'Curry who provided Mangan with a literal translation of Mac Liag's "Kincora." As for "The Clown with the Grey Coat," it is not known who supplied Mangan with his model.

17. For this translation, see Patrick C. Power, *The Story of Anglo-Irish Poetry 1800-1922,* (Cork: Mercier Press, 1967), p. 57.

18. Quoted by O'Donoghue, op. cit., p. 121.

19. On 27 March the *Journal* published "Slighted Love" (from the Spanish, by M.), but this was a reprint from the *Dublin University Magazine* for January and acknowledged as such.

20. *Irish Penny Journal,* 1 May 1841.

21. 1841 does not seem to have been a productive year for Mangan anyway. Whereas he wrote seven articles for the *Dublin University Magazine* in 1838 and five (plus two isolated poems) in 1839, he only published two articles there in 1840, and two again in 1841. This, by the way, even taking into account what Mangan wrote during those two years for the *Belfast Vindicator* and the *Irish Penny Journal,* contradicts my former assertion that "while employed in the Ordnance Survey office Mangan's production did not abate in the slightest" ("A Further Glance at Mangan and the Library," *Long Room,* Bulletin of the Friends of the Library, Trinity College, Dublin, No. 5, Spring 1972).

22. Taking leave of his readers, Petrie complained that "the sale of the Journal in London alone has exceeded that in the four provinces of Ireland, not including Dublin."

23. *Dublin University Magazine,* February 1847, p. 239.

24. Quoted by O'Donoghue, op. cit., p. 172. Mangan's biographer does not give any date, but it is clear from other matters discussed in the letter that it was written sometime in 1847.

25. *Dublin University Magazine,* July 1847, p. 66.

26. Like the "Ode to the Maguire," this poem was first published in H. R. Montgomery's *Specimens of the Early Native Poetry of Ireland* (Dublin:—, 1846). How closely Mangan followed Petrie can be seen from a comparison between these two stanzas:

    Petrie: O solitary fort that standest yonder,
    What desolation dost thou not reveal!
    How tarnished is the beauty of thine aspect,
    Thou mansion of the chaste and gentle melodies!

    Mangan: O mournful, O forsaken pile,
    What desolation dost thou dree!
    How tarnished is the beauty that was thine erewhile,
    Thou mansion of chaste melody!

27. *Dublin University Magazine,* July 1847, p. 66.

28. These are: "Sarsfield," *The Nation,* 24 October 1846; "A Cry for Ireland," ibid., 31 October 1846; "The Sorrows of Innisfail," ibid., 5 December 1846; and "The Vision of Egan O'Reilly," *The Irishman,* 27 January 1849.

29. National Library of Ireland, MS. 138. The poem referred to is said to comprise sixteen stanzas and must therefore be "Sarsfield." This in turn makes it possible to date the letter as having been written on 23, possibly 16, October 1846.

30. O'Donoghue, op. cit., p. 168.

31. Douglas Hyde, *Love Songs of Connacht* (Dublin: Gill, 1893), pp. 84-85.

32. Hyde's italics. The sound [ei] appears in every line.

33. The same remark applies to many other pieces in the volume such as, for instance, "Black-haired Fair Rose," a translation of "Rois gheal Dubh," which opens with the lines:

    Since last night's star, afar, afar, Heaven saw my speed,
    I seem'd to fly o'er mountains high, on magic steed.

    It seems clear that through the use of assonance and interlinear rhyming (star—afar—afar; night—fly—high; speed—seem'd—steed), Mangan endeavoured to render the musicality of his Irish model, the first two lines of which read:

    Is fada an réim do thug me féin ó n-de go 'niugh,
    An imioll sléibh 'muich go h-iniollta, éadtrom, mar b'eólach dam.

34. *The Tribes of Ireland* (Dublin: John O'Daly, 1852), p. 92.

35. O'Donoghue, op. cit., p. 216.

Peter MacMahon (essay date 1978)

SOURCE: MacMahon, Peter. "James Clarence Mangan, the Irish Language, and the Strange Case of *The Tribes of Ireland.*" *Irish University Review* 8.2 (1978): 209-22. Print.

[*In the following essay, MacMahon contends that Mangan did not learn Irish well enough to translate anything on his own, including* The Tribes of Ireland. *In translating the work, MacMahon argues, Mangan worked primarily from John O'Daly's prose translation of the satire, altering some parts and versifying the whole.*]

In the course of an article published recently in the *Irish University Review,* Mr Jacques Chuto has raised once again the question of James Clarence Mangan's knowledge of the Irish language. Mr Chuto presents evidence to show "that towards the end of his life Mangan earnestly tried to fulfil his early ambition to learn Irish." In connection with *The Tribes of Ireland* by Aenghus Ó Dálaigh, he remarks, "it can be safely concluded that Mangan translated this work on his own."[1] In the present article, I should like to challenge Mr Chuto's evidence and to offer the view that Mangan's knowledge of Irish was negligible, and remained so until his death.

It is, indeed, true that Mangan liked to convey the impression that he translated directly from original texts, and, in the case of **"My Three Plagues,"** acknowledged only that Eugene O'Curry had provided him with "the original of this song."[2] Likewise he makes mention only of "the originals" when expressing gratitude to John O'Daly for his help with four poems mentioned by Mr Chuto.[3] We cannot, however, infer from this that Mangan translated his originals independently, for we have O'Daly's own words for it that he did not. In a biographical notice of Mangan introducing ***The Poets and Poetry of Munster,*** O'Daly remarks:

> We may here observe, that all of his versions of Gaelic poetry were made from literal translations furnished him by Irish scholars, as he was totally unacquainted with the original language.[4]

Mangan was dead when O'Daly wrote this notice, which incorporates a sort of advertisement for the future publication of his translation of ***The Tribes of Ireland.*** It is, in any case, improbable that he should have in the last few dissipated years of his life achieved a command of Irish sufficient to cope, even roughly, with the original text of the work in question. Nor can one argue that apparent echoes of Gaelic prosody in some of his translations indicate a knowledge of the language. His "ghazels" in the Turkish style are much closer to original patterns than any of his Irish translations are to the metrical structure of their sources,[5] yet it would be unwise to infer that he knew the Turkish language well.

Mr Chuto's remarks on Mangan's translation of ***The Tribes of Ireland*** lead us into something of a literary puzzle. Briefly, he points out that footnotes to Mangan's verse translation of the work criticise his interpretation of the original. Such divergences might be simply the result of Mangan's employing a translator's licence. However, one instance looks obviously like a case of straightforward mistranslation.

Mangan's stanza in question reads:

> My curse on Drumsnaghta, that beggarly hole,
> Without meat-stall or fish-shop—priest, vicar, or bishop!
> I saw in their temple and Oh! my sick soul!
> A profound Irish feeling of shame stirs
> Thy depths at the thought, playing hookey, two
> gamesters.[6]

The footnote to this stanza is as follows:

> *Gamesters* This is incorrect. Aenghus merely complains that the church of Drumsnat had no Herenach, and that there were only two *cáirnigh* or priests, (not *cearbhaigh* or gamesters) at the church. He expected a regular parish establishment; and every parish of any wealth had an Herenach, and three priests at the least.

Mr Chuto points out that the note "clearly contradicts O'Donoghue's assertion that while translating ***The Tribes of Ireland*** Mangan had 'a version by John O'Donovan before him.'" Where then did Mangan find the literal translation upon which he worked? Mr Chuto concludes that he must have translated the work on his own, since John O'Daly would not have made such an error in translation.[7]

We may object to this, firstly, that O'Daly's testimony precludes the possibility; secondly, that Mangan might have obtained a version from someone else altogether; and, thirdly, that, as will become apparent, O'Daly was quite capable of approving and publishing, and almost certainly originating, even worse misinterpretations of Aengus Ó Dálaigh's text.

The satire now known to us as *The Tribes of Ireland* was composed by Aenghus Ó Dálaigh in the early seventeenth century. It lampoons many of the Gaelic and Anglo-Norman—"Old English"—aristocratic families of the time, chiefly by accusing them of poverty, niggardliness and inhospitality. In the opinion of John O'Donovan, it was written at the instigation of agents of Lord Mountjoy and Sir George Carew in order to infuriate and demoralise the victims.[8] Aenghus na nAor Ó Dálaigh, also known as the Bard Ruadh, was stabbed to death by a member of the O'Meagher family, so we are told, while in the course of lampooning them in similar vein in 1617.[9] The poem—or series of quatrains—, as we possess it, winds up with an account of the incident, together with an extempore verse of recantation of his satires said to have been uttered by the dying poet. This would indicate that the work as it has reached us is at least, to some extent, of a composite character. O'Donovan suspected that its text, of which no very old copy had survived, had been subjected to corruptions and interpolations at the hands of various scribes. He put together his own text for publication from a number of sources, some of which proved to contain material new to him, and rearranged the quatrains of the work under the headings of the four provinces of Ireland.[10] It is important to note that, as we shall see, John O'Daly had access to a version which differs somewhat from O'Donovan's published text.

The volume published by O'Daly in 1852 opens with a lengthy introduction by John O'Donovan dealing with the history of the Ó Dálaigh sept and introducing the poem. This is followed by O'Donovan's edited text with footnotes and parallel literal translation. Lastly comes Mangan's verse rendering. It is headed as follows:

> [*A versified paraphrase,* or imitation, of *Aenghus O'Daly's Satires,* by *James Clarence Mangan,* arranged to agree with the Stanzas as they now stand in the original Irish—with the *ranns* omitted by J. C. M. pointed out in foot notes, by J. O'D.][11]

Since "J. O'D." was obliged to arrange Mangan's stanzas to agree with O'Donovan's edited sequence, it follows that the former must have been prepared at an earlier date than the latter. Which "J. O'D." have we here? In most of the footnotes, we can recognise O'Donovan's scholarly, discursive style, already familiar from his annotation of the Bárd Ruadh's text. The pervading lack of enthusiasm for Mangan's rendering is certainly not characteristic of the publisher O'Daly. Misinterpretations, including the *cáirnigh/ cearbhaigh* error mentioned above, are sternly noted. Where Mangan's lines are praised, it is for fidelity to the literal meaning of the original:

> Knocked down by a *pig* I fell into their den,
> Such an upset I hadn't got, *Munster knows when*;
> I looked round quite bewildered, and heard *Kian* squall out,
> "Fall out again, friend, or perhaps you and I may fall out!"

Although Mangan has in fact altered and embellished the original here, the fact that he preserves the command of the original to "fall out again" attracts the curious gloss:

> *Fall out again.* This is in the true style of the satirist and the best stanza in the whole of this translation.[12]

However, O'Donovan cannot be regarded as the sole contributor of the footnotes signed "J. O'D." A note to Mangan's verses glosses the placename "Burrin" thus:

> *Burrin* "Boirind," i.e., rocky, a barony in the north of the Country of Clare, adjoining Clanrickard.[13]

O'Donovan's notes to the original contain a differing derivation of the name:

> *Burren* "Buirrin." from "Borr," great, and "onn" a stone, i.e., rocky district, now Burren, a barony forming the northern portion of the County of Clare, remarkable for its limestone rocks.[14]

It is unlikely that O'Donovan would have perpetrated such differences in spelling and interpretation within the same volume.

Another discrepancy relates to "J. O'D.'s" note:

> *O'Hanlon* of Mullagh or Tandragee, in the County of Armagh.[15]

The identification of "Mullagh" with Tandragee would appear to originate in a misreading of a lengthy footnote of O'Donovan's, which points out that the head of this family in Ó Dálaigh's time was "Sir Eochy O'Hanlon of Tandragee." "Mullagh" is located elsewhere:

> *Mullagh* i.e. the summit or hill-top. This was the name of O'Hanlon's house at Mullagh, near Forkhill, in the County of Armagh.[16]

The indications are that John O'Daly added to O'Donovan's footnotes a few of his own, and used the initials "J. O'D." as a conveniently ambiguous ascription of authorship.

Not only did O'Daly expand the footnotes to Mangan's stanzas: there is ample evidence to show that he altered the stanzas themselves. In the biographical notice prefixed to ***The Poets and Poetry of Munster,*** published shortly after Mangan's death, he offered the public some samples from the poet's translation of Ó Dálaigh satires. (There is no mention of an edition of the original poem. At this stage, it would appear, O'Daly intended only to publish Mangan's version.) I quote extensively from his remarks:

> For two years before Mangan's death, we were in constant intercourse with him, and induced him to undertake the versification of some of the native poetry of Ireland, of which the the songs here printed form part. The remainder of his translations from the Irish, including the satires of Angus O'Daly (known to Irish scholars as "Aongus na n-Aor," "Angus the Satirist"; or "Bárd Ruadh," "Red Bard"), a poem of the seventeenth century, we hope soon to present to the public; and in giving this an English dress, we beg to assure our readers that the original lost none of its beauty in poor Mangan's hands, as may be seen by the following specimen:
>
> CLANN N-DÁLAIGH
>
> Dá n-Aorainn clann n-Dálaigh,
> Níor dhion dham síol sean-Adhaimh;
> Clann n-Dálaigh ba dhíon dham,
> Agus síol Adhaimh do Aoradh.
>
> **THE CLAN DALY**
>
> By me the Clan Daly shall never be snubbed:
> I say nothing about them.
> For, were I to flout them,
> The world wouldn't save me from getting well drubbed;
> While with *them* at my beck (or my back) I
> Might drub the world well without fear of one black eye!
>
> MUINTIR ARA
>
> Muintir Ara, bualta beaga,
> Finne iad nár chosain clú;
> Is é is ceól dóibh, ceól na cuile,
> Ampall a m-beól gach duine dhiu!
>
> **THE GOOD PEOPLE (NOT THE FAIRIES) OF ARA**
>
> The good people of Ara are four feet in height;
> They are soldiers, and really stand stoutly in fight;
> But they don't sacrifice overmuch to the graces,
> And hunger stares forth from their fly-bitten faces.
>
> Tigh fada fairsing air lár bealaidh,
> 'S gan sáith seangáin ann do bhiadh;

Cúradh a chroidhe air an g-ceatharnach gortach,
Nach dearnadh tigh crom-shlaite air shliabh!

There is one waste, wide, void, bleak, blank, black, cold
odd pile
On the highway: its length is one-third of a mile:
Whose is it I don't know, but you hear the rats gnawing
Its timbers inside, while its owner keeps sawing.

Mangan's acquaintance with the modern tongues was very extensive, as may be seen by his translations from almost every language in the world. His powers of versification were extraordinary. Many of his most beautiful poems were written in an incredibly short period, and with such accuracy, that they never required revision. . . .

We may here observe, that all his versions of Gaelic poetry were made from literal translations furnished him by Irish scholars, as he was totally unacquainted with the original language.[17]

The laudatory tone of O'Daly's words, which speak of Mangan's "accuracy" and his preservation of the originals' "beauty," is very much at variance with the attitude expressed most frequently by "J. O'D." It is worth examining these examples of Mangan's work presented by O'Daly. The Irish text differs considerably in spelling and in one or two grammatical points from the O'Donovan version. This is not particularly surprising: both texts are modernised and probably popularised versions of what we should expect from an early seventeenth-century *file*; and thirty years earlier, according to O'Reilly, copies were "in the hands of every Irish scholar."[18] Mangan's rendering of the first quatrain quoted is reasonably faithful, and of the third extremely and obviously free, for which "J. O'D." was later to censure him.[19] His version of the second, however, is a remarkably clear case of downright misinterpretation. *Muintir Ara, (Muintir Eaghra* in O'Donovan's text), means the O'Hara sept, and neither the "Good People" nor the "Fairies" of "Ara." *Bualta beaga, (buailte* in O'Donovan's version), means small booleys or dairies, often associated with summer pastures. Mangan's collaborator seems to have taken it to mean something like *"buachaillí beaga,"* "small fellows." The second line of the quatrain, *"Finne iad nár chosain clú,"* is completely misconstrued. Its literal meaning is: "They are a tribe who did not earn (or, perhaps, "maintain"), a reputation." The translator has taken *Finne* (usually spelt *Fine*), to mean the same thing as *"Fianna,"* and misunderstood the rest of the line. These solecisms are even more surprising than the confusion between *cáirnigh* and *cearbhaigh* referred to above.

When we recall that Mangan was dead when O'Daly published this specimen stanza, it is instructive to compare it with the version in the eventually published text. We find that it has been thoroughly revised in order to eliminate the more obvious misinterpretations:

The tribe of O'Hara are men of some height,
But they've never been known to stand stoutly in fight;
They have no other music but the hum of the flies,
And hunger stares forth from their deep-sunken eyes.[20]

Indeed, an examination of the verse translation of ***The Tribes of Ireland*** reveals evidence that John O'Daly may be the author of a significant proportion of it. We know, for instance, that Mangan's stanzas were rearranged after his death to tally with O'Donovan's division of the original into sections under the headings of the four provinces of Ireland. Yet we are presented with lines, purportedly of Mangan's, composed to act as links in this arrangement. In one instance—that ending the Ulster section—the interpolation is admitted to; but this is not so in the case of the opening lines of the Leinster section:

Escaping from Connacht I came to Leinster,
Where I met neither Esquire, dame, chieftain, or spinster[21]

There is no mention in the original of "escaping from Connacht." These two lines, which begin the longest stanza in the verse translation, are clearly an unacknowledged interpolation on the part of "J. O'D."—here, obviously, O'Daly.

Occasionally "J. O'D." offers an alternative translation to that of Mangan's in the footnotes, although this is not done consistently as a response to the degree of divergence from the original. It may be relevant to look at one or two examples. Here is Mangan's stanza on the Burke:

The Burkes of Cloghstookin are a niggardly crew,
They are rough Turks in temper,—and turf-sticks in hue;
They make the few guests they admit, rich and poor fast,
On half nothing a day; they make also their door fast!

This draws the note:

Cloghstookin. A few words of Mangan's are here altered.

It might be more literally rendered as follows:—

At Clough-an-stookin, 'mong the Burkes,
Dire starvation ever lurks;
The child, with hunger, ever bawls!
Within their drear and roofless walls![22]

O'Donovan's corresponding text and translation read:

A Chloch an stuaicín! a Chúirt gan cheann!
Le'r mheasas no chúl do chur;
D'a h-ionnsaighe níor dholta dham,
An Chloch 'na m-bí an ghorta ar gor!

O Cloch an stuaicín! O Court without a roof!
To which I had intended to turn my back;
To visit it I should not have gone,
The stone fortress in which famine was hatching![23]

"J. O'D.'s" version is indeed a relatively closer loose translation of the original than Mangan's, but it is inconceivable that John O'Donovan should have produced it, and we can take this literary effort as an example of O'Daly's preparedness to try his hand at translation in Mangan's style. Another piece of alternative translation offered in these footnotes reads oddly like a production of the poet himself, with its heavy-handed, grotesque humour so characteristic of Mangan's treatment of *The Tribes of Ireland.* A certain clumsiness of rhythm and syntax, such as the use of the redundant auxiliary verb in the third line, however, leads me to think that this is an attempt at imitation on O'Daly's part rather than, say, plagiarism of a discarded version of Mangan's. Here is Mangan's stanza, followed by the footnote:

> O'Conor brags much of his cattle; their milk
> Ne'ertheless, is enough to half poison that ilk;
> They are poor, skinny, hunger-starved sots, the same cattle,
> When they walk you can hear their dry bones creak and rattle!
>
> *O'Conor,* i.e., Calvagh O'Conor Faly. The translator is wide of Aenghus's meaning here. Take the following:—
>
> A handful of meal in a trough in his house!
> Lord save them from hunger, 'twould starve a good mouse!
> The Minstrels the harp-strings, do rattle and flitter,
> With noise like the sow's singing bass to her litter.[24]

This offering is closer to the original than Mangan's, but itself remains rather "wide." O'Donovan's literal translation runs:

> A handful of seed in a deep trough,
> In the house of the the red-headed Calbhach:
> Such tearing of discordant [harp] strings!
> Which would raise the dead from the grave.[25]

It has been seen that Mangan cannot have worked up his version from O'Donovan's translation. Indeed, since O'Daly made no mention of an edition by O'Donovan when he advertised Mangan's poetic rendering in 1849, shortly after the poet's death, it would appear that the volume incorporating the work of both was a project conceived subsequently. It has been established that O'Daly was the author of interpolation and revisions both acknowledged and unacknowledged in the final versified text. The first two stanzas of this text amplify the original's simple reference to:

> Muintir Fhiodhnacha na mionn,
> A bh-fuil díobh fionn, agus dubh,[26]
>
> "The people of Fenagh of the relics,
> Those of them who are fair, and dark-haired,"

with the information that they are the "Roddys," "Coarbs of Fenagh," "Who talk of St. Kallin's miraculous powers." These facts can be gleaned from O'Donovan's notes to Aenghus's text,[27] but are unlikely to have been in either O'Daly's or Mangan's possession when the latter was versifying his translation. (Against O'Daly's undoubted familiarity with such subjects as eighteenth-century Munster poetry we must take into account his responsibility for such errors as the misinterpretation of the phrase *Muintir Ara* discussed above.) The metrical ineptitude of these two stanzas reinforces the probability that they were composed substantially, if not wholly, by John O'Daly after his receipt of O'Donovan's text for publication. It is tempting, if irrelevant, to speculate that O'Daly was obliged to replace a version by Mangan based upon a mistranslation of the word *mionn.* Its secondary meaning of "curse" would probably have been more familiar to O'Daly, who was, I believe, the interpreter of his own text to Mangan.

We are fortunate to have several accounts of Mangan's relationship with John O'Daly which help to illuminate the puzzling history of his version of ***The Tribes of Ireland.*** The notice by O'Daly quoted above tells us that it was worked upon during the same period as ***The Poets and Poetry of Munster.*** Mangan's friend the Revd C. P. Meehan tells us that after leaving St Vincent's Hospital in May 1848, the poet "worked by fits and starts at the 'Poems and Poetry' [sic] which was not published till November 1849. His remuneration was scant, but it was as much as O'Daly could afford—some few pounds at long intervals, and a seat by a fire in the Anglesea Street back parlour."[28] Another friend of Mangan's, Joseph Brenan, published a review of ***The Poets and Poetry of Munster*** in the *Irishman* of 3 November 1849, which describes the relationship as follows:

> Yes, but there was another who never shunned or fled you, even when you lay bleeding, wounded, and robbed of right reason by those most accursed of all freebooters, whisky and despair! This good Samaritan was the publisher of the volume before us, and he, poor fellow, little richer than yourself in this world's goods, did give, with a kind hand, such as well becomes the true Celt's generous nature, the little he could afford. What was that little?—a seat at his humble hearth—half the poor meal that an occasional profitable speculation in some old book enabled him to purchase, a few pens, an ink-bottle, candle, and a literal prose version of those old songs, whose melting pathos, and quaint wit, would not lose a particle of one or the other when mated to English verse by such a man as Mangan.[29]

Douglas Hyde has actually preserved for us O'Daly's own account of their informal joint *modus operandi.* In his book of memoirs, *Mise agus an Connradh,* Hyde mentions O'Daly as a manuscript collector, and continues:

> Is dóigh gurbh é féin do chruinnigh na h-abhráin do thug sé amach in ***Poets and Poetry of Munster,*** agus thug sé don Mhongánach iad le filidheacht Béarla do chur orra. Dubhairt se liom nach raibh Gaedhilg ag an Mongánach agus go mba ghnáth leis a chorp do shíneadh leath-bhealaigh treasna an chúntair, agus d'aistrigheadh Seán féin an t-abhrán Gaedhilge dhó, agus chuireadh seisean bhéarsuigheacht air, agus a leath de 'na shuidhe agus a leath de 'na luidhe ar an gcúntar.[30]
>
> It seems that he himself collected the songs which he brought out in ***Poets and Poetry of Munster,*** and gave them to Mangan to versify in English. He told me that Mangan did not know Irish, and that it was his custom to stretch his body halfway across the counter, while John would translate the Irish song to him and would versify it, half-sitting and half-lying on the counter.

The picture which emerges is of a friendly, casual collaboration, proceeding by "fits and starts," with Mangan composing his verse in an impromptu fashion from O'Daly's prose renderings. This body of verse included both ***The Poets and Poetry of Munster*** and ***The Tribes of Ireland.*** The odd thing is that O'Daly published the latter as if the work of translation was purely and independently Mangan's. Even if not O'Daly but some other "Irish scholar" had provided assistance, we should have expected some allusion to the circumstances of composition. All the evidence points to O'Daly as the one who furnished Mangan with a literal translation, and this view is supported by the very fact of its obvious imperfection, since a scholar like Eugene O'Curry, say, would never have made the errors discussed above, while O'Daly, versed though he was in the songs and lore of eighteenth-century Munster, might easily have done so. While Irish speakers were common in contemporary Dublin, scholars capable of precise interpretation of the Bárd Ruadh were not.

The best hypothesis is that Mangan versified, piecemeal and hurriedly, O'Daly's prose translation of the copy of Aenghus's satires available to him. The translation may have been conveyed merely verbally and without much preparation, increasing the possibility of error. Mangan never completed the work, hence the many omissions pointed out by "J. O'D." When O'Daly came to prepare the stanzas for publication, he revised and added to them as we have seen, with O'Donovan's scholarly edition in the office to aid him. Nevertheless O'Donovan later observed and noted a number of inaccuracies stemming from mistranslation (e.g. the *cáirnigh/cearbhaigh* error), as well as from poetic license. O'Daly allowed these mistakes to appear as Mangan's, although he had elsewhere denied that Mangan knew the original language and was to repeat the fact to the young Douglas Hyde in later years. He himself amplified O'Donovan's footnotes to the verse translation and attributed them, with convenient equivocation, to "J. O'D."

It might be objected that O'Daly's behaviour in tampering with Mangan's words calls into question his integrity as a witness to Mangan's ignorance of the Irish language. This is hardly the case: contemporary editorial practice differed considerably from our own, and indeed O'Daly may have felt that he was performing a service to the memory of his dead friend by tidying-up and improving upon his unfinished last work. We might remember that D. J. O'Donoghue, who was to edit much of Mangan's poetry a half-century or so later, did not hesitate to revise and trim where he considered it appropriate. In any case, O'Daly's word is supported by that of others who knew Mangan during his last years, including, most importantly, the Revd C. P. Meehan[31] and John Mitchel.[32]

One mystery which remains unclear is John O'Donovan's attitude to the affair. One can only guess that he agreed that O'Daly should add to his notes on Mangan's stanzas and attribute them, collectively, to those ambiguous initials. It appears, in any case, that O'Donovan was not particularly interested in the verse translation.

Mangan's ***The Tribes of Ireland*** does not, of course, rank with his best work, though it is unfortunately characteristic of much of his output. It is hack-work undertaken on the initiative, without doubt, of John O'Daly. Aenghus Ó Dálaigh's terse, sour quatrains are transported into a wordy, facetious, jocular vein, owing much to the tradition of heavy-handed humour to which Mangan apprenticed himself years before in the pages of the *Comet* and the almanacs. It is what Gavan Duffy would approvingly have called "Manganesque."[33] Yet, in spite of the desperate clowning and overacting, we are forced to admire the performer's inventiveness and dexterity. Its unintended pathos makes it an appropriate enough finish to the career of this flawed and gifted man.

Notes

1. Jacques Chuto, "Mangan, Petrie, O'Donovan, and a Few Others: The Poet and the Scholars," *Irish University Review,* VI (Autumn, 1976), 169-187.

2. Chuto, p. 183.

3. Chuto, pp. 183-184.

4. *The Poets and Poetry of Munster* (Dublin: John O'Daly, 1849), p. xvi.

5. For advice on this matter I am indebted to Mr Peter Hird.

6. *The Tribes of Ireland* (Dublin: John O'Daly, 1852), p. 92.

7. Chuto, p. 187.

8. *Tribes,* pp. 22-23, 26. "Nothing has been discovered to prove directly that our Bard was employed by the Government, but it looks very likely that he received a small portion of the secret service money, which was at the disposal of Crosbie, Fox, and others."

9. *Tribes,* p. 23.

10. *Tribes,* p. 33.

11. *Tribes,* p. 87.

12. *Tribes,* p. 102.

13. *Tribes,* p. 88.

14. *Tribes,* p. 39.

15. *Tribes,* p. 95.

16. *Tribes,* p. 62.

17. *Poets and Poetry,* pp. xiv-xvi.

18. Edward O'Reilly, *A Chronological Account of Nearly Four Hundred Irish Writers* (Dublin: 1820; reprinted Shannon: Irish University Press, 1970), p. clxxvii.
19. *Tribes,* p. 95.
20. *Tribes,* p. 95.
21. *Tribes,* p. 91.
22. *Tribes,* p. 89.
23. *Tribes,* pp. 40-41.
24. *Tribes,* p. 91.
25. *Tribes,* p. 47.
26. *Tribes,* p. 34.
27. loc. cit.
28. *Poets and Poetry* (fourth edition, Dublin: James Duffy and Sons, n.d.) p. xxv.
29. Reprinted in op. cit., pp. lvii-lviii.
30. Dubhghlas de hÍde, (Douglas Hyde), *Mise agus an Connradh* (Dublin: Oifig Díolta Foilseacháin Rialtais, 1937), p. 16.
31. "... he never learnt Gaelic ..." *Poets and Poetry* (fourth edition), p. viii.
32. See John Mitchel (editor), *Poems by James Clarence Mangan* (New York: P. M Haverty, 1870), p. 18.
33. See Sir Charles Gavan Duffy, *My Life in Two Hemispheres* (second edition, London: T. Fisher Unwin, 1898), I, 56.

David C. Lloyd (essay date 1982)

SOURCE: Lloyd, David C. "Translator as Refractor: Towards a Re-reading of James Clarence Mangan as Translator." *Dispositio* 7.19-21 (1982): 141-62. Print.

[*In the following essay, Lloyd takes issue with previous characterizations of Mangan's translations as original poems, faithful renderings, or rewritten versions, contending that the concept of refraction—an alteration meant to convey the original in a different language or culture—is a more correct way of viewing the revised poems.*]

I

The greater part of the writings of the nineteenth century Irish poet James Clarence Mangan (1803-1849) go under, if not by, the name of translations, the majority of which appeared in a series of articles for the *Dublin University Magazine* from 1834 to 1849, and—particularly in the case of Irish translations—in such contemporary periodicals as *The Nation* and the *Irish Penny Journal.* It is clear that Mangan was an excellent reader of German and French, almost certainly of Italian, Spanish and Portuguese[1] while it seems reasonable to attribute him adequate knowledge of Gaelic, though this remains a vexed question among his critics and biographers.[2] However, the difficulty of allowing this principally self-educated Dubliner, who was not known to have left his native land, a competence in up to fourteen languages, including Turkish, Coptic, Persian, Arabic, Hindu and Chinese, raised justifiable doubts, even among his contemporaries, as to the 'authenticity' of his translations. His first editor, Mitchel, classified his oriental translations as 'Apocrypha' (***Poems*** 1859), while O'Donoghue in 1903 entitled them 'Oriental Versions and Perversions' (***Poems*** [***Poems of James Clarence Mangan***] 1903), emphasizing the humoristic vein of many of these oversettings. Only recently has the source of the majority of such as do have sources been traced to J. von Hammer Purgstall's monumental *Geschichte der osmanischen Dichtkunst* (1836-1838) by M. Jacques Chuto, confirming that Mangan's 'orientalism' is in fact a branch of his Germanism.[3] Not surprisingly, he has been accused of considerably more than 'traditore': been labelled a mystifier, a transvestite of sorts, unable to produce himself except when disguised as German or Bedouin in a degraded version of 'negative capability'[4] and—a description he accepted with pleasure in a posthumously published pseudonymous 'Life' (*Irishman* August 17, 1850)—'a complete literary Proteus' (*Dublin Satirist* Dec. 1845, p. 313). An anonymous review of the ***German Anthology*** [***Anthologia Germanica = German Anthology***] (published in that year) is scandalized by the liberties (by no means the most excessive for that matter) taken by Mangan with Uhland's 'Auf der Ueberfahrt' (cf. Uhland, pp. 66; Mangan: ***Poems*** 1859 p. 94):

> He takes many unwarrantable liberties with his authors, mutilates and interpolates, and falsifies them by an exaggeration that not seldom produces a burlesque effect where a grave one was intended.
>
> (*Foreign Quarterly Review,* October 1845, p. 239)

Despite its outraged moral tone, the passage is a fair enough description of some, though certainly not all, of Mangan's practices as translator. In more recent times, the notorious difficulties of tracing Mangan's sources and of handling the various degrees of authenticity in the relation of the translation to its purported source have been generally resolved by the expedient of such classifications as that of Eoin McKiernan in his discussions of Mangan's German translations: 'original poems,' 'oversettings,' and 'faithful renderings' (cf. McKiernan pp. 54-8). Such a classification has a certain descriptive value, but for the purposes of a more stringent analysis of the function of translation in Mangan's writings it is nevertheless ultimately limited and even obscuring in its effects. To begin with, one is faced immediately with the familiar problem of the definition of 'a faithful rendering' of 'a correct/accurate translation,' and further with the problem of drawing border lines in the continuum between these and 'oversettings/perversions,' and again between the latter and so-called original poems. Such problems of definition are almost necessarily overcome by impressionistic readings of the source texts in pursuit of rough equivalents which provide a recognizable formal and verbal image of the translation on hand. Such readings—while effectively reversing the process of translating—inevitably fail to consider the possibility that an apparently close translation may, even by its 'original,' reveal far more significant divergences from the source text than a poem which is openly a variation on themes offered by another. Ironically, the sliding scale of 'originality' becomes inadequate for the analysis of the quite complex relationships between the original and translated poems of this writer.

At bottom, the inadequacy of such classifications lies in the very notion of 'equivalence' which—explicitly or implicitly—underlies the theory of translation to which they adhere. For to suppose that a given text might be translated into another linguistic and cultural axis 'without loss of value' demands the presupposition of a certain linguistic and cultural transparency, permitting, in an ideal domain, a perfect mirroring of original in translation. The idealism of such a concept, always latently operative in the sense that it is never necessary to assume that the perfect translation has or might be achieved, further demands that source and translated text be considered, in practice, in isolation from their respective literary systems. The comparison of the two texts in isolation permits the play of ultimately unquantifiable value terms, such as (frequently enough in the case of Mangan) translations which are 'better' poems than their 'originals,' while the more detailed, and more verifiable, study of what is taking place in the gap between the ideal 'equivalent' and the actual 'adequate' translations is neglected.[5]

The metaphor most frequently used in Mangan's own time by favourable critics of his translations was metallurgical:

> (the originals) became melted and fused in his imagination and flowed out into something very different often far richer and more poetical.
>
> (*Nation,* Sept. 8 1849, p. 26)[6]

a metaphor that might tempt one to coin the term *metamorphusis.* More apt, however, to both Mangan and to the broader field of Irish writing in the nineteenth century, is the metaphor of 'refraction' introduced by Andre Lefevere to describe effects of translation strictly speaking and of other forms of inter-cultural transference (cf. Lefevere 1980a & 1981). The optical root of the metaphor provides already a useful corrective to the mirror imaging of equivalence, and Lefevere's papers provide several characteristic examples of the ways in which canonized texts are refracted—and 'known'—through series of adaptations and versions within a cultural system, or in which 'foreign' texts are refracted through translation. Most important, particularly to the context of nineteenth century Ireland, is the contention that it is impossible to consider the process of refraction and the function of the refracted text (whether at the level of the motivation of the choice of text or at that of the particular strategies used in its refraction) apart from the set of ideological constraints that produce the cultural system in question.

In common with many states in which the sense of a national identity—or, to speak more accurately, the lack of one—is beginning to become articulate, the Ireland of Mangan's lifetime saw a particularly intense activity of refraction. A number of factors were influential on the intensification of this activity. The most important of these was the Union with England in 1800, which, by dissolving the Irish parliament in Dublin, accentuated the sense of a lost identity[7] while simultaneously, by offering hope of Catholic emancipation after a century of Penal Laws, aggravated the sense of a divided nation, the unification of which within the folds of a common identity became a priority both for the conservative unionist in the interest of stability, and for the nationalist in the interest of national resurgence. It should be noted in passing that this initial overlapping of interests has been productive of many of the ironies of Irish political and cultural history. So too has the fact that the material for refraction was initially of foreign extraction, deriving as it did in the first place from the British and European fashion for Celticism, inspired by Macpherson's spurious *Ossian,* and in the second from the massive influx of German *Sturm und Drang* and Romantic writings into the British Isles, two movements which were clearly intimately related.[8] The necessity, and the irony, of the activity of refraction is compacted by the fact that the year 1800 is taken to mark the beginning of the extremely rapid decline of Gaelic as the vernacular of the majority of the Irish population.[9] Thus, if the terms of the refraction were provided by European romanticism mediated through English (nationalism is, after all, a product of romanticism rather than Gaelic culture[10]), so also the initial impetus to the research that provided the material (later to be synthesized into 'the Irish cultural heritage') was governed by English requirements. Those requirements ranged from the needs of the tourist, satisfied by a large output of guide books to Irish countryside and customs, to those of a new centralized bureaucracy in Dublin, giving rise to the national educational system or to the nationwide Ordnance Survey conducted by the military with the assistance of those scholars primarily responsible for the 're-discovery of Ireland's past,' Petrie, O'Donovan, Ferguson and O'Curry among others.[11] The net result of this complex of activities has been an anglicization of Irish culture, for better or worse, not only in its medium but also in its modes of apperception. Consequently Irish discussions of the literary tradition from Mangan to Thomas Kinsella are afflicted with a considerable sense of loss, a sense of division which the nationalist leader Thomas Davis anticipated in graphic terms as early as 1843:

> The language, which grows up with a people, is conformed to their organs, descriptive of their climate, constitution and

manners, mingled inseparably with their history and their soil, fitted beyond any other language to express their most prevalent thoughts in the most natural and efficient way.

To impose another language on such a people is to set their history adrift among the accidents of translations—'tis to tear their identity from all places—'tis to substitute arbitrary signs for picturesque and suggestive names—'tis to cut off the entail of feeling, and separate the people from their forefathers by a deep gulf—'tis to corrupt their very organs, and abridge their power of expression.

(*Nation* April 1, 1843, p. 394)[12]

In the almost visceral rhetoric of this outcry, it is possible to find the echo of that seminal nationalist text, Fichte's *Addresses to the German Nation.* Fichte, one in a line of German thinkers through which the idea that language is identical with the nation developed,[13] argues the superiority of a language whose development from origin to actual state has been 'a continuous transition without a leap' (Fichte p. 57) to one in which the language has been formed in the abandonment of the original language of the people and the adoption of a foreign one (the superiority, that is, of the Germanic languages over French). Internal to the language, the continuity of development is parallelled by the continuity between its 'sensuous' and 'supersensuous' elements, between its designations of concrete objects and the metaphors for concepts derived from those designations:

The new designation which thus arises, together with all the new clearness which sensuous perception itself acquires by this extended use of the sign, is now deposited in the language, and the supersensuous perception possible in the future is now designated in accordance with its relation to the total supersensuous and sensuous perception deposited in the whole language. So it goes on without interruption, and so the immediate clearness and comprehensibility of the images is never broken off, but remains a continuous stream. ... ... So, in this respect also, the continuous progress of language, which broke forth in the beginning as a force of nature, remains uninterrupted, and into the stream of designation no arbitrariness enters. For the same reason the supersensuous part of a language thus continuously developed cannot lose its power of stimulating life in him who but sets his mental instrument in motion.

(ibid. pp. 60-1)

On the other hand, the essential discontinuity that Fichte regards as characterizing the development of French out of the dead language, Latin, implies that for speakers of that language

this advent of history, and nothing but history, as expositor, makes the language dead and closed in respect of its whole sphere of imagery, and its continuous onward flow is broken off.

(ibid. p. 63)

Obviously for Davis and other nationalists of the time, the interruption had already taken place in Ireland, and their project became—as the banner of their paper, *The Nation,* had it—'to create and foster public opinion in Ireland and make it racy of the soil.' For them, as for Fichte, the essential part of that work was to be the work of education,[14] an education which would produce an ideal unity out of an Irish history which had in fact actually seen its disintegration:

Rightly understood, the history of Ireland abounded in noble lessons, and had the unity and purpose of an epic poem.

(Duffy 1880, p. 153)[15]

It might be considered one of those ironies of Irish history referred to above, that perhaps the most coherent statement of the unifying project of education that was to become that of the nationalists in the 1840s had already been elaborated by Samuel Ferguson in the *Dublin University Magazine* of 1834, though with the interests of Tory unionists in mind. It represents also a quite classic case of the process of refraction at work in accordance with ideological constraints. The series of four articles in question constituted a review of James Hardiman's collection of Irish poetry, *Irish Minstrelsy* (London 1831), attacking the editor for his anti-English sentiments, and his translators for their

morbid desire, neither healthy nor honest, to elevate the tone of the original to a pitch of refined poetic art altogether foreign from the whole genius and *rationale* of its composition.

(*D.U.M.* October 1834, p. 453n.)

Though one might again locate in that 'morbid desire' and the 'genius' of the composition (the latter term being frequently used in nineteenth century English in contexts where German would use 'Geist') an echo of Fichtean nationalism, it is not the case that Ferguson is intending to protect the spirit of Gaelic poetry intact from an English cultural imperialism that might be seen in the renderings of that poetry in the outmoded diction of eighteenth century sentimentalism. In a more sophisticated move, Ferguson achieves a far more thorough appropriation of the Gaelic originals than Hardiman's own national sentiments. Turning initially to an unversified translation from the Gaelic offered by Hardiman, he remarks

Here are the words, and unmutilated thoughts, and turn, and expression of the original; only observe, that the idiomatic differences of the two languages give to the translation an uncouth and difficult hesitation, which in the original did not affect the Irishman.

(*D.U.M.* April 1834, p. 460)

Though at this point Ferguson recognizes that the 'uncouthness' derives from the linguistic differences,[16] throughout the course of the articles such uncouthness is absorbed and reproduced as the index of the untutored simplicity of the Irish 'genius,' the index, that is, of the less civilized stage of development which the native Irish have attained in comparison with their Anglo-Irish countrymen. It is the 'pathetic sentiment' that is the dominant characteristic of the Irish racial genius, and which gives rise to the fierce 'tribal' attachments which vitiate Irish politics. Consequently it becomes the task of the Anglo-Irish to come closer in the spirit of unity to their Gaelic fellows through research into Irish ways, and, through education to lead them forward from a spirit of feudal loyalty to constitutional government along English lines:

> To supply the lost links, to carry forward the untutored loyalty of the clansman, till the whole country becomes his faction and the king his chief, and to withdraw the utilitarian aspirations of the economist from severe and sometimes sordid speculation, and carry back his kindlier sentiments in charitable appreciation of human nature, till he can revert to a common ground of sympathy with his less intellectual but more enthusiastic and devoted countryman: in one word, to make Irishmen know themselves and one another; this is the want, the worthiest labour of the age. Education, in its fullest sense, is the engine by whose agency we hope to see the great work yet effected. . . .
>
> (*D.U.M.* October 1834, p. 451)

In the belief in an education in feeling capable of reunifying the two elements which threaten the stability of Irish society, the new Catholic bourgeoisie ('Utilitarians') and the Catholic peasantry; in the very belief that such a 'felt' knowledge performs a unifying function; in the evolutionary historiography; the articles indicate their saturation with conservative English romanticism, in particular with Coleridge's *Church and State,* an avowed influence on Ferguson and many of the *D.U.M.*'s Protestant contributors. In the same way, the poetic which underlies the translations which Ferguson provides in order to support his criticisms of Hardiman's translators (*D.U.M.* November 1834, pp. 530-542) indicates clearly the lessons absorbed from the Preface to Wordsworth's *Lyrical Ballads.* The poems follow the language of common men in programmatic opposition to Hardiman, only preferring that a certain eccentricity of turn of phrase should come through the translation than that it should be cast in the 'classic language of Pope.' If it must be said that the persisting 'quaintness' is to a large extent determined by the problems of rendering Irish syntax and idiom appropriately in English,[17] it must also be stressed that the choice practically made in producing those translations was as much determined by the need of a refraction that would conform to the whole system of conservative Romanticism, a system which could no longer be satisfied with a diction that it had superseded. The desire to produce an 'equivalent' in which the spirit of the Irish race would be translucent is intrinsic to that project, and, even given an updating of the poetic through the influence of imagism in the present century, it is Ferguson's example which has dominated the English reader's image of Gaelic Irish writing since the 1830s.

II

Given the seminal importance of translation and other less easily observed forms of refraction in the evolution of Irish culture since 1800, and the way in which refraction itself might well be taken to be one of the most appropriate metaphors for that evolution, it might seem surprising that the fact Mangan gave so much of his energy to translation has generally been lamented as one of the factors that prevented him from consistently producing work adequate to his 'genius.' It is of course probable that Mangan was to a large extent encouraged to engage in translation work for economic reasons, in that the *D.U.M.* permitted the inclusion of any number of translations but only three 'original poems' per issue. It is also not unlikely that with Mangan as with a substantial number of other poets, translation was a means of overcoming a psychic incapacity to write, whether one regards this, as does Welch (p. 95), as being aimed at finding an alternative tradition to that offered with stifling proximity by English writing, or, as again does Welch (ibid.) and also Chuto (1977 p. 2), as a means of evading confrontation with the self. The latter criticism, however, indicates what is at stake in the subjection of translation to a secondary role. Just as serious considerations of Mangan's translations have tended to classify on the basis of degrees of 'equivalence,' so in broader discussions of his writing, the persistence of attitudes of romantic derivation continues to privilege work that can be termed 'original.'[18] As a result, sustained attention to the understanding of Mangan's interest in German writing is neglected.

The case of Ferguson indicates valuably the degree to which translation involves not a rendering but an appropriation of material; even more, in this specific case it is the very claim to render the Gaelic translucent in English, the negative capability with regard to alien material, which is the most effective device for ideological refraction. Through that posture, the appropriation of the Gaelic text appears to occur only at the secondary, discursive level of the use that Ferguson intends to be made of the material of the 'genius' of the Irish people which has been as objectively supplied as language permits. In fact that appropriation has already taken place in the act of presenting the translations. The effectiveness with which the ideal of the translator as a purely transparent medium who permits an unrefracted passage of source text into equivalent masks the ideological function of translation is apparent in such an appraisal of Ferguson and Mangan as follows, by a critic who is fully aware of the political aims of the former:

> So that when Ferguson turns to versifying a selection of poems from Hardiman's collection, his intention is in no way that of Mangan, who always wished to make his originals as expressive of himself as possible. Ferguson is not interested in that kind of coercion of his material. To him, such self-appropriation would be an insolence to the proper spirit of inquiry. Ferguson had that kind of personality which expresses itself in impersonality, in a kind of

> self-effacement, so that he remains an excellent translator, remaining absolutely true in as many particulars as possible, to the spirit, tone, and rhythm of his originals, and to their curious, if at times chaotic, image sequences.
>
> We get, in the appendix affixed to the four Hardiman articles, twenty translations which are as faithful to their Irish originals as it is possible to get in English versions. Here, the act of the imagination is one of transparency, of self-denial, curiously analogous in its self-surrender to that 'negative capability' of which Mangan was incapable.
>
> (Welch p. 130)

True as it is that Mangan rarely exhibits anything that might pass for 'negative capability,' it seems, reading through the articles that contain his poetic translations, that this is less a question of incapacity (McKiernan, p. 58, even remarks that one finds among his German work 'almost perfect examples of the translator's art') as it is one of disinterest, ranging through to almost explicit criticism of the strategy. In his introductions to the **'Anthologia Germanica'** [***Anthologia Germanica = German Anthology***] series of articles and translations Mangan is quite disingenuous about the variety of possible strategies open to the translator, ranging from the attempt to render Bürger's 'Ballad of Leonore' 'faithfully' and 'With corresponding imitations of the rhythmical peculiarities of the original' (*D.U.M.* Nov. 1834, p. 509) to the translation from Heyden, 'The Last Words of Al Hassan,' of which Mangan remarks

> Of course we do not pledge our honour that our version of it is at all a faithful one, in the translatorial sense of the word. About the term *Wechabite,* in the second stanza, we entertain some doubt: possibly it may not mean "Wahabee." The Wahabee fanatics, we believe, displayed rather too much than too little zeal in defence of the "holy places."
>
> (ibid. January 1845, p. 98)

The latter sentence, placed as it is, suggests one of Mangan's frequent and typically concealed jests at the expense of the solemn and scholarly: his own role is indeed that of the virtuoso but disrespectful translator, the 'truculent Wahabee' 'profaning' the veiled stone of the Kaaba. Beyond such play made with original texts come those impositions on the public, the pseudo-translations by such writers as 'Drechsler' (= 'Turner,' or, perhaps more appropriately, 'Elaborator') and 'Selber' (= 'Self'), through which he disguises his own 'original' writings. And, though Mangan at no point espouses any systematic theory of translation, producing rather several various and often apparently contradictory assertions about his practice, the notions of 'disguise' and of 'elaboration' (in the two senses of fanciful embroidery and of producing in greater detail) recur with some consistency, sufficient at least to provoke attention. Thus, introducing some translations from Schiller, he remarks that

> We have (for no base purpose) disguised them to the best of our poor ability; but we should, after all, be loath to hear that they had forfeited their identity.
>
> (*D.U.M.* Jan. 1835, p. 41)

Among the translations so referred to is Schiller's 'Die Ideale' (Schiller I pp. 92-95), and a comparison of source text with translation (often considered as one of Mangan's most faithful and 'successful') provides a valuable instance of the nature and intent of Mangan's 'disguising' of poems. 'Die Ideale' ('So willst du treulos von mir scheiden') is an elegiac account of the loss of youth's 'innocent' intoxication with nature, of the passage—through disappointment in the incommensurability of the actual with desire—from the 'naive' to the 'sentimental,' to use the terms of Schiller's celebrated essay. That youthful intoxication is described by Schiller as a very real interpenetration of youth and nature, a reciprocation of desires:

> So schlang ich mich mit Liebesarmen
> Um die Natur, mit Jugendlust,
> Bis sie zu atmen, zu erwarmen
> Begann an meiner Dichterbrust,
>
> Und teilend meine Flammentriebe
> Die Stumme eine Sprache fand,
> Mir wiedergab den Kuss der Liebe
> Und meines Herzens Klang verstand;
> Da lebte mir der Bau, die Rose,
> Mir sang der Quellen Silberfall,
> Es fühlte selbst das Seelenlose
> Von meines Lebens Widerhall.

It is in the course of a life's unfolding that nature comes to appear insufficient to the longing of youth to encompass the Whole:

> Wie gross war diese Welt gestaltet,
> Solang die Knospe sie noch barg,
> Wie wenig, ach! hat sich entfaltet,
> Dies wenige, wie klein und karg.

Successively, the train of Fortune, Love and Fame desert him, as the ideal fails to be met by the real. Friendship and 'Beschäftigung' (Occupation) alone remain to console him. In the context of such writings as 'On Naive and Sentimental Poetry' and 'On the Connection between the Animal and the Spiritual in Man,' this course of events would appear as the natural consequence of the dual nature of man, and, moreover, the condition of this moral freedom, the freedom, that is, to submit freely his independent will to the laws of necessity (cf. 'On Naive and Sentimental Poetry' Schiller *Essays* p. 264). Nature and Childhood, on the contrary, represent to us the idea of 'existence in all its freedom':

> These objects which captivate us *are* what we *were,* what we *must be* again some day. We were nature as they are; and culture following the way of reason and of liberty, must bring us back to nature. Accordingly these objects are an image of our infancy irrecoverably past—of our infancy which will remain eternally very dear to us, and they infuse a certain melancholy into us; they are also the image of our highest perfection in the ideal world, whence they excite a sublime emotion in us.
>
> (ibid. pp. 263-4)

In effect, the form of Schiller's appropriation of Nature and Childhood as representations and as images for the mature adult of his former state, and as a means to projecting a future ideal, is not so different from Ferguson's equally Romantic appropriation of the *idea* of Gaelic natural piety. They belong of course in the same intellectual tradition, in so far as Schiller's ideas are mediated into English thought through Coleridge.

It is, however, exactly this appropriation that Mangan in his translation implicitly highlights. In the same article he had earlier remarked on a quality of Schiller's lyric poems:

> Their great hallowing charm is the captivating, rather than faithful resemblance they bear with the realities they profess to be images of.
>
> (*D.U.M.* Jan. 1835, p. 42)[19]

The captivation of which Schiller spoke is here in a sense reversed—the real is captured in the service of images of the poet's own production. Mangan's translation is, accordingly, entitled **'The Unrealities'** (ib. pp. 55-6), and in a process which can perhaps best be described as a 'platonization' of 'Die Ideale,' he manages, while remaining notionally 'faithful,' to insert the extra remove from the real which he seems to be identifying as characteristic of Schiller in the passage above, and which Plato had regarded as the critical feature of the poet-as-liar (*Republic* X 595-8). So in the first lines (a little as Plato regards art as the imitation of phantasms and not of the real (X 598)) Mangan, taking his cue from the possibilities offered by the German 'Phantasien,' translates:

> And dost thou faithlessly abandon me?
> Must thy cameleon phantasies depart?

where 'cameleon,' with its connotations of that which takes colour from that on which it lives, replaces the German 'holden,' charming. In the second stanza, Schiller's sense only of an intoxication is displaced by the more sinister sense of imagination as entrapment in delusion (one should probably not underestimate in Mangan the more sinister quality of 'Faerie' that persists in the Irish imagination):

> Die Ideale sind zerronnen,
> Die einst das trunkne Herz geschwellt.
>
> Those fairy bands Imagination spun
> Around my heart have long been rent asunder.

Thus, the 'Stein' of Schiller's Pygmalion is emphasized to be 'The lovely statue' of the 'enthusiastic Prince's' own making, while the 'Dichterbrust' of the same stanza becomes the '*bounding* brest' with a full awareness of the ambiguity of that adjective. The narcissistic implications of the poet's activity, and the 'platonization' of the poem continue in the stanza already quoted from Schiller ('Und teilend meine Flammentriebe').

> Then sparkled hues of Life on tree and flower,
> Sweet music from the silver fountain flowed;
> All soulless images in that brief hour
> The Echo of my Life divinely glowed!

The 'Da lebte mir' of Schiller becomes the superficial sparkle of light, the 'seelenlose' the 'soulless *images,*' which in turn glow *as* rather than *from* his life's Echo. One of the most radical transformtions of the poem appears to derive from a single word—'entfaltet'—in the German of the fourth stanza. The idea of unfurling, here applied to the bud, 'Knospe,' is transferred to the unfurling of a theatre curtain, underlining once more the aesthetic appropriation of nature:

> This human theatre, how fair it beamed
> While yet the curtain hung before the scene!
> Uprolled, how little then the arena seemed!
> That little how contemptible and mean!

These comparisons could be extended line for line through the two poems, to underline the extensive linking of a vocabulary of enchanted illusion and dreamt imagery throughout Mangan's version which is scarcely even latent in Schiller.

Were it not for the consistency with which this train of distancing vocabulary is sustained, not only in this poem but throughout Mangan's translated and 'original' work, to perform time and again almost identical functions,[20] it would be a quite simple matter to dismiss such effects as symptoms of romanticism in decadence jerking automatically to a stock rhythm and vocabulary, or as symptoms of Mangan's own incapacity at an individual level to step beyond the repetition of certain conventional tropes of loss and melancholy into an authentic confrontation with himself. But to read attentively Mangan's work as a whole leads one to understand that, however much of the symptomatic there may be in the personal inhibitions explored in his still insufficiently read ***Autobiography*** or in the hesitations of a colonial writer *vis-à-vis* a practice of writing that is alien yet dominating, there is a knowingness in the persistent platonization exemplified in **'The Unrealities'** which at least objectifies and explores those symptoms even where unable to transcend them. It belongs indeed with a rudimentary psychological theory which, in its context and in its time, has a certain polemic weight. This theory is sketched in the **'Chapters on Ghostcraft'** (*D.U.M.* Jan. 1842, pp. 1-17), a synthetic review of several texts in German on animal magnetism and in particular Dr. Justinus Kerner's 'Ghost-Seeress of Prevorst.' Here it appears that man, in consequence of the fall, has suffered not just the traditional dualistic split into soul and body, but a tripartite one into spirit, soul and body:

> By its connection with the body the soul receives impressions from the senses, and by its connection with the spirit it conveys these impressions, by means of the imagination and memory, to the spirit, as materials for its operation.
>
> (op. cit. p. 7)

This process, in which, in effect, the soul performs the function of language, is however vitiated by the persistence of the effects of the fall, due to which the soul, in its passage towards the bodily, partakes, as it were, of a further fall, and comes in opposition to the spirit which it is supposed to serve:

> Both soul and spirit were in perfect harmony with each other before the Fall of Man; but since the occurence of that tremendous calamity they have ever stood in a relation of mutual hostility.
>
> (ibid.)

This, again, might appear mere pious Jansenism (and Pascal was certainly a major influence on Mangan's thinking, according to his ***Autobiography***), were it not for the refractive aspect of Mangan's handling of the material. For the 'Chapters on Ghostcraft' appear to have been written with a series of articles by the pseudonymous 'Irys Herfner' with the *D.U.M.* in mind. The Herfner articles use a similar body of material derived from researches in mesmerism, animal magnetism and spiritualism, but to develop other, far more harmonious conclusions as to the nature of the cosmos, man's psychology and, significantly, poetry. Though several of the articles in question come after Mangan's own, those that precede it ('German Ghosts and Ghost Seers' I and II, *D.U.M.* Jan. and Feb. 1841) already contain the outline of the theory of cosmic unity developed throughout the series on the basis of the supposed 'Nervengeist' or 'shaping spirit' in man and universe (Jan. 1841 p. 44). With explicit reference to Coleridge's *Aids to Reflection* 'Herfner' develops his theory of the imagination as a unifying principle, assimilating and re-uniting that which knowledge ruptures. Though 'animal magnetism' is scarcely considered at present, it was in the early nineteenth century a reasonably respectable body of science, and provided at least a groundswell of metaphoric references in discussions of poetics and psychology even in thinkers like Caryle and Coleridge. In any case, the 'Herfner' articles establish Mangan's own as a quite specific intervention, with the polemic effect of replacing the harmonious continuum of body and spirit with a tripartite split in which the soul appears as a kind of representing agent or language, unable to suture the unredeemed post-lapsarian psyche.

The idea that the soul could be identified with the processes of language was certainly not original to Mangan: in England, the radical Horne Tooke had already argued as much in his *Diversions of Purley,*[21] but perhaps more important is the growth of the idea of an identification of language and 'Geist' in the German tradition both at the level of the individual, and at the level of the race.[22] As Schlegel has it in his *Lectures on the Philosophy of Life* of 1827-8:

> Now, the soul furnishes the cognitive mind with language for the expression of its cognitions and it is even the distinctive character of human knowledge, that it depends on language, which not only forms an essential constituent of it, but is also its indispensable organ. Language, however, the discursive, but at the same time also the vividly figurative language of man, is entirely the product of soul, which in its production first of all, and preeminently, manifests its fruitful and creative energy.
>
> (Quoted Brown, p. 92)

But, while as here for Schlegel and earlier with Fichte, language tended to be seen as a creative medium, clarifying perception and structuring it in accord with the physical impressions of the being or race which it informs, the soul or language remains for Mangan an obscuring or refractory medium. Its being is bound up in the problematic expressed in Schiller's epigram 'Sprache':

> Warum kann der lebendige Geist dem Geist nicht erscheinen!
> *Spricht* die Seele, so spricht, ach! schon die *Seele* nicht mehr,
>
> (Schiller I, p. 125)

which Mangan translates—with full awareness of the complexity of the word 'Geist'—as follows:

> Why are all efforts failures when we seek
> Communion with the soul, the ghost, *sans corps*?
> Is't not that when the soul begins to *speak*
> It seems—alas! and is—the *soul* no more?
>
> (*D.U.M.* July 1838, p. 64)

Representation is for Mangan fundamentally bound up with such processes of alienation: his 'Geist' is more in the image of the Irishman alienated from his original language into the deathly world described by Fichte and Davis as that of adopted or imposed languages than that of the German living in vital interchange of language and perception.

In such a way, indeed, one could analyze or explain away the nostalgia for childhood and the 'golden summer of existence' that appears to afflict Mangan himself as he writes. Thus Welch criticizes him for mocking such writers as the sentimental Ludwig Tieck while translating from him a poem entitled 'Life is the Desert and the Solitude'

> which states unequivocally one of his central preoccupations, the desire to be out of time, away from the personality, which, in its everchangingness, is subject at all times to unpredictable surges from the unconscious, and so is essentially unknowable.
>
> (Welch, p. 90)

One is immediately suspicious of the notion of any translation of Mangan's being "unequivocal," and rightly so, as a comparison of translation with source shows. Welch's description of Mangan's poem as "a clear and direct statement of the German *Sehnsucht,* the yearning to be out of the process of time, and to find some paradisal sweetness" (Welch, p. 89) is an accurate, even tautologically accurate description of the poem by Tieck, who was indeed one of the central figures among the German *Frühromantiker,* and one of the principal figures in the pursuit of "the truly subjective expression of the forlorn melancholy of the transitory."[23] Tieck's "Sehnsucht" (Tieck I, 1-2) is an almost schematic rendering of the striving for the distance ("trachten / Weit nach Ferne") and its tension with the stern bonds ("ernste Bande") that hold the poet from the undiscovered distant land ("Unentdeckte ferne Lande"). As he perceives its shores shimmering in the twilight of his dreams, and some ambiguous figure appears, an unspecified power holds him back and all sinks again:

> Nur wen Träume um mich dämmern,
> Seh' ich deine Ufer schimmern,
> Seh' von dorther mir was winken,—
> Ist es Freund, ist's Menschgestalt?
> Schnell mus alles untersinken,
> Rückwärts hält mich die Gewalt.

The cycle of languishing in longing begins again in exact repetition of the opening lines. Mangan's translation seems at first to follow closely the opening lines of Tieck's poem, removing only the solecism by which it is the poet's tears ("Tränen") which do the striving. One shortly begins to perceive how Mangan transforms the idiom "weit nach Ferne" into one in which, far from "striving," the longings "roam" after stars which "wander" as if in a never-closing process, which is echoed in the syntax:

> Ah! for ever,
> Ever turning,
> Ever thronging
> Tow'rds the Distance,
> Roams each fonder
> Yearning yonder,
> Golden stars in blest existence!

The nominal presences which Tieck attributes to his far land—which include the very substantial "Klüfte," ravines,—are softened out into "What fragrant / Airs," "What rich vagrant / Music," and "Angel-voices" calling to "win" the yearner. This softening of the vision into a vague "phantasmagoria of the mind" into "fairy / Bowers and palace gardens" becomes an "undeveloped Land," a phrase which condenses neatly both the "undeveloped," vague nature of its forms and the tendency by which, "wanting what we do not have, cannot have," we make of the "undiscovered" ("unentdeckte") a zone which we can appropriate for our own projections.

Thus the power that restrained Tieck is only appealed to here to "*break* each band / That keeps my soul from thee," while the "wenn Träume um mich dämmern" of the German (which implies the breaking of a dawn as well as the "twilight" of the dream's shadows) becomes the "spectral sky" that lights "shifting dreams" such as are produced by yearnings that "roam" rather than "strive." Nor is it the power that restrains, but the yearner's attempt to realize his unreal projection that causes the vision to fade:

> Ah! what fair form, flitting through yon green glades,
> Dazes mine eye? Spirit, oh! rive my chain!
> Woe is my soul! Swiftly the vision fades . . .[24]

In Mangan's version, however, the issue is not an unambiguous return to the cycle of "Sehnsucht": a slight shift maintains an ambivalence as to whether the "longing" derives from some actual distant, "undeveloped Land," or from the frustrated attempt of the yearner to grasp a shadow of his own projection:

> Hence this fever;
> Hence this burning.
> Love and Longing:
> Hence for ever,
> Ever turning,
> Ever thronging
> Tow'rds the Distance. . . .

This ironic development is legible within the translation itself, but it is the process of translation—as the comparison with the original confirms—which introduces that development into a notion of "Sehnsucht" which is caught in its own cyclical forms, just as it maintains the distance necessary for the production of that irony with regard to the "fancy" ("wähnen") that sustains such longing.

III

The sort of suspension of desire in ceaseless repetition that is remarkable in **'Life Is the Desert and the Solitude'** sustains constantly the 'authentic' rhetoric that Jacques Chuto has analyzed in Mangan's translated and original writing (Chuto 1977). Much has been written by both critics and biographers to offer explanations psychological and sociological for the sense of suffering and entrapment that may have induced what appears as a state of paralysis of the will. There is no space here, unfortunately, to discuss these assertions, and it seems more important to indicate the effects of Mangan's psyche, however constituted, as they appear to inform his writing.[25] The most frequent assertion about Mangan is that he was obsessed with the image of a golden age of the past, in himself or for Ireland, which haunted him with the effect of inducing a sense of terror at the passage of time and producing in turn the rhetorical stasis of his most characteristic poems. Even apart from the evidence of his own ***Autobiography***—evidence that is about his own interpretation of his life, and not the 'objective facts'—that from his boyhood he was 'haunted by an indescribable feeling of something terrible' (A. p. 9), attentive reading of such poems as **'Life Is the Desert'** and **'The Unrealities'** demonstrates how far that obsession involves an ironic distance from the idea of such original states of harmony. It should be remembered, furthermore, to how great an extreme such myths—whether projected into past or future—structured the unifying drives of the Romantic movement, and in particular the movements of nationalism and unionism in Ireland.

For Mangan, it seems, such myths of origin were distinctly suspicious. The very opening epigraph of his ***Autobiography***—

> . . . A heavy shadow lay
> On that boy's spirit; he was not of his fathers.

denies his origins, while the last reference of the text (which is full of references to types and models of his experiences as if again to deny 'originality') is to Pascal, whose theology, apparently an important influence on Mangan's thinking, involves among other things a rejection of all Edenic nostalgia as 'divertissement': the idea of a paradisial origin is the symbol of man's wretched state, no more. It is, then, of some interest to note how, in that frequently cited poem **'And Then No More,'** translated from the German of Rückert, 'Und Dann Nicht Mehr,' Mangan transforms the slight original (itself a translation from the Persian) into a metaphoric study of fixation of considerable power. The original is the brief tale of the poet's vision of a young girl, and of her subsequent early death:

> Im Saal des Festes sah ich sie entschleiern sich;
> Da war das Paradies im Saal, und dann nicht mehr.
>
> (Rückert, *Gedichte,* p. 381)

Whatever biographical reasons underlay Mangan's interest in the themes of the poem, in translating it he chooses to pick up Rückert's quite casual references to 'einen Himmelstrahl' and 'Paradies,' and to construct from them a progress of increasingly unreal apotheosis of the original vision, from 'Eden's light,' through Paradise and 'Earth looked like Heaven,' to the 'Peri-land' of the final stanza. Counterpointing that movement is a gradual decline of the poet's persona towards death, replacing that of the girl in the German text. The poem again revolves around the static repetitive rhetoric so familiar in Mangan, but the counterpointing suggests that the stasis is to be viewed with ironic distance, as the image of a certain condition rather the personal lament of the writer. In part, that ironic distance is supported by the objective distance which separates the translator from his original.

The most cogent critique of the obsession with origins comes, however, in Mangan's first article in the series **'Literae Orientales.'** The appositeness of this extended critique, of which only part is here quoted, can best be appreciated in the context of a whole series of quite serious discussions on the origins of mankind and of language, which concluded by suggesting that the Gaelic tongue and the Gaelic people were that origin, through the devious routes of impressionistic etymology and archaeology.[26] It is probably also worth considering the extent to which such writings on Orientalism as Sir William Jones' *Anniversary Discourses* were involved in extending the domain of 'an *imperial,* but, which is a character of equal dignity, a *commercial* people' (op. cit. pp. 13-14). Mangan writes as follows:

> If the East is really accessible, so may be at last—the reverse who dares to prophesy?—"the unreached paradise of our despair"; and so long as the Wonderful Lamp, the dazzler of our boyhood, can be dreamed of as still lying *perdu* in some corner of the Land of Wonders, so long must we continue captives to the hope that a lovelier light than any now diffused over the dusky pathway of our existence will yet be borne to us across the blue Mediterranean. Alas! wanting that which we have not, cannot have, we mould that which we really have into an ill-defined counterfeit of that which we want, and then, casting a veil over it, we contemplate the creature of our own fancy with much the same sort of emotion that may be supposed to have dilated the breast of Mareses, the artist of Sais, when he first surveyed the outlines of the gigantic statue himself had curtained from human view. Yet it is on the whole fortunate that speculation can fall back upon such resources. Slender and shifting though they seem, they serve as barriers against Insanity.
>
> (*D.U.M.* Sept. 1837, p. 275)

Mangan's critique of the pursuit of origins here is disturbing both for the steadiness with which it describes the process of appropriation and for the clarity with which it is capable of containing within it an ostensible undermining of its argument, in that final avowal of the probable necessity of such an activity. Both recognitions extend right through his practice as a translator, in his constant recognition of the opacity of one culture to another and in his lack of hesitation in refracting translated texts to his own purposes. Thus it is in fact no contradiciton that he should argue in separate places two apparently opposed cases concerning the nature of translation, on the one hand, that in translating, everything is practicable (cf. *D.U.M.* Dec. 1836, p. 721), and on the other, that oriental poems are quite untranslatable for a European (ib. April 1840, p. 377). In a certain sense, the acceptance of the opacity of foreign language and culture that is involved in the latter assertion is the condition of the arrogation involved in the former. For Mangan, translation ceases to pretend to be a transparency seeking identification with some supposed original moment contained within the genius of or behind the text which is its object:

> But nobody knows what he conceals, or whether he conceals anything or not, and so nobody can give him credit for his concealments. If a man writes anything he must write something, and the something that he does write is *prima facie* the unabridged and perfect exposition of his thought.
>
> (*D.U.M.* July 1838, p. 60)

Given that it is thus a surface and not an authentic anterior experience or speech which is to be rendered, what will always be of concern in the reading of the translation will be not the clarity of transference into an 'equivalent' of an 'original,' but exactly the degree of refraction which takes place, through the opacity of the translator. Seen in this aspect, translation, eschewing the passivity of a negative capability, which would seek to efface all traces of distancing irony, in favour of an activity of full critical involvement, must be regarded not as an unfortunate detour in Mangan's career, but as a metaphor and a practice of central importance to the understanding of his writing as a whole, in its achievements as in its impasses.

Notes

1. O'Donoghue (*Life,* p. 15) says that Mangan was taught modern and classical languages by a Father Graham, lately returned from Salamanca. Mangan himself, in the 'impersonal autobiography' (*Irishman,* Aug. 1850) claims knowledge of only eight languages.

2. Although Mangan expressed interest in the Irish language as early as 1832 (cf. *Dublin Penny Journal,* 15 Sept. 1832, p. 93), comments such as O'Daly's in his introduction to *The Poets and Poetry of Munster* (p. xvi) that 'all his versions of Gaelic poetry were made from literal translations furnished to him by Irish scholars, as he was totally unacquainted with the original language' continue to cloud the issue of Mangan' Irish.

3. Cf. Chuto, 'The Sources of James Clarence Mangan's Oriental Writings' (1980) to appear in *Notes and Queries.*

4. Cf. Welch pp. 84-5 for an argument to this effect.

5. For a fuller discussion of the question of 'equivalence,' see Lefevere (1979) pp. 90-4.

6. Cf. also the *Dublin Review* Dec. 1845, p. 313: With him translation is a mere process of fusion; but the metal is recast in precisely the same mould, and preserves not alone the substance, but the most minute and delicate peculiarities of form which characterized its original structure.

7. A fact which Maria Edgeworth notes in her introduction to *Castle Rackrent,* though then in optimistic terms. (Edgeworth 1964, p. 5).

8. The most comprehensive account of these factors is given in Rafroidi chaps I and V, and, for the German influence, in McKiernan.

9. Akenson (pp. 378-80) provides some statistical evidence from census returns for this widely accepted dating.

10. Cf. in particular Kamenka and Kedourie for extended accounts of the Romantic origins of nationalism.

11. Akenson provides a full account of the 'Irish educational experiment,' and Andrews a history of the early days of the Ordnance Survey. Chuto 1976 is an interesting account of Mangan's involvement with the Survey.

12. Cf. especially Kinsella (ed) *Davis, Mangan, Ferguson? Tradition and the Irish Writer.*

13. In the early 1800's that line can be traced from Herder's *Essay on the Origin of Language* (1772) through to Humboldt's various writings on philology, in particular his *Uber die Verschiedenheit des menschlichen Sprachbaues und ihren Einfluss auf die geistige Entwicklung des Menschengeschlechts* (1836). The cultural relativism implicit in the latter is not embodied in such theories as offered earlier by nationalists such as Fichte. For accounts of this strand of German language theory, see Jesperson 1946, and Brown, Chap. 5.

14. For Fichte's discussion of the importance of national education to the rebuilding of a German Nation, which had profound implications for cultural theory in Britain and Ireland as in Germany, see Fichte, *Addresses to the German Nation,* Addresses 9-11.

15. As Duffy and the *Nation* projected an education in which unity and purpose would be each other's means and end in Ireland's 'epic' history, so Fichte writes in 1808:

    > By means of the new education we want to mould the Germans into a corporate body, which shall be stimulated and animated in all its individual members by the same interest.
    >
    > (*Addresses,* p. 15)

    This ideology of education is common to nationalist thought; cf. for example, Mazzini, Chap. 9.

16. The poem here in question is 'The County Mayo,' translated with George Fox, often regarded as a classic in catching the Gaelic 'note' in English.

17. As Welch has argued, p. 131.

18. Cf. Welch, pp. 101-2: Poetic freedom in the Romantic period (and in the modern too) involves a going out from the self, a 'negative capability.' Only then can the joy intrinsic to true creation come about.

    In fact, it would probably be more accurate to say that poetic freedom involves, for the Romantics, the production of the self, a notion fundamental to such central texts as *Naive and Sentimental Poetry* or *Biographia Literaria.*

19. Welch remarks on this passage, but claims not to appreciate its meaning fully. He also regards Mangan's translation of 'Die Ideale' as 'one of Mangan's finest poems and also one of his most faithful translations' (p. 86).

20. See for example such poems as 'Drechsler''s 'Stanzas to . . .' (*D.U.M.* August 1836, p. 163); 'Life Is the Desert and the Solitude' (*Comet* July 21 1833, p. 517); or 'A Vision of Connaught in the Thirteenth Century' (*Nation* July 11, 1846, p. 619).

21. Cf. Tooke p. 25. Mangan was certainly aware of Tooke's linguistic work, as is evidenced by reference to him, *D.U.M.* March 1837, p. 285.

22. For accounts, see again Jesperson 1946 and 1947, and Brown ch. 5 and 6.

23. This comment is translated from an article in a standard German history of literature, Werner Kohlschmidt's "Die Romantik" in Boesch, 1961, p. 311.

24. Cf. this process in, for example, 'A Vision of Connaught' (n. 20 above) or in 'The Dream of John MacDonnell,' (*Nation* May 16, 1846, p. 489). The disappearence of the visionary Lady on being approached is a familiar feature of the Gaelic 'aisling' or dream poem.

25. For biographical material, see especially Mangan's own brief autobiography, Mitchel's introduction to *Poems* 1859, O'Donoghue's *Life* and Welch, pp. 76-85 in particular. It is probably necessary to counsel against too naive an acceptance of accounts of suffering that are certainly in part strategic in Mangan and his biographers.

26. Cf. for example, Charles Vallancey 1772, and O'Brien 1834.

Bibliography

Note: due to the general unavailability of collected editions of Mangan's poetry (there exists to date no complete edition) I have referred to the poems in their original journal publication locations throughout. Most of them can, however, be found in one or other collection. For reasons which this article should have begun to make clear, it is always wiser to read Mangan's writings in their contexts, be that the context of the articles in which they appear, or the wider cultural and historical context of his life and writings.

Akenson, D. H. 1970 *The Irish Educational Experiment. The National System of Education in Nineteenth Century Ireland.* London.

Andrews, J. H. 1975 *A Paper Landscape: The Ordnance Survey in Nineteenth Century Ireland.* Oxford.

Boesch, B. 1961 (ed) *Deutsche Literaturgeschichte in Grundzügen. Die Epochen Deutscher Dichtung,* 2nd edn. Berne.

Brower, R. L. 1966 (ed) *On Translation.* New York.

Chuto, J. 1976 'Mangan, Petrie, O'Donovan and a Few Others: The Poet and the Scholars' in the *Irish University Review* Autumn 1976, pp. 169-87.

———. 1977 'Rhétorique et Autheticité chez J. C. Mangan'—paper presented to the Congrès de la S. A. E. S., Tours (unpublished).

Coleridge, S. T. 1976 *On the Constitution of Church and State.* Ed. J. Colmer. Princeton.

Edgeworth, M. 1964 *Castle Rackrent.* Ed. G. Watson. Oxford.

Even-Zohar, L. 1979 'Polysystem Theory' in *Poetics Today* Vol. I No. 1-2. Autumn 1979.

Fichte, J. G. 1922 *Addresses to the German Nation,* trans. R. F. Jones and G. H. Turnbull. Chicago.

Hardiman, J. 1831 *Irish Minstrelsy.* London.

Herder, J. G. 1966 'Essay on the Origin of Language.' Trans. A. Gode. in *Rousseau and Herder: Essays on the Origin of Language.* New York.

Jesperson, O. 1946 *Mankind, Nation and Individual from a Linguistic Point of View.* London.

———. 1947 *Language. Its Nature, Development and Origin.* London.

Kamenka, E. 1973 *Nationalism: The Nature and Evolution of an Idea.* London.

Kedourie, E. 1961 *Nationalism.* London.

Lefèvere, A., Van Den Broeck, R. 1979 *Uitnodiging tot de Vertaalwetenschap.* Muiderberg.

Lefèvere, A. 1977 (ed. and trans.) *Translating Literature: The German Tradition.* Amsterdam.

———. 1981 'Translated Literature: Towards an Integrated Theory' in *Bulletin of the Midwest Modern Language Association* Vol. 14 No. 1 Spring 1981, pp. 68-77.

———. 1984 'That Structure in the Dialect of Men Interpreted' in *Comparative Criticism* (forthcoming).

Mangan, J. C. 1845 *Anthologia Germanica.* London.

———. 1968 *Autobiography.* Ed. J. Kilroy. Dublin.

———. 1859 *Poems*; with biographical introduction by J. Mitchel. New York.

———. 1903 *Poems.* Edited by D. J. O'Donoghue. Dublin.

Mazzini, J. 1929 *The Duties of Man and Other Essays.* London.

O'Brien, H. 1834 *The Round Towers of Ireland.* London.

O'Daly, J. 1849 (ed.) *The Poets and Poetry of Munster.* Translated by J. C. Mangan. Dublin.

O'Donoghue, D. J. 1898 *The Life and Writings of James Clarence Mangan.* Dublin.

Plato 1898 *The Republic.* Trans. J. L. Davies and D. J. Vaughan. London.

Rafroidi, P. 1980 *Irish Literature in English. The Romantic Period.* Gerrards Cross and Atlantic Highlands, N.J.

Rückert, F. 1872 *Gedichte.* Frankfurt-am-Main.

Schiller, F. 1974 *Werke in fünf Bänden. Band I.* Berlin und Weimar.

———. 1845 *Essays Aesthetical and Philosophical.* Trans. A. Morrison.

Steiner, G. 1975 *After Babel.* London.

Tieck, L. 1821 *Gedichte.* 3 vols. Dresden.

Tooke, J. H. 1840 *Epea Pteroenta or The Diversions of Purley.* ed. revised by R. Taylor. London.

Uhland, L. 1835 *Gedichte.* Stuttgart und Tübingen.

Vallancey, C. 1772 *An Essay on the Antiquity of the Irish Language.* Dublin.

Welch, R. 1980 *Irish Poetry from Moore to Yeats.* Gerrards Cross.

David C. Lloyd (essay date 1984)

SOURCE: Lloyd, David C. "Great Gaps in Irish Song: James Clarence Mangan and the Ideology of the Nationalist Ballad." *Irish University Review* 14.2 (1984): 178-90. Print.

[*In the following essay, Lloyd examines the importance of ballad poetry to Irish nationalism and Mangan's work in that form. According to Lloyd, Mangan failed to "conform his rhetoric to nationalist prescriptions," not because he was frustrated in his attempts to join the nationalist movement but because of his general tendency to refuse to "integrate and identify with the greater whole."*]

When Charles Gavan Duffy suggested that the history of Ireland, once fully known, would be perceived to have "the unity and purpose of an epic poem,"[1] he was intimating a connection between research into the history of Ireland and its reproduction in literature that was fundamental to the programme of the Young Ireland movement as expressed in their newspaper, the *Nation.* Where the drive of the one activity aimed at the revival of a vital continuity with the nation's past, the ideal task of the other was to carry that continuity forward into the future. Even where the nationalist is forced to consider the divisions that characterize the idea of Irish history as opposed to that of England, his saving grace is still located in literature, conceived of as providing that unifying institution which Ireland lacks constitutionally. Thus, for example, John Mitchel's reconstitution of his identity for the future reader, himself and others, through writing his *Jail Journal* is an act typical of the nationalist which repeats in the individual a process projected elsewhere for the nation as a whole:

> One of the great social bonds which England—in fact every other nation but ours—possesses, is the existence of some *institution* or *idea,* towards the completion of which all have toiled in common, which comprehends all, and renders them respectable in each other's eyes. Thus her *history* knits together all ranks and sects of England. . . . Each has erected a story of the constitution. They value each other and acknowledge a connection. There are bright spots in our history; but of how few is the story common! and the contemplation of it, *as a whole,* does not tend to harmony, unless the conviction of past error produces wisdom for the future. We have no institution or idea that comprehends all, that has been produced by all. We must look to the present or future for the foundation of concord and nationality. We must set ourselves to erect some such institution or idea. A national literature is in its very essence amalgamating, and may eventually become the great temple of concord. . . .[2]

In this sense, "literature is practical . . . and the writer is a man of action,"[3] participating in the construction of the nation within which he will be "comprehended." The mutual interdependence of writer and nation in nationalist theory was expressed by the *Nation*'s critic and reviewer D. F. McCarthy: "A great literature . . . was either the creation or the creator of a great people."[4] The ambivalence of that formulation expresses exactly the problem with which the Irish nationalist is faced when appealing to literature as a national institution. If the function of literature is to form and unite a people not yet in existence, how will a writer of sufficient stature arise, given that it is from the people he must arise if he is to express the spirit of the nation?

The problem here expressed is one that has in various ways confronted all nation states on their assumption of a distinct identity, and which has been theoretically resolved in equally various ways. The most apposite parallel to the Irish context would be the deliberate attempts in Germany to construct a literary language through the combined methods of translation from other languages and research into medieval Germanic poetry in a tradition which stretches from Luther's translation of the Bible to the researches of scholars like Karl Simrock and the brothers Grimm in the nineteenth century.[5] Allusion to the German tradition, however, reminds one forcibly of the anomaly of the Irish situation, in which the virtual loss of the Irish language creates a double break in the continuity of that process. In the first place, simple ignorance of the Gaelic tradition permitted the assumption, rooted in centuries of indifference on the part of the English-speaking community, that that tradition could not in itself constitute a national literature, was too primitive and unsophisticated to do so. "There are," remarked Davis with something of the air of a mason assessing the monumental work to be performed, "great gaps in Irish song to be filled up," gaps which he attributes to "ignorance, disorder, and every kind of oppression."[6] In the second place, even the use of that rubble of the Gaelic tradition for the foundations of the institution of national literature will have to be permitted by research and translation. Unlike the German nationalist, who can conceive the translation of foreign material as assimilation, and research as revivifying, thus retaining effortlessly an organic idea of continuity, the Irish nationalist's work of research and translation is determined by a gap, and involves the assimilation of the native to the foreign, Irish into English, thus incurring the risk of being "set adrift among the accidents of translation."[7] The uneasy shifts here between opposed models of the organic evolution or creative interdependence of nation and writer and of the architectural construction of a monumental institution is symptomatic of a radical unease in the Irish nationalist's projection of a national literature as a unifying idea.

The theoretical resolution of these difficulties entails an almost exact repetition of the forms of the nationalist recourse to history, elaborated this time in the idea of the "ballad." If the national literature is to be "the very flowering of the soul" of the nation,[8] rather than an institution arbitrarily imposed upon it, it will, like the nationalist himself, need to be made "racy of the soil," and to absorb the spirit of the people. By the time McCarthy assembled his *Book of Irish Ballads* in 1846, the idea that ballads represented the original and primitive poetry of a people was a critical commonplace. McCarthy's introduction to the anthology, however, recasts this notion in order to appropriate it to specifically Irish concerns. For him, an understanding of a people's character is incomplete "unless it be based upon the revelations they themselves have made, or the confessions they have uttered," and his belief that "Hesiod and Homer built their beautiful and majestic structures on the original ballads that were probably floating among the people"[9] leads him to a formulation of the need for a ballad poetry in Ireland to form the basis of a literature which, deriving from such ballads, will be—as they are—filled with the "distinct character and peculiar charm" of the Irish genius.[10] What is of most importance to McCarthy is the belief that the contact with the Irish spirit, which a knowledge of the ballad poetry provides, will give a distinctive character back to an Irish literature which will perforce be written in English:

> To those among us, and to the generations who are yet to be among us, whose mother tongue is, and of necessity must be, the English and not the Irish, the establishing of this fact is of the utmost importance, and of the greatest consolation:—that we can be thoroughly Irish in our writings without ceasing to be English; that we can be faithful to the land of our birth without being unfaithful to that literature which has been "the nursing mother of our minds"; that we can develop the intellectual resources of our country, and establish for ourselves a distinct and separate existence in the world of letters, without depriving ourselves of the widely-diffused and genius-consecrated language of England, are facts that I conceive cannot be too widely disseminated.[11]

Thus through a thorough knowledge of the *spirit* of the Irish ballad, translation in the widest sense becomes assimilation, and the language that might have been the badge of conquest is reinfused as a national as well as an individual "mother tongue."

A parallel argument in an anonymous *Nation* article on Elizabeth Barrett Browning and Alfred Tennyson clarifies even further the historical principles involved, and the demand made upon the Irish writer by the nationalists. Lamenting the fact that "the healthy growth of an Irish literature" has been "thwarted and impeded" by the English tie, the writer continues with a sketch of the ideal evolution of a literature:

> The different stages of social development have their distinct characters written in the development of mind. First there is the ballad, simple, direct, and unadorned; then lyric poetry, the epic, the drama, history, philosophy, each growing naturally out of the other. So are all great national literatures built; … so must it be here, if we are ever to have a literature of our own.[12]

This being the natural course of development, the very fact that English literature is "the nursing mother of our minds" constitutes an impediment to healthy growth, introducing the refinements of a fully developed national literature to force the growth of a plant whose first shoots are scarcely apparent. The remedy is characteristic:

> The philosophical tone of a high civilisation does not suit us; we have our history to make, and our writings must help to make it. We want strength, earnestness, passion, the song and the ballad, all that fires and nerves the minds of men. Perfection in this is to be attained, not by studying English cotemporary [*sic*] poets, but by becoming saturated as it were with Irish feeling, by learning the Irish language, sympathising in every beat of an Irish peasant's pulse, by being filled with knowledge of Ireland's past and of boundless hope in her future. …[13]

Once again the nationalist is called to a total identification with the nation, evacuating himself of the subjectivisim of an English civilization in order to be "saturated" and "filled" with the Irish spirit, his present only part of an arc that stretches continuously from past to future. That spiritual identification serves to conceal—or suture, as one's point of view may be—the gap which derives one artificially to "make" a history, whether national or literary.

The demand made by *Nation* writers like Davis and McCarthy for the full-scale production of ballad poetry is not then simply a call to the work of propaganda through direct statement or appeal, a kind of "poster art" as Padraic Fallon has suggested, which might most effectively have been achieved through the sort of street ballad that the *Nation* writers despised as an Anglo-Gaelic hybrid.[14] Far more important than the present for the nationalist is the future, and in calling the Irish to the labour of ballad writing, the Young Irelander is looking to lay the foundations of a national literature which has yet to arise. The lack of individuality in the ballads published in nationalist journals, and reprinted in the enormously successful anthology deliberately entitled *The Spirit of the Nation,* is thus a part of the programme rather than a failing.[15] Total immersion of the writer's identity in that of the nation was seen as the first condition of a process which sought to fabricate effectively a foreshortened literary history in which the development which had hitherto been thwarted might speedily be made up. For, if in the first stage of that missed development the ballad would have been the anonymous voice of the people, in the attempt to forge the trace of a never-existent literary history, an *impersonal* balladry becomes the necessary first step, that the spirit of the nation may manifest itself uncontaminated by a subjectivism which would be the mark of English civilization, and thus kept pure for future emergence in a fuller growth of the literary tradition. And, implicitly, the more intense the production of ballads, the more rapidly might the gaps be filled in and this perhaps rather ignominious stage be passed on from.

As an established poet, James Clarence Mangan was not exempt from the demand to produce Irish ballads. Duffy seems, for example, to have attempted to induce him to embark on the unlikely project of a series of historical romances.[16] More pointedly, Thomas Davis exclaimed in the course of a *Nation* article, "A Ballad History of Ireland":

> How we wish the author of **"The Barmecides"** [**"The Time of the Barmecides"**] would lend his help to an Irish ballad history! His power of making verses racy of the soil cannot be doubted by anyone who reads his **"Paraphrase of Katheleen [*sic*] ny Houlahan"** and his **"Elegy on the Princes"** [**"An Elegy on the Tyronian and Tyrconnellian Princes"**], in the *Dublin Penny Magazine.*[17]

In an unpublished paper, "Rhétorique et authenticité chez J. C. Mangan," Jacques Chuto has finely analysed the "inauthenticity" of the rhetoric of the nationalist verse which Mangan produced in response to such demands. Having analysed what he regards as Mangan's authentic "rhetoric of lamentation" in terms of an opposition, fundamentally between the grammatical past and present, and repetition, of syntactic forms and devices such as the refrain, Chuto turns to a consideration of the effect on his rhetoric of Mangan's attempts to adopt the style of the Young Irelanders:

> Here is a poet, introverted by nature, and, most often, protected by his masks, who steps forward with uncovered face to address an auditorium. Incapable of relating immediately to others on account of the fissure in his own self, Mangan has recourse to the exhortatory formulas current among Young Ireland's rhymers.[18]

The result, according to Chuto, is the production of a rhetoric characterized by the accumulation of imperatives, gathered in a syntax without resilience:

> Deprived of any internal necessity, it rests on contingence, that is, it arranges side by side a certain number of propositions linked merely by a profusion of question and exclamation marks. . . .[19]

This description seems on the face of it accurate with regard to a large number of the exhortatory nationalist poems that Mangan produced for various Young Ireland journals, the *Nation,* the *United Irishman,* and the *Irishman* in particular. To compare passages of such poems with examples selected at random from *The Spirit of the Nation,* or even from the prose of Mitchel's editorials is to confirm Chuto's remarks:

> Know then your true lot,
>   Ye faithful, though few!
>   Understand your position,
>   Remember your mission,
> And vacillate not,
>   Whatsoever ensue!
> Alter not! Falter not!
>   Palter not with your own living souls!
>
> For a Sword that never spared
>   Stand prepared!
> Though that glory Sword be bared
>   Be not scared!
> Do not blench and dare not falter!
> For the axe and for the halter
>   Stand prepared!
>
> Stand together, brothers all,
>   Close together, close together!
> Be Ireland's might a brazen wall—
>   Close up together, tight together!
> Peace! no noise!—but, hand in hand,
> Let calm resolve pervade your band. . . .
>
> Yes! with our fellow citizens rests now the fate of Ireland. If they quail, or shrink, vacillate, pause, postpone, or exhibit the slightest weakness—if they balk the hopes of a single Irishman, or give one enemy another chance to scoff, 'twere better they had remained slaves, contented in their slavery, or, being discontented, had hanged themselves.[20]

But, even when abstracted from their full context, these brief passages of Mangan's exhortatory verse (the first two quoted) exhibit a quality, which might be described as a certain nervous tension, that is generally absent from Young Ireland balladry. In part, that tension derives locally from the taut metrics and internal rhymes that underpin the accumulation of imperatives. Replaced in the total context of the poems, the tension that underlies the exhortation can be shown to repeat a tension that subsists between an imperative voice that mimes nationalist projections into the future, and a present in which an accumulation of substantives mimes the situation that evokes that projection, the perpetual *imminence,* that is, of the realization of the *immanent* idea of the nation, which makes of the nationalist's present a perpetual labour in perpetual suspension. For each generation of readers of **"The Warning Voice,"** that suspension is to be reasserted:

To *this* generation
The sore tribulation,
The stormy commotion,
And foam of the Popular Ocean,
The struggle of class against class;
The Dearth and the Sadness,
The Sword and the War-vest;
To the *next,* the Repose and the Gladness,
"The Sea of clear glass,"
And the rich Golden Harvest.[21]

The final lines of **"A Voice of Encouragement"** conclude, after eight stanzas of exhortatory rhetoric in a strikingly unwieldy metre, with an image and a syntax which crystallize the common form of these "nationalist" poems of Mangan's:

Cloaked in the Hall, the Envoy stands, his mission unspoken, While the pale, banquetless guests await in trembling to hear it.[22]

Pace Chuto, it is always in this "masked" form that Mangan approaches his nationalist audience, offering them an unspoken event as the limit of the labour to which he exhorts them. If, as at the end of the **"Irish National Hymn,"** he continually assumes the privilege of "one whom some have called a Seer,"[23] he is most typically a prophet who intimates but does not see, stressing the gap which persists between expectation and event:

And I heard, as I guessed,
The far-echoing sound
Of a trumpet, with tones,
And lightning and thunders,
As ye read of in John's
Revelation of Wonders.
What meant they? I trow not.
What next might befal?
And how ended All?
This, too, friends, I know not—
For here were my cords
Of sleep suddenly broken,
The bell booming Three;
But there seemed in mine ears,
As I started up, woken,
A noise like fierce cheers,
Blent with clashing of swords,
And the roar of the sea![24]

With that refusal to endow his vision with the expected full meaning, Mangan introduces a disarming and distancing irony, compacted by the shadings of "as I guessed," "seemed in mine ears," "a noise like," into a poem whose dream is initially posed in terms of "a Stream / That in vain seeks the light," and which "mocks our control." Exactly at the point where the meaning of the vision—final defeat or final victory, hell or apocalyptic prelude to the new earth—seems about to be grasped and controlled, the vision is interrupted. The seer who does not see remains outside his "vision," in the position of the "human eyes" of the oriental fable which intrudes into the **"Irish National Hymn"**:

Deep, saith the Eastern story,
Burns in Iran's mines a gem,
For its dazzling hues and glory
Worth a Sultan's diadem.
But from human eyes
Hidden there it ever lies!
The aye-travailing gnomes alone,
Who toil to form the mountain's treasure,
May gaze and gloat with pleasure, without measure,
Upon the lustrous beauty of that wonder-stone.
. . . .
Strangers who travail
To lay bare the gem, shall fail.

If, as the poem suggests, the Young Irelanders are to be seen as the "aye-travailing gnomes," labouring "hour by hour" for "That bright pearl, self-liberation," a possible reading is that they remain so gazing and gloating at this alchemical stone, which they themselves may even have "formed," but may never actually grasp. Such ironies can be traced throughout Mangan's "nationalist" ballads, seeding the positive rhetoric of exhortation with doubts as to the real status of those nationalist "Dreams that almost outshone Realities while they were cherished":

Such see the rainbow's glory where Heaven looms darkest and sternest;
Such in the storm wind hear but the music of pipe and of tabor.[25]

"A Voice of Encouragement" begins expressly with the assertion that the speaker is "a man unworthy to rank in your number," "his music and diction / Rather . . . fitted, alas! to lull to than startle from, slumber." The uneven, faltering "numbers" of Mangan's nationalist poems repeatedly subtend the poet's self-subtraction from the nationalist vision—which can, perhaps, only be seen in the "chords / Of Sleep." As Chuto points out, it is at these moments of self-subtraction that the clash of rhetorics becomes most apparent, the poet's appearance on the scene being—it should be added—the moment of his departure:

This cleavage is particularly evident, and
lived as such by Mangan, when he himself appears
on the scene in this category of poems. . . .
And albeit I hasten home,
I, a nameless child of thine,
To the last, the lampless dome,
Though I die and make no sign,
My last thoughts shall be of thee.[26]

Accurate as Chuto's descriptions are, however, it is difficult to assent to the tendency of his article which suggests that Mangan's inability to conform his rhetoric to nationalist prescriptions represents the frustration of a sincere desire to integrate with that movement. His feelings with regard to the nationalist project seem more adequately reflected in the sentiments of the German tragedian Zacharias Werner on "Seeing afar the golden booty / Which I dare not hope to share," as rendered in Mangan's translation **"The Coming Time,"** which appeared in a number of the **"Anthologia Germanica"** [***Anthologia Germanica* = *German Anthology***] in which Mangan also castigates Freiligrath for his adoption of political commitment in place of poetic indifference.[27] Like Werner, Mangan's apprehension of the nationalist dream is always from the perspective of one about to die, not of one seeking his future life in incorporation in the greater life of the nation. The clash of rhetorics in his nationalist poems stands as symbolic of a more general refusal on Mangan's part to integrate and identify with the greater whole.

Exactly because the nationalist call to the writing of ballad poetry demands an effacement of the self in the interests of founding the literary institution essential to the nation's existence and unity, Mangan's political writing bears in it patterns which work quite radically against the nationalist programme. In writing as the medium, so to speak, of the spirit of the nation, the Irish writer was to become "a man of action," his words becoming actions, as the sign, transfused with spirit, becomes the thing itself. Hence, confronted with the writer whom they wished to be able to hail as a great national poet, contemporary nationalist commentators on Mangan's life and work manifest a certain unease in relation to the very inaction that characterizes his life—his failure, in the words of Joseph Brenan, "To live his poetry—to act his rhyme."[28] In his introduction to his edition of Mangan's poetry, Mitchel was obliged to indulge in considerable flights of rhetoric and systematic distortion in order to make of Mangan the image of suffering Ireland. Duffy, later and more honestly, records his failure to get Mangan to identify fully with the Young Ireland movement:

> I thought the gifted and gallant young men associated in the enterprise, who were afterwards known as "Young Irelanders," would bring him companions for his mind and heart for the first time and that his slumbering nationality would be awakened by their design to raise up their country anew and place a sceptre in her hands. But his habit of isolation had hardened; he shuddered at the idea of social intercourse.[29]

The *Nation* itself, in an obituary appreciation of Mangan's life and writings, makes a comment which summarizes nationalist difficulty in assimilating this writer:

> Melancholy in any one, most tragic in a man of genius is it to see the separation between the speculative and active powers, the curse of the fall, become an utter divorce, and the will lie prostrate and impotent beneath the feet of tyrannic habit—to see fancy, imagination, poetic susceptibility still subsisting, and at a breath giving forth music to delight and benefit mankind, while the Man, the lord of these, is drifting hopeless and powerless to ruin and death.[30]

Not only is this a representative statement of the strictures received by Mangan particularly from nationalist quarters, but it at the same time demonstrates how the nationalist is able to overcome those hesitations and reappropriate Mangan for nationalism, exactly by maintaining a separation between life and writings which effectively allows the spirit to remain pure in the latter while the "fall" is manifested in the former. Mitchel's dualistic view of Mangan—"one well known to the Muses, the other to the police"—is only an extreme version of this procedure, which can be perceived as reflecting on a small scale the nationalist reconstitution of Irish history.

But the associated images of "gaps" and "separation," in which the "curse of the fall" plays no small part, structures Mangan's writings—and not only his overtly political ones—at a level which is absolutely fundamental, and persistently raises problems in exactly those domains that a nationalist reading is driven to conceal. It is perhaps an index of the objective efficacy of nationalist ideology in Ireland that that aspect of Mangan's writings which appears assimilable to the nationalist literary programme has been so highlighted as to occlude those problematic elements of his writing which time and again refuse "neatness of identification," to borrow Samuel Beckett's apt formulation. Indeed, already written into the "official history" of Irish literature as that of a progressive production of literary institution which articulates more and more a specifically Irish identity and voice, and written in from the very inception of nationalist theories of literature to resurge time and again in a precisely "gapped" and obscured genealogy, is another history which, at times even by means of apparent failure, calls that official model into question. In the case of Mangan, in his nationalist ballads as elsewhere in his translations and original writings, the possible forms of that resistance are already becoming apparent, and at the very points where, from Mitchel on, his "failure" has been identified as distressing and accidental.

Notes

1. Charles Gavan Duffy, *Young Ireland—A Fragment of Irish History, 1840-50* (London, 1880), p. 153.

2. "The Individuality of a Native Literature," *Nation,* 21 August 1847, p. 731.

3. Ibid.

4. Quoted by Charles Gavan Duffy in *Four Years of Irish History, 1845-1849* (London 1883), p. 72. Daniel Corkery confronts a similar problem in Chapter I of *Synge and Anglo-Irish Literature* (Cork: Cork University Press, 1931), pp. 1-7.

5. On the German tradition, see Lefevere, *Translating Literature: The German Tradition* (Amsterdam: Van Gorcum, 1977), and W. W. Chambers, "Language and Nationality in German Pre-Romantic and Romantic Thought," *MLR,* XLI, (1946), 382-92.

6. Thomas Davis, "Irish Songs," *Nation,* 4 January 1845, p. 202.

7. Thomas Davis, "Our National Language," *Nation,* 1 April 1843, p. 394.

8. "Ballad Poetry of Ireland, *Nation,* 2 August 1845, p. 698.

9. D. F. McCarthy, ed., *The Book of Irish Ballads* (Dublin, 1846), p. 12.

10. Ibid., pp. 21-22.

11. Ibid., pp. 22-23.

12. "Recent English Poets No. 1.—Alfred Tennyson and E. B. Barrett" *Nation,* 15 February 1845, p. 314.

13. Ibid.

14. Padraic Fallon, "The Poetry of Thomas Davis," in *Thomas Davis and Young Ireland,* ed. M. J. MacManus (Dublin: Stationery Office, 1945), p. 25. On the scorn in which the street ballad was held, see Duffy, *Young Ireland,* p. 756, and generally, on these topics, Patrick C. Power, *The Story of Anglo-Irish Poetry, 1800-1922* (Cork: Mercier Press, 1967), pp. 16-25.

15. According to Duffy, *Young Ireland,* p. 285, a new edition was required every year between 1843 and 1880. The edition of 1882 is already the fifty-first.

16. Letter of Mangan to Duffy, 10 November 1846: NLI MS 138, fol. 9.

17. Thomas Davis, "A Ballad History of Ireland," *Nation,* 16 November 1844, p. 91. Davis in fact means the *Irish Penny Journal*: see this periodical, 16 January 1841, pp. 228-29 and 17 October 1840, pp. 123-25, respectively.

18. Jacques Chuto, "Rhétorique et Authenticité chez J. C. Mangan," unpublished paper delivered to the Congrès de la S.A.E.S., Tours, 1977, TS pp. 10-11. Translation by the present writer.

19. Ibid., p. 12.

20. See, respectively, Mangan's "The Warning Voice," *Nation,* 21 February 1846, p. 297, and "The Peal of Another Trumpet," *Nation,* 2 May 1846, p. 47; "Stand Together!" by "Theta," in *The Spirit of the Nation,* 51st edn., (Dublin, 1882), p. 27; John Mitchel, "The Coming Meeting," *United Irishman,* 18 March 1848, p. 88.

21. "The Warning Voice," Mangan's emphasis.

22. "A Voice of Encouragement: A New Year's Lay," *Nation,* 1 January 1848, p. 9.

23. "Irish National Hymn," *United Irishman,* 13 May 1848, p. 211. See also similar references in "The Funerals," *Irishman,* 31 March 1849, p. 203, and "A Vision: 1848," *United Irishman,* 26 February 1848, p. 43.

24. "A Vision: 1848."

25. "A Voice of Encouragement," stanzas 3 and 5.

26. "Rhétorique et Authenticité," p. 11; "Still a Nation," *Irishman,* 8 September 1849, p. 571, also cited by Chuto.

27. "Anthologia Germanica. No. 21. The Later German Poets," *Dublin University Magazine* XXVI, No. 153 (September 1845), pp. 294-95, and 287-90.

28. "A Word to James Clarence Mangan," *Irishman,* 26 May 1849, p. 331. Brenan also refers to Mangan in this poem as a "seer of visions."

29. John Mitchel, ed., *Poems by James Clarence Mangan* (New York: Haverty, 1859), p. 15, and passim; Charles Gavan Duffy, "Personal Memoirs of James Clarence Mangan," *Dublin Review,* CXLII (1908), 287.

30. "Clarence Mangan" *Nation* (New Series), 8 September 1849, p. 27.

Kevin J. H. Dettmar (essay date 1986)

SOURCE: Dettmar, Kevin J. H. "Martyr without a Cause: James Clarence Mangan and the Ideology of Irish Nationalism." *Ideology in Literature.* Spec. issue of *Quarterly Journal of Ideology* 10.3 (1986): 33-53. Print.

[*In the following essay, Dettmar discusses Mangan's ambiguous politics. He emphasizes divisions within the poet's mind about the work of the Young Irelanders and the rightness of English rule, noting that Mangan "with his right hand wrote poems of rousing nationalism while his left subverted their logic." Dettmar also comments on Mangan's relative obscurity outside of Ireland, attributing it to his determination to publish only in Irish periodicals rather than in the wider English press.*]

Tears, idle tears, I know not what they mean,
Tears from the depth of some divine despair
Rise in the heart, and gather to the eyes,
In looking on the happy autumn-fields,
And thinking of the days that are no more.

Tennyson

Scholars frequently observe that the Romantic movement in English poetry was slow in coming to the United States. If Romantic poetry can be said to have found its voice in England with Wordsworth's *Lyrical Ballads* of 1798, no corresponding American Romantic poetry was written before William Cullen Bryant, the "first American Romantic poet," whose poems were published beginning in 1917. But what is surely more remarkable, and far less often remarked upon, is that it took just as long for Romanticism to cross the tiny Irish Sea as it did to span the vast Atlantic: Thomas Moore's *Lalla Rookh: An Oriental Romance,* the first collection of Irish Romantic poetry, was also published in 1917.

Although Romanticism did finally have an impact on Irish poetry, the standard American- and English-edited anthologies of the period give the impression that Ireland is "The Land That Romanticism Forgot." The primary reason for this critical bias is plain enough: Ireland never produced a Romantic poet the stature of Wordsworth, Coleridge, Keats, or Shelley. In the minds of most of the English-speaking world, Ireland simply had no English-language poet before Yeats. Since Yeats in "September 1913" announced that "Romantic Ireland's dead and gone, / It's with O'Leary in the grave," and proclaimed in "Coole Park and Ballylee, 1931" that he and his fellow poets were "the last Romantics," (*Collected Poems* 121, 276), the Anglo-American academy's ignorance of Irish Romantic poetry is easily explained.

Given this background, it is not hard to understand why the foremost of the Irish Romantic poets, James Clarence Mangan, is virtually unknown outside his own country. And yet regarding his preeminence in "Romantic Ireland" there can be little serious question. If Mangan is not Ireland's greatest Romantic poet, who better deserves the title? The most obvious alternative candidate would be the writer of Ireland's first collection of Romantic verse, Thomas Moore. Yeats, however, seems not to have thought Moore an important literary presence; when he names the poets in whose footsteps he wished to follow in "To Ireland in the Coming Times," Yeats does not name Moore:

> Know, that I would accounted be
> True brother of a company
> That sang, to sweeten Ireland's wrong,
> Ballad and story, rann and song;
>
> . . . .
>
> Nor may I less be counted one
> With Davis, Mangan, Ferguson, . . .
>
> (*CP* 56)

Although Yeats has conspicuously omitted Moore's name from his list, he does propose two others besides Mangan for consideration: Thomas Davis, leader of the "Young Ireland" movement and founder of its official mouthpiece, *The Nation,* and Sir Samuel Ferguson, perhaps the most perfect technically of Ireland's Romantic poets. But while Yeats does seem genuinely to admire the Republican fervor of Davis's verse, and the prosodic achievement of Ferguson's, the Irish poet he most often invokes as his Romantic ideal is James Clarence Mangan:

> The most passionate [Irish poetry of the nineteenth century] was made by Clarence Mangan, that strange visionary ruined by drink and narcotics, who wrought some half-dozen lyrics of indescribable, vehement beauty . . .
>
> (*Uncollected Prose* 1:363)

Yeats elsewhere calls Mangan one of the "masters of Irish song" (*UP* 1:333). And although his enthusiasm waned in later years, Yeat's praise was promptly picked up in the next generation by James Joyce, who seems to have believed that *he* had discovered Mangan. Joyce's brother Stanislaus tells us that Joyce, who is said to have had a beautiful tenor voice, "set two or three of Mangan's poems to pretty airs with appropriate lilts" (112). Joyce describes Mangan as having

> . . . an exalted lyrical music and a burning idealism that revealed themselves in rhythms of extraordinary and unpremeditated beauty, to be found, perhaps, nowhere else in the range of English literature except in the inspired songs of Shelley.
>
> (*Critical Writings* 177)

Later in this same address Joyce calls Mangan ". . . the man I consider the most significant poet of the modern Celtic world, and one of the most inspired singers that ever used the lyric form in any country" (179).

Although Joyce's and Yeats' early praise of Mangan now seems rather hyperbolic, there was clearly something in his work which sparked the imaginations of both men. The non-Irish world has largely ignored the poetry of Mangan, but we have done so against the express warnings of Yeats and Joyce. When they looked back to the Romantic period of Irish literature, Mangan's was the poetic achievement which towered above all others.

Given Mangan's preeminence among the Irish poets of the nineteenth century, and the later championship of Yeats and Joyce, why is his name so little known outside his own country? When his poetry is read today, some of Mangan's idiosyncrasies irritate the modern reader. His "exoticism" and his exuberant punning now seems dated; as an example of the latter, he glossed Spenser's line "The wretched man 'gan grinning horridlie" as "The wretched Mangan grinning? Horrid lie!" (O'Donoghue, *Life* 86). But the primary reason for Mangan's relative obscurity lies not in the poetry itself, but rather in the manner in which he chose to publish his poetry. In the 1840's, as today, an Irish writer who wished to reach a wide reading public had necessarily to publish his work in the English press. English publishers and English periodicals have always enjoyed a vastly greater circulation and readership than their Irish counterparts, and Irish writers, even into the twentieth century (witness Yeats, Kavanagh, and Beckett), have found it necessary to move to London in order to further their careers. Tom Moore did so, and thereby established himself as a "West Briton" in the minds of many contemporary and subsequent Irish writers. Mangan, however, was never willing to avail himself of the power of the English press. Mangan's long-time friend John Mitchel puts it this way:

> Mangan was not only an Irishman—not only an Irish Papist, not only an Irish papist rebel, but throughout his whole literary life he never deigned to submit to English criticism, never published a line in any English

> periodical, or through any English bookseller, and never seemed to be aware that there was an English public to please.
>
> (O'Donoghue, *Life* XX)

Although Mangan may not have "*seemed*" to be aware of the English public, his disregard of that public was certainly a conscious choice. In making that decision, Mangan tacitly accepted the fact that his poetry would never enjoy the popularity of that of some of his English (and one of his Irish) contemporaries. The very fact that we today think of Tom Moore as Ireland's greatest Romantic poet, despite the wealth of evidence to the contrary, shows just how large an influence the English press could (and can) exert. Although never the nationalist revolutionary some of his friends were, Mangan always thought of the English as "the enemy," and could not in good conscience submit his (mildly) revolutionary verse to their presses for publication. The enemy controlled the means of production, and on that basis Mangan decided that his work would be circulated only locally. That decision, more than any other single factor, is responsible for Mangan's obscure role in the history of Romantic poetry.

Mangan's early decision not to publish in the English press is but the first example of what was to be a lifelong, though half-hearted, devotion to the cause of Irish Nationalism. The single largest event in the shaping of this nationalist consciousness, indeed the most powerful and poignant historical event of Mangan's life and of the life of the Irish people in the first half of the nineteenth century, was the "Great Famine" of 1845-50.[1] In order to understand the impact of the Famine on the national spirit of the Irish people, and on the poetic sensibility of Mangan, one must first understand the rather specific way in which the Irish "read" the historical facts of the Famine. For the Irish, the Famine was not an act of God, but of man—the latest chapter in the ongoing saga of British imperialist repression of Ireland.

The raw "facts" of the Famine, if indeed such raw facts can be said to exist, read something like this:

> Because of their poverty, most of the Irish people depended on potatoes for food. But from 1845 to 1847, Ireland's potato crop failed because of a plant disease. About 750,000 persons died of starvation or disease, and hundreds of thousands more left the country.
>
> (*World Book* X:337)

In *Capital,* Marx gives a more complete reckoning of the Famine's toll:

> The population of Ireland had, in 1841, reached 8,222,664; in 1851, it had dwindled to 6,623,985; in 1861, to 5,850,309; in 1866, to 5 1/2 million, nearly to its level in 1801. The diminution began with the famine year, 1846, so that Ireland, in less than twenty years, lost more than 5/16ths of its people. Its total emigration from May, 1851, to July, 1865, numbered 1,591,487; the emigration during the years 1861-1865 was more than half a million.
>
> (Marx 99)

Some more- or less-elaborated version of this account forms the basis of most Anglo-Americans' knowledge of the Famine. In one of the standard works of Irish history, J. C. Beckett's *A Short History of Ireland,* the account of the Famine, although slightly more complete than the encyclopedia version, relates essentially the same facts. What is of particular interest in analyzing the Famine and its effects on the Irish who survived it is the way that these Anglo-American histories distort by their omission of some salient information regarding the shortage of food. As T. A. Jackson puts it,

> A second set of facts must be set in comparison with the foregoing: (1) In the "famine" years Ireland produced foodstuffs (grain, cattle, dairy-produce, etc.) in abundance; (2) No disease (except that of the tillers) afflicted either the corn harvest, which was superabundant, or the cattle; (3) The landlord and the tax collector not merely took their tribute as usual but also took the occasion to squeeze out arrears due; (4) The amount of corn, cattle, etc., exported from Ireland in these years would have fed all those who hungered twice over.
>
> (243-44)

This set of facts, most often kept out of bourgeois Anglo-American histories, is an unsettling revelation. The hegemony of the Anglo-American writing of history has effectively kept these facts from the general non-Irish public. But although that discourse neatly circumvents any mention of the massive exports of food during time of famine, one passage from the autobiography of a Catholic priest who lived through the Famine, *An t-Athair Peadar O Laoghaire* (Father Peter O'Leary), serves as a corrective to the established histories' distortions:

> That is how things were then, ugly, hateful, nauseating, around the place where I was born. I believe that the situation was the same everywhere in Ireland. And the worst of it was that it was not really the will of God that things were so. They were so by the will of man. In that year enough corn was sent out of Ireland as would feed the people of Ireland twice over. The harbours of Ireland were full of Irish corn, leaving the harbours while the people all through Ireland were dying of hunger.
>
> "Why was the corn not kept?" someone will say, perhaps. It was not kept because it had to be sold to pay the rent, it and the butter and meat and every other scrap of farm produce, save the potato. The blight snatched away the potato, so that no food was left for the people.
>
> "Why," someone will say perhaps, "was no law enacted to protect the people from the injustice that compelled them to sell the corn and to keep nothing for themselves?"
>
> God help your foolish head! "A law to protect the people," you say. Why, if at that time you mentioned a law to protect the people to the English gentlemen, they would say you were mad.

> In those days the English did not make laws for the protection of the people, but to grind them down and impoverish them and kill them . . .
>
> (13-14)

Although the exact amounts of grain exported can be shown to be smaller than implied by O Laoghaire, what is significant in his account is not the accuracy or inaccuracy of his data, but rather the frame of mind with which those facts are interpreted. Whether or not Father O Laoghaire's version of the Famine is in some abstract sense "true," it accurately depicts the way that the Famine was seen and felt by the people who lived through it.

The Famine as a "natural phenomenon," when interpreted against the backdrop of six hundred years of British usurpation, became just one more example of the dispossession of the Irish people by the English. The Irish Nationalist radical John Mitchell, a friend of Mangan's, declared that "The Almighty indeed sent the potato blight, but the English created the Famine" (Mitchel 75). Even as "Anglicized" an Irishman as George Benard Shaw was convinced of the English's complicity in the events of '47:

MALONE:

> . . . Me father died of starvation in Ireland in the black 47. Maybe youve heard of it.

VIOLET:

> . . . The Famine?

MALONE:

> . . . [*with smouldering passion*]: No, the starvation. When a country is full of food, and exporting it, there can be no famine. Me father was starved to death; and I was starved out to America in me mother's arms. English rule drove me and mine out of Ireland.
>
> (185)

At least as important as the apparent English "orchestration" of the famine was the insensitive English reaction in the wake of Ireland's national disaster. As Sydney Smith put it, "the moment the very name of Ireland is mentioned, the English seem to bid adieu to common feeling, common prudence, and common sense, and to act with the barbarity of tyrants and the fatuity of idiots" (Woodham-Smith 411). Barbarity and fatuity were well in evidence during the famine years; Father Matthew, an English cleric, pronounced that "Divine Providence in its inscrutable ways has poured out upon Ireland the vials of wrath" (Rafroidi 90), and an English Royal Duke "solved" the Famine this way:

> I understand that rotten potatoes and seaweed—or even grass—properly mixed, afford a very wholesome and nutritious food. We all know that Irishmen can live upon anything, and there is plenty of grass in the fields even if the potatoes should fail.
>
> (Jackson 245)

Comments like these, added to belief in the English complicity in the famine, raised the anger of the Irish to a feverish pitch. As we have seen, the reaction of Father O Laoghaire, one of the common people, was quite bitter; for the most part, the literary reaction was equally vituperative:

> Weary men, what reap ye?—Golden corn for the stranger.
> What sow ye?—Human corpses that wait the avenger.
> Fainting forms, hunger-stricken, what see you in the offing?
> Stately ships to bear our food away, amid the stranger's scoffing.
>
> Speranza (Lady Wilde) (Rafroidi 93)

The Famine, as well as profoundly affecting the way Mangan subsequently viewed Anglo-Irish relations, was the occasion of some of his most angry verse:

> Gaunt Famine rideth in the van,
> And Pestilence, with myriad arrows,
> Followeth in fiery guise: they spare
> Nor Woman, child, nor Man!
> The stricken Dead lie without barrows
> By roadsides black and bare . . .
>
> (Rafroidi 138)

> Friends! the gloom on our land, in our bright land, grows deeper,
> Suffering, even to death in its horriblest form, aboundeth;
> Thro' our black harvestless fields, the peasants' faint wail resoundeth.
> Hark to it, even now! . . . The nightmare-oppressed sleeper
> Gasping and struggling for life beneath his hideous bestrider
> Seeth not, dreeth not, sight or terror more fearful or ghastly
> Than that poor paralysed slave! Want, Homelessness, Famine, and lastly
> Death in a thousand-corpsed grave, the momently waxeth wider.
>
> (Rafroidi 138)

Ultimately, however, the Famine's most profound effect on Mangan's poetry was on its formal qualities rather than on its subject matter. In 1842, three years prior to the famine that was to change forever the hearts and minds of the Irish nation, Mangan became loosely associated with the Young Ireland movement and began publishing his poetry in their paper, *The Nation.* The Young Irelanders, led by Irish Nationalist Thomas Davis, was a group of Irish rebels who had dedicated themselves to the task of setting Ireland free from British domination. The men of Young Ireland were the nineteenth-century inheritors of what has become a long tradition of Irish resistance to British rule.

Inspired by the French Revolution, Wolfe Tone and his Society of United Irishmen led an uprising against British imperialist domination in 1798. That uprising in some sense marked the birth of Ireland's republican movement.

Wolfe Tone's Society of United Irishmen was the first republican group—"republican" in the sense elaborated by Sean Cronin:

> In Ireland, a republican has come to mean one who maintains that England will not abdicate her role in Irish affairs unless forced to do so by superior power. . . . The lesson of Irish history, this view holds, is that England never yields to right, reason or justice, only to force. Consequently, armed rebellion is an essential element in any attempt to win Irish independence.
>
> (Cronin 1)

The birth of Ireland's republican movement proved, however, to be a painful one; Wolfe Tone was easily defeated, resulting in the Act of Union of 1800. After Tone's defeat, the Irish were actually in a worse position than before the revolt. Lord Byron, in one of his rare addresses to Parliament, described the Union in vivid terms: "If it must be called a Union, it is the union of the shark with its prey; the spoiler swallows up his victim, and thus they become one and indivisible" (Rafroidi 80). Tone's rebellion had been put down, but the nationalistic sentiment that he and his group had stirred lived on.

Although Mangan later became more enthusiastic about the patriotic cause sponsored by Duffy and Mitchel, his early writing for *The Nation* was for the most part ostensibly "apolitical." Writing for *The Nation,* Mangan worked in close contact with John Mitchel, James Fintan Lawlor, and Thomas Davis, Nationalistic radicals whose revolutionary ideals to some extent rubbed off on him over the years. When *The Nation* began publication in 1842, the more radical members of the group were writing openly treasonable essays, such as this anonymous piece:

> We say to you then, People of Ireland—Work for your freedom. If you work there is no fear but you will get it. THE POWER, WE REPEAT, IS IN YOUR HANDS.
>
> Recollect your own strength. Recollect that you have with you, in the first place, the might—the majestic might—of TRUTH. It is not more true that two and two make four, than that every nation has the sole and indefeasible right to make her own laws for the government of her own affairs. It is right derived from the ALMIGHTY. It is perfectly true that this right may be modified on the part of one nation by compact, or treaty, with some *other* nation; *but this is not the case of Ireland.* The Irish nation indignantly disclaim having ever, by treaty or compact, surrendered one tittle of their sole and exclusive right to make their own laws to govern themselves. The Union was not the act of the Irish people. The tyrant's ruthless gripe was on Ireland's throat; and during the moment of her weakness her ruin was achieved by her enemies. . . .
>
> But GOD has raised up honest men in Ireland—ay, and strong men, too. GOD has implanted an indomitable hatred of oppression and tyranny, and an inextinguishable love of justice, in the hearts of the Irish millions . . . They *will* struggle with him [Daniel O'Connell], and they *will* be free.
>
> (Davis 44)

Although Mangan was in sympathy with *The Nation*'s nationalistic sentiments, his reserve never allowed him to share their republican advocacy of violence. He expressed his reticence to Gavan Duffy in a letter of 1843:

> I would express to you, my dear friend, my sincere regret that you are compelled to devote such a larger proportion of your space to frothy speeches. . . . Believe me, that until you remedy this defect the great mass of your readers will peruse even the *Nation* with some degree of indifference.
>
> (Sheridan 90)

Mangan seems to have wanted to endorse the views of his friends on *The Nation,* but some of their more radical ideas offended the sensibilities.

As time went on, however, Mangan's poetry was increasingly involved with the Irish political situation. As Mangan's poetry became increasingly nationalistic, due to the events of 1845-50, he searched for a new form to body forth the new political content; the combination of the Famine, and the resurgence of Irish Nationalism that the Famine helped to create, impelled Mangan to find a way "to sing, to sweeten Ireland's wrong." Whether or not he experimented with the new poetic forms is no longer clear; a large portion of Mangan's more experimental poetry was written anonymously or under a series of pseudonyms. What is clear, however, is that when Mangan sought for a way in which to voice his hatred of British oppression, his mind went back to the dispossession of the Irish *filid* (ancient poets) of the thirteenth through the eighteenth centuries; he ultimately found the forms for his new poetry ready-made in the revolutionary Gaelic poetry of the *filid.* He felt the parallel between their situation and his own to be compelling, and made it his ongoing project to adapt the ancient Irish bardic forms to poetry of the contemporary Irish political situation. Mangan set himself the task, as Joyce did in *Dubliners,* of writing a chapter in the moral history of his country.

In his attempt to revive the ancient Irish bardic forms, Mangan ran up against at least one major obstacle—like Thomas Davis before him, and Yeats after him, he believed that the Irish language should be restored to Ireland; but, like them, he was never able to learn Irish. Mangan's most productive years coincided with a renaissance of interest in Irish literature and the Irish language, and a great number of scholars were at work on translations of the masterpieces of Irish Gaelic literature. Mangan's greatest poems, the poems for which he is remembered in Ireland today, are what he called "translations" from the Irish. We would probably do better to call these poems "versions" of the Irish, for although he did do some (quite good) translations from the German poets,[2] he based all his Irish poetry on the translations of others.

Although Mangan's Irish "versions" are almost without exception improvements over the rather pedestrian prose "translations" from which he worked, his inability to learn Irish bothered and embarrassed him. Of all the legacies of English colonial rule, the hegemony of the English language was surely the most oppressive and odious to Mangan. These feelings were never proclaimed in a public manner, but are instead to be found in some of his mock-translations from Oriental languages. Unlike his second-hand translations of Irish poetry, these "Oriental translations" are purely original writing; when we see Mangan claiming one of his poems to be translated "from the Ottoman," we are probably to understand not the Turkish language, but rather a piece of sitting-room furniture. The short verse **"Lamii's Apology for His Nonsense (from the Ottoman)"** is perhaps Mangan's most poignant statement of his guilt over using language of his captors:

> I was a parrot mute and happy, till
> Once upon a time,
> The fowler pierced the wood and caught me.
> Then blame me not; for I but echo still
> In wayward rhyme
> The melancholy wit they taught me.
>
> (O'Donoghue, ***Poems*** **[*Poems of James Clarence Mangan*]** 226)

The poem offers a pithy metaphor for the subjugation of Irish speakers by the English conquerors. From the perspective of the fowlers, the parrot was "mute" before their tutelage. This, of course, was not the case; the parrot did not previously speak their language, but it surely *sang*. The "rhyme" he now echoes sounds to the ear "wayward," for the majority of ancient Irish poetry was unrhymed, relying heavily on assonance and alliteration for its effects. The poet asks not to be "blamed" for using the conqueror's tongue, but makes his tone clear that he cannot forgive himself. Hence, the poem is called an "apology," not in the sense of a defense, but rather an excuse. His feelings are the same as those of Stephen Dedalus three-quarters of a century later, when speaking with the dean of his school:

> The little word ["tundish"/"funnel"] seemed to have turned a rapier point of his sensitiveness against this courteous and vigilant foe. He felt with a smart of dejection that the man to whom he was speaking was a countryman of Ben Jonson. He thought:
>
> —The language in which we are speaking is his before it is mine. How different are the words *home, Christ, ale, master,* on his lips and on mine! I cannot speak or write these words without unrest of spirit. His language, so familiar and so foreign, will always be for me an acquired speech. I have not made or accepted its words. My voice holds them at bay. My soul frets in the shadow of his language.
>
> (Joyce, *Portrait* 189)

Like Mangan, Joyce was never able to learn the native tongue of his land, and the English language served as an ever-present reminder of the subjugation of the Irish by the English.

Due to his ignorance of Irish, Mangan's stylistic borrowings from the bardic poetry were limited to those devices which made their way into the English translations. One of the most popular bardic forms, the *deibhidh* ("cut in two"), is not amenable to use in English verse:

> The *debide* (cut in two) was essentially a quatrain composed of two couplets, generally heptasyllabic or octosyllabic, and regularly containing a very difficult bardic technique, the *aird-rinn.* In this device, the rhyming word of the second line contained a syllable more than that of the first line; likewise, the fourth line's rhyming word contained one more than the third's. Also, if the accent fell on the penultimate syllable in the first line, it would fall on the antepenult in the second.
>
> (Donaghy 72-73)

Rather than try to reproduce such a complicated metrical pattern in English, Mangan used the more ancient alliterative one line of the *filid,* adding rhyme to give the line a sense of urgency. This adaptation is probably the most commonly used of the ancient Irish metrical forms in Mangan's poetry. At its best, this technique gives his verse a driving insistency, as in **"O'Hussey's Ode to the Maguire"**:

> Where is my Chief, my Master, this bleak night, *mavrone!*
> O, cold, cold, miserably cold is this bleak night for Hugh,
> Its showery, arrowy,
> speary sleet pierceth one through and through, Pierceth one to the very bone!
>
> Rolls real thunder? Or was that red, livid light
> Only a meteor? I scarce know; but through the midnight dim
> The pitiless ice-wind streams. Except the hate that persecutes *him*
> Nothing hath crueller venomy might.
>
> An awful, a tremendous night is this, meseems!
> The flood-gates of the rivers of heaven, I think, have been burst wide—
> Down from the overcharged clouds, like unto headlong ocean's tide,
> Descends grey rain in roaring streams.
>
> . . . .
>
> And though frost glaze to-night the clear dew of his eyes,
> And white ice-gauntlets glove his noble fine fair fingers o'er,
> A warm dress is to him that lightning-garb he ever wore,
> The lightning of the soul, not skies.
>
> *AVRAN*
>
> Hugh marched forth to the fight—I grieved to see him depart;
> And lo! to-night he wanders frozen, rain-drenched, sad, betrayed—
> *But the memory of the lime-white mansions his right hand hath laid*
> *In ashes, warms the hero's heart!*
>
> (***Selected Poems*** **[*Selected Poems of James Clarence Mangan*]** 18-20)

Through the poem's rather free meter, Mangan is able to recreate the "wild, lashing fury of the elements as they strike this Lear figure and make him feel the coldness and rejection of his fellow chieftains" (Donaghy 73). Padraic Colum has described the poem as "like a storm that spends its fury the chieftain addressed; it rises and falls, pauses and lashes out" (36).

On first reading, there is some confusion as to the identity of the enemy that Hugh fights. The poem is addressed to the Maguire's fellow chieftains, whose cowardice prevented them from coming to his aid. But they are not the enemy who is spoken of. In one sense, of course, the enemy is the elements against which Hugh is fighting—"the blackened heavens," "the tempestuous winds" (1.26). But there is, we are told, something which "hath crueller venomy might" than this "bleak night"—his unnamed persecutors. Since the historical Hugh Maguire was killed by an English captain, St. Leger, we might guess that it is the English who persecute Hugh; two pieces of internal evidence support such a reading. Lines 18-20 are a textbook example of what Ruskin called the "pathetic fallacy"; it is surely not the wind, but rather the speaker's pursuer, who is filled with "tyrannous anger," and in Mangan's poetic vocabulary "tyrannous" is virtually synonymous with "English." In addition, the final two lines of the *avran* ("a concluding stanza, generally intended as a recapitulation of the entire poem" [Kennelly 154]), italicized, speak of the "lime-white mansions" which Hugh has demolished. In Ireland during the English Plantation, it was the English landlords who lived in the "lime-white mansions," known as the "big houses" to this day. The destruction of the English usurpers' homes "warms the hero's heart"; Hugh Maguire in Mangan's poem becomes an early forbear of Irish Republicanism.

In **"O'Hussey's Ode,"** [**"O'Hussey's Ode to the Maguire"**] we see Mangan employing the alliterative long line of the *filid* to great effect. Individual lines build up an inexorable movement, aided by alliteration's quickening effect:

> This sharp, sore sleet, these howling floods. . . .
> Blow fiercely over and round him, and smiting sleet
> shower blinds . . .
> Should this chill, churlish night, perchance, be paralysed
> by frost—

Another device which speeds up the poem's long lines is the frequent assonance:

> Its showery, arrowy, speary sleet pierceth one through and
> through,
> O, mournful is my soul this night for Hugh Maguire! . . .
> It overflows the low banks of the rivulets and ponds—

Mangan's addition to the formula is the *abba* rhyme scheme, which itself adds to the poem's momentum. By using the metrics and historical material of the *filid*, Mangan made connection with the nationalist poets of the thirteenth century, implicitly drawing a parallel between their political situation and his own. In rehearsing the events of the famine years and making poetry of them, Mangan hoped, as Stephen Dedalus would later, to forge in the smithy of his soul the uncreated conscience of his race.

A second poetic form common in the verse of the *filid* is the *caoine* ("keen"). The *caoine* is the elegy or lament sung for the death of a loved one at an Irish wake. In the English-speaking world, the dead are eulogized by piling praise upon praise until the mourners have constructed a monument to the deceased; in the *caoine* tradition, the focus is on the deceased's survivors, and sorrow is added to sorrow in a vast song of grief. As a result, the *caoine* poetry tends to be very long and repetitive. Mangan's best-constructed *caoine*, **"Woman of the Piercing Wail,"** runs to 216 lines; I quote the first and last two stanzas here:

> O Woman of the Piercing Wail,
> Who mournest o'er yon mound of clay
> With sigh and groan,
> Would God thou wert among the Gael!
> Thou wouldst not then from day to day
> Weep thus alone,
> 'Twere long before, around a grave
> In green Tirconnell, one could find
> This loneliness;
> Near where Beann-Roirche's banners wave
> Such grief as thine could ne'er have pined
> Companionless.
>
> Beside the wave, in Donegal,
> In Antrim's glens, or fair Dromore,
> Or Killilee,
> Or where the sunny waters fall,
> At Assaroe, near Erna's shore,
> This could not be.
> On Derry's plains—in rich Drumclieff—
> Throughout Armagh the Great, renowned
> In olden years,
> No day could pass but Woman's grief
> Would rain upon the burial-ground
> Fresh floods of tears!
>
> . . . .
>
> Look not, nor sigh for earthly throne,
> Nor place thy trust in arm of clay—
> But on thy knees
> Uplift thy would to God alone,
> For all things go their destined way
> As he decrees.
> Embrace the faithful Crucifix,
> And seek the path of pain and prayer
> Thy savior trod;
> Nor let they spirit intermix
> With earthly hope and worldly care
> Its groans to God!
>
> And thou, O mighty Lord! whose ways
> Are far above our feeble minds
> To understand,
> Sustain us in these doleful days,
> And render light the chain that binds
> Our fallen land!
> Look down upon our dreary state,
> And through the ages that may still

Roll sadly on,
Watch Thou o'er hapless Erin's fate,
And shield at least from darker ill
The blood of Conn!

(O'Donoghue, *Life,* 17-24)

In sharp contrast to the quickness of the alliterative long line of the *filid,* these typographically shorter lines paradoxically read more slowly. For instance, an iambic septameter like "It penetrates and fills the cottagers' dwellings far and wide" moves at a much brisker pace than some of the monosyllable-packed lines of **"Woman of the Piercing Wail"**:

O Woman of the Piercing Wail,
Who mourneth o'er yon mound of clay,
With sigh and groan,
Would God thou wert among the Gael!
Thou wouldst not then from day to day
Weep thus alone.

The abundance of open vowel sounds, characteristic of Irish poetry, also slows the line. What is perhaps the slowest sestet of the entire poem occurs in the penultimate stanza, an unenthusiastic statement of what Nietzsche has called "Christian nihilism":

Look not, nor sigh for earthly throne,
Nor place thy trust in arm of clay—
But on thy knees
Uplift thy soul to God alone,
For all things go their destined way
As He decrees.

The forty syllables of those six lines contain only five disyllabic words. At points like this in the poem, the line slows down to a dirge-like pace, seemingly wallowing in its own grief. The one exception to this plodding rhythm is the section where the poet lists the famous Irish place-names which would mourn the dead. Whether intentional or not, when Mangan invokes the Irish place-names—Tirconnel, Beann-Roirche, Donegal, Antrim, Dromore, Killilee, Assaroe . . .—the polysyllables have the effect of picking up the pace of the verse, as if the Irish landscape is the only thing capable of removing the sombre cast of the poem. These place-names have the added efficacy of having many long vowel sounds, which serve to lighten the color of the verse (Shapiro 12). In the structure of the poem, the few relics of the Irish language function as the only rays of hope in an otherwise bleak sky.

The third Irish poetic form used by Mangan, and by far the most productive for him, is the *aisling* ("vision"). Patrick Power describes Aogan O Rathaille's use of the *aisling*:

> O Rathaille is also noted for his use of what is known as the *aisling* in Gaelic poetry. If any form of verse can be described as typically 18th century, then the *aisling* deserves this title. Essentially, the *aisling* means vision and the poetry written and known as "*aisling*" are essentially vision poems. The first poems of this kind appeared during the end of the 16th century but it must be stressed that the 18th century *aisling* was composed to set a formula as follows: The poet goes out walking and meets a beautiful lady. He then describes her dress and appearance and asks her who she is. She is generally the personification of Ireland and she promises early deliverance from the foreign yoke and the return of the Stuarts to the English throne. Sometimes, the lady is comforted in this manner by the poet. *Aisling*-poetry was always closely connected with the Jacobite movement and is mainly escapist in mood.
>
> (97)

Aogan O Rathaille is the preeminent figure in the history of Gaelic Irish poetry, the last great poet of the Irish language before the virtual eradication of Irish by the English. To turn to O Rathaille's poetry as a source of inspiration was for Mangan to be aware of just how far the place of the poet in Ireland had fallen under English rule.

Mangan's best-remembered poem, still memorized by schoolchildren in Ireland, is **"Dark Rosaleen."** It is a translation of a folk *aisling* poem, in which Ireland is represented by the beautiful *Roisin Dubh* (Dark [-haired] Rosaleen). Despite its length, I quote it here in full, due to its masterfully structured argument:

O My Dark Rosaleen,
Do not sigh, do not weep!
The priests are on the ocean green,
They march along the Deep.
There's wine . . . from the royal Pope
Upon the ocean green;
And Spanish ale shall give you hope,
My Dark Rosaleen!
My own Rosaleen!
Shall glad your heart, shall give you hope,
Shall give you health, and help and hope,
My Dark Rosaleen.

Over hills and through dales
Have I roamed for your sake;
All yesterday I sailed with sails
On river and on lake.
The Erne . . . at its highest flood
I dashed across unseen,
For there was lightning in my blood,
My Dark Rosaleen!
My own Rosaleen!
Oh! there was lightning in my blood,
Red lightning lightened through my blood,
My Dark Rosaleen!

All day long in unrest
To and fro do I move,
The very soul within my breast
Is wasted for you, love!
The heart . . . in my bosom faints
To think of you, my Queen,
My life of life, my saint of saints,
My Dark Rosaleen!
My own Rosaleen!
To hear your sweet and sad complaints,
My life, my love, my saint of saints,
My Dark Rosaleen!

Woe and pain, pain and woe,
Are my lot night and noon,
To see your bright face clouded so,
Like to the mournful moon.
But yet . . . will I rear your throne
Again in golden sheen;
'Tis you shall reign, shall reign alone,
My Dark Rosaleen!
My own Rosaleen!
'Tis you shall have the golden throne,
'Tis you shall reign, and reign alone,
My Dark Rosaleen!

Over dews, over sands
Will I fly for your weal;
Your holy delicate white hands
Shall girdle me with steel.
At home . . . in your emerald bowers,
From morning's dawn till e'en,
You'll pray for me, my flower of flowers,
My Dark Rosaleen!
My fond Rosaleen!
You'll think of me through Daylight's hours,
My virgin flower, my flower of flowers,
My Dark Rosaleen!

I could scale the blue air,
I could plough the high hills,
Oh, I could kneel all night in prayer,
To heal your many ills!
And one . . . beamy smile from you
Would float like light between
My toils and me, my own, my true,
My Dark Rosaleen!
My fond Rosaleen!
Would give me life and soul anew,
A second life, a soul anew,
My Dark Rosaleen!

O! the Erne shall run red
With redundance of blood,
The earth shall rock beneath our tread,
And flames wrap hill and wood,
And gun-peal, and slogan cry,
Wake many a glen serene,
Ere you shall fade, ere you shall die,
My Dark Rosaleen!
My own Rosaleen!
The judgement Hour must first be nigh,
Ere you can fade, ere you can die,
My Dark Rosaleen!

(***SP*** [***Selected Poems of James Clarence Mangan***] 15-17)

It is impossible to read this poem without remarking the religious stature ascribed to Rosaleen. She is regal, the speaker's "Queen," to whom he pays homage as a knight. But in stark contrast to the Protestant Queen of England, this Queen is Catholic, and an object herself of religious adoration much like the Virgin Mary: she is "my saint of saints," with "holy delicate white hands"; "my virgin flower, my flower of flowers." Along with language suggestive of the Madonna, Mangan employs the Hebraic form of the superlative, "life of life," "saint of saints," "flower of flowers"; such a construction in English immediately reminds one of the Hebrew love poetry of the Song of Solomon ("Song of Songs"). The speaker even asks for her intercession using a variation on the traditional Catholic formula: "At home . . . in your emerald bowers, / From morning's dawn til e'en, / You'll pray for me, my flower of flowers." Mangan has transformed the Queen of Heaven into the Queen of Ireland, transporting her to an "emerald bower."

Like any good knight, the speaker appears ready, even eager, to make any sacrifice for his Queen: he has "dashed across" the Erne, roamed "over hills and through dales," all for her sake; "the very soul within [his] heart is wasted for [her]"; the speaker would even be willing, were it necessary, "to kneel all night in prayer, to heal [her] many ills." The one thing that this knight does not seem willing to do, which knights traditionally offer to their queens, is to lay down his life for her. Compared with an offer to fight to the death, if need be, the speaker's claim that he "could kneel all night in prayer" sounds rather ludicrous. The upheaval described in the last stanza, if it is to happen at all, will happen without the assistance of the speaker; the events there are described without the speaker ever acting as a subject:

O! the Erne shall run red
With redundance of blood,
The earth shall rock beneath our tread,
And flames wrap hill and wood,
And gun-peal, and slogan cry,
Wake many a glen serene . . .

The apocalyptic tone of the stanza is combined with a certain teleological elusiveness: just how are these events to come about? By whose agency? Mangan's appears to be a revolution without any revolutionaries.

Mangan's other major poem written in the *aisling* form is **"Kathaleen Ny-Houlahan."** In it, the name has been changed, Kathaleen Ny-Houlahan (*Caitlin Ni Hullachain*) substituted for Dark Rosaleen (*Roisin Dubh*), but the song remains the same:

Long they pine in weary woe, the nobles of our land,
Long they wander to and fro, proscribed, alas! and banned;
Feastless, houseless, altarless, they bear the exile's brand,
But their hope is in the coming-to of Kathaleen Ny-Houlahan!

Think her not a ghostly hag, too hideous to be seen,
Call her not unseemly names, our matchless Kathaleen;
Young she is, and fair she is, and would be crowned a queen
Were the king's son at home here with Kathaleen Ny-Houlahan!

Sweet and mild would look her face, O, none so sweet and mild.
Could she crush the foes by whom her beauty is reviled;

Woolen plaids would grace herself and robes of silk her child,
If the king's son were living here with Kathaleen Ny-Houlahan!

Sore disgrace it is to see the Arbitress of thrones,
Vassal to a *Saxoneen* of cold and sapless bones!
Bitter anguish wrings our souls—with heavy sighs and groans
We wait the Young Deliverer of Kathaleen Ny-Houlahan!

Let us pray to Him who holds Life's issues in His hand—
Him who formed the mighty globe, with all its thousand lands;
Girding them with seas and mountains, rivers deep, and strands,
To cast a look of pity upon Kathaleen Ny-Houlahan!

He, who over sands and waves led Israel along—
He, who fed, with heavenly bread, that chosen tribe and throng—
He, who stood by Moses, when his foes were fierce and strong—
May He show forth His might in saving Kathaleen Ny-Houlahan.

(O'Donoghue, *Life* 16-17)

The poem looks forward to Kathaleen's deliverance, as **"Dark Rosaleen"** does Rosaleen's, but like most Irish Jacobite poems, it does so without a great deal of optimism. The poem consists primarily of complaints regarding Ireland's unfair treatment at the hands of the *Saxoneen,* but describes little if any action directed at correcting the situation. In place of the apocalyptic annunciation at the close of **"Dark Rosaleen," "Kathaleen Ny-Houlahan"** posits a pathetic prayer for pity. That the poem's close is not an optimistic one is manifest even in its punctuation; the last quatrain is the only one in the poem that ends in a period rather than an exclamation point, as if to suggest that the groundless optimism of the first five stanzas can no longer be maintained.

These two women, Rosaleen and Kathaleen, were to become for Mangan the center of a sort of surrogate religion. He was, to all outward appearances, an orthodox, devout Catholic, and as to his sincere religious faith we should have no doubt. In a footnote to his ***Autobiography,*** Mangan apologizes to his reader for his constant use of the words "God" and "Providence," which he fears may be growing noisome:

> My reader will pardon the frequent allusion to GOD and Providence which occur in the course of these Memoirs. But, as Malebranche saw all things in GOD, so I see GOD in all things. GOD is *the* idea of my mind.
>
> (15)

Though God was "*the*" idea of his mind, it was the vengeful God of the Old Testament, rather than the sacrificing Christ of the New Testament, that arrested Mangan's imagination. Mangan, like other Romantic poets, found the Christian sacrifice intractable poetic material. Even as devout a Christian as Coleridge found it impossible to treat Christ's death on the cross in his poetry; and for his part, Mangan not only does not deal with the crucifixion in his poetry, but conspicuously avoids any mention, in poetry or prose, of his own specific religious affiliations. In Ireland in the 1840's, the refusal of a "public" poet of Mangan's stature to take a religious stance was a self-consciously defiant act. Take, for example, the religious lyric **"Life, Death, and Eternity"**:

How shalt thou, then, find best escape
From all the ills that so beset
Life's drear exile?
Gold, Glory, even the tempting grape,
At most but aid thee to forget
Thy state awhile!
Where, when the warring world's alarms
Ring loud around thee, shalt thou find
True peace of soul?
Oh, where, but in Religion's arms.
Where, but with Faith, which wings the mind
To Heaven, its goal.

(Sheridan 88)

A religious view of life is in evidence here, but its formulation is extremely vague. Mention is made of the soul, Religion, Faith, and Heaven, but this could just as easily be a statement of Jewish belief as Catholic. "With Faith"—faith in what? The faith described is a faith without an object, without content. The object of faith in the Christian religion is "Jesus Christ and Him crucified" (I Cor. 2:2)—where is Christ in this poem, and where the sacrifice? Similarly, what is the end of this faith? Apparently, it is to find "true peace of soul" by having one's mind transported to heaven. This is perhaps a tenable religious posture for a monk, but certainly not for a political poet; it is another version of Nietzsche's "Christian nihilism," which denies this world, its pleasures and troubles, for a vision of the afterlife.

Like the majority of the Romantic poets, Mangan was "by Calvary's turbulence unsatisfied" (Yeats, *CP* 141); at the same time, he was tormented his entire life with a sense of his own guilt and sinfulness. That a crime had been committed was clear enough to Mangan, but he could not accept Christ's taking on the punishment which should rightly fall to him. In his personal religious system, Christ's sacrificial death, the central even of the Christian religion, is circumvented. In order to perform this operation, Mangan substituted the figure of the Virgin (and those of Rosaleen and Kathaleen) for that of Christ as the object of religious devotion, and replaced Christ's sacrificial death with another ritual death—his own.

The substitution of the Virgin Mary for Christ as the central figure of religious adoration is not an unheard-of phenomenon. Thus, on 20 June, 1849, Mangan died with the words "O Mary, Queen of Mercy" on his lips (Donaghy 38). Why did Mangan make this substitution? One reason, as has already been suggested, is that he found Christ's sacrificial death difficult to accept. Another more complex and personal reason may have to do with Mangan's relationship with his father. Mangan's childhood relationship with his father, as chronicled in the ***Autobiography,*** was certainly one which would have left a mark on a child. One early paragraph gives an especially vivid description:

> My father . . . never established any of the qualities of a guardian towards his children. His temper was not merely quick and irascible, but it also embodied much of that calm concentrated spirit of Milesian fierceness, . . . He was of an ardent and forward-bounding disposition, and, though deeply religious by nature he hated the restraints of social life, and seemed to think that all feelings with regard to family connections, and the obligations imposed by them, were totally beneath his notice. Me, my two brothers, and my sister, he treated habitually as a huntsman would treat refractory hounds. It was his boast, uttered in pure glee, that we "would run into a mouse-hole" to shun him. While my mother lived he made her miserable—he led my only sister such a life that she was obligated to leave our house—he kept up a succession of continual hostilities with my brothers—and if he spared me more than others it was perhaps because I displayed a greater contempt of life and everything connected with it than the thought was shown by the other members of his family. If any one can imagine such an idea as a human boaconstrictor *without his alimentive propensities* he will be able to form some notion of the character of my father. May GOD assoil his great and mistaken soul and grant him eternal peace and forgiveness!—but I have an inward feeling that to him I owe all my misfortunes.
>
> (13-14)

One need not read between the lines to realize that Mangan was not close to his father. For his mother, on the other hand, he seems to have felt genuine sympathy: "I scarcely regarded my own sufferings when I reflected on those of my relatives, my mother especially, whose fortitude was admirable . . ." (***Auto*** [***Autobiography***] 19). This emotional pattern which emerged in Mangan's childhood, one of sympathy for his mother and antipathy toward his father, love of the feminine principle and hatred of the masculine, found its way into both his religion and his politics.

Historically, Ireland and England have been imagined as representing the feminine and masculine, respectively. In Irish writing the *aisling* tradition, as we have seen, represented Ireland as a woman (Rosaleen, Kathaleen Ny-Houlahan) from the thirteenth century to the present day. Sir Walter Raleigh, in "Ocean's Love to Cynthia," took advantage of geography to construct an elaborate conceit of England (the male) taking his pleasure of Ireland (the female). In the English/Irish literary tradition, and especially in Mangan's imagination, England was associated with the masculine, aggressive, and violent, Ireland with the feminine, passive, and life-giving; England was John Bull, Ireland Kathaleen Ny-Houlahan; England the father, Ireland the mother; England Christ, Ireland the Virgin. Mangan, owing in part to his hatred of his father, hated as well John Bull/England and Christ, and took Ireland/Kathaleen and the Virgin to his bosom.

Having thus turned the personification of Ireland into the primary object of religious worship, Mangan set out to make himself a sacrifice wholly acceptable to her, hoping that his suffering would somehow prove efficacious in bringing about a new, free nation. To one familiar with the details of Mangan's biography, his suffering is quite evident; he lived out the Thomas Chatterton myth of the tortured Romantic artist. What is not apparent is how that suffering could possibly have any positive effect on Ireland's future.

As Anthony Cronin has pointed out, Mangan was a man ahead of his time, being both the precursor and prototype of what Rimbaud was to call *le poet maudit*:

> Some twenty years or so after James Clarence Mangan's death, the young Arthur Rimbaud, who, of course, had never heard of him, invented the notion of the poet as *maudit,* "accursed." Suffering was an essential part of his role, and it was actually necessary for the poet to deliberately become "*le grand malade, le grand criminal, le grand maudit.*" Part of the concept, subsequently developed by Verlaine, and adopted, consciously or otherwise, by many poets, (the "otherwise" often leading to strange results) was that of the poet as scapegoat, who, by sin and circumstance, getting himself into trouble and generally bashed around, atoned in some way for the sins and hypocrisies of bourgeois society, which was felt by both parties to the contract to be deeply in need of such an animal as a scapegoat. One says both parties for, of course, society gleefully, if inchoately, adopted the idea.
>
> (11)

Mangan took on the role of scapegoat quite self-consciously. Although he seems not to have had a fully articulated sense of his "mission" at any point in his career, he did, from a very early age, have an acute feeling that he had been somehow "set apart." He opens his ***Autobiography*** with an epigraph from Massinger, "A heavy shadow lay / On that boy's spirit: he was not of his fathers," and proceeds in the first page to describe this feeling of separateness in his own boyhood:

> At a very early period of my life I became impressed by the conviction that it is the imperative duty of every man who has deeply sinned and deeply suffered to place upon record some memorial of his wretched experiences for the benefit of his fellow-creatures, and by way of a beacon to them to avoid, in their voyage of existence, the rocks and shoals upon which his own peace of soul has undergone shipwreck. This conviction continually gained strength within me, until it assumed all the importance of a paramount idea in my mind. It was in its nature, alas! a sort of dark anticipation, a species of melancholy foreboding of

the task which Providence and my own disastrous destiny would one day call upon myself to undertake.

(9)

The tone of this passage is not simply fatalistic, although it most certainly is that; Mangan's conception of his "imperative duty" is described in terms that are also pointedly Messianic. His language sounds like that of Christ, faced with the knowledge of his impending death: "the Son of Man shall be delivered into the hands of men" (Lk. 9:44).

That Mangan thought of himself as a Christ-figure, a "man of sorrows, and acquainted with grief" (Isa. 53:3), is also evidenced in his adopted middle name; born without one, Mangan took on the middle name Clarence (literally, "famous, illustrious one"), and became "J. C." Mangan, Ireland's self-appointed Savior. Like John Keats before him, Mangan seems to have had a "death wish" from a very early age. Keats expressed his occasional desire to die this way:

... for many a time
I have been half in love with easeful Death,
Called to him soft names in many a mused rhyme,
To take into the air my quiet breath;
Now more than ever seems it rich to die, ...

(347)

Mangan, rather than being "half in love" with death, instead accepted its inevitability with fatalistic resignation. Mangan hankered after death, but as Cronin says of the *poet maudit* in general, he believed he had a great deal of suffering to do here on earth before he could be allowed to die.

All the available evidence would seem to indicate that Mangan's longing for death antedated his mission to save Ireland. His earliest extant poem, **"Genius,"** written at age sixteen, introduces the theme of the man of genius sacrificed to brutish society:

O Genius! Genius! all thou dost endure
First from thyself, and finally from those
The Earth-bound and the Blind, who cannot feel
That there be souls with purpose as pure
And lofty as the mountain-snows, and zeal
All quenchless as the spirit whence it flows!—
In whom that fire, struck but like spark from steel
In other bosoms, ever lives and glows!
Of such, thrice-blest are they whom, ere mature
Life generate woes which God alone can heal
His mercy calls to a loftier sphere than this—
For the mind's conflicts are the worst of woes,
And fathomless and fearful yawns the Abyss
Of Darkness thenceforth under all who inherit
That melancholy, changeless hue of heart,
Which flings its pale gloom o'er the years of Youth—
Those most—or least—illumined by the spirit
Of the Eternal Archetypes of Truth.—
For such as these there is no peace within
Either in Action or in Contemplation,
From first to last,—but, even as they begin,
They close, the dim night of their tribulation,
Worn by the torture of the untiring breast,
Which, scorning all, and shunned of all, by turns,
Upheld in solitary strength begot
By its own unshared shroudedness of lot,
Through years and years of crushed hopes throbs and burns,
And burns and throbs, and will not be at rest,
Searching a desolate Earth for that it findeth not!

(***Auto*** 20-21)

Rather gloomy musings for a sixteen-year-old! He describes his condition elsewhere in the ***Autobiography*** as "a lingering living martyrdom" (22). And yet we must still ask, martyr to what cause? Mangan's was an inward-looking suffering; the punishment to which he was subjected affected no one but himself. It was not until he had reached middle age, and become associated with the members of Young Ireland, that he began to think of himself as sacrifice in the struggle for Irish freedom. Mangan's national martyrdom was clearly an afterthought.

Ironically enough, even though Mangan identified his *raison d'etre* only shortly before his death, that death was in keeping with the scenario he had established: Mangan died of cholera, a complication of the English-sent Famine. The process of martyrdom and canonization that was begun by Mangan was promptly picked up and furthered by others after his death. In Irish art and literature, Mangan was assimilated into nationalist and poetic sainthood. The only extant drawing of Mangan that was made in his presence is the deathbed portrait drawn by Sir Frederick William Burton. Burton described Mangan as looking almost beatific in death, the cares and pain of life having fled his countenance. The very form of the portrait itself puts one in mind of Severn's deathbed portrait of Keats, a drawing which was well-known and widely circulated in Mangan's day. Mangan was described by others as looking like the young Byron and Schiller, having something in his looks common to all Romantic poets. Perhaps the most important portrait iconographically in the process of making Mangan an Irish poetic saint is the frontispiece portrait to O'Donoghue's *The Life and Writings of James Clarence Mangan,* in which the poet is drawn in the apparel of the 1890's, looking remarkably like Yeats in his pre-Raphaelite days. Seemingly, the generations following Mangan's own updated his image to that of the reigning poetic clique in an ongoing project to promote Mangan to his proper position in the annals of Romantic poetry.

Parallel to this iconographic sainthood was canonization in poetry. Poets beginning with Sir Samuel Ferguson, Anne Hildebrand, and Thomas MacDonnagh, and continuing all the way up to the contemporary Irish poets Brendan Kennelly and Thomas Kinsella, have written poems occasioned by Burton's deathbed portrait. The poem most humorously illustrative of the poetic canonization process is Hildebrand's "Clarence Mangan":

I give thee tears, I give thee tears,
'Tis all I have to give,
Thy soul, perchance, my mourning hears,
Where thou at last dost live;
Here, on a sea of storm and strife,
Thy life was but a death in life.

(15)

It is oddly appropriate that the latter-day poet is able to do little more for the dead Mangan than Mangan was able to do for his beloved Rosaleen/Kathaleen while he was alive; it would seem that the best either has to offer is "tears, idle tears." In the third stanza, Hildebrand openly speaks of Mangan as a "martyr'd saint":

I kneel before thee, as before
Some pallid, martyr'd saint,
And muse thy chequer'd story o'er,
With anguish'd heart and faint:
To think of all the sorrow prest
Into one fated human beast.

But despite the admiration of his worshipers, which, as we have noted, included such luminaries as James Joyce and W. B. Yeats, one final question looms large: What was the actual substance of Mangan's nationalism? The republican men of Young Ireland did not consider him to be one of them; while Mangan at his best was a powerful lyricist, he was never an effective political propagandist. Lines like "And render light the chain that binds / Our fallen Land!" and "And shield at least from darker ill / The blood of Conn!" reek of nationalist "Uncle Tom"-ism.

The root cause of these ideological discrepancies, which plague a great deal of Mangan's work, is a deeply divided political mind. On the one hand, he had no doubt that his Young Ireland compatriots and the things that they were fighting for were right; on the other hand, his mind seems to have been tainted by the propaganda of the English usurpers he wished to banish. Patrick Rafroidi has noted that "... he published at one and the same time Germano-Gothic fantasies in the Tory *Dublin University Magazine* and patriotic poems in the columns of the revolutionary *Nation*" (Rafroidi 139). Mangan was a man deeply divided, a man who with his right hand wrote poems of rousing nationalism while his left subverted their logic. The result is a body of poetry which stands as a unique document to the ideology of Irish nationalism.

Notes

1. There is necessarily some haziness about these dates. The "rack rents" charged by the majority of the English landlords kept their Irish tenants always on the edge of starvation, and any fluctuation in the potato harvest was bound to have dire consequences for the native population. The blight that hit in 1845 was relatively minor, but those of '46 and '47 severe, followed again by a lesser blight in 1848, and the residual effects of crop loss lingered into 1849 and '50. See T. A. Jackson, *Ireland Her Own: An Outline of History of the Irish Struggle,* p. 243.

2. One of Mangan's favorite and most protracted puns involves one of his many pseudonyms—"Selber." He claimed that many of his poems were translated from an obscure German poet called Selber, and once commented on the difficulty of translating him properly:

> It is fortunate for us that we are not required to criticize as well as translate, for we should scarcely know what judgement to pronounce on this eccentric writer. ... He appears to have begun the world with a redundance of enthusiasm. ... Nobody can translate Selber to advantage. His particular idiosyncrasy unfortunately betrays itself in every line he writes, and there exists, moreover, an evident wish to show the world that he possesses a life within himself.
>
> (O'Donoghue 119-20)

In fact, Mangan's translations from "Selber" were no translations at all, "Selber" being a version of the German word for "self," and Mangan himself having written the poems.

References

Beckett, J. C. *A Short History of Ireland.* London: Hutchinson and Co., 1979.

Colum, Padraic. "James Clarence Mangan." *Dublin Magazine,* VIII (1933), p. 36.

Cronin, Anthony. "Foreword." *Selected Poems of James Clarence Mangan.* Ed. Michael Smith. Dublin: Gallery Press, 1974. 1-11.

Cronin, Sean. *Irish Nationalism: A History of Its Roots and Ideology.* Dublin: The Academy Press, 1980.

Davis, Thomas, ed. *The Voice of The Nation.* Dublin: James Duffy, 1844.

Donaghy, Henry J. *James Clarence Mangan.* New York: Twayne Publishers Inc., 1974.

Hildebrand, Anna Louisa. *Lays from the Land of the Gael.* Belfast: M'Caw, Stevenson & Orr, Linenhall Works, n.d. [1879].

Jackson, T. A. *Ireland Her Own: An Outline History of the Irish Struggle.* New York: International Publishers, 1947.

Joyce, James. *The Critical Writings of James Joyce.* New York: Viking Press, 1959.

———. *A Portrait of the Artist as a Young Man.* New York: Penguin Books, 1977.

Joyce, Stanislaus. *My Brother's Keeper.* London: Faber and Faber, 1958.

Keats, John. *John Keats: The Complete Poems*. New York: Penguin Books, 1977.

Kennelly, Brendan, ed. *The Penguin Book of Irish Verse*. Harmondsworth, England: Penguin Books, 1970.

Mangan, James Clarence. *The Autobiography of James Clarence Mangan*. Ed. James Kilroy. Dublin: Dolmen Press, 1968.

———. *Selected Poems of James Clarence Mangan*. Ed. Michael Smith. Dublin: Gallery Press, 1974.

Marx, Karl, and Frederick Engels. *Ireland and the Irish Question*. Moscow: Progress Publishers, 1971.

Mitchel, John. *The Last Conquest of Ireland (Perhaps)*. New York, n.p., 1876.

O'Donoghue, D. J. *The Life and Writings of James Clarence Mangan*. Dublin: M. H. Gill, 1897.

———. *Poems of James Clarence Mangan*. Dublin: M. H. Gill, 1903.

O Laoghaire, An t-Athair Peadar. *My Own Story*. Trans. Sheila O Sullivan. Dublin: Gill and Macmillan, 1973.

Power, Patrick. *A Literary History of Ireland*. Cork: Mercier Press, 1969.

Rafroidi, Patrick. *Irish Literature in English: The Romantic Period* (1789-1850). Gerrards Cross: Colin Smythe, 1980.

Shapiro, Karl. *A Prosody Handbook*. New York: Harper and Row, 1965.

Shaw, George Bernard. *Man and Superman*. Middlesex, England: Penguin Books, 1980.

Sheridan, John. *James Clarence Mangan*. Dublin: Talbot Press, 1937.

Tennyson, Alfred, Lord. *Tennyson's Poetry*. Ed. Robert W. Hill, Jr. New York: W. W. Norton, 1971.

Woodham-Smith, Cecil. *The Great Hunger: Ireland 1845-49*. New York: Harper and Row, 1962.

World Book Encyclopedia. Chicago: World Book, Inc., 1984.

Yeats, William Butler. *Collected Poems*. London: Macmillan, 1979.

———. *Uncollected Prose*. 2 vols. New York: Columbia UP, 1970.

Patricia A. Coughlan (essay date 1986)

SOURCE: Coughlan, Patricia A. "'Fold over Fold, Inveterately Convolv'd': Some Aspects of Mangan's Intertextuality." *Anglo-Irish and Irish Literature: Aspects of Language and Culture; Proceedings of the Ninth International Congress of the International Association for the Study of Anglo-Irish Literature Held at Uppsala University, 4-7 August, 1986*. Ed. Birgit Bramsbäck and Martin Croghan. Vol. 2. Uppsala: U of Uppsala, 1988. 191-200. Print.

[In the following essay, originally presented at a congress in 1986, Coughlan evaluates the influence of Mangan's writing on the works he revered and referenced often, particularly Lord Byron's poetry and the novel St. Leon *(1799) by William Godwin. Coughlan sees in Mangan's work a "perpetually recurring contest between the quotidian and the transcendent," resulting in a "bifocal" style of writing that, for her, is among his strengths as an author.]*

My intention in this paper is to examine the significance in Mangan's work of a small number of texts by other writers, works which were evidently of great importance to him, and to which he refers so often that they are virtually part of the fabric of his own writing. The principal subjects of my discussion will be the poetry of Byron and William Godwin's novel *St. Leon*; but individual motifs and character types from other authors also crop up in the argument.

I propose to argue that in Mangan's writing there is a perpetually recurring contest between the quotidian and the transcendent, and a constant problem in effecting the necessary transactions between them. This tension is well defined in Schiller's discussions of aesthetics. In his essay entitled "Thoughts Upon the Common and Low in Art," the following passages appear:

> Everything is Common which does not address the spirit, and which excites only a sensuous interest . . . A portrait painter can treat his subject in a style both *Common* and *Great*; *Common*, if he sets forth the contingent as carefully as the necessary, if he neglects the great, and solicitously brings out the little; *Great*, if he knows how to discover the most interesting traits, separating the accidental from the necessary, bringing out the greater and only indicating the little. But nothing is Great, except the expression of soul in actions, features and positions . . . The *Low* stands yet one degree below the common, and is distinguished from it by the fact that it indicates not only something *negative*, not only a want of the spiritual and noble, but something *positive*—namely, rudeness of feeling, bad manners, and degraded sentiments . . . The low always indicates something coarse and clownish . . . In works of art, the low *may be apparent*, not only by selecting low objects, which a sense of fitness and propriety forbids, but also by treating *them in a low way* . . . Low incidents occur in the life of the greatest man, but only a low taste would select and portray them.[1]

What I have called the transcendent in Mangan is comparable to that which "addresses the spirit," the "Great," in Schiller. It is an imagined state of limitless power, energy and life, whose possessors are suffused with a "woundrous excess of light," and exist in a condition of grandeur and suffering. Its types in Mangan's imagination are the following. First: Byron's Childe Harold and Manfred; second, the Faustian heroes of two Gothic novels, Godwin's *St. Leon* (published in 1799) and the Irish writer C. R. Maturin's *Melmoth the Wanderer* (published in 1820). Both St. Leon and Melmoth have contracted demonic bargains of an obscure kind, and both as a result possess immortality and the capacity to wander widely over space and time. Both are grandly tormented, glamorous and isolated souls, like Byron's Manfred, defying the spirits in "thrilling monologues" (Mangan's phrase) from his Alpine peak, and like Childe Harold, who picturesquely exhibits his existential despair against a backdrop of sublime Mediterranean scenery. A third version of the eternal and eternally grieving spirit is the Wandering Jew, whose legend Mangan found in German poetry, and reworked in two different versions, one from Schubart and one from F. V. Schlegel.[2]

I shall first examine the uses to which Mangan puts Byron, taking the tones and techniques of Byron's work as of equal importance with the subject-matter and characters of the poems. In Mangan's work, taking prose and poetry together, Byron is quoted, paraphrased or mentioned more than a score of times. The pattern of these references reveals a strong emphasis on *Childe Harold,* from which Mangan quotes at least six times, but there are also quotations from *Don Juan, Beppo, The Giaour,* and *The Vision of Judgment,* a reference to *Mazeppa,* and several mentions and an important discussion of *Manfred.*[3]

Byron's *Childe Harold* is, in the sense which has been defined by Mikhail Bakhtin, monological: it uses one kind of language, a grand lyric tone which by comparison with the wry variousness of *Don Juan* is a simple affair.[4] The narrative poems, too, though full of vigour, deal in relatively simple versions of passion and heroism, in a diction unshadowed by irony. *Don Juan, Beppo* and *The Vision of Judgment* are quite another matter, with their sardonic colloquialism and virtuoso comic rhymes. It is important to recognize that though passages of *Childe Harold* are the most obvious trace of Byronic influence in Mangan's work, in fact both Byrons had their effect on him. His lifelong supple and delightful experiments with stanza-forms and the effects of rhyme must surely have their origins in his early absorption of the quizzically comic Byron, what Bakhtin calls the "novelized" texts, which play tone against tone, and "Common" (or even "Low") against "Great" in the Schillerian sense.[5] Byron achieves his dialogical quality in various ways; I shall look at two of his methods. One is to draw attention to his medium. Here he is doing it in *Beppo,* stanza 63:

> To turn—and to return;—the devil take it,
> This story slips for ever through my fingers,
> Because, just as the stanza likes to make it,
> It needs must be—and so it rather lingers;
> This form of verse begun, I can't well break it,
> But must keep time and tune like public singers;
> But if I once get through my present measure,
> I'll take another when I'm next at leisure.[6]

In this passage for a moment the reader can see, because of Byron's laughing disclaimer itself, how the leisurely, digressive narration is intimately bound up with, is indeed a product of, the "measure"; and thus the story, and by implication all poetic speech, is shown as mediated through the enabling conventions of language and metre. No absolute lyric feeling can continue to present itself as such in the presence of this genially ironic tone.

In the following stanza from *Don Juan,* we can see another of Byron's mediating touches, in the juxtaposition of the sun-chariot of Phaeton with "the York mail":

> What a delightful thing's a turnpike road!
> So smooth, so level, such a mode of shaving
> The earth, as scarce the eagle in the broad
> Air can accomplish, with his wide wings waving;
> Had such been cut in Phaeton's time, the god
> Had told his son to satisfy his craving
> With the York mail . . .
>
> (Canto X. stanza 78)

In this stanza the transcendent, Promethean aspirations of Phaeton doubly come a cropper: the framework of the Greek legend is wrenched to accommodate the turnpike road, and on it, the York mail, or in other words, the everyday world of contemporary England. No such quotidian fact is allowed to complicate the tone in the poetic drama *Manfred,* written somewhat earlier.

As I have said, the most immediately obvious element of Byronic influence on Mangan's poetry is the figure of tormented grief and puzzlement from *Childe Harold.* Again and again Mangan quotes snatches of the third canto, which is a *locus classicus* of extreme Romantic despair. Stanza 34 alone feeds several passages of Mangan:

> There is a very life in our despair,
> Vitality of poison,—a quick root
> Which feeds these deadly branches; for it were
> As nothing did we die; but Life will suit
> Itself to Sorrow's most detested fruit,
> Like to the apples on the Dead Sea's shore,
> All ashes to the taste: Did man compute
> Existence by enjoyment, and count o'er
> Such hours 'gainst years of life,—say, would he name threescore?

But in his use of this material he evinces a bewildering variety of moods. In the prose piece **"A Sixty-Drop Dose of Laudanum"** he solemnly employs the last two syllables of the last two lines of the stanza for one of his epigraphs, complete with full reference, giving:

> - - - - - - - - - - Count o'er
> - - - - - - - - - - threescore!
>
> *Childe Harold,* c. iii. st. xxxiv[7]

This, with its very Mangan-like emphasis on the rhyme at the expense of the meaning and the syntax, would seem to make fun of the gloom in Byron's passage. On the other hand, in his English version of a poem by the German poet Ferdinand Freiligrath, the ghost of the stanza seems to appear in its original, gloomy attire:

> But no long voyagings,—oh, no more
> Of the wary East or South—no more of the Simoom—
> No apples from the Dead Sea shore—
> No fierce volcanoes,
> All fire and gloom!

—Or so, at least, it seems, until the final two lines:

> Or else, at most, sing *basso,* we implore,
> Of Orient sands, while Europe's sands monopolise thy *Sopranos*![8]

At the end of his prose piece **"My Bugle, and How I Blow It"** (1841), Mangan weaves stanza 60 of *Childe Harold* into a similar crisscrossing of tones. In a voice of self-mockery he sketches himself as doomed isolate, by virtue of his genius:

> But for me there is no hope; at home or abroad I tarry not. Like Schubart's *Wandering Jew,* I am "scourged by unrest through many climes." Like Coleridge's *Ancient Mariner,* "I pass like Night, from land to land" . . . A fearful voice, to all but me inaudible, for ever thunders in mine ear, "Pack up thy duds!—push along!—keep moving! I see no prospect before me but an eternity of peripateticalism—
>
> The race of Life becomes a hopeless flight
> To those that walk in darkness—on the sea
> The boldest steer but where their ports invite,
> But there are wanderers o'er eternity
> Whose bark drives on and on, and anchored ne'er shall be.
>
> Once again, Reader, farewell, but forget not—THE MAN IN THE CLOAK.[9]

The demotic expression "pack up thy duds!" comically undercuts the grand gloom of the legendary and lyric wanderers who are also involved: an encounter is staged between the narrator of *Don Juan* or *Beppo,* and the figure of Childe Harold himself: that is, between the quotidian world, which guarantees no separation of pathetic and comic effects, and the high simplicity of cosmic disillusionment.

Turning to the influence of the Gothic novels, *Melmoth the Wanderer* and *St. Leon,* we find that Mangan's attitude to this prose material is characterized by an equivalent complexity. Melmoth is a type of Promethean, almost superhuman, power, like Goethe's *Faust,* another work often mentioned by Mangan, though he finds Byron's drama of transgressive individual will, *Manfred,* to be superior to Goethe's.[10] As is clear especially from his prose work, Mangan's passionate imaginative interest in such figures always involves a lively sense of their ridiculousness when brought into relation with modernity, and particularly with urban life. I have argued elsewhere that he shows this by choosing to translate Balzac's continuation of *Melmoth the Wanderer,* his story *Melmoth réconcilié,* which brings the Wanderer into the city and shows the buying and selling of the demonic powers, at an ever-accelerating rate, and their resultant trivialization.[11]

Insofar as this transcendent figure who has won extraordinary powers is a type of the poet, Mangan mocks him by bringing him up against the actualities of life for a writer in the magazines; as he says in his "Grand and Transcendent Ode . . . to *The Comet,*" in 1833: "Magazines are ('tis said) but shifts for buttering bread."[12] Writing about fame in the teasing and relentlessly allusive **"Sixty-Drop Dose of Laudanum"** (1839), he links St. Leon with two other supernatural literary figures:

> Yes: fame, like Mrs Shelley's Frankenstein, is a genuine production, of the sepulchre. "The nightmare Life-in-Death is she." She springs up from the dust of him who seeks her no more, as the phoenix rises from its own ashes. "The grave-dews winnowing through the rotting clay" are distilled into an *elixir vitae* which, unlike St. Leon's, turns out no burden to its possessor."[13]

In ***Anthologia Germanica*** **[*Anthologia Germanica = German Anthology*]** No. XIII, in 1838, he self-mockingly uses St. Leon to describe his own "capability of expatiating to eternity upon a single topic":

> Give us but one pull from St. Leon's elixir-bottle, and ages might elapse, until the grass grew over the forgotten tombs of those who shall still be unborn in the days of our grandchildren, before our monotonous drawl should cease to astound and mystify mankind.[14]

The elixir appears elsewhere in a serio-comic list of marvels:

> Had we Aladdin's lamp—Gyges' ring—the wishing-cap of Fortunatus—Paganini's violin—the lyre of Orpheus—the collar of Moran—the sword of Harlequin—Prospero's wand—St. Leon's *elixir vitae*—the finger of Midas—the wings of Icarus—the talisman of Camaralzaman—the flying horse of Prince Firouz Schah . . .[15]

The collocation here of the collar of Moran and Paganini's violin with Orpheus' lyre resembles that of Phaeton and the York mail, in *Don Juan.*

And yet Mangan was evidently not immune to the grand romance of St. Leon and his dark bargain. In a poem from his nationalist phase, three years before his own death, he imagines the patriotic "Youths of Ireland" as "the new St. Leons, who . . . conquer Time and Fate" by their sacrifice of self to the cause.[16] He footnotes this reference in the poem with a quotation from *St. Leon* itself, from the moment of crisis in the book when St. Leon actually gains knowledge of the secret:

> For me the laws of nature are suspended, the eternal wheels of the universe roll backward; I am destined to be triumphant over Fate and Time.

Much of Mangan's best work is written as if the lyric speaker in fact possessed some such powers as Melmoth's or St. Leon's. It is a discourse which puts itself outside the framework of history, if history is understood as a continuing process. Its viewpoint on the everyday doings and habitations of men is often Olympian—that of a prophet or an exile, or of the last representative of a dead caste or nation (the pair of poems called **"Khidder"** and **"The World's Changes"** use a prophet-figure; and last survivors abound, from Mac Liag, poet of Kincora, to the Ottoman student remembering his "Daunishmend"). In these poems glory has always already departed, or can at best be dreamed of (as in **"A Vision of Connacht"** [**"A Vision of Connaught in the Thirteenth Century"**]). The setting of these poems is an elsewhere, whether of time or space—a splendid past, for the construction of which Mangan made an imaginative pillage of other periods and other cultures: the time of the Barmecides, Karaman, Connaught in the thirteenth century, twenty golden years ago, or the reign of a score of euphoniously-named sheikhs, caliphs and khans. All cultures are thus deprived of their historical particularity and reconstituted as a single one, within which men suffer identical pains and mourn the loss of identical joys. The poem called **"Advice (from the Ottoman)"** puts it especially clearly:

Moor, Chinese, Egyptian, Russian, Roman,
Tread one common downhill path of doom:
Everywhere the names are Man and Woman,
Everywhere the old sad sins find room.[17]

(At the same time, however, this poem is itself an exercise in verbal inventiveness, the first word of each stanza being a palindrome of the last, which puts theme and form in a fairly incongruous relationship).

The single realm which Mangan has by these means invented for himself becomes *the* realm of poetry, and within that realm all deeds are either heroically noble, or grandly evil, as in **"The Howling Song of Al-Mohara,"** which begins:

My heart is as a House of Groans
From dusky eve to dawning grey;
Allah, Allah hu!
The glazed flesh on my staring bones
Grows black and blacker with decay;
Allah, Allah hu!
Yet am I none whom Death may slay;
I am spared to suffer and to warn;
Allah, Allah hu![18]

Life as proposed within these poems is a matter of swords and swift steeds, of the perfect good fellowship usually of a warrior group, now destroyed and departed. It is all a long way from the robust quotidian life of Dublin in the eighteen-thirties and eighteen-forties, and from Mangan's own actual life as a professional writer for a clutch of magazines of various political opinions, producing contributions for which he was paid by the line, never very flush with money, frequently drunk, drugged, or melancholic.[19] Mangan was a second-generation Romantic poet, who had perforce to renegotiate the Byronic and Shelleyan absolutes of Romantic will and feeling. His Schillerian "low" and "common" conditions of production do find their way into his writings, though one has to look fairly hard to discover them in the tidied-up Mangan of the anthologies. In spite of his fascination with the spirit of poetry and his commitment to its beautiful sad sentiments, Mangan's work is shot through with comic moments, instants of ironic self-debasement and attention to the "accidental" in Schiller's terms. If one looks, for instance, at his treatment of time, one finds not only the absolute and vanished past (Kincora, Karaman), whose date is left unstated or vague, but also more precisely indicated moments: as in the poem **"Eighteen-Hundred Fifty,"** by Mangan's invented German alter ego "Selber"[20] or the year 1833, in **"A Verye Splendidde and Ryghte Conceited Dittie of ande Concernyinge the Newe Yeare."**[21]

Even in those poems which look as if they mean to remain within the privileged domain of pure lyric feeling, Mangan cannot always sustain his own power to imagine it with a straight face (or perhaps he does not sufficiently wish to). In the poems of loss and grief which form such a large proportion of his work, what the reader finds is the set of formal elements—the stanza, the refrain, the persona of a sorrowing isolate—but somehow the whole is lacking in semantic weight. In the narrative poems, many of them versions from the German—for example, **"The Diver," "The Spectre-Caravan," "Alexander and the Tree"**—the impetus of the tale carries the reader on and unifies the poem in the mind.[22] But in many of the lament-poems there is a sensation of slackness; the refrain so fills out the metrical space which is set up at the start, that it can end by mesmerizing the reader. The result is the actual immobilization of the lyric persona, who becomes locked in an attitude of grief, imprisoned like Prometheus on the cliff, like St. Leon and Melmoth in their frightful immortality, or like the Wandering Jew within his recurring visionary nightmare.

I would argue that this effect can be read as an interrogation by the poet of the adequacy of the available poetic forms, but in a way more radical and ultimately more disturbing than Byron's genial advertence to his stanza or his rhyme. In Byron the strong narrative interest carries the poems on, sufficiently distracting attention from the palpable poetic mechanism. But Mangan seems deliberately to seek to foreground the devices of his work. This mischievous quizzing of the medium can be seen easily in his evident spoofing poems, such as some of his German alter egos' *Selber*'s and *Drechsler*'s work. But one may also discover it in apparently serious pieces, such as **"The Wail of the Three Khalendeers"** [**"The Wail and Warning of the Three Khalendeers"**], with its relentless treble rhymes. Here is the first stanza:

La'laha, il Allah!
Here we meet, we three, at length,
Amrab, Osman, Perizad,
Shorn of all our grace and strength,
Poor, and old, and very sad!

We have lived, but live no more;
Life has lost its gloss for us,
Since the days we spent of yore
Boating down the Bosphorus!
La'laha, il Allah!
The Bosphorus, the Bosphorus!
Old Time brought home no loss for us.
We felt full of health and heart
Upon the foamy Bosphorus!

And so it goes on, for a further six stanzas.[23] The word "Bosphorus" quickly comes to exert a magnetic influence on the reader, all but obliterating any particularities in the earlier part of each successive stanza. It is hard not to feel that what Mangan is doing here is primarily diverting himself by the application of the resources of Walker's *Rhyming Lexicon* (a work he often mentions) to an utterly conventional kit of poetic sentiments, including wine, roses, and all the usual paraphernalia.

In his enterprise as a poet in the fourth and fifth decades of the nineteenth century, Mangan had to attempt the reconciliation of two strongly antipathetic sets of conditions. These were, on the one hand, the quotidian scenery of a provincial city under strong political tensions, experienced from a precarious social and financial position; and on the other, the grand literary inheritance of high Romanticism, with its imperatives arising from the force of the individual will and sensibility. Throughout his work Mangan is remarkable for the doubleness of his tone: at one instant he is expressing the depths of gloom and despair, at the next punning and building up crazy comic edifices by his rhyme-schemes and elaborate metrical games. This bewildering changeableness is familiar to all readers of Mangan who have got beyond the few familiar anthology pieces, and one could multiply examples of it almost endlessly. His Victorian biographer, D. J. O'Donoghue, regretted Mangan's facetiousness, and indeed did his best to remove it surgically from his edition of the poems.[24] But merely to deplore the joking and the incessant shifting of tones—irritating and arid though they may sometimes seem—is, I would argue, to miss the point of Mangan. Mangan's work is *both* "clownish," in Schiller's word, *and* intensely serious and lyrical. But he is always bifocal, never letting the reader rest for long in either mode, and it is his resolute maintenance of the tension between the two which gives his work its fullest energy. And as I have tried to show, one of the clearest ways of perceiving this doubleness is in his incessant transvaluations of the Promethean images of Romanticism, from transcendent to ridiculous and back again.

Notes

1. *Philosophical and Aesthetic Letters and Essays* (1795), trans. J. Weiss (London: John Chapman, 1845), 266-67. Mangan thought highly of Schiller; he preferred him to Goethe, and had been translating him from the beginning of his career. He chose to begin his *Anthologia Germanica* in the *Dublin University Magazine* (henceforth *D.U.M.*), in 1835 with versions of Schiller's poems.
2. F. V. Schlegel, "The Everlasting Jew," *D.U.M.*, XXXIII (Jan. 1849), 92-94; and Schubert, "The Wandering Jew," in J. C. Mangan, *Essays in Prose and Verse,* ed. C. Meehan (Dublin: Duffy, 1884), 269-75. Mangan presumably makes the capital "V" stand for "von."
3. The stereotype 'Byronic' Byron, spectacularly moody representative sinner of the period, plays only a minor role in Mangan's writing. See *D.U.M.*, XII (Aug. 1838), p. 177, and, XIV (July 1839), p. 72, the only disparaging references to Byron I have found in Mangan.
4. Mikhail Bakhtin, *The Dialogical Imagination* (Austin: University of Texas Press, 1981).
5. Ibid., pp. 6 & 33; see also the longer discussion of Pushkin.
6. *Poetical Works of Lord Byron* (London: Frederick Warne, 1890).
7. *D.U.M.*, XIII (March 1839), 269-78.
8. "My Themes," *D.U.M.*, XXI (Jan. 1843), 41.
9. "My Bugle and How I Blow It," *Belfast Vindicator,* II (March 1841).
10. See his discussion, *D.U.M.*, VII (March 1836), 278-79.
11. See my "The Recycling of Melmoth: 'A Very German Story,'" in *Literary Interrelations. Ireland, England and the World. Vol. III,* ed. W. Zach and H. Kosok (Tübingen: G. H. Narr, 1987).
12. *The Comet,* III (June 1833), p. 494.
13. Ibid.; and, "Drop 47," *D.U.M.*, XIII (March 1839).
14. *D.U.M.*, XII (August 1838), 168.
15. "Anthologia Germanica No. VI," *D.U.M.*, VI (May 1836), 518.
16. "The Peal of Another Trumpet," *The Nation,* IV (May 1846), p. 457.
17. "Advice (from the Ottoman)," J. C. Mangan, *Poems,* ed. D. J. O'Donoghue (Dublin: O'Donoghue and M. H. Gill, 1903), p. 209.
18. *D.U.M.*, XV (April 1840), 383.
19. See the excellent discussion of Mangan's life and circumstances by David Lloyd, *The Writings of James Clarence Mangan: A Case Study in Nationalism and Writings,* Diss. Cambridge 1982.
20. *D.U.M.*, XXV (January 1845), 104-06.

21. Meehan, p. 129.

22. "The Diver," from Schiller, *D.U.M.*, V (May 1835), 590-93; "The Spectre-Caravan," from Freiligrath, *D.U.M.*, XIX (Feb. 1842), 203-05; "Alexander and the Tree," *Irish Penny Journal*, I (July 1840), p. 28.

23. *D.U.M.*, XXIII (May 1845), 538-40.

24. See *The Life and Writings of James Clarence Mangan* (Dublin: M. H. Gill, 1897). The most glaring example of O'Donoghue's tampering with a text is probably his silent omission of the wryly optimistic final stanza from the poem "Broken-Hearted Lay, No. I," from his edition of the poems, op. cit., 124-35.

Jean Andrews (essay date 1989)

SOURCE: Andrews, Jean. "James Clarence Mangan and Romantic Stereotypes: 'Old and Hoary at Thirty-Nine.'" *Irish University Review* 19.2 (1989): 240-63. Print.

[*In the following essay, Andrews argues that Mangan's religious orthodoxy, detachment from society, and celibacy contributed to his being a less successful Romantic author than he aspired to be. She also notes the impact of Mangan's limited experience on the political and philosophical dimensions of his work.*]

Among the Irish writers of the nineteenth century, James Clarence Mangan stands out as the most gifted, the most individual. His life was a history of one misery after another and, at the end of it, he was a physical wreck. He was very much an eccentric; a loner who became isolated from those around him with relative ease but who found it difficult to communicate and make friends. Though he made many translations from the Irish and was stirred to write some original poems about the condition of Ireland during the Famine he actually made no political commitments or overt statements during his life. Indeed Jacques Chuto has already cast doubt on the nationalism of these poems.[1] Equally, Mangan's writing does not appear to convey any particular philosophy except what may be inferred from idiosyncratic prose pieces such as ***A Sixty-Drop Dose of Laudanum.***[2] Clarence Mangan, as he styled himself, perennially escapes definition; he was a calculated and enigmatic blend of reality and fiction.

He perpetuated the myth he created about his own person in his unfinished ***Autobiography*** and in a biography of himself he attributed to the translator, Edward Walsh.[3] In the ***Autobiography*** Mangan paints a nightmarish picture of his childhood: he describes his parents' house as two holes occupied by spiders and beetles, the environment he lived in was one of "curses and intemperance, of cruelty, infidelity and blasphemy—and of both secret and open hatred towards the moral government of GOD." He even claims he had to share a bed with a leper and contracted a peculiar "hypochondriasis" as a result. In the E. W. biography he makes the even more extravagant admission that he remained blind from the age of five to the age of thirteen because a servant girl sent him out in the rain. Mangan hints significantly at the "dark secret" at the heart of his malaise. He explains that he had an unusually strongly-marked nervous temperament and hastens to add that the reason for this must be a "something sore and very heavy on his conscience."

It is clear from the *paysage dâme* presented in the two biographies that Mangan identified himself with the great Romantic *poètes maudits*: Werther, Childe Harold, Manfred, even the Ancient Mariner, and with the real doomed poets who were their creators.[4] His "Werther" was a combination of Romantic *angst* and Byronic humour: a small withered man with an ashen face, blond wig, a curious half-length cloak and an odd hat who sat in ale-house corners writing poetry on sheets of paper cadged from the landlord. To complete the mystique he drank to addition, was frequently ill, always penniless, probably dabbled in opium and certainly died in the same High Romantic fashion as Chatterton and Beddoes. A minor poet himself, his closest affinity is surely with the lesser English Romantics, Darley, Hood and Beddoes, poets who wasted their gifts trying to live out an impossible literary role.

To some extent Mangan succeeded in imitating the lives of the poets and Romantic heroes he admired. However, his lonely, celibate existence passed in the taverns of Dublin, the scrivener's office, Trinity College Library and with the Ordnance Survey is quite tame in comparison with the turbulent and adventurous lives and loves of the major Romantics. Yet theirs was the literature he chose to imitate. It is my intention to show, because of his religious orthodoxy and his apparent lack of sexual initiation, Mangan was unable to comprehend in his work the basic elements of blasphemy and eroticism central to the kind of High Romanticism he espoused. He seems to have concentrated his efforts in three specific areas: in prose he explored the Gothic genre, while in poetry he associated himself first with the persona of the forsaken lover and later with the figure of the outcast, living in a bleak wasteland.

Mario Praz isolates death, the flesh and the devil as the most important components of the dark side of Romanticism in his classic work *The Romantic Agony.*[5] He shows how this nexus provides the energy and the inspiration behind the imaginative and narrative production of Romanticism and its descendants. One only has to think of Schiller, Tieck, Coleridge, Byron, Rimbaud, Baudelaire and so on to span three cultures and almost three generations. Praz claims that the passionate interest of these poets in exotic places, dreams, fantasy and unusual mental states and their preoccupation with suffering, death and salvation all stem from this conjunction. Elsewhere he traces the origin of these concerns from the eighteenth century:

> Why in the most polite and effeminate of centuries, in the century of *bergeries* and *fêtes galantes* and idyllic conversation pieces, the century of Watteau and Boucher and Zoffaany, should people have begun to feel the horrible fascination of dark forests and lugubrious caverns and cemeteries and thunderstorms? The answer is just because of its feminine character. In no other century was woman such a dominating figure, the very essence of rococco being a feminine delicacy—just because of this the eighteenth century had *les nerfs à fleur de peau.* They discovered the *mal de vivre* and the *vapeurs.*[6]

What Praz denominates as the essential femininity of the eighteenth century was of course carried forward to the literature of Romanticism and the later nineteenth century. The emphasis was always on a basic feminine quality of sensibility; sensitivity and emotion acquired a new importance. As emotion was granted a dignified status in literature, it was only natural that one of the most powerful expressions of emotions, sexual passion, should also be more prominent though rarely expressed overtly. Praz elaborates:

> . . . a love of the exotic is usually an imaginative projection of a sexual desire. This is very clear in such cases as those of Gautier and Flaubert, whose dreams carry them to an atmosphere of barbaric and oriental antiquity, where all the most unbridled desires can be indulged and the cruellest fantasies take form.[7]

Nowhere is this love of the exotic indulged to a greater degree than in the Gothic novel, in many ways a cruder and more basic rendering of the preoccupations of Romantic poetry. Rape, pillage, incest, sacrilege, pacts with the devil, the torture of the innocents; these are all elements of such notable novels as *Vathek, Melmoth the Wanderer* and *St. Leon.* According to O'Donoghue, Mangan was well-acquainted with such works:

> . . . the writers, however who . . . had the most marked effect upon Mangan were William Godwin and Charles Robert Maturin. For them and their gloomy school Mangan always had a notable fancy. Godwin's *St. Leon* he knew almost by heart, and there are many evidences of his knowledge and appreciation of, or at any rate interest in, Maturin's works.[8]

Be that as it may, Mangan's two most notable attempts at the Gothic genre, ***The Thirty Flasks*** and ***The Man in the Cloak*** deviate in significant and characteristic ways from mainstream Gothic fiction.

The first and longest of these tales is set in a comic opera-style Germany. It concerns a young nobleman who having got himself into debt, goes to a mysterious nabob three feet six inches in height and enters into a kind of loan arrangement with him. The nabob claims to be the hero's long lost brother and offers him one thousand ducats for every flask of a black liquid he drinks. This "Black Elixir" sensationally robs Basil of one inch of his height for every draught he swallows and transfers it to the nabob. Before he drinks the irreversible thirtieth flask however, Basil's stature is saved by the intervention of the curiously named Rubadub Snooksnacker Slickwitz. This newcomer exposes the nabob as none other than the evil Maugraby (a magician). He quickly restores Basil's inches and bestows on him the fortune he needs to marry the beautiful Aurelia.[9]

The Thirty Flasks is quite evidently a pastiche of the Gothic genre. It includes a typical episode, that of Basil's pact with the nabob, without approaching the sex-death-devil nexus that is so central to mainstream Gothic fiction. The comic nabob plays the role of the devil and the loss of three feet in height is put in place of the usual horrible fate: damnation. Sexual passion is also outside the range of ***The Thirty Flasks.*** The exchanges between Basil and Aurelia are extremely forced and stilted without having the saving grace of mannerism. Indeed Mangan's touch is generally unsure. The tale oscillates uncertainly between light ironic whimsy and the seriousness of a moral fable. It is quite undisciplined; often the exuberance of the language interrupts the flow of the narrative to no telling effect. The best that can be said of the story is that it is a Gothic horror tale subverted by its own humour.

The Man in the Cloak, Mangan's other major attempt at the Gothic genre, contains less of a humourous nature. He considered Maturin's *Melmoth the Wanderer* "a bore of the first magnitude," perhaps this is why he decided to rework the tale to his own liking. This story is also set in comic opera land and tells of an ineffectual bank cashier whose embezzlement is about to be discovered. He is warned by a mysterious stranger with piercing eyes who turns out to be Melmoth himself. He offers to save Braunbrock, the cashier, if he takes the talisman from him. Braunbrock accepts and, as the holder of the talisman, he is condemned to an isolation none of the evil talisman's wealth can compensate for. He leads a dissipate life for a time but soon tires of the empty luxuries the talisman brings. He tries to find a victim to give the talisman to. In a vision he sees Melmoth at the church of St Sulpice in Paris and finds that the outcast repented of his sins and died at peace with God. He then finds someone to take the talisman from him, makes his confession and is shriven.

As with ***The Thirty Flasks,*** Mangan's touch in this tale is unsure. Until Braunbrock makes his pact with Melmoth the piece is replete with the same kind of verbal humour, wordplay and punning as the former story. Braunbrock is blatantly cuckolded by his mistress, Livonia, and is very much a figure of fun in his long interview with her. Then the tone of the story immediately changes when Braunbrock becomes the outcast. Mangan dwells very seriously on the misery of Braunbrock's position:

> . . . all the resources of human nature, aided even by infernal agency, are insufficient to battle against the mighty agony of that despair which the prospect of an eternity of

woe, incessantly before the mind's eye, must of necessity generate.[10]

As soon as Braunbrock passes the talisman on, the story returns to the quirky banter of the early part and the report of "mon cher courier belge" relates the subsequent history of the talisman. The very seriousness of the central part of this piece indicates a sincere concern with the salvation of the protagonists' souls. This is contrary to the whole Gothic tradition and betrays a deep religious orthodoxy.

Mangan's religious beliefs were strong, orthodox and relatively simple as his ***Autobiography*** and the testimony of Fr Meehan shows.[11] Henry J. Donaghy claims that Mangan was interested in Swedenborg and spiritualism and only returned to the Catholic church in the eighteen forties.[12] This theory, though plausible, is belied by these stories both of which were written in 1838 and appeared in the *Dublin University Magazine* for that year. Indeed all of Mangan's work is so deeply imbued with what can only be described as an orthodox Catholic sensibility that it is easier to believe, with Whitcomb Hess, that he never strayed far from the fold.[13] It is no surprise therefore that he could not bring himself to engage in the acts of blasphemy the Gothic genre demanded without at least bringing his characters to complete repentance and acceptance into the Church. Neither could he indulge in the kind of titillation of the senses while ostensibly telling a moral fable which filled the novels of respectable clergymen such as Horace Walpole.

The Man in the Cloak and the humourous ***My Bugle and How I Blow It*** have the same central character, "the man in the cloak." Though ***My Bugle and How I Blow It*** is a nonsense piece, it does imply that Mangan himself was the last recipient of the talisman. The image Mangan cultivated was, to a certain degree, an attempt to imitate the notable eccentric Robert Maturin but he must also have realised how incongrous a figure he would cut as a Dublin version of Maturin's Melmoth.

Mangan's foray into the realm of the Gothic horror story reveals two important traits in his writing: that he was strongly attracted to the figure of the damned outcast central to the genre and that he desperately wanted to identify himself with that literary type; that his enthusiasm was confounded by a latent inability to grasp the fundamental elements of sexual passion and religious blasphemy leading to damnation implicit in the Gothic form. He was therefore forced, in a manner of speaking, to cast a cloak of humour over his inadequacies, with varying degrees of success. Though his prose is definitely not of the same calibre as his poetry, it does provide a macroscopic illustration of the problems he encountered as a poet. Here also it is evident that he tried to take his inspiration from a source he could not fully comprehend. In this case, too, his work was ultimately salvaged by the quaint charm of his humour.

II

Mangan himself is the subject of all his poetry, translated or original. Indeed his original poems have so many borrowings in them and his translations are so personalised that the entire canon of his verse must be surveyed as a homogenous whole. Though Byron, Shelley and Keats were dead before Mangan began to publish his poetry in Dublin magazines, his strongest poetic affinity is with the second generation Romantics. P. M. Diskin believes that Byron was the chief influence on Mangan's poetry; that the rhetorical side of Mangan's work was mainly derived from him while the lyrical aspects owed a great deal to Shelley, and later, to a lesser degree, to the early Tennyson.[14] Mangan was of course dead before the great Victorians came into their own. Chronologically, thematically and temperamentally he belongs to the intermediate years, between the deaths of the younger Romantics and the flowering of Victorian poetry in the second half of the century.

He shares these years with the English minor Romantics. They lived on after the deaths of their great contemporaries, more tragic still because they each dissipated what could have been a great talent. Thomas Hood turned from lyric poetry to comic verse before a combination of poverty and tuberculosis killed him. An even more striking parallel can be drawn between Mangan and Thomas Lovell Beddoes.[15] He and Mangan died in the same year, both at the age of forty-six. Beddoes, however, after a series of failed attempts committed suicide. A skilled anatomist, he was also fascinated by the Gothic genre and his last and finest work, *Death's Jest Book* is firmly in that tradition. These poets and the others of their company, John Clare, George Darley and Hartley Coleridge, pursued the same doomed quest as Byron and Shelley but their visionary powers were not strong enough to sustain them and they outlived their time. They abandoned themselves to misery and became living embodiments of the Romantic myth of failure, as indeed did Mangan in a less spectacular fashion. It is nonetheless also true that the melancholia of these poets was partly a "cultivated literary attitude," one which Mangan also assumed.[16]

Mangan does not appear to have been ideologically influenced by his contact with the writing of such as Byron, Shelley and Keats in England, and Fichte and AW Schlegel in Germany. This is mostly owing to the fact, already referred to, that his religious orthodoxy remained unaffected at a time when the Romantic poets and thinkers were evolving new concepts of religion. The elements Mangan took from them were more superficial; he borrowed subjects, modes of expression, patterns. He took motifs without having a profound understanding of their connotations. The most important theme he took from Romanticism is that of the poet as hero and forsaken outcast. But Mangan's outcast is not separated from the rest of society either by ideology or by an overwhelming quest for an unachievable goal like the doomed heroes of contemporary literature.

Quite often he simply choses to be apart because that is his preferred state. His inherent lack of confidence leads him to conclude that he is either unfit for society or cannot be understood by it. This is at once true of Mangan's fictional outcast and of himself. In his poetry the presentation of this motif takes two forms: the more particular one of the deserted or deceived lover, and the more general one of the solitary isolated in a barren wasteland.

Generally speaking, in Romantic love poetry the lover who has been rejected by his loved one or separated from her by death has had an intense relationship with her. On the other hand, Mangan's lovers admire from a distance and feel themselves spurned without ever having declared their love. At a time when the erotic was as important to poetry as to Gothic fiction, Mangan's work is unique in its lack of a sexual awareness. This is not to suggest that all the literature of the period was highly-charged sexually, far from it. The portrayal of relations between lovers in the novels of Sir Walter Scott, for example, is stilted and, to modern eyes, overly circumspect. However there is no distortion involved. For Mangan, every woman was an untouchable goddess or a proven (or potential) traitress. Perhaps only in Edgar Allan Poe can a true parallel for Mangan's treatment of love, sexuality and women be found. Yet Poe's work is replete with sexual implication as Marie Bonaparte's classic psychoanalytical study has shown.[17] She suggests that the most important forces behind Poe's work are sadism and necrophilia. She notes how often he presents the situation of "some ideal woman who sickens and dies, yet does not really die since she lives on in unearthly radiance, putrescent and ethereal at one and the same time." According to Bonaparte, chastity was the only means he could employ to curb his sado-necrophilic tendencies and so she believes he lived with his wife as brother and sister.

Bonaparte deals mainly with Poe's stories but the same tendencies can be identified in his poetry. The poems inspired by his love for his wife are always addressed to a pure, gentle young woman. His Eulalie, a paragon of the maidenly virtues, is pictured in perfect filial devotion to Astarte in the poem of the same name.[18] Her relations with the maternal figure of Astarte in fact supersede her relations with her groom. In "Annabel Lee" the lovers are imagined as children who "loved with a love that was more than love." It was "stronger by far than the love / of those who were older." In another poem, "For Annie," the poet's relationship to his beloved is more like that of mother and child:

> She tenderly kissed me,
> She fondly caressed,
> And then I fell gently
> To sleep on her breast—
> Deep to sleep
> From the haven of her breast.[19]

At the other extreme Poe wrote an address to Helen of Troy, not to the legendary beauty but to her statue, a cold stone effigy.[20] The women are all either petrified and unreal like Helen, pure and childlike like Eulalie/Annabel Lee, or maternal like Annie. No woman is an adult lover. Often the flesh and blood women are separated even further from the poet by the grave: Annabel Lee is envisioned in her "sepulchre by the sea" for example.

The women portrayed in Mangan's poetry cannot be as neatly classified as Poe's. Nevertheless, the relationship of lover and beloved shows a similar type of distortion. It is as if Mangan in his innocence touched the tip of an erotic dilemma he could not possibly comprehend. As Marie Bonaparte's study has shown, Poe's attitude to women and sex is the result of deep-rooted psychological problems. As yet there is no psychoanalytical study of Mangan to suggest he was the victim of a similar type of disorder. This seems unlikely though his ***Autobiography*** does contain what might be construed as an indication of a lifelong Oedipal complex, possibly brought on by his father's brutality. This naturally would have inhibited his relations with women other than his mother. Equally, his constant penury and nomadic lifestyle could easily have made it impossible for him to contemplate marriage. Whatever the reason it is most likely that Mangan had no sexual experience.

He does claim to have fallen in love once, however. As usual with Mangan, there are conflicting reports of this event. Sir Charles Gavan Duffy asserts that Mangan met a Margaret Stackpole when he was in his early thirties and fell in love with her.[21] Mangan told Duffy that when he proposed she told him that she was already married and was living under her maiden name while waiting for her husband to come back from a business speculation abroad. Since this is Mangan's uncorroborated assertion it can hardly be trusted. ***My Transformation—A Wonderful Tale*** is a veiled but self-indulgent account of his unhappy experience.[22] Mangan's biographer, D. J. O'Donoghue quotes another source of information on this subject, James Price:

> He (Mangan) once, with unusual bitterness of manner, alluded to the priceless argosy of the heart's first affections, tossed amid the quicksands of a woman's caprice, to a love, fresh, pure, fervent and beautiful as ever lighted passion's flame in human bosom, its jealous agony derided and its first rapturous declaration chilled by cruel and bitter scorn.[23]

Price includes an extract from a letter Mangan wrote to him about his unrequited love. The love affair, if such it was, seems to have been a feeble one at best:

> I often longed for death. Death, however came not, but in its place came something worse than death—love. I formed an attachment to a young lady who gave me every encouragement for some months, and then appeared to take delight in exciting me to jealousy. One evening—I well remember it—she openly slighted me and shunned me. I escaped marriage with this girl, but it was at the expense of my health and mind.[24]

Poor Mangan uses all the Romantic imagery on a very tenuous affection. In fact, O'Donoghue believes he hardly knew Margaret Stackpole and certainly never mentioned his feelings to her.[25] It seems infinitely more likely that the whole episode took place in Mangan's imagination. To have a broken heart to allude to added to the mystique of the miserable poet-lover. Whatever the seriousness of the affair, Mangan extracted the maximum of agony and distress of soul from it in the poems of 1832-33.

Though Mangan identified himself with the Romantic figure of the forsaken lover, he did not have either the personality, the experience or the imagination to portray very powerful heroes. It seems that in Romantic poetry, because of its highly personal nature, the poet had to be an extraordinary person himself in order to project and sustain an heroic persona. The real lives of Byron and Shelley, for instance, were as adventurous and turbulent as their poetry. When Byron presents the hero of *Lara,* he creates a character only as potent as he was (or believed himself to be):

> In him inexplicably mixed appeared
> Much to be loved and hated, sought and feared;
> Opinion varying o'er his hidden lot,
> In praise or railing n'er his name forgot:
> His silence formed a theme for other's prat
> They guessed—they gazed—they fain would know his
> fate.[26]

This is the model Mangan sought to emulate but his real personality was certainly not of the right type to make his chosen literary personae very imposing. Perhaps realising this he frequently lapses into humour and mocks his own pretentions, as in **"Twenty Golden Years Ago."**

Only a handful of the 1832-33 poems deals with the theme of love directly. **"To Laura"** is a vitriolic attack on the woman who deceived him:

> . . . versed in every witching art
> That even the warmest love would dare,
> First having gained her victim's heart
> Then turns him over to despair.[27]

Interestingly, the lover in this poem implies that he never declared his love but perversely asserts that "the love is deepest oft and truest / that burns within the breast untold." At the end of the poem he detaches himself from this hopeless love and looks into the future. He sees himself in lonely isolation, his only relief coming with death:

> But when shall rest be mine? Alas!
> When first the winter winds shall wave
> The pale wild flowers and long dark grass
> Above mine unremembered grave.[28]

"Lines on the death of a beloved friend," written in 1832, is presumed to be about the death of Catherine Hayes, a girl to whom Mangan gave German lessons.[29] In this poem it is obvious that there had been a real friendship between them. He celebrates the innocent, happy life of the dead girl but then switches self-consciously to his own plight. He spends the greater part of the poem bemoaning his own position and dwelling on his own sense of isolation. Through her death Catherine has become an image of lost happiness for him.

Mangan wrote many poems about his own miserable condition in 1832-33. However only in these two pieces and in a short sonnet, **"Love,"** is his unhappy affair referred to.[30] This sonnet underlines the fragility of pure young love and the sorrow that must be endured by the undeceived. Again, Mangan is far more interested in exploring the words of the unsatisfied lover. It is evident that disappointed love is important only as the apparent cause of his desolation. The recurrent pattern is one where the poet establishes as quickly as possible that he is the victim of an unhappy love affair and then proceeds to dwell at length on his own sufferings. It is not surprising therefore that the majority of the 1832-33 poems deal with Mangan's inner torment without mentioning its supposed cause.

After this Mangan's original poetry never returned to the theme of unrequited love and the heart-broken lover. The motif, nevertheless, recurs in his translations. In the ballad **"Lonely from home I come,"** taken from the Irish, the poet is separated from his beloved by death but it is his own miserable condition which concerns him most.[31] He pulls back from a contemplation of her grave to concentrate on his own misery: "in my soul doth darkness dwell" he wails. In **"The Miller's Daughter,"** taken from the German, the lover has been deserted by his lady and is therefore free to devote all his attention to his own sufferings:

> I'll don the willow, and till grim
> Death shall at length arrest my career
> I'll wander about as a pilgrim.[32]

Yet in **"The Lover's Farewell,"** also from the German, though it is the lover who must leave he seems more perturbed by the "tomb-still" streets he must pass through on his journey than by the loss of his beloved.[33] Even in Mangan's "Oriental Versions and Perversions," taken supposedly from the most exotic corpus of work generally available to the nineteenth century, the lovers betray no passion for their mistresses. The women in these poems are out of reach and the lover must look in from outside: as an unrequited lover in the **"Ghazel,"** as an impartial observer in **"To Mihri."**[34] Even **"Jealousy,"** where the speaker promises his "darling, tiny little girl" all sorts of delicacies if she will only admit she has been unfaithful, sounds more like a father coaxing a spoilt child.[35]

Certainly Mangan's love poetry, such as it is, is a failure. It contains nothing that is either erotic or passionate and centres to an extraordinary degree on the condition of the lover himself. It is only when he deliberately employs a form resembling the aphorism that he achieves a modicum of success. His oriental poems are interspersed with a few short, pithy couplets in which he is able to exercise his wit and his flair for wordplay. Because of the brevity of these pieces the poet's melancholia cannot be indulged. One such comment is **"Double Trouble"**:

I am blinded by thy hair and thy tears together
The dark night and the rain come down on me together.[36]

Another couplet is untitled and makes the following cryptic observation:

My heart is a monk, and thy bosom is cloister
So sleeps the bright pearl in the shell of the oyster.[37]

If Mangan could have maintained the same level of detachment throughout the rest of his "love poetry" he might have produced a more significant body of work. As it is, he states wearily at the end of **"What is love?"**:

But the end of it all is Sadness
Desolation, Devastation
Spoliation and uprooting.[38]

He could not resist the urge to wallow in his own despair and beat his breast in the most prolix manner. Though his actual melancholia was quite real, the supposed cause of it in the 1832-33 poems (unrequited love) was largely taken from literary sources. Significantly there exists in his poetry no passionate experience of love or consciousness of sexuality which would, of itself, justify the extent of the deserted lover's devastation. Mangan's unhappiness was probably rooted in more mundane territory: an unsettled family background, financial difficulties, chronic bad health. His identification with the figure of the forsaken lover is another attempt to work within a literary genre that was not suited to his talents or experience. As with the Gothic tradition, he finds a compromise in humour. Irony provides a space behind which he can hide his inadequacies.

III

So far Mangan has shown himself untouched by two of the three elements of Mario Praz's death-flesh-devil nexus. His love poetry and certain of his Gothic stories have proven him innocent of any tinge of carnality; the prose tales themselves are evidence of his inability to deny orthodox religion. In the 1832-33 poems and in certain of his translations, Mangan's lover moves into a world of spiritual and physical discomfort after his separation from the loved one. The landscape which provides the backdrop for the lover is always desolate. Padraic Colum found this bleakness of external nature remarkable in Mangan's poetry; he saw him "looking out on lands that are all waste, in which there is no green or familiar thing."[39] The wasteland is the most common motif in all of Mangan's personal poetry and in many of his translations, especially in his versions from the Irish. In Mangan's work it corresponds to the element of death identified by Praz as part of his three-way nexus. Mangan's employment of the wasteland metaphor is often as derivative as the rest of his chosen themes but it is only in this area that he begins to achieve some semblance of an individual vision; only here he shows his real talent.

The presentation of the wasteland in Romantic poetry varies considerably. Both Wordsworth and Coleridge describe personal wastelands; most notably in *Dejection: An Ode* and its response, *Resolution and Independence.* In these two poems the poets' crises are associated with a stormy night. Coleridge's "grief without a pang, void, dark and drear" is echoed in the "dull sobbing draft, that moans and rakes / Upon the strings of this Aeolian lute." He hopes for a storm to lift him out of his mood. Wordsworth, on the other hand, is lifted out of his depression by his meeting with the old leech-gatherer. He expected to see the old man "pace / about the weary moors continually / wandering about alone and silently," a tired and decrepit specimen of humanity. Instead the old man is a figure of hope for Wordsworth. His solitary moors are a place of contentment for him and, by implication, for the poet. In a similar way, Coleridge looks forward to that most terrible manifestation of external nature, the storm, for some kind of relief. For both these poets, the wasteland or the harshness of nature has a positive value, as indeed it had for Shelley. His Julian exclaims:

. . . I love all waste
and solitary places; where we taste
The pleasure of believing what we are
Is boundless, as we wish our souls to be.[40]

The therapeutic value of waste and solitary places is more equivocal in the daemonic Coleridge. The wasteland that comes on the Ancient Mariner after he kills the albatross is gratuitous, since the slaying of the bird of good omen was an involuntary act. The Ancient Mariner is delivered of the wasteland through another involuntary act; he blesses the sea snakes unaware. Yet he is never free of his experience but doomed to tell it over and over again to such as the wedding guest. Browning's *Childe Roland to the Dark Tower Came* is more enigmatic still. The wasteland through which the quaestor passes is nightmarish in the extreme, like the enchanted sea in the *Ancient Mariner.* The bitter knight's jaundiced eye beholds a diseased and deformed nature as he goes along the dark path to the consummation of victory or defeat at the dark tower. The wasteland of Sir Percivale in *The Holy Grail* does not have the same phantasmagoric quality or the same mounting hysteria as *Childe Roland.* Sir Percivale's torment consists of a set of pleaures which fade away and crumble at the touch.

The Ancient Mariner, Childe Roland and Sir Percivale have come through deserts which are nothing like the passive solitary places of Wordsworth's solitaries or Shelley's Julian. The wastelands become active and malevolent as the century progresses. The poet-protagonists of the famous crisis lyrics were literary representations of Wordsworth and Coleridge's actual experience; Shelley's *Julian and Maddalo* was quite blatantly based on his relationship with Byron. The Ancient Mariner and Childe Roland however, are much more sharply distinguished from their poet-creators. So too are all of Tennyson's protagonists. Later again the wasteland image became something more complex than just a stage in the life or journey of the protagonist. The Ancient Mariner, Childe Roland and Sir Percivale all pass through the wasteland. They have achieved something at the end of their ordeals, however questionable. The desert and the solitude depicted in *Mariana, Tithonus, St. Simeon Stylites* and *Ulysses,* though less nightmarish than that of *Childe Roland* for instance, is one out of which there is no escape. All four characters are trapped in their suffering; their situations remain static and there is no issue for them. Although the protagonists do retain some shadowy hope of deliverance, the value of the wastelands they inhabit is ultimately negative.

Mangan's treatment of the wasteland motif is more assured than his employment of other Romantic conventions. The actual misery of his own life gives a ring of authenticity to his groans of despair. Indeed he uses the same level of sophistication at times as Tennyson or Browning and perhaps somewhat anticipates the greater poets. His protagonists, while not so clearly distinct from the poet's own persona as Childe Roland or Mariana, are still removed from Mangan himself by a series of distancing mechanisms. In Mangan too the value of the wastelands is ultimately negative. His sufferers do not move through a desert in a learning process. Interestingly they are not trapped against their own will either. They choose the wastelands voluntarily as a place of retreat from an alien or hostile society, but they become prisoners there for ever, like Tennyson's incarcerated sufferers.

In the majority of the 1832-33 poems the poet is always shown alone and despairing in a desolate landscape. **"Life is the desert and the solitude"** echoes Coleridge's *Dejection: An Ode.* The speaker looks out on a beautiful scene but cannot appreciate its beauty:

> Yet I am far—Oh! far from feeling
> The life, the thrilling glow, the power.[41]

Instead he wails, affliction is his "doom and dower," he is a member of an unfortunate elite:

> . . . those who stand alone—
> The shrouded few who feel and know
> What none beside have felt and known.

The final image in the poem rivals the horror of the ford crossed by Childe Roland. The poet likens his misery to a terrible disease:

> A cankering worm whose work is slow,
> But gnaws the heart strings one by one,
> And drains the bosom's blood till the last drop be gone.

In similar vein the poems **"The Dying Enthusiast"** [**"The Dying Enthusiast to Hist Friend"**], **"Disaster," "A Broken-Hearted Lay"** and **"The One Mystery,"** as their titles suggest, all lament lost illusions and the pitiful plight of the protagonist.[42] In each poem, life for the poet is "all times dark with tragedy and woe," "care and pain build their lampless dwelling in the brain" and "the flood of life runs dark—dark clouds make lampless night around its shore." These poems are generally trite and all couched in the same highly derivative language.[43] The poems written between 1840 and Mangan's death, however, are more profound and better crafted. He no longer concentrates exclusively on his own misery. There lies behind the poems written in the years 1845-46 an acute awareness of the terrible effects of the Famine. This poetry is also more sophisticated and the subjects are to some degree removed from Mangan's own persona.

"Twenty Golden Years Ago" is set in Germany and given a cosmopolitan air by the inclusion of French and German phrases.[44] The German poet laments the loss of youth and happiness like the Mangan of the early poems but the general atmosphere of doom is relieved by the occasional burst of self-deprecatory humour. This poem is narrated in the third person and uses all the conventions of the popular ballad, devices which prevent its falling into trite self-indulgence. Mangan also uses the third person in **"The Nameless One."**[45] Here the protagonist does not move from society into isolation. Unlike the subjects of the 1832-33 poems who are forced into exile, the nameless one is already in the figurative world of his own choosing. His innocence is long lost and he has inhabited the bleak world of disillusion ever since. The outsider lives in the same state of misery as the poet of the early poems, only it is intensified:

> . . . this Nameless, condemned for years long
> To herd with demons from hell beneath,
> Saw things that made him, with groans and tears, long
> For even death.
>
> . . . now, amid wreck and sorrow,
> And want, and sickness, and houseless nights,
> He bides in calmness the silent morros,
> That no ray lights.

The speaker in **"The Groans of Despair"** is the poet, Mangan.[46] Here another distancing mechanism is employed, that of addressing the poem as a plea to an anonymous friend. The reader is not confronted directly, rather a conversation is overheard. The condition of the protagonist is as bad as ever; he appears to be locked in some kind of drug or alcohol-induced delirium:

> I see black dragons mount the sky,
> I see the earth yawn beneath my feet—
> I feel within the asp, the worm
> That will not sleep and cannot die,
> Fair though may show the winding sheet!
> I hear all night as though a storm,
> Hoarse voices calling, calling
> My name upon the wind—
> All omens monstrous and appaling,
> Affright my guilty mind.

Even death, courted in the early poems, is no longer a refuge for the sufferer:

> But for myself, I nightly die—
> In dreams I see that black gate open
> That shows my future doom to me
> In pictured forms that cannot lie.

One must assume that the suffering in this poem was exacerbated either by alcohol or opium. The question of whether Mangan took opium has long puzzled his critics. However, it is really quite irrelevant in this instance since, as Alethea Hayter has pointed out, opium could not stimulate a poetic gift that was not there, it merely compounded the poet's torment.[47] The lasting impression given by this poem is one of overwhelming guilt. His error has been such that it merits the curse of eternal damnation. It must be due, in part, to a sense of having dissipated his talents needlessly. Mangan claims that he wrote the poem **"Genius"** at the age of sixteen.[48] If this is indeed the case, then he was convinced at an early age that he had quite a considerable poetic gift. The disappointment he must have experienced as this great promise was stifled by external circumstances and his own weakness for alcohol would have been immense, almost Coleridgean in effect.

"Siberia" is by far the most effective of the personal poems written during this period.[49] In the poem the wasteland image takes over completely. The suffering poet, who was the all-pervading subject of the other poems, is referred to only once and in a very general way:

> And the exile there
> Is one with those;
> They are part and he is part,
> For the sands are in his heart,
> And the killing snows.

He is part of a multitude of fellow sufferers, exiles in the Siberian cold. He is no longer one set apart by an exclusive fate and a deeper sensibility. The wasteland dominates the entire poem. Siberia is cold, dark, blighted; full of death, frozen pain, barreness. The exile is not a quaestor passing through a freezing desert. He accepts the wasteland as his fate. It is within him.

The wastes of Siberia provide the ultimate metaphor, the most complete objective correlative for Mangan's personal misery. It is the very distance created between the anonymous exile and the suffering poet, Mangan, which makes **"Siberia"** such a powerful poem. The banished outcast has even less hope than Tennyson's sufferers trapped in a static wasteland: Mariana still hopes her lover will come, Tithonus and St Simeon Stylites can look forward to a release from their wasted bodies in death, and Ulysses at least talks about facing outward on his voyage. However, as in the **"Groans of Despair,"** death holds no hope for the Siberian exile. The frozen desert is living death.

It is not just in Mangan's personal poems that the motif of the wasteland is to be found. Whether by coincidence or design many of the Irish language poems Mangan translated contain images of a wasteland. Amongst his "original poems" there is one other striking evocation of a wasteland which, as it were bridges the divide between his personal condition and his translations. **"A Vision of Connaught in the Thirteenth Century"** presents the demise of the old Gaelic civilisation in apocalyptic terms.[50] There is a strong Coleridgean influence in this poem. It is resonant of "Kubla Khan" in its movement from scene to unconnected scene, in its evocation of a resplendent countryside, in the use of the word "khan" for leader, in the lack of explanation. Suddenly in the last two stanzas the land of plenty is turned to waste. The sky is dotted with blood and a skeleton is visible through the rays of an alien sun. The parallels with *The Ancient Mariner* are quite evident. The mariner speaks of a "Bloody sun" and in part three of the poem the sun shines through the skeleton of the "spectre woman." It is interesting that the wasteland here should be the complete opposite of the Siberian cold so favoured by Mangan. It is either a unique homage to the oriental poets he translated or an indication of how great a debt he owes to Coleridge; perhaps both. Here the sun is the dominant element instead of the cold darkness. It suggests desert heat as opposed to frozen winter. The blood-flecked sky carries with it connotations of violence and mutilation which contrast with the slow decaying process of the personal poems. Another difference, and a significant one, is that Mangan is exclusively concerned with the condition of his country in this poem.

The metaphor of **"A Vision of Connaught in the Thirteenth Century"** is quite an apt one for the violent upheaval that overtook Irish society thereafter. In the translations Mangan made from Irish language ballads however, the emphasis once again is on a solitary: the miserable retainer left isolated and cold in the wake of his lord's defeat. The wasteland in these poems is predictably cold and wet. There is none of the exotic imagery Mangan purloined to fashion his oriental impression of thirteenth century Connaught in these versions. It is evident however, that Mangan felt a close affinity with the lone bard from the number of translations which deal with this theme. The originals were composed out of bitter experience by poets within a Gaelic tradition who knew very little of European culture and most of them predate Romanticism by at least fifty years. For Mangan, who came upon these laments with a very deep awareness of certain aspects of European Romanticism, the work of translation was more an exercise in reinterpretation.

In **"O'Hussey's Ode to the Maguire"** the isolated retainer imagines his lord out on a cold bleak night with nobody to look after him.[51] He is an outlaw and the land through which he wanders is laid waste by winter, seen in its most awful guise in the terrible storm:

> The tempest-driven torrent deluges the mead,
> It overflows the low banks of the rivulets and ponds—
> The lawns and pasture grounds lie locked in icy bonds
> So that the cattle cannot feed.

In **"The Lamentation of MacLiag for Kincora"** the bard himself is the focus of the poem.[52] He draws attention to the desolation around him by asking repeatedly where all the warriors and their glories have gone. The palace of Kincora, the fulcrum of this vanished world, is now "that place whose beauty is fled" and MacLiag must live on in a barren reality. In the same way the ruins of Donegal Castle symbolise the Gaelic society that once was and what it has been reduced to:

Demolished lie thy towers and halls;
A dark, unsightly, earthen mound
Defaces the pure whiteness of thy shining walls,
And solitude doth girth thee round.[53]

The **"Lament over the Ruins of the Abbey of Teach Molaga"** has all the hallmarks of the crisis lyric including a very Romantic ruin for the poet to sigh over.[54] The depressed poet goes out at night and finds that the countryside he beholds complements his mood:

I wandered forth at night alone
Along the dreary, shingly, billow-beaten shore;
Sadness that night was in my bosom's core,
My soul and strength lay prone.

The moon sheds "funeral beams" on the scene and the wind howls mournfully. Then he comes upon the ruined abbey and uses the Shelleyan word "pile" to describe it. (He uses the same word to describe Donegal Castle). The ruined abbey conjures up a picture of a holy, idyllic past, a paradisiacal other world in stark contrast to the unsavoury present:

The unity of Work and Will
Blent hundreds into one: no jealousies or jars
Troubled their placid lives: their fortune
Had triumphed o'er all Ill!

In his translations from the Irish, Mangan concentrates on the elegiac nature of these ballads. In his versions the bards' natural and very practical lament for the only way of life they knew becomes suffused with a whole system of Romantic clichés and a weight of indefinable longing for a lost paradise which would have puzzled the pragmatic poets of the Irish eighteenth century and earlier. Unlike these Irish ballads, the poems Mangan translated from the German were written by contemporary poets, most of them in the vanguard of German Romanticism and already imbued with a Romantic sensibility. Mangan's selection is interesting for the number of lyrics which dwell on the transience of all things beautiful. The song **"Oh Strew the Way with Rosy Flowers"** is one such example.[55] The poet exhorts the reader to "taste the joys that God bestows" because he will soon be dead. The concern with transience, decay and death in these poems is mainly lyrical, as opposed to the elegiac nature of the ballads taken from the Irish tradition. **"Gone in the Wind"** emphasises over and over again the transience of all things human and the peculiar position of those who have been unfortunate on Earth: their misfortune makes them the only ones who will be happy in death.[56] **"Ichabod! Thy Glory Has Departed"** is perhaps the only real evocation of a wasteland in Mangan's German translations.[57] Because his beloved is dead the poet lives in a bleak world of darkness. He rides through "a dark, dark land by night" with the "Mantle of Age" on his shoulders, only death awaits him. These two lyrics are the most elegiac of Mangan's German "oversettings." That they are also quite oriental in flavour should not be surprising since Mangan went to German sources for most of his so-called oriental poems.[58]

The oriental pieces which deal with the themes of death, transience and decay are even more lyrical than their German counterparts. A great number of these are elegiac and, like the Irish poems, they feature a lone speaker remembering a time of glory: he contrasts it to his present condition and looks forward only to the grave. Perhaps the two best examples from the oriental work are **"The Lament"** (from the *Farewell Book of Ahi*) and **"The Howling Song of Al Mohara."**[59] The first poem has a lone isolated protagonist. He uses three similes to illustrate his condition: the cypress tree in a land which bears no fruit, the bee in a cold climate, and the abandoned boat drifting towards a deserted shore. All three similes depict wastelands, external deserts which correspond to the poet's inner desolation. Like all Mangan's protagonists he longs for death as a release. In **"The Howling Song of Al Mohara"** the singer is like any of Tennyson's wasting old men, his body decays but he cannot die. Like Tithonus and the Ancient Mariner he is being punished for a transgression. He lives on, his body wasted, in a wasteland:

I wander among graves where rot
The carcasses of leprous men;
Allah, Allah hu!
I house me in the dragon's den
Till evening darkens grove and grot;
Allah, Allah hu!
But bootless all!—Who penance dress
Must dree it his life through;
My heartwrung cry is still therefore
All night long, on my knees,
Evermore,
Allah, Allah hy!

Mangan's motley troop of old men, deserted retainers, forsaken lovers and failed Byronic poets have one important thing in common: their absolute adoration of the god of misery. It is their religion to be desolate and depressed. The forsaken lover of the early original poems deliberately seeks out a place where he can be free to wallow in his own unhappiness, without it appears, giving his love affair a reasonable chance. The failed genius of the later poems is as addicted to his misfortune as to any other drug. The personae of the German and oriental poems are preoccupied with melancholy thoughts of the brevity of life and of happiness, and the orientals also mourn a lost world in common with their Irish brethren. Although these characters see their only chance of relief from pain in death, more often than not death itself is an unsatisfactory solution. In **"Siberia"** death will not bring a respite, only the eternal suffering of damnation. **"Siberia"** is Mangan's best poem and must be accepted as his definitive vision of the wasteland. In this poem, death ceases to be the object of the outcast's longing: suffering is its own end and the only end for the exile.

IV

It is obvious from this examination of Romantic stereotypes in Mangan's work that he tried very earnestly to assimilate Romanticism into his work and that he tried himself to be the very embodiment of a Romantic poet. In this he is no different from the minor English Romantics who are his undoubted spiritual mates. Mangan is different however, in that he was Irish, practically never left Dublin, hardly knew any other poets in Ireland let alone English Romantics and never sent any of his work to England. He is also different in that his need to imitate led him to plagiarism of a much more concrete sort than any of the minor Romantics were guilty of. At best he took from other poets' work and fashioned what now count as outstanding originals, such as **"My Dark Rosaleen"**; at worst he failed to grasp the essentials of the conventions within which he worked. It is hardly necessary to add that he failed more often than not. Unfortunately most of his personal poetry lapses into whinging self-pity and his venture into the realm of the Gothic horror story is quite naive.

More than anything else it is Mangan's religious orthodoxy which prevents him being admitted to the inner circle of Romanticism. Because of his innocence and childlike belief he could never have fathomed the darker depths of Romanticism though he assumed its outward trappings. His Gothic stories become pastiche, rescued from utter failure by mischievous humour; his attempts at love poetry too are occasionally saved by the distancing effect of irony, while a spark of sincere but inconstant patriotism makes **"My Dark Rosaleen"** great. Only in his employment of the wasteland theme does he achieve something approaching a personal interpretation of one of the Romantic stereotypes. Significantly this work is written out of a genuine experience of actual bodily misery. The Mangan who succeeds at last in **"Siberia"** was himself "old and hoary at thirty-nine" because of a tragic commitment to a Romanticism he never fully understood.

Notes

1. Jacques Chuto, "Rhetorique et Authenticité chez J. C. Mangan," Unpublished paper delivered to the Congrès de la S.A.E.S. (Tours 1977), quoted in David C. Lloyd, "Great Gaps in Irish Song: James Clarence Mangan and the Ideology of the Nationalist Ballad," *Irish University Review,* Autumn 1984, pp. 182-183.
2. D. J. O'Donoghue, *The Prose Writings of James Clarence Mangan* (Dublin: M. H. Gill & Son, 1904), pp. 199-299.
3. James Kilroy, ed., *The Autobiography of James Clarence Mangan* (Dublin: The Dolman Press, 1968); and see also "Sketches and Reminiscences of Irish Writers: No. 10, James Clarence Mangan," *The Irishman* New Series, No. 2, (7 Aug. 1850), pp. 27-28.
4. Anthony Cronin, *Heritage Now* (Dublin: Brandon, 1982), pp. 47-50.
5. Mario Praz, *The Romantic Agony* (London: Oxford University Press, 1933).
6. Mario Praz, *The Gothic Novels* (Penguin English Library, 1968), p. 9.
7. *The Romantic Agony,* p. 197.
8. *The Prose Writings of James Clarence Mangan,* p. vii.
9. Ibid., pp. 1-98.
10. Ibid., p. 134.
11. James Clarence Mangan, *Poets and Poetry of Munster* (Dublin: James Duffy, 1925), Preface.
12. Henry J. Donaghy, *James Clarence Mangan* (New York: Twayne, 1974), pp. 20, 99, 102.
13. M. Whitcomb Hess, "James Clarence Mangan: A Story of Triumph," *Catholic World,* CLXIX, (June 1949), pp. 185-190.
14. Patrick Diskin, "The Poetry of James Clarence Mangan," *University Review,* 2, No. 1, (n.d.) pp. 22-23.
15. James Kilroy, *James Clarence Mangan* (Lewisburgh: Bucknell University Press, 1970), p. 22.
16. Patrick Diskin, op. cit., p. 22.
17. Marie Bonaparte, *The Life and Works of Edgar Allan Poe* (London: Imago, 1949), pp. 222-223.
18. Edgar Allan Poe, *The Poems of Edgar Allan Poe* (London: Dent, 1927), pp. 20, 88.
19. Ibid., p. 83.
20. Ibid., p. 1.
21. Sir Charles Gavan Duffy, "Personal Memoirs of James Clarence Mangan," *Dublin Review,* CXLII (1908), pp. 285-286.
22. James Clarence Mangan, "My Transformation—A Wonderful Tale," *The Dublin Satirist,* (Oct. 19, 1833).
23. D. J. O'Donoghue, *The Life and Writings of James Clarence Mangan* (Dublin: M. H. Gill, 1897), p. 52.
24. Ibid.
25. Ibid., p. 63.
26. Thomas Moore, ed., *Works of Lord Byron,* Vol. X (London: Murray, 1843), p. 32.
27. D. J. O'Donoghue, ed., *The Poems of James Clarence Mangan* (Dublin: M. H. Gill, 1910), p. 32. All subsequent quotations from the poems are from this edition and page references will be given in the text parenthetically.

28. Ibid., p. 133.
29. Ibid.
30. Ibid., p. 158.
31. Ibid., p. 65.
32. Ibid., p. 280.
33. Ibid.
34. Ibid., pp. 222, 216.
35. Ibid., p. 223.
36. Ibid., p. 229.
37. Ibid., p. 322.
38. Ibid., p. 223.
39. Padraic Colum, "James Clarence Mangan," *Dublin Magazine,* VIII, No. 2 (1933), p. 33.
40. Edward Dowden, *The Poetical Works of Percy Bysshe Shelley* (London: Macmillan, 1908), p. 233.
41. *The Poems,* p. 137.
42. Ibid., pp. 119, 127, 124, 122.
43. Patrick Diskin, p. 22.
44. *The Poems,* p. 142.
45. Ibid., p. 120.
46. Ibid., p. 125.
47. Alethea Hayter, *Opium and the Romantic Imagination* (London: Faber and Faber, 1968), p. 46.
48. *The Autobiography,* pp. 20-21.
49. *The Poems,* p. 151.
50. Ibid., p. 94.
51. Ibid., p. 8.
52. Ibid., p. 49.
53. Ibid., p. 78.
54. Ibid., p. 24.
55. Ibid., p. 262.
56. Ibid., p. 249.
57. Ibid., p. 260.
58. Jacques Chuto, "The Sources of James Clarence Mangan's Oriental Writings," *Notes and Queries,* 29, No.3 (June 1982), pp. 224-228.
59. *The Poems,* pp. 124, 207.

Melissa Fegan (essay date 2005)

SOURCE: Fegan, Melissa. "'Like a Wail from the Tomb, / But of World-Waking Power': James Clarence Mangan's 'A Vision: A.D. 1848,' the Great Famine, and the Young Ireland Rising." *1848: The Year the World Turned?* Ed. Kay Boardman and Christine Kinealy. Newcastle upon Tyne: Cambridge Scholars, 2007. 210-24. Print.

[In the following essay, originally presented at a conference in 2005, Fegan discusses Mangan's many famine-related poems in relation to his nationalism, highlighting connections between the poet's growing political awareness and his apocalyptic and prophetic poetry. Fegan stresses Mangan's consciousness of his shortcomings as a revolutionary—and its expression in his poems—but also draws attention to the esteem in which Mangan was held by his contemporaries and later writers, including James Joyce.]

On 1 January 1848, the *Nation,* the leading Dublin nationalist newspaper, reviewed the horrors of 1847, the second full year of the Great Famine, which was to kill more than a million people. The *Nation* spoke of 'massacres,' 'the temporary prostration of the Irish people before its executioner, like a victim on the scaffold,' and the Coercion Bill (9). The one bright light, it continued, had been the growth of national feeling, both among the higher classes, and among Young Irelanders, who had broken away from O'Connell's Repeal movement and founded the Irish Confederation. The article was accompanied by a poem, **'A Voice of Encouragement: A New Year's Lay,'** by one of the *Nation*'s stalwarts, James Clarence Mangan. It would be difficult to imagine a less encouraging poem, or indeed one less like a lay. The second stanza outlines the horrors of the present:

Friends! the gloom in the land, in our once bright land,
grows deeper.
Suffering, even to Death in its horriblest form, aboundeth;
Through our black harvestless fields the peasant's faint
wail resoundeth.
Hark to it even now! The nightmare-oppressed sleeper
Gasping and struggling for life beneath his hideous
bestrider,
Seeth not, dreeth not, sight or terror more fearful or
ghastly
Than that poor paralysed slave!

(9-15)

Even so, things are about to get worse; the Trustful and Firm, Sage and Saintly, Patriots, Orators and Prophets of Ireland have lost faith, and sunk into degradation and abasement. Denied progress by centuries of colonization, the Irish are in fact degenerating:

Slavery debases the soul, yea reverses its primal nature.
Long were our fathers bowed to the earth by fetters of
iron—
And, alas! WE inherit the failings and ills that environ
Slaves like a dungeon-wall, and dwarf their natural
stature.

(49-52)

The speaker calls on his compatriots to reverse the backward slide: 'Follow your destiny up!' (41). By working, writing and preaching they can redeem their countrymen. But the final stanza is ominous and apocalyptic:

Omen-full, arched with gloom, and laden with many a presage,
Many a portent of woe, looms the Impending Era.
Not, as of old, by Comet-sword, Gorgon, or ghastly Chimera,
Scarcely by Lightning and Thunder, Heaven to-day sends its message.
Into the secret heart—down through the caves of the spirit,
Pierces the silent Shaft—sinks the invisible Token—
Cloaked in the Hall the Envoy stands, his mission unspoken,
While the pale banquetless guests await in trembling to hear it.

(65-72)

In many ways **'A Voice of Encouragement'** is typical of Mangan's poems of exhortation in the *Nation.* He rarely foresees success for his friends and compatriots; instead, they must be prepared to fulfil their predestined role as sacrificial victims to pave the way for possible success in a future generation of Irish nationalists. In **'The Warning Voice,'** published in the *Nation* in February 1846, he forecasts a coming era of Knowledge and Peace, but warns the present generation:

On *you* its beams glow not—
For *you* its flowers blow not!
You cannot rejoice in its light,
But in darkness and suffering instead
You go down to the place of the Dead!
To *this* generation,
The stormy commotion,
And foam of the Popular Ocean,
The struggle of class against class;
The Dearth and the Sadness,
The Sword and the War-vest;
To the *next,* the Repose and the Gladness,
"The sea of clear glass,"
And the rich Golden Harvest!

(61-75)

The next generation will achieve the 'sea of clear glass' of the Book of Revelation: 'and I saw as it were a sea of glass mingled with fire: and them that had gotten the victory over the beast, and over his image, and over his mark, and over the number of his name, stand on the sea of glass' (Rev. 15:2). But this generation must accept merely the 'foam of the Popular Ocean,' do their duty and die.

'A Voice of Encouragement' also acknowledges Mangan's own position on the periphery of the struggle for liberty. In the first stanza he admits his unfitness for the role of rebel:

You, young men, would a man unworthy to rank in your number,
Yet with a heart that bleeds for his country's wrongs and affliction,
Fain raise a Voice to in Song, albeit his music and diction
Rather be fitted, alas! to lull to, than startle from, slumber.

(5-8)

His desire to play a part, and very real sense of pain at the horrors he had witnessed over the years of Famine, are balanced against the realisation that the 'young men' of Young Ireland outrank him. In the autobiographical **'The Nameless One,'** published posthumously but written in 1848, Mangan describes himself as 'Old and hoary / At thirty-nine' (49-50); he was in fact forty-five, reflecting his consistent excision of six years from his age. Three years earlier he wrote to James McGlashan, editor of the *Dublin University Magazine*: 'I suppose, *en passant,* that you imagine me an old man. I am 36 years of age in point of time' (**'Correspondence'** 277). Mangan's biographer, Ellen Shannon-Mangan, has argued that the loss of six years from his age was due to a suppressed childhood trauma (12), but it is clearly also related to the uncomfortable proximity of the virile youths of Young Ireland. His own physical weakness is often foregrounded in poems in which he calls on the Youth of Ireland to rise: in **'For Soul and Country,'** published in 1849, he cries:

My countrymen! my words are weak,
My health is gone, my soul is dark,
My heart is chill—.

(49-51)

Any role he could play was going to be limited.

Mangan knew he was an unlikely rebel. While some of his earliest poems were published in the *Comet,* founded as part of the nationalist anti-tithe campaign, this was in part a matter of necessity, given how few publishing opportunities were available, and Mangan's contributions tended to be comic charades and enigmas. In the 1830s and 1840s he worked for some of the bastions of the Union in Ireland: the *Dublin University Magazine,* Trinity College Dublin, and the Ordnance Survey. In 1832 the twenty-nine year old Mangan wrote a long letter to his friend Tynan, meditating on his political apathy:

> [M]y conclusion is this: that political liberty is not worth a bag of chaff. [. . .] If I were to-morrow to enter into possession of all the advantages that the best of good governments have been able to bestow, I would feel precisely as an individual would, who, suffering under a complication of maladies, gout, palsy, stone, phythisis, scrofula, cancer, dropsy, cholic, catarrh, epilepsy, erysipelas, &c. &c. should find himself one morning freed from a little wen upon his thumb. [. . .] I should myself like a revolution better than you think, especially if it produced a general transfer of property and I had any prospect of robbing somebody, for my finances are too low for my ideas, which are of the princeliest. A revolution, besides, creates an extensive hubbub, a thing I am occasionally partial to, and exceedingly so whenever I see any likelihood of making anything by it.

(**'Correspondence'** 246-8)

At this stage, he can see nothing altruistic in revolution; it is merely another form of self-absorption: 'I think the man who labours to earn the price of a pair of boots for himself proportionally entitled to as many encomiums as the man who kills other people that he may procure freedom for himself. Depend upon it that Self is at the bottom of every struggle' (245). In 1840 he wrote to Charles Gavan Duffy, then editor of the Belfast *Vindicator,* later editor of *The Nation* and one of the leaders of Young Ireland: 'Don't ask me for political articles just now. I have had no experience in that *genre d'écrire* and I should infallibly blunder' (**'Correspondence'** 258). Duffy later commented: 'At this time he knew nothing of politics and cared nothing for them, and he averted his eyes from Irish history as from a painful and humiliating spectacle' ('Personal Memories' 286).

If Mangan was clear about his lack of credentials for rebel status, so were his friends and colleagues. The son of a failed grocer, Mangan was forced to leave school at fifteen in order to support his parents and brothers by working as a clerk; he was a prodigious auto-didact, but did not share the social backgrounds of the Young Irelanders, many of whom were lawyers and doctors moonlighting as poets and journalists. Mangan was also an eccentric figure. Duffy recalled: 'When he emerged into daylight, he was dressed in a blue cloak, midsummer or midwinter, and a hat of fantastic shape, under which golden hair, as fine and silky as a woman's, hung in unkempt tangles, and deep blue eyes lighted a face as colourless as parchment. He looked like the spectre of some German romance rather than a living creature' ('Personal Memories' 278). John Mitchel, who worked alongside Duffy in *The Nation,* before seceding to found the *United Irishman,* described his first encounter with Mangan in Trinity College Library:

> It was an unearthly and ghostly figure, in a brown garment; the same garment (to all appearance) which lasted till the day of his death. The blanched hair was totally unkempt; the corpse-like features still as marble; a large book was in his arms, and all his soul was in the book. I had never heard of Clarence Mangan before, and knew not for what he was celebrated; whether as a magician, a poet, or a murderer; yet took a volume and spread it on a table, not to read, but with pretence of reading to gaze on the spectral creature upon the ladder.
>
> (xxxiv-xxxv)

Added to his weird appearance was his undoubted alcoholism and (probably untrue) rumours that he was addicted to opium; Mitchel cruelly commented: 'There were [. . .] two Mangans; one well known to the Muses, the other to the police; one soared through the empyrean and sought the stars—the other lay too often in gutters of Peter Street and Bride Street' (xxxv). While Duffy disputed this, saying 'he was never at any period of his life in the hands of the police,' Mangan's appearance and intemperance clearly counted against him with the nationalist cause; when he applied for membership of the newly-formed Irish Confederation in 1847 Duffy refused: 'he could not be of the slightest use to the Confederation; he had none of the qualities that make a man at home in a political assembly; he was shy, timid, and eccentric, always clothed in a manner which excited curiosity and perhaps ridicule' ('Personal Memories' 288, 293). While Mangan could do the Irish Confederation no good, Duffy argued, he could do himself immeasurable wrong, and needed to be protected against himself: 'Self-sacrifice is natural and proper in a revolutionary movement, but one would scarcely think pushing a woman or a child into the fire was a permissible sacrifice' (293). Mangan was not only not accepted as one of the virile young revolutionaries, he was seen as equivalent to a woman or a child, to be kept in safety while the fire of revolution spread.

The very fact that Mangan put himself forward for membership of the Irish Confederation shows how far his political awareness had developed; the man who in 1832 had joked that 'political liberty was not worth a bag of chaff' was attempting to align himself with the future leaders of an uprising. The major turning point was, of course, the start of the Famine in 1845; by February 1846 Mangan was warning Duffy: 'we are on the verge of the most tremendous calamity of ancient times or modern' (**'Correspondence'** 259). If he had averted his gaze from Irish history and politics before, he could not do so now, and he began to make increasingly strident statements about his commitment to Irish liberty. In April 1846, he wrote to Duffy of 'my determination to devote myself almost exclusively to the interests of my country in future' (261); the 'almost exclusively' harks back to his previous stance of political apathy. But by 1847 he was declaring—in the *Dublin University Magazine*—that: 'Slender as our talents are, we have become exceedingly desirous to dedicate them henceforward exclusively to the service of our country' (**'Anthologia Hibernica'** [**'Anthologia Hibernica 1'**] 160); his now exclusive dedication, publicly expressed in a conservative unionist publication, says much both about how far Mangan has moved politically, and how much national feeling had penetrated unionist strongholds as a result of the Famine. By June 1847, Mangan was describing himself as a 'patriot':

> I will begin in earnest to labour for my country henceforward, and [. . .] come weal or woe, life or death, glory or shame, the triumphal chariot or the gallows, I will adhere to the fortunes of my fellow patriots. And I invoke the vengeance of hell upon me if I ever prove false to this promise!
>
> (**'Correspondence'** 269)

But self was to an extent at the bottom of this struggle too. The onset of Famine worsened Mangan's already precarious social position. As an urban intellectual, he did not face the immediate dire straits of the potato-reliant rural peasant, but his alcoholism and his reticence about pressing for payment for his poems and translations, combined with responsibility for his elderly mother and often unemployed brother, left him frequently distressed. In April 1846 he asked Duffy for five pounds, adding: 'Could you see my condition at this moment—could you look into my heart and read my anxiety, my anguish—and above all could you understand the causes of these, you would pity me' (**'Correspondence'** 261). He told John O'Daly in late 1847: 'you will save me from a doom that I dread to contemplate. I shall be obliged to leave my lodgings, and perhaps will die in the streets. [...] If you can get me those ten shillings they will prove my salvation' (271-2). In both cases he was not begging, but asking for advance payment, and his appeals reflect the terrible anticipations he was labouring under.

This apprehension of doom and dread, apparent in the final stanza of **'A Voice of Encouragement,'** with its omens and portents, its mysterious Envoy (identified in an earlier poem, **'The Two Envoys,'** as Death) and 'pale banquetless guests,' while obviously a response to the horrors Mangan was witnessing in the Famine, was in part temperamental. As a child he felt 'an indescribable feeling of something terrible' lurking in his future, and he was drawn to 'the wonderful and terrible in art, nature and society. Descriptions of battles and histories of revolutions; accounts of earthquakes, inundations and tempests [...] possessed a charm for me which I could neither resist nor explain' (**'Autobiography'** 226, 236). The conjunction of time and temperament led Mangan to become 'the Banshee of the famine' (O'Donoghue 234) for the *Nation,* contributing apocalyptic visions of blight and bloodshed. Mangan was one of the first Irish writers to insist on the uniqueness of the Famine. The failure of the potato crop was not unusual; Roy Foster notes there were fourteen partial or complete failures between 1816-1842 (320). In retrospect, poems like **'The Warning Voice'** and **'The Peal of Another Trumpet'** seemed terrifyingly prescient, and Mangan began to enjoy a reputation as a visionary: an editorial note attached to 'Ireland's Resurrection,' published in the *Nation* on 30 October 1847, comments: 'the poet, who is a true *Vates,* reads the aspect of coming events, still blank to common men' (888). Perhaps humiliated by being denied membership of the Confederation, it is unsurprising that Mangan embraced his prophet status, referring to himself proudly in **'Irish National Hymn'** in May 1848 as: '*one whom some have called a Seer*' (60).

Many of Mangan's poems employ visions and dreams to explain the Famine, to urge for action, or to obliquely criticise the government. **'A Vision of Connaught in the Thirteenth Century,'** published in the *Nation* in July 1846, contrasts the dearth of food in the present with the abundance Ireland enjoyed under Cáthal Mór. Mangan notes: 'The Irish and Oriental poets both agree in attributing favorable or unfavorable weather and abundant or deficient harvests to the good or bad qualities of the reigning monarch. What the character of Cahal was will be seen below' (455); the character of Queen Victoria, he implies, can equally be seen in the sufferings of her Irish subjects. **'The Funerals,'** published in the *Irishman* in March 1849, recounts a recurring nightmare that haunts the speaker for ten years:

> A vision of dim FUNERALS that passed
> In troubled sleep before my sight,
> With dirges and deep wails of woe,
> That never died upon the blast!
>
> (3-6)

Each funeral hearse is attended by a crowd of skeletons, marching first towards the West, then the South—the areas of Ireland worst affected by the Famine. The Famine is never explicitly referred to, but is the obvious fulfilment of the speaker's dark anticipations of the coming Apocalypse: 'it gives / Dread witness of a JUDGEMENT HOUR!' (59-60).

Mangan was not alone in his use of visionary and apocalyptic imagery; the Famine answered or inspired millenarian feeling in many observers. Richard D'Alton Williams's 'The Vision: A National Ode' foresees the destruction of the oppressor nation (clearly England), and 'A Prophecy' sees the tyrant crushed and dragged to hell (18). Jane Francesca Elgee, the future mother of Oscar Wilde, who wrote for the *Nation* as 'Speranza,' predicted in 'The Famine Year' that the starving would triumph over their oppressors on the Day of Judgment:

> Now is your hour of pleasure—bask ye in the world's
> caress;
> But our whitening bones against ye will rise as witnesses,
> From the cabins and the ditches, in their charred,
> uncoffin'd masses,
> For the Angel of the Trumpet will know them when he
> passes.
> A ghastly, spectral army, before the great God we'll stand,
> And arraign ye as our murderers, the spoilers of our land.
>
> (43-8)

More widely, this apocalyptic interest reflects a pervasive providentialist reading of the Famine as the wrath of God. For Hugh McNeile, Canon of Chester, it was punishment for Irishmen's perverse clinging to Roman Catholicism and the government's grant to Maynooth seminary: 'the famine and pestilence which are at present sweeping thousands of our fellow-subjects into untimely graves, are punishments righteously inflicted by the hand of God for the sins of the nation' (19). Peter Gray has argued that providentialism was a powerful factor in the British government's relief policy: 'official conceptions of the famine in Ireland were shaped by established linguistic systems, such as providentialism' (viii). Charles Trevelyan, Chief Secretary to the Treasury, declared of the Famine: 'on this, as on many other occasions, Supreme Wisdom has educed permanent good out of transient evil' (89). The *Nation* also saw the blight as providential, suggesting it was a punishment for Irishmen's abdication of nationality, internal wrangling and acquiescence in slavery, but argued that the Famine itself was man-made: 'The potato blight is the dispensation of Providence—the famine is the work of a foreign Government' (30 Jan. 1847, 265).

'A Vision: A. D. 1848' is one of the most striking of Mangan's apocalyptic Famine poems. Mangan looks to both past and future, re-reading events since 1839 as predestined and necessary for Ireland's eventual freedom. He is also with this poem staking his meagre political capital in the prospect of a violent uprising. At the end of 1847, John Mitchel had broken with the *Nation* and Young Ireland, and on 12 February 1848 he published the first issue of the *United Irishman.* Mangan's **'A Vision: A. D. 1848'** appeared on 26 February, in the third issue. He was allying himself openly with the man the *Times* described as: 'the most devoted disciple of bloodshed and blunderbusses' (14 Feb. 1848, 8).

The dreamer of **'A Vision: A. D. 1848'** is wandering in 'the Valley of Dream,' prey to uncontrollable thoughts that sweep 'The lone paths of the soul' (2, 7). His situation echoes Dante's in the opening of *Inferno*:

> Half way along the road we have to go,
> I found myself obscured in a great forest,
> Bewildered, and I knew I had lost the way.
>
> (Canto I: 1-3)

This dreamer's guide is not Virgil, but a mysterious Voice, like the 'great voice, as of a trumpet' of Revelation 1:10:

> In that spectralest hour,
> In that Valley of Gloom,
> Fell a Voice on mine ear,
> Like a wail from the tomb,
> Or that dread cry which Fear
> Gives our Angels of Doom,
> But of world-waking power.
>
> (11-17)

Mangan identified the 'Angels of Doom' in a note as 'The Banshees' (274), and later refers to the Voice as '*the Oracle,*' merging Revelation with classical and Irish mythology. The banshee, from the Irish 'bean sídhe,' woman of the fairies, is a portentous figure whose cry of lamentation foretells an approaching death. But this Voice is not merely sounding the alert; it is 'Like a wail from the tomb / [. . .] / But of world-waking power (14, 17), implying its role is to rouse not just Irish nationalists, but the whole world in fury at the fate of Ireland. The gender of the Voice is not disclosed—it is referred to as 'it' throughout—but the banshee simile, and the Voice's role in provoking a response in dreamer and reader, suggest that Mangan may have been modelling his vision poem on the traditional *aisling,* a form particularly prevalent in eighteenth-century Irish political poetry, in which the speaker meets a lovely but sorrowful woman, revealed in the end as the incarnation of Ireland, who laments her woes and looks forward to the return of her rightful husband (Charles Stuart) with the help of brave Irishmen like the speaker. Mangan's translation of Egan O'Rahilly's aisling 'Gile na gile' (**"The Brightest of the Bright"**), ends:

> Oh, my misery, my woe, my sorrow and my anguish,
> My bitter source of dolor is evermore that she
> The Loveliest of the Lovely should thus be left to languish
> Amid a ruffian horde till the Heroes cross the sea.
>
> (33-36)

Mangan had used this form already in his most famous poem, **'Dark Rosaleen,'** a version of the Irish 'Roisin Dubh,' which he noted was: 'an allegorical address [. . .] to Ireland' (450), and he was translating several aislingí, including Timothy O'Sullivan's 'Sighile ni Ghadharadh,' Conor O'Riordan's 'Vision,' and several versions of 'Moirin ni Chuillionnain,' for John O'Daly's *The Poets and Poetry of Munster,* which would be published after Mangan's death. But if **'A Vision: A. D. 1848'** is an aisling, the Voice is not the lovely, vulnerable, erotically charged yet unattainable figure of tradition, but a dominant, omniscient and awe-inspiring invisible presence, reminiscent of the cloaked Envoy of **'A Voice of Encouragement'**—making the dreamer one of the 'pale banquetless guests' trembling with anticipation. While the Envoy's mission is 'unspoken,' the identification of the Voice as 'the Oracle' reflects not just its prophetic status, but also the etymology of 'oracle' from *orare,* speak. The poem's purpose is to make audible the message of Heaven left silent in **'A Voice of Encouragement.'**

The Oracle explains to the dreamer that the tumultuous events of the last ten years have been a providential preparation for Irish freedom. The first stage is 'The Anointing: 1839-1842'; the Irish had been drowning their sorrows and shame in 'the soul-killing cup' (22) until God raised a Man to break the 'red bowl' (34) and free their minds. Mangan thus begins his prophecy of Irish freedom with the temperance campaigner Father Theobald Mathew, whose success in persuading more than five million people—more than half the population—to sign his total abstinence pledge boosted nationalist leaders' belief that Irishmen had the self-discipline necessary for a sustained attempt for Repeal of the Union; Daniel O'Connell took the pledge himself in 1840. Mangan did not, at least in 1840, later telling his friend Fr Meehan that he 'could not be induced to take the pledge, simply because he doubted his ability to keep it' (qtd. in Shannon-Mangan 232). He later took, and broke the pledge several times, and was racked by guilt at this, and the disapproval of his nationalist friends. In June 1847, he sent a letter to Duffy, asking him to circulate it among his literary friends, promising: 'to live soberly, abstemiously, and regularly in all respects [. . .] I will constantly advocate the cause of Temperance—the interests of Knowledge—and the duties of Patriotism' (**'Correspondence'** 269).

Temperance and Patriotism were inherently linked for him—after all his lack of temperance was to exclude him from the Confederation. Undoubtedly aware that he could not keep this promise, Duffy did not circulate the letter.

The second phase of Irish freedom was 'The Muster: 1842-1845,' O'Connell's campaign for Repeal and his Monster Meetings. There had been a great deal of antipathy between O'Connell's Repeal Association and Young Ireland, and Mangan himself had referred to O'Connell as a 'shuffling sneaker' in a letter to Duffy in July 1846 (265). But O'Connell had died in May 1847; Mangan contemplated writing an elegy on the Liberator for the *Nation,* and called him: 'as great a prophet as a politician' (**'Correspondence'** 273). O'Connell is canonized in the poem as a saint of the coming struggle.

A more striking revision emerges in the third phase, 'The Famine 1845-1848.' The year 1847 had been the worst year of the Famine, and deaths were to continue into the next decade, yet Mangan in February 1848 was asserting that it would end that year. Furthermore, the Famine emerges not as a cataclysmic avoidable tragedy, but as a necessary purgation of 'The Weak Ones' before the coming battle:

> For that scene must behold
> But stern spirits and bold,
> When the Lord takes the field.
> Therefore Famine first came
> And then Pestilence came,
> And careered through the land
> Like twin giants of Flame—
> And men's hearts were updried,
> And a seventh of that Band,
> Who are still to be tried,
> Fell in death, mute, unmanned,
> And with names writ in sand.
> There fell One for each Seven—
> Pray thou peace for their souls
> In the homesteads of Heaven!
>
> (68-82)

By this stark account, more than a million people must die, or exchange their hovels for the 'homesteads of Heaven,' in order that the strong can remain and prevail; the Famine is not just a providential punishment, but a necessary forerunner of the apocalypse. Mangan may also have been reflecting on a *Nation* leading article published the previous month:

> We stand thus: In this accursed Imperial famine we have lost, or will lose a million of our brave people. But we must not lose a whole generation. The seven millions must be saved to avenge the one, and to redeem the island out of bondage and this valley of the shadow of death, in which it now sits sorrowing.
>
> (22 Jan. 1848, 56)

The death-knell for the Famine victims mutates at the end of this section into 'an omenful peal' (86) of 'the Tocsin of War!' (90). The dismissal of Famine victims as 'The Weak Ones' may seem callous, but not compared to contemporary providentialist rhetoric, or the pronouncements of later nationalists; the Land League leader Michael Davitt, born in 1846, declared: 'as the peasants had chosen to die like sheep rather than retain that food in a fight for life, to live or die like men, their loss to the Irish nation need not occasion many pangs of racial regret' (66). Mangan is prepared to sacrifice 'The Weak Ones,' but only because he recognises he is one of them.

The Oracle falls silent in 1848; rather than predicting the future, it has exhumed the past, leaving the dreamer to interpret the omens and signs of the coming apocalypse. 'The End,' dated '1848-185*' is ambiguous: it is certainly not going to happen this year—the end will take place some time in the 1850s; and it is not exactly clear what the end will be: the freedom of Ireland, heralded by 'A noise like fierce cheers, / Blent with clashings of swords' (114-5); or the end of the world, 'lightnings and thunders, / As ye read of in John's / Revelation of Wonders' (102-4)? The dreamer wakes to the sound of 'The bell booming Three' (111), and cannot tell.

If Mangan could not prophesize what 1848 would bring for Ireland, he could foresee what would come of his alliance with Mitchel and the *United Irishman.* The February Revolution in France had released Mitchel into militancy; Duffy peevishly commented: 'he demeaned himself as if the French Revolution and the new opportunities it furnished were his personal achievements' (*My Life* 261). From now on Mitchel was on a collision course with the government, telling his readers on 4 March: 'Above all, let the man amongst you who has no gun, *sell his garment, and buy one*' (*United Irishman* 4 Mar. 1848 56). On 25 March 1848, a letter from Mangan to Mitchel was published in the *United Irishman*:

> There is a rumour in circulation, that the government intend to commence a prosecution against you. Insignificant an individual as I am, and unimportant to society as my political opinions may be, I, nevertheless, owe it, not merely to the kindness you have shown me, but to the cause of my country, to assure you that I thoroughly sympathize with your sentiments, that I identify my views of public affairs with yours, and that I am prepared to go all lengths with you and your intrepid friend, Devin Reilly, for the achievement of our national independence.
>
> (**'Correspondence'** 168)

It was a brave, if rather futile act; Mangan was in no condition to 'to go all lengths' for national independence; the effects of the Famine, his alcoholism, and haphazard lifestyle had told on his physical and mental health, and he was admitted to St Vincent's Hospital in May 1848, writing ruefully to McGlashan: 'Here it is I am at last—here, where I shall have ample time for repentance and reflection, for I cannot probably leave for some months, and during all that time I shall be rigorously denied everything in the shape of stimulants' (**'Correspondence'** 285). Mitchel was characteristically derogatory about Mangan's support: 'Welcome as the letter was, and not a little touching as coming from him the truth of history compels me to declare that it did not intimidate the British Government much' (xxxviii). Yet he published it, which suggests either respect for Mangan's opinion, or Mitchel's complete isolation. On 13 May, Mitchel was arrested, convicted of treason-felony by a packed jury, and on 27 May transported. Young Ireland's bravado was crushed in an abortive rising in July, ridiculed ever since as 'the Battle of Widow McCormick's cabbage-patch.' Several of Mangan's fellow poets had their parts to play in the rebellion: Richard D'Alton Williams was tried for treason-felony for his writings in the *Irish Tribune* in 1848; Jane Francesca Elgee (Speranza), edited *The Nation* while Duffy was imprisoned, telling its readers: 'One instant to take breath, and then a rising; a rush, a charge from north, south, east, and west upon the English garrison, *and the land is ours*' (*Jacta Alea Est* 488); Thomas D'Arcy McGee had to flee the country disguised as a priest to avoid capture.

There was never any question of arresting Mangan, who had discharged himself from hospital in June, unable to cope with the doctors' refusal of stimulants. He was in Richmond Surgical Hospital a few days later, having (probably while drunk) fallen the previous night fifteen feet into the foundations of a house (Shannon-Mangan 388-9). Mangan may not have had a direct role in the failed rising, but it sealed his fate nonetheless. His friends and employers on nationalist newspapers like the *Nation, United Irishman* and *Irishman* were transported, in prison or in hiding, and the newspapers themselves were suppressed; without anyone to turn to Mangan went into speedy decline. He wrote to the Irish scholar James Hardiman on 4 December to ask for a loan of £1: 'It is a positive fact that there is not, at this juncture in my affairs, a single soul in Dublin to whom I could make a similar application' (**'Correspondence'** 272). John O'Donovan, Mangan's former colleague on the Ordnance Survey, told Hardiman: 'I never saw any man in such a state of destitution [. . .] His present condition is a scandal to Ireland starving as it is, and a disgrace to literature and to human nature' (qtd. in Shannon-Mangan 397). In January 1849, the state prisoners in Kilmainham gaol, including Mangan's friend, the poet Joseph Brenan, subscribed £3 10s for Mangan—'as much as they (thanks to their paternal government) can afford'—stating their belief that he was 'a man of the highest and purest genius' (qtd. in Shannon-Mangan 402). In May 1849 he contracted cholera; he was discovered by William Wilde, future father of Oscar, in a garret in Bride Street and brought to the Meath Hospital, where he died on 20 June. He was forty-six. In spite of his sufferings, and the disasters of 1848, his political zeal—or at least his conviction in a providential outcome—remained intact until the last. A few days before he died, his poem **'The Famine'** appeared in *The Irishman*:

Ye True, ye Noble, who unblenching stand
Amid the storms and ills of this dark Day,
Still hold your ground! Yourselves, your Fatherland,
Have in the Powers above a surest stay!
Though Famine, Pest, Want, Sickness of the Heart,
Be now your lot—all these shall soon depart—
And Heaven be yet at your command!

(36-42)

His transmutation of pain into poetry made him, for James Joyce, 'the spiritual focus of his age [. . .] a romantic, a would-be herald, a prototype for a would-be nation' (134). He was an unlikely rebel, spurred by time and circumstance to take a stand, and while his voice had more in common with 'the wail from the tomb' than 'world-waking power,' his poetry provides a remarkable reflection of Ireland in 1848, a year of famine and failed rebellion.

Works Cited

Dante. *The Divine Comedy.* Trans. C. H. Sisson. Oxford and New York: Oxford U P, 1998.

Davitt, Michael. *The Fall of Feudalism in Ireland; or The Story of the Land League Revolution.* London and New York: Harper and Brothers, 1904.

Duffy, Charles Gavan. *My Life in Two Hemispheres.* London: T. Fisher Unwin, 1898. Vol. I.

———. 'Personal Memories of James C. Mangan.' *Dublin Review* 142 (1908): 278-94.

Elgee, Jane Francesca. 'Jacta Alea Est.' *Nation* 29 Jul. 1848: 488.

———. 'The Famine Year.' *Poems by Speranza.* Dublin: James Duffy, 1864.

Foster, Roy. *Modern Ireland 1600-1972.* London: Penguin, 1989.

Gray, Peter. *Famine, Land and Politics: British Government and Irish Society 1843-1850.* Dublin and Portland, Oregon: Irish Academic Press, 1999.

Joyce, James. 'James Clarence Mangan (1907).' *Occasional, Critical and Political Writing.* Oxford: Oxford U P, 2000. 127-36.

Mangan, James Clarence. 'The Warning Voice'; 'The Peal of Another Trumpet'; 'A Vision of Connaught in the Thirteenth Century'; 'Dark Rosaleen.' *The Collected Works of James Clarence Mangan: Poems: 1845-1847.* Eds. Jacques Chuto, Rudolf Patrick Holzapfel, Ellen Shannon-Mangan. Dublin and Portland, Oregon: Irish Academic Press, 1997.

———. 'A Voice of Encouragement: A New Year's Lay'; 'The Nameless One'; 'For Soul and Country'; 'Irish National Hymn'; 'The Funerals'; 'A Vision: A.D. 1848'; 'The Brightest of the Bright'; 'The Famine.' *The Collected Works of James Clarence Mangan: Poems: 1848-1912.*

Eds. Jacques Chuto, Tadhg Ó Dúshláine, Peter van de Kamp. Dublin and Portland, Oregon: Irish Academic Press, 1999.

———. 'Correspondence'; 'Anthologia Hibernica. No 1'; 'Autobiography.' *The Collected Works of James Clarence Mangan: Prose: 1840-1882; Correspondence.* Eds. Jacques Chuto, Peter van de Kamp, Augustine Martin, Ellen Shannon-Mangan. Dublin and Portland, Oregon: Irish Academic Press, 2002.

McNeile, Hugh. 'The Famine: A Rod of God: Its Provoking Cause—Its Merciful Design. A Sermon.' London and Liverpool: Seeley, Burnside, and Seeley; Arthur Newling, 1847.

Mitchel, John, ed. *Poems by James Clarence Mangan; with a Biographical Introduction by John Mitchel.* New York: P. M. Haverty, 1859.

O'Donoghue, D. J. *The Life and Writings of James Clarence Mangan.* Edinburgh, Dublin, Chicago and Peabody: Patrick Geddes & Co., M. H. Gill & Son, T. G. O'Donoghue, P. V. Fitzpatrick, Nugent Bros., 1897.

Shannon-Mangan, Ellen. *James Clarence Mangan: A Biography.* Dublin and Portland, Oregon: Irish Academic Press, 1996.

Trevelyan, Charles. *The Irish Crisis.* London: Longman, Brown, Green and Longmans, 1848.

Williams, Richard D'Alton. *The Poems of Richard Dalton Williams.* Dublin: T. D. Sullivan, 1883.

Richard Haslam (essay date 2006)

SOURCE: Haslam, Richard. "'Broad Farce and Thrilling Tragedy': Mangan's Fiction and Irish Gothic." *Éire-Ireland* 41.3-4 (2006): 215-44. Print.

[*In the following essay, Haslam argues that Mangan's work demonstrates an Irish Gothic mode and, though he identifies several other Irish Gothic writers, does not see it as a subgenre of its own. Haslam outlines critical definitions of Catholic and Protestant Gothic literature in the nineteenth century and compares them with Gothicism in other countries.*]

Deane's Mangan and Irish-Catholic-Nationalist Gothic

Respected in his lifetime as a gifted poet and translator, James Clarence Mangan (1803-49) nonetheless died in obscure poverty, the victim of cholera and alcoholism.[1] Early biographers like John Mitchel soon began to mythologize him, speculating that the poet's "history and fate were indeed a type and shadow of the land he loved so well" (cited in O'Donoghue xxxvi). When Mangan's unfinished ***Autobiography*** was published in 1882, thirty-three years after his death, it contained no evidence that he viewed himself as an avatar of suffering Ireland, but its speaker did reveal didactic intentions: "My desire is to leave after me a work that may not merely inform but instruct … [unveiling] for the thinking the more hidden springs of human frailty … [and functioning] as a warning to the uneducated votary of Vice" (***Prose 2*** [***The Collected Works of James Clarence Mangan: Prose, 1840-1882***] 227).[2] However, the temptation to make Mangan's life and work didactic in a different way proved hard to resist, as could be seen in James Joyce's representation of him as "the type of his race," in whom "a narrow and hysterical nationality receives a last justification" (81-82). James Kilroy, introducing the 1968 edition of ***Autobiography,*** also followed the Mangan Ni Houlihan route, claiming that "more than any other poet of the nineteenth century, and probably more than any poet since then as well, Mangan represents Ireland, and the suffering of his life can be seen as symbolizing the miseries of his country in the middle of the last century" (9). In a later and more sophisticated version of such emblematizing, Seamus Deane argued that Mangan possessed the "ability to internalize … [cultural] crises, to see history as an expression of his own life, to recognize within himself the psychic stress of the country's political and social condition" (*Short History* 80-81).

The longstanding critical tendency to treat Mangan as a holographic shard of Irish historical experience provides a possible context for Deane's subsequent, radical claim that Mangan's ***Autobiography*** "introduces us to a new genre—what we may call Catholic or Catholic-nationalist Gothic" (*Strange Country* 126). In order to understand why the claim is radical, we need to consider briefly the history of the term "Irish Gothic." During the past two and a half decades, it has become a widely used category in both Irish and Gothic studies. Although some critics have used it to classify a group of novels and short stories by Charles Maturin (1780-1824), Joseph Sheridan Le Fanu (1814-73), and Bram Stoker (1847-1912), others have extended the label to encompass work by Sydney Owenson (1776?-1859), Oscar Wilde (1854-1900), W. B. Yeats (1865-1939), and Elizabeth Bowen (1899-1973).[3] By the early 1990s, opinions may have diverged about whether Irish Gothic was a tradition or a sub-genre, but agreement about its denominational traits appeared nonetheless to be imminent. As W. J. McCormack remarked, "At the risk of paradox, it has to be said that while Irish gothic writing does not amount to a tradition, it is a distinctly Protestant tradition" ("Irish Gothic and After" 837).

However, any consensus on this confessional aspect was challenged by Deane's aforementioned representation of ***Autobiography*** as the initiator of "Catholic or Catholic-nationalist Gothic" (*Strange Country* 126). Deane substantiated his assertion by first listing what he saw as the work's "standard elements" of Gothic content:

> an overpowering sense of doom, related to criminality; reference to German romances; dream-sequences and

ruins; a terrifying father-figure whose shadow falls over and dominates the narrator's life; isolating illness; spiritual hauntings and world-weariness; Promethean ambitions and humiliating rebukes; appeals to a select audience for sympathy and contempt for the mass of mankind; religious longings and the refusal of conventional religious consolations.

(126)

Deane also identified in ***Autobiography*** formal devices and rhetorical styles frequently found in Gothic texts, most notably the "fragment" (126-27) and "the mode of melodramatic excess" (127). He then located the distinctively "Catholic" features of Mangan's Gothic in its "autobiographical internalization of the whole Gothic apparatus, the incorporation into the history of an individual of a series of protocols that belong to the historical sequences that characterize the plots of Gothic novels" (129). Yet Deane's reader is left unclear as to why this is a particularly Catholic feature of ***Autobiography.*** After all, what he refers to as "the discrepancy between a Gothic experience of intense formlessness and a Catholic account of the shape a life should have" (129) operates just as vividly in the Scottish Presbyterian milieu of James Hogg's 1824 *The Private Memoirs and Confessions of a Justified Sinner.* Furthermore, with respect to the eschatological musings that terminate ***Autobiography,*** Deane admits, "if the work does merit the title of Catholic Gothic," its references to Bishop Massillon and Blaise Pascal indicate that "it is only Catholic in as Protestant form of Catholicism as possible" (130).[4] One last puzzle in Deane's analysis of ***Autobiography*** is its lack of any substantial exploration of the "nationalist" component in Mangan's "Catholic-nationalist Gothic" (126). That Deane hesitates about terming Mangan's Gothic "Catholic or Catholic-nationalist" (126) suggests his uncertainty about where, precisely, to locate the "nationalist" dimension—if there is one. On the other hand, since Deane accepts that the "figure" of Mangan created through his autobiography and the later biographies becomes "a figure for Ireland itself, trying to emerge from its history and from the clasp of the degraded national character" (131), he may view the "nationalist" factor in Mangan as self-evident.

In what follows, I argue that Deane's innovative claims about Catholic-nationalist Gothic are valid but can only be fully substantiated if we go beyond ***Autobiography*** and scrutinize Mangan's earlier fiction, especially works like **"Love, Mystery, and Murder. A Tale (Foundered on Facts)"** (1834) and **"The Man in the Cloak. A Very German Story"** (1838). The examination of these stories leads in turn to a modification of Deane's claim that ***Autobiography*** "introduces us to a new genre" (*Strange Country* 126). As we shall see, Mangan's Catholic-nationalist Gothic is not a "genre" (126) but a supernaturalist mode that interacts with specific narrative tones to create distinctive rhetorical effects. In addition, ***Autobiography*** does not "introduce" something "new" so much as alert us to something that was already there, but overlooked: the presence of characteristically Gothic motifs and devices in the fiction of earlier nineteenth-century Irish Catholic writers, such as John and Michael Banim, Gerald Griffin, and the Catholic-turned-Protestant William Carleton. Once we recognize that Catholic Gothic establishes a substantial counterclaim to Protestant Gothic, we are impelled to rethink not only Irish Gothic but also the literary history of nineteenth-century Ireland.

Mangan's Maturin: How Jansen Met Calvin

An appropriate place to begin investigating the complexity of Mangan's Gothic is his depiction of Charles Maturin and his work.[5] Toward the end of his life, Mangan chose Maturin as the first subject in a series of **"Sketches and Reminiscences of Irish Writers."** In his youth, he recalls, he saw Maturin on three occasions but never summoned the courage to speak to "this marvellous man" (***Prose 2*** 193). Quoting from Byron's *Manfred,* Mangan describes Maturin as one whose nature was "averse from life"; he also compares "the great Irishman" to Hamlet, who "had that within him which passed show" (***Prose 2*** 192-93). However, Mangan's representation of Maturin as an isolated, misunderstood, and intellectually superior individual is selective; he plays up those characteristics that seem to correspond to the lonely *hauteur* of a Byronic protagonist and plays down Maturin's well-attested uxoriousness and gregariousness.[6] Self-representation through the medium of another is a hallmark of Mangan's writings; sometimes, it is achieved through a literary style, such as his poetic "versions" and "translations" from the Arabian, Persian, German, or Irish; at other times, it is pursued through a persona, or the depiction of a real person, as in the Maturin "Sketch."[7] We can see the process in operation when he describes Maturin as one who had an "impatience of existence"; in ***Autobiography,*** by comparison, the narrator depicts his own "grand moral malady" as "an impatience of life and its commonplace pursuits" (***Prose 2*** 192, 236).[8]

These techniques of selection and self-representation become more complicated when Mangan turns to Maturin's fiction. He believes that Maturin has produced "three works of unsurpassable interest and power" (***Prose 2*** 194): *Fatal Revenge* (1807), *The Milesian Chief* (1812), and *Women* (1818). However, Mangan is much less enthusiastic about *Melmoth the Wanderer* (1820)—a novel now viewed as Maturin's masterpiece and one never omitted when critics construct a lineage of Irish Gothic. Despite praising the work's "energetic writing and magnificent description," Mangan argues that its Faustian-pact plot is "at once hackneyed and monstrous" (194). Such ambivalence is initially perplexing because the imagery and themes of ***Autobiography*** often echo *Melmoth,* especially in the evocation of a mood of eschatological fatalism. For example, the speaker claims that as a youth he "was haunted by an indescribable feeling of something terrible," which surfaced in his "imagination like one of those dreadful ideas which are said by some German writers of romance to infest the soul of a man apparently foredoomed to the commission of murder" (***Prose 2*** 226). He then hastens to gloss (and gloss over) this simile: "I say apparently, for I may here, in the outset, state that I have no faith in the theory of predestination, and that I believe every individual to be the architect of his own happiness or misery . . ." (226). Nonetheless, the narrative immediately reverts to his youthful perspective on the matter: ". . . but I did feel that a period would arrive when I should look back upon the Past with horror, and should say to myself, Now the Great Tree of my Existence is blasted, and will never more put forth fruit or blossom" (226). Thus, in the present moment, the indicative mood, and the literal sense, predestination is repudiated; but, in the past moment, the subjunctive mood, and the figurative sense, it is once more sanctioned.

The Catholic Mangan never mentions reading the works of John Calvin, but the imagery of ***Autobiography*** is fraught—in every sense—with the kind of aestheticized Calvinism that pervades Maturin's *Melmoth.* For example, Mangan's narrator requests in the first sentence that the text should be viewed as a "beacon" "for the benefit of his fellow-creatures" to help them "avoid, in their voyage of existence, the rocks and shoals upon which his own peace of soul has undergone shipwreck" (***Prose 2*** 226). This figure of speech recalls one of the few metaphors that Calvin permits himself in his *Institutes of the Christian Religion* (1536-59), when he depicts predestination as an ocean journey and compares the lack of an assurance of salvation to shipwreck.[9] Mangan's speaker has endured "melancholy foreboding," "disastrous destiny," and "nightmare loads lying most heavily on my spirit" (226). He recalls his youth in order to comprehend how "the seeds of . . . moral insanity were developed within me which afterwards grew up into a tree of giant altitude" (229)—the same tree that would eventually be "blasted" (226). Grandiloquently, he describes himself as a "ruined soul in a wasted frame:—the very *ideal* and perfection of moral and physical evil combined in one individual" (234). As his thoughts turn once again to predestination, the grammatical mood turns once again to the subjunctive: "I began to think, with Buffon, that it is not impossible that some beings may have been created expressly for unhappiness; and I knew that Cowper had lived, and perhaps died, in the dreadful belief that he himself was a cast-away, and a 'vessel of wrath, fitted for destruction'" (237).[10] As a result, the author notes, "[my] mind became a chaos of horrors, and all the fires of Pandaemonium seemed to burn in my brain" (237). In his "deplorable inner state," he believes that the "gates of Heaven" are "barred" against him: "its floor and walls, of brass and triple adamant, repelled my cries; and I appeared to myself to be sending a voice of agony into some interminable chasm" (237).[11] Despite the speaker's earlier intimation that "[b]y-and-by" he "may invite . . . [the reader's] attention to more cheerful and consolatory matter" (235), the fragmented work never reaches that goal. As a result, ***Autobiography*** exudes inconsolability.

The thematic affinities between *Melmoth* and ***Autobiography*** may lie in a theological overlap between the Jansenistic Irish Catholicism of Mangan and the Calvinistic Irish Anglicanism of the Huguenot-descended Maturin. The "deplorable inner state" of Mangan's narrator deforms his perception of the outside world, as he experiences what Patrick Kavanagh would later term "the sharp knife of Jansen" that "cuts all the green branches."[12] In the closing paragraphs of ***Autobiography,*** he declares, "I have pleasure in nothing, and I admire nothing . . . I hate scenery and suns. I see nothing in Creation but what is fallen and ruined" (239). This Jansenist tendency shadows Mangan's account in the "Sketch" of trailing Maturin "into the porch of St. Peter's Church" in order to hear him "read the burial service" (***Prose 2*** 192). Mangan revealingly confesses that "the force of the impulse which urged" him "to follow the author of 'Melmoth'" into an alien church arose in part because he was "strongly imbued with a belief in those doctrines of my Church which seem (and only seem) to savour of what is theologically called 'exclusiveness'" (192). The "seem (and only seem)" formulation is strongly reminiscent of the "I say apparently [foredoomed]" qualification in ***Autobiography*** (226), and the reference to "exclusiveness" foreshadows the last incident in ***Autobiography,*** in which the "reader" is asked "to imagine" the young narrator "reclining" and reflecting on "*Les Pensées de Pascal*" (238). He encounters another young Catholic man, who criticizes the section in *Pensées* "in which Pascal compares the world to a dungeon, and its inhabitants to condemned criminals, awaiting the hour that shall summon them to execution" (239). In response, Mangan's speaker cites Bishop Massillon's sermon "The Small Number of the Saved," arguing that the church's "holiest and most learned theologians" conclude that "the majority of mankind will be irrevocably consigned to eternal misery" (239).[13] The other young man counters, "I take the judgment of no one individual even in my own church . . . as my guide. The goodness—the justice of GOD—" (239). He is then "interrupted" by the narrator: "'Stop,' said I. 'What do you'" (239). At this moment, ***Autobiography*** abruptly ceases—interrupting the interruption—and the "goodness" and "justice" of God are left hanging in the balance with the "eternal misery" of "the majority of mankind."[14]

In addition to echoing the reprobation-haunted acoustics of Maturin's novel, Mangan's speaker consciously or unconsciously draws upon the tone and figurative language in which the soul-sold Melmoth expresses his lethal love for the naïve Isidora, object both of his desire and persecution:

> "But I feel another pride," answered Melmoth, and in a proud tone he spoke it,—"a pride, which, like that of the storm that visited the ancient cities, whose destruction you may have read of, while it blasts, withers, and encrusts paintings, gems, music, and festivity, grasping them in its talons of annihilation, exclaims, Perish to all the world, perhaps beyond the period of its existence, but live to me in darkness and corruption! Preserve all the exquisite modulation of your forms! all the indestructible brilliancy

> of your colouring!—but preserve it for me alone!—me, the single, pulseless, eyeless, heartless embracer of an unfertile bride,—the brooder over the dark and unproductive nest of eternal sterility,—the mountain whose lava of internal fire has stifled, and indurated, and inclosed for ever, all that was the joy of earth, the felicity of life, and the hope of futurity!"
>
> (*Melmoth* 354)

Fragments of this magniloquent extravaganza reverberate through ***Autobiography,*** in passages that describe "the outbreakings of that rebellious and gloomy spirit that smouldered like a volcano within me" (***Prose 2*** 233) and announce that "the Pompeii and Herculaneum of my soul have been dug up from their ancient sepulchers" (238). The "dominant passion" of Mangan's speaker—like that of Melmoth—"was Pride; and this was to be overcome by pain of every description and the continual sense of self-helplessness" (233). Previously in the narrative, he had described how he "felt or fancied that between me and those who approached me no species of sympathy could exist; and I shrank from communion with them as from somewhat alien to my nature" (230). He diagnoses this feeling, which "became one of the grand and terrible miseries of my existence," as "a morbid product of the pride and presumption which, almost hidden from myself, constituted even from my childhood, governing traits in my character, and have so often contributed to render me repulsive in the eyes of others" (230). To overcome the results of this pride, the narrator's "spiritual director" forces him "to perform my very penances . . . in darkness and subterranean places—wheresoever I could bury myself from the face of living man" (233). Whereas Melmoth torments others as a means to save himself from a literal hell, Mangan's speaker punishes himself in order "to lift me out of the hell of my own nature" (233). In this zone between literal and figurative damnation, the Calvinist aesthetics of Maturin and the Jansenist aesthetics of Mangan intersect.

Modes and Tones in Mangan's Gothic

Given these many correspondences between Maturin's novel and ***Autobiography,*** it comes as a shock to learn from the "Sketch" that Mangan regarded Melmoth as "a bore of the first magnitude, who is always talking grandiloquent fustian, and folding his cloak about him" (***Prose 2*** 194).[15] How can we explain the discrepancy? And how might it relate to the peculiar proportions of Mangan's Gothic? For answers, we must turn to **"Love, Mystery, and Murder. A Tale (Foundered on Facts),"** which caricatures the "grandiloquent fustian" of apparently outmoded Gothic conventions. Published in the *Weekly Dublin Satirist* of 1834 (fifteen years before the "Sketch" of Maturin), this fast-paced parody takes the form of a miniature Gothic romance, comprising (and compressing) fourteen chapters within thirteen pages. Throughout the story, Mangan displays his familiarity with the thematic and narrative motifs of Gothic fiction, which he defamiliarizes through sarcasm, exaggeration, and groan-inducing puns. For example, the narrator laments that the wealth of Conde Ugolino di Bulbruzzi "sprang from assassination and pillage—these being the modes by which Italian noblemen generally make out a subsistence, as I clearly find in Mrs. Radcliffe's romances" (***Prose 1*** [***The Collected Works of James Clarence Mangan: Prose, 1832-1839***] 52). The Conde, we learn, has "murdered several hundreds of persons,—suppose we say coolly, in round numbers, 700 . . ." (52). Although the "unappeased spirits" of these victims haunt "the tapestried chambers and winding galleries of the castle in swarms" (52), they are not numbered among the castle's inmates because the narrator regards "the ghosts as nobodies" (53). The Conde's designated assassin—a refugee from Radcliffe's *The Italian* (1797)—is a monk called Hugh Gundalpho, who "wore a cowl over his face, and generally carried a dagger in one hand and a lamp in the other. He never either ate or drank; so that in fact it was a sort of miracle how he subsisted" (***Prose 1*** 53). The heroine Amelrosa is attacked by a buffalo, but "a young man . . . stepped up (of course precisely at the critical moment)" to dispatch the animal, who "magnanimously expired without a groan" (54). Amelrosa then suffers incarceration in a subterranean dungeon, a perilous ocean journey, a storm at sea, shipwreck, and the revelation that her lover has been unfaithful, before the high-speed narrative terminates in a double-murder-double-suicide bloodbath at the royal court.

"Love, Mystery, and Murder" aims to amuse the reader by satirizing Gothic conventions, but might it have anything to tell us about a possible Irish-Catholic-nationalist Gothic? As his most recent editors note, Mangan gestures to an Irish political context when he explains why Amelrosa's love affair has been interrupted: "Thus, they met on ten successive nights. But, after the tenth night, the Lord Lieutenant of the Castle issued a proclamation, and they met no more!" (56, 337). We may also find allusions to Irish political discord behind the story's opening claim that it is "a bad thing, on the whole, to be a tyrant and a throat-cutter, at least in these times; and why? Because every body reads the DUBLIN SATIRIST" (52). Similar hints appear in the story's concluding suggestion that the king could be forced to wear the "*bonnet rouge*" of the French revolutionaries (64). Intimations about Irish religious division also underlie the scene in which Amelrosa begs to be saved from the menacing monk and is answered by "a small philosopher": "Who talks of Monks? . . . We have no Monks in this country. This is the land of philosophy, of universal benevolence and humanity. We have pillaged all the monasteries and expelled all the Monks" (62). Cumulatively, **"Love, Mystery, and Murder"** undermines some of the anti-Catholic stereotypes that recur in Gothic fiction, but its specific allusions are too sporadic and insubstantial to constitute compelling evidence for a coherent Irish-Catholic-nationalist-Gothic dimension in the story.[16]

Nevertheless, if we juxtapose **"Love, Mystery, and Murder"** with ***Autobiography,*** we can identify two distinctive aspects of Mangan's employment of Gothic motifs. Firstly, both narratives select different thematic and stylistic elements from the capacious repertoire established in the first phase of the Gothic mode, which reaches from Walpole's *The Castle of Otranto* (1764) to James Hogg's *The Private Memoirs and Confessions of a Justified Sinner* (1824).[17] In his introduction to *Melmoth,* Chris Baldick establishes a rough but useful working distinction relating to novels of this phase, which are all "concerned with extreme states of mental disturbance" (x). Baldick differentiates between "'full-dress' Gothic," which "decks out its essential psychological tremors in a uniform costume of lurid effects and trappings," and a "second unorthodox group," which "carries a much lighter cargo of chains and cowls, so that its similar obsessions with persecution and delusion stand out more clearly" (x). According to Baldick, novels in the second group (such as *Caleb Williams* [1794], *Frankenstein* [1818, 1831], and *Justified Sinner*) "tend to rely less on the evocation of atmosphere from a monastic or castellar setting than on a fabulous principle of transgression, usually involving the Faustian acquisition of forbidden knowledge" (x). Although *Melmoth* makes some use of monastic "trappings," Baldick persuasively locates it in the more psychologically inflected group. In terms of Baldick's division, then, **"Love, Mystery, and Murder"** clearly belongs in the first category and ***Autobiography*** in the second. The plot of **"Love, Mystery, and Murder"** is focused on sensational events and sinister settings—in this case, a Catholic Italy populated with evil aristocrats and monks, where a "persecuted maiden" is "incarcerated in a horrible dungeon" (***Prose 1*** 57), people are "trampled to death by the crowd" (59), and a "ghastly and bloody spectacle" finally erupts "in all its horrors" (64). In contrast, the thematic focus of ***Autobiography*** is upon guilt-haunted consciousness, as the narrator broods upon the possibility of predestined damnation, as do the protagonists of Maturin's *Melmoth* and Hogg's *Justified Sinner.* However, the second—and crucial—distinction between Mangan's two texts involves *tone.* Unlike the deftly disparaging tone of **"Love, Mystery, and Murder,"** the earnest tone of ***Autobiography*** never undermines its Gothic apparatus. In ***Autobiography,*** Mangan's narrator describes human life as "a drama that so strangely united the two extremes of broad farce and thrilling tragedy" (***Prose 2*** 236), yet the narrative itself consistently maintains a tragic tone, excluding any hints of the farcical tone of **"Love, Mystery, and Murder."**[18]

Such a strict separation of tones is not always the case with Mangan's writing. In fact, as Patricia Coughlan has noted, any reader who goes "beyond the few familiar anthology pieces" soon discovers that many of Mangan's poems, stories, and essays exhibit an "incessant shifting of tones . . . incessant transvaluations of the Promethean images of Romanticism, from transcendent to ridiculous and back again" ("Fold over Fold" 199). **"Love, Mystery, and Murder"** and ***Autobiography*** are, in fact, at opposite ends of a tonal register that ranges from irony to sincerity. In between are works of fiction that exhibit varying degrees of tonal shift, such as **"An Extraordinary Adventure in the Shades"** (1833), **"My Transformation: A Wonderful Tale"** (1833), **"The Thirty Flasks"** (1838), and **"The Threefold Prediction. A Psychological Narrative"** (1845). Some of Mangan's most flamboyant experiments in tonal fluctuation occur in **"The Man in the Cloak. A Very German Story"** (1838), a work that is—as we shall see—central to the case for an Irish-Catholic-nationalist Gothic.

"Smoking with Mangan": Romantic Irony and Contraband Nationalism

"The Man in the Cloak" plagiaristically adapts Honoré de Balzac's *Melmoth Réconcilié* (1835).[19] Since Balzac's novella is itself a satirical appendix to Maturin's *Melmoth the Wanderer,* Mangan's story is an intertextual palimpsest—an Irish (Catholic) "Germanizing" of a French reworking of an Irish (Protestant) novel that itself incorporated both French sources (such as Diderot's *La Religieuse* [1796]) and German and English elements (from the Faust tradition).[20] Although he retains much of the Satanic pride and world-weary disdain of Maturin's creation, Balzac employs Melmoth principally as a prop to satirize the pretensions and self-deceptions of early nineteenth-century Paris, where the omnipotence of money divests modernity of spirituality. The narrator declares that this "city of fiery ordeals and branch establishment of hell" (Balzac 293) is one of "the real plague spots of our civilization" because it has "since 1815 . . . been moved by the spirit of gain rather than by principles of honor" (296). Unlike Maturin's original, Balzac's Melmoth finds it fairly easy to identify someone willing to sell his soul for superhuman powers.[21] When, in his turn, the cashier Castanier repents his demonic bargain, he heads for the Stock Exchange and soon discovers a merchant prepared to sell his "share of paradise": "It is a matter of business like anything else, isn't it? We all hold shares in the great Speculation of Eternity" (Balzac 338-39). The soul-trading continues, each time for a lower price, until the death of a syphilitic notary's clerk from a mercury overdose prohibits any further transactions. A further irony emerges in the story's final words, uttered by a German demonologist, who visits Paris in order to investigate the clerk's death. Oblivious to the sarcasm and sexual innuendo of the clerk's workmates, he concludes, "Education is making strides in France" (344).

Just as Balzac adapts Maturin's novel for his own ends, Mangan reshapes and repurposes the work of both authors. He edits out Balzac's screeds on the victory of greed over integrity, the moral deficiencies of Napoleon's army, and the involutions of human motivation; he also excises any licentiousness. At the same time, Mangan retains a crucial, Balzacian plot point, one that would have horrified the anti-Catholic Maturin: not only does Balzac's Melmoth successfully find someone who will trade fates, but he also dies a good, Catholic death, surrounded by candles and superintended by priests. By heightening the devout atmosphere of Melmoth's obsequies, Mangan outdoes Balzac in the Catholicizing of Maturin's Protestant anti-hero. Unlike Balzac's Castanier, Braunbrock (Mangan's German substitute) locates Melmoth's corpse not at home but in "the Church of St. Sulpice"; the remains are attended not by two but a "number" of priests, who are "singing the office for a departed soul" (***Prose 1*** 260). One priest informs Braunbrock that Melmoth "died within the precincts of this church only last week; and his soul, I trust, if not already in heaven, is on its way thither" (261). Remarking that the deceased "made a pious and penitent end," the priest prays for Braunbrock to do the same: "And that it may please thee, O Lord . . . to soften the hard heart of the living, and make of it a heart of flesh!" (261).

In order to intensify the Catholic ambience, Mangan removes the heterodox mockery that often counterpoints apparent orthodoxy in *Melmoth Réconcilié.* For example, Balzac's narrator alleges that the "faith of the peasant . . . varies inversely with the amount of use . . . made of his reasoning faculties" (333); that religious conversion is analogous to social climbing (334-35); and that the stock market is a place "where God Himself, in a manner, borrows on the security of His revenue of souls, for the Pope has a running account there" (337). Expunging such barbs, Mangan replaces them with an extended conversion scene that both anticipates the spiritual yearnings in ***Autobiography*** and provides a very good public relations moment for the Catholic Church:

> "Invoke the assistance of God, unhappy man!" said the priest.
>
> "Impossible," answered Braunbrock.
>
> "Can you not call upon God for mercy?"
>
> "I do not know what to say," replied the German.
>
> "Repeat after me, and with as much sincerity and unction as you can command, O, God, be merciful to me a sinner!"
>
> And Braunbrock repeated the words, *O, God, be merciful to me a sinner!*
>
> "It is enough," said the priest. "Rise!"
>
> Braunbrock rose up.
>
> "Go now in peace," said the priest; "but return hither, and be here again on this day week, a changed man—a man who need no longer shroud himself *in a cloak.*"
>
> The sequel of our tale may easily be divined by the penetrating. Religion and Hope from that hour found their way slowly into the heart of Braunbrock. Still he was not able to disembarrass himself of the fatal gift that had been bestowed on him. But an invisible agency was at length operating in his behalf.
>
> (***Prose 1*** 261-62)

"The Man in the Cloak" is crucial to the formation of an Irish-Catholic-nationalist Gothic not only because it reverses the fervently anti-Catholic attitude of *Melmoth the Wanderer,* but also because—like a Gothic Trojan horse—the story first appears in the pages of the *Dublin University Magazine.* During the 1830s, this intensely pro-Anglican, pro-unionist organ referred to "POPERY" as "the most finished and most abominable superstition on this earth," a "monstrous and incestuous offspring of infidelity and superstition" (cited in Hall 39). The magazine's editorials bellowed that "all the maxims of political wisdom, and all the sanctions of religious duty" required the political administration to "employ every means which the spirit of Christianity will recognize, to destroy and exterminate Popery in Ireland" because it is "the worst tyranny, civil or religious, that ever trampled upon the slaves of superstition" (54).[22]

How, then, did Mangan get away with sneaking in contraband pro-Catholicism? The answer may lie in the way that the story's capacity for fictional proselytism is disguised by its swift alternations of tone.[23] Whereas Balzac satirizes social and religious conventions and leaves Gothic conventions relatively unscathed, Mangan does the opposite. The uniting of "the two extremes of broad farce and thrilling tragedy" (***Prose 2*** 236), briefly acknowledged in ***Autobiography*** at the level of content, is repeatedly enacted in **"The Man in the Cloak"** at the level of form. For example, the mysterious stranger who first appears before Braunbrock "has a strange and hollow voice, the accents of which thrilled through every nerve and fibre of the cashier" (***Prose 1*** 240), but the unhomely mood of their encounter is soon dissipated by the introduction of the non-Balzacian Baron Queerkopf, who gives a lengthy disquisition on phrenology (242-43). Braunbrock's second confrontation with the Man in the Cloak is still alarming (if brief), but at their third meeting the narrative tone suddenly shifts, by means of another non-Balzacian situation:

> "What do you mean, Sir?" asked Braunbrock.
>
> "I mean to smoke," replied the Irishman, as he drew a long pipe, already ignited, from beneath the folds of his cloak.
>
> "Come, come, Sir," cried Braunbrock, "I don't understand this buffoonery. Let me pass, or take the consequences! . . .
>
> . . . "So serious a matter as forgery, I fancy, has unfitted you for relishing buffoonery," said the Irishman, aloud, and in the hearing of all.
>
> (***Prose 1*** 247)

As Patricia Coughlan has noted, one *O.E.D.* definition of "to smoke" is "to make fun of, to jest at, to ridicule, banter, or quiz a person" ("Recycling" 186).[24] Through the character of the Man in the Cloak, Mangan smokes both Maturin's Melmoth, the spouter of "grandiloquent fustian" (***Prose 2*** 194), and the expectations of readers who assume tonal consistency. Consider, for example, the following declamation by the Man in the Cloak:

> "Poor handful of dust!" he here exclaimed [to Braunbrock]—"did *you* think to resist ME? As well might you attempt to pluck the planets from their spheres. Know that on this vile ball of earth all that man can dream of in the shape of Power is mine. I wield, or if I chose, could wield, all the engines of governments and systems. I read every heart; I see into the future; I know the past. I am here; and yet I may be elsewhere, for I am independent of time and place and distance. . . .
>
> (***Prose 1*** 248)

This outburst, which issues for another thirteen lines, is largely adapted from Balzac, who in turn modeled it on dialogue in Maturin's novel. But the rhetorical force of the rodomontade is unsettled in Mangan's version by the pipe-episode that immediately precedes it. For the rest of the narrative, Mangan alternates scenes of "terror" (249), such as Braunbrock's experience at the theater, and scenes of religious devotion, such as Braunbrock's repentance, with exchanges and incidents that ridicule the story's Gothic credentials:

> . . . [The Man in the Cloak:] "No human power can rescue you."
>
> "Why? How?" cried the agitated betrayer of trust.
>
> "Why?" said the Man in the Cloak, seizing the arm of Braunbrock. "Dunce! Because the adamantine hand that grasps you thus will not relinquish its grasp until you are delivered up to justice. Is that German or not?"
>
> "Cursed be the day that I was born!" exclaimed Braunbrock, in a paroxysm of despair. . . .
>
> (***Prose 1*** 252)[25]

The "adamantine hand" sentence is from Balzac (320), but by adding "Is that German or not?" Mangan mocks Balzac's (and Maturin's) "fustian" (***Prose 2*** 194). "German" is used here in a pejorative sense, unlike the neutral, descriptive sense in which it is used in ***Autobiography,*** where (as we have seen) the speaker describes being "haunted" in his youth "by an indescribable feeling" that "rose on my imagination like one of those dreadful ideas which are said by some German writers of romance to infest the soul of a man apparently foredoomed to the commission of murder" (***Prose 2*** 226). The use of "German" as a self-reflexive term to undermine Gothic conventions can also be found in the subtitle of the work—"A Very German Story"—and in Mangan's **"The Thirty Flasks,"** when the evil magician Maugraby stages a diversion in order to escape:

> . . . [H]e snatched up his snuff-box, which had been lying on the table, and shook its contents into the fire. The effect of this apparently insignificant act was tremendously terrible and German. An explosion instantly followed, louder than the roar of ten parks of artillery together, *à qui mieux mieux.*
>
> (***Prose 1*** 237)

In **"Anthologia Germanica, VII"** (1836), Mangan makes a distinction between poetry in "the style German," of which he approves, and poetry in "the style Germanesque," of which he disapproves. The former hovers between "the Sublime and the Misty" and "elevates . . . to the clouds" its seeker, whereas the latter perches precariously between "the Sublime and the Ridiculous" and "infallibly prostrates a stalker, no matter how good an understanding he may have been on with his stilts the moment before" (***Prose 1*** 105). In his fiction, poetry, and criticism, however, Mangan sometimes deliberately employs "the style Germanesque" in order to pull the stilts from under the reader. In an essay published a year after **"The Man in the Cloak,"** Mangan writes, "If a combination of the Sublime and Sarcastic be possible, I fancy I find it in two lines by [Johann] Gleim" (***Prose 1*** 285). In many lines of **"The Man in the Cloak"** readers will find just such a "combination."

For certain contemporaries, the sudden intrusions of irony were disconcerting. When Mangan produced his magical pipe and began smoking, some readers were put in the position of Braunbrock, who exclaimed, "I don't understand this buffoonery" (***Prose 1*** 247). For example, John Mitchel diagnosed the tendency as a "grotesque" and "burlesque" expression of authorial self-hatred.[26] Against this psychologizing and censuring critique, however, we can place the suggestion by the German Romantic Friedrich Schlegel that "a real transcendental *buffoonery*" inhabits certain "ancient and modern poems which breathe, in their entirety and in every detail, the divine breath of irony" (126; my italics). According to Schlegel, although the "exterior form" of such works may exhibit "the histrionic style of an ordinary good Italian buffo," their "interior is permeated by the mood which surveys everything and rises infinitely above everything limited, even above the poet's own art, virtue, and genius" (126). Elsewhere, Schlegel uses the term "arabesque" to describe such works, praising their "artfully ordered confusion . . . charming symmetry of contradictions . . . [and] wonderfully perennial alternation of enthusiasm and irony which lives even in the smallest parts of the whole" (86). A "perennial alternation of enthusiasm and irony" is, of course, another way of describing the kind of tonal fluctuation we find in works like **"The Man in the Cloak."** Thus, combining the terminology of Mangan, Mitchel, and Schlegel, we can classify **"The Man in the Cloak"** as an example of the arabesque-burlesque-Germanesque-grotesque branch of Irish-Catholic-nationalist Gothic.

Less Manganesquely, we might describe it as an experiment in Irish Romantic irony.[27] Such a linkage, however, has been challenged by David Lloyd, who, in order to demonstrate that Mangan is a precociously modernist practitioner of "minor writing" (4), is anxious to distance him from "that nebulous concept, Romantic irony" (208). According to Lloyd, just as Mangan refuses the cultural nationalism of his Irish contemporaries and the cultural imperialism of British Romantic and Victorian writers, he "equally eludes the political aesthetic through which, precisely in its notorious undecidability, Romantic irony emerges as instrumental in the production of a subjectivity assimilable to the state" (209). But even if one accepts the highly debatable premise that the "undecidability" of romantic irony is somehow always "instrumental" in the manner stated, it is difficult to grasp from Lloyd's argument the precise way in which Mangan's "subjectivity" was unassimilable to "the state." In fact, if we remove from Mangan the burden of being a representative of anti-imperial, anti-cultural nationalist, proto-modernist, radically "minor" inauthenticity, then it seems a more plausible critical move to associate him with romantic irony.[28] This is not, however, a simple (or simplistic) move, since, as Lloyd Bishop reminds us, romantic irony is "a complex phenomenon":

> It is . . . not simply a local device (e.g., antiphrasis). It is a structural principle, in fact a combination, often, of several different structural principles: the self-conscious, unreliable, or nescient narrator; the intrusive author; the multiple point of view; the deflation of a hero who is ambivalently admired and ridiculed; the fragmentation of time into a series of discrete, independent, isolated moments; the eschewal of closure in favor of an open-ended dénouement; textual self-reflexiveness with metafiction often overtaking the fiction; frequent recourse to oxymoron, paradox, parabasis, parataxis, montage, or other staccato effects such as sudden changes of mood, theme, or stylistic register. And when it pervades an entire text, as it usually does, it becomes . . . the expression of a philosophical stance, either ethical (e.g., ambivalence or skepticism regarding traditional values), ontological (intimating that paradox is inherent in human nature and even in the "nature of things"), and/or epistemological (often stating and always implying the question: "What can we really know for sure?").
>
> (17)

Many of these elements—especially "textual self-reflexiveness" and "sudden changes of mood, theme, or stylistic register"—are at work in **"The Man in the Cloak,"** in a manner that transfuses the spirit of German romantic irony into the mainstream of nineteenth-century Irish literature in English.[29]

Thus, Mangan's dismissive claim in the Maturin "Sketch" that Melmoth is "a bore of the first magnitude, who is always talking grandiloquent fustian, and folding his cloak about him" (***Prose 2*** 194), is itself a kind of cloak for a much more ambivalent attitude. To the best of my knowledge, only once in the 542 pages of *Melmoth* does Maturin describe the protagonist as wearing a cloak (441). Mangan, on the other hand, changed the character's name from Melmoth to the Man in the Cloak for his eponymous adaptation of Maturin and Balzac, used the term as a sobriquet for some of his own writings, and was famous for his own bizarre blue cloak.[30] Although **"My Bugle, and How I Blow It"** (1841), signed by **"The Man in the Cloak,"** represents an ironic take on self-representation, the priestly admonition in **"The Man in the Cloak"** to "return . . . a changed man—a man who need no longer shroud himself *in a cloak*" (***Prose 1*** 262; Mangan's italics) is voiced in the more pious and remorseful tone of potentially autobiographical allusion. In an early work like **"Love, Mystery, and Murder,"** Mangan delights in exposing the outmodedness of the Gothic idiom. In a late work like ***Autobiography,*** he is drawn to the rhetoric of Gothic because it appears to offer a vocabulary that is sufficiently ostentatious to do artistic justice to the "interminable chasm" (***Prose 2*** 237) he perceives in his own consciousness—the chasm which engulfs all of his exertions to fabricate for himself a stable psychological and theological identity. But the techniques of Romantic irony that are at work and at play in **"The Man in the Cloak,"** alternating between tones of religious earnestness and stylistic parody, permit Mangan to take a deliberate aesthetic stance toward the character of Melmoth (in particular) and to Gothic conventions (in general), a stance that is encapsulated in his observation on the poetry of Ludwig Tieck: "Every stanza is a basilisk which we at once abhor and are fascinated by. One half of our sensations are at war with the other half" (***Prose 1*** 146).

Rethinking Irish Gothic

How, then, might this perusal of **"The Man in the Cloak"** lead us to revise the concept of "Irish Gothic"? Firstly, I have argued that "Irish-Catholic-nationalist Gothic" only becomes a valid critical term when we examine texts by Mangan in addition to ***Autobiography.*** Secondly, rather than "a new *genre*" (Deane, *Strange Country* 126; my italics), Mangan's Gothic should be regarded as a mode whose rhetorical effects are decisively modulated by variations in tone. ***Autobiography***'s tone of sincerity places it at the opposite pole of the register from the tone of irony in **"Love, Mystery, and Murder,"** whereas the Romantic irony at work in **"The Man in the Cloak"** generates a deliberate fluctuation between these poles.[31] Thirdly, I have pointed out that the Catholic-nationalist components of Irish Gothic in **"The Man in the Cloak"** derive as much from the story's first place of publication as from its thematic concerns and formal devices. Under the smoke screen of Romantic irony, Mangan successfully smuggles a Catholic agenda into the pages of the *Dublin University Magazine* and thereby performs a nationalist maneuver.[32]

I want to conclude by sketching out a couple of questions for future investigation. How might the particular intersections of mode and tone at work in Mangan's fiction relate to the supernaturalist modes, narrative tones, and rhetorical effects at work in later Irish Gothic texts, such as Oscar Wilde's *The Picture of Dorian Gray* (1890; 1891) and "The Canterville Ghost" (1891) and Flann O'Brien's *The Third Policeman* (1939-40; 1967)?[33] And how might Mangan's fiction alert us to the recognition of Gothic motifs in the fiction of other early nineteenth-century Irish Catholic writers? In the period between the publication of Maturin's *Melmoth* (1820) and Le Fanu's *The Purcell Papers* (1838-40), John Banim published "The Fetches" (1825) and "The Ace of Clubs" (1838), Michael Banim published "Crohoore of the Bill-Hook" (1825) and *The Ghost Hunter and His Family* (1833), Gerald Griffin published "The Barber of Bantry" (1835), and William Carleton (a Catholic-turned-Protestant writer) published "The Lianhan Shee" (1830/1833): all of these narratives—like Mangan's—experiment in intriguing ways with aspects of the Gothic mode.[34] Therefore, in order to establish firmly the category of an Irish-Catholic-nationalist Gothic mode, critics need to range beyond Mangan's fiction. And Irish Gothic itself should be re-conceptualized as one of several supernaturalist modes at work in Irish fiction, including—among others—the ghost-story, the folkloric, the historicized, the sensational, and the theological. Each of these supernaturalist modes is modulated by narrative tones that range from the polemical to the parodic, in order to generate a range of rhetorical effects.[35] For example, the Faustian-pact plots in John Banim's "The Ace of Clubs" and Griffin's "The Barber of Bantry" are both narrated in tones that hesitate between piety and anxiety, and the combination of Gothic, folkloric, and Catholic theological supernaturalist modes in the former provides a subtle contrast with the interaction of Gothic, psychological, and Catholic theological modes in the latter. Griffin's and Banim's stories, in turn, counterpoint the blend of Gothic and folkloric supernaturalist modes with sarcastic and sensational narrative tones that can be found in the opening, Irish-set chapters of Maturin's *Melmoth* and in his posthumously published "Leixlip Castle" (1825).

The challenge for critics of Irish Gothic is encapsulated in the first paragraph of Gerald Griffin's folkloric supernaturalist tale, "The Brown Man" (1827):

> If one were disposed to be fancifully metaphysical upon the subject, it might not be amiss to compare credulity to a sort of mental prism, by which the great volume of the light of speculative superstition is refracted in a manner precisely similar to that of the material, every day sun, the great refractor thus showing only *blue* devils to the dwellers in the good city of London, *orange* and *green* devils to the inhabitants of the sister (or rather step-daughter), island, and so forward until the seven component hues are made out, through the other nations of the earth. But what has this to do with the story? In order to answer that question, the story must be told.
>
> (297-98)

Our examination of Mangan's fiction suggests that many parts of the story about the relationship between a country's expression of "speculative superstition" and its religious, social, and political structures remain to be told, and many other "component hues" await spectrum (and specter) analysis.

Notes

1. Ellen Shannon-Mangan has written the most comprehensive biography: *James Clarence Mangan: A Biography* (1996).

2. I refer to the "speaker" or "narrator," rather than "Mangan," since *Autobiography* is very much a histrionic embellishment on the known facts of Mangan's life (see Kilroy 7 and Shannon-Mangan 6-13). The work was written at the request of a priest, Father Meehan, who initially deprecated it as "the merest Reve d'une Vie, with here and there some filaments of reality in its texture." According to Meehan, Mangan admitted that he had "dreamed it" (Shannon-Mangan 394).

3. The critical designation "Irish Gothic" (along with the variations "Anglo-Irish Gothic" and "Protestant Gothic") began to circulate in the 1980s, principally through the work of Julian Moynahan, Seamus Deane (*Short History* 99-101; 205), and Roy Foster (217-22). In the early 1990s, the term achieved greater visibility with W. J. McCormack's lengthy "Irish Gothic and After" section in *The Field Day Anthology* and Siobhán Kilfeather's exploration of eighteenth-century "Irish Female Gothic." Terry Eagleton went on to redefine the concept through a provocative methodological amalgam of psychoanalysis and Marxism, a reading that risked reductionism because it did not distinguish clearly between allegory, which is a form of textual production, and allegoresis, which is a form of textual exegesis (see Haslam, "Joseph Sheridan," 275-77.) Toward the end of the 1990s, Margot Backus produced the first book-length analysis of Irish Gothic, extending the range of authors examined even beyond the wide sweep of the *Field Day* assortment. Recent extended studies include Luke Gibbons's analysis of the mobilization of Gothic tropes in political discourse concerning Ireland, and Jarlath Killeen's investigation of the eighteenth-century cultural contexts that foreshadowed the emergence of nineteenth-century Gothic. For a detailed genealogy of the term, see Haslam ("Irish Gothic").

4. Blaise Pascal (1623-62) is one of the more famous adherents of Jansenism, a seventeenth-century, Calvinistically influenced Catholic movement. Jean Baptiste Massillon (1663-1742) was the Bishop of Clermont in France; Mangan cites the sermon, "The Small Number of the Saved," at the close of *Autobiography* (*Prose 2* 239).

5. Maturin was born in Dublin, educated at Trinity College, and ordained as a Church of Ireland clergyman in 1803. After spending three years as a curate in Loughrea, Co. Galway, he was appointed a curate at St. Peter's, Dublin, where he served until his death. Although his play *Bertram* (1816) brought initial fame and temporary financial relief, he is remembered today for the novel *Melmoth the Wanderer* (1820), a sprawling Gothic masterpiece. Published as the campaign for Catholic Emancipation accelerated, *Melmoth* (like Maturin's novel *Women* [1818] and his sermons) repeatedly exhibits an appalled fascination with both Catholicism and Calvinism.

6. See, for example, Lougy (15).

7. With respect to such self-representation, I am grateful to my anonymous peer reviewer for suggesting that Mangan's "marvellous man" (*Prose 2* 193) reference to Maturin may contain echoes of William Wordsworth's description in "Resolution and Independence" (1807) of the eighteenth-century poet Thomas Chatterton as "the marvellous Boy" (Greenblatt and Abrams 1534). Like Mangan, Chatterton had an interest in disguised identities, and Mangan may have believed that Wordsworth's reflection on Chatterton and Robert Burns was relevant to his own plight: "We Poets in our youth begin in gladness; / But thereof come in the end despondency and madness" (1534). Similarly, Mangan's references to Byron and Hamlet in his portrait of Maturin speak more to his image of himself than to his image of his subject. On Mangan's response to Byron, see Coughlan ("Fold over Fold" 191-94). Ellen Shannon-Mangan notes that Mangan's dying words included allusions to *Hamlet* (421).

8. As Ellen Shannon-Mangan notes, the following excerpt from the "Sketch" is more plausible as a description of what we know of Mangan's own life, than as a comprehensive assessment of Maturin (64):

> An inhabitant of one of the stars, dropped upon our planet, could hardly feel more bewildered than Maturin habitually felt in his consociation with the beings around him. He had no friend—companion—brother; he, and the "Lonely Man of Shiraz" might have shaken hands, and then—parted. He—in his own dark way—understood many people; but nobody understood him in *any* way. And therefore it was that he, this man of highest genius, Charles Robert Maturin, lived unappreciated—and died unsympathized with, uncared for, unenquired after—and only *not* forgotten, because he had never been thought about.
>
> (*Prose 2* 192)

9. According to Calvin, "if we dread shipwreck, let us anxiously beware of this rock, on which none ever strike without being destroyed." He notes that although "the discussion of predestination may be compared to a dangerous ocean, yet, in traversing over it, the navigation is safe and serene, and I will also add pleasant, unless anyone freely wishes to expose himself to danger" (cited in Boulger 33).

10. Mangan may be hearkening back to the astringent, Augustinian idea of predestination that was cited so often by Calvin and muffled in later Catholic theology (Boulger 28). The "vessels of wrath" verse that Mangan cites from Saint Paul's Epistle to the Romans (9:22) comes immediately after two verses that Calvin frequently drew upon in the *Institutes* in order to silence queries and fears about the workings of predestination: "O man, who art thou that repliest against God? Shall the thing formed say to him that formed it, Why hast thou made me thus? Hath not the potter power over the clay, of the same lump, to make one vessel unto honour, and another unto dishonour?" (Romans 9:20-21). For discussion of both Maturin's youthful flirtations with hard-line Calvinism and the "Calvinist aesthetics" at work in *Melmoth,* see Haslam, "Maturin and the 'Calvinist Sublime.'"

11. Mangan's imagery picks up on an issue confronted by Calvin in *Concerning the Eternal Predestination of God* (1552), a work he was forced to produce in response to the controversy generated by the theory of predestination outlined in Book III of the *Institutes.* Calvin defensively states that "if those who attribute the hardening of men to His eternal counsel invest God with the character of a tyrant, we are certainly not the author of this opinion" (*Concerning* 60). With respect to Mangan's image of an "interminable chasm," compare Calvin's claim in the *Institutes* that "those who, in order to gain an assurance of their election, examine into the eternal counsel of God without the word, plunge themselves into a fatal abyss . . . [whereas those] who investigate it in a regular and orderly manner, as it is contained in the word, derive from such enquiry the benefit of peculiar consolation . . ." (cited in Boulger 33).

12. In "Lough Derg" (Kennelly 360). The speaker of *Autobiography* appears to be a card-carrying member of what Denis Devlin, in his poem "Lough Derg," calls "Clan Jansen" (Ibid., 370).

13. In the sermon, Massillon seeks to convince his audience that it is necessary for salvation to be "*singulier*" and to separate oneself from the masses—advice that Mangan appears to have taken to heart (Massillon, III, 540).

14. One question that shadows attempts, such as Deane's, to read the fragmentary form of *Autobiography* as a Gothic element is whether or not the abrupt ending is a deliberate artistic decision by Mangan or a contingent circumstance. The available evidence suggests the latter (see Shannon-Mangan 394).

15. It is hard to tell whether or not Mangan is making an intentional pun when he remarks of *Melmoth* that "the impossibility of feeling a genuine human interest in the characters, *damns* the book, despite of its many beauties" (*Prose 2* 194; my italics).

16. For an early study of anti-Catholic Gothic stereotyping, see Tarr. For a concise and astute analysis of the "essentially Whiggish" treatment of Catholicism in much early Gothic fiction (7), see Mighall (1-26).

17. As Robert Hume noted many years ago, "there is in an objective sense no such thing as *The Gothic Novel*; rather there are a variety of novels from different periods and countries which, on the basis of similarities, we may want to categorize as a group" (Platzner and Hume 273). He thus recommends referring to "a

very loosely defined *mode*" rather than presuming that "Gothic and Romantic are discrete entities which have an essential nature and real existence" (ibid. 273; my italics). More recently, Fred Botting has reasserted this point, arguing that it is less accurate to refer to a gothic genre or tradition than to a gothic "mode," one that "exceeds genre and categories" and is "restricted neither to a literary school nor to a historical period" (14).

18. The heartfelt tone of *Autobiography,* however, does include a variety of subtones that range from the homiletic to the histrionic, the resigned to the resentful, and the petitionary to the posturing. The closest the narrator comes to the facetious tone of "Love, Mystery, and Murder" is when the pains of his apprenticeship, undergone in order to support his poverty-stricken family, lead him to question "why it was that I should be called upon to sacrifice the Immortal for the Mortal—to give away irrevocably the Promethean fire within me for the cooking of a beefsteak—to destroy and damn my own soul that I might preserve for a few miserable months or years the bodies of others" (233).

19. As Patricia Coughlan notes in "The Recycling of *Melmoth.*" This essay and her aforementioned "Fold over Fold" are pioneering and invaluable analyses of tonal shifts and intertextuality in Mangan's fiction and poetry.

20. W. J. McCormack has used Balzac's *Melmoth Réconcilié* as part of a project to salvage Joseph Sheridan Le Fanu from a "so-called" and "doubtful" "Irish gothic tradition" (*Dissolute Characters* 3). However, the omission of any discussion of Mangan's "The Man in the Cloak" renders McCormack's attempt rather problematic.

21. In the last hours of his life, Maturin's Melmoth declares, "No one has ever exchanged destinies with Melmoth the Wanderer. *I have traversed the world in the search, and no one, to gain that world, would lose his own soul!*" (538). However, a never fully-confronted question haunts the novel—and undermines the doctrinal defensiveness of Maturin's preface: why did Melmoth make the original bargain?

22. Wayne Hall notes that when the London *Sun* concluded that the *Dublin University Magazine* "desired simply to do away with all Catholics," the magazine hastily rejoined that "it had carefully defined the problem, not as Catholics, but as Catholicism" (54).

23. Ironically, the magazine enthusiastically supported proselytism to convert Catholics. See Hall 57-58.

24. Coughlan also observes that the malevolent monk in "Love, Mystery, and Murder" permits himself for "recreation ... the occasional use of a tobacco pipe, the smoke of which drove away the ghosts" (Coughlan, "Recycling" 186; Mangan, *Prose 1* 53).

25. As we can see, the tone quickly switches here again, via Braunbrock's allusion to the Book of Job. Other examples of tone shifts (which often take the form of obtrusive puns) can be found on pages 250, 253, 254, 257, 258, and 264-66. Mangan retains Balzac's bathetic coda, but he turns the German demonologist into an astrologer and cuts out the reference to syphilis.

26. Mitchel referred to a "grotesque, bitter" humor that "leaves an unpleasant impression, as if he were grimly sneering at himself and at all the world; purposely spoiling and marring the effect of fine poetry by turning it into burlesque, and showing how meanly he regarded everything, even his Art, wherein he lived and had his being, when he compared his own exalted ideal of Art and Life with the bitterness of all his experiences and performances" (cited in O'Donoghue, xliv).

As Patricia Coughlan notes, a vivid example of critical frustration and editorial intervention produced by Mangan's work can be found in the last stanza of "Broken-Hearted Lays—No. 1," which was excised by D. J. O'Donoghue in his centenary edition of the poems ("Recycling" 190-91). In his notes to the poem, O'Donoghue comments that the "portion of the *absurd and perverse* tag has been omitted" (328; my italics).

27. We can find a relevant link here with Edgar Allan Poe, who entitled his 1840 collection of stories *Tales of the Grotesque and Arabesque.* In his famous "Preface" to the two volumes, Poe states that the "epithets 'Grotesque' and 'Arabesque' will be found to indicate with sufficient precision the prevalent tenor of the tales here published" (*Collected Works* 473). He is keen to refute critical assertions of "'Germanism' and gloom" (473), declaring that "there is no one of these stories in which the scholar should recognize the distinctive features of that species of pseudo-horror which we are taught to call Germanic, for no better reason than that some of the secondary names of German literature have become identified with its folly" (473); "terror," he insists, "is not of Germany, but of the soul" (473). One of Poe's editors, G. R. Thompson, has noted the techniques of Romantic irony at work in both his explicitly comic and his supposedly more serious stories (*Great Short Works* 9-11, 18-45). Like Mangan, Poe worked both within and against the Gothic mode: for an example of outright parody, see "How to Write a Blackwood Article. A Predicament" (1838; 1845); for a more subtle parody, which—like Mangan's "The Man in the

Cloak"—critiques Gothic "fustian" (429), see "The Premature Burial" (1844; 1845); for an apparently straight treatment that incorporates sudden tone shifts, see "The Fall of the House of Usher" (1839; 1845). I am grateful to my colleague Dr. Richard Fusco for alerting me to these similarities.

28. Paul Muldoon offers another possible category. Referring to the recurrent appearance in Irish writing of a "discrepancy between outward appearance and inward reality," he remarks that he is "tempted" to term it "Eriny" (6). I should be tempted to call "The Man in the Cloak" an example of "Romantic Eriny," were it not for Muldoon's assertion that the device constitutes "a central tenet" of a rather doubtful entity entitled "the Irish imagination" (6).

29. Lack of space precludes a detailed discussion of the "philosophical stance"—to use Bishop's term—at work within "The Man in the Cloak." Suffice to say, at present, that it is "ontological" and "epistemological" rather than "ethical."

30. See Coughlan ("Fold over Fold" 194; "Recycling" 187-88) and Shannon-Mangan (163, 195-98, 245-47, 288).

31. Space restrictions prevent for the moment a detailed consideration of the tonal shifts and intensities and the supernaturalist modes (from mentalist to orientalist) in other examples of Mangan's fiction, such as "An Extraordinary Adventure in the Shades," "My Transformation: A Wonderful Tale," "The Thirty Flasks," and "The Threefold Prediction. A Psychological Narrative."

32. Mangan signs "The Man in the Cloak" with the sobriquet "B.A.M." As Patricia Coughlan notes—again, via the *O.E.D.*—to bam "was a slang word meaning 'to hoax, practice on the credulity of, deceive, impose, cozen,' and a 'bam' was 'a story intended to impose on the credulous'" ("Recycling" 183). With respect to the Catholic and nationalist dimensions of "The Man in the Cloak," Mangan successfully bams the editors of the *D.U.M.*

33. For a preliminary exploration of the merging and montaging of literary modes in *Dorian Gray,* see Haslam, "Melmoth (OW)."

34. W. J. McCormack includes Carleton's "Wildgoose Lodge" in his influential *Field Day* section on Irish Gothic but highlights those elements in the story that "reflect" the author's "conversion to the Church of Ireland" ("Irish Gothic and After" 873). Siobhán Kilfeather has suggested that the Gothic and denominational affiliations of Carleton's story may be more complex ("Terrific Register" 59-60), a claim that I believe is reinforced by a reading of "The Lianhan Shee." I am grateful to Dr. Kilfeather for sharing with me her forthcoming essay on Irish Gothic for *The Cambridge Companion to the Irish Novel,* in which she discusses Gothic motifs in the work of Irish Catholic authors like Mangan and the Banims and poses a pertinent question: "Is the Gothic always the nightmare of the oppressor, or can it be a vehicle for dissent from below?"

35. As Robert Hume notes, it is "evident the serious Gothic works were written with effect very much in mind—terror, horror, mystery in a more than frivolous sense—and hence 'affective' groupings have some justification" (Platzner and Hume 274). Hume also makes the important qualification that there is a "vast difference between reading one's responses back into a work" (W. K. Wimsatt and Monroe Beardsley's so-called "affective fallacy") and the procedure of "seeking, on *internal* evidence, to determine the response it is apparently designed to elicit" (274).

Works Cited

Backus, Margot Gayle. *The Gothic Family Romance: Heterosexuality, Child Sacrifice, and the Anglo-Irish Colonial Order.* Durham: Duke University Press, 1999.

Baldick, Chris. "Introduction." *Melmoth the Wanderer,* by Charles Maturin. Oxford: Oxford University Press, 1989. vii-xix.

Balzac, Honoré de. *Melmoth Reconciled.* In *The Magic Skin, The Quest of the Absolute, and Other Stories.* Intro. George Saintsbury. Boston: Jefferson Press, 1901. 293-344.

Bishop, Lloyd. *Romantic Irony in French Literature from Diderot to Beckett.* Nashville: Vanderbilt University Press, 1989.

Botting, Fred. *Gothic.* London: Routledge, 1996.

Boulger, James. *The Calvinist Temper in English Poetry.* The Hague: Moulton, 1980.

Calvin, John. *Concerning the Eternal Predestination of God.* Trans. J. K. S. Reid. London: James Clarke, 1961.

Coughlan, Patricia. "'Fold over Fold, Inveterately Convolv'd': Some Aspects of Mangan's Intertextuality." In *Anglo-Irish and Irish Literature: Aspects of Language and Culture.* Ed. Birgit Bramsbäck and Martin Croghan. 2 vols. Stockholm: Almqvist and Wiksell International, 1988. II, 191-200.

———. "The Recycling of *Melmoth*: 'A Very German Story.'" In *Literary Interrelations: Ireland, England and the World.* 3 vols. Ed. Wolfgang Zach and Heinz Kosok. Tübingen: Gunter Narr Verlag, 1987. II, 181-99.

Deane, Seamus. *A Short History of Irish Literature.* London: Hutchinson, 1986.

———. *Strange Country: Modernity and Nationhood in Irish Writing since 1790.* Oxford: Clarendon Press, 1997.

Eagleton, Terry. *Heathcliff and the Great Hunger: Studies in Irish Culture.* London: Verso, 1995.

Foster, R. F. *Paddy and Mr Punch: Connections in Irish and English History.* London: Penguin, 1993.

Gibbons, Luke. *Gaelic Gothic: Race, Colonization, and Irish Culture.* Galway, Ireland: Arlen House, 2004.

Greenblatt, Stephen, and M. H. Abrams, eds. *The Norton Anthology of English Literature: The Major Authors.* Eighth ed. New York: W. W. Norton, 2006.

Griffin, Gerald. *Holland-Tide; or, Munster Popular Tales.* London: Simpkin and Marshall, 1827.

Hall, Wayne E. *Dialogues in the Margin: A Study of the Dublin University Magazine.* Washington, D.C.: The Catholic University Press, 1999.

Haslam, Richard. "Irish Gothic." *The Routledge Companion to Gothic.* Ed. Catherine Spooner and Emma McEvoy. London: Routledge, forthcoming 2007.

———. "Joseph Sheridan Le Fanu and the Fantastic Semantics of Ghost-Colonial Ireland." *That Other World: The Supernatural and the Fantastic in Irish Literature and Its Contexts.* 2 vols. Ed. Bruce Stewart. Gerrards Cross: Colin Smythe, 1998. I, 268-86.

———. "Maturin and the 'Calvinist Sublime.'" *Gothick Origins and Innovations.* Ed. Allan Lloyd Smith and Victor Sage. Amsterdam/Atlanta: Editions Rodopi, 1994. 44-56.

———. "Melmoth (OW): Gothic Modes in *The Picture of Dorian Gray.*" *Irish Studies Review* 12:3 (December 2004): 303-14.

Hogg, James. *The Private Memoirs and Confessions of a Justified Sinner* (1824). Oxford World's Classics: Oxford and New York, Oxford University Press (rev. ed.), 1999.

Joyce, James. *The Critical Writings of James Joyce.* Ed. Ellsworth Mason and Richard Ellmann. London: Faber and Faber, 1959.

Kennelly, Brendan, ed. *The Penguin Book of Irish Verse.* Second Ed. London: Penguin, 1981.

Kilfeather, Siobhán. "Gothic Novel." *The Cambridge Companion to the Irish Novel.* Ed. J. W. Foster. Cambridge: Cambridge University Press, 2006.

———. "Origins of the Irish Female Gothic." *Bullán* 1:2 (Autumn 1994): 35-45.

———. "Terrific Register: The Gothicization of Atrocity in Irish Romanticism." *Boundary 2,* 31:1 (Spring 2004): 49-71.

Killeen, Jarlath. *Gothic Ireland: Horror and the Irish Anglican Imagination in the Long Eighteenth Century.* Dublin: Four Courts Press, 2005.

Kilroy, James, ed. *Autobiography.* James Clarence Mangan. Dublin: The Dolmen Press, 1968.

Lloyd, David. *Nationalism and Minor Literature: James Clarence Mangan and the Emergence of Irish Cultural Nationalism.* Berkeley: University of California Press, 1987.

Lougy, Robert E. *Charles Robert Maturin.* Lewisburg: Bucknell University Press, 1975.

Mangan, James Clarence. *Prose 1832-1839.* [*Prose 1.*] Blackrock: Irish Academic Press, 2002.

———. *Prose 1840-1882.* [*Prose 2.*] Blackrock: Irish Academic Press, 2002.

Massillon, Jean Baptiste. *Oeuvres.* 3 vols. Paris: Gaume Frères et J. Duprey, 1864.

Maturin, Charles. *Melmoth the Wanderer.* Oxford: Oxford University Press, 1989.

McCormack, W. J. *Dissolute Characters: Irish Literary History through Balzac, Sheridan Le Fanu, Yeats and Bowen.* Manchester: Manchester University Press, 1993.

———. "Irish Gothic and After (1820-1945)." *The Field Day Anthology of Irish Writing.* Ed. Seamus Deane. 3 vols. Derry: Field Day, 1991. II, 831-949.

Mighall, Robert. *A Geography of Victorian Gothic Fiction: Mapping History's Nightmares.* Oxford: Oxford University Press, 1999.

Moynahan, Julian. "The Politics of Anglo-Irish Gothic: Maturin, Le Fanu and the Return of the Repressed." *Studies in Anglo-Irish Literature.* Ed. Heinz Kosok. Bonn: Bouvier Verlag, 1982. 43-53.

Muldoon, Paul. *To Ireland, I.* Oxford: Oxford University Press, 2000.

O'Donoghue, D. J., ed. *Poems of James Clarence Mangan.* Dublin: M. H. Gill & Son, 1903.

Platzner, Robert L., and Robert D. Hume. "'Gothic Versus Romantic': A Rejoinder." *PMLA* 86 (1971): 266-74.

Poe, Edgar Allan. *Collected Works of Edgar Allan Poe: Tales and Sketches, 1831-1842.* Ed. Thomas Ollive Mabbott, et al. Cambridge, Mass.: The Belknap Press, 1978.

———. *Great Short Works of Edgar Allan Poe: Poems, Tales, Criticism.* Ed. G. R. Thompson. New York: Harper & Row, 1970.

Schlegel, Friedrich. *Dialogue on Poetry and Literary Aphorisms.* Trans. E. Behler and R. Strug. University Park: Pennsylvania State University Press, 1968.

Shannon-Mangan, Ellen. *James Clarence Mangan: A Biography.* Blackrock: Irish Academic Press, 1996.

Tarr, Sister Mary Muriel. *Catholicism in Gothic Fiction: A Study of the Nature and Function of Catholic Materials in Gothic Fiction in England (1762-1820).* Washington: The Catholic University of America Press, 1946.

Aingeal Clare (essay date 2009)

SOURCE: Clare, Aingeal. "'Pseudostylic Shamiana': James Joyce and James Clarence Mangan." *Joyce Studies Annual* (2009): 248-65. Print.

[*In the following essay, Clare identifies a trend among critics of Mangan to discuss him mostly as part of the Young Irelanders. She describes Joyce's efforts to praise Mangan's writing outside of that historical context and analyzes Mangan's own impact on Joyce's writing.*]

David Lloyd begins an article on the Oriental translations of James Clarence Mangan with an explication of the two dominant readings of Mangan's literary status in Ireland. One sees him as the prodigy of the Young Ireland movement, contributing rabble-rousing lyrics to Nationalist journals, while the other classes him as the bridge between British high Romanticism and Anglo-Irish Revivalism, a peer of Coleridge and Shelley and a precursor of Yeats and Joyce. Consequently, writes Lloyd, Mangan has been read in terms of his "failure to meet the standards of either of the poles between which [he] is located"; his patriotism was insufficiently fervent, his poetic muse too fanciful for him to adequately represent the Nationalist movement, while his dubious status as a "bridge" between Romanticism and Revivalism is problematic in that it defines the poet only in terms of what he is not: As a Romantic, he limps belatedly past the finishing post with little that is new to contribute, while his "misfired attempt to forge an Irish idiom" inevitably finds him languishing in the "oblivion" Joyce tentatively identified as the poet's final resting place.[1] The broadness of historical generalization in both the Nationalist and Romantic-Revivalist readings makes for two very narrow critical appreciations of Mangan. The overlap between them means that the Anglo-Irish reading is more often implied than fully expounded, but the view of Mangan as the banner-waving *Wunderkind* of the Nationalist cause has persisted. For this reason, Mangan rarely meets with critical engagement outside of this political-historical context.

An early enemy of this line of criticism was James Joyce, who in two lectures on the poet attempted to free Mangan from this restricting public role as sometime creature of the Young Ireland movement. This essay will assess Joyce's critical position *vis-à-vis* Mangan, before broadening into an exploration of the artistic influence of Mangan over Joyce, an influence often overlooked by Joyce scholars. References to Mangan abound in Joyce's prose; there are several Mangan cuttings in *Ulysses,* most conspicuously the word "contransmagnificandjewbangtantiality," taken from a coinage Mangan used to describe an elegy he had written in a letter to Charles Gavan Duffy.[2] *Finnegans Wake* (mis)quotes the poems and prose with abandon, and bases a substantial slice of narrative (Shem's "Portrait") partly on Mangan's famous ***Autobiography.*** All of these respectful salutes toward Mangan invite critical attention that, strangely, Joyce scholarship has scarcely recognized.[3]

In 1902, the young Joyce wrote an address to the Literary and Historical Society of University College, Dublin, entitled "James Clarence Mangan." In it, Joyce introduces Mangan, "the most significant poet of the modern Celtic world," to an Irish audience that, according to Joyce, has all but forgotten him. The essay's style is ornamental to the point of conceitedness, and the argument accordingly difficult to follow. Paterian flourishes of rhetoric warn the reader that the essay is as much an exercise in dramatic presentation as an attempt to restore Mangan to the Irish consciousness; an over-long introduction to the Romantic school makes no mention of Mangan, and when Joyce finally does settle on his subject, Mangan often finds himself upstaged and displaced by Joyce's stylistic experiments:

> Vittoria Colonna and Laura and Beatrice—even she upon whose face many lives have cast that shadowy delicacy, as of one who broods upon distant terrors and riotous dreams, and that strange stillness before which love is silent, Mona Lisa—embody one chivalrous idea, which is no mortal thing, bearing it bravely above the accidents of lust and faithlessness and weariness; and she whose white and holy hands have the virtue of enchanted hands, his virgin flower, and flower of flowers, is no less than these an embodiment of that idea.[4]

That a version of this essay, with all mention of Mangan erased, found its way into the fledgling novel *Stephen Hero* is a good indication of Joyce's priorities at this time: The young author wanted to carve a reputation as a stylish polemicist, an opinionated and thoroughly modern innovator; the task of rescuing Mangan from obscurity took a deliberate second place to these ambitions.

Five years later, Joyce translated and revised "James Clarence Mangan" for the purpose of a series of Irish-themed lectures he had been commissioned to give at Trieste's *Università del Popolo.* While this essay has tended to be treated as a later version of the original 1902 essay, "Giacomo Clarenzio Mangan" in fact stands up as an interesting critical document in its own right. It is more readable, both critically and stylistically, than its template, and provides us with some helpful insights into Joyce's changing critical attitudes toward Ireland since his voluntary exile nearly five years earlier. A comparative analysis between the two essays, as the critic Eric Bulson has noted, can provide a "barometer" to gauge Joyce's development as a prose stylist writing in another language and as an ambitious writer testing out aesthetic theories.[5] But more than this, Bulson argues, self-translation affords the opportunity for a more radical self-revision, and Joyce's less kind attitude toward Mangan's prose essays in 1907 (the charge shifts up a notch from "pretty fooling" to "insipid efforts") recasts Mangan less as a victim of Ireland's lack of "native tradition" than as a contributor to that condition. Failing to represent an adequate solution, Mangan's prose becomes part of the problem:

> His writings, which have never been collected in a definitive edition, show no order whatsoever and often very little thought. His prose essays may perhaps be interesting on the first reading, but, in truth, they are but insipid efforts. Their style is conceited, in the worst sense of the word, contorted and banal, their argument crude and inflated, and, finally, their prose belongs to the style in which trivial items of news in a provincial newspaper are published.
>
> (132-3)[6]

Bulson interprets this passage as an indicator of Joyce's less forgiving attitude toward Ireland's struggling writers; in 1902, Joyce included himself in that group, whereas in 1907 he is able to look down from his Continental vantage point as one who made the necessary sacrifices for his art, as Mangan and others had failed to do. The shift in Joyce's sympathy toward Mangan, writes Bulson, "makes manifest Joyce's adamant refusal to accept complacency and victimhood as excuses for his race" (433). It is an attractive argument, and one that fits in very neatly with our idea of Joyce flying by the nets of an artistically stunted and self-pitying Ireland, but it is somewhat discredited by Joyce's decision to follow up his harsh judgment with a list of just such "excuses," as he had done in 1902:

> It must be remembered, however, that Mangan wrote with no native literary tradition, for a public which cared for the matters of the day, and believed that the poet's only task was to illustrate these facts. He could not, unless in exceptional circumstances, correct his work . . .
>
> (133)

These excuses were still legitimate for Joyce; we have to look deeper if we are to understand Joyce's relationship with Mangan and his apparent dismissal of the prose.

What is conspicuous in both essays is the extent to which Joyce credits himself with discovering Mangan, and the bravado with which he appoints himself as the poet's posthumous literary agent, effectively marketing him in Dublin and Trieste. In fact, Joyce was by no means the first of his contemporaries to be attracted by the eccentric, solipsistic figure cut by Mangan. Yeats was quick to recognize his greatness, and if Mangan was appropriated to the national cause by Yeats as much as by the Mitchels and O'Dalys of his own time, the purpose was only to install him on the pedestal typically reserved for his more heroically flag-waving peers: "Nor would I less be counted one / With Davis, Mangan, Ferguson."[7] Yeats was a passionate advocate of Mangan's lyric virtuosity, calling his poetry in an "impromptu speech" to the Irish Literary Society "as near to perfection as anything that has ever been written,"[8] and in a sympathetic phrase accounting for the disapproval Mangan often encountered: "If you tie a red ribbon to the leg of a sea-gull, the other gulls will peck it to death. To the soul of Clarence Mangan was tied the burning ribbon of genius."[9]

The important thing to say about Joyce's Mangan is that he was not at all the dutiful creature of Irish Nationalism that many self-serving critics and contemporaries made him out to be. The Mangan of Joyce's two lectures is admired for his depth and intensity of feeling, his outlandish (and Oriental) literary leanings, and the scope of his poetic imagination. While patriotic idealism was far from Joyce's list of admirable literary habits, the two Mangan essays do betray an uncertainty about just how nationalist Mangan actually was, branding him by turns the "national poet" not yet accepted as such, then "little of a patriot." Joyce noted his refusal to publish in English journals, but also his refusal to "prostitute himself to the rabble or become a mouthpiece for politicians" ("Giacomo Clarenzio Mangan" 134). We can forgive Joyce his wavering on this subject, as it is indeed difficult to work out what Mangan himself thought of the Nationalist cause. We know that toward the end of the 1840s he became radicalized, writing to the vehement Young Irelander John Mitchel that "I thoroughly sympathise with your sentiments, that I identify my views of public affairs with yours, and that I am prepared to go to all lengths with you . . . for the achievement of our national independence" (***Collected Works: Prose 1840-1882*** [***The Collected Works of James Clarence Mangan: Prose, 1840-1882***] 168). In an 1832 letter to his friend Tynan, however, Mangan comically distanced himself from political activity of any kind, blaming laziness for his chronic apathy and ignorance of political affairs. He notes that "Nothing occurs in Ireland. No prospect of a Revolution," and concedes that a revolution might be propitious on the condition that "it produced a general transfer of property and I had any prospect of robbing somebody, for my finances are too low for my ideas, which are of the princeliest" (248-9).[10]

Mangan's politics at this time, if he had any, constituted both a romantic despotism, where fairy tales filled with autocratic kings and queens were lauded as perfected versions of reality, and a "pseudo-patriotism," as he might have called it.[11] This was hardly the committed nationalism of so many biographical portraits and second-hand stories. Even Mitchel's miniature biography of his friend acknowledges that Mangan took little interest in party meetings, though "when he . . . believed that a mortal struggle was approaching . . . he became vehemently excited." In any case, it could be argued, contemporary Irish nationalism was not without an element of fairytale escapism in its own right. I have mentioned Mangan's Orientalism, and among the more eccentric strands in nineteenth-century antiquarianism was Charles Vallancey's belief that the Irish language was descended from ancient Phoenician. Mangan refers to Vallancey in an 1839 epigraph as "Prov[ing] us mere Irish to be Orientals,"[12] and no doubt it was the same spirit of the exotic East that drove Joyce to make "Mangan's sister" the love-object of the protagonist of "Araby" in *Dubliners.* When Duffy and Mitchel condemned Mangan's translations as "Apocrypha" and "Perversions," they were holding him to a concept of purity and cultural exclusivism that he failed to recognize, not just in his translations but also in his "original" poems and politics. The exotic is domesticated under the veil of Irishness, but Irishness, too, is estranged and refreshed in the process.

Mitchel annexes Mangan's identity, in typical nationalist style, to that of his race and nation: "Whatever relic of manly vigour and force of character was still left living amid the wrecks and ruins of the man seemed to flame up; for his history and fate were indeed a type and shadow of the land he loved so well."[13] The strategy, David Lloyd has noted, is "fundamental to nationalist ideology."[14] Joyce, who gathered much of his biographical information about Mangan from Mitchel's introduction to the ***Poems*** [***Poems of James Clarence Mangan***], draws the same conclusion, painting Mangan as an individual embodiment of the national struggle: "Love of sorrow, desperation, high-sounding threats, these are the great traditions of James Clarence Mangan's race; and, in that miserable, reedy, feeble figure, a hysteric nationalism receives its final justification" ("Giacomo Clarenzio Mangan" 136). It is perhaps a little disappointing that Joyce allowed himself to fall back on these Romantic tropes, although the shift into mawkish martyrdom is at least more understated than in the 1902 original: "With Mangan a narrow and hysterical nationality receives a last justification, for when this feeble-bodied figure departs dusk begins to veil the train of the gods, and he who listens may hear their footsteps leaving the world" (60). Here Joyce risks crediting Mangan with creating or defining the same nationalist cause from whose association Joyce is also trying to free Mangan; his argument seems to swallow its own tail, ouroboros-fashion. If Joyce doesn't want Mangan to be viewed eternally as the creature of the Nationalist cause, he chooses a perverse way of making his point.

Mangan is rarely read or written about today, and when he is, it is almost always with the aim of restoring him to the Nationalist tradition, historicizing his patriotic poetry, and examining his (rather uneven) connections to the Young Ireland movement. This would seem to be the reason why, though his poetry retains its place in anthologies of Irish literature, his prose languishes in what Joyce rather dramatically called "profound obscurity" (127). As illustrated previously, Joyce's own attitude to the prose was dismissive:

> His writings . . . show no order and sometimes very little thought. Many of his essays are pretty fooling when read once, but one cannot but discern some fierce energy beneath the banter . . . and there is a likeness between the desperate writer, himself the victim of too dexterous torture, and the contorted writing.
>
> (56)

It would be tempting to trace an anxiety of influence in Joyce's essay that prevents him, perhaps, from giving Mangan's prose its due; but in fairness, it is uncertain how much of the prose Joyce would have had the opportunity to read, there being published (as he notes) only "some pages of prose" in C. P. Meehan's 1884 ***Essays in Prose and Verse.*** Nevertheless, Meehan's book does contain some of the most brilliant examples of Mangan's exuberant prose style, including **"The Two Flats: Our Quackstitution,"** an extended piece of satirical paranomasia on the House of Commons (or "Clamours") and the House of Lords (or "Words"), the latter populated by a grotesque menagerie of "ducks, Mere-quizzes, Erralls, Wise-counts, and Barrens." The collection also includes **"A Treatise on a Pair of Tongs,"** a delightfully prolix panegyric to that necessary tool, and **"An Extraordinary Adventure in the Shades,"** a hallucinatory and Sternean account of an afternoon's drinking in a Dublin pub. Even this edition, however, offers a striking reminder of the process of refashioning and reconfiguring performed on Mangan by his admirers, omitting as it does the ***Autobiography,*** which had originally been written at Meehan's request, only to be dismissed as "the merest Reve d'une Vie, with here and there some filaments of reality in its texture" (a crestfallen Mangan offered to destroy the manuscript).[15] In the case of John Mitchel, whose edition, complete with long martyrological introduction, appeared in 1859, this refashioning took the form of editing out of the picture the apolitical younger Mangan found in the 1832 letter, any evidence of imaginative connection between Mangan and his English Romantic contemporaries, and to some extent the Mangan of wilder Orientalist flights of fancy, none of which was to Mitchel's more urgently propagandistic purpose.[16]

What is important to note, however, is that Joyce too, despite his evidently superior and more sensitive response to Mangan, engages in the same process of refashioning, in his way. If we leave Meehan and Mitchel aside for the moment, Mangan has already been laid claim to by the far more important figure of Yeats, in "to Ireland in the Coming Times." The enjoyable prospect of wresting him back from Yeats's embrace is not the least of the benefits accruing to the young Joyce from choosing Mangan as a precursor figure. But the shift in tone from the 1902 to the 1907 essay lays bare the important limits of this identification: Mangan is first a victim of and later a conniver in the culture of self-pitying nationalism that condemns his work to minor status. He rises up out of the conflagration and tragedy of post-Famine Ireland but never achieves the Dedalean exit velocity required to fly by the nets of nationality, language, and religion. What he fatally fails to achieve is the individuation of the modern artist who will represent the national drama of his people without becoming their creature and victim in the process. Mangan is thus both honored precursor and negative exemplar, whose shortcomings Joyce can project accusingly onto the Revivalist culture of his day. It is in the light of this ambivalence, on Joyce's part, that we should read his otherwise baffling negative comments on Mangan's prose (by far the most Joycean part of the *oeuvre*), whether or not he read the ***Autobiography*** during the Trieste years. He is recruiting the precursor to his private agon of tradition and influence, in which Mangan is allowed just so much overlap with Joyce's own work, but no more, or at least not until several decades have passed and we reach the gracious salutes to Mangan's prose in *Finnegans Wake.* James F. Wurtz notices this side of Joyce's response to Mangan in his "Famine Memory and Representations of the Gothic in *Ulysses,*" when he describes how "Joyce simultaneously praises and condemns the poet" and takes from him "an emphasis on guilt," coupled with what Wurtz terms Mangan's Gothic troping of sin, guilt, and the ghostly.[17] Out of this thematic nexus, Joyce developed a unique version of Catholic or post-Catholic Gothic in the spectres and sinners of *A Portrait* and *Ulysses.*[18] Wurtz's reading is an illuminating one, as it shows how the young Joyce, less obvious in his verbal play than the writer of *Finnegans Wake* and the later chapters of *Ulysses,* is influenced initially by the Gothic in Mangan, and then by the more ludic, proto-modernistic qualities of his prose squibs second. In demonstrating this link, Wurtz prepares the ground for investigations into the relationship between modernism and the Gothic, a relationship that is "manifest in Joyce's writing," and thus in which Joyce plays a central role (103). That these two strands of Joyce's style are both influenced by Mangan suggests that a re-reading of Mangan in relation to the Gothic-modernist axis may prove especially rewarding. I shall return to this topic at a later stage in my argument, in reference to Seamus Deane's influential reading of the Catholic Gothic in his study *Strange Country.*

For all the nationalist appropriation of Mangan as a figurehead for a would-be monolithic tradition, the true Mangan condition is one of mongrelization and impurity, serial textual fakery speaking from behind the arras of hoax translations, and it is in this version of Mangan, rather than the Young Ireland balladeer, that we find a way around Joyce's misgivings. The true Mangan is a mongrelized alter ego of Mitchel's nationalist martyr, and the truth of Joyce's Mangan too may require a blending of the claims made about him in the 1902 and 1907 essays. As an antecedent for the Joyce of *Finnegans Wake,* Mangan as cunning and punning autobiographer is at a far remove from the patriotic martyr portrayed in Joyce's early essays. For Mangan to become the serious artist of the ***Autobiography*** and his handful of great poems, he had to transcend the demands on his genius of nation and nationalists, and for Joyce to put the "Mangan inheritance" (to adopt the title of a Brian Moore novel) to creative use, he too had to transcend the nationalist template of his early essays. "The danger is in the neatness of identifications,"[19] Samuel Beckett warned at the beginning of his 1929 essay on Joyce's *Work in Progress,* and to read Mangan, Joyce on Mangan, and Joyce himself, a careful sieving out of premature assumptions and identifications is vital.

It is doubtful, in any case, that Mangan would have objected to Joyce's description of his prose as "fooling"; he himself calls his prose works "facetiæ"—in fact he aspires to this condition.[20] The prose pieces do, however, have a great deal in common with Joyce's later writing, a shared style and sensibility that goes far beyond merely reveling in puns and riddles (though there is plenty of this too), and was far stronger than the young Joyce was prepared to acknowledge or anticipate. Robert Welch has compared the neurotically interrogative passages of "An Extraordinary Adventure in the Shades" with the "Ithaca" chapter of *Ulysses,* pointing out that the difference between them lies in the fact that "Joyce's minutiae are a celebration of the multiplicity of things, and the variety of angles from which they can be looked at; [in Mangan] the complexity of external things, their mysteriousness, is a kind of threat to the existence of the psyche itself."[21] The "tortured torturer of reluctant rhymes," as Mangan described himself in the anthology favorite **"Twenty Golden Years Ago,"** would not have disagreed with this statement;[22] the suspicion and anxiety aroused by the world of objects in **"An Extraordinary Adventure in the Shades"** are comparable in force to Samuel Beckett's *Watt,* where attempts to control and order the external world bring about the collapse not only of the psyche but of language itself.

What is peculiar about Joyce's dismissal of Mangan's prose, and what reveals more than anything else the age and inexperience of the writer of the two essays, is the lack of self-recognition. We see this not only in his description of the contorted prose of the "desperate writer," but also in Mangan's prose itself, where what Joyce describes as "pretty fooling" flippancy is more often a tantalizing display of ludic, witty, wordy bravura, a species of the tradition of "that siamixed twoatalk used twist stern swift and jolly roger"—and also De Quincey, Lewis Carroll, and Edward Lear (*FW* 66.18-21). The ultimate inheritor of this tradition was, of course, Joyce himself. The passage from *Finnegans Wake* in which Joyce applauds the Sternean and Swiftian line in his literary heritage (the "jolly roger" refers to Swift's clerk, Roger Cox), follows a reference to a Mangan poem written "in seven divers stages of ink," and forms part of the question: "Will whatever will be written in lappish language with inbursts of Maggyer always seem semposed … in that siamixed twoatalk used twist stern swift and jolly roger?"[23] A half-authentic multilingualism ("lappish language with inbursts of Maggyer"), as well as a literary inheritance from Sterne and Swift, is shared by Joyce and Mangan; that these multilingual scraps of text are "semposed" on the Sterne/Swift axis suggests that the mature Joyce aligned Mangan's prose with that tradition.

Aside from Ronald McHugh's suggestions of "superimposed" and "symposium" in his *Annotations,* "semposed" also calls to mind Shem the Penman, whose "Portrait" we come across in Chapter VII.[24] There is a strong case to be made for reading Shem's "Portrait" as a perversion (Manganesque word) of Mangan's ***Autobiography,*** a text Joyce had certainly read at this point in his career. The chapter begins by itemizing Shem's "bodily getup" and his "low" tastes (169.11, 170.25), and unfolds into a sequence full of "thump and swagger and syrupy self-pity," as Louis MacNeice characterized Mangan.[25] Alienation and a lingering defeatism capture the mood both of the ***Autobiography*** and of Shem's "Portrait," and a number of references overlap: the "heavy downpour" that "blinds" the young Mangan; his family's rapid sink from an already low status to destitution ("the pleb was born a Quicklow and sank alowing till he stank out of sight") (174.23; 175.3-4); and Mangan's striking description of his father as "a human boa-constrictor *without his alimentive properties*" (***Collected Works: Prose 1840-1882*** 228), which resurfaces in Shem as "mynfadher was a boer constructor" (180.38).[26] Shem, like Mangan, takes a pseudonym, "maistre Sheames de la Plume," in order to write highly original works of fiction. As with the ***Autobiography,*** the reliability of the narrator must be called into question, and Shem self-reflexively addresses the problem:

> But would anyone, short of a madhouse, believe it? Neither of those clean little cherubim, Nero or Nobookisonester himself, ever nursed such a spoiled opinion of his monstrous marvellosity as did this mental and moral defective.
>
> (177.13-16)

Mangan self-diagnoses his "moral insanity" (***Collected Works: Prose 1840-1882*** 299) in the ***Autobiography,*** and certainly there is an almost intrusive insistence on his own "monstrous marvellosity" throughout that recalls Yeats's description of the unusual attraction of Mangan's work: "He does not say look at yourself in this mirror; but rather, 'Look at me—I am so strange, so exotic, so different.'"[27] Mangan's "look at me" approach to autobiography often strays into outrageous melodrama when, for example—and as Joyce notes in his 1902 essay ("James Clarence Mangan" 55)—the "tottering old fragment of a house, or … hovel" illustrated in Chapter III is described at a pitch of lurid overmuchness: "It consisted of two wretched rooms, or rather holes … Door or window was there none to the lower chamber—the place of the latter being supplied, not very elegantly, by a huge chasm in the bare and broken brick wall" (***Collected Works: Prose 1840-1882*** 231). When asked about the accuracy of this description, Mangan replied that he had dreamt the whole thing, a confession that gives marvelous clout to Shem's punning description of himself (or of Mangan, who admits to his "incurable hypochondriasis") as a "Ballade Imaginaire" (177.27-8).[27] In his analysis of this passage of the ***Autobiography,*** D. J. O'Donoghue cites Mangan's sketch of George Petrie, where the poet describes his method of forming an opinion:

> I take a few facts, not caring to be overwhelmed by too many proofs that they are facts; with them I mix up a dish of the marvellous—perhaps an old wife's tale—perhaps a half-remembered dream or mesmeric experience of my own—and the business is done.[28]

That Mangan's ***Autobiography,*** like Shem's self-portrait, is based on half-remembered dreams is wonderfully apt (*Finnegans Wake* itself being a dream), and if Shem wins his case against the implausibility of Mangan's memoir, it only underlines Shem's own reluctance to "look facts in their face" (179.7). Amid these charges of dishonesty and melodrama, Joyce cunningly slots a voice of defense ("Nobookisonester"), and in a broader sense this proves the more sympathetic reading, for in its encapsulation of a romantic sensibility, in its confession of incurable melancholy, "no book is honester" than Mangan's ***Autobiography.***

Mangan's many pseudonyms are also a fruitful topic of discussion for Shem:

> Who can say how many pseudostylic shamiana, how few or how many of the most venerated public impostures, how very many piously forged palimpsests slipped in the first place by this morbid process from his pelagiarist pen?
>
> (181.36-182.3)

It is interesting that where Joyce is at his most self-reflexive, the theme is Mangan. Joyce, a confessed plagiarist (or "scissors and paste man," as he prefers), refers after this passage to Shem "[stippling] endlessly inartistic portraits of himself," an unveiled intertextual reference to *A Portrait of the Artist as a Young Man.* The endlessly evasive nature of Mangan's personality found its reverse in the self-reflexive quality of so much of his writing (one thinks of **"The Nameless One"** and **"Neither One Thing Nor t'Other"**). His various public incarnations ranged from the shadowy "man in the Cloak" to the turban-donning "Hafiz" of his Oriental "shamiana," and included the self-pitying "poor Mangan" only as one member of a copious cast of possible personae. In a third-person sketch of himself written as part of his series of "Reminiscences" of Irish notables, Mangan wrote that "people have called him a singular man, but he is rather a plural one—a Proteus, as the *Dublin Review* designates him."[29] Mangan's multiple personalities or "venerated public impostures" help to "drown his singularity in literary plurality," as Jacques Chuto has written, and to snuff out the oppressive sense of failure and self-loathing that penetrates so much of his autobiographical writing.[30] Mangan is comparable in this instance to other cosmopolitan-provincial writers, such as Søren Kierkegaard and Fernando Pessoa, each living in capital cities (Dublin, Copenhagen, Lisbon), which nonetheless seem peripheral and belated in comparison to the capitals of Continental culture (London, Paris, Berlin). Each suffered from intense feelings of isolation, amplified by their state of provincial exile from the cultural capitals of Europe, and existential and spiritual angst, which prompted them to publish under a sequence of pseudonyms (or "heteronyms" as Pessoa called them), and which in turn enabled an escape from and rejection of the self and its many shortcomings.

Aside from the few draft versions of *Dubliners* stories published under the name of Stephen Dedalus in 1904, Joyce never felt the need to acquire the pseudonyms that unlocked so much literary freedom for his predecessors and compatriots. (I am thinking in particular of Brian O'Nolan's "Flann O'Brien" and "Myles na gCopaleen.") This didn't stop him, however, from sporting a number of different guises and personae to ferment the mystique that had been steadily gathering around him since the publication of *A Portrait of the Artist as a Young Man.* Like Bloom in "Circe," Joyce was a master shape-shifter; in a letter of 1921, he listed with a mixture of satisfaction and annoyance the circulating rumors of what had become of him during the logomanic years of his writing *Ulysses*:

> A man from Liverpool told me he had heard that I was the owner of several cinema theatres all over Switzerland. In America [there are] two versions: one that I was almost blind, emaciated and consumptive, the other that I am an austere mixture of the Dalai Lama and sir Rabindranath Tagore. Mr Pound described me as a dour Aberdeen minister. Mr Lewis told me he was told that I was a crazy fellow who always carried four watches and rarely spoke except to ask my neighbour what o'clock it was. Mr Yeats [described me] as a kind of Dick Swiveller.
>
> (*SL* 282)

The report of an Oriental Joyce, half Dalai Lama, half Tagore, is particularly pleasing, especially given how many of Mangan's pseudo-personalities were cultivated from Arabic and Persian poets via his prolific collection of "anti-plagiaristic" translations. In his third-person self-portrait written as part of a series of "sketches of Modern Irish Writers," Mangan writes that "my poor friend Clarence has perpetrated a great many singular literary sins, which, taken together, … would appear to be 'the antithesis of plagiarism'" (***Collected Works: Prose 1840-1882*** 223). The sin was his "addiction," as he put it, to "fathering upon other writers the offspring of his own brain." His reasons for such practice, he claims, are twofold: first, Mangan "entertained a deep diffidence of his own capacity to amuse or attract others, by anything emanating from himself" (223); second, in order to maintain the façade of authenticity, the author explains:

> I once asked Mangan why he did not prefix his own name to his anti-plagiaristic productions, and his reply was characteristic of the man: "that would be no go; nohow you fixed it: I must write in a variety of styles; and it wouldn't do for me to don the turban, and open my poem with a Bismillah."
>
> (224)

Here the poet replaces one species of imposture with another, more radical kind: Not wanting fraudulently to "don the turban" himself, or to pretend that he, an untraveled Catholic Dubliner, can cry to Allah, he does away with his own poetic identity altogether and adopts another, more "authentic" one. The motive is "parrydocksickle" (255);[31] the poet swaps second-hand inauthenticity for first-hand masquerade, and fails to hide another, more urgent motive: his impish affection for the literary hoax.

David Lloyd has written in an article on Mangan's Orientalism of the labyrinths of scholarly reference the poet would construct around his translations. What John Mitchel called "Apocrypha," and D. J. O'Donoghue "Oriental Versions and Perversions," Lloyd calls unceremonious "spoofs."[32] Mangan's "parodistic" translation style, writes Lloyd, picks fun at the Oriental scholar's preoccupation with sources. In an article on Mangan's own sources, Jacques Chuto showed us that a large amount of Mangan's material originates from Joseph von Hammer-Purgstall's *Geschichte der Osmanischen Dichtkunst,* for which Mangan professes a great degree of respect in his **"Literæ Orientales"** article on Turkish poetry, where he praises Hammer-Purgstall as "one man in a million … the first Orientalist of his era" (***Collected Works: Prose 1840-1882*** 150).[33] Throughout the **"Literæ Orientales,"** Mangan lifts from Hammer-Purgstall freely, "distorts or appropriates [his scholarly passages] with varying degrees of disguise as his own, and frequently sets up blind trails with false or inaccurate references" ("Mangan's Oriental Translations" 26). Moreover, those sources that are full enough to be pursued often yield originals that are "nonexistent, misattributed," or unrecognizable (26). If Hammer-Purgstall is "one man in a million," Mangan aspires to be the reverse, a million men in one (the *Dublin Review*'s "complete literary Proteus"), bestowing his own original poems on fake authors, and tracing his liberal perversions of poems to erroneous or invisible sources. Chuto suggests that such practice forms an elaborate practical joke "at the expense of Hammer-Purgstall and scholars in general," and also of any reader committed or gullible enough to attempt to take up Mangan's perplexing trail of references ("The Sources of James Clarence Mangan's Oriental Writings" 227). His strategy strongly recalls Joyce's (aptly unsourced) remark to one of his translators about *Ulysses*: "I've put in so many enigmas and puzzles that it will keep the professors busy for centuries arguing over what I meant, and that's the only way of insuring one's immortality" (*JJ* 521). The same is even truer of *Finnegans Wake,* the very existence of which throws down the gauntlet to any intrepid scholar who thinks he or she can trace every last source.

For Mangan, however, such trickery was not enough to cement his "immortality." If anything, the nebulousness of his pseudo-scholarly endeavors contributed to Mangan's present status as minor poet and Gothic curiosity. It is interesting and not a little ironic that the literary effects Joyce learned from, or at the very least shared with, his predecessor served him far better than they did Mangan: the playful, multilingual puzzles; the skits and jokes played on academic seriousness; the self-mythologizing and endless writerly self-reinvention; the subtle subversions of the notions of plagiarism and "anti-plagiarism." These games and experiments are distinctly modernist in flavor; they had no place in the world of the patriotic purpose and righteous balladeering that characterized Victorian Dublin. I have quoted the "Portrait of Shem the Penman" chapter of *Finnegans Wake* and its reference to Shem's "pelagiarist pen." Joyce's work, and in particular *Ulysses,* abounds in heretics; Pelagius's heresy was to deny original sin and state that good works alone could lead man to God. Mangan's commitment to Young Ireland nationalism may be a kind of original sin in the eyes of the Joyce of 1902 and 1907, but the creative use to which Joyce puts him constitutes sufficient good works to redeem this stigma. Mangan, in any case, appears as much an "anti-pelagiarist" as an "anti-plagiarist," as he writes toward the end of the ***Autobiography***: "From the days of Adam in Eden to our own we purchase Knowledge at the price of Innocence" (***Collected Works: Prose 1840-1882*** 238). Ever contradictory though, Mangan's "anti-pelagiarism" by no means makes him a faithful Catholic, but rather finds him stranded between "a Gothic experience of intense formlessness and a Catholic account of the shape a life should have," as Seamus Deane writes.[34] When the "Catholic Christian" stranger accosts him outside Rathfarnham, Mangan takes issue with the stranger's optimism, borne, he says, out of ignorance of his religion. Mangan, unchristian in his reading of unhealthy literature and his pessimistic view of the world, proves himself more Catholic than the upbeat stranger when he discovers the latter's Catholicism and asks:

> "Then," said I, "you know that it is the belief of the holiest and most learned theologians of your church that the majority of mankind will be irrevocably consigned to eternal misery?"
>
> "I know no such thing," he replied.
>
> "Have you never read Massillon," I asked, "on 'The Small Number of the Saved'?"
>
> "I take the judgment of no one individual even in my own church," he answered, "as my guide. The goodness—the justice of GOD—"
>
> I interrupted him. "Stop," said I. "What do you
>
> (***Collected Works: Prose 1840-1882*** 239)

Here the ***Autobiography*** ends in abrupt aposiopesis, as much a Romantic ruin as its author and subject. Mangan's own "*non serviam*" is cut short, fragmented before it has a chance to mean something, and the same could be said not only of his "pseudo-patriotic" Nationalism, but of his whole career and reputation as a writer both of rabble-rousing ballads and more decadent "pseudostylic shamiana." Mangan's arguments with himself, and Joyce's with Mangan, are suspended before certain "identifications" can acquire any "neatness" (to quote Beckett once more). It is the critic's responsibility, therefore, to fill the gaps in a textual relationship that asserts itself in scraps and fragments over time and throughout Joyce's *oeuvre.* Joyce wonders, in his 1907 essay, whether "the undisturbed peace in which [Mangan] lies has become so welcome to him that he will take umbrage . . . at hearing his spectral quietude disturbed by an exiled fellow-countryman delivering an unskilled lecture" ("Giacomo Clarenzio Mangan" 127). This uncharacteristic self-effacement says a great deal about Joyce's respect for his predecessor, and it is unlikely that any umbrage would have been taken against the service Joyce did Mangan in his writing. Through Mangan, we learn more about Joyce, and through Joyce we discover new ways of reading Mangan: It is a mutually rewarding exchange, more complex and subtle than it first seems. As I have shown, Joyce is not entirely truthful with himself in his dismissal of Mangan's prose, and if, as I suggested earlier, the truth of Joyce's Mangan requires a balancing of the claims made about him, then perhaps by "putting truth and untruth together a shot may be made at what this hybrid actually was like to look at" (*FW* 169.9-10).

Notes

1. David Lloyd, "James Clarence Mangan's Oriental Translations and the Question of Origins," *Comparative Literature* 38, no. 1 (Winter 1986): 20-35, 20. See James Joyce, "James Clarence Mangan," 1902, and "Giacomo Clarenzio Mangan," 1907, in *Occasional, Critical, and Political Writing,* ed. Kevin Barry (Oxford: Oxford University Press, 2000).

2. James Clarence Mangan, *The Collected Works of James Clarence Mangan: Prose 1840-1882,* ed. Jacques Chuto (Dublin: Irish Academic Press, 2002), 275. As Jacques Chuto writes in an endnote, it is possible that the word in the letter, "transmagnificanbandancial," is a mistranscription for "transmagnificandubandanciality," which appears in "The Editor's Room. Third Conclave," *Vindicator,* August 8, 1840, the latter seeming the most likely source for Joyce's "contransmagnificandjewbangtantiality" in *Ulysses* 3.51 (43-44). Subsequent references to this work will be cited parenthetically in the text.

3. This is no exaggeration; very few articles exist on the subject of Joyce and Mangan, and while passing reference is often made to the connection, it has yet to be explored in any great depth. Such essays on Joyce and Mangan that do exist are typically on the

subject of Joyce's Orientalism. See Heyward Ehrlich, "'Araby' in Context: The 'splendid Bazaar,' Irish Orientalism, and James Clarence Mangan," *James Joyce Quarterly* 35, no. 2/3 (Winter/Spring 1998): 309-31.

4. James Joyce, "James Clarence Mangan," 1902, in *Occasional, Critical, and Political Writing,* 57. Subsequent references to this work will be cited parenthetically in the text.
5. Eric Bulson, "On Joyce's Figura: A Requiem for Giacomo Clarenzio Mangan," *James Joyce Quarterly* 38, no. 3/4 (Spring/Summer 2001): 431-51, 432. Subsequent references to this work will be cited parenthetically in the text.
6. James, Joyce, "Giacomo Clarenzio Mangan," 1907, *Occasional, Critical, and Political Writing.* Subsequent references to this work will be cited parenthetically in the text.
7. W. B. Yeats, "To Ireland in the Coming Times," *Collected Poems* (London: Macmillan, 1950), 57, lines 17-18.
8. Roy Foster, *W. B. Yeats: A Life, Vol. I: The Apprentice Mage* (Oxford: Oxford University Press, 1997), 90.
9. W. B. Yeats, "Clarence Mangan's Love Affair," *United Ireland* 11, no. 520 (August 22, 1891): 5-6.
10. Letter to Tynan, April or May 1832, *Collected Works: Prose 1840-1882,* 248-49.
11. See Mangan's 1840 letter to Charles Gavan Duffy, *Collected Works: Prose 1840-1882*: 255.
12. Mangan, "Though Laughter Seems," *Collected Works: Poems 1838-1844,* 102.
13. Mangan, *Poems,* ed. John Mitchel (New York: Haverty, 1859), 15.
14. David Lloyd, *Nationalism and Minor Literature* (Berkeley: University of California Press, 1987), 47.
15. Ellen Shannon-Mangan, *James Clarence Mangan: A Biography* (Dublin: Irish Academic Press, 1994): 394. Joyce's reference in his 1902 lecture to Mangan's father as a "boa constrictor" strongly suggests that he had read the *Autobiography* by that stage. The *Autobiography* was first published in the *Irish Monthly* in 1882, and was reprinted in subsequent editions of C. P. Meehan's *The Poets and Poetry of Munster,* for which Mangan provided "poetical translations." See Jacques Chuto, *James Clarence Mangan: A Bibliography* (Dublin: Irish Academic Press, 1999), 64, 71.
16. Mitchel's edition is divided into four parts, entitled "German Anthology," "Irish Anthology," "Apocrypha," and "Miscellaneous." Needless to say, the second part is afforded greater space than the third, which contains four (chaotically edited) Oriental-style poems, and whose title "Apocrypha" seems rather distancing and dismissive. (See *Poems,* ed. John Mitchel.)
17. James F. Wurtz, "Famine Memory and Representations of the Gothic in *Ulysses,*" *Journal of Modern Literature* 29, no. 1 (2005): 102-17, 102.
18. For an excellent study of the relationship between Catholicism and the Gothic, see Patrick O'Malley, *Catholicism, Sexual Deviance, and Victorian Gothic Culture* (Cambridge: Cambridge University Press, 2006).
19. Samuel Beckett, "Dante ... Bruno. Vico ... Joyce," in *Disjecta: Miscellaneous Writings and a Dramatic Fragment* (London: John Calder, 1983): 19.
20. In a letter to Charles Gavan Duffy, *The Collected Works of James Clarence Mangan: Prose 1840-1882,* "I send you six pages. Our Budget—Pokeriana—Pokerisms—Flim-Flams and Whim-Whams—Scraps and Scrapings—Attic Stories etc ... etc ... etc ... [...] They are facetiæ (at least I hope so)" (254).
21. Robert Welch, *Irish Poetry from Moore to Yeats* (Gerrards Cross: Colin Smythe, 1980).
22. Mangan, *Poems,* ed. David Wheatley (Oldcastle: Gallery Press, 2003), 51.
23. Joyce's Mangan reference here is to a passage in Imogen Guiney, *James Clarence Mangan* (John Lane: London, 1897), 22. "O'Daly also had said that the versions of the Munster poets were often brought to him in different-coloured inks indicative of different public houses in which they were composed." See also James Atherton, *Books at the Wake* (London: Faber, 1959), 266.
24. See Ronald McHugh, *Annotations to Finnegans Wake* (Baltimore: Johns Hopkins University Press 1980), 66.
25. Louis MacNeice, *The Poetry of W. B. Yeats* (London: Faber and Faber, 1967), 55.
26. This phrase clearly caught Joyce's attention, as he also quotes it in his 1902 essay on Mangan. Atherton misses this "boer constructor" Mangan reference in *Books at the Wake.*
27. Further on, he is called a "drumchondriac" (181.35).
28. D. J. O'Donoghue, *The Life and Writings of James Clarence Mangan,* ed. James Kilroy (New York: Johnson Reprint Corp., 1972), 226.
29. The *Dublin Review* referred to Mangan as "a complete literary Proteus" in a review of his *German Anthology* in December 1845. Review of German

Anthology. Dublin Review (London), Vol. XIX, No. 38, December 1845, 312-31.

30. Chuto (unpublished conference paper) quoted in Robert Welch, *Irish Poetry from Moore to Yeats* (Gerrards Cross: Colin Smythe, 1980), 84.

31. Letter to Charles Gavan Duffy, 1840.

32. See Mangan, *Poems,* ed. John Mitchel; Mangan, *Poems,* ed. D. J. O'Donoghue; and David Lloyd, "James Clarence Mangan's Oriental Translations and the Question of Origins."

33. Jacques Chuto, "The Sources of James Clarence Mangan's Oriental Writings," *Notes and Queries* 29, no. 3 (June 1982): 224-8.

34. Seamus Deane, *Strange Country: Modernity and Nationhood in Irish Writing since 1790* (Oxford: Oxford University Press, 1997), 129-30.

Ciara Hogan (essay date 2010)

SOURCE: Hogan, Ciara. "'Lost Hero of the Past': Ruin, Wound, and the Failure of Idealism in the Poetry of James Clarence Mangan." *Études irlandaises* 35.1 (2010): 131-46. Print.

[*In the following essay, Hogan argues that as a poet, Mangan was a supporter of Irish cultural nationalism, disagreeing with critics who have found him unsympathetic to literary nationalism. She finds in his work, however, a pervasive "strain between the quotidian and the transcendent" that undermines any high Romantic ideals or complete acceptance of cultural nationalism.*]

James Clarence Mangan and the Critical Canon

From early contributions by John Mitchel, W. B. Yeats, and James Joyce to contemporary studies by Robert Welsh, Ellen Shannon-Mangan, and David Lloyd the field of Mangan studies has been dominated by debates about canonicity and the extent to which Mangan can be said to lie inside the canonical boundaries of Irish cultural nationalism. A predominantly middle-brow movement which dominated Irish letters in the first half of the nineteenth century, cultural nationalism was premised on joint principles of cultural unity, spiritual essence, and national identity, common to all European romantic and nationalist movements. In Ireland the ideology of respectable nationalism established itself around Thomas Davis and the Young Irelanders, whose *Nation* newspaper became the axis of romantic-nationalist publishing in the country. Its literature provided a unifying grammar for their governing ideology: evoking the authentic and timeless spirit of the Irish nation, it sought to conquer "sectarian and social differences" in Irish society, and to nationalise consciousness around the ideal of a discreet and harmonious cultural identity.[1] Although based on an ideal, rather than a material or economic definition of Irish culture, the Young-Ireland ethos not altogether twee. Its schema, linking "language, culture and national destiny," marked out a serious "political and cultural project[2]"; and its literature aimed to be both mentally bracing and socially improving. "Vibrant," in Arthur Griffith's words, "with manliness and passion," it was "written deliberately to re-awaken and strengthen the national spirit and inflame the national mind.[3]" Against this earnest, ethical patriotism, then, press Mangan's familiar problems with ideological commitment, ethical debility, and the endurance of faith. And discussions of Mangan's intersection with cultural nationalism typically focus on his ambiguous submission to its idealist agenda, as well as his willingness to deploy (reliably) key signifiers of Irish identity in a universalising aesthetic.

The most significant aspects of the debate have crystallised in or around the discussion laid out by David Lloyd in *Nationalism and Minor Literature.* Lloyd's Mangan is anti-establishment. He defines the poet according to his "recalcitrance to the demands of nationalist [...] aesthetics" to construct "a major writing [...] whose function is to produce identity.[4]" This recalcitrance manifests itself in Mangan's deliberate non-conformity with nationalist poetics. Styles and subjects are so various in Mangan; postures so multiple; parody so commonplace; irony and ambiguity such standard structural features of the verse, that any single interpretation of the poet in terms of a romantic-national school is unsustainable. By refusing to fix himself in any one subject position, Lloyd argues, Mangan rejects the privileged subjectivity of the poet of literary romanticism. By refusing to merge his voice with that of the "nation," Mangan resists assimilation into the cultural-nationalist canon.

While Lloyd's larger point that Mangan challenges the homogeneity of literary nationalism is crucial, it may, however, be overstated in terms of the poet's resistance to aesthetic or political labels. For Mangan variously displays a comically incongruous and unambiguously poignant relationship to romantic canons, nationalist politics, and romantic poet types. As Seán Ryder points out, Mangan's Catholic lower middle-class background meant that nationalism was part of his cultural grammar; and the poet has, by turn, been linked to the literatures of Catholic and working-class nationalism, as well as to that of Davis and Young Ireland.[5] Patricia Coughlan, meanwhile, has traced the influence of English romanticism on Mangan's work, finding that many of his best poems on heroic themes (Irish and otherwise) are spoken "as if" voiced by a Byronic poet type. Their mobilisation may involve "a sense of their ridiculousness when brought into relation with [modern ...] life," but Mangan's work nonetheless evidences a "perpetually recurring contest between the quotidian and the transcendent" in romantic poetics.[6]

The same strain between the quotidian and the transcendent characterises Mangan's bearing towards romantic nationalism and the romantic bardic role. Ideally, and ideologically, the bard of nineteenth-century nationalism functioned as the spokesman of culturally unambiguous experience, often figured as the mythic (primordial and supra-historical) spirit of the nation. However, in Mangan a consciousness of material everyday contexts disrupts the possibility of any correspondence with the high-romantic ideal or any full merging with cultural nationalism; the role of romantic bard is problematic for him in consequence. As I argue at length elsewhere, Mangan's attitude to ideals of cultural authority was strongly inflected by his economic and class experience; and in the poetry a class-based scepticism leads directly to the questioning of authority and the utility of poetry in real life. Mangan's lower-class experience bred a degree of cynicism about the material advantages a national literature, or indeed national sovereignty, could offer a man at his end of the social spectrum; as such, they deeply affected his ability to construct himself as a poet in the largely bourgeois tradition of the *Nation* authors.[7]

Nevertheless, while Mangan is critical of received platitudes about the transcendent romantic imagination and the general benefits of Young-Ireland nationalism, his writing continues to give evidence of a later-romantic poet with nationalist sympathies. The problem that remains in Mangan studies, then, lies not in rejecting but in rebalancing Mangan's uneasy fit in romantic-nationalist canons. This article seeks to do just that, in an analysis of the poetry written in the 1840s, the period that witnessed the ascendancy of the cultural-nationalist movement as well as its imminent collapse as it coincided with the Great Famine of 1845-1849.

My aim is to locate Mangan's writing with respect to larger currents of thought governing cultural discourse at mid-century. I will be paying particular attention to a literature of cultural improvement, common across the Victorian period, whose themes of perfectionism and exemplarity were a defining, if under-explored, influence on the culture-building discourse of Irish nationalists. If Mangan's attraction to romantic nationalism can be explained by the movement's intellectual and cultural authority, his discomfort with the perfectionist tradition can similarly be traced to his social and class experience, where a healthy suspicion of improving discourse was active and commonplace. The following pages explore Mangan's personal engagement with this perfectionist tradition, then, teasing out evidence of his uneasy but visible attachment to national culture-building, and analysing its ramifications for the mainstream nationalist canon. Throughout, my analysis is guided by the view that Mangan's uneven relation with romantic nationalism is representative in terms of his class and cultural background: the overwhelming occurrence of tropes of ruin and rupture in the verse formalise his sense of social dislocation, in my view. This paper will also look at moments of ruin, wounding, and formal rupture in Mangan, reading them as a means of figuring his philosophical breakage from the governing ideology of the nationalist establishment. A final word: although there will be much in the way of echoing and overlapping, my discussion does not absolutely seek to bond stray elements of Mangan, so much as to weigh them up in their incongruous relationship with each other. In tracing the path of Mangan's own irresolute nationalism, the following essay will also, therefore, contain much in the way of necessary qualification, contradiction, and questioning.

"I Dreamed in My Folly": Mangan's Faltering Perfectionism

As Seán Ryder points out, in spite of his waywardness, Mangan does in fact frequently voice a sense of "artistic responsibility." His work regularly presents poetry in terms of its "deep moral purpose" to "elevate" the reader's "spirit."[8] Many of the poems from the end of Mangan's life address readers in terms that exhort, entreat, and advise. **"A Voice of Encouragement"** (1848), **"For Soul and Country"** (1849), **"Bear Up"** (1849)—all Famine poems—seek to bolster Irish culture in a time of national crisis. **"The Nameless One"** (1849) speaks in terms of a more general philosophy. There, Mangan explicitly bequeaths his song "to after-ages" to "tell how . . . / He would have taught Men, from Wisdom's pages, / The way to live.[9]" Meanwhile his ***Autobiography*** seeks to present his own life to after-ages as a cautionary moral case:

> At a very early period in my life I became impressed by the conviction that it is the imperative duty of every man who has sinned deeply and suffered deeply to place upon record some memorial of his wretched experience for the benefit of his fellow creatures, and by way of a beacon to them, to avoid, in their voyage of existence, the rocks and shoals upon which his own peace of soul has undergone shipwreck.[10]

The modes of ethical presentation visible in these last two texts particularly, correspond with a literature of responsibility and moral purpose widespread in the Victorian period. More specifically, they conform to a mode of Victorian perfectionist writing, visible in the ideological hero-worship of British as well as Irish authors, and concretised in the literature of moral exemplars.

The concept of the cultural exemplar arose in Germany and England around 1800, and its influence is felt in the Irish cultural-nationalist schools in which Mangan moved. In all contexts the exemplar was a crucial figure in discourses that sought to construct, codify, and perfect culture.[11] Exemplarity of an ethical or cultural-specific kind was central to the construction of the romantic-nationalist canon. The exemplary men who peopled Young-Ireland ballads played a central role in the formation of cultural-nationalist philosophy as ideal or aspirational types that putatively embodied what Davis might call *the spirit of the nation.*[12] The ballad itself, which tends to raise its content to a universal level, was the ideal medium for acculturation. Within cultural-nationalist ballads, verse narratives functioned as representative anecdotes, from which an idealised history of the country could be constructed. They instanced cases of national heroism from which an ideal, heroic, national self could be learned. In this context cultural perfectionism comes to be understood as the achievement of a new self through the contemplation of exemplary others who, in demonstrating excellence, inspire it. Thus, just as the ideal Young-Ireland poet should merge his identity with that of the nation by writing within universal ballad forms, the average reader should merge his moral identity with that of the ballad hero by reproducing spirited nationalism in everyday contexts.

While Mangan did not buy wholesale into the myth of Irish nationality, considerations of ethical exemplarity emerge strongly in his verse. He shows himself to be attentive to the function of ancient heroes as exemplary types from whom an ethical self could be constructed; and he registers his own relationship to them through pedestrian patterns of engagement and imitation, as well as by donning the mantle of bardic exemplar, the traditional mouthpiece for cultural-nationalist values. Hence Mangan's formal contribution to the canons of cultural-nationalist poetry, in texts that valorise the heroism of patriot endeavour and celebrate a catalogue of exemplars of Irish nationalism. **"The Lamentation of Mac Liag for Kincora"** (1841) commemorates Brian Boru, his blood descendants, and his martial sept, the "Dalcassians of the Golden Swords." The **"Testament of Cathaeir Mor"** (1846) and **"A Vision of Connaught"** [**"A Vision of Connaught in the Thirteenth Century"**] (1846) celebrate Cáhal Mór, king of Connaught, of "the Wine-red Hand." The **"Elegy on the Tironian and Tirconnellian Princes"** (1840) laments the passing of the O'Donnells and the O'Neills. **"O'Hussey's Ode to the Maguire"** (1846) honours the adversity endured by Hugh Maguire in the 1600-1601 Munster campaigns with Hugh O'Neill.

Robert Welsh finds the "surging waves of energy and excitement" conveyed in these poems an index of their importance for Mangan: "what was Irish, was, in some sense or other, his by right of inheritance. [. . .] Because these poems [. . .] were somehow his, he may have felt that through them he would escape from himself into knowledge of himself, as part of some kind of national being."[13] Yet, in spite of a demonstrable attraction to mythic heroes of the national imaginary, Mangan is also demonstrably inconstant in his attachments to them. His Irish poems are haunted by shades of alienation and the national bard is often presented as a figure in pained isolation. Moreover, such accounts of exemplary Irishmen as these poems provide are rarely offered in a manner that promises any national unity of vision, or, indeed, any real access to moral or historical aspiration. As nearly all commentators have pointed out, the heroic times the poems evoke have passed, and their visions of exemplary heroism are therefore either past utterly or spectrally alive in an unstable, visionary present.

In the **"Tironian and Tirconnellian Princes"** [**"An Elegy on the Tyronian and Tyrconnellian Princes"**] the larger tragedy sung by the poet is the fact that Nuala O'Donnell must mourn Hugh O'Neill and Rury and Cathbar O'Donnell alone and in exile—her solitude is heightened by an ideal, imaginary home-scene wherein "one wail would rise from Crucahan's walls / To Tara's Hill." At home, the bards themselves are sickening and ailing in their inherited contexts. In the **"Lament over the Ruins of the Abbey of Teach Molaga"** (1846) the poet closes noting, "If change is here, / Is it not o'er the land?—Is it not too in me? / Yes I am changed even more than what I see." Change leads to foolishness and doubt, doubt in one's choice of exemplar and doubt in one's ability to judge. The **"Teach Molaga"** poet can only say, at last, "*I thought*" (my emphasis) that "Piety and Peace; Virtue and Truth" were housed in the saint's abbey, or embodied in the brotherhood gathered there. When Mangan reanimates the historical bard, he habitually animates a world of impoverished isolation. "Culture" in this context is one of loss and fragmentation, implying a fragmenting or lost system of idealised belief. The spokesman of national culture appears a faltering orator, meanwhile, possessed of doubtful authority and insight. In Mangan's idiosyncratic version of "Gile na Gile," **"The Vision of Egan O'Reilly"** (1849), the poet dreams "*in my folly*" (my emphasis) of a "glorious mansion on the brow of Slieve Cruachra." Thus the poem expresses scepticism about a once sustaining nationalist vision and, implicitly, about the philosophical sustenance provided by the formulas of the *aisling,* as one among a range of traditional genres preserved in the cultural-nationalist canon.

As we shall see, Mangan's scepticism and qualified alienation from culture-building programmes take strikingly personal form, but they are also inflected by a species of philosophical questioning peculiar to his time and directly disruptive of Young Ireland's literary ideology. "Such scepticism concerning the worth of the ideals or internal models to which we have entrusted our hopes, their ability to bear the weight of our vulnerable belief, is chronic in perfectionism," Andrew H. Miller observes.[14] Theories of exemplarity, and of representative cultural heroes themselves emerged at a time where none existed, and they were expressly designed to unite cultures already undergoing ideological and social fragmentation.[15] From the perspective of the cultural-nationalist dream, Mangan's poetics of diminishing faith was particularly destabilising. For his work lays bare the historical yearning that the figure of the national exemplar was designed to anneal or occlude, as well as the peculiar cultural anxieties attached to that yearning. A perfectionist crisis in Mangan inevitably leads to a crisis in cultural-nationalist perfectionism. Vulnerability of belief is far removed from the "true ecstatic spirit of the Irish muse" vaunted by the nationalist ideologue Charles Gavin

Duffy.[16] And it is a result of a form of theoretical misgiving that the *Nation* deemed antithetical to a national literature, because putatively belonging to "high" (that is, belated and English) civilisation:

> Differing from England as we do in almost everything in which one people can differ from another, in nothing do we differ so widely as in our literary wants. The philosophical tone of a high civilisation does not suit us; we have our history to make, and our writings must help to make it. We want strength, earnestness, passion, the song and the ballad, all that fires and nerves the minds of men.[17]

Mangan's writing on heroic nationalism is not only ideologically unstable, it is unsuitable (even "un-Irish") in revealing the distinguishing psychological features of Victorian perfectionism, in representing perfectionist hope at its most attenuated.

Of course, much of Mangan's angular relationship to national perfectionism can be explained by his sense of cultural difference from the largely bourgeois institution from which it sprang. By the 1840s the poet was living in penury. However, even in the decade prior to this Mangan's movement between the high and low worlds of Dublin publishing and the Dublin back street, respectively, made for a pronounced personal anxiety about his ability to adopt the role of national poet and social mentor. A cultural barrier also prohibits conscientious possession of or identification with the Irish nationalist poetic that he recites, and thus with the idealised nation that it normatively represents. Unsurprisingly, the same obstacle elucidates many of Mangan's characteristic themes and poetic mannerisms or forms. Themes of discomfort, exposure, alienation, and loss, for instance, seem deliberately to figure a sense of dislocation from the national culture-building enterprise. Forms of fragmentation and inarticulacy in Mangan produce an aesthetic of self-doubt and ideological disillusionment, which stems principally from his experience of social alienation.

In Andrew H. Miller's extensive studies of Victorian perfectionism, both the original desire for perfection, and the uncertain self-esteem that comes from evaluating oneself against cultural exemplars, "forces an uneasy sensitivity to exposure"—exposure to oneself and to one's audience.[18] In Mangan, such sensations are multiply felt, and thematised in relation to two main tropes: pained and/or guilty memory; feelings of dis-ease and unworthiness. His texts constantly betray these to be intermingled with the sense of "exposure" and "inarticulacy" thematised in Victorian perfectionist discourse.[19] Thus his canon registers combinations of self-abasement and guilt before the exemplary model of the public national poet.

In the 1837 **"My Adieu to the Muse"** Mangan's search for "nobleness and truth" is stimulated by perfectionist models but offset by his experience of private pain. Hence "the reveil-call which on Fame's drum Time's / Hands beat for some lost hero of the Past" is offset by self-hate and self-defeat—"all the javelin memories that pierce me now." Humility before his "Fatherland," in his capacity as a poet, is mingled with a desire for some vague forgiveness by it:

> I owe
> Ye much, and would not seem ungrateful now;
> And if the laurel decorate my brow,
> Be that set-off against so much woe
> As Man's applause hath power to mitigate.

Such feelings do not dissipate with time. The posthumously published **"The Nameless One"** (1849) reiterates the theme. It expressly represses both the poet's name and detail of his personal history, while openly grieving for having endured "what future Story / will never know," and it begs his public to guard a kind memory of him in spite of his failings.

Elsewhere irony softens the blow of reality and undercuts the force of exemplary paradigms. **"Twenty Golden Years Ago"** (1840) evokes the speaker's "grand Byronian soul" in its state of "anticlimax," or depressed pastness. Thus it erodes the speaker's character as an exemplary poet type with self-deprecating irony. Such irony takes the form of parodic self-exposure in "Andrew Magrath's Reply to John O'Tuomy" (1849), which jokingly restates the unstable relations between the public poet and his private moods of pessimism and deceit: "Old Bards never vainly shall woo me, / But your tricks and your capers O'Tuomy, / Have nought in them winning— / You jest and keep grinning, / But your thoughts are all guileful and gloomy." Verbal irony is the product of skepticism; scepticism is itself impossible, however, except in relation to disappointed or disrupted idealism. Romantic ideals still played a strong part in Mangan's notion of the model poet, and these texts suggest that he felt some degree of fraudulence in his capacity to satisfy the bardic standard.[20]

Again, this internal conflict is characteristic of the consciousness of a poet in uneasy relation to the lower and middle-class cultures in which he doubly moved. As we shall see, when not breaking out in laughing skepticism, the Irish poetry is "wounded" by moments of voicelessness and self-doubt. Ideological disjunction and perfectionist anguish—intellectual alienation and feelings of social exclusion—thus mean that inarticulacy becomes a dominant formal feature of Mangan's verse. It is to this point I now turn.

Ruin and Wound: Dialogues in Responsibility and Inarticulacy

Figures and forms of silence in Mangan mark out an awkward presence in the romantic canon, at once opening onto and foreclosing upon strikingly nationalist sentiments of cultural ruin. In concluding, I want to examine how tropes of piercing and wounding, associated with personal and perfectionist crisis in Mangan, can be located in the cultural-nationalist poetics of the Famine years. Linked to this is the question of how forms of piercing—gasps, silences, moments of breathlessness and unspeakability—coincide with patterns of representation in Famine writing, ambiguously functioning as a synecdoche of national history, but also of the cultural-nationalist enterprise on the point of its collapse.

Romantic ideologues valorised ruins on the Irish landscape as a visible sign of a lost cultural order. Emotional focal points, they were sites of remembrance that substituted for memory of a distant Gaelic past.[21] Analogous to the ruin on the landscape is the scar or wound on the human body, a visible remnant of former suffering and a figure for emotional trauma. Luke Gibbons has demonstrated that, in the literary and visual culture of late-eighteenth and nineteenth-century Ireland, the wounded body functions as a type or substitute national narrative.[22] The wounded subject reconnects to a violent and violating colonial history at a political-allegorical level; indeed, in Gibbon's post-colonial calculus, allegory is the grammatical type of the "semantic wound.[23]"

Ruins are everywhere in Mangan's poetry and, formally, they betray their affinity to the memorialising paradigms of cultural-nationalist narrative. In **"Teach Molaga"** [**"Lament over the Ruins of the Abbey of Teach Molaga"**] and **"Kilcash"** [**"Lament for Kilcash"**] (both 1849), the abbey and castle ruins are sites where mourning for national culture occurs. In **"O'Hussey's Ode"** [**"O'Hussey's Ode to the Maguire"**], acts of political ruin are guarded in remembrance to inspire politically: "*memory of the lime-white mansions*" Hugh Maguire "*hath laid / In ashes warms the hero's heart!*" Nonetheless, it is truer to say that scars in Mangan are more commonly found on mental than physical geographies. The "arrowy, speary, sleet" that "Pierceth to the very bone" in **"O'Hussey"** [**"O'Hussey's Ode to the Maguire"**], though referable to the poem's dramatic context, in fact crystallises the ode's pained if ecstatic temper. In a parallel spirit, in the **"Lamentation for Maurice FitzGerald"** (1846) the mourner's "*keen*" is "piercing"—emotion, sensation, and song mingle in the national context, but they meet in the air, not on the ground. In the poetry images of piercing, wounding, and stabbing are figurative vehicles for emotional pain used to intensify key emotional states that Mangan typically fails to excavate. These openings are vacant spaces that typically evacuate any meaning they moodily evoke. Resisting explication, they equally defy attachment to philosophical-historical narrative whether of a perfectionist or nationalist kind.

In **"Farewell to the Maig"** (1847), the exiled poet, "Without help, without hope, without friends, without treasure, / And thorough-pierced with arrows from Fate's laden quiver" is conveyed to be utterly "lost," "lone," "[pining]," and "[dying]." His isolation is utter. As **"My Adieu to the Muse"** showed, the "arrows" of "Fate" in Mangan are commonly associated with the sting of guilty memory. Accordingly such figures point up the poet's peculiar moral solipsism, an existential crisis which triggers his isolation from nation and society. In **"Siberia"** (1846) Mangan makes wounded seclusion into a mannered aesthetic:

In Siberia's wastes
The Ice-wind's breath
Woundeth like toothèd steel.

The use of the stiletto capital and cutting hyphen in "Ice-wind," and the sharp backward glance of the accented e in "toothèd steel," effect a visible incision on the page that mimics the scars on the speaker's mind. Meanwhile, the typological presentation of the text, the wide blank spaces against which the stanzas press, enforce the impression of claustrophobic, solitary emptiness. Particularly in emotional contexts, Mangan is slow to grant authority to the word. Thus his writing can appear peculiarly non-communicative. When psychological pain infects his nationalist poetics, therefore, it patently deflects them from their ostensible ideological goal; the labouring emotion rather appears to evoke a radically other narrative beside its nationalist shadow.[24]

Of considerable interest is the peculiar gasping, rasping, breathlessness which enters the poems of 1846. These poems strike up profoundly nationalist themes, in the first years of the Great Famine. Indeed, it is tempting to read in their suffocating breath some sensible evocation of the intensely sultry weather that had spread across the country with the Famine. Some are poems of national fervour, others of national failure; all ostensibly connect to the public space; yet their emotions are so synthetically devised as to persist in suggesting remoteness from the real.

Mangan's **"Pulse of the Bards,"** a version of O'Toumy, speaks out on the subject of bardic inarticulateness, itself the result of social and political impasse in native culture. Here silence coincides with political decay, political decay with spiritual bondage:

Poets are no more, . . . and Storyists are mute.
Nought is ever heard . . . through tale, or lay, or lute
Of the Youth of the old kingly line.
Oh! For Erin, for Erin, my spirit lies in bondage long!

Mangan's self-consciously literary response to social stasis and bardic silence is built into the poem's structure. The pulse of the bard, rendered as an ellipsis—". . ."—, mimics the inarticulate gasp of Poets and Storyists as the text's rhythmic pulse.

Similar gasping breathlessness is found in the *aisling* **"Shane Bwee; or, The Captivity of the Gaels"** (1846) which knits the poet's sadness to general social declension:

Sunk in sadness, . . . I darkly pondered
All the wrongs our . . . lost land endures.

It is found again in **"A Cry for Ireland"** (1846):

Oh, my land! . . . oh, my love!
What a woe, . . . and how deep,
Is thy death to my long-mourning soul!

Pausing declensions such as these are consonant with Mangan's tendency to deploy forms that enact the subjective experience of blocked desire; all figure a context where social and economic progress has deliberately been arrested. In their very self-consciousness, they doubtless illustrate an ironic use of form unsuited to a poetics that openly seeks to communicate national sentiment to its readership—though, again, the empty moans of these texts do appear to turn into literal phrasing in **"Teach Molaga"** (1846). There the poet wanders out along upon a "funereal" and "billow-beaten shore": "While in low tones, with many a pause between, / The mournful night-wind wailed." When finally legible, the pausing moan is shown to signify absence in plural directions: the death of patriot history as the source of inspiration and the death, in the present moment, of the dull promise of a nationalist future. Mangan's national poetics in the Famine years are characterised by formal evasion, therefore, and philosophical betrayal.

The romantic-national consciousness succeeds through the operation of saving analogy; likenesses breed universals, and the universal transcends the particular world. Ideally, by attaching oneself to the universal one saves oneself; transcending oneself, one leaves national history to join with nationalist myth.[25] However, Mangan refuses to merge with this mythic national consciousness. Instead he skirts it, as echo, shade, or perversion, or else operates as a ruined presence within it. His aesthetics of wounding, loss, and impasse inject scepticism into the conceptual framework of bardic poetry at the very level of sentence. Such analogy as emerges is not with myth, but with no-myth; not with transcendence, but with immanent failure and social crisis. It is a formula that marks the tentative emergence of another national poetic, anti-idealist in spirit, and in tune with Famine history.

The Great Famine of 1845-49 did not just implicate the ruin of the population or the national economy; it also bankrupted the cultural-nationalist dream of spiritual cohesion. The political and economic consequences of the Famine (not to speak of Famine mortality) showed up the naked differences between diverse human communities in Ireland. Making social distinction vital and vivid, the Famine produced at once more radical forms of political nationalism and more extreme forms of cultural despair. Clearly, all were antithetical to the unifying, perfectionist grammar of national culture-building. Famine history beggared the romantic consciousness before historical fact; and in consequence the late 1840s saw the "evaporation" of the idealist ethos that characterised Davisite cultural nationalism.[26]

Historical awareness, writes Octavio Paz, is coincident with "the knowledge of death." Where such consciousness enters romantic aesthetics, it corrupts both its characteristic idealism and its poetic poise, leading to a "breaking away from analogy through irony or anguish.[27]" Gaps, gasps, and lacunae in Mangan—whether conceived as formal irony or anguished wail—constitute what Paz would call the "disintegrating word," a sign of this philosophical breakage. They entail a falling away from the normative philosophical order of romantic nationalism, in a manner that co-implicates the norm and the fall. Mangan's breached aesthetic, then, figures a vision of cultural perfection punctured by the particular floundering emotion of Famine history. The poetry evokes an understanding of discourse's powerlessness to effect cultural progress, as Mangan uses poetic form to explore the individual experience of futility in the face of history.

This fall, or turn, from perfectionist history, clearly marks out Mangan's alienation from Young-Ireland idealism, and is itself the result of his experience of social disempowerment.[28] What Mangan's Famine poetry produces is nationalist void. Emerging forcefully in the writing is both the poet's want of an object of hope, an explicating narrative, or some saving solidarity—as well as his material faithlessness in them. Hence in the poems of the late forties there is a tentatively romantic seeking for some larger correspondence in varieties of the historical particular. From the destruction of Pompeii, Mangan turns to the Albanian war of independence from Turkey, where scenes of distant devastation and famine evoke the local. His seeking takes curiously agitated forms. **"The Song of the Albanian"** (1847) is apocalyptic and calls down eschatological violence:

> Gaunt Famine rideth in the van,
> And Pestilence, with myriad arrows,
> Followeth in fiery guise: they spare
> Nor Woman, Child, nor Man!
> The stricken Dead lie without barrows
> By roadsides, black and bare!
> Down on the burnt-up cottage roofs
> The sick sun all the long day flashes.

Evoking Irish Famine dearth, by analogy, the poem goes on to call for revolution, by example: "Were there a land whose people could / Lie down beneath the Heaven's blue pavilions / And gasp, and perish, famished slaves!— / While the ripe golden food / That might and should have fed their millions / Rotted above their graves— / That land were doomed! . . ." The poem betrays a radical-nationalist consciousness informed by earlier theories of heroic exemplarity. Here, however, the heroes are the starving revolutionary masses in the Albanian war, whose example at once urges and chastises phantasmal Famine anti-heroes at home, gasping and prone. It is a very caustic evocation of the national perfectionist paradigm, and, in its mode of figuration—its "myriad arrows"—it appears both self-implicating and self-lacerating.

Martin MacDermott wrote that the poems of prophesy and apocalypse that Mangan produced, "full of awful feeling of impending doom," were more "dreadful" than "any even Ireland has ever passed through."[29] In **"Pompeii"** (1847) the speaker "rave[s]," while turning through forms of "Conjectural Dread" he imagines swept over the lost city. The conjectural dread is consonant with

Mangan's attachment to a poetry of outermost mood. Where high emotion ascends it is hysterical and apocalyptic. His famous **"Dark Rosaleen"** (1846) presents a contemporary apocalyptical vision in a characteristically personal manner. The gasp and gap mimic the passionate intensity of the speaker's state of mind; and his fevered apostrophe to **"Rosaleen,"** the allegorical figure of Irish nationalism, shows the limits to which Mangan takes the cultural-nationalist dream:

All day long, in unrest,
To and for, do I move.
The very soul within my breast
Is wasted for you, love!
The heart . . . in my bosom faints
To think of you, my Queen,
My life of life, my saint of saints,
My dark Rosaleen!
My own Rosaleen!

John Mitchel would subsequently try to recuperate Mangan for the nationalist tradition, merging the poet's ruin with Ireland's.[30] Where his apocalyptic strains become knit with nationalist figures and themes, the result can, indeed, be extraordinarily powerful, in spite of the disorienting influence of Mangan's iconoclasm. However, such panting agitation as is found here is temperamentally agnostic to the cultural-nationalist canon: its very emotional excess destabilises the cultural authority upon which habitual bardic verse, and thus nationalist ideology, depend. Faith, so voiced, and in a context that endangers its eclipse, forces the questioning of nationalist sentiment and aspiration. Itself beyond even the discipline of doubt, "**Rosaleen**'s" clipped, ritual phrases rather evidence desperation for a cause—any cause—to absorb the otherwise unreckonable longing. What truly distinguishes the poem, however, is the image of the national poet that it presents, for the speaker of **"Dark Rosaleen"** is a craven nationalist exemplar. Neither properly present nor transcendent, he is simply beside himself.

Conclusion

While attracted to Young Ireland's idealist ethos, Mangan's marginal social status meant that his faith in a future perfected culture was always short-lived and frequently ironised, interrupted, or undermined. Such ideological irregularity on his part is consonant with his position on the periphery of romantic-nationalist circles in which he also, erratically, assisted. The texts studied in this paper illustrate the problems that both Mangan's darkening idealism and enlivening scepticism posed to heroic song in bourgeois culture-building. The darker existential moments in Mangan fit unevenly in a canon they also intensify, his cynical flashes render cultural nationalism uneven by exaggerating its ideals and goals. He takes things too far. Yet while his irresolution and emotional excess evidently problematise Mangan's ability to fulfil the role of exemplary national poet, he stands inside romantic nationalism sufficiently to be able to take cultural-nationalist aspiration to an anticlimax. Reading Mangan in light of the foundational tradition of nationalist perfectionism, heroic exemplarity, and girding patriotism therefore allows us to reconceptualise the later-nationalist poems as (often penetrating) excurses into the failure of cultural-nationalist idealism.

Notes

1. Joep Leerssen, *Remembrance and Imagination: Patterns in the Historical and Literary Representation of Ireland in the Nineteenth Century,* Cork, Cork University Press, 1996, p. 4.
2. Seamus Deane, (ed.), "Poetry and Song, 1800-1890," *The Field Day Anthology of Irish Writing, Vol. 2,* Derry, Field Day, 1991, p. 1-9, p. 3.
3. Quoted in Matthew Campbell, "Poetry in English, 1830-1890: From Catholic Emancipation to the Fall of Parnell," Margaret Kelleher and Philip O'Leary (eds.), *The Cambridge History of Irish Literature, Vol. I,* Cambridge, Cambridge University Press, 2006, p. 500-54, p. 515.
4. David Lloyd, *Nationalism and Minor Literature: James Clarence Mangan and the Emergence of Irish Cultural Nationalism,* London and Berkeley, University of California Press, 1987, p. xi.
5. Seán Ryder, "Introduction," Ryder, S. (ed.); *James Clarence Mangan: Selected Writings,* Dublin, Dublin University Press, 2004, p. 1-13, p. 8; Richard Haslam, "'Broad Farce and Thrilling Tragedy': Mangan's Fiction and Irish Gothic," Éire-Ireland, 41: 3&4, Fall/Winter, 2006, p. 215-44; Christopher Morash, *Writing the Irish Famine,* Oxford, Oxford University Press, 1995, p. 122-24.
6. Patricia Coughlan, "'Fold over Fold, Inveterately Convolv'd': Some Aspects of Mangan's Intertextuality," Birgit Bamsbäck and Martin Croghan (eds.), *Anglo-Irish and Irish Literature: Aspects of Language and Culture, Proceedings of the Ninth International Congress of the International Association for the Study of Anglo-Irish Literature, Held at Uppsala University, 4-7 August, 1986, Vol. 2, Studia Anglistica,* University Presspsala, 1988, p. 191-200, p. 195, p. 191. Further, Matthew Campbell points to Mangan's affinities with Keats, Browning, and Tennyson, and concludes that his poetry stands confidently (and sometimes reprovingly) within late-romantic and Victorian verse cultures. See "Lyrical Unions: Mangan, O'Hussey and Ferguson," *Irish Studies Review* 8:3, Dec. 2000, p. 325-38, p. 327.
7. Ciara Hogan, "Cultural Nationalism and the 'Cashless Bard': Class and Nation in the Poetry of James Clarence Mangan," Olivier Coquelin, Patrick Galliou, and Thierry Robin, (eds.), *Political Ideology in Ireland: From the Enlightenment to the Present,* Newcastle, Cambridge Scholars Press, 2009, p. 82-102.

8. S. Ryder, *op. cit.,* p. 6.

9. All quotations from Mangan's poetry are taken from Jacques Chuto *et al.* (eds.), *The Collected Works of James Clarence Mangan,* 6 vols, Dublin and Portland, Or., Irish Academic Press, 1996-2002.

10. John Kilroy (ed.), *The Autobiography of James Clarence Mangan,* Dublin, Dolmen, 1969, p. 8.

11. For studies of the exemplar in the historical development of cultural identity see A. Dwight Culler, *The Victorian Mirror of History,* New Haven, Yale University Press, 1985, p. 20-73. See also the following works by Andrew H. Miller, which have been a central influence on this study: "Reading Thoughts: Victorian Perfectionism and the Display of Thinking," *Studies in the Literary Imagination,* 35:2, Fall 2002, p. 79-98; "John Henry Newman, Knowingness, and Victorian Perfectionism," *Texas Studies in Literature and Language,* 45:1, Spring 2003, p. 92-113; "Bruising, Laceration, and Lifelong Maiming; or, How We Encourage Research," *ELH* 70:1, Spring 2003, p. 301-18.

12. The title of Davis's seminal collection of nationalist verse. See Thomas Osborne Davis (ed.), *The Spirit of the Nation. Ballads and Songs by the Writers of "The Nation," with Original and Ancient Music, Arranged for the Voice and Piano Forte,* Dublin, J. Duffy, 1845.

13. Robert Welsh, *Irish Poetry from Moore to Yeats,* Gerrards Cross, Colin Smythe, 1980, p. 96.

14. Andrew H. Miller, "Bruising," *op. cit.,* p. 310.

15. James Chandler notes that Emerson, Mill, and Carlyle developed their theories of representative men in an age where none existed and in a culture characterised by their absence. See *England in 1819: The Politics of Literary Culture and the Case of Romantic Historicism,* Chicago, University of Chicago Press, 1998, p. 176.

16. The quotation is from Duffy's "Introduction to the Fifth Edition," Charles Gavin Duffy (ed.), *The Ballad Poetry of Ireland,* 5th rev. ed., Dublin, 1845, p. xi-xlvii, p. xiii.

17. Anon, "Current English Poets: No. 1 Alfred Tennyson and E. B. Browning," *The Nation,* 15 Feb. 1845, p. 314.

18. Andrew H. Miller, "Bruising," *op. cit.,* p. 310.

19. Andrew H. Miller, "Newman," *op. cit.,* p. 92.

20. While it is not within the parameters of this study to address Mangan's character as a translator *per se,* a similar strain is felt when he seeks to present himself to his readership in the capacity of public poet/literary translator. The use of pseudonyms such as Selber (or self) and Clarence, for instance, show Mangan evading exposure for insufficient literary authority through parodic self-exposure—hence too his tendency to undermine the concept of literary authority itself. His comment that his writing was "the antithesis of plagiarism" clearly mocks up the charge of authorial irresponsibility he consciously felt at some level. (Quoted in D. J. Donoghue, *The Life and Times of James Clarence Mangan,* Dublin, Patrick Geddes, 1897, p. 19. Mangan refers to a writing practice he adopted, fabricating imaginary poets and poems, which then he claimed to "translate" for his readers' improvement and culture.)

21. Although she does not locate her discussion in a single chapter, Katie Trumpener's *Bardic Nationalism* offers a fairly comprehensive discussion of the role of ruins in romantic-national contexts. See, for example, *Bardic Nationalism: The Romantic Novel and the British Empire,* Princeton, Princeton University Press, 1997, p. 69-70; 82-84; 102-04; 123-24; 143-45.

22. Luke Gibbons, *Edmund Burke and Ireland: Aesthetics, Politics and the Colonial Sublime,* Cambridge, Cambridge University Press, 2003, p. 39-82.

23. *Ibid.,* p. 77.

24. This tendency has caused readers to judge Mangan's poetic as selfish, not social or national. Ellen Shannon-Mangan finds that Mangan exploited the Famine to develop themes of "personal dissolution," *James Clarence Mangan: A Biography,* Dublin and Portland, Or: Irish Academic P, 1996, p. 206. See also Jacques Chuto's comments on the ambiguous "nationalism" of Mangan's Famine verse, "Rhétorique et Authenticité chez J. C. Mangan," unpublished conference paper delivered to the Congrès S.A.E.S. (Tours, 1977), cited in D. Lloyd, "Great Gaps in Irish Song: James Clarence Mangan and the Ideology of the Nationalist Ballad," *Irish University Review,* 14, Autumn 1984, p. 182-83.

25. My discussion of nationalist myth here is influenced by Richard Kearney's analysis of "utopian myth" in *Postnationalist Ireland: Politics, Culture, Philosophy,* London, Routledge, 1997, p. 122-24.

26. Seamus Deane, "The Famine and Young Ireland," *Field Day Anthology, op. cit.* p. 115-20, p. 117.

27. Octavio Paz, *Children of the Mire: Modern Poetry from Romanticism to the Avant-Garde,* trans. Rachel Phillips, London and Cambridge, MA., Harvard University Press, 1974, p. 57.

28. Christopher Morash places Mangan's Famine writing beside that of a generation of working-class poets such as Francis Davis, John de Jean Frazer, and John Keegan, all of whom work in forms of apocalyptic verse, a poetry of impasse and disintegration, to voice proletarian disaffect with bourgeois nationalism. See Christopher Morash, *op. cit.,* p. 122-24. It is an index of the general weakness

of class politics and poetics in mid-century Ireland that this protesting consciousness ultimately finds no stable vocabulary or ideological resting ground. Crucial to Mangan's rehearsal of poetic futility in the face of historical crisis, for instance, is an often frenzied longing for the forms and philosophies he undermines.

29. Martin MacDermott, (ed.), *The New Spirit of the Nation; or, Ballads and Songs by the Writers of "The Nation," Containing Songs and Ballads Published since 1845,* 2nd ed., Dublin, T. Fisher Unwin, 1896, p. XXII.

30. "His history and fate were indeed a type and shadow of the land he loved so well." John Mitchel, "Biographical Introduction," *Poems by James Clarence Mangan,* New York, P. M. Laverty, 1859. p. 7-31, p. 15.

Andrew Cusack (essay date 2012)

SOURCE: Cusack, Andrew. "Cultural Transfer in the *Dublin University Magazine*: James Clarence Mangan and the German Gothic." *Popular Revenants: The German Gothic and Its International Reception, 1800-2000.* Ed. Cusack and Barry Murnane. Rochester: Camden House, 2012. 87-104. Print.

[*In the following essay, Cusack argues that Mangan's translations from German and promotion of Germanic literary traditions, such as the Gothic, in the* Dublin University Magazine *were central to bringing German literature into Great Britain in the nineteenth century. Cusack also suggests that Mangan, unlike many contributors to the magazine, often used humor to reveal the Germanic roots of his works.*]

Together with its peers, the Edinburgh-based *Blackwood's Magazine* and *Fraser's Magazine* in London, the *Dublin University Magazine* (*DUM*) was the principal conduit for German literature into the British Isles in the Victorian Age. In the following I will consider the part played by the *DUM* in propagating German gothic in Ireland and Britain between 1833 and 1850. One indication that the founders of the *DUM* had a taste for the gothic is the choice of the name "Anthony Poplar" for the editorial voice—a name recalling the "Anthony Evergreen" of the earlier New York magazine *Salmagundi,* which possessed its own exponent of German gothic in Washington Irving. There were numerous purveyors of the gothic among the contributors to the magazine, although Joseph Sheridan Le Fanu is the only one to enjoy a significant posthumous reputation. The group of gothic contributors to the *DUM* overlapped—but was not identical with—those authors engaged in propagating German literature in Ireland. Within this group James Clarence Mangan occupied an outstanding position, both as a practitioner of the gothic and as an interpreter of German literature.

In order to understand the significance of the *DUM* as an organ of cultural transfer between Germany and the British Isles, it is necessary to clarify the position occupied by that publication in the cultural and political life of the Irish nineteenth century, which in turn requires knowledge of the origins of the magazine and the goals of its editors.[1] The *DUM* was established by a group of six Trinity College men, including four undergraduates, the first monthly issue appearing in January 1833. One of the undergraduates, Isaac Butt, subsequently a barrister and much later "the Father of Home Rule," would edit the magazine during the period of its most intense commerce with German letters. The immediate impetus for founding the magazine came from the establishment of the Reform Parliament in Westminster in that year, a development that the conservative Anglicans then governing Ireland regarded with alarm. The extension of the franchise, together with the Catholic Emancipation achieved in 1829, were perceived as significant threats by this elite, the intellectual vanguard of Anglo-Irish society.

Out of the galvanizing effect of such anxieties on a coterie of literary men was born the *DUM.* Until 1877, when it ceased publication, the magazine remained true to its conservative credentials, pouring scorn on opponents of the 1800 Act of Union that abolished Ireland's parliament—the demagogue Daniel O'Connell and the poet Thomas Moore were singled out for particular opprobrium. But despite the anti-Catholic invective of its editorials the *DUM* was a great stimulator of interest in Irish history and literature, gathering together a considerable body of Irish poetry in translation and in the original language. So great were its merits in this area that it may justly be considered to have paved the way for the Celtic literary revival in the late nineteenth century. The magazine's original cover motifs of a round tower, a harp, and a tomb signaled the editors' interests in Irish history, poetry, and biography. This cover was soon replaced, however, by a portrait of Elizabeth I, a less ambiguous icon for an organ of conservative and unionist opinion.

The explanation for the "Ireland-first" attitude of the *DUM* lay in the opinion of its contributors that the best way of securing the Union was by putting Ireland on an equal footing with Britain. This could only be achieved by a combination of cultural and economic rehabilitation that would restore a country demoralized by its relegation to subaltern status by the Act of Union. The Protestant Ascendancy then populating Trinity believed that if they could lead such change, their position as an elite could be preserved, even in the face of growing Catholic populism. While the progressive moment in this conservatism was reflected in calls for economic development, the emphasis on the cultural distinctiveness of Ireland as a partner in the British Empire necessitated the rediscovery and propagation of a distinctly Irish literature and culture, which in turn required antiquarian studies. Thus, contributions on educational reform and the railways appeared alongside Samuel Ferguson's series "By-Ways of Irish History," which opened with the programmatic statement that "to render the present intelligible, the past must be consulted."[2]

From its foundation the *DUM* was modeled on *Blackwood's* in Edinburgh and *Fraser's* in London, literary magazines whose conservative political tendency did not prevent them from advocating German literature to their readers. Indeed, these magazines led the revival of British interest in German literature from 1820 onward.[3] That revival affected Ireland, but in ways that differed from the reception of German literature in Britain. The bookish founders of the *DUM* were attracted by the special prominence that literature appeared to enjoy in the national life of Germany. The idea expressed in a lecture on the German educational system, that Germany was "incontestably the most literary nation in existence," chimed with hopes that literature could play a significant role in the intellectual regeneration of Ireland.[4] The nationalists of the Young Ireland movement were slower to realize the ideological potential of German literature than the unionists of Trinity College. By 1840, however, they had begun to do so. In that year Thomas Davis gave an address to the Historical Society at Trinity that was peppered with references to Herder. Davis's most resonant phrase, "think wrongly if you will, but think for yourselves," was borrowed from Lessing.[5] Two years later Davis helped establish *The Nation,* the weekly newspaper of the Young Ireland movement whose name indicated filiations with *La Giovine Italia* and *Junges Deutschland.* In its second issue *The Nation* set about overcoming Irish ignorance of modern European literature, remarking that "some of the greatest works that have ever seen the light have, within the last few years, been published in Germany and France."[6]

Despite competition from the *Nation,* the *DUM* was the most important conduit for German literature into Ireland. Among the magazine's Germanizing contributors Mangan was by far the most prolific, though the Victorian practice of appending abbreviated or pseudonymous signatures to periodical contributions meant that his identity was known only to a few. The heyday of Irish interest in German literature between 1833 and 1850 coincided substantially with the period in which Mangan was active as a translator and critic. He is principally remembered in this context for his ***Anthologia Germanica*** [***Anthologia Germanica = German Anthology***], a series of critical translations that appeared in the *DUM* in twenty-two installments from 1835 to 1846 and published as a single volume in 1845. Schiller is the best-represented poet, but many others are present: from Bürger, Hölty, and Matthison to Goethe, Kerner, Heine, and Uhland. In all, Mangan translated over five hundred poems from the German, a veritable torrent of verse. Writing in the 1980s, Patrick O'Neill could say of the ***Anthologia Germanica,*** "Mangan's anthology is still, after nearly a century and a half, the most representative selection of German verse ever published in Ireland."[7]

Who was James Clarence Mangan and how did he develop into such an ardent and successful promoter of German literature? Tantalizing though these questions are, they elude answers. Not only are the documentary traces scant, the nineteenth-century myth of the *poète maudit* whose sufferings were symbolically linked to those of his country has acted powerfully to obscure our image of the poet. The picture is further complicated by the willingness of Mangan's biographers to endow their subject with a distinctly gothic physiognomy, as if taking their cue from Mangan's fictions themselves:

> The first time the present biographer saw Clarence Mangan, it was in this wise: Being in the college library, and having occasion for a book in that gloomy apartment of the institution called the "Fagel Library," which is the innermost recess of the stately building, an acquaintance pointed out to me a man perched on the top of a ladder, with the whispered information that the figure was Clarence Mangan. It was an unearthly and ghostly figure, in a brown garment; the same garment (to all appearance) which lasted till the day of his death. The bleached hair was totally unkempt; the corpse-like features still as marble; a large book was in his hands, and all his soul was in the book. I had never heard of Clarence Mangan before, and I knew not for what he was celebrated; whether as a magician, a poet, or a murderer; yet I took a volume and spread it on a table, not to read, but with a pretence of reading to gaze upon the spectral creature on the ladder.[8]

James Mangan—Clarence was a *nom de plume*—was born on 1 May 1803 in Fishamble Street on the edge of Dublin's Liberties, not a fashionable area. He was the second son of a grocer, who figures in Mangan's fragmentary ***Autobiography*** as a volatile domestic tyrant.[9] Mangan attended four schools, including a Jesuit Latin school; the frequent moves suggest an unsettled childhood. He appears to have acquired some French, Spanish, and Italian, but German was not taught at any of his schools. Where he gained his German is unknown, but he was apparently self-taught; there is no substantial evidence that he ever left Dublin. At the age of fifteen he was apprenticed to be a scrivener, the trade of Herman Melville's Bartleby, which brought him into contact with some of Dublin's minor literati, and he was soon publishing rebus and riddling poems in *The Dublin Satirist* and other periodicals. From that time on, Mangan's earnings from the magazines supplemented his income from various employments in a legal office and at the Ordnance Survey and, later, as a catalogue clerk in the library of Trinity College. Mangan first became visible as a translator through his association with Charles Lever, a gregarious medical student, later a popular novelist and, from 1842 until 1845, a Germanophile editor of the *DUM.* During a sojourn at Göttingen University Lever became so enamored of the patriotic German student associations that, on returning to Dublin, he established a "Burschen Club" of his own. As editor of the *Dublin Literary Gazette and National Magazine,* Lever published Mangan's first translation (of Schiller's "An die Freude") in 1830, and he may have secured Mangan for the *DUM* in 1833. For his part, Mangan may never have traveled beyond his native Dublin, but as a reader he ranged far and wide, plumbing the historical depths of Gaelic poetry and European mysticism—and moving outward to embrace the literature of contemporary Germany.

In his history of the *DUM* Wayne Hall remarks that "stories and novels with a strain of Gothic fantasy form one of the most enduring genres" and "the attention to translation is yet another manifestation of the same phenomenon, especially in the work of such Poe-like writers as James Clarence Mangan."[10] At its most superficial level the relationship between translation and the gothic was manifest in the "from the German" labels worn by tales that may or may not have been translations.[11] I will consider the relationship between these two terms in Mangan's work presently.

At this point a review of Mangan's gothic contributions to the *DUM* and other periodicals seems necessary. Gothic tropes were already present in **"An Extraordinary Adventure in the Shades"** in the *Comet* (1833), and in **"Love, Mystery and Murder: A Tale (Foundered on Facts)"** in the *Dublin Satirist* (1834). These set the pattern for the *DUM* tales **"The Thirty Flasks," "The Man in the Cloak: A Very German Story"** (both 1838), and **"The Threefold Prediction: A Psychological Narrative"** (1845). Also relevant to a consideration of the gothic Mangan are a translation of Zacharias Werner's verse melodrama *Der vierundzwanzigste Februar* (**The Twenty-Fourth of February, 1837**), a curious metaphysical essay—the fragmentary **"Chapters on Ghostcraft"** (1842), and the posthumously published ***Autobiography.***

"The Thirty Flasks" is, in O'Neill's concise summary, "a tale set in Saxony, a burlesque variation on the theme of the diabolical pact, related to Chamisso's *Schlemiel* [*sic*], Goethe's *Faust,* and Maturin's *Melmoth*: the hero Basil Theodore von Rosenwald, impoverished through gambling, contracts to sell his stature by inches to a (short) sorcerer."[12] It is on the face of it a slight piece, but it rewards further attention for the insights it gives us into Mangan's fictional procedures. His handling of the devil's pact motif, which also supplies the basic situation in **"The Man in the Cloak,"** refers parodically to Maturin's gothic novel *Melmoth the Wanderer* (1820) and to Balzac's "sequel," *Melmoth Réconcilié* (*Melmoth Reconciled,* 1833). While Maturin's hero sells his soul for boundless knowledge, Mangan's sells his stature—not all at once, but by inches, and not for superhuman powers, but to clear a gambling debt. The effect is to trivialize the Faustian pact by reducing it from a unique tragic act to a reversible series of transactions. This is part of Mangan's reckoning with the brand of gothic peddled by Maturin. In his sketch of Maturin, Mangan praised *Melmoth* for its "energetic writing and magnificent description" before damning the book's central idea as "hackneyed and monstrous" and traducing the hero as "a bore of the first magnitude, who is always talking grandiloquent fustian, and folding his cloak about him."[13]

The superficiality of the German references in **"The Thirty Flasks"** and **"The Man in the Cloak"** seems to indicate that Mangan's gothic is less than fertile ground for a study of cultural exchange. John Hennig concludes that the quantity and scope of knowledge about Germany in Mangan's prose works is limited, especially in the fiction, but allows that Mangan did assume reader familiarity with aspects of the German cultural scene.[14] Yet for all their superficiality of reference, German or pseudo-German tales were just as much part of the intercultural economy of the *DUM* as Mangan's prolific translations of German verse. Such tales appear to have functioned as a low-culture complement to the high-culture project of translation and criticism—one that may have appealed to beginning students of German who could take pleasure in the surface differences of the language, and to literary insiders who delighted in the punning allusiveness.

As far as Mangan was concerned, such productions belonged to "the style Germanesque" (***Prose 1*** [***The Collected Works of James Clarence Mangan: Prose, 1832-1839***], 105), which is closer to the ridiculous than to the sublime; his poetical translations belonged to what he called "the style German." Mangan also reflected ironically on the literary labels "from the German" and "a German tale," frequently used to mark the ostensible sources of gothic tales in the *DUM,* as in **"The Thirty Flasks,"** where the effect of an explosion caused by the sorcerer shaking his snuff-box into the fire is described as "tremendously terrible and German" (***Prose 1,*** 237), and in the threat uttered by the Man in the Cloak to the forger Braunbrock: "the adamantine hand that grasps you thus will not relinquish its grasp until you are delivered up to justice. Is that German or not?" (***Prose 1,*** 252). In the same tale—which is subtitled "A Very German Story"—Braunbrock predicts the trial and execution of his mistress's lover, declaring it "too true for a German ballad" (***Prose 1,*** 256). Patricia Coughlan has remarked that in such contexts "the word 'German' is the locus of a teasing piece of word-play, which draws on another of its meanings: 'genuine, true, thorough.' "[15]

Mangan's play on ideas of authenticity refers the reader to the origins of the gothic and to the conditions under which it was still being produced during the revival of the 1830s. Barry Murnane has recently described the "wave of uncanny texts [that] emerges at the close of the 1780s and holds readers in its thralls across Western Europe" as "the result of a furious process of translation and cultural exchange," observing that "the cultural practices involved in this exchange are highly dubious: novels purporting to be translations turn out to be original works; supposedly original novels turn out to be either adaptations, unauthorized translations or simply acts of unashamed plagiarism."[16]

Forgery features prominently in the figure of Johann Braunbrock, the protagonist of **"The Man in the Cloak."** The beginning of the story finds him, a cashier in a Viennese bank, putting the finishing touches to a series of counterfeit letters of credit and contemplating fleeing the country with two passports and two disguises. But the tongue-in-cheek claim to authenticity of the subtitle—"A Very German Story"—alerts the reader to counterfeiting as a literary technique, and one especially associated with translation. Seen in this light the following description of Braunbrock acquires a self-reflexive dimension: "the eye of the forger glanced rapidly but scrutinisingly over the work of his hands, to enable him to decide which of the counterfeits before him was least liable to awake suspicion" (***Prose 1,*** 240).

The theme of literary forgery had a particular historical resonance in early nineteenth-century Dublin. Before the Act of Union the city's book trade had thrived on making pirated copies of editions published in England. Legislative union in 1801 ended this lucrative practice overnight, dealing a blow from which Irish publishing took decades to recover. Among the pirated titles was a translation of Schiller's *Der Geisterseher* from the pen of a certain divine, the Reverend W. Render.[17] It is tempting to think that Mangan's tale **"Love, Mystery and Murder: A Tale (Foundered on Facts)"** specifically echoes Render's subtitle, "A History Founded on Fact." Indeed, Mangan could well have stumbled upon Render's work in the popular lending library that he frequented in D'Olier Street, close by Trinity College. There German works in translation were stocked alongside such gothic titles as Charles Brockden Brown's 1798 novel *Wieland, or The Transformation.*[18] But the irony of Mangan's subtitle was more likely aimed at a common early nineteenth-century designation for fictions, including those of a gothic hue.[19]

Mangan did not abstain from the dubious practices of cultural exchange described above, nor did he confine them to his work in the "Germanesque" mode; his work as a "serious" translator was also affected—indeed, so much so that in the case of his translations the *Wellesley Index of Victorian Periodicals* has found itself unable to take his attributions to original authors at face value, noting, "Mangan exercised extreme freedom as a translator, falsely claimed knowledge of esoteric languages, and on occasion fabricated both documents and original authors. . . ."[20] This false-flagging of translations was motivated by pecuniary considerations as Mangan himself indicated in a characteristically punning rejoinder recorded in John Mitchel's 1859 memoir of the poet: "Somebody asked him why he gave credit to Hafiz for such exquisite gems of his own poetry; because, he said, Hafiz paid better than Mangan—and any critic could see that they were only *half his*."[21]

The theme of forgery is amplified in **"The Man in The Cloak"** by the introduction of "the Baron Queerkopf, a determined thick-and-thin, anti-loophole phrenologist" (***Prose 1,*** 242) who, perusing Braunbrock's "characteristic head," diagnoses "Secretiveness" and "Acquisitiveness." Queerkopf's interlocutor, however, insists on the "classic head" of "our honest cash-keeper." This exchange ironizes the modish pseudo-science of phrenology, which fascinated Mangan, drawing attention to the discrepancy between outward form and concealed intention. Together with the pointed use of the label "German" and the previously mentioned reference to forgery, it represents another decidedly self-reflexive moment in the text.

Here it is necessary to distinguish between Mangan and the other gothic contributors to the *DUM,* none of whom matched him for depth of critical engagement with German literature. Mangan was demonstratively and self-consciously intertextual and intercultural in a way that Maturin, Lever, and Le Fanu were not. Moreover, his prose flaunts its apparent inauthenticity and in so doing lays bare the hybrid roots of the gothic. In his twin capacities of translator and critic Mangan had ample exposure to the techniques of romantic irony in the works of Tieck, Hoffmann, and Heine. His criticism of these writers was always astringent and occasionally damning, but it invariably showed a thorough knowledge of their works and an unerring sense of style.

The discussion so far may give the impression that Mangan's own gothic, parodying as it did the fossilized conventions of the mode, stemmed from a repudiation of all belief in transcendental phenomena. John Hennig finds just such an "Abhub von Lehren des deutschen Idealismus" in passages like the following from **"The Thirty Flasks"**:[22] "While at college, it is true, he had perused with some diligence certain abstruse treatises *Ueber die Natur des Geistes*; but being completely satisfied with the great proficiency which these works had enabled him to make in the knowledge of nothing at all on the subject, he had thought it better to devote himself to studies of a more practical description" (***Prose 1,*** 218). Such an interpretation is only possible if we see Mangan's gothic as confined to a handful of tales written in parody of "the style Germanesque." But to do so is to ignore the fragmentary ***Autobiography,*** the **"Chapters on Ghostcraft,"** and the poetry, especially ballads on supernatural themes by Bürger (two versions of **"Lenore"**[23]) and Goethe (**"The Erl-King"**), his version of Schubart's poem "Der ewige Jude" (**"The Wandering Jew"**), and—his longest translation—of Zacharias Werner's verse melodrama *Der vierundzwanzigste Februar.*

In all of these works the tone of Mangan's gothic is largely or wholly sincere, with little in the way of irony or tongue-in-cheek subversion. Indeed, he was first recognized as a gothic author (in 1997!) on the strength of the "sincere" gothic of his ***Autobiography.***[24] The **"Chapters on Ghostcraft"** (1842) are an impassioned defence of the spiritualist investigations of Justinus Kerner in the face of a flippant account of German ghosts and ghost-seers published one year previously in the *DUM.*

Like many of the German Romantics, Justinus Kerner combined literary production with the philosophical study of nature, taking a special interest in what Gotthilf Heinrich Schubert notoriously termed the "dark side" of the natural sciences, such phenomena as magnetism, somnambulism, clairvoyance, and siderism.[25] A key figure in the Swabian School of lyric poets, Kerner was celebrated as the physician and biographer of the somnambulist Friederike Hauffe, the "Seeress of Prevorst." His account of Hauffe's mysterious afflictions, which he treated using mesmerism, her reported visions of the spirit world, and her musings on salvation and the afterlife created an uproar in Germany when they were published in 1829.[26]

An article published by Henry Ferris under the anagrammatic pseudonym "Irys Herfner" (a pun on the German for "Irish harpist") expressed alarm at the heterodox views espoused by Kerner and his supporters, who affirmed the possibility of communication with the dead in a spirit world that bore an uncomfortable resemblance to the purgatory of Catholic dogma. Like the better-known Le Fanu, a contributor of supernatural tales to the *DUM,* Ferris complained: "ghost-seers generally, and those who believe in their revelations, including no small part of the Lutheran clergy of Middle Germany, particularly of Wirtemberg [*sic*], admit a kind of purgatory, though not exactly the popish one; admit it, too, on worse grounds than those alleged by the Papists, namely not on the authority of the church, but on that of ghosts."[27] He was equally dismissive of mesmerism, or animal magnetism, the technique used by Kerner to alleviate the sufferings of Friederike Hauffe. Kerner's claim that his magnetized patient was susceptible to visions of the spirit world scandalized Ferris. As conservatives and unionists Ferris's fellow Anglicans were committed to maintaining the primacy of the Church of Ireland; as Protestants, they regarded themselves as the natural heirs of the European Enlightenment, whose origins they habitually traced to the Reformation.

This group derived its claim to authority from its espousal of Enlightenment values, to which the Catholic majority were gradually to be assimilated by conversion and education. Conventional gothic fictions catered to the prejudices of the wider Anglo-Irish class by representing Catholicism as the abject other. From Radcliffe and Lewis to Maturin's *Melmoth,* the favored locus of the gothic had been a superstitious, feudal, and unreasonable Catholic Southern Europe.[28] However, Kerner's revelations about the spirit world showed Lutheranism itself to be divided between the orthodox and the heterodox. In spatial terms there was a troubling irruption of the South into the North.[29] The former self-identification with Germany as the source of Enlightenment culture being threatened, Ferris had no option but to redraw the boundaries, excluding Germany to emphasize a British identity: "Germans are of all men most magnetizable. Has the reader any theory to account for the fact, that in Germany magnetism is as generally held to be a reality, as in our British lands it is believed to be a humbug?"[30]

Here the British national character is strongly aligned with the empirical and skeptical, the German with the metaphysical and speculative. Ferris's further development of this distinction reveals a nervous preoccupation with the stability of personal identity: "Your Briton has too fast a hold on the actual, or it on him; he is too much in the world, a man altogether too 'wide awake,' too strong in the faith that no other number is number one, to be very easily charmed out of his identity, meshed and spell-bound in soul by airy net-weaving of mesmerite fingers." Particularly disturbing was the image of the magnetized subject, devoid of consciousness and will, a plaything in the hands of the mesmerist—the very antithesis of the self-possessed subject of Enlightenment. Susceptibility to mesmerism was also gendered: "Thus women are more magnetizable than men; and among men those chiefly are magnetizable who are fitted rather to be guided than guides—to be under headship than to be heads."[31] For Ferris the importation of German ideas—a project to which the *DUM* was committed—appeared to harbor dangerously heterodox, anti-rational, and feminizing influences.

Mangan opened his response, the **"Chapters on Ghostcraft,"** with a striking rhetorical move: by characterizing Kerner's opponents as "Credulists," he turned their weapons upon themselves. In typically punning fashion he referred his "spectacled reader" (bespectacled and specter-haunted) to "the classics of German Supernaturalism"—Kerner's *Die Seherin von Prevorst* (The Seeress of Prevorst, Mangan's main source), Gotthilf Heinrich Schubert's *Geschichte der Seele* (History of the Soul), Johann Heinrich Jung-Stilling's *Theorie der Geister-Kunde* (Theory of Spiritology), and Joseph Görres's *Die christliche Mystik* (Christian Mysticism)—before claiming that the skeptical forces of empiricism and materialism were in full flight in Germany, and that it was only a matter of time before "the anti-ghostial creed of the Credulists" (***Prose 2*** [***The Collected Works of James Clarence Mangan: Prose, 1840-1882***], 72) would finally be defeated.[32] Mangan's picture of the intellectual situation in Germany was a distortion: if anything, by the 1840s the tide was turning against the speculative philosophy of nature and toward empiricism, while religious faith was being demysticized and psychologized by the historical criticism of Ludwig Feuerbach and David Friedrich Strauß. Nevertheless, the 1830s and 1840s were marked by the countervailing trend of a growing fascination with mysticism, a point I will return to presently.

Ignoring these complexities, Mangan represented the antimythic tendencies of the Enlightenment as the "eclipse of generations" that was "passing from the fair face of Truth" and claimed that men "are again standing on the ancient ways, again turning into the old ghost-haunted pasts trodden by their grandfathers" (***Prose 2,*** 71). The supernaturalist movement stood poised to defeat its opponents "after a century and a half of bitterest battle on their part, armed as they were with all the weapons which the magazines of Materialism could furnish (including of course the pick-axes of Geology)" (***Prose 2,*** 72). He clinched his argument with a reference to the gains made by spiritualism in Germany: "it is to this complexion that the face of things has come at length, and that too in the most intellectual country in Europe" (***Prose 2,*** 72).

The **"Chapters on Ghostcraft"** is a curious document: it proclaims itself a first part, but there is no sequel; it deploys a battery of references in a way that both copies and parodies a scholarly essay; and it banks on the intellectual prestige of Germany to attack a self-confident rationalism. In the Irish context such an attack implied a confrontation with Anglicanism, but for obvious reasons Mangan did not argue on sectarian lines. His principal concern seems rather to have been with a general decline in religious feeling and observance, and with a philistinism that was inimical to poetry. Whereas Ferris was concerned with the heterodox implications of ghost-seeing, Mangan broadened the religious dimension of the debate to include such matters as man's yearning for transcendence and his need for salvation, as well as speculation on the afterlife.

Mangan's secondary aim in the **"Chapters on Ghostcraft"** was to uphold the dignity of Catholicism in the face of the ideological onslaught mounted on it in the pages of the *DUM.* Haslam has identified a similar strategy operating in the **"Man in the Cloak,"** which "reverses the fervently anti-Catholic attitude of *Melmoth the Wanderer,*" appearing "like a Gothic Trojan horse" in the *DUM.* Taken together with such fictions, the **"Chapters on Ghostcraft"** was another instance of Mangan's use of the gothic as a vessel of "contraband pro-Catholicism."[33] Techniques of the uncanny played their part in unsettling the assumptions of the *DUM*'s ideologues. By confronting the magazine's readership with Kerner's "evidence" of a communion between the spirits of the living and those who had died, and Friederike Hauffe's testimony concerning a "Purgatorial Realm" in which spirits linger after death, Mangan was reacquainting them with the uncanny in Freud's definition as "something that is secretly familiar [*heimlich-heimisch*], which has undergone repression and then returned from it."[34]

Mangan was keenly aware that gothic fictions, from Schiller's *Der Geisterseher* via Lewis's *The Monk* to Maturin's *Melmoth,* depended on a dialectic of superstition on the one hand and of reason, or right belief, on the other—and that this dialectic was coded geographically and distinguished an enlightened, rational, and Protestant Northern Europe from a superstitious, unreasonable, and Catholic Southern Europe. Sir Walter Scott provided the exemplary account of such constructions of the Catholic South in his 1824 essay on Ann Radcliffe:

> [Radcliffe] uniformly (except in her first effort) selected for her place of action the south of Europe, where the human passions, like the weeds of the climate, are supposed to attain portentous growth under the fostering sun; which abounds with ruined monuments of antiquity, as well as the more massive remnants of the middle ages; and where feudal tyranny and Catholic superstition still continue to exercise their sway over the slave and bigot, and to indulge to the haughty lord, or more haughty priest, that sort of despotic power, the exercise of which seldom fails to deprave the heart, and disorder the judgment. These circumstances are skilfully selected, to give probability to events which could not, without great violation of truth, be represented as having taken place in England.[35]

In the parody **"Love, Mystery and Murder"** Mangan undermined reader confidence in the gothic's conventional constructions of Catholic Europe. The narrator deplores the fact that the wealth of the Conde Ugolino di Bulbruzzi "sprang from assassination and pillage—these being the modes by which Italian noblemen generally make out a subsistence, as I clearly find in Mrs. Radcliffe's romances" (***Prose 1,*** 52). In the same tale the heroine refers to a monk only to be answered by "a small philosopher" in the following words: "Who talks of Monks? . . . We have no monks in this country. This is the land of philosophy, of universal benevolence and humanity. We have pillaged all the monasteries and expelled all the Monks" (***Prose 1,*** 62).

The story of Friederike Hauffe resembles the *vita* of a nineteenth-century mystic; and it is worth recalling that Kerner and Joseph Görres, Hauffe's advocates, were both members of German Romanticism, a movement that had "rediscovered" the German mystics as part of its rehabilitation of the Middle Ages in defiance of the Enlightenment definition of the medieval as the "other" of reason. In 1807 Friedrich Schlegel had called Meister Eckhart of Hochheim "vielleicht der tiefsinnigste Philosoph, den Deutschland je gehabt hat" (perhaps the profoundest philosopher that Germany has ever known).[36] Such pronouncements paved the way for an event that transformed German literary history. In 1836 Karl Rosenkranz, a thirty-one-year-old philosophy professor at the University of Königsberg who had studied under Hegel in Berlin, launched a term that neatly encapsulated a hitherto unrecognized phenomenon of German intellectual history: "Deutsche Mystik" (German mysticism).[37] With the invention of this term and building on Hegel's work, Rosenkranz was able to redraw the genealogy of German idealism by pointing to a philosophical current in the Middle Ages that was in many respects highly individualistic and therefore "modern." For Rosenkranz the mystics—chief among them Meister Eckhart—were the true forerunners of the German idealism that had reached its recent apogee in the thinking of Kant and Hegel.

The principal source for the chapter on German mysticism in Rosenkranz's history of German literature was Melchior Diepenbrock's 1829 edition of the writings of Heinrich Seuse (lat. Suso), a fourteenth-century Dominican theologian who defended Eckhart's teachings in the face of official church condemnation.[38] Diepenbrock's edition contained a lengthy introduction written by Joseph Görres in which a connection is made between the ecstatic visions of the mystic Seuse and those of the Seeress of Prevorst. There the visions of the magnetized and the beatific visions of saints are seen as distinct but analogous phenomena. Rosenkranz was more careful to distinguish between the two, objecting to the shutting-down of consciousness—"diese Aufhebung der selbstbewussten Objectivität der Intelligenz"—described by Görres and Kerner as the condition of mystic seeing.[39] For the Young Hegelian philosopher, mysticism was an intellectual performance involving *willed* acts of self-transcendence.

In **"Chapters on Ghostcraft"** Mangan displayed his familiarity with German mysticism by referring directly to the Diepenbrock edition of Seuse's writings and specifically to the introduction by Görres. He concurred with Görres's distinction between the "Lucid Vision of Magnetisees" as a "connatural exoteric phenomenon" and the "Beatific Vision of Saints" as a "supernal and esoteric mystery" (***Prose 2,*** 82). The latter are granted "only to those who through faith and prayer, long-continued penances, and severe crucifixion of the Psychical Man in themselves, have become in some degree worthy to enjoy so exceeding great a glory" (***Prose 2,*** 82-83). Such lines contained a double irritant and provocation for readers like Ferris: not only was the possibility of magnetic vision allowed, but the "perverse" monastic asceticism of *DUM* editorials and conventional gothic fictions was reconfigured as a path to sanctity.

More perilous than these provocations to the *DUM* project of appropriating German literature and ideas to the project of national renewal under Anglican leadership was Mangan's reference to the newly discovered field of German mysticism. The creation of the term "German mysticism" entailed resituating the roots of intellectual inquiry in the formerly reviled Middle Ages. The Young Hegelian Rosenkranz had sketched a genealogy of German philosophy that began not with Luther, but with Heinrich Seuse, a fourteenth-century Dominican elevated to the status of "blessed" in 1831. Mangan played on this idea of a renewed link between medieval thought and contemporary philosophy by teasingly identifying the sources of **"Ghostcraft"** [**"Chapters on Ghostcraft"**] as "mystical and modern" (***Prose 2,*** 71). The discovery of mysticism rewrote the intellectual history of German idealism in a way that made the *DUM* project of assimilating prestigious German letters and ideas to a conservative-progressive project of national renewal under Anglican leadership precarious by destabilizing the claim to represent "Enlightenment."

Divining the seriousness of Mangan's intent in **"Ghostcraft"** is not a straightforward matter. I have described that essay as an example of Mangan's "sincere" gothic, with little in the way of outright irony. But not even **"Ghostcraft"** asks to be taken entirely seriously: while wearing the outward form of a scholarly essay, it banters with the "spectacled" reader. In a pragmatic sense the question of sincerity is irrelevant with regard to such a highly performative and allusive text; indeed, its potency as an irritant to *DUM* readers of Ferris's stamp was heightened rather than lessened by its parodic qualities.[40]

Mangan's fictions were distinguished from those of other contributors by precisely this disconcerting alternation between somber pathos and flashes of irony. In support of his claim that such works as **"The Man in the Cloak"** represented "an experiment in Irish Romantic irony," Haslam observes that such tonal fluctuations in Mangan's work closely resemble the "perennial alternation of enthusiasm and irony" identified by Friedrich Schlegel as the hallmark of the "arabesque" in literature, citing as a prime example of Mangan's romantic irony the following exchange in **"The Man in the Cloak"** between the eponymous Irishman and the forger Braunbrock:[41]

> "What do you mean, Sir?" asked Braunbrock.
>
> "I mean to smoke," replied the Irishman, as he drew a long pipe, already ignited, from beneath the folds of his cloak.
>
> "Come, come, Sir," cried Braunbrock, "I don't understand this buffoonery. Let me pass, or take the consequences!" . . .
>
> "So serious a matter as forgery, I fancy, has unfitted you for relishing buffoonery," said the Irishman, aloud, and in the hearing of all.
>
> (***Prose 1,*** 247)

Irony is indicated by the gesture of smoking, which in the literary parlance of the nineteenth-century literary meant "to make fun of, to jest at; to ridicule, banter, or quiz (a person)."[42] Following this exchange, which takes place in a theater, the Man in the Cloak accompanies Braunbrock and Braunbrock's faithless fiancée, Livonia, to their box. While the rest of the audience enjoys the advertised play, a series of rather different scenes unfolds to Braunbrock's appalled gaze. First he glimpses a "private room, into which he had been more than once introduced" (***Prose 1,*** 249). There his host is engaged in conversation with the Chief of Police about Braunbrock's imminent arrest and unmasking for forgery. The scene then shifts to the interior of Livonia's house, where a "sergeant-major of cavalry in a Bavarian regiment" awaits his assignation with Braunbrock's beloved (***Prose 1,*** 250). The young officer disappears into a closet, and Braunbrock is horrified to see himself ushered into the anteroom, where his fiancée receives him with feigned affection, silently laughing over his shoulder at her maid, who is party to the deception. Braunbrock's horror and revulsion is intensified by the fact that he alone is the witness of these scenes; Livonia and the rest of the audience are meanwhile convulsed with mirth at a crude farce featuring "a gouty old English alderman . . . devouring an entire haunch of venison." The theater episode in **"The Man in the Cloak"** evinces a kind of climactic development of a thoroughly Hoffmannesque character, from the initial rupture in narrated reality presented by the play-in-the-play, via the appearance of the doppelgänger, to scenes of flight and arrest, trial and punishment. In the flight scene Braunbrock witnesses his double's attempt to escape Vienna in a postchaise rented under a false name. His hopes are raised as the carriage rolls unhindered through the streets—only to be dashed when he sees the vehicle stopped at the barrier of the city and his double taken prisoner and fettered. These uncanny representations are the means by which Braunbrock is brought to enter into a Faustian pact with the Irishman, Melmoth, exchanging places with him, and accepting his talisman, which guarantees unlimited wealth and inhuman isolation in equal measure.

The meta-fictional ramifications of the theater episode extend beyond the suggestive resemblance to techniques of romantic irony, for the episode refers to the conditions of production of the gothic itself. We have seen how prominent the theme of forgery is in **"The Man in The Cloak"** and that reader attention is drawn via physiognomics to a discrepancy between outward form and inward intention. The poetological implications of this are apparent: straight-faced gothic fictions were in Mangan's view forgeries because they concealed their derivativeness. His own gothic fictions distinguished themselves by thematizing their indebtedness to other fictions and ironizing the conditions of their production. Forgery was the mode by which the "German" tales of the *DUM* were made, buffoonery the mode of ironic disclosure—Mangan's mode. Buffoonery, in the person of Mangan's cloaked Irishman, decisively trumps forgery represented by Braunbrock, who, in the gothic surroundings of Saint Sulpice, repents of his counterfeiting and is exhorted by a priest to return "a changed man—a man who need no longer shroud himself *in a cloak*" (***Prose 1,*** 262).

Notes

1. The periodical introduction in *The Wellesley Index to Victorian Periodicals* provides a useful overview of the history of the *Dublin University Magazine*: http://gateway.proquest.com/openurl?url_ver=Z39.88-2004&res_dat=xri:wellesley&rft_dat=xri:wellesley:intro:JID-DUM (accessed 10 January 2011). See also Wayne E. Hall, *Dialogues in the Margin: A Study of the Dublin University Magazine* (Buckinghamshire: Colin Smythe, 2000).

2. Samuel Ferguson, "By-Ways of Irish History," *Dublin University Magazine* 10 (1837): 207 (subsequent references to the *Dublin University Magazine* in text).

3. John Anster's 1820 translation of Goethe's *Faust* (1808) in *Blackwood's* was a significant spur to the upturn in interest in German literature in Britain. Anster, a Dublin lawyer, was one of the founders of the *DUM* in 1833.

4. See [John Francis Waller], "Herr Zander's lectures on German literature," *Dublin University Magazine* 1 (1833): 335; this is an account of seven public lectures on German literature recently given in Dublin by "Herr Zander of Berlin."

5. Mary M. Colum, *From These Roots: The Ideas That Have Made Modern Literature* (London: Cape, 1938), 241.

6. *The Nation,* 22 October 1842; quoted in Patrick O'Neill, *Ireland and Germany: A Study in Literary Relations* (New York: Peter Lang, 1985), 100.

7. O'Neill, *Ireland and Germany,* 97. O'Neill has calculated that the *DUM* contained 137 references to German literature in the period from 1833 to 1850, an average of eight references per twelve monthly issues, or an average of sixty-five pages per year. Of these an average of thirty-one pages per year was contributed by Mangan, whose total contribution amounted to at least 558 of the 1179 pages devoted to German literature in this period. See Patrick O'Neill, "German Literature and the *Dublin University Magazine,* 1833-50: A Checklist and Commentary," *Long Room* 14/15 (Autumn 1976-Spring/Summer 1977): 20-21.

8. John Mitchel, Introduction, in *Poems by James Clarence Mangan,* ed. David James O'Donoghue (Dublin: [n.p.], 1904), xxxiv-xxxv.

9. The standard biography is Ellen Shannon-Mangan, *James Clarence Mangan: A Biography* (Dublin: Irish Academic Press, 1996).

10. Hall, *Dialogues in the Margin,* 212.

11. Barry Murnane, "Importing Home-Grown Horrors? The English Reception of the Schauerroman and Schiller's *Der Geisterseher,*" *Angermion: Yearbook for Anglo-German Literary Criticism, Intellectual History and Cultural Transfers/Jahrbuch für britisch-deutsche Kulturbeziehungen* 1 (2008): 51-82.

12. O'Neill, "German Literature and the *Dublin University Magazine,*" 26.

13. *The Collected Works of James Clarence Mangan,* ed. Augustine Martin, Jacques Chuto et al., 6 vols. (Dublin: Irish Academic Press, 1996-2002). This edition contains Mangan's collected prose in two vols.: *Prose 1, 1832-39,* and *Prose 2, 1840-82* (hereafter cited in text).

14. John Hennig, "Deutschlandkunde in James Clarence Mangan's Prosawerken," *Deutsche Vierteljahrsschrift für Literaturwissenschaft und Geistesgeschichte* 44 (1970): 505.

15. Patricia Coughlan, "The Recycling of *Melmoth*: 'A Very German Story,'" in *Literary Interrelations: Ireland, England and the World,* ed. Wolfgang Zach and Heinz Kosok, 3 vols. (Tübingen: Narr, 1987), 2:184.

16. Murnane, "Importing Home-Grown Horrors," 52-53.

17. *The Armenian; or, The Ghost Seer, a History Founded on Fact. Translated from the German of F. Schiller, Author of The Robbers, Don Carlos &c., by the Rev. W. Render,* 2 vols. (Dublin: William Folds, 1800). The authorized edition of Render's text was published by H. D. Symonds of London in 1800. The latter part of volume 1 and volume 2 is taken up by a translation of the continuation of Schiller's *Der Geisterseher* by Ernst Friedrich Follenius.

18. Ellen Shannon Mangan, *James Clarence Mangan,* 48.

19. A quick search of the *Eighteenth Century Collections Online* database turned up thirty-five works of fiction with this subtitle: http://find.galegroup.com.elib.tcd.ie/ecco/ (accessed 15 January 2011).

20. *The Wellesley Index to Victorian Periodicals,* "Periodical Introduction: The Dublin University Magazine," para. 10.

21. John Mitchel, Introduction, xliii.

22. See Hennig, "Deutschlandkunde," 503.

23. Gottfried August Bürger's ballad "Lenore" was repeatedly translated into English in the mid-1790s during the first flourishing of the gothic in Britain.

24. Seamus Deane, *Strange Country: Modernity and Nationhood in Irish Writing since 1790* (Oxford: Clarendon, 1997), 122-39. Deane identifies Mangan as an exponent of "what we may call Catholic or Catholic-nationalist Gothic" (126), a claim that was new because Irish gothic had previously been identified with such Protestant writers as Charles Maturin, J. S. Le Fanu, and Bram Stoker. Thus W. J. McCormack: "At the risk of paradox, it has to be said that while Irish gothic writing does not amount to a tradition, it is a distinctly Protestant tradition"; see W. J. McCormack, "Irish Gothic and After (1820-1945)," in *The Field Day Anthology of Irish Writing,* ed. Seamus Deane, 3 vols. (Derry: Field Day, 1991), 2:837.

25. Gotthilf Heinrich Schubert, *Ansichten von der Nachtseite der Naturwissenschaft* (Dresden: Arnold, 1808).

26. Justinus Kerner, *Die Seherin von Prevorst: Eröffnungen über das innere Leben der Menschen und über das Hereinragen einer Geisterwelt in die unsere* (Stuttgart: Cotta, 1829). Jürgen Barkhoff emphasizes Kerner's importance in sustaining and promoting German interest in mesmerism (or animal magnetism), a phenomenon that preoccupied the speculative *Naturphilosophie* of romanticism: "für die weitere Rezeption und Transformation des Mesmerismus im 19. Jahrhundert ist er von weit größerer Bedeutung als Schlegel und Brentano, geraden wegen seiner populären, mit Anschaulichkeit, Anteilnahme und frommem Pathos formulierten Schriften"; see Jürgen Barkhoff, *Magnetische Fiktionen: Literarisierung des Mesmerismus in der Romantik* (Stuttgart: Metzler, 1995), 310.

27. [Henry Ferris], "German Ghosts and Ghost-Seers," by Irys Herfner, *DUM* 17 (1841): 37.

28. See Robert Mighall, *A Geography of Victorian Gothic Fiction: Mapping History's Nightmares* (Oxford: Oxford UP, 1999), xiv-xix.

29. On the favored geographical settings of British gothic tales between 1770 and 1840, see Franco Moretti, *Atlas of the European Novel, 1800-1900* (London: Verso, 1999), 12-31. According to Moretti, "the highest concentration of Gothic tales is to be found in the triangle comprised between the Rhine, the Black Forest, and the Harz (the region of the pact with the Devil)" (16). Thanks to Marion Dalvai for this information.

30. Ferris, "German Ghosts and Ghost-Seers," 37.

31. Ferris, "German Ghosts and Ghost-Seers," 38.

32. Gotthilf Heinrich Schubert, *Die Geschichte der Seele* (Stuttgart: Cotta, 1830); Johann Heinrich Jung-Stilling, *Theorie der Geister-Kunde: In einer Natur-, Vernunft- und Bibelmäßigen Beantwortung der Frage: Was von Ahnungen, Gesichten und Geistererscheinungen geglaubt und nicht geglaubt werden müße* (Nuremberg: Raw'sche Buchhandlung, 1808); Joseph von Görres, *Die christliche Mystik,* 5 vols. (Regensburg: Manz, 1836-42).

33. Richard Haslam, "'Broad Farce and Thrilling Tragedy': Mangan's Fiction and Irish Gothic," *Éire-Ireland* 41 (2006): 231-32.

34. Sigmund Freud, "The 'Uncanny'" (1919), in *The Standard Edition of the Complete Psychological Works of Sigmund Freud,* tr. and ed. James Strachey, Anna Freud et al., 24 vols. (London: Hogarth Press, 1953-74), 17:245.

35. Sir Walter Scott, "Ann Radcliffe," in *Sir Walter Scott on Novelists and Fiction,* ed. Ioan Williams (London: Routledge, 1968), 114.

36. Friedrich Schlegel to August Wilhelm Schlegel, Cologne, 22 Dec. 1807, in Josef Körner, ed., *Krisenjahre der Frühromantik,* 2 vols., 2nd ed. (Bern: Francke, 1969), 1:489.

37. Karl Rosenkranz, *Zur Geschichte der deutschen Literatur* (Königsberg: Bornträger, 1836), 37-57 (chapter 4).

38. Melchior Diepenbrock, *Heinrich Suso's genannt Amandus Leben und Schriften* (Regensburg: Pustet, 1829).

39. Rosenkranz, *Zur Geschichte der deutschen Literatur,* 53.

40. Since Avril Horner and Sue Zlosnic's landmark publication it has become more common to acknowledge an ironic and even parodic nature of the gothic; see their *Gothic and the Comic Turn* (Basingstoke: Palgrave Macmillan, 2005).

41. See Friedrich Schlegel, *Dialogue on Poetry and Literary Aphorisms,* tr. E. Behler and R. Strug (University Park: Pennsylvania State UP, 1968), 86 (quoted in Haslam, 235), and Haslam, "Broad Farce and Thrilling Tragedy," 236.

42. *Oxford English Dictionary,* http://www.oed.com:80/Entry/182699 (accessed 6 February 2011). Patricia Coughlan is the first scholar to have pointed to this usage (now obsolete) of the term "to smoke" in Mangan's works; see Coughlan, "The Recycling of *Melmoth,*" 186. Compare also the prefatory motto of "Psalmanazar" in the New York magazine *Salmagundi*: "In hoc est hoax, cum quiz et jokesez, / Et smokem, toastem, roastem folksez, / Fee, faw, fum. / With baked, and broiled, and stewed, and toasted; / And fried, and boiled, and smoked, and roasted, / We treat the town"; see *Salmagundi; or, The Whim-Whams and Opinions of Launcelot Langstaff, Esq. and Others,* 3rd. ed. (New York: Longworth, 1820), 5.

Work Cited

Primary Literature

Houghton, Walter E., ed. *The Wellesley Index to Victorian Periodicals.* 5 vols. Toronto: U of Toronto P, 1965-88. CD-ROM, Routledge, 1999.

Melissa Fegan (essay date 2013)

SOURCE: Fegan, Melissa. "'Every Irishman Is an Arab': James Clarence Mangan's Eastern 'Translations.'" *Translation and Literature* 22.2 (2013): 195-214. Print.

[*In the following essay, Fegan takes issue with the idea, circulated by Mangan himself, that he translated Eastern poetry exclusively for money. She finds that Mangan wrote much original poetry under the guise of translating minor poets and used the ruse of translation to confront the English colonial government.*]

If the vagrant Imagination is at home anywhere, it is the East, proclaimed James Clarence Mangan (1803-49)—even if its conception of the East is somewhat illusory, and dominated by 'images of Geniiland' rather than a realistic Orient.[1] Mangan—unkindly described by Valentine Cunningham as the 'archetypical drunken-Irish poet'[2]—is chiefly remembered for stirring nationalist anthems like **'Dark Rosaleen,'** or his depictions of the horrors of the Great Famine. The young James Joyce described him as 'the national poet,'[3] but Mangan's leanings were international, and his delight in the East emerged in a series of six articles on Oriental poetry, titled **'Literæ Orientales,'** published in the *Dublin University Magazine* between September 1837 and January 1846. Mangan had already published several **'Anthologia Germanica'** [***Anthologia Germanica = German Anthology***], articles in the same magazine, and his fascination with the East, rooted in childhood encounters with the *Arabian Nights' Entertainments,* was deepened by his work on German poets including Rückert and Goethe, themselves heavily influenced by Oriental literature. In an article on ***'Faust* and the Minor Poems of Goethe'** in March 1836, Mangan comments that Goethe, 'skilled in the languages of the East,' had rightly avoided feeding 'the popular appetite for those monstrous fictions with which the stores of Oriental literature abound,' suggesting Mangan's disapproval of the typical imaginative excess of Western visions of the East (***Prose* [*The Collected Works of James Clarence Mangan: Prose*]**, I, 94). Yet Mangan himself would soon begin to exploit the popular appetite for Oriental literature in his **'Literæ Orientales,'** and, unlike Goethe, Mangan could claim little or no knowledge of the languages of the East. The *Dublin University Magazine* limited contributors to a maximum of three original poems per issue, but there were no limits on the number of translations,[4] so it made financial sense for the penurious Mangan to translate Persian and Turkish poems rather than submit his own original work. One friend, Charles Gavan Duffy, lamented that Mangan, 'goaded by necessity' (and a prodigious thirst) had squandered his talent by producing too many 'poetical pot-boilers (or, alas! flask-fillers),'[5] while another, John Mitchel, reported Mangan as explaining that 'Hafiz paid better than Mangan.'[6]

The financial incentive is for several critics the most obvious and significant motivation for Mangan's writings on the East; Haideh Ghomi repeats that Mangan believed '(quite rightly too) that Hafez pays better than Mangan,' and Hasan Javadi and John D. Yohannan also quote Mitchel to suggest that Mangan sought to trade on the name of the well-known Persian poet.[7] The phenomenal success of Byron's Eastern poems *Childe Harold's Pilgrimage* (1812-18), *The Giaour* (1813), and *The Bride of Abydos* (1813), Beckford's *Vathek* (1786), and his countryman Thomas Moore's *Lalla Rookh* (1817), confirmed for Mangan the appetite for Oriental literature, as did the current vogue for Eastern travels and letters. From its foundation in 1833, the *Dublin University Magazine,* 'the supreme archive of Irish Victorian experience,'[8] reflected the demand for representations of the East, publishing articles on Oriental travel and reviews of books including Robert Walsh's 'Turkey and Greece: the Sultan and Capo d'Istrias' in July 1833, Lord Lindsay's *Letters on Egypt, Edom, and the Holy Land* in November 1838,

James B. Fraser's *A Winter Journey from Constantinople to Tehran* in January 1839, Wilbraham's *Travels in Caucasus, Georgia and Persia* in August 1839, Malcolm's *Travels in South-Eastern Asia* in February 1840, and Colonel Dennie's letters from the Afghan War in 1842. Warburton's *The Crescent and the Cross,* one of the most successful travel books of the nineteenth century, appeared in the *Dublin University Magazine* as 'Episodes of Eastern Travel' in October 1843 and January 1844, and was reviewed in January 1845.

However, in spite of the fame and marketability of Hafiz, and Mangan's claim in the first of his articles that 'no poet has as yet made his appearance in Arabia, China, Tartary, India, or the Ottoman Empire, who has succeeded in transferring the laurel from the brows of Shemseddin Mohammed Hafiz to his own,'[9] Mangan only translated four lines of Hafiz's poetry in his **'Literæ Orientales'** articles, and even these are attributed not to Hafiz but to Servi.[10] Indeed, as the editors of Mangan's ***Collected Works*** [***The Collected Works of James Clarence Mangan: Poems***] note, the only poem he offers as a translation from Hafiz appeared in the *Dublin University Magazine* in 1848 as **'An Ode of Hafiz,'** and is, in fact, not a translation at all, but an original poem;[11] when rebuked by his friend, the translator John Anster, Mangan is said to have replied: 'Ah, it is only *Half-his.*'[12] This suggests that the motivation behind Mangan's Oriental translations was not entirely mercenary; if the only incentive was financial, Mangan could easily have presented numerous translations from Hafiz. Hafiz might pay better than Mangan, but Mesihi, Nedschati, Chuffi, and the other poets Mangan chose to translate instead were riskier prospects. What they offered was greater licence creatively; Mangan's early biographer, D. J. O'Donoghue, wrote:

> It is curious that he nowhere translates, or professes to translate, the famous Eastern poets. Omar, Sadi, Hafiz, to mention only three, are left severely alone. This would seem to imply that when he wished to mystify his readers—which he generally did—he found the smaller writers much more useful for the purpose.[13]

Lesser-known writers provided a convenient cover for the fact that many of his 'translations' were originals masquerading as translations. But Mangan desires to do more than simply 'mystify his readers'; his **'Literae Orientales'** articles and translations demonstrate the growth of an anti-imperialist—if not postcolonial—feeling in his work long before the tragedy of the Great Famine forced him into more direct confrontation with colonial authority. Mangan's essays on and translations of Eastern poetry underline his status as a 'minor' writer whose radical inauthenticity and critique of canonical aesthetics, as David Lloyd argues, 'opens out continually onto a critique of the assumptions that support the bourgeois state and legitimate its domestic and imperial hegemony.'[14]

Mangan's self-association with the impostor Al Mokanna, the Veiled Prophet of Khorassan of Moore's *Lalla Rookh,* is alluded to by the editors of the ***Collected Works,*** who choose to end their General Introduction with one of the 'translations' from Mangan's **'Literæ Orientales,'** attributed to the Turkish poet Lamii. This emphasizes both Mangan's deliberate mystification and his compulsive hint-dropping about his practices:

> Mine inkstand is the Well of NAKSHEB;—and from each
> Imperishable drop I spread along the page
> Another Veilèd Prophet utters mystic speech,
> To be translated only by a future age.[15]

Lamii is one of the real poets Mangan uses to veil his fake translations; in the third of his articles Lamii is taken over almost wholesale. Mangan had done much the same thing with his German translations; of four poems attributed to Salis in his article on 'The Poems of Matthison [sic] and Salis' in 1835, two are by poets other than Salis, and two are original poems by Mangan.[16] Mangan also invented two German alter-egos, Drechsler and Selber ('turner' or 'translator,' and 'myself'), whose poems he 'translated' in his **'Anthologia Germanica'** articles. A piece on Mangan (probably written by himself in the third person), which appeared posthumously in *The Irishman* (**'Sketches of Modern Irish Writers. James Clarence Mangan'**), explains that his translations are 'anti-plagiaristic,' 'fathering upon other writers the offspring of his own brain' (***Prose*** [***The Collected Works of James Clarence Mangan: Prose***], II, 224). The sketch states this is due to lack of confidence: 'It is a strange fault ... that Mangan should entertain a deep diffidence of his own capacity to amuse or attract others, by anything emanating from himself' (223). But it also quotes Mangan as offering a different reason:

> I *must* write in a variety of styles; and it wouldn't do for me to don the turban, and open my poem with a *Bismillah*; when I write a poem to the Arab Mohir-Ibn-Mohir—Ibn Khalakan is the man from whom it should come; and to him I give it ... When I write as a Persian, I feel as a Persian, and am transported back to the days of Diemsheed and the Genii ...
>
> (224)

The fourth **'Literæ Orientales'** article suggests this self-negation is a necessity for any translator of Oriental literature: 'He must for a season renounce his country, divest himself of his educational prejudices, forego his individuality, and become, like Alfred Tennyson, "a Mussulman true and sworn"' (***Prose,*** II, 1-2). Mangan is of course being ironic; Tennyson's speaker in 'Recollections of the Arabian Nights' self-consciously dons the turban as obvious fantasy.[17] Part of Mangan's project in **'Literæ Orientales,'** as in his German translations, is to engage in the contemporary debate about originality and fidelity in translation—and in poetry more generally; but in **'Literæ Orientales'** this is complicated by Mangan's critique of imperialism and cultural appropriation. As Mangan was aware, few contemporary translators were interested in becoming 'a Mussulman true and sworn'; indeed, too many were derisory about not only the literature, but the entire culture. Two years before Mangan began his series, Thomas Macaulay, in his famous 'Minute on Indian Education,' admitting he had 'no knowledge of either Sanscrit or Arabic' himself, used his reading of translations and conversations with 'men distinguished by their proficiency in the Eastern tongues' as evidence of European superiority: 'I have never found one among them who could deny that a single shelf of a good European library was worth the whole native literature of India and Arabia.'[18] George Sale, whose translation of the *Koran* Mangan uses in his articles, wanted 'to undeceive those who, from the ignorant or unfair translations which have appeared, have entertained too favourable an opinion of the original, and also to enable us effectually to expose the imposture [of Mohammed].'[19] Robert Southey prefaces his *The Curse of Kehama* (1810) with an assertion that 'of all false religions' Hinduism is 'the most monstrous in its fables, and the most fatal in its effects,'[20] while the notes to *Thalaba the Destroyer* (1801) confidently dismiss 'the little of their literature that has reached us' as 'equally worthless.' Southey scoffs at the '*barbarian* scholars' who compared Ferdusi to Homer: 'To make this Iliad of the East, as they have sacrilegiously stiled it, a good poem, would be realizing the dreams of Alchemy, and transmuting lead into gold.'[21] Walter Savage Landor, in his notes to his hoax translations from the Arabic and Persian, written in response to a challenge from a friend, derides 'the heady spirits and high-seasoned garbage of Barbarians': 'It must surely result from the weakest or from the most perverted understanding that the *gazal* has ever been preferred to the pure and almost perfect, though utterly dissimilar, pieces of Anacreon and Tibullus.'[22] The Romantics may have found an imaginative landscape and new poetic vocabulary in the East, but as Yohannan argues:

> There was something frankly exploitative about the way they made use of the materials of Oriental literature, something curiously analogous to the relations between England and her Asian empire. The riches of Oriental expression were gaudily displayed and frequently gilded with the colors of false imagination. It is doubtful whether any of the authors had a serious regard for the subjects they were adapting.[23]

Mangan was able to exploit his familiarity with the *Arabian Nights' Entertainments* and the Oriental fictions of his contemporaries to create the appropriate atmosphere: 'To an acquaintance who objected that a particular translation was not Moorish, he replied: "Well, never mind, it's *Tom Moorish*."'[24] He is quite capable of presenting his readers with the image of the East that he knows they want to buy—the 'Land of Wonders,' rose and bulbul, exotic scenery, despots, battles, veiled maidens. Mangan offers glimpses of alluring Oriental women, bearing names such as Amine, Gulnare, Zelica and Leila, drawn from the heroines of Moore, Byron, and the *Arabian Nights' Entertainments,* who are alternately called upon to unveil or to refrain from unveiling: 'My starlight, my moonlight, my midnight, my noonlight, | Unveil not, unveil not, or millions must pine' (***Poems*** [***The Collected Works of James Clarence Mangan: Poems***], II, 7). For those who seek spiritual enlightenment, proverbs and epigrams abound:

> The world is one Vast Caravanserai,
> Where none may stay,
> BUT WHERE EACH GUEST WRITES ON THE WALL THIS WORD,
> O, MIGHTY LORD!
>
> (***Poems,*** I, 365)

Many of the poems are elegiac, lamenting exile from a beloved homeland, or the decay of cities such as Palmyra, Balbec, Babylon and Persepolis: 'Where flourished gardens then, it is true, we stray in wildernesses now; where palaces rose we find roofless walls and broken columns' (***Prose,*** I, 131). Others, such as **'The Daunishmend's Lamentation,' 'The Time of the Barmecides,'** or **'The Lament of Leeah Rewaan,'** mourn the loss of youth and vitality. These are all major concerns of Mangan's poetry in general—indeed the editors of the ***Collected Works*** suggest **'The Lament of Leeah Rewaan'** is an 'oriental' version of Mangan's purported German 'translation' **'Twenty Golden Years Ago'** (***Poems,*** III, 131). Instead of rehearsing the stereotypes of cruelty and licentiousness, or the magical aspect of the 'Land of Wonders,' the East Mangan presents in his 'translations' is distant in time—the poems he purports to translate are from the fifteenth, sixteenth, and seventeenth centuries—but often realistic, familiar, and accessible, sympathetically realized and inhabited by complex emotional beings. Mangan's interest in the East seems to accord with the strand of Orientalism Mohammed Sharaffudin identifies as an alternative to straightforward cultural exploitation: 'namely that orientalism which, because it proved receptive to the radical energies liberated by the French Revolution, offered an effective vantage point from which to condemn the reactionary forces at home and the prevailing spirit of intolerance reflected in relations with a culture such as that of Islam.'[25] Indeed, Mangan identifies the French Revolution as a turning point in the representation of the East, sweeping away those he termed the 'old Orientalists':

> Time has trodden them down, them, their works, their memory; their light . . . could burn only in an atmosphere of darkness;—directly the *Appian Way* of the human mind was upbroken by the first pickaxes and crowbars of the French Revolutionists, it died, day-extinguished, storm-destroyed. They have passed away, and bolder enquirers occupy their places.
>
> (***Prose,*** I, 133)

Mangan uses **'Literæ Orientales'** to challenge the ignorance, prejudice, racism and essentialism of the 'old Orientalists,' and those who read, commented on, and indeed translated, Oriental literature with very little knowledge of the languages or cultures of the East. Mangan's title, **'Literæ Orientales,'** suggests a broad correspondence between the literature of diverse nations; while these articles focus on the poetry of Persia and Turkey, elsewhere Mangan's capacious East seems capable of accommodating swathes of geographical space from Albania to China, Siberia to India. Yet Mangan is careful to point out that 'The Arabian, Persian and Turkish poetries do not constitute one literature' (***Prose,*** II, 5), and he reproves the superficiality of the Western version of the Orient, with its recurring imagery and stories: 'It is a great mistake to fancy that the Orientals know nothing about any body except Haroun Alraschid and Sinbad the sailor' (***Prose,*** I, 135). Mangan criticizes the chauvinism that prevented the 'old Orientalists' from recognizing worth in the literature of the East:

> They regarded the Asiatics as a subordinate and degraded caste of mortals, without troubling themselves to anatomise with too much curiousness the reasonings they had arrived at their conclusions by . . . They tested the genius, habits, and prejudices of one continent by the genius, habits and prejudices of another; and because the two continents differed—because the moral character of Europe was reckoned austerer than that of Asia—because Asia was not Europe, the literature of Asia was pronounced unworthy of a comparison with the literature of Europe.
>
> (***Prose,*** I, 132)

More than six decades before Joseph Conrad's 'And this also . . . has been one of the dark places of the earth,'[26] Mangan undermines the West's self-consoling imagery of darkness and light, civilization and savagery, with a chastening reminder of Britain's own history of subordination: 'The old Roman, as he looked with contempt on the barbarian Teuton and Briton, could scarcely have imagined a period when Germany and England would contest the victory of intellectual pre-eminence with the majestic Mistress of the World' (***Prose,*** I, 132). Mangan's articles are often playful, parodic, and flamboyantly artificial, but they are also fiercely anti-imperialist in their examination of the politics and aesthetics of translation.

The very concept of translation of Oriental literature is bound up with conquest and commerce. Hafiz paid better than Mangan partly because of the importance of Persian literature in India, and the importance to the sahibs of the East India Company of possessing at least a superficial familiarity with Indian culture. As Sir William Jones recognized, the languages and literature of the East would have continued to be despised or overlooked by the nations of Europe had it not been for the powerful incentive of commerce: 'interest was the charm which gave to the languages of the East a real and solid importance.'[27] Mangan recognizes that translation is implicated in the colonial enterprise. Cataloguing and translating is 'the preliminary step towards rendering available, that is, transferable into our own land's language, all that may be really valuable in the literature of the East' (***Prose,*** I, 137). Translation is a form of plunder:

> It is our policy, roamers as we are through the Enchanted Caverns of Oriental Poetry, to commence our scheme of operations . . . by picking up from the ground a few stray jewels of slight weight and no very brilliant water, before we proceed to ransack the coffers and carry off the ponderous golden vases that lie piled about us.
>
> (***Prose,*** I, 143)

The translator—particularly the translator of Oriental poetry—is a hawker of stolen or counterfeit goods, valuing only what he can sell to an undiscriminating audience.

Mangan exposes the essential spuriousness of the Western experience of Oriental poetry, making little effort to hide his own fakery—in fact constantly inviting discovery. In order to construct an adequate literary history of the Oriental nations, he asserts in the first article, he would have to be proficient in the languages, travel to the East to compare rare manuscripts, and spend perhaps a quarter of a century growing old over his desk, before he was ready to pronounce an authoritative opinion. 'The work,' he announces blithely, 'need not be more voluminous than the *Bibliothèque Orientale*' (***Prose,*** I, 137); this would be no mean feat, as d'Herbelot's dictionary, published posthumously in 1697, was still the standard reference work on Oriental literature, and according to Said, 'Its scope was truly epochal.'[28] Mangan pretends he has travelled to see illuminated manuscripts and quibbles with the translations of Sir William Jones and Edward Lane, yet he had little or no knowledge of Eastern tongues, and had hardly been outside Dublin, and never outside Ireland, in his life. The poems he translated were German rather than Persian or Turkish; the main source for **'Literæ Orientales'** was the Austrian Joseph Von Hammer-Purgstall's German translations of Persian and Turkish poems. Mangan did not need to hide the fact that his source material was in German: 'relay translation,'[29] translating Oriental literature into English via French or German translations, was an entirely acceptable practice in the early nineteenth century, and some of the most successful translations of Persian poetry in this period were made by writers who did not know the language, including Emerson, Edwin Arnold, Matthew Arnold, and Louise Costello. Emerson, like Mangan, used Von Hammer-Purgstall rather than Persian originals. But by pretending to a greater familiarity with the language and manuscripts than he actually possessed, Mangan is clearly questioning the authority and authenticity of other translators of Oriental poetry.

In the first article, Mangan presents the translator as a flower-seller, who is 'stifled, smothered, trampled into powder' by the hordes of ladies and gentlemen crowding for his merchandise; however, his gaudy flowers look suspiciously 'like ancient acquaintances' disguised:

> Wherefore a misgiving masters us, on the sudden, that not all are exotics. The deuce a matter, nathless, good folks. We shall await with decorous gravity the decision of the horticulturalists. They know a vast deal about the matter indeed.
>
> (***Prose,*** I, 142)

Mangan flaunts his falsity in **'Literæ Orientales,'** courting exposure, aware that the 'horticulturalists' knew as little about Persian or Turkish poetry as he did. References to the Island of Quackquack, 'so called because the fruits on the trees of the island are birds which, by an instinctive intelligence, cry out *Quack, quack,* whenever a traveller visits the place,' or the 'fable of a cock and a bull' (***Prose,*** I, 158-9), should have alerted even the most credulous readers, as should the translation of **'Treacherous Black Guards'** by 'Ali Baba, a Persian' (***Poems,*** II, 11). Of his 'translation' **'The Time of the Barmecides,'** Mangan admits that he had already published it a few months before, 'but in such suspicious company that it probably remained unread, except by the few—very few—persons who have always believed us too honourable to attempt imposing on or mystifying the public,' and he promises 'that if any lady or gentleman wish to have a copy of the original—or indeed of any original of any of our oversettings—we are quite ready to come forward and treat: terms cash, except to young ladies' (***Poems,*** II, 393-4). The poem, of course, is a Mangan original. O'Donoghue claims that Mangan's contemporaries (apart of course from experts like Anster) do not seem to have detected the invented poems.[30] It was up to Mangan to point them out, and expose his own imposture.

For many of Mangan's contemporaries, the primary duty of the translator was accuracy and fidelity to the original. George Moir noted in the *Edinburgh Review* in 1835: 'it seems now to be pretty generally felt that the main object of a translator should be to exhibit his author and not himself. If a work is worth translating at all it is worth translating *literally.*'[31] Mangan was in profound disagreement with this, describing his translations as 'perversions' (***Poems,*** II, 174) or 'oversettings' (as just quoted), suggesting the translation superseded the original. The translation, he argues, could be a more significant work than the original text: Mangan says of Anster as a translator of Goethe: 'He sees through his author, as through glass, but corrects all the distortions produced by the refraction of the substance through which he looks ... he is, in short, *the real author of* "Faust"' (***Prose,*** II, 201). In **'Anthologia Germanica'** Mangan argues that the translator cannot be held responsible for his author's deficiencies—'We cannot, like the experimentalist in Gulliver, undertake to extract a greater number of sunbeams from a cucumber than it is in the habit of yielding'—but the translator must polish and improve where he can: 'it is our business to cast a veil over his blemishes, and bring forward nothing but his excellences, or what we presume to be such' (***Prose,*** I, 112). The impostor's veil could therefore spare the original author's blushes as much as hide the translator's 'perversions.' The problem he finds with the translations of Jones and Von Hammer-Purgstall is that their 'panegyrics on the peculiar beauty of Persian poetry' are followed only by 'a few starveling verses from Hafez and others, rather more prosaic than ordinary prose' (***Prose,*** I, 150). Mangan hopes 'to exhibit the Ottoman Muse in apparel somewhat more attractive' (***Prose,*** I, 152). If the originals are lacking, the translator is within his rights in 'giving them a lift and a shove': 'If I receive two or three dozen of sherry for a dinner-party, and by some chemical process can convert the sherry into champagne, my friends are all the merrier, and nobody is a loser' (***Prose,*** I, 288). The authenticity of the text is less significant than the pleasure its transformation affords to translator and reader.

Mangan also explodes the notion that the translator is impartial and objective. The translator is much more powerful than that, choosing and discriminating, selecting certain poems, discarding others, consciously shaping the reader's responses. In his notes to **'Lines on the Launching of the Bashtardah,'** Mangan says:

> In ransacking the Divan of Moostafa Tchelibi ... we have lighted on a few samples of very intolerable versification indeed, which we beg all our readers to read and reprobate vehemently. It is a matter pretty notorious at present, that we have our share of *l'esprit malin*; the detection of faults never failing to afford us deep gratification, while the discovery of beauties agonises us. In accordance with our sentiments we pass with contempt over the greater part of the volume before us, inlaid as it is with melodies worthy of the Nightingale himself, to grapple with the following shabby impostures—palmed upon Us for poetry—but which We thus expose publicly in our Magazine.
>
> (***Poems,*** II, 378)

The translator is not an invisible honest broker between author and reader, and in the context of Oriental poetry this may mean reinforcing stereotypes of racial or cultural inferiority. Having ransacked a culture, he has the power to distort it for his own base purposes, inviting 'all' his readers to denigrate a civilization on the basis of a 'few' paltry poems, while deliberately ignoring those providing evidence of a threatening artistic wealth.

Mangan had stated confidently in his articles on German poetry: 'We have never yet met with a Spanish, French, Italian, Dutch, or German line, which we found it impracticable to render by a corresponding English line' (***Prose,*** I, 117). The second **'Literæ Orientales'** article added: 'We believe that that which is good poetry in any one of these languages may be made to appear equally as good poetry in any other of them, if the translator be possessed of skill enough to make it appear so' (***Prose,*** I, 152-3). However, the fourth article questions whether any European translator is capable of adequately translating an Oriental text:

> we state, and we challenge the entire world of linguists and littérateurs to refute the statement, that Oriental Poetry is not fairly readable in an English translation,—that there is no practicability of idiomatically translating it with effect into our language—perhaps into any of our languages.
>
> (***Prose,*** II, 1)

He denies that this has anything to do with any innate superiority in European languages: Persian is 'coeval with the earliest dawn of civilization among mankind,' Arabic 'as a language, is entitled to every deference' (***Prose,*** I, 138). The problem is not language but the confinements of culture; Oriental poetry is not 'fairly' readable, nor can it be translated 'with effect' into the language of a culture inclined to disparage it. The only way a European can appreciate Oriental poetry is to 'disencumber himself of all the old rags of his Europeanism and scatter them to the winds' (***Prose,*** II, 2). Mangan argues that the pervading character of Oriental poetry is mysticism, and its obscurity can never be truly accepted by a European reader—particularly by the English reader:

> The truth is that the Mooslem has more *faith,* humanly speaking, than the Englishman. It is an easier task to satisfy him. He reverences with deeper emotion, cherishes sympathies more comprehensive, has a roomier capacity for the reception of mysteries of all sorts ... He is a philosopher—not a purblind analyst of some incontrovertible axiom—not a groping investigator into noon-day facts—but a genuine, generous, downright, unsophisticated, catholic philosopher.
>
> (***Prose,*** II, 3-4)

Mangan's comparison of the 'Mooslem' and the Englishman covertly raises the question how Oriental poetry would be translated and read by an Irishman; Mangan's reference to 'Mooslems' as 'catholic' philosophers is teasingly suggestive in the (largely Protestant and Unionist) context of the *Dublin University Magazine,* and reminiscent of Abdallah's description of Papists as 'only Sunnites with a brogue' in Moore's *Intercepted Letters* (1813).[32] Mangan and Moore were working within a long tradition of associating Ireland with the East. Joseph Lennon notes that the connection between Asia and Ireland was established in ancient Greco-Roman texts 'amid connections between Ireland and all borderlands.'[33] In the fourth article, encouraging other Irishmen to come forward to second his translation efforts, Mangan refers tongue-in-cheek to the theories of Charles Vallancey, who argued that the Irish language had an Oriental origin: 'According to Vallancey every Irishman is an Arab' (***Prose,*** II, 7).

But the Irish were also Europeans, and many Irishmen were active participants in the subjection of the East. Joep Leerssen warns that Irish critics have tended to apply Said's theories to Ireland too partially and simplistically:

> Anglo-Irish orientalism flourished against the background of a cultural self-estrangement and self-exoticization which is linked to the country's subjection by English hegemony; but on the other hand, authors like Moore, Ferguson and Yeats were comfortable middle-class or upper-middle-class members of the literary establishment whom it would be unconvincing to cast in the role of downtrodden natives.[34]

Irish Orientalists could be collusive or subversive in their imaginative appropriation of the East: 'Irish Orientalism developed both imperial and anticolonial strains, mirroring the Irish population in their participation in and resistance to the British Empire.'[35] Mangan was writing for the conservative Unionist *Dublin University Magazine*; modelling itself on *Blackwood's Magazine,* it was clearly aligned with the British discourse of orientalism, and not averse to viewing the majority Catholic nationalist population, agitating in the 1830s and 1840s for a repeal of the Union, as exotic and troublesome Others. In 'Thuggee in India, and Ribandism in Ireland, compared,' a long review of Taylor's *Confessions of a Thug,* published in January 1840, one of the magazine's prominent controversialists, Samuel O'Sullivan, drew grisly parallels between Thugs and Irish Ribbonmen, arguing that both were degraded and brutalized by their false religion, and both devoted to the destruction of their fellow loyal subjects.[36] O'Sullivan's article 'Successes in the East,' in January 1843, hailed England's triumphs in Afghanistan and China as major blows to both Daniel O'Connell and Young Ireland, and O'Sullivan took the opportunity to remind readers that

> if there are Affghans abroad in the punishment of whose barbarous treachery we have reason to exult, *there are Affghans at home,* for whose distresses at the mischances of their defeated kindred, as they may well be called, we are bound, in common humanity, to feel a due commiseration ... The sudden and unhoped-for blaze of England's victories in the East, has startled into an unwary manifestation of its hidden virulence that latent treason against our Protestant state, which is engrained in the hearts of a servilely popish population.[37]

While Mangan was a Catholic, and had contributed poetry to the Young Ireland journal *The Nation* from its first number in October 1842, and so was potentially one of the 'Irish Affghans' O'Sullivan feared, he had yet to be radicalized when he began his Oriental translations in 1837. Duffy, cofounder and editor of *The Nation,* said that in 1840 Mangan 'knew nothing of politics and cared nothing for them, and he averted his eyes from Irish history as from a painful and humiliating spectacle.'[38] However, **'Literæ Orientales'** suggests a growing awareness of political injustice in Ireland and elsewhere, and of poets' (and translators') roles in reinforcing or challenging it. In his notes to his translation of Kerimi's 'Justice Alone is Eternal,' in the third article in 1838, Mangan writes: 'These lines were addressed by the poet Kheremi to a corrupt and tyrannical Cadi in Constantinople, who had amassed immense riches by his private and public robberies.' The tyrant is warned:

> Only those Gates which no soul nears
> Except by Penance' road and over Sorrow's flood,
> Those gates through which *thou* canst not find thy way,
> Those only, *and the burning marble piers*
> *Of* IBLIS' *halls—as they have stood*
> *From immemorial time*—shall stand for aye.
>
> (***Poems,*** II, 75)

The editors of the ***Collected Works*** note that these lines are not in Mangan's German source (***Poems,*** II, 378). He also inserted a reference to the Liberty Trees, planted in America and France during their Revolutions, and adopted by the United Irishmen as a symbol of their revolutionary aspirations, into 'Lament,' supposedly by Mulheed, helpfully alerting the reader: 'Sentiments like the following are rare in Eastern poetry' (***Poems,*** II, 367):

The stately Tree of Liberty,
  Which, when the storms of tyrant Power rage,
Might yet lend shelter to the Free,
  Is shrunken and decayed in *our* age!

(***Poems,*** II, 13)

Similarly, **'The Thugs' Ditty,'** which appeared in the fifth article in 1844, Mangan notes, is 'of questionable authenticity' due to its 'unoriental' expression—'We tipple and smoke; we hocus and cozen, | And that sort of thing'—and might indeed offer a satiric riposte to blood-curdling comparisons, such as O'Sullivan's, of the Irish and the Oriental (***Poems,*** II, 353; 421n.). The Eastern veil may have provided him with the means of contemplating that reality from which he only apparently 'averted his eyes,' and of inscribing it in coded form within the pages of the journal of Anglo-Irish cultural hegemony.

In her discussion of Mangan's incorporation of an epigraph from Shelley's *Adonais* in his early poem **'The Dying Enthusiast to His Friend,'** Fiona Stafford notes the uncanny ease with which Mangan makes the transition from Shelley's poem to his own: 'There is no immediate sense of disjunction, nor of the earlier poem being part of a culture fundamentally alien to that of the new composition.'[39] This is all the more remarkable in that Mangan's poem was composed and first published without the epigraph, suggesting the Irish poet's immersion in and internalization of English Romantic values and aesthetics at a time when other Irish writers, such as Samuel Ferguson and William Carleton, were attempting to define and promote an Irish literature not written with an English audience in mind. Yet, as Stafford suggests, Mangan's foregrounding of *Adonais* is less an attempt by an unknown provincial poet to provide an authorizing stamp for his poem, than a complex provocation. Given Shelley's support for Catholic Emancipation and Repeal, the use of his name, even posthumously, in a poem published in a Dublin journal colours it politically. But Stafford also intriguingly suggests that in **'The Dying Enthusiast'** Mangan is 'exhibit[ing] a similar kind of ventriloquism to that practised in many of his Oriental poems,'[40] in that the speaker might be imagined to be the dying Keats, preemptively challenging his friend's elegy. Mangan resurrects Shelley in the epigraph, only to resurrect Keats as his speaker to object to the way the meaning of Keats' death had been shaped. In **'The Dying Enthusiast,'** Mangan proves himself more than capable of mimicking English Romantic poetry; but **'Literæ Orientales,'** rather than employing the 'double vision' of mimicry, which 'in disclosing the ambivalence of colonial discourse also disrupts its authority,'[41] offers instead a triple vision of ventriloquism, in which the Irish poet mimics not the colonial usurper but other colonized, dispossessed, and denigrated denizens who have been denied the opportunity to speak.

The habit of veiling seems so persistent that Mangan continues it even when an overt comparison between the Oriental and the Irish colonized might be welcomed. In April 1846, during the first full year of the Great Famine, Mangan published what he described as a 'particularly genuine Persian poem'—clearly entirely original—**'To the Ingleezee Khafir, Calling Himself Djaun Bool Djenkinzun,'** in *The Nation,* one of the organs most vociferously critical of British government inaction in the face of starvation. The sentiments of the speaker, Meer Djafrit, for John Bull were unlikely to be disputed in this forum:

  I hate thee, Djaun Bool,
Worse than Márid or Afrit,
  Or corpse-eating Ghool.
I hate thee like Sin,
  For thy mop-head of hair,
Thy snub nose and bald chin,
  And thy turkeycock air.

(***Poems,*** III, 159)

Yet the explicit analogy between Persia and Ireland is restricted to the notes and the lightly disguised name. In his notes Mangan compares the tendency of Oriental and Irish poets to introduce their own names into their poems, and explains his use of the phrase 'Thou dog' by the similarity between the Persian 'Ei G[i]aour' and 'the Irish *A Gadar,*' meaning 'dog.' Mangan observes that the poem uses the ancient 'Iran' rather than 'Persia'; the editors of the ***Collected Works*** are surely right to suggest that Mangan is 'inviting his readers to remember that, as Iran is the ancient name of Persia, so Erin is the ancient name of Ireland' (***Poems,*** III, 449). But Mangan also notes that Persia was known as 'the Land of Djem'; knowing Mangan's fondness for puns, it is hard to resist reading this as a pun on his own name, 'the Land of Jim.'

Perhaps significantly, one of his **'Literæ Orientales'** translations, **'Ghazel by Djim,'** identifies this king (whose name is spelt 'Dschem' by Von Hammer-Purgstall and 'Giam' by d'Herbelot—'Djim' is Mangan's creation) as having been born in Caramania (***Poems,*** II, 4, 364). Caramania seems to have held a particular attraction for Mangan. In the first article he noted the 'tendency to homonymousness' of Oriental poets: 'D'Herbelot has recorded no fewer than fourteen Persian writers, all of whom pass under the common cognomen of Karamani, from their province, Karaman. Here is perspicuity!' (***Prose,*** I, 136-7). Mangan, exploiting this homonymity, takes on a Caramanian identity in several of his 'translations.' He may have been remembering Shelley's *Alastor* (1816), in which the poet wanders 'through Arabie | And Persia, and the wild

Carmanian waste' (140-1). But Caramania's military history is its major attraction; the speaker of **'The Time of the Barmecides'** recalls how in his youth 'my tried Karamanian sword I Lay always bright and bare' (***Poems,*** I, 168). In the fifth article, Mangan describes its history:

> Caramania was the last province of Asia Minor that submitted to the Ottoman yoke; and long and gallant and bloody was the resistance it first offered to the conquering arms of its invaders. A history of that memorable struggle, by the way, is much wanted. Why should not some one of the first-rate men of our era—Dr. Wilde, for instance,—undertake it?
>
> (***Prose,*** II, 108)

The suggestion of an affinity with Ireland in its history of resistance to colonization is reinforced by the naming of William Wilde (future father of Oscar), an amateur Irish antiquarian, as the ideal man to write of Caramania's 'memorable struggle' with the Ottoman Empire. In Mangan's 'translation' **'The Caramanian Exile,'** which follows, the speaker, once 'mild as milk,' is maddened by the invasion of his homeland and his exile from it:

> *Now* my breast is as a den,
> Karaman!
> Foul with blood and bones of men,
> Karaman!
> With blood and bones of slaughtered men,
> Karaman! O, Karaman!
>
> (***Poems,*** II, 346)

Mangan comments: 'One is not often electrified by such bursts of passion and feeling in Ottoman poetry' (***Prose,*** II, 108); not surprisingly, as it is an Irish poem, one of Mangan's originals. In Mangan, as Joyce noted: 'East and West meet . . . and whether the song is of Ireland or of Istambol, it has the same refrain.'[42]

Another poem of 1846, **'To the Pens of *The Nation,*'** puns shamelessly in calling on Irish writers to praise the Sikhs in their opposition to English rule in India: 'Sing of British overthrow— I SING A SONG OF SIKHS, PENS!' (***Poems,*** III, 151). In **'A Vision of Connaught in the Thirteenth Century,'** published in *The Nation* in July 1846, Mangan invites several comparisons, most obviously between the wealth of thirteenth-century Ireland under the benevolent Cáhal Mór, and its famine-stricken state in 1846. Cáhal Mór is referred to in the poem using the oriental 'Khan.' Mangan explains that this is 'identical with the Irish *Ceann,* Head, or Chief; but I the rather gave him the Oriental title, as really fancying myself in one of the regions of Araby the Blest.' He also notes: 'The Irish and Oriental poets both agree in attributing favorable or unfavorable weather and abundant or deficient harvests to the good or bad qualities of the reigning monarch. What the character of Cahal was will be seen below' (***Poems,*** III, 455). The implication, of course, is that the character of Victoria could be equally well judged from the present state of Ireland.

The East functions for Mangan not as an escape from reality—Ireland prior to and during the Famine—but a way of reimagining and reengaging with it. The belief that 'the Wonderful Lamp, the dazzler of our boyhood' is 'still lying perdu in some corner of the Land of Wonders' serves as a barrier against insanity:

> From amid the lumber of the actual world prize is made of a safety-valve which carries off from the surface of our reveries the redundant smoke and vapour that, suffered to continue pent up within us, would suffocate every healthier volition and energy of the spirit.
>
> (***Prose,*** I, 129-30)

It is difficult to read a poem like **'Elegy on the Death of Sultan Suleimaun the Magnificent,'** which appeared in the *Dublin University Magazine* in 1848, without thinking of the situation in Ireland at the time Mangan wrote it. Once again, Mangan attributes the poem to Lamii, but, since he died before Sultan Suleimaun, it is a safe assumption that it is a Mangan original:

> We who remain behind, we wither all from day to day,
> Wulla-hu!
> The sight hath left our eyes; our very beards show crisped and grey,
> Wulla-hu!
> For Plague, and Thirst, and Famine
> Have come down on the land:
> Each of us, black-skinned as a Brahmin,
> Sits weeping; scarce a few
> Take even the Koran now in hand—
> Wull-wullahu! Wull-wullahu!
>
> (***Poems,*** IV, 82-3)

Mangan died of cholera at the age of forty-six in June 1849, one of the million-and-a-half victims of the Great Famine of 1845-52. During the Famine he transformed himself into an Irish poet of great stature, and it is largely for his Famine poems that he is remembered. The last poem to be published before he died is the explicitly Irish **'The Famine'**—no averting of the eyes is possible anymore, and the displaced and dispossessed 'Caramanian Exile' is replaced by 'The Irish serf,' 'a Being banned— I Life-exiled as none ever was before.' Yet the Eastern analogy encroaches even here:

> Even as the dread Simoom of Araby
> Sweeps o'er the desert through the pathless air,
> So came, 'mid Ireland's joy and revelry,
> That cloud of gloom above her visions fair.
>
> (***Poems,*** IV, 137)

The affinity between the East and Ireland may be no less illusory than that between the Orient and Genii-land, but it offered Mangan the opportunity of exposing the cultural insularity and the religious and racial intolerance that cankered relations between Ireland and England, Irish and Anglo-Irish, no less than between Caramania and the Ottoman Empire, or East and West. 'This is my own, my native land!' (***Prose,*** I, 131), exclaims Mangan in **'Literæ Orientales'**—and sometimes it is.

Notes

Mangan's work is collected in six volumes under the general editorship of Jacques Chuto (Dublin, 1996-2002). These are referred to in this paper as follows:

Poems, I-IV: I. *Poems 1818-1837* (1996) II. *Poems 1838-1844* (1996) III. *Poems 1845-1847* (1997) IV. *Poems 1848-1912* (1999).

Prose, I-II: I. *Prose 1832-1839* (2002) II. *Prose 1840-1882* (2002).

1. *Prose,* I, 129.
2. *The Victorians: An Anthology of Poetry and Poetics,* edited by Valentine Cunningham (Oxford, 2000), p. 125.
3. James Joyce, 'James Clarence Mangan,' in *Occasional, Critical, and Political Writing,* edited by Kevin Barry (Oxford, 2000), p. 128.
4. David Lloyd, 'Translator as Refractor: Towards a Rereading of James Clarence Mangan as Translator,' *Dispositio,* 7 (1982), 141-62 (p. 148).
5. Charles Gavan Duffy, 'Personal Memories of James C. Mangan,' *Dublin Review,* 142 (1908), 278-94 (p. 294).
6. John Mitchel, 'Introduction,' *Poems of James Clarence Mangan,* edited by D. J. O'Donoghue (Dublin, 1903), p. xliii.
7. Haideh Ghomi, *The Fragrance of the Rose: The Transmission of Religion, Culture, and Tradition through the Translation of Persian Poetry* (Göteborg, 1993), p. 53; Hasan Javadi, *Persian Literary Influence on English Literature with Special Reference to the Nineteenth Century* (Costa Mesa, CA, 2005), p. 69; John D. Yohannan, *Persian Poetry in England and America* (Delmar, NY, 1977), p. 64.
8. W. J. McCormack, 'The Intellectual Revival (1830-50),' in *The Field Day Anthology of Irish Writing,* edited by Seamus Deane *et al.,* 5 vols (Cork, 1991-2002), I, 1173-7 (p. 1176).
9. Mangan, 'Literæ Orientales. Persian and Turkish Poetry—First Article,' *Prose,* I, 140.
10. Mangan, 'Relic of Servi,' *Poems,* II, 367.
11. Mangan, 'An Ode of Hafiz,' *Poems,* IV, 278.
12. Note by the editor of the *Irishman* in 'Sketches of Modern Irish Writers. James Clarence Mangan,' *Prose,* II, 342.
13. *Poems of James Clarence Mangan* (n. 6), p. xxi.
14. David Lloyd, *Nationalism and Minor Literature: James Clarence Mangan and the Emergence of Irish Cultural Nationalism* (Berkeley, CA, 1987), p. 23.
15. Mangan, 'A Well-Delivered Speech,' *Poems,* II, 70.
16. Mangan, 'To Childhood,' 'The Exile,' 'Silence,' and 'Hope,' *Poems,* I, 404 (editorial note).
17. Alfred Tennyson, 'Recollections of the Arabian Nights,' in *Poems and Plays,* edited by T. Herbert Warren (Oxford, 1971), pp. 9-10.
18. Thomas Macaulay, 'Minute on Indian Education,' in *Revolutions in Romantic Literature: An Anthology of Print Culture, 1780-1832,* edited by Paul Keen (Peterborough, ON, 2004), p. 313.
19. George Sale, *The Koran* (London, 1844), p. v.
20. Robert Southey, *The Curse of Kehama* (London, 1810), p. vii.
21. Robert Southey, *Thalaba the Destroyer* (London, 1801), p. 10.
22. Walter Savage Landor, *Poems from the Arabic and Persian* (Warwick, 1800), p. 1.
23. Yohannan (n. 7), pp. 33-4.
24. Duffy (n. 5), p. 290.
25. Mohammed Sharafuddin, *Islam and Romantic Orientalism: Literary Encounters with the Orient* (London, 1994), p. ix.
26. Joseph Conrad, *Heart of Darkness,* edited by Robert Hampson (Harmondsworth, 1995), p. 18.
27. Sir William Jones, *A Grammar of the Persian Language* (London, 1828), p. vi.
28. Edward Said, *Orientalism* (London, 1995), p. 64.
29. For the term see Margaret Lesser, 'Professionals,' in *The Oxford History of Literary Translation in English,* Vol 4: *1790-1900,* edited by Peter France and Kenneth Haynes (Oxford, 2006), pp. 85-97 (p. 91).
30. D. J. O'Donoghue, *The Life and Writings of James Clarence Mangan* (Edinburgh, 1897), p. 87.
31. Cited in *Oxford History of Literary Translation,* IV, 65.
32. Thomas Moore, 'Letter VI. From Abdallah, in London, to Mohassan, in Ispahan,' *Intercepted Letters; or, the Twopenny Post-Bag* (London, 1813), p. 29.

33. Joseph Lennon, *Irish Orientalism: A Literary and Intellectual History* (Syracuse, NY, 2004), p. 8.

34. Joep Leerssen, 'Irish Studies and *Orientalism*: Ireland and the Orient,' in *Oriental Prospects: Western Literature and the Lure of the East,* edited by C. C. Barfoot and Theo D'haen (Amsterdam, 1998), pp. 161-73 (p. 171).

35. Lennon, p. 123.

36. [Samuel O'Sullivan], 'Thuggee in India, and Ribandism in Ireland, Compared,' *Dublin University Magazine,* 15 (1840), 50-65.

37. [Samuel O'Sullivan], 'Successes in the East—Affghanistan—China,' *Dublin University Magazine,* 21 (1843), 125-42 (p. 131).

38. Duffy, 'Personal Memories' (n. 5), p. 286.

39. Fiona Stafford, *Starting Lines in Scottish, Irish, and English Poetry from Burns to Heaney* (Oxford, 2000), p. 147.

40. Stafford, p. 180.

41. Homi K. Bhabha, *The Location of Culture* (London, 2007), p. 126.

42. Joyce, 'James Clarence Mangan' (n. 3), p. 133.

FURTHER READING

Bibliography

Chuto, Jacques. *James Clarence Mangan: A Bibliography.* Dublin: Irish Academic P, 1999. Print.

Provides a comprehensive bibliography of Mangan's contributions to periodicals and books, as well as works about the author, collected by the leading Mangan scholar.

Biographies

Duffy, Charles Gavan. "Personal Memories of James C. Mangan." *Dublin Review* 142 (1908): 278-94. Print.

Comments on the exaggerations in Mangan's autobiography, disputes rumors of his addiction to opium, and criticizes descriptions of Mangan by those who never saw or knew him. Duffy, as the editor of the *Nation* and thus someone who published many of Mangan's poems, was a close colleague and friend of Mangan and received many of his letters.

O'Donoghue, D. J. *The Life and Writings of James Clarence Mangan.* Edinburgh: Geddes, 1897. Print.

Examines Mangan as the most neglected and misunderstood Irishman of genius, according to O'Donoghue, who saw Mangan in danger of being forgotten for a variety of reasons but especially due to British government policy of excluding him from the national schoolbooks. O'Donoghue's account is the most significant of the early biographies on the author. An excerpt from this book is included in the entry above.

Shannon-Mangan, Ellen. *James Clarence Mangan: A Biography.* Dublin: Irish Academic P, 1996. Print.

Presents the definitive biography of Mangan, by one of the editors of his *Collected Works.*

W., E. "Sketches of Modern Irish Writers. James Clarence Mangan." *The Collected Works of James Clarence Mangan: Prose, 1840-1882.* Ed. Jacques Chuto et al. Dublin: Irish Academic P, 2002. 222-25. Print.

Argues that Mangan has been called a "singular man" but is in fact "a plural one—a Proteus" and an antiplagiarist, "addicted to . . . fathering upon other writers the offspring of his own brain." E. W. is widely believed to be a pseudonym of Mangan, making this essay a useful companion to Mangan's unfinished autobiography, which is reprinted in the same volume. This essay was first published in the *Irishman* in August 1850.

Criticism

Bessai, Diane E. "'Dark Rosaleen' as Image of Ireland." *Éire-Ireland* 10.4 (1975): 62-84. Print.

Discusses how the association of Ireland with the symbol of the rose is frequently considered a centuries-old tradition but is in fact primarily an Anglo-Irish invention. Bessai considers the various versions of "Roisin Dubh" by James Hardiman, Samuel Ferguson, Thomas Furlong, and Mangan as creating, rather than recovering, a political allegory, which later poets, such as William Butler Yeats, then take up. [Excerpted in *NCLC,* Vol. 27.]

Campbell, Matthew. "Mangan's Golden Years." *Irish Poetry under the Union, 1801-1924.* Cambridge: Cambridge UP, 2013. 95-131. Print.

Claims that Mangan "writes a poetry of the perpetual middle," trapped between the desolation of the past and the intractable personal and political problems of his present, between Irish and English verse forms, Gothic and Oriental influences, and between repetition and originality.

Kilroy, James. *James Clarence Mangan.* Lewisburg: Bucknell UP, 1970. Print.

Considers how Mangan's life is both "a parable of the damned poet, alienated, lonesome and driven nearly to madness by his poetic vision and sensitive nature," and a symbol of the miseries of Ireland in the mid-nineteenth century. Kilroy connects Mangan beyond provincial borders to the works of Thomas Lovell Beddoes and Edgar Allan Poe. [Excerpted in *NCLC,* Vol. 27.]

Lloyd, David. *Nationalism and Minor Literature: James Clarence Mangan and the Emergence of Irish Cultural Nationalism.* Berkeley: U of California P, 1987. Print.

Provides the most significant book-length study on Mangan. Lloyd argues that Mangan's work is minor in the positive sense of actively resisting assimilation into a canon designed to legitimate nationalist or imperialist hegemony. [Excerpted in *NCLC,* Vol. 27.]

MacCarthy, Anne. *James Clarence Mangan, Edward Walsh and Nineteenth-Century Irish Literature in English.* Lewiston: Mellen, 2000. Print.

Evaluates the work of Mangan and his fellow Irish poet and translator Edward Walsh. MacCarthy draws on the theories of Itamar Even-Zohar and André A. Lefevere to argue that Mangan and Walsh were marginalized as a result of ideological and cultural, rather than purely aesthetic, judgments.

Morash, Christopher. "Sins of the Nation." *Writing the Irish Famine.* Oxford: Clarendon P, 1995. 99-127. Print.

Examines Mangan's poetry written during the Great Famine alongside that of his contemporaries. Faced with the famine, even the nationalist poets, says Morash, employ the language of apocalypse and national sin more familiar to Evangelical millenarianism. He suggests that poems such as "The Warning Voice" also reflect the generational and class difference between the older and poorer poets of the *Nation,* such as John De Jean Frazer and Mangan, and younger, middle-class ones, such as Denis Florence MacCarthy, Thomas D'Arcy McGee, Richard D'Alton Williams, and Jane Elgee, better known as "Speranza."

Parsons, Cóilín. "The Archive in Ruins: James Clarence Mangan and Colonial Cartography." *Interventions* 13.3 (2011): 464-82. Print.

Looks at Mangan's translations of Gaelic ruin poems—including "Lament over the Ruins of the Abbey of Teach Molaga," "Lamentation of Mac Liag for Kincora," and "The Vision of Egan O'Reilly"—as both contemporary critiques of the archival practice of the Ordnance Survey and as key components of that archive's preservation of vanishing originals.

Sturgeon, Sinéad. *Essays on James Clarence Mangan: The Man in the Cloak.* Basingstoke: Palgrave Macmillan, 2014. Print.

Collects essays on Mangan, including contributions on the author and his legacy by Sturgeon, David Lloyd, David Wheatley, Joseph Lennon, Cóilín Parsons, John McCourt, Richard Haslam, Anne Jamison, Sean Ryder, and Matthew Campbell. It also contains a foreword by Jacques Chuto, an afterword by Ciaran Carson, Paul Muldoon's poem "A Night on the Tiles with J. C. Mangan," and a useful bibliography.

Welch, Robert. "'In Wreathèd Swell': James Clarence Mangan, Translator from the Irish." *Éire-Ireland* 11.2 (1976): 36-55. Print.

Reflects on Mangan's translations from Irish in the context of his work with George Petrie, John O'Donovan, and Eugene O'Curry at the Ordnance Survey, as well as with John O'Daly on *The Poets and Poetry of Munster.* Welch argues that Mangan's Irish translations were liberating, both for himself and for Irish poetry, freeing the "old verse to new uses and experiences." [Reprinted in *NCLC,* Vol. 27.]

Yeats, W[illiam]. B[utler]. "Clarence Mangan (1803-1849)." *Uncollected Prose by W. B. Yeats.* Ed. John P. Frayne. Vol. 1. New York: Columbia UP, 1970. 114-19. Print.

Emphasizes the misery of Mangan's life but finds in his poetry "electric flashes" and "a certain radiant energy," particularly in "Dark Rosaleen," "Twenty Golden Years Ago," "The Nameless One," and "Siberia." Yeats's essay was first published in the *Irish Fireside* in March 1887. [Excerpted in *NCLC,* Vol. 27.]

Additional information on Mangan's life and works is contained in the following sources published by Gale: *British Writers Supplement,* Vol. 13; *Literature Resource Center; Nineteenth-Century Literature Criticism,* Vol. 27; and *Reference Guide to English Literature,* Ed. 2.

How to Use This Index

The main references

Calvino, Italo 1923-1985 .... **CLC 5, 8, 11, 22, 33, 39, 73; SSC 3, 48**

list all author entries in the following Gale Literary Criticism series:

AAL = *Asian American Literature*
BG = *The Beat Generation: A Gale Critical Companion*
BLC = *Black Literature Criticism*
BLCS = *Black Literature Criticism Supplement*
CLC = *Contemporary Literary Criticism*
CLR = *Children's Literature Review*
CMLC = *Classical and Medieval Literature Criticism*
DC = *Drama Criticism*
FL = *Feminism in Literature: A Gale Critical Companion*
GL = *Gothic Literature: A Gale Critical Companion*
HLC = *Hispanic Literature Criticism*
HLCS = *Hispanic Literature Criticism Supplement*
HR = *Harlem Renaissance: A Gale Critical Companion*
LC = *Literature Criticism from 1400 to 1800*
NCLC = *Nineteenth-Century Literature Criticism*
NNAL = *Native North American Literature*
PC = *Poetry Criticism*
SSC = *Short Story Criticism*
TCLC = *Twentieth-Century Literary Criticism*
WLC = *World Literature Criticism, 1500 to the Present*
WLCS = *World Literature Criticism Supplement*

The cross-references

See also CA 85-88, 116; CANR 23, 61; DAM NOV; DLB 196; EW 13; MTCW 1, 2; RGSF 2; RGWL 2; SFW 4; SSFS 12

list all author entries in the following Gale biographical and literary sources:

AAYA = *Authors & Artists for Young Adults*
AFAW = *African American Writers*
AFW = *African Writers*
AITN = *Authors in the News*
AMW = *American Writers*
AMWR = *American Writers Retrospective Supplement*
AMWS = *American Writers Supplement*
ANW = *American Nature Writers*
AW = *Ancient Writers*
BEST = *Bestsellers*
BPFB = *Beacham's Encyclopedia of Popular Fiction: Biography and Resources*
BRW = *British Writers*
BRWS = *British Writers Supplement*
BW = *Black Writers*
BYA = *Beacham's Guide to Literature for Young Adults*
CA = *Contemporary Authors*
CAAS = *Contemporary Authors Autobiography Series*
CABS = *Contemporary Authors Bibliographical Series*
CAD = *Contemporary American Dramatists*
CANR = *Contemporary Authors New Revision Series*
CAP = *Contemporary Authors Permanent Series*
CBD = *Contemporary British Dramatists*
CCA = *Contemporary Canadian Authors*

CD = *Contemporary Dramatists*
CDALB = *Concise Dictionary of American Literary Biography*
CDALBS = *Concise Dictionary of American Literary Biography Supplement*
CDBLB = *Concise Dictionary of British Literary Biography*
CMW = *St. James Guide to Crime & Mystery Writers*
CN = *Contemporary Novelists*
CP = *Contemporary Poets*
CPW = *Contemporary Popular Writers*
CSW = *Contemporary Southern Writers*
CWD = *Contemporary Women Dramatists*
CWP = *Contemporary Women Poets*
CWRI = *St. James Guide to Children's Writers*
CWW = *Contemporary World Writers*
DA = *DISCovering Authors*
DA3 = *DISCovering Authors 3.0*
DAB = *DISCovering Authors: British Edition*
DAC = *DISCovering Authors: Canadian Edition*
DAM = *DISCovering Authors: Modules*
DRAM: *Dramatists Module;* ***MST:*** Most-studied Authors Module;
MULT: *Multicultural Authors Module;* ***NOV:*** Novelists Module;
POET: *Poets Module;* ***POP:*** Popular Fiction and Genre Authors Module
DFS = *Drama for Students*
DLB = *Dictionary of Literary Biography*
DLBD = *Dictionary of Literary Biography Documentary Series*
DLBY = *Dictionary of Literary Biography Yearbook*
DNFS = *Literature of Developing Nations for Students*
EFS = *Epics for Students*
EW = *European Writers*
EWL = *Encyclopedia of World Literature in the 20th Century*
EXPN = *Exploring Novels*
EXPP = *Exploring Poetry*
EXPS = *Exploring Short Stories*
FANT = *St. James Guide to Fantasy Writers*
FW = *Feminist Writers*
GFL = *Guide to French Literature, Beginnings to 1789; 1789 to the Present*
GLL = *Gay and Lesbian Literature*
HGG = *St. James Guide to Horror, Ghost & Gothic Writers*
HW = *Hispanic Writers*
IDFW = *International Dictionary of Films and Filmmakers: Writers and Production Artists*
IDTP = *International Dictionary of Theatre: Playwrights*
LAIT = *Literature and Its Times*
LAW = *Latin American Writers*
JRDA = *Junior DISCovering Authors*
MAICYA = *Major Authors and Illustrators for Children and Young Adults*
MAICYAS = *Major Authors and Illustrators for Children and Young Adults Supplement*
MAWW = *Modern American Women Writers*
MJW = *Modern Japanese Writers*
MTCW = *Major 20th-Century Writers*
NCFS = *Nonfiction Classics for Students*
NFS = *Novels for Students*
PAB = *Poets: American and British*
PFS = *Poetry for Students*
RGAL = *Reference Guide to American Literature*
RGEL = *Reference Guide to English Literature*
RGSF = *Reference Guide to Short Fiction*
RGWL = *Reference Guide to World Literature*
RHW = *Twentieth-Century Romance and Historical Writers*
SAAS = *Something about the Author Autobiography Series*
SATA = *Something about the Author*
SFW = *St. James Guide to Science Fiction Writers*
SSFS = *Short Stories for Students*
TCWW = *Twentieth-Century Western Writers*
WLIT = *World Literature and Its Times*
WP = *World Poets*
YABC = *Yesterday's Authors of Books for Children*

Literary Criticism Series Cumulative Author Index

20/1631
See Upward, Allen

A/C Cross
See Lawrence, T. E.

A. M.
See Megged, Aharon

A. Uthor
See Breytenbach, Breyten

Aaron, Sidney
See Chayefsky, Paddy

Abani, Chris 1966- .... **CLC 361**
See also CA 241; CANR 176; DLB 347; NFS 35

Abasiyanik, Sait Faik 1906-1954 ... **TCLC 23**
See also CA 123; 231

Abbey, Edward 1927-1989 .... **CLC 36, 59; TCLC 160**
See also AAYA 75; AMWS 13; ANW; CA 45-48; 128; CANR 2, 41, 131; DA3; DLB 256, 275; LATS 1:2; MTCW 2; MTFW 2005; NFS 43; TCWW 1, 2

Abbott, Edwin A. 1838-1926 .... **SSC 135; TCLC 139**
See also DLB 178

Abbott, Lee K. 1947- .... **CLC 48**
See also CA 124; CANR 51, 101, 210; DLB 130

Abbott, Lee Kittredge
See Abbott, Lee K.

Abe, Kōbō 1924-1993 .... **CLC 8, 22, 53, 81; SSC 61; TCLC 131, 297**
See also CA 65-68; 140; CANR 24, 60; DAM NOV; DFS 14; DLB 182; EWL 3; MJW; MTCW 1, 2; MTFW 2005; NFS 22; RGWL 3; SFW 4

Abe Kobo
See Abe, Kōbō

Abelard, Peter
c. 1079-c. 1142 ...... **CMLC 11, 77, 162**
See also DLB 115, 208

Abell, Kjeld 1901-1961 .... **CLC 15**
See also CA 191; 111; DLB 214; EWL 3

Abercrombie, Lascelles
1881-1938 .... **TCLC 141**
See also BRWS 16; CA 112; DLB 19; RGEL 2

Abhavananda
See Crowley, Edward Alexander

Abish, Walter 1931- ... **CLC 22, 246; SSC 44**
See also CA 101; CANR 37, 114, 153; CN 3, 4, 5, 6; DLB 130, 227; MAL 5; RGHL

Abrahams, Peter (Henry) 1919- .... **CLC 4**
See also AFW; BW 1; CA 57-60; CANR 26, 125; CDWLB 3; CN 1, 2, 3, 4, 5, 6; DLB 117, 225; EWL 3; MTCW 1, 2; RGEL 2; WLIT 2

Abrams, M(eyer) H(oward)
1912- .... **CLC 24**
See also CA 57-60; CANR 13, 33; DLB 67

Abse, Dannie 1923- .... **CLC 7, 29, 266; PC 41**
See also CA 53-56; CAAS 1; CANR 4, 46, 74, 124; CBD; CN 1, 2, 3; CP 1, 2, 3, 4, 5, 6, 7; DAB; DAM POET; DLB 27, 245; MTCW 2

Abutsu 1222(?)-1283 .... **CMLC 46**
See also DLB 203

Abutsu-ni
See Abutsu

Achebe, Albert Chinualumogu
See Achebe, Chinua

Achebe, Chinua 1930-2013 .... **BLC 1:1, 2:1; CLC 1, 3, 5, 7, 11, 26, 51, 75, 127, 152, 272, 278, 325, 370; SSC 105; WLC 1**
See also AAYA 15; AFW; BPFB 1; BRWC 2; BW 2, 3; CA 1-4R; CANR 6, 26, 47, 124, 220; CDWLB 3; CLR 20, 156; CN 1, 2, 3, 4, 5, 6, 7; CP 2, 3, 4, 5, 6, 7; CWRI 5; DA; DA3; DAB; DAC; DAM MST, MULT, NOV; DLB 117; DNFS 1; EWL 3; EXPN; EXPS; LAIT 2; LATS 1:2; MAICYA 1, 2; MTCW 1, 2; MTFW 2005; NFS 2, 33; RGEL 2; RGSF 2; SATA 38, 40; SATA-Brief 38; SSFS 3, 13, 30, 37; TWA; WLIT 2; WWE 1

Acker, Kathy 1948-1997 .... **CLC 45, 111; TCLC 191**
See also AMWS 12; CA 117; 122; 162; CANR 55; CN 5, 6; MAL 5

Ackroyd, Peter 1949- .... **CLC 34, 52, 140, 256**
See also BRWS 6; CA 123; 127; CANR 51, 74, 99, 132, 175, 229; CN 4, 5, 6, 7; DLB 155, 231; HGG; INT CA-127; MTCW 2; MTFW 2005; RHW; SATA 153; SUFW 2

Acorn, Milton 1923-1986 .... **CLC 15**
See also CA 103; CCA 1; CP 1, 2, 3, 4; DAC; DLB 53; INT CA-103

Adam de la Halle
c. 1250-c. 1285 .... **CMLC 80**

Adamic, Louis 1899?-1951 .... **TCLC 285**
See also CA 109; 177; DLB 9

Adamic, Louis 1899?-1951 .... **TCLC 285**
See also CA 77, 109; DLB 9

Adamov, Arthur 1908-1970 .... **CLC 4, 25; TCLC 189**
See also CA 17-18; 25-28R; CAP 2; DAM DRAM; DLB 321; EWL 3; GFL 1789 to the Present; MTCW 1; RGWL 2, 3

Adams, Alice 1926-1999 .... **CLC 6, 13, 46; SSC 24**
See also CA 81-84; 179; CANR 26, 53, 75, 88, 136; CN 4, 5, 6; CSW; DLB 234; DLBY 1986; INT CANR-26; MTCW 1, 2; MTFW 2005; SSFS 14, 21

Adams, Andy 1859-1935 .... **TCLC 56**
See also TCWW 1, 2; YABC 1

Adams, (Henry) Brooks 1848-1927 ... **TCLC 80**
See also CA 123; 193

Adams, Douglas 1952-2001 .... **CLC 27, 60**
See also AAYA 4, 33; BEST 89:3; BYA 14; CA 106; 197; CANR 34, 64, 124; CPW; DA3; DAM POP; DLB 261; DLBY 1983; JRDA; MTCW 2; MTFW 2005; NFS 7; SATA 116; SATA-Obit 128; SFW 4

Adams, Douglas Noel
See Adams, Douglas

Adams, Francis 1862-1893 .... **NCLC 33**

Adams, Henry 1838-1918 ... **TCLC 4, 52, 309**
See also AMW; CA 104; 133; CANR 77; DA; DAB; DAC; DAM MST; DLB 12, 47, 189, 284; EWL 3; MAL 5; MTCW 2; NCFS 1; RGAL 4; TUS

Adams, Henry Brooks
See Adams, Henry

Adams, John 1735-1826 .... **NCLC 106**
See also DLB 31, 183

Adams, John Quincy 1767-1848 ... **NCLC 175**
See also DLB 37

Adams, Mary
See Phelps, Elizabeth Stuart

Adams, Richard 1920- .... **CLC 4, 5, 18, 357**
See also AAYA 16; AITN 1, 2; BPFB 1; BYA 5; CA 49-52; CANR 3, 35, 128; CLR 20, 121; CN 4, 5, 6, 7; DAM NOV; DLB 261; FANT; JRDA; LAIT 5; MAICYA 1, 2; MTCW 1, 2; NFS 11; SATA 7, 69; YAW

Adams, Richard George
See Adams, Richard

Adamson, Joy(-Friederike Victoria)
1910-1980 .... **CLC 17**
See also CA 69-72; 93-96; CANR 22; MTCW 1; SATA 11; SATA-Obit 22

Adcock, Fleur 1934- .... **CLC 41**
See also BRWS 12; CA 25-28R, 182; CAAE 182; CAAS 23; CANR 11, 34, 69, 101; CP 1, 2, 3, 4, 5, 6, 7; CWP; DLB 40; FW; WWE 1

Addams, Charles 1912-1988 .... **CLC 30**
See also CA 61-64; 126; CANR 12, 79

Addams, Charles Samuel
See Addams, Charles

Addams, (Laura) Jane
1860-1935 .... **TCLC 76, 299**
See also AMWS 1; CA 194; DLB 303; FW

Addison, Joseph 1672-1719 .... **LC 18, 146**
See also BRW 3; CDBLB 1660-1789; DLB 101; RGEL 2; WLIT 3

Ade, George 1866-1944 .... **TCLC 307**
See also CA 110, 238; DLB 11, 25; RGAL 4

Adelard of Bath c. 1070-c. 1150 .. **CMLC 119**

Adichie, Chimamanda Ngozi
1977- .... **BLC 2:1; CLC 364**
See also AAYA 80; CA 231; CANR 217

Adiga, Aravind 1974- .... **CLC 280**
See also CA 282; CANR 235

Adler, Alfred (F.) 1870-1937 .... **TCLC 61**
See also CA 119; 159

Adler, C. S. 1932- .... **CLC 35**
See also AAYA 4, 41; CA 89-92; CANR 19, 40, 101; CLR 78; JRDA; MAICYA 1, 2; SAAS 15; SATA 26, 63, 102, 126; YAW
Adler, Carole Schwerdtfeger
See Adler, C. S.
Adler, Renata 1938- .... **CLC 8, 31**
See also CA 49-52; CANR 95; CN 4, 5, 6; MTCW 1
Adorno, Theodor W(iesengrund)
1903-1969 .... **TCLC 111**
See also CA 89-92; 25-28R; CANR 89; DLB 242; EWL 3
Ady, Endre 1877-1919 .... **TCLC 11, 253**
See also CA 107; CDWLB 4; DLB 215; EW 9; EWL 3
A.E.
See Russell, George William
Aelfric c. 955-c. 1010 ... **CMLC 46, 128, 148**
See also DLB 146
Aelred of Rievaulx 1110-1167 ... **CMLC 123**
Aeschines
c. 390B.C.-c. 320B.C. .... **CMLC 47**
See also DLB 176
Aeschylus
525(?)B.C.-456(?)B.C. .... **CMLC 11, 51, 94; DC 8; WLCS**
See also AW 1; CDWLB 1; DA; DAB; DAC; DAM DRAM, MST; DFS 5, 10, 26; DLB 176; LMFS 1; RGWL 2, 3; TWA; WLIT 8
Aesop 620(?)B.C.-560(?)B.C. .... **CMLC 24, 158; SSC 164**
See also CLR 14; MAICYA 1, 2; SATA 64
Affable Hawk
See MacCarthy, Sir (Charles Otto) Desmond
Africa, Ben
See Bosman, Herman Charles
Afrika, Jan
See Breytenbach, Breyten
Afton, Effie
See Harper, Frances Ellen Watkins
Agamben, Giorgio 1942- .... **CLC 355**
Agapida, Fray Antonio
See Irving, Washington
Agar, Emile
See Kacew, Romain
Agee, James 1909-1955 ..... **TCLC 1, 19, 180**
See also AAYA 44; AITN 1; AMW; CA 108; 148; CANR 131; CDALB 1941-1968; DAM NOV; DLB 2, 26, 152; DLBY 1989; EWL 3; LAIT 3; LATS 1:2; MAL 5; MTCW 2; MTFW 2005; NFS 22; RGAL 4; TUS
Agee, James Rufus
See Agee, James
A Gentlewoman in New England
See Bradstreet, Anne
A Gentlewoman in Those Parts
See Bradstreet, Anne
Aghill, Gordon
See Silverberg, Robert
Agnon, S. Y. 1888-1970 .... **CLC 4, 8, 14; SSC 30, 120; TCLC 151**
See also CA 17-18; 25-28R; CANR 60, 102, 211; CAP 2; DLB 329; EWL 3; MTCW 1, 2; RGHL; RGSF 2; RGWL 2, 3; WLIT 6
Agnon, Shmuel Yosef Halevi
See Agnon, S. Y.
Agrippa von Nettesheim, Henry Cornelius
1486-1535 .... **LC 27**
Aguilera Malta, Demetrio
1909-1981 .... **HLCS 1**
See also CA 111; 124; CANR 87; DAM MULT, NOV; DLB 145; EWL 3; HW 1; RGWL 3
Agustín, José 1944- .... **CLC 357**
See also CA 179; EWL 3
Agustini, Delmira 1886-1914 .... **HLCS 1**
See also CA 166; DLB 290; HW 1, 2; LAW
Aherne, Owen
See Cassill, R(onald) V(erlin)
Ai 1947-2010 .... **CLC 4, 14, 69; PC 72**
See also CA 85-88; CAAS 13; CANR 70; CP 6, 7; DLB 120; PFS 16
Aichinger, Ilse 1921- .... **CLC 383**
See also CA 85-88; CWW 2; DLB 85, 299; EWL 3; RGHL; RGSF
Aickman, Robert (Fordyce)
1914-1981 .... **CLC 57**
See also CA 5-8R; CANR 3, 72, 100; DLB 261; HGG; SUFW 1, 2
Aidoo, (Christina) Ama Ata (Ejinma)
1942- ... **BLCS; CLC 177, 314; SSC 178**
See also AFW; BRWS 15; BW 1; CA 101; CANR 62, 144; CD 5, 6; CDWLB 3; CN 6, 7; CWD; CWP; DLB 117; DNFS 1, 2; EWL 3; FW; WLIT 2
Aiken, Conrad 1889-1973 .... **CLC 1, 3, 5, 10, 52; PC 26; SSC 9, 166**
See also AMW; CA 5-8R; 45-48; CANR 4, 60; CDALB 1929-1941; CN 1; CP 1; DAM NOV, POET; DLB 9, 45, 102; EWL 3; EXPS; HGG; MAL 5; MTCW 1, 2; MTFW 2005; PFS 24; RGAL 4; RGSF 2; SATA 3, 30; SSFS 8, 34; TUS
Aiken, Conrad Potter
See Aiken, Conrad
Aiken, Joan 1924-2004 .... **CLC 35**
See also AAYA 1, 25; CA 9-12R, 182; 223; CAAE 182; CANR 4, 23, 34, 64, 121, 238; CLR 1, 19, 90; DLB 161; FANT; HGG; JRDA; MAICYA 1, 2; MTCW 1; RHW; SAAS 1; SATA 2, 30, 73; SATA-Essay 109; SATA-Obit 152; SSFS 33; SUFW 2; WYA; YAW
Aiken, Joan Delano
See Aiken, Joan
Ainsworth, William Harrison
1805-1882 .... **NCLC 13**
See also DLB 21; HGG; RGEL 2; SATA 24; SUFW 1
Aitmatov, Chingiz 1928-2008 .... **CLC 71; SSC 131**
See also CA 103; CANR 38; CWW 2; DLB 302; EWL 3; MTCW 1; RGSF 2; SATA 56
Aitmatov, Chingiz Torekulovich
See Aitmatov, Chingiz
Ajar, Emile
See Kacew, Romain
Akenside, Mark 1721-1770 .... **LC 239**
See also DLB 109; RGEL 2
Akers, Floyd
See Baum, L. Frank
Akhmadulina, Bella
1937-2010 .... **CLC 53; PC 43**
See also CA 65-68; CWP; CWW 2; DAM POET; DLB 359; EWL 3
Akhmadulina, Bella Akhatovna
See Akhmadulina, Bella
Akhmatova, Anna 1888-1966 .... **CLC 11, 25, 64, 126; PC 2, 55**
See also CA 19-20; 25-28R; CANR 35; CAP 1; DA3; DAM POET; DLB 295; EW 10; EWL 3; FL 1:5; MTCW 1, 2; PFS 18, 27, 32, 36, 44; RGWL 2, 3
Akhtiorskaya, Yelena 1985- .... **CLC 389**
See also CA 366
Aksakov, Sergei Timofeevich
1791-1859 .... **NCLC 2, 181**
See also DLB 198
Aksenov, Vasilii
See Aksyonov, Vasily
Aksenov, Vasilii Pavlovich
See Aksyonov, Vasily
Aksenov, Vassily
See Aksyonov, Vasily
Akst, Daniel 1956- .... **CLC 109**
See also CA 161; CANR 110
Aksyonov, Vasily 1932-2009 .. **CLC 22, 37, 101**
See also CA 53-56; CANR 12, 48, 77; CWW 2; DLB 302; EWL 3
Aksyonov, Vassily Pavlovich
See Aksyonov, Vasily
Akutagawa Ryunosuke
1892-1927 .... **SSC 44; TCLC 16, 259**
See also CA 117; 154; DLB 180; EWL 3; MJW; RGSF 2; RGWL 2, 3; SSFS 35
Alabaster, William 1568-1640 .... **LC 90**
See also DLB 132; RGEL 2
Alain 1868-1951 .... **TCLC 41**
See also CA 163; EWL 3; GFL 1789 to the Present
Alain de Lille
c. 1116-c. 1203 .... **CMLC 53, 138**
See also DLB 208
Alain-Fournier 1886-1914 .... **TCLC 6**
See also CA 104; 179; DLB 65; EWL 3; GFL 1789 to the Present; RGWL 2, 3
Al-Amin, Jamil Abdullah 1943- .... **BLC 1:1**
See also BW 1, 3; CA 112; 125; CANR 82; DAM MULT
al-Tabari 839-923 .... **CMLC 161**
See also DLB 311
Alan of Lille
See Alain de Lille
Alanus de Insluis
See Alain de Lille
Alarcon, Pedro Antonio de
1833-1891 .... **NCLC 1, 219; SSC 64**
Alas (y Urena), Leopoldo (Enrique Garcia)
1852-1901 .... **TCLC 29; SSC 171**
See also CA 113; 131; HW 1; RGSF 2
Albee, Edward (III) 1928- ..... **CLC 1, 2, 3, 5, 9, 11, 13, 25, 53, 86, 113; DC 11; WLC 1**
See also AAYA 51; AITN 1; AMW; CA 5-8R; CABS 3; CAD; CANR 8, 54, 74, 124; CD 5, 6; CDALB 1941-1968; DA; DA3; DAB; DAC; DAM DRAM, MST; DFS 25; DLB 7, 266; EWL 3; INT CANR-8; LAIT 4; LMFS 2; MAL 5; MTCW 1, 2; MTFW 2005; RGAL 4; TUS
Albee, Edward Franklin
See Albee, Edward (III)
Alberti, Leon Battista 1404-1472 .... **LC 173**
Alberti, Rafael 1902-1999 .. **CLC 7; TCLC 286**
See also CA 85-88; 185; CANR 81; CWW 2; DLB 108; EWL 3; HW 2; RGWL 2, 3
Alberti Merello, Rafael
See Alberti, Rafael
Albert of Saxony c. 1316-1390 ... **CMLC 110**
Albert the Great
1193(?)-1280 .... **CMLC 16, 155**
See also DLB 115
Alcaeus c. 620B.C. .... **CMLC 65**
See also DLB 176
Alcala-Galiano, Juan Valera y
See Valera y Alcala-Galiano, Juan
Alcayaga, Lucila Godoy
See Mistral, Gabriela
Alciato, Andrea 1492-1550 .... **LC 116, 235**
Alcott, Amos Bronson
1799-1888 .... **NCLC 1, 167**
See also DLB 1, 223
Alcott, Louisa May 1832-1888 .... **NCLC 6, 58, 83, 218; SSC 27, 98, 164; WLC 1**
See also AAYA 20; AMWS 1; BPFB 1; BYA 2; CDALB 1865-1917; CLR 1, 38, 109, 195, 196; DA; DA3; DAB; DAC; DAM MST, NOV; DLB 1, 42, 79, 223, 239, 242; DLBD 14; FL 1:2; FW; JRDA; LAIT 2; MAICYA 1, 2; NFS 12; RGAL 4; SATA 100; TUS; WCH; WYA; YABC 1; YAW
Alcuin c. 730-804 .... **CMLC 69, 139**
See also DLB 148
Aldanov, M. A.
See Aldanov, Mark (Alexandrovich)

Aldanov, Mark (Alexandrovich) 1886-1957 .... **TCLC 23**
See also CA 118; 181; DLB 317
Alden, Jean François
See Twain, Mark
Aldhelm c. 639-709 .... **CMLC 90**
Aldington, Richard 1892-1962 .... **CLC 49; PC 134; TCLC 296**
See also CA 85-88; CANR 45; DLB 20, 36, 100, 149; LMFS 2; RGEL 2
Aldiss, Brian W. 1925- .... **CLC 5, 14, 40, 290; SSC 36**
See also AAYA 42; BRWS 19; CA 5-8R, 190; CAAE 190; CAAS 2; CANR 5, 28, 64, 121, 168; CLR 197; CN 1, 2, 3, 4, 5, 6, 7; DAM NOV; DLB 14, 261, 271; MTCW 1, 2; MTFW 2005; SATA 34; SCFW 1, 2; SFW 4
Aldiss, Brian Wilson
See Aldiss, Brian W.
Aldrich, Ann
See Meaker, Marijane
Aldrich, Bess Streeter 1881-1954 .... **TCLC 125**
See also CLR 70; TCWW 2
Alegria, Claribel 1924- .... **CLC 75; HLCS 1; PC 26, 150**
See also CA 131; CAAS 15; CANR 66, 94, 134; CWW 2; DAM MULT; DLB 145, 283; EWL 3; HW 1; MTCW 2; MTFW 2005; PFS 21
Alegria, Claribel Joy
See Alegria, Claribel
Alegria, Fernando 1918-2005 .... **CLC 57**
See also CA 9-12R; CANR 5, 32, 72; EWL 3; HW 1, 2
Aleichem, Sholom 1859-1916 .. **SSC 33, 125; TCLC 1, 35**
See also CA 104; DLB 333; TWA
Aleixandre, Vicente 1898-1984 ...... **HLCS 1; TCLC 113**
See also CANR 81; DLB 108, 329; EWL 3; HW 2; MTCW 1, 2; RGWL 2, 3
Alekseev, Konstantin Sergeivich
See Stanislavsky, Constantin
Alekseyer, Konstantin Sergeyevich
See Stanislavsky, Constantin
Alemán, Mateo 1547-1615(?) ..... **LC 81, 234**
Alencar, Jose de 1829-1877 .... **NCLC 157**
See also DLB 307; LAW; WLIT 1
Alencon, Marguerite d'
See de Navarre, Marguerite
Alepoudelis, Odysseus
See Elytis, Odysseus
Aleramo, Sibilla 1876-1960 .... **TCLC 312**
See also DLB 114, 264; WLIT 7
Aleshkovsky, Joseph
See Aleshkovsky, Yuz
Aleshkovsky, Yuz 1929- .... **CLC 44**
See also CA 121; 128; DLB 317
Alexander, Barbara
See Ehrenreich, Barbara
Alexander, Lloyd 1924-2007 .... **CLC 35**
See also AAYA 1, 27; BPFB 1; BYA 5, 6, 7, 9, 10, 11; CA 1-4R; 260; CANR 1, 24, 38, 55, 113; CLR 1, 5, 48; CWRI 5; DLB 52; FANT; JRDA; MAICYA 1, 2; MAICYAS 1; MTCW 1; SAAS 19; SATA 3, 49, 81, 129, 135; SATA-Obit 182; SUFW; TUS; WYA; YAW
Alexander, Lloyd Chudley
See Alexander, Lloyd
Alexander, Meena 1951- .... **CLC 121, 335**
See also CA 115; CANR 38, 70, 146; CP 5, 6, 7; CWP; DLB 323; FW
Alexander, Rae Pace
See Alexander, Raymond Pace
Alexander, Raymond Pace 1898-1974 .... **SSC 62**
See also CA 97-100; SATA 22; SSFS 4
Alexander, Samuel 1859-1938 .... **TCLC 77**
Alexander of Hales c. 1185-1245 .... **CMLC 128**
Alexeiev, Konstantin
See Stanislavsky, Constantin
Alexeyev, Constantin Sergeivich
See Stanislavsky, Constantin
Alexeyev, Konstantin Sergeyevich
See Stanislavsky, Constantin
Alexie, Sherman 1966- ... **CLC 96, 154, 312; NNAL; PC 53; SSC 107, 189**
See also AAYA 28, 85; BYA 15; CA 138; CANR 65, 95, 133, 174; CLR 179; CN 7; DA3; DAM MULT; DLB 175, 206, 278; LATS 1:2; MTCW 2; MTFW 2005; NFS 17, 31, 38; PFS 39; SSFS 18, 36
Alexie, Sherman Joseph, Jr.
See Alexie, Sherman
al-Farabi 870(?)-950 .... **CMLC 58**
See also DLB 115
Alfau, Felipe 1902-1999 .... **CLC 66**
See also CA 137
Alfieri, Vittorio 1749-1803 .... **NCLC 101**
See also EW 4; RGWL 2, 3; WLIT 7
Alfonso X 1221-1284 .... **CMLC 78**
Alfred, Jean Gaston
See Ponge, Francis
Alger, Horatio, Jr. 1832-1899 .... **NCLC 8, 83, 260**
See also CLR 87, 170; DLB 42; LAIT 2; RGAL 4; SATA 16; TUS
Al-Ghazali, Muhammad ibn Muhammad 1058-1111 .... **CMLC 50, 149**
See also DLB 115
Algren, Nelson 1909-1981 .... **CLC 4, 10, 33; SSC 33**
See also AMWS 9; BPFB 1; CA 13-16R; 103; CANR 20, 61; CDALB 1941-1968; CN 1, 2; DLB 9; DLBY 1981, 1982, 2000; EWL 3; MAL 5; MTCW 1, 2; MTFW 2005; RGAL 4; RGSF 2
al-Hamadhani 967-1007 .... **CMLC 93**
See also WLIT 6
al-Hariri, al-Qasim ibn 'Ali Abu Muhammad al-Basri 1054-1122 .... **CMLC 63**
See also RGWL 3
Ali, Ahmed 1908-1998 .... **CLC 69**
See also CA 25-28R; CANR 15, 34; CN 1, 2, 3, 4, 5; DLB 323; EWL 3
Ali, Monica 1967- .... **CLC 304**
See also AAYA 67; BRWS 13; CA 219; CANR 158, 205, 240; DLB 323
Ali, Tariq 1943- .... **CLC 173, 323**
See also CA 25-28R; CANR 10, 99, 161, 196
Alighieri, Dante
See Dante
Alkali, Zaynab 1950- .... **CLC 381**
See also CA 172; DLB 360
al-Kindi, Abu Yusuf Ya'qub ibn Ishaq c. 801-c. 873 .... **CMLC 80**
Allan, John B.
See Westlake, Donald E.
Allan, Sidney
See Hartmann, Sadakichi
Allan, Sydney
See Hartmann, Sadakichi
Allard, Janet .... **CLC 59**
Allen, Betsy
See Harrison, Elizabeth (Allen) Cavanna
Allen, Edward 1948- .... **CLC 59**
Allen, Fred 1894-1956 .... **TCLC 87**
Allen, Paula Gunn 1939-2008 .... **CLC 84, 202, 280; NNAL**
See also AMWS 4; CA 112; 143; 272; CANR 63, 130; CWP; DA3; DAM MULT; DLB 175; FW; MTCW 2; MTFW 2005; RGAL 4; TCWW 2
Allen, Roland
See Ayckbourn, Alan
Allen, Sarah A.
See Hopkins, Pauline Elizabeth
Allen, Sidney H.
See Hartmann, Sadakichi
Allen, Woody 1935- ... **CLC 16, 52, 195, 288**
See also AAYA 10, 51; AMWS 15; CA 33-36R; CANR 27, 38, 63, 128, 172; DAM POP; DLB 44; MTCW 1; SSFS 21
Allende, Isabel 1942- ... **CLC 39, 57, 97, 170, 264, 350; HLC 1; SSC 65, 209; WLCS**
See also AAYA 18, 70; CA 125; 130; CANR 51, 74, 129, 165, 208; CDWLB 3; CLR 99, 171; CWW 2; DA3; DAM MULT, NOV; DLB 145; DNFS 1; EWL 3; FL 1:5; FW; HW 1, 2; INT CA-130; LAIT 5; LAWS 1; LMFS 2; MTCW 1, 2; MTFW 2005; NCFS 1; NFS 6, 18, 29; RGSF 2; RGWL 3; SATA 163; SSFS 11, 16; WLIT 1
Alleyn, Ellen
See Rossetti, Christina
Alleyne, Carla D. .... **CLC 65**
Allingham, Margery (Louise) 1904-1966 .... **CLC 19**
See also CA 5-8R; 25-28R; CANR 4, 58; CMW 4; DLB 77; MSW; MTCW 1, 2
Allingham, William 1824-1889 ..... **NCLC 25**
See also DLB 35; RGEL 2
Allison, Dorothy E. 1949- .... **CLC 78, 153, 290**
See also AAYA 53; CA 140; CANR 66, 107; CN 7; CSW; DA3; DLB 350; FW; MTCW 2; MTFW 2005; NFS 11; RGAL 4
Alloula, Malek .... **CLC 65**
Allston, Washington 1779-1843 ...... **NCLC 2**
See also DLB 1, 235
Almedingen, E. M. 1898-1971 .... **CLC 12**
See also CA 1-4R; CANR 1; SATA 3
Almedingen, Martha Edith von
See Almedingen, E. M.
Almodovar, Pedro 1949(?)- ... **CLC 114, 229; HLCS 1**
See also CA 133; CANR 72, 151; HW 2
Almqvist, Carl Jonas Love 1793-1866 .... **NCLC 42**
al-Mutanabbi, Ahmad ibn al-Husayn Abu al-Tayyib al-Jufi al-Kindi 915-965 .... **CMLC 66**
See also RGWL 3; WLIT 6
Alonso, Dámaso 1898-1990 .... **CLC 14; PC 158; TCLC 245**
See also CA 110; 131; 130; CANR 72; DLB 108; EWL 3; HW 1, 2
Alov
See Gogol, Nikolai
al'Sadaawi, Nawal
See El Saadawi, Nawal
al-Shaykh, Hanan
See Shaykh, Hanan al-
Al Siddik
See Rolfe, Frederick (William Serafino Austin Lewis Mary)
Alta 1942- .... **CLC 19**
See also CA 57-60
Alter, Robert B. 1935- .... **CLC 34**
See also CA 49-52; CANR 1, 47, 100, 160, 201
Alter, Robert Bernard
See Alter, Robert B.
Alther, Lisa 1944- .... **CLC 7, 41**
See also BPFB 1; CA 65-68; CAAS 30; CANR 12, 30, 51, 180; CN 4, 5, 6, 7; CSW; GLL 2; MTCW 1
Althusser, L.
See Althusser, Louis
Althusser, Louis 1918-1990 .... **CLC 106**
See also CA 131; 132; CANR 102; DLB 242

Altman, Robert 1925-2006 .... **CLC 16, 116, 242**
See also CA 73-76; 254; CANR 43
Alurista 1947- .... **HLCS 1; PC 34**
See also CA 45-48R; CANR 2, 32; DLB 82; HW 1; LLW
Alvarez, A. 1929- .... **CLC 5, 13**
See also CA 1-4R; CANR 3, 33, 63, 101, 134; CN 3, 4, 5, 6; CP 1, 2, 3, 4, 5, 6, 7; DLB 14, 40; MTFW 2005
Alvarez, Alejandro Rodriguez 1903-1965 .... **CLC 49; DC 32; TCLC 199**
See also CA 131; 93-96; EWL 3; HW 1
Alvarez, Julia 1950- ... **CLC 93, 274; HLCS 1**
See also AAYA 25, 85; AMWS 7; CA 147; CANR 69, 101, 133, 166; DA3; DLB 282; LATS 1:2; LLW; MTCW 2; MTFW 2005; NFS 5, 9, 42; PFS 39, 44; SATA 129; SSFS 27, 31; WLIT 1
Alvaro, Corrado 1896-1956 .... **TCLC 60**
See also CA 163; DLB 264; EWL 3
Amado, Jorge 1912-2001 .... **CLC 13, 40, 106, 232; HLC 1**
See also CA 77-80; 201; CANR 35, 74, 135; CWW 2; DAM MULT, NOV; DLB 113, 307; EWL 3; HW 2; LAW; LAWS 1; MTCW 1, 2; MTFW 2005; RGWL 2, 3; TWA; WLIT 1
Ambler, Eric 1909-1998 .... **CLC 4, 6, 9**
See also BRWS 4; CA 9-12R; 171; CANR 7, 38, 74; CMW 4; CN 1, 2, 3, 4, 5, 6; DLB 77; MSW; MTCW 1, 2; TEA
Ambrose c. 339-c. 397 .... **CMLC 103**
Ambrose, Stephen E. 1936-2002 ... **CLC 145**
See also AAYA 44; CA 1-4R; 209; CANR 3, 43, 57, 83, 105; MTFW 2005; NCFS 2; SATA 40, 138
Amichai, Yehuda 1924-2000 ... **CLC 9, 22, 57, 116; PC 38**
See also CA 85-88; 189; CANR 46, 60, 99, 132; CWW 2; EWL 3; MTCW 1, 2; MTFW 2005; PFS 24, 39; RGHL; WLIT 6
Amichai, Yehudah
See Amichai, Yehuda
Amiel, Henri Frederic 1821-1881 ... **NCLC 4**
See also DLB 217
Amis, Kingsley 1922-1995 .... **CLC 1, 2, 3, 5, 8, 13, 40, 44, 129**
See also AAYA 77; AITN 2; BPFB 1; BRWS 2; CA 9-12R; 150; CANR 8, 28, 54; CDBLB 1945-1960; CN 1, 2, 3, 4, 5, 6; CP 1, 2, 3, 4; DA; DA3; DAB; DAC; DAM MST, NOV; DLB 15, 27, 100, 139, 326, 352; DLBY 1996; EWL 3; HGG; INT CANR-8; MTCW 1, 2; MTFW 2005; RGEL 2; RGSF 2; SFW 4
Amis, Martin 1949- .... **CLC 4, 9, 38, 62, 101, 213, 329; SSC 112**
See also BEST 90:3; BRWS 4; CA 65-68; CANR 8, 27, 54, 73, 95, 132, 166, 208; CN 5, 6, 7; DA3; DLB 14, 194; EWL 3; INT CANR-27; MTCW 2; MTFW 2005
Amis, Martin Louis
See Amis, Martin
Ammianus Marcellinus c. 330-c. 395 .... **CMLC 60**
See also AW 2; DLB 211
Ammons, A.R. 1926-2001 .... **CLC 2, 3, 5, 8, 9, 25, 57, 108, 339; PC 16, 139**
See also AITN 1; AMWS 7; CA 9-12R; 193; CANR 6, 36, 51, 73, 107, 156; CP 1, 2, 3, 4, 5, 6, 7; CSW; DAM POET; DLB 5, 165, 342; EWL 3; MAL 5; MTCW 1, 2; PFS 19; RGAL 4; TCLE 1:1
Ammons, Archie Randolph
See Ammons, A.R.
Amo, Tauraatua i
See Adams, Henry
Amory, Thomas 1691(?)-1788 .... **LC 48**
See also DLB 39
Anand, Mulk Raj 1905-2004 .... **CLC 23, 93, 237**
See also CA 65-68; 231; CANR 32, 64; CN 1, 2, 3, 4, 5, 6, 7; DAM NOV; DLB 323; EWL 3; MTCW 1, 2; MTFW 2005; RGSF 2
Anatol
See Schnitzler, Arthur
Anaximander c. 611B.C.-c. 546B.C. .... **CMLC 22**
Anaya, Rudolfo 1937- .... **CLC 23, 148, 255, 362; HLC 1**
See also AAYA 20; BYA 13; CA 45-48; CAAS 4; CANR 1, 32, 51, 124, 169; CLR 129; CN 4, 5, 6, 7; DAM MULT, NOV; DLB 82, 206, 278; HW 1; LAIT 4; LLW; MAL 5; MTCW 1, 2; MTFW 2005; NFS 12; RGAL 4; RGSF 2; TCWW 2; WLIT 1
Anaya, Rudolfo A.
See Anaya, Rudolfo
Anaya, Rudolpho Alfonso
See Anaya, Rudolfo
Anchieta, José de 1534-1597 .... **LC 219**
Andersen, Hans Christian 1805-1875 .... **NCLC 7, 79, 214; SSC 6, 56, 196; WLC 1**
See also AAYA 57; CLR 6, 113; DA; DA3; DAB; DAC; DAM MST, POP; EW 6; MAICYA 1, 2; RGSF 2; RGWL 2, 3; SATA 100; TWA; WCH; YABC 1
Anderson, C. Farley
See Mencken, H. L.; Nathan, George Jean
Anderson, Jessica (Margaret) Queale 1916- .... **CLC 37**
See also CA 9-12R; CANR 4, 62; CN 4, 5, 6, 7; DLB 325
Anderson, Jon (Victor) 1940- .... **CLC 9**
See also CA 25-28R; CANR 20; CP 1, 3, 4, 5; DAM POET
Anderson, Lindsay (Gordon) 1923-1994 .... **CLC 20**
See also CA 125; 128; 146; CANR 77
Anderson, Maxwell 1888-1959 .... **DC 43; TCLC 2, 144**
See also CA 105; 152; DAM DRAM; DFS 16, 20; DLB 7, 228; MAL 5; MTCW 2; MTFW 2005; RGAL 4
Anderson, Poul 1926-2001 .... **CLC 15**
See also AAYA 5, 34; BPFB 1; BYA 6, 8, 9; CA 1-4R, 181; 199; CAAE 181; CAAS 2; CANR 2, 15, 34, 64, 110; CLR 58; DLB 8; FANT; INT CANR-15; MTCW 1, 2; MTFW 2005; SATA 90; SATA-Brief 39; SATA-Essay 106; SCFW 1, 2; SFW 4; SUFW 1, 2
Anderson, R. W.
See Anderson, Robert
Anderson, Robert 1917-2009 .... **CLC 23**
See also AITN 1; CA 21-24R; 283; CANR 32; CD 6; DAM DRAM; DLB 7; LAIT 5
Anderson, Robert W.
See Anderson, Robert
Anderson, Robert Woodruff
See Anderson, Robert
Anderson, Roberta Joan
See Mitchell, Joni
Anderson, Sherwood 1876-1941 .... **SSC 1, 46, 91, 142; TCLC 1, 10, 24, 123; WLC 1**
See also AAYA 30; AMW; AMWC 2; BPFB 1; CA 104; 121; CANR 61; CDALB 1917-1929; DA; DA3; DAB; DAC; DAM MST, NOV; DLB 4, 9, 86; DLBD 1; EWL 3; EXPS; GLL 2; MAL 5; MTCW 1, 2; MTFW 2005; NFS 4; RGAL 4; RGSF 2; SSFS 4, 10, 11, 37; TUS
Anderson, Wes 1969- .... **CLC 227**
See also CA 214
Andier, Pierre
See Desnos, Robert
Andouard
See Giraudoux, Jean
Andrade, Carlos Drummond de
See Drummond de Andrade, Carlos
Andrade, Mario de 1892-1945 .... **PC 148; TCLC 43**
See also CA 178; DLB 307; EWL 3; HW 2; LAW; RGWL 2, 3
Andreae, Johann V(alentin) 1586-1654 .... **LC 32**
See also DLB 164
Andreas Capellanus fl. c. 1185 .... **CMLC 45, 135**
See also DLB 208
Andreas-Salome, Lou 1861-1937 ... **TCLC 56**
See also CA 178; DLB 66
Andreev, Leonid
See Andreyev, Leonid
Andress, Lesley
See Sanders, Lawrence
Andrew, Joseph Maree
See Occomy, Marita (Odette) Bonner
Andrewes, Lancelot 1555-1626 .... **LC 5**
See also DLB 151, 172
Andrews, Cicily Fairfield
See West, Rebecca
Andrews, Elton V.
See Pohl, Frederik
Andrews, Peter
See Soderbergh, Steven
Andrews, Raymond 1934-1991 ...... **BLC 2:1**
See also BW 2; CA 81-84; 136; CANR 15, 42
Andreyev, Leonid 1871-1919 ... **TCLC 3, 221**
See also CA 104; 185; DLB 295; EWL 3
Andreyev, Leonid Nikolaevich
See Andreyev, Leonid
Andrezel, Pierre
See Blixen, Karen
Andric, Ivo 1892-1975 ...... **CLC 8; SSC 36; TCLC 135**
See also CA 81-84; 57-60; CANR 43, 60; CDWLB 4; DLB 147, 329; EW 11; EWL 3; MTCW 1; RGSF 2; RGWL 2, 3
Androvar
See Prado (Calvo), Pedro
Angela of Foligno 1248(?)-1309 ... **CMLC 76**
Angelique, Pierre
See Bataille, Georges
Angell, Judie
See Angell, Judie
Angell, Judie 1937- .... **CLC 30**
See also AAYA 11, 71; BYA 6; CA 77-80; CANR 49; CLR 33; JRDA; SATA 22, 78; WYA; YAW
Angell, Roger 1920- .... **CLC 26**
See also CA 57-60; CANR 13, 44, 70, 144; DLB 171, 185
Angelou, Maya 1928-2014 ... **BLC 1:1; CLC 12, 35, 64, 77, 155, 389; PC 32; WLCS**
See also AAYA 7, 20; AMWS 4; BPFB 1; BW 2, 3; BYA 2; CA 65-68; CANR 19, 42, 65, 111, 133, 204; CDALBS; CLR 53, 184; CP 4, 5, 6, 7; CPW; CSW; CWP; DA; DA3; DAB; DAC; DAM MST, MULT, POET, POP; DLB 38; EWL 3; EXPN; EXPP; FL 1:5; LAIT 4; MAICYA 2; MAICYAS 1; MAL 5; MBL; MTCW 1, 2; MTFW 2005; NCFS 2; NFS 2; PFS 2, 3, 33, 38, 42; RGAL 4; SATA 49, 136; TCLE 1:1; WYA; YAW
Angouleme, Marguerite d'
See de Navarre, Marguerite
Anna Comnena 1083-1153 .... **CMLC 25**
Annensky, Innokentii Fedorovich
See Annensky, Innokenty (Fyodorovich)
Annensky, Innokenty (Fyodorovich) 1856-1909 .... **TCLC 14**
See also CA 110; 155; DLB 295; EWL 3

Annunzio, Gabriele d'
See D'Annunzio, Gabriele
Anodos
See Coleridge, Mary E(lizabeth)
Anon, Charles Robert
See Pessoa, Fernando
Anouilh, Jean 1910-1987 .... **CLC 1, 3, 8, 13, 40, 50; DC 8, 21; TCLC 195**
See also AAYA 67; CA 17-20R; 123; CANR 32; DAM DRAM; DFS 9, 10, 19; DLB 321; EW 13; EWL 3; GFL 1789 to the Present; MTCW 1, 2; MTFW 2005; RGWL 2, 3; TWA
Anouilh, Jean Marie Lucien Pierre
See Anouilh, Jean
Ansa, Tina McElroy 1949- .... **BLC 2:1**
See also BW 2; CA 142; CANR 143; CSW
Anselm of Canterbury
1033(?)-1109 .... **CMLC 67**
See also DLB 115
Anthony, Florence
See Ai
Anthony, John
See Ciardi, John (Anthony)
Anthony, Peter
See Shaffer, Anthony; Shaffer, Peter
Anthony, Piers 1934- .... **CLC 35**
See also AAYA 11, 48; BYA 7; CA 200; CAAE 200; CANR 28, 56, 73, 102, 133, 202; CLR 118; CPW; DAM POP; DLB 8; FANT; MAICYA 2; MAICYAS 1; MTCW 1, 2; MTFW 2005; SAAS 22; SATA 84, 129; SATA-Essay 129; SFW 4; SUFW 1, 2; YAW
Anthony, Susan B(rownell)
1820-1906 .... **TCLC 84**
See also CA 211; FW
Antin, David 1932- .... **PC 124**
See also CA 73-76; CP 1, 3, 4, 5, 6, 7; DLB 169
Antin, Mary 1881-1949 .... **TCLC 247**
See also AMWS 20; CA 118; 181; DLB 221; DLBY 1984
Antiphon
c. 480B.C.-c. 411B.C. .... **CMLC 55**
Antoine, Marc
See Proust, Marcel
Antoninus, Brother
See Everson, William
Antonioni, Michelangelo
1912-2007 .... **CLC 20, 144, 259**
See also CA 73-76; 262; CANR 45, 77
Antschel, Paul
See Celan, Paul
Anwar, Chairil 1922-1949 .... **TCLC 22**
See also CA 121; 219; EWL 3; RGWL 3
Anyidoho, Kofi 1947- .... **BLC 2:1**
See also BW 3; CA 178; CP 5, 6, 7; DLB 157; EWL 3
Anzaldúa, Gloria (Evanjelina)
1942-2004 ...... **CLC 200, 350; HLCS 1**
See also CA 175; 227; CSW; CWP; DLB 122; FW; LLW; RGAL 4; SATA-Obit 154
Apess, William 1798-1839(?) .... **NCLC 73; NNAL**
See also DAM MULT; DLB 175, 243
Apollinaire, Guillaume 1880-1918 ...... **PC 7; TCLC 3, 8, 51**
See also CA 104; 152; DAM POET; DLB 258, 321; EW 9; EWL 3; GFL 1789 to the Present; MTCW 2; PFS 24; RGWL 2, 3; TWA; WP
Apollonius of Rhodes
See Apollonius Rhodius
Apollonius Rhodius
c. 300B.C.-c. 220B.C. .... **CMLC 28**
See also AW 1; DLB 176; RGWL 2, 3
Appelfeld, Aharon 1932- .... **CLC 23, 47, 317; SSC 42**
See also CA 112; 133; CANR 86, 160, 207; CWW 2; DLB 299; EWL 3; RGHL; RGSF 2; WLIT 6
Appelfeld, Aron
See Appelfeld, Aharon
Apple, Max 1941- .... **CLC 9, 33; SSC 50**
See also AMWS 17; CA 81-84; CANR 19, 54, 214; DLB 130
Apple, Max Isaac
See Apple, Max
Appleman, Philip (Dean) 1926- ...... **CLC 51**
See also CA 13-16R; CAAS 18; CANR 6, 29, 56
Appleton, Lawrence
See Lovecraft, H. P.
Apteryx
See Eliot, T. S.
Apuleius, (Lucius Madaurensis)
c. 125-c. 164 .... **CMLC 1, 84**
See also AW 2; CDWLB 1; DLB 211; RGWL 2, 3; SUFW; WLIT 8
Aquin, Hubert 1929-1977 .... **CLC 15**
See also CA 105; DLB 53; EWL 3
Aquinas, Thomas 1224(?)-1274 ... **CMLC 33, 137**
See also DLB 115; EW 1; TWA
Aragon, Louis 1897-1982 .... **CLC 3, 22; PC 155; TCLC 123**
See also CA 69-72; 108; CANR 28, 71; DAM NOV, POET; DLB 72, 258; EW 11; EWL 3; GFL 1789 to the Present; GLL 2; LMFS 2; MTCW 1, 2; RGWL 2, 3
Arany, Janos 1817-1882 .... **NCLC 34**
Aranyos, Kakay 1847-1910
See Mikszath, Kalman
Aratus of Soli
c. 315B.C.-c. 240B.C. .... **CMLC 64, 114**
See also DLB 176
Arbuthnot, John 1667-1735 .... **LC 1**
See also BRWS 16; DLB 101
Archer, Herbert Winslow
See Mencken, H. L.
Archer, Jeffrey 1940- .... **CLC 28**
See also AAYA 16; BEST 89:3; BPFB 1; CA 77-80; CANR 22, 52, 95, 136, 209; CPW; DA3; DAM POP; INT CANR-22; MTFW 2005
Archer, Jeffrey Howard
See Archer, Jeffrey
Archer, Jules 1915- .... **CLC 12**
See also CA 9-12R; CANR 6, 69; SAAS 5; SATA 4, 85
Archer, Lee
See Ellison, Harlan
Archilochus c. 7th cent. B.C. .... **CMLC 44**
See also DLB 176
Ard, William
See Jakes, John
Ardelia
See Finch, Anne
Arden, Constance
See Naden, Constance
Arden, John 1930-2012 .... **CLC 6, 13, 15**
See also BRWS 2; CA 13-16R; CAAS 4; CANR 31, 65, 67, 124; CBD; CD 5, 6; DAM DRAM; DFS 9; DLB 13, 245; EWL 3; MTCW 1
Arenas, Reinaldo 1943-1990 .... **CLC 41; HLC 1; TCLC 191**
See also CA 124; 128; 133; CANR 73, 106; DAM MULT; DLB 145; EWL 3; GLL 2; HW 1; LAW; LAWS 1; MTCW 2; MTFW 2005; RGSF 2; RGWL 3; WLIT 1
Arendt, Hannah 1906-1975 .... **CLC 66, 98; TCLC 193**
See also CA 17-20R; 61-64; CANR 26, 60, 172; DLB 242; MTCW 1, 2
Aretino, Pietro 1492-1556 .... **LC 12, 165**
See also RGWL 2, 3
Arghezi, Tudor 1880-1967 .... **CLC 80**
See also CA 167; 116; CDWLB 4; DLB 220; EWL 3
Arguedas, Jose Maria 1911-1969 ... **CLC 10, 18; HLCS 1; TCLC 147**
See also CA 89-92; CANR 73; DLB 113; EWL 3; HW 1; LAW; RGWL 2, 3; WLIT 1
Argueta, Manlio 1936- .... **CLC 31**
See also CA 131; CANR 73; CWW 2; DLB 145; EWL 3; HW 1; RGWL 3
Arias, Ron 1941- .... **HLC 1**
See also CA 131; CANR 81, 136; DAM MULT; DLB 82; HW 1, 2; MTCW 2; MTFW 2005
Ariosto, Lodovico
See Ariosto, Ludovico
Ariosto, Ludovico 1474-1533 .... **LC 6, 87, 206; PC 42**
See also EW 2; RGWL 2, 3; WLIT 7
Aristides
See Epstein, Joseph
Aristides Quintilianus
fl. c. 100-fl. c. 400 .... **CMLC 122**
Aristophanes 450B.C.-385B.C. ...... **CMLC 4, 51, 138, 164; DC 2; WLCS**
See also AW 1; CDWLB 1; DA; DA3; DAB; DAC; DAM DRAM, MST; DFS 10; DLB 176; LMFS 1; RGWL 2, 3; TWA; WLIT 8
Aristotle 384B.C.-322B.C. .... **CMLC 31, 123; WLCS**
See also AW 1; CDWLB 1; DA; DA3; DAB; DAC; DAM MST; DLB 176; RGWL 2, 3; TWA; WLIT 8
Arlt, Roberto 1900-1942 .... **HLC 1; TCLC 29, 255**
See also CA 123; 131; CANR 67; DAM MULT; DLB 305; EWL 3; HW 1, 2; IDTP; LAW
Arlt, Roberto Godofredo Christophersen
See Arlt, Roberto
Armah, Ayi Kwei
1939- ... **BLC 1:1, 2:1; CLC 5, 33, 136**
See also AFW; BRWS 10; BW 1; CA 61-64; CANR 21, 64; CDWLB 3; CN 1, 2, 3, 4, 5, 6, 7; DAM MULT, POET; DLB 117; EWL 3; MTCW 1; WLIT 2
Armatrading, Joan 1950- .... **CLC 17**
See also CA 114; 186
Armin, Robert 1568(?)-1615(?) .... **LC 120**
Armitage, Frank
See Carpenter, John
Armstrong, Gillian 1950- .... **CLC 385**
See also AAYA 74; CA 173
Armstrong, Jeannette (C.) 1948- .... **NNAL**
See also CA 149; CCA 1; CN 6, 7; DAC; DLB 334; SATA 102
Armytage, R.
See Watson, Rosamund Marriott
Arnauld, Antoine 1612-1694 .... **LC 169**
See also DLB 268
Arnette, Robert
See Silverberg, Robert
Arnim, Achim von (Ludwig Joachim von Arnim) 1781-1831 .... **NCLC 5, 159; SSC 29**
See also DLB 90
Arnim, Bettina von
1785-1859 .... **NCLC 38, 123**
See also DLB 90; RGWL 2, 3
Arnold, Matthew 1822-1888 .... **NCLC 6, 29, 89, 126, 218; PC 5, 94; WLC 1**
See also BRW 5; CDBLB 1832-1890; DA; DAB; DAC; DAM MST, POET; DLB 32, 57; EXPP; PAB; PFS 2; TEA; WP
Arnold, Thomas 1795-1842 .... **NCLC 18**
See also DLB 55
Arnow, Harriette (Louisa) Simpson
1908-1986 .... **CLC 2, 7, 18; TCLC 196**

Author Index

See also BPFB 1; CA 9-12R; 118; CANR 14; CN 2, 3, 4; DLB 6; FW; MTCW 1, 2; RHW; SATA 42; SATA-Obit 47

Arouet, Francois-Marie
See Voltaire

Arp, Hans
See Arp, Jean

Arp, Jean 1887-1966 .... **CLC 5; PC 156; TCLC 115**
See also CA 81-84; 25-28R; CANR 42, 77; EW 10

Arrabal
See Arrabal, Fernando

Arrabal, Fernando
1932- .... **CLC 2, 9, 18, 58; DC 35**
See also CA 9-12R; CANR 15; CWW 2; DLB 321; EWL 3; LMFS 2

Arrabal Teran, Fernando
See Arrabal, Fernando

Arreola, Juan Jose 1918-2001 ..... **CLC 147; HLC 1; SSC 38**
See also CA 113; 131; 200; CANR 81; CWW 2; DAM MULT; DLB 113; DNFS 2; EWL 3; HW 1, 2; LAW; RGSF 2

Arrian c. 89(?)-c. 155(?) .... **CMLC 43**
See also DLB 176

Arrick, Fran
See Angell, Judie

Arrley, Richmond
See Delany, Samuel R., Jr.

Artaud, Antonin
1896-1948 .... **DC 14; TCLC 3, 36**
See also CA 104; 149; DA3; DAM DRAM; DFS 22; DLB 258, 321; EW 11; EWL 3; GFL 1789 to the Present; MTCW 2; MTFW 2005; RGWL 2, 3

Artaud, Antonin Marie Joseph
See Artaud, Antonin

Artemidorus fl. 2nd cent. .... **CMLC 129**

Arthur, Ruth M(abel) 1905-1979 ... **CLC 12**
See also CA 9-12R; 85-88; CANR 4; CWRI 5; SATA 7, 26

Artsybashev, Mikhail (Petrovich)
1878-1927 .... **TCLC 31**
See also CA 170; DLB 295

Arundel, Honor (Morfydd)
1919-1973 .... **CLC 17**
See also CA 21-22; 41-44R; CAP 2; CLR 35; CWRI 5; SATA 4; SATA-Obit 24

Arzner, Dorothy 1900-1979 .... **CLC 98**

Asch, Sholem 1880-1957 .... **TCLC 3, 251**
See also AMWS 23; CA 105; DLB 333; EWL 3; GLL 2; RGHL

Ascham, Roger 1516(?)-1568 .... **LC 101**
See also DLB 236

Ash, Shalom
See Asch, Sholem

Ashbery, John 1927- .... **CLC 2, 3, 4, 6, 9, 13, 15, 25, 41, 77, 125, 221; PC 26, 159**
See also AMWS 3; CA 5-8R; CANR 9, 37, 66, 102, 132, 170, 230; CP 1, 2, 3, 4, 5, 6, 7; DA3; DAM POET; DLB 5, 165; DLBY 1981; EWL 3; GLL 1; INT CANR-9; MAL 5; MTCW 1, 2; MTFW 2005; PAB; PFS 11, 28; RGAL 4; TCLE 1:1; WP

Ashbery, John Lawrence
See Ashbery, John

Ashbridge, Elizabeth 1713-1755 ...... **LC 147**
See also DLB 200

Ashdown, Clifford
See Freeman, R(ichard) Austin

Ashe, Gordon
See Creasey, John

Ashton-Warner, Sylvia (Constance)
1908-1984 .... **CLC 19**
See also CA 69-72; 112; CANR 29; CN 1, 2, 3; MTCW 1, 2

Asimov, Isaac 1920-1992 .... **CLC 1, 3, 9, 19, 26, 76, 92; SSC 148**
See also AAYA 13; BEST 90:2; BPFB 1; BYA 4, 6, 7, 9; CA 1-4R; 137; CANR 2, 19, 36, 60, 125; CLR 12, 79; CMW 4; CN 1, 2, 3, 4, 5; CPW; DA3; DAM POP; DLB 8; DLBY 1992; INT CANR-19; JRDA; LAIT 5; LMFS 2; MAICYA 1, 2; MAL 5; MTCW 1, 2; MTFW 2005; NFS 29; RGAL 4; SATA 1, 26, 74; SCFW 1, 2; SFW 4; SSFS 17, 33; TUS; YAW

Askew, Anne 1521(?)-1546 .... **LC 81, 219**
See also DLB 136

Asser -c. 909 .... **CMLC 117**

Assis, Joaquim Maria Machado de
See Machado de Assis, Joaquim Maria

Astell, Mary 1666-1731 .... **LC 68, 183**
See also DLB 252, 336; FW

Astley, Thea (Beatrice May)
1925-2004 .... **CLC 41, 332**
See also CA 65-68; 229; CANR 11, 43, 78; CN 1, 2, 3, 4, 5, 6, 7; DLB 289; EWL 3

Astley, William 1855-1911 .... **TCLC 45**
See also DLB 230; RGEL 2

Aston, James
See White, T(erence) H(anbury)

Asturias, Miguel Angel 1899-1974 .... **CLC 3, 8, 13; HLC 1; TCLC 184**
See also CA 25-28; 49-52; CANR 32; CAP 2; CDWLB 3; DA3; DAM MULT, NOV; DLB 113, 290, 329; EWL 3; HW 1; LAW; LMFS 2; MTCW 1, 2; RGWL 2, 3; WLIT 1

Atares, Carlos Saura
See Saura (Atares), Carlos

Athanasius c. 295-c. 373 .... **CMLC 48**

Atheling, William
See Pound, Ezra

Atheling, William, Jr.
See Blish, James

Atherton, Gertrude (Franklin Horn)
1857-1948 .... **TCLC 2**
See also CA 104; 155; DLB 9, 78, 186; HGG; RGAL 4; SUFW 1; TCWW 1, 2

Atherton, Lucius
See Masters, Edgar Lee

Atkins, Jack
See Harris, Mark

Atkinson, Kate 1951- .... **CLC 99**
See also CA 166; CANR 101, 153, 198, 231; DLB 267

'Aṭṭār, Farid al-Din Abu Hamid Mohammad
1145?-1221? .... **CMLC 157**
See also RGWL 2,3; WLIT 6

'Aṭṭār, Farīd al-Dīn
1145?-1221? .... **CMLC 157**
See also RGWL 2, 3; WLIT 6

Attaway, William (Alexander)
1911-1986 .... **BLC 1:1; CLC 92**
See also BW 2, 3; CA 143; CANR 82; DAM MULT; DLB 76; MAL 5

Atticus
See Fleming, Ian; Wilson, (Thomas) Woodrow

Atwood, Margaret 1939- ..... **CLC 2, 3, 4, 8, 13, 15, 25, 44, 84, 135, 232, 239, 246, 342, 371, 382; PC 8, 123; SSC 2, 46, 142; WLC 1**
See also AAYA 12, 47; AMWS 13; BEST 89:2; BPFB 1; CA 49-52; CANR 3, 24, 33, 59, 95, 133; CN 2, 3, 4, 5, 6, 7; CP 1, 2, 3, 4, 5, 6, 7; CPW; CWP; DA; DA3; DAB; DAC; DAM MST, NOV, POET; DLB 53, 251, 326; EWL 3; EXPN; FL 1:5; FW; GL 2; INT CANR-24; LAIT 5; MTCW 1, 2; MTFW 2005; NFS 4, 12, 13, 14, 19, 39; PFS 7, 37; RGSF 2; SATA 50, 170; SSFS 3, 13; TCLE 1:1; TWA; WWE 1; YAW

Atwood, Margaret Eleanor
See Atwood, Margaret

Aubigny, Pierre d'
See Mencken, H. L.

Aubin, Penelope 1685-1731(?) .... **LC 9**
See also DLB 39

Auchincloss, Louis 1917-2010 ...... **CLC 4, 6, 9, 18, 45, 318; SSC 22**
See also AMWS 4; CA 1-4R; CANR 6, 29, 55, 87, 130, 168, 202; CN 1, 2, 3, 4, 5, 6, 7; DAM NOV; DLB 2, 244; DLBY 1980; EWL 3; INT CANR-29; MAL 5; MTCW 1; RGAL 4

Auchincloss, Louis Stanton
See Auchincloss, Louis

Auden, W. H. 1907-1973 .... **CLC 1, 2, 3, 4, 6, 9, 11, 14, 43, 123; PC 1, 92, 161; TCLC 223; WLC 1**
See also AAYA 18; AMWS 2; BRW 7; BRWR 1; CA 9-12R; 45-48; CANR 5, 61, 105; CDBLB 1914-1945; CP 1, 2; DA; DA3; DAB; DAC; DAM DRAM, MST, POET; DLB 10, 20; EWL 3; EXPP; MAL 5; MTCW 1, 2; MTFW 2005; PAB; PFS 1, 3, 4, 10, 27; TUS; WP

Auden, Wystan Hugh
See Auden, W. H.

Audiberti, Jacques 1899-1965 .... **CLC 38**
See also CA 252; 25-28R; DAM DRAM; DLB 321; EWL 3

Audubon, John James 1785-1851 .. **NCLC 47**
See also AAYA 76; AMWS 16; ANW; DLB 248

Auel, Jean
See Auel, Jean M.

Auel, Jean M. 1936- .... **CLC 31, 107**
See also AAYA 7, 51; BEST 90:4; BPFB 1; CA 103; CANR 21, 64, 115; CPW; DA3; DAM POP; INT CANR-21; NFS 11; RHW; SATA 91

Auel, Jean Marie
See Auel, Jean M.

Auerbach, Berthold
1812-1882 .... **NCLC 171**
See also DLB 133

Auerbach, Erich
1892-1957 .... **TCLC 43**
See also CA 118; 155; EWL 3

Augier, Emile 1820-1889 .... **NCLC 31**
See also DLB 192; GFL 1789 to the Present

August, John
See De Voto, Bernard (Augustine)

Augustine, St.
354-430 .... **CMLC 6, 95; WLCS**
See also DA; DA3; DAB; DAC; DAM MST; DLB 115; EW 1; RGWL 2, 3; WLIT 8

Aunt Belinda
See Braddon, Mary Elizabeth

Aunt Weedy
See Alcott, Louisa May

Aurelius
See Bourne, Randolph S(illiman)

Aurelius, Marcus 121-180 .... **CMLC 45**
See also AW 2; RGWL 2, 3

Aureoli, Petrus c. 1280-1322 ...... **CMLC 174**

Aurobindo, Sri
See Ghose, Aurabinda

Aurobindo Ghose
See Ghose, Aurabinda

Ausonius, Decimus Magnus
c. 310-c. 394 .... **CMLC 88**
See also RGWL 2, 3

Austen, Jane 1775-1817 .... **NCLC 1, 13, 19, 33, 51, 81, 95, 119, 150, 207, 210, 222, 242, 271, 314, 316; WLC 1**
See also AAYA 19; BRW 4; BRWC 1; BRWR 2; BYA 3; CDBLB 1789-1832; DA; DA3; DAB; DAC; DAM MST, NOV; DLB 116, 363, 365, 366; EXPN; FL 1:2; GL 2; LAIT 2; LATS 1:1; LMFS 1; NFS 1, 14, 18, 20, 21, 28, 29, 33; TEA; WLIT 3; WYAS 1

Auster, Paul 1947- .... **CLC 47, 131, 227, 339, 356**
See also AMWS 12; CA 69-72; CANR 23, 52, 75, 129, 165; CMW 4; CN 5, 6, 7;

DA3; DLB 227; MAL 5; MTCW 2; MTFW 2005; SUFW 2; TCLE 1:1
Austin, Frank
See Faust, Frederick
Austin, Mary Hunter 1868-1934 ... **SSC 104; TCLC 25, 249**
See also ANW; CA 109; 178; DLB 9, 78, 206, 221, 275; FW; TCWW 1, 2
Avellaneda, Gertrudis Gomez de
See Gomez de Avellaneda, Gertrudis
Averroes 1126-1198 .... **CMLC 7, 104**
See also DLB 115
Avicenna 980-1037 .... **CMLC 16, 110**
See also DLB 115
Avison, Margaret 1918-2007 .... **CLC 2, 4, 97; PC 148**
See also CA 17-20R; CANR 134; CP 1, 2, 3, 4, 5, 6, 7; DAC; DAM POET; DLB 53; MTCW 1
Avison, Margaret Kirkland
See Avison, Margaret
Axton, David
See Koontz, Dean
Ayala, Francisco 1906-2009 .... **SSC 119**
See also CA 208; CWW 2; DLB 322; EWL 3; RGSF 2
Ayala, Francisco de Paula y Garcia Duarte
See Ayala, Francisco
Ayckbourn, Alan 1939- .... **CLC 5, 8, 18, 33, 74; DC 13**
See also BRWS 5; CA 21-24R; CANR 31, 59, 118; CBD; CD 5, 6; DAB; DAM DRAM; DFS 7; DLB 13, 245; EWL 3; MTCW 1, 2; MTFW 2005
Aydy, Catherine
See Tennant, Emma
Ayme, Marcel (Andre)
1902-1967 .... **CLC 11; SSC 41**
See also CA 89-92; CANR 67, 137; CLR 25; DLB 72; EW 12; EWL 3; GFL 1789 to the Present; RGSF 2; RGWL 2, 3; SATA 91
Ayrton, Michael 1921-1975 .... **CLC 7**
See also CA 5-8R; 61-64; CANR 9, 21
Aytmatov, Chingiz
See Aitmatov, Chingiz
Azorin
See Martinez Ruiz, Jose
Azuela, Mariano 1873-1952 .... **HLC 1; TCLC 3, 145, 217**
See also CA 104; 131; CANR 81; DAM MULT; EWL 3; HW 1, 2; LAW; MTCW 1, 2; MTFW 2005
Ba, Mariama 1929-1981 .... **BLC 2:1; BLCS**
See also AFW; BW 2; CA 141; CANR 87; DLB 360; DNFS 2; WLIT 2
Baastad, Babbis Friis
See Friis-Baastad, Babbis Ellinor
Bab
See Gilbert, W(illiam) S(chwenck)
Babbis, Eleanor
See Friis-Baastad, Babbis Ellinor
Babel, Isaac
See Babel, Isaak (Emmanuilovich)
Babel, Isaak (Emmanuilovich)
1894-1941(?) .... **SSC 16, 78, 161; TCLC 2, 13, 171**
See also CA 104; 155; CANR 113; DLB 272; EW 11; EWL 3; MTCW 2; MTFW 2005; RGSF 2; RGWL 2, 3; SSFS 10; TWA
Babits, Mihaly 1883-1941 .... **TCLC 14**
See also CA 114; CDWLB 4; DLB 215; EWL 3
Babur 1483-1530 .... **LC 18**
Babylas
See Ghelderode, Michel de
Baca, Jimmy Santiago
1952- .... **HLC 1; PC 41**
See also CA 131; CANR 81, 90, 146, 220; CP 6, 7; DAM MULT; DLB 122; HW 1, 2; LLW; MAL 5; PFS 40
Baca, Jose Santiago
See Baca, Jimmy Santiago
Bacchelli, Riccardo 1891-1985 .... **CLC 19**
See also CA 29-32R; 117; DLB 264; EWL 3
Bacchylides
c. 520B.C.-c. 452B.C. .... **CMLC 119**
Bach, Richard 1936- .... **CLC 14**
See also AITN 1; BEST 89:2; BPFB 1; BYA 5; CA 9-12R; CANR 18, 93, 151; CPW; DAM NOV, POP; FANT; MTCW 1; SATA 13
Bach, Richard David
See Bach, Richard
Bache, Benjamin Franklin
1769-1798 .... **LC 74**
See also DLB 43
Bachelard, Gaston 1884-1962 ..... **TCLC 128**
See also CA 97-100; 89-92; DLB 296; GFL 1789 to the Present
Bachman, Richard
See King, Stephen
Bachmann, Ingeborg 1926-1973 ... **CLC 69; PC 151; TCLC 192**
See also CA 93-96; 45-48; CANR 69; DLB 85; EWL 3; RGHL; RGWL 2, 3
Bacigalupi, Paolo 1973- .... **CLC 309**
See also AAYA 86; CA 317; SATA 230
Bacon, Delia 1811-1859 .... **NCLC 315**
See also DLB 1, 243
Bacon, Francis 1561-1626 .... **LC 18, 32, 131, 239**
See also BRW 1; CDBLB Before 1660; DLB 151, 236, 252; RGEL 2; TEA
Bacon, Roger
1214(?)-1294 .... **CMLC 14, 108, 155**
See also DLB 115
Bacovia, G.
See Bacovia, George
Bacovia, George 1881-1957 .... **TCLC 24**
See Bacovia, George
See also CA 123; 189; CDWLB 4; DLB 220; EWL 3
Badanes, Jerome 1937-1995 .... **CLC 59**
See also CA 234
Badiou, Alain 1937- .... **CLC 326**
See also CA 261
Baena, Juan Alfonso de
c. 1375-c. 1434 .... **LC 239**
Bage, Robert 1728-1801 .... **NCLC 182**
See also DLB 39; RGEL 2
Bagehot, Walter 1826-1877 .... **NCLC 10**
See also DLB 55
Bagnold, Enid 1889-1981 .... **CLC 25**
See also AAYA 75; BYA 2; CA 5-8R; 103; CANR 5, 40; CBD; CN 2; CWD; CWRI 5; DAM DRAM; DLB 13, 160, 191, 245; FW; MAICYA 1, 2; RGEL 2; SATA 1, 25
Bagritsky, Eduard
See Dzyubin, Eduard Georgievich
Bagritsky, Edvard
See Dzyubin, Eduard Georgievich
Bagrjana, Elisaveta
See Belcheva, Elisaveta Lyubomirova
Bagryana, Elisaveta
See Belcheva, Elisaveta Lyubomirova
Bail, Murray 1941- .... **CLC 353**
See also CA 127; CANR 62; CN 4, 5, 6, 7; DLB 325
Bailey, Paul 1937- .... **CLC 45**
See also CA 21-24R; CANR 16, 62, 124; CN 1, 2, 3, 4, 5, 6, 7; DLB 14, 271; GLL 2
Baillie, Joanna 1762-1851 .... **NCLC 71, 151; PC 151**
See also DLB 93, 344; GL 2; RGEL 2
Bainbridge, Beryl 1934-2010 .... **CLC 4, 5, 8, 10, 14, 18, 22, 62, 130, 292**
See also BRWS 6; CA 21-24R; CANR 24, 55, 75, 88, 128; CN 2, 3, 4, 5, 6, 7; DAM NOV; DLB 14, 231; EWL 3; MTCW 1, 2; MTFW 2005
Baker, Carlos (Heard) 1909-1987 ... **TCLC 119**
See also CA 5-8R; 122; CANR 3, 63; DLB 103
Baker, Elliott 1922-2007 .... **CLC 8**
See also CA 45-48; 257; CANR 2, 63; CN 1, 2, 3, 4, 5, 6, 7
Baker, Elliott Joseph
See Baker, Elliott
Baker, Nicholson 1957- .... **CLC 61, 165**
See also AMWS 13; CA 135; CANR 63, 120, 138, 190, 237; CN 6; CPW; DA3; DAM POP; DLB 227; MTFW 2005
Baker, Ray Stannard 1870-1946 ... **TCLC 47**
See also CA 118; DLB 345
Baker, Russell 1925- .... **CLC 31**
See also BEST 89:4; CA 57-60; CANR 11, 41, 59, 137; MTCW 1, 2; MTFW 2005
Baker, Russell Wayne
See Baker, Russell
Bakhtin, M.
See Bakhtin, Mikhail Mikhailovich
Bakhtin, M. M.
See Bakhtin, Mikhail Mikhailovich
Bakhtin, Mikhail
See Bakhtin, Mikhail Mikhailovich
Bakhtin, Mikhail Mikhailovich
1895-1975 .... **CLC 83; TCLC 160**
See Bakhtin, Mikhail Mikhailovich
See also CA 128; 113; DLB 242; EWL 3
Bakshi, Ralph 1938(?)- .... **CLC 26**
See also CA 112; 138; IDFW 3
Bakunin, Mikhail (Alexandrovich)
1814-1876 .... **NCLC 25, 58**
See also DLB 277
Bal, Mieke 1946- .... **CLC 252**
See also CA 156; CANR 99
Bal, Mieke Maria Gertrudis
See Bal, Mieke
Baldwin, James 1924-1987 .... **BLC 1:1, 2:1; CLC 1, 2, 3, 4, 5, 8, 13, 15, 17, 42, 50, 67, 90, 127; DC 1; SSC 10, 33, 98, 134, 199; TCLC 229; WLC 1**
See also AAYA 4, 34; AFAW 1, 2; AMWR 2; AMWS 1; BPFB 1; BW 1; CA 1-4R; 124; CABS 1; CAD; CANR 3, 24; CDALB 1941-1968; CLR 191; CN 1, 2, 3, 4; CPW; DA; DA3; DAB; DAC; DAM MST, MULT, NOV, POP; DFS 11, 15; DLB 2, 7, 33, 249, 278; DLBY 1987; EWL 3; EXPS; LAIT 5; MAL 5; MTCW 1, 2; MTFW 2005; NCFS 4; NFS 4; RGAL 4; RGSF 2; SATA 9; SATA-Obit 54; SSFS 2, 18; TUS
Baldwin, William c. 1515-1563 ... **LC 113, 209**
See also DLB 132
Bale, John 1495-1563 .... **LC 62, 228**
See also DLB 132; RGEL 2; TEA
Ball, Hugo 1886-1927 .... **TCLC 104**
Ballard, James G.
See Ballard, J.G.
Ballard, James Graham
See Ballard, J.G.
Ballard, J.G. 1930-2009 .... **CLC 3, 6, 14, 36, 137, 299; SSC 1, 53, 146**
See also AAYA 3, 52; BRWS 5; CA 5-8R; 285; CANR 15, 39, 65, 107, 133, 198; CN 1, 2, 3, 4, 5, 6, 7; DA3; DAM NOV, POP; DLB 14, 207, 261, 319; EWL 3; HGG; MTCW 1, 2; MTFW 2005; NFS 8; RGEL 2; RGSF 2; SATA 93; SATA-Obit 203; SCFW 1, 2; SFW 4
Ballard, Jim G.
See Ballard, J.G.
Balmont, Konstantin (Dmitriyevich)
1867-1943 .... **PC 149; TCLC 11**
See also CA 109; 155; DLB 295; EWL 3

Ballantyne, R. M. 1825-1894 ...... **NCLC 301**
See also CLR 137; DLB 163; JRDA; RGEL 2; SATA 24

Baltausis, Vincas 1847-1910
See Mikszath, Kalman

Balwhidder, Rev. Micah
See Galt, John

Balzac, Guez de (?)-
See Balzac, Jean-Louis Guez de

Balzac, Honore de 1799-1850 .... **NCLC 5, 35, 53, 153, 273, 311; SSC 5, 59, 102, 153; WLC 1**
See also DA; DA3; DAB; DAC; DAM MST, NOV; DLB 119; EW 5; GFL 1789 to the Present; LMFS 1; NFS 33; RGSF 2; RGWL 2, 3; SSFS 10; SUFW; TWA

Balzac, Jean-Louis Guez de 1597-1654 .... **LC 162**
See also DLB 268; GFL Beginnings to 1789

Bambara, Toni Cade 1939-1995 .... **BLC 1:1, 2:1; CLC 19, 88; SSC 35, 107; TCLC 116; WLCS**
See also AAYA 5, 49; AFAW 2; AMWS 11; BW 2, 3; BYA 12, 14; CA 29-32R; 150; CANR 24, 49, 81; CDALBS; DA; DA3; DAC; DAM MST, MULT; DLB 38, 218; EXPS; MAL 5; MTCW 1, 2; MTFW 2005; RGAL 4; RGSF 2; SATA 112; SSFS 4, 7, 12, 21

Bamdad, A.
See Shamlu, Ahmad

Bamdad, Alef
See Shamlu, Ahmad

Banat, D. R.
See Bradbury, Ray

Bancroft, Laura
See Baum, L. Frank

Bandello, Matteo 1485-1562 .. **LC 212; SSC 143**

Banim, John 1798-1842 .... **NCLC 13**
See also DLB 116, 158, 159; RGEL 2

Banim, Michael 1796-1874 .... **NCLC 13**
See also DLB 158, 159

Banjo, The
See Paterson, A(ndrew) B(arton)

Banks, Iain 1954-2013 .... **CLC 34, 356**
See also BRWS 11; CA 123; 128; CANR 61, 106, 180; DLB 194, 261; EWL 3; HGG; INT CA-128; MTFW 2005; SFW 4

Banks, Iain M.
See Banks, Iain

Banks, Iain Menzies
See Banks, Iain

Banks, Lynne Reid
See Reid Banks, Lynne

Banks, Russell 1940- .... **CLC 37, 72, 187; SSC 42**
See also AAYA 45; AMWS 5; CA 65-68; CAAS 15; CANR 19, 52, 73, 118, 195, 240; CN 4, 5, 6, 7; DLB 130, 278; EWL 3; MAL 5; MTCW 2; MTFW 2005; NFS 13

Banks, Russell Earl
See Banks, Russell

Banti, Anna 1895-1985 .... **TCLC 303**
See also CA 202; DLB 177; WLIT 7

Banville, John 1945- .... **CLC 46, 118, 224, 315**
See also CA 117; 128; CANR 104, 150, 176, 225; CN 4, 5, 6, 7; DLB 14, 271, 326; INT CA-128

Banville, Theodore (Faullain) de 1832-1891 .... **NCLC 9**
See also DLB 217; GFL 1789 to the Present

Baraka, Amiri 1934-2014 ...... **BLC 1:1, 2:1; CLC 1, 2, 3, 5, 10, 14, 33, 115, 213, 389; DC 6; PC 4, 113; WLCS**
See also AAYA 63; AFAW 1, 2; AMWS 2; BW 2, 3; CA 21-24R; CABS 3; CAD; CANR 27, 38, 61, 133, 172; CD 3, 5, 6; CDALB 1941-1968; CN 1, 2; CP 1, 2, 3, 4, 5, 6, 7; CPW; DA; DA3; DAC; DAM MST, MULT, POET, POP; DFS 3, 11, 16; DLB 5, 7, 16, 38; DLBD 8; EWL 3; MAL 5; MTCW 1, 2; MTFW 2005; PFS 9; RGAL 4; TCLE 1:1; TUS; WP

Baratynsky, Evgenii Abramovich 1800-1844 .... **NCLC 103**
See also DLB 205

Barbauld, Anna Laetitia 1743-1825 .... **NCLC 50, 185; PC 149**
See also CLR 160; DLB 107, 109, 142, 158, 336; RGEL 2

Barbellion, W. N. P.
See Cummings, Bruce F.

Barber, Benjamin R. 1939- .... **CLC 141**
See also CA 29-32R; CANR 12, 32, 64, 119

Barbera, Jack 1945- .... **CLC 44**
See also CA 110; CANR 45

Barbera, Jack Vincent
See Barbera, Jack

Barbey d'Aurevilly, Jules-Amédée 1808-1889 ... **NCLC 1, 213; SSC 17, 218**
See also DLB 119; GFL 1789 to the Present

Barbour, John c. 1316-1395 .... **CMLC 33**
See also DLB 146

Barbusse, Henri 1873-1935 .... **TCLC 5**
See also CA 105; 154; DLB 65; EWL 3; RGWL 2, 3

Barclay, Alexander c. 1475-1552 ..... **LC 109**
See also DLB 132

Barclay, Bill
See Moorcock, Michael

Barclay, William Ewert
See Moorcock, Michael

Barclay, William Ewert
See Moorcock, Michael

Barea, Arturo 1897-1957 .... **TCLC 14**
See also CA 111; 201

Barfoot, Joan 1946- .... **CLC 18**
See also CA 105; CANR 141, 179

Barham, Richard Harris 1788-1845 .... **NCLC 77**
See also DLB 159

Baring, Maurice 1874-1945 .... **TCLC 8**
See also CA 105; 168; DLB 34; HGG

Baring-Gould, Sabine 1834-1924 ... **TCLC 88**
See also DLB 156, 190

Barker, Clive 1952- .... **CLC 52, 205; SSC 53**
See also AAYA 10, 54; BEST 90:3; BPFB 1; CA 121; 129; CANR 71, 111, 133, 187; CPW; DA3; DAM POP; DLB 261; HGG; INT CA-129; MTCW 1, 2; MTFW 2005; SUFW 2

Barker, George Granville 1913-1991 .... **CLC 8, 48; PC 77**
See also CA 9-12R; 135; CANR 7, 38; CP 1, 2, 3, 4, 5; DAM POET; DLB 20; EWL 3; MTCW 1

Barker, Harley Granville
See Granville-Barker, Harley

Barker, Howard 1946- .... **CLC 37; DC 51**
See also CA 102; CBD; CD 5, 6; DLB 13, 233

Barker, Jane 1652-1732 ...... **LC 42, 82, 216; PC 91**
See also DLB 39, 131

Barker, Pat 1943- .... **CLC 32, 94, 146**
See also BRWS 4; CA 117; 122; CANR 50, 101, 148, 195; CN 6, 7; DLB 271, 326; INT CA-122

Barker, Patricia
See Barker, Pat

Barlach, Ernst (Heinrich) 1870-1938 .... **TCLC 84**
See also CA 178; DLB 56, 118; EWL 3

Barlow, Joel 1754-1812 .... **NCLC 23, 223**
See also AMWS 2; DLB 37; RGAL 4

Barnard, Mary (Ethel) 1909- .... **CLC 48**
See also CA 21-22; CAP 2; CP 1

Barnes, Djuna 1892-1982 .... **CLC 3, 4, 8, 11, 29, 127; SSC 3, 163; TCLC 212**
See also AMWS 3; CA 9-12R; 107; CAD; CANR 16, 55; CN 1, 2, 3; CWD; DLB 4, 9, 45; EWL 3; GLL 1; MAL 5; MTCW 1, 2; MTFW 2005; RGAL 4; TCLE 1:1; TUS

Barnes, Jim 1933- .... **NNAL**
See also CA 108, 175, 272; CAAE 175, 272; CAAS 28; DLB 175

Barnes, Julian 1946- .... **CLC 42, 141, 315**
See also BRWS 4; CA 102; CANR 19, 54, 115, 137, 195; CN 4, 5, 6, 7; DAB; DLB 194; DLBY 1993; EWL 3; MTCW 2; MTFW 2005; SSFS 24

Barnes, Julian Patrick
See Barnes, Julian

Barnes, Peter 1931-2004 .... **CLC 5, 56**
See also CA 65-68; 230; CAAS 12; CANR 33, 34, 64, 113; CBD; CD 5, 6; DFS 6; DLB 13, 233; MTCW 1

Barnes, William 1801-1886 ... **NCLC 75, 283**
See also DLB 32

Barnfield, Richard 1574-1627 .... **LC 192; PC 152**
See also DLB 172

Baroja, Pio 1872-1956 ..... **HLC 1; SSC 112; TCLC 8, 240**
See also CA 104; 247; EW 9

Baroja y Nessi, Pio
See Baroja, Pio

Baron, David
See Pinter, Harold

Baron Corvo
See Rolfe, Frederick (William Serafino Austin Lewis Mary)

Barondess, Sue K. 1926-1977 .... **CLC 3, 8**
See also CA 1-4R; 69-72; CANR 1

Barondess, Sue Kaufman
See Barondess, Sue K.

Baron de Teive
See Pessoa, Fernando

Baroness Von S.
See Zangwill, Israel

Barreto, Afonso Henrique de Lima
See Lima Barreto, Afonso Henrique de

Barrett, Andrea 1954- .... **CLC 150**
See also CA 156; CANR 92, 186; CN 7; DLB 335; SSFS 24

Barrett, Michele
See Barrett, Michele

Barrett, Michele 1949- .... **CLC 65**
See also CA 280

Barrett, Roger Syd
See Barrett, Syd

Barrett, Syd 1946-2006 .... **CLC 35**

Barrett, William (Christopher) 1913-1992 .... **CLC 27**
See also CA 13-16R; 139; CANR 11, 67; INT CANR-11

Barrett Browning, Elizabeth 1806-1861 .... **NCLC 1, 16, 61, 66, 170; PC 6, 62; WLC 1**
See also AAYA 63; BRW 4; CDBLB 1832-1890; DA; DA3; DAB; DAC; DAM MST, POET; DLB 32, 199; EXPP; FL 1:2; PAB; PFS 2, 16, 23; TEA; WLIT 4; WP

Barrie, Baronet
See Barrie, J. M.

Barrie, J. M. 1860-1937 .... **TCLC 2, 164**
See also BRWS 3; BYA 4, 5; CA 104; 136; CANR 77; CDBLB 1890-1914; CLR 16, 124; CWRI 5; DA3; DAB; DAM DRAM; DFS 7; DLB 10, 141, 156, 352; EWL 3; FANT; MAICYA 1, 2; MTCW 2; MTFW 2005; SATA 100; SUFW; WCH; WLIT 4; YABC 1

Barrie, James Matthew
See Barrie, J. M.

Barrington, Michael
See Moorcock, Michael
Barrol, Grady
See Bograd, Larry
Barres, (Auguste-)Maurice
1862-1923 .... **TCLC 47**
See also CA 164; DLB 123; GFL 1789 to the Present
Barry, Mike
See Malzberg, Barry N(athaniel)
Barry, Philip 1896-1949 .... **TCLC 11**
See also CA 109; 199; DFS 9; DLB 7, 228; MAL 5; RGAL 4
Barry, Sebastian 1955- .... **CLC 282**
See also CA 117; CANR 122, 193, 243; CD 5, 6; DLB 245
Bart, Andre Schwarz
See Schwarz-Bart, Andre
Barth, John 1930- ...... **CLC 1, 2, 3, 5, 7, 9, 10, 14, 27, 51, 89, 214; SSC 10, 89, 207**
See also AITN 1, 2; AMW; BPFB 1; CA 1-4R; CABS 1; CANR 5, 23, 49, 64, 113, 204; CN 1, 2, 3, 4, 5, 6, 7; DAM NOV; DLB 2, 227; EWL 3; FANT; MAL 5; MTCW 1; RGAL 4; RGSF 2; RHW; SSFS 6; TUS
Barth, John Simmons
See Barth, John
Barthelme, Donald 1931-1989 .... **CLC 1, 2, 3, 5, 6, 8, 13, 23, 46, 59, 115; SSC 2, 55, 142**
See also AMWS 4; BPFB 1; CA 21-24R; 129; CANR 20, 58, 188; CN 1, 2, 3, 4; DA3; DAM NOV; DLB 2, 234; DLBY 1980, 1989; EWL 3; FANT; LMFS 2; MAL 5; MTCW 1, 2; MTFW 2005; RGAL 4; RGSF 2; SATA 7; SATA-Obit 62; SSFS 17
Barthelme, Frederick 1943- .... **CLC 36, 117**
See also AMWS 11; CA 114; 122; CANR 77, 209; CN 4, 5, 6, 7; CSW; DLB 244; DLBY 1985; EWL 3; INT CA-122
Barthes, Roland 1915-1980 ...... **CLC 24, 83; TCLC 135**
See also CA 130; 97-100; CANR 66, 237; DLB 296; EW 13; EWL 3; GFL 1789 to the Present; MTCW 1, 2; TWA
Barthes, Roland Gerard
See Barthes, Roland
Bartram, William 1739-1823 ...... **NCLC 145**
See also ANW; DLB 37
Barzun, Jacques 1907-2012 ..... **CLC 51, 145**
See also CA 61-64; CANR 22, 95
Barzun, Jacques Martin
See Barzun, Jacques
Bashevis, Isaac
See Singer, Isaac Bashevis
Bashevis, Yitskhok
See Singer, Isaac Bashevis
Bashkirtseff, Marie 1859-1884 ...... **NCLC 27**
Basho, Matsuo
See Matsuo Basho
Basil of Caesaria c. 330-379 .... **CMLC 35**
Basket, Raney
See Edgerton, Clyde
Bass, Kingsley B., Jr.
See Bullins, Ed
Bass, Rick 1958- .... **CLC 79, 143, 286; SSC 60**
See also AMWS 16; ANW; CA 126; CANR 53, 93, 145, 183; CSW; DLB 212, 275
Bassani, Giorgio 1916-2000 .... **CLC 9**
See also CA 65-68; 190; CANR 33; CWW 2; DLB 128, 177, 299; EWL 3; MTCW 1; RGHL; RGWL 2, 3
Bassine, Helen
See Yglesias, Helen
Bastian, Ann .... **CLC 70**
Bastos, Augusto Roa
See Roa Bastos, Augusto
Bataille, Georges
1897-1962 .... **CLC 29; TCLC 155**
See also CA 101; 89-92; EWL 3
Bates, H(erbert) E(rnest)
1905-1974 .... **CLC 46; SSC 10**
See also CA 93-96; 45-48; CANR 34; CN 1; DA3; DAB; DAM POP; DLB 162, 191; EWL 3; EXPS; MTCW 1, 2; RGSF 2; SSFS 7
Batiushkov, Konstantin Nikolaevich
1787-1855 .... **NCLC 254**
See also DLB 205
Bauchart
See Camus, Albert
Baudelaire, Charles 1821-1867 .... **NCLC 6, 29, 55, 155, 303; PC 1, 106, 150; SSC 18; WLC 1**
See also DA; DA3; DAB; DAC; DAM MST, POET; DLB 217; EW 7; GFL 1789 to the Present; LMFS 2; PFS 21, 38; RGWL 2, 3; TWA
Baudouin, Marcel
See Peguy, Charles (Pierre)
Baudouin, Pierre
See Peguy, Charles (Pierre)
Baudrillard, Jean 1929-2007 .... **CLC 60**
See also CA 252; 258; DLB 296
Baum, L. Frank 1856-1919 .... **TCLC 7, 132**
See also AAYA 46; BYA 16; CA 108; 133; CLR 15, 107, 175; CWRI 5; DLB 22; FANT; JRDA; MAICYA 1, 2; MTCW 1, 2; NFS 13; RGAL 4; SATA 18, 100; WCH
Baum, Louis F.
See Baum, L. Frank
Baum, Lyman Frank
See Baum, L. Frank
Bauman, Zygmunt 1925- .... **CLC 314**
See also CA 127; CANR 205
Baumbach, Jonathan 1933- .... **CLC 6, 23**
See also CA 13-16R, 284; CAAE 284; CAAS 5; CANR 12, 66, 140; CN 3, 4, 5, 6, 7; DLBY 1980; INT CANR-12; MTCW 1
Baumgarten, Alexander Gottlieb
1714-1762 .... **LC 199**
Bausch, Richard 1945- .... **CLC 51**
See also AMWS 7; CA 101; CAAS 14; CANR 43, 61, 87, 164, 200; CN 7; CSW; DLB 130; MAL 5
Bausch, Richard Carl
See Bausch, Richard
Baxter, Charles 1947- .... **CLC 45, 78**
See also AMWS 17; CA 57-60; CANR 40, 64, 104, 133, 188, 238; CPW; DAM POP; DLB 130; MAL 5; MTCW 2; MTFW 2005; TCLE 1:1
Baxter, Charles Morley
See Baxter, Charles
Baxter, George Owen
See Faust, Frederick
Baxter, James K(eir) 1926-1972 ... **CLC 14; PC 164; TCLC 249**
See also CA 77-80; CP 1; EWL 3
Baxter, John
See Hunt, E. Howard
Bayer, Sylvia
See Glassco, John
Bayle, Pierre 1647-1706 .... **LC 126**
See also DLB 268, 313; GFL Beginnings to 1789
Baynton, Barbara
1857-1929 ..... **SSC 213; TCLC 57, 211**
See also DLB 230; RGSF 2
Buchner, (Karl) Georg 1813-1837 .... **DC 35; NCLC 26, 146; SSC 131**
See also CDWLB 2; DLB 133; EW 6; RGSF 2; RGWL 2, 3; TWA
Becquer, Gustavo Adolfo 1836-1870 .... **HLCS 1; NCLC 106, 285; PC 113**
See also DAM MULT
Bodker, Cecil 1927- .... **CLC 21**
See also CA 73-76; CANR 13, 44, 111; CLR 23; MAICYA 1, 2; SATA 14, 133
Beagle, Peter S. 1939- .... **CLC 7, 104**
See also AAYA 47; BPFB 1; BYA 9, 10, 16; CA 9-12R; CANR 4, 51, 73, 110, 213; DA3; DLBY 1980; FANT; INT CANR-4; MTCW 2; MTFW 2005; SATA 60, 130; SUFW 1, 2; YAW
Beagle, Peter Soyer
See Beagle, Peter S.
Bean, Normal
See Burroughs, Edgar Rice
Beard, Charles A(ustin)
1874-1948 .... **TCLC 15**
See also CA 115; 189; DLB 17; SATA 18
Beardsley, Aubrey 1872-1898 .... **NCLC 6**
Beatrice of Nazareth 1200-1268 ... **CMLC 124**
Beattie, Ann 1947- .... **CLC 8, 13, 18, 40, 63, 146, 293; SSC 11, 130**
See also AMWS 5; BEST 90:2; BPFB 1; CA 81-84; CANR 53, 73, 128, 225; CN 4, 5, 6, 7; CPW; DA3; DAM NOV, POP; DLB 218, 278; DLBY 1982; EWL 3; MAL 5; MTCW 1, 2; MTFW 2005; RGAL 4; RGSF 2; SSFS 9; TUS
Beattie, James 1735-1803 .... **NCLC 25**
See also DLB 109
Beauchamp, Katherine Mansfield
See Mansfield, Katherine
Beaumarchais, Pierre-Augustin Caron de
1732-1799 .... **DC 4; LC 61, 192**
See also DAM DRAM; DFS 14, 16; DLB 313; EW 4; GFL Beginnings to 1789; RGWL 2, 3
Beaumont, Francis 1584(?)-1616 .... **DC 6; LC 33, 222**
See also BRW 2; CDBLB Before 1660; DLB 58; TEA
Beauvoir, Simone de 1908-1986 ...... **CLC 1, 2, 4, 8, 14, 31, 44, 50, 71, 124; SSC 35; TCLC 221; WLC 1**
See also BPFB 1; CA 9-12R; 118; CANR 28, 61; DA; DA3; DAB; DAC; DAM MST, NOV; DLB 72; DLBY 1986; EW 12; EWL 3; FL 1:5; FW; GFL 1789 to the Present; LMFS 2; MTCW 1, 2; MTFW 2005; RGSF 2; RGWL 2, 3; TWA
Beauvoir, Simone Lucie Ernestine Marie Bertrand de
See Beauvoir, Simone de
Bechdel, Alison 1960- .... **CLC 364**
See also AAYA 83; CA 138; CANR 97, 159, 248; DLB 345; GLL 2
Becker, Carl (Lotus) 1873-1945 .... **TCLC 63**
See also CA 157; DLB 17
Becker, Jurek 1937-1997 .... **CLC 7, 19; TCLC 287**
See also CA 85-88; 157; CANR 60, 117; CWW 2; DLB 75, 299; EWL 3; RGHL
Becker, Walter 1950- .... **CLC 26**
Becket, Thomas a 1118(?)-1170 ... **CMLC 83**
Beckett, Samuel 1906-1989 ..... **CLC 1, 2, 3, 4, 6, 9, 10, 11, 14, 18, 29, 57, 59, 83; DC 22; PC 153; SSC 16, 74, 161, 218; TCLC 145; WLC 1**
See also BRWC 2; BRWR 1; BRWS 1; CA 5-8R; 130; CANR 33, 61; CBD; CDBLB 1945-1960; CN 1, 2, 3, 4; CP 1, 2, 3, 4; DA; DA3; DAB; DAC; DAM DRAM, MST, NOV; DFS 2, 7, 18; DLB 13, 15, 233, 319, 321, 329; DLBY 1990; EWL 3; GFL 1789 to the Present; LATS 1:2; LMFS 2; MTCW 1, 2; MTFW 2005; RGSF 2; RGWL 2, 3; SSFS 15; TEA; WLIT 4
Beckett, Samuel Barclay
See Beckett, Samuel
Beckford, William
1760-1844 .... **NCLC 16, 214, 291**

See also BRW 3; DLB 39, 213; GL 2; HGG; LMFS 1; SUFW
Beckham, Barry 1944- .... **BLC 1:1**
See also BW 1; CA 29-32R; CANR 26, 62; CN 1, 2, 3, 4, 5, 6; DAM MULT; DLB 33
Beckman, Gunnel 1910- .... **CLC 26**
See also CA 33-36R; CANR 15, 114; CLR 25; MAICYA 1, 2; SAAS 9; SATA 6
Becque, Henri 1837-1899 ..... **DC 21; NCLC 3**
See also DLB 192; GFL 1789 to the Present
Beddoes, Thomas Lovell 1803-1849 ...... **DC 15; NCLC 3, 154; PC 164**
See also BRWS 11; DLB 96
Bede c. 673-735 .... **CMLC 20, 130**
See also DLB 146; TEA
Bedford, Denton R. 1907-(?) .... **NNAL**
Bedford, Donald F.
See Fearing, Kenneth
Beecher, Catharine Esther 1800-1878 .... **NCLC 30**
See also DLB 1, 243
Beecher, John 1904-1980 .... **CLC 6**
See also AITN 1; CA 5-8R; 105; CANR 8; CP 1, 2, 3
Beer, Johann 1655-1700 .... **LC 5**
See also DLB 168
Beer, Patricia 1924- .... **CLC 58**
See also BRWS 14; CA 61-64; 183; CANR 13, 46; CP 1, 2, 3, 4, 5, 6; CWP; DLB 40; FW
Beerbohm, Max
See Beerbohm, (Henry) Max(imilian)
Beerbohm, (Henry) Max(imilian) 1872-1956 .... **TCLC 1, 24**
See also BRWS 2; CA 104; 154; CANR 79; DLB 34, 100; FANT; MTCW 2
Beer-Hofmann, Richard 1866-1945 .... **TCLC 60**
See also CA 160; DLB 81
Beethoven, Ludwig van 1770(?)-1827 .... **NCLC 227**
Beg, Shemus
See Stephens, James
Begiebing, Robert J(ohn) 1946- ..... **CLC 70**
See also CA 122; CANR 40, 88
Begley, Louis 1933- .... **CLC 197**
See also CA 140; CANR 98, 176, 210; DLB 299; RGHL; TCLE 1:1
Behan, Brendan 1923-1964 .... **CLC 1, 8, 11, 15, 79**
See also BRWS 2; CA 73-76; CANR 33, 121; CBD; CDBLB 1945-1960; DAM DRAM; DFS 7; DLB 13, 233; EWL 3; MTCW 1, 2
Behan, Brendan Francis
See Behan, Brendan
Behn, Aphra 1640(?)-1689 .... **DC 4; LC 1, 30, 42, 135, 237; PC 13, 88; WLC 1**
See also BRWR 3; BRWS 3; DA; DA3; DAB; DAC; DAM DRAM, MST, NOV, POET; DFS 16, 24; DLB 39, 80, 131; FW; NFS 35; TEA; WLIT 3
Behrman, S(amuel) N(athaniel) 1893-1973 .... **CLC 40**
See also CA 13-16; 45-48; CAD; CAP 1; DLB 7, 44; IDFW 3; MAL 5; RGAL 4
Bei Dao 1949- .... **PC 130**
See also CA 139; CANR 69; CWW 2; EWL 3; PFS 38; RGWL 3; SSFS 35
Bekederemo, J. P. Clark
See Clark-Bekederemo, J. P.
Belasco, David 1853-1931 .... **TCLC 3**
See also CA 104; 168; DLB 7; MAL 5; RGAL 4
Belben, Rosalind 1941- .... **CLC 280**
See also CA 291
Belben, Rosalind Loveday
See Belben, Rosalind
Belcheva, Elisaveta Lyubomirova 1893-1991 .... **CLC 10**
See also CA 178; CDWLB 4; DLB 147; EWL 3
Beldone, Phil "Cheech"
See Ellison, Harlan
Beleno
See Azuela, Mariano
Belinski, Vissarion Grigoryevich 1811-1848 .... **NCLC 5**
See also DLB 198
Belitt, Ben 1911- .... **CLC 22**
See also CA 13-16R; CAAS 4; CANR 7, 77; CP 1, 2, 3, 4, 5, 6; DLB 5
Belknap, Jeremy 1744-1798 .... **LC 115**
See also DLB 30, 37
Bell, Gertrude (Margaret Lowthian) 1868-1926 .... **TCLC 67**
See also CA 167; CANR 110; DLB 174, 366
Bell, J. Freeman
See Zangwill, Israel
Bell, James Madison 1826-1902 ... **BLC 1:1; TCLC 43**
See also BW 1; CA 122; 124; DAM MULT; DLB 50
Bell, Madison Smartt 1957- .... **CLC 41, 102, 223**
See also AMWS 10; BPFB 1; CA 111, 183; CAAE 183; CANR 28, 54, 73, 134, 176, 223; CN 5, 6, 7; CSW; DLB 218, 278; MTCW 2; MTFW 2005
Bell, Marvin 1937- .... **CLC 8, 31; PC 79**
See also CA 21-24R; CAAS 14; CANR 59, 102, 206; CP 1, 2, 3, 4, 5, 6, 7; DAM POET; DLB 5; MAL 5; MTCW 1; PFS 25
Bell, Marvin Hartley
See Bell, Marvin
Bell, W. L. D.
See Mencken, H. L.
Bellamy, Atwood C.
See Mencken, H. L.
Bellamy, Edward 1850-1898 .... **NCLC 4, 86, 147**
See also DLB 12; NFS 15; RGAL 4; SFW 4
Belli, Gioconda 1949- .... **HLCS 1**
See also CA 152; CANR 143, 209; CLC 359; CWW 2; DLB 290; EWL 3; RGWL 3
Bellin, Edward J.
See Kuttner, Henry
Bello, Andres 1781-1865 .... **NCLC 131**
See also LAW
Belloc, Hilaire 1870-1953 .... **PC 24; TCLC 7, 18**
See also CA 106; 152; CLR 102; CWRI 5; DAM POET; DLB 19, 100, 141, 174; EWL 3; MTCW 2; MTFW 2005; SATA 112; WCH; YABC 1
Belloc, Joseph Hilaire Pierre Sebastien Rene Swanton
See Belloc, Hilaire
Belloc, Joseph Peter Rene Hilaire
See Belloc, Hilaire
Belloc, Joseph Pierre Hilaire
See Belloc, Hilaire
Belloc, M. A.
See Lowndes, Marie Adelaide (Belloc)
Belloc-Lowndes, Mrs.
See Lowndes, Marie Adelaide (Belloc)
Bellow, Saul 1915-2005 .... **CLC 1, 2, 3, 6, 8, 10, 13, 15, 25, 33, 34, 63, 79, 190, 200, 342; SSC 14, 101; WLC 1**
See also AITN 2; AMW; AMWC 2; AMWR 2; BEST 89:3; BPFB 1; CA 5-8R; 238; CABS 1; CANR 29, 53, 95, 132; CDALB 1941-1968; CN 1, 2, 3, 4, 5, 6, 7; DA; DA3; DAB; DAC; DAM MST, NOV, POP; DLB 2, 28, 299, 329; DLBD 3; DLBY 1982; EWL 3; MAL 5; MTCW 1, 2; MTFW 2005; NFS 4, 14, 26, 33; RGAL 4; RGHL; RGSF 2; SSFS 12, 22; TUS
Belser, Reimond Karel Maria de 1929- .... **CLC 14**
See also CA 152
Bely, Andrey
See Bugayev, Boris Nikolayevich
Belyi, Andrei
See Bugayev, Boris Nikolayevich
Bembo, Pietro 1470-1547 .... **LC 79**
See also RGWL 2, 3
Benary, Margot
See Benary-Isbert, Margot
Benary-Isbert, Margot 1889-1979 ... **CLC 12**
See also CA 5-8R; 89-92; CANR 4, 72; CLR 12; MAICYA 1, 2; SATA 2; SATA-Obit 21
Benavente, Jacinto 1866-1954 .... **DC 26; HLCS 1; TCLC 3**
See also CA 106; 131; CANR 81; DAM DRAM, MULT; DLB 329; EWL 3; GLL 2; HW 1, 2; MTCW 1, 2
Benavente y Martinez, Jacinto
See Benavente, Jacinto
Benchley, Peter 1940-2006 .... **CLC 4, 8**
See also AAYA 14; AITN 2; BPFB 1; CA 17-20R; 248; CANR 12, 35, 66, 115; CPW; DAM NOV, POP; HGG; MTCW 1, 2; MTFW 2005; SATA 3, 89, 164
Benchley, Peter Bradford
See Benchley, Peter
Benchley, Robert (Charles) 1889-1945 .... **TCLC 1, 55**
See also CA 105; 153; DLB 11; MAL 5; RGAL 4
Benda, Julien 1867-1956 .... **TCLC 60**
See also CA 120; 154; GFL 1789 to the Present
Benedetti, Mario 1920-2009 .... **CLC 299; SSC 135**
See also CA 152; 286; DAM MULT; DLB 113; EWL 3; HW 1, 2; LAW
Benedetti, Mario Orlando Hardy Hamlet Brenno
See Benedetti, Mario
Benedetti Farrugia, Mario
See Benedetti, Mario
Benedetti Farrugia, Mario Orlando Hardy Hamlet Brenno
See Benedetti, Mario
Benedict, Ruth 1887-1948 .... **TCLC 60**
See also CA 158; CANR 146; DLB 246
Benedict, Ruth Fulton
See Benedict, Ruth
Benedikt, Michael 1935- .... **CLC 4, 14**
See also CA 13-16R; CANR 7; CP 1, 2, 3, 4, 5, 6, 7; DLB 5
Benet, Juan 1927-1993 .... **CLC 28**
See also CA 143; EWL 3
Benford, Gregory 1941- .... **CLC 52**
See also BPFB 1; CA 69-72, 175, 268; CAAE 175, 268; CAAS 27; CANR 12, 24, 49, 95, 134; CN 7; CSW; DLBY 1982; MTFW 2005; SCFW 2; SFW 4
Benford, Gregory Albert
See Benford, Gregory
Bengtsson, Frans (Gunnar) 1894-1954 .... **TCLC 48**
See also CA 170; EWL 3
Benjamin, David
See Slavitt, David R.
Benjamin, Lois
See Gould, Lois
Benjamin, Walter 1892-1940 .... **TCLC 39**
See also CA 164; CANR 181; DLB 242; EW 11; EWL 3
Ben Jelloun, Tahar 1944- ...... **CLC 180, 311**
See also CA 135, 162; CANR 100, 166, 217; CWW 2; EWL 3; RGWL 3; WLIT 2
Benn, Gottfried 1886-1956 .... **PC 35; TCLC 3, 256**

See also CA 106; 153; DLB 56; EWL 3; RGWL 2, 3
Bennett, Alan 1934- .... **CLC 45, 77, 292**
See also BRWS 8; CA 103; CANR 35, 55, 106, 157, 197, 227; CBD; CD 5, 6; DAB; DAM MST; DLB 310; MTCW 1, 2; MTFW 2005
Bennett, (Enoch) Arnold
1867-1931 .... **TCLC 5, 20, 197**
See also BRW 6; CA 106; 155; CDBLB 1890-1914; DLB 10, 34, 98, 135; EWL 3; MTCW 2
Bennett, Elizabeth
See Mitchell, Margaret
Bennett, George Harold 1930- .... **CLC 5**
See also BW 1; CA 97-100; CAAS 13; CANR 87; DLB 33
Bennett, Gwendolyn B. 1902-1981 ... **HR 1:2**
See also BW 1; CA 125; DLB 51; WP
Bennett, Hal
See Bennett, George Harold
Bennett, Jay 1912- .... **CLC 35**
See also AAYA 10, 73; CA 69-72; CANR 11, 42, 79; JRDA; SAAS 4; SATA 41, 87; SATA-Brief 27; WYA; YAW
Bennett, Louise 1919-2006 .... **BLC 1:1; CLC 28**
See also BW 2, 3; CA 151; 252; CDWLB 3; CP 1, 2, 3, 4, 5, 6, 7; DAM MULT; DLB 117; EWL 3
Bennett, Louise Simone
See Bennett, Louise
Bennett-Coverley, Louise
See Bennett, Louise
Benoit de Sainte-Maure
fl. 12th cent. .... **CMLC 90**
Benson, A. C. 1862-1925 .... **TCLC 123**
See also DLB 98
Benson, E(dward) F(rederic)
1867-1940 .... **TCLC 27**
See also CA 114; 157; DLB 135, 153; HGG; SUFW 1
Benson, Jackson J. 1930- .... **CLC 34**
See also CA 25-28R; CANR 214; DLB 111
Benson, Sally 1900-1972 .... **CLC 17**
See also CA 19-20; 37-40R; CAP 1; SATA 1, 35; SATA-Obit 27
Benson, Stella 1892-1933 .... **TCLC 17**
See also CA 117; 154, 155; DLB 36, 162; FANT; TEA
Benet, Stephen Vincent 1898-1943 ... **PC 64; SSC 10, 86; TCLC 7**
See also AMWS 11; CA 104; 152; DA3; DAM POET; DLB 4, 48, 102, 249, 284; DLBY 1997; EWL 3; HGG; MAL 5; MTCW 2; MTFW 2005; RGAL 4; RGSF 2; SSFS 22, 31; SUFW; WP; YABC 1
Benet, William Rose 1886-1950 .... **TCLC 28**
See also CA 118; 152; DAM POET; DLB 45; RGAL 4
Bentham, Jeremy
1748-1832 .... **NCLC 38, 237**
See also DLB 107, 158, 252
Bentley, E(dmund) C(lerihew)
1875-1956 .... **TCLC 12**
See also CA 108; 232; DLB 70; MSW
Bentley, Eric 1916- .... **CLC 24**
See also CA 5-8R; CAD; CANR 6, 67; CBD; CD 5, 6; INT CANR-6
Bentley, Eric Russell
See Bentley, Eric
ben Uzair, Salem
See Horne, Richard Henry Hengist
Beolco, Angelo 1496-1542 .... **LC 139**
Beranger, Pierre Jean de
1780-1857 .... **NCLC 34; PC 112**
Berceo, Gonzalo de
c. 1190-c. 1260 .... **CMLC 151**
See also DLB 337
Berdyaev, Nicolas
See Berdyaev, Nikolai (Aleksandrovich)
Berdyaev, Nikolai (Aleksandrovich)
1874-1948 .... **TCLC 67**
See also CA 120; 157
Berdyayev, Nikolai (Aleksandrovich)
See Berdyaev, Nikolai (Aleksandrovich)
Berendt, John 1939- .... **CLC 86**
See also CA 146; CANR 75, 83, 151
Berendt, John Lawrence
See Berendt, John
Berengar of Tours
c. 1000-1088 .... **CMLC 124**
Beresford, J(ohn) D(avys)
1873-1947 .... **TCLC 81**
See also CA 112; 155; DLB 162, 178, 197; SFW 4; SUFW 1
Bergelson, David (Rafailovich)
1884-1952 .... **TCLC 81**
See also CA 220; DLB 333; EWL 3
Bergelson, Dovid
See Bergelson, David (Rafailovich)
Berger, Colonel
See Malraux, Andre
Berger, John 1926- .... **CLC 2, 19, 375**
See also BRWS 4; CA 81-84; CANR 51, 78, 117, 163, 200; CN 1, 2, 3, 4, 5, 6, 7; DLB 14, 207, 319, 326
Berger, John Peter
See Berger, John
Berger, Melvin H. 1927- .... **CLC 12**
See also CA 5-8R; CANR 4, 142; CLR 32; SAAS 2; SATA 5, 88, 158; SATA-Essay 124
Berger, Thomas 1924- .... **CLC 3, 5, 8, 11, 18, 38, 259**
See also BPFB 1; CA 1-4R; CANR 5, 28, 51, 128; CN 1, 2, 3, 4, 5, 6, 7; DAM NOV; DLB 2; DLBY 1980; EWL 3; FANT; INT CANR-28; MAL 5; MTCW 1, 2; MTFW 2005; RHW; TCLE 1:1; TCWW 1, 2
Bergman, Ernst Ingmar
See Bergman, Ingmar
Bergman, Ingmar
1918-2007 .... **CLC 16, 72, 210**
See also AAYA 61; CA 81-84; 262; CANR 33, 70; CWW 2; DLB 257; MTCW 2; MTFW 2005
Bergson, Henri(-Louis)
1859-1941 .... **TCLC 32**
See also CA 164; DLB 329; EW 8; EWL 3; GFL 1789 to the Present
Bergstein, Eleanor 1938- .... **CLC 4**
See also CA 53-56; CANR 5
Berkeley, George 1685-1753 .... **LC 65**
See also DLB 31, 101, 252
Berkoff, Steven 1937- .... **CLC 56**
See also CA 104; CANR 72; CBD; CD 5, 6
Berlin, Isaiah 1909-1997 .... **TCLC 105**
See also CA 85-88; 162
Bermant, Chaim (Icyk)
1929-1998 .... **CLC 40**
See also CA 57-60; CANR 6, 31, 57, 105; CN 2, 3, 4, 5, 6
Bern, Victoria
See Fisher, M. F. K.
Bernanos, (Paul Louis) Georges
1888-1948 .... **TCLC 3, 267**
See also CA 104; 130; CANR 94; DLB 72; EWL 3; GFL 1789 to the Present; RGWL 2, 3
Bernard, April 1956- .... **CLC 59**
See also CA 131; CANR 144, 230
Bernard, Mary Ann
See Soderbergh, Steven
Bernard of Clairvaux
1090-1153 .... **CMLC 71, 170**
See also DLB 208
Bernard Silvestris
fl. c. 1130-fl. c. 1160 .... **CMLC 87**
See also DLB 208
Bernardin de Saint-Pierre, Jacques-Henri
1737-1814 .... **NCLC 297**
See also DLB 313; GFL
Bernart de Ventadorn
c. 1130-c. 1190 .... **CMLC 98**
Berne, Victoria
See Fisher, M. F. K.
Bernhard, Thomas 1931-1989 .... **CLC 3, 32, 61; DC 14; TCLC 165**
See also CA 85-88; 127; CANR 32, 57; CDWLB 2; DLB 85, 124; EWL 3; MTCW 1; RGHL; RGWL 2, 3
Bernhardt, Sarah (Henriette Rosine)
1844-1923 .... **TCLC 75**
See also CA 157
Berni, Francesco c. 1497-1536 .... **LC 210**
Bernstein, Charles 1950- .. **CLC 142; PC 152**
See also CA 129; CAAS 24; CANR 90; CP 4, 5, 6, 7; DLB 169
Bernstein, Ingrid
See Kirsch, Sarah
Béroul fl. c. 12th cent. .... **CMLC 75, 148; PC 151**
Berriault, Gina 1926-1999 ...... **CLC 54, 109; SSC 30**
See also CA 116; 129; 185; CANR 66; DLB 130; SSFS 7,11
Berrigan, Daniel 1921- .... **CLC 4**
See also CA 33-36R, 187; CAAE 187; CAAS 1; CANR 11, 43, 78, 219; CP 1, 2, 3, 4, 5, 6, 7; DLB 5
Berrigan, Edmund Joseph Michael, Jr.
1934-1983 .... **CLC 37; PC 103**
See also CA 61-64; 110; CANR 14, 102; CP 1, 2, 3; DLB 5, 169; WP
Berrigan, Ted
See Berrigan, Edmund Joseph Michael, Jr.
Berry, Charles Edward Anderson
See Berry, Chuck
Berry, Chuck 1931- .... **CLC 17**
See also CA 115
Berry, Jonas
See Ashbery, John
Berry, Wendell 1934- .... **CLC 4, 6, 8, 27, 46, 279; PC 28**
See also AITN 1; AMWS 10; ANW; CA 73-76; CANR 50, 73, 101, 132, 174, 228; CP 1, 2, 3, 4, 5, 6, 7; CSW; DAM POET; DLB 5, 6, 234, 275, 342; MTCW 2; MTFW 2005; PFS 30; TCLE 1:1
Berry, Wendell Erdman
See Berry, Wendell
Berry, William
See Harwood, Gwen
Berryman, John 1914-1972 ..... **CLC 1, 2, 3, 4, 6, 8, 10, 13, 25, 62; PC 64**
See also AMW; CA 13-16; 33-36R; CABS 2; CANR 35; CAP 1; CDALB 1941-1968; CP 1; DAM POET; DLB 48; EWL 3; MAL 5; MTCW 1, 2; MTFW 2005; PAB; PFS 27; RGAL 4; WP
Berssenbrugge, Mei-mei 1947- .... **PC 115**
See also CA 104; DLB 312
Bertolucci, Bernardo 1940- ..... **CLC 16, 157**
See also CA 106; CANR 125
Berton, Pierre (Francis de Marigny)
1920-2004 .... **CLC 104**
See also CA 1-4R; 233; CANR 2, 56, 144; CPW; DLB 68; SATA 99; SATA-Obit 158
Bertrand, Aloysius 1807-1841 .... **NCLC 31**
See also DLB 217
Bertrand, Louis oAloysiusc
See Bertrand, Aloysius
Bertran de Born c. 1140-1215 .... **CMLC 5**
Berwick, Mary
See Adelaide Anne Procter

Author Index

Besant, Annie (Wood) 1847-1933 ... **TCLC 9**
See also CA 105; 185
Bessie, Alvah 1904-1985 .... **CLC 23**
See also CA 5-8R; 116; CANR 2, 80; DLB 26
Bestuzhev, Aleksandr Aleksandrovich 1797-1837 .... **NCLC 131**
See also DLB 198
Bethlen, T.D.
See Silverberg, Robert
Beti, Mongo
1932-2001 .... **BLC 1:1; CLC 27, 380**
See also AFW; BW 1, 3; CA 114; 124; CANR 81; DA3; DAM MULT; DLB 360; EWL 3; MTCW 1, 2
Betjeman, John 1906-1984 .... **CLC 2, 6, 10, 34, 43; PC 75**
See also BRW 7; CA 9-12R; 112; CANR 33, 56; CDBLB 1945-1960; CP 1, 2, 3; DA3; DAB; DAM MST, POET; DLB 20; DLBY 1984; EWL 3; MTCW 1, 2
Bettelheim, Bruno 1903-1990 .... **CLC 79; TCLC 143**
See also CA 81-84; 131; CANR 23, 61; DA3; MTCW 1, 2; RGHL
Betti, Ugo 1892-1953 .... **TCLC 5**
See also CA 104; 155; EWL 3; RGWL 2, 3
Betts, Doris 1932-2012 .. **CLC 3, 6, 28, 275; SSC 45**
See also CA 13-16R; CANR 9, 66, 77; CN 6, 7; CSW; DLB 218; DLBY 1982; INT CANR-9; RGAL 4
Betts, Doris Waugh
See Betts, Doris
Bevan, Alistair
See Roberts, Keith (John Kingston)
Bey, Pilaff
See Douglas, (George) Norman
Beyala, Calixthe 1961- ... **BLC 2:1; CLC 329**
See also EWL 3
Beynon, John
See Harris, John (Wyndham Parkes Lucas) Beynon
Bhabha, Homi K. 1949- .... **CLC 285**
Bohme, Jakob 1575-1624 .... **LC 178**
See also DLB 164
Bi Shang-guan
See Shen Congwen
Bialik, Chaim Nachman 1873-1934 ... **TCLC 25, 201**
See also CA 170; EWL 3; WLIT 6
Bialik, Hayyim Nahman
See Bialik, Chaim Nachman
Bickerstaff, Isaac
See Swift, Jonathan
Bidart, Frank 1939- .... **CLC 33**
See also AMWS 15; CA 140; CANR 106, 215; CP 5, 6, 7; PFS 26
Bienek, Horst 1930- .... **CLC 7, 11**
See also CA 73-76; DLB 75
Bierce, Ambrose 1842-1914(?) .... **SSC 9, 72, 124, 169; TCLC 1, 7, 44; WLC 1**
See also AAYA 55; AMW; BYA 11; CA 104; 139; CANR 78; CDALB 1865-1917; DA; DA3; DAC; DAM MST; DLB 11, 12, 23, 71, 74, 186; EWL 3; EXPS; HGG; LAIT 2; MAL 5; RGAL 4; RGSF 2; SSFS 9, 27; SUFW 1
Bierce, Ambrose Gwinett
See Bierce, Ambrose
Biggers, Earl Derr 1884-1933 .... **TCLC 65**
See also CA 108; 153; DLB 306
Bilek, Anton F. 1919-
See Rankin, Ian
See also CA 304
Billiken, Bud
See Motley, Willard (Francis)
Billings, Josh
See Shaw, Henry Wheeler
Billington, Lady Rachel Mary
See Billington, Rachel
Billington, Rachel 1942- .... **CLC 43**
See also AITN 2; CA 33-36R; CANR 44, 196, 242; CN 4, 5, 6, 7
Binchy, Maeve 1940-2012 .... **CLC 153**
See also BEST 90:1; BPFB 1; CA 127; 134; CANR 50, 96, 134, 208; CN 5, 6, 7; CPW; DA3; DAM POP; DLB 319; INT CA-134; MTCW 2; MTFW 2005; RHW
Binyon, T(imothy) J(ohn)
1936-2004 .... **CLC 34**
See also CA 111; 232; CANR 28, 140
Bion 335B.C.-245B.C. .... **CMLC 39**
Bioy Casares, Adolfo 1914-1999 ..... **CLC 4, 8, 13, 88; HLC 1; SSC 17, 102**
See also CA 29-32R; 177; CANR 19, 43, 66; CWW 2; DAM MULT; DLB 113; EWL 3; HW 1, 2; LAW; MTCW 1, 2; MTFW 2005; RGSF 2
Birch, Allison .... **CLC 65**
Bird, Cordwainer
See Ellison, Harlan
Bird, Robert Montgomery
1806-1854 .... **NCLC 1, 197**
See also DLB 202; RGAL 4
Birdwell, Cleo
See DeLillo, Don
Birkerts, Sven 1951- .... **CLC 116**
See also CA 128; 133, 176; CAAE 176; CAAS 29; CANR 151, 243; INT CA-133
Birney, (Alfred) Earle
1904-1995 .... **CLC 1, 4, 6, 11; PC 52**
See also CA 1-4R; CANR 5, 20; CN 1, 2, 3, 4; CP 1, 2, 3, 4, 5, 6; DAC; DAM MST, POET; DLB 88; MTCW 1; PFS 8; RGEL 2
Biruni, al 973-1048(?) .... **CMLC 28**
Bishop, Elizabeth 1911-1979 .... **CLC 1, 4, 9, 13, 15, 32; PC 3, 34, 150; SSC 151; TCLC 121**
See also AMWR 2; AMWS 1; CA 5-8R; 89-92; CABS 2; CANR 26, 61, 108; CDALB 1968-1988; CP 1, 2, 3; DA; DA3; DAC; DAM MST, POET; DLB 5, 169; EWL 3; GLL 2; MAL 5; MBL; MTCW 1, 2; PAB; PFS 6, 12, 27, 31, 44; RGAL 4; SATA-Obit 24; TUS; WP
Bishop, George Archibald
See Crowley, Edward Alexander
Bishop, John 1935- .... **CLC 10**
See also CA 105
Bishop, John Peale 1892-1944 .... **TCLC 103**
See also CA 107; 155; DLB 4, 9, 45; MAL 5; RGAL 4
Bissett, Bill 1939- .... **CLC 18; PC 14**
See also CA 69-72; CAAS 19; CANR 15; CCA 1; CP 1, 2, 3, 4, 5, 6, 7; DLB 53; MTCW 1
Bissoondath, Neil 1955- .... **CLC 120, 285**
See also CA 136; CANR 123, 165; CN 6, 7; DAC
Bissoondath, Neil Devindra
See Bissoondath, Neil
Bitov, Andrei (Georgievich) 1937- ... **CLC 57, 361**
See also CA 142; DLB 302
Biyidi, Alexandre
See Beti, Mongo
Bjarme, Brynjolf
See Ibsen, Henrik
Bjoernson, Bjoernstjerne (Martinius)
1832-1910 .... **TCLC 7, 37**
See also CA 104
Blab, W. Epaminondas Adrastus
See Twain, Mark
Black, Benjamin
See Banville, John
Black, Robert
See Holdstock, Robert
Blackburn, Paul 1926-1971 .... **CLC 9, 43**
See also BG 1:2; CA 81-84; 33-36R; CANR 34; CP 1; DLB 16; DLBY 1981
Black Elk 1863-1950 .... **NNAL; TCLC 33**
See also CA 144; DAM MULT; MTCW 2; MTFW 2005; WP
Black Hawk 1767-1838 .... **NNAL**
Black Hobart
See Sanders, Ed
Blacklin, Malcolm
See Chambers, Aidan
Blackmore, R(ichard) D(oddridge)
1825-1900 .... **TCLC 27**
See also CA 120; DLB 18; RGEL 2
Blackmur, R(ichard) P(almer)
1904-1965 .... **CLC 2, 24**
See also AMWS 2; CA 11-12; 25-28R; CANR 71; CAP 1; DLB 63; EWL 3; MAL 5
Black Tarantula
See Acker, Kathy
Blackwood, Algernon
1869-1951 .... **SSC 107, 220; TCLC 5**
See also AAYA 78; CA 105; 150; CANR 169; DLB 153, 156, 178; HGG; SUFW 1
Blackwood, Algernon Henry
See Blackwood, Algernon
Blackwood, Caroline (Maureen)
1931-1996 .... **CLC 6, 9, 100**
See also BRWS 9; CA 85-88; 151; CANR 32, 61, 65; CN 3, 4, 5, 6; DLB 14, 207; HGG; MTCW 1
Blade, Alexander
See Hamilton, Edmond; Silverberg, Robert
Blaga, Lucian 1895-1961 .... **CLC 75**
See also CA 157; DLB 220; EWL 3
Blair, Eric
See Orwell, George
Blair, Eric Arthur
See Orwell, George
Blair, Hugh 1718-1800 .... **NCLC 75**
See also DLB 356
Blais, Marie-Claire 1939- .... **CLC 2, 4, 6, 13, 22**
See also CA 21-24R; CAAS 4; CANR 38, 75, 93; CWW 2; DAC; DAM MST; DLB 53; EWL 3; FW; MTCW 1, 2; MTFW 2005; TWA
Blaise, Clark 1940- .... **CLC 29, 261**
See also AITN 2; CA 53-56, 231; CAAE 231; CAAS 3; CANR 5, 66, 106; CN 4, 5, 6, 7; DLB 53; RGSF 2
Blake, Fairley
See De Voto, Bernard (Augustine)
Blake, Nicholas
See Day Lewis, C.
Blake, Sterling
See Benford, Gregory
Blake, William 1757-1827 .... **NCLC 13, 37, 57, 127, 173, 190, 201; PC 12, 63, 157, 171; WLC 1**
See also AAYA 47; BRW 3; BRWR 1; CDBLB 1789-1832; CLR 52; DA; DA3; DAB; DAC; DAM MST, POET; DLB 93, 154, 163; EXPP; LATS 1:1; LMFS 1; MAICYA 1, 2; PAB; PFS 2, 12, 24, 34, 40; SATA 30; TEA; WCH; WLIT 3; WP
Blanchot, Maurice 1907-2003 ... **CLC 135, 381**
See also CA 117; 144; 213; CANR 138; DLB 72, 296; EWL 3
Blanco White, Joseph 1775-1841 .. **NCLC 305**
Blasco Ibanez, Vicente
1867-1928 .... **TCLC 12**
See also BPFB 1; CA 110; 131; CANR 81; DA3; DAM NOV; DLB 322; EW 8; EWL 3; HW 1, 2; MTCW 1
Blatty, William Peter 1928- .... **CLC 2**
See also CA 5-8R; CANR 9, 124, 226; DAM POP; HGG

Bleeck, Oliver
See Thomas, Ross (Elmore)
Bleecker, Ann Eliza 1752-1783 .... **LC 161**
See also DLB 200
Blessing, Lee 1949- .... **CLC 54**
See also CA 236; CAD; CD 5, 6; DFS 23, 26
Blessing, Lee Knowlton
See Blessing, Lee
Blessington, Marguerite, Countess of 1789-1849 .... **NCLC 297**
See also DLB 166
Blight, Rose
See Greer, Germaine
Blind, Mathilde 1841-1896 .... **NCLC 202**
See also DLB 199
Blish, James 1921-1975 .... **CLC 14**
See also BPFB 1; CA 1-4R; 57-60; CANR 3; CN 2; DLB 8; MTCW 1; SATA 66; SCFW 1, 2; SFW 4
Blish, James Benjamin
See Blish, James
Bliss, Frederick
See Card, Orson Scott
Bliss, Gillian
See Paton Walsh, Jill
Bliss, Reginald
See Wells, H. G.
Blixen, Karen 1885-1962 .... **CLC 10, 29, 95; SSC 7, 75, 191; TCLC 255**
See also CA 25-28; CANR 22, 50; CAP 2; DA3; DLB 214; EW 10; EWL 3; EXPS; FW; GL 2; HGG; LAIT 3; LMFS 1; MTCW 1; NCFS 2; NFS 9; RGSF 2; RGWL 2, 3; SATA 44; SSFS 3, 6, 13; WLIT 2
Blixen, Karen Christentze Dinesen
See Blixen, Karen
Boll, Heinrich
See Boell, Heinrich
Bloch, Robert (Albert) 1917-1994 ... **CLC 33**
See also AAYA 29; CA 5-8R, 179; 146; CAAE 179; CAAS 20; CANR 5, 78; DA3; DLB 44; HGG; INT CANR-5; MTCW 2; SATA 12; SATA-Obit 82; SFW 4; SUFW 1, 2
Blok, Alexander (Alexandrovich) 1880-1921 .... **PC 21; TCLC 5**
See also CA 104; 183; DLB 295; EW 9; EWL 3; LMFS 2; RGWL 2, 3
Blom, Jan
See Breytenbach, Breyten
Bloom, Harold 1930- .... **CLC 24, 103, 221**
See also CA 13-16R; CANR 39, 75, 92, 133, 181, 238; DLB 67; EWL 3; MTCW 2; MTFW 2005; RGAL 4
Bloomfield, Aurelius
See Bourne, Randolph S(illiman)
Bloomfield, Robert 1766-1823 .... **NCLC 145; PC 160**
See also DLB 93
Blount, Roy, Jr. 1941- .... **CLC 38**
See also CA 53-56; CANR 10, 28, 61, 125, 176; CSW; INT CANR-28; MTCW 1, 2; MTFW 2005
Blount, Roy Alton
See Blount, Roy, Jr.
Blowsnake, Sam 1875-(?) .... **NNAL**
Bloy, Leon 1846-1917 .... **TCLC 22**
See also CA 121; 183; DLB 123; GFL 1789 to the Present
Blue Cloud, Peter (Aroniawenrate) 1933- .... **NNAL**
See also CA 117; CANR 40; DAM MULT; DLB 342
Bluggage, Oranthy
See Alcott, Louisa May
Blume, Judy 1938- .... **CLC 12, 30, 325**
See also AAYA 3, 26; BYA 1, 8, 12; CA 29-32R; CANR 13, 37, 66, 124, 186; CLR 2, 15, 69, 176; CPW; DA3; DAM NOV, POP; DLB 52; JRDA; MAICYA 1, 2; MAICYAS 1; MTCW 1, 2; MTFW 2005; NFS 24; SATA 2, 31, 79, 142, 195; WYA; YAW
Blume, Judy Sussman
See Blume, Judy
Blunden, Edmund (Charles) 1896-1974 .... **CLC 2, 56; PC 66**
See also BRW 6; BRWS 11; CA 17-18; 45-48; CANR 54; CAP 2; CP 1, 2; DLB 20, 100, 155; MTCW 1; PAB
Bly, Robert 1926- .... **CLC 1, 2, 5, 10, 15, 38, 128, 325; PC 39**
See also AMWS 4; CA 5-8R; CANR 41, 73, 125, 235; CP 1, 2, 3, 4, 5, 6, 7; DA3; DAM POET; DLB 5, 342; EWL 3; MAL 5; MTCW 1, 2; MTFW 2005; PFS 6, 17; RGAL 4
Bly, Robert Elwood
See Bly, Robert
Boas, Franz 1858-1942 .... **TCLC 56**
See also CA 115; 181
Bobette
See Simenon, Georges
Bobrowski, Johannes 1917-1965 ... **TCLC 319**
See also CA 77-80; CANR 33; DLB 75; EWL 3; RGWL 2, 3
Boccaccio, Giovanni 1313-1375 ... **CMLC 13, 57, 140; PC 162; SSC 10, 87, 167**
See also EW 2; RGSF 2; RGWL 2, 3; SSFS 28; TWA; WLIT 7
Bochco, Steven 1943- .... **CLC 35**
See also AAYA 11, 71; CA 124; 138
Bock, Charles 1970- .... **CLC 299**
See also CA 274
Bode, Sigmund
See O'Doherty, Brian
Bodel, Jean 1167(?)-1210 ..... **CMLC 28, 162**
Bodenheim, Maxwell 1892-1954 ... **TCLC 44**
See also CA 110; 187; DLB 9, 45; MAL 5; RGAL 4
Bodenheimer, Maxwell
See Bodenheim, Maxwell
Bodin, Jean 1529/30?-1596 .... **LC 242**
See also GFL
Bodker, Cecil
See Bodker, Cecil
Boell, Heinrich 1917-1985 .... **CLC 2, 3, 6, 9, 11, 15, 27, 32, 72; SSC 23; TCLC 185; WLC 1**
See also BPFB 1; CA 21-24R; 116; CANR 24; CDWLB 2; DA; DA3; DAB; DAC; DAM MST, NOV; DLB 69, 329; DLBY 1985; EW 13; EWL 3; MTCW 1, 2; MTFW 2005; RGHL; RGSF 2; RGWL 2, 3; SSFS 20; TWA
Boell, Heinrich Theodor
See Boell, Heinrich
Boerne, Alfred
See Doeblin, Alfred
Boethius c. 480-c. 524 .... **CMLC 15, 136**
See also DLB 115; RGWL 2, 3; WLIT 8
Boff, Leonardo (Genezio Darci) 1938- .... **CLC 70; HLC 1**
See also CA 150; DAM MULT; HW 2
Bogan, Louise 1897-1970 .... **CLC 4, 39, 46, 93; PC 12**
See also AMWS 3; CA 73-76; 25-28R; CANR 33, 82; CP 1; DAM POET; DLB 45, 169; EWL 3; MAL 5; MBL; MTCW 1, 2; PFS 21, 39; RGAL 4
Bogarde, Dirk 1921-1999 .... **CLC 14**
See also CA 77-80; 179; DLB 14
Bogat, Shatan
See Kacew, Romain
Bogomolny, Robert L. 1938- .... **SSC 41; TCLC 11**
See also CA 121, 164; DLB 182; EWL 3; MJW; RGSF 2; RGWL 2, 3; TWA
Bogomolny, Robert Lee
See Bogomolny, Robert L.
Bogosian, Eric 1953- .... **CLC 45, 141**
See also CA 138; CAD; CANR 102, 148, 217; CD 5, 6; DLB 341
Bograd, Larry 1953- .... **CLC 35**
See also CA 93-96; CANR 57; SAAS 21; SATA 33, 89; WYA
Boiardo, Matteo Maria 1441-1494 **LC 6, 168**
Boileau-Despreaux, Nicolas 1636-1711 .... **LC 3, 164**
See also DLB 268; EW 3; GFL Beginnings to 1789; RGWL 2, 3
Boissard, Maurice
See Leautaud, Paul
Bojer, Johan 1872-1959 .... **TCLC 64**
See also CA 189; EWL 3
Bok, Edward W(illiam) 1863-1930 .... **TCLC 101**
See also CA 217; DLB 91; DLBD 16
Boker, George Henry 1823-1890 ... **NCLC 125**
See also RGAL 4
Boland, Eavan 1944- .... **CLC 40, 67, 113; PC 58**
See also BRWS 5; CA 143, 207; CAAE 207; CANR 61, 180; CP 1, 6, 7; CWP; DAM POET; DLB 40; FW; MTCW 2; MTFW 2005; PFS 12, 22, 31, 39
Boland, Eavan Aisling
See Boland, Eavan
Bolano, Roberto 1953-2003 .... **CLC 294**
See also CA 229; CANR 175
Bolingbroke, Viscount
See St. John, Henry
Bolt, Lee
See Faust, Frederick
Bolt, Robert (Oxton) 1924-1995 .... **CLC 14; TCLC 175**
See also CA 17-20R; 147; CANR 35, 67; CBD; DAM DRAM; DFS 2; DLB 13, 233; EWL 3; LAIT 1; MTCW 1
Bolivar, Simon 1783-1830 .... **NCLC 266**
Bombal, Maria Luisa 1910-1980 ... **HLCS 1; SSC 37; TCLC 296**
See also CA 127; CANR 72; EWL 3; HW 1; LAW; RGSF 2; SSFS 36
Bombet, Louis-Alexandre-Cesar
See Stendhal
Bomkauf
See Kaufman, Bob (Garnell)
Bonaventura .... **NCLC 35, 252**
See also DLB 90
Bonaventure 1217(?)-1274 .... **CMLC 79**
See also DLB 115; LMFS 1
Bond, Edward 1934- ...... **CLC 4, 6, 13, 23; DC 45**
See also AAYA 50; BRWS 1; CA 25-28R; CANR 38, 67, 106; CBD; CD 5, 6; DAM DRAM; DFS 3, 8; DLB 13, 310; EWL 3; MTCW 1
Bonham, Frank 1914-1989 .... **CLC 12**
See also AAYA 1, 70; BYA 1, 3; CA 9-12R; CANR 4, 36; JRDA; MAICYA 1, 2; SAAS 3; SATA 1, 49; SATA-Obit 62; TCWW 1, 2; YAW
Bonnefoy, Yves 1923- .... **CLC 9, 15, 58; PC 58**
See also CA 85-88; CANR 33, 75, 97, 136; CWW 2; DAM MST, POET; DLB 258; EWL 3; GFL 1789 to the Present; MTCW 1, 2; MTFW 2005
Bonner, Marita
See Occomy, Marita (Odette) Bonner
Bonnin, Gertrude 1876-1938 .... **NNAL**
See also CA 150; DAM MULT; DLB 175
Bontemps, Arna 1902-1973 .... **BLC 1:1; CLC 1, 18; HR 1:2; TCLC 292**
See also BW 1; CA 1-4R; 41-44R; CANR 4, 35; CLR 6; CP 1; CWRI 5; DA3; DAM

Author Index

MULT, NOV, POET; DLB 48, 51; JRDA; MAICYA 1, 2; MAL 5; MTCW 1, 2; PFS 32; SATA 2, 44; SATA-Obit 24; WCH; WP

Bontemps, Arnaud Wendell
See Bontemps, Arna

Boot, William
See Stoppard, Tom

Booth, Irwin
See Hoch, Edward D.

Booth, Martin 1944-2004 .... **CLC 13**
See also CA 93-96, 188; 223; CAAE 188; CAAS 2; CANR 92; CP 1, 2, 3, 4

Booth, Philip 1925-2007 .... **CLC 23**
See also CA 5-8R; 262; CANR 5, 88; CP 1, 2, 3, 4, 5, 6, 7; DLBY 1982

Booth, Philip Edmund
See Booth, Philip

Booth, Wayne C. 1921-2005 .... **CLC 24**
See also CA 1-4R; 244; CAAS 5; CANR 3, 43, 117; DLB 67

Booth, Wayne Clayson
See Booth, Wayne C.

Borchert, Wolfgang 1921-1947 .... **DC 42; TCLC 5**
See also CA 104; 188; DLB 69, 124; EWL 3

Borel, Petrus 1809-1859 .... **NCLC 41**
See also DLB 119; GFL 1789 to the Present

Borges, Jorge Luis 1899-1986 ..... **CLC 1, 2, 3, 4, 6, 8, 9, 10, 13, 19, 44, 48, 83; HLC 1; PC 22, 32; SSC 4, 41, 100, 159, 170, 183, 187, 191, 215; TCLC 109, 320; WLC 1**
See also AAYA 26; BPFB 1; CA 21-24R; CANR 19, 33, 75, 105, 133; CDWLB 3; DA; DA3; DAB; DAC; DAM MST, MULT; DLB 113, 283; DLBY 1986; DNFS 1, 2; EWL 3; HW 1, 2; LAW; LMFS 2; MSW; MTCW 1, 2; MTFW 2005; PFS 27; RGHL; RGSF 2; RGWL 2, 3; SFW 4; SSFS 17; TWA; WLIT 1

Borowski, Tadeusz 1922-1951 .... **SSC 48; TCLC 9**
See also CA 106; 154; CDWLB 4; DLB 215; EWL 3; RGHL; RGSF 2; RGWL 3; SSFS 13

Borrow, George (Henry) 1803-1881 .. **NCLC 9**
See also BRWS 12; DLB 21, 55, 166

Bosch (Gavino), Juan 1909-2001 .... **HLCS 1**
See also CA 151; 204; DAM MST, MULT; DLB 145; HW 1, 2

Bosman, Herman Charles
1905-1951 .... **TCLC 49**
See also CA 160; DLB 225; RGSF 2

Bosschere, Jean de 1878(?)-1953 ... **TCLC 19**
See also CA 115; 186

Boswell, James 1740-1795 .... **LC 4, 50, 182; WLC 1**
See also BRW 3; CDBLB 1660-1789; DA; DAB; DAC; DAM MST; DLB 104, 142; TEA; WLIT 3

Boto, Eza
See Beti, Mongo

Bottomley, Gordon 1874-1948 .... **TCLC 107**
See also CA 120; 192; DLB 10

Bottoms, David 1949- .... **CLC 53; PC 158**
See also CA 105; CANR 22; CSW; DLB 120; DLBY 1983

Boucicault, Dion 1820-1890 ... **NCLC 41, 306**
See also DLB 344

Boucolon, Maryse
See Conde, Maryse

Boullosa, Carmen 1954- .... **CLC 350**
See also CA 190; CANR 159

Bourcicault, Dion
See Boucicault, Dion

Bourdieu, Pierre 1930-2002 ... **CLC 198, 296**
See also CA 130; 204

Bourget, Paul (Charles Joseph)
1852-1935 .... **TCLC 12**
See also CA 107; 196; DLB 123; GFL 1789 to the Present

Bourjaily, Vance 1922-2010 .... **CLC 8, 62**
See also CA 1-4R; CAAS 1; CANR 2, 72; CN 1, 2, 3, 4, 5, 6, 7; DLB 2, 143; MAL 5

Bourjaily, Vance Nye
See Bourjaily, Vance

Bourne, Randolph S(illiman)
1886-1918 .... **TCLC 16**
See also AMW; CA 117; 155; DLB 63; MAL 5

Boursiquot, Dionysius
See Boucicault, Dion

Bova, Ben 1932- .... **CLC 45**
See also AAYA 16; CA 5-8R; CAAS 18; CANR 11, 56, 94, 111, 157, 219; CLR 3, 96; DLBY 1981; INT CANR-11; MAICYA 1, 2; MTCW 1; SATA 6, 68, 133; SFW 4

Bova, Benjamin William
See Bova, Ben

Bowen, Elizabeth 1899-1973 .... **CLC 1, 3, 6, 11, 15, 22, 118; SSC 3, 28, 66, 193; TCLC 148**
See also BRWS 2; CA 17-18; 41-44R; CANR 35, 105; CAP 2; CDBLB 1945-1960; CN 1; DA3; DAM NOV; DLB 15, 162; EWL 3; EXPS; FW; HGG; MTCW 1, 2; MTFW 2005; NFS 13; RGSF 2; SSFS 5, 22; SUFW 1; TEA; WLIT 4

Bowen, Elizabeth Dorothea Cole
See Bowen, Elizabeth

Bowering, George 1935- .... **CLC 15, 47**
See also CA 21-24R; CAAS 16; CANR 10; CN 7; CP 1, 2, 3, 4, 5, 6, 7; DLB 53

Bowering, Marilyn R(uthe) 1949- .. **CLC 32**
See also CA 101; CANR 49; CP 4, 5, 6, 7; CWP; DLB 334

Bowers, Edgar 1924-2000 .... **CLC 9**
See also CA 5-8R; 188; CANR 24; CP 1, 2, 3, 4, 5, 6, 7; CSW; DLB 5

Bowers, Mrs. J. Milton
See Bierce, Ambrose

Bowie, David 1947- .... **CLC 17**
See also CA 103; CANR 104

Bowles, Jane (Sydney)
1917-1973 .... **CLC 3, 68; TCLC 275**
See also CA 19-20; 41-44R; CAP 2; CN 1; EWL 3; MAL 5

Bowles, Jane Auer
See Bowles, Jane (Sydney)

Bowles, Paul 1910-1999 .... **CLC 1, 2, 19, 53; SSC 3, 98, 214; TCLC 209**
See also AMWS 4; CA 1-4R; 186; CAAS 1; CANR 1, 19, 50, 75; CN 1, 2, 3, 4, 5, 6; DA3; DLB 5, 6, 218; EWL 3; MAL 5; MTCW 1, 2; MTFW 2005; RGAL 4; SSFS 17

Bowles, William Lisle 1762-1850 .. **NCLC 103**
See also DLB 93

Box, Edgar
See Vidal, Gore

Boyd, James 1888-1944 .... **TCLC 115**
See also CA 186; DLB 9; DLBD 16; RGAL 4; RHW

Boyd, Nancy
See Millay, Edna St. Vincent

Boyd, Thomas (Alexander)
1898-1935 .... **TCLC 111**
See also CA 111; 183; DLB 9; DLBD 16, 316

Boyd, William 1952- .... **CLC 28, 53, 70**
See also BRWS 16; CA 114; 120; CANR 51, 71, 131, 174; CN 4, 5, 6, 7; DLB 231

Boyesen, Hjalmar Hjorth
1848-1895 .... **NCLC 135**
See also DLB 12, 71; DLBD 13; RGAL 4

Boyle, Kay 1902-1992 ...... **CLC 1, 5, 19, 58, 121; SSC 5, 102**
See also CA 13-16R; 140; CAAS 1; CANR 29, 61, 110; CN 1, 2, 3, 4, 5; CP 1, 2, 3, 4, 5; DLB 4, 9, 48, 86; DLBY 1993; EWL 3; MAL 5; MTCW 1, 2; MTFW 2005; RGAL 4; RGSF 2; SSFS 10, 13, 14

Boyle, Mark
See Kienzle, William X.

Boyle, Patrick 1905-1982 .... **CLC 19**
See also CA 127

Boyle, Roger 1621-1679 .... **LC 198**
See also DLB 80; RGEL 2

Boyle, T.C. 1948- .... **CLC 36, 55, 90, 284; SSC 16, 127**
See also AAYA 47; AMWS 8, 20; BEST 90:4; BPFB 1; CA 120; CANR 44, 76, 89, 132, 224; CN 6, 7; CPW; DA3; DAM POP; DLB 218, 278; DLBY 1986; EWL 3; MAL 5; MTCW 2; MTFW 2005; NFS 41; SSFS 13, 19, 34

Boyle, T.Coraghessan
See Boyle, T.C.

Boyle, Thomas Coraghessan
See Boyle, T.C.

Boz
See Dickens, Charles

bpNichol
See Nichol, B(arrie) P(hillip)

Brackenridge, Hugh Henry
1748-1816 .... **NCLC 7, 227**
See also DLB 11, 37; RGAL 4

Bradbury, Edward P.
See Moorcock, Michael

Bradbury, Malcolm 1932-2000 ... **CLC 32, 61**
See also BRWS 17; CA 1-4R; CANR 1, 33, 91, 98, 137; CN 1, 2, 3, 4, 5, 6, 7; CP 1; DA3; DAM NOV; DLB 14, 207; EWL 3; MTCW 1, 2; MTFW 2005

Bradbury, Ray 1920-2012 ... **CLC 1, 3, 10, 15, 42, 98, 235, 333; SSC 29, 53, 157; WLC 1**
See also AAYA 15, 84; AITN 1, 2; AMWS 4; BPFB 1; BYA 4, 5, 11; CA 1-4R; CANR 2, 30, 75, 125, 186; CDALB 1968-1988; CLR 174; CN 1, 2, 3, 4, 5, 6, 7; CPW; DA; DA3; DAB; DAC; DAM MST, NOV, POP; DLB 2, 8; EXPN; EXPS; HGG; LAIT 3, 5; LATS 1:2; LMFS 2; MAL 5; MTCW 1, 2; MTFW 2005; NFS 1, 22, 29, 42; RGAL 4; RGSF 2; SATA 11, 64, 123; SCFW 1, 2; SFW 4; SSFS 1, 20, 28, 37; SUFW 1, 2; TUS; YAW

Bradbury, Ray Douglas
See Bradbury, Ray

Braddon, Mary Elizabeth
1837-1915 .... **TCLC 111**
See also BRWS 8; CA 108; 179; CMW 4; DLB 18, 70, 156; HGG

Bradfield, Scott 1955- .... **SSC 65**
See also CA 147; CANR 90; HGG; SUFW 2

Bradfield, Scott Michael
See Bradfield, Scott

Bradford, Gamaliel 1863-1932 ..... **TCLC 36**
See also CA 160; DLB 17

Bradford, William 1590-1657 .... **LC 64**
See also DLB 24, 30; RGAL 4

Bradley, David, Jr. 1950- .... **BLC 1:1; CLC 23, 118**
See also BW 1, 3; CA 104; CANR 26, 81; CN 4, 5, 6, 7; DAM MULT; DLB 33

Bradley, David Henry, Jr.
See Bradley, David, Jr.

Bradley, John Ed 1958- .... **CLC 55**
See also CA 139; CANR 99; CN 6, 7; CSW

Bradley, John Edmund, Jr.
See Bradley, John Ed

Bradley, Marion Zimmer
1930-1999 .... **CLC 30**
See also AAYA 40; BPFB 1; CA 57-60; 185; CAAS 10; CANR 7, 31, 51, 75, 107; CLR 158; CPW; DA3; DAM POP; DLB 8; FANT; FW; GLL 1; MTCW 1, 2; MTFW 2005; NFS 40; SATA 90, 139; SATA-Obit 116; SFW 4; SUFW 2; YAW

Bradshaw, John 1933- .... **CLC 70**
See also CA 138; CANR 61, 216

Bradshaw, John Elliot
See Bradshaw, John

Bradstreet, Anne 1612(?)-1672 .... **LC 4, 30, 130; PC 10, 139, 155**
See also AMWS 1; CDALB 1640-1865; DA; DA3; DAC; DAM MST, POET; DLB 24; EXPP; FW; PFS 6, 33, 42; RGAL 4; TUS; WP
Brady, Joan 1939- .... **CLC 86**
See also CA 141
Bragg, Melvyn 1939- .... **CLC 10**
See also BEST 89:3; CA 57-60; CANR 10, 48, 89, 158; CN 1, 2, 3, 4, 5, 6, 7; DLB 14, 271; RHW
Bragg, Rick 1959- .... **CLC 296**
See also CA 165; CANR 112, 137, 194; MTFW 2005
Bragg, Ricky Edward
See Bragg, Rick
Brahe, Tycho 1546-1601 .... **LC 45**
See also DLB 300
Braine, John (Gerard)
1922-1986 .... **CLC 1, 3, 41**
See also CA 1-4R; 120; CANR 1, 33; CDBLB 1945-1960; CN 1, 2, 3, 4; DLB 15; DLBY 1986; EWL 3; MTCW 1
Braithwaite, William Stanley (Beaumont)
1878-1962 .... **BLC 1:1; HR 1:2; PC 52**
See also BW 1; CA 125; DAM MULT; DLB 50, 54; MAL 5
Bramah, Ernest 1868-1942 .... **TCLC 72**
See also CA 156; CMW 4; DLB 70; FANT
Brammer, Billy Lee
See Brammer, William
Brammer, William 1929-1978 .... **CLC 31**
See also CA 235; 77-80
Brancati, Vitaliano 1907-1954 ...... **TCLC 12**
See also CA 109; DLB 264; EWL 3
Brancato, Robin F. 1936- .... **CLC 35**
See also AAYA 9, 68; BYA 6; CA 69-72; CANR 11, 45; CLR 32; JRDA; MAICYA 2; MAICYAS 1; SAAS 9; SATA 97; WYA; YAW
Brancato, Robin Fidler
See Brancato, Robin F.
Brand, Dionne 1953- .... **CLC 192**
See also BW 2; CA 143; CANR 143, 216; CWP; DLB 334
Brand, Max
See Faust, Frederick
Brand, Millen 1906-1980 .... **CLC 7**
See also CA 21-24R; 97-100; CANR 72
Branden, Barbara 1929- .... **CLC 44**
See also CA 148
Brandes, Georg (Morris Cohen)
1842-1927 .... **TCLC 10, 264**
See also CA 105; 189; DLB 300
Brandys, Kazimierz 1916-2000 .... **CLC 62**
See also CA 239; EWL 3
Branley, Franklyn M(ansfield)
1915-2002 .... **CLC 21**
See also CA 33-36R; 207; CANR 14, 39; CLR 13; MAICYA 1, 2; SAAS 16; SATA 4, 68, 136
Brant, Beth (E.) 1941- .... **NNAL**
See also CA 144; FW
Brant, Sebastian 1457-1521 ..... **LC 112, 206**
See also DLB 179; RGWL 2, 3
Brathwaite, Edward Kamau
1930- .... **BLC 2:1; BLCS; CLC 11, 305; PC 56**
See also BRWS 12; BW 2, 3; CA 25-28R; CANR 11, 26, 47, 107; CDWLB 3; CP 1, 2, 3, 4, 5, 6, 7; DAM POET; DLB 125; EWL 3
Brathwaite, Kamau
See Brathwaite, Edward Kamau
Braun, Volker 1939- .... **CLC 356**
See also CA 194; CWW 2; DLB 75, 124; EWL 3
Brautigan, Richard 1935-1984 .... **CLC 1, 3, 5, 9, 12, 34, 42; PC 94; TCLC 133**
See also BPFB 1; CA 53-56; 113; CANR 34; CN 1, 2, 3; CP 1, 2, 3, 4; DA3; DAM NOV; DLB 2, 5, 206; DLBY 1980, 1984; FANT; MAL 5; MTCW 1; RGAL 4; SATA 56
Brautigan, Richard Gary
See Brautigan, Richard
Brave Bird, Mary
See Crow Dog, Mary
Braverman, Kate 1950- .... **CLC 67**
See also CA 89-92; CANR 141; DLB 335
Brecht, Bertolt 1898-1956 ... **DC 3; TCLC 1, 6, 13, 35, 169; WLC 1**
See also CA 104; 133; CANR 62; CDWLB 2; DA; DA3; DAB; DAC; DAM DRAM, MST; DFS 4, 5, 9; DLB 56, 124; EW 11; EWL 3; IDTP; MTCW 1, 2; MTFW 2005; RGHL; RGWL 2, 3; TWA
Brecht, Eugen Berthold Friedrich
See Brecht, Bertolt
Brecht, Eugen Bertolt Friedrich
See Brecht, Bertolt
Bremer, Fredrika 1801-1865 .... **NCLC 11**
See also DLB 254
Brennan, Christopher John
1870-1932 .... **TCLC 17**
See also CA 117; 188; DLB 230; EWL 3
Brennan, Maeve 1917-1993 .... **CLC 5; TCLC 124**
See also CA 81-84; CANR 72, 100
Brenner, Jozef 1887-1919 .... **TCLC 13**
See also CA 111; 240
Brent, Linda
See Jacobs, Harriet A.
Brentano, Clemens (Maria)
1778-1842 .... **NCLC 1, 191; SSC 115**
See also DLB 90; RGWL 2, 3
Brent of Bin Bin
See Franklin, (Stella Maria Sarah) Miles (Lampe)
Brenton, Howard 1942- .... **CLC 31**
See also CA 69-72; CANR 33, 67; CBD; CD 5, 6; DLB 13; MTCW 1
Breslin, James
See Breslin, Jimmy
Breslin, Jimmy 1930- .... **CLC 4, 43**
See also CA 73-76; CANR 31, 75, 139, 187, 237; DAM NOV; DLB 185; MTCW 2; MTFW 2005
Bresson, Robert 1901(?)-1999 .... **CLC 16; TCLC 287**
See also CA 110; 187; CANR 49
Breton, Andre 1896-1966 ...... **CLC 2, 9, 15, 54; PC 15; TCLC 247**
See also CA 19-20; 25-28R; CANR 40, 60; CAP 2; DLB 65, 258; EW 11; EWL 3; GFL 1789 to the Present; LMFS 2; MTCW 1, 2; MTFW 2005; RGWL 2, 3; TWA; WP
Breton, Nicholas c. 1554-c. 1626 ..... **LC 133**
See also DLB 136
Breytenbach, Breyten
1939(?)- .... **CLC 23, 37, 126**
See also CA 113; 129; CANR 61, 122, 202; CWW 2; DAM POET; DLB 225; EWL 3
Bridgers, Sue Ellen 1942- .... **CLC 26**
See also AAYA 8, 49; BYA 7, 8; CA 65-68; CANR 11, 36; CLR 18, 199; DLB 52; JRDA; MAICYA 1, 2; SAAS 1; SATA 22, 90; SATA-Essay 109; WYA; YAW
Bridges, Robert (Seymour)
1844-1930 .... **PC 28; TCLC 1**
See also BRW 6; CA 104; 152; CDBLB 1890-1914; DAM POET; DLB 19, 98
Bridie, James
See Mavor, Osborne Henry
Brin, David 1950- .... **CLC 34**
See also AAYA 21; CA 102; CANR 24, 70, 125, 127; INT CANR-24; SATA 65; SCFW 2; SFW 4
Brink, Andre 1935- .... **CLC 18, 36, 106**
See also AFW; BRWS 6; CA 104; CANR 39, 62, 109, 133, 182; CN 4, 5, 6, 7; DLB 225; EWL 3; INT CA-103; LATS 1:2; MTCW 1, 2; MTFW 2005; WLIT 2
Brink, Andre Philippus
See Brink, Andre
Brinsmead, H. F(ay)
See Brinsmead, H(esba) F(ay)
Brinsmead, H. F.
See Brinsmead, H(esba) F(ay)
Brinsmead, H(esba) F(ay) 1922- .... **CLC 21**
See also CA 21-24R; CANR 10; CLR 47; CWRI 5; MAICYA 1, 2; SAAS 5; SATA 18, 78
Brittain, Vera (Mary)
1893(?)-1970 .... **CLC 23; TCLC 228**
See also BRWS 10; CA 13-16; 25-28R; CANR 58; CAP 1; DLB 191; FW; MTCW 1, 2
Broch, Hermann
1886-1951 ...... **TCLC 20, 204, 304, 307**
See also CA 117; 211; CDWLB 2; DLB 85, 124; EW 10; EWL 3; RGWL 2, 3
Brock, Rose
See Hansen, Joseph
Brod, Max 1884-1968 .... **TCLC 115, 305**
See also CA 5-8R; 25-28R; CANR 7; DLB 81; EWL 3
Brodber, Erna 1940- .... **CLC 379**
See also BW 2; CA 143; CN 6, 7; DLB 157
Brodkey, Harold (Roy)
1930-1996 .... **CLC 56; TCLC 123**
See also CA 111; 151; CANR 71; CN 4, 5, 6; DLB 130
Brodskii, Iosif
See Brodsky, Joseph
Brodskii, Iosif Alexandrovich
See Brodsky, Joseph
Brodsky, Iosif Alexandrovich
See Brodsky, Joseph
Brodsky, Joseph 1940-1996 .... **CLC 4, 6, 13, 36, 100; PC 9; TCLC 219**
See also AAYA 71; AITN 1; AMWS 8; CA 41-44R; 151; CANR 37, 106; CWW 2; DA3; DAM POET; DLB 285, 329; EWL 3; MTCW 1, 2; MTFW 2005; PFS 35; RGWL 2, 3
Brodsky, Michael 1948- .... **CLC 19**
See also CA 102; CANR 18, 41, 58, 147; DLB 244
Brodsky, Michael Mark
See Brodsky, Michael
Brodzki, Bella .... **CLC 65**
Brome, Richard 1590(?)-1652 ... **DC 50; LC 61**
See also BRWS 10; DLB 58
Bromell, Henry 1947- .... **CLC 5**
See also CA 53-56; CANR 9, 115, 116
Bromfield, Louis (Brucker)
1896-1956 .... **TCLC 11**
See also CA 107; 155; DLB 4, 9, 86; RGAL 4; RHW
Broner, E. M. 1930-2011 .... **CLC 19**
See also CA 17-20R; CANR 8, 25, 72, 216; CN 4, 5, 6; DLB 28
Broner, Esther Masserman
See Broner, E. M.
Bronk, William 1918-1999 .... **CLC 10**
See also AMWS 21; CA 89-92; 177; CANR 23; CP 3, 4, 5, 6, 7; DLB 165
Bronstein, Lev Davidovich
See Trotsky, Leon
Bronte, Anne 1820-1849 .... **NCLC 4, 71, 102, 235**
See also BRW 5; BRWR 1; DA3; DLB 21, 199, 340; NFS 26; TEA

Bronte, (Patrick) Branwell 1817-1848 .... **NCLC 109**
See also DLB 340

Bronte, Charlotte 1816-1855 .... **NCLC 3, 8, 33, 58, 105, 155, 217, 229, 280; SSC 167; WLC 1**
See also AAYA 17; BRW 5; BRWC 2; BRWR 1; BYA 2; CDBLB 1832-1890; DA; DA3; DAB; DAC; DAM MST, NOV; DLB 21, 159, 199, 340; EXPN; FL 1:2; GL 2; LAIT 2; NFS 4, 36; TEA; WLIT 4

Bronte, Emily 1818-1848 .... **NCLC 16, 35, 165, 244; PC 8; WLC 1**
See also AAYA 17; BPFB 1; BRW 5; BRWC 1; BRWR 1; BYA 3; CDBLB 1832-1890; DA; DA3; DAB; DAC; DAM MST, NOV, POET; DLB 21, 32, 199, 340; EXPN; FL 1:2; GL 2; LAIT 1; NFS 2; PFS 33, 43; TEA; WLIT 3

Bronte, Emily Jane
See Bronte, Emily

Brontes
See Bronte, Anne; Bronte, (Patrick) Branwell; Bronte, Charlotte; Bronte, Emily

Brooke, Frances 1724-1789 .... **LC 6, 48**
See also DLB 39, 99

Brooke, Henry 1703(?)-1783 .... **LC 1**
See also DLB 39

Brooke, Rupert 1887-1915 .... **PC 24; TCLC 2, 7; WLC 1**
See also BRWS 3; CA 104; 132; CANR 61; CDBLB 1914-1945; DA; DAB; DAC; DAM MST, POET; DLB 19, 216; EXPP; GLL 2; MTCW 1, 2; MTFW 2005; PFS 7; TEA

Brooke, Rupert Chawner
See Brooke, Rupert

Brooke-Haven, P.
See Wodehouse, P. G.

Brooke-Rose, Christine 1923-2012 .... **CLC 40, 184, 338**
See also BRWS 4; CA 13-16R; CANR 58, 118, 183; CN 1, 2, 3, 4, 5, 6, 7; DLB 14, 231; EWL 3; SFW 4

Brookner, Anita 1928- .... **CLC 32, 34, 51, 136, 237**
See also BRWS 4; CA 114; 120; CANR 37, 56, 87, 130, 212; CN 4, 5, 6, 7; CPW; DA3; DAB; DAM POP; DLB 194, 326; DLBY 1987; EWL 3; MTCW 1, 2; MTFW 2005; NFS 23; TEA

Brooks, Cleanth 1906-1994 .. **CLC 24, 86, 110**
See also AMWS 14; CA 17-20R; 145; CANR 33, 35; CSW; DLB 63; DLBY 1994; EWL 3; INT CANR-35; MAL 5; MTCW 1, 2; MTFW 2005

Brooks, George
See Baum, L. Frank

Brooks, Gwendolyn 1917-2000 ..... **BLC 1:1, 2:1; CLC 1, 2, 4, 5, 15, 49, 125, 349; PC 7, 138; WLC 1**
See also AAYA 20; AFAW 1, 2; AITN 1; AMWS 3; BW 2, 3; CA 1-4R; 190; CANR 1, 27, 52, 75, 132; CDALB 1941-1968; CLR 27; CP 1, 2, 3, 4, 5, 6, 7; CWP; DA; DA3; DAC; DAM MST, MULT, POET; DLB 5, 76, 165; EWL 3; EXPP; FL 1:5; MAL 5; MBL; MTCW 1, 2; MTFW 2005; PFS 1, 2, 4, 6, 32, 40; RGAL 4; SATA 6; SATA-Obit 123; SSFS 35; TUS; WP

Brooks, Gwendolyn Elizabeth
See Brooks, Gwendolyn

Brooks, Mel 1926- .... **CLC 12, 217**
See also AAYA 13, 48; CA 65-68; CANR 16; DFS 21; DLB 26

Brooks, Peter 1938- .... **CLC 34**
See also CA 45-48; CANR 1, 107, 182

Brooks, Peter Preston
See Brooks, Peter

Brooks, Van Wyck 1886-1963 .... **CLC 29**
See also AMW; CA 1-4R; CANR 6; DLB 45, 63, 103; MAL 5; TUS

Brophy, Brigid 1929-1995 .... **CLC 6, 11, 29, 105**
See also CA 5-8R; 149; CAAS 4; CANR 25, 53; CBD; CN 1, 2, 3, 4, 5, 6; CWD; DA3; DLB 14, 271; EWL 3; MTCW 1, 2

Brophy, Brigid Antonia
See Brophy, Brigid

Brosman, Catharine Savage 1934- ... **CLC 9**
See also CA 61-64; CANR 21, 46, 149, 222

Brossard, Nicole 1943- .... **CLC 115, 169; PC 80**
See also CA 122; CAAS 16; CANR 140; CCA 1; CWP; CWW 2; DLB 53; EWL 3; FW; GLL 2; RGWL 3

Brother Antoninus
See Everson, William

Brothers Grimm
See Grimm, Jacob Ludwig Karl; Grimm, Wilhelm Karl

The Brothers Quay
See Quay, Stephen; Quay, Timothy

Broughton, T(homas) Alan 1936- .... **CLC 19**
See also CA 45-48; CANR 2, 23, 48, 111

Broumas, Olga 1949- .... **CLC 10, 73**
See also CA 85-88; CANR 20, 69, 110; CP 5, 6, 7; CWP; GLL 2

Broun, Heywood 1888-1939 .... **TCLC 104**
See also DLB 29, 171

Brown, Alan 1950- .... **CLC 99**
See also CA 156

Brown, Charles Brockden 1771-1810 .... **NCLC 22, 74, 122, 246**
See also AMWS 1; CDALB 1640-1865; DLB 37, 59, 73; FW; GL 2; HGG; LMFS 1; RGAL 4; TUS

Brown, Christy 1932-1981 .... **CLC 63**
See also BYA 13; CA 105; 104; CANR 72; DLB 14

Brown, Claude 1937-2002 .... **BLC 1:1; CLC 30**
See also AAYA 7; BW 1, 3; CA 73-76; 205; CANR 81; DAM MULT

Brown, Dan 1964- .... **CLC 209**
See also AAYA 55; CA 217; CANR 223; LNFS 1; MTFW 2005

Brown, Dee 1908-2002 .... **CLC 18, 47**
See also AAYA 30; CA 13-16R; 212; CAAS 6; CANR 11, 45, 60, 150; CPW; CSW; DA3; DAM POP; DLBY 1980; LAIT 2; MTCW 1, 2; MTFW 2005; NCFS 5; SATA 5, 110; SATA-Obit 141; TCWW 1, 2

Brown, Dee Alexander
See Brown, Dee

Brown, George
See Wertmueller, Lina

Brown, George Douglas 1869-1902 .... **TCLC 28**
See also CA 162; RGEL 2

Brown, George Mackay 1921-1996 .... **CLC 5, 48, 100**
See also BRWS 6; CA 21-24R; 151; CAAS 6; CANR 12, 37, 67; CN 1, 2, 3, 4, 5, 6; CP 1, 2, 3, 4, 5, 6; DLB 14, 27, 139, 271; MTCW 1; RGSF 2; SATA 35

Brown, James Wllie
See Komunyakaa, Yusef

Brown, James Wllie, Jr.
See Komunyakaa, Yusef

Brown, Larry 1951-2004 .... **CLC 73, 289**
See also AMWS 21; CA 130; 134; 233; CANR 117, 145; CSW; DLB 234; INT CA-134

Brown, Moses
See Barrett, William (Christopher)

Brown, Rita Mae 1944- .... **CLC 18, 43, 79, 259**
See also BPFB 1; CA 45-48; CANR 2, 11, 35, 62, 95, 138, 183, 232; CN 5, 6, 7; CPW; CSW; DA3; DAM NOV, POP; FW; INT CANR-11; MAL 5; MTCW 1, 2; MTFW 2005; NFS 9; RGAL 4; TUS

Brown, Roderick (Langmere) Haig-
See Haig-Brown, Roderick (Langmere)

Brown, Rosellen 1939- .... **CLC 32, 170**
See also CA 77-80; CAAS 10; CANR 14, 44, 98; CN 6, 7; PFS 41

Brown, Sterling Allen 1901-1989 .... **BLC 1; CLC 1, 23, 59; HR 1:2; PC 55**
See also AFAW 1, 2; BW 1, 3; CA 85-88; 127; CANR 26; CP 3, 4; DA3; DAM MULT, POET; DLB 48, 51, 63; MAL 5; MTCW 1, 2; MTFW 2005; RGAL 4; WP

Brown, Will
See Ainsworth, William Harrison

Brown, William Hill 1765-1793 .... **LC 93**
See also DLB 37

Brown, William Larry
See Brown, Larry

Brown, William Wells 1814(?)-1884 .... **BLC 1:1; DC 1; NCLC 2, 89, 247**
See also DAM MULT; DLB 3, 50, 183, 248; RGAL 4

Browne, Clyde Jackson
See Browne, Jackson

Browne, Jackson 1948(?)- .... **CLC 21**
See also CA 120

Browne, Sir Thomas 1605-1682 ...... **LC 111**
See also BRW 2; DLB 151

Browne of Tavistock, William 1590-1645 .... **LC 192**
See also DLB 121

Browning, Robert 1812-1889 .... **NCLC 19, 79; PC 2, 61, 97; WLCS**
See also BRW 4; BRWC 2; BRWR 3; CDBLB 1832-1890; CLR 97; DA; DA3; DAB; DAC; DAM MST, POET; DLB 32, 163; EXPP; LATS 1:1; PAB; PFS 1, 15, 41; RGEL 2; TEA; WLIT 4; WP; YABC 1

Browning, Tod 1882-1962 .... **CLC 16**
See also CA 141; 117

Brownmiller, Susan 1935- .... **CLC 159**
See also CA 103; CANR 35, 75, 137; DAM NOV; FW; MTCW 1, 2; MTFW 2005

Brownson, Orestes Augustus 1803-1876 .... **NCLC 50**
See also DLB 1, 59, 73, 243

Bruccoli, Matthew J. 1931-2008 ..... **CLC 34**
See also CA 9-12R; 274; CANR 7, 87; DLB 103

Bruccoli, Matthew Joseph
See Bruccoli, Matthew J.

Bruce, Lenny 1925-1966 .... **CLC 21**
See also CA 89-92

Bruchac, Joseph 1942- .... **NNAL**
See also AAYA 19; CA 33-36R, 256; CAAE 256; CANR 13, 47, 75, 94, 137, 161, 204; CLR 46; CWRI 5; DAM MULT; DLB 342; JRDA; MAICYA 2; MAICYAS 1; MTCW 2; MTFW 2005; PFS 36; SATA 42, 89, 131, 176, 228; SATA-Essay 176

Bruin, John
See Brutus, Dennis

Brulard, Henri
See Stendhal

Brulls, Christian
See Simenon, Georges

Brunetto Latini c. 1220-1294 ... **CMLC 73, 151**

Bruni, Leonardo 1370-1444 .... **LC 212**

Brunner, John (Kilian Houston) 1934-1995 .... **CLC 8, 10**
See also CA 1-4R; 149; CAAS 8; CANR 2, 37; CPW; DAM POP; DLB 261; MTCW 1, 2; SCFW 1, 2; SFW 4

Bruno, Giordano 1548-1600 .... **LC 27, 167**
See also RGWL 2, 3

Brutus, Dennis 1924-2009 .... **BLC 1:1; CLC 43; PC 24**

See also AFW; BW 2, 3; CA 49-52; CAAS 14; CANR 2, 27, 42, 81; CDWLB 3; CP 1, 2, 3, 4, 5, 6, 7; DAM MULT, POET; DLB 117, 225; EWL 3
Bryan, C.D.B. 1936-2009 .... **CLC 29**
See also CA 73-76; CANR 13, 68; DLB 185; INT CANR-13
Bryan, Courtlandt Dixon Barnes
See Bryan, C.D.B.
Bryan, Michael
See Moore, Brian
Bryan, William Jennings
1860-1925 .... **TCLC 99**
See also DLB 303
Bryant, William Cullen
1794-1878 ..... **NCLC 6, 46, 284; PC 20**
See also AMWS 1; CDALB 1640-1865; DA; DAB; DAC; DAM MST, POET; DLB 3, 43, 59, 189, 250; EXPP; PAB; PFS 30; RGAL 4; TUS
Bryusov, Valery Yakovlevich
1873-1924 .... **TCLC 10**
See also CA 107; 155; EWL 3; SFW 4
Buchan, John 1875-1940 .... **TCLC 41**
See also CA 108; 145; CMW 4; DAB; DAM POP; DLB 34, 70, 156; HGG; MSW; MTCW 2; RGEL 2; RHW; YABC 2
Buchanan, George 1506-1582 ...... **LC 4, 179**
See also DLB 132
Buchanan, Robert 1841-1901 ...... **TCLC 107**
See also CA 179; DLB 18, 35
Buchheim, Lothar-Guenther
1918-2007 .... **CLC 6**
See also CA 85-88; 257
Buchwald, Art 1925-2007 .... **CLC 33**
See also AITN 1; CA 5-8R; 256; CANR 21, 67, 107; MTCW 1, 2; SATA 10
Buchwald, Arthur
See Buchwald, Art
Buck, Pearl S.
1892-1973 .... **CLC 7, 11, 18, 127**
See also AAYA 42; AITN 1; AMWS 2; BPFB 1; CA 1-4R; 41-44R; CANR 1, 34; CDALBS; CN 1; DA; DA3; DAB; DAC; DAM MST, NOV; DLB 9, 102, 329; EWL 3; LAIT 3; MAL 5; MTCW 1, 2; MTFW 2005; NFS 25; RGAL 4; RHW; SATA 1, 25; SSFS 33; TUS
Buck, Pearl Sydenstricker
See Buck, Pearl S.
Buckler, Ernest 1908-1984 .... **CLC 13**
See also CA 11-12; 114; CAP 1; CCA 1; CN 1, 2, 3; DAC; DAM MST; DLB 68; SATA 47
Buckley, Christopher 1952- .... **CLC 165**
See also CA 139; CANR 119, 180
Buckley, Christopher Taylor
See Buckley, Christopher
Buckley, Vincent (Thomas)
1925-1988 .... **CLC 57**
See also CA 101; CP 1, 2, 3, 4; DLB 289
Buckley, William F., Jr.
See Buckley, William F.
Buckley, William F. 1925-2008 ... **CLC 7, 18, 37**
See also AITN 1; BPFB 1; CA 1-4R; 269; CANR 1, 24, 53, 93, 133, 185; CMW 4; CPW; DA3; DAM POP; DLB 137; DLBY 1980; INT CANR-24; MTCW 1, 2; MTFW 2005; TUS
Buckley, William Frank
See Buckley, William F.
Buckley, William Frank, Jr.
See Buckley, William F.
Buechner, Frederick 1926- ... **CLC 2, 4, 6, 9**
See also AMWS 12; BPFB 1; CA 13-16R; CANR 11, 39, 64, 114, 138, 213; CN 1, 2, 3, 4, 5, 6, 7; DAM NOV; DLBY 1980; INT CANR-11; MAL 5; MTCW 1, 2; MTFW 2005; TCLE 1:1
Buell, John (Edward) 1927- .... **CLC 10**
See also CA 1-4R; CANR 71; DLB 53
Buero Vallejo, Antonio 1916-2000 ... **CLC 15, 46, 139, 226; DC 18**
See also CA 106; 189; CANR 24, 49, 75; CWW 2; DFS 11; EWL 3; HW 1; MTCW 1, 2
Bufalino, Gesualdo 1920-1996 .... **CLC 74**
See also CA 209; CWW 2; DLB 196
Buffon, Georges-Louis Leclerc
1707-1788 .... **LC 186**
See also DLB 313; GFL Beginnings to 1789
Bugayev, Boris Nikolayevich
1880-1934 .... **PC 11; TCLC 7**
See also CA 104; 165; DLB 295; EW 9; EWL 3; MTCW 2; MTFW 2005; RGWL 2, 3
Bukowski, Charles 1920-1994 .... **CLC 2, 5, 9, 41, 82, 108; PC 18; SSC 45**
See also CA 17-20R; 144; CANR 40, 62, 105, 180; CN 4, 5; CP 1, 2, 3, 4, 5; CPW; DA3; DAM NOV, POET; DLB 5, 130, 169; EWL 3; MAL 5; MTCW 1, 2; MTFW 2005; PFS 28
Bulawayo, NoViolet 1981- .... **CLC 370**
See also CA 351
Bulawayo, NoViolet Mkha
See Bulawayo, NoViolet
Bulgakov, Mikhail 1891-1940 .... **SSC 18; TCLC 2, 16, 159, 288**
See also AAYA 74; BPFB 1; CA 105; 152; DAM DRAM, NOV; DLB 272; EWL 3; MTCW 2; MTFW 2005; NFS 8; RGSF 2; RGWL 2, 3; SFW 4; TWA
Bulgakov, Mikhail Afanasevich
See Bulgakov, Mikhail
Bulgya, Alexander Alexandrovich
1901-1956 .... **TCLC 53**
See also CA 117; 181; DLB 272; EWL 3
Bullins, Ed 1935- .... **BLC 1:1; CLC 1, 5, 7; DC 6**
See also BW 2, 3; CA 49-52; CAAS 16; CAD; CANR 24, 46, 73, 134; CD 5, 6; DAM DRAM, MULT; DLB 7, 38, 249; EWL 3; MAL 5; MTCW 1, 2; MTFW 2005; RGAL 4
Bulosan, Carlos 1911-1956 .... **AAL**
See also CA 216; DLB 312; RGAL 4
Bulwer-Lytton, Edward
1803-1873 .... **NCLC 1, 45, 238**
See also DLB 21; RGEL 2; SATA 23; SFW 4; SUFW 1; TEA
Bulwer-Lytton, Edward George Earle Lytton
See Bulwer-Lytton, Edward
Bunin, Ivan
See Bunin, Ivan Alexeyevich
Bunin, Ivan 1870-1953 .... **TCLC 253**
Bunin, Ivan Alekseevich
See Bunin, Ivan Alexeyevich
Bunin, Ivan Alexeyevich
1870-1953 .... **SSC 5; TCLC 6, 253**
See also CA 104; DLB 317, 329; EWL 3; RGSF 2; RGWL 2, 3; TWA
Bunting, Basil
1900-1985 ..... **CLC 10, 39, 47; PC 120**
See also BRWS 7; CA 53-56; 115; CANR 7; CP 1, 2, 3, 4; DAM POET; DLB 20; EWL 3; RGEL 2
Bunuel, Luis 1900-1983 .... **CLC 16, 80; HLC 1**
See also CA 101; 110; CANR 32, 77; DAM MULT; HW 1
Bunyan, John 1628-1688 ...... **LC 4, 69, 180; WLC 1**
See also BRW 2; BYA 5; CDBLB 1660-1789; CLR 124; DA; DAB; DAC; DAM MST; DLB 39; NFS 32; RGEL 2; TEA; WCH; WLIT 3
Buonarroti, Michelangelo
1568-1646 .... **PC 103**
See also DLB 339
Buravsky, Alexandr .... **CLC 59**
Burchill, Julie 1959- .... **CLC 238**
See also CA 135; CANR 115, 116, 207
Burckhardt, Jacob (Christoph)
1818-1897 .... **NCLC 49**
See also EW 6
Burford, Eleanor
See Hibbert, Eleanor Alice Burford
Burgess, Anthony 1917-1993 .... **CLC 1, 2, 4, 5, 8, 10, 13, 15, 22, 40, 62, 81, 94; TCLC 316, 319**
See also AAYA 25; AITN 1; BRWS 1; CA 1-4R; 143; CANR 2, 46; CDBLB 1960 to Present; CN 1, 2, 3, 4, 5; DA3; DAB; DAC; DAM NOV; DLB 14, 194, 261; DLBY 1998; EWL 3; MTCW 1, 2; MTFW 2005; NFS 15; RGEL 2; RHW; SFW 4; TEA; YAW
Buridan, John c. 1295-c. 1358 .... **CMLC 97**
Burke, Edmund 1729(?)-1797 .... **LC 7, 36, 146; WLC 1**
See also BRW 3; DA; DA3; DAB; DAC; DAM MST; DLB 104, 252, 336; RGEL 2; TEA
Burke, James Lee 1936- .... **CLC 322**
See also AAYA 84; AMWS 14; CA 13-16R; CAAS 19; CANR 7, 22, 41, 64, 106, 176, 219; CMW 4; CN 6, 7; CSW; DLB 226, 350
Burke, Kenneth (Duva)
1897-1993 .... **CLC 2, 24; TCLC 286**
See also AMW; CA 5-8R; 143; CANR 39, 74, 136; CN 1, 2; CP 1, 2, 3, 4, 5; DLB 45, 63; EWL 3; MAL 5; MTCW 1, 2; MTFW 2005; RGAL 4
Burke, Leda
See Garnett, David
Burke, Ralph
See Silverberg, Robert
Burke, Thomas
1886-1945 .... **SSC 158; TCLC 63**
See also CA 113; 155; CMW 4; DLB 197
Burke, Valenza Pauline
See Marshall, Paule
Burney, Fanny 1752-1840 .... **NCLC 12, 54, 107, 251, 299, 306**
See also BRWS 3; DLB 39; FL 1:2; NFS 16; RGEL 2; TEA
Burney, Frances
See Burney, Fanny
Burns, Robert 1759-1796 .... **LC 3, 29, 40, 190; PC 6, 114; WLC 1**
See also AAYA 51; BRW 3; CDBLB 1789-1832; DA; DA3; DAB; DAC; DAM MST, POET; DLB 109; EXPP; PAB; RGEL 2; TEA; WP
Burns, Tex
See L'Amour, Louis
Burnshaw, Stanley 1906-2005 .... **CLC 3, 13, 44**
See also CA 9-12R; 243; CP 1, 2, 3, 4, 5, 6, 7; DLB 48; DLBY 1997
Burr, Anne 1937- .... **CLC 6**
See also CA 25-28R
Burroughs, Augusten 1965- .... **CLC 277**
See also AAYA 73; CA 214; CANR 168, 218
Burroughs, Augusten Xon
See Burroughs, Augusten
Burroughs, Edgar Rice
1875-1950 .... **TCLC 2, 32**
See also AAYA 11; BPFB 1; BYA 4, 9; CA 104; 132; CANR 131; CLR 157; DA3; DAM NOV; DLB 8, 364; FANT; MTCW 1, 2; MTFW 2005; RGAL 4; SATA 41; SCFW 1, 2; SFW 4; TCWW 1, 2; TUS; YAW
Burroughs, William S. 1914-1997 ... **CLC 1, 2, 5, 15, 22, 42, 75, 109; TCLC 121 WLC 1**
See also AAYA 60; AITN 2; AMWS 3; BG 1:2; BPFB 1; CA 9-12R; 160; CANR 20, 52, 104; CN 1, 2, 3, 4, 5, 6; CPW; DA; DA3;

DAB; DAC; DAM MST, NOV, POP; DLB 2, 8, 16, 152, 237; DLBY 1981, 1997; EWL 3; GLL 1; HGG; LMFS 2; MAL 5; MTCW 1, 2; MTFW 2005; RGAL 4; SFW 4
Burroughs, William Seward
See Burroughs, William S.
Burton, Sir Richard F(rancis) 1821-1890 .... **NCLC 42**
See also DLB 55, 166, 184, 366; SSFS 21
Burton, Robert 1577-1640 .... **LC 74, 195**
See also DLB 151; RGEL 2
Buruma, Ian 1951- .... **CLC 163**
See also CA 128; CANR 65, 141, 195
Bury, Stephen
See Stephenson, Neal
Busch, Frederick 1941-2006 .... **CLC 7, 10, 18, 47, 166**
See also CA 33-36R; 248; CAAS 1; CANR 45, 73, 92, 157; CN 1, 2, 3, 4, 5, 6, 7; DLB 6, 218
Busch, Frederick Matthew
See Busch, Frederick
Bush, Barney (Furman) 1946- .... **NNAL**
See also CA 145
Bush, Ronald 1946- .... **CLC 34**
See also CA 136
Busia, Abena, P. A. 1953- .... **BLC 2:1**
Bustos, Francisco
See Borges, Jorge Luis
Bustos Domecq, Honorio
See Bioy Casares, Adolfo; Borges, Jorge Luis
Butler, Octavia 1947-2006 .... **BLC 2:1; BLCS; CLC 38, 121, 230, 240**
See also AAYA 18, 48; AFAW 2; AMWS 13; BPFB 1; BW 2, 3; CA 73-76; 248; CANR 12, 24, 38, 73, 145, 240; CLR 65, 186; CN 7; CPW; DA3; DAM MULT, POP; DLB 33; LATS 1:2; MTCW 1, 2; MTFW 2005; NFS 8, 21, 34; SATA 84; SCFW 2; SFW 4; SSFS 6; TCLE 1:1; YAW
Butler, Octavia E.
See Butler, Octavia
Butler, Octavia Estelle
See Butler, Octavia
Butler, Robert Olen, Jr.
See Butler, Robert Olen
Butler, Robert Olen 1945- ...... **CLC 81, 162; SSC 117, 219**
See also AMWS 12; BPFB 1; CA 112; CANR 66, 138, 194, 236; CN 7; CSW; DAM POP; DLB 173, 335; INT CA-112; MAL 5; MTCW 2; MTFW 2005; SSFS 11, 22
Butler, Samuel 1612-1680 .... **LC 16, 43, 173; PC 94**
See also DLB 101, 126; RGEL 2
Butler, Samuel 1835-1902 .... **TCLC 1, 33; WLC 1**
See also BRWS 2; CA 143; CDBLB 1890-1914; DA; DA3; DAB; DAC; DAM MST, NOV; DLB 18, 57, 174; RGEL 2; SFW 4; TEA
Butler, Walter C.
See Faust, Frederick
Butor, Michel (Marie Francois) 1926- .... **CLC 1, 3, 8, 11, 15, 161**
See also CA 9-12R; CANR 33, 66; CWW 2; DLB 83; EW 13; EWL 3; GFL 1789 to the Present; MTCW 1, 2; MTFW 2005
Butt, Nathan
See Galt, John
Butts, Mary 1890(?)-1937 .... **SSC 124; TCLC 77**
See also CA 148; DLB 240
Buxton, Ralph
See Silverstein, Alvin; Silverstein, Virginia B.
Buzo, Alex
See Buzo, Alex
Buzo, Alex 1944- .... **CLC 61**
See also CA 97-100; CANR 17, 39, 69; CD 5, 6; DLB 289
Buzo, Alexander John
See Buzo, Alex
Buzzati, Dino 1906-1972 .... **CLC 36**
See also CA 160; 33-36R; DLB 177; RGWL 2, 3; SFW 4
Byars, Betsy 1928- .... **CLC 35**
See also AAYA 19; BYA 3; CA 33-36R, 183; CAAE 183; CANR 18, 36, 57, 102, 148; CLR 1, 16, 72; DLB 52; INT CANR-18; JRDA; MAICYA 1, 2; MAICYAS 1; MTCW 1; SAAS 1; SATA 4, 46, 80, 163, 223; SATA-Essay 108; WYA; YAW
Byars, Betsy Cromer
See Byars, Betsy
Byatt, A. S. 1936- .... **CLC 19, 65, 136, 223, 312; SSC 91, 214**
See also BPFB 1; BRWC 2; BRWS 4; CA 13-16R; CANR 13, 33, 50, 75, 96, 133, 205; CN 1, 2, 3, 4, 5, 6; DA3; DAM NOV, POP; DLB 14, 194, 319, 326; EWL 3; MTCW 1, 2; MTFW 2005; RGSF 2; RHW; SSFS 26; TEA
Byatt, Antonia Susan Drabble
See Byatt, A. S.
Byrd, William II 1674-1744 .... **LC 112**
See also DLB 24, 140; RGAL 4
Byrne, David 1952- .... **CLC 26**
See also CA 127; CANR 215
Byrne, John Joseph
See Leonard, Hugh
Byrne, John Keyes
See Leonard, Hugh
Byron, George Gordon
See Lord Byron
Byron, George Gordon Noel
See Lord Byron
Byron, Robert 1905-1941 .... **TCLC 67**
See also CA 160; DLB 195
C. 3. 3.
See Wilde, Oscar
C. A.
See Naden, Constance
Caballero, Fernan 1796-1877 .. **NCLC 10, 262**
Cabell, Branch
See Cabell, James Branch
Cabell, James Branch 1879-1958 ... **TCLC 6, 314**
See also CA 105; 152; DLB 9, 78; FANT; MAL 5; MTCW 2; RGAL 4; SUFW 1
Cabeza de Vaca, Alvar Nunez 1490-1557(?) .... **LC 61**
Cable, George Washington 1844-1925 .... **SSC 4, 155; TCLC 4**
See also CA 104; 155; DLB 12, 74; DLBD 13; RGAL 4; TUS
Cabral de Melo Neto, Joao 1920-1999 .... **CLC 76**
See also CA 151; CWW 2; DAM MULT; DLB 307; EWL 3; LAW; LAWS 1
Cabrera, Lydia 1900-1991 .... **TCLC 223**
See also CA 178; DLB 145; EWL 3; HW 1; LAWS 1
Cabrera Infante, G. 1929-2005 .... **CLC 5, 25, 45, 120, 291; HLC 1; SSC 39**
See also CA 85-88; 236; CANR 29, 65, 110; CDWLB 3; CWW 2; DA3; DAM MULT; DLB 113; EWL 3; HW 1, 2; LAW; LAWS 1; MTCW 1, 2; MTFW 2005; RGSF 2; WLIT 1
Cabrera Infante, Guillermo
See Cabrera Infante, G.
Cadalso y Vázquez, José de 1741-1782 .... **LC 238**
Cade, Toni
See Bambara, Toni Cade
Cadmus and Harmonia
See Buchan, John
Caedmon fl. 658-680 .... **CMLC 7, 133**
See also DLB 146
Caeiro, Alberto
See Pessoa, Fernando
Caesar, Julius
See Julius Caesar
Cage, John (Milton), (Jr.) 1912-1992 .... **CLC 41; PC 58**
See also CA 13-16R; 169; CANR 9, 78; DLB 193; INT CANR-9; TCLE 1:1
Cahan, Abraham 1860-1951 .... **TCLC 71**
See also CA 108; 154; DLB 9, 25, 28; MAL 5; RGAL 4
Cain, Christopher
See Fleming, Thomas
Cain, G.
See Cabrera Infante, G.
Cain, Guillermo
See Cabrera Infante, G.
Cain, James M(allahan) 1892-1977 .... **CLC 3, 11, 28**
See also AITN 1; BPFB 1; CA 17-20R; 73-76; CANR 8, 34, 61; CMW 4; CN 1, 2; DLB 226; EWL 3; MAL 5; MSW; MTCW 1; RGAL 4
Caine, Hall 1853-1931 .... **TCLC 97**
See also RHW
Caine, Mark
See Raphael, Frederic
Calasso, Roberto 1941- .... **CLC 81**
See also CA 143; CANR 89, 223
Calderon de la Barca, Pedro 1600-1681 .... **DC 3; HLCS 1; LC 23, 136**
See also DFS 23; EW 2; RGWL 2, 3; TWA
Caldwell, Erskine 1903-1987 .... **CLC 1, 8, 14, 50, 60; SSC 19, 147; TCLC 117**
See also AITN 1; AMW; BPFB 1; CA 1-4R; 121; CAAS 1; CANR 2, 33; CN 1, 2, 3, 4; DA3; DAM NOV; DLB 9, 86; EWL 3; MAL 5; MTCW 1, 2; MTFW 2005; RGAL 4; RGSF 2; TUS
Caldwell, Gail 1951- .... **CLC 309**
See also CA 313
Caldwell, (Janet Miriam) Taylor (Holland) 1900-1985 .... **CLC 2, 28, 39**
See also BPFB 1; CA 5-8R; 116; CANR 5; DA3; DAM NOV, POP; DLBD 17; MTCW 2; RHW
Calhoun, John Caldwell 1782-1850 .... **NCLC 15**
See also DLB 3, 248
Calisher, Hortense 1911-2009 ...... **CLC 2, 4, 8, 38, 134; SSC 15**
See also CA 1-4R; 282; CANR 1, 22, 117; CN 1, 2, 3, 4, 5, 6, 7; DA3; DAM NOV; DLB 2, 218; INT CANR-22; MAL 5; MTCW 1, 2; MTFW 2005; RGAL 4; RGSF 2
Callaghan, Morley 1903-1990 .... **CLC 3, 14, 41, 65; TCLC 145, 292**
See also CA 9-12R; 132; CANR 33, 73; CN 1, 2, 3, 4; DAC; DAM MST; DLB 68; EWL 3; MTCW 1, 2; MTFW 2005; RGEL 2; RGSF 2; SSFS 19
Callaghan, Morley Edward
See Callaghan, Morley
Callahan, S. Alice 1868-1894 .... **NCLC 315**
See also DLB 175, 221; RGAL 4
Callimachus c. 305B.C.-c. 240B.C. ... **CMLC 18**
See also AW 1; DLB 176; RGWL 2, 3
Calprenede
See La Calprenede, Gautier de Costes
Calvin, Jean
See Calvin, John
Calvin, John 1509-1564 .... **LC 37, 215**
See also DLB 327; GFL Beginnings to 1789
Calvino, Italo 1923-1985 .... **CLC 5, 8, 11, 22, 33, 39, 73; SSC 3, 48, 179; TCLC 183, 306, 313**

See also AAYA 58; CA 85-88; 116; CANR 23, 61, 132; DAM NOV; DLB 196; EW 13; EWL 3; MTCW 1, 2; MTFW 2005; RGHL; RGSF 2; RGWL 2, 3; SFW 4; SSFS 12, 31; WLIT 7
Camara Laye
See Laye, Camara
Cambridge, A Gentleman of the University of
See Crowley, Edward Alexander
Camden, William 1551-1623 .... **LC 77**
See also DLB 172
Cameron, Carey 1952- .... **CLC 59**
See also CA 135
Cameron, Peter 1959- .... **CLC 44**
See also AMWS 12; CA 125; CANR 50, 117, 188, 239; DLB 234; GLL 2
Camoes, Luis de 1524(?)-1580 .... **HLCS 1; LC 62, 191; PC 31**
See also DLB 287; EW 2; RGWL 2, 3
Camoens, Luis Vaz de 1524(?)-1580
See Camoes, Luis de
Camp, Madeleine L'Engle
See L'Engle, Madeleine
Campana, Dino 1885-1932 .... **TCLC 20**
See also CA 117; 246; DLB 114; EWL 3
Campanella, Tommaso 1568-1639 ..... **LC 32**
See also RGWL 2, 3
Campbell, Bebe Moore
1950-2006 .... **BLC 2:1; CLC 246**
See also AAYA 26; BW 2, 3; CA 139; 254; CANR 81, 134; DLB 227; MTCW 2; MTFW 2005
Campbell, John Ramsey
See Campbell, Ramsey
Campbell, John W. 1910-1971 .... **CLC 32**
See also CA 21-22; 29-32R; CANR 34; CAP 2; DLB 8; MTCW 1; SCFW 1, 2; SFW 4
Campbell, John Wood, Jr.
See Campbell, John W.
Campbell, Joseph
1904-1987 .... **CLC 69; TCLC 140**
See also AAYA 3, 66; BEST 89:2; CA 1-4R; 124; CANR 3, 28, 61, 107; DA3; MTCW 1, 2
Campbell, Maria 1940- ...... **CLC 85; NNAL**
See also CA 102; CANR 54; CCA 1; DAC
Campbell, Ramsey 1946- ... **CLC 42; SSC 19**
See also AAYA 51; CA 57-60, 228; CAAE 228; CANR 7, 102, 171; DLB 261; HGG; INT CANR-7; SUFW 1, 2
Campbell, (Ignatius) Roy (Dunnachie)
1901-1957 .... **TCLC 5**
See also AFW; CA 104; 155; DLB 20, 225; EWL 3; MTCW 2; RGEL 2
Campbell, Thomas
1777-1844 .... **NCLC 19, 314**
See also DLB 93, 144; RGEL 2
Campbell, Wilfred
See Campbell, William
Campbell, William 1858(?)-1918 .... **TCLC 9**
See also CA 106; DLB 92
Campbell, William Edward March
See March, William
Campion, Jane 1954- .... **CLC 95, 229**
See also AAYA 33; CA 138; CANR 87
Campion, Thomas 1567-1620 .... **LC 78, 221; PC 87**
See also BRWS 16; CDBLB Before 1660; DAM POET; DLB 58, 172; RGEL 2
Camus, Albert 1913-1960 .... **CLC 1, 2, 4, 9, 11, 14, 32, 63, 69, 124; DC 2; SSC 9, 76, 129, 146; WLC 1**
See also AAYA 36; AFW; BPFB 1; CA 89-92; CANR 131; DA; DA3; DAB; DAC; DAM DRAM, MST, NOV; DLB 72, 321, 329; EW 13; EWL 3; EXPN; EXPS; GFL 1789 to the Present; LATS 1:2; LMFS 2; MTCW 1, 2; MTFW 2005; NFS 6, 16; RGHL; RGSF 2; RGWL 2, 3; SSFS 4; TWA
Canby, Vincent 1924-2000 .... **CLC 13**
See also CA 81-84; 191
Cancale
See Desnos, Robert
Canetti, Elias 1905-1994 ...... **CLC 3, 14, 25, 75, 86; TCLC 157**
See also CA 21-24R; 146; CANR 23, 61, 79; CDWLB 2; CWW 2; DA3; DLB 85, 124, 329; EW 12; EWL 3; MTCW 1, 2; MTFW 2005; RGWL 2, 3; TWA
Canfield, Dorothea F.
See Fisher, Dorothy (Frances) Canfield
Canfield, Dorothea Frances
See Fisher, Dorothy (Frances) Canfield
Canfield, Dorothy
See Fisher, Dorothy (Frances) Canfield
Canin, Ethan 1960- .... **CLC 55; SSC 70**
See also CA 131; 135; CANR 193; DLB 335, 350; MAL 5
Cankar, Ivan 1876-1918 .... **TCLC 105**
See also CDWLB 4; DLB 147; EWL 3
Cannon, Curt
See Hunter, Evan
Cao, Lan 1961- .... **CLC 109**
See also CA 165
Cape, Judith
See Page, P.K.
Capek, Karel 1890-1938 ...... **DC 1; SSC 36; TCLC 6, 37, 192; WLC 1**
See also CA 104; 140; CDWLB 4; DA; DA3; DAB; DAC; DAM DRAM, MST, NOV; DFS 7, 11; DLB 215; EW 10; EWL 3; MTCW 2; MTFW 2005; RGSF 2; RGWL 2, 3; SCFW 1, 2; SFW 4
Capella, Martianus fl. 4th cent. ... **CMLC 84**
Capote, Truman 1924-1984 ..... **CLC 1, 3, 8, 13, 19, 34, 38, 58; SSC 2, 47, 93; TCLC 164; WLC 1**
See also AAYA 61; AMWS 3; BPFB 1; CA 5-8R; 113; CANR 18, 62, 201; CDALB 1941-1968; CN 1, 2, 3; CPW; DA; DA3; DAB; DAC; DAM MST, NOV, POP; DLB 2, 185, 227; DLBY 1980, 1984; EWL 3; EXPS; GLL 1; LAIT 3; MAL 5; MTCW 1, 2; MTFW 2005; NCFS 2; RGAL 4; RGSF 2; SATA 91; SSFS 2; TUS
Capra, Frank 1897-1991 .... **CLC 16**
See also AAYA 52; CA 61-64; 135
Caputo, Philip 1941- .... **CLC 32**
See also AAYA 60; CA 73-76; CANR 40, 135; YAW
Caragiale, Ion Luca 1852-1912 .... **TCLC 76**
See also CA 157
Card, Orson Scott
1951- .... **CLC 44, 47, 50, 279**
See also AAYA 11, 42; BPFB 1; BYA 5, 8; CA 102; CANR 27, 47, 73, 102, 106, 133, 184; CLR 116; CPW; DA3; DAM POP; FANT; INT CANR-27; MTCW 1, 2; MTFW 2005; NFS 5; SATA 83, 127, 241; SCFW 2; SFW 4; SUFW 2; YAW
Cardenal, Ernesto 1925- .... **CLC 31, 161; HLC 1; PC 22**
See also CA 49-52; CANR 2, 32, 66, 138, 217; CWW 2; DAM MULT, POET; DLB 290; EWL 3; HW 1, 2; LAWS 1; MTCW 1, 2; MTFW 2005; RGWL 2, 3
Cardinal, Marie 1929-2001 .... **CLC 189**
See also CA 177; CWW 2; DLB 83; FW
Cardozo, Benjamin N(athan)
1870-1938 .... **TCLC 65**
See also CA 117; 164
Carducci, Giosue (Alessandro Giuseppe)
1835-1907 .... **PC 46; TCLC 32**
See also CA 163; DLB 329; EW 7; RGWL 2, 3
Carew, Thomas 1595(?)-1640 ... **LC 13, 159; PC 29**
See also BRW 2; DLB 126; PAB; RGEL 2
Carey, Ernestine Gilbreth
1908-2006 .... **CLC 17**
See also CA 5-8R; 254; CANR 71; SATA 2; SATA-Obit 177
Carey, Peter 1943- .... **CLC 40, 55, 96, 183, 294, 384; SSC 133**
See also BRWS 12; CA 123; 127; CANR 53, 76, 117, 157, 185, 213; CN 4, 5, 6, 7; DLB 289, 326; EWL 3; INT CA-127; LNFS 1; MTCW 1, 2; MTFW 2005; RGSF 2; SATA 94
Carey, Peter Philip
See Carey, Peter
Carleton, William 1794-1869 ... **NCLC 3, 199**
See also DLB 159; RGEL 2; RGSF 2
Carlisle, Henry 1926-2011 .... **CLC 33**
See also CA 13-16R; CANR 15, 85
Carlisle, Henry Coffin
See Carlisle, Henry
Carlsen, Chris
See Holdstock, Robert
Carlson, Ron 1947- .... **CLC 54**
See also CA 105, 189; CAAE 189; CANR 27, 155, 197; DLB 244
Carlson, Ronald F.
See Carlson, Ron
Carlyle, Jane Welsh
1801-1866 .... **NCLC 181**
See also DLB 55
Carlyle, Thomas
1795-1881 .... **NCLC 22, 70, 248**
See also BRW 4; CDBLB 1789-1832; DA; DAB; DAC; DAM MST; DLB 55, 144, 254, 338, 366; RGEL 2; TEA
Carman, (William) Bliss
1861-1929 .... **PC 34; TCLC 7**
See also CA 104; 152; DAC; DLB 92; RGEL 2
Carnegie, Dale 1888-1955 .... **TCLC 53**
See also CA 218
Caro Mallén de Soto, Ana
c. 1590-c. 1650 .... **LC 175**
Carossa, Hans 1878-1956 .... **TCLC 48**
See also CA 170; DLB 66; EWL 3
Carpenter, Don(ald Richard)
1931-1995 .... **CLC 41**
See also CA 45-48; 149; CANR 1, 71
Carpenter, Edward 1844-1929 ...... **TCLC 88**
See also BRWS 13; CA 163; GLL 1
Carpenter, John 1948- .... **CLC 161**
See also AAYA 2, 73; CA 134; SATA 58
Carpenter, John Howard
See Carpenter, John
Carpenter, Johnny
See Carpenter, John
Carpentier, Alejo 1904-1980 ...... **CLC 8, 11, 38, 110; HLC 1; SSC 35; TCLC 201, 294, 316**
See also CA 65-68; 97-100; CANR 11, 70; CDWLB 3; DAM MULT; DLB 113; EWL 3; HW 1, 2; LAW; LMFS 2; RGSF 2; RGWL 2, 3; WLIT 1
Carpentier y Valmont, Alejo
See Carpentier, Alejo
Carr, Caleb 1955- .... **CLC 86**
See also CA 147; CANR 73, 134; DA3; DLB 350
Carr, Emily 1871-1945 .... **TCLC 32, 260**
See also CA 159; DLB 68; FW; GLL 2
Carr, H. D.
See Crowley, Edward Alexander
Carr, John Dickson 1906-1977 .... **CLC 3**
See also CA 49-52; 69-72; CANR 3, 33, 60; CMW 4; DLB 306; MSW; MTCW 1, 2
Carr, Philippa
See Hibbert, Eleanor Alice Burford
Carr, Virginia Spencer 1929-2012 ... **CLC 34**
See also CA 61-64; CANR 175; DLB 111
Carrier, Roch 1937- .... **CLC 13, 78**
See also CA 130; CANR 61, 152; CCA 1; DAC; DAM MST; DLB 53; SATA 105, 166

Carroll, James Dennis
See Carroll, Jim
Carroll, James P. 1943(?)- .... **CLC 38**
See also CA 81-84; CANR 73, 139, 209; MTCW 2; MTFW 2005
Carroll, Jim 1949-2009 .... **CLC 35, 143**
See also AAYA 17; CA 45-48; 290; CANR 42, 115, 233; NCFS 5
Carroll, Lewis 1832-1898 .... **NCLC 2, 53, 139, 258, 308; PC 18, 74; WLC 1**
See also AAYA 39; BRW 5; BYA 5, 13; CDBLB 1832-1890; CLR 18, 108; DA; DA3; DAB; DAC; DAM MST, NOV, POET; DLB 18, 163, 178; DLBY 1998; EXPN; EXPP; FANT; JRDA; LAIT 1; MAICYA 1, 2; NFS 27; PFS 11, 30; RGEL 2; SATA 100; SUFW 1; TEA; WCH; YABC 2
Carroll, Paul Vincent 1900-1968 .... **CLC 10**
See also CA 9-12R; 25-28R; DLB 10; EWL 3; RGEL 2
Carrere, Emmanuel 1957- .... **CLC 89**
See also CA 200
Carruth, Hayden 1921-2008 .... **CLC 4, 7, 10, 18, 84, 287; PC 10**
See also AMWS 16; CA 9-12R; 277; CANR 4, 38, 59, 110, 174; CP 1, 2, 3, 4, 5, 6, 7; DLB 5, 165; INT CANR-4; MTCW 1, 2; MTFW 2005; PFS 26; SATA 47; SATA-Obit 197
Carson, Anne 1950- .... **CLC 185; PC 64**
See also AMWS 12; CA 203; CANR 209; CP 7; DLB 193; PFS 18; TCLE 1:1
Carson, Ciaran 1948- .... **CLC 201**
See also BRWS 13; CA 112; 153; CANR 113, 189; CP 6, 7; PFS 26
Carson, Rachel 1907-1964 .... **CLC 71; TCLC 314**
See also AAYA 49; AMWS 9; ANW; CA 77-80; CANR 35; DA3; DAM POP; DLB 275; FW; LAIT 4; MAL 5; MTCW 1, 2; MTFW 2005; NCFS 1; SATA 23
Carson, Rachel Louise
See Carson, Rachel
Cartagena, Teresa de 1425(?)- .... **LC 155**
See also DLB 286
Carter, Angela 1940-1992 .... **CLC 5, 41, 76; SSC 13, 85, 151; TCLC 139, 321**
See also BRWS 3; CA 53-56; 136; CANR 12, 36, 61, 106; CN 3, 4, 5; DA3; DLB 14, 207, 261, 319; EXPS; FANT; FW; GL 2; MTCW 1, 2; MTFW 2005; RGSF 2; SATA 66; SATA-Obit 70; SFW 4; SSFS 4, 12; SUFW 2; WLIT 4
Carter, Angela Olive
See Carter, Angela
Carter, Elizabeth 1717-1806 .... **NCLC 277**
See also DLB 109
Carter, Martin (Wylde) 1927- .... **BLC 2:1**
See also BW 2; CA 102; CANR 42; CDWLB 3; CP 1, 2, 3, 4, 5, 6; DLB 117; EWL 3
Carter, Nick
See Smith, Martin Cruz
Carter, Nick
See Smith, Martin Cruz
Carver, Raymond 1938-1988 .... **CLC 22, 36, 53, 55, 126; PC 54; SSC 8, 51, 104, 213**
See also AAYA 44; AMWS 3; BPFB 1; CA 33-36R; 126; CANR 17, 34, 61, 103; CN 4; CPW; DA3; DAM NOV; DLB 130; DLBY 1984, 1988; EWL 3; MAL 5; MTCW 1, 2; MTFW 2005; PFS 17; RGAL 4; RGSF 2; SSFS 3, 6, 12, 13, 23, 32; TCLE 1:1; TCWW 2; TUS
Carvosso, Alan
See Harwood, Gwen
Cary, Elizabeth, Lady Falkland 1585-1639 .... **LC 30, 141**
Cary, (Arthur) Joyce (Lunel) 1888-1957 .... **TCLC 1, 29, 196**
See also BRW 7; CA 104; 164; CDBLB 1914-1945; DLB 15, 100; EWL 3; MTCW 2; RGEL 2; TEA
Casal, Julian del 1863-1893 .... **NCLC 131**
See also DLB 283; LAW
Casanova, Giacomo
See Casanova de Seingalt, Giovanni Jacopo
Casanova, Giovanni Giacomo
See Casanova de Seingalt, Giovanni Jacopo
Casanova de Seingalt, Giovanni Jacopo 1725-1798 .... **LC 13, 151**
See also WLIT 7
Casares, Adolfo Bioy
See Bioy Casares, Adolfo
Casas, Bartolome de las 1474-1566
See Las Casas, Bartolome de
Case, John
See Hougan, Carolyn
Casely-Hayford, J(oseph) E(phraim) 1866-1903 .... **BLC 1:1; TCLC 24**
See also BW 2; CA 123; 152; DAM MULT
Casey, John 1939- .... **CLC 59**
See also BEST 90:2; CA 69-72; CANR 23, 100, 225
Casey, John Dudley
See Casey, John
Casey, Michael 1947- .... **CLC 2**
See also CA 65-68; CANR 109; CP 2, 3; DLB 5
Casey, Patrick
See Thurman, Wallace (Henry)
Casey, Warren 1935-1988 .... **CLC 12**
See also CA 101; 127; INT CA-101
Casey, Warren Peter
See Casey, Warren
Casona, Alejandro
See Alvarez, Alejandro Rodriguez
Cassavetes, John 1929-1989 .... **CLC 20**
See also CA 85-88; 127; CANR 82
Cassian, Nina 1924- .... **PC 17**
See also CA 298; CWP; CWW 2
Cassill, R(onald) V(erlin) 1919-2002 .... **CLC 4, 23**
See also CA 9-12R; 208; CAAS 1; CANR 7, 45; CN 1, 2, 3, 4, 5, 6, 7; DLB 6, 218; DLBY 2002
Cassiodorus, Flavius Magnus Aurelius c. 490(?)-c. 583(?) .... **CMLC 43, 122**
Cassirer, Ernst 1874-1945 .... **TCLC 61**
See also CA 157
Cassity, (Allen) Turner 1929- ..... **CLC 6, 42**
See also CA 17-20R, 223; CAAE 223; CAAS 8; CANR 11; CSW; DLB 105
Cassius Dio c. 155-c. 229 .... **CMLC 99, 167**
See also DLB 176
Castaneda, Carlos (Cesar Aranha) 1931(?)-1998 .... **CLC 12, 119**
See also CA 25-28R; CANR 32, 66, 105; DNFS 1; HW 1; MTCW 1
Castedo, Elena 1937- .... **CLC 65**
See also CA 132
Castedo-Ellerman, Elena
See Castedo, Elena
Castellanos, Rosario 1925-1974 ..... **CLC 66; HLC 1; SSC 39, 68; TCLC 285**
See also CA 131; 53-56; CANR 58; CDWLB 3; DAM MULT; DLB 113, 290; EWL 3; FW; HW 1; LAW; MTCW 2; MTFW 2005; RGSF 2; RGWL 2, 3
Castelvetro, Lodovico 1505-1571 .... **LC 12**
Castiglione, Baldassare 1478-1529 .... **LC 12, 165**
See also EW 2; LMFS 1; RGWL 2, 3; WLIT 7
Castiglione, Baldesar
See Castiglione, Baldassare
Castillo, Ana 1953- .... **CLC 151, 279**
See also AAYA 42; CA 131; CANR 51, 86, 128, 172; CWP; DLB 122, 227; DNFS 2; FW; HW 1; LLW; PFS 21
Castillo, Ana Hernandez Del
See Castillo, Ana
Castle, Robert
See Hamilton, Edmond
Castro (Ruz), Fidel 1926(?)- .... **HLC 1**
See also CA 110; 129; CANR 81; DAM MULT; HW 2
Castro, Guillen de 1569-1631 .... **LC 19**
Castro, Rosalia de 1837-1885 ... **NCLC 3, 78; PC 41**
See also DAM MULT
Castro Alves, Antonio de 1847-1871 .... **NCLC 205**
See also DLB 307; LAW
Cather, Willa 1873-1947 ..... **SSC 2, 50, 114, 186, 207; TCLC 1, 11, 31, 99, 132, 152, 264, 308; WLC 1**
See also AAYA 24; AMW; AMWC 1; AMWR 1; BPFB 1; CA 104; 128; CDALB 1865-1917; CLR 98; DA; DA3; DAB; DAC; DAM MST, NOV; DLB 9, 54, 78, 256; DLBD 1; EWL 3; EXPN; EXPS; FL 1:5; LAIT 3; LATS 1:1; MAL 5; MBL; MTCW 1, 2; MTFW 2005; NFS 2, 19, 33, 41; RGAL 4; RGSF 2; RHW; SATA 30; SSFS 2, 7, 16, 27; TCWW 1, 2; TUS
Cather, Willa Sibert
See Cather, Willa
Catherine II
See Catherine the Great
Catherine, Saint 1347-1380 .. **CMLC 27, 116**
Catherine the Great 1729-1796 ... **LC 69, 208**
See also DLB 150
Cato, Marcus Porcius 234B.C.-149B.C. .... **CMLC 21**
See also DLB 211
Cato, Marcus Porcius, the Elder
See Cato, Marcus Porcius
Cato the Elder
See Cato, Marcus Porcius
Catton, (Charles) Bruce 1899-1978 ... **CLC 35**
See also AITN 1; CA 5-8R; 81-84; CANR 7, 74; DLB 17; MTCW 2; MTFW 2005; SATA 2; SATA-Obit 24
Catullus c. 84B.C.-54B.C. ..... **CMLC 18, 141**
See also AW 2; CDWLB 1; DLB 211; RGWL 2, 3; WLIT 8
Cauldwell, Frank
See King, Francis
Caunitz, William J. 1933-1996 .... **CLC 34**
See also BEST 89:3; CA 125; 130; 152; CANR 73; INT CA-130
Causley, Charles (Stanley) 1917-2003 ... **CLC 7**
See also CA 9-12R; 223; CANR 5, 35, 94; CLR 30; CP 1, 2, 3, 4, 5; CWRI 5; DLB 27; MTCW 1; SATA 3, 66; SATA-Obit 149
Caute, (John) David 1936- .... **CLC 29**
See also CA 1-4R; CAAS 4; CANR 1, 33, 64, 120; CBD; CD 5, 6; CN 1, 2, 3, 4, 5, 6, 7; DAM NOV; DLB 14, 231
Cavafy, C. P.
See Cavafy, Constantine
Cavafy, Constantine 1863-1933 .... **PC 36; TCLC 2, 7**
See also CA 104; 148; DA3; DAM POET; EW 8; EWL 3; MTCW 2; PFS 19; RGWL 2, 3; WP
Cavafy, Constantine Peter
See Cavafy, Constantine
Cavalcanti, Guido c. 1250-c. 1300 ... **CMLC 54, 162; PC 114**
See also RGWL 2, 3; WLIT 7
Cavallo, Evelyn
See Spark, Muriel

Cavanna, Betty
See Harrison, Elizabeth (Allen) Cavanna
Cavanna, Elizabeth
See Harrison, Elizabeth (Allen) Cavanna
Cavanna, Elizabeth Allen
See Harrison, Elizabeth (Allen) Cavanna
Cave, Nick 1957- .... **CLC 379**
See also CA 303
Cavendish, Margaret
1623-1673 .... **LC 30, 132; PC 134**
See also DLB 131, 252, 281; RGEL 2
Cavendish, Margaret Lucas
See Cavendish, Margaret
Caxton, William 1421(?)-1491(?) ... **LC 17, 236**
See also DLB 170
Cayer, D. M.
See Duffy, Maureen
Cayrol, Jean 1911-2005 .... **CLC 11**
See also CA 89-92; 236; DLB 83; EWL 3
Cela, Camilo Jose
See Cela, Camilo Jose
Cela, Camilo Jose 1916-2002 ..... **CLC 4, 13, 59, 122; HLC 1; SSC 71**
See also BEST 90:2; CA 21-24R; 206; CAAS 10; CANR 21, 32, 76, 139; CWW 2; DAM MULT; DLB 322; DLBY 1989; EW 13; EWL 3; HW 1; MTCW 1, 2; MTFW 2005; RGSF 2; RGWL 2, 3
Celan, Paul 1920-1970 .... **CLC 10, 19, 53, 82; PC 10**
See also CA 85-88; CANR 33, 61; CDWLB 2; DLB 69; EWL 3; MTCW 1; PFS 21; RGHL; RGWL 2, 3
Cela y Trulock, Camilo Jose
See Cela, Camilo Jose
Celati, Gianni 1937- .... **CLC 373**
See also CA 251; CWW 2; DLB 196
Cellini, Benvenuto 1500-1571 .... **LC 7**
See also WLIT 7
Cendrars, Blaise
See Sauser-Hall, Frederic
Centlivre, Susanna 1669(?)-1723 ...... **DC 25; LC 65, 221**
See also DLB 84; RGEL 2
Cernuda, Luis 1902-1963 .... **CLC 54; PC 62; TCLC 286**
See also CA 131; 89-92; DAM POET; DLB 134; EWL 3; GLL 1; HW 1; RGWL 2, 3
Cernuda y Bidon, Luis
See Cernuda, Luis
Cervantes, Lorna Dee 1954- ... **HLCS 1; PC 35**
See also CA 131; CANR 80; CP 7; CWP; DLB 82; EXPP; HW 1; LLW; PFS 30
Cervantes, Miguel de 1547-1616 ...... **HLCS; LC 6, 23, 93; SSC 12, 108; WLC 1**
See also AAYA 56; BYA 1, 14; DA; DAB; DAC; DAM MST, NOV; EW 2; LAIT 1; LATS 1:1; LMFS 1; NFS 8; RGSF 2; RGWL 2, 3; TWA
Cervantes Saavedra, Miguel de
See Cervantes, Miguel de
Cesaire, Aime 1913-2008 .... **BLC 1:1; CLC 19, 32, 112, 280; DC 22; PC 25**
See also BW 2, 3; CA 65-68; 271; CANR 24, 43, 81; CWW 2; DA3; DAM MULT, POET; DLB 321; EWL 3; GFL 1789 to the Present; MTCW 1, 2; MTFW 2005; WP
Cesaire, Aime Fernand
See Cesaire, Aime
Cha, Louis
See Jin Yong
Cha Leung-yung, Louis
See Jin Yong
Cha, Theresa Hak Kyung
1951-1982 .... **TCLC 307**
See also CA 217; DLB 312
Chaadaev, Petr Iakovlevich
1794-1856 .... **NCLC 197**
See also DLB 198
Chabon, Michael 1963- .... **CLC 55, 149, 265; SSC 59**
See also AAYA 45; AMWS 11; CA 139; CANR 57, 96, 127, 138, 196; DLB 278; MAL 5; MTFW 2005; NFS 25; SATA 145; SSFS 36
Chabrol, Claude 1930-2010 .... **CLC 16**
See also CA 110
Chacel, Rosa 1898-1994 .... **TCLC 298**
See also CA 243; CANR 216; CWW 2; DLB 134, 322; EWL 3
Chairil Anwar
See Anwar, Chairil
Challans, Mary
See Renault, Mary
Challis, George
See Faust, Frederick
Chambers, Aidan 1934- .... **CLC 35**
See also AAYA 27, 86; CA 25-28R; CANR 12, 31, 58, 116; CLR 151; JRDA; MAICYA 1, 2; SAAS 12; SATA 1, 69, 108, 171; WYA; YAW
Chambers, James .... **CLC 21**
See also CA 124; 199
Chambers, Jessie
See Lawrence, D. H.
Chambers, Maria Cristina
See Mena, Maria Cristina
Chambers, Robert W(illiam)
1865-1933 .... **SSC 92; TCLC 41**
See also CA 165; DLB 202; HGG; SATA 107; SUFW 1
Chambers, (David) Whittaker
1901-1961 .... **TCLC 129**
See also CA 89-92; DLB 303
Chamisso, Adelbert von
1781-1838 .... **NCLC 82; SSC 140**
See also DLB 90; RGWL 2, 3; SUFW 1
Chamoiseau, Patrick 1953- ... **CLC 268, 276**
See also CA 162; CANR 88; EWL 3; RGWL 3
Chance, James T.
See Carpenter, John
Chance, John T.
See Carpenter, John
Chand, Munshi Prem
See Srivastava, Dhanpat Rai
Chand, Prem
See Srivastava, Dhanpat Rai
Chandler, Raymond 1888-1959 ...... **SSC 23; TCLC 1, 7, 179**
See also AAYA 25; AMWC 2; AMWS 4; BPFB 1; CA 104; 129; CANR 60, 107; CDALB 1929-1941; CMW 4; DA3; DLB 226, 253; DLBD 6; EWL 3; MAL 5; MSW; MTCW 1, 2; MTFW 2005; NFS 17; RGAL 4; TUS
Chandler, Raymond Thornton
See Chandler, Raymond
Chandra, Vikram 1961- .... **CLC 302**
See also CA 149; CANR 97, 214; SSFS 16
Chang, Diana 1934-2009 .... **AAL**
See also CA 228; CWP; DLB 312; EXPP; PFS 37
Chang, Eileen 1920-1995 ...... **AAL; SSC 28, 169; TCLC 184**
See also CA 166; CANR 168; CWW 2; DLB 328; EWL 3; RGSF 2
Chang, Jung 1952- .... **CLC 71**
See also CA 142
Chang Ai-Ling
See Chang, Eileen
Channing, William Ellery
1780-1842 .... **NCLC 17**
See also DLB 1, 59, 235; RGAL 4
Channing, William Ellery II
1817-1901 .... **TCLC 306**
See also CA 215; DLB 1, 223
Chao, Patricia 1955- .... **CLC 119**
See also CA 163; CANR 155
Chaplin, Charles Spencer
1889-1977 .... **CLC 16**
See also AAYA 61; CA 81-84; 73-76; DLB 44
Chaplin, Charlie
See Chaplin, Charles Spencer
Chapman, George 1559(?)-1634 .... **DC 19; LC 22, 116; PC 96**
See also BRW 1; DAM DRAM; DLB 62, 121; LMFS 1; RGEL 2
Chapman, Graham 1941-1989 .... **CLC 21**
See also AAYA 7; CA 116; 129; CANR 35, 95
Chapman, John Jay 1862-1933 ...... **TCLC 7**
See also AMWS 14; CA 104; 191
Chapman, Lee
See Bradley, Marion Zimmer
Chapman, Maile .... **CLC 318**
Chapman, Walker
See Silverberg, Robert
Chappell, Fred 1936- .... **CLC 40, 78, 162, 293; PC 105**
See also CA 5-8R, 198; CAAE 198; CAAS 4; CANR 8, 33, 67, 110, 215; CN 6; CP 6, 7; CSW; DLB 6, 105; HGG
Chappell, Fred Davis
See Chappell, Fred
Char, Rene 1907-1988 ... **CLC 9, 11, 14, 55; PC 56**
See also CA 13-16R; 124; CANR 32; DAM POET; DLB 258; EWL 3; GFL 1789 to the Present; MTCW 1, 2; RGWL 2, 3
Char, Rene-Emile
See Char, Rene
Charby, Jay
See Ellison, Harlan
Chardin, Pierre Teilhard de
See Teilhard de Chardin, (Marie Joseph) Pierre
Chariton fl. 1st cent. (?) .... **CMLC 49**
Charke, Charlotte 1713-1760 .... **LC 236**
Charlemagne 742-814 .... **CMLC 37**
Charles I 1600-1649 .... **LC 13, 194, 237**
Charrière, Isabelle de
1740-1805 .... **NCLC 66, 314**
See also DLB 313
Charron, Pierre 1541-1603 .... **LC 174**
See also GFL Beginnings to 1789
Chartier, Alain c. 1392-1430 .... **LC 94**
See also DLB 208
Chartier, Emile-Auguste
See Alain
Charyn, Jerome 1937- .... **CLC 5, 8, 18**
See also CA 5-8R; CAAS 1; CANR 7, 61, 101, 158, 199; CMW 4; CN 1, 2, 3, 4, 5, 6, 7; DLBY 1983; MTCW 1
Chase, Adam
See Marlowe, Stephen
Chase, Mary (Coyle) 1907-1981 .... **DC 1**
See also CA 77-80; 105; CAD; CWD; DFS 11; DLB 228; SATA 17; SATA-Obit 29
Chase, Mary Ellen 1887-1973 .... **CLC 2; TCLC 124**
See also CA 13-16; 41-44R; CAP 1; SATA 10
Chase, Nicholas
See Hyde, Anthony
Chase-Riboud, Barbara (Dewayne Tosi)
1939- .... **BLC 2:1**
See also BW 2; CA 113; CANR 76; DAM MULT; DLB 33; MTCW 2
Chateaubriand, Francois Rene de
1768-1848 .... **NCLC 3, 134**
See also DLB 119, 366; EW 5; GFL 1789 to the Present; RGWL 2, 3; TWA
Chatterje, Saratchandra -(?)
See Chatterji, Sarat Chandra
Chatterji, Bankim Chandra
1838-1894 .... **NCLC 19**

Author Index

Chatterji, Sarat Chandra 1876-1936 .... **TCLC 13**
See also CA 109; 186; EWL 3
Chatterton, Thomas 1752-1770 ... **LC 3, 54; PC 104**
See also DAM POET; DLB 109; RGEL 2
Chatwin, Bruce 1940-1989 ... **CLC 28, 57, 59**
See also AAYA 4; BEST 90:1; BRWS 4; CA 85-88; 127; CANR 228; CPW; DAM POP; DLB 194, 204; EWL 3; MTFW 2005
Chatwin, Charles Bruce
See Chatwin, Bruce
Chaucer, Daniel
See Ford, Ford Madox
Chaucer, Geoffrey 1340(?)-1400 .... **LC 17, 56, 173, 210, 213; PC 19, 58, 155; WLCS**
See also BRW 1; BRWC 1; BRWR 2; CDBLB Before 1660; DA; DA3; DAB; DAC; DAM MST, POET; DLB 146; LAIT 1; PAB; PFS 14; RGEL 2; TEA; WLIT 3; WP
Chaudhuri, Nirad C(handra) 1897-1999 .... **TCLC 224**
See also CA 128; 183; DLB 323
Chaviaras, Strates 1935- .... **CLC 33**
See also CA 105
Chayefsky, Paddy 1923-1981 .... **CLC 23**
See also CA 9-12R; 104; CAD; CANR 18; DAM DRAM; DFS 26; DLB 23; DLBY 7, 44; RGAL 4
Chayefsky, Sidney
See Chayefsky, Paddy
Chedid, Andree 1920-2011 .... **CLC 47**
See also CA 145; CANR 95; EWL 3
Cheever, John 1912-1982 ... **CLC 3, 7, 8, 11, 15, 25, 64; SSC 1, 38, 57, 120; WLC 2**
See also AAYA 65; AMWS 1; BPFB 1; CA 5-8R; 106; CABS 1; CANR 5, 27, 76; CDALB 1941-1968; CN 1, 2, 3; CPW; DA; DA3; DAB; DAC; DAM MST, NOV, POP; DLB 2, 102, 227; DLBY 1980, 1982; EWL 3; EXPS; INT CANR-5; MAL 5; MTCW 1, 2; MTFW 2005; RGAL 4; RGSF 2; SSFS 2, 14; TUS
Cheever, Susan 1943- .... **CLC 18, 48**
See also CA 103; CANR 27, 51, 92, 157, 198, 232; DLBY 1982; INT CANR-27
Chekhonte, Antosha
See Chekhov, Anton
Chekhov, Anton 1860-1904 ... **DC 9; SSC 2, 28, 41, 51, 85, 102, 155; TCLC 3, 10, 31, 55, 96, 163; WLC 2**
See also AAYA 68; BYA 14; CA 104; 124; DA; DA3; DAB; DAC; DAM DRAM, MST; DFS 1, 5, 10, 12, 26; DLB 277; EW 7; EWL 3; EXPS; LAIT 3; LATS 1:1; RGSF 2; RGWL 2, 3; SATA 90; SSFS 5, 13, 14, 26, 29, 33; TWA
Chekhov, Anton Pavlovich
See Chekhov, Anton
Chen Jia
See Shen Congwen
Cheney, Lynne V. 1941- .... **CLC 70**
See also CA 89-92; CANR 58, 117, 193; SATA 152
Cheney, Lynne Vincent
See Cheney, Lynne V.
Chernyshevsky, Nikolai Gavrilovich
See Chernyshevsky, Nikolay Gavrilovich
Chernyshevsky, Nikolay Gavrilovich 1828-1889 .... **NCLC 1**
See also DLB 238
Cherry, Carolyn Janice
See Cherryh, C.J.
Cherryh, C.J. 1942- .... **CLC 35**
See also AAYA 24; BPFB 1; CA 65-68; CANR 10, 147, 179; DLBY 1980; FANT; SATA 93, 172; SCFW 2; YAW
Chesler, Phyllis 1940- .... **CLC 247**
See also CA 49-52; CANR 4, 59, 140, 189; FW
Chesnut, Mary 1823-1886 .... **NCLC 250**
See also DLB 239
Chesnut, Mary Boykin
See Chesnut, Mary
Chesnutt, Charles W(addell) 1858-1932 .... **BLC 1; SSC 7, 54, 139, 184; TCLC 5, 39**
See also AFAW 1, 2; AMWS 14; BW 1, 3; CA 106; 125; CANR 76; DAM MULT; DLB 12, 50, 78; EWL 3; MAL 5; MTCW 1, 2; MTFW 2005; RGAL 4; RGSF 2; SSFS 11, 26
Chester, Alfred 1929(?)-1971 .... **CLC 49**
See also CA 196; 33-36R; DLB 130; MAL 5
Chesterton, G. K. 1874-1936 .... **PC 28; SSC 1, 46, 148; TCLC 1, 6, 64**
See also AAYA 57; BRW 6; CA 104; 132; CANR 73, 131; CDBLB 1914-1945; CMW 4; DAM NOV, POET; DLB 10, 19, 34, 70, 98, 149, 178; EWL 3; FANT; MSW; MTCW 1, 2; MTFW 2005; RGEL 2; RGSF 2; SATA 27; SUFW 1
Chesterton, Gilbert Keith
See Chesterton, G. K.
Chettle, Henry 1560-1607(?) .... **LC 112**
See also DLB 136; RGEL 2
Chiang, Pin-chin 1904-1986 .... **CLC 68**
See also CA 118; DLB 328; EWL 3; RGWL 3
Chiang Ping-chih
See Chiang, Pin-chin
Chief Joseph 1840-1904 .... **NNAL**
See also CA 152; DA3; DAM MULT
Chief Seattle 1786(?)-1866 .... **NNAL**
See also DA3; DAM MULT
Ch'ien, Chung-shu
See Qian, Zhongshu
Chikamatsu Monzaemon 1653-1724 ... **LC 66**
See also RGWL 2, 3
Child, Francis James 1825-1896 ... **NCLC 173**
See also DLB 1, 64, 235
Child, L. Maria
See Child, Lydia Maria
Child, Lydia Maria 1802-1880 .... **NCLC 6, 73, 289**
See also DLB 1, 74, 243; RGAL 4; SATA 67
Child, Mrs.
See Child, Lydia Maria
Child, Philip 1898-1978 .... **CLC 19, 68**
See also CA 13-14; CAP 1; CP 1; DLB 68; RHW; SATA 47
Childers, Erskine 1870-1922 .... **TCLC 65**
See also BRWS 17; CA 113; 153; DLB 70
Childress, Alice 1920-1994 .... **BLC 1:1; CLC 12, 15, 86, 96; DC 4; TCLC 116**
See also AAYA 8; BW 2, 3; BYA 2; CA 45-48; 146; CAD; CANR 3, 27, 50, 74; CLR 14; CWD; DA3; DAM DRAM, MULT, NOV; DFS 2, 8, 14, 26; DLB 7, 38, 249; JRDA; LAIT 5; MAICYA 1, 2; MAICYAS 1; MAL 5; MTCW 1, 2; MTFW 2005; RGAL 4; SATA 7, 48, 81; TUS; WYA; YAW
Chin, Frank 1940- ... **AAL; CLC 135; DC 7**
See also CA 33-36R; CAD; CANR 71; CD 5, 6; DAM MULT; DLB 206, 312; LAIT 5; NFS 41; RGAL 4
Chin, Frank Chew, Jr.
See Chin, Frank
Chin, Marilyn 1955- .... **PC 40**
See also CA 129; CANR 70, 113, 218; CWP; DLB 312; PFS 28, 41
Chin, Marilyn Mei Ling
See Chin, Marilyn
Chislett, (Margaret) Anne 1943- .... **CLC 34**
See also CA 151
Chitty, Thomas Willes
See Hinde, Thomas
Chivers, Thomas Holley 1809-1858 .... **NCLC 49**
See also DLB 3, 248; RGAL 4
Chlamyda, Jehudil
See Gorky, Maxim
Chenier, Andre-Marie de 1762-1794 ... **LC 174**
See also EW 4; GFL Beginnings to 1789; TWA
Ch'o, Chou
See Shu-Jen, Chou
Choi, Susan 1969- .... **CLC 119**
See also CA 223; CANR 188
Chomette, Rene Lucien 1898-1981 ... **CLC 20**
See also CA 103
Chomsky, Avram Noam
See Chomsky, Noam
Chomsky, Noam 1928- .... **CLC 132**
See also CA 17-20R; CANR 28, 62, 110, 132, 179; DA3; DLB 246; MTCW 1, 2; MTFW 2005
Chona, Maria 1845(?)-1936 .... **NNAL**
See also CA 144
Chopin, Kate 1851-1904 ..... **SSC 8, 68, 110, 171, 211; TCLC 127; WLCS**
See also AAYA 33; AMWR 2; BYA 11, 15; CA 104; 122; CDALB 1865-1917; DA3; DAB; DAC; DAM MST, NOV; DLB 12, 78; EXPN; EXPS; FL 1:3; FW; LAIT 3; MAL 5; MBL; NFS 3; RGAL 4; RGSF 2; SSFS 2, 13, 17, 26, 35; TUS
Chopin, Katherine
See Chopin, Kate
Christie
See Ichikawa, Kon
Christie, Agatha 1890-1976 ..... **CLC 1, 6, 8, 12, 39, 48, 110; DC 39**
See also AAYA 9; AITN 1, 2; BPFB 1; BRWS 2; CA 17-20R; 61-64; CANR 10, 37, 108; CBD; CDBLB 1914-1945; CMW 4; CN 1, 2; CPW; CWD; DA3; DAB; DAC; DAM NOV; DFS 2; DLB 13, 77, 245; MSW; MTCW 1, 2; MTFW 2005; NFS 8, 30, 33; RGEL 2; RHW; SATA 36; SSFS 31, 34; TEA; YAW
Christie, Agatha Mary Clarissa
See Christie, Agatha
Christie, Ann Philippa
See Pearce, Philippa
Christie, Philippa
See Pearce, Philippa
Christine de Pisan
See Christine de Pizan
Christine de Pizan 1365(?)-1431(?) .... **LC 9, 130, 235; PC 68**
See also DLB 208; FL 1:1; FW; RGWL 2, 3
Chretien de Troyes c. 12th cent. .... **CMLC 10, 135**
See also DLB 208; EW 1; RGWL 2, 3; TWA
Chatelet, Gabrielle-Emilie Du
See du Chatelet, Emilie
Chuang-Tzu c. 369B.C.-c. 286B.C. .... **CMLC 57, 134**
Chubb, Elmer
See Masters, Edgar Lee
Chudleigh, Lady Mary 1656-1710 .... **LC 217**
Chulkov, Mikhail Dmitrievich 1743-1792 .... **LC 2**
See also DLB 150
Chung, Sonya .... **CLC 318**
See also CA 307
Churchill, Caryl 1938- .... **CLC 31, 55, 157; DC 5**
See also BRWS 4; CA 102; CANR 22, 46, 108; CBD; CD 5, 6; CWD; DFS 25; DLB 13, 310; EWL 3; FW; MTCW 1; RGEL 2
Churchill, Charles 1731-1764 .... **LC 3**
See also DLB 109; RGEL 2
Churchill, Chick
See Churchill, Caryl

Churchill, Sir Winston 1874-1965 .... **TCLC 113**
See also BRW 6; CA 97-100; CDBLB 1890-1914; DA3; DLB 100, 329; DLBD 16; LAIT 4; MTCW 1, 2
Churchill, Sir Winston Leonard Spencer
See Churchill, Sir Winston
Churchyard, Thomas 1520(?)-1604 ... **LC 187**
See also DLB 132; RGEL 2
Chute, Carolyn 1947- .... **CLC 39, 322**
See also CA 123; CANR 135, 213; CN 7; DLB 350
Ciardi, John (Anthony) 1916-1986 .. **CLC 10, 40, 44, 129; PC 69**
See also CA 5-8R; 118; CAAS 2; CANR 5, 33; CLR 19; CP 1, 2, 3, 4; CWRI 5; DAM POET; DLB 5; DLBY 1986; INT CANR-5; MAICYA 1, 2; MAL 5; MTCW 1, 2; MTFW 2005; RGAL 4; SAAS 26; SATA 1, 65; SATA-Obit 46
Cibber, Colley 1671-1757 .... **LC 66, 211**
See also DLB 84; RGEL 2
Cicero, Marcus Tullius 106B.C.-43B.C. .... **CMLC 3, 81, 121, 175**
See also AW 1; CDWLB 1; DLB 211; RGWL 2, 3; WLIT 8
Cimino, Michael 1943- .... **CLC 16**
See also CA 105
Cioran, E(mil) M. 1911-1995 .... **CLC 64**
See also CA 25-28R; 149; CANR 91; DLB 220; EWL 3
Circus, Anthony
See Hoch, Edward D.
Cisneros, Sandra 1954- .... **CLC 69, 118, 193, 305, 352; HLC 1; PC 52; SSC 32, 72, 143, 187**
See also AAYA 9, 53; AMWS 7; CA 131; CANR 64, 118; CLR 123; CN 7; CWP; DA3; DAM MULT; DLB 122, 152; EWL 3; EXPN; FL 1:5; FW; HW 1, 2; LAIT 5; LATS 1:2; LLW; MAICYA 2; MAL 5; MTCW 2; MTFW 2005; NFS 2; PFS 19; RGAL 4; RGSF 2; SSFS 3, 13, 27, 32; WLIT 1; YAW
Cixous, Helene 1937- .... **CLC 92, 253**
See also CA 126; CANR 55, 123; CWW 2; DLB 83, 242; EWL 3; FL 1:5; FW; GLL 2; MTCW 1, 2; MTFW 2005; TWA
Clair, Rene
See Chomette, Rene Lucien
Clampitt, Amy 1920-1994 ... **CLC 32; PC 19**
See also AMWS 9; CA 110; 146; CANR 29, 79; CP 4, 5; DLB 105; MAL 5; PFS 27, 39
Clancy, Thomas L., Jr.
See Clancy, Tom
Clancy, Tom 1947-2013 .... **CLC 45, 112**
See also AAYA 9, 51; BEST 89:1, 90:1; BPFB 1; BYA 10, 11; CA 125; 131; CANR 62, 105, 132; CMW 4; CPW; DA3; DAM NOV, POP; DLB 227; INT CA-131; MTCW 1, 2; MTFW 2005
Clare, John 1793-1864 .... **NCLC 9, 86, 259; PC 23**
See also BRWS 11; DAB; DAM POET; DLB 55, 96; RGEL 2
Clare of Assisi 1194-1253 .... **CMLC 149**
Clarin
See Alas (y Urena), Leopoldo (Enrique Garcia)
Clark, Al C.
See Goines, Donald
Clark, Brian (Robert)
See Clark, (Robert) Brian
Clark, (Robert) Brian 1932- .... **CLC 29**
See also CA 41-44R; CANR 67; CBD; CD 5, 6
Clark, Curt
See Westlake, Donald E.
Clark, Eleanor 1913-1996 .... **CLC 5, 19**
See also CA 9-12R; 151; CANR 41; CN 1, 2, 3, 4, 5, 6; DLB 6
Clark, J. P.
See Clark-Bekederemo, J. P.
Clark, John Pepper
See Clark-Bekederemo, J. P.
Clark, Kenneth (Mackenzie) 1903-1983 .... **TCLC 147**
See also CA 93-96; 109; CANR 36; MTCW 1, 2; MTFW 2005
Clark, M. R.
See Clark, Mavis Thorpe
Clark, Mavis Thorpe 1909-1999 .... **CLC 12**
See also CA 57-60; CANR 8, 37, 107; CLR 30; CWRI 5; MAICYA 1, 2; SAAS 5; SATA 8, 74
Clark, Rev. T.
See Galt, John
Clark, Walter Van Tilburg 1909-1971 .... **CLC 28**
See also CA 9-12R; 33-36R; CANR 63, 113; CN 1; DLB 9, 206; LAIT 2; MAL 5; NFS 40; RGAL 4; SATA 8; TCWW 1, 2
Clark-Bekederemo, J. P. 1935- ..... **BLC 1:1; CLC 38; DC 5**
See also AAYA 79; AFW; BW 1; CA 65-68; CANR 16, 72; CD 5, 6; CDWLB 3; CP 1, 2, 3, 4, 5, 6, 7; DAM DRAM, MULT; DFS 13; DLB 117; EWL 3; MTCW 2; MTFW 2005; RGEL 2
Clark-Bekederemo, John Pepper
See Clark-Bekederemo, J. P.
Clark Bekederemo, Johnson Pepper
See Clark-Bekederemo, J. P.
Clarke, Arthur
See Clarke, Arthur C.
Clarke, Arthur C. 1917-2008 ...... **CLC 1, 4, 13, 18, 35, 136; SSC 3**
See also AAYA 4, 33; BPFB 1; BYA 13; CA 1-4R; 270; CANR 2, 28, 55, 74, 130, 196; CLR 119; CN 1, 2, 3, 4, 5, 6, 7; CPW; DA3; DAM POP; DLB 261; JRDA; LAIT 5; MAICYA 1, 2; MTCW 1, 2; MTFW 2005; SATA 13, 70, 115; SATA-Obit 191; SCFW 1, 2; SFW 4; SSFS 4, 18, 29, 36; TCLE 1:1; YAW
Clarke, Arthur Charles
See Clarke, Arthur C.
Clarke, Austin 1896-1974 .... **CLC 6, 9; PC 112**
See also BRWS 15; CA 29-32; 49-52; CAP 2; CP 1, 2; DAM POET; DLB 10, 20; EWL 3; RGEL 2
Clarke, Austin 1934- .... **BLC 1:1; CLC 8, 53; SSC 45, 116**
See also BW 1; CA 25-28R; CAAS 16; CANR 14, 32, 68, 140, 220; CN 1, 2, 3, 4, 5, 6, 7; DAC; DAM MULT; DLB 53, 125; DNFS 2; MTCW 2; MTFW 2005; RGSF 2
Clarke, Gillian 1937- .... **CLC 61**
See also CA 106; CP 3, 4, 5, 6, 7; CWP; DLB 40
Clarke, Marcus (Andrew Hislop) 1846-1881 .... **NCLC 19, 258; SSC 94**
See also DLB 230; RGEL 2; RGSF 2
Clarke, Shirley 1925-1997 .... **CLC 16**
See also CA 189
Clash, The
See Headon, (Nicky) Topper; Jones, Mick; Simonon, Paul; Strummer, Joe
Claudel, Paul (Louis Charles Marie) 1868-1955 .... **TCLC 2, 10, 268**
See also CA 104; 165; DLB 192, 258, 321; EW 8; EWL 3; GFL 1789 to the Present; RGWL 2, 3; TWA
Claudian 370(?)-404(?) .... **CMLC 46**
See also RGWL 2, 3
Claudius, Matthias 1740-1815 ...... **NCLC 75**
See also DLB 97
Clausewitz, Carl von 1780-1831 ... **NCLC 296**
Clavell, James 1925-1994 ..... **CLC 6, 25, 87**
See also BPFB 1; CA 25-28R; 146; CANR 26, 48; CN 5; CPW; DA3; DAM NOV, POP; MTCW 1, 2; MTFW 2005; NFS 10; RHW
Clayman, Gregory .... **CLC 65**
Cleage, Pearl 1948- .... **DC 32**
See also BW 2; CA 41-44R; CANR 27, 148, 177, 226; DFS 14, 16; DLB 228; NFS 17
Cleage, Pearl Michelle
See Cleage, Pearl
Cleaver, (Leroy) Eldridge 1935-1998 ... **BLC 1:1; CLC 30, 119**
See also BW 1, 3; CA 21-24R; 167; CANR 16, 75; DA3; DAM MULT; MTCW 2; YAW
Cleese, John (Marwood) 1939- .... **CLC 21**
See also CA 112; 116; CANR 35; MTCW 1
Cleishbotham, Jebediah
See Scott, Sir Walter
Cleland, John 1710-1789 .... **LC 2, 48, 235**
See also DLB 39; RGEL 2
Clemens, Samuel
See Twain, Mark
Clemens, Samuel Langhorne
See Twain, Mark
Clement of Alexandria 150(?)-215(?) .... **CMLC 41**
Cleophil
See Congreve, William
Clerihew, E.
See Bentley, E(dmund) C(lerihew)
Clerk, N. W.
See Lewis, C. S.
Cleveland, John 1613-1658 .... **LC 106**
See also DLB 126; RGEL 2
Cliff, Jimmy
See Chambers, James
Cliff, Michelle 1946- .... **BLCS; CLC 120**
See also BW 2; CA 116; CANR 39, 72; CDWLB 3; DLB 157; FW; GLL 2
Clifford, Lady Anne 1590-1676 .... **LC 76**
See also DLB 151
Clifton, Lucille 1936-2010 ..... **BLC 1:1, 2:1; CLC 19, 66, 162, 283; PC 17, 148**
See also AFAW 2; BW 2, 3; CA 49-52; CANR 2, 24, 42, 76, 97, 138; CLR 5; CP 2, 3, 4, 5, 6, 7; CSW; CWP; CWRI 5; DA3; DAM MULT, POET; DLB 5, 41; EXPP; MAICYA 1, 2; MTCW 1, 2; MTFW 2005; PFS 1, 14, 29, 41; SATA 20, 69, 128; SSFS 34; WP
Clifton, Thelma Lucille
See Clifton, Lucille
Celine, Louis-Ferdinand 1894-1961 .... **CLC 1, 3, 4, 7, 47, 124**
See also CA 85-88; CANR 28; DLB 72; EW 11; EWL 3; GFL 1789 to the Present; MTCW 1; RGWL 2, 3
Clinton, Dirk
See Silverberg, Robert
Clough, Arthur Hugh 1819-1861 .... **NCLC 27, 163; PC 103**
See also BRW 5; DLB 32; RGEL 2
Clouts, Sydney 1926-1982 .... **TCLC 318**
See also CA 207; CP 1, 2, 3; DLB 225
Clutha, Janet
See Frame, Janet
Clutha, Janet Paterson Frame
See Frame, Janet
Clyne, Terence
See Blatty, William Peter
C. N.
See Naden, Constance
Cobalt, Martin
See Mayne, William
Cobb, Irvin S(hrewsbury) 1876-1944 .... **TCLC 77**
See also CA 175; DLB 11, 25, 86

Cobbett, William 1763-1835 .. **NCLC 49, 288**
See also DLB 43, 107, 158; RGEL 2
Coben, Harlan 1962- .... **CLC 269**
See also AAYA 83; CA 164; CANR 162, 199, 234
Coburn, D(onald) L(ee) 1938- .... **CLC 10**
See also CA 89-92; DFS 23
Cockburn, Catharine Trotter
See Trotter, Catharine
Cocteau, Jean 1889-1963 .... **CLC 1, 8, 15, 16, 43; DC 17; TCLC 119; WLC 2**
See also AAYA 74; CA 25-28; CANR 40; CAP 2; DA; DA3; DAB; DAC; DAM DRAM, MST, NOV; DFS 24; DLB 65, 258, 321; EW 10; EWL 3; GFL 1789 to the Present; MTCW 1, 2; RGWL 2, 3; TWA
Cocteau, Jean Maurice Eugene Clement
See Cocteau, Jean
Codrescu, Andrei 1946- .... **CLC 46, 121**
See also CA 33-36R; CAAS 19; CANR 13, 34, 53, 76, 125, 223; CN 7; DA3; DAM POET; MAL 5; MTCW 2; MTFW 2005
Coe, Max
See Bourne, Randolph S(illiman)
Coe, Tucker
See Westlake, Donald E.
Coelho, Paulo 1947- .... **CLC 258**
See also CA 152; CANR 80, 93, 155, 194; NFS 29
Coen, Ethan 1957- .... **CLC 108, 267**
See also AAYA 54; CA 126; CANR 85
Coen, Joel 1954- .... **CLC 108, 267**
See also AAYA 54; CA 126; CANR 119
Coetzee, J. M. 1940- .... **CLC 23, 33, 66, 117, 161, 162, 305**
See also AAYA 37; AFW; BRWS 6; CA 77-80; CANR 41, 54, 74, 114, 133, 180; CN 4, 5, 6, 7; DA3; DAM NOV; DLB 225, 326, 329; EWL 3; LMFS 2; MTCW 1, 2; MTFW 2005; NFS 21; WLIT 2; WWE 1
Coetzee, John Maxwell
See Coetzee, J. M.
Coffey, Brian
See Koontz, Dean
Coffin, Robert P. Tristram
1892-1955 .... **TCLC 95**
See also CA 123; 169; DLB 45
Coffin, Robert Peter Tristram
See Coffin, Robert P. Tristram
Cohan, George M. 1878-1942 .... **TCLC 60**
See also CA 157; DLB 249; RGAL 4
Cohan, George Michael
See Cohan, George M.
Cohen, Arthur A(llen)
1928-1986 .... **CLC 7, 31**
See also CA 1-4R; 120; CANR 1, 17, 42; DLB 28; RGHL
Cohen, Leonard 1934- .... **CLC 3, 38, 260; PC 109**
See also CA 21-24R; CANR 14, 69; CN 1, 2, 3, 4, 5, 6; CP 1, 2, 3, 4, 5, 6, 7; DAC; DAM MST; DLB 53; EWL 3; MTCW 1
Cohen, Leonard Norman
See Cohen, Leonard
Cohen, Matt(hew) 1942-1999 .... **CLC 19**
See also CA 61-64; 187; CAAS 18; CANR 40; CN 1, 2, 3, 4, 5, 6; DAC; DLB 53
Cohen-Solal, Annie 1948- .... **CLC 50**
See also CA 239
Colegate, Isabel 1931- .... **CLC 36**
See also CA 17-20R; CANR 8, 22, 74; CN 4, 5, 6, 7; DLB 14, 231; INT CANR-22; MTCW 1
Coleman, Emmett
See Reed, Ishmael
Coleridge, Hartley 1796-1849 ... **NCLC 90, 283**
See also DLB 96
Coleridge, M. E.
See Coleridge, Mary E(lizabeth)
Coleridge, Mary E(lizabeth)
1861-1907 .... **TCLC 73**
See also CA 116; 166; DLB 19, 98
Coleridge, Samuel Taylor
1772-1834 .... **NCLC 9, 54, 99, 111, 177, 197, 231; PC 11, 39, 67, 100; WLC 2**
See also AAYA 66; BRW 4; BRWR 2; BYA 4; CDBLB 1789-1832; DA; DA3; DAB; DAC; DAM MST, POET; DLB 93, 107; EXPP; LATS 1:1; LMFS 1; PAB; PFS 4, 5, 39; RGEL 2; TEA; WLIT 3; WP
Coleridge, Sara 1802-1852 .... **NCLC 31**
See also DLB 199
Coles, Don 1928- .... **CLC 46**
See also CA 115; CANR 38; CP 5, 6, 7
Coles, Robert 1929- .... **CLC 108**
See also CA 45-48; CANR 3, 32, 66, 70, 135, 225; INT CANR-32; SATA 23
Coles, Robert Martin
See Coles, Robert
Colette 1873-1954 .... **SSC 10, 93; TCLC 1, 5, 16, 272**
See also CA 104; 131; DA3; DAM NOV; DLB 65; EW 9; EWL 3; GFL 1789 to the Present; GLL 1; MTCW 1, 2; MTFW 2005; RGWL 2, 3; TWA
Colette, Sidonie-Gabrielle
See Colette
Collett, (Jacobine) Camilla (Wergeland)
1813-1895 .... **NCLC 22**
See also DLB 354
Collier, Christopher 1930- .... **CLC 30**
See also AAYA 13; BYA 2; CA 33-36R; CANR 13, 33, 102; CLR 126; JRDA; MAICYA 1, 2; NFS 38; SATA 16, 70; WYA; YAW 1
Collier, James Lincoln 1928- .... **CLC 30**
See also AAYA 13; BYA 2; CA 9-12R; CANR 4, 33, 60, 102, 208; CLR 3, 126; DAM POP; JRDA; MAICYA 1, 2; NFS 38; SAAS 21; NFS 38; SATA 8, 70, 166; WYA; YAW 1
Collier, Jeremy 1650-1726 .... **LC 6, 157**
See also DLB 336
Collier, John 1901-1980 .. **SSC 19; TCLC 127**
See also CA 65-68; 97-100; CANR 10; CN 1, 2; DLB 77, 255; FANT; SUFW 1
Collier, John Payne 1789-1883 ... **NCLC 286**
See also DLB 184
Collier, Mary 1688?-1762 .... **LC 86, 214**
See also DLB 95
Collingwood, R(obin) G(eorge)
1889(?)-1943 .... **TCLC 67**
See also CA 117; 155; DLB 262
Collins, Billy 1941- .... **PC 68**
See also AAYA 64; AMWS 21; CA 151; CANR 92, 211; CP 7; MTFW 2005; PFS 18, 42
Collins, Hunt
See Hunter, Evan
Collins, Linda 1931- .... **CLC 44**
See also CA 125
Collins, Merle 1950- .... **BLC 2:1**
See also BW 3; CA 175; DLB 157
Collins, Suzanne 1952- .... **CLC 355**
See also AAYA 86; CA 258; CANR 207; SATA 180, 224
Collins, Tom
See Furphy, Joseph
Collins, Wilkie 1824-1889 .... **NCLC 1, 18, 93, 255, 272; SSC 93, 209**
See also BRWS 6; CDBLB 1832-1890; CMW 4; DFS 28; DLB 18, 70, 159; GL 2; MSW; NFS 39; RGEL 2; RGSF 2; SUFW 1; WLIT 4
Collins, William 1721-1759 .. **LC 4, 40; PC 72**
See also BRW 3; DAM POET; DLB 109; RGEL 2
Collins, William Wilkie
See Collins, Wilkie
Collodi, Carlo 1826-1890 ...... **NCLC 54, 299**
See also CLR 5, 120; MAICYA 1,2; SATA 29, 100; WCH; WLIT 7
Colman, George
See Glassco, John
Colman, George, the Elder
1732-1794 .... **LC 98**
See also RGEL 2
Colman, George, the Younger
1762-1836 .... **NCLC 302**
See also DLB 89; RGEL 2
Colonna, Vittoria 1492-1547 ...... **LC 71, 224**
See also RGWL 2, 3
Colt, Winchester Remington
See Hubbard, L. Ron
Colter, Cyrus J. 1910-2002 .... **CLC 58**
See also BW 1; CA 65-68; 205; CANR 10, 66; CN 2, 3, 4, 5, 6; DLB 33
Colton, James
See Hansen, Joseph
Colum, Padraic 1881-1972 .. **CLC 28; PC 137**
See also BYA 4; CA 73-76; 33-36R; CANR 35; CLR 36; CP 1; CWRI 5; DLB 19; MAICYA 1, 2; MTCW 1; RGEL 2; SATA 15; WCH
Colvin, James
See Moorcock, Michael
Colwin, Laurie (E.)
1944-1992 .... **CLC 5, 13, 23, 84**
See also CA 89-92; 139; CANR 20, 46; DLB 218; DLBY 1980; MTCW 1
Comfort, Alex(ander) 1920-2000 ...... **CLC 7**
See also CA 1-4R; 190; CANR 1, 45; CN 1, 2, 3, 4; CP 1, 2, 3, 4, 5, 6, 7; DAM POP; MTCW 2
Comfort, Montgomery
See Campbell, Ramsey
Comnena, Anna 1083-c. 1153 .... **CMLC 151**
Compton-Burnett, I. 1892(?)-1969 ... **CLC 1, 3, 10, 15, 34; TCLC 180**
See also BRW 7; CA 1-4R; 25-28R; CANR 4; DAM NOV; DLB 36; EWL 3; MTCW 1, 2; RGEL 2
Compton-Burnett, Ivy
See Compton-Burnett, I.
Comstock, Anthony 1844-1915 ..... **TCLC 13**
See also CA 110; 169
Comte, Auguste 1798-1857 .... **NCLC 54**
Conan Doyle, Arthur
See Doyle, Sir Arthur Conan
Conde, Maryse 1937- .... **BLC 2:1; BLCS; CLC 52, 92, 247**
See also BW 2, 3; CA 110, 190; CAAE 190; CANR 30, 53, 76, 171; CWW 2; DAM MULT; EWL 3; MTCW 2; MTFW 2005
Conde (Abellan), Carmen
1901-1996 .... **HLCS 1**
See also CA 177; CWW 2; DLB 108; EWL 3; HW 2
Condillac, Etienne Bonnot de
1714-1780 .... **LC 26**
See also DLB 313
Condon, Richard 1915-1996 ... **CLC 4, 6, 8, 10, 45, 100**
See also BEST 90:3; BPFB 1; CA 1-4R; 151; CAAS 1; CANR 2, 23, 164; CMW 4; CN 1, 2, 3, 4, 5, 6; DAM NOV; INT CANR-23; MAL 5; MTCW 1, 2
Condon, Richard Thomas
See Condon, Richard
Condorcet
See Condorcet, marquis de Marie-Jean-Antoine-Nicolas Caritat
Condorcet, marquis de Marie-Jean-Antoine-Nicolas Caritat 1743-1794 .... **LC 104**
See also DLB 313; GFL Beginnings to 1789
Confucius 551B.C.-479B.C. ... **CMLC 19, 65, 159; WLCS**
See also DA; DA3; DAB; DAC; DAM MST

Congreve, William 1670-1729 .... **DC 2; LC 5, 21, 170; WLC 2**
See also BRW 2; CDBLB 1660-1789; DA; DAB; DAC; DAM DRAM, MST, POET; DFS 15; DLB 39, 84; RGEL 2; WLIT 3
Conley, Robert J. 1940- .... **NNAL**
See also CA 41-44R, 295; CAAE 295; CANR 15, 34, 45, 96, 186; DAM MULT; TCWW 2
Connell, Evan S. 1924-2013 ... **CLC 4, 6, 45**
See also AAYA 7; AMWS 14; CA 1-4R; CAAS 2; CANR 2, 39, 76, 97, 140, 195; CN 1, 2, 3, 4, 5, 6; DAM NOV; DLB 2, 335; DLBY 1981; MAL 5; MTCW 1, 2; MTFW 2005
Connell, Evan Shelby, Jr.
See Connell, Evan S.
Connelly, Marc(us Cook) 1890-1980 ... **CLC 7**
See also CA 85-88; 102; CAD; CANR 30; DFS 12; DLB 7; DLBY 1980; MAL 5; RGAL 4; SATA-Obit 25
Connelly, Michael 1956- .... **CLC 293**
See also AMWS 21; CA 158; CANR 91, 180, 234; CMW 4; LNFS 2
Connolly, Paul
See Wicker, Tom
Connor, Ralph
See Gordon, Charles William
Conrad, Joseph 1857-1924 ... **SSC 9, 67, 69, 71, 153, 169, 171, 174, 175, 177, 178, 185, 188, 189, 193, 194, 197, 201, 203, 204, 206, 219, 221; TCLC 1, 6, 13, 25, 43, 57, 291, 293, 295, 297, 298, 301, 303; WLC 2, 193**
See also AAYA 26; BPFB 1; BRW 6; BRWC 1; BRWR 2; BYA 2; CA 104; 131; CANR 60; CDBLB 1890-1914; DA; DA3; DAB; DAC; DAM MST, NOV; DLB 10, 34, 98, 156; EWL 3; EXPN; EXPS; LAIT 2; LATS 1:1; LMFS 1; MTCW 1, 2; MTFW 2005; NFS 2, 16; RGEL 2; RGSF 2; SATA 27; SSFS 1, 12, 31; TEA; WLIT 4
Conrad, Robert Arnold
See Hart, Moss
Conroy, Donald Patrick
See Conroy, Pat
Conroy, Pat 1945- .... **CLC 30, 74**
See also AAYA 8, 52; AITN 1; BPFB 1; CA 85-88; CANR 24, 53, 129, 233; CN 7; CPW; CSW; DA3; DAM NOV, POP; DLB 6; LAIT 5; MAL 5; MTCW 1, 2; MTFW 2005
Consolo, Vincenzo 1933-2012 .... **CLC 371**
See also CA 232; DLB 196
Constant (de Rebecque), (Henri) Benjamin
1767-1830 .... **NCLC 6, 182**
See also DLB 119; EW 4; GFL 1789 to the Present
Conway, Jill K. 1934- .... **CLC 152**
See also CA 130; CANR 94
Conway, Jill Ker
See Conway, Jill K.
Conybeare, Charles Augustus
See Eliot, T. S.
Cook, Michael 1933-1994 .... **CLC 58**
See also CA 93-96; CANR 68; DLB 53
Cook, Robin 1940- .... **CLC 14**
See also AAYA 32; BEST 90:2; BPFB 1; CA 108; 111; CANR 41, 90, 109, 181, 219; CPW; DA3; DAM POP; HGG; INT CA-111
Cook, Roy
See Silverberg, Robert
Cooke, Elizabeth 1948- .... **CLC 55**
See also CA 129
Cooke, John Esten 1830-1886 .... **NCLC 5**
See also DLB 3, 248; RGAL 4
Cooke, John Estes
See Baum, L. Frank
Cooke, M. E.
See Creasey, John
Cooke, Margaret
See Creasey, John
Cooke, Rose Terry 1827-1892 ... **NCLC 110; SSC 149**
See also DLB 12, 74
Cook-Lynn, Elizabeth 1930- **CLC 93; NNAL**
See also CA 133; DAM MULT; DLB 175
Cooney, Ray .... **CLC 62**
See also CBD
Cooper, Anthony Ashley 1671-1713 **LC 107**
See also DLB 101, 336
Cooper, Dennis 1953- .... **CLC 203**
See also CA 133; CANR 72, 86, 204; GLL 1; HGG
Cooper, Douglas 1960- .... **CLC 86**
Cooper, Henry St. John
See Creasey, John
Cooper, J. California (?)- .... **CLC 56**
See also AAYA 12; BW 1; CA 125; CANR 55, 207; CLR 188; DAM MULT; DLB 212
Cooper, James Fenimore
1789-1851 .... **NCLC 1, 27, 54, 203, 279, 312**
See also AAYA 22; AMW; BPFB 1; CDALB 1640-1865; CLR 105, 188; DA3; DLB 3, 183, 250, 254; LAIT 1; NFS 25; RGAL 4; SATA 19; TUS; WCH
Cooper, Joan California
See Cooper, J. California
Cooper, Susan Fenimore
1813-1894 .... **NCLC 129**
See also ANW; DLB 239, 254
Coover, Robert 1932- .... **CLC 3, 7, 15, 32, 46, 87, 161, 306; SSC 15, 101**
See also AMWS 5; BPFB 1; CA 45-48; CANR 3, 37, 58, 115, 228; CN 1, 2, 3, 4, 5, 6, 7; DAM NOV; DLB 2, 227; DLBY 1981; EWL 3; MAL 5; MTCW 1, 2; MTFW 2005; RGAL 4; RGSF 2
Copeland, Stewart 1952- .... **CLC 26**
See also CA 305
Copeland, Stewart Armstrong
See Copeland, Stewart
Copernicus, Nicolaus 1473-1543 .... **LC 45**
Coppard, A(lfred) E(dgar)
1878-1957 .... **SSC 21; TCLC 5**
See also BRWS 8; CA 114; 167; DLB 162; EWL 3; HGG; RGEL 2; RGSF 2; SUFW 1; YABC 1
Coppee, Francois 1842-1908 .... **TCLC 25**
See also CA 170; DLB 217
Coppola, Francis Ford 1939- ... **CLC 16, 126**
See also AAYA 39; CA 77-80; CANR 40, 78; DLB 44
Copway, George 1818-1869 .... **NNAL**
See also DAM MULT; DLB 175, 183
Corbiere, Tristan 1845-1875 .... **NCLC 43**
See also DLB 217; GFL 1789 to the Present
Corcoran, Barbara (Asenath)
1911-2003 .... **CLC 17**
See also AAYA 14; CA 21-24R, 191; CAAE 191; CAAS 2; CANR 11, 28, 48; CLR 50; DLB 52; JRDA; MAICYA 2; MAICYAS 1; RHW; SAAS 20; SATA 3, 77; SATA-Essay 125
Cordelier, Maurice
See Giraudoux, Jean
Cordier, Gilbert
See Rohmer, Eric
Corelli, Marie
See Mackay, Mary
Corinna c. 225B.C.-c. 305B.C. ..... **CMLC 72**
Corman, Cid 1924-2004 .... **CLC 9**
See also CA 85-88; 225; CAAS 2; CANR 44; CP 1, 2, 3, 4, 5, 6, 7; DAM POET; DLB 5, 193
Corman, Sidney
See Corman, Cid
Cormier, Robert 1925-2000 .... **CLC 12, 30**
See also AAYA 3, 19; BYA 1, 2, 6, 8, 9; CA 1-4R; CANR 5, 23, 76, 93; CDALB 1968-1988; CLR 12, 55, 167; DA; DAB; DAC; DAM MST, NOV; DLB 52; EXPN; INT CANR-23; JRDA; LAIT 5; MAICYA 1, 2; MTCW 1, 2; MTFW 2005; NFS 2, 18; SATA 10, 45, 83; SATA-Obit 122; WYA; YAW
Cormier, Robert Edmund
See Cormier, Robert
Corn, Alfred (DeWitt III) 1943- .... **CLC 33**
See also CA 179; CAAE 179; CAAS 25; CANR 44; CP 3, 4, 5, 6, 7; CSW; DLB 120, 282; DLBY 1980
Corneille, Pierre 1606-1684 .... **DC 21; LC 28, 135, 212, 217**
See also DAB; DAM MST; DFS 21; DLB 268; EW 3; GFL Beginnings to 1789; RGWL 2, 3; TWA
Cornwell, David
See le Carre, John
Cornwell, David John Moore
See le Carre, John
Cornwell, Patricia 1956- .... **CLC 155**
See also AAYA 16, 56; BPFB 1; CA 134; CANR 53, 131, 195; CMW 4; CPW; CSW; DAM POP; DLB 306; MSW; MTCW 2; MTFW 2005
Cornwell, Patricia Daniels
See Cornwell, Patricia
Cornwell, Smith
See Smith, David (Jeddie)
Corso, Gregory 1930-2001 .... **CLC 1, 11; PC 33, 108**
See also AMWS 12; BG 1:2; CA 5-8R; 193; CANR 41, 76, 132; CP 1, 2, 3, 4, 5, 6, 7; DA3; DLB 5, 16, 237; LMFS 2; MAL 5; MTCW 1, 2; MTFW 2005; WP
Cortes, Hernan 1485-1547 .... **LC 31, 213**
Cortez, Jayne 1936- .... **BLC 2:1**
See also BW 2, 3; CA 73-76; CANR 13, 31, 68, 126; CWP; DLB 41; EWL 3
Cortázar, Julio 1914-1984 .... **CLC 2, 3, 5, 10, 13, 15, 33, 34, 92; HLC 1; SSC 7, 76, 156, 210; TCLC 252**
See also AAYA 85; BPFB 1; CA 21-24R; CANR 12, 32, 81; CDWLB 3; DA3; DAM MULT, NOV; DLB 113; EWL 3; EXPS; HW 1, 2; LAW; MTCW 1, 2; MTFW 2005; RGSF 2; RGWL 2, 3; SSFS 3, 20, 28, 31, 34; TWA; WLIT 1
Corvinus, Jakob
See Raabe, Wilhelm (Karl)
Corwin, Cecil
See Kornbluth, C(yril) M.
Coryate, Thomas 1577(?)-1617 .... **LC 218**
See also DLB 151, 172
Cosic, Dobrica 1921- .... **CLC 14**
See also CA 122; 138; CDWLB 4; CWW 2; DLB 181; EWL 3
Costain, Thomas B(ertram)
1885-1965 .... **CLC 30**
See also BYA 3; CA 5-8R; 25-28R; DLB 9; RHW
Costantini, Humberto 1924(?)-1987 ... **CLC 49**
See also CA 131; 122; EWL 3; HW 1
Costello, Elvis 1954(?)- .... **CLC 21**
See also CA 204
Costenoble, Philostene
See Ghelderode, Michel de
Cotes, Cecil V.
See Duncan, Sara Jeannette
Cotter, Joseph Seamon Sr.
1861-1949 .... **BLC 1:1; TCLC 28**
See also BW 1; CA 124; DAM MULT; DLB 50
Cotton, John 1584-1652 .... **LC 176**
See also DLB 24; TUS
Couch, Arthur Thomas Quiller
See Quiller-Couch, Sir Arthur (Thomas)
Coulton, James
See Hansen, Joseph

Couperus, Louis (Marie Anne) 1863-1923 .... **TCLC 15**
See also CA 115; EWL 3; RGWL 2, 3

Coupland, Douglas 1961- .... **CLC 85, 133**
See also AAYA 34; CA 142; CANR 57, 90, 130, 172, 213; CCA 1; CN 7; CPW; DAC; DAM POP; DLB 334

Coupland, Douglas Campbell
See Coupland, Douglas

Court, Wesli
See Turco, Lewis

Courtenay, Bryce 1933- .... **CLC 59**
See also CA 138; CPW; NFS 32

Courtney, Robert
See Ellison, Harlan

Cousteau, Jacques 1910-1997 .... **CLC 30**
See also CA 65-68; 159; CANR 15, 67, 201; MTCW 1; SATA 38, 98

Cousteau, Jacques-Yves
See Cousteau, Jacques

Couto, Mia 1955- .... **CLC 367**
See also AFW; CA 245; CANR 213; DLB 360, 367

Coventry, Francis 1725-1754 .... **LC 46**
See also DLB 39

Coverdale, Miles c. 1487-1569 .... **LC 77**
See also DLB 167

Cowan, Peter (Walkinshaw) 1914-2002 .... **SSC 28**
See also CA 21-24R; CANR 9, 25, 50, 83; CN 1, 2, 3, 4, 5, 6, 7; DLB 260; RGSF 2

Coward, Noel 1899-1973 .... **CLC 1, 9, 29, 51; DC 45**
See also AITN 1; BRWS 2; CA 17-18; 41-44R; CANR 35, 132, 190; CAP 2; CBD; CDBLB 1914-1945; DA3; DAM DRAM; DFS 3, 6; DLB 10, 245; EWL 3; IDFW 3, 4; MTCW 1, 2; MTFW 2005; RGEL 2; TEA

Coward, Noel Peirce
See Coward, Noel

Cowley, Abraham 1618-1667 .... **LC 43, 236; PC 90**
See also BRW 2; DLB 131, 151; PAB; RGEL 2

Cowley, Malcolm 1898-1989 .... **CLC 39**
See also AMWS 2; CA 5-8R; 128; CANR 3, 55; CP 1, 2, 3, 4; DLB 4, 48; DLBY 1981, 1989; EWL 3; MAL 5; MTCW 1, 2; MTFW 2005

Cowper, William 1731-1800 .... **NCLC 8, 94; PC 40**
See also BRW 3; BRWR 3; DA3; DAM POET; DLB 104, 109; RGEL 2

Cox, William Trevor
See Trevor, William

Coyle, William
See Keneally, Thomas

Coyne, P. J.
See Masters, Hilary

Cozzens, James Gould 1903-1978 .... **CLC 1, 4, 11, 92**
See also AMW; BPFB 1; CA 9-12R; 81-84; CANR 19; CDALB 1941-1968; CN 1, 2; DLB 9, 294; DLBD 2; DLBY 1984, 1997; EWL 3; MAL 5; MTCW 1, 2; MTFW 2005; RGAL 4

Crabbe, George 1754-1832 .... **NCLC 26, 121; PC 97**
See also BRW 3; DLB 93; RGEL 2

Crace, Jim 1946- .... **CLC 157; SSC 61**
See also BRWS 14; CA 128; 135; CANR 55, 70, 123, 180; CN 5, 6, 7; DLB 231; INT CA-135

Craddock, Charles Egbert
See Murfree, Mary Noailles

Craig, A. A.
See Anderson, Poul

Craik, Mrs.
See Craik, Dinah Maria (Mulock)

Craik, Dinah Maria (Mulock) 1826-1887 .... **NCLC 38; 286**
See also DLB 35, 163; MAICYA 1, 2; RGEL 2; SATA 34

Cram, Ralph Adams 1863-1942 .... **TCLC 45**
See also CA 160

Cranch, Christopher Pearse 1813-1892 .... **NCLC 115**
See also DLB 1, 42, 243

Crane, Harold Hart
See Crane, Hart

Crane, Hart 1899-1932 .... **PC 3, 99; TCLC 2, 5, 80; WLC 2**
See also AAYA 81; AMW; AMWR 2; CA 104; 127; CDALB 1917-1929; DA; DA3; DAB; DAC; DAM MST, POET; DLB 4, 48; EWL 3; MAL 5; MTCW 1, 2; MTFW 2005; RGAL 4; TUS

Crane, R(onald) S(almon) 1886-1967 .... **CLC 27**
See also CA 85-88; DLB 63

Crane, Stephen 1871-1900 .... **PC 80; SSC 7, 56, 70, 129, 194; TCLC 11, 17, 32, 216; WLC 2**
See also AAYA 21; AMW; AMWC 1; BPFB 1; BYA 3; CA 109; 140; CANR 84; CDALB 1865-1917; CLR 132; DA; DA3; DAB; DAC; DAM MST, NOV, POET; DLB 12, 54, 78, 357; EXPN; EXPS; LAIT 2; LMFS 2; MAL 5; NFS 4, 20; PFS 9; RGAL 4; RGSF 2; SSFS 4, 28, 34; TUS; WYA; YABC 2

Crane, Stephen Townley
See Crane, Stephen

Cranmer, Thomas 1489-1556 .... **LC 95**
See also DLB 132, 213

Cranshaw, Stanley
See Fisher, Dorothy (Frances) Canfield

Crase, Douglas 1944- .... **CLC 58**
See also CA 106; CANR 204

Crashaw, Richard 1612(?)-1649 .... **LC 24, 200; PC 84**
See also BRW 2; DLB 126; PAB; RGEL 2

Cratinus c. 519B.C.-c. 422B.C. .... **CMLC 54**
See also LMFS 1

Craven, Margaret 1901-1980 .... **CLC 17**
See also BYA 2; CA 103; CCA 1; DAC; LAIT 5

Crawford, F(rancis) Marion 1854-1909 .... **TCLC 10**
See also CA 107; 168; DLB 71; HGG; RGAL 4; SUFW 1

Crawford, Isabella Valancy 1850-1887 .... **NCLC 12, 127**
See also DLB 92; RGEL 2

Crayon, Geoffrey
See Irving, Washington

Crebillon, Claude Prosper Jolyot de (fils) 1707-1777 .... **LC 1, 28**
See also DLB 313; GFL Beginnings to 1789

Creasey, John 1908-1973 .... **CLC 11**
See also CA 5-8R; 41-44R; CANR 8, 59; CMW 4; DLB 77; MTCW 1

Credo
See Creasey, John

Credo, Alvaro J. de
See Prado (Calvo), Pedro

Creeley, Robert 1926-2005 .... **CLC 1, 2, 4, 8, 11, 15, 36, 78, 266; PC 73**
See also AMWS 4; CA 1-4R; 237; CAAS 10; CANR 23, 43, 89, 137; CP 1, 2, 3, 4, 5, 6, 7; DA3; DAM POET; DLB 5, 16, 169; DLBD 17; EWL 3; MAL 5; MTCW 1, 2; MTFW 2005; PFS 21; RGAL 4; WP

Creeley, Robert White
See Creeley, Robert

Crenne, Helisenne de 1510-1560 .... **LC 113**
See also DLB 327

Crevel, Rene 1900-1935 .... **TCLC 112**
See also GLL 2

Crews, Harry 1935-2012 **CLC 6, 23, 49, 277**
See also AITN 1; AMWS 11; BPFB 1; CA 25-28R; CANR 20, 57; CN 3, 4, 5, 6, 7; CSW; DA3; DLB 6, 143, 185; MTCW 1, 2; MTFW 2005; RGAL 4

Crichton, John Michael
See Crichton, Michael

Crichton, Michael 1942-2008 .... **CLC 2, 6, 54, 90, 242**
See also AAYA 10, 49; AITN 2; BPFB 1; CA 25-28R; 279; CANR 13, 40, 54, 76, 127, 179; CMW 4; CN 2, 3, 6, 7; CPW; DA3; DAM NOV, POP; DLB 292; DLBY 1981; INT CANR-13; JRDA; LNFS 1; MTCW 1, 2; MTFW 2005; NFS 34; SATA 9, 88; SATA-Obit 199; SFW 4; YAW

Crispin, Edmund
See Montgomery, Bruce

Cristina of Sweden 1626-1689 .... **LC 124**

Cristofer, Michael 1945(?)- .... **CLC 28**
See also CA 110; 152; CAD; CANR 150; CD 5, 6; DAM DRAM; DFS 15; DLB 7

Cristofer, Michael Ivan
See Cristofer, Michael

Criton
See Alain

Croce, Benedetto 1866-1952 .... **TCLC 37**
See also CA 120; 155; EW 8; EWL 3; WLIT 7

Crockett, David
See Crockett, Davy

Crockett, Davy 1786-1836 .... **NCLC 8**
See also DLB 3, 11, 183, 248

Crofts, Freeman Wills 1879-1957 .... **TCLC 55**
See also CA 115; 195; CMW 4; DLB 77; MSW

Croker, John Wilson 1780-1857 .... **NCLC 10**
See also DLB 110

Crommelynck, Fernand 1885-1970 .. **CLC 75**
See also CA 189; 89-92; EWL 3

Cromwell, Oliver 1599-1658 .... **LC 43**

Cronenberg, David 1943- .... **CLC 143**
See also CA 138; CCA 1

Cronin, A(rchibald) J(oseph) 1896-1981 .... **CLC 32**
See also BPFB 1; CA 1-4R; 102; CANR 5; CN 2; DLB 191; SATA 47; SATA-Obit 25

Cross, Amanda
See Heilbrun, Carolyn G.

Crothers, Rachel 1878-1958 .... **TCLC 19**
See also CA 113; 194; CAD; CWD; DLB 7, 266; RGAL 4

Croves, Hal
See Traven, B.

Crow Dog, Mary (?)- .... **CLC 93; NNAL**
See also CA 154

Crowfield, Christopher
See Stowe, Harriet Beecher

Crowley, Aleister
See Crowley, Edward Alexander

Crowley, Edward Alexander 1875-1947 .... **TCLC 7**
See also CA 104; GLL 1; HGG

Crowley, John 1942- .... **CLC 57**
See also AAYA 57; BPFB 1; CA 61-64; CANR 43, 98, 138, 177; DLBY 1982; FANT; MTFW 2005; SATA 65, 140; SFW 4; SUFW 2

Crowne, John 1641-1712 .... **LC 104**
See also DLB 80; RGEL 2

Crud
See Crumb, R.

Crumarums
See Crumb, R.

Crumb, R. 1943- .... **CLC 17**
See also CA 106; CANR 107, 150, 218

Crumb, Robert
See Crumb, R.
Crumbum
See Crumb, R.
Crumski
See Crumb, R.
Crum the Bum
See Crumb, R.
Crunk
See Crumb, R.
Crustt
See Crumb, R.
Crutchfield, Les
See Trumbo, Dalton
Cruz, Victor Hernandez 1949- .... **HLC 1; PC 37**
See also BW 2; CA 65-68, 271; CAAE 271; CAAS 17; CANR 14, 32, 74, 132; CP 1, 2, 3, 4, 5, 6, 7; DAM MULT, POET; DLB 41; DNFS 1; EXPP; HW 1, 2; LLW; MTCW 2; MTFW 2005; PFS 16; WP
Crevecoeur, J. Hector St. John de 1735-1813 .... **NCLC 105**
See also AMWS 1; ANW; DLB 37
Crevecoeur, Michel Guillaume Jean de
See Crevecoeur, J. Hector St. John de
Cryer, Gretchen (Kiger) 1935- .... **CLC 21**
See also CA 114; 123
Csath, Geza
See Brenner, Jozef
Cudlip, David R(ockwell) 1933- ..... **CLC 34**
See also CA 177
Cuervo, Talia
See Vega, Ana Lydia
Cullen, Countee 1903-1946 ... **BLC 1:1; HR 1:2; PC 20; TCLC 4, 37, 220; WLCS**
See also AAYA 78; AFAW 2; AMWS 4; BW 1; CA 108; 124; CDALB 1917-1929; DA; DA3; DAC; DAM MST, MULT, POET; DLB 4, 48, 51; EWL 3; EXPP; LMFS 2; MAL 5; MTCW 1, 2; MTFW 2005; PFS 3, 42; RGAL 4; SATA 18; WP
Culleton, Beatrice 1949- .... **NNAL**
See also CA 120; CANR 83; DAC
Culver, Timothy J.
See Westlake, Donald E.
Cum, R.
See Crumb, R.
Cumberland, Richard 1732-1811 .... **NCLC 167**
See also DLB 89; RGEL 2
Cummings, Bruce F. 1889-1919 ... **TCLC 24**
See also CA 123
Cummings, Bruce Frederick
See Cummings, Bruce F.
Cummings, E. E. 1894-1962 ... **CLC 1, 3, 8, 12, 15, 68; PC 5; TCLC 137; WLC 2**
See also AAYA 41; AMW; CA 73-76; CANR 31; CDALB 1929-1941; DA; DA3; DAB; DAC; DAM MST, POET; DLB 4, 48; EWL 3; EXPP; MAL 5; MTCW 1, 2; MTFW 2005; PAB; PFS 1, 3, 12, 13, 19, 30, 34, 40; RGAL 4; TUS; WP
Cummings, Edward Estlin
See Cummings, E. E.
Cummins, Maria Susanna 1827-1866 .... **NCLC 139**
See also DLB 42; YABC 1
Cunha, Euclides (Rodrigues Pimenta) da 1866-1909 .... **TCLC 24**
See also CA 123; 219; DLB 307; LAW; WLIT 1
Cunningham, E. V.
See Fast, Howard
Cunningham, J. Morgan
See Westlake, Donald E.
Cunningham, J(ames) V(incent) 1911-1985 .... **CLC 3, 31; PC 92**
See also CA 1-4R; 115; CANR 1, 72; CP 1, 2, 3, 4; DLB 5
Cunningham, Julia (Woolfolk) 1916- .. **CLC 12**
See also CA 9-12R; CANR 4, 19, 36; CWRI 5; JRDA; MAICYA 1, 2; SAAS 2; SATA 1, 26, 132
Cunningham, Michael 1952- ... **CLC 34, 243**
See also AMWS 15; CA 136; CANR 96, 160, 227; CN 7; DLB 292; GLL 2; MTFW 2005; NFS 23
Cunninghame Graham, R. B.
See Cunninghame Graham, Robert Bontine
Cunninghame Graham, Robert Bontine 1852-1936 .... **TCLC 19**
See also CA 119; 184; DLB 98, 135, 174; RGEL 2; RGSF 2
Cunninghame Graham, Robert Gallnigad Bontine
See Cunninghame Graham, Robert Bontine
Curnow, (Thomas) Allen (Monro) 1911-2001 .... **PC 48**
See also CA 69-72; 202; CANR 48, 99; CP 1, 2, 3, 4, 5, 6, 7; EWL 3; RGEL 2
Currie, Ellen 19(?)- .... **CLC 44**
Curtin, Philip
See Lowndes, Marie Adelaide (Belloc)
Curtin, Phillip
See Lowndes, Marie Adelaide (Belloc)
Curtis, Price
See Ellison, Harlan
Cusanus, Nicolaus 1401-1464
See Nicholas of Cusa
Cutrate, Joe
See Spiegelman, Art
Cynewulf fl. 9th cent. .... **CMLC 23, 117; PC 158**
See also DLB 146; RGEL 2
Cyprian, St. c. 200-258 .... **CMLC 127**
Cyrano de Bergerac, Savinien de 1619-1655 .... **LC 65**
See also DLB 268; GFL Beginnings to 1789; RGWL 2, 3
Cyril of Alexandria c. 375-c. 430 ... **CMLC 59**
Czaczkes, Shmuel Yosef Halevi
See Agnon, S. Y.
Dabrowska, Maria (Szumska) 1889-1965 .... **CLC 15**
See also CA 106; CDWLB 4; DLB 215; EWL 3
Dabydeen, David 1955- .... **CLC 34, 351**
See also BW 1; CA 125; CANR 56, 92; CN 6, 7; CP 5, 6, 7; DLB 347
Dacey, Philip 1939- .... **CLC 51**
See also CA 37-40R, 231; CAAE 231; CAAS 17; CANR 14, 32, 64; CP 4, 5, 6, 7; DLB 105
Dacre, Charlotte c. 1772-1825(?) .... **NCLC 151**
Dafydd ap Gwilym c. 1320-c. 1380 ... **PC 56**
Dagerman, Stig (Halvard) 1923-1954 .... **TCLC 17**
See also CA 117; 155; DLB 259; EWL 3
D'Aguiar, Fred 1960- ... **BLC 2:1; CLC 145**
See also CA 148; CANR 83, 101; CN 7; CP 5, 6, 7; DLB 157; EWL 3
Dahl, Roald 1916-1990 ... **CLC 1, 6, 18, 79; TCLC 173, 312**
See also AAYA 15; BPFB 1; BRWS 4; BYA 5; CA 1-4R; 133; CANR 6, 32, 37, 62; CLR 1, 7, 41, 111; CN 1, 2, 3, 4; CPW; DA3; DAB; DAC; DAM MST, NOV, POP; DLB 139, 255; HGG; JRDA; MAICYA 1, 2; MTCW 1, 2; MTFW 2005; RGSF 2; SATA 1, 26, 73; SATA-Obit 65; SSFS 4, 30; TEA; YAW
Dahlberg, Edward 1900-1977 ...... **CLC 1, 7, 14; TCLC 208**
See also CA 9-12R; 69-72; CANR 31, 62; CN 1, 2; DLB 48; MAL 5; MTCW 1; RGAL 4
Dahlie, Michael 1970(?)- .... **CLC 299**
See also CA 283
Daitch, Susan 1954- .... **CLC 103**
See also CA 161
Dale, Colin
See Lawrence, T. E.
Dale, George E.
See Asimov, Isaac
d'Alembert, Jean Le Rond 1717-1783 .... **LC 126**
Dalton, Roque 1935-1975(?) .... **HLCS 1; PC 36**
See also CA 176; DLB 283; HW 2
Daly, Elizabeth 1878-1967 .... **CLC 52**
See also CA 23-24; 25-28R; CANR 60; CAP 2; CMW 4
Daly, Mary 1928-2010 .... **CLC 173**
See also CA 25-28R; CANR 30, 62, 166; FW; GLL 1; MTCW 1
Daly, Maureen 1921-2006 .... **CLC 17**
See also AAYA 5, 58; BYA 6; CA 253; CANR 37, 83, 108; CLR 96; JRDA; MAICYA 1, 2; SAAS 1; SATA 2, 129; SATA-Obit 176; WYA; YAW
Damas, Leon-Gontran 1912-1978 .... **CLC 84; TCLC 204**
See also BW 1; CA 125; 73-76; EWL 3
Damocles
See Benedetti, Mario
Dana, Richard Henry Sr. 1787-1879 .... **NCLC 53**
Dangarembga, Tsitsi 1959- .... **BLC 2:1**
See also BW 3; CA 163; DLB 360; NFS 28; WLIT 2
Daniel, Samuel 1562(?)-1619 ...... **LC 24, 171**
See also DLB 62; RGEL 2
Danielewski, Mark Z. 1966- .... **CLC 360**
See also CA 194; CANR 170
Daniels, Brett
See Adler, Renata
Dannay, Frederic 1905-1982 .... **CLC 3, 11**
See also BPFB 3; CA 1-4R; 107; CANR 1, 39; CMW 4; DAM POP; DLB 137; MSW; MTCW 1; RGAL 4
D'Annunzio, Gabriele 1863-1938 .... **TCLC 6, 40, 215**
See also CA 104; 155; EW 8; EWL 3; RGWL 2, 3; TWA; WLIT 7
Danois, N. le
See Gourmont, Remy(-Marie-Charles) de
Dante 1265-1321 .... **CMLC 3, 18, 39, 70, 142; PC 21, 108; WLCS**
See also DA; DA3; DAB; DAC; DAM MST, POET; EFS 1:1, 2:1; EW 1; LAIT 1; RGWL 2, 3; TWA; WLIT 7; WP
d'Antibes, Germain
See Simenon, Georges
Danticat, Edwidge 1969- .... **BLC 2:1; CLC 94, 139, 228; SSC 100**
See also AAYA 29, 85; CA 152, 192; CAAE 192; CANR 73, 129, 179; CN 7; DLB 350; DNFS 1; EXPS; LATS 1:2; LNFS 3; MTCW 2; MTFW 2005; NFS 28, 37; SSFS 1, 25, 37; YAW
Danvers, Dennis 1947- .... **CLC 70**
Danziger, Paula 1944-2004 .... **CLC 21**
See also AAYA 4, 36; BYA 6, 7, 14; CA 112; 115; 229; CANR 37, 132; CLR 20; JRDA; MAICYA 1, 2; MTFW 2005; SATA 36, 63, 102, 149; SATA-Brief 30; SATA-Obit 155; WYA; YAW
Dao, Bei
See Bei Dao

Da Ponte, Lorenzo 1749-1838 .... **NCLC 50**
d'Aragona, Tullia 1510(?)-1556 .... **LC 121**
Darko, Amma 1956- .... **BLC 2:1; CLC 341**
Darley, George 1795-1846 ... **NCLC 2; PC 125**
See also DLB 96; RGEL 2
Dario, Ruben 1867-1916 ..... **HLC 1; PC 15; TCLC 4, 265**
See also CA 131; CANR 81; DAM MULT; DLB 290; EWL 3; HW 1, 2; LAW; MTCW 1, 2; MTFW 2005; RGWL 2, 3
Darrow, Clarence (Seward) 1857-1938 .... **TCLC 81**
See also CA 164; DLB 303
Darwin, Charles 1809-1882 .... **NCLC 57**
See also BRWS 7; DLB 57, 166; LATS 1:1; RGEL 2; TEA; WLIT 4
Darwin, Erasmus 1731-1802 .... **NCLC 106**
See also BRWS 16; DLB 93; RGEL 2
Darwish, Mahmoud 1941-2008 .... **PC 86**
See also CA 164; CANR 133; CWW 2; EWL 3; MTCW 2; MTFW 2005
Darwish, Mahmud -2008
See Darwish, Mahmoud
Daryush, Elizabeth 1887-1977 .... **CLC 6, 19**
See also CA 49-52; CANR 3, 81; DLB 20
Das, Kamala 1934-2009 .... **CLC 191; PC 43**
See also CA 101; 287; CANR 27, 59; CP 1, 2, 3, 4, 5, 6, 7; CWP; DLB 323; FW
Dasgupta, Surendranath 1887-1952 .... **TCLC 81**
See also CA 157
Dashwood, Edmee Elizabeth Monica de la Pasture 1890-1943 .... **TCLC 61**
See also CA 119; 154; DLB 34; RHW
d'Aubignac, François Hédelin, abbé 1604-1676 .... **LC 222**
Daudet, (Louis Marie) Alphonse 1840-1897 .... **NCLC 1, 312**
See also DLB 123; GFL 1789 to the Present; RGSF 2
Daudet, Alphonse Marie Leon 1867-1942 .... **SSC 94**
See also CA 217
d'Aulnoy, Marie-Catherine c. 1650-1705 .... **LC 100, 216**
Daumal, Rene 1908-1944 .... **TCLC 14**
See also CA 114; 247; EWL 3
Davenant, William 1606-1668 .... **DC 48; LC 13, 166; PC 99**
See also DLB 58, 126; RGEL 2
Davenport, Guy (Mattison, Jr.) 1927-2005 .... **CLC 6, 14, 38, 241; SSC 16**
See also CA 33-36R; 235; CANR 23, 73; CN 3, 4, 5, 6; CSW; DLB 130
David, Robert
See Nezval, Vitezslav
Davidson, Donald (Grady) 1893-1968 .... **CLC 2, 13, 19**
See also CA 5-8R; 25-28R; CANR 4, 84; DLB 45
Davidson, Hugh
See Hamilton, Edmond
Davidson, John 1857-1909 .... **TCLC 24**
See also CA 118; 217; DLB 19; RGEL 2
Davidson, Sara 1943- .... **CLC 9**
See also CA 81-84; CANR 44, 68; DLB 185
Davie, Donald (Alfred) 1922-1995 ... **CLC 5, 8, 10, 31; PC 29**
See also BRWS 6; CA 1-4R; 149; CAAS 3; CANR 1, 44; CP 1, 2, 3, 4, 5, 6; DLB 27; MTCW 1; RGEL 2
Davie, Elspeth 1918-1995 .... **SSC 52**
See also CA 120; 126; 150; CANR 141; DLB 139
Davies, Ray 1944- .... **CLC 21**
See also CA 116; 146; CANR 92
Davies, Raymond Douglas
See Davies, Ray
Davies, Rhys 1901-1978 .... **CLC 23**
See also CA 9-12R; 81-84; CANR 4; CN 1, 2; DLB 139, 191
Davies, Robertson 1913-1995 .... **CLC 2, 7, 13, 25, 42, 75, 91; WLC 2**
See also BEST 89:2; BPFB 1; CA 1, 33-36R; 150; CANR 17, 42, 103; CN 1, 2, 3, 4, 5, 6; CPW; DA; DA3; DAB; DAC; DAM MST, NOV, POP; DLB 68; EWL 3; HGG; INT CANR-17; MTCW 1, 2; MTFW 2005; RGEL 2; TWA
Davies, Sir John 1569-1626 .... **LC 85**
See also DLB 172
Davies, Walter C.
See Kornbluth, C(yril) M.
Davies, William Henry 1871-1940 ... **TCLC 5**
See also BRWS 11; CA 104; 179; DLB 19, 174; EWL 3; RGEL 2
Davies, William Robertson
See Davies, Robertson
Da Vinci, Leonardo 1452-1519 .... **LC 12, 57, 60**
See also AAYA 40
Daviot, Gordon
See Mackintosh, Elizabeth
Davis, Angela Y. 1944- .... **CLC 77**
See also BW 2, 3; CA 57-60; CANR 10, 81; CSW; DA3; DAM MULT; FW
Davis, Angela Yvonne
See Davis, Angela Y.
Davis, B. Lynch
See Bioy Casares, Adolfo; Borges, Jorge Luis
Davis, Frank Marshall 1905-1987 .. **BLC 1:1**
See also BW 2, 3; CA 125; 123; CANR 42, 80; DAM MULT; DLB 51
Davis, Gordon
See Hunt, E. Howard
Davis, H(arold) L(enoir) 1896-1960 .... **CLC 49**
See also ANW; CA 178; 89-92; DLB 9, 206; SATA 114; TCWW 1, 2
Davis, Hart
See Poniatowska, Elena
Davis, Lydia 1947- .... **CLC 306, 370**
See also CA 139; CANR 120, 171, 222; DLB 130
Davis, Natalie Zemon 1928- .... **CLC 204**
See also CA 53-56; CANR 58, 100, 174
Davis, Rebecca Blaine Harding
See Davis, Rebecca Harding
Davis, Rebecca Harding 1831-1910 ... **SSC 38, 109, 192; TCLC 6, 267**
See also AMWS 16; CA 104; 179; DLB 74, 239; FW; NFS 14; RGAL 4; SSFS 26; TUS
Davis, Richard Harding 1864-1916 .... **TCLC 24**
See also CA 114; 179; DLB 12, 23, 78, 79, 189; DLBD 13; RGAL 4
Davison, Frank Dalby 1893-1970 ... **CLC 15**
See also CA 217; 116; DLB 260
Davison, Lawrence H.
See Lawrence, D. H.
Davison, Peter (Hubert) 1928-2004 .... **CLC 28**
See also CA 9-12R; 234; CAAS 4; CANR 3, 43, 84; CP 1, 2, 3, 4, 5, 6, 7; DLB 5
Davys, Mary 1674-1732 .... **LC 1, 46, 217**
See also DLB 39
Dawe, Bruce 1930- .... **PC 159**
See also CA 69-72; CANR 11, 27, 52, 83; CP 1, 2, 3, 4, 5, 6, 7; DLB 289; PFS 10
Dawson, (Guy) Fielding (Lewis) 1930-2002 .... **CLC 6**
See also CA 85-88; 202; CANR 108; DLB 130; DLBY 2002
Day, Clarence (Shepard, Jr.) 1874-1935 .... **TCLC 25**
See also CA 108; 199; DLB 11
Day, John 1574(?)-1640(?) .... **LC 70**
See also DLB 62, 170; RGEL 2
Day, Thomas 1748-1789 .... **LC 1**
See also DLB 39; YABC 1
Day Lewis, C. 1904-1972 ...... **CLC 1, 6, 10; PC 11; TCLC 261**
See also BRWS 3; CA 13-16; 33-36R; CANR 34; CAP 1; CN 1; CP 1; CWRI 5; DAM POET; DLB 77; EWL 3; MSW; MTCW 1, 2; RGEL 2
Day Lewis, Cecil
See Day Lewis, C.
Diaz, Junot 1968- .... **CLC 258; SSC 144**
See also AAYA 83; BYA 12; CA 161; CANR 119, 183; LLW; NFS 36; SSFS 20
Diaz del Castillo, Bernal c. 1496-1584 .... **HLCS 1; LC 31**
See also DLB 318; LAW
Doblin, Alfred 1878-1957 ..... **TCLC 13, 269**
See also CA 110; 141; CDWLB 2; DLB 66; EWL 3; RGWL 2, 3
de Andrade, Carlos Drummond
See Drummond de Andrade, Carlos
de Andrade, Mario (?)-
See Andrade, Mario de
Deane, Norman
See Creasey, John
Deane, Seamus (Francis) 1940- .... **CLC 122**
See also CA 118; CANR 42
de Athayde, Alvaro Coelho
See Pessoa, Fernando
Deaver, Jeff
See Deaver, Jeffery
Deaver, Jeffery 1950- .... **CLC 331**
See also AAYA 41; CA 163; CANR 105, 151, 178, 236
Deaver, Jeffery Wilds
See Deaver, Jeffery
de Beauvoir, Simone
See Beauvoir, Simone de
de Beer, P.
See Bosman, Herman Charles
De Botton, Alain 1969- .... **CLC 203**
See also CA 159; CANR 96, 201
de Brissac, Malcolm
See Dickinson, Peter
de Campos, Álvaro
See Pessoa, Fernando
de Chardin, Pierre Teilhard
See Teilhard de Chardin, (Marie Joseph) Pierre
de Conte, Sieur Louis
See Twain, Mark
de Crenne, Helisenne c. 1510-c. 1560 .... **LC 113, 218**
Dee, John 1527-1608 .... **LC 20**
See also DLB 136, 213
Deer, Sandra 1940- .... **CLC 45**
See also CA 186
De Ferrari, Gabriella 1941- .... **CLC 65**
See also CA 146
de Filippo, Eduardo 1900-1984 ... **TCLC 127**
See also CA 132; 114; EWL 3; MTCW 1; RGWL 2, 3
Defoe, Daniel 1660(?)-1731 .... **LC 1, 42, 108, 180, 238; WLC 2**
See also AAYA 27; BRW 3; BRWR 1; BYA 4; CDBLB 1660-1789; CLR 61, 164; DA; DA3; DAB; DAC; DAM MST, NOV; DLB 39, 95, 101, 336; JRDA; LAIT 1; LMFS 1; MAICYA 1, 2; NFS 9, 13, 30; RGEL 2; SATA 22; TEA; WCH; WLIT 3
de Gouges, Olympe
See Gouges, Olympe de

de Gouges, Olympe 1748-1793 .. **LC 127, 214**
See also DLB 313
de Gourmont, Remy(-Marie-Charles)
See Gourmont, Remy(-Marie-Charles) de
de Gournay, Marie le Jars
1566-1645 .... **LC 98, 244**
See also DLB 327; FW
de Hartog, Jan 1914-2002 .... **CLC 19**
See also CA 1-4R; 210; CANR 1, 192; DFS 12
de Hostos, E. M.
See Hostos (y Bonilla), Eugenio Maria de
de Hostos, Eugenio M.
See Hostos (y Bonilla), Eugenio Maria de
Deighton, Len
See Deighton, Leonard Cyril
Deighton, Leonard Cyril 1929- ... **CLC 4, 7, 22, 46**
See also AAYA 57, 6; BEST 89:2; BPFB 1; CA 9-12R; CANR 19, 33, 68; CDBLB 1960- Present; CMW 4; CN 1, 2, 3, 4, 5, 6, 7; CPW; DA3; DAM NOV, POP; DLB 87; MTCW 1, 2; MTFW 2005
Dekker, Thomas 1572(?)-1632 .... **DC 12; LC 22, 159**
See also CDBLB Before 1660; DAM DRAM; DLB 62, 172; LMFS 1; RGEL 2
de Laclos, Pierre Ambroise Franois
See Laclos, Pierre-Ambroise Francois
Delacroix, (Ferdinand-Victor-)Eugene
1798-1863 .... **NCLC 133**
See also EW 5
Delafield, E. M.
See Dashwood, Edmee Elizabeth Monica de la Pasture
de la Mare, Walter (John)
1873-1956 .... **PC 77; SSC 14; TCLC 4, 53; WLC 2**
See also AAYA 81; CA 163; CDBLB 1914-1945; CLR 23, 148; CWRI 5; DA3; DAB; DAC; DAM MST, POET; DLB 19, 153, 162, 255, 284; EWL 3; EXPP; HGG; MAICYA 1, 2; MTCW 2; MTFW 2005; PFS 39; RGEL 2; RGSF 2; SATA 16; SUFW 1; TEA; WCH
de Lamartine, Alphonse
See Lamartine, Alphonse de
Deland, Margaret(ta Wade Campbell)
1857-1945 .... **SSC 162**
See also CA 122; DLB 78; RGAL 4
Delaney, Franey
See O'Hara, John
Delaney, Shelagh 1939-2011 ... **CLC 29; DC 45**
See also CA 17-20R; CANR 30, 67; CBD; CD 5, 6; CDBLB 1960 to Present; CWD; DAM DRAM; DFS 7; DLB 13; MTCW 1
Delany, Martin Robison 1812-1885 .. **NCLC 93**
See also DLB 50; RGAL 4
Delany, Mary (Granville Pendarves)
1700-1788 .... **LC 12, 220**
Delany, Samuel R., Jr. 1942- .... **BLC 1:1; CLC 8, 14, 38, 141, 313**
See also AAYA 24; AFAW 2; BPFB 1; BW 2, 3; CA 81-84; CANR 27, 43, 116, 172; CN 2, 3, 4, 5, 6, 7; DAM MULT; DLB 8, 33; FANT; MAL 5; MTCW 1, 2; RGAL 4; SATA 92; SCFW 1, 2; SFW 4; SUFW 2
Delany, Samuel Ray
See Delany, Samuel R., Jr.
de la Parra, Ana Teresa Sonojo
See de la Parra, Teresa
de la Parra, Teresa
1890(?)-1936 .... **HLCS 2; TCLC 185**
See also CA 178; HW 2; LAW
Delaporte, Theophile
See Green, Julien
De La Ramee, Marie Louise
1839-1908 .... **TCLC 43**
See also CA 204; DLB 18, 156; RGEL 2; SATA 20
de la Roche, Mazo 1879-1961 .... **CLC 14**
See also CA 85-88; CANR 30; DLB 68; RGEL 2; RHW; SATA 64
De La Salle, Innocent
See Hartmann, Sadakichi
de Laureamont, Comte
See Lautreamont
Delbanco, Nicholas 1942- ... **CLC 6, 13, 167**
See also CA 17-20R, 189; CAAE 189; CAAS 2; CANR 29, 55, 116, 150, 204, 237; CN 7; DLB 6, 234
Delbanco, Nicholas Franklin
See Delbanco, Nicholas
del Castillo, Michel 1933- .... **CLC 38**
See also CA 109; CANR 77
Deledda, Grazia (Cosima) 1875 (?)-1936 .... **TCLC 23**
See also CA 123; 205; DLB 264, 329; EWL 3; RGWL 2, 3; WLIT 7
Deleuze, Gilles 1925-1995 .... **TCLC 116**
See also DLB 296
Delgado, Abelardo (Lalo) B(arrientos)
1930-2004 .... **HLC 1**
See also CA 131; 230; CAAS 15; CANR 90; DAM MST, MULT; DLB 82; HW 1, 2
Delibes, Miguel
See Delibes Setien, Miguel
Delibes Setien, Miguel 1920-2010 ... **CLC 8, 18**
See also CA 45-48; CANR 1, 32; CWW 2; DLB 322; EWL 3; HW 1; MTCW 1
DeLillo, Don 1936- .... **CLC 8, 10, 13, 27, 39, 54, 76, 143, 210, 213, 336**
See also AMWC 2; AMWS 6; BEST 89:1; BPFB 1; CA 81-84; CANR 21, 76, 92, 133, 173, 240; CN 3, 4, 5, 6, 7; CPW; DA3; DAM NOV, POP; DLB 6, 173; EWL 3; MAL 5; MTCW 1, 2; MTFW 2005; NFS 28; RGAL 4; TUS
de Lisser, H. G.
See De Lisser, H(erbert) G(eorge)
De Lisser, H(erbert) G(eorge)
1878-1944 .... **TCLC 12**
See also BW 2; CA 109; 152; DLB 117
Della Casa, Giovanni 1503-1556 ..... **LC 220**
Deloire, Pierre
See Peguy, Charles (Pierre)
Deloney, Thomas 1543(?)-1600 .... **LC 41; PC 79**
See also DLB 167; RGEL 2
Deloria, Ella (Cara) 1889-1971(?) ..... **NNAL**
See also CA 152; DAM MULT; DLB 175
Deloria, Vine, Jr. 1933-2005 ... **CLC 21, 122; NNAL**
See also CA 53-56; 245; CANR 5, 20, 48, 98; DAM MULT; DLB 175; MTCW 1; SATA 21; SATA-Obit 171
Deloria, Vine Victor, Jr.
See Deloria, Vine, Jr.
del Valle-Inclan, Ramon
See Valle-Inclan, Ramon del
Del Vecchio, John M(ichael) 1947- ... **CLC 29**
See also CA 110; DLBD 9
de Man, Paul (Adolph Michel)
1919-1983 .... **CLC 55**
See also CA 128; 111; CANR 61; DLB 67; MTCW 1, 2
de Mandiargues, Andre Pieyre
See Pieyre de Mandiargues, Andre
DeMarinis, Rick 1934- .... **CLC 54**
See also CA 57-60, 184; CAAE 184; CAAS 24; CANR 9, 25, 50, 160; DLB 218; TCWW 2
de Maupassant, Guy
See Maupassant, Guy de
Dembry, R. Emmet
See Murfree, Mary Noailles
Demby, William 1922- ... **BLC 1:1; CLC 53**
See also BW 1, 3; CA 81-84; CANR 81; DAM MULT; DLB 33
de Menton, Francisco
See Chin, Frank
Demetrius of Phalerum
c. 307B.C. .... **CMLC 34**
Demijohn, Thom
See Disch, Thomas M.
De Mille, James 1833-1880 .... **NCLC 123**
See also DLB 99, 251
Democritus
c. 460B.C.-c. 370B.C. .... **CMLC 47, 136**
de Montaigne, Michel
See Montaigne, Michel de
de Montherlant, Henry
See Montherlant, Henry de
Demosthenes
384B.C.-322B.C. .... **CMLC 13**
See also AW 1; DLB 176; RGWL 2, 3; WLIT 8
de Musset, (Louis Charles) Alfred
See Musset, Alfred de
de Natale, Francine
See Malzberg, Barry N(athaniel)
de Navarre, Marguerite
1492-1549 .... **LC 61, 167; SSC 85, 211**
See also DLB 327; GFL Beginnings to 1789; RGWL 2, 3
Denby, Edwin (Orr) 1903-1983 ...... **CLC 48**
See also CA 138; 110; CP 1
de Nerval, Gerard
See Nerval, Gerard de
Denfeld, Rene 1967- .... **CLC 389**
See also CA 259
Denham, John 1615-1669 ... **LC 73; PC 166**
See also DLB 58, 126; RGEL 2
Denis, Claire 1948- .... **CLC 286**
See also CA 249
Denis, Julio
See Cortázar, Julio
Denmark, Harrison
See Zelazny, Roger
Dennie, Joseph 1768-1812 .... **NCLC 249**
See also DLB 37, 43, 59, 73
Dennis, John 1658-1734 .... **LC 11, 154**
See also DLB 101; RGEL 2
Dennis, Nigel (Forbes) 1912-1989 .... **CLC 8**
See also CA 25-28R; 129; CN 1, 2, 3, 4; DLB 13, 15, 233; EWL 3; MTCW 1
Dent, Lester 1904-1959 .... **TCLC 72**
See also CA 112; 161; CMW 4; DLB 306; SFW 4
Dentinger, Stephen
See Hoch, Edward D.
De Palma, Brian 1940- .... **CLC 20, 247**
See also CA 109
De Palma, Brian Russell
See De Palma, Brian
de Pizan, Christine
See Christine de Pizan
De Quincey, Thomas
1785-1859 .... **NCLC 4, 87, 198**
See also BRW 4; CDBLB 1789-1832; DLB 110, 144; RGEL 2
De Ray, Jill
See Moore, Alan
Deren, Eleanora 1908(?)-1961 ... **CLC 16, 102**
See also CA 192; 111
Deren, Maya
See Deren, Eleanora
Derleth, August (William)
1909-1971 .... **CLC 31**
See also BPFB 1; BYA 9, 10; CA 1-4R; 29-32R; CANR 4; CMW 4; CN 1; DLB 9; DLBD 17; HGG; SATA 5; SUFW 1
Der Nister 1884-1950 .... **TCLC 56**
See also DLB 333; EWL 3
de Routisie, Albert
See Aragon, Louis

Derrida, Jacques 1930-2004 .... **CLC 24, 87, 225**
See also CA 124; 127; 232; CANR 76, 98, 133; DLB 242; EWL 3; LMFS 2; MTCW 2; TWA
Derry Down Derry
See Lear, Edward
Dershowitz, Alan 1938- .... **CLC 298**
See also CA 25-28R; CANR 11, 44, 79, 159, 227
Dershowitz, Alan Morton
See Dershowitz, Alan
Dersonnes, Jacques
See Simenon, Georges
Der Stricker c. 1190-c. 1250 .... **CMLC 75**
See also DLB 138
der Vogelweide, Walther von
See Walther von der Vogelweide
Derzhavin, Gavriil Romanovich 1743-1816 .... **NCLC 215**
See also DLB 150
Desai, Anita 1937- .... **CLC 19, 37, 97, 175, 271; SSC 168**
See also AAYA 85; BRWS 5; CA 81-84; CANR 33, 53, 95, 133; CN 1, 2, 3, 4, 5, 6, 7; CWRI 5; DA3; DAB; DAM NOV; DLB 271, 323; DNFS 2; EWL 3; FW; MTCW 1, 2; MTFW 2005; SATA 63, 126; SSFS 28, 31
Desai, Kiran 1971- .... **CLC 119**
See also BRWS 15; BYA 16; CA 171; CANR 127; NFS 28
de Saint-Luc, Jean
See Glassco, John
de Saint Roman, Arnaud
See Aragon, Louis
Desbordes-Valmore, Marceline 1786-1859 .... **NCLC 97, 293**
See also DLB 217
Descartes, Rene 1596-1650 .... **LC 20, 35, 150, 202**
See also DLB 268; EW 3; GFL Beginnings to 1789
Deschamps, Eustache 1340(?)-1404 ... **LC 103**
See also DLB 208
De Sica, Vittorio 1901(?)-1974 .... **CLC 20**
See also CA 117
Desnos, Robert 1900-1945 .... **TCLC 22, 241**
See also CA 121; 151; CANR 107; DLB 258; EWL 3; LMFS 2
Des Périers, Bonaventure 1510?-1543? .... **LC 243**
See also DLB 327
des Roches, Catherine 1542-1587 ... **LC 117, 206**
See also DLB 327
des Roches, Madeleine 1520(?)-1587(?) .... **LC 206**
See also DLB 327
Destouches, Louis-Ferdinand
See Celine, Louis-Ferdinand
Desvignes, Lucette 1926- .... **CLC 372**
See also DLB 321
De Teran, Lisa St. Aubin
See St. Aubin de Teran, Lisa
de Teran, Lisa St. Aubin
See St. Aubin de Teran, Lisa
de Tolignac, Gaston
See Griffith, D.W.
de Tyard, Pontus
See Tyard, Pontus de
Deutsch, Babette 1895-1982 .... **CLC 18**
See also BYA 3; CA 1-4R; 108; CANR 4, 79; CP 1, 2, 3; DLB 45; SATA 1; SATA-Obit 33
de Vere, Edward 1550-1604 .... **LC 193**
See also DLB 172
Devi, Mahasweta 1926- .... **CLC 290; SSC 165**
Deville, Rene
See Kacew, Romain
Devkota, Laxmiprasad 1909-1959 ... **TCLC 23**
See also CA 123
Devlin, Denis 1908-1959 .... **PC 122**
See also RGEL 2
De Voto, Bernard (Augustine) 1897-1955 .... **TCLC 29**
See also CA 113; 160; DLB 9, 256; MAL 5; TCWW 1, 2
De Vries, Peter 1910-1993 ... **CLC 1, 2, 3, 7, 10, 28, 46**
See also CA 17-20R; 142; CANR 41; CN 1, 2, 3, 4, 5; DAM NOV; DLB 6; DLBY 1982; MAL 5; MTCW 1, 2; MTFW 2005
Dewey, John 1859-1952 .... **TCLC 95**
See also CA 114; 170; CANR 144; DLB 246, 270; RGAL 4
Dexter, John
See Bradley, Marion Zimmer
Dexter, Martin
See Faust, Frederick
Dexter, Pete 1943- .... **CLC 34, 55**
See also BEST 89:2; CA 127; 131; CANR 129, 219; CPW; DAM POP; INT CA-131; MAL 5; MTCW 1; MTFW 2005
Dhuoda 805?-after 843 .... **CMLC 155**
See also DLB 148
Diamano, Silmang
See Senghor, Leopold Sedar
Diamant, Anita 1951- .... **CLC 239**
See also CA 145; CANR 126, 219; NFS 36
Diamond, Neil 1941- .... **CLC 30**
See also CA 108
Dias, B. H.
See Pound, Ezra
di Bassetto, Corno
See Shaw, George Bernard
Dick, Philip K. 1928-1982 .... **CLC 10, 30, 72; SSC 57, 219**
See also AAYA 24; BPFB 1; BYA 11; CA 49-52; 106; CANR 2, 16, 132; CN 2, 3; CPW; DA3; DAM NOV, POP; DLB 8; MTCW 1, 2; MTFW 2005; NFS 5, 26; SCFW 1, 2; SFW 4
Dick, Philip Kindred
See Dick, Philip K.
Dickens, Charles 1812-1870 ...... **NCLC 3, 8, 18, 26, 37, 50, 86, 105, 113, 161, 187, 203, 206, 211, 217, 219, 230, 231, 239, 285, 307; SSC 17, 49, 88, 215; WLC 2**
See also AAYA 23; BRW 5; BRWC 1, 2; BYA 1, 2, 3, 13, 14; CDBLB 1832-1890; CLR 95, 162; CMW 4; DA; DA3; DAB; DAC; DAM MST, NOV; DLB 21, 55, 70, 159, 166; EXPN; GL 2; HGG; JRDA; LAIT 1, 2; LATS 1:1; LMFS 1; MAICYA 1, 2; NFS 4, 5, 10, 14, 20, 25, 30, 33, 41; RGEL 2; RGSF 2; SATA 15; SUFW 1; TEA; WCH; WLIT 4; WYA
Dickens, Charles John Huffam
See Dickens, Charles
Dickey, James 1923-1997 .... **CLC 1, 2, 4, 7, 10, 15, 47, 109; PC 40; TCLC 151**
See also AAYA 50; AITN 1, 2; AMWS 4; BPFB 1; CA 9-12R; 156; CABS 2; CANR 10, 48, 61, 105; CDALB 1968-1988; CP 1, 2, 3, 4, 5, 6; CPW; CSW; DA3; DAM NOV, POET, POP; DLB 5, 193, 342; DLBD 7; DLBY 1982, 1993, 1996, 1997, 1998; EWL 3; INT CANR-10; MAL 5; MTCW 1, 2; NFS 9; PFS 6, 11; RGAL 4; TUS
Dickey, James Lafayette
See Dickey, James
Dickey, William 1928-1994 .... **CLC 3, 28**
See also CA 9-12R; 145; CANR 24, 79; CP 1, 2, 3, 4; DLB 5
Dickinson, Charles 1951- .... **CLC 49**
See also CA 128; CANR 141
Dickinson, Emily 1830-1886 .... **NCLC 21, 77, 171; PC 1, 131; WLC 2**
See also AAYA 22; AMW; AMWR 1; CDALB 1865-1917; DA; DA3; DAB; DAC; DAM MST, POET; DLB 1, 243; EXPP; FL 1:3; MBL; PAB; PFS 1, 2, 3, 4, 5, 6, 8, 10, 11, 13, 16, 28, 32, 35, 42; RGAL 4; SATA 29; TUS; WP; WYA
Dickinson, Emily Elizabeth
See Dickinson, Emily
Dickinson, Mrs. Herbert Ward
See Phelps, Elizabeth Stuart
Dickinson, Peter 1927- .... **CLC 12, 35**
See also AAYA 9, 49; BYA 5; CA 41-44R; CANR 31, 58, 88, 134, 195; CLR 29, 125; CMW 4; DLB 87, 161, 276; JRDA; MAICYA 1, 2; SATA 5, 62, 95, 150, 229; SFW 4; WYA; YAW
Dickinson, Peter Malcolm de Brissac
See Dickinson, Peter
Dickson, Carr
See Carr, John Dickson
Dickson, Carter
See Carr, John Dickson
Diderot, Denis 1713-1784 .. **LC 26, 126, 224**
See also DLB 313; EW 4; GFL Beginnings to 1789; LMFS 1; RGWL 2, 3
Didion, Joan 1934- .... **CLC 1, 3, 8, 14, 32, 129**
See also AITN 1; AMWS 4; CA 5-8R; CANR 14, 52, 76, 125, 174, 236; CDALB 1968-1988; CN 2, 3, 4, 5, 6, 7; DA3; DAM NOV; DLB 2, 173, 185; DLBY 1981, 1986; EWL 3; MAL 5; MBL; MTCW 1, 2; MTFW 2005; NFS 3; RGAL 4; TCLE 1:1; TCWW 2; TUS
di Donato, Pietro 1911-1992 .... **TCLC 159**
See also AMWS 20; CA 101; 136; DLB 9
Dietrich, Robert
See Hunt, E. Howard
Difusa, Pati
See Almodovar, Pedro
di Lampedusa, Giuseppe Tomasi
See Lampedusa, Giuseppe di
Dillard, Annie 1945- ... **CLC 9, 60, 115, 216**
See also AAYA 6, 43; AMWS 6; ANW; CA 49-52; CANR 3, 43, 62, 90, 125, 214; DA3; DAM NOV; DLB 275, 278; DLBY 1980; LAIT 4, 5; MAL 5; MTCW 1, 2; MTFW 2005; NCFS 1; RGAL 4; SATA 10, 140; TCLE 1:1; TUS
Dillard, R(ichard) H(enry) W(ilde) 1937- .... **CLC 5**
See also CA 21-24R; CAAS 7; CANR 10; CP 2, 3, 4, 5, 6, 7; CSW; DLB 5, 244
Dillon, Eilis 1920-1994 .... **CLC 17**
See also CA 9-12R, 182; 147; CAAE 182; CAAS 3; CANR 4, 38, 78; CLR 26; MAICYA 1, 2; MAICYAS 1; SATA 2, 74; SATA-Essay 105; SATA-Obit 83; YAW
Dilthey, Wilhelm 1833-1911 .... **TCLC 320**
See also DLB 129
Dimont, Penelope
See Mortimer, Penelope (Ruth)
Dinesen, Isak
See Blixen, Karen
Ding Ling
See Chiang, Pin-chin
Diodorus Siculus c. 90B.C.-c. 31B.C. .... **CMLC 88**
Dionysius of Halicarnassus c. 60B.C.-c. 7B.C. .... **CMLC 126**
Diop, Boubacar Boris 1946- .... **CLC 323**
See also CA 266
Diphusa, Patty
See Almodovar, Pedro
Disch, Thomas M. 1940-2008 .... **CLC 7, 36, 325**
See also AAYA 17; BPFB 1; CA 21-24R; 274; CAAS 4; CANR 17, 36, 54, 89; CLR 18; CP 5, 6, 7; DA3; DLB 8, 282; HGG; MAICYA 1, 2; MTCW 1, 2; MTFW 2005;

SAAS 15; SATA 92; SATA-Obit 195; SCFW 1, 2; SFW 4; SUFW 2
Disch, Thomas Michael
See Disch, Thomas M.
Disch, Tom
See Disch, Thomas M.
d'Isly, Georges
See Simenon, Georges
Disraeli, Benjamin 1804-1881 .... **NCLC 2, 39, 79, 272**
See also BRW 4; DLB 21, 55; RGEL 2
D'Israeli, Isaac 1766-1848 .... **NCLC 217**
See also DLB 107
Ditcum, Steve
See Crumb, R.
Divakaruni, Chitra Banerjee 1956- **CLC 316**
See also CA 182; CANR 127, 189, 226; CN 7; DLB 323; NFS 38; PFS 34; SATA 160, 222; SSFS 18, 24, 36
Dixon, Paige
See Corcoran, Barbara (Asenath)
Dixon, Stephen 1936- .... **CLC 52; SSC 16**
See also AMWS 12; CA 89-92; CANR 17, 40, 54, 91, 175; CN 4, 5, 6, 7; DLB 130; MAL 5
Dixon, Thomas, Jr. 1864-1946 .... **TCLC 163**
See also RHW
Djebar, Assia 1936- ..... **BLC 2:1; CLC 182, 296; SSC 114**
See also CA 188; CANR 169; DLB 346; EWL 3; RGWL 3; WLIT 2
Doak, Annie
See Dillard, Annie
Dobell, Sydney Thompson 1824-1874 .... **NCLC 43; PC 100**
See also DLB 32; RGEL 2
Doblado, Don Leucadio
See Blanco White, Joseph
Dobroliubov, Nikolai Aleksandrovich
See Dobrolyubov, Nikolai Alexandrovich
Dobrolyubov, Nikolai Alexandrovich 1836-1861 .... **NCLC 5**
See also DLB 277
Dobson, Austin 1840-1921 .... **TCLC 79**
See also DLB 35, 144
Dobyns, Stephen 1941- .... **CLC 37, 233**
See also AMWS 13; CA 45-48; CANR 2, 18, 99; CMW 4; CP 4, 5, 6, 7; PFS 23
Doctorow, Cory 1971- .... **CLC 273**
See also AAYA 84; CA 221; CANR 203; CLR 194
Doctorow, E. L. 1931- .... **CLC 6, 11, 15, 18, 37, 44, 65, 113, 214, 324, 363, 366**
See also AAYA 22; AITN 2; AMWS 4; BEST 89:3; BPFB 1; CA 45-48; CANR 2, 33, 51, 76, 97, 133, 170, 218; CDALB 1968-1988; CN 3, 4, 5, 6, 7; CPW; DA3; DAM NOV, POP; DLB 2, 28, 173; DLBY 1980; EWL 3; LAIT 3; MAL 5; MTCW 1, 2; MTFW 2005; NFS 6; RGAL 4; RGHL; RHW; SSFS 27; TCLE 1:1; TCWW 1, 2; TUS
Doctorow, Edgar Lawrence
See Doctorow, E. L.
Dodgson, Charles Lutwidge
See Carroll, Lewis
Dodsley, Robert 1703-1764 .... **LC 97**
See also DLB 95, 154; RGEL 2
Dodson, Owen (Vincent) 1914-1983 .... **BLC 1:1; CLC 79**
See also BW 1; CA 65-68; 110; CANR 24; DAM MULT; DLB 76
Doeblin, Alfred
See Doblin, Alfred
Doerr, Harriet 1910-2002 .... **CLC 34**
See also CA 117; 122; 213; CANR 47; INT CA-122; LATS 1:2
Domecq, Honorio Bustos
See Bioy Casares, Adolfo; Borges, Jorge Luis
Domini, Rey
See Lorde, Audre
Dominic, R. B.
See Hennissart, Martha
Dominique
See Proust, Marcel
Don, A
See Stephen, Sir Leslie
Donaldson, Stephen R. 1947- .... **CLC 46, 138**
See also AAYA 36; BPFB 1; CA 89-92; CANR 13, 55, 99, 228; CPW; DAM POP; FANT; INT CANR-13; SATA 121; SFW 4; SUFW 1, 2
Donleavy, J(ames) P(atrick) 1926- .... **CLC 1, 4, 6, 10, 45**
See also AITN 2; BPFB 1; CA 9-12R; CANR 24, 49, 62, 80, 124; CBD; CD 5, 6; CN 1, 2, 3, 4, 5, 6, 7; DLB 6, 173; INT CANR-24; MAL 5; MTCW 1, 2; MTFW 2005; RGAL 4
Donnadieu, Marguerite
See Duras, Marguerite
Donne, John 1572-1631 .... **LC 10, 24, 91, 216; PC 1, 43, 145; WLC 2**
See also AAYA 67; BRW 1; BRWC 1; BRWR 2; CDBLB Before 1660; DA; DAB; DAC; DAM MST, POET; DLB 121, 151; EXPP; PAB; PFS 2, 11, 35, 41; RGEL 3; TEA; WLIT 3; WP
Donnell, David 1939(?)- .... **CLC 34**
See also CA 197
Donoghue, Denis 1928- .... **CLC 209**
See also CA 17-20R; CANR 16, 102, 206
Donoghue, Emma 1969- .... **CLC 239**
See also CA 155; CANR 103, 152, 196; DLB 267; GLL 2; SATA 101
Donoghue, P.S.
See Hunt, E. Howard
Donoso, Jose 1924-1996 ... **CLC 4, 8, 11, 32, 99; HLC 1; SSC 34; TCLC 133**
See also CA 81-84; 155; CANR 32, 73; CDWLB 3; CWW 2; DAM MULT; DLB 113; EWL 3; HW 1, 2; LAW; LAWS 1; MTCW 1, 2; MTFW 2005; RGSF 2; WLIT 1
Donoso Yanez, Jose
See Donoso, Jose
Donovan, John 1928-1992 .... **CLC 35**
See also AAYA 20; CA 97-100; 137; CLR 3, 183; MAICYA 1, 2; SATA 72; SATA-Brief 29; YAW
Don Roberto
See Cunninghame Graham, Robert Bontine
Doolittle, Hilda 1886-1961 ..... **CLC 3, 8, 14, 31, 34, 73; PC 5, 127; WLC 3**
See also AAYA 66; AMWS 1; CA 97-100; CANR 35, 131; DA; DAC; DAM MST, POET; DLB 4, 45; EWL 3; FL 1:5; FW; GLL 1; LMFS 2; MAL 5; MBL; MTCW 1, 2; MTFW 2005; PFS 6, 28; RGAL 4
Doppo
See Kunikida Doppo
Doppo, Kunikida
See Kunikida Doppo
Dorfman, Ariel 1942- .... **CLC 48, 77, 189; HLC 1**
See also CA 124; 130; CANR 67, 70, 135; CWW 2; DAM MULT; DFS 4; EWL 3; HW 1, 2; INT CA-130; PFS 43; WLIT 1
Dorn, Edward 1929-1999 .... **CLC 10, 18; PC 115**
See also CA 93-96; 187; CANR 42, 79; CP 1, 2, 3, 4, 5, 6, 7; DLB 5; INT CA-93-96; WP
Dorn, Edward Merton
See Dorn, Edward
Dor-Ner, Zvi .... **CLC 70**
Dorris, Michael 1945-1997 .... **CLC 109; NNAL**
See also AAYA 20; BEST 90:1; BYA 12; CA 102; 157; CANR 19, 46, 75; CLR 58; DA3; DAM MULT, NOV; DLB 175; LAIT 5; MTCW 2; MTFW 2005; NFS 3; RGAL 4; SATA 75; SATA-Obit 94; TCWW 2; YAW
Dorris, Michael A.
See Dorris, Michael
Dorris, Michael Anthony
See Dorris, Michael
Dorsan, Luc
See Simenon, Georges
Dorsange, Jean
See Simenon, Georges
Dorset
See Sackville, Thomas
Dos Passos, John 1896-1970 ... **CLC 1, 4, 8, 11, 15, 25, 34, 82; TCLC 268, 291, 300, 306; WLC 2**
See also AMW; BPFB 1; CA 1-4R; 29-32R; CANR 3; CDALB 1929-1941; DA; DA3; DAB; DAC; DAM MST, NOV; DLB 4, 9, 274, 316; DLBD 1, 15; DLBY 1996; EWL 3; MAL 5; MTCW 1, 2; MTFW 2005; NFS 14; RGAL 4; TUS
Dos Passos, John Roderigo
See Dos Passos, John
Dossage, Jean
See Simenon, Georges
Dostoevsky, Fedor
See Dostoevsky, Fyodor
Dostoevsky, Fedor Mikhailovich
See Dostoevsky, Fyodor
Dostoevsky, Fyodor 1821-1881 ...... **NCLC 2, 7, 21, 33, 43, 119, 167, 202, 238, 268, 273; SSC 2, 33, 44, 134, 181; WLC 2**
See also AAYA 40; DA; DA3; DAB; DAC; DAM MST, NOV; DLB 238; EW 7; EXPN; LATS 1:1; LMFS 1, 2; NFS 28; RGSF 2; RGWL 2, 3; SSFS 8, 30; TWA
Doty, Mark 1953(?)- .. **CLC 176, 334; PC 53**
See also AMWS 11; CA 161, 183; CAAE 183; CANR 110, 173; CP 7; PFS 28, 40
Doty, Mark A.
See Doty, Mark
Doty, Mark Alan
See Doty, Mark
Doty, M.R.
See Doty, Mark
Doughty, Charles M(ontagu) 1843-1926 .... **TCLC 27**
See also CA 115; 178; DLB 19, 57, 174, 366
Douglas, Ellen 1921- .... **CLC 73, 335**
See also CA 115; CANR 41, 83; CN 5, 6, 7; CSW; DLB 292
Douglas, Gavin 1475(?)-1522 .... **LC 20**
See also DLB 132; RGEL 2
Douglas, George
See Brown, George Douglas
Douglas, Keith (Castellain) 1920-1944 .... **PC 106; TCLC 40**
See also BRW 7; CA 160; DLB 27; EWL 3; PAB; RGEL 2
Douglas, Leonard
See Bradbury, Ray
Douglas, Michael
See Crichton, Michael
Douglas, (George) Norman 1868-1952 .... **TCLC 68**
See also BRW 6; CA 119; 157; DLB 34, 195; RGEL 2
Douglas, William
See Brown, George Douglas
Douglass, Frederick 1817(?)-1895 .... **BLC 1:1; NCLC 7, 55, 141, 235; WLC 2**
See also AAYA 48; AFAW 1, 2; AMWC 1; AMWS 3; CDALB 1640-1865; DA; DA3; DAC; DAM MST, MULT; DLB 1, 43, 50, 79, 243; FW; LAIT 2; NCFS 2; RGAL 4; SATA 29

Dourado, (Waldomiro Freitas) Autran 1926- .... **CLC 23, 60**
See also CA 25-28R, 179; CANR 34, 81; DLB 145, 307; HW 2
Dourado, Waldomiro Freitas Autran
See Dourado, (Waldomiro Freitas) Autran
Dove, Rita 1952- .... **BLC 2:1; BLCS; CLC 50, 81, 349; PC 6, 140**
See also AAYA 46; AMWS 4; BW 2; CA 109; CAAS 19; CANR 27, 42, 68, 76, 97, 132, 217; CDALBS; CP 5, 6, 7; CSW; CWP; DA3; DAM MULT, POET; DLB 120; EWL 3; EXPP; MAL 5; MTCW 2; MTFW 2005; PFS 1, 15, 37; RGAL 4
Dove, Rita Frances
See Dove, Rita
Doveglion
See Villa, Jose Garcia
Dowell, Coleman 1925-1985 .... **CLC 60**
See also CA 25-28R; 117; CANR 10; DLB 130; GLL 2
Downing, Major Jack
See Smith, Seba
Dowson, Ernest (Christopher) 1867-1900 .... **PC 163; TCLC 4**
See also CA 105; 150; DLB 19, 135; RGEL 2
Doyle, A. Conan
See Doyle, Sir Arthur Conan
Doyle, Sir Arthur Conan 1859-1930 .... **SSC 12, 83, 95, 196; TCLC 7, 287, 289; WLC 2**
See also AAYA 14; BPFB 1; BRWS 2; BYA 4, 5, 11; CA 104; 122; CANR 131; CDBLB 1890-1914; CLR 106; CMW 4; DA; DA3; DAB; DAC; DAM MST, NOV; DLB 18, 70, 156, 178; EXPS; HGG; LAIT 2; MSW; MTCW 1, 2; MTFW 2005; NFS 28; RGEL 2; RGSF 2; RHW; SATA 24; SCFW 1, 2; SFW 4; SSFS 2; TEA; WCH; WLIT 4; WYA; YAW
Doyle, Conan
See Doyle, Sir Arthur Conan
Doyle, John
See Graves, Robert
Doyle, Roddy 1958- .... **CLC 81, 178**
See also AAYA 14; BRWS 5; CA 143; CANR 73, 128, 168, 200, 235; CN 6, 7; DA3; DLB 194, 326; MTCW 2; MTFW 2005
Doyle, Sir A. Conan
See Doyle, Sir Arthur Conan
Dr. A
See Asimov, Isaac; Silverstein, Alvin; Silverstein, Virginia B.
Drabble, Margaret 1939- ..... **CLC 2, 3, 5, 8, 10, 22, 53, 129**
See also BRWS 4; CA 13-16R; CANR 18, 35, 63, 112, 131, 174, 218; CDBLB 1960 to Present; CN 1, 2, 3, 4, 5, 6, 7; CPW; DA3; DAB; DAC; DAM MST, NOV, POP; DLB 14, 155, 231; EWL 3; FW; MTCW 1, 2; MTFW 2005; RGEL 2; SATA 48; TEA
Drakulic, Slavenka 1949- .... **CLC 173**
See also CA 144; CANR 92, 198, 229; DLB 353
Drakulic, Slavenka
See Drakulic, Slavenka
Drakulic-Ilic, Slavenka
See Drakulic, Slavenka
Drakulic-Ilic, Slavenka
See Drakulic, Slavenka
Drapier, M. B.
See Swift, Jonathan
Drayham, James
See Mencken, H. L.
Drayton, Michael 1563-1631 ...... **LC 8, 161; PC 98**
See also DAM POET; DLB 121; RGEL 2
Dreadstone, Carl
See Campbell, Ramsey
Drechsler, Johann Theodor
See Mangan, James Clarence
Dreiser, Theodore 1871-1945 .... **SSC 30, 114; TCLC 10, 18, 35, 83, 277; WLC 2**
See also AMW; AMWC 2; AMWR 2; BYA 15, 16; CA 106; 132; CDALB 1865-1917; DA; DA3; DAC; DAM MST, NOV; DLB 9, 12, 102, 137, 361, 368; DLBD 1; EWL 3; LAIT 2; LMFS 2; MAL 5; MTCW 1, 2; MTFW 2005; NFS 8, 17; RGAL 4; TUS
Dreiser, Theodore Herman Albert
See Dreiser, Theodore
Drexler, Rosalyn 1926- .... **CLC 2, 6**
See also CA 81-84; CAD; CANR 68, 124; CD 5, 6; CWD; MAL 5
Dreyer, Carl Theodor 1889-1968 ... **CLC 16**
See also CA 116
Drieu la Rochelle, Pierre 1893-1945 .... **TCLC 21**
See also CA 117; 250; DLB 72; EWL 3; GFL 1789 to the Present
Drieu la Rochelle, Pierre-Eugene 1893-1945
See Drieu la Rochelle, Pierre
Drinkwater, John 1882-1937 .... **TCLC 57**
See also CA 109; 149; DLB 10, 19, 149; RGEL 2
Drop Shot
See Cable, George Washington
Droste-Hulshoff, Annette Freiin von 1797-1848 .... **NCLC 3, 133, 273**
See also CDWLB 2; DLB 133; RGSF 2; RGWL 2, 3
Drummond, Walter
See Silverberg, Robert
Drummond, William Henry 1854-1907 .... **TCLC 25**
See also CA 160; DLB 92
Drummond de Andrade, Carlos 1902-1987 .... **CLC 18; TCLC 139**
See also CA 132; 123; DLB 307; EWL 3; LAW; RGWL 2, 3
Drummond of Hawthornden, William 1585-1649 .... **LC 83**
See also DLB 121, 213; RGEL 2
Drury, Allen (Stuart) 1918-1998 .... **CLC 37**
See also CA 57-60; 170; CANR 18, 52; CN 1, 2, 3, 4, 5, 6; INT CANR-18
Druse, Eleanor
See King, Stephen
Dryden, John 1631-1700 ... **DC 3; LC 3, 21, 115, 188; PC 25; WLC 2**
See also BRW 2; BRWR 3; CDBLB 1660-1789; DA; DAB; DAC; DAM DRAM, MST, POET; DLB 80, 101, 131; EXPP; IDTP; LMFS 1; RGEL 2; TEA; WLIT 3
du Aime, Albert
See Wharton, William
du Aime, Albert William
See Wharton, William
Du Bellay, Joachim 1524-1560 .... **LC 92; PC 144**
See also DLB 327; GFL Beginnings to 1789; RGWL 2, 3
Duberman, Martin 1930- .... **CLC 8**
See also CA 1-4R; CAD; CANR 2, 63, 137, 174, 233; CD 5, 6
Dubie, Norman (Evans) 1945- .... **CLC 36**
See also CA 69-72; CANR 12, 115; CP 3, 4, 5, 6, 7; DLB 120; PFS 12
Du Bois, W. E. B. 1868-1963 .... **BLC 1:1; CLC 1, 2, 13, 64, 96; HR 1:2; TCLC 169; WLC 2**
See also AAYA 40; AFAW 1, 2; AMWC 1; AMWS 2; BW 1, 3; CA 85-88; CANR 34, 82, 132; CDALB 1865-1917; DA; DA3; DAC; DAM MST, MULT, NOV; DLB 47, 50, 91, 246, 284; EWL 3; EXPP; LAIT 2; LMFS 2; MAL 5; MTCW 1, 2; MTFW 2005; NCFS 1; PFS 13; RGAL 4; SATA 42
Du Bois, William Edward Burghardt
See Du Bois, W. E. B.
Dubos, Jean-Baptiste 1670-1742 ...... **LC 197**
Dubus, Andre 1936-1999 .... **CLC 13, 36, 97; SSC 15, 118**
See also AMWS 7; CA 21-24R; 177; CANR 17; CN 5, 6; CSW; DLB 130; INT CANR-17; RGAL 4; SSFS 10, 36; TCLE 1:1
Duca Minimo
See D'Annunzio, Gabriele
Ducharme, Rejean 1941- .... **CLC 74**
See also CA 165; DLB 60
du Chatelet, Emilie 1706-1749 .... **LC 96**
See also DLB 313
Duchen, Claire .... **CLC 65**
Duck, Stephen 1705(?)-1756 .... **PC 89**
See also DLB 95; RGEL 2
Duclos, Charles Pinot- 1704-1772 .... **LC 1**
See also GFL Beginnings to 1789
Ducornet, Erica 1943- .... **CLC 232**
See also CA 37-40R; CANR 14, 34, 54, 82, 236; SATA 7
Ducornet, Rikki
See Ducornet, Erica
Dudek, Louis 1918-2001 .... **CLC 11, 19**
See also CA 45-48; 215; CAAS 14; CANR 1; CP 1, 2, 3, 4, 5, 6, 7; DLB 88
Duerrenmatt, Friedrich
See Dürrenmatt, Friedrich
Duff Gordon, Lucie 1821-1869 ... **NCLC 262**
See also DLB 166
Duffle, Thomas
See Galt, John
Duffy, Bruce 1951- .... **CLC 50**
See also CA 172; CANR 238
Duffy, Carol Ann 1955- ... **CLC 337; PC 166**
See also CA 119; CANR 70, 120, 203; CP 5, 6, 7; CWP; PFS 25; SATA 95, 165
Duffy, Maureen 1933- .... **CLC 37**
See also CA 25-28R; CANR 33, 68; CBD; CN 1, 2, 3, 4, 5, 6, 7; CP 5, 6, 7; CWD; CWP; DFS 15; DLB 14, 310; FW; MTCW 1
Duffy, Maureen Patricia
See Duffy, Maureen
Du Fu
See Tu Fu
Dugan, Alan 1923-2003 .... **CLC 2, 6**
See also CA 81-84; 220; CANR 119; CP 1, 2, 3, 4, 5, 6, 7; DLB 5; MAL 5; PFS 10
du Gard, Roger Martin
See Martin du Gard, Roger
du Guillet, Pernette 1520(?)-1545 .... **LC 190**
See also DLB 327
Duhamel, Georges 1884-1966 .... **CLC 8**
See also CA 81-84; 25-28R; CANR 35; DLB 65; EWL 3; GFL 1789 to the Present; MTCW 1
du Hault, Jean
See Grindel, Eugene
Dujardin, Edouard (Emile Louis) 1861-1949 .... **TCLC 13**
See also CA 109; DLB 123
Duke, Raoul
See Thompson, Hunter S.
Dulles, John Foster 1888-1959 ..... **TCLC 72**
See also CA 115; 149
Dumas, Alexandre (père) 1802-1870 .... **NCLC 11, 71, 271; WLC 2**
See also AAYA 22; BYA 3; CLR 134; DA; DA3; DAB; DAC; DAM MST, NOV; DLB 119, 192; EW 6; GFL 1789 to the Present; LAIT 1, 2; NFS 14, 19, 41; RGWL 2, 3; SATA 18; TWA; WCH
Dumas, Alexandre (fils) 1824-1895 .... **DC 1; NCLC 9**
See also DLB 192; GFL 1789 to the Present; RGWL 2, 3

Dumas, Claudine
See Malzberg, Barry N(athaniel)
Dumas, Henry L. 1934-1968 .... **BLC 2:1; CLC 6, 62; SSC 107**
See also BW 1; CA 85-88; DLB 41; RGAL 4
du Maurier, Daphne 1907-1989 ...... **CLC 6, 11, 59; SSC 18, 129; TCLC 209**
See also AAYA 37; BPFB 1; BRWS 3; CA 5-8R; 128; CANR 6, 55; CMW 4; CN 1, 2, 3, 4; CPW; DA3; DAB; DAC; DAM MST, POP; DLB 191; GL 2; HGG; LAIT 3; MSW; MTCW 1, 2; NFS 12; RGEL 2; RGSF 2; RHW; SATA 27; SATA-Obit 60; SSFS 14, 16; TEA
Du Maurier, George 1834-1896 .... **NCLC 86**
See also DLB 153, 178; RGEL 2
Dummett, Michael 1925-2011 .... **CLC 384**
See also CA 102; CANR 224; DLB 262
Dunbar, Alice
See Nelson, Alice Ruth Moore Dunbar
Dunbar, Alice Moore
See Nelson, Alice Ruth Moore Dunbar
Dunbar, Paul Laurence 1872-1906 ...... **BLC 1:1; PC 5; SSC 8; TCLC 2, 12; WLC 2**
See also AAYA 75; AFAW 1, 2; AMWS 2; BW 1, 3; CA 104; 124; CANR 79; CDALB 1865-1917; DA; DA3; DAC; DAM MST, MULT, POET; DLB 50, 54, 78; EXPP; MAL 5; PFS 33, 40; RGAL 4; SATA 34
Dunbar, William 1460(?)-1520(?) .... **LC 20; PC 67**
See also BRWS 8; DLB 132, 146; RGEL 2
Dunbar-Nelson, Alice
See Nelson, Alice Ruth Moore Dunbar
Dunbar-Nelson, Alice Moore
See Nelson, Alice Ruth Moore Dunbar
Duncan, Dora Angela
See Duncan, Isadora
Duncan, Isadora 1877(?)-1927 ...... **TCLC 68**
See also CA 118; 149
Duncan, Lois 1934- .... **CLC 26**
See also AAYA 4, 34; BYA 6, 8; CA 1-4R; CANR 2, 23, 36, 111; CLR 29, 129; JRDA; MAICYA 1, 2; MAICYAS 1; MTFW 2005; SAAS 2; SATA 1, 36, 75, 133, 141, 219; SATA-Essay 141; WYA; YAW
Duncan, Robert 1919-1988 .... **CLC 1, 2, 4, 7, 15, 41, 55; PC 2, 75**
See also BG 1:2; CA 9-12R; 124; CANR 28, 62; CP 1, 2, 3, 4; DAM POET; DLB 5, 16, 193; EWL 3; MAL 5; MTCW 1, 2; MTFW 2005; PFS 13; RGAL 4; WP
Duncan, Sara Jeannette 1861-1922 ... **TCLC 60**
See also CA 157; DLB 92
Dunlap, William 1766-1839 .... **NCLC 2, 244**
See also DLB 30, 37, 59; RGAL 4
Dunn, Douglas (Eaglesham) 1942- .. **CLC 6, 40**
See also BRWS 10; CA 45-48; CANR 2, 33, 126; CP 1, 2, 3, 4, 5, 6, 7; DLB 40; MTCW 1
Dunn, Katherine 1945- .... **CLC 71**
See also CA 33-36R; CANR 72; HGG; MTCW 2; MTFW 2005
Dunn, Stephen 1939- .... **CLC 36, 206**
See also AMWS 11; CA 33-36R; CANR 12, 48, 53, 105; CP 3, 4, 5, 6, 7; DLB 105, 238; PFS 21
Dunn, Stephen Elliott
See Dunn, Stephen
Dunne, Finley Peter 1867-1936 .... **TCLC 28**
See also CA 108; 178; DLB 11, 23; RGAL 4
Dunne, John Gregory 1932-2003 ... **CLC 28**
See also CA 25-28R; 222; CANR 14, 50; CN 5, 6, 7; DLBY 1980
Dunne, Mary Chavelita
See Egerton, George
Duns Scotus, John
See Scotus, John Duns
Dunton, John 1659-1733 .... **LC 219**
See also DLB 170
Duong, Thu Huong 1947- .... **CLC 273**
See also CA 152; CANR 106, 166; DLB 348; NFS 23
Duong Thu Huong
See Duong, Thu Huong
du Perry, Jean
See Simenon, Georges
Durang, Christopher 1949- .... **CLC 27, 38**
See also CA 105; CAD; CANR 50, 76, 130; CD 5, 6; MTCW 2; MTFW 2005
Durang, Christopher Ferdinand
See Durang, Christopher
Duras, Claire de 1777-1832 ... **NCLC 154, 304**
Duras, Marguerite 1914-1996 ...... **CLC 3, 6, 11, 20, 34, 40, 68, 100; DC 51; SSC 40, 206**
See also BPFB 1; CA 25-28R; 151; CANR 50; CWW 2; DFS 21; DLB 83, 321; EWL 3; FL 1:5; GFL 1789 to the Present; IDFW 4; MTCW 1, 2; RGWL 2, 3; TWA
Durban, (Rosa) Pam 1947- .... **CLC 39**
See also CA 123; CANR 98; CSW
Durcan, Paul 1944- .... **CLC 43, 70**
See also CA 134; CANR 123; CP 1, 5, 6, 7; DAM POET; EWL 3
d'Urfe, Honore
See Urfe, Honore d'
Durfey, Thomas 1653-1723 .... **LC 94**
See also DLB 80; RGEL 2
Durkheim, Emile 1858-1917 .... **TCLC 55**
See also CA 249
Durrell, Lawrence 1912-1990 .... **CLC 1, 4, 6, 8, 13, 27, 41; PC 142**
See also BPFB 1; BRWR 3; BRWS 1; CA 9-12R; 132; CANR 40, 77; CDBLB 1945-1960; CN 1, 2, 3, 4; CP 1, 2, 3, 4, 5; DAM NOV; DLB 15, 27, 204; DLBY 1990; EWL 3; MTCW 1, 2; RGEL 2; SFW 4; TEA
Durrell, Lawrence George
See Durrell, Lawrence
Dürrenmatt, Friedrich 1921-1990 ... **CLC 1, 4, 8, 11, 15, 43, 102**
See also CA 17-20R; CANR 33; CDWLB 2; CMW 4; DAM DRAM; DLB 69, 124; EW 13; EWL 3; MTCW 1, 2; RGHL; RGWL 2, 3
Dutt, Michael Madhusudan 1824-1873 .... **NCLC 118**
Dutt, Toru 1856-1877 .... **NCLC 29**
See also DLB 240
Dwight, Timothy 1752-1817 ... **NCLC 13, 245**
See also DLB 37; RGAL 4
Dworkin, Andrea 1946-2005 ... **CLC 43, 123**
See also CA 77-80; 238; CAAS 21; CANR 16, 39, 76, 96; FL 1:5; FW; GLL 1; INT CANR-16; MTCW 1, 2; MTFW 2005
Dwyer, Deanna
See Koontz, Dean
Dwyer, K.R.
See Koontz, Dean
Dybek, Stuart 1942- .... **CLC 114; SSC 55**
See also AMWS 23; CA 97-100; CANR 39; DLB 130; SSFS 23
Dye, Richard
See De Voto, Bernard (Augustine)
Dyer, Geoff 1958- .... **CLC 149**
See also CA 125; CANR 88, 209, 242
Dyer, George 1755-1841 .... **NCLC 129**
See also DLB 93
Dylan, Bob 1941- .... **CLC 3, 4, 6, 12, 77, 308; PC 37**
See also AMWS 18; CA 41-44R; CANR 108; CP 1, 2, 3, 4, 5, 6, 7; DLB 16
Dyson, John 1943- .... **CLC 70**
See also CA 144
Dzyubin, Eduard Georgievich 1895-1934 .... **TCLC 60**
See also CA 170; DLB 359; EWL 3
E. V. L.
See Lucas, E(dward) V(errall)
E. W.
See Mangan, James Clarence
Eagleton, Terence
See Eagleton, Terry
Eagleton, Terence Francis
See Eagleton, Terry
Eagleton, Terry 1943- .... **CLC 63, 132**
See also CA 57-60; CANR 7, 23, 68, 115, 198, 243; DLB 242; LMFS 2; MTCW 1, 2; MTFW 2005
Earl of Orrey
See Boyle, Roger
Early, Jack
See Scoppettone, Sandra
Early, Tom
See Kelton, Elmer
East, Michael
See West, Morris L(anglo)
Eastaway, Edward
See Thomas, (Philip) Edward
Eastlake, William (Derry) 1917-1997 ... **CLC 8**
See also CA 5-8R; 158; CAAS 1; CANR 5, 63; CN 1, 2, 3, 4, 5, 6; DLB 6, 206; INT CANR-5; MAL 5; TCWW 1, 2
Eastland, Sam
See Watkins, Paul
Eastman, Charles A(lexander) 1858-1939 .... **NNAL; TCLC 55**
See also CA 179; CANR 91; DAM MULT; DLB 175; YABC 1
Eaton, Edith Maude 1865-1914 ... **AAL; SSC 157; TCLC 232**
See also CA 154; DLB 221, 312; FW
Eaton, (Lillie) Winnifred 1875-1954 .... **AAL**
See also CA 217; DLB 221, 312; RGAL 4
Eberhart, Richard 1904-2005 .... **CLC 3, 11, 19, 56; PC 76**
See also AMW; CA 1-4R; 240; CANR 2, 125; CDALB 1941-1968; CP 1, 2, 3, 4, 5, 6, 7; DAM POET; DLB 48; MAL 5; MTCW 1; RGAL 4
Eberhart, Richard Ghormley
See Eberhart, Richard
Eberstadt, Fernanda 1960- .... **CLC 39**
See also CA 136; CANR 69, 128
Ebner, Margaret c. 1291-1351 .... **CMLC 98**
Echegaray (y Eizaguirre), Jose (Maria Waldo) 1832-1916 .... **HLCS 1; TCLC 4**
See also CA 104; CANR 32; DLB 329; EWL 3; HW 1; MTCW 1
Echeverría, (Jose) Esteban (Antonino) 1805-1851 .... **NCLC 18, 309**
See also LAW
Echo
See Proust, Marcel
Eckert, Allan W. 1931- .... **CLC 17**
See also AAYA 18; BYA 2; CA 13-16R; CANR 14, 45; INT CANR-14; MAICYA 2; MAICYAS 1; SAAS 21; SATA 29, 91; SATA-Brief 27
Eckhart, Meister 1260(?)-1327(?) .... **CMLC 9, 80, 131**
See also DLB 115; LMFS 1
Eckmar, F. R.
See de Hartog, Jan
Eco, Umberto 1932- .... **CLC 28, 60, 142, 248, 360**
See also BEST 90:1; BPFB 1; CA 77-80; CANR 12, 33, 55, 110, 131, 195, 234; CPW; CWW 2; DA3; DAM NOV, POP; DLB 196, 242; EWL 3; MSW; MTCW 1, 2; MTFW 2005; NFS 22; RGWL 3; WLIT 7

Eddison, E(ric) R(ucker) 1882-1945 .... **TCLC 15**
See also CA 109; 156; DLB 255; FANT; SFW 4; SUFW 1

Eddy, Mary (Ann Morse) Baker 1821-1910 .... **TCLC 71**
See also CA 113; 174

Edel, (Joseph) Leon 1907-1997 .. **CLC 29, 34**
See also CA 1-4R; 161; CANR 1, 22, 112; DLB 103; INT CANR-22

Eden, Emily 1797-1869 .... **NCLC 10**

Edgar, David 1948- .... **CLC 42; DC 44**
See also CA 57-60; CANR 12, 61, 112; CBD; CD 5, 6; DAM DRAM; DFS 15; DLB 13, 233; MTCW 1

Edgerton, Clyde 1944- .... **CLC 39**
See also AAYA 17; CA 118; 134; CANR 64, 125, 195, 238; CN 7; CSW; DLB 278; INT CA-134; TCLE 1:1; YAW

Edgerton, Clyde Carlyle
See Edgerton, Clyde

Edgeworth, Maria 1768-1849 .... **NCLC 1, 51, 158, 279; SSC 86**
See also BRWS 3; CLR 153; DLB 116, 159, 163; FL 1:3; FW; RGEL 2; SATA 21; TEA; WLIT 3

Edmonds, Paul
See Kuttner, Henry

Edmonds, Walter D(umaux) 1903-1998 .... **CLC 35**
See also BYA 2; CA 5-8R; CANR 2; CWRI 5; DLB 9; LAIT 1; MAICYA 1, 2; MAL 5; RHW; SAAS 4; SATA 1, 27; SATA-Obit 99

Edmondson, Wallace
See Ellison, Harlan

Edson, Margaret 1961- .... **CLC 199; DC 24**
See also AMWS 18; CA 190; DFS 13; DLB 266

Edson, Russell 1935- .... **CLC 13**
See also CA 33-36R; CANR 115; CP 2, 3, 4, 5, 6, 7; DLB 244; WP

Edwards, Bronwen Elizabeth
See Rose, Wendy

Edwards, Eli
See McKay, Claude

Edwards, G(erald) B(asil) 1899-1976 .... **CLC 25**
See also CA 201; 110

Edwards, Gus 1939- .... **CLC 43**
See also CA 108; INT CA-108

Edwards, Jonathan 1703-1758 .... **LC 7, 54**
See also AMW; DA; DAC; DAM MST; DLB 24, 270; RGAL 4; TUS

Edwards, Marilyn
See French, Marilyn

Edwards, Sarah Pierpont 1710-1758 .. **LC 87**
See also DLB 200

Efron, Marina Ivanovna Tsvetaeva
See Tsvetaeva, Marina

Egan, Jennifer 1962- .... **CLC 326**
See also CA 154; CANR 112, 166, 219

Egeria fl. 4th cent. .... **CMLC 70**

Egerton, George 1859-1945 .... **SSC 182**

Eggers, Dave 1970- .... **CLC 241, 318**
See also AAYA 56; CA 198; CANR 138; MTFW 2005

Egill Skallagrimsson 900(?)-983(?) .... **CMLC 150**

Egoyan, Atom 1960- .... **CLC 151, 291**
See also AAYA 63; CA 157; CANR 151

Ehle, John (Marsden, Jr.) 1925- .... **CLC 27**
See also CA 9-12R; CSW

Ehrenbourg, Ilya
See Ehrenburg, Ilya

Ehrenbourg, Ilya Grigoryevich
See Ehrenburg, Ilya

Ehrenburg, Ilya 1891-1967 ... **CLC 18, 34, 62**
See also CA 102; 25-28R; DLB 272; EWL 3

Ehrenburg, Ilya Grigoryevich
See Ehrenburg, Ilya

Ehrenburg, Ilyo
See Ehrenburg, Ilya

Ehrenburg, Ilyo Grigoryevich
See Ehrenburg, Ilya

Ehrenreich, Barbara 1941- ... **CLC 110, 267**
See also BEST 90:4; CA 73-76; CANR 16, 37, 62, 117, 167, 208; DLB 246; FW; LNFS 1; MTCW 1, 2; MTFW 2005

Ehrlich, Gretel 1946- .... **CLC 249**
See also ANW; CA 140; CANR 74, 146; DLB 212, 275; TCWW 2

Eich, Gunter 1907-1972 .... **CLC 15**
See also CA 111; 93-96; DLB 69, 124; EWL 3; RGWL 2, 3

Eich, Gunter
See Eich, Gunter

Eichendorff, Joseph 1788-1857 .... **NCLC 8, 225, 246**
See also DLB 90; RGWL 2, 3

Eigner, Larry
See Eigner, Laurence (Joel)

Eigner, Laurence (Joel) 1927-1996 ... **CLC 9**
See also CA 9-12R; 151; CAAS 23; CANR 6, 84; CP 1, 2, 3, 4, 5, 6, 7; DLB 5; WP

Eilhart von Oberge c. 1140-c. 1195 ... **CMLC 67**
See also DLB 148

Einhard c. 770-840 .... **CMLC 50**
See also DLB 148

Einstein, Albert 1879-1955 .... **TCLC 65**
See also CA 121; 133; MTCW 1, 2

Eiseley, Loren
See Eiseley, Loren Corey

Eiseley, Loren Corey 1907-1977 ...... **CLC 7; TCLC 310**
See also AAYA 5; ANW; CA 1-4R; 73-76; CANR 6; DLB 275; DLBD 17

Eisenstadt, Jill 1963- .... **CLC 50**
See also CA 140

Eisenstein, Sergei (Mikhailovich) 1898-1948 .... **TCLC 57**
See also CA 114; 149

Eisler, Steve
See Holdstock, Robert

Eisner, Simon
See Kornbluth, C(yril) M.

Eisner, Will 1917-2005 .... **CLC 237**
See also AAYA 52; CA 108; 235; CANR 114, 140, 179; MTFW 2005; SATA 31, 165

Eisner, William Erwin
See Eisner, Will

Ekelof, Gunnar 1907-1968 .... **CLC 27; PC 23**
See also CA 123; 25-28R; DAM POET; DLB 259; EW 12; EWL 3

Ekeloef, Bengt Gunnar
See Ekelof, Gunnar

Ekeloef, Gunnar
See Ekelof, Gunnar

Ekelund, Vilhelm 1880-1949 .... **TCLC 75**
See also CA 189; EWL 3

Ekman, Kerstin 1933- .... **CLC 279**
See also CA 154; CANR 124, 214; DLB 257; EWL 3

Ekman, Kerstin Lillemor
See Ekman, Kerstin

Ekwensi, C. O. D.
See Ekwensi, Cyprian

Ekwensi, Cyprian 1921-2007 .... **BLC 1:1; CLC 4**
See also AFW; BW 2, 3; CA 29-32R; CANR 18, 42, 74, 125; CDWLB 3; CN 1, 2, 3, 4, 5, 6; CWRI 5; DAM MULT; DLB 117; EWL 3; MTCW 1, 2; RGEL 2; SATA 66; WLIT 2

Ekwensi, Cyprian Odiatu Duaka
See Ekwensi, Cyprian

Elaine
See Leverson, Ada Esther

El Conde de Pepe
See Mihura, Miguel

El Crummo
See Crumb, R.

Elder, Lonne III 1931-1996 .... **BLC 1:1; DC 8**
See also BW 1, 3; CA 81-84; 152; CAD; CANR 25; DAM MULT; DLB 7, 38, 44; MAL 5

Eleanor of Aquitaine 1122-1204 ... **CMLC 39**

Elia
See Lamb, Charles

Eliade, Mircea 1907-1986 .... **CLC 19; TCLC 243**
See also CA 65-68; 119; CANR 30, 62; CDWLB 4; DLB 220; EWL 3; MTCW 1; RGWL 3; SFW 4

Eliot, A. D.
See Jewett, Sarah Orne

Eliot, Alice
See Jewett, Sarah Orne

Eliot, Dan
See Silverberg, Robert

Eliot, George 1819-1880 ... **NCLC 4, 13, 23, 41, 49, 89, 118, 183, 199, 209, 233; PC 20; SSC 72, 139; WLC 2**
See also BRW 5; BRWC 1, 2; BRWR 2; CDBLB 1832-1890; CN 7; CPW; DA; DA3; DAB; DAC; DAM MST, NOV; DLB 21, 35, 55, 366; FL 1:3; LATS 1:1; LMFS 1; NFS 17, 20, 34; RGEL 2; RGSF 2; SSFS 8; TEA; WLIT 3

Eliot, John 1604-1690 .... **LC 5**
See also DLB 24

Eliot, T. S. 1888-1965 .... **CLC 1, 2, 3, 6, 9, 10, 13, 15, 24, 34, 41, 55, 57, 113; DC 28; PC 5, 31, 90, 234; TCLC 236; WLC 2**
See also AAYA 28; AMW; AMWC 1; AMWR 1; BRW 7; BRWR 2; CA 5-8R; 25-28R; CANR 41; CBD; CDALB 1929-1941; DA; DA3; DAB; DAC; DAM DRAM, MST, POET; DFS 4, 13, 28; DLB 7, 10, 45, 63, 245, 329; DLBY 1988; EWL 3; EXPP; LAIT 3; LATS 1:1; LMFS 2; MAL 5; MTCW 1, 2; MTFW 2005; NCFS 5; PAB; PFS 1, 7, 20, 33; RGAL 4; RGEL 2; TUS; WLIT 4; WP

Eliot, Thomas Stearns
See Eliot, T. S.

Elisabeth of Schonau c. 1129-1165 .... **CMLC 82**

Elizabeth 1866-1941 .... **TCLC 41**

Elizabeth I, Queen of England 1533-1603 .... **LC 118**
See also BRWS 16; DLB 136

Elkin, Stanley L. 1930-1995 .... **CLC 4, 6, 9, 14, 27, 51, 91; SSC 12**
See also AMWS 6; BPFB 1; CA 9-12R; 148; CANR 8, 46; CN 1, 2, 3, 4, 5, 6; CPW; DAM NOV, POP; DLB 2, 28, 218, 278; DLBY 1980; EWL 3; INT CANR-8; MAL 5; MTCW 1, 2; MTFW 2005; RGAL 4; TCLE 1:1

Elledge, Scott .... **CLC 34**

Eller, Scott
See Shepard, Jim

Elliott, Don
See Silverberg, Robert

Elliott, Ebenezer 1781-1849 .... **PC 96**
See also DLB 96, 190; RGEL 2

Elliott, George P(aul) 1918-1980 ...... **CLC 2**
See also CA 1-4R; 97-100; CANR 2; CN 1, 2; CP 3; DLB 244; MAL 5

Elliott, Janice 1931-1995 .... **CLC 47**
See also CA 13-16R; CANR 8, 29, 84; CN 5, 6, 7; DLB 14; SATA 119

Elliott, Sumner Locke 1917-1991 .... **CLC 38**
See also CA 5-8R; 134; CANR 2, 21; DLB 289
Elliott, William
See Bradbury, Ray
Ellis, A. E. .... **CLC 7**
Ellis, Alice Thomas
See Haycraft, Anna
Ellis, Bret Easton 1964- .... **CLC 39, 71, 117, 229, 345**
See also AAYA 2, 43; CA 118; 123; CANR 51, 74, 126, 226; CN 6, 7; CPW; DA3; DAM POP; DLB 292; HGG; INT CA-123; MTCW 2; MTFW 2005; NFS 11
Ellis, (Henry) Havelock 1859-1939 .... **TCLC 14**
See also CA 109; 169; DLB 190
Ellis, Landon
See Ellison, Harlan
Ellis, Trey 1962- .... **CLC 55**
See also CA 146; CANR 92; CN 7
Ellison, Harlan 1934- .... **CLC 1, 13, 42, 139; SSC 14**
See also AAYA 29; BPFB 1; BYA 14; CA 5-8R; CANR 5, 46, 115; CPW; DAM POP; DLB 8, 335; HGG; INT CANR-5; MTCW 1, 2; MTFW 2005; SCFW 2; SFW 4; SSFS 13, 14, 15, 21; SUFW 1, 2
Ellison, Ralph 1914-1994 .... **BLC 1:1, 2:2; CLC 1, 3, 11, 54, 86, 114; SSC 26, 79; TCLC 308; WLC 2**
See also AAYA 19; AFAW 1, 2; AMWC 2; AMWR 2; AMWS 2; BPFB 1; BW 1, 3; BYA 2; CA 9-12R; 145; CANR 24, 53; CDALB 1941-1968; CLR 197; CN 1, 2, 3, 4, 5; CSW; DA; DA3; DAB; DAC; DAM MST, MULT, NOV; DLB 2, 76, 227; DLBY 1994; EWL 3; EXPN; EXPS; LAIT 4; MAL 5; MTCW 1, 2; MTFW 2005; NCFS 3; NFS 2, 21; RGAL 4; RGSF 2; SSFS 1, 11; YAW
Ellison, Ralph Waldo
See Ellison, Ralph
Ellmann, Lucy 1956- .... **CLC 61**
See also CA 128; CANR 154
Ellmann, Lucy Elizabeth
See Ellmann, Lucy
Ellmann, Richard (David) 1918-1987 .... **CLC 50**
See also BEST 89:2; CA 1-4R; 122; CANR 2, 28, 61; DLB 103; DLBY 1987; MTCW 1, 2; MTFW 2005
Ellroy, James 1948- .... **CLC 215**
See also BEST 90:4; CA 138; CANR 74, 133, 219; CMW 4; CN 6, 7; DA3; DLB 226; MTCW 2; MTFW 2005
Ellroy, Lee Earle
See Ellroy, James
Elman, Richard (Martin) 1934-1997 .... **CLC 19**
See also CA 17-20R; 163; CAAS 3; CANR 47; TCLE 1:1
Elron
See Hubbard, L. Ron
El Saadawi, Nawal 1931- .... **BLC 2:2; CLC 196, 284**
See also AFW; CA 118; CAAS 11; CANR 44, 92; CWW 2; DLB 360; EWL 3; FW; WLIT 2
El-Shabazz, El-Hajj Malik
See Malcolm X
Elstob, Elizabeth 1683-1756 .... **LC 205**
Eltit, Diamela 1949- .... **CLC 294**
See also CA 253
Eluard, Paul
See Grindel, Eugene
Elyot, Thomas 1490(?)-1546 .... **LC 11, 139**
See also DLB 136; RGEL 2
Elytis, Odysseus 1911-1996 .... **CLC 15, 49, 100; PC 21**
See also CA 102; 151; CANR 94; CWW 2; DAM POET; DLB 329; EW 13; EWL 3; MTCW 1, 2; RGWL 2, 3
Emecheta, Buchi 1944- .... **BLC 1:2; CLC 14, 48, 128, 214**
See also AAYA 67; AFW; BW 2, 3; CA 81-84; CANR 27, 81, 126; CDWLB 3; CLR 158; CN 4, 5, 6, 7; CWRI 5; DA3; DAM MULT; DLB 117; EWL 3; FL 1:5; FW; MTCW 1, 2; MTFW 2005; NFS 12, 14, 41; SATA 66; WLIT 2
Emecheta, Florence Onye Buchi
See Emecheta, Buchi
Emerson, Mary Moody 1774-1863 ... **NCLC 66**
Emerson, Ralph Waldo 1803-1882 **NCLC 1, 38, 98, 252; PC 18; WLC 2**
See also AAYA 60; AMW; ANW; CDALB 1640-1865; DA; DA3; DAB; DAC; DAM MST, POET; DLB 1, 59, 73, 183, 223, 270, 351, 366; EXPP; LAIT 2; LMFS 1; NCFS 3; PFS 4, 17, 34; RGAL 4; TUS; WP
Eminem 1972- .... **CLC 226**
See also CA 245
Eminescu, Mihail 1850-1889 .... **NCLC 33, 131**
Empedocles 5th cent. B.C. ... **CMLC 50, 171**
See also DLB 176
Empson, William 1906-1984 .... **CLC 3, 8, 19, 33, 34; PC 104**
See also BRWS 2; CA 17-20R; 112; CANR 31, 61; CP 1, 2, 3; DLB 20; EWL 3; MTCW 1, 2; RGEL 2
Enchi, Fumiko 1905-1986 .... **CLC 31**
See also CA 129; 121; DLB 182; EWL 3; FW; MJW
Enchi, Fumiko Ueda
See Enchi, Fumiko
Enchi Fumiko
See Enchi, Fumiko
Ende, Michael (Andreas Helmuth) 1929-1995 .... **CLC 31**
See also BYA 5; CA 118; 124; 149; CANR 36, 110; CLR 14, 138; DLB 75; MAICYA 1, 2; MAICYAS 1; SATA 61, 130; SATA-Brief 42; SATA-Obit 86
Endo, Shusaku 1923-1996 ... **CLC 7, 14, 19, 54, 99; SSC 48; TCLC 152**
See also CA 29-32R; 153; CANR 21, 54, 131; CWW 2; DA3; DAM NOV; DLB 182; EWL 3; MTCW 1, 2; MTFW 2005; RGSF 2; RGWL 2, 3
Endo Shusaku
See Endo, Shusaku
Engel, Marian 1933-1985 .... **CLC 36; TCLC 137**
See also CA 25-28R; CANR 12; CN 2, 3; DLB 53; FW; INT CANR-12
Engelhardt, Frederick
See Hubbard, L. Ron
Engels, Friedrich 1820-1895 .... **NCLC 85, 114**
See also DLB 129; LATS 1:1
Ennius, Quintus 239-169 BC ..... **CMLC 169**
See also DLB 211; RGWL 1, 2
Enquist, Per Olov 1934- .... **CLC 257**
See also CA 109; 193; CANR 155; CWW 2; DLB 257; EWL 3
Enright, D(ennis) J(oseph) 1920-2002 .... **CLC 4, 8, 31; PC 93**
See also CA 1-4R; 211; CANR 1, 42, 83; CN 1, 2; CP 1, 2, 3, 4, 5, 6, 7; DLB 27; EWL 3; SATA 25; SATA-Obit 140
Ensler, Eve 1953- .... **CLC 212; DC 47**
See also CA 172; CANR 126, 163; DFS 23
Enzensberger, Hans Magnus 1929- .... **CLC 43; PC 28**
See also CA 116; 119; CANR 103, 235; CWW 2; EWL 3
Ephron, Nora 1941- .... **CLC 17, 31**
See also AAYA 35; AITN 2; CA 65-68; CANR 12, 39, 83, 161, 236; DFS 22
Epictetus c. 55-c. 135 .... **CMLC 126**
See also AW 2; DLB 176
Epicurus 341B.C.-270B.C. ... **CMLC 21, 165**
See also DLB 176
Epinay, Louise d' 1726-1783 .... **LC 138**
See also DLB 313
Epsilon
See Betjeman, John
Epstein, Daniel Mark 1948- .... **CLC 7**
See also CA 49-52; CANR 2, 53, 90, 193, 236
Epstein, Jacob 1956- .... **CLC 19**
See also CA 114
Epstein, Jean 1897-1953 .... **TCLC 92**
Epstein, Joseph 1937- .... **CLC 39, 204**
See also AMWS 14; CA 112; 119; CANR 50, 65, 117, 164, 190, 225
Epstein, Leslie 1938- .... **CLC 27**
See also AMWS 12; CA 73-76, 215; CAAE 215; CAAS 12; CANR 23, 69, 162; DLB 299; RGHL
Equiano, Olaudah 1745(?)-1797 ... **BLC 1:2; LC 16, 143**
See also AFAW 1, 2; AMWS 17; CDWLB 3; DAM MULT; DLB 37, 50; WLIT 2
Erasmus, Desiderius 1469(?)-1536 .... **LC 16, 93, 228, 231**
See also DLB 136; EW 2; LMFS 1; RGWL 2, 3; TWA
Ercilla y Zuniga, Don Alonso de 1533-1594 .... **LC 190; PC 161**
See also LAW
Erdman, Paul E. 1932-2007 .... **CLC 25**
See also AITN 1; CA 61-64; 259; CANR 13, 43, 84
Erdman, Paul Emil
See Erdman, Paul E.
Erdrich, Karen Louise
See Erdrich, Louise
Erdrich, Louise 1954- .... **CLC 39, 54, 120, 176, 327, 354; NNAL; PC 52; SSC 121**
See also AAYA 10, 47; AMWS 4; BEST 89:1; BPFB 1; CA 114; CANR 41, 62, 118, 138, 190; CDALBS; CN 5, 6, 7; CP 6, 7; CPW; CWP; DA3; DAM MULT, NOV, POP; DLB 152, 175, 206; EWL 3; EXPP; FL 1:5; LAIT 5; LATS 1:2; MAL 5; MTCW 1, 2; MTFW 2005; NFS 5, 37, 40; PFS 14, 43; RGAL 4; SATA 94, 141; SSFS 14, 22, 30, 37; TCWW 2
Erenburg, Ilya
See Ehrenburg, Ilya
Erenburg, Ilya Grigoryevich
See Ehrenburg, Ilya
Erickson, Stephen Michael
See Erickson, Steve
Erickson, Steve 1950- .... **CLC 64**
See also CA 129; CANR 60, 68, 136, 195; MTFW 2005; SFW 4; SUFW 2
Erickson, Walter
See Fast, Howard
Ericson, Walter
See Fast, Howard
Eriksson, Buntel
See Bergman, Ingmar
Eriugena, John Scottus c. 810-877 .... **CMLC 65**
See also DLB 115
Ernaux, Annie 1940- .... **CLC 88, 184, 330**
See also CA 147; CANR 93, 208; MTFW 2005; NCFS 3, 5
Erskine, John 1879-1951 .... **TCLC 84**
See also CA 112; 159; DLB 9, 102; FANT
Erwin, Will
See Eisner, Will

Eschenbach, Wolfram von
See von Eschenbach, Wolfram

Eseki, Bruno
See Mphahlele, Es'kia

Esekie, Bruno
See Mphahlele, Es'kia

Esenin, S.A.
See Esenin, Sergei

Esenin, Sergei 1895-1925 .... **TCLC 4**
See also CA 104; EWL 3; RGWL 2, 3

Esenin, Sergei Aleksandrovich
See Esenin, Sergei

Eshleman, Clayton 1935- .... **CLC 7**
See also CA 33-36R, 212; CAAE 212; CAAS 6; CANR 93; CP 1, 2, 3, 4, 5, 6, 7; DLB 5

Espada, Martin 1957- .... **PC 74**
See also CA 159; CANR 80, 241; CP 7; EXPP; LLW; MAL 5; PFS 13, 16, 43

Espriella, Don Manuel Alvarez
See Southey, Robert

Espriu, Salvador 1913-1985 .... **CLC 9**
See also CA 154; 115; DLB 134; EWL 3

Espronceda, Jose de 1808-1842 ... **NCLC 39, 276**

Esquivel, Laura
1950- .... **CLC 141, 351; HLCS 1**
See also AAYA 29; CA 143; CANR 68, 113, 161; DA3; DNFS 2; LAIT 3; LMFS 2; MTCW 2; MTFW 2005; NFS 5; WLIT 1

Esse, James
See Stephens, James

Esterbrook, Tom
See Hubbard, L. Ron

Esterhazy, Peter 1950- .... **CLC 251**
See also CA 140; CANR 137, 223; CDWLB 4; CWW 2; DLB 232; EWL 3; RGWL 3

Estleman, Loren D. 1952- .... **CLC 48**
See also AAYA 27; CA 85-88; CANR 27, 74, 139, 177, 240; 240; CMW 4; CPW; DA3; DAM NOV, POP; DLB 226; INT CANR-27; MTCW 1, 2; MTFW 2005; TCWW 1, 2

Etherege, Sir George
1636-1692 .... **DC 23; LC 78**
See also BRW 2; DAM DRAM; DLB 80; PAB; RGEL 2

Euclid 306B.C.-283B.C. .... **CMLC 25, 172**

Eugenides, Jeffrey 1960- ... **CLC 81, 212, 312**
See also AAYA 51; CA 144; CANR 120, 237; DLB 350; MTFW 2005; NFS 24

Euripides c. 484B.C.-406B.C. ...... **CMLC 23, 51, 169, 174; DC 4; WLCS**
See also AW 1; CDWLB 1; DA; DA3; DAB; DAC; DAM DRAM, MST; DFS 1, 4, 6, 25, 27; DLB 176; LAIT 1; LMFS 1; RGWL 2, 3; WLIT 8

Eusebius c. 263-c. 339 .... **CMLC 103**

Evan, Evin
See Faust, Frederick

Evans, Caradoc
1878-1945 .... **SSC 43; TCLC 85**
See also DLB 162

Evans, Evan
See Faust, Frederick

Evans, Marian
See Eliot, George

Evans, Mary Ann
See Eliot, George

Evaristo, Bernardine 1959- .... **CLC 355**
See also CA 212, 275; CP 7; DLB 347

Evarts, Esther
See Benson, Sally

Evelyn, John 1620-1706 .... **LC 144**
See also BRW 2; RGEL 2

Everett, Percival 1956- .... **CLC 57, 304**
See also AMWS 18; BW 2; CA 129; CANR 94, 134, 179, 219; CN 7; CSW; DLB 350; MTFW 2005

Everett, Percival L.
See Everett, Percival

Everson, R(onald) G(ilmour)
1903-1992 .... **CLC 27**
See also CA 17-20R; CP 1, 2, 3, 4; DLB 88

Everson, William 1912-1994 .... **CLC 1, 5, 14; PC 169**
See also BG 1:2; CA 9-12R; 145; CANR 20; CP 1; DLB 5, 16, 212; MTCW 1

Everson, William Oliver
See Everson, William

Evtushenko, Evgenii Aleksandrovich
See Yevtushenko, Yevgenyn

Ewart, Gavin (Buchanan)
1916-1995 .... **CLC 13, 46**
See also BRWS 7; CA 89-92; 150; CANR 17, 46; CP 1, 2, 3, 4, 5, 6; DLB 40; MTCW 1

Ewers, Hanns Heinz 1871-1943 .... **TCLC 12**
See also CA 109; 149

Ewing, Frederick R.
See Sturgeon, Theodore (Hamilton)

Exley, Frederick 1929-1992 .... **CLC 6, 11**
See also AITN 2; AMWS 23; BPFB 1; CA 81-84; 138; CANR 117; DLB 143; DLBY 1981

Eynhardt, Guillermo
See Quiroga, Horacio (Sylvestre)

Ezekiel, Nissim (Moses) 1924-2004 ... **CLC 61**
See also CA 61-64; 223; CP 1, 2, 3, 4, 5, 6, 7; DLB 323; EWL 3

Ezekiel, Tish O'Dowd 1943- .... **CLC 34**
See also CA 129

Fadeev, Aleksandr Aleksandrovich
See Bulgya, Alexander Alexandrovich

Fadeev, Alexandr Alexandrovich
See Bulgya, Alexander Alexandrovich

Fadeyev, A.
See Bulgya, Alexander Alexandrovich

Fadeyev, Alexander
See Bulgya, Alexander Alexandrovich

Fagen, Donald 1948- .... **CLC 26**

Fagunwa, D. O. 1903-1963 .... **TCLC 295**
See also CA 116

Fainzil'berg, Il'ia Arnol'dovich
See Fainzilberg, Ilya Arnoldovich

Fainzilberg, Ilya Arnoldovich
1897-1937 .... **TCLC 21**
See also CA 120; 165; DLB 272; EWL 3

Fair, Ronald L. 1932- .... **CLC 18**
See also BW 1; CA 69-72; CANR 25; DLB 33

Fairbairn, Roger
See Carr, John Dickson

Fairbairns, Zoe (Ann) 1948- .... **CLC 32**
See also CA 103; CANR 21, 85; CN 4, 5, 6, 7

Fairfield, Flora
See Alcott, Louisa May

Falco, Gian
See Papini, Giovanni

Falconer, James
See Kirkup, James

Falconer, Kenneth
See Kornbluth, C(yril) M.

Falkland, Samuel
See Heijermans, Herman

Fallaci, Oriana 1930-2006 .... **CLC 11, 110**
See also CA 77-80; 253; CANR 15, 58, 134; FW; MTCW 1

Faludi, Susan 1959- .... **CLC 140**
See also CA 138; CANR 126, 194; FW; MTCW 2; MTFW 2005; NCFS 3

Faludy, George
See Faludy, Gyorgy

Faludy, Gyorgy 1913-2006 .... **CLC 42**
See also CA 21-24R; CANR 243

Fanon, Frantz 1925-1961 .... **BLC 1:2; CLC 74; TCLC 188**
See also BW 1; CA 116; 89-92; DAM MULT; DLB 296; LMFS 2; WLIT 2

Fanshawe, Ann 1625-1680 .... **LC 11**

Fante, John (Thomas)
1911-1983 .... **CLC 60; SSC 65**
See also AMWS 11; CA 69-72; 109; CANR 23, 104; DLB 130; DLBY 1983

Farah, Nuruddin 1945- .... **BLC 1:2, 2:2; CLC 53, 137, 344**
See also AFW; BW 2, 3; CA 106; CANR 81, 148, 243; CDWLB 3; CN 4, 5, 6, 7; DAM MULT; DLB 125; EWL 3; WLIT 2

Fardusi
See Ferdowsi, Abu'l Qasem

Fargue, Leon-Paul 1876(?)-1947 ... **TCLC 11**
See also CA 109; CANR 107; DLB 258; EWL 3

Farigoule, Louis
See Romains, Jules

Farina, Richard 1936(?)-1966 .... **CLC 9**
See also CA 81-84; 25-28R

Farley, Walter (Lorimer)
1915-1989 .... **CLC 17**
See also AAYA 58; BYA 14; CA 17-20R; CANR 8, 29, 84; DLB 22; JRDA; MAICYA 1, 2; SATA 2, 43, 132; YAW

Farmer, Philipe Jos
See Farmer, Philip Jose

Farmer, Philip Jose 1918-2009 .... **CLC 1, 19, 299**
See also AAYA 28; BPFB 1; CA 1-4R; 283; CANR 4, 35, 111, 220; CLR 201; DLB 8; MTCW 1; SATA 93; SATA-Obit 201; SCFW 1, 2; SFW 4

Farmer, Philip Jose
See Farmer, Philip Jose

Farquhar, George 1677-1707 .... **DC 38; LC 21**
See also BRW 2; DAM DRAM; DLB 84; RGEL 2

Farrell, James Gordon
See Farrell, J.G.

Farrell, James T(homas)
1904-1979 .... **CLC 1, 4, 8, 11, 66; SSC 28; TCLC 228**
See also AMW; BPFB 1; CA 5-8R; 89-92; CANR 9, 61; CN 1, 2; DLB 4, 9, 86; DLBD 2; EWL 3; MAL 5; MTCW 1, 2; MTFW 2005; RGAL 4

Farrell, J.G. 1935-1979 .... **CLC 6**
See also CA 73-76; 89-92; CANR 36; CN 1, 2; DLB 14, 271, 326; MTCW 1; RGEL 2; RHW; WLIT 4

Farrell, M. J.
See Keane, Mary Nesta

Farrell, Warren (Thomas) 1943- .... **CLC 70**
See also CA 146; CANR 120

Farren, Richard J.
See Betjeman, John

Farren, Richard M.
See Betjeman, John

Farrugia, Mario Benedetti
See Bentley, Eric

Farrugia, Mario Orlando Hardy Hamlet Brenno Benedetti
See Benedetti, Mario

Fassbinder, Rainer Werner
1946-1982 .... **CLC 20**
See also CA 93-96; 106; CANR 31

Fast, Howard 1914-2003 .... **CLC 23, 131**
See also AAYA 16; BPFB 1; CA 1-4R, 181; 214; CAAE 181; CAAS 18; CANR 1, 33, 54, 75, 98, 140; CMW 4; CN 1, 2, 3, 4, 5, 6, 7; CPW; DAM NOV; DLB 9; INT CANR-33; LATS 1:1; MAL 5; MTCW 2; MTFW 2005; NFS 35; RHW; SATA 7; SATA-Essay 107; TCWW 1, 2; YAW

Faulcon, Robert
See Holdstock, Robert

Faulkner, William 1897-1962 .... **CLC 1, 3, 6, 8, 9, 11, 14, 18, 28, 52, 68; SSC 1, 35, 42, 92, 97, 191, 200, 204, 209; TCLC 141; WLC 2**
See also AAYA 7; AMW; AMWR 1; BPFB 1; BYA 5, 15; CA 81-84; CANR 33; CDALB 1929-1941; DA; DA3; DAB; DAC; DAM MST, NOV; DLB 9, 11, 44, 102, 316, 330; DLBD 2; DLBY 1986, 1997; EWL 3; EXPN; EXPS; GL 2; LAIT 2; LATS 1:1; LMFS 2; MAL 5; MTCW 1, 2; MTFW 2005; NFS 4, 8, 13, 24, 33, 38; RGAL 4; RGSF 2; SSFS 2, 5, 6, 12, 27; TUS

Faulkner, William Cuthbert
See Faulkner, William

Fauset, Jessie Redmon 1882(?)-1961 .... **BLC 1:2; CLC 19, 54; HR 1:2**
See also AFAW 2; BW 1; CA 109; CANR 83; DAM MULT; DLB 51; FW; LMFS 2; MAL 5; MBL

Faust, Frederick 1892-1944 .... **TCLC 49**
See also BPFB 1; CA 108; 152; CANR 143; DAM POP; DLB 256; TCWW 1, 2; TUS

Faust, Frederick Schiller
See Faust, Frederick

Faust, Irvin 1924-2012 .... **CLC 8**
See also CA 33-36R; CANR 28, 67; CN 1, 2, 3, 4, 5, 6, 7; DLB 2, 28, 218, 278; DLBY 1980

Faverón Patriau, Gustavo 1966- .... **CLC 389**
See also CA 368

Fawkes, Guy
See Benchley, Robert (Charles)

Fearing, Kenneth 1902-1961 .... **CLC 51**
See also CA 93-96; CANR 59; CMW 4; DLB 9; MAL 5; RGAL 4

Fearing, Kenneth Flexner
See Fearing, Kenneth

Fecamps, Elise
See Creasey, John

Federman, Raymond 1928-2009 ... **CLC 6, 47**
See also CA 17-20R, 208; 292; CAAE 208; CAAS 8; CANR 10, 43, 83, 108; CN 3, 4, 5, 6; DLBY 1980

Federspiel, J.F. 1931-2007 .... **CLC 42**
See also CA 146; 257

Federspiel, Jurg F.
See Federspiel, J.F.

Federspiel, Juerg F.
See Federspiel, J.F.

Feiffer, Jules 1929- .... **CLC 2, 8, 64**
See also AAYA 3, 62; CA 17-20R; CAD; CANR 30, 59, 129, 161, 192; CD 5, 6; DAM DRAM; DLB 7, 44; INT CANR-30; MTCW 1; SATA 8, 61, 111, 157, 201, 243

Feiffer, Jules Ralph
See Feiffer, Jules

Feige, Hermann Albert Otto Maximilian
See Traven, B.

Fei-Kan, Li
See Jin, Ba

Feinberg, David B. 1956-1994 .... **CLC 59**
See also CA 135; 147

Feinstein, Elaine 1930- .... **CLC 36**
See also CA 69-72; CAAS 1; CANR 31, 68, 121, 162; CN 3, 4, 5, 6, 7; CP 2, 3, 4, 5, 6, 7; CWP; DLB 14, 40; MTCW 1

Feke, Gilbert David .... **CLC 65**

Feldman, Irving (Mordecai) 1928- ... **CLC 7**
See also CA 1-4R; CANR 1; CP 1, 2, 3, 4, 5, 6, 7; DLB 169; TCLE 1:1

Felix-Tchicaya, Gerald
See Tchicaya, Gerald Felix

Fellini, Federico 1920-1993 .... **CLC 16, 85**
See also CA 65-68; 143; CANR 33

Felltham, Owen 1602(?)-1668 .... **LC 92**
See also DLB 126, 151

Felsen, Henry Gregor 1916-1995 ... **CLC 17**
See also CA 1-4R; 180; CANR 1; SAAS 2; SATA 1

Felski, Rita .... **CLC 65**

Fenno, Jack
See Calisher, Hortense

Fenollosa, Ernest (Francisco)
1853-1908 .... **TCLC 91**

Fenton, James 1949- .... **CLC 32, 209**
See also CA 102; CANR 108, 160; CP 2, 3, 4, 5, 6, 7; DLB 40; PFS 11

Fenton, James Martin
See Fenton, James

Fenwick, Eliza 1766-1840 .... **NCLC 301**

Ferber, Edna 1887-1968 .... **CLC 18, 93**
See also AITN 1; CA 5-8R; 25-28R; CANR 68, 105; DLB 9, 28, 86, 266; MAL 5; MTCW 1, 2; MTFW 2005; RGAL 4; RHW; SATA 7; TCWW 1, 2

Ferdousi
See Ferdowsi, Abu'l Qasem

Ferdovsi
See Ferdowsi, Abu'l Qasem

Ferdowsi
See Ferdowsi, Abu'l Qasem

Ferdowsi, Abolghasem Mansour
See Ferdowsi, Abu'l Qasem

Ferdowsi, Abolqasem
See Ferdowsi, Abu'l Qasem

Ferdowsi, Abol-Qasem
See Ferdowsi, Abu'l Qasem

Ferdowsi, Abu'l Qasem
940-1020(?) .... **CMLC 43**
See also CA 276; RGWL 2, 3; WLIT 6

Ferdowsi, A.M.
See Ferdowsi, Abu'l Qasem

Ferdowsi, Hakim Abolghasem
See Ferdowsi, Abu'l Qasem

Ferguson, Helen
See Kavan, Anna

Ferguson, Niall 1964- .... **CLC 134, 250**
See also CA 190; CANR 154, 200

Ferguson, Niall Campbell
See Ferguson, Niall

Ferguson, Samuel 1810-1886 .... **NCLC 33**
See also DLB 32; RGEL 2

Fergusson, Robert 1750-1774 .... **LC 29; PC 157**
See also DLB 109; RGEL 2

Ferling, Lawrence
See Ferlinghetti, Lawrence

Ferlinghetti, Lawrence 1919(?)- .... **CLC 2, 6, 10, 27, 111; PC 1**
See also AAYA 74; BG 1:2; CA 5-8R; CAD; CANR 3, 41, 73, 125, 172; CDALB 1941-1968; CP 1, 2, 3, 4, 5, 6, 7; DA3; DAM POET; DLB 5, 16; MAL 5; MTCW 1, 2; MTFW 2005; PFS 28, 41; RGAL 4; WP

Ferlinghetti, Lawrence Monsanto
See Ferlinghetti, Lawrence

Fern, Fanny
See Parton, Sara Payson Willis

Fernandez, Vicente Garcia Huidobro
See Huidobro Fernandez, Vicente Garcia

Fernández Cubas, Cristina 1945- ... **SSC 205**
See also CA 211; EWL 3

Fernandez de Lizardi, Jose Joaquin
See Lizardi, Jose Joaquin Fernandez de

Fernandez-Armesto, Felipe 1950- .... **CLC 70**
See also CA 142; CANR 93, 153, 189

Fernandez-Armesto, Felipe Fermin Ricardo
See Fernandez-Armesto, Felipe

Ferre, Rosario 1938- .... **CLC 139, 328; HLCS 1; SSC 36, 106**
See also CA 131; CANR 55, 81, 134; CWW 2; DLB 145; EWL 3; HW 1, 2; LAWS 1; MTCW 2; MTFW 2005; WLIT 1

Ferrer, Gabriel (Francisco Victor) Miro
See Miro (Ferrer), Gabriel (Francisco Victor)

Ferrier, Susan (Edmonstone)
1782-1854 .... **NCLC 8**
See also DLB 116; RGEL 2

Ferrigno, Robert 1947- .... **CLC 65**
See also CA 140; CANR 125, 161

Ferris, Joshua 1974- .... **CLC 280**
See also CA 262

Ferron, Jacques 1921-1985 .... **CLC 94**
See also CA 117; 129; CCA 1; DAC; DLB 60; EWL 3

Feuchtwanger, Lion
1884-1958 .... **TCLC 3, 321**
See also CA 104; 187; DLB 66; EWL 3; RGHL

Feuerbach, Ludwig 1804-1872 .... **NCLC 139**
See also DLB 133

Feuillet, Octave 1821-1890 .... **NCLC 45**
See also DLB 192

Feydeau, Georges 1862-1921 .... **TCLC 22**
See also CA 113; 152; CANR 84; DAM DRAM; DLB 192; EWL 3; GFL 1789 to the Present; RGWL 2, 3

Feydeau, Georges Leon JulesMarie
See Feydeau, Georges

Fichte, Johann Gottlieb
1762-1814 .... **NCLC 62, 261**
See also DLB 90

Ficino, Marsilio 1433-1499 .... **LC 12, 152**
See also LMFS 1

Fiedeler, Hans
See Doblin, Alfred

Fiedler, Leslie A(aron)
1917-2003 .... **CLC 4, 13, 24**
See also AMWS 13; CA 9-12R; 212; CANR 7, 63; CN 1, 2, 3, 4, 5, 6; DLB 28, 67; EWL 3; MAL 5; MTCW 1, 2; RGAL 4; TUS

Field, Andrew 1938- .... **CLC 44**
See also CA 97-100; CANR 25

Field, Eugene 1850-1895 .... **NCLC 3**
See also DLB 23, 42, 140; DLBD 13; MAICYA 1, 2; RGAL 4; SATA 16

Field, Gans T.
See Wellman, Manly Wade

Field, Kate 1838-1896 .... **NCLC 307**

Field, Michael 1915-1971 .... **TCLC 43**
See also CA 29-32R

Fielding, Helen 1958- .... **CLC 146, 217**
See also AAYA 65; CA 172; CANR 127; DLB 231; MTFW 2005

Fielding, Henry 1707-1754 ..... **LC 1, 46, 85, 151, 154; WLC 2**
See also BRW 3; BRWR 1; CDBLB 1660-1789; DA; DA3; DAB; DAC; DAM DRAM, MST, NOV; DFS 28; DLB 39, 84, 101; NFS 18, 32; RGEL 2; TEA; WLIT 3

Fielding, Sarah 1710-1768 ..... **LC 1, 44, 223**
See also DLB 39; RGEL 2; TEA

Fields, W. C. 1880-1946 .... **TCLC 80**
See also DLB 44

Fierstein, Harvey 1954- .... **CLC 33**
See also CA 123; 129; CAD; CD 5, 6; CPW; DA3; DAM DRAM, POP; DFS 6; DLB 266; GLL; MAL 5

Fierstein, Harvey Forbes
See Fierstein, Harvey

Figes, Eva 1932- .... **CLC 31**
See also CA 53-56; CANR 4, 44, 83, 207; CN 2, 3, 4, 5, 6, 7; DLB 14, 271; FW; RGHL

Filippo, Eduardo de
See de Filippo, Eduardo

Finch, Anne
1661-1720 .... **LC 3, 137; PC 21, 156**
See also BRWS 9; DLB 95; PFS 30; RGEL 2

Finch, Robert (Duer Claydon)
1900-1995 .... **CLC 18**
See also CA 57-60; CANR 9, 24, 49; CP 1, 2, 3, 4, 5, 6; DLB 88

Findley, Timothy 1930-2002 ... **CLC 27, 102; SSC 145**
See also AMWS 20; CA 25-28R; 206; CANR 12, 42, 69, 109; CCA 1; CN 4, 5, 6, 7; DAC; DAM MST; DLB 53; FANT; RHW
Fink, William
See Mencken, H. L.
Firbank, Louis
See Reed, Lou
Firbank, (Arthur Annesley) Ronald 1886-1926 .... **TCLC 1**
See also BRWS 2; CA 104; 177; DLB 36; EWL 3; RGEL 2
Firdaosi
See Ferdowsi, Abu'l Qasem
Firdausi
See Ferdowsi, Abu'l Qasem
Firdavsii, Abulqosimi
See Ferdowsi, Abu'l Qasem
Firdavsi, Abulqosimi
See Ferdowsi, Abu'l Qasem
Firdawsi, Abu al-Qasim
See Ferdowsi, Abu'l Qasem
Firdosi
See Ferdowsi, Abu'l Qasem
Firdousi, Abu'l-Qasim
See Ferdowsi, Abu'l Qasem
Firdousi
See Ferdowsi, Abu'l Qasem
Firdovsi, A.
See Ferdowsi, Abu'l Qasem
Firdovsi, Abulgasim
See Ferdowsi, Abu'l Qasem
Firdusi
See Ferdowsi, Abu'l Qasem
Fish, Stanley 1938- .... **CLC 142, 343**
See also CA 112; 132; CANR 90; DLB 67
Fish, Stanley E.
See Fish, Stanley
Fish, Stanley Eugene
See Fish, Stanley
Fisher, Dorothy (Frances) Canfield 1879-1958 .... **TCLC 87**
See also CA 114; 136; CANR 80; CLR 71; CWRI 5; DLB 9, 102, 284; MAICYA 1, 2; MAL 5; YABC 1
Fisher, Mary Frances Kennedy
See Fisher, M.F.K.
Fisher, M. F. K. 1908-1992 .... **CLC 76, 87**
See also AMWS 17; CA 77-80; 138; CANR 44, 241; MTCW 2
Fisher, Roy 1930- .... **CLC 25; PC 121**
See also CA 81-84; CAAS 10; CANR 16; CP 1, 2, 3, 4, 5, 6, 7; DLB 40
Fisher, Rudolph 1897-1934 .... **BLC 1:2; HR 1:2; SSC 25; TCLC 11, 255**
See also BW 1, 3; CA 107; 124; CANR 80; DAM MULT; DLB 51, 102
Fisher, Vardis (Alvero) 1895-1968 ... **CLC 7; TCLC 140**
See also CA 5-8R; 25-28R; CANR 68; DLB 9, 206; MAL 5; RGAL 4; TCWW 1, 2
Fishman, Boris 1979- .... **CLC 389**
See also CA 362
Fiske, Tarleton
See Bloch, Robert (Albert)
Fitch, Clarke
See Sinclair, Upton
Fitch, John IV
See Cormier, Robert
Fitzgerald, Captain Hugh
See Baum, L. Frank
FitzGerald, Edward 1809-1883 .... **NCLC 9, 153; PC 79**
See also BRW 4; DLB 32; RGEL 2
Fitzgerald, F. Scott 1896-1940 .... **SSC 6, 31, 75, 143; TCLC 1, 6, 14, 28, 55, 157, 280, 311; WLC 2**
See also AAYA 24; AITN 1; AMW; AMWC 2; AMWR 1; BPFB 1; CA 110; 123; CDALB 1917-1929; CLR 176; DA; DA3; DAB; DAC; DAM MST, NOV; DLB 4, 9, 86, 219, 273; DLBD 1, 15, 16; DLBY 1981, 1996; EWL 3; EXPN; EXPS; LAIT 3; MAL 5; MTCW 1, 2; MTFW 2005; NFS 2, 19, 20; RGAL 4; RGSF 2; SSFS 4, 15, 21, 25, 36; TUS
Fitzgerald, Francis Scott Key
See Fitzgerald, F. Scott
Fitzgerald, Penelope 1916-2000 .... **CLC 19, 51, 61, 143**
See also BRWS 5; CA 85-88; 190; CAAS 10; CANR 56, 86, 131; CN 3, 4, 5, 6, 7; DLB 14, 194, 326; EWL 3; MTCW 2; MTFW 2005
Fitzgerald, Robert (Stuart) 1910-1985 .... **CLC 39**
See also CA 1-4R; 114; CANR 1; CP 1, 2, 3, 4; DLBY 1980; MAL 5
FitzGerald, Robert D(avid) 1902-1987 .... **CLC 19**
See also CA 17-20R; CP 1, 2, 3, 4; DLB 260; RGEL 2
Fitzgerald, Zelda (Sayre) 1900-1948 .... **TCLC 52**
See also AMWS 9; CA 117; 126; DLBY 1984
Flagg, Fannie 1941- .... **CLC 297**
See also CA 111; CANR 40, 238; CPW; CSW; DA3; DAM POP; NFS 7
Flanagan, Richard 1961- .... **CLC 389**
See also CA 195; CANR 169, 213
Flanagan, Thomas (James Bonner) 1923-2002 .... **CLC 25, 52**
See also CA 108; 206; CANR 55; CN 3, 4, 5, 6, 7; DLBY 1980; INT CA-108; MTCW 1; RHW; TCLE 1:1
Flashman, Harry Paget
See Fraser, George MacDonald
Flaubert, Gustave 1821-1880 .... **NCLC 2, 10, 19, 62, 66, 135, 179, 185, 251; SSC 11, 60, 182, 187; WLC 2**
See also DA; DA3; DAB; DAC; DAM MST, NOV; DLB 119, 301, 366; EW 7; EXPS; GFL 1789 to the Present; LAIT 2; LMFS 1; NFS 14; RGSF 2; RGWL 2, 3; SSFS 6; TWA
Flavius Josephus
See Josephus, Flavius
Flecker, Herman Elroy
See Flecker, (Herman) James Elroy
Flecker, (Herman) James Elroy 1884-1915 .... **TCLC 43**
See also CA 109; 150; DLB 10, 19; RGEL 2
Fleming, Ian 1908-1964 .... **CLC 3, 30; TCLC 193**
See also AAYA 26; BPFB 1; BRWS 14; CA 5-8R; CANR 59; CDBLB 1945-1960; CMW 4; CPW; DA3; DAM POP; DLB 87, 201; MSW; MTCW 1, 2; MTFW 2005; RGEL 2; SATA 9; TEA; YAW
Fleming, Ian Lancaster
See Fleming, Ian
Fleming, Thomas 1927- .... **CLC 37**
See also CA 5-8R; CANR 10, 102, 155, 197; INT CANR-10; SATA 8
Fleming, Thomas James
See Fleming, Thomas
Fletcher, John 1579-1625 .... **DC 6; LC 33, 151**
See also BRW 2; CDBLB Before 1660; DLB 58; RGEL 2; TEA
Fletcher, John Gould 1886-1950 ... **TCLC 35**
See also CA 107; 167; DLB 4, 45; LMFS 2; MAL 5; RGAL 4
Fleur, Paul
See Pohl, Frederik
Flieg, Helmut
See Heym, Stefan
Flooglebuckle, Al
See Spiegelman, Art
Flying Officer X
See Bates, H(erbert) E(rnest)
Fenelon, Francois de Pons de Salignac de la Mothe- 1651-1715 .... **LC 134**
See also DLB 268; EW 3; GFL Beginnings to 1789
Fo, Dario 1926- ... **CLC 32, 109, 227; DC 10**
See also CA 116; 128; CANR 68, 114, 134, 164; CWW 2; DA3; DAM DRAM; DFS 23; DLB 330; DLBY 1997; EWL 3; MTCW 1, 2; MTFW 2005; WLIT 7
Foden, Giles 1967- .... **CLC 231**
See also CA 240; DLB 267; NFS 15
Foer, Jonathan Safran 1977- .... **CLC 301**
See also AAYA 57; CA 204; CANR 160; MTFW 2005; NFS 36
Fogarty, Jonathan Titulescu Esq.
See Farrell, James T(homas)
Follett, Ken 1949- .... **CLC 18**
See also AAYA 6, 50; BEST 89:4; BPFB 1; CA 81-84; CANR 13, 33, 54, 102, 156, 197, 229; CMW 4; CPW; DA3; DAM NOV, POP; DLB 87; DLBY 1981; INT CANR-33; LNFS 3; MTCW 1
Follett, Kenneth Martin
See Follett, Ken
Fondane, Benjamin 1898-1944 ... **TCLC 159**
Fontane, Theodor 1819-1898 **NCLC 26, 163**
See also CDWLB 2; DLB 129; EW 6; RGWL 2, 3; TWA
Fonte, Moderata 1555-1592 .... **LC 118**
Fontenelle, Bernard Le Bovier de 1657-1757 .... **LC 140**
See also DLB 268, 313; GFL Beginnings to 1789
Fontenot, Chester .... **CLC 65**
Fonvizin, Denis Ivanovich 1744(?)-1792 .... **LC 81**
See also DLB 150; RGWL 2, 3
Foote, Albert Horton
See Foote, Horton
Foote, Horton 1916-2009 .... **CLC 51, 91; DC 42**
See also AAYA 82; CA 73-76; 284; CAD; CANR 34, 51, 110; CD 5, 6; CSW; DA3; DAM DRAM; DFS 20; DLB 26, 266; EWL 3; INT CANR-34; MTFW 2005
Foote, Mary Hallock 1847-1938 ... **SSC 150; TCLC 108**
See also DLB 186, 188, 202, 221; TCWW 2
Foote, Samuel 1721-1777 .... **LC 106**
See also DLB 89; RGEL 2
Foote, Shelby 1916-2005 .... **CLC 75, 224**
See also AAYA 40; CA 5-8R; 240; CANR 3, 45, 74, 131; CN 1, 2, 3, 4, 5, 6, 7; CPW; CSW; DA3; DAM NOV, POP; DLB 2, 17; MAL 5; MTCW 2; MTFW 2005; RHW
Forbes, Cosmo
See Lewton, Val
Forbes, Esther 1891-1967 .... **CLC 12**
See also AAYA 17; BYA 2; CA 13-14; 25-28R; CAP 1; CLR 27, 147; DLB 22; JRDA; MAICYA 1, 2; RHW; SATA 2, 100; YAW
Forche, Carolyn 1950- .... **CLC 25, 83, 86; PC 10**
See also CA 109; 117; CANR 50, 74, 138; CP 4, 5, 6, 7; CWP; DA3; DAM POET; DLB 5, 193; INT CA-117; MAL 5; MTCW 2; MTFW 2005; PFS 18, 43; RGAL 4
Forche, Carolyn Louise
See Forche, Carolyn
Ford, Elbur
See Hibbert, Eleanor Alice Burford

Ford, Ford Madox 1873-1939 .... **TCLC 1, 15, 39, 57, 172, 308, 309**
See also BRW 6; CA 104; 132; CANR 74; CDBLB 1914-1945; DA3; DAM NOV; DLB 34, 98, 162; EWL 3; MTCW 1, 2; NFS 28; RGEL 2; RHW; TEA
Ford, Helen
See Garner, Helen
Ford, Henry 1863-1947 .... **TCLC 73**
See also CA 115; 148
Ford, Jack
See Ford, John
Ford, John 1586-1639 .... **DC 8; LC 68, 153**
See also BRW 2; CDBLB Before 1660; DA3; DAM DRAM; DFS 7; DLB 58; IDTP; RGEL 2
Ford, John 1895-1973 .... **CLC 16**
See also AAYA 75; CA 187; 45-48
Ford, Richard 1944- .... **CLC 46, 99, 205, 277; SSC 143**
See also AMWS 5; CA 69-72; CANR 11, 47, 86, 128, 164; CN 5, 6, 7; CSW; DLB 227; EWL 3; MAL 5; MTCW 2; MTFW 2005; NFS 25; RGAL 4; RGSF 2
Ford, Webster
See Masters, Edgar Lee
Foreman, Richard 1937- .... **CLC 50**
See also CA 65-68; CAD; CANR 32, 63, 143; CD 5, 6
Forester, C. S. 1899-1966 .... **CLC 35; TCLC 152**
See also CA 73-76; 25-28R; CANR 83; DLB 191; RGEL 2; RHW; SATA 13
Forester, Cecil Scott
See Forester, C. S.
Forez
See Mauriac, Francois (Charles)
Forman, James
See Forman, James D.
Forman, James D. 1932-2009 .... **CLC 21**
See also AAYA 17; CA 9-12R; CANR 4, 19, 42; JRDA; MAICYA 1, 2; SATA 8, 70; YAW
Forman, James Douglas
See Forman, James D.
Forman, Milos 1932- .... **CLC 164**
See also AAYA 63; CA 109
Fornes, Maria Irene 1930- .... **CLC 39, 61, 187; DC 10; HLCS 1**
See also CA 25-28R; CAD; CANR 28, 81; CD 5, 6; CWD; DFS 25; DLB 7, 341; HW 1, 2; INT CANR-28; LLW; MAL 5; MTCW 1; RGAL 4
Forrest, Leon (Richard) 1937-1997 .... **BLCS; CLC 4**
See also AFAW 2; BW 2; CA 89-92; 162; CAAS 7; CANR 25, 52, 87; CN 4, 5, 6; DLB 33
Forster, E. M. 1879-1970 .... **CLC 1, 2, 3, 4, 9, 10, 13, 15, 22, 45, 77; SSC 27, 96, 201; TCLC 125, 264; WLC 2**
See also AAYA 2, 37; BRW 6; BRWR 2; BYA 12; CA 13-14; 25-28R; CANR 45; CAP 1; CDBLB 1914-1945; DA; DA3; DAB; DAC; DAM MST, NOV; DLB 34, 98, 162, 178, 195; DLBD 10; EWL 3; EXPN; LAIT 3; LMFS 1; MTCW 1, 2; MTFW 2005; NCFS 1; NFS 3, 10, 11; RGEL 2; RGSF 2; SATA 57; SUFW 1; TEA; WLIT 4
Forster, Edward Morgan
See Forster, E. M.
Forster, John 1812-1876 .... **NCLC 11**
See also DLB 144, 184
Forster, Margaret 1938- .... **CLC 149**
See also CA 133; CANR 62, 115, 175; CN 4, 5, 6, 7; DLB 155, 271
Forsyth, Frederick 1938- .... **CLC 2, 5, 36**
See also BEST 89:4; CA 85-88; CANR 38, 62, 115, 137, 183, 242; CMW 4; CN 3, 4, 5, 6, 7; CPW; DAM NOV, POP; DLB 87; MTCW 1, 2; MTFW 2005
Fort, Paul
See Stockton, Francis Richard
Forten, Charlotte
See Grimke, Charlotte L. Forten
Forten, Charlotte L. 1837-1914
See Grimke, Charlotte L. Forten
Fortinbras
See Grieg, (Johan) Nordahl (Brun)
Foscolo, Ugo 1778-1827 ... **NCLC 8, 97, 274**
See also EW 5; WLIT 7
Fosse, Bob 1927-1987 .... **CLC 20**
See also AAYA 82; CA 110; 123
Fosse, Robert L.
See Fosse, Bob
Foster, Hannah Webster 1758-1840 .... **NCLC 99, 252**
See also DLB 37, 200; RGAL 4
Foster, Stephen Collins 1826-1864 .. **NCLC 26**
See also RGAL 4
Foucault, Michel 1926-1984 .... **CLC 31, 34, 69**
See also CA 105; 113; CANR 34; DLB 242; EW 13; EWL 3; GFL 1789 to the Present; GLL 1; LMFS 2; MTCW 1, 2; TWA
Fountain, Ben 1958- .... **CLC 354**
See also CA 254; CANR 254
Fouqué, Caroline de la Motte 1774-1831 .... **NCLC 307**
See also DLB 90; RGWL 2, 3
Fouque, Friedrich (Heinrich Karl) de la Motte 1777-1843 .... **NCLC 2**
See also DLB 90; RGWL 2, 3; SUFW 1
Fourier, Charles 1772-1837 .... **NCLC 51**
Fournier, Henri-Alban
See Alain-Fournier
Fournier, Pierre 1916-1997 .... **CLC 11**
See also CA 89-92; CANR 16, 40; EWL 3; RGHL
Fowles, John 1926-2005 .... **CLC 1, 2, 3, 4, 6, 9, 10, 15, 33, 87, 287; SSC 33, 128**
See also BPFB 1; BRWS 1; CA 5-8R; 245; CANR 25, 71, 103; CDBLB 1960 to Present; CN 1, 2, 3, 4, 5, 6, 7; DA3; DAB; DAC; DAM MST; DLB 14, 139, 207; EWL 3; HGG; MTCW 1, 2; MTFW 2005; NFS 21; RGEL 2; RHW; SATA 22; SATA-Obit 171; TEA; WLIT 4
Fowles, John Robert
See Fowles, John
Fox, Norma Diane
See Mazer, Norma Fox
Fox, Paula 1923- .... **CLC 2, 8, 121**
See also AAYA 3, 37; BYA 3, 8; CA 73-76; CANR 20, 36, 62, 105, 200, 237; CLR 1, 44, 96; DLB 52; JRDA; MAICYA 1, 2; MTCW 1; NFS 12; SATA 17, 60, 120, 167; WYA; YAW
Fox, William Price, Jr.
See Fox, William Price
Fox, William Price 1926- .... **CLC 22**
See also CA 17-20R; CAAS 19; CANR 11, 142, 189; CSW; DLB 2; DLBY 1981
Foxe, John 1517(?)-1587 .... **LC 14, 166**
See also DLB 132
Frame, Janet 1924-2004 .... **CLC 2, 3, 6, 22, 66, 96, 237; SSC 29, 127**
See also CA 1-4R; 224; CANR 2, 36, 76, 135, 216; CN 1, 2, 3, 4, 5, 6, 7; CP 2, 3, 4; CWP; EWL 3; MTCW 1,2; RGEL 2; RGSF 2; SATA 119; TWA
Frame, Janet Paterson
See Frame, Janet
France, Anatole 1844-1924 .... **TCLC 9**
See also CA 106; 127; DA3; DAM NOV; DLB 123, 330; EWL 3; GFL 1789 to the Present; MTCW 1, 2; RGWL 2, 3; SUFW 1; TWA
Francis, Claude .... **CLC 50**
See also CA 192
Francis, Dick 1920-2010 .... **CLC 2, 22, 42, 102**
See also AAYA 5, 21; BEST 89:3; BPFB 1; CA 5-8R; CANR 9, 42, 68, 100, 141, 179; CDBLB 1960 to Present; CMW 4; CN 2, 3, 4, 5, 6; DA3; DAM POP; DLB 87; INT CANR-9; MSW; MTCW 1, 2; MTFW 2005
Francis, Paula Marie
See Allen, Paula Gunn
Francis, Richard Stanley
See Francis, Dick
Francis, Robert (Churchill) 1901-1987 .... **CLC 15; PC 34**
See also AMWS 9; CA 1-4R; 123; CANR 1; CP 1, 2, 3, 4; EXPP; PFS 12; TCLE 1:1
Francis, Lord Jeffrey
See Jeffrey, Francis
Franco, Veronica 1546-1591 .... **LC 171**
See also WLIT 7
Frank, Anne 1929-1945 .... **TCLC 17; WLC 2**
See also AAYA 12; BYA 1; CA 113; 133; CANR 68; CLR 101, 189; DA; DA3; DAB; DAC; DAM MST; LAIT 4; MAICYA 2; MAICYAS 1; MTCW 1, 2; MTFW 2005; NCFS 2; RGHL; SATA 87; SATA-Brief 42; WYA; YAW
Frank, Annelies Marie
See Frank, Anne
Frank, Bruno 1887-1945 .... **TCLC 81**
See also CA 189; DLB 118; EWL 3
Frank, Elizabeth 1945- .... **CLC 39**
See also CA 121; 126; CANR 78, 150; INT CA-126
Frankl, Viktor E(mil) 1905-1997 .... **CLC 93**
See also CA 65-68; 161; RGHL
Franklin, Benjamin
See Hasek, Jaroslav
Franklin, Benjamin 1706-1790 .... **LC 25, 134; WLCS**
See also AMW; CDALB 1640-1865; DA; DA3; DAB; DAC; DAM MST; DLB 24, 43, 73, 183; LAIT 1; RGAL 4; TUS
Franklin, Madeleine
See L'Engle, Madeleine
Franklin, Madeleine L'Engle
See L'Engle, Madeleine
Franklin, Madeleine L'Engle Camp
See L'Engle, Madeleine
Franklin, (Stella Maria Sarah) Miles (Lampe) 1879-1954 .... **TCLC 7**
See also CA 104; 164; DLB 230; FW; MTCW 2; RGEL 2; TWA
Franzen, Jonathan 1959- .... **CLC 202, 309**
See also AAYA 65; AMWS 20; CA 129; CANR 105, 166, 219; NFS 40;
Fraser, Antonia 1932- .... **CLC 32, 107**
See also AAYA 57; CA 85-88; CANR 44, 65, 119, 164, 225; CMW; DLB 276; MTCW 1, 2; MTFW 2005; SATA-Brief 32
Fraser, George MacDonald 1925-2008 .... **CLC 7**
See also AAYA 48; CA 45-48, 180; 268; CAAE 180; CANR 2, 48, 74, 192; DLB 352; MTCW 2; RHW
Fraser, Sylvia 1935- .... **CLC 64**
See also CA 45-48; CANR 1, 16, 60; CCA 1
Frater Perdurabo
See Crowley, Edward Alexander
Frayn, Michael 1933- .... **CLC 3, 7, 31, 47, 176, 315; DC 27**
See also AAYA 69; BRWC 2; BRWS 7; CA 5-8R; CANR 30, 69, 114, 133, 166, 229; CBD; CD 5, 6; CN 1, 2, 3, 4, 5, 6, 7; DAM

DRAM, NOV; DFS 22, 28; DLB 13, 14, 194, 245; FANT; MTCW 1, 2; MTFW 2005; SFW 4
Fraze, Candida 1945- .... **CLC 50**
See also CA 126
Fraze, Candida Merrill
See Fraze, Candida
Frazer, Andrew
See Marlowe, Stephen
Frazer, J(ames) G(eorge)
1854-1941 .... **TCLC 32**
See also BRWS 3; CA 118; NCFS 5
Frazer, Robert Caine
See Creasey, John
Frazer, Sir James George
See Frazer, J(ames) G(eorge)
Frazier, Charles 1950- .... **CLC 109, 224**
See also AAYA 34; CA 161; CANR 126, 170, 235; CSW; DLB 292; MTFW 2005; NFS 25
Frazier, Charles R.
See Frazier, Charles
Frazier, Charles Robinson
See Frazier, Charles
Frazier, Ian 1951- .... **CLC 46**
See also CA 130; CANR 54, 93, 193, 227
Frederic, Harold
1856-1898 .... **NCLC 10, 175**
See also AMW; DLB 12, 23; DLBD 13; MAL 5; NFS 22; RGAL 4
Frederick, John
See Faust, Frederick
Frederick the Great 1712-1786 .... **LC 14**
Fredro, Aleksander 1793-1876 .... **NCLC 8**
Freeling, Nicolas 1927-2003 .... **CLC 38**
See also CA 49-52; 218; CAAS 12; CANR 1, 17, 50, 84; CMW 4; CN 1, 2, 3, 4, 5, 6; DLB 87
Freeman, Douglas Southall
1886-1953 .... **TCLC 11**
See also CA 109; 195; DLB 17; DLBD 17
Freeman, Judith 1946- .... **CLC 55**
See also CA 148; CANR 120, 179; DLB 256
Freeman, Mary E(leanor) Wilkins
1852-1930 ..... **SSC 1, 47, 113; TCLC 9**
See also CA 106; 177; DLB 12, 78, 221; EXPS; FW; HGG; MBL; RGAL 4; RGSF 2; SSFS 4, 8, 26; SUFW 1; TUS
Freeman, R(ichard) Austin
1862-1943 .... **TCLC 21**
See also CA 113; CANR 84; CMW 4; DLB 70
French, Albert 1943- .... **CLC 86**
See also BW 3; CA 167
French, Antonia
See Kureishi, Hanif
French, Marilyn 1929-2009 ...... **CLC 10, 18, 60, 177**
See also BPFB 1; CA 69-72; 286; CANR 3, 31, 134, 163, 220; CN 5, 6, 7; CPW; DAM DRAM, NOV, POP; FL 1:5; FW; INT CANR-31; MTCW 1, 2; MTFW 2005
French, Paul
See Asimov, Isaac
Freneau, Philip Morin
1752-1832 .... **NCLC 1, 111, 253**
See also AMWS 2; DLB 37, 43; RGAL 4
Freud, Sigmund 1856-1939 .... **TCLC 52**
See also CA 115; 133; CANR 69; DLB 296; EW 8; EWL 3; LATS 1:1; MTCW 1, 2; MTFW 2005; NCFS 3; TWA
Freytag, Gustav 1816-1895 .... **NCLC 109**
See also DLB 129
Friedan, Betty 1921-2006 .... **CLC 74**
See also CA 65-68; 248; CANR 18, 45, 74; DLB 246; FW; MTCW 1, 2; MTFW 2005; NCFS 5
Friedan, Betty Naomi
See Friedan, Betty
Friedlander, Saul
See Friedlander, Saul
Friedlander, Saul 1932- .... **CLC 90**
See also CA 117; 130; CANR 72, 214; RGHL
Friedman, Bernard Harper
See Friedman, B.H.
Friedman, B.H. 1926-2011 .... **CLC 7**
See also CA 1-4R; CANR 3, 48
Friedman, Bruce Jay 1930- ... **CLC 3, 5, 56**
See also CA 9-12R; CAD; CANR 25, 52, 101, 212; CD 5, 6; CN 1, 2, 3, 4, 5, 6, 7; DLB 2, 28, 244; INT CANR-25; MAL 5; SSFS 18
Friel, Brian 1929- .... **CLC 5, 42, 59, 115, 253; DC 8, 49; SSC 76**
See also BRWS 5; CA 21-24R; CANR 33, 69, 131; CBD; CD 5, 6; DFS 11; DLB 13, 319; EWL 3; MTCW 1; RGEL 2; TEA
Friis-Baastad, Babbis Ellinor
1921-1970 .... **CLC 12**
See also CA 17-20R; 134; SATA 7
Frisch, Max 1911-1991 .... **CLC 3, 9, 14, 18, 32, 44; TCLC 121**
See also CA 85-88; 134; CANR 32, 74; CDWLB 2; DAM DRAM, NOV; DFS 25; DLB 69, 124; EW 13; EWL 3; MTCW 1, 2; MTFW 2005; RGHL; RGWL 2, 3
Frischmuth, Barbara 1941- .... **CLC 372**
See also CA 178; DLB 85; SATA 114
Froehlich, Peter
See Gay, Peter
Fromentin, Eugene (Samuel Auguste)
1820-1876 .... **NCLC 10, 125**
See also DLB 123, 366; GFL 1789 to the Present
Frost, Frederick
See Faust, Frederick
Frost, Robert 1874-1963 ...... **CLC 1, 3, 4, 9, 10, 13, 15, 26, 34, 44; PC 1, 39, 71; TCLC 236; WLC 2**
See also AAYA 21; AMW; AMWR 1; CA 89-92; CANR 33; CDALB 1917-1929; CLR 67; DA; DA3; DAB; DAC; DAM MST, POET; DLB 54, 284, 342; DLBD 7; EWL 3; EXPP; MAL 5; MTCW 1, 2; MTFW 2005; PAB; PFS 1, 2, 3, 4, 5, 6, 7, 10, 13, 32, 35, 41; RGAL 4; SATA 14; TUS; WP; WYA
Frost, Robert Lee
See Frost, Robert
Froude, James Anthony
1818-1894 .... **NCLC 43, 311**
See also DLB 18, 57, 144
Froy, Herald
See Waterhouse, Keith
Fry, Christopher 1907-2005 .... **CLC 2, 10, 14; DC 36**
See also BRWS 3; CA 17-20R; 240; CAAS 23; CANR 9, 30, 74, 132; CBD; CD 5, 6; CP 1, 2, 3, 4, 5, 6, 7; DAM DRAM; DLB 13; EWL 3; MTCW 1, 2; MTFW 2005; RGEL 2; SATA 66; TEA
Frye, (Herman) Northrop
1912-1991 ...... **CLC 24, 70; TCLC 165**
See also CA 5-8R; 133; CANR 8, 37; DLB 67, 68, 246; EWL 3; MTCW 1, 2; MTFW 2005; RGAL 4; TWA
Fuchs, Daniel 1909-1993 .... **CLC 8, 22**
See also CA 81-84; 142; CAAS 5; CANR 40; CN 1, 2, 3, 4, 5; DLB 9, 26, 28; DLBY 1993; MAL 5
Fuchs, Daniel 1934-2012 .... **CLC 34**
See also CA 37-40R; CANR 14, 48
Fuentes, Carlos 1928- ...... **CLC 3, 8, 10, 13, 22, 41, 60, 113, 288, 354; HLC 1; SSC 24, 125; WLC 2**
See also AAYA 4, 45; AITN 2; BPFB 1; CA 69-72; CANR 10, 32, 68, 104, 138, 197; CDWLB 3; CWW 2; DA; DA3; DAB; DAC; DAM MST, MULT, NOV; DLB 113; DNFS 2; EWL 3; HW 1, 2; LAIT 3; LATS 1:2; LAW; LAWS 1; LMFS 2; MTCW 1, 2; MTFW 2005; NFS 8; RGSF 2; RGWL 2, 3; TWA; WLIT 1
Fuentes, Gregorio Lopez y
See Lopez y Fuentes, Gregorio
Fuentes Macias, Carlos Manuel
See Fuentes, Carlos
Fuertes, Gloria
1918-1998 .... **PC 27; TCLC 271**
See also CA 178, 180; DLB 108; HW 2; SATA 115
Fugard, Athol 1932- .... **CLC 5, 9, 14, 25, 40, 80, 211; DC 3**
See also AAYA 17; AFW; BRWS 15; CA 85-88; CANR 32, 54, 118; CD 5, 6; DAM DRAM; DFS 3, 6, 10, 24; DLB 225; DNFS 1, 2; EWL 3; LATS 1:2; MTCW 1; MTFW 2005; RGEL 2; WLIT 2
Fugard, Harold Athol
See Fugard, Athol
Fugard, Sheila 1932- .... **CLC 48**
See also CA 125
Fuguet, Alberto 1964- .... **CLC 308**
See also CA 170; CANR 144
Fujiwara no Teika 1162-1241 ...... **CMLC 73**
See also DLB 203
Fukuyama, Francis 1952- ...... **CLC 131, 320**
See also CA 140; CANR 72, 125, 170, 233
Fuller, Charles (H.), (Jr.) 1939- .... **BLC 1:2; CLC 25; DC 1**
See also BW 2; CA 108; 112; CAD; CANR 87; CD 5, 6; DAM DRAM, MULT; DFS 8; DLB 38, 266; EWL 3; INT CA-112; MAL 5; MTCW 1
Fuller, Henry Blake 1857-1929 ... **TCLC 103**
See also CA 108; 177; DLB 12; RGAL 4
Fuller, John (Leopold) 1937- .... **CLC 62**
See also CA 21-24R; CANR 9, 44; CP 1, 2, 3, 4, 5, 6, 7; DLB 40
Fuller, Margaret
1810-1850 .... **NCLC 5, 50, 211**
See also AMWS 2; CDALB 1640-1865; DLB 1, 59, 73, 183, 223, 239; FW; LMFS 1; SATA 25
Fuller, Roy (Broadbent)
1912-1991 .... **CLC 4, 28**
See also BRWS 7; CA 5-8R; 135; CAAS 10; CANR 53, 83; CN 1, 2, 3, 4, 5; CP 1, 2, 3, 4, 5; CWRI 5; DLB 15, 20; EWL 3; RGEL 2; SATA 87
Fuller, Sarah Margaret
See Fuller, Margaret
Fuller, Thomas 1608-1661 .... **LC 111**
See also DLB 151
Fulton, Alice 1952- .... **CLC 52**
See also CA 116; CANR 57, 88, 200; CP 5, 6, 7; CWP; DLB 193; PFS 25
Fundi
See Baraka, Amiri
Furey, Michael
See Ward, Arthur Henry Sarsfield
Furphy, Joseph 1843-1912 .... **TCLC 25**
See also CA 163; DLB 230; EWL 3; RGEL 2
Furst, Alan 1941- .... **CLC 255**
See also CA 69-72; CANR 12, 34, 59, 102, 159, 193; DLB 350; DLBY 01
Fuson, Robert H(enderson) 1927- ... **CLC 70**
See also CA 89-92; CANR 103
Fussell, Paul 1924- .... **CLC 74**
See also BEST 90:1; CA 17-20R; CANR 8, 21, 35, 69, 135; INT CANR-21; MTCW 1, 2; MTFW 2005
Futabatei, Shimei 1864-1909 .... **TCLC 44**
See also CA 162; DLB 180; EWL 3; MJW
Futabatei Shimei
See Futabatei, Shimei
Futrelle, Jacques 1875-1912 .... **TCLC 19**
See also CA 113; 155; CMW 4

GAB
See Russell, George William

Gaberman, Judie Angell
See Angell, Judie

Gaboriau, Emile 1835-1873 .... **NCLC 14**
See also CMW 4; MSW

Gadamer, Hans-Georg
1900-2002 .... **CLC 376**
See also CA 85-88, 206; DLB 296

Gadda, Carlo Emilio 1893-1973 .... **CLC 11; TCLC 144**
See also CA 89-92; DLB 177; EWL 3; WLIT 7

Gaddis, William 1922-1998 ..... **CLC 1, 3, 6, 8, 10, 19, 43, 86**
See also AMWS 4; BPFB 1; CA 17-20R; 172; CANR 21, 48, 148; CN 1, 2, 3, 4, 5, 6; DLB 2, 278; EWL 3; MAL 5; MTCW 1, 2; MTFW 2005; RGAL 4

Gage, Walter
See Inge, William (Motter)

Gaiman, Neil 1960- .... **CLC 319**
See also AAYA 19, 42, 82; CA 133; CANR 81, 129, 188; CLR 109, 177; DLB 261; HGG; MTFW 2005; SATA 85, 146, 197, 228; SFW 4; SUFW 2

Gaiman, Neil Richard
See Gaiman, Neil

Gaines, Ernest J. 1933- .... **BLC 1:2; CLC 3, 11, 18, 86, 181, 300; SSC 68, 137**
See also AAYA 18; AFAW 1, 2; AITN 1; BPFB 2; BW 2, 3; BYA 6; CA 9-12R; CANR 6, 24, 42, 75, 126; CDALB 1968-1988; CLR 62; CN 1, 2, 3, 4, 5, 6, 7; CSW; DA3; DAM MULT; DLB 2, 33, 152; DLBY 1980; EWL 3; EXPN; LAIT 5; LATS 1:2; MAL 5; MTCW 1, 2; MTFW 2005; NFS 5, 7, 16; RGAL 4; RGSF 2; RHW; SATA 86; SSFS 5; YAW

Gaines, Ernest James
See Gaines, Ernest J.

Gaitskill, Mary 1954- .... **CLC 69, 300; SSC 213**
See also CA 128; CANR 61, 152, 208; DLB 244; TCLE 1:1

Gaitskill, Mary Lawrence
See Gaitskill, Mary

Gaius Suetonius Tranquillus
See Suetonius

Galdos, Benito Perez
See Perez Galdos, Benito

Gale, Zona 1874-1938 ...... **DC 30; SSC 159; TCLC 7**
See also CA 105; 153; CANR 84; DAM DRAM; DFS 17; DLB 9, 78, 228; RGAL 4

Galeano, Eduardo 1940- .... **CLC 72; HLCS 1**
See also CA 29-32R; CANR 13, 32, 100, 163, 211; HW 1

Galeano, Eduardo Hughes
See Galeano, Eduardo

Galiano, Juan Valera y Alcala
See Valera y Alcala-Galiano, Juan

Galilei, Galileo 1564-1642 .... **LC 45, 188**

Gallagher, Tess 1943- ..... **CLC 18, 63; PC 9**
See also CA 106; CP 3, 4, 5, 6, 7; CWP; DAM POET; DLB 120, 212, 244; PFS 16

Gallant, Mavis 1922- .... **CLC 7, 18, 38, 172, 288; SSC 5, 78**
See also CA 69-72; CANR 29, 69, 117; CCA 1; CN 1, 2, 3, 4, 5, 6, 7; DAC; DAM MST; DLB 53; EWL 3; MTCW 1, 2; MTFW 2005; RGEL 2; RGSF 2

Gallant, Roy A(rthur) 1924- .... **CLC 17**
See also CA 5-8R; CANR 4, 29, 54, 117; CLR 30; MAICYA 1, 2; SATA 4, 68, 110

Gallico, Paul 1897-1976 .... **CLC 2**
See also AITN 1; CA 5-8R; 69-72; CANR 23; CN 1, 2; DLB 9, 171; FANT; MAICYA 1, 2; SATA 13

Gallico, Paul William
See Gallico, Paul

Gallo, Max Louis 1932- .... **CLC 95**
See also CA 85-88

Gallois, Lucien
See Desnos, Robert

Gallup, Ralph
See Whitemore, Hugh (John)

Galsworthy, John 1867-1933 .... **SSC 22; TCLC 1, 45; WLC 2**
See also BRW 6; CA 104; 141; CANR 75; CDBLB 1890-1914; DA; DA3; DAB; DAC; DAM DRAM, MST, NOV; DLB 10, 34, 98, 162, 330; DLBD 16; EWL 3; MTCW 2; RGEL 2; SSFS 3; TEA

Galt, John 1779-1839 ..... **NCLC 1, 110, 296**
See also DLB 99, 116, 159; RGEL 2; RGSF 2

Galvin, James 1951- .... **CLC 38**
See also CA 108; CANR 26

Gambaro, Griselda 1928- .... **CLC 380**
See also CA 131; CWW 2; DLB 305; EWL 3; HW 1; LAW

Gamboa, Federico 1864-1939 .... **TCLC 36**
See also CA 167; HW 2; LAW

Gandhi, M. K.
See Gandhi, Mohandas Karamchand

Gandhi, Mahatma
See Gandhi, Mohandas Karamchand

Gandhi, Mohandas Karamchand
1869-1948 .... **TCLC 59**
See also CA 121; 132; DA3; DAM MULT; DLB 323; MTCW 1, 2

Gann, Ernest Kellogg 1910-1991 .... **CLC 23**
See also AITN 1; BPFB 2; CA 1-4R; 136; CANR 1, 83; RHW

Gao Xingjian
See Xingjian, Gao

Garber, Eric
See Holleran, Andrew

Garber, Esther
See Lee, Tanith

Garcia Lorca, Federico 1898-1936 ..... **DC 2; HLC 2; PC 3, 130; TCLC 1, 7, 49, 181, 197; WLC 2**
See also AAYA 46; CA 104; 131; CANR 81; DA; DA3; DAB; DAC; DAM DRAM, MST, MULT, POET; DFS 4; DLB 108; EW 11; EWL 3; HW 1, 2; LATS 1:2; MTCW 1, 2; MTFW 2005; PFS 20, 31, 38; RGWL 2, 3; TWA; WP

García Márquez, Gabriel
1927/28-2014 .... **CLC 2, 3, 8, 10, 15, 27, 47, 55, 68, 170, 254, 389; HLC 1; SSC 8, 83, 162, 217; WLC 3**
See also AAYA 3, 33; BEST 89:1, 90:4; BPFB 2; BYA 12, 16; CA 33-36R; CANR 10, 28, 50, 75, 82, 128, 204; CDWLB 3; CPW; CWW 2; DA; DA3; DAB; DAC; DAM MST, MULT, NOV, POP; DLB 113, 330; DNFS 1, 2; EWL 3; EXPN; EXPS; HW 1, 2; LAIT 2; LATS 1:2; LAW; LAWS 1; LMFS 2; MTCW 1, 2; MTFW 2005; NCFS 3; NFS 1, 5, 10; RGSF 2; RGWL 2, 3; SSFS 1, 6, 16, 21, 37; TWA; WLIT 1

García Márquez, Gabriel Jose
See Garcia Marquez, Gabriel

Garcia, Cristina 1958- .... **CLC 76**
See also AMWS 11; CA 141; CANR 73, 130, 172, 243; CN 7; DLB 292; DNFS 1; EWL 3; HW 2; LLW; MTFW 2005; NFS 38; SATA 208

Garcilaso de la Vega, El Inca
1539-1616 .... **HLCS 1; LC 127**
See also DLB 318; LAW

Gard, Janice
See Latham, Jean Lee

Gard, Roger Martin du
See Martin du Gard, Roger

Gardam, Jane 1928- .... **CLC 43**
See also CA 49-52; CANR 2, 18, 33, 54, 106, 167, 206; CLR 12; DLB 14, 161, 231; MAICYA 1, 2; MTCW 1; SAAS 9; SATA 39, 76, 130; SATA-Brief 28; YAW

Gardam, Jane Mary
See Gardam, Jane

Gardens, S. S.
See Snodgrass, W. D.

Gardner, Herb(ert George)
1934-2003 .... **CLC 44**
See also CA 149; 220; CAD; CANR 119; CD 5, 6; DFS 18, 20

Gardner, John, Jr. 1933-1982 ...... **CLC 2, 3, 5, 7, 8, 10, 18, 28, 34; SSC 7; TCLC 195**
See also AAYA 45; AITN 1; AMWS 6; BPFB 2; CA 65-68; 107; CANR 33, 73; CDALBS; CN 2, 3; CPW; DA3; DAM NOV, POP; DLB 2; DLBY 1982; EWL 3; FANT; LATS 1:2; MAL 5; MTCW 1, 2; MTFW 2005; NFS 3; RGAL 4; RGSF 2; SATA 40; SATA-Obit 31; SSFS 8

Gardner, John 1926-2007 .... **CLC 30**
See also CA 103; 263; CANR 15, 69, 127, 183; CMW 4; CPW; DAM POP; MTCW 1

Gardner, John Champlin, Jr.
See Gardner, John, Jr.

Gardner, John Edmund
See Gardner, John

Gardner, Miriam
See Bradley, Marion Zimmer

Gardner, Noel
See Kuttner, Henry

Gardons, S.S.
See Snodgrass, W. D.

Garfield, Leon 1921-1996 .... **CLC 12**
See also AAYA 8, 69; BYA 1, 3; CA 17-20R; 152; CANR 38, 41, 78; CLR 21, 166; DLB 161; JRDA; MAICYA 1, 2; MAICYAS 1; SATA 1, 32, 76; SATA-Obit 90; TEA; WYA; YAW

Garland, (Hannibal) Hamlin
1860-1940 ... **SSC 18, 117; TCLC 3, 256**
See also CA 104; DLB 12, 71, 78, 186; MAL 5; RGAL 4; RGSF 2; TCWW 1, 2

Garneau, (Hector de) Saint-Denys
1912-1943 .... **TCLC 13**
See also CA 111; DLB 88

Garner, Alan 1934- .... **CLC 17**
See also AAYA 18; BYA 3, 5; CA 73-76, 178; CAAE 178; CANR 15, 64, 134; CLR 20, 130; CPW; DAB; DAM POP; DLB 161, 261; FANT; MAICYA 1, 2; MTCW 1, 2; MTFW 2005; SATA 18, 69; SATA-Essay 108; SUFW 1, 2; YAW

Garner, Helen 1942- .... **SSC 135**
See also CA 124; 127; CANR 71, 206; CN 4, 5, 6, 7; DLB 325; GLL 2; RGSF 2

Garner, Hugh 1913-1979 .... **CLC 13**
See also CA 69-72; CANR 31; CCA 1; CN 1, 2; DLB 68

Garnett, David 1892-1981 .... **CLC 3**
See also CA 5-8R; 103; CANR 17, 79; CN 1, 2; DLB 34; FANT; MTCW 2; RGEL 2; SFW 4; SUFW 1

Garnier, Robert c. 1545-1590 .... **LC 119**
See also DLB 327; GFL Beginnings to 1789

Garrett, Almeida 1799-1854 .... **NCLC 316**
See also DLB 287

Garrett, George 1929-2008 .... **CLC 3, 11, 51; SSC 30**
See also AMWS 7; BPFB 2; CA 1-4R, 202; 272; CAAE 202; CAAS 5; CANR 1, 42, 67, 109, 199; CN 1, 2, 3, 4, 5, 6, 7; CP 1, 2, 3, 4, 5, 6, 7; CSW; DLB 2, 5, 130, 152; DLBY 1983

Garrett, George P.
See Garrett, George

Garrett, George Palmer
See Garrett, George
Garrett, George Palmer, Jr.
See Garrett, George
Garrick, David 1717-1779 .... **DC 50; LC 15, 156**
See also DAM DRAM; DLB 84, 213; RGEL 2
Garrigue, Jean 1914-1972 .... **CLC 2, 8**
See also CA 5-8R; 37-40R; CANR 20; CP 1; MAL 5
Garrison, Frederick
See Sinclair, Upton
Garrison, William Lloyd
1805-1879 .... **NCLC 149**
See also CDALB 1640-1865; DLB 1, 43, 235
Garro, Elena 1920(?)-1998 .... **HLCS 1; SSC 203; TCLC 153**
See also CA 131; 169; CWW 2; DLB 145; EWL 3; HW 1; LAWS 1; WLIT 1
Garshin, Vsevolod Mikhailovich
1855-1888 .... **NCLC 257**
See also DLB 277
Garth, Will
See Hamilton, Edmond; Kuttner, Henry
Garvey, Marcus (Moziah, Jr.)
1887-1940 .... **BLC 1:2; HR 1:2; TCLC 41**
See also BW 1; CA 120; 124; CANR 79; DAM MULT; DLB 345
Gary, Romain
See Kacew, Romain
Gascar, Pierre
See Fournier, Pierre
Gascoigne, George 1539-1577 .... **LC 108**
See also DLB 136; RGEL 2
Gascoyne, David (Emery)
1916-2001 .... **CLC 45**
See also CA 65-68; 200; CANR 10, 28, 54; CP 1, 2, 3, 4, 5, 6, 7; DLB 20; MTCW 1; RGEL 2
Gaskell, Elizabeth Cleghorn
1810-1865 .... **NCLC 5, 70, 97, 137, 214, 264; SSC 25, 97, 218**
See also AAYA 80; BRW 5; BRWR 3; CDBLB 1832-1890; DAB; DAM MST; DLB 21, 144, 159; RGEL 2; RGSF 2; TEA
Gass, William H. 1924- ..... **CLC 1, 2, 8, 11, 15, 39, 132; SSC 12**
See also AMWS 6; CA 17-20R; CANR 30, 71, 100; CN 1, 2, 3, 4, 5, 6, 7; DLB 2, 227; EWL 3; MAL 5; MTCW 1, 2; MTFW 2005; RGAL 4
Gassendi, Pierre 1592-1655 .... **LC 54**
See also GFL Beginnings to 1789
Gasset, Jose Ortega y
See Ortega y Gasset, Jose
Gates, Henry Louis, Jr.
1950- .... **BLCS; CLC 65**
See also AMWS 20; BW 2, 3; CA 109; CANR 25, 53, 75, 125, 203; CSW; DA3; DAM MULT; DLB 67; EWL 3; MAL 5; MTCW 2; MTFW 2005; RGAL 4
Gatos, Stephanie
See Katz, Steve
Gauden, John 1605-1662 .... **LC 237**
Gautier, Theophile 1811-1872 .... **NCLC 1, 59, 243, 267; PC 18; SSC 20**
See also DAM POET; DLB 119, 366; EW 6; GFL 1789 to the Present; RGWL 2, 3; SUFW; TWA
Gautreaux, Tim 1947- ... **CLC 270; SSC 125**
See also CA 187; CANR 207; CSW; DLB 292
Gautreaux, Tim Martin
See Gautreaux, Tim
Gay, John 1685-1732 .. **DC 39, 48; LC 49, 176**
See also BRW 3; DAM DRAM; DLB 84, 95; RGEL 2; WLIT 3
Gay, Oliver
See Gogarty, Oliver St. John
Gay, Peter 1923- .... **CLC 158**
See also CA 13-16R; CANR 18, 41, 77, 147, 196; INT CANR-18; RGHL
Gay, Peter Jack
See Gay, Peter
Gaye, Marvin (Pentz, Jr.) 1939-1984 .. **CLC 26**
See also CA 195; 112
Gebler, Carlo 1954- .... **CLC 39**
See also CA 119; 133; CANR 96, 186; DLB 271
Gebler, Carlo Ernest
See Gebler, Carlo
Gee, Maggie 1948- .... **CLC 57**
See also CA 130; CANR 125; CN 4, 5, 6, 7; DLB 207; MTFW 2005
Gee, Maurice 1931- .... **CLC 29**
See also AAYA 42; CA 97-100; CANR 67, 123, 204; CLR 56; CN 2, 3, 4, 5, 6, 7; CWRI 5; EWL 3; MAICYA 2; RGSF 2; SATA 46, 101, 227
Gee, Maurice Gough
See Gee, Maurice
Geiogamah, Hanay 1945- .... **NNAL**
See also CA 153; DAM MULT; DLB 175
Gelbart, Larry 1928-2009 .... **CLC 21, 61**
See also CA 73-76; 290; CAD; CANR 45, 94; CD 5, 6
Gelbart, Larry Simon
See Gelbart, Larry
Gelber, Jack 1932-2003 .... **CLC 1, 6, 14, 79**
See also CA 1-4R; 216; CAD; CANR 2; DLB 7, 228; MAL 5
Gellhorn, Martha 1908-1998 ..... **CLC 14, 60**
See Gellhorn, Martha Ellis
See also CA 77-80; 164; CANR 44; CN 1, 2, 3, 4, 5, 6 7; DLB 364; DLBY 1982, 1998
Gellhorn, Martha Ellis
See Gellhorn, Martha
Gellius, Aulus c. 125-170/180? ... **CMLC 153**
See also DLB 211
Genet, Jean 1910-1986 .... **CLC 1, 2, 5, 10, 14, 44, 46; DC 25; TCLC 128**
See also CA 13-16R; CANR 18; DA3; DAM DRAM; DFS 10; DLB 72, 321; DLBY 1986; EW 13; EWL 3; GFL 1789 to the Present; GLL 1; LMFS 2; MTCW 1, 2; MTFW 2005; RGWL 2, 3; TWA
Genette, Gérard 1930- .... **CLC 372**
See also CA 238; DLB 242
Genlis, Stephanie-Felicite Ducrest
1746-1830 .... **NCLC 166**
See also DLB 313
Gent, Peter 1942-2011 .... **CLC 29**
See also AITN 1; CA 89-92; DLBY 1982
Gentile, Giovanni 1875-1944 .... **TCLC 96**
See also CA 119
Geoffrey of Monmouth
c. 1100-c. 1155 .... **CMLC 44, 164; PC 140**
See also DLB 146; TEA
Geoffrey of Vinsauf
fl. c. 12th cent. .... **CMLC 129**
George, Jean
See George, Jean Craighead
George, Jean C.
See George, Jean Craighead
George, Jean Craighead 1919- .... **CLC 35**
See also AAYA 8, 69; BYA 2, 4; CA 5-8R; CANR 25, 198; CLR 1, 80, 136; DLB 52; JRDA; MAICYA 1, 2; SATA 2, 68, 124, 170, 226; WYA; YAW
George, Stefan (Anton)
1868-1933 .... **TCLC 2, 14**
See also CA 104; 193; EW 8; EWL 3
Georges, Georges Martin
See Simenon, Georges
Gerald of Wales
c. 1146-c. 1223 .... **CMLC 60, 144**
Gerhardi, William Alexander
See Gerhardie, William Alexander
Gerhardie, William Alexander
1895-1977 .... **CLC 5**
See also CA 25-28R; 73-76; CANR 18; CN 1, 2; DLB 36; RGEL 2
Germain, Sylvie 1954- .... **CLC 283**
See also CA 191
Gerome
See France, Anatole
Gerson, Jean 1363-1429 .... **LC 77**
See also DLB 208
Gersonides 1288-1344 .... **CMLC 49**
See also DLB 115
Gerstler, Amy 1956- .... **CLC 70**
See also CA 146; CANR 99
Gertler, T. .... **CLC 34**
See also CA 116; 121
Gertrude of Helfta
c. 1256-c. 1301 .... **CMLC 105**
Gertsen, Aleksandr Ivanovich
See Herzen, Aleksandr Ivanovich
Gervase of Melkley
c. 1185-c. 1216 .... **CMLC 121**
Geyer, Francis
See Harwood, Gwen
Ghalib
See Ghalib, Asadullah Khan
Ghelderode, Michel de 1898-1962 ... **CLC 6, 11; DC 15; TCLC 187**
See also CA 85-88; CANR 40, 77; DAM DRAM; DLB 321; EW 11; EWL 3; TWA
Ghiselin, Brewster 1903-2001 .... **CLC 23**
See also CA 13-16R; CAAS 10; CANR 13; CP 1, 2, 3, 4, 5, 6, 7
Ghalib, Asadullah Khan
1797-1869 .... **NCLC 39, 78**
See also DAM POET; RGWL 2, 3
Ghose, Aurabinda 1872-1950 .... **TCLC 63**
See also CA 163; EWL 3
Ghose, Aurobindo
See Ghose, Aurabinda
Ghose, Zulfikar 1935- .... **CLC 42, 200**
See also CA 65-68; CANR 67; CN 1, 2, 3, 4, 5, 6, 7; CP 1, 2, 3, 4, 5, 6, 7; DLB 323; EWL 3
Ghosh, Amitav 1956- ...... **CLC 44, 153, 300**
See also CA 147; CANR 80, 158, 205; CN 6, 7; DLB 323; WWE 1
Giacosa, Giuseppe 1847-1906 .... **TCLC 7**
See also CA 104
Gibb, Lee
See Waterhouse, Keith
Gibbon, Edward 1737-1794 .... **LC 97**
See also BRW 3; DLB 104, 336; RGEL 2
Gibbon, Lewis Grassic
See Mitchell, James Leslie
Gibbons, Kaye 1960- .... **CLC 50, 88, 145**
See also AAYA 34; AMWS 10; CA 151; CANR 75, 127; CN 7; CSW; DA3; DAM POP; DLB 292; MTCW 2; MTFW 2005; NFS 3; RGAL 4; SATA 117
Gibran, Kahlil 1883-1931 ... **PC 9; TCLC 1, 9, 205**
See also AMWS 20; CA 104; 150; DA3; DAM POET, POP; DLB 346; EWL 3; MTCW 2; WLIT 6
Gibran, Khalil
See Gibran, Kahlil
Gibson, Mel 1956- .... **CLC 215**
See also AAYA 80
Gibson, William 1914-2008 .... **CLC 23**
See also CA 9-12R; 279; CAD; CANR 9, 42, 75, 125; CD 5, 6; DA; DAB; DAC; DAM DRAM, MST; DFS 2, 28; DLB 7; LAIT 2; MAL 5; MTCW 2; MTFW 2005; SATA 66; SATA-Obit 199; YAW
Gibson, William 1948- ..... **CLC 39, 63, 186, 192, 333; SSC 52**

See also AAYA 12, 59; AMWS 16; BPFB 2; CA 126; 133; CANR 52, 90, 106, 172, 229; CN 6, 7; CPW; DA3; DAM POP; DLB 251; MTCW 2; MTFW 2005; NFS 38; SCFW 2; SFW 4; SSFS 26
Gibson, William Ford
See Gibson, William
Gide, Andre 1869-1951 .... **SSC 13; TCLC 5, 12, 36, 177; WLC 3**
See also CA 104; 124; DA; DA3; DAB; DAC; DAM MST, NOV; DLB 65, 321, 330; EW 8; EWL 3; GFL 1789 to the Present; MTCW 1, 2; MTFW 2005; NFS 21; RGSF 2; RGWL 2, 3; TWA
Gide, Andre Paul Guillaume
See Gide, Andre
Gifford, Barry 1946- .... **CLC 34**
See also CA 65-68; CANR 9, 30, 40, 90, 180
Gifford, Barry Colby
See Gifford, Barry
Gilbert, Frank
See De Voto, Bernard (Augustine)
Gilbert, W(illiam) S(chwenck)
1836-1911 .... **TCLC 3**
See also CA 104; 173; DAM DRAM, POET; DLB 344; RGEL 2; SATA 36
Gilbert of Poitiers c. 1085-1154 ... **CMLC 85**
Gilbreth, Frank B., Jr. 1911-2001 ... **CLC 17**
See also CA 9-12R; SATA 2
Gilbreth, Frank Bunker
See Gilbreth, Frank B., Jr.
Gilchrist, Ellen 1935- .... **CLC 34, 48, 143, 264; SSC 14, 63**
See also BPFB 2; CA 113; 116; CANR 41, 61, 104, 191; CN 4, 5, 6, 7; CPW; CSW; DAM POP; DLB 130; EWL 3; EXPS; MTCW 1, 2; MTFW 2005; RGAL 4; RGSF 2; SSFS 9
Gilchrist, Ellen Louise
See Gilchrist, Ellen
Gildas fl. 6th cent. .... **CMLC 99**
Giles, Molly 1942- .... **CLC 39**
See also CA 126; CANR 98
Gill, Arthur Eric Rowton Peter Joseph
See Gill, Eric
Gill, Eric 1882-1940 .... **TCLC 85**
See Gill, Arthur Eric Rowton Peter Joseph
See also CA 120; DLB 98
Gill, Patrick
See Creasey, John
Gillette, Douglas .... **CLC 70**
Gilliam, Terry 1940- .... **CLC 21, 141**
See also AAYA 19, 59; CA 108; 113; CANR 35; INT CA-113
Gilliam, Terry Vance
See Gilliam, Terry
Gillian, Jerry
See Gilliam, Terry
Gilliatt, Penelope (Ann Douglass)
1932-1993 .... **CLC 2, 10, 13, 53**
See also AITN 2; CA 13-16R; 141; CANR 49; CN 1, 2, 3, 4, 5; DLB 14
Gilligan, Carol 1936- .... **CLC 208**
See also CA 142; CANR 121, 187; FW
Gilman, Caroline 1794-1888 .... **NCLC 302**
See also DLB 3, 73
Gilman, Charlotte Anna Perkins Stetson
See Gilman, Charlotte Perkins
Gilman, Charlotte Perkins
1860-1935 .. **SSC 13, 62, 182; TCLC 9, 37, 117, 201**
See also AAYA 75; AMWS 11; BYA 11; CA 106; 150; DLB 221; EXPS; FL 1:5; FW; HGG; LAIT 2; MBL; MTCW 2; MTFW 2005; NFS 36; RGAL 4; RGSF 2; SFW 4; SSFS 1, 18
Gilmore, Mary (Jean Cameron)
1865-1962 .... **PC 87**
See also CA 114; DLB 260; RGEL 2; SATA 49
Gilmour, David 1946- .... **CLC 35**
Gilpin, William 1724-1804 .... **NCLC 30**
Gilray, J. D.
See Mencken, H. L.
Gilroy, Frank D(aniel) 1925- .... **CLC 2**
See also CA 81-84; CAD; CANR 32, 64, 86; CD 5, 6; DFS 17; DLB 7
Gilstrap, John 1957(?)- .... **CLC 99**
See also AAYA 67; CA 160; CANR 101, 229
Ginsberg, Allen 1926-1997 ...... **CLC 1, 2, 3, 4, 6, 13, 36, 69, 109; PC 4, 47; TCLC 120; WLC 3**
See also AAYA 33; AITN 1; AMWC 1; AMWS 2; BG 1:2; CA 1-4R; 157; CANR 2, 41, 63, 95; CDALB 1941-1968; CP 1, 2, 3, 4, 5, 6; DA; DA3; DAB; DAC; DAM MST, POET; DLB 5, 16, 169, 237; EWL 3; GLL 1; LMFS 2; MAL 5; MTCW 1, 2; MTFW 2005; PAB; PFS 29; RGAL 4; TUS; WP
Ginzburg, Eugenia
See Ginzburg, Evgeniia
Ginzburg, Evgeniia 1904-1977 .... **CLC 59**
See also DLB 302
Ginzburg, Natalia 1916-1991 .... **CLC 5, 11, 54, 70; SSC 65; TCLC 156**
See also CA 85-88; 135; CANR 33; DFS 14; DLB 177; EW 13; EWL 3; MTCW 1, 2; MTFW 2005; RGHL; RGWL 2, 3
Gioia, (Michael) Dana
1950- .... **CLC 251**
See also AMWS 15; CA 130; CANR 70, 88; CP 6, 7; DLB 120, 282; PFS 24
Giono, Jean 1895-1970 .... **CLC 4, 11; TCLC 124**
See also CA 45-48; 29-32R; CANR 2, 35; DLB 72, 321; EWL 3; GFL 1789 to the Present; MTCW 1; RGWL 2, 3
Giovanni, Nikki 1943- ..... **BLC 1:2; CLC 2, 4, 19, 64, 117; PC 19; WLCS**
See also AAYA 22, 85; AITN 1; BW 2, 3; CA 29-32R; CAAS 6; CANR 18, 41, 60, 91, 130, 175; CDALBS; CLR 6, 73; CP 2, 3, 4, 5, 6, 7; CSW; CWP; CWRI 5; DA; DA3; DAB; DAC; DAM MST, MULT, POET; DLB 5, 41; EWL 3; EXPP; INT CANR-18; MAICYA 1, 2; MAL 5; MTCW 1, 2; MTFW 2005; PFS 17, 28, 35, 42; RGAL 4; SATA 24, 107, 208; TUS; YAW
Giovanni, Yolanda Cornelia
See Giovanni, Nikki
Giovanni, Yolande Cornelia
See Giovanni, Nikki
Giovanni, Yolande Cornelia, Jr.
See Giovanni, Nikki
Giovene, Andrea 1904-1998 .... **CLC 7**
See also CA 85-88
Gippius, Zinaida 1869-1945 ... **TCLC 9, 273**
See also CA 106; 212; DLB 295; EWL 3
Gippius, Zinaida Nikolaevna
See Gippius, Zinaida
Guiraldes, Ricardo (Guillermo)
1886-1927 .... **TCLC 39**
See also CA 131; EWL 3; HW 1; LAW; MTCW 1
Giraldi, Giovanni Battista
1504-1573 .... **LC 220**
Giraldi, William .... **CLC 334**
See also CA 329
Giraudoux, Jean 1882-1944 .... **DC 36; TCLC 2, 7**
See also CA 104; 196; DAM DRAM; DFS 28; DLB 65, 321; EW 9; EWL 3; GFL 1789 to the Present; RGWL 2, 3; TWA
Giraudoux, Jean-Hippolyte
See Giraudoux, Jean
Giraut de Bornelh
c. 1140-c. 1200 .... **CMLC 175**
Gironella, Jose Maria (Pous)
1917-2003 .... **CLC 11**
See also CA 101; 212; EWL 3; RGWL 2, 3
Gissing, George (Robert) 1857-1903 ..... **SSC 37, 113; TCLC 3, 24, 47; TCLC 310, 313**
See also BRW 5; CA 105; 167; DLB 18, 135, 184; RGEL 2; TEA
Gitlin, Todd 1943- .... **CLC 201**
See also CA 29-32R; CANR 25, 50, 88, 179, 227
Giurlani, Aldo
See Palazzeschi, Aldo
Gladkov, Fedor Vasil'evich
See Gladkov, Fyodor (Vasilyevich)
Gladkov, Fyodor (Vasilyevich)
1883-1958 .... **TCLC 27**
See also CA 170; DLB 272; EWL 3
Gladstone, William Ewart
1809-1898 .... **NCLC 213**
See also DLB 57, 184
Glancy, Diane 1941- .... **CLC 210; NNAL**
See also CA 136, 225; CAAE 225; CAAS 24; CANR 87, 162, 217; DLB 175
Glanville, Brian (Lester) 1931- .... **CLC 6**
See also CA 5-8R; CAAS 9; CANR 3, 70; CN 1, 2, 3, 4, 5, 6, 7; DLB 15, 139; SATA 42
Glasgow, Ellen 1873-1945 .... **SSC 34, 130; TCLC 2, 7, 239**
See also AMW; CA 104; 164; DLB 9, 12; MAL 5; MBL; MTCW 2; MTFW 2005; RGAL 4; RHW; SSFS 9; TUS
Glasgow, Ellen Anderson Gholson
See Glasgow, Ellen
Glaspell, Susan 1882(?)-1948 .... **DC 10; SSC 41, 132; TCLC 55, 175**
See also AMWS 3; CA 110; 154; DFS 8, 18, 24; DLB 7, 9, 78, 228; MBL; RGAL 4; SSFS 3; TCWW 2; TUS; YABC 2
Glassco, John 1909-1981 .... **CLC 9**
See also CA 13-16R; 102; CANR 15; CN 1, 2; CP 1, 2, 3; DLB 68
Glasscock, Amnesia
See Steinbeck, John
Glasser, Ronald J. 1940(?)- .... **CLC 37**
See also CA 209; CANR 240
Glassman, Joyce
See Johnson, Joyce
Gluck, Louise 1943- .... **CLC 7, 22, 44, 81, 160, 280; PC 16, 159**
See also AMWS 5; CA 33-36R; CANR 40, 69, 108, 133, 182; CP 1, 2, 3, .4, 5, 6, 7; CWP; DA3; DAM POET; DLB 5; MAL 5; MTCW 2; MTFW 2005; PFS 5, 15; RGAL 4; TCLE 1:1
Gluck, Louise Elisabeth
See Gluck, Louise
Gleick, James 1954- .... **CLC 147**
See also CA 131; 137; CANR 97, 236; INT CA-137
Gleick, James W.
See Gleick, James
Glendinning, Victoria 1937- .... **CLC 50**
See also CA 120; 127; CANR 59, 89, 166; DLB 155
Glissant, Edouard 1928-2011 ... **CLC 10, 68, 337**
See also CA 153; CANR 111; CWW 2; DAM MULT; EWL 3; RGWL 3
Glissant, Edouard Mathieu
See Glissant, Edouard
Gloag, Julian 1930- .... **CLC 40**
See also AITN 1; CA 65-68; CANR 10, 70; CN 1, 2, 3, 4, 5, 6
Glowacki, Aleksander
See Prus, Boleslaw
Glyn, Elinor 1864-1943 .... **TCLC 72**
See also DLB 153; RHW

Gomez de Avellaneda, Gertrudis 1814-1873 .... **NCLC 111, 264**
See also LAW

Gongora (y Argote), Luis de 1561-1627 .... **LC 72**
See also RGWL 2, 3

Gunter, Erich
See Eich, Gunter

Gobineau, Joseph-Arthur 1816-1882 .... **NCLC 17, 259**
See also DLB 123; GFL 1789 to the Present

Godard, Jean-Luc 1930- .... **CLC 20**
See also CA 93-96

Godden, (Margaret) Rumer 1907-1998 .... **CLC 53**
See also AAYA 6; BPFB 2; BYA 2, 5; CA 5-8R; 172; CANR 4, 27, 36, 55, 80; CLR 20; CN 1, 2, 3, 4, 5, 6; CWRI 5; DLB 161; MAICYA 1, 2; RHW; SAAS 12; SATA 3, 36; SATA-Obit 109; TEA

Godoy Alcayaga, Lucila
See Mistral, Gabriela

Godwin, Gail 1937- .... **CLC 5, 8, 22, 31, 69, 125, 331**
See also BPFB 2; CA 29-32R; CANR 15, 43, 69, 132, 218; CN 3, 4, 5, 6, 7; CPW; CSW; DA3; DAM POP; DLB 6, 234, 350; INT CANR-15; MAL 5; MTCW 1, 2; MTFW 2005

Godwin, Gail Kathleen
See Godwin, Gail

Godwin, William 1756-1836 .. **NCLC 14, 130, 287**
See also BRWS 15; CDBLB 1789-1832; CMW 4; DLB 39, 104, 142, 158, 163, 262, 336; GL 2; HGG; RGEL 2

Goebbels, Josef
See Goebbels, (Paul) Joseph

Goebbels, (Paul) Joseph 1897-1945 .... **TCLC 68**
See also CA 115; 148

Goebbels, Joseph Paul
See Goebbels, (Paul) Joseph

Goethe, Johann Wolfgang von 1749-1832 ..... **DC 20; NCLC 4, 22, 34, 90, 154, 247, 266, 270, 284, 287; PC 5, 147; SSC 38, 141; WLC 3**
See also CDWLB 2; DA; DA3; DAB; DAC; DAM DRAM, MST, POET; DLB 94; EW 5; GL 2; LATS 1; LMFS 1:1; RGWL 2, 3; TWA

Gogarty, Oliver St. John 1878-1957 .... **PC 121; TCLC 15**
See also CA 109; 150; DLB 15, 19; RGEL 2

Gogol, Nikolai 1809-1852 .. **DC 1; NCLC 5, 15, 31, 162, 281, 315; SSC 4, 29, 52, 145; WLC 3**
See also DA; DAB; DAC; DAM DRAM, MST; DFS 12; DLB 198; EW 6; EXPS; RGSF 2; RGWL 2, 3; SSFS 7, 32; TWA

Gogol, Nikolai Vasilyevich
See Gogol, Nikolai

Goines, Donald 1937(?)-1974 .... **BLC 1:2; CLC 80**
See also AITN 1; BW 1, 3; CA 124; 114; CANR 82; CMW 4; DA3; DAM MULT, POP; DLB 33

Gold, Herbert 1924- .... **CLC 4, 7, 14, 42, 152**
See also CA 9-12R; CANR 17, 45, 125, 194; CN 1, 2, 3, 4, 5, 6, 7; DLB 2; DLBY 1981; MAL 5

Goldbarth, Albert 1948- .... **CLC 5, 38**
See also AMWS 12; CA 53-56; CANR 6, 40, 206; CP 3, 4, 5, 6, 7; DLB 120

Goldberg, Anatol 1910-1982 .... **CLC 34**
See also CA 131; 117

Goldemberg, Isaac 1945- .... **CLC 52**
See also CA 69-72; CAAS 12; CANR 11, 32; EWL 3; HW 1; WLIT 1

Golding, Arthur 1536-1606 .... **LC 101**
See also DLB 136

Golding, William 1911-1993 .... **CLC 1, 2, 3, 8, 10, 17, 27, 58, 81; WLC 3**
See also AAYA 5, 44; BPFB 2; BRWR 1; BRWS 1; BYA 2; CA 5-8R; 141; CANR 13, 33, 54; CD 5; CDBLB 1945-1960; CLR 94, 130; CN 1, 2, 3, 4; DA; DA3; DAB; DAC; DAM MST, NOV; DLB 15, 100, 255, 326, 330; EWL 3; EXPN; HGG; LAIT 4; MTCW 1, 2; MTFW 2005; NFS 2, 36; RGEL 2; RHW; SFW 4; TEA; WLIT 4; YAW

Golding, William Gerald
See Golding, William

Goldman, Emma 1869-1940 .... **TCLC 13**
See also CA 110; 150; DLB 221; FW; RGAL 4; TUS

Goldman, Francisco 1954- ...... **CLC 76, 298**
See also CA 162; CANR 185, 233

Goldman, William 1931- .... **CLC 1, 48**
See also BPFB 2; CA 9-12R; CANR 29, 69, 106; CN 1, 2, 3, 4, 5, 6, 7; DLB 44; FANT; IDFW 3, 4; NFS 31

Goldman, William W.
See Goldman, William

Goldmann, Lucien 1913-1970 .... **CLC 24**
See also CA 25-28; CAP 2

Goldoni, Carlo 1707-1793 .... **DC 47; LC 4, 152**
See also DAM DRAM; DFS 27; EW 4; RGWL 2, 3; WLIT 7

Goldsberry, Steven 1949- .... **CLC 34**
See also CA 131

Goldsmith, Oliver 1730(?)-1774 .... **DC 8; LC 2, 48, 122; PC 77; WLC 3**
See also BRW 3; CDBLB 1660-1789; DA; DAB; DAC; DAM DRAM, MST, NOV, POET; DFS 1; DLB 39, 89, 104, 109, 142, 336; IDTP; RGEL 2; SATA 26; TEA; WLIT 3

Goldsmith, Peter
See Priestley, J(ohn) B(oynton)

Goldstein, Rebecca 1950- .... **CLC 239**
See also CA 144; CANR 99, 165, 214; TCLE 1:1

Goldstein, Rebecca Newberger
See Goldstein, Rebecca

Gombrowicz, Witold 1904-1969 ...... **CLC 4, 7, 11, 49; TCLC 247**
See also CA 19-20; 25-28R; CANR 105; CAP 2; CDWLB 4; DAM DRAM; DLB 215; EW 12; EWL 3; RGWL 2, 3; TWA

Gomez de la Serna, Ramon 1888-1963 .... **CLC 9**
See also CA 153; 116; CANR 79; EWL 3; HW 1, 2

Gomez-Pena, Guillermo 1955- ...... **CLC 310**
See also CA 147; CANR 117

Goncharov, Ivan Alexandrovich 1812-1891 .... **NCLC 1, 63**
See also DLB 238; EW 6; RGWL 2, 3

Goncourt, Edmond de 1822-1896 ... **NCLC 7**
See also DLB 123; EW 7; GFL 1789 to the Present; RGWL 2, 3

Goncourt, Edmond Louis Antoine Huot de
See Goncourt, Edmond de

Goncourt, Jules Alfred Huot de
See Goncourt, Jules de

Goncourt, Jules de 1830-1870 .... **NCLC 7**
See Goncourt, Jules de
See also DLB 123; EW 7; GFL 1789 to the Present; RGWL 2, 3

Gontier, Fernande 19(?)- .... **CLC 50**

Gonzalez Martinez, Enrique 1871-1952 .... **TCLC 72**
See also CA 166; CANR 81; DLB 290; EWL 3; HW 1, 2

Gonzalez Martinez, Enrique
See Gonzalez Martinez, Enrique

Goodison, Lorna 1947- ...... **BLC 2:2; PC 36**
See also CA 142; CANR 88, 189; CP 5, 6, 7; CWP; DLB 157; EWL 3; PFS 25

Goodman, Allegra 1967- .... **CLC 241**
See also CA 204; CANR 162, 204; DLB 244, 350

Goodman, Paul 1911-1972 ... **CLC 1, 2, 4, 7**
See also CA 19-20; 37-40R; CAD; CANR 34; CAP 2; CN 1; DLB 130, 246; MAL 5; MTCW 1; RGAL 4

Goodweather, Hartley
See King, Thomas

GoodWeather, Hartley
See King, Thomas

Googe, Barnabe 1540-1594 .... **LC 94**
See also DLB 132; RGEL 2

Gordimer, Nadine 1923-2014 .... **CLC 3, 5, 7, 10, 18, 33, 51, 70, 123, 160, 161, 263, 389; SSC 17, 80, 154; WLCS**
See also AAYA 39; AFW; BRWS 2; CA 5-8R; CANR 3, 28, 56, 88, 131, 195, 219; CN 1, 2, 3, 4, 5, 6, 7; DA; DA3; DAB; DAC; DAM MST, NOV; DLB 225, 326, 330; EWL 3; EXPS; INT CANR-28; LATS 1:2; MTCW 1, 2; MTFW 2005; NFS 4; RGEL 2; RGSF 2; SSFS 2, 14, 19, 28, 31; TWA; WLIT 2; YAW

Gordon, Adam Lindsay 1833-1870 .. **NCLC 21**
See also DLB 230

Gordon, Caroline 1895-1981 ...... **CLC 6, 13, 29, 83; SSC 15; TCLC 241**
See also AMW; CA 11-12; 103; CANR 36; CAP 1; CN 1, 2; DLB 4, 9, 102; DLBD 17; DLBY 1981; EWL 3; MAL 5; MTCW 1, 2; MTFW 2005; RGAL 4; RGSF 2

Gordon, Charles William 1860-1937 .... **TCLC 31**
See also CA 109; DLB 92; TCWW 1, 2

Gordon, Lucie Duff
See Duff Gordon, Lucie

Gordon, Mary 1949- .... **CLC 13, 22, 128, 216; SSC 59**
See also AMWS 4; BPFB 2; CA 102; CANR 44, 92, 154, 179, 222; CN 4, 5, 6, 7; DLB 6; DLBY 1981; FW; INT CA-102; MAL 5; MTCW 1

Gordon, Mary Catherine
See Gordon, Mary

Gordon, N. J.
See Bosman, Herman Charles

Gordon, Sol 1923- .... **CLC 26**
See also CA 53-56; CANR 4; SATA 11

Gordone, Charles 1925-1995 .... **BLC 2:2; CLC 1, 4; DC 8**
See also BW 1, 3; CA 93-96, 180; 150; CAAE 180; CAD; CANR 55; DAM DRAM; DLB 7; INT CA-93-96; MTCW 1

Gore, Catherine 1800-1861 .... **NCLC 65**
See also DLB 116, 344; RGEL 2

Gorenko, Anna Andreevna
See Akhmatova, Anna

Gor'kii, Maksim
See Gorky, Maxim

Gorky, Maxim 1868-1936 .... **SSC 28; TCLC 8; WLC 3**
See also CA 105; 141; CANR 83; DA; DAB; DAC; DAM DRAM, MST, NOV; DFS 9; DLB 295; EW 8; EWL 3; MTCW 2; MTFW 2005; RGSF 2; RGWL 2, 3; TWA

Gorriti, Juana Manuela 1818-1892 ... **NCLC 298**

Goryan, Sirak
See Saroyan, William

Gosse, Edmund (William)
1849-1928 .... **TCLC 28**
See also CA 117; DLB 57, 144, 184; RGEL 2
Goto, Hiromi 1966- .... **CLC 338**
See also CA 165; CANR 142
Gotlieb, Phyllis 1926-2009 .... **CLC 18**
See also CA 13-16R; CANR 7, 135; CN 7; CP 1, 2, 3, 4; DLB 88, 251; SFW 4
Gotlieb, Phyllis Fay Bloom
See Gotlieb, Phyllis
Gottesman, S. D.
See Kornbluth, C(yril) M.; Pohl, Frederik
Gottfried von Strassburg
fl. c. 1170-1215 ...... **CMLC 10, 96, 132**
See also CDWLB 2; DLB 138; EW 1; RGWL 2, 3
Gotthelf, Jeremias 1797-1854 ...... **NCLC 117**
See also DLB 133; RGWL 2, 3
Gottschalk c. 804-c. 866 .... **CMLC 130**
See also DLB 148
Gottschalk, Laura Riding
See Jackson, Laura
Gottsched, Johann Christoph
1700-1766 .... **LC 207**
See also DLB 97
Gottsched, Luise Adelgunde Victoria
1713-1762 .... **LC 211**
Gouges, Olympe de
1748-1793 .... **LC 127, 214**
See also DLB 313
Gould, Lois 1932(?)-2002 .... **CLC 4, 10**
See also CA 77-80; 208; CANR 29; MTCW 1
Gould, Stephen Jay 1941-2002 ..... **CLC 163**
See also AAYA 26; BEST 90:2; CA 77-80; 205; CANR 10, 27, 56, 75, 125; CPW; INT CANR-27; MTCW 1, 2; MTFW 2005
Gourmont, Remy(-Marie-Charles) de
1858-1915 .... **TCLC 17**
See also CA 109; 150; GFL 1789 to the Present; MTCW 2
Gournay, Marie le Jars de
See de Gournay, Marie le Jars
Govier, Katherine 1948- .... **CLC 51**
See also CA 101; CANR 18, 40, 128; CCA 1
Gower, John c. 1330-1408 .... **LC 76; PC 59**
See also BRW 1; DLB 146; RGEL 2
Goyen, (Charles) William
1915-1983 .... **CLC 5, 8, 14, 40**
See also AITN 2; CA 5-8R; 110; CANR 6, 71; CN 1, 2, 3; DLB 2, 218; DLBY 1983; EWL 3; INT CANR-6; MAL 5
Goytisolo, Juan 1931- .... **CLC 5, 10, 23, 133; HLC 1**
See also CA 85-88; CANR 32, 61, 131, 182; CWW 2; DAM MULT; DLB 322; EWL 3; GLL 2; HW 1, 2; MTCW 1, 2; MTFW 2005
Gozzano, Guido 1883-1916 .... **PC 10**
See also CA 154; DLB 114; EWL 3
Gozzi, (Conte) Carlo 1720-1806 ... **NCLC 23**
Grabbe, Christian Dietrich
1801-1836 .... **NCLC 2**
See also DLB 133; RGWL 2, 3
Grace, Patricia 1937- .... **CLC 56, 337; SSC 199**
See also CA 176; CANR 118; CN 4, 5, 6, 7; EWL 3; RGSF 2; SSFS 33
Grace, Patricia Frances
See Grace, Patricia
Gracian, Baltasar 1601-1658 ..... **LC 15, 160**
Gracian y Morales, Baltasar
See Gracian, Baltasar
Gracq, Julien 1910-2007 ... **CLC 11, 48, 259**
See also CA 122; 126; 267; CANR 141; CWW 2; DLB 83; GFL 1789 to the present
Grade, Chaim 1910-1982 .... **CLC 10**
See also CA 93-96; 107; DLB 333; EWL 3; RGHL
Grade, Khayim
See Grade, Chaim
Graduate of Oxford, A
See Ruskin, John
Grafton, Garth
See Duncan, Sara Jeannette
Grafton, Sue 1940- .... **CLC 163, 299**
See also AAYA 11, 49; BEST 90:3; CA 108; CANR 31, 55, 111, 134, 195; CMW 4; CPW; CSW; DA3; DAM POP; DLB 226; FW; MSW; MTFW 2005
Graham, John
See Phillips, David Graham
Graham, Jorie 1950- **CLC 48, 118, 352; PC 59**
See also AAYA 67; CA 111; CANR 63, 118, 205; CP 4, 5, 6, 7; CWP; DLB 120; EWL 3; MTFW 2005; PFS 10, 17; TCLE 1:1
Graham, R. B. Cunninghame
See Cunninghame Graham, Robert Bontine
Graham, Robert
See Haldeman, Joe
Graham, Robert Bontine Cunninghame
See Cunninghame Graham, Robert Bontine
Graham, Tom
See Lewis, Sinclair
Graham, W(illiam) S(ydney)
1918-1986 .... **CLC 29; PC 127**
See also BRWS 7; CA 73-76; 118; CP 1, 2, 3, 4; DLB 20; RGEL 2
Graham, Winston (Mawdsley)
1910-2003 .... **CLC 23**
See also CA 49-52; 218; CANR 2, 22, 45, 66; CMW 4; CN 1, 2, 3, 4, 5, 6, 7; DLB 77; RHW
Grahame, Kenneth 1859-1932 ... **TCLC 64, 136**
See also BYA 5; CA 108; 136; CANR 80; CLR 5, 135; CWRI 5; DA3; DAB; DLB 34, 141, 178; FANT; MAICYA 1, 2; MTCW 2; NFS 20; RGEL 2; SATA 100; TEA; WCH; YABC 1
Granger, Darius John
See Marlowe, Stephen
Granin, Daniil 1918- .... **CLC 59**
See also DLB 302
Grannec, Yannick 1969- .... **CLC 389**
Granovsky, Timofei Nikolaevich
1813-1855 .... **NCLC 75**
See also DLB 198
Grant, Anne MacVicar
1755-1838 .... **NCLC 302**
See also DLB 200
Grant, Skeeter
See Spiegelman, Art
Granville-Barker, Harley 1877-1946 ... **TCLC 2**
See also CA 104; 204; DAM DRAM; DLB 10; RGEL 2
Granzotto, Gianni
See Granzotto, Giovanni Battista
Granzotto, Giovanni Battista
1914-1985 .... **CLC 70**
See also CA 166
Grasemann, Ruth Barbara
See Rendell, Ruth
Grass, Gunter 1927- ..... **CLC 1, 2, 4, 6, 11, 15, 22, 32, 49, 88, 207; WLC 3**
See also BPFB 2; CA 13-16R; CANR 20, 75, 93, 133, 174, 229; CDWLB 2; CWW 2; DA; DA3; DAB; DAC; DAM MST, NOV; DLB 330; EW 13; EWL 3; MTCW 1, 2; MTFW 2005; RGHL; RGWL 2, 3; TWA
Grass, Gunter Wilhelm
See Grass, Gunter
Grass, Guenter
See Grass, Gunter
Gratton, Thomas
See Hulme, T(homas) E(rnest)
Grau, Shirley Ann 1929- ..... **CLC 4, 9, 146; SSC 15**
See also CA 89-92; CANR 22, 69; CN 1, 2, 3, 4, 5, 6, 7; CSW; DLB 2, 218; INT CA-89-92; CANR-22; MTCW 1
Gravel, Fern
See Hall, James Norman
Graver, Elizabeth 1964- .... **CLC 70**
See also CA 135; CANR 71, 129
Graves, Richard Perceval
1895-1985 .... **CLC 44**
See also CA 65-68; CANR 9, 26, 51
Graves, Robert 1895-1985 .... **CLC 1, 2, 6, 11, 39, 44, 45; PC 6**
See also BPFB 2; BRW 7; BYA 4; CA 5-8R; 117; CANR 5, 36; CDBLB 1914-1945; CN 1, 2, 3; CP 1, 2, 3, 4; DA3; DAB; DAC; DAM MST, POET; DLB 20, 100, 191; DLBD 18; DLBY 1985; EWL 3; LATS 1:1; MTCW 1, 2; MTFW 2005; NCFS 2; NFS 21; RGEL 2; RHW; SATA 45; TEA
Graves, Robert von Ranke
See Graves, Robert
Graves, Valerie
See Bradley, Marion Zimmer
Gray, Alasdair 1934- .... **CLC 41, 275, 388**
See also BRWS 9; CA 126; CANR 47, 69, 106, 140; CN 4, 5, 6, 7; DLB 194, 261, 319; HGG; INT CA-126; MTCW 1, 2; MTFW 2005; RGSF 2; SUFW 2
Gray, Amlin 1946- .... **CLC 29**
See also CA 138
Gray, Francine du Plessix
1930- .... **CLC 22, 153**
See also BEST 90:3; CA 61-64; CAAS 2; CANR 11, 33, 75, 81, 197; DAM NOV; INT CANR-11; MTCW 1, 2; MTFW 2005
Gray, John (Henry) 1866-1934 ..... **TCLC 19**
See also CA 119; 162; RGEL 2
Gray, John Lee
See Jakes, John
Gray, Simon 1936-2008 .... **CLC 9, 14, 36**
See also AITN 1; CA 21-24R; 275; CAAS 3; CANR 32, 69, 208; CBD; CD 5, 6; CN 1, 2, 3; DLB 13; EWL 3; MTCW 1; RGEL 2
Gray, Simon James Holliday
See Gray, Simon
Gray, Spalding 1941-2004 ...... **CLC 49, 112; DC 7**
See also AAYA 62; CA 128; 225; CAD; CANR 74, 138; CD 5, 6; CPW; DAM POP; MTCW 2; MTFW 2005
Gray, Thomas 1716-1771 ..... **LC 4, 40, 178; PC 2, 80; WLC 3**
See also BRW 3; CDBLB 1660-1789; DA; DA3; DAB; DAC; DAM MST; DLB 109; EXPP; PAB; PFS 9; RGEL 2; TEA; WP
Grayson, David
See Baker, Ray Stannard
Grayson, Richard (A.) 1951- .... **CLC 38**
See also CA 85-88, 210; CAAE 210; CANR 14, 31, 57; DLB 234
Greeley, Andrew M. 1928-2013 ...... **CLC 28**
See also BPFB 2; CA 5-8R; CAAS 7; CANR 7, 43, 69, 104, 136, 184; CMW 4; CPW; DA3; DAM POP; MTCW 1, 2; MTFW 2005
Green, Anna Katharine
1846-1935 .... **TCLC 63**
See also CA 112; 159; CMW 4; DLB 202, 221; MSW
Green, Brian
See Card, Orson Scott
Green, Hannah
See Greenberg, Joanne (Goldenberg)
Green, Hannah 1927(?)-1996 .... **CLC 3**
See also CA 73-76; CANR 59, 93; NFS 10
Green, Henry
See Yorke, Henry Vincent

Green, Julian
See Green, Julien

Green, Julien 1900-1998 .... **CLC 3, 11, 77**
See also CA 21-24R; 169; CANR 33, 87; CWW 2; DLB 4, 72; EWL 3; GFL 1789 to the Present; MTCW 2; MTFW 2005

Green, Julien Hartridge
See Green, Julien

Green, Paul (Eliot) 1894-1981 .... **CLC 25; DC 37**
See also AITN 1; CA 5-8R; 103; CAD; CANR 3; DAM DRAM; DLB 7, 9, 249; DLBY 1981; MAL 5; RGAL 4

Greenaway, Peter 1942- .... **CLC 159**
See also CA 127

Greenberg, Ivan 1908-1973 .... **CLC 24**
See also CA 85-88; DLB 137; MAL 5

Greenberg, Joanne (Goldenberg) 1932- .... **CLC 7, 30**
See also AAYA 12, 67; CA 5-8R; CANR 14, 32, 69; CN 6, 7; DLB 335; NFS 23; SATA 25; YAW

Greenberg, Richard 1959(?)- .... **CLC 57**
See also CA 138; CAD; CD 5, 6; DFS 24

Greenblatt, Stephen J. 1943- .. **CLC 70, 334**
See also CA 49-52; CANR 115; LNFS 1

Greenblatt, Stephen Jay
See Greenblatt, Stephen J.

Greene, Bette 1934- .... **CLC 30**
See also AAYA 7, 69; BYA 3; CA 53-56; CANR 4, 146; CLR 2, 140; CWRI 5; JRDA; LAIT 4; MAICYA 1, 2; NFS 10; SAAS 16; SATA 8, 102, 161; WYA; YAW

Greene, Gael .... **CLC 8**
See also CA 13-16R; CANR 10, 166

Greene, Graham 1904-1991 .... **CLC 1, 3, 6, 9, 14, 18, 27, 37, 70, 72, 125; DC 41; SSC 29, 121, 212; WLC 3**
See also AAYA 61; AITN 2; BPFB 2; BRWR 2; BRWS 1; BYA 3; CA 13-16R; 133; CANR 35, 61, 131; CBD; CDBLB 1945-1960; CMW 4; CN 1, 2, 3, 4; DA; DA3; DAB; DAC; DAM MST, NOV; DLB 13, 15, 77, 100, 162, 201, 204; DLBY 1991; EWL 3; MSW; MTCW 1, 2; MTFW 2005; NFS 16, 31, 36; RGEL 2; SATA 20; SSFS 14, 35; TEA; WLIT 4

Greene, Graham Henry
See Greene, Graham

Greene, Robert 1558-1592 ... **DC 53; LC 41, 185**
See also BRWS 8; DLB 62, 167; IDTP; RGEL 2; TEA

Greer, Germaine 1939- .... **CLC 131**
See also AITN 1; CA 81-84; CANR 33, 70, 115, 133, 190; FW; MTCW 1, 2; MTFW 2005

Greer, Richard
See Silverberg, Robert

Gregor, Arthur 1923- .... **CLC 9**
See also CA 25-28R; CAAS 10; CANR 11; CP 1, 2, 3, 4, 5, 6, 7; SATA 36

Gregor, Lee
See Pohl, Frederik

Gregory, Lady Isabella Augusta (Persse) 1852-1932 .... **TCLC 1, 176**
See also BRW 6; CA 104; 184; DLB 10; IDTP; RGEL 2

Gregory, J. Dennis
See Williams, John A(lfred)

Gregory of Nazianzus, St. 329-389 .... **CMLC 82**

Gregory of Nyssa c. 335-c. 394 ... **CMLC 126**

Gregory of Rimini 1300(?)-1358 **CMLC 109**
See also DLB 115

Gregory of Tours 538?-594 .... **CMLC 158**

Gregory the Great c. 540-604 ... **CMLC 124**

Grekova, I.
See Ventsel, Elena Sergeevna

Grekova, Irina
See Ventsel, Elena Sergeevna

Grendon, Stephen
See Derleth, August (William)

Grenville, Kate 1950- .... **CLC 61**
See also CA 118; CANR 53, 93, 156, 220; CN 7; DLB 325

Grenville, Pelham
See Wodehouse, P. G.

Greve, Felix Paul (Berthold Friedrich) 1879-1948 .... **TCLC 4, 248**
See also CA 104; 141, 175; CANR 79; DAC; DAM MST; DLB 92; RGEL 2; TCWW 1, 2

Greville, Fulke 1554-1628 .... **LC 79**
See also BRWS 11; DLB 62, 172; RGEL 2

Grey, Lady Jane 1537-1554 .... **LC 93**
See also DLB 132

Grey, Zane 1872-1939 .... **TCLC 6**
See also BPFB 2; CA 104; 132; CANR 210; DA3; DAM POP; DLB 9, 212; MTCW 1, 2; MTFW 2005; RGAL 4; TCWW 1, 2; TUS

Griboedov, Aleksandr Sergeevich 1795(?)-1829 .... **NCLC 129**
See also DLB 205; RGWL 2, 3

Grieg, (Johan) Nordahl (Brun) 1902-1943 .... **TCLC 10**
See also CA 107; 189; EWL 3

Grieve, C. M. 1892-1978 .... **CLC 2, 4, 11, 19, 63; PC 9, 122**
See also BRWS 12; CA 5-8R; 85-88; CANR 33, 107; CDBLB 1945-1960; CP 1, 2; DAM POET; DLB 20; EWL 3; MTCW 1; RGEL 2

Grieve, Christopher Murray
See Grieve, C. M.

Griffin, Gerald 1803-1840 .... **NCLC 7**
See also DLB 159; RGEL 2

Griffin, John Howard 1920-1980 ... **CLC 68**
See also AITN 1; CA 1-4R; 101; CANR 2

Griffin, Peter 1942- .... **CLC 39**
See also CA 136

Griffith, David Lewelyn Wark
See Griffith, D.W.

Griffith, D.W. 1875(?)-1948 .... **TCLC 68**
See also AAYA 78; CA 119; 150; CANR 80

Griffith, Lawrence
See Griffith, D.W.

Griffiths, Trevor 1935- .... **CLC 13, 52**
See also CA 97-100; CANR 45; CBD; CD 5, 6; DLB 13, 245

Griggs, Sutton (Elbert) 1872-1930 .... **TCLC 77**
See also CA 123; 186; DLB 50

Grigson, Geoffrey (Edward Harvey) 1905-1985 .... **CLC 7, 39**
See also CA 25-28R; 118; CANR 20, 33; CP 1, 2, 3, 4; DLB 27; MTCW 1, 2

Grile, Dod
See Bierce, Ambrose

Grillparzer, Franz 1791-1872 .... **DC 14; NCLC 1, 102, 245; SSC 37**
See also CDWLB 2; DLB 133; EW 5; RGWL 2, 3; TWA

Grimble, Reverend Charles James
See Eliot, T. S.

Grimke, Angelina Emily Weld
See Grimke, Angelina Weld

Grimke, Angelina Weld 1880-1958 .... **DC 38; HR 1:2**
See also BW 1; CA 124; DAM POET; DLB 50, 54; FW

Grimke, Charlotte L. Forten 1837(?)-1914 .... **BLC 1:2; TCLC 16**
See also BW 1; CA 117; 124; DAM MULT, POET; DLB 50, 239

Grimke, Charlotte Lottie Forten
See Grimke, Charlotte L. Forten

Grimm, Jacob Ludwig Karl 1785-1863 .. **NCLC 3, 77, 288; SSC 36, 88, 179**
See also CLR 112; DLB 90; MAICYA 1, 2; RGSF 2; RGWL 2, 3; SATA 22; WCH

Grimm, Wilhelm Karl 1786-1859 .. **NCLC 3, 77, 288; SSC 36, 88, 179**
See also CDWLB 2; CLR 112; DLB 90; MAICYA 1, 2; RGSF 2; RGWL 2, 3; SATA 22; WCH

Grimm and Grimm
See Grimm, Jacob Ludwig Karl; Grimm, Wilhelm Karl

Grimm Brothers
See Grimm, Jacob Ludwig Karl; Grimm, Wilhelm Karl

Grimmelshausen, Hans Jakob Christoffel von
See Grimmelshausen, Johann Jakob Christoffel von

Grimmelshausen, Johann Jakob Christoffel von 1621-1676 .... **LC 6, 209**
See also CDWLB 2; DLB 168; RGWL 2, 3

Grindel, Eugene 1895-1952 .... **PC 38; TCLC 7, 41**
See also CA 104; 193; EWL 3; GFL 1789 to the Present; LMFS 2; RGWL 2, 3

Grisham, John 1955- .... **CLC 84, 273**
See also AAYA 14, 47; BPFB 2; CA 138; CANR 47, 69, 114, 133; CMW 4; CN 6, 7; CPW; CSW; DA3; DAM POP; LNFS 1; MSW; MTCW 2; MTFW 2005

Grosseteste, Robert 1175(?)-1253 .... **CMLC 62, 172**
See also DLB 115

Grossman, David 1954- .... **CLC 67, 231**
See also CA 138; CANR 114, 175; CWW 2; DLB 299; EWL 3; RGHL; WLIT 6

Grossman, Vasilii Semenovich
See Grossman, Vasily

Grotius, Hugo 1583-1645 .... **LC 203**

Grossman, Vasily 1905-1964 .... **CLC 41**
See also CA 124; 130; DLB 272; MTCW 1; RGHL

Grossman, Vasily Semenovich
See Grossman, Vasily

Grove, Frederick Philip
See Greve, Felix Paul (Berthold Friedrich)

Grubb
See Crumb, R.

Grumbach, Doris 1918- ...... **CLC 13, 22, 64**
See also CA 5-8R; CAAS 2; CANR 9, 42, 70, 127; CN 6, 7; INT CANR-9; MTCW 2; MTFW 2005

Grumbler
See Twain, Mark

Grundtvig, Nikolai Frederik Severin 1783-1872 .... **NCLC 1, 158**
See also DLB 300

Grunge
See Crumb, R.

Grunwald, Lisa 1959- .... **CLC 44**
See also CA 120; CANR 148

Gryphius, Andreas 1616-1664 ... **LC 89, 223**
See also CDWLB 2; DLB 164; RGWL 2, 3

Guare, John 1938- .... **CLC 8, 14, 29, 67; DC 20**
See also CA 73-76; CAD; CANR 21, 69, 118; CD 5, 6; DAM DRAM; DFS 8, 13; DLB 7, 249; EWL 3; MAL 5; MTCW 1, 2; RGAL 4

Guarini, Battista 1538-1612 ... **DC 48; LC 102**
See also DLB 339

Gubar, Susan 1944- .... **CLC 145**
See also CA 108; CANR 45, 70, 139, 179; FW; MTCW 1; RGAL 4
Gubar, Susan David
See Gubar, Susan
Gudjonsson, Halldor Kiljan
1902-1998 .... **CLC 25**
See also CA 103; 164; CWW 2; DLB 293, 331; EW 12; EWL 3; RGWL 2, 3
Guedes, Vincente
See Pessoa, Fernando
Guenter, Erich
See Eich, Gunter
Guest, Barbara 1920-2006 .... **CLC 34; PC 55**
See also BG 1:2; CA 25-28R; 248; CANR 11, 44, 84; CP 1, 2, 3, 4, 5, 6, 7; CWP; DLB 5, 193
Guest, Edgar A(lbert)
1881-1959 .... **TCLC 95**
See also CA 112; 168
Guest, Judith 1936- .... **CLC 8, 30**
See also AAYA 7, 66; CA 77-80; CANR 15, 75, 138; DA3; DAM NOV, POP; EXPN; INT CANR-15; LAIT 5; MTCW 1, 2; MTFW 2005; NFS 1, 33
Guest, Judith Ann
See Guest, Judith
Guevara, Che 1928-1967 .. **CLC 87; HLC 1**
See also CA 127; 111; CANR 56; DAM MULT; HW 1
Guevara (Serna), Ernesto
See Guevara, Che
Guicciardini, Francesco 1483-1540 ... **LC 49**
Guido delle Colonne
c. 1215-c. 1290 .... **CMLC 90**
Guild, Nicholas M. 1944- .... **CLC 33**
See also CA 93-96
Guillemin, Jacques
See Sartre, Jean-Paul
Guillen y Alvarez, Jorge
See Guillen, Jorge
Guillevic, (Eugene) 1907-1997 .... **CLC 33**
See also CA 93-96; CWW 2
Guillen, Jorge 1893-1984 .... **CLC 11; HLCS 1; PC 35; TCLC 233**
See also CA 89-92; 112; DAM MULT, POET; DLB 108; EWL 3; HW 1; RGWL 2, 3
Guillen, Nicolas 1902-1989 .... **BLC 1:2; CLC 48, 79; HLC 1; PC 23**
See also BW 2; CA 116; 125; 129; CANR 84; DAM MST, MULT, POET; DLB 283; EWL 3; HW 1; LAW; RGWL 2, 3; WP
Guillen, Nicolas Cristobal
See Guillen, Nicolas
Guillois
See Desnos, Robert
Guillois, Valentin
See Desnos, Robert
Guimaraes Rosa, Joao
1908-1967 .... **CLC 23; HLCS 1**
See also CA 175; 89-92; DLB 113, 307; EWL 3; LAW; RGSF 2; RGWL 2, 3; WLIT 1
Guiney, Louise Imogen
1861-1920 .... **TCLC 41**
See also CA 160; DLB 54; RGAL 4
Guinizelli, Guido c. 1230-1276 .... **CMLC 49**
See also WLIT 7
Guinizzelli, Guido
See Guinizelli, Guido
Guma, Alex La
See La Guma, Alex
Gumilev, Nikolai (Stepanovich)
1886-1921 .... **TCLC 60**
See also CA 165; DLB 295; EWL 3
Gumilyov, Nikolay Stepanovich
See Gumilev, Nikolai (Stepanovich)
Gump, P.Q.
See Card, Orson Scott
Gunesekera, Romesh 1954- ..... **CLC 91, 336**
See also BRWS 10; CA 159; CANR 140, 172; CN 6, 7; DLB 267, 323
Gunn, Bill
See Gunn, William Harrison
Gunn, Thom 1929-2004 .... **CLC 3, 6, 18, 32, 81; PC 26**
See also BRWR 3; BRWS 4; CA 17-20R; 227; CANR 9, 33, 116; CDBLB 1960 to Present; CP 1, 2, 3, 4, 5, 6, 7; DAM POET; DLB 27; INT CANR-33; MTCW 1; PFS 9; RGEL 2
Gunn, William Harrison
1934(?)-1989 .... **CLC 5**
See also AITN 1; BW 1, 3; CA 13-16R; 128; CANR 12, 25, 76; DLB 38
Gunn Allen, Paula
See Allen, Paula Gunn
Gunnars, Kristjana 1948- .... **CLC 69**
See also CA 113; CCA 1; CP 6, 7; CWP; DLB 60
Gurdjieff, G(eorgei) I(vanovich)
1877(?)-1949 .... **TCLC 71**
See also CA 157
Gurganus, Allan 1947- .... **CLC 70**
See also BEST 90:1; CA 135; CANR 114; CN 6, 7; CPW; CSW; DAM POP; DLB 350; GLL 1
Gurnah, Abdulrazak 1948- .... **CLC 368**
See also CA 179; CANR 153; CN 7; EWL 3
Gurney, A. R.
See Gurney, A(lbert) R(amsdell), Jr.
Gurney, A(lbert) R(amsdell), Jr.
1930- .... **CLC 32, 50, 54**
See also AMWS 5; CA 77-80; CAD; CANR 32, 64, 121; CD 5, 6; DAM DRAM; DLB 266; EWL 3
Gurney, Ivor (Bertie) 1890-1937 ... **TCLC 33**
See also BRW 6; CA 167; DLBY 2002; PAB; RGEL 2
Gurney, Peter
See Gurney, A(lbert) R(amsdell), Jr.
Guro, Elena (Genrikhovna)
1877-1913 .... **TCLC 56**
See also DLB 295
Gustafson, James M(oody) 1925- ... **CLC 100**
See also CA 25-28R; CANR 37
Gustafson, Ralph (Barker)
1909-1995 .... **CLC 36**
See also CA 21-24R; CANR 8, 45, 84; CP 1, 2, 3, 4, 5, 6; DLB 88; RGEL 2
Gut, Gom
See Simenon, Georges
Guterson, David 1956- .... **CLC 91**
See also CA 132; CANR 73, 126, 194; CN 7; DLB 292; MTCW 2; MTFW 2005; NFS 13
Guthrie, A(lfred) B(ertram), Jr.
1901-1991 .... **CLC 23**
See also CA 57-60; 134; CANR 24; CN 1, 2, 3; DLB 6, 212; MAL 5; SATA 62; SATA-Obit 67; TCWW 1, 2
Guthrie, Isobel
See Grieve, C. M.
Gutierrez Najera, Manuel
1859-1895 .... **HLCS 2; NCLC 133**
See also DLB 290; LAW
Guy, Rosa 1925- .... **CLC 26**
See also AAYA 4, 37; BW 2; CA 17-20R; CANR 14, 34, 83; CLR 13, 137; DLB 33; DNFS 1; JRDA; MAICYA 1, 2; SATA 14, 62, 122; YAW
Guy, Rosa Cuthbert
See Guy, Rosa
Gwendolyn
See Bennett, (Enoch) Arnold
H. D.
See Doolittle, Hilda
H. de V.
See Buchan, John
Haavikko, Paavo Juhani 1931- ... **CLC 18, 34**
See also CA 106; CWW 2; EWL 3
Habbema, Koos
See Heijermans, Herman
Habermas, Jurgen
See Habermas, Juergen
Habermas, Juergen 1929- ..... **CLC 104, 345**
See also CA 109; CANR 85, 162; DLB 242
Hacker, Marilyn 1942- .... **CLC 5, 9, 23, 72, 91; PC 47**
See also CA 77-80; CANR 68, 129; CP 3, 4, 5, 6, 7; CWP; DAM POET; DLB 120, 282; FW; GLL 2; MAL 5; PFS 19
Hackleskinner, Fred
See Harwood, Gwen
Hadewijch of Antwerp
fl. 1250 .... **CMLC 61**
See also RGWL 3
Hadrian 76-138 .... **CMLC 52**
Haeckel, Ernst Heinrich (Philipp August)
1834-1919 .... **TCLC 83**
See also CA 157
Hafiz c. 1326-1389(?) .... **CMLC 34, 156; PC 116**
See also RGWL 2, 3; WLIT 6
Hagedorn, Jessica 1949- .... **CLC 185**
See also CA 139; CANR 69, 231; CWP; DLB 312; RGAL 4
Hagedorn, Jessica Tarahata
See Hagedorn, Jessica
Hagendoor, W. W.
See Harwood, Gwen
Haggard, H(enry) Rider
1856-1925 .... **TCLC 11**
See also AAYA 81; BRWS 3; BYA 4, 5; CA 108; 148; CANR 112; DLB 70, 156, 174, 178; FANT; LMFS 1; MTCW 2; NFS 40; RGEL 2; RHW; SATA 16; SCFW 1, 2; SFW 4; SUFW 1; WLIT 4
Hagiosy, L.
See Larbaud, Valery (Nicolas)
Hagiwara, Sakutaro 1886-1942 .... **PC 18; TCLC 60**
See also CA 154; EWL 3; RGWL 3
Hagiwara Sakutaro
See Hagiwara, Sakutaro
Haig, Fenil
See Ford, Ford Madox
Haig-Brown, Roderick (Langmere)
1908-1976 .... **CLC 21**
See also CA 5-8R; 69-72; CANR 4, 38, 83; CLR 31; CWRI 5; DLB 88; MAICYA 1, 2; SATA 12; TCWW 2
Haight, Rip
See Carpenter, John
Haij, Vera
See Jansson, Tove (Marika)
Hailey, Arthur 1920-2004 .... **CLC 5**
See also AITN 2; BEST 90:3; BPFB 2; CA 1-4R; 233; CANR 2, 36, 75; CCA 1; CN 1, 2, 3, 4, 5, 6, 7; CPW; DAM NOV, POP; DLB 88; DLBY 1982; MTCW 1, 2; MTFW 2005
Hailey, Elizabeth Forsythe 1938- ... **CLC 40**
See also CA 93-96, 188; CAAE 188; CAAS 1; CANR 15, 48; INT CANR-15
Haines, John 1924-2011 .... **CLC 58**
See also AMWS 12; CA 17-20R; CANR 13, 34; CP 1, 2, 3, 4, 5; CSW; DLB 5, 212; TCLE 1:1
Haines, John Meade
See Haines, John

Hakluyt, Richard 1552-1616 .... **LC 31**
See also DLB 136; RGEL 2

Haldeman, Joe 1943- .... **CLC 61**
See also AAYA 38; CA 53-56, 179; CAAE 179; CAAS 25; CANR 6, 70, 72, 130, 171, 224; DLB 8; INT CANR-6; SCFW 2; SFW 4

Haldeman, Joe William
See Haldeman, Joe

Hale, Janet Campbell 1947- .... **NNAL**
See also CA 49-52; CANR 45, 75; DAM MULT; DLB 175; MTCW 2; MTFW 2005

Hale, Sarah Josepha (Buell)
1788-1879 .... **NCLC 75**
See also DLB 1, 42, 73, 243

Haley, Alex 1921-1992 .... **BLC 1:2; CLC 8, 12, 76; TCLC 147**
See also AAYA 26; BPFB 2; BW 2, 3; CA 77-80; 136; CANR 61; CDALBS; CLR 192; CPW; CSW; DA; DA3; DAB; DAC; DAM MST, MULT, POP; DLB 38; LAIT 5; MTCW 1, 2; NFS 9

Haley, Alexander Murray Palmer
See Haley, Alex

Haliburton, Thomas Chandler
1796-1865 .... **NCLC 15, 149**
See also DLB 11, 99; RGEL 2; RGSF 2

Hall, Donald 1928- .... **CLC 1, 13, 37, 59, 151, 240; PC 70**
See also AAYA 63; CA 5-8R; CAAS 7; CANR 2, 44, 64, 106, 133, 196; CP 1, 2, 3, 4, 5, 6, 7; DAM POET; DLB 5, 342; MAL 5; MTCW 2; MTFW 2005; RGAL 4; SATA 23, 97

Hall, Donald Andrew, Jr.
See Hall, Donald

Hall, Frederic Sauser
See Sauser-Hall, Frederic

Hall, James
See Kuttner, Henry

Hall, James Norman 1887-1951 ... **TCLC 23**
See also CA 123; 173; LAIT 1; RHW 1; SATA 21

Hall, Joseph 1574-1656 .... **LC 91**
See also DLB 121, 151; RGEL 2

Hall, Marguerite Radclyffe
See Hall, Radclyffe

Hall, Radclyffe 1880-1943 .... **TCLC 12, 215**
See also BRWS 6; CA 110; 150; CANR 83; DLB 191; MTCW 2; MTFW 2005; RGEL 2; RHW

Hall, Rodney 1935- .... **CLC 51**
See also CA 109; CANR 69; CN 6, 7; CP 1, 2, 3, 4, 5, 6, 7; DLB 289

Hallam, Arthur Henry
1811-1833 .... **NCLC 110**
See also DLB 32

Halldor Laxness
See Gudjonsson, Halldor Kiljan

Halleck, Fitz-Greene 1790-1867 .... **NCLC 47**
See also DLB 3, 250; RGAL 4

Halliday, Michael
See Creasey, John

Halpern, Daniel 1945- .... **CLC 14**
See also CA 33-36R; CANR 93, 174; CP 3, 4, 5, 6, 7

Halevy, Elie 1870-1937 .... **TCLC 104**

Hamann, Johann Georg
1730-1788 .... **LC 198**
See also DLB 97

Hamburger, Michael 1924-2007 ... **CLC 5, 14**
See also CA 5-8R, 196; 261; CAAE 196; CAAS 4; CANR 2, 47; CP 1, 2, 3, 4, 5, 6, 7; DLB 27

Hamburger, Michael Peter Leopold
See Hamburger, Michael

Hamill, Pete 1935- .... **CLC 10, 261**
See also CA 25-28R; CANR 18, 71, 127, 180, 235

Hamill, William Peter
See Hamill, Pete

Hamilton, Alexander 1712-1756 ...... **LC 150**
See also DLB 31

Hamilton, Alexander 1755(?)-1804 ... **NCLC 49**
See also DLB 37

Hamilton, Clive
See Lewis, C. S.

Hamilton, Edmond 1904-1977 .... **CLC 1**
See also CA 1-4R; CANR 3, 84; DLB 8; SATA 118; SFW 4

Hamilton, Elizabeth
1756/58-1816 .... **NCLC 153, 309**
See also DLB 116, 158

Hamilton, Eugene (Jacob) Lee
See Lee-Hamilton, Eugene (Jacob)

Hamilton, Franklin
See Silverberg, Robert

Hamilton, Gail
See Corcoran, Barbara (Asenath)

Hamilton, (Robert) Ian
1938-2001 .... **CLC 191**
See also CA 106; 203; CANR 41, 67; CP 1, 2, 3, 4, 5, 6, 7; DLB 40, 155

Hamilton, Jane 1957- .... **CLC 179**
See also CA 147; CANR 85, 128, 214; CN 7; DLB 350; MTFW 2005

Hamilton, Mollie
See Kaye, M.M.

Hamilton, Patrick 1904-1962 .... **CLC 51**
See also BRWS 16; CA 176; 113; DLB 10, 191

Hamilton, Virginia 1936-2002 .... **CLC 26**
See also AAYA 2, 21; BW 2, 3; BYA 1, 2, 8; CA 25-28R; 206; CANR 20, 37, 73, 126; CLR 1, 11, 40, 127; DAM MULT; DLB 33, 52; DLBY 2001; INT CANR-20; JRDA; LAIT 5; MAICYA 1, 2; MAICYAS 1; MTCW 1, 2; MTFW 2005; SATA 4, 56, 79, 123; SATA-Obit 132; WYA; YAW

Hamilton, Virginia Esther
See Hamilton, Virginia

Hammett, Dashiell 1894-1961 ...... **CLC 3, 5, 10, 19, 47; SSC 17; TCLC 187**
See also AAYA 59; AITN 1; AMWS 4; BPFB 2; CA 81-84; CANR 42; CDALB 1929-1941; CMW 4; DA3; DLB 226, 280; DLBD 6; DLBY 1996; EWL 3; LAIT 3; MAL 5; MSW; MTCW 1, 2; MTFW 2005; NFS 21; RGAL 4; RGSF 2; TUS

Hammett, Samuel Dashiell
See Hammett, Dashiell

Hammon, Jupiter
1720(?)-1800(?) .... **BLC 1:2; NCLC 5; PC 16**
See also DAM MULT, POET; DLB 31, 50

Hammond, Keith
See Kuttner, Henry

Hamner, Earl (Henry), Jr. 1923- ..... **CLC 12**
See also AITN 2; CA 73-76; DLB 6

Hampton, Christopher 1946- .... **CLC 4**
See also CA 25-28R; CD 5, 6; DLB 13; MTCW 1

Hampton, Christopher James
See Hampton, Christopher

Hamsun, Knut
See Pedersen, Knut

Hamsund, Knut Pedersen
See Pedersen, Knut

Handke, Peter 1942- .... **CLC 5, 8, 10, 15, 38, 134; DC 17**
See also CA 77-80; CANR 33, 75, 104, 133, 180, 236; CWW 2; DAM DRAM, NOV; DLB 85, 124; EWL 3; MTCW 1, 2; MTFW 2005; TWA

Handler, Chelsea 1975(?)- .... **CLC 269**
See also CA 243; CANR 230

Handy, W(illiam) C(hristopher)
1873-1958 .... **TCLC 97**
See also BW 3; CA 121; 167

Haneke, Michael 1942- .... **CLC 283**

Hanif, Mohammed 1965- .... **CLC 299**
See also CA 283

Hanley, James 1901-1985 .... **CLC 3, 5, 8, 13**
See also BRWS 19; CA 73-76; 117; CANR 36; CBD; CN 1, 2, 3; DLB 191; EWL 3; MTCW 1; RGEL 2

Hannah, Barry 1942-2010 .... **CLC 23, 38, 90, 270, 318; SSC 94**
See also BPFB 2; CA 108; 110; CANR 43, 68, 113, 236; CN 4, 5, 6, 7; CSW; DLB 6, 234; INT CA-110; MTCW 1; RGSF 2

Hannon, Ezra
See Hunter, Evan

Hanrahan, Barbara 1939-1991 ... **TCLC 219**
See also CA 121; 127; CN 4, 5; DLB 289

Hansberry, Lorraine 1930-1965 ... **BLC 1:2, 2:2; CLC 17, 62; DC 2; TCLC 192**
See also AAYA 25; AFAW 1, 2; AMWS 4; BW 1, 3; CA 109; 25-28R; CABS 3; CAD; CANR 58; CDALB 1941-1968; CWD; DA; DA3; DAB; DAC; DAM DRAM, MST, MULT; DFS 2, 29; DLB 7, 38; EWL 3; FL 1:6; FW; LAIT 4; MAL 5; MTCW 1, 2; MTFW 2005; RGAL 4; TUS

Hansberry, Lorraine Vivian
See Hansberry, Lorraine

Hansen, Joseph 1923-2004 .... **CLC 38**
See also BPFB 2; CA 29-32R; 233; CAAS 17; CANR 16, 44, 66, 125; CMW 4; DLB 226; GLL 1; INT CANR-16

Hansen, Karen V. 1955- .... **CLC 65**
See also CA 149; CANR 102

Hansen, Martin A(lfred)
1909-1955 .... **TCLC 32**
See also CA 167; DLB 214; EWL 3

Hanson, Kenneth O. 1922- .... **CLC 13**
See also CA 53-56; CANR 7; CP 1, 2, 3, 4, 5

Hanson, Kenneth Ostlin
See Hanson, Kenneth O.

Han Yu 768-824 .... **CMLC 122**

Harbach, Chad .... **CLC 334**
See also CA 327

Hardwick, Elizabeth 1916-2007 ...... **CLC 13**
See also AMWS 3; CA 5-8R; 267; CANR 3, 32, 70, 100, 139; CN 4, 5, 6; CSW; DA3; DAM NOV; DLB 6; MBL; MTCW 1, 2; MTFW 2005; TCLE 1:1

Hardwick, Elizabeth Bruce
See Hardwick, Elizabeth

Hardy, Thomas 1840-1928 .... **PC 8, 92; SSC 2, 60, 113; TCLC 4, 10, 18, 32, 48, 53, 72, 143, 153, 229, 284; WLC 3**
See also AAYA 69; BRW 6; BRWC 1, 2; BRWR 1; CA 104; 123; CDBLB 1890-1914; DA; DA3; DAB; DAC; DAM MST, NOV, POET; DLB 18, 19, 135, 284; EWL 3; EXPN; EXPP; LAIT 2; MTCW 1, 2; MTFW 2005; NFS 3, 11, 15, 19, 30; PFS 3, 4, 18, 42; RGEL 2; RGSF 2; TEA; WLIT 4

Hare, David 1947- .... **CLC 29, 58, 136; DC 26**
See also BRWS 4; CA 97-100; CANR 39, 91; CBD; CD 5, 6; DFS 4, 7, 16; DLB 13, 310; MTCW 1; TEA

Harewood, John
See Van Druten, John (William)

Harford, Henry
See Hudson, W(illiam) H(enry)

Hargrave, Leonie
See Disch, Thomas M.

Hariri, Al- al-Qasim ibn 'Ali Abu Muhammad al-Basri
See al-Hariri, al-Qasim ibn 'Ali Abu Muhammad al-Basri

Harjo, Joy 1951- ... **CLC 83; NNAL; PC 27**
See also AMWS 12; CA 114; CANR 35, 67, 91, 129; CP 6, 7; CWP; DAM MULT; DLB 120, 175, 342; EWL 3; MTCW 2; MTFW 2005; PFS 15, 32, 44; RGAL 4

Harlan, Louis R. 1922-2010 .... **CLC 34**
See also CA 21-24R; CANR 25, 55, 80

Harlan, Louis Rudolph
See Harlan, Louis R.

Harlan, Louis Rudolph
See Harlan, Louis R.

Harling, Robert 1951(?)- .... **CLC 53**
See also CA 147

Harmon, William (Ruth) 1938- ...... **CLC 38**
See also CA 33-36R; CANR 14, 32, 35; SATA 65

Harper, Edith Alice Mary
See Wickham, Anna

Harper, F. E. W.
See Harper, Frances Ellen Watkins

Harper, Frances E. W.
See Harper, Frances Ellen Watkins

Harper, Frances E. Watkins
See Harper, Frances Ellen Watkins

Harper, Frances Ellen
See Harper, Frances Ellen Watkins

Harper, Frances Ellen Watkins
1825-1911 .... **BLC 1:2; PC 21; TCLC 14, 217**
See also AFAW 1, 2; BW 1, 3; CA 111; 125; CANR 79; DAM MULT, POET; DLB 50, 221; MBL; PFS 44; RGAL 4

Harper, Michael S. 1938- .... **BLC 2:2; CLC 7, 22; PC 130**
See also AFAW 2; BW 1; CA 33-36R, 224; CAAE 224; CANR 24, 108, 212; CP 2, 3, 4, 5, 6, 7; DLB 41; RGAL 4; TCLE 1:1

Harper, Michael Steven
See Harper, Michael S.

Harper, Mrs. F. E. W.
See Harper, Frances Ellen Watkins

Harpur, Charles 1813-1868 .... **NCLC 114**
See also DLB 230; RGEL 2

Harris, Christie
See Harris, Christie (Lucy) Irwin

Harris, Christie (Lucy) Irwin
1907-2002 .... **CLC 12**
See also CA 5-8R; CANR 6, 83; CLR 47; DLB 88; JRDA; MAICYA 1, 2; SAAS 10; SATA 6, 74; SATA-Essay 116

Harris, E. Lynn 1955-2009 .... **CLC 299**
See also CA 164; 288; CANR 111, 163, 206; MTFW 2005

Harris, Everett Lynn
See Harris, E. Lynn

Harris, Everette Lynn
See Harris, E. Lynn

Harris, Frank 1856-1931 .... **TCLC 24**
See also CA 109; 150; CANR 80; DLB 156, 197; RGEL 2

Harris, George Washington
1814-1869 .... **NCLC 23, 165**
See also DLB 3, 11, 248; RGAL 4

Harris, Joel Chandler 1848-1908 .... **SSC 19, 103; TCLC 2**
See also CA 104; 137; CANR 80; CLR 49, 128; DLB 11, 23, 42, 78, 91; LAIT 2; MAICYA 1, 2; RGSF 2; SATA 100; WCH; YABC 1

Harris, John (Wyndham Parkes Lucas) Beynon 1903-1969 .... **CLC 19**
See also BRWS 13; CA 102; 89-92; CANR 84; CLR 190; DLB 255; SATA 118; SCFW 1, 2; SFW 4

Harris, MacDonald
See Heiney, Donald (William)

Harris, Mark 1922-2007 .... **CLC 19**
See also CA 5-8R; 260; CAAS 3; CANR 2, 55, 83; CN 1, 2, 3, 4, 5, 6, 7; DLB 2; DLBY 1980

Harris, Norman .... **CLC 65**

Harris, (Theodore) Wilson 1921- ... **BLC 2:2; CLC 25, 159, 297**
See also BRWS 5; BW 2, 3; CA 65-68; CAAS 16; CANR 11, 27, 69, 114; CDWLB 3; CN 1, 2, 3, 4, 5, 6, 7; CP 1, 2, 3, 4, 5, 6, 7; DLB 117; EWL 3; MTCW 1; RGEL 2

Harris, Thomas 1940- .... **CLC 356**
See also AAYA 34; BPFB 2; CMTFW; CA 113; CANR 35, 73, 106; CMW 4; CPW; CSW; DAM POP; HGG; MTFW

Harrison, Barbara Grizzuti
1934-2002 .... **CLC 144**
See also CA 77-80; 205; CANR 15, 48; INT CANR-15

Harrison, Elizabeth (Allen) Cavanna
1909-2001 .... **CLC 12**
See also CA 9-12R; 200; CANR 6, 27, 85, 104, 121; JRDA; MAICYA 1; SAAS 4; SATA 1, 30; YAW

Harrison, Harry 1925- .... **CLC 42**
See also CA 1-4R; CANR 5, 21, 84, 225; DLB 8; SATA 4; SCFW 2; SFW 4

Harrison, Harry Max
See Harrison, Harry

Harrison, James
See Harrison, Jim

Harrison, James Thomas
See Harrison, Jim

Harrison, Jim 1937- .... **CLC 6, 14, 33, 66, 143, 348; SSC 19**
See also AMWS 8; CA 13-16R; CANR 8, 51, 79, 142, 198, 229; CN 5, 6; CP 1, 2, 3, 4, 5, 6; DLBY 1982; INT CANR-8; RGAL 4; TCWW 2; TUS

Harrison, Kathryn 1961- .... **CLC 70, 151**
See also CA 144; CANR 68, 122, 194

Harrison, Tony 1937- .... **CLC 43, 129; PC 168**
See also BRWS 5; CA 65-68; CANR 44, 98; CBD; CD 5, 6; CP 2, 3, 4, 5, 6, 7; DLB 40, 245; MTCW 1; RGEL 2

Harriss, Will(ard Irvin) 1922- .... **CLC 34**
See also CA 111

Hart, Ellis
See Ellison, Harlan

Hart, Josephine 1942-2011 .... **CLC 70**
See also CA 138; CANR 70, 149, 220; CPW; DAM POP

Hart, Moss 1904-1961 .... **CLC 66**
See also CA 109; 89-92; CANR 84; DAM DRAM; DFS 1; DLB 7, 266; RGAL 4

Harte, Bret 1836-1902 .... **SSC 8, 59, 207; TCLC 1, 25; WLC 3**
See also AMWS 2; CA 104; 140; CANR 80; CDALB 1865-1917; DA; DA3; DAC; DAM MST; DLB 12, 64, 74, 79, 186; EXPS; LAIT 2; RGAL 4; RGSF 2; SATA 26; SSFS 3; TUS

Harte, Francis Brett
See Harte, Bret

Hartley, L(eslie) P(oles)
1895-1972 .... **CLC 2, 22; SSC 125**
See also BRWS 7; CA 45-48; 37-40R; CANR 33; CN 1; DLB 15, 139; EWL 3; HGG; MTCW 1, 2; MTFW 2005; RGEL 2; RGSF 2; SUFW 1

Hartman, Geoffrey H. 1929- .... **CLC 27**
See also CA 117; 125; CANR 79, 214; DLB 67

Hartmann, Sadakichi
1869-1944 .... **TCLC 73**
See also CA 157; DLB 54

Hartmann von Aue
c. 1170-c. 1210 .... **CMLC 15, 131**
See also CDWLB 2; DLB 138; RGWL 2, 3

Hartog, Jan de
See de Hartog, Jan

Haruf, Kent 1943- .... **CLC 34**
See also AAYA 44; CA 149; CANR 91, 131

Harvey, Caroline
See Trollope, Joanna

Harvey, Gabriel 1550(?)-1631 .... **LC 88**
See also DLB 167, 213, 281

Harvey, Jack
See Rankin, Ian

Harwood, Gwen 1920-1995 .... **PC 160**
See also CA 97-100; CP 1, 2, 3, 4, 5, 6; DLB 289

Harwood, Ronald 1934- .... **CLC 32**
See also CA 1-4R; CANR 4, 55, 150; CBD; CD 5, 6; DAM DRAM, MST; DLB 13

Hasegawa Tatsunosuke
See Futabatei, Shimei

Hasek, Jaroslav 1883-1923 .... **SSC 69; TCLC 4, 261**
See also CA 104; 129; CDWLB 4; DLB 215; EW 9; EWL 3; MTCW 1, 2; RGSF 2; RGWL 2, 3

Hasek, Jaroslav Matej Frantisek
See Hasek, Jaroslav

Haslett, Adam 1970- .... **CLC 334**
See also CA 216; SSFS 24

Hass, Robert
1941- .... **CLC 18, 39, 99, 287; PC 16**
See also AMWS 6; CA 111; CANR 30, 50, 71, 187; CP 3, 4, 5, 6, 7; DLB 105, 206; EWL 3; MAL 5; MTFW 2005; PFS 37; RGAL 4; SATA 94; TCLE 1:1

Hassan, Ihab 1925- .... **CLC 365**
See also CA 5-8R; CAAS 12; CANR 3, 19, 41

Hassler, Jon 1933-2008 .... **CLC 263**
See also CA 73-76; 270; CANR 21, 80, 161; CN 6, 7; INT CANR-21; SATA 19; SATA-Obit 191

Hassler, Jon Francis
See Hassler, Jon

Hastings, Hudson
See Kuttner, Henry

Hastings, Selina 1945- .... **CLC 44**
See also CA 257; CANR 225

Hastings, Selina Shirley
See Hastings, Selina

Hastings, Lady Selina Shirley
See Hastings, Selina

Hastings, Victor
See Disch, Thomas M.

Hathorne, John 1641-1717 .... **LC 38**

Hatteras, Amelia
See Mencken, H. L.

Hatteras, Owen
See Mencken, H. L.; Nathan, George Jean

Hauff, Wilhelm 1802-1827 .... **NCLC 185**
See also CLR 155; DLB 90; SUFW 1

Hauptmann, Gerhart 1862-1946 ... **DC 34, 52; SSC 37; TCLC 4, 300**
See also CA 104; 153; CDWLB 2; DAM DRAM; DLB 66, 118, 330; EW 8; EWL 3; RGSF 2; RGWL 2, 3; TWA

Hauptmann, Gerhart Johann Robert
See Hauptmann, Gerhart

Havel, Vaclav 1936-2011 .... **CLC 25, 58, 65, 123, 314; DC 6**
See also CA 104; CANR 36, 63, 124, 175; CDWLB 4; CWW 2; DA3; DAM DRAM; DFS 10; DLB 232; EWL 3; LMFS 2; MTCW 1, 2; MTFW 2005; RGWL 3

Haviaras, Stratis
See Chaviaras, Strates

Hawes, Stephen 1475(?)-1529(?) .... **LC 17**
See also DLB 132; RGEL 2

Hawk, Alex
See Kelton, Elmer
Hawkes, John 1925-1998 ..... **CLC 1, 2, 3, 4, 7, 9, 14, 15, 27, 49**
See also BPFB 2; CA 1-4R; 167; CANR 2, 47, 64; CN 1, 2, 3, 4, 5, 6; DLB 2, 7, 227; DLBY 1980, 1998; EWL 3; MAL 5; MTCW 1, 2; MTFW 2005; RGAL 4
Hawking, S. W.
See Hawking, Stephen W.
Hawking, Stephen W. 1942- .... **CLC 63, 105**
See also AAYA 13; BEST 89:1; CA 126; 129; CANR 48, 115; CPW; DA3; MTCW 2; MTFW 2005
Hawking, Stephen William
See Hawking, Stephen W.
Hawkins, Anthony Hope
See Hope, Anthony
Hawthorne, Julian 1846-1934 .... **TCLC 25**
See also CA 165; HGG
Hawthorne, Nathaniel 1804-1864 .... **NCLC 2, 10, 17, 23, 39, 79, 95, 158, 171, 191, 226; SSC 3, 29, 39, 89, 130, 166, 176, 185, 190, 195, 214; WLC 3**
See also AAYA 18; AMW; AMWC 1; AMWR 1; BPFB 2; BYA 3; CDALB 1640-1865; CLR 103, 163; DA; DA3; DAB; DAC; DAM MST, NOV; DLB 1, 74, 183, 223, 269; EXPN; EXPS; GL 2; HGG; LAIT 1; NFS 1, 20; RGAL 4; RGSF 2; SSFS 1, 7, 11, 15, 30, 35; SUFW 1; TUS; WCH; YABC 2
Hawthorne, Sophia Peabody 1809-1871 .... **NCLC 150**
See also DLB 183, 239
Haxton, Josephine Ayres 1921-
See Douglas, Ellen
Hayaseca y Eizaguirre, Jorge
See Echegaray (y Eizaguirre), Jose (Maria Waldo)
Hayashi, Fumiko 1904-1951 .... **TCLC 27**
See also CA 161; DLB 180; EWL 3
Hayashi Fumiko
See Hayashi, Fumiko
Haycraft, Anna 1932-2005 .... **CLC 40**
See also CA 122; 237; CANR 90, 141; CN 4, 5, 6; DLB 194; MTCW 2; MTFW 2005
Haycraft, Anna Margaret
See Haycraft, Anna
Hayden, Robert
See Hayden, Robert Earl
Hayden, Robert E.
See Hayden, Robert Earl
Hayden, Robert Earl 1913-1980 ... **BLC 1:2; CLC 5, 9, 14, 37; PC 6, 123**
See also AFAW 1, 2; AMWS 2; BW 1, 3; CA 69-72; 97-100; CABS 2; CANR 24, 75, 82; CDALB 1941-1968; CP 1, 2, 3; DA; DAC; DAM MST, MULT, POET; DLB 5, 76; EWL 3; EXPP; MAL 5; MTCW 1, 2; PFS 1, 31; RGAL 4; SATA 19; SATA-Obit 26; WP
Haydon, Benjamin Robert 1786-1846 .... **NCLC 146**
See also DLB 110
Hayek, F(riedrich) A(ugust von) 1899-1992 .... **TCLC 109**
See also CA 93-96; 137; CANR 20; MTCW 1, 2
Hayford, J(oseph) E(phraim) Casely
See Casely-Hayford, J(oseph) E(phraim)
Hayley, William 1745-1820 .... **NCLC 286**
See also DLB 142
Hayman, Ronald 1932- .... **CLC 44**
See also CA 25-28R; CANR 18, 50, 88; CD 5, 6; DLB 155
Hayne, Paul Hamilton 1830-1886 .... **NCLC 94**
See also DLB 3, 64, 79, 248; RGAL 4
Haynes, Todd 1961- .... **CLC 313**
See also CA 220
Hays, Mary 1760-1843 .... **NCLC 114**
See also DLB 142, 158; RGEL 2
Haywood, Eliza (Fowler) 1693(?)-1756 .... **LC 1, 44, 177**
See also BRWS 12; DLB 39; RGEL 2
Hazlitt, William 1778-1830 ..... **NCLC 29, 82**
See also BRW 4; DLB 110, 158; RGEL 2; TEA
Hazzard, Shirley 1931- ... **CLC 18, 218, 325**
See also BRWS 19; CA 9-12R; CANR 4, 70, 127, 212; CN 1, 2, 3, 4, 5, 6, 7; DLB 289; DLBY 1982; MTCW 1
Hébert, Anne 1916-2000 ...... **CLC 4, 13, 29, 246; PC 126**
See also CA 85-88; 187; CANR 69, 126; CCA 1; CWP; CWW 2; DA3; DAC; DAM MST, POET; DLB 68; EWL 3; GFL 1789 to the Present; MTCW 1, 2; MTFW 2005; PFS 20
Head, Bessie 1937-1986 .... **BLC 1:2, 2:2; CLC 25, 67; SSC 52**
See also AFW; BW 2, 3; CA 29-32R; 119; CANR 25, 82; CDWLB 3; CN 1, 2, 3, 4; DA3; DAM MULT; DLB 117, 225; EWL 3; EXPS; FL 1:6; FW; MTCW 1, 2; MTFW 2005; NFS 31; RGSF 2; SSFS 5, 13, 30, 33; WLIT 2; WWE 1
Headley, Elizabeth
See Harrison, Elizabeth (Allen) Cavanna
Headon, (Nicky) Topper 1956(?)- ... **CLC 30**
Heaney, Seamus 1939-2013 .... **CLC 5, 7, 14, 25, 37, 74, 91, 171, 225, 309, 370; PC 18, 100; WLCS**
See also AAYA 61; BRWR 1; BRWS 2; CA 85-88; CANR 25, 48, 75, 91, 128, 184, 241; CDBLB 1960 to Present; CP 1, 2, 3, 4, 5, 6, 7; DA3; DAB; DAM POET; DLB 40, 330; DLBY 1995; EWL 3; EXPP; MTCW 1, 2; MTFW 2005; PAB; PFS 2, 5, 8, 17, 30, 41; RGEL 2; TEA; WLIT 4
Heaney, Seamus Justin
See Heaney, Seamus
Hearn, Lafcadio 1850-1904 .... **SSC 158; TCLC 9, 263**
See also AAYA 79; CA 105; 166; DLB 12, 78, 189; HGG; MAL 5; RGAL 4
Hearn, Patricio Lafcadio Tessima Carlos
See Hearn, Lafcadio
Hearne, Samuel 1745-1792 .... **LC 95**
See also DLB 99
Hearne, Vicki 1946-2001 .... **CLC 56**
See also CA 139; 201
Hearon, Shelby 1931- .... **CLC 63**
See also AITN 2; AMWS 8; CA 25-28R; CAAS 11; CANR 18, 48, 103, 146; CSW
Heat-Moon, William Least 1939- ... **CLC 29**
See also AAYA 9, 66; ANW; CA 115; 119; CANR 47, 89, 206; CPW; INT CA-119
Hebbel, Friedrich 1813-1863 .... **DC 21; NCLC 43, 287**
See also CDWLB 2; DAM DRAM; DLB 129; EW 6; RGWL 2, 3
Hebreo, Leon c. 1460-1520 .... **LC 193**
See also DLB 318
Hecht, Anthony (Evan) 1923-2004 .... **CLC 8, 13, 19; PC 70**
See also AMWS 10; CA 9-12R; 232; CANR 6, 108; CP 1, 2, 3, 4, 5, 6, 7; DAM POET; DLB 5, 169; EWL 3; PFS 6; WP
Hecht, Ben 1894-1964 ... **CLC 8; TCLC 101**
See also CA 85-88; DFS 9; DLB 7, 9, 25, 26, 28, 86; FANT; IDFW 3, 4; RGAL 4
Hedayat, Sadeq 1903-1951 .... **SSC 131; TCLC 21**
See also CA 120; EWL 3; RGSF 2
Hoeg, Peter 1957- .... **CLC 95, 156**
See also CA 151; CANR 75, 202; CMW 4; DA3; DLB 214; EWL 3; MTCW 2; MTFW 2005; NFS 17; RGWL 3; SSFS 18
Hegel, Georg Wilhelm Friedrich 1770-1831 .... **NCLC 46, 151**
See also DLB 90, 366; TWA
Heidegger, Martin 1889-1976 .... **CLC 24**
See also CA 81-84; 65-68; CANR 34; DLB 296; MTCW 1, 2; MTFW 2005
Heidenstam, (Carl Gustaf) Verner von 1859-1940 .... **TCLC 5**
See also CA 104; DLB 330
Heidi Louise
See Erdrich, Louise
Heifner, Jack 1946- .... **CLC 11**
See also CA 105; CANR 47
Heijermans, Herman 1864-1924 ... **TCLC 24**
See also CA 123; EWL 3
Heilbrun, Carolyn G. 1926-2003 ... **CLC 25, 173, 303**
See also BPFB 1; CA 45-48; 220; CANR 1, 28, 58, 94; CMW; CPW; DLB 306; FW; MSW
Heilbrun, Carolyn Gold
See Heilbrun, Carolyn G.
Hein, Christoph 1944- .... **CLC 154**
See also CA 158; CANR 108, 210; CDWLB 2; CWW 2; DLB 124
Heine, Heinrich 1797-1856 ...... **NCLC 4, 54, 147, 249; PC 25**
See also CDWLB 2; DLB 90; EW 5; PFS 37; RGWL 2, 3; TWA
Heinemann, Larry 1944- .... **CLC 50**
See also CA 110; CAAS 21; CANR 31, 81, 156; DLBD 9; INT CANR-31
Heinemann, Larry Curtiss
See Heinemann, Larry
Heiney, Donald (William) 1921-1993 .. **CLC 9**
See also CA 1-4R; 142; CANR 3, 58; FANT
Heinlein, Robert A. 1907-1988 .... **CLC 1, 3, 8, 14, 26, 55; SSC 55**
See also AAYA 17; BPFB 2; BYA 4, 13; CA 1-4R; 125; CANR 1, 20, 53; CLR 75; CN 1, 2, 3, 4; CPW; DA3; DAM POP; DLB 8; EXPS; JRDA; LAIT 5; LMFS 2; MAICYA 1, 2; MTCW 1, 2; MTFW 2005; NFS 40; RGAL 4; SATA 9, 69; SATA-Obit 56; SCFW 1, 2; SFW 4; SSFS 7; YAW
Heinrich von dem Tuerlin fl. c. 1230- .... **CMLC 133**
See also DLB 138
Heinse, Wilhelm 1746-1803 .... **NCLC 289**
See also DLB 94
Hejinian, Lyn 1941- .... **PC 108**
See also CA 153; CANR 85, 214; CP 4, 5, 6, 7; CWP; DLB 165; PFS 27; RGAL 4
Held, Peter
See Vance, Jack
Heldris of Cornwall fl. 13th cent. ... **CMLC 97**
Helforth, John
See Doolittle, Hilda
Heliodorus fl. 3rd cent. .... **CMLC 52**
See also WLIT 8
Helisenne de Crenne
See Crenne, Helisenne de
Hellenhofferu, Vojtech Kapristian z
See Hasek, Jaroslav
Heller, Joseph 1923-1999 .... **CLC 1, 3, 5, 8, 11, 36, 63; TCLC 131, 151; WLC 3**
See also AAYA 24; AITN 1; AMWS 4; BPFB 2; BYA 1; CA 5-8R; 187; CABS 1; CANR 8, 42, 66, 126; CN 1, 2, 3, 4, 5, 6; CPW; DA; DA3; DAB; DAC; DAM MST, NOV, POP; DLB 2, 28, 227; DLBY 1980, 2002; EWL 3; EXPN; INT CANR-8; LAIT 4; MAL 5; MTCW 1, 2; MTFW 2005; NFS 1; RGAL 4; TUS; YAW
Heller, Peter 1959- .... **CLC 354**
See also CA 276; CANR 256

Hellman, Lillian 1905-1984 .... **CLC 2, 4, 8, 14, 18, 34, 44, 52; DC 1; TCLC 119**
See also AAYA 47; AITN 1, 2; AMWS 1; CA 13-16R; 112; CAD; CANR 33; CWD; DA3; DAM DRAM; DFS 1, 3, 14; DLB 7, 228; DLBY 1984; EWL 3; FL 1:6; FW; LAIT 3; MAL 5; MBL; MTCW 1, 2; MTFW 2005; RGAL 4; TUS

Hellman, Lillian Florence
See Hellman, Lillian

Heloise c. 1095-c. 1164 .... **CMLC 122**

Helprin, Mark 1947- .... **CLC 7, 10, 22, 32**
See also CA 81-84; CANR 47, 64, 124, 222; CDALBS; CN 7; CPW; DA3; DAM NOV, POP; DLB 335; DLBY 1985; FANT; MAL 5; MTCW 1, 2; MTFW 2005; SSFS 25; SUFW 2

Helvetius, Claude-Adrien 1715-1771 ... **LC 26**
See also DLB 313

Helyar, Jane Penelope Josephine 1933- .... **CLC 17**
See also CA 21-24R; CANR 10, 26; CWRI 5; SAAS 2; SATA 5; SATA-Essay 138

Hemans, Felicia 1793-1835 .... **NCLC 29, 71, 291; PC 170**
See also DLB 96; RGEL 2

Hemingway, Ernest 1899-1961 .... **CLC 1, 3, 6, 8, 10, 13, 19, 30, 34, 39, 41, 44, 50, 61, 80; SSC 1, 25, 36, 40, 63, 117, 137, 168, 189, 190, 212; TCLC 115, 203; WLC 3**
See also AAYA 19; AMW; AMWC 1; AMWR 1; BPFB 2; BYA 2, 3, 13, 15; CA 77-80; CANR 34; CDALB 1917-1929; CLR 168, 201; DA; DA3; DAB; DAC; DAM MST, NOV; DLB 4, 9, 102, 210, 308, 316, 330; DLBD 1, 15, 16; DLBY 1981, 1987, 1996, 1998; EWL 3; EXPN; EXPS; LAIT 3, 4; LATS 1:1; MAL 5; MTCW 1, 2; MTFW 2005; NFS 1, 5, 6, 14; RGAL 4; RGSF 2; SSFS 17; TUS; WYA

Hemingway, Ernest Miller
See Hemingway, Ernest

Hempel, Amy 1951- .... **CLC 39**
See also AMWS 21; CA 118; 137; CANR 70, 166; DA3; DLB 218; EXPS; MTCW 2; MTFW 2005; SSFS 2

Henderson, Eleanor .... **CLC 334**
See also CA 324

Henderson, F. C.
See Mencken, H. L.

Henderson, Mary
See Mavor, Osborne Henry

Henderson, Smith 1972- .... **CLC 389**

Henderson, Sylvia
See Ashton-Warner, Sylvia (Constance)

Henderson, Zenna (Chlarson) 1917-1983 .... **SSC 29**
See also CA 1-4R; 133; CANR 1, 84; DLB 8; SATA 5; SFW 4

Henisch, Peter 1943- .... **CLC 385**
See also CA 177; DLB 85

Henkin, Joshua 1964- .... **CLC 119**
See also CA 161; CANR 186; DLB 350

Henley, Beth 1952- .... **CLC 23, 255; DC 6, 14**
See also AAYA 70; CA 107; CABS 3; CAD; CANR 32, 73, 140; CD 5, 6; CSW; CWD; DA3; DAM DRAM, MST; DFS 2, 21, 26; DLBY 1986; FW; MTCW 1, 2; MTFW 2005

Henley, Elizabeth Becker
See Henley, Beth

Henley, William Ernest 1849-1903 .... **PC 127; TCLC 8**
See also CA 105; 234; DLB 19; PFS 43; RGEL 2

Hennissart, Martha 1929- .... **CLC 2**
See also BPFB 2; CA 85-88; CANR 64; CMW 4; DLB 306

Henry VIII 1491-1547 .... **LC 10**
See also DLB 132

Henry, O. 1862-1910 .... **SSC 5, 49, 117; TCLC 1, 19; WLC 3**
See also AAYA 41; AMWS 2; CA 104; 131; CDALB 1865-1917; DA; DA3; DAB; DAC; DAM MST; DLB 12, 78, 79; EXPS; MAL 5; MTCW 1, 2; MTFW 2005; RGAL 4; RGSF 2; SSFS 2, 18, 27, 31; TCWW 1, 2; TUS; YABC 2

Henry, Oliver
See Henry, O.

Henry, Patrick 1736-1799 .... **LC 25, 225**
See also LAIT 1

Henryson, Robert 1430(?)-1506(?) .... **LC 20, 110; PC 65**
See also BRWS 7; DLB 146; RGEL 2

Henschke, Alfred
See Klabund

Henson, Lance 1944- .... **NNAL**
See also CA 146; DLB 175

Hentoff, Nat(han Irving) 1925- ...... **CLC 26**
See also AAYA 4, 42; BYA 6; CA 1-4R; CAAS 6; CANR 5, 25, 77, 114; CLR 1, 52; DLB 345; INT CANR-25; JRDA; MAICYA 1, 2; SATA 42, 69, 133; SATA-Brief 27; WYA; YAW

Hentz, Caroline Lee 1800-1856 .... **NCLC 281**
See also DLB 3, 248

Heppenstall, (John) Rayner 1911-1981 .... **CLC 10**
See also CA 1-4R; 103; CANR 29; CN 1, 2; CP 1, 2, 3; EWL 3

Heraclitus c. 540B.C.-c. 450B.C. ... **CMLC 22**
See also DLB 176

Herber, William
See Everson, William

Herbert, Edward 1583-1648 .... **LC 177**
See also DLB 121, 151, 252; RGEL 2

Herbert, Frank 1920-1986 .... **CLC 12, 23, 35, 44, 85**
See also AAYA 21; BPFB 2; BYA 4, 14; CA 53-56; 118; CANR 5, 43; CDALBS; CPW; DAM POP; DLB 8; INT CANR-5; LAIT 5; MTCW 1, 2; MTFW 2005; NFS 17, 31; SATA 9, 37; SATA-Obit 47; SCFW 1, 2; SFW 4; YAW

Herbert, George 1593-1633 ...... **LC 24, 121; PC 4, 145**
See also BRW 2; BRWR 2; CDBLB Before 1660; DAB; DAM POET; DLB 126; EXPP; PFS 25, 43; RGEL 2; TEA; WP

Herbert, Zbigniew 1924-1998 .... **CLC 9, 43; PC 50; TCLC 168**
See also CA 89-92; 169; CANR 36, 74, 177; CDWLB 4; CWW 2; DAM POET; DLB 232; EWL 3; MTCW 1; PFS 22

Herbert of Cherbury, Lord
See Herbert, Edward

Herbst, Josephine (Frey) 1897-1969 .... **CLC 34; TCLC 243**
See also CA 5-8R; 25-28R; DLB 9

Herder, Johann Gottfried von 1744-1803 .... **NCLC 8, 186**
See also DLB 97; EW 4; TWA

Heredia, Jose Maria 1803-1839 ..... **HLCS 2; NCLC 209**
See also LAW

Hergesheimer, Joseph 1880-1954 ... **TCLC 11**
See also CA 109; 194; DLB 102, 9; RGAL 4

Herlihy, James Leo 1927-1993 .... **CLC 6**
See also CA 1-4R; 143; CAD; CANR 2; CN 1, 2, 3, 4, 5

Herman, William
See Bierce, Ambrose

Hermogenes fl. c. 175 .... **CMLC 6**

Hernandez, Felisberto 1902-1964 ... **SSC 152**
See also CA 213; EWL 3; LAWS 1

Hernandez, Gilbert 1957- .... **CLC 378**
See also CA 37-40R, 171, 224; CANR 134, 211, 221, 268

Hernandez, Jaime 1959- .... **CLC 378**
See also CA 37-40R, 171, 224; CANR 134, 211, 221, 268

Hernandez, Jose 1834-1886 .... **NCLC 17, 269; PC 141**
See also LAW; RGWL 2, 3; WLIT 1

Hernandez, Mario 1953- .... **CLC 378**
See also CA 37-40R, 171, 224; CANR 134, 211, 221, 268

Herodotus c. 484B.C.-c. 420B.C. .... **CMLC 17, 163**
See also AW 1; CDWLB 1; DLB 176; RGWL 2, 3; TWA; WLIT 8

Herr, Michael 1940(?)- .... **CLC 231**
See also CA 89-92; CANR 68, 142; DLB 185; MTCW 1

Herrick, Robert 1591-1674 .... **LC 13, 145; PC 9, 138**
See also BRW 2; BRWC 2; DA; DAB; DAC; DAM MST, POP; DLB 126; EXPP; PFS 13, 29, 39; RGAL 4; RGEL 2; TEA; WP

Herring, Guilles
See Somerville, Edith Oenone

Herriot, James 1916-1995 .... **CLC 12**
See also AAYA 1, 54; BPFB 2; CA 77-80; 148; CANR 40; CLR 80; CPW; DAM POP; LAIT 3; MAICYA 2; MAICYAS 1; MTCW 2; SATA 86, 135; SATA-Brief 44; TEA; YAW

Herris, Violet
See Hunt, Violet

Herrmann, Dorothy 1941- .... **CLC 44**
See also CA 107

Herrmann, Taffy
See Herrmann, Dorothy

Hersey, John 1914-1993 .... **CLC 1, 2, 7, 9, 40, 81, 97**
See also AAYA 29; BPFB 2; CA 17-20R; 140; CANR 33; CDALBS; CN 1, 2, 3, 4, 5; CPW; DAM POP; DLB 6, 185, 278, 299, 364; MAL 5; MTCW 1, 2; MTFW 2005; NFS 41; RGHL; SATA 25; SATA-Obit 76; TUS

Hersey, John Richard
See Hersey, John

Hervent, Maurice
See Grindel, Eugene

Herzen, Aleksandr Ivanovich 1812-1870 .... **NCLC 10, 61**
See also DLB 277

Herzen, Alexander
See Herzen, Aleksandr Ivanovich

Herzl, Theodor 1860-1904 .... **TCLC 36**
See also CA 168

Herzog, Werner 1942- .... **CLC 16, 236**
See also AAYA 85; CA 89-92; CANR 215

Hesiod fl. 8th cent. B.C. .... **CMLC 5, 102**
See also AW 1; DLB 176; RGWL 2, 3; WLIT 8

Hesse, Hermann 1877-1962 ..... **CLC 1, 2, 3, 6, 11, 17, 25, 69; SSC 9, 49; TCLC 148, 196; WLC 3**
See also AAYA 43; BPFB 2; CA 17-18; CAP 2; CDWLB 2; DA; DA3; DAB; DAC; DAM MST, NOV; DLB 66, 330; EW 9; EWL 3; EXPN; LAIT 1; MTCW 1, 2; MTFW 2005; NFS 6, 15, 24; RGWL 2, 3; SATA 50; TWA

Hewes, Cady
See De Voto, Bernard (Augustine)

Heyen, William 1940- .... **CLC 13, 18**
See also CA 33-36R, 220; CAAE 220; CAAS 9; CANR 98, 188; CP 3, 4, 5, 6, 7; DLB 5; RGHL

Heyerdahl, Thor 1914-2002 .... **CLC 26**
See also CA 5-8R; 207; CANR 5, 22, 66, 73; LAIT 4; MTCW 1, 2; MTFW 2005; SATA 2, 52
Heym, Georg (Theodor Franz Arthur) 1887-1912 .... **TCLC 9**
See also CA 106; 181
Heym, Stefan 1913-2001 .... **CLC 41**
See also CA 9-12R; 203; CANR 4; CWW 2; DLB 69; EWL 3
Heyse, Paul (Johann Ludwig von) 1830-1914 .... **TCLC 8**
See also CA 104; 209; DLB 129, 330
Heyward, (Edwin) DuBose 1885-1940 ... **HR 1:2; TCLC 59**
See also CA 108; 157; DLB 7, 9, 45, 249; MAL 5; SATA 21
Heywood, John 1497(?)-1580(?) .... **LC 65**
See also DLB 136; RGEL 2
Heywood, Thomas 1573(?)-1641 .... **DC 29; LC 111**
See also DAM DRAM; DLB 62; LMFS 1; RGEL 2; TEA
Hiaasen, Carl 1953- .... **CLC 238**
See also CA 105; CANR 22, 45, 65, 113, 133, 168; CMW 4; CPW; CSW; DA3; DLB 292; LNFS 2, 3; MTCW 2; MTFW 2005; SATA 208
Hibbert, Eleanor Alice Burford 1906-1993 .... **CLC 7**
See also BEST 90:4; BPFB 2; CA 17-20R; 140; CANR 9, 28, 59; CMW 4; CPW; DAM POP; MTCW 2; MTFW 2005; RHW; SATA 2; SATA-Obit 74
Hichens, Robert (Smythe) 1864-1950 .... **TCLC 64**
See also CA 162; DLB 153; HGG; RHW; SUFW
Higgins, Aidan 1927- .... **SSC 68**
See also CA 9-12R; CANR 70, 115, 148; CN 1, 2, 3, 4, 5, 6, 7; DLB 14
Higgins, George V(incent) 1939-1999 .... **CLC 4, 7, 10, 18**
See also BPFB 2; CA 77-80; 186; CAAS 5; CANR 17, 51, 89, 96; CMW 4; CN 2, 3, 4, 5, 6; DLB 2; DLBY 1981, 1998; INT CANR-17; MSW; MTCW 1
Higginson, Thomas Wentworth 1823-1911 .... **TCLC 36**
See also CA 162; DLB 1, 64, 243
Higgonet, Margaret .... **CLC 65**
Highet, Helen
See MacInnes, Helen (Clark)
Highsmith, Mary Patricia
See Highsmith, Patricia
Highsmith, Patricia 1921-1995 ..... **CLC 2, 4, 14, 42, 102**
See also AAYA 48; BRWS 5; CA 1-4R; 147; CANR 1, 20, 48, 62, 108; CMW 4; CN 1, 2, 3, 4, 5; CPW; DA3; DAM NOV, POP; DLB 306; GLL 1; MSW; MTCW 1, 2; MTFW 2005; NFS 27; SSFS 25
Highwater, Jamake (Mamake) 1942(?)-2001 .... **CLC 12**
See also AAYA 7, 69; BPFB 2; BYA 4; CA 65-68; 199; CAAS 7; CANR 10, 34, 84; CLR 17; CWRI 5; DLB 52; DLBY 1985; JRDA; MAICYA 1, 2; SATA 32, 69; SATA-Brief 30
Highway, Tomson 1951- .... **CLC 92, 333; DC 33; NNAL**
See also CA 151; CANR 75; CCA 1; CD 5, 6; CN 7; DAC; DAM MULT; DFS 2; DLB 334; MTCW 2
Hijuelos, Oscar 1951-2013 ... **CLC 65; HLC 1**
See also AAYA 25; AMWS 8; BEST 90:1; CA 123; CANR 50, 75, 125, 205, 239; CPW; DA3; DAM MULT, POP; DLB 145; HW 1, 2; LLW; MAL 5; MTCW 2; MTFW 2005; NFS 17; RGAL 4; WLIT 1
Hikmet, Nazim 1902-1963 .... **CLC 40**
See also CA 141; 93-96; EWL 3; PFS 38, 41; WLIT 6
Hildegard von Bingen 1098-1179 .... **CMLC 20, 118**
See also DLB 148
Hildesheimer, Wolfgang 1916-1991 .... **CLC 49**
See also CA 101; 135; DLB 69, 124; EWL 3; RGHL
Hill, Aaron 1685-1750 .... **LC 148**
See also DLB 84; RGEL 2
Hill, Geoffrey 1932- .... **CLC 5, 8, 18, 45, 251; PC 125**
See also BRWR 3; BRWS 5; CA 81-84; CANR 21, 89; CDBLB 1960 to Present; CP 1, 2, 3, 4, 5, 6, 7; DAM POET; DLB 40; EWL 3; MTCW 1; RGEL 2; RGHL
Hill, George Roy 1921-2002 .... **CLC 26**
See also CA 110; 122; 213
Hill, John
See Koontz, Dean
Hill, Susan 1942- .... **CLC 4, 113**
See also BRWS 14; CA 33-36R; CANR 29, 69, 129, 172, 201; CN 2, 3, 4, 5, 6, 7; DAB; DAM MST, NOV; DLB 14, 139; HGG; MTCW 1; RHW; SATA 183
Hill, Susan Elizabeth
See Hill, Susan
Hillard, Asa G. III .... **CLC 70**
Hillerman, Anthony Grove
See Hillerman, Tony
Hillerman, Tony 1925-2008 ..... **CLC 62, 170**
See also AAYA 40; BEST 89:1; BPFB 2; CA 29-32R; 278; CANR 21, 42, 65, 97, 134; CMW 4; CPW; DA3; DAM POP; DLB 206, 306; MAL 5; MSW; MTCW 2; MTFW 2005; RGAL 4; SATA 6; SATA-Obit 198; TCWW 2; YAW
Hillesum, Etty 1914-1943 .... **TCLC 49**
See also CA 137; RGHL
Hilliard, Noel (Harvey) 1929-1996 ... **CLC 15**
See also CA 9-12R; CANR 7, 69; CN 1, 2, 3, 4, 5, 6
Hillis, Rick 1956- .... **CLC 66**
See also CA 134
Hilton, James 1900-1954 .... **TCLC 21**
See also AAYA 76; CA 108; 169; DLB 34, 77; FANT; SATA 34
Hilton, Walter 1343-1396(?) ... **CMLC 58, 141**
See also DLB 146; RGEL 2
Himes, Chester (Bomar) 1909-1984 .... **BLC 1:2; CLC 2, 4, 7, 18, 58, 108; TCLC 139**
See also AFAW 2; AMWS 16; BPFB 2; BW 2; CA 25-28R; 114; CANR 22, 89; CMW 4; CN 1, 2, 3; DAM MULT; DLB 2, 76, 143, 226; EWL 3; MAL 5; MSW; MTCW 1, 2; MTFW 2005; RGAL 4
Himmelfarb, Gertrude 1922- .... **CLC 202**
See also CA 49-52; CANR 28, 66, 102, 166
Hinde, Thomas 1926- .... **CLC 6, 11**
See also CA 5-8R; CN 1, 2, 3, 4, 5, 6; EWL 3
Hine, (William) Daryl 1936- .... **CLC 15**
See also CA 1-4R; CAAS 15; CANR 1, 20; CP 1, 2, 3, 4, 5, 6, 7; DLB 60
Hinkson, Katharine Tynan
See Tynan, Katharine
Hinojosa, Rolando 1929- .... **HLC 1**
See also CA 131; CAAS 16; CANR 62; DAM MULT; DLB 82; EWL 3; HW 1, 2; LLW; MTCW 2; MTFW 2005; RGAL 4
Hinton, S. E. 1950- .... **CLC 30, 111**
See also AAYA 2, 33; BPFB 2; BYA 2, 3; CA 81-84; CANR 32, 62, 92, 133; CDALBS; CLR 3, 23; CPW; DA; DA3; DAB; DAC; DAM MST, NOV; JRDA; LAIT 5; MAICYA 1, 2; MTCW 1, 2; MTFW 2005; NFS 5, 9, 15, 16, 35; SATA 19, 58, 115, 160; WYA; YAW
Hinton, Susan Eloise
See Hinton, S. E.
Hippius, Zinaida
See Gippius, Zinaida
Hiraoka, Kimitake 1925-1970 ...... **CLC 2, 4, 6, 9, 27; DC 1; SSC 4; TCLC 161; WLC 4**
See Mishima, Yukio
See also AAYA 50; BPFB 2; CA 97-100; 29-32R; DA3; DAM DRAM; DLB 182; EWL 3; GLL 1; MJW; MTCW 1, 2; RGSF 2; RGWL 2, 3; SSFS 5, 12
Hirsch, E.D., Jr. 1928- .... **CLC 79**
See also CA 25-28R; CANR 27, 51, 146, 181; DLB 67; INT CANR-27; MTCW 1
Hirsch, Edward 1950- .... **CLC 31, 50**
See also CA 104; CANR 20, 42, 102, 167, 229; CP 6, 7; DLB 120; PFS 22
Hirsch, Eric Donald, Jr.
See Hirsch, E.D., Jr.
Hitchcock, Alfred (Joseph) 1899-1980 .... **CLC 16**
See also AAYA 22; CA 159; 97-100; SATA 27; SATA-Obit 24
Hitchens, Christopher 1949-2011 ... **CLC 157**
See also CA 152; CANR 89, 155, 191
Hitchens, Christopher Eric
See Hitchens, Christopher
Hitler, Adolf 1889-1945 .... **TCLC 53**
See also CA 117; 147
Holderlin, (Johann Christian) Friedrich 1770-1843 ... **NCLC 16, 187, 263; PC 4**
See also CDWLB 2; DLB 90; EW 5; RGWL 2, 3
Hoagland, Edward (Morley) 1932- .... **CLC 28**
See also ANW; CA 1-4R; CANR 2, 31, 57, 107; CN 1, 2, 3, 4, 5, 6, 7; DLB 6; SATA 51; TCWW 2
Hoban, Russell 1925-2011 .... **CLC 7, 25**
See also BPFB 2; CA 5-8R; CANR 23, 37, 66, 114, 138, 218; CLR 3, 69, 139; CN 4, 5, 6, 7; CWRI 5; DAM NOV; DLB 52; FANT; MAICYA 1, 2; MTCW 1, 2; MTFW 2005; SATA 1, 40, 78, 136; SFW 4; SUFW 2; TCLE 1:1
Hoban, Russell Conwell
See Hoban, Russell
Hobbes, Thomas 1588-1679 .... **LC 36, 142, 199**
See also DLB 151, 252, 281; RGEL 2
Hobbs, Perry
See Blackmur, R(ichard) P(almer)
Hobson, Laura Z(ametkin) 1900-1986 .... **CLC 7, 25**
See also BPFB 2; CA 17-20R; 118; CANR 55; CN 1, 2, 3, 4; DLB 28; SATA 52
Hoccleve, Thomas c. 1368-c. 1437 ... **LC 75; PC 146**
See also DLB 146; RGEL 2
Hoch, Edward D. 1930-2008 .... **SSC 119**
See also CA 29-32R; CANR 11, 27, 51, 97; CMW 4; DLB 306; SFW 4
Hoch, Edward Dentinger
See Hoch, Edward D.
Hochhuth, Rolf 1931- .... **CLC 4, 11, 18**
See also CA 5-8R; CANR 33, 75, 136; CWW 2; DAM DRAM; DLB 124; EWL 3; MTCW 1, 2; MTFW 2005; RGHL
Hochman, Sandra 1936- .... **CLC 3, 8**
See also CA 5-8R; CP 1, 2, 3, 4, 5; DLB 5
Hochwaelder, Fritz 1911-1986 .... **CLC 36**
See also CA 29-32R; 120; CANR 42; DAM DRAM; EWL 3; MTCW 1; RGWL 2, 3
Hochwalder, Fritz
See Hochwaelder, Fritz

Hocking, Mary 1921- .... **CLC 13**
See also CA 101; CANR 18, 40
Hocking, Mary Eunice
See Hocking, Mary
Hodge, Merle 1944- .... **BLC 2:2**
See also EWL 3
Hodgins, Jack 1938- .... **CLC 23; SSC 132**
See also CA 93-96; CN 4, 5, 6, 7; DLB 60
Hodgson, William Hope
1877(?)-1918 .... **TCLC 13**
See also CA 111; 164; CMW 4; DLB 70, 153, 156, 178; HGG; MTCW 2; SFW 4; SUFW 1
Hoeg, Peter
See Hoeg, Peter
Hoffman, Alice 1952- .... **CLC 51**
See also AAYA 37; AMWS 10; CA 77-80; CANR 34, 66, 100, 138, 170, 237; CN 4, 5, 6, 7; CPW; DAM NOV; DLB 292; MAL 5; MTCW 1, 2; MTFW 2005; TCLE 1:1
Hoffman, Daniel (Gerard)
1923- .... **CLC 6, 13, 23**
See also CA 1-4R; CANR 4, 142; CP 1, 2, 3, 4, 5, 6, 7; DLB 5; TCLE 1:1
Hoffman, Eva 1945- .... **CLC 182**
See also AMWS 16; CA 132; CANR 146, 209
Hoffman, Stanley 1944- .... **CLC 5**
See also CA 77-80
Hoffman, William 1925-2009 .... **CLC 141**
See also AMWS 18; CA 21-24R; CANR 9, 103; CSW; DLB 234; TCLE 1:1
Hoffman, William M.
See Hoffman, William M(oses)
Hoffman, William M(oses) 1939- ... **CLC 40**
See also CA 57-60; CAD; CANR 11, 71; CD 5, 6
Hoffmann, E(rnst) T(heodor) A(madeus)
1776-1822 ... **NCLC 2, 183; SSC 13, 92**
See also CDWLB 2; CLR 133; DLB 90; EW 5; GL 2; RGSF 2; RGWL 2, 3; SATA 27; SUFW 1; WCH
Hofmann, Gert 1931-1993 .... **CLC 54**
See also CA 128; CANR 145; EWL 3; RGHL
Hofmannsthal, Hugo von
1874-1929 .... **DC 4; TCLC 11**
See also CA 106; 153; CDWLB 2; DAM DRAM; DFS 17; DLB 81, 118; EW 9; EWL 3; RGWL 2, 3
Hoffmannswaldau, Christian Hoffmann von
1616-1679 .... **LC 237**
See also DLB 168
Hogan, Linda 1947- .... **CLC 73, 290; NNAL; PC 35**
See also AMWS 4; ANW; BYA 12; CA 120, 226; CAAE 226; CANR 45, 73, 129, 196; CWP; DAM MULT; DLB 175; SATA 132; TCWW 2
Hogarth, Charles
See Creasey, John
Hogarth, Emmett
See Polonsky, Abraham (Lincoln)
Hogarth, William 1697-1764 .... **LC 112**
See also AAYA 56
Hogg, James 1770-1835 .... **NCLC 4, 109, 260; SSC 130**
See also BRWS 10; DLB 93, 116, 159; GL 2; HGG; RGEL 2; SUFW 1
Holbach, Paul-Henri Thiry 1723-1789 .. **LC 14**
See also DLB 313
Holberg, Ludvig 1684-1754 .... **LC 6, 208**
See also DLB 300; RGWL 2, 3
Holbrook, John
See Vance, Jack
Holcroft, Thomas 1745-1809 .... **NCLC 85**
See also DLB 39, 89, 158; RGEL 2
Holden, Ursula 1921- .... **CLC 18**
See also CA 101; CAAS 8; CANR 22
Holdstock, Robert 1948-2009 .... **CLC 39**
See also CA 131; CANR 81, 207; DLB 261; FANT; HGG; SFW 4; SUFW 2
Holdstock, Robert P.
See Holdstock, Robert
Holinshed, Raphael fl. 1580 .... **LC 69, 217**
See also DLB 167; RGEL 2
Holland, Isabelle (Christian)
1920-2002 .... **CLC 21**
See also AAYA 11, 64; CA 21-24R; 205; CAAE 181; CANR 10, 25, 47; CLR 57; CWRI 5; JRDA; LAIT 4; MAICYA 1, 2; SATA 8, 70; SATA-Essay 103; SATA-Obit 132; WYA
Holland, Marcus
See Caldwell, (Janet Miriam) Taylor (Holland)
Hollander, John 1929-2013 ..... **CLC 2, 5, 8, 14; PC 117**
See also CA 1-4R; CANR 1, 52, 136; CP 1, 2, 3, 4, 5, 6, 7; DLB 5; MAL 5; SATA 13
Hollander, Paul
See Silverberg, Robert
Holleran, Andrew 1943(?)- .... **CLC 38**
See also CA 144; CANR 89, 162; GLL 1
Holley, Marietta 1836(?)-1926 .... **TCLC 99**
See also CA 118; DLB 11; FL 1:3
Hollinghurst, Alan 1954- ... **CLC 55, 91, 329**
See also BRWS 10; CA 114; CN 5, 6, 7; DLB 207, 326; GLL 1
Hollis, Jim
See Summers, Hollis (Spurgeon, Jr.)
Holly, Buddy 1936-1959 .... **TCLC 65**
See also CA 213
Holmes, Gordon
See Shiel, M. P.
Holmes, John
See Souster, (Holmes) Raymond
Holmes, John Clellon 1926-1988 .... **CLC 56**
See also BG 1:2; CA 9-12R; 125; CANR 4; CN 1, 2, 3, 4; DLB 16, 237
Holmes, Oliver Wendell, Jr.
1841-1935 .... **TCLC 77**
See also CA 114; 186
Holmes, Oliver Wendell
1809-1894 .... **NCLC 14, 81; PC 71**
See also AMWS 1; CDALB 1640-1865; DLB 1, 189, 235; EXPP; PFS 24; RGAL 4; SATA 34
Holmes, Raymond
See Souster, (Holmes) Raymond
Holt, Elliott 1974- .... **CLC 370**
See also CA 351
Holt, Samuel
See Westlake, Donald E.
Holt, Victoria
See Hibbert, Eleanor Alice Burford
Holub, Miroslav 1923-1998 .... **CLC 4**
See also CA 21-24R; 169; CANR 10; CDWLB 4; CWW 2; DLB 232; EWL 3; RGWL 3
Holz, Detlev
See Benjamin, Walter
Homer c. 8th cent. B.C. .... **CMLC 1, 16, 61, 121, 166; PC 23; WLCS**
See also AW 1; CDWLB 1; DA; DA3; DAB; DAC; DAM MST, POET; DLB 176; EFS 1:1, 2:1,2; LAIT 1; LMFS 1; RGWL 2, 3; TWA; WLIT 8; WP
Hong, Maxine Ting Ting
See Kingston, Maxine Hong
Hongo, Garrett Kaoru 1951- .... **PC 23**
See also CA 133; CAAS 22; CP 5, 6, 7; DLB 120, 312; EWL 3; EXPP; PFS 25, 33, 43; RGAL 4
Honig, Edwin 1919-2011 .... **CLC 33**
See also CA 5-8R; CAAS 8; CANR 4, 45, 144; CP 1, 2, 3, 4, 5, 6, 7; DLB 5
Hood, Hugh (John Blagdon)
1928- .... **CLC 15, 28, 273; SSC 42**
See also CA 49-52; CAAS 17; CANR 1, 33, 87; CN 1, 2, 3, 4, 5, 6, 7; DLB 53; RGSF 2
Hood, Thomas 1799-1845 .... **NCLC 16, 242; PC 93**
See also BRW 4; DLB 96; RGEL 2
Hooft, Pieter Corneliszoon
1581-1647 .... **LC 214**
See also RGWL 2, 3
Hooker, (Peter) Jeremy 1941- .... **CLC 43**
See also CA 77-80; CANR 22; CP 2, 3, 4, 5, 6, 7; DLB 40
Hooker, Richard 1554-1600 .... **LC 95**
See also BRW 1; DLB 132; RGEL 2
Hooker, Thomas 1586-1647 .... **LC 137**
See also DLB 24
hooks, bell 1952(?)- .... **BLCS; CLC 94**
See also BW 2; CA 143; CANR 87, 126, 211; DLB 246; MTCW 2; MTFW 2005; SATA 115, 170
Hooper, Johnson Jones
1815-1862 .... **NCLC 177**
See also DLB 3, 11, 248; RGAL 4
Hope, A(lec) D(erwent)
1907-2000 .... **CLC 3, 51; PC 56**
See also BRWS 7; CA 21-24R; 188; CANR 33, 74; CP 1, 2, 3, 4, 5; DLB 289; EWL 3; MTCW 1, 2; MTFW 2005; PFS 8; RGEL 2
Hope, Anthony 1863-1933 .... **TCLC 83**
See also CA 157; DLB 153, 156; RGEL 2; RHW
Hope, Brian
See Creasey, John
Hope, Christopher 1944- .... **CLC 52**
See also AFW; CA 106; CANR 47, 101, 177; CN 4, 5, 6, 7; DLB 225; SATA 62
Hope, Christopher David Tully
See Hope, Christopher
Hopkins, Gerard Manley
1844-1889 .... **NCLC 17, 189; PC 15; WLC 3**
See also BRW 5; BRWR 2; CDBLB 1890-1914; DA; DA3; DAB; DAC; DAM MST, POET; DLB 35, 57; EXPP; PAB; PFS 26, 40; RGEL 2; TEA; WP
Hopkins, John (Richard) 1931-1998 ... **CLC 4**
See also CA 85-88; 169; CBD; CD 5, 6
Hopkins, Pauline Elizabeth
1859-1930 ..... **BLC 1:2; TCLC 28, 251**
See also AFAW 2; BW 2, 3; CA 141; CANR 82; DAM MULT; DLB 50
Hopkinson, Francis 1737-1791 .... **LC 25**
See also DLB 31; RGAL 4
Hopkinson, Nalo 1960- .... **CLC 316**
See also AAYA 40; CA 196, 219; CAAE 219; CANR 173; DLB 251
Hopley, George
See Hopley-Woolrich, Cornell George
Hopley-Woolrich, Cornell George
1903-1968 .... **CLC 77**
See also CA 13-14; CANR 58, 156; CAP 1; CMW 4; DLB 226; MSW; MTCW 2
Horace 65B.C.-8B.C. .... **CMLC 39, 125; PC 46**
See also AW 2; CDWLB 1; DLB 211; RGWL 2, 3; WLIT 8
Horatio
See Proust, Marcel
Horgan, Paul (George Vincent O'Shaughnessy)
1903-1995 .... **CLC 9, 53**
See also BPFB 2; CA 13-16R; 147; CANR 9, 35; CN 1, 2, 3, 4, 5; DAM NOV; DLB 102, 212; DLBY 1985; INT CANR-9; MTCW 1, 2; MTFW 2005; SATA 13; SATA-Obit 84; TCWW 1, 2
Horkheimer, Max 1895-1973 ...... **TCLC 132**
See also CA 216; 41-44R; DLB 296
Horn, Peter
See Kuttner, Henry

Hornby, Nicholas Peter John
See Hornby, Nick

Hornby, Nick 1957(?)- .... **CLC 243**
See also AAYA 74; BRWS 15; CA 151; CANR 104, 151, 191; CN 7; DLB 207, 352

Horne, Frank 1899-1974 .... **HR 1:2**
See also BW 1; CA 125; 53-56; DLB 51; WP

Horne, Richard Henry Hengist 1802(?)-1884 .... **NCLC 127**
See also DLB 32; SATA 29

Hornem, Horace Esq.
See Lord Byron

Horne Tooke, John 1736-1812 .... **NCLC 195**

Horney, Karen (Clementine Theodore Danielsen) 1885-1952 .... **TCLC 71**
See also CA 114; 165; DLB 246; FW

Hornung, E(rnest) W(illiam) 1866-1921 .... **TCLC 59**
See also CA 108; 160; CMW 4; DLB 70

Horovitz, Israel 1939- .... **CLC 56**
See also CA 33-36R; CAD; CANR 46, 59; CD 5, 6; DAM DRAM; DLB 7, 341; MAL 5

Horton, George Moses 1797(?)-1883(?) .... **NCLC 87**
See also DLB 50

Horvath, Oedoen von
See Horvath, Odon von

Horvath, Odon von 1901-1938 ..... **TCLC 45**
See also CA 118; 184, 194; DLB 85, 124; EWL 3; RGWL 2, 3

Horwitz, Julius 1920-1986 .... **CLC 14**
See also CA 9-12R; 119; CANR 12

Horwitz, Ronald
See Harwood, Ronald

Hospital, Janette Turner 1942- .... **CLC 42, 145, 321**
See also CA 108; CANR 48, 166, 200; CN 5, 6, 7; DLB 325; DLBY 2002; RGSF 2

Hosseini, Khaled 1965- .... **CLC 254**
See also CA 225; LNFS 1, 3; SATA 156

Hostos, E. M. de
See Hostos (y Bonilla), Eugenio Maria de

Hostos, Eugenio M. de
See Hostos (y Bonilla), Eugenio Maria de

Hostos, Eugenio Maria
See Hostos (y Bonilla), Eugenio Maria de

Hostos (y Bonilla), Eugenio Maria de 1839-1903 .... **TCLC 24**
See also CA 123; 131; HW 1

Houdini
See Lovecraft, H. P.

Houellebecq, Michel 1958- .... **CLC 179, 311**
See also CA 185; CANR 140, 231; MTFW 2005

Hougan, Carolyn 1943-2007 .... **CLC 34**
See also CA 139; 257

Household, Geoffrey 1900-1988 ...... **CLC 11**
See also BRWS 17; CA 77-80; 126; CANR 58; CMW 4; CN 1, 2, 3, 4; DLB 87; SATA 14; SATA-Obit 59

Housman, A. E. 1859-1936 .... **PC 2, 43; TCLC 1, 10; WLCS**
See also AAYA 66; BRW 6; CA 104; 125; DA; DA3; DAB; DAC; DAM MST, POET; DLB 19, 284; EWL 3; EXPP; MTCW 1, 2; MTFW 2005; PAB; PFS 4, 7, 40; RGEL 2; TEA; WP

Housman, Alfred Edward
See Housman, A. E.

Housman, Laurence 1865-1959 ...... **TCLC 7**
See also CA 106; 155; DLB 10; FANT; RGEL 2; SATA 25

Houston, Jeanne Wakatsuki 1934- .... **AAL**
See also AAYA 49; CA 103, 232; CAAE 232; CAAS 16; CANR 29, 123, 167; LAIT 4; SATA 78, 168; SATA-Essay 168

Houth, Eduardo
See Barker, Howard

Hove, Chenjerai 1956- .... **BLC 2:2**
See also CP 7; DLB 360

Howard, E. J.
See Howard, Elizabeth Jane

Howard, Elizabeth Jane 1923- ... **CLC 7, 29**
See also BRWS 11; CA 5-8R; CANR 8, 62, 146, 210; CN 1, 2, 3, 4, 5, 6, 7

Howard, Maureen 1930- .... **CLC 5, 14, 46, 151**
See also CA 53-56; CANR 31, 75, 140, 221; CN 4, 5, 6, 7; DLBY 1983; INT CANR-31; MTCW 1, 2; MTFW 2005

Howard, Richard 1929- .... **CLC 7, 10, 47; PC 168**
See also AITN 1; CA 85-88; CANR 25, 80, 154, 217; CP 1, 2, 3, 4, 5, 6, 7; DLB 5; INT CANR-25; MAL 5

Howard, Robert E. 1906-1936 ...... **SSC 202; TCLC 8**
See also AAYA 80; BPFB 2; BYA 5; CA 105; 157; CANR 155; FANT; SUFW 1; TCWW 1, 2

Howard, Robert Ervin
See Howard, Robert E.

Howard, Sidney (Coe) 1891-1939 ..... **DC 42**
See also CA 198; DFS 29; DLB 7, 26, 249; IDFW 3, 4; MAL 5; RGAL 4

Howard, Warren F.
See Pohl, Frederik

Howe, Fanny 1940- .... **CLC 47**
See also CA 117, 187; CAAE 187; CAAS 27; CANR 70, 116, 184, 240; CP 6, 7; CWP; SATA-Brief 52

Howe, Fanny Quincy
See Howe, Fanny

Howe, Irving 1920-1993 .... **CLC 85**
See also AMWS 6; CA 9-12R; 141; CANR 21, 50; DLB 67; EWL 3; MAL 5; MTCW 1, 2; MTFW 2005

Howe, Julia Ward 1819-1910 .... **PC 81; TCLC 21**
See also CA 117; 191; DLB 1, 189, 235; FW

Howe, Susan 1937- ..... **CLC 72, 152; PC 54**
See also AMWS 4; CA 160; CANR 209; CP 5, 6, 7; CWP; DLB 120; FW; RGAL 4

Howe, Tina 1937- .... **CLC 48; DC 43**
See also CA 109; CAD; CANR 125; CD 5, 6; CWD; DLB 341

Howell, James 1594(?)-1666 .... **LC 13**
See also DLB 151

Howells, W. D.
See Howells, William Dean

Howells, William D.
See Howells, William Dean

Howells, William Dean 1837-1920 ... **SSC 36, TCLC 7, 17, 41**
See also AMW; CA 104; 134; CDALB 1865-1917; DLB 12, 64, 74, 79, 189; LMFS 1; MAL 5; MTCW 2; NFS 43; RGAL 4; TUS

Howes, Barbara 1914-1996 .... **CLC 15**
See also CA 9-12R; 151; CAAS 3; CANR 53; CP 1, 2, 3, 4, 5, 6; SATA 5; TCLE 1:1

Hrabal, Bohumil 1914-1997 ..... **CLC 13, 67; TCLC 155**
See also CA 106; 156; CAAS 12; CANR 57; CWW 2; DLB 232; EWL 3; RGSF 2

Hrabanus Maurus 776(?)-856 ...... **CMLC 78**
See also DLB 148

Hroswitha of Gandersheim
See Hrotsvit of Gandersheim

Hrotsvit of Gandersheim c. 935-c. 1000 .... **CMLC 29, 123**
See also DLB 148

Hsi, Chu 1130-1200 .... **CMLC 42**

Hsun, Lu
See Shu-Jen, Chou

Huan Yue
See Shen Congwen

Hubbard, L. Ron 1911-1986 .... **CLC 43**
See also AAYA 64; CA 77-80; 118; CANR 52; CPW; DA3; DAM POP; FANT; MTCW 2; MTFW 2005; SFW 4

Hubbard, Lafayette Ronald
See Hubbard, L. Ron

Huch, Ricarda (Octavia) 1864-1947 .... **TCLC 13**
See also CA 111; 189; DLB 66; EWL 3

Huddle, David 1942- .... **CLC 49**
See also CA 57-60, 261; CAAS 20; CANR 89; DLB 130

Hudson, Jeffery
See Crichton, Michael

Hudson, Jeffrey
See Crichton, Michael

Hudson, W(illiam) H(enry) 1841-1922 .... **TCLC 29**
See also CA 115; 190; DLB 98, 153, 174; RGEL 2; SATA 35

Hueffer, Ford Madox
See Ford, Ford Madox

Hughart, Barry 1934- .... **CLC 39**
See also CA 137; FANT; SFW 4; SUFW 2

Hughes, Colin
See Creasey, John

Hughes, David (John) 1930-2005 ... **CLC 48**
See also CA 116; 129; 238; CN 4, 5, 6, 7; DLB 14

Hughes, Edward James
See Hughes, Ted

Hughes, James Langston
See Hughes, Langston

Hughes, Langston 1902-1967 .... **BLC 1:2; CLC 1, 5, 10, 15, 35, 44, 108; DC 3; HR 1:2; PC 1, 53; SSC 6, 90; WLC 3**
See also AAYA 12; AFAW 1, 2; AMWR 1; AMWS 1; BW 1, 3; CA 1-4R; 25-28R; CANR 1, 34, 82; CDALB 1929-1941; CLR 17; DA; DA3; DAB; DAC; DAM DRAM, MST, MULT, POET; DFS 6, 18; DLB 4, 7, 48, 51, 86, 228, 315; EWL 3; EXPP; EXPS; JRDA; LAIT 3; LMFS 2; MAICYA 1, 2; MAL 5; MTCW 1, 2; MTFW 2005; NFS 21; PAB; PFS 1, 3, 6, 10, 15, 30, 38; RGAL 4; RGSF 2; SATA 4, 33; SSFS 4, 7, 29; TUS; WCH; WP; YAW

Hughes, Richard (Arthur Warren) 1900-1976 .... **CLC 1, 11; TCLC 204**
See also CA 5-8R; 65-68; CANR 4; CN 1, 2; DAM NOV; DLB 15, 161; EWL 3; MTCW 1; RGEL 2; SATA 8; SATA-Obit 25

Hughes, Ted 1930-1998 ...... **CLC 2, 4, 9, 14, 37, 119; PC 7, 89**
See also BRWC 2; BRWR 2; BRWS 1; CA 1-4R; 171; CANR 1, 33, 66, 108; CLR 3, 131; CP 1, 2, 3, 4, 5, 6; DA3; DAB; DAC; DAM MST, POET; DLB 40, 161; EWL 3; EXPP; MAICYA 1, 2; MTCW 1, 2; MTFW 2005; PAB; PFS 4, 19, 32; RGEL 2; SATA 49; SATA-Brief 27; SATA-Obit 107; TEA; YAW

Hughes, Thomas 1822-1896 .... **NCLC 207**
See also BYA 3; CLR 160; DLB 18, 163; LAIT 2; RGEL 2; SATA 31

Hugo, Richard
See Huch, Ricarda (Octavia)

Hugo, Richard F(ranklin) 1923-1982 .... **CLC 6, 18, 32; PC 68**
See also AMWS 6; CA 49-52; 108; CANR 3; CP 1, 2, 3; DAM POET; DLB 5, 206; EWL 3; MAL 5; PFS 17; RGAL 4

Hugo, Victor 1802-1885 ... **DC 38; NCLC 3, 10, 21, 161, 189, 303; PC 17; WLC 3**
See also AAYA 28; DA; DA3; DAB; DAC; DAM DRAM, MST, NOV, POET; DLB 119, 192, 217; EFS 1:2, 2:1; EW 6; EXPN; GFL 1789 to the Present; LAIT 1, 2; NFS 5, 20; RGWL 2, 3; SATA 47; TWA

Hugo, Victor Marie
See Hugo, Victor
Huidobro, Vicente
1893-1948 .... **PC 147; TCLC 31**
See also DLB 283
See also Huidobro Fernandez, Vicente Garcia
Huidobro Fernandez, Vicente Garcia
1893-1948 .... **PC 147; TCLC 31**
See also CA 131; DLB 283; EWL 3; HW 1; LAW
Hulme, Keri 1947- .... **CLC 39, 130, 339**
See also CA 125; CANR 69; CN 4, 5, 6, 7; CP 6, 7; CWP; DLB 326; EWL 3; FW; INT CA-125; NFS 24
Hulme, T(homas) E(rnest)
1883-1917 .... **TCLC 21**
See also BRWS 6; CA 117; 203; DLB 19
Humboldt, Alexander von
1769-1859 .... **NCLC 170**
See also DLB 90, 366
Humboldt, Wilhelm von
1767-1835 .... **NCLC 134, 256**
See also DLB 90
Hume, David 1711-1776 .... **LC 7, 56, 156, 157, 197**
See also BRWS 3; DLB 104, 252, 336; LMFS 1; TEA
Hum-ishu-ma
See Mourning Dove
Humphrey, William 1924-1997 .... **CLC 45**
See also AMWS 9; CA 77-80; 160; CANR 68; CN 1, 2, 3, 4, 5, 6; CSW; DLB 6, 212, 234, 278; TCWW 1, 2
Humphreys, Emyr Owen 1919- ..... **CLC 47**
See also CA 5-8R; CANR 3, 24; CN 1, 2, 3, 4, 5, 6, 7; DLB 15
Humphreys, Josephine 1945- .... **CLC 34, 57, 335**
See also CA 121; 127; CANR 97; CSW; DLB 292; INT CA-127
Huneker, James Gibbons
1860-1921 .... **TCLC 65**
See also CA 193; DLB 71; RGAL 4
Hungerford, Hesba Fay
See Brinsmead, H(esba) F(ay)
Hungerford, Pixie
See Brinsmead, H(esba) F(ay)
Hunt, E. Howard 1918-2007 .... **CLC 3**
See also AITN 1; CA 45-48; 256; CANR 2, 47, 103, 160; CMW 4
Hunt, Everette Howard, Jr.
See Hunt, E. Howard
Hunt, Francesca
See Holland, Isabelle (Christian)
Hunt, Howard
See Hunt, E. Howard
Hunt, Kyle
See Creasey, John
Hunt, (James Henry) Leigh
1784-1859 .... **NCLC 1, 70; PC 73**
See also DAM POET; DLB 96, 110, 144; RGEL 2; TEA
Hunt, Marsha 1946- .... **CLC 70**
See also BW 2, 3; CA 143; CANR 79
Hunt, Violet 1866(?)-1942 .... **TCLC 53**
See also CA 184; DLB 162, 197
Hunter, E. Waldo
See Sturgeon, Theodore (Hamilton)
Hunter, Evan 1926-2005 .... **CLC 11, 31**
See also AAYA 39; BPFB 2; CA 5-8R; 241; CANR 5, 38, 62, 97, 149; CMW 4; CN 1, 2, 3, 4, 5, 6, 7; CPW; DAM POP; DLB 306; DLBY 1982; INT CANR-5; MSW; MTCW 1; SATA 25; SATA-Obit 167; SFW 4
Hunter, Kristin
See Lattany, Kristin Hunter
Hunter, Mary
See Austin, Mary Hunter
Hunter, Mollie 1922- .... **CLC 21**
See also AAYA 13, 71; BYA 6; CANR 37, 78; CLR 25; DLB 161; JRDA; MAICYA 1, 2; SAAS 7; SATA 2, 54, 106, 139; SATA-Essay 139; WYA; YAW
Hunter, Robert (?)-1734 .... **LC 7**
Hurston, Zora Neale 1891-1960 ... **BLC 1:2; CLC 7, 30, 61; DC 12; HR 1:2; SSC 4, 80, 219; TCLC 121, 131, 285; WLCS**
See also AAYA 15, 71; AFAW 1, 2; AMWS 6; BW 1, 3; BYA 12; CA 85-88; CANR 61; CDALBS; CLR 177; DA; DA3; DAC; DAM MST, MULT, NOV; DFS 6, 30; DLB 51, 86; EWL 3; EXPN; EXPS; FL 1:6; FW; LAIT 3; LATS 1:1; LMFS 2; MAL 5; MBL; MTCW 1, 2; MTFW 2005; NFS 3; RGAL 4; RGSF 2; SSFS 1, 6, 11, 19, 21; TUS; YAW
Husserl, E. G.
See Husserl, Edmund (Gustav Albrecht)
Husserl, Edmund (Gustav Albrecht)
1859-1938 .... **TCLC 100**
See also CA 116; 133; DLB 296
Huston, John (Marcellus) 1906-1987 **CLC 20**
See also CA 73-76; 123; CANR 34; DLB 26
Huston, Nancy 1953- .... **CLC 357**
See also CA 145; CANR 102, 198
Hustvedt, Siri 1955- .... **CLC 76**
See also CA 137; CANR 149, 191, 223
Hutcheson, Francis 1694-1746 .... **LC 157**
See also DLB 252
Hutchinson, Lucy 1620-1675 .... **LC 149**
Hutten, Ulrich von 1488-1523 .... **LC 16**
See also DLB 179
Huxley, Aldous 1894-1963 .... **CLC 1, 3, 4, 5, 8, 11, 18, 35, 79; SSC 39; WLC 3**
See also AAYA 11; BPFB 2; BRW 7; CA 85-88; CANR 44, 99; CDBLB 1914-1945; CLR 151; DA; DA3; DAB; DAC; DAM MST, NOV; DLB 36, 100, 162, 195, 255; EWL 3; EXPN; LAIT 5; LMFS 2; MTCW 1, 2; MTFW 2005; NFS 6; RGEL 2; SATA 63; SCFW 1, 2; SFW 4; TEA; YAW
Huxley, Aldous Leonard
See Huxley, Aldous
Huxley, T(homas) H(enry)
1825-1895 .... **NCLC 67**
See also DLB 57; TEA
Huygens, Constantijn 1596-1687 ..... **LC 114**
See also RGWL 2, 3
Huysmans, Charles Marie Georges
See Huysmans, Joris-Karl
Huysmans, Joris-Karl
1848-1907 .... **TCLC 7, 69, 212**
See also CA 104; 165; DLB 123; EW 7; GFL 1789 to the Present; LMFS 2; RGWL 2, 3
Hwang, David Henry 1957- .... **CLC 55, 196; DC 4, 23**
See also AMWS 21; CA 127; 132; CAD; CANR 76, 124; CD 5, 6; DA3; DAM DRAM; DFS 11, 18, 29; DLB 212, 228, 312; INT CA-132; MAL 5; MTCW 2; MTFW 2005; RGAL 4
Hyatt, Daniel
See James, Daniel (Lewis)
Hyde, Anthony 1946- .... **CLC 42**
See also CA 136; CCA 1
Hyde, Margaret O. 1917- .... **CLC 21**
See also CA 1-4R; CANR 1, 36, 137, 181; CLR 23; JRDA; MAICYA 1, 2; SAAS 8; SATA 1, 42, 76, 139
Hyde, Margaret Oldroyd
See Hyde, Margaret O.
Hynes, James 1956(?)- .... **CLC 65**
See also CA 164; CANR 105
Hypatia c. 370-415 .... **CMLC 35**
Ian, Janis 1951- .... **CLC 21**
See also CA 105; 187; CANR 206
Ibanez, Vicente Blasco
See Blasco Ibanez, Vicente
Ibarbourou, Juana de
1895(?)-1979 .... **HLCS 2**
See also DLB 290; HW 1; LAW
Ibarguengoitia, Jorge 1928-1983 ... **CLC 37; TCLC 148**
See also CA 124; 113; EWL 3; HW 1
Ibn Arabi 1165-1240 .... **CMLC 105**
Ibn Battuta, Abu Abdalla
1304-1368(?) .... **CMLC 57**
See also WLIT 2
Ibn Hazm 994-1064 .... **CMLC 64**
Ibn Zaydun 1003-1070 .... **CMLC 89**
Ibsen, Henrik 1828-1906 .... **DC 2, 30; TCLC 2, 8, 16, 37, 52; WLC 3**
See also AAYA 46; CA 104; 141; DA; DA3; DAB; DAC; DAM DRAM, MST; DFS 1, 6, 8, 10, 11, 15, 16, 25; DLB 354; EW 7; LAIT 2; LATS 1:1; MTFW 2005; RGWL 2, 3
Ibsen, Henrik Johan
See Ibsen, Henrik
Ibuse, Masuji 1898-1993 .... **CLC 22**
See also CA 127; 141; CWW 2; DLB 180; EWL 3; MJW; RGWL 3
Ibuse Masuji
See Ibuse, Masuji
Ichikawa, Kon 1915-2008 .... **CLC 20**
See also CA 121; 269
Ichiyo, Higuchi 1872-1896 .... **NCLC 49**
See also MJW
Idle, Eric 1943- .... **CLC 21**
See also CA 116; CANR 35, 91, 148; DLB 352
Idler, An
See Mangan, James Clarence
Idris, Yusuf 1927-1991 .... **SSC 74; TCLC 232**
See also AFW; DLB 346; EWL 3; RGSF 2, 3; RGWL 3; WLIT 2
Ignatieff, Michael 1947- .... **CLC 236**
See also CA 144; CANR 88, 156; CN 6, 7; DLB 267
Ignatieff, Michael Grant
See Ignatieff, Michael
Ignatow, David 1914-1997 ..... **CLC 4, 7, 14, 40; PC 34**
See also CA 9-12R; 162; CAAS 3; CANR 31, 57, 96; CP 1, 2, 3, 4, 5, 6; DLB 5; EWL 3; MAL 5
Ignotus
See Strachey, (Giles) Lytton
Ihimaera, Witi (Tame) 1944- .... **CLC 46, 329**
See also CA 77-80; CANR 130; CN 2, 3, 4, 5, 6, 7; RGSF 2; SATA 148
Il'f, Il'ia
See Fainzilberg, Ilya Arnoldovich
Ilf, Ilya
See Fainzilberg, Ilya Arnoldovich
Illyes, Gyula 1902-1983 .... **PC 16**
See also CA 114; 109; CDWLB 4; DLB 215; EWL 3; RGWL 2, 3
Imalayen, Fatima-Zohra
See Djebar, Assia
Immermann, Karl (Lebrecht)
1796-1840 .... **NCLC 4, 49**
See also DLB 133
Ince, Thomas H. 1882-1924 .... **TCLC 89**
See also IDFW 3, 4
Inchbald, Elizabeth 1753-1821 .... **NCLC 62, 276**
See also BRWS 15; DLB 39, 89; RGEL 2
Inclan, Ramon del Valle
See Valle-Inclan, Ramon del
Incogniteau, Jean-Louis
See Kerouac, Jack
Infante, Guillermo Cabrera
See Cabrera Infante, G.

Author Index

Ingalls, Rachel 1940- .... **CLC 42**
See also CA 123; 127; CANR 154
Ingalls, Rachel Holmes
See Ingalls, Rachel
Ingamells, Reginald Charles
See Ingamells, Rex
Ingamells, Rex 1913-1955 .... **TCLC 35**
See also CA 167; DLB 260
Inge, William (Motter) 1913-1973 ... **CLC 1, 8, 19; DC 37; TCLC 283**
See also CA 9-12R; CAD; CDALB 1941-1968; DA3; DAM DRAM; DFS 1, 3, 5, 8; DLB 7, 249; EWL 3; MAL 5; MTCW 1, 2; MTFW 2005; RGAL 4; TUS
Ingelow, Jean 1820-1897 ...... **NCLC 39, 107; PC 119**
See also DLB 35, 163; FANT; SATA 33
Ingram, Willis J.
See Harris, Mark
Innaurato, Albert (F.) 1948(?)- ... **CLC 21, 60**
See also CA 115; 122; CAD; CANR 78; CD 5, 6; INT CA-122
Innes, Michael
See Stewart, J(ohn) I(nnes) M(ackintosh)
Innis, Harold Adams 1894-1952 ... **TCLC 77**
See also CA 181; DLB 88
Insluis, Alanus de
See Alain de Lille
Iola
See Wells-Barnett, Ida B(ell)
Ionesco, Eugene 1909-1994 ... **CLC 1, 4, 6, 9, 11, 15, 41, 86; DC 12; TCLC 232; WLC 3**
See also CA 9-12R; 144; CANR 55, 132; CWW 2; DA; DA3; DAB; DAC; DAM DRAM, MST; DFS 4, 9, 25; DLB 321; EW 13; EWL 3; GFL 1789 to the Present; LMFS 2; MTCW 1, 2; MTFW 2005; RGWL 2, 3; SATA 7; SATA-Obit 79; TWA
Iqbal, Muhammad 1877-1938 .... **TCLC 28**
See also CA 215; EWL 3
Ireland, Patrick
See O'Doherty, Brian
Irenaeus St. 130- .... **CMLC 42**
Irigaray, Luce 1930- .... **CLC 164, 326**
See also CA 154; CANR 121; FW
Irish, William
See Hopley-Woolrich, Cornell George
Irland, David
See Green, Julien
Iron, Ralph
See Schreiner, Olive
Irving, John 1942- .... **CLC 13, 23, 38, 112, 175**
See also AAYA 8, 62; AMWS 6; BEST 89:3; BPFB 2; CA 25-28R; CANR 28, 73, 112, 133, 223; CN 3, 4, 5, 6, 7; CPW; DA3; DAM NOV, POP; DLB 6, 278; DLBY 1982; EWL 3; MAL 5; MTCW 1, 2; MTFW 2005; NFS 12, 14; RGAL 4; TUS
Irving, John Winslow
See Irving, John
Irving, Washington 1783-1859 .... **NCLC 2, 19, 95, 242; SSC 2, 37, 104, 197, 210, 211; WLC 3**
See also AAYA 56; AMW; CDALB 1640-1865; CLR 97; DA; DA3; DAB; DAC; DAM MST; DLB 3, 11, 30, 59, 73, 74, 183, 186, 250, 254; EXPS; GL 2; LAIT 1; RGAL 4; RGSF 2; SSFS 1, 8, 16; SUFW 1; TUS; WCH; YABC 2
Irwin, P. K.
See Page, P.K.
Isaacs, Jorge Ricardo 1837-1895 .. **NCLC 70**
See also LAW
Isaacs, Susan 1943- .... **CLC 32**
See also BEST 89:1; BPFB 2; CA 89-92; CANR 20, 41, 65, 112, 134, 165, 226; CPW; DA3; DAM POP; INT CANR-20; MTCW 1, 2; MTFW 2005
Isherwood, Christopher 1904-1986 . **CLC 1, 9, 11, 14, 44; SSC 56; TCLC 227**
See also AMWS 14; BRW 7; CA 13-16R; 117; CANR 35, 97, 133; CN 1, 2, 3; DA3; DAM DRAM, NOV; DLB 15, 195; DLBY 1986; EWL 3; IDTP; MTCW 1, 2; MTFW 2005; RGAL 4; RGEL 2; TUS; WLIT 4
Isherwood, Christopher William Bradshaw
See Isherwood, Christopher
Ishiguro, Kazuo 1954- .... **CLC 27, 56, 59, 110, 219**
See also AAYA 58; BEST 90:2; BPFB 2; BRWR 3; BRWS 4; CA 120; CANR 49, 95, 133; CN 5, 6, 7; DA3; DAM NOV; DLB 194, 326; EWL 3; MTCW 1, 2; MTFW 2005; NFS 13, 35, 39; WLIT 4; WWE 1
Ishikawa, Hakuhin
See Ishikawa, Takuboku
Ishikawa, Takuboku 1886(?)-1912 .... **PC 10; TCLC 15**
See Ishikawa Takuboku
See also CA 113; 153; DAM POET
Isidore of Seville c. 560-636 .... **CMLC 101**
Iskander, Fazil (Abdulovich) 1929- **CLC 47**
See also CA 102; DLB 302; EWL 3
Iskander, Fazil' Abdulevich
See Iskander, Fazil (Abdulovich)
Islas, Arturo 1938-1991 .... **TCLC 321**
See also CA 131, 140; DLB 122; HW 1
Isler, Alan (David) 1934- .... **CLC 91**
See also CA 156; CANR 105
Ivan IV 1530-1584 .... **LC 17**
Ivanov, V.I.
See Ivanov, Vyacheslav
Ivanov, Vyacheslav 1866-1949 ...... **TCLC 33**
See also CA 122; EWL 3
Ivanov, Vyacheslav Ivanovich
See Ivanov, Vyacheslav
Ivask, Ivar Vidrik 1927-1992 .... **CLC 14**
See also CA 37-40R; 139; CANR 24
Ives, Morgan
See Bradley, Marion Zimmer
Ivo of Chartres c. 1040-1115 ..... **CMLC 116**
Izumi Shikibu c. 973-c. 1034 .... **CMLC 33**
J. R. S.
See Gogarty, Oliver St. John
Jabès, Edmond 1912-1991 .... **TCLC 304**
See also CA 127, 133; EWL 3; RGHL
Jabran, Kahlil
See Gibran, Kahlil
Jabran, Khalil
See Gibran, Kahlil
Jaccottet, Philippe 1925- .... **PC 98**
See also CA 116; 129; CWW 2; GFL 1789 to the Present
Jackson, Daniel
See Wingrove, David
Jackson, Helen Hunt
1830-1885 .... **NCLC 90, 256**
See also DLB 42, 47, 186, 189; RGAL 4
Jackson, Jesse 1908-1983 .... **CLC 12**
See also BW 1; CA 25-28R; 109; CANR 27; CLR 28; CWRI 5; MAICYA 1, 2; SATA 2, 29; SATA-Obit 48
Jackson, Laura 1901-1991 .... **CLC 3, 7; PC 44; TCLC 240**
See also CA 65-68; 135; CANR 28, 89; CP 1, 2, 3, 4, 5; DLB 48; RGAL 4
Jackson, Laura Riding
See Jackson, Laura
Jackson, Sam
See Trumbo, Dalton
Jackson, Sara
See Wingrove, David
Jackson, Shirley 1916-1965 ...... **CLC 11, 60, 87; SSC 9, 39, 213; TCLC 187; WLC 3**
See also AAYA 9; AMWS 9; BPFB 2; CA 1-4R; 25-28R; CANR 4, 52; CDALB 1941-1968; DA; DA3; DAC; DAM MST; DLB 6, 234; EXPS; HGG; LAIT 4; MAL 5; MTCW 2; MTFW 2005; NFS 37; RGAL 4; RGSF 2; SATA 2; SSFS 1, 27, 30, 37; SUFW 1, 2
Jacob, (Cyprien-)Max 1876-1944 ... **TCLC 6**
See also CA 104; 193; DLB 258; EWL 3; GFL 1789 to the Present; GLL 2; RGWL 2, 3
Jacobs, Harriet A.
1813(?)-1897 .... **NCLC 67, 162**
See also AFAW 1, 2; DLB 239; FL 1:3; FW; LAIT 2; RGAL 4
Jacobs, Harriet Ann
See Jacobs, Harriet A.
Jacobs, Jim 1942- .... **CLC 12**
See also CA 97-100; INT CA-97-100
Jacobs, W(illiam) W(ymark)
1863-1943 .... **SSC 73; TCLC 22**
See also CA 121; 167; DLB 135; EXPS; HGG; RGEL 2; RGSF 2; SSFS 2; SUFW 1
Jacobsen, Jens Peter
1847-1885 .... **NCLC 34, 237**
Jacobsen, Josephine (Winder)
1908-2003 .... **CLC 48, 102; PC 62**
See also CA 33-36R; 218; CAAS 18; CANR 23, 48; CCA 1; CP 2, 3, 4, 5, 6, 7; DLB 244; PFS 23; TCLE 1:1
Jacobson, Dan 1929- .... **CLC 4, 14; SSC 91**
See also AFW; CA 1-4R; CANR 2, 25, 66, 170; CN 1, 2, 3, 4, 5, 6, 7; DLB 14, 207, 225, 319; EWL 3; MTCW 1; RGSF 2
Jacopone da Todi 1236-1306 .... **CMLC 95**
Jacqueline
See Carpentier, Alejo
Jacques de Vitry
c. 1160-1240 .... **CMLC 63, 152**
See also DLB 208
Jagger, Michael Philip
See Jagger, Mick
Jagger, Mick 1943- .... **CLC 17**
See also CA 239
Jahiz, al- c. 780-c. 869 .... **CMLC 25**
See also DLB 311
Jakes, John 1932- .... **CLC 29**
See also AAYA 32; BEST 89:4; BPFB 2; CA 57-60, 214; CAAE 214; CANR 10, 43, 66, 111, 142, 171; CPW; CSW; DA3; DAM NOV, POP; DLB 278; DLBY 1983; FANT; INT CANR-10; MTCW 1, 2; MTFW 2005; RHW; SATA 62; SFW 4; TCWW 1, 2
Jakes, John William
See Jakes, John
James I 1394-1437 .... **LC 20**
See also RGEL 2
James, Alice 1848-1892 .... **NCLC 206**
See also DLB 221
James, Andrew
See Kirkup, James
James, C.L.R. 1901-1989 .... **BLCS; CLC 33**
See also AMWS 21; BW 2; CA 117; 125; 128; CANR 62; CN 1, 2, 3, 4; DLB 125; MTCW 1
James, Daniel (Lewis) 1911-1988 ... **CLC 33**
See also CA 174; 125; DLB 122
James, Dynely
See Mayne, William
James, Henry Sr. 1811-1882 .... **NCLC 53**
James, Henry 1843-1916 .... **DC 41; SSC 8, 32, 47, 108, 150, 196, 201, 205; TCLC 2, 11, 24, 40, 47, 64, 171; WLC 3**
See also AAYA 84; AMW; AMWC 1; AMWR 1; BPFB 2; BRW 6; CA 104; 132; CDALB 1865-1917; CLR 189; DA; DA3; DAB; DAC; DAM MST, NOV; DLB 12, 71, 74, 189; DLBD 13; EWL 3; EXPS; GL 2; HGG; LAIT 2; MAL 5; MTCW 1, 2; MTFW 2005; NFS 12, 16, 19, 32, 37; RGAL 4; RGEL 2; RGSF 2; SSFS 9; SUFW 1; TUS

James, M. R.
See James, Montague
James, Mary
See Meaker, Marijane
James, Montague 1862-1936 ..... **SSC 16, 93, 214; TCLC 6**
See also CA 104; 203; DLB 156, 201; HGG; RGEL 2; RGSF 2; SUFW 1
James, Montague Rhodes
See James, Montague
James, P. D. 1920- .... **CLC 18, 46, 122, 226, 345**
See also BEST 90:2; BPFB 2; BRWS 4; CA 21-24R; CANR 17, 43, 65, 112, 201, 231; CDBLB 1960 to Present; CMW 4; CN 4, 5, 6, 7; CPW; DA3; DAM POP; DLB 87, 276; DLBD 17; MSW; MTCW 1, 2; MTFW 2005; TEA
James, Philip
See Moorcock, Michael
James, Samuel
See Stephens, James
James, Seumas
See Stephens, James
James, Stephen
See Stephens, James
James, T. F.
See Fleming, Thomas
James, William 1842-1910 ...... **TCLC 15, 32**
See also AMW; CA 109; 193; DLB 270, 284; MAL 5; NCFS 5; RGAL 4
Jameson, Anna 1794-1860 .... **NCLC 43, 282**
See also DLB 99, 166
Jameson, Fredric 1934- .... **CLC 142**
See also CA 196; CANR 169; DLB 67; LMFS 2
Jameson, Fredric R.
See Jameson, Fredric
James VI of Scotland 1566-1625 .... **LC 109**
See also DLB 151, 172
Jami, Nur al-Din 'Abd al-Rahman 1414-1492 .... **LC 9**
Jammes, Francis 1868-1938 .... **TCLC 75**
See also CA 198; EWL 3; GFL 1789 to the Present
Jandl, Ernst 1925-2000 .... **CLC 34**
See also CA 200; EWL 3
Janowitz, Tama 1957- .... **CLC 43, 145**
See also CA 106; CANR 52, 89, 129; CN 5, 6, 7; CPW; DAM POP; DLB 292; MTFW 2005
Jansson, Tove (Marika) 1914-2001 ... **SSC 96**
See also CA 17-20R; 196; CANR 38, 118; CLR 2, 125; CWW 2; DLB 257; EWL 3; MAICYA 1, 2; RGSF 2; SATA 3, 41
Japrisot, Sebastien 1931-
See Rossi, Jean-Baptiste
Jarrell, Randall 1914-1965 ...... **CLC 1, 2, 6, 9, 13, 49; PC 41; TCLC 177**
See also AMW; BYA 5; CA 5-8R; 25-28R; CABS 2; CANR 6, 34; CDALB 1941-1968; CLR 6, 111; CWRI 5; DAM POET; DLB 48, 52; EWL 3; EXPP; MAICYA 1, 2; MAL 5; MTCW 1, 2; PAB; PFS 2, 31; RGAL 4; SATA 7
Jarry, Alfred 1873-1907 ...... **DC 49; SSC 20; TCLC 2, 14, 147**
See also CA 104; 153; DA3; DAM DRAM; DFS 8; DLB 192, 258; EW 9; EWL 3; GFL 1789 to the Present; RGWL 2, 3; TWA
Jarvis, E. K.
See Ellison, Harlan; Silverberg, Robert
Jawien, Andrzej
See John Paul II, Pope
Jaynes, Roderick
See Coen, Ethan
Jeake, Samuel, Jr.
See Aiken, Conrad
Jean-Louis
See Kerouac, Jack
Jean Paul 1763-1825 .... **NCLC 7, 268**
Jefferies, (John) Richard 1848-1887 .... **NCLC 47**
See also BRWS 15; DLB 98, 141; RGEL 2; SATA 16; SFW 4
Jefferies, William
See Deaver, Jeffery
Jeffers, John Robinson
See Jeffers, Robinson
Jeffers, Robinson 1887-1962 .... **CLC 2, 3, 11, 15, 54; PC 17; WLC 3**
See also AMWS 2; CA 85-88; CANR 35; CDALB 1917-1929; DA; DAC; DAM MST, POET; DLB 45, 212, 342; EWL 3; MAL 5; MTCW 1, 2; MTFW 2005; PAB; PFS 3, 4; RGAL 4
Jefferson, Janet
See Mencken, H. L.
Jefferson, Thomas 1743-1826 ... **NCLC 11, 103**
See also AAYA 54; ANW; CDALB 1640-1865; DA3; DLB 31, 183; LAIT 1; RGAL 4
Jeffrey, Francis 1773-1850 .... **NCLC 33**
See also DLB 107
Jelakowitch, Ivan
See Heijermans, Herman
Jelinek, Elfriede 1946- .... **CLC 169, 303; DC 53**
See also AAYA 68; CA 154; CANR 169; DLB 85, 330; FW
Jellicoe, (Patricia) Ann 1927- .... **CLC 27**
See also CA 85-88; CBD; CD 5, 6; CWD; CWRI 5; DLB 13, 233; FW
Jelloun, Tahar ben
See Ben Jelloun, Tahar
Jemyma
See Holley, Marietta
Jen, Gish 1955- ..... **AAL; CLC 70, 198, 260**
See also AAYA 85; AMWC 2; CA 135; CANR 89, 130, 231; CN 7; DLB 312; NFS 30; SSFS 34
Jen, Lillian
See Jen, Gish
Jenkins, (John) Robin 1912- .... **CLC 52**
See also CA 1-4R; CANR 1, 135; CN 1, 2, 3, 4, 5, 6, 7; DLB 14, 271
Jennings, Elizabeth (Joan) 1926-2001 .... **CLC 5, 14, 131**
See also BRWS 5; CA 61-64; 200; CAAS 5; CANR 8, 39, 66, 127; CP 1, 2, 3, 4, 5, 6, 7; CWP; DLB 27; EWL 3; MTCW 1; SATA 66
Jennings, Waylon 1937-2002 .... **CLC 21**
Jensen, Johannes V(ilhelm) 1873-1950 .... **TCLC 41**
See also CA 170; DLB 214, 330; EWL 3; RGWL 3
Jensen, Laura 1948- .... **CLC 37**
See also CA 103
Jensen, Laura Linnea
See Jensen, Laura
Jensen, Wilhelm 1837-1911 .... **SSC 140**
Jerome, Saint 345-420 .... **CMLC 30, 157**
See also RGWL 3
Jerome, Jerome K(lapka) 1859-1927 .... **TCLC 23**
See also CA 119; 177; DLB 10, 34, 135; RGEL 2
Jerrold, Douglas William 1803-1857 .... **NCLC 2**
See also DLB 158, 159, 344; RGEL 2
Jewett, Sarah Orne 1849-1909 ... **SSC 6, 44, 110, 138; TCLC 1, 22, 253**
See also AAYA 76; AMW; AMWC 2; AMWR 2; CA 108; 127; CANR 71; DLB 12, 74, 221; EXPS; FL 1:3; FW; MAL 5; MBL; NFS 15; RGAL 4; RGSF 2; SATA 15; SSFS 4
Jewett, Theodora Sarah Orne
See Jewett, Sarah Orne
Jewsbury, Geraldine (Endsor) 1812-1880 .... **NCLC 22**
See also DLB 21
Jhabvala, Ruth Prawer 1927-2013 ... **CLC 4, 8, 29, 94, 138, 284; SSC 91**
See also BRWS 5; CA 1-4R; CANR 2, 29, 51, 74, 91, 128; CN 1, 2, 3, 4, 5, 6, 7; DAB; DAM NOV; DLB 139, 194, 323, 326; EWL 3; IDFW 3, 4; INT CANR-29; MTCW 1, 2; MTFW 2005; RGSF 2; RGWL 2; RHW; TEA
Jibran, Kahlil
See Gibran, Kahlil
Jibran, Khalil
See Gibran, Kahlil
Jiles, Paulette 1943- .... **CLC 13, 58**
See also CA 101; CANR 70, 124, 170; CP 5; CWP
Jimenez, Juan Ramon 1881-1958 ... **HLC 1; PC 7; TCLC 4, 183**
See also CA 104; 131; CANR 74; DAM MULT, POET; DLB 134, 330; EW 9; EWL 3; HW 1; MTCW 1, 2; MTFW 2005; NFS 36; RGWL 2, 3
Jimenez, Ramon
See Jimenez, Juan Ramon
Jimenez Mantecon, Juan
See Jimenez, Juan Ramon
Jimenez Mantecon, Juan Ramon
See Jimenez, Juan Ramon
Jin, Ba 1904-2005 .... **CLC 18**
See Cantu, Robert Clark
See also CA 105; 244; CWW 2; DLB 328; EWL 3
Jin, Ha 1956- .... **CLC 109, 262**
See also AMWS 18; CA 152; CANR 91, 130, 184; DLB 244, 292; MTFW 2005; NFS 25; SSFS 17, 32
Jin, Xuefei
See Jin, Ha
Jin Ha
See Jin, Ha
Jin Yong 1924- .... **CLC 358**
See also DLB 370
Junger, Ernst
See Juenger, Ernst
Jobbry, Archibald
See Galt, John
Jodelle, Etienne 1532-1573 .... **LC 119**
See also DLB 327; GFL Beginnings to 1789
Joel, Billy 1949- .... **CLC 26**
See also CA 108
Joel, William Martin
See Joel, Billy
John, St.
See John of Damascus, St.
John of Damascus, St. c. 675-749 .... **CMLC 27, 95**
John of Salisbury c. 1120-1180 .... **CMLC 63, 128**
John of the Cross, St. 1542-1591 .... **LC 18, 146**
See also RGWL 2, 3
John Paul II, Pope 1920-2005 ...... **CLC 128**
See also CA 106; 133; 238
Johnson, B(ryan) S(tanley William) 1933-1973 .... **CLC 6, 9**
See also CA 9-12R; 53-56; CANR 9; CN 1; CP 1, 2; DLB 14, 40; EWL 3; RGEL 2
Johnson, Benjamin F., of Boone
See Riley, James Whitcomb
Johnson, Charles (Richard) 1948- .... **BLC 1:2, 2:2; CLC 7, 51, 65, 163; SSC 160**

See also AFAW 2; AMWS 6; BW 2, 3; CA 116; CAAS 18; CANR 42, 66, 82, 129; CN 5, 6, 7; DAM MULT; DLB 33, 278; MAL 5; MTCW 2; MTFW 2005; NFS 43; RGAL 4; SSFS 16
Johnson, Charles S(purgeon) 1893-1956 .... **HR 1:3**
See also BW 1, 3; CA 125; CANR 82; DLB 51, 91
Johnson, Denis 1949- .... **CLC 52, 160; SSC 56**
See also CA 117; 121; CANR 71, 99, 178; CN 4, 5, 6, 7; DLB 120
Johnson, Diane 1934- .... **CLC 5, 13, 48, 244**
See also BPFB 2; CA 41-44R; CANR 17, 40, 62, 95, 155, 198; CN 4, 5, 6, 7; DLB 350; DLBY 1980; INT CANR-17; MTCW 1
Johnson, E(mily) Pauline 1861-1913 ... **NNAL**
See also CA 150; CCA 1; DAC; DAM MULT; DLB 92, 175; TCWW 2
Johnson, Eyvind (Olof Verner) 1900-1976 .... **CLC 14**
See also CA 73-76; 69-72; CANR 34, 101; DLB 259, 330; EW 12; EWL 3
Johnson, Fenton 1888-1958 .... **BLC 1:2**
See also BW 1; CA 118; 124; DAM MULT; DLB 45, 50
Johnson, Georgia Douglas (Camp) 1880-1966 .... **HR 1:3**
See also BW 1; CA 125; DLB 51, 249; WP
Johnson, Helene 1907-1995 .... **HR 1:3**
See also CA 181; DLB 51; WP
Johnson, J. R.
See James, C.L.R.
Johnson, James Weldon 1871-1938 ...... **BLC 1:2; HR 1:3; PC 24; TCLC 3, 19, 175**
See also AAYA 73; AFAW 1, 2; BW 1, 3; CA 104; 125; CANR 82; CDALB 1917-1929; CLR 32; DA3; DAM MULT, POET; DLB 51; EWL 3; EXPP; LMFS 2; MAL 5; MTCW 1, 2; MTFW 2005; NFS 22; PFS 1; RGAL 4; SATA 31; TUS
Johnson, Joyce 1935- .... **CLC 58**
See also BG 1:3; CA 125; 129; CANR 102
Johnson, Judith 1936- .... **CLC 7, 15**
See also CA 25-28R, 153; CANR 34, 85; CP 2, 3, 4, 5, 6, 7; CWP
Johnson, Judith Emlyn
See Johnson, Judith
Johnson, Lionel (Pigot) 1867-1902 .... **TCLC 19**
See also CA 117; 209; DLB 19; RGEL 2
Johnson, Marguerite Annie
See Angelou, Maya
Johnson, Mel
See Malzberg, Barry N(athaniel)
Johnson, Pamela Hansford 1912-1981 .... **CLC 1, 7, 27**
See also CA 1-4R; 104; CANR 2, 28; CN 1, 2, 3; DLB 15; MTCW 1, 2; MTFW 2005; RGEL 2
Johnson, Paul 1928- .... **CLC 147**
See also BEST 89:4; CA 17-20R; CANR 34, 62, 100, 155, 197, 241
Johnson, Paul Bede
See Johnson, Paul
Johnson, Robert .... **CLC 70**
Johnson, Robert 1911(?)-1938 ...... **TCLC 69**
See also BW 3; CA 174
Johnson, Samuel 1709-1784 .... **LC 15, 52, 128, 249; PC 81; WLC 3**
See also BRW 3; BRWR 1; CDBLB 1660-1789; DA; DAB; DAC; DAM MST; DLB 39, 95, 104, 142, 213; LMFS 1; RGEL 2; TEA
Johnson, Stacie
See Myers, Walter Dean
Johnson, Uwe 1934-1984 ..... **CLC 5, 10, 15, 40; TCLC 249**
See also CA 1-4R; 112; CANR 1, 39; CDWLB 2; DLB 75; EWL 3; MTCW 1; RGWL 2, 3
Johnston, Basil H. 1929- .... **NNAL**
See also CA 69-72; CANR 11, 28, 66; DAC; DAM MULT; DLB 60
Johnston, George (Benson) 1913- .... **CLC 51**
See also CA 1-4R; CANR 5, 20; CP 1, 2, 3, 4, 5, 6, 7; DLB 88
Johnston, Jennifer (Prudence) 1930- .... **CLC 7, 150, 228**
See also CA 85-88; CANR 92; CN 4, 5, 6, 7; DLB 14
Joinville, Jean de 1224(?)-1317 ... **CMLC 38, 152**
Jolley, Elizabeth 1923-2007 .... **CLC 46, 256, 260; SSC 19**
See also CA 127; 257; CAAS 13; CANR 59; CN 4, 5, 6, 7; DLB 325; EWL 3; RGSF 2
Jolley, Monica Elizabeth
See Jolley, Elizabeth
Jones, Arthur Llewellyn 1863-1947 .... **SSC 20, 206; TCLC 4**
See also CA 104; 179; DLB 36; HGG; RGEL 2; SUFW 1
Jones, D(ouglas) G(ordon) 1929- ... **CLC 10**
See also CA 29-32R; CANR 13, 90; CP 1, 2, 3, 4, 5, 6, 7; DLB 53
Jones, David (Michael) 1895-1974 ... **CLC 2, 4, 7, 13, 42; PC 116**
See also BRW 6; BRWS 7; CA 9-12R; 53-56; CANR 28; CDBLB 1945-1960; CP 1, 2; DLB 20, 100; EWL 3; MTCW 1; PAB; RGEL 2
Jones, David Robert
See Bowie, David
Jones, Diana Wynne 1934-2011 ..... **CLC 26**
See also AAYA 12; BYA 6, 7, 9, 11, 13, 16; CA 49-52; CANR 4, 26, 56, 120, 167; CLR 23, 120; DLB 161; FANT; JRDA; MAICYA 1, 2; MTFW 2005; SAAS 7; SATA 9, 70, 108, 160, 234; SFW 4; SUFW 2; YAW
Jones, Edward P. 1950- .... **BLC 2:2; CLC 76, 223**
See also AAYA 71; BW 2, 3; CA 142; CANR 79, 134, 190; CSW; LNFS 2; MTFW 2005; NFS 26
Jones, Edward Paul
See Jones, Edward P.
Jones, Ernest Charles 1819-1869 .... **NCLC 222**
See also DLB 32
Jones, Everett LeRoi
See Baraka, Amiri
Jones, Gail 1955- .... **CLC 386**
See also CA 188; CANR 193
Jones, Gayl 1949- .... **BLC 1:2; CLC 6, 9, 131, 270**
See also AFAW 1, 2; BW 2, 3; CA 77-80; CANR 27, 66, 122; CN 4, 5, 6, 7; CSW; DA3; DAM MULT; DLB 33, 278; MAL 5; MTCW 1, 2; MTFW 2005; RGAL 4
Jones, James 1921-1977 .... **CLC 1, 3, 10, 39**
See also AITN 1, 2; AMWS 11; BPFB 2; CA 1-4R; 69-72; CANR 6; CN 1, 2; DLB 2, 143; DLBD 17; DLBY 1998; EWL 3; MAL 5; MTCW 1; RGAL 4
Jones, John J.
See Lovecraft, H. P.
Jones, LeRoi
See Baraka, Amiri
Jones, Louis B. 1953- .... **CLC 65**
See also CA 141; CANR 73
Jones, Madison 1925- .... **CLC 4**
See also CA 13-16R; CAAS 11; CANR 7, 54, 83, 158; CN 1, 2, 3, 4, 5, 6, 7; CSW; DLB 152
Jones, Madison Percy, Jr.
See Jones, Madison
Jones, Mervyn 1922-2010 .... **CLC 10, 52**
See also CA 45-48; CAAS 5; CANR 1, 91; CN 1, 2, 3, 4, 5, 6, 7; MTCW 1
Jones, Mick 1956(?)- .... **CLC 30**
Jones, Nettie (Pearl) 1941- .... **CLC 34**
See also BW 2; CA 137; CAAS 20; CANR 88
Jones, Peter 1802-1856 .... **NNAL**
Jones, Preston 1936-1979 .... **CLC 10**
See also CA 73-76; 89-92; DLB 7
Jones, Robert F(rancis) 1934-2003 ... **CLC 7**
See also CA 49-52; CANR 2, 61, 118
Jones, Rod 1953- .... **CLC 50**
See also CA 128
Jones, Terence Graham Parry 1942- .... **CLC 21**
See also CA 112; 116; CANR 35, 93, 173; INT CA-116; SATA 67, 127; SATA-Brief 51
Jones, Terry
See Jones, Terence Graham Parry
Jones, Thom (Douglas) 1945(?)- .... **CLC 81; SSC 56**
See also CA 157; CANR 88; DLB 244; SSFS 23
Jones, Sir William 1746-1794 .... **LC 191**
See also DLB 109
Jong, Erica 1942- .... **CLC 4, 6, 8, 18, 83**
See also AITN 1; AMWS 5; BEST 90:2; BPFB 2; CA 73-76; CANR 26, 52, 75, 132, 166, 212; CN 3, 4, 5, 6, 7; CP 2, 3, 4, 5, 6, 7; CPW; DA3; DAM NOV, POP; DLB 2, 5, 28, 152; FW; INT CANR-26; MAL 5; MTCW 1, 2; MTFW 2005
Jonson, Ben 1572(?)-1637 .... **DC 4; LC 6, 33, 110, 158, 196, 227, 240, 248; PC 17, 146; WLC 3**
See also BRW 1; BRWC 1; BRWR 1; CDBLB Before 1660; DA; DAB; DAC; DAM DRAM, MST, POET; DFS 4, 10; DLB 62, 121; LMFS 1; PFS 23, 33; RGEL 2; TEA; WLIT 3
Jonson, Benjamin
See Jonson, Ben
Jordan, June 1936-2002 ...... **BLCS; CLC 5, 11, 23, 114, 230; PC 38**
See also AAYA 2, 66; AFAW 1, 2; BW 2, 3; CA 33-36R; 206; CANR 25, 70, 114, 154; CLR 10; CP 3, 4, 5, 6, 7; CWP; DAM MULT, POET; DLB 38; GLL 2; LAIT 5; MAICYA 1, 2; MTCW 1; SATA 4, 136; YAW
Jordan, June Meyer
See Jordan, June
Jordan, Neil 1950- .... **CLC 110; SSC 180**
See also CA 124; 130; CANR 54, 154; CN 4, 5, 6, 7; GLL 2; INT CA-130
Jordan, Neil Patrick
See Jordan, Neil
Jordan, Pat(rick M.) 1941- .... **CLC 37**
See also CA 33-36R; CANR 121
Jorgensen, Ivar
See Ellison, Harlan
Jorgenson, Ivar
See Silverberg, Robert
Joseph, George Ghevarughese ...... **CLC 70**
Josephson, Mary
See O'Doherty, Brian
Josephus, Flavius c. 37-100 ... **CMLC 13, 93**
See also AW 2; DLB 176; WLIT 8
Josh
See Twain, Mark
Josiah Allen's Wife
See Holley, Marietta

Josipovici, Gabriel 1940- .... **CLC 6, 43, 153**
See also CA 37-40R, 224; CAAE 224; CAAS 8; CANR 47, 84; CN 3, 4, 5, 6, 7; DLB 14, 319
Josipovici, Gabriel David
See Josipovici, Gabriel
Joubert, Joseph 1754-1824 .... **NCLC 9**
Jouve, Pierre Jean 1887-1976 .... **CLC 47**
See also CA 252; 65-68; DLB 258; EWL 3
Jovine, Francesco 1902-1950 .... **TCLC 79**
See also DLB 264; EWL 3
Joyaux, Julia
See Kristeva, Julia
Joyce, James 1882-1941 .... **DC 16; PC 22; SSC 3, 26, 44, 64, 118, 122, 172, 186, 188, 198; TCLC 3, 8, 16, 35, 52, 159, 280; WLC 3**
See also AAYA 42; BRW 7; BRWC 1; BRWR 3; BYA 11, 13; CA 104; 126; CDBLB 1914-1945; DA; DA3; DAB; DAC; DAM MST, NOV, POET; DLB 10, 19, 36, 162, 247; EWL 3; EXPN; EXPS; LAIT 3; LMFS 1, 2; MTCW 1, 2; MTFW 2005; NFS 7, 26; RGSF 2; SSFS 1, 19, 32; TEA; WLIT 4
Joyce, James Augustine Aloysius
See Joyce, James
Joyce, Rachel 1962- .... **CLC 354**
Jozsef, Attila 1905-1937 .... **TCLC 22**
See also CA 116; 230; CDWLB 4; DLB 215; EWL 3
Juana Inés de la Cruz, Sor
1651(?)-1695 .... **HLCS 1; LC 5, 136; PC 24, 166**
See also DLB 305; FW; LAW; PFS 43; RGWL 2, 3; WLIT 1
Juana Inez de La Cruz, Sor
See Juana Inés de la Cruz, Sor
Juan Manuel, Don 1282-1348 .... **CMLC 88**
Judd, Cyril
See Kornbluth, C(yril) M.; Pohl, Frederik
Juenger, Ernst 1895-1998 .... **CLC 125**
See also CA 101; 167; CANR 21, 47, 106; CDWLB 2; DLB 56; EWL 3; RGWL 2, 3
Julian of Norwich
1342(?)-1416(?) .... **LC 6, 52**
See also BRWS 12; DLB 146; LMFS 1
Julius Caesar 100B.C.-44B.C. ..... **CMLC 47, 173**
See also AW 1; CDWLB 1; DLB 211; RGWL 2, 3; WLIT 8
Jung, Patricia B.
See Hope, Christopher
Junger, Sebastian 1962- .... **CLC 109**
See also AAYA 28; CA 165; CANR 130, 171, 228; MTFW 2005
Juniper, Alex
See Hospital, Janette Turner
Junius
See Luxemburg, Rosa
Junzaburo, Nishiwaki
See Nishiwaki, Junzaburo
Just, Ward 1935- .... **CLC 4, 27**
See also CA 25-28R; CANR 32, 87, 219; CN 6, 7; DLB 335; INT CANR-32
Just, Ward S.
See Just, Ward
Just, Ward Swift
See Just, Ward
Justice, Donald 1925-2004 .... **CLC 6, 19, 102; PC 64**
See also AMWS 7; CA 5-8R; 230; CANR 26, 54, 74, 121, 122, 169; CP 1, 2, 3, 4, 5, 6, 7; CSW; DAM POET; DLBY 1983; EWL 3; INT CANR-26; MAL 5; MTCW 2; PFS 14; TCLE 1:1
Justice, Donald Rodney
See Justice, Donald
Juvenal c. 55-c. 127 .... **CMLC 8, 115**
See also AW 2; CDWLB 1; DLB 211; RGWL 2, 3; WLIT 8
Juvenis
See Bourne, Randolph S(illiman)
K., Alice
See Knapp, Caroline
Kabakov, Sasha .... **CLC 59**
Kabir 1398(?)-1448(?) .... **LC 109; PC 56**
See also RGWL 2, 3
Kacew, Romain 1914-1980 .... **CLC 25**
See also CA 108; 102; DLB 83, 299; RGHL
Kacew, Roman
See Kacew, Romain
Kadare, Ismail 1936- ...... **CLC 52, 190, 331**
See also CA 161; CANR 165, 212; DLB 353; EWL 3; RGWL 3
Kadohata, Cynthia 1956(?)- .... **CLC 59, 122**
See also AAYA 71; CA 140; CANR 124, 205; CLR 121; LNFS 1; SATA 155, 180, 228
Kadohata, Cynthia L.
See Kadohata, Cynthia
Kafu
See Nagai, Kafu
Kafka, Franz 1883-1924 .... **SSC 5, 29, 35, 60, 128, 184, 186; TCLC 2, 6, 13, 29, 47, 53, 112, 179, 288; WLC 3**
See also AAYA 31; BPFB 2; CA 105; 126; CDWLB 2; CLR 193; DA; DA3; DAB; DAC; DAM MST, NOV; DLB 81; EW 9; EWL 3; EXPS; LATS 1:1; LMFS 2; MTCW 1, 2; MTFW 2005; NFS 7, 34; RGSF 2; RGWL 2, 3; SFW 4; SSFS 3, 7, 12, 33; TWA
Kahanovitch, Pinchas
See Der Nister
Kahanovitsch, Pinkhes
See Der Nister
Kahanovitsh, Pinkhes
See Der Nister
Kahn, Roger 1927- .... **CLC 30**
See also CA 25-28R; CANR 44, 69, 152; DLB 171; SATA 37
Kain, Saul
See Sassoon, Siegfried
Kaiser, Georg 1878-1945 .... **TCLC 9, 220**
See also CA 106; 190; CDWLB 2; DLB 124; EWL 3; LMFS 2; RGWL 2, 3
Kaledin, Sergei .... **CLC 59**
Kaletski, Alexander 1946- .... **CLC 39**
See also CA 118; 143
Kallman, Chester (Simon)
1921-1975 .... **CLC 2**
See also CA 45-48; 53-56; CANR 3; CP 1, 2
Kaminsky, Melvin
See Brooks, Mel
Kaminsky, Stuart
See Kaminsky, Stuart M.
Kaminsky, Stuart M. 1934-2009 .... **CLC 59**
See also CA 73-76; 292; CANR 29, 53, 89, 161, 190; CMW 4
Kaminsky, Stuart Melvin
See Kaminsky, Stuart M.
Kamo no Chomei 1153(?)-1216 ... **CMLC 66**
See also DLB 203
Kamo no Nagaakira
See Kamo no Chomei
Kandinsky, Wassily 1866-1944 ..... **TCLC 92**
See also AAYA 64; CA 118; 155
Kane, Francis
See Robbins, Harold
Kane, Paul
See Simon, Paul
Kane, Sarah 1971-1999 .... **DC 31**
See also BRWS 8; CA 190; CD 5, 6; DLB 310
Kanin, Garson 1912-1999 .... **CLC 22**
See also AITN 1; CA 5-8R; 177; CAD; CANR 7, 78; DLB 7; IDFW 3, 4
Kaniuk, Yoram 1930- .... **CLC 19**
See also CA 134; DLB 299; RGHL
Kant, Immanuel 1724-1804 .... **NCLC 27, 67, 253**
See also DLB 94
Kant, Klerk
See Copeland, Stewart
Kantor, MacKinlay 1904-1977 .... **CLC 7**
See also CA 61-64; 73-76; CANR 60, 63; CN 1, 2; DLB 9, 102; MAL 5; MTCW 2; RHW; TCWW 1, 2
Kanze Motokiyo
See Zeami
Kaplan, David Michael 1946- .... **CLC 50**
See also CA 187
Kaplan, James 1951- .... **CLC 59**
See also CA 135; CANR 121, 228
Karadzic, Vuk Stefanovic
1787-1864 .... **NCLC 115**
See also CDWLB 4; DLB 147
Karageorge, Michael
See Anderson, Poul
Karamzin, Nikolai Mikhailovich
1766-1826 .... **NCLC 3, 173**
See also DLB 150; RGSF 2
Karapanou, Margarita 1946- .... **CLC 13**
See also CA 101
Karinthy, Frigyes 1887-1938 .... **TCLC 47**
See also CA 170; DLB 215; EWL 3
Karl, Frederick R(obert) 1927-2004 .. **CLC 34**
See also CA 5-8R; 226; CANR 3, 44, 143
Karnad, Girish 1938- .... **CLC 367**
See also CA 65-68; CD 5, 6; DLB 323
Karr, Mary 1955- .... **CLC 188**
See also AMWS 11; CA 151; CANR 100, 191, 241; MTFW 2005; NCFS 5
Kastel, Warren
See Silverberg, Robert
Kataev, Evgeny Petrovich
1903-1942 .... **TCLC 21**
See also CA 120; DLB 272
Kataphusin
See Ruskin, John
Katz, Steve 1935- .... **CLC 47**
See also CA 25-28R; CAAS 14, 64; CANR 12; CN 4, 5, 6, 7; DLBY 1983
Kauffman, Janet 1945- .... **CLC 42**
See also CA 117; CANR 43, 84; DLB 218; DLBY 1986
Kaufman, Bob (Garnell)
1925-1986 .... **CLC 49; PC 74**
See also BG 1:3; BW 1; CA 41-44R; 118; CANR 22; CP 1; DLB 16, 41
Kaufman, George S. 1889-1961 .... **CLC 38; DC 17**
See also CA 108; 93-96; DAM DRAM; DFS 1, 10; DLB 7; INT CA-108; MTCW 2; MTFW 2005; RGAL 4; TUS
Kaufman, Moises 1963- .... **DC 26**
See also AAYA 85; CA 211; DFS 22; MTFW 2005
Kaufman, Sue
See Barondess, Sue K.
Kavafis, Konstantinos Petrov
See Cavafy, Constantine
Kavan, Anna 1901-1968 .... **CLC 5, 13, 82**
See also BRWS 7; CA 5-8R; CANR 6, 57; DLB 255; MTCW 1; RGEL 2; SFW 4
Kavanagh, Dan
See Barnes, Julian
Kavanagh, Julie 1952- .... **CLC 119**
See also CA 163; CANR 186
Kavanagh, Patrick (Joseph)
1904-1967 .... **CLC 22; PC 33, 105**
See also BRWS 7; CA 123; 25-28R; DLB 15, 20; EWL 3; MTCW 1; RGEL 2
Kawabata, Yasunari 1899-1972 ... **CLC 2, 5, 9, 18, 107; SSC 17**

See also CA 93-96; 33-36R; CANR 88; DAM MULT; DLB 180, 330; EWL 3; MJW; MTCW 2; MTFW 2005; NFS 42; RGSF 2; RGWL 2, 3; SSFS 29, 37
Kawabata Yasunari
See Kawabata, Yasunari
Kaye, Mary Margaret
See Kaye, M.M.
Kaye, M.M. 1908-2004 .... **CLC 28**
See also CA 89-92; 223; CANR 24, 60, 102, 142; MTCW 1, 2; MTFW 2005; RHW; SATA 62; SATA-Obit 152
Kaye, Mollie
See Kaye, M.M.
Kaye-Smith, Sheila 1887-1956 ...... **TCLC 20**
See also CA 118; 203; DLB 36
Kaymor, Patrice Maguilene
See Senghor, Leopold Sedar
Kazakov, Iurii Pavlovich
See Kazakov, Yuri Pavlovich
Kazakov, Yuri Pavlovich 1927-1982 ... **SSC 43**
See also CA 5-8R; CANR 36; DLB 302; EWL 3; MTCW 1; RGSF 2
Kazakov, Yury
See Kazakov, Yuri Pavlovich
Kazan, Elia 1909-2003 .... **CLC 6, 16, 63**
See also AAYA 83; CA 21-24R; 220; CANR 32, 78
Kazanjoglou, Elia
See Kazan, Elia
Kazantzakis, Nikos 1883(?)-1957 .... **PC 126; TCLC 2, 5, 33, 181**
See also AAYA 83; BPFB 2; CA 105; 132; DA3; EW 9; EWL 3; MTCW 1, 2; MTFW 2005; RGWL 2, 3
Kazin, Alfred 1915-1998 ... **CLC 34, 38, 119**
See also AMWS 8; CA 1-4R; CAAS 7; CANR 1, 45, 79; DLB 67; EWL 3
Koda Rohan
See Koda Shigeyuki
Keane, Mary Nesta 1904-1996 .... **CLC 31**
See also CA 108; 114; 151; CN 5, 6; INT CA-114; RHW; TCLE 1:1
Keane, Mary Nesta Skrine
See Keane, Mary Nesta
Keane, Molly
See Keane, Mary Nesta
Keates, Jonathan 1946(?)- .... **CLC 34**
See also CA 163; CANR 126
Keaton, Buster 1895-1966 .... **CLC 20**
See also AAYA 79; CA 194
Keats, John 1795-1821 .... **NCLC 8, 73, 121, 225; PC 1, 96, 157; WLC 3**
See also AAYA 58; BRW 4; BRWR 1; CDBLB 1789-1832; DA; DA3; DAB; DAC; DAM MST, POET; DLB 96, 110; EXPP; LMFS 1; PAB; PFS 1, 2, 3, 9, 17, 32, 36; RGEL 2; TEA; WLIT 3; WP
Keble, John 1792-1866 .... **NCLC 87**
See also DLB 32, 55; RGEL 2
Keene, Donald 1922- .... **CLC 34**
See also CA 1-4R; CANR 5, 119, 190
Kees, Weldon 1914-1955? .... **PC 166**
See also AMWS 15
Keillor, Garrison 1942- ... **CLC 40, 115, 222**
See also AAYA 2, 62; AMWS 16; BEST 89:3; BPFB 2; CA 111; 117; CANR 36, 59, 124, 180; CPW; DA3; DAM POP; DLBY 1987; EWL 3; MTCW 1, 2; MTFW 2005; SATA 58; TUS
Keillor, Gary Edward
See Keillor, Garrison
Keith, Carlos
See Lewton, Val
Keith, Michael
See Hubbard, L. Ron
Kell, Joseph
See Burgess, Anthony
Keller, Gottfried 1819-1890 ... **NCLC 2, 277; SSC 26, 107**
See also CDWLB 2; DLB 129; EW; RGSF 2; RGWL 2, 3
Keller, Nora Okja 1965- .... **CLC 109, 281**
See also CA 187
Kellerman, Jonathan 1949- .... **CLC 44**
See also AAYA 35; BEST 90:1; CA 106; CANR 29, 51, 150, 183, 236; CMW 4; CPW; DA3; DAM POP; INT CANR-29
Kelley, William Melvin 1937- .... **BLC 2:2; CLC 22**
See also BW 1; CA 77-80; CANR 27, 83; CN 1, 2, 3, 4, 5, 6, 7; DLB 33; EWL 3
Kellock, Archibald P.
See Mavor, Osborne Henry
Kellogg, Marjorie 1922-2005 .... **CLC 2**
See also CA 81-84; 246
Kellow, Kathleen
See Hibbert, Eleanor Alice Burford
Kelly, Lauren
See Oates, Joyce Carol
Kelly, M(ilton) T(errence) 1947- .... **CLC 55**
See also CA 97-100; CAAS 22; CANR 19, 43, 84; CN 6
Kelly, Robert 1935- .... **SSC 50**
See also CA 17-20R; CAAS 19; CANR 47; CP 1, 2, 3, 4, 5, 6, 7; DLB 5, 130, 165
Kelman, James 1946- .... **CLC 58, 86, 292**
See also BRWS 5; CA 148; CANR 85, 130, 199; CN 5, 6, 7; DLB 194, 319, 326; RGSF 2; WLIT 4
Kelton, Elmer 1926-2009 .... **CLC 299**
See also AAYA 78; AITN 1; BYA 9; CA 21-24R; 289; CANR 12, 36, 85, 149, 173, 209; DLB 256; TCWW 1, 2
Kelton, Elmer Stephen
See Kelton, Elmer
Kemal, Yasar
See Kemal, Yashar
Kemal, Yashar 1923(?)- .... **CLC 14, 29**
See also CA 89-92; CANR 44; CWW 2; EWL 3; WLIT 6
Kemble, Fanny 1809-1893 .... **NCLC 18**
See also DLB 32
Kemelman, Harry 1908-1996 .... **CLC 2**
See also AITN 1; BPFB 2; CA 9-12R; 155; CANR 6, 71; CMW 4; DLB 28
Kempe, Margery 1373(?)-1440(?) .... **LC 6, 56, 224**
See also BRWS 12; DLB 146; FL 1:1; RGEL 2
Kempis, Thomas a 1380-1471 .... **LC 11**
Kenan, Randall (G.) 1963- .... **BLC 2:2**
See also BW 2, 3; CA 142; CANR 86; CN 7; CSW; DLB 292; GLL 1
Kendall, Henry 1839-1882 .... **NCLC 12**
See also DLB 230
Keneally, Thomas 1935- .... **CLC 5, 8, 10, 14, 19, 27, 43, 117, 279**
See also BRWS 4; CA 85-88; CANR 10, 50, 74, 130, 165, 198, 240; CN 1, 2, 3, 4, 5, 6, 7; CPW; DA3; DAM NOV; DLB 289, 299, 326; EWL 3; MTCW 1, 2; MTFW 2005; NFS 17, 38; RGEL 2; RGHL; RHW
Keneally, Thomas Michael
See Keneally, Thomas
Keneally, Tom
See Keneally, Thomas
Kennedy, A. L. 1965- .... **CLC 188**
See also CA 168, 213; CAAE 213; CANR 108, 193; CD 5, 6; CN 6, 7; DLB 271; RGSF 2
Kennedy, Adrienne (Lita) 1931- .... **BLC 1:2; CLC 66, 308; DC 5**
See also AFAW 2; BW 2, 3; CA 103; CAAS 20; CABS 3; CAD; CANR 26, 53, 82; CD 5, 6; DAM MULT; DFS 9, 28; DLB 38, 341; FW; MAL 5
Kennedy, Alison Louise
See Kennedy, A. L.
Kennedy, Cate 1963- .... **CLC 334**
See also CA 279
Kennedy, John Pendleton 1795-1870 .... **NCLC 2**
See also DLB 3, 248, 254; RGAL 4
Kennedy, Joseph Charles
See Kennedy, X. J.
Kennedy, William 1928- ...... **CLC 6, 28, 34, 53, 239**
See also AAYA 1, 73; AMWS 7; BPFB 2; CA 85-88; CANR 14, 31, 76, 134; CN 4, 5, 6, 7; DA3; DAM NOV; DLB 143; DLBY 1985; EWL 3; INT CANR-31; MAL 5; MTCW 1, 2; MTFW 2005; SATA 57
Kennedy, William Joseph
See Kennedy, William
Kennedy, X. J. 1929- ..... **CLC 8, 42; PC 93**
See also AMWS 15; CA 1-4R, 201; CAAE 201; CAAS 9; CANR 4, 30, 40, 214; CLR 27; CP 1, 2, 3, 4, 5, 6, 7; CWRI 5; DLB 5; MAICYA 2; MAICYAS 1; SAAS 22; SATA 14, 86, 130; SATA-Essay 130
Kenny, Maurice 1929- .... **CLC 87; NNAL**
See also AMWS 23; CA 144; CAAS 22; CANR 143; DAM MULT; DLB 175
Kent, Kathleen .... **CLC 280**
See also CA 288
Kent, Kelvin
See Kuttner, Henry
Kent, Klark
See Copeland, Stewart
Kenton, Maxwell
See Southern, Terry
Kenyon, Jane 1947-1995 .... **PC 57; TCLC 269**
See also AAYA 63; AMWS 7; CA 118; 148; CANR 44, 69, 172; CP 6, 7; CWP; DLB 120; PFS 9, 17, 39; RGAL 4
Kenyon, Robert O.
See Kuttner, Henry
Kepler, Johannes 1571-1630 .... **LC 45**
Ker, Jill
See Conway, Jill K.
Kerkow, H. C.
See Lewton, Val
Kerouac, Jack 1922-1969 .... **CLC 1, 2, 3, 5, 14, 61; TCLC 117; WLC**
See also AAYA 25; AITN 1; AMWC 1; AMWS 3; BG 3; BPFB 2; CA 5-8R; 25-28R; CANR 26, 54, 95, 184; CDALB 1941-1968; CP 1; CPW; DA; DA3; DAB; DAC; DAM MST, NOV, POET, POP; DLB 2, 16, 237; DLBY 1995; EWL 3; GLL 1; LATS 1:2; LMFS 2; MAL 5; MTCW 1, 2; MTFW 2005; NFS 8; RGAL 4; TUS; WP
Kerouac, Jean-Louis le Brisde
See Kerouac, Jack
Kerouac, John
See Kerouac, Jack
Kerr, (Bridget) Jean (Collins) 1923(?)-2003 .... **CLC 22**
See also CA 5-8R; 212; CANR 7; INT CANR-7
Kerr, M. E.
See Meaker, Marijane
Kerr, Robert .... **CLC 55**
Kerrigan, (Thomas) Anthony 1918- .. **CLC 4, 6**
See also CA 49-52; CAAS 11; CANR 4
Kerry, Lois
See Duncan, Lois
Kesey, Ken 1935-2001 .... **CLC 1, 3, 6, 11, 46, 64, 184, 341; WLC 3**
See also AAYA 25; BG 1:3; BPFB 2; CA 1-4R; 204; CANR 22, 38, 66, 124; CDALB 1968-1988; CLR 170; CN 1, 2, 3, 4, 5, 6, 7; CPW; DA; DA3; DAB; DAC; DAM MST, NOV, POP; DLB 2, 16, 206; EWL

3; EXPN; LAIT 4; MAL 5; MTCW 1, 2; MTFW 2005; NFS 2; RGAL 4; SATA 66; SATA-Obit 131; TUS; YAW
Kesselring, Joseph (Otto) 1902-1967 .... **CLC 45**
See also CA 150; DAM DRAM, MST; DFS 20
Kessler, Jascha (Frederick) 1929- .... **CLC 4**
See also CA 17-20R; CANR 8, 48, 111; CP 1
Kettelkamp, Larry (Dale) 1933- ..... **CLC 12**
See also CA 29-32R; CANR 16; SAAS 3; SATA 2
Key, Ellen (Karolina Sofia) 1849-1926 .... **TCLC 65**
See also DLB 259
Keyber, Conny
See Fielding, Henry
Keyes, Daniel 1927- .... **CLC 80**
See also AAYA 23; BYA 11; CA 17-20R, 181; CAAE 181; CANR 10, 26, 54, 74; DA; DA3; DAC; DAM MST, NOV; EXPN; LAIT 4; MTCW 2; MTFW 2005; NFS 2; SATA 37; SFW 4
Keynes, John Maynard 1883-1946 .... **TCLC 64**
See also CA 114; 162, 163; DLBD 10; MTCW 2; MTFW 2005
Khanshendel, Chiron
See Rose, Wendy
Khatibi, Abdelkebir 1938- .... **CLC 327**
See also CA 250; EWL 3; RGWL 3
Khayyam, Omar 1048-1131 .... **CMLC 11, 137; PC 8**
See also DA3; DAM POET; RGWL 2, 3; WLIT 6
Kherdian, David 1931- .... **CLC 6, 9**
See also AAYA 42; CA 21-24R, 192; CAAE 192; CAAS 2; CANR 39, 78; CLR 24; JRDA; LAIT 3; MAICYA 1, 2; SATA 16, 74; SATA-Essay 125
Khlebnikov, Velimir
See Khlebnikov, Viktor Vladimirovich
Khlebnikov, Viktor Vladimirovich 1885-1922 .... **TCLC 20**
See also CA 117; 217; DLB 295; EW 10; EWL 3; RGWL 2, 3
Khodasevich, V.F.
See Khodasevich, Vladislav
Khodasevich, Vladislav 1886-1939 .... **TCLC 15**
See also CA 115; DLB 317; EWL 3
Khodasevich, Vladislav Felitsianovich
See Khodasevich, Vladislav
Khoury, Elias 1948- .... **CLC 338**
See also CA 248; CANR 189
Kis, Danilo 1935-1989 .... **CLC 57**
See also CA 109; 118; 129; CANR 61; CDWLB 4; DLB 181; EWL 3; MTCW 1; RGSF 2; RGWL 2, 3
Kiarostami, Abbas 1940- .... **CLC 295**
See also CA 204
Kidd, Sue Monk 1948- .... **CLC 267**
See also AAYA 72; CA 202; LNFS 1; MTFW 2005; NFS 27
Kielland, Alexander Lange 1849-1906 .... **TCLC 5**
See also CA 104; DLB 354
Kiely, Benedict 1919-2007 .... **CLC 23, 43; SSC 58, 184**
See also CA 1-4R; 257; CANR 2, 84; CN 1, 2, 3, 4, 5, 6, 7; DLB 15, 319; TCLE 1:1
Kienzle, William X. 1928-2001 .... **CLC 25**
See also CA 93-96; 203; CAAS 1; CANR 9, 31, 59, 111; CMW 4; DA3; DAM POP; INT CANR-31; MSW; MTCW 1, 2; MTFW 2005
Kierkegaard, Soren 1813-1855 .... **NCLC 34, 78, 125, 265**
See also DLB 300; EW 6; LMFS 2; RGWL 3; TWA
Kieslowski, Krzysztof 1941-1996 ... **CLC 120**
See also CA 147; 151
Killens, John Oliver 1916-1987 .... **BLC 2:2; CLC 10**
See also BW 2; CA 77-80; 123; CAAS 2; CANR 26; CN 1, 2, 3, 4; DLB 33; EWL 3
Killigrew, Anne 1660-1685 .... **LC 4, 73, 221**
See also DLB 131
Killigrew, Thomas 1612-1683 .... **LC 57**
See also DLB 58; RGEL 2
Kim
See Simenon, Georges
Kincaid, Jamaica 1949- .... **BLC 1:2, 2:2; CLC 43, 68, 137, 234; SSC 72, 180**
See also AAYA 13, 56; AFAW 2; AMWS 7; BRWS 7; BW 2, 3; CA 125; CANR 47, 59, 95, 133; CDALBS; CDWLB 3; CLR 63; CN 4, 5, 6, 7; DA3; DAM MULT, NOV; DLB 157, 227; DNFS 1; EWL 3; EXPS; FW; LATS 1:2; LMFS 2; MAL 5; MTCW 2; MTFW 2005; NCFS 1; NFS 3; SSFS 5, 7; TUS; WWE 1; YAW
King, Francis 1923-2011 ..... **CLC 8, 53, 145**
See also CA 1-4R; CANR 1, 33, 86; CN 1, 2, 3, 4, 5, 6, 7; DAM NOV; DLB 15, 139; MTCW 1
King, Francis Henry
See King, Francis
King, Grace 1852-1932 .... **SSC 195**
See also CA 116; DLB 12, 78
King, Kennedy
See Brown, George Douglas
King, Martin Luther, Jr. 1929-1968 ... **BLC 1:2; CLC 83; WLCS**
See also BW 2, 3; CA 25-28; CANR 27, 44; CAP 2; DA; DA3; DAB; DAC; DAM MST, MULT; LAIT 5; LATS 1:2; MTCW 1, 2; MTFW 2005; SATA 14
King, Stephen 1947- ..... **CLC 12, 26, 37, 61, 113, 228, 244, 328, 378; SSC 17, 55**
See also AAYA 1, 17, 82; AMWS 5; BEST 90:1; BPFB 2; CA 61-64; CANR 1, 30, 52, 76, 119, 134, 168, 227; CLR 124, 194; CN 7; CPW; DA3; DAM NOV, POP; DLB 143, 350; DLBY 1980; HGG; JRDA; LAIT 5; LNFS 1; MTCW 1, 2; MTFW 2005; RGAL 4; SATA 9, 55, 161; SSFS 30; SUFW 1, 2; WYAS 1; YAW
King, Stephen Edwin
See King, Stephen
King, Steve
See King, Stephen
King, Thomas 1943- .... **CLC 89, 171, 276; NNAL**
See also CA 144; CANR 95, 175; CCA 1; CN 6, 7; DAC; DAM MULT; DLB 175, 334; SATA 96
King, Thomas Hunt
See King, Thomas
Kingman, Lee
See Natti, Lee
Kingsley, Charles 1819-1875 .... **NCLC 35**
See also BRWS 16; CLR 77, 167; DLB 21, 32, 163, 178, 190; FANT; MAICYA 2; MAICYAS 1; RGEL 2; WCH; YABC 2
Kingsley, Henry 1830-1876 .... **NCLC 107**
See also DLB 21, 230; RGEL 2
Kingsley, Sidney 1906-1995 .... **CLC 44**
See also CA 85-88; 147; CAD; DFS 14, 19; DLB 7; MAL 5; RGAL 4
Kingsolver, Barbara 1955- .... **CLC 55, 81, 130, 216, 269, 342**
See also AAYA 15; AMWS 7; CA 129; 134; CANR 60, 96, 133, 179; CDALBS; CN 7; CPW; CSW; DA3; DAM POP; DLB 206; INT CA-134; LAIT 5; MTCW 2; MTFW 2005; NFS 5, 10, 12, 24; RGAL 4; TCLE 1:1
Kingston, Maxine Hong 1940- ... **AAL; CLC 12, 19, 58, 121, 271; SSC 136; WLCS**
See also AAYA 8, 55; AMWS 5; BPFB 2; CA 69-72; CANR 13, 38, 74, 87, 128, 239; CDALBS; CN 6, 7; DA3; DAM MULT, NOV; DLB 173, 212, 312; DLBY 1980; EWL 3; FL 1:6; FW; INT CANR-13; LAIT 5; MAL 5; MBL; MTCW 1, 2; MTFW 2005; NFS 6; RGAL 4; SATA 53; SSFS 3; TCWW 2
Kingston, Maxine Ting Ting Hong
See Kingston, Maxine Hong
Kinnell, Galway 1927- ... **CLC 1, 2, 3, 5, 13, 29, 129; PC 26**
See also AMWS 3; CA 9-12R; CANR 10, 34, 66, 116, 138, 175; CP 1, 2, 3, 4, 5, 6, 7; DLB 5, 342; DLBY 1987; EWL 3; INT CANR-34; MAL 5; MTCW 1, 2; MTFW 2005; PAB; PFS 9, 26, 35; RGAL 4; TCLE 1:1; WP
Kinsella, John 1963- .... **CLC 384**
See also CA 189; CP 7; DLB 325; WWE 1
Kinsella, Thomas 1928- ..... **CLC 4, 19, 138, 274; PC 69**
See also BRWS 5; CA 17-20R; CANR 15, 122; CP 1, 2, 3, 4, 5, 6, 7; DLB 27; EWL 3; MTCW 1, 2; MTFW 2005; RGEL 2; TEA
Kinsella, William Patrick
See Kinsella, W.P.
Kinsella, W.P. 1935- .... **CLC 27, 43, 166**
See also AAYA 7, 60; BPFB 2; CA 97-100, 222; CAAE 222; CAAS 7; CANR 21, 35, 66, 75, 129; CN 4, 5, 6, 7; CPW; DAC; DAM NOV, POP; DLB 362; FANT; INT CANR-21; LAIT 5; MTCW 1, 2; MTFW 2005; NFS 15; RGSF 2; SSFS 30
Kinsey, Alfred C(harles) 1894-1956 .... **TCLC 91**
See also CA 115; 170; MTCW 2
Kipling, Joseph Rudyard
See Kipling, Rudyard
Kipling, Rudyard 1865-1936 .... **PC 3, 91; SSC 5, 54, 110, 207, 217; TCLC 8, 17, 167; WLC 3**
See also AAYA 32; BRW 6; BRWC 1, 2; BRWR 3; BYA 4; CA 105; 120; CANR 33; CDBLB 1890-1914; CLR 39, 65, 199; CWRI 5; DA; DA3; DAB; DAC; DAM MST, POET; DLB 19, 34, 141, 156, 330; EWL 3; EXPS; FANT; LAIT 3; LMFS 1; MAICYA 1, 2; MTCW 1, 2; MTFW 2005; NFS 21; PFS 22; RGEL 2; RGSF 2; SATA 100; SFW 4; SSFS 8, 21, 22, 32, 42; SUFW 1; TEA; WCH; WLIT 4; YABC 2
Kircher, Athanasius 1602-1680 .... **LC 121**
See also DLB 164
Kirk, Richard
See Holdstock, Robert
Kirk, Russell (Amos) 1918-1994 ... **TCLC 119**
See also AITN 1; CA 1-4R; 145; CAAS 9; CANR 1, 20, 60; HGG; INT CANR-20; MTCW 1, 2
Kirkham, Dinah
See Card, Orson Scott
Kirkland, Caroline M. 1801-1864 .... **NCLC 85, 309**
See also DLB 3, 73, 74, 250, 254; DLBD 13
Kirkup, James 1918-2009 .... **CLC 1**
See also CA 1-4R; CAAS 4; CANR 2; CP 1, 2, 3, 4, 5, 6, 7; DLB 27; SATA 12
Kirkwood, James 1930(?)-1989 .... **CLC 9**
See also AITN 2; CA 1-4R; 128; CANR 6, 40; GLL 2
Kirsch, Sarah 1935- .... **CLC 176**
See also CA 178; CWW 2; DLB 75; EWL 3
Kirshner, Sidney
See Kingsley, Sidney
Kissinger, Henry A. 1923- .... **CLC 137**
See also CA 1-4R; CANR 2, 33, 66, 109; MTCW 1

Kissinger, Henry Alfred
See Kissinger, Henry A.

Kittel, Frederick August
See Wilson, August

Kivi, Aleksis 1834-1872 .... **NCLC 30**

Kizer, Carolyn 1925- .. **CLC 15, 39, 80; PC 66**
See also CA 65-68; CAAS 5; CANR 24, 70, 134; CP 1, 2, 3, 4, 5, 6, 7; CWP; DAM POET; DLB 5, 169; EWL 3; MAL 5; MTCW 2; MTFW 2005; PFS 18; TCLE 1:1

Klabund 1890-1928 .... **TCLC 44**
See also CA 162; DLB 66

Klappert, Peter 1942- .... **CLC 57**
See also CA 33-36R; CSW; DLB 5

Klausner, Amos
See Oz, Amos

Klay, Phil 1983- .... **CLC 389**
See also CA 358

Klein, A. M. 1909-1972 .... **CLC 19**
See also CA 101; 37-40R; CP 1; DAB; DAC; DAM MST; DLB 68; EWL 3; RGEL 2; RGHL

Klein, Abraham Moses
See Klein, A. M.

Klein, Joe
See Klein, Joseph

Klein, Joseph 1946- .... **CLC 154**
See also CA 85-88; CANR 55, 164

Klein, Norma 1938-1989 .... **CLC 30**
See also AAYA 2, 35; BPFB 2; BYA 6, 7, 8; CA 41-44R; 128; CANR 15, 37; CLR 2, 19, 162; INT CANR-15; JRDA; MAICYA 1, 2; SAAS 1; SATA 7, 57; WYA; YAW

Klein, T.E.D. 1947- .... **CLC 34**
See also CA 119; CANR 44, 75, 167; HGG

Klein, Theodore Eibon Donald
See Klein, T.E.D.

Kleinzahler, August 1949- .... **CLC 320**
See also CA 125; CANR 51, 101, 153, 210

Kleist, Heinrich von 1777-1811 .... **DC 29; NCLC 2, 37, 222, 293, 313; SSC 22**
See also CDWLB 2; DAM DRAM; DLB 90; EW 5; RGSF 2; RGWL 2, 3

Kalidasa fl. c. 400-455 ...... **CMLC 9; PC 22**
See also RGWL 2, 3

Klima, Ivan 1931- .... **CLC 56, 172**
See also CA 25-28R; CANR 17, 50, 91; CDWLB 4; CWW 2; DAM NOV; DLB 232; EWL 3; RGWL 3

Klimentev, Andrei Platonovich
See Klimentov, Andrei Platonovich

Klimentov, Andrei Platonovich 1899-1951 .... **SSC 42; TCLC 14**
See also CA 108; 232; DLB 272; EWL 3

Kline, T. F.
See Harwood, Gwen

Klinger, Friedrich Maximilian von 1752-1831 .... **NCLC 1**
See also DLB 94

Klingsor the Magician
See Hartmann, Sadakichi

Klopstock, Friedrich Gottlieb 1724-1803 .... **NCLC 11, 225**
See also DLB 97; EW 4; RGWL 2, 3

Kluge, Alexander 1932- .... **SSC 61**
See also CA 81-84; CANR 163; DLB 75

Knapp, Caroline 1959-2002 .... **CLC 99, 309**
See also CA 154; 207

Knebel, Fletcher 1911-1993 .... **CLC 14**
See also AITN 1; CA 1-4R; 140; CAAS 3; CANR 1, 36; CN 1, 2, 3, 4, 5; SATA 36; SATA-Obit 75

Kung, Hans 1928- .... **CLC 130**
See also CA 53-56; CANR 66, 134; MTCW 1, 2; MTFW 2005

Knickerbocker, Diedrich
See Irving, Washington

Knight, Etheridge 1931-1991 .... **BLC 1:2; CLC 40; PC 14**
See also BW 1, 3; CA 21-24R; 133; CANR 23, 82; CP 1, 2, 3, 4, 5; DAM POET; DLB 41; MTCW 2; MTFW 2005; PFS 36; RGAL 4; TCLE 1:1

Knight, Sarah Kemble 1666-1727 .... **LC 7**
See also DLB 24, 200

Knister, Raymond 1899-1932 .... **TCLC 56**
See also CA 186; DLB 68; RGEL 2

Knowles, John 1926-2001 .. **CLC 1, 4, 10, 26**
See also AAYA 10, 72; AMWS 12; BPFB 2; BYA 3; CA 17-20R; 203; CANR 40, 74, 76, 132; CDALB 1968-1988; CLR 98; CN 1, 2, 3, 4, 5, 6, 7; DA; DAC; DAM MST, NOV; DLB 6; EXPN; MTCW 1, 2; MTFW 2005; NFS 2; RGAL 4; SATA 8, 89; SATA-Obit 134; YAW

Knox, Calvin M.
See Silverberg, Robert

Knox, John c. 1505-1572 .... **LC 37**
See also DLB 132

Knye, Cassandra
See Disch, Thomas M.

Koch, C(hristopher) J(ohn) 1932- ... **CLC 42**
See also CA 127; CANR 84; CN 3, 4, 5, 6, 7; DLB 289

Koch, Christopher
See Koch, C(hristopher) J(ohn)

Koch, Kenneth 1925-2002 ..... **CLC 5, 8, 44; PC 80**
See also AMWS 15; CA 1-4R; 207; CAD; CANR 6, 36, 57, 97, 131; CD 5, 6; CP 1, 2, 3, 4, 5, 6, 7; DAM POET; DLB 5; INT CANR-36; MAL 5; MTCW 2; MTFW 2005; PFS 20; SATA 65; WP

Kochanowski, Jan 1530-1584 ..... **LC 10, 229**
See also RGWL 2, 3

Kock, Charles Paul de 1794-1871 .... **NCLC 16**

Koda Rohan
See Koda Shigeyuki

Koda Shigeyuki 1867-1947 .... **TCLC 22**
See also CA 121; 183; DLB 180

Koestler, Arthur 1905-1983 ..... **CLC 1, 3, 6, 8, 15, 33; TCLC 283**
See also BRWS 1; CA 1-4R; 109; CANR 1, 33; CDBLB 1945-1960; CN 1, 2, 3; DLBY 1983; EWL 3; MTCW 1, 2; MTFW 2005; NFS 19; RGEL 2

Kogawa, Joy 1935- ... **CLC 78, 129, 262, 268**
See also AAYA 47; CA 101; CANR 19, 62, 126; CN 6, 7; CP 1; CWP; DAC; DAM MST, MULT; DLB 334; FW; MTCW 2; MTFW 2005; NFS 3; SATA 99

Kogawa, Joy Nozomi
See Kogawa, Joy

Kohout, Pavel 1928- .... **CLC 13**
See also CA 45-48; CANR 3

Koizumi, Yakumo
See Hearn, Lafcadio

Kolmar, Gertrud 1894-1943 .... **TCLC 40**
See also CA 167; EWL 3; RGHL

Komunyakaa, Yusef 1947- .... **BLC 2:2; BLCS; CLC 86, 94, 207, 299; PC 51**
See also AFAW 2; AMWS 13; CA 147; CANR 83, 164, 211, 241; CP 6, 7; CSW; DLB 120; EWL 3; PFS 5, 20, 30, 37; RGAL 4

Kong Shangren 1648-1718 .... **LC 210**

Konigsberg, Alan Stewart
See Allen, Woody

Konrad, George
See Konrad, Gyorgy

Konrad, George
See Konrad, Gyorgy

Konrad, Gyorgy 1933- .... **CLC 4, 10, 73**
See also CA 85-88; CANR 97, 171; CDWLB 4; CWW 2; DLB 232; EWL 3

Konwicki, Tadeusz 1926- .... **CLC 8, 28, 54, 117**
See also CA 101; CAAS 9; CANR 39, 59; CWW 2; DLB 232; EWL 3; IDFW 3; MTCW 1

Koontz, Dean 1945- .... **CLC 78, 206**
See Koontz, Dean R.
See also AAYA 9, 31; BEST 89:3, 90:2; CA 108; CANR 19, 36, 52, 95, 138, 176; CMW 4; CPW; DA3; DAM NOV, POP; DLB 292; HGG; MTCW 1; MTFW 2005; SATA 92, 165; SFW 4; SUFW 2; YAW

Koontz, Dean R.
See Koontz, Dean
See also SATA 225

Koontz, Dean Ray
See Koontz, Dean

Kooser, Ted 1939- .... **PC 162**
See also AAYA 69; CMTFW; CA 33-36R; CANR 15, 136, 220; CP 7; DLB 105; LNFS 2; PFS 8, 24

Kopernik, Mikolaj
See Copernicus, Nicolaus

Kopit, Arthur 1937- .... **CLC 1, 18, 33; DC 37**
See also AITN 1; CA 81-84; CABS 3; CAD; CD 5, 6; DAM DRAM; DFS 7, 14, 24; DLB 7; MAL 5; MTCW 1; RGAL 4

Kopit, Arthur Lee
See Kopit, Arthur

Kopitar, Jernej (Bartholomaus) 1780-1844 .... **NCLC 117**

Kops, Bernard 1926- .... **CLC 4**
See also CA 5-8R; CANR 84, 159; CBD; CN 1, 2, 3, 4, 5, 6, 7; CP 1, 2, 3, 4, 5, 6, 7; DLB 13; RGHL

Kornbluth, C(yril) M. 1923-1958 ... **TCLC 8**
See also CA 105; 160; DLB 8; SCFW 1, 2; SFW 4

Korolenko, V.G.
See Korolenko, Vladimir G.

Korolenko, Vladimir
See Korolenko, Vladimir G.

Korolenko, Vladimir G. 1853-1921 ... **TCLC 22**
See also CA 121; DLB 277

Korolenko, Vladimir Galaktionovich
See Korolenko, Vladimir G.

Korzybski, Alfred (Habdank Skarbek) 1879-1950 .... **TCLC 61**
See also CA 123; 160

Kosinski, Jerzy 1933-1991 ... **CLC 1, 2, 3, 6, 10, 15, 53, 70**
See also AMWS 7; BPFB 2; CA 17-20R; 134; CANR 9, 46; CN 1, 2, 3, 4; DA3; DAM NOV; DLB 2, 299; DLBY 1982; EWL 3; HGG; MAL 5; MTCW 1, 2; MTFW 2005; NFS 12; RGAL 4; RGHL; TUS

Kostelanetz, Richard 1940- .... **CLC 28**
See also CA 13-16R; CAAS 8; CANR 38, 77; CN 4, 5, 6; CP 2, 3, 4, 5, 6, 7

Kostelanetz, Richard Cory
See Kostelanetz, Richard

Kostrowitzki, Wilhelm Apollinaris de 1880-1918
See Apollinaire, Guillaume

Kotlowitz, Robert 1924- .... **CLC 4**
See also CA 33-36R; CANR 36

Kotzebue, August (Friedrich Ferdinand) von 1761-1819 .... **DC 51; NCLC 25, 260**
See also DLB 94

Kotzwinkle, William 1938- ... **CLC 5, 14, 35**
See also BPFB 2; CA 45-48; CANR 3, 44, 84, 129; CLR 6; CN 7; DLB 173; FANT; MAICYA 1, 2; SATA 24, 70, 146; SFW 4; SUFW 2; YAW

Kourouma, Ahmadou 1927-2003 .. **CLC 347**
See also BW 2; CA 143, 224; CA 128; DLB 360; EWL 3; RGWL 3

Kowna, Stancy
See Szymborska, Wislawa
Kozol, Jonathan 1936- .... **CLC 17**
See also AAYA 46; CA 61-64; CANR 16, 45, 96, 178; MTFW 2005
Kozoll, Michael 1940(?)- .... **CLC 35**
Krakauer, Jon 1954- .... **CLC 248**
See also AAYA 24; AMWS 18; BYA 9; CA 153; CANR 131, 212; MTFW 2005; SATA 108
Kramer, Kathryn 19(?)- .... **CLC 34**
Kramer, Larry 1935- .... **CLC 42; DC 8**
See also CA 124; 126; CANR 60, 132; DAM POP; DLB 249; GLL 1
Krasicki, Ignacy 1735-1801 .... **NCLC 8**
Krasinski, Zygmunt 1812-1859 .... **NCLC 4**
See also RGWL 2, 3
Kraus, Karl 1874-1936 .... **TCLC 5, 263**
See also CA 104; 216; DLB 118; EWL 3
Kraynay, Anton
See Gippius, Zinaida
Kreve (Mickevicius), Vincas
1882-1954 .... **TCLC 27**
See also CA 170; DLB 220; EWL 3
Kristeva, Julia 1941- .. **CLC 77, 140, 340, 367**
See also CA 154; CANR 99, 173; DLB 242; EWL 3; FW; LMFS 2
Kristofferson, Kris 1936- .... **CLC 26**
See also CA 104
Krizanc, John 1956- .... **CLC 57**
See also CA 187
Krleza, Miroslav 1893-1981 ...... **CLC 8, 114**
See also CA 97-100; 105; CANR 50; CDWLB 4; DLB 147; EW 11; RGWL 2, 3
Kroetsch, Robert 1927-2011 ...... **CLC 5, 23, 57, 132, 286; PC 152**
See also CA 17-20R; CANR 8, 38; CCA 1; CN 2, 3, 4, 5, 6, 7; CP 6, 7; DAC; DAM POET; DLB 53; MTCW 1
Kroetsch, Robert Paul
See Kroetsch, Robert
Kroetz, Franz
See Kroetz, Franz Xaver
Kroetz, Franz Xaver 1946- .... **CLC 41**
See also CA 130; CANR 142; CWW 2; EWL 3
Krog, Antjie 1952- .... **CLC 373**
See also CA 194
Kroker, Arthur (W.) 1945- .... **CLC 77**
See also CA 161
Kroniuk, Lisa
See Berton, Pierre (Francis de Marigny)
Kropotkin, Peter
1842-1921 .... **TCLC 36**
See also CA 119; 219; DLB 277
Kropotkin, Peter Aleksieevich
See Kropotkin, Peter
Kropotkin, Petr Alekseevich
See Kropotkin, Peter
Krotkov, Yuri 1917-1981 .... **CLC 19**
See also CA 102
Krumb
See Crumb, R.
Krumgold, Joseph (Quincy)
1908-1980 .... **CLC 12**
See also BYA 1, 2; CA 9-12R; 101; CANR 7; MAICYA 1, 2; SATA 1, 48; SATA-Obit 23; YAW
Krumwitz
See Crumb, R.
Krutch, Joseph Wood
1893-1970 .... **CLC 24**
See also ANW; CA 1-4R; 25-28R; CANR 4; DLB 63, 206, 275
Krutzch, Gus
See Eliot, T. S.
Krylov, Ivan Andreevich
1768(?)-1844 .... **NCLC 1**
See also DLB 150
Kubin, Alfred (Leopold Isidor)
1877-1959 .... **TCLC 23**
See also CA 112; 149; CANR 104; DLB 81
Kubrick, Stanley 1928-1999 .... **CLC 16; TCLC 112**
See also AAYA 30; CA 81-84; 177; CANR 33; DLB 26
Kueng, Hans
See Kung, Hans
Kumin, Maxine 1925- .... **CLC 5, 13, 28, 164; PC 15**
See also AITN 2; AMWS 4; ANW; CA 1-4R, 271; CAAE 271; CAAS 8; CANR 1, 21, 69, 115, 140; CP 2, 3, 4, 5, 6, 7; CWP; DA3; DAM POET; DLB 5; EWL 3; EXPP; MTCW 1, 2; MTFW 2005; PAB; PFS 18, 38; SATA 12
Kumin, Maxine Winokur
See Kumin, Maxine
Kundera, Milan 1929- ..... **CLC 4, 9, 19, 32, 68, 115, 135, 234; SSC 24**
See also AAYA 2, 62; BPFB 2; CA 85-88; CANR 19, 52, 74, 144, 223; CDWLB 4; CWW 2; DA3; DAM NOV; DLB 232; EW 13; EWL 3; MTCW 1, 2; MTFW 2005; NFS 18, 27; RGSF 2; RGWL 3; SSFS 10
Kunene, Mazisi 1930-2006 .... **CLC 85**
See also BW 1, 3; CA 125; 252; CANR 81; CP 1, 6, 7; DLB 117
Kunene, Mazisi Raymond
See Kunene, Mazisi
Kunene, Mazisi Raymond Fakazi Mngoni
See Kunene, Mazisi
Kunert, Günter 1929- .... **CLC 377**
See also CA 178; CANR 149; CWW 2; DLB 75; EWL 3
Kung, Hans
See Kung, Hans
K'ung Shang-jen
See Kong Shangren
Kunikida, Tetsuo
See Kunikida Doppo
Kunikida Doppo 1869(?)-1908 ...... **TCLC 99**
See also DLB 180; EWL 3
Kunikida Tetsuo
See Kunikida Doppo
Kunitz, Stanley 1905-2006 ... **CLC 6, 11, 14, 148, 293; PC 19**
See also AMWS 3; CA 41-44R; 250; CANR 26, 57, 98; CP 1, 2, 3, 4, 5, 6, 7; DA3; DLB 48; INT CANR-26; MAL 5; MTCW 1, 2; MTFW 2005; PFS 11; RGAL 4
Kunitz, Stanley Jasspon
See Kunitz, Stanley
Kunt, Klerk
See Copeland, Stewart
Kunze, Reiner 1933- .... **CLC 10**
See also CA 93-96; CWW 2; DLB 75; EWL 3
Kuprin, Aleksander Ivanovich
1870-1938 .... **TCLC 5**
See also CA 104; 182; DLB 295; EWL 3
Kuprin, Aleksandr Ivanovich
See Kuprin, Aleksander Ivanovich
Kuprin, Alexandr Ivanovich
See Kuprin, Aleksander Ivanovich
Kureishi, Hanif 1954- .... **CLC 64, 135, 284; DC 26**
See also BRWS 11; CA 139; CANR 113, 197; CBD; CD 5, 6; CN 6, 7; DLB 194, 245, 352; GLL 2; IDFW 4; WLIT 4; WWE 1
Kurosawa, Akira 1910-1998 ... **CLC 16, 119**
See also AAYA 11, 64; CA 101; 170; CANR 46; DAM MULT
Kushner, Tony 1956- ...... **CLC 81, 203, 297; DC 10, 50**
See also AAYA 61; AMWS 9; CA 144; CAD; CANR 74, 130; CD 5, 6; DA3; DAM DRAM; DFS 5; DLB 228; EWL 3; GLL 1; LAIT 5; MAL 5; MTCW 2; MTFW 2005; RGAL 4; RGHL; SATA 160
Kuttner, Henry 1915-1958 .... **TCLC 10**
See also CA 107; 157; DLB 8; FANT; SCFW 1, 2; SFW 4
Kutty, Madhavi
See Das, Kamala
Kuzma, Greg 1944- .... **CLC 7**
See also CA 33-36R; CANR 70
Kuzmin, Mikhail (Alekseevich)
1872(?)-1936 .... **TCLC 40**
See also CA 170; DLB 295; EWL 3
Kyd, Thomas 1558-1594 ... **DC 3; LC 22, 125**
See also BRW 1; DAM DRAM; DFS 21; DLB 62; IDTP; LMFS 1; RGEL 2; TEA; WLIT 3
Kyprianos, Iossif
See Samarakis, Antonis
L. S.
See Stephen, Sir Leslie
Labé, Louise
1521-1566 .... **LC 120, 222; PC 154**
See also DLB 327
Labrunie, Gerard
See Nerval, Gerard de
La Bruyere, Jean de 1645-1696 .... **LC 17, 168**
See also DLB 268; EW 3; GFL Beginnings to 1789
LaBute, Neil 1963- .... **CLC 225**
See also CA 240
La Calprenede, Gautier de Costes 1610(?)-1663 .... **LC 215**
See also DLB 268; GFL Beginnings to 1789
Lacan, Jacques (Marie Emile)
1901-1981 .... **CLC 75**
See also CA 121; 104; DLB 296; EWL 3; TWA
La Ceppède, Jean de c. 1550-1623 ... **LC 249**
See also DLB 327
Laclos, Pierre-Ambroise Francois
1741-1803 .... **NCLC 4, 87, 239**
See also DLB 313; EW 4; GFL Beginnings to 1789; RGWL 2, 3
Lacolere, Francois
See Aragon, Louis
La Colere, Francois
See Aragon, Louis
Lactantius c. 250-c. 325 .... **CMLC 118**
La Deshabilleuse
See Simenon, Georges
Lady Gregory
See Gregory, Lady Isabella Augusta (Persse)
Lady of Quality, A
See Bagnold, Enid
La Fayette, Marie-(Madelaine Pioche de la Vergne) 1634-1693 .... **LC 2, 144**
See also DLB 268; GFL Beginnings to 1789; RGWL 2, 3
Lafayette, Marie-Madeleine
See La Fayette, Marie-(Madelaine Pioche de la Vergne)
Lafayette, Rene
See Hubbard, L. Ron
La Flesche, Francis 1857(?)-1932 ...... **NNAL**
See also CA 144; CANR 83; DLB 175
La Fontaine, Jean de
1621-1695 .... **LC 50, 184**
See also DLB 268; EW 3; GFL Beginnings to 1789; MAICYA 1, 2; RGWL 2, 3; SATA 18
LaForet, Carmen 1921-2004 .... **CLC 219**
See also CA 246; CWW 2; DLB 322; EWL 3
LaForet Diaz, Carmen
See LaForet, Carmen
Laforgue, Jules 1860-1887 ...... **NCLC 5, 53, 221; PC 14; SSC 20**
See also DLB 217; EW 7; GFL 1789 to the Present; RGWL 2, 3

Lagerkvist, Paer 1891-1974 .... **CLC 7, 10, 13, 54; SSC 12; TCLC 144**
See also CA 85-88; 49-52; DA3; DAM DRAM, NOV; DLB 259, 331; EW 10; EWL 3; MTCW 1, 2; MTFW 2005; RGSF 2; RGWL 2, 3; SSFS 33; TWA

Lagerkvist, Paer Fabian
See Lagerkvist, Paer

Lagerkvist, Par
See Lagerkvist, Paer

Lagerlof, Selma 1858-1940 .... **TCLC 4, 36**
See also CA 108; 188; CLR 7; DLB 259, 331; MTCW 2; RGWL 2, 3; SATA 15; SSFS 18, 35

Lagerloef, Selma
See Lagerlof, Selma

Lagerloef, Selma Ottiliana Lovisa
See Lagerlof, Selma

Lagerlof, Selma Ottiliana Lovisa
See Lagerlof, Selma

La Calprènede, Gautier de Costes 1609/1610-1663 .... **LC 215**
See also DLB 268, GFL

La Guma, Alex 1925-1985 .... **BLCS; CLC 19; TCLC 140**
See also AFW; BW 1, 3; CA 49-52; 118; CANR 25, 81; CDWLB 3; CN 1, 2, 3; CP 1; DAM NOV; DLB 117, 225; EWL 3; MTCW 1, 2; MTFW 2005; WLIT 2; WWE 1

La Guma, Justin Alexander
See La Guma, Alex

Lahiri, Jhumpa 1967- .... **CLC 282, 335; SSC 96**
See also AAYA 56; AMWS 21; CA 193; CANR 134, 184; DLB 323; MTFW 2005; NFS 31; SSFS 19, 27, 37

Laidlaw, A. K.
See Grieve, C. M.

Lainez, Manuel Mujica
See Mujica Lainez, Manuel

Laing, R(onald) D(avid) 1927-1989 .. **CLC 95**
See also CA 107; 129; CANR 34; MTCW 1

Laishley, Alex
See Booth, Martin

Lamartine, Alphonse de 1790-1869 ... **NCLC 11, 190; PC 16**
See also DAM POET; DLB 217; GFL 1789 to the Present; RGWL 2, 3

Lamartine, Alphonse Marie Louis Prat de
See Lamartine, Alphonse de

Lamb, Charles 1775-1834 ... **NCLC 10, 113, 298; SSC 112; WLC 3**
See also BRW 4; CDBLB 1789-1832; DA; DAB; DAC; DAM MST; DLB 93, 107, 163; RGEL 2; SATA 17; TEA

Lamb, Lady Caroline 1785-1828 .... **NCLC 38, 261**
See also DLB 116

Lamb, Mary Ann 1764-1847 ..... **NCLC 125, 285; SSC 112**
See also DLB 163; SATA 17

Lame Deer 1903(?)-1976 .... **NNAL**
See also CA 69-72

La Mettrie, Julien Offroy de 1709-1751 .... **LC 202**
See also DLB 313

Lamming, George 1927- .... **BLC 1:2, 2:2; CLC 2, 4, 66, 144**
See also BW 2, 3; CA 85-88; CANR 26, 76; CDWLB 3; CN 1, 2, 3, 4, 5, 6, 7; CP 1; DAM MULT; DLB 125; EWL 3; MTCW 1, 2; MTFW 2005; NFS 15; RGEL 2

Lamming, George William
See Lamming, George

L'Amour, Louis 1908-1988 .... **CLC 25, 55**
See also AAYA 16; AITN 2; BEST 89:2; BPFB 2; CA 1-4R; 125; CANR 3, 25, 40; CPW; DA3; DAM NOV, POP; DLB 206; DLBY 1980; MTCW 1, 2; MTFW 2005; RGAL 4; TCWW 1, 2

Lampedusa, Giuseppe di 1896-1957 .... **TCLC 13**
See also CA 111; 164; DLB 177; EW 11; EWL 3; MTCW 2; MTFW 2005; RGWL 2, 3; WLIT 7

Lampman, Archibald 1861-1899 .... **NCLC 25, 194**
See also DLB 92; RGEL 2; TWA

Lancaster, Bruce 1896-1963 .... **CLC 36**
See also CA 9-10; CANR 70; CAP 1; SATA 9

Lanchester, John 1962- .... **CLC 99, 280**
See also CA 194; DLB 267

Landau, Mark Alexandrovich
See Aldanov, Mark (Alexandrovich)

Landau-Aldanov, Mark Alexandrovich
See Aldanov, Mark (Alexandrovich)

Landis, Jerry
See Simon, Paul

Landis, John 1950- .... **CLC 26**
See also CA 112; 122; CANR 128

Landolfi, Tommaso 1908-1979 ... **CLC 11, 49**
See also CA 127; 117; DLB 177; EWL 3

Landon, Letitia Elizabeth 1802-1838 .... **NCLC 15, 266; PC 163**
See also DLB 96

Landor, Walter Savage 1775-1864 ... **NCLC 14**
See also BRW 4; DLB 93, 107; RGEL 2

Landwirth, Heinz
See Lind, Jakov

Lane, Patrick 1939- .... **CLC 25**
See also CA 97-100; CANR 54; CP 3, 4, 5, 6, 7; DAM POET; DLB 53; INT CA-97-100

Lane, Rose Wilder 1887-1968 .... **TCLC 177**
See also CA 102; CANR 63; SATA 29; SATA-Brief 28; TCWW 2

Lang, Andrew 1844-1912 .... **TCLC 16**
See also CA 114; 137; CANR 85; CLR 101, 174; DLB 98, 141, 184; FANT; MAICYA 1, 2; RGEL 2; SATA 16; WCH

Lang, Fritz 1890-1976 .... **CLC 20, 103**
See also AAYA 65; CA 77-80; 69-72; CANR 30

Lange, John
See Crichton, Michael

Langer, Elinor 1939- .... **CLC 34**
See also CA 121

Langland, William 1332(?)-1400(?) .... **LC 19, 120**
See also BRW 1; DA; DAB; DAC; DAM MST, POET; DLB 146; RGEL 2; TEA; WLIT 3

Langstaff, Launcelot
See Irving, Washington

Langton, Stephen c. 1165-1228 ... **CMLC 125**

Lanier, Sidney 1842-1881 ...... **NCLC 6, 118; PC 50**
See also AMWS 1; DAM POET; DLB 64; DLBD 13; EXPP; MAICYA 1; PFS 14; RGAL 4; SATA 18

Lanyer, Aemilia 1569-1645 ... **LC 10, 30, 83, 232; PC 60**
See also DLB 121

Lao-Tzu
See Lao Tzu

Lao Tzu c. 6th cent. B.C.-3rd cent. B.C. .... **CMLC 7, 125**

Lapine, James (Elliot) 1949- .... **CLC 39**
See also CA 123; 130; CANR 54, 128; DFS 25; DLB 341; INT CA-130

La Ramee, Pierre de 1515(?)-1572 ... **LC 174**
See also DLB 327

Larbaud, Valery (Nicolas) 1881-1957 .... **TCLC 9**
See also CA 106; 152; EWL 3; GFL 1789 to the Present

Larcom, Lucy 1824-1893 .... **NCLC 179**
See also AMWS 13; DLB 221, 243

Lardner, Ring 1885-1933 .... **SSC 32, 118; TCLC 2, 14**
See also AMW; BPFB 2; CA 104; 131; CDALB 1917-1929; DLB 11, 25, 86, 171; DLBD 16; MAL 5; MTCW 1, 2; MTFW 2005; RGAL 4; RGSF 2; TUS

Lardner, Ring W., Jr.
See Lardner, Ring

Lardner, Ringold Wilmer
See Lardner, Ring

Laredo, Betty
See Codrescu, Andrei

Larkin, Maia
See Wojciechowska, Maia (Teresa)

Larkin, Philip 1922-1985 ..... **CLC 3, 5, 8, 9, 13, 18, 33, 39, 64; PC 21, 144**
See also BRWR 3; BRWS 1; CA 5-8R; 117; CANR 24, 62; CDBLB 1960 to Present; CP 1, 2, 3, 4; DA3; DAB; DAM MST, POET; DLB 27; EWL 3; MTCW 1, 2; MTFW 2005; PFS 3, 4, 12, 42; RGEL 2

Larkin, Philip Arthur
See Larkin, Philip

La Roche, Sophie von 1730-1807 .... **NCLC 121, 262**
See also DLB 94

La Rochefoucauld, Francois 1613-1680 .... **LC 108, 172**
See also DLB 268; EW 3; GFL Beginnings to 1789; RGWL 2, 3

Larra (y Sanchez de Castro), Mariano Jose de 1809-1837 .... **NCLC 17, 130**

Larsen, Eric 1941- .... **CLC 55**
See also CA 132

Larsen, Nella 1893(?)-1963 .... **BLC 1:2; CLC 37; HR 1:3; TCLC 200**
See also AFAW 1, 2; AMWS 18; BW 1; CA 125; CANR 83; DAM MULT; DLB 51; FW; LATS 1:1; LMFS 2

Larson, Charles R(aymond) 1938- .... **CLC 31**
See also CA 53-56; CANR 4, 121

Larson, Jonathan 1960-1996 .... **CLC 99**
See also AAYA 28; CA 156; DFS 23; MTFW 2005

La Sale, Antoine de c. 1386-1460(?) ... **LC 104**
See also DLB 208

Lasarus, B. B.
See Breytenbach, Breyten

Las Casas, Bartolome de 1474-1566 .... **HLCS; LC 31, 203**
See also DLB 318; LAW; WLIT 1

Lasch, Christopher 1932-1994 ...... **CLC 102**
See also CA 73-76; 144; CANR 25, 118; DLB 246; MTCW 1, 2; MTFW 2005

Lasker-Schüler, Else
See Lasker-Schueler, Else

Lasker-Schueler, Else 1869-1945 ..... **PC 156; TCLC 57**
See also CA 183; DLB 66, 124; EWL 3

Laski, Harold J(oseph) 1893-1950 .. **TCLC 79**
See also CA 188

Latham, Jean Lee 1902-1995 .... **CLC 12**
See also AITN 1; BYA 1; CA 5-8R; CANR 7, 84; CLR 50; MAICYA 1, 2; SATA 2, 68; YAW

Latham, Mavis
See Clark, Mavis Thorpe

Lathen, Emma
See Hennissart, Martha

Lathrop, Francis
See Leiber, Fritz (Reuter, Jr.)

Latini, Brunetto
See Brunetto Latini

Lattany, Kristin
See Lattany, Kristin Hunter

Lattany, Kristin Elaine Eggleston Hunter
See Lattany, Kristin Hunter
Lattany, Kristin Hunter 1931-2008 ... **CLC 35**
See also AITN 1; BW 1; BYA 3; CA 13-16R; CANR 13, 108; CLR 3; CN 1, 2, 3, 4, 5, 6; DLB 33; INT CANR-13; MAICYA 1, 2; SAAS 10; SATA 12, 132; YAW
Lattimore, Richmond (Alexander) 1906-1984 .... **CLC 3**
See also CA 1-4R; 112; CANR 1; CP 1, 2, 3; MAL 5
Laughlin, James 1914-1997 .... **CLC 49**
See also CA 21-24R; 162; CAAS 22; CANR 9, 47; CP 1, 2, 3, 4, 5, 6; DLB 48; DLBY 1996, 1997
Launko, Okinba
See Osofisan, Femi
Laurence, Jean Margaret Wemyss
See Laurence, Margaret
Laurence, Margaret 1926-1987 ... **CLC 3, 6, 13, 50, 62; SSC 7, 220**
See also BYA 13; CA 5-8R; 121; CANR 33; CN 1, 2, 3, 4; DAC; DAM MST; DLB 53; EWL 3; FW; MTCW 1, 2; MTFW 2005; NFS 11; RGEL 2; RGSF 2; SATA-Obit 50; TCWW 2
Laurent, Antoine 1952- .... **CLC 50**
Lauscher, Hermann
See Hesse, Hermann
Leautaud, Paul 1872-1956 .... **TCLC 83**
See also CA 203; DLB 65; GFL 1789 to the Present
Lautreamont 1846-1870 .... **NCLC 12, 194; SSC 14**
See also DLB 217; GFL 1789 to the Present; RGWL 2, 3
Lautreamont, Isidore Lucien Ducasse
See Lautreamont
Lavater, Johann Kaspar 1741-1801 .... **NCLC 142**
See also DLB 97
Laverty, Donald
See Blish, James
Lavin, Mary 1912-1996 .... **CLC 4, 18, 99; SSC 4, 67, 137; TCLC 271**
See also BRWS 19; CA 9-12R; 151; CANR 33; CN 1, 2, 3, 4, 5, 6; DLB 15, 319; FW; MTCW 1; RGEL 2; RGSF 2; SSFS 23
Lavond, Paul Dennis
See Kornbluth, C(yril) M.; Pohl, Frederik
Lawes, Henry 1596-1662 .... **LC 113**
See also DLB 126
Lawler, Ray
See Lawler, Raymond Evenor
Lawler, Raymond Evenor 1922- .... **CLC 58, 353**
See also CA 103; CD 5, 6; DLB 289; RGEL 2
Lawrence, D. H. 1885-1930 .... **DC 44; PC 54; SSC 4, 19, 73, 149, 221; TCLC 2, 9, 16, 33, 48, 61, 93; WLC 3**
See also BPFB 2; BRW 7; BRWR 2; CA 104; 121; CANR 131; CDBLB 1914-1945; DA; DA3; DAB; DAC; DAM MST, NOV, POET; DLB 10, 19, 36, 98, 162, 195; EWL 3; EXPP; EXPS; GLL 1; LAIT 2, 3; MTCW 1, 2; MTFW 2005; NFS 18, 26; PFS 6; RGEL 2; RGSF 2; SSFS 2, 6, 36; TEA; WLIT 4; WP
Lawrence, David Herbert Richards
See Lawrence, D. H.
Lawrence, T. E. 1888-1935 ... **TCLC 18, 204**
See also BRWS 2; CA 115; 167; DLB 195, 366
Lawrence, Thomas Edward
See Lawrence, T. E.
Lawrence of Arabia
See Lawrence, T. E.
Lawson, Henry (Archibald Hertzberg) 1867-1922 .... **SSC 18; TCLC 27**
See also CA 120; 181; DLB 230; RGEL 2; RGSF 2
Lawton, Dennis
See Faust, Frederick
Laxness, Halldor (Kiljan)
See Gudjonsson, Halldor Kiljan
Layamon fl. c. 1200 .... **CMLC 10, 105**
See also DLB 146; RGEL 2
Laye, Camara 1928-1980 .... **BLC 1:2; CLC 4, 38**
See also AFW; BW 1; CA 85-88; 97-100; CANR 25; DAM MULT; DLB 360; EWL 3; MTCW 1, 2; WLIT 2
Layton, Irving 1912-2006 ... **CLC 2, 15, 164**
See also CA 1-4R; 247; CANR 2, 33, 43, 66, 129; CP 1, 2, 3, 4, 5, 6, 7; DAC; DAM MST, POET; DLB 88; EWL 3; MTCW 1, 2; PFS 12; RGEL 2
Layton, Irving Peter
See Layton, Irving
Lazarus, Emma 1849-1887 .... **NCLC 8, 109; PC 136**
See also PFS 37
Lazarus, Felix
See Cable, George Washington
Lazarus, Henry
See Slavitt, David R.
Lea, Joan
See Neufeld, John (Arthur)
Leacock, Stephen (Butler) 1869-1944 ... **SSC 39, 185; TCLC 2, 263**
See also CA 104; 141; CANR 80; DAC; DAM MST; DLB 92; EWL 3; MTCW 2; MTFW 2005; RGEL 2; RGSF 2
Lead, Jane Ward 1623-1704 .... **LC 72**
See also DLB 131
Leapor, Mary 1722-1746 ...... **LC 80; PC 85**
See also DLB 109
Lear, Edward 1812-1888 .... **NCLC 3; PC 65**
See also AAYA 48; BRW 5; CLR 1, 75, 169; DLB 32, 163, 166; MAICYA 1, 2; RGEL 2; SATA 18, 100; WCH; WP
Lear, Norman (Milton) 1922- .... **CLC 12**
See also CA 73-76
Least Heat-Moon, William
See Heat-Moon, William Least
Leavis, F(rank) R(aymond) 1895-1978 .... **CLC 24**
See also BRW 7; CA 21-24R; 77-80; CANR 44; DLB 242; EWL 3; MTCW 1, 2; RGEL 2
Leavitt, David 1961- .... **CLC 34**
See also CA 116; 122; CANR 50, 62, 101, 134, 177; CPW; DA3; DAM POP; DLB 130, 350; GLL 1; INT CA-122; MAL 5; MTCW 2; MTFW 2005
Leblanc, Maurice (Marie Emile) 1864-1941 .... **TCLC 49**
See also CA 110; CMW 4
Lebowitz, Fran 1951(?)- .... **CLC 11, 36**
See also CA 81-84; CANR 14, 60, 70; INT CANR-14; MTCW 1
Lebowitz, Frances Ann
See Lebowitz, Fran
Lebrecht, Peter
See Tieck, (Johann) Ludwig
le Cagat, Benat
See Whitaker, Rod
le Carre, John 1931- .... **CLC 9, 15**
See also AAYA 42; BEST 89:4; BPFB 2; BRWR 3; BRWS 2; CA 5-8R; CANR 13, 33, 59, 107, 132, 172; CDBLB 1960 to Present; CMW 4; CN 1, 2, 3, 4, 5, 6, 7; CPW; DA3; DAM POP; DLB 87; EWL 3; MSW; MTCW 1, 2; MTFW 2005; RGEL 2; TEA
le Carre, John
See le Carre, John
Le Clezio, J. M.G. 1940- .... **CLC 31, 155, 280; SSC 122**
See also CA 116; 128; CANR 147; CWW 2; DLB 83; EWL 3; GFL 1789 to the Present; RGSF 2
Le Clezio, Jean Marie Gustave
See Le Clezio, J. M.G.
Leconte de Lisle, Charles-Marie-Rene 1818-1894 .... **NCLC 29**
See also DLB 217; EW 6; GFL 1789 to the Present
Le Coq, Monsieur
See Simenon, Georges
Leduc, Violette 1907-1972 .... **CLC 22**
See also CA 13-14; 33-36R; CANR 69; CAP 1; EWL 3; GFL 1789 to the Present; GLL 1
Ledwidge, Francis 1887(?)-1917 ... **TCLC 23**
See also CA 123; 203; DLB 20
Lee, Andrea 1953- .... **BLC 1:2; CLC 36**
See also BW 1, 3; CA 125; CANR 82, 190; DAM MULT; SSFS 37
Lee, Andrew
See Auchincloss, Louis
Lee, Chang-rae 1965- ..... **CLC 91, 268, 274**
See also CA 148; CANR 89; CN 7; DLB 312; LATS 1:2; NFS 42
Lee, Don L.
See Madhubuti, Haki R.
Lee, George W(ashington) 1894-1976 .... **BLC 1:2; CLC 52**
See also BW 1; CA 125; CANR 83; DAM MULT; DLB 51
Lee, Harper 1926- .... **CLC 12, 60, 194; WLC 4**
See also AAYA 13; AMWS 8; BPFB 2; BYA 3; CA 13-16R; CANR 51, 128; CDALB 1941-1968; CLR 169; CSW; DA; DA3; DAB; DAC; DAM MST, NOV; DLB 6; EXPN; LAIT 3; MAL 5; MTCW 1, 2; MTFW 2005; NFS 2, 32; SATA 11; WYA; YAW
Lee, Helen Elaine 1959(?)- .... **CLC 86**
See also CA 148
Lee, John .... **CLC 70**
Lee, Julian
See Latham, Jean Lee
Lee, Larry
See Lee, Lawrence
Lee, Laurie 1914-1997 .... **CLC 90**
See also CA 77-80; 158; CANR 33, 73; CP 1, 2, 3, 4, 5, 6; CPW; DAB; DAM POP; DLB 27; MTCW 1; RGEL 2
Lee, Lawrence 1941-1990 .... **CLC 34**
See also CA 131; CANR 43
Lee, Li-Young 1957- .... **CLC 164; PC 24**
See also AMWS 15; CA 153; CANR 118, 206; CP 6, 7; DLB 165, 312; LMFS 2; PFS 11, 15, 17, 37
Lee, Manfred B. 1905-1971 .... **CLC 11**
See also CA 1-4R; 29-32R; CANR 2, 150; CMW 4; DLB 137
Lee, Manfred Bennington
See Lee, Manfred B.
Lee, Nathaniel 1645(?)-1692 .... **LC 103**
See also DLB 80; RGEL 2
Lee, Nelle Harper
See Lee, Harper
Lee, Shelton Jackson
See Lee, Spike
Lee, Sophia 1750-1824 .... **NCLC 191**
See also DLB 39
Lee, Spike 1957(?)- ... **BLCS; CLC 105, 281**
See also AAYA 4, 29; BW 2, 3; CA 125; CANR 42, 164; DAM MULT
Lee, Stan 1922- .... **CLC 17**
See also AAYA 5, 49; CA 108; 111; CANR 129; INT CA-111; MTFW 2005

Lee, Tanith 1947- .... **CLC 46**
See also AAYA 15; CA 37-40R; CANR 53, 102, 145, 170; DLB 261; FANT; SATA 8, 88, 134, 185; SFW 4; SUFW 1, 2; YAW

Lee, Vernon
See Paget, Violet

Lee, William
See Burroughs, William S.

Lee, Willy
See Burroughs, William S.

Lee-Hamilton, Eugene (Jacob)
1845-1907 .... **TCLC 22**
See also CA 117; 234

Leet, Judith 1935- .... **CLC 11**
See also CA 187

Le Fanu, Joseph Sheridan
1814-1873 .... **NCLC 9, 58, 282; SSC 14, 84, 200, 220**
See also BRWS 19; CMW 4; DA3; DAM POP; DLB 21, 70, 159, 178; GL 3; HGG; RGEL 2; RGSF 2; SUFW 1

Leffland, Ella 1931- .... **CLC 19**
See also CA 29-32R; CANR 35, 78, 82; DLBY 1984; INT CANR-35; SATA 65; SSFS 24

Leger, Alexis
See Leger, Alexis Saint-Leger

Leger, Alexis Saint-Leger
1887-1975 .... **CLC 4, 11, 46; PC 23**
See also CA 13-16R; 61-64; CANR 43; DAM POET; DLB 258, 331; EW 10; EWL 3; GFL 1789 to the Present; MTCW 1; RGWL 2, 3

Leger, Marie-Rene Auguste Alexis Saint-Leger
See Leger, Alexis Saint-Leger

Leger, Saintleger
See Leger, Alexis Saint-Leger

Le Guin, Ursula K. 1929- .... **CLC 8, 13, 22, 45, 71, 136, 310; SSC 12, 69, 217**
See also AAYA 9, 27, 84; AITN 1; BPFB 2; BYA 5, 8, 11, 14; CA 21-24R; CANR 9, 32, 52, 74, 132, 192; CDALB 1968-1988; CLR 3, 28, 91, 173; CN 2, 3, 4, 5, 6, 7; CPW; DA3; DAB; DAC; DAM MST, POP; DLB 8, 52, 256, 275; EXPS; FANT; FW; INT CANR-32; JRDA; LAIT 5; MAICYA 1, 2; MAL 5; MTCW 1, 2; MTFW 2005; NFS 6, 9; SATA 4, 52, 99, 149, 194; SCFW 1, 2; SFW 4; SSFS 2; SUFW 1, 2; WYA; YAW

Le Guin, Ursula Kroeber
See Le Guin, Ursula K.

Lehane, Dennis 1965- .... **CLC 320**
See also AAYA 56; CA 154; CANR 72, 112, 136, 168, 219; LNFS 1; MTFW 2005

Lehmann, Rosamond (Nina)
1901-1990 .... **CLC 5**
See also CA 77-80; 131; CANR 8, 73; CN 1, 2, 3, 4; DLB 15; MTCW 2; RGEL 2; RHW

Lehmann, Walter
See Harwood, Gwen

Leiber, Fritz (Reuter, Jr.)
1910-1992 .... **CLC 25**
See also AAYA 65; BPFB 2; CA 45-48; 139; CANR 2, 40, 86; CN 2, 3, 4, 5; DLB 8; FANT; HGG; MTCW 1, 2; MTFW 2005; SATA 45; SATA-Obit 73; SCFW 1, 2; SFW 4; SUFW 1, 2

Leibniz, Gottfried Wilhelm von
1646-1716 .... **LC 35, 196**
See also DLB 168

Leino, Eino
See Lonnbohm, Armas Eino Leopold

Leiris, Michel (Julien) 1901-1990 ... **CLC 61**
See also CA 119; 128; 132; EWL 3; GFL 1789 to the Present

Leithauser, Brad 1953- .... **CLC 27**
See also CA 107; CANR 27, 81, 171; CP 5, 6, 7; DLB 120, 282

le Jars de Gournay, Marie
See de Gournay, Marie le Jars

Lelchuk, Alan 1938- .... **CLC 5**
See also CA 45-48; CAAS 20; CANR 1, 70, 152; CN 3, 4, 5, 6, 7

Lem, Stanislaw 1921-2006 .... **CLC 8, 15, 40, 149; SSC 177**
See also AAYA 75; CA 105; 249; CAAS 1; CANR 32; CWW 2; MTCW 1; SCFW 1, 2; SFW 4

Lemann, Nancy (Elise) 1956- .... **CLC 39**
See also CA 118; 136; CANR 121

Lemonnier, (Antoine Louis) Camille
1844-1913 .... **TCLC 22**
See also CA 121

Leñero, Vicente 1933-2014 .... **CLC 378**
See also CA 180; DLB 305; EWL 3

Leon, Luis de 1527-1591 .... **LC 182**
See also DLB 318

Lenau, Nikolaus 1802-1850 .... **NCLC 16**

L'Engle, Madeleine 1918-2007 .... **CLC 12**
See also AAYA 28; AITN 2; BPFB 2; BYA 2, 4, 5, 7; CA 1-4R; 264; CANR 3, 21, 39, 66, 107, 207; CLR 1, 14, 57, 172; CPW; CWRI 5; DA3; DAM POP; DLB 52; JRDA; MAICYA 1, 2; MTCW 1, 2; MTFW 2005; NFS 32; SAAS 15; SATA 1, 27, 75, 128; SATA-Obit 186; SFW 4; WYA; YAW

L'Engle, Madeleine Camp Franklin
See L'Engle, Madeleine

Lengyel, Jozsef 1896-1975 .... **CLC 7**
See also CA 85-88; 57-60; CANR 71; RGSF 2

Lenin, N.
See Lenin, Vladimir

Lenin, Nikolai
See Lenin, Vladimir

Lenin, V. I.
See Lenin, Vladimir

Lenin, Vladimir 1870-1924 .... **TCLC 67**
See also CA 121; 168

Lenin, Vladimir I.
See Lenin, Vladimir

Lenin, Vladimir Ilyich
See Lenin, Vladimir

Lennon, John 1940-1980 .... **CLC 12, 35**
See also CA 102; SATA 114

Lennon, John Ono
See Lennon, John

Lennox, Charlotte
1729(?)-1804 .... **NCLC 23, 134, 263**
See also BRWS 17; DLB 39; RGEL 2

Lentricchia, Frank, Jr.
See Lentricchia, Frank

Lentricchia, Frank 1940- .... **CLC 34, 387**
See also CA 25-28R; CANR 19, 106, 148; DLB 246

Lenz, Gunter .... **CLC 65**

Lenz, Jakob Michael Reinhold
1751-1792 .... **LC 100, 226**
See also DLB 94; RGWL 2, 3

Lenz, Siegfried 1926- .... **CLC 27; SSC 33**
See also CA 89-92; CANR 80, 149; CWW 2; DLB 75; EWL 3; RGSF 2; RGWL 2, 3

Leo Africanus, Johannes
c. 1490-1550(?) .... **LC 215**

Leon, David
See Jacob, (Cyprien-)Max

Leonard, Dutch
See Leonard, Elmore

Leonard, Elmore 1925-2013 ..... **CLC 28, 34, 71, 120, 222, 370**
See also AAYA 22, 59; AITN 1; BEST 89:1, 90:4; BPFB 2; CA 81-84; CANR 12, 28, 53, 76, 96, 133, 176, 219; CMW 4; CN 5, 6, 7; CPW; DA3; DAM POP; DLB 173, 226; INT CANR-28; MSW; MTCW 1, 2; MTFW 2005; RGAL 4; SATA 163; TCWW 1, 2

Leonard, Elmore John, Jr.
See Leonard, Elmore

Leonard, Hugh 1926-2009 .... **CLC 19**
See also CA 102; 283; CANR 78, 140; CBD; CD 5, 6; DFS 13, 24; DLB 13; INT CA-102

Leonard, Tom 1944- .... **CLC 289**
See also CA 77-80; CANR 13, 31; CP 2, 3, 4, 5, 6, 7

Leonov, Leonid 1899-1994 .... **CLC 92**
See also CA 129; CANR 76; DAM NOV; DLB 272; EWL 3; MTCW 1, 2; MTFW 2005

Leonov, Leonid Maksimovich
See Leonov, Leonid

Leonov, Leonid Maximovich
See Leonov, Leonid

Leopardi, (Conte) Giacomo
1798-1837 .... **NCLC 22, 129; PC 37**
See also EW 5; RGWL 2, 3; WLIT 7; WP

Le Reveler
See Artaud, Antonin

Lerman, Eleanor 1952- .... **CLC 9**
See also CA 85-88; CANR 69, 124, 184

Lerman, Rhoda 1936- .... **CLC 56**
See also CA 49-52; CANR 70

Lermontov, Mikhail Iur'evich
See Lermontov, Mikhail Yuryevich

Lermontov, Mikhail Yuryevich
1814-1841 .... **NCLC 5, 47, 126, 288; PC 18**
See also DLB 205; EW 6; RGWL 2, 3; TWA

Leroux, Gaston 1868-1927 .... **TCLC 25**
See also CA 108; 136; CANR 69; CMW 4; MTFW 2005; NFS 20; SATA 65

Lesage, Alain-René 1668-1747 ...... **LC 2, 28, 233**
See also DLB 313; EW 3; GFL Beginnings to 1789; RGWL 2, 3

Leskov, N(ikolai) S(emenovich) 1831-1895
See Leskov, Nikolai (Semyonovich)

Leskov, Nikolai (Semyonovich)
1831-1895 .... **NCLC 25, 174; SSC 34, 96**
See also DLB 238

Leskov, Nikolai Semenovich
See Leskov, Nikolai (Semyonovich)

Lesser, Milton
See Marlowe, Stephen

Lessing, Doris 1919-2013 ..... **CLC 1, 2, 3, 6, 10, 15, 22, 40, 94, 170, 254, 370; SSC 6, 61, 160; WLCS**
See also AAYA 57; AFW; BRWS 1; CA 9-12R; CAAS 14; CANR 33, 54, 76, 122, 179; CBD; CD 5, 6; CDBLB 1960 to Present; CN 1, 2, 3, 4, 5, 6, 7; CWD; DA; DA3; DAB; DAC; DAM MST, NOV; DFS 20; DLB 15, 139; DLBY 1985; EWL 3; EXPS; FL 1:6; FW; LAIT 4; MTCW 1, 2; MTFW 2005; NFS 27, 38; RGEL 2; RGSF 2; SFW 4; SSFS 1, 12, 20, 26, 30, 35; TEA; WLIT 2, 4

Lessing, Doris May
See Lessing, Doris

Lessing, Gotthold Ephraim
1729-1781 .... **DC 26; LC 8, 124, 162**
See also CDWLB 2; DLB 97; EW 4; RGWL 2, 3

Lester, Julius 1939- .... **BLC 2:2**
See also AAYA 12, 51; BW 2; BYA 3, 9, 11, 12; CA 17-20R; CANR 8, 23, 43, 129, 174; CLR 2, 41, 143; JRDA; MAICYA 1, 2; MAICYAS 1; MTFW 2005; SATA 12, 74, 112, 157; YAW

Lester, Richard 1932- .... **CLC 20**

Lethem, Jonathan 1964- .... **CLC 295**
See also AAYA 43; AMWS 18; CA 150; CANR 80, 138, 165; CN 7; MTFW 2005; SFW 4

Lethem, Jonathan Allen
See Lethem, Jonathan

Letts, Tracy 1965- .... **CLC 280**
See also CA 223; CANR 209
Levenson, Jay .... **CLC 70**
Lever, Charles (James)
1806-1872 .... **NCLC 23**
See also DLB 21; RGEL 2
Leverson, Ada Esther
1862(?)-1933(?) .... **TCLC 18**
See also CA 117; 202; DLB 153; RGEL 2
Levertov, Denise 1923-1997 ..... **CLC 1, 2, 3, 5, 8, 15, 28, 66; PC 11, 164**
See also AMWS 3; CA 1-4R, 178; 163; CAAE 178; CAAS 19; CANR 3, 29, 50, 108; CDALBS; CP 1, 2, 3, 4, 5, 6; CWP; DAM POET; DLB 5, 165, 342; EWL 3; EXPP; FW; INT CANR-29; MAL 5; MTCW 1, 2; PAB; PFS 7, 17, 31, 42; RGAL 4; RGHL; TUS; WP
Levi, Carlo 1902-1975 .... **TCLC 125**
See also CA 65-68; 53-56; CANR 10; EWL 3; RGWL 2, 3
Levi, Jonathan .... **CLC 76**
See also CA 197
Levi, Peter (Chad Tigar)
1931-2000 .... **CLC 41**
See also CA 5-8R; 187; CANR 34, 80; CP 1, 2, 3, 4, 5, 6, 7; DLB 40
Levi, Primo 1919-1987 .... **CLC 37, 50; SSC 12, 122; TCLC 109**
See also CA 13-16R; 122; CANR 12, 33, 61, 70, 132, 171; DLB 177, 299; EWL 3; MTCW 1, 2; MTFW 2005; RGHL; RGWL 2, 3; WLIT 7
Levin, Ira 1929-2007 .... **CLC 3, 6**
See also CA 21-24R; 266; CANR 17, 44, 74, 139; CMW 4; CN 1, 2, 3, 4, 5, 6, 7; CPW; DA3; DAM POP; HGG; MTCW 1, 2; MTFW 2005; SATA 66; SATA-Obit 187; SFW 4
Levin, Ira Marvin
See Levin, Ira
Levin, Meyer 1905-1981 .... **CLC 7**
See also AITN 1; CA 9-12R; 104; CANR 15; CN 1, 2, 3; DAM POP; DLB 9, 28; DLBY 1981; MAL 5; RGHL; SATA 21; SATA-Obit 27
Levine, Albert Norman
See Levine, Norman
Levine, Norman 1923-2005 .... **CLC 54**
See also CA 73-76; 240; CAAS 23; CANR 14, 70; CN 1, 2, 3, 4, 5, 6, 7; CP 1; DLB 88
Levine, Norman Albert
See Levine, Norman
Levine, Philip
1928- .... **CLC 2, 4, 5, 9, 14, 33, 118; PC 22**
See also AMWS 5; CA 9-12R; CANR 9, 37, 52, 116, 156; CP 1, 2, 3, 4, 5, 6, 7; DAM POET; DLB 5; EWL 3; MAL 5; PFS 8
Levinson, Deirdre 1931- .... **CLC 49**
See also CA 73-76; CANR 70
Levitin, Sonia 1934- .... **CLC 17**
See also AAYA 13, 48; CA 29-32R; CANR 14, 32, 79, 182; CLR 53; JRDA; MAICYA 1, 2; SAAS 2; SATA 4, 68, 119, 131, 192; SATA-Essay 131; YAW
Levon, O. U.
See Kesey, Ken
Levy, Amy 1861-1889 .... **NCLC 59, 203, PC 126**
See also DLB 156, 240
Lewald, Fanny 1811-1889 .... **NCLC 275**
See also DLB 129
Lewees, John
See Stockton, Francis Richard
Lewes, George Henry
1817-1878 .... **NCLC 25, 215**
See also DLB 55, 144
Lewis, Alun 1915-1944 .... **SSC 40; TCLC 3**
See also BRW 7; CA 104; 188; DLB 20, 162; PAB; RGEL 2
Lewis, C. S. 1898-1963 ...... **CLC 1, 3, 6, 14, 27, 124; WLC 4**
See also AAYA 3, 39; BPFB 2; BRWS 3; BYA 15, 16; CA 81-84; CANR 33, 71, 132; CDBLB 1945-1960; CLR 3, 27, 109, 173; CWRI 5; DA; DA3; DAB; DAC; DAM MST, NOV, POP; DLB 15, 100, 160, 255; EWL 3; FANT; JRDA; LMFS 2; MAICYA 1, 2; MTCW 1, 2; MTFW 2005; NFS 24; RGEL 2; SATA 13, 100; SCFW 1, 2; SFW 4; SUFW 1; TEA; WCH; WYA; YAW
Lewis, Clive Staples
See Lewis, C. S.
Lewis, Harry Sinclair
See Lewis, Sinclair
Lewis, Janet 1899-1998 .... **CLC 41**
See also CA 9-12R; 172; CANR 29, 63; CAP 1; CN 1, 2, 3, 4, 5, 6; DLBY 1987; RHW; TCWW 2
Lewis, Matthew Gregory
1775-1818 .... **NCLC 11, 62**
See also DLB 39, 158, 178; GL 3; HGG; LMFS 1; RGEL 2; SUFW
Lewis, Sinclair 1885-1951 .... **TCLC 4, 13, 23, 39, 215; WLC 4**
See also AMW; AMWC 1; BPFB 2; CA 104; 133; CANR 132; CDALB 1917-1929; DA; DA3; DAB; DAC; DAM MST, NOV; DLB 9, 102, 284, 331; DLBD 1; EWL 3; LAIT 3; MAL 5; MTCW 1, 2; MTFW 2005; NFS 15, 19, 22, 34; RGAL 4; TUS
Lewis, (Percy) Wyndham
1884(?)-1957 .... **SSC 34; TCLC 2, 9, 104, 216**
See also AAYA 77; BRW 7; CA 104; 157; DLB 15; EWL 3; FANT; MTCW 2; MTFW 2005; RGEL 2
Lewisohn, Ludwig 1883-1955 .... **TCLC 19**
See also CA 107; 203; DLB 4, 9, 28, 102; MAL 5
Lewton, Val 1904-1951 .... **TCLC 76**
See also CA 199; IDFW 3, 4
Leyner, Mark 1956- .... **CLC 92**
See also CA 110; CANR 28, 53; DA3; DLB 292; MTCW 2; MTFW 2005
Leyton, E. K.
See Campbell, Ramsey
Lezama Lima, Jose 1910-1976 ... **CLC 4, 10, 101; HLCS 2**
See also CA 77-80; CANR 71; DAM MULT; DLB 113, 283; EWL 3; HW 1, 2; LAW; RGWL 2, 3
L'Heureux, John (Clarke) 1934- .... **CLC 52**
See also CA 13-16R; CANR 23, 45, 88; CP 1, 2, 3, 4; DLB 244
Li, Fei-kan
See Jin, Ba
Li Ch'ing-chao 1081(?)-1141(?) ... **CMLC 71**
Lichtenberg, Georg Christoph
1742-1799 .... **LC 162**
See also DLB 94
Liddell, C. H.
See Kuttner, Henry
Lie, Jonas (Lauritz Idemil)
1833-1908(?) .... **TCLC 5**
See also CA 115
Lieber, Joel 1937-1971 .... **CLC 6**
See also CA 73-76; 29-32R
Lieber, Stanley Martin
See Lee, Stan
Lieberman, Laurence (James)
1935- .... **CLC 4, 36**
See also CA 17-20R; CANR 8, 36, 89; CP 1, 2, 3, 4, 5, 6, 7
Lieh Tzu fl. 7th cent. B.C.-5th cent. B.C. .... **CMLC 27**
Lieksman, Anders
See Haavikko, Paavo Juhani
Lifton, Robert Jay 1926- .... **CLC 67**
See also CA 17-20R; CANR 27, 78, 161, 239; INT CANR-27; SATA 66
Lightfoot, Gordon 1938- .... **CLC 26**
See also CA 109; 242
Lightfoot, Gordon Meredith
See Lightfoot, Gordon
Lightman, Alan P. 1948- .... **CLC 81**
See also CA 141; CANR 63, 105, 138, 178; MTFW 2005; NFS 29
Lightman, Alan Paige
See Lightman, Alan P.
Ligotti, Thomas 1953- .... **CLC 44; SSC 16**
See also CA 123; CANR 49, 135; HGG; SUFW 2
Ligotti, Thomas Robert
See Ligotti, Thomas
Li Ho 791-817 .... **PC 13**
Li Ju-chen c. 1763-c. 1830 .... **NCLC 137**
Liking, Werewere 1950- .... **BLC 2:2**
See also CA 293; DLB 360; EWL 3
Lilar, Francoise
See Mallet-Joris, Francoise
Liliencron, Detlev
See Liliencron, Detlev von
Liliencron, Detlev von 1844-1909 ... **TCLC 18**
See also CA 117
Liliencron, Friedrich Adolf Axel Detlev von
See Liliencron, Detlev von
Liliencron, Friedrich Detlev von
See Liliencron, Detlev von
Lille, Alain de
See Alain de Lille
Lillo, George 1691-1739 .... **LC 131**
See also DLB 84; RGEL 2
Lilly, William 1602-1681 .... **LC 27**
Lima, Jose Lezama
See Lezama Lima, Jose
Lima Barreto, Afonso Henrique de
1881-1922 .... **TCLC 23**
See also CA 117; 181; DLB 307; LAW
Lima Barreto, Afonso Henriques de
See Lima Barreto, Afonso Henrique de
Limonov, Eduard
See Limonov, Edward
Limonov, Edward 1944- .... **CLC 67**
See also CA 137; DLB 317
Lin, Frank
See Atherton, Gertrude (Franklin Horn)
Lin, Yutang 1895-1976 .... **TCLC 149**
See also CA 45-48; 65-68; CANR 2; RGAL 4
Lincoln, Abraham 1809-1865 .... **NCLC 18, 201**
See also LAIT 2
Lincoln, Geoffrey
See Mortimer, John
Lind, Jakov
1927-2007 .... **CLC 1, 2, 4, 27, 82**
See also CA 9-12R; 257; CAAS 4; CANR 7; DLB 299; EWL 3; RGHL
Lindbergh, Anne Morrow
1906-2001 .... **CLC 82**
See also BPFB 2; CA 17-20R; 193; CANR 16, 73; DAM NOV; MTCW 1, 2; MTFW 2005; SATA 33; SATA-Obit 125; TUS
Lindbergh, Anne Spencer Morrow
See Lindbergh, Anne Morrow
Lindgren, Astrid 1907-2002 .... **CLC 361**
See also BYA 5; CLR 1, 39, 119; CA 13-16R, 204; CANR 39, 80, 117; CWW 2; DLB 257; MAICYA 1, 2; SATA 2, 38, 118; TWA
Lindholm, Anna Margaret
See Haycraft, Anna

Author Index

Lindsay, David 1878(?)-1945 .... **TCLC 15**
See also CA 113; 187; DLB 255; FANT; SFW 4; SUFW 1
Lindsay, Nicholas Vachel
See Lindsay, Vachel
Lindsay, Vachel 1879-1931 .... **PC 23, 139; TCLC 17; WLC 4**
See also AMWS 1; CA 114; 135; CANR 79; CDALB 1865-1917; DA; DA3; DAC; DAM MST, POET; DLB 54; EWL 3; EXPP; MAL 5; RGAL 4; SATA 40; WP
Linke-Poot
See Doblin, Alfred
Linney, Romulus 1930-2011 .... **CLC 51**
See also CA 1-4R; CAD; CANR 40, 44, 79; CD 5, 6; CSW; RGAL 4
Linton, Eliza Lynn 1822-1898 ...... **NCLC 41**
See also DLB 18
Li Po 701-763 .... **CMLC 2, 86; PC 29**
See also PFS 20, 40; WP
Lippard, George 1822-1854 .... **NCLC 198**
See also AMWS 23; DLB 202
Lipsius, Justus 1547-1606 .... **LC 16, 207**
Lipsyte, Robert 1938- .... **CLC 21**
See also AAYA 7, 45; CA 17-20R; CANR 8, 57, 146, 189; CLR 23, 76; DA; DAC; DAM MST, NOV; JRDA; LAIT 5; MAICYA 1, 2; NFS 35; SATA 5, 68, 113, 161, 198; WYA; YAW
Lipsyte, Robert Michael
See Lipsyte, Robert
Lish, Gordon 1934- .... **CLC 45; SSC 18**
See also CA 113; 117; CANR 79, 151; DLB 130; INT CA-117
Lish, Gordon Jay
See Lish, Gordon
Lispector, Clarice 1920-1977 .... **CLC 43; HLCS 2; SSC 34, 96, 215; TCLC 305**
See also CA 139; 116; CANR 71; CDWLB 3; DLB 113, 307; DNFS 1; EWL 3; FW; HW 2; LAW; RGSF 2; RGWL 2, 3; WLIT 1
Liszt, Franz 1811-1886 .... **NCLC 199**
Littell, Jonathan 1967- .... **CLC 383**
See also CA 259; CANR 207
Littell, Robert 1935(?)- .... **CLC 42**
See also CA 109; 112; CANR 64, 115, 162, 217; CMW 4
Little, Malcolm
See Malcolm X
Littlewit, Humphrey Gent.
See Lovecraft, H. P.
Litwos
See Sienkiewicz, Henryk (Adam Alexander Pius)
Liu, E. 1857-1909 .... **TCLC 15**
See also CA 115; 190; DLB 328
Lively, Penelope 1933- ...... **CLC 32, 50, 306**
See also BPFB 2; CA 41-44R; CANR 29, 67, 79, 131, 172, 222; CLR 7, 159; CN 5, 6, 7; CWRI 5; DAM NOV; DLB 14, 161, 207, 326; FANT; JRDA; MAICYA 1, 2; MTCW 1, 2; MTFW 2005; SATA 7, 60, 101, 164; TEA
Lively, Penelope Margaret
See Lively, Penelope
Livesay, Dorothy (Kathleen) 1909-1996 .... **CLC 4, 15, 79**
See also AITN 2; CA 25-28R; CAAS 8; CANR 36, 67; CP 1, 2, 3, 4, 5; DAC; DAM MST, POET; DLB 68; FW; MTCW 1; RGEL 2; TWA
Livius Andronicus c. 284B.C.-c. 204B.C. .... **CMLC 102**
Livy c. 59B.C.-c. 12 .... **CMLC 11, 154**
See also AW 2; CDWLB 1; DLB 211; RGWL 2, 3; WLIT 8
Li Yaotang
See Jin, Ba
Liyong, Taban lo 1939- .... **CLC 359**
See also BW 2; CA 105; CANR 79; CP 2, 3, 4, 5, 6, 7; DLB 125
Li-Young, Lee
See Lee, Li-Young
Lizardi, Jose Joaquin Fernandez de 1776-1827 .... **NCLC 30**
See also LAW
Llewellyn, Richard
See Llewellyn Lloyd, Richard Dafydd Vivian
Llewellyn Lloyd, Richard Dafydd Vivian 1906-1983 .... **CLC 7, 80**
See also CA 53-56; 111; CANR 7, 71; DLB 15; NFS 30; SATA 11; SATA-Obit 37
Llosa, Jorge Mario Pedro Vargas
See Vargas Llosa, Mario
Llosa, Mario Vargas
See Vargas Llosa, Mario
Lloyd, Manda
See Mander, (Mary) Jane
Lloyd Webber, Andrew 1948- .... **CLC 21**
See also AAYA 1, 38; CA 116; 149; DAM DRAM; DFS 7; SATA 56
Llull, Ramon c. 1235-c. 1316 .... **CMLC 12, 114**
Lonnbohm, Armas Eino Leopold 1878-1926 .... **TCLC 24**
See also CA 123; EWL 3
Lobb, Ebenezer
See Upward, Allen
Lochhead, Liz 1947- .... **CLC 286**
See also BRWS 17; CA 81-84; CANR 79; CBD; CD 5, 6; CP 2, 3, 4, 5, 6, 7; CWD; CWP; DLB 310
Lock, Anne c. 1530-c. 1595 .... **PC 135**
Locke, Alain Leroy 1885-1954 ... **BLCS; HR 1:3; TCLC 43**
See also AMWS 14; BW 1, 3; CA 106; 124; CANR 79; DLB 51; LMFS 2; MAL 5; RGAL 4
Locke, John 1632-1704 .... **LC 7, 35, 135**
See also DLB 31, 101, 213, 252; RGEL 2; WLIT 3
Locke-Elliott, Sumner
See Elliott, Sumner Locke
Lockhart, John Gibson 1794-1854 ... **NCLC 6**
See also DLB 110, 116, 144
Lockridge, Ross (Franklin), Jr. 1914-1948 .... **TCLC 111**
See also CA 108; 145; CANR 79; DLB 143; DLBY 1980; MAL 5; RGAL 4; RHW
Lockwood, Robert
See Johnson, Robert
Lodge, David 1935- .... **CLC 36, 141, 293**
See also BEST 90:1; BRWS 4; CA 17-20R; CANR 19, 53, 92, 139, 197, 243; CN 1, 2, 3, 4, 5, 6, 7; CPW; DAM POP; DLB 14, 194; EWL 3; INT CANR-19; MTCW 1, 2; MTFW 2005
Lodge, David John
See Lodge, David
Lodge, Thomas 1558-1625 .... **LC 41**
See also DLB 172; RGEL 2
Loewinsohn, Ron(ald William) 1937- .... **CLC 52**
See also CA 25-28R; CANR 71; CP 1, 2, 3, 4
Logan, Jake
See Smith, Martin Cruz
Logan, John (Burton) 1923-1987 ..... **CLC 5**
See also CA 77-80; 124; CANR 45; CP 1, 2, 3, 4; DLB 5
Lohenstein, Daniel Casper von 1635-1683 .... **LC 240**
See also DLB 168
Lo-Johansson, (Karl) Ivar 1901-1990 .... **TCLC 216**
See also CA 102; 131; CANR 20, 79, 137; DLB 259; EWL 3; RGWL 2, 3
Lo Kuan-chung
See Luo Guanzhong
Lomax, Pearl
See Cleage, Pearl
Lomax, Pearl Cleage
See Cleage, Pearl
Lombard, Nap
See Johnson, Pamela Hansford
Lombard, Peter 1100(?)-1160(?) ... **CMLC 72**
Lombino, Salvatore
See Hunter, Evan
London, Jack 1876-1916 .... **SSC 4, 49, 133; TCLC 9, 15, 39; WLC 4**
See also AAYA 13, 75; AITN 2; AMW; BPFB 2; BYA 4, 13; CA 110; 119; CANR 73; CDALB 1865-1917; CLR 108; DA; DA3; DAB; DAC; DAM MST, NOV; DLB 8, 12, 78, 212; EWL 3; EXPS; JRDA; LAIT 3; MAICYA 1, 2,; MAL 5; MTCW 1, 2; MTFW 2005; NFS 8, 19, 35; RGAL 4; RGSF 2; SATA 18; SFW 4; SSFS 7, 35; TCWW 1, 2; TUS; WYA; YAW
London, John Griffith
See London, Jack
Long, Emmett
See Leonard, Elmore
Longbaugh, Harry
See Goldman, William
Longfellow, Henry Wadsworth 1807-1882 .... **NCLC 2, 45, 101, 103, 235; PC 30; WLCS**
See also AMW; AMWR 2; CDALB 1640-1865; CLR 99; DA; DA3; DAB; DAC; DAM MST, POET; DLB 1, 59, 235; EXPP; PAB; PFS 2, 7, 17, 31, 39; RGAL 4; SATA 19; TUS; WP
Longinus c. 1st cent. .... **CMLC 27**
See also AW 2; DLB 176
Longley, Michael 1939- ..... **CLC 29; PC 118**
See also BRWS 8; CA 102; CP 1, 2, 3, 4, 5, 6, 7; DLB 40
Longstreet, Augustus Baldwin 1790-1870 .... **NCLC 159**
See also DLB 3, 11, 74, 248; RGAL 4
Longus fl. c. 2nd cent. .... **CMLC 7**
Longway, A. Hugh
See Lang, Andrew
Lonnbohm, Armas Eino Leopold
See Lonnbohm, Armas Eino Leopold
Lonsdale, Roger .... **CLC 65**
Lopate, Phillip 1943- .... **CLC 29**
See also CA 97-100; CANR 88, 157, 196; DLBY 1980; INT CA-97-100
Lopez, Barry 1945- .... **CLC 70, 359**
See also AAYA 9, 63; ANW; CA 65-68; CANR 7, 23, 47, 68, 92; DLB 256, 275, 335; INT CANR-7, CANR-23; MTCW 1; RGAL 4; SATA 67
Lopez, Barry Holstun
See Lopez, Barry
Lopez y Fuentes, Gregorio 1897(?)-1966 .... **CLC 32**
See also CA 131; EWL 3; HW 1
Lorca, Federico Garcia
See Garcia Lorca, Federico
Lord, Audre
See Lorde, Audre
Lord, Bette Bao 1938- .... **AAL; CLC 23**
See also BEST 90:3; BPFB 2; CA 107; CANR 41, 79; CLR 151; INT CA-107; SATA 58
Lord Auch
See Bataille, Georges
Lord Brooke
See Greville, Fulke
Lord Byron 1788-1824 .... **DC 24; NCLC 2, 12, 109, 149, 256; PC 16, 95; WLC 1**

See also AAYA 64; BRW 4; BRWC 2; CDBLB 1789-1832; DA; DA3; DAB; DAC; DAM MST, POET; DLB 96, 110; EXPP; LMFS 1; PAB; PFS 1, 14, 29, 35; RGEL 2; TEA; WLIT 3; WP
Lord Dunsany 1878-1957 .... **TCLC 2, 59**
See also CA 104; 148; DLB 10, 77, 153, 156, 255; FANT; MTCW 2; RGEL 2; SFW 4; SUFW 1
Lorde, Audre 1934-1992 .... **BLC 1:2, 2:2; CLC 18, 71; PC 12, 141; TCLC 173, 300**
See also AFAW 1, 2; BW 1, 3; CA 25-28R; 142; CANR 16, 26, 46, 82; CP 2, 3, 4, 5; DA3; DAM MULT, POET; DLB 41; EWL 3; FW; GLL 1; MAL 5; MTCW 1, 2; MTFW 2005; PFS 16, 32; RGAL 4
Lorde, Audre Geraldine
See Lorde, Audre
Lord Houghton
See Milnes, Richard Monckton
Lord Jeffrey
See Jeffrey, Francis
Loreaux, Nichol .... **CLC 65**
Lorenzo, Heberto Padilla
See Padilla (Lorenzo), Heberto
Loris
See Hofmannsthal, Hugo von
Loti, Pierre
See Viaud, Julien
Lottie
See Grimke, Charlotte L. Forten
Lou, Henri
See Andreas-Salome, Lou
Louie, David Wong 1954- .... **CLC 70**
See also CA 139; CANR 120
Louis, Adrian C. .... **NNAL**
See also CA 223
Louis, Father M.
See Merton, Thomas
Louise, Heidi
See Erdrich, Louise
Lounsbury, Ruth Ozeki
See Ozeki, Ruth L.
Lovecraft, H. P. 1890-1937 .... **SSC 3, 52, 165, 200; TCLC 4, 22**
See also AAYA 14; BPFB 2; CA 104; 133; CANR 106; DA3; DAM POP; HGG; MTCW 1, 2; MTFW 2005; RGAL 4; SCFW 1, 2; SFW 4; SUFW
Lovecraft, Howard Phillips
See Lovecraft, H. P.
Lovelace, Earl 1935- .... **CLC 51; SSC 141**
See also BW 2; CA 77-80; CANR 41, 72, 114; CD 5, 6; CDWLB 3; CN 1, 2, 3, 4, 5, 6, 7; DLB 125; EWL 3; MTCW 1
Lovelace, Richard
1618-1658 .... **LC 24, 158; PC 69**
See also BRW 2; DLB 131; EXPP; PAB; PFS 32, 34; RGEL 2
Low, Penelope Margaret
See Lively, Penelope
Lowe, Pardee 1904- .... **AAL**
Lowell, Amy 1874-1925 .... **PC 13, 168; TCLC 1, 8, 259**
See also AAYA 57; AMW; CA 104; 151; DAM POET; DLB 54, 140; EWL 3; EXPP; LMFS 2; MAL 5; MBL; MTCW 2; MTFW 2005; PFS 30, 42; RGAL 4; TUS
Lowell, James Russell
1819-1891 .... **NCLC 2, 90**
See also AMWS 1; CDALB 1640-1865; DLB 1, 11, 64, 79, 189, 235; RGAL 4
Lowell, Robert 1917-1977 ... **CLC 1, 2, 3, 4, 5, 8, 9, 11, 15, 37, 124; PC 3, 132; WLC 4**
See also AMW; AMWC 2; AMWR 2; CA 9-12R; 73-76; CABS 2; CAD; CANR 26, 60; CDALBS; CP 1, 2; DA; DA3; DAB; DAC; DAM MST, NOV; DLB 5, 169; EWL 3; MAL 5; MTCW 1, 2; MTFW 2005; PAB; PFS 6, 7, 36; RGAL 4; WP
Lowell, Robert Trail Spence, Jr.
See Lowell, Robert
Lowenthal, Michael 1969- .... **CLC 119**
See also CA 150; CANR 115, 164
Lowenthal, Michael Francis
See Lowenthal, Michael
Lowndes, Marie Adelaide (Belloc)
1868-1947 .... **TCLC 12**
See also CA 107; CMW 4; DLB 70; RHW
Lowry, (Clarence) Malcolm
1909-1957 ... **SSC 31; TCLC 6, 40, 275**
See also BPFB 2; BRWS 3; CA 105; 131; CANR 62, 105; CDBLB 1945-1960; DLB 15; EWL 3; MTCW 1, 2; MTFW 2005; RGEL 2
Lowry, Mina Gertrude
1882-1966 .... **CLC 28; PC 16**
See also CA 113; DAM POET; DLB 4, 54; PFS 20
Lowry, Sam
See Soderbergh, Steven
Loxsmith, John
See Brunner, John (Kilian Houston)
Loy, Mina
See Lowry, Mina Gertrude
Loyson-Bridet
See Schwob, Marcel (Mayer Andre)
Lopez de Mendoza, Inigo
See Santillana, Inigo Lopez de Mendoza, Marques de
Lopez Portillo (y Pacheco), Jose
1920-2004 .... **CLC 46**
See also CA 129; 224; HW 1
Eluard, Paul
See Grindel, Eugene
Lucan 39-65 .... **CMLC 33, 112, 160**
See also AW 2; DLB 211; EFS 1:2, 2:2; RGWL 2, 3
Lucas, Craig 1951- .... **CLC 64**
See also CA 137; CAD; CANR 71, 109, 142; CD 5, 6; GLL 2; MTFW 2005
Lucas, E(dward) V(errall)
1868-1938 .... **TCLC 73**
See also CA 176; DLB 98, 149, 153; SATA 20
Lucas, George 1944- .... **CLC 16, 252**
See also AAYA 1, 23; CA 77-80; CANR 30; SATA 56
Lucas, Hans
See Godard, Jean-Luc
Lucas, Victoria
See Plath, Sylvia
Lucian c. 125-c. 180 .... **CMLC 32, 144**
See also AW 2; DLB 176; RGWL 2, 3
Lucilius c. 180B.C.-102B.C. .... **CMLC 82**
See also DLB 211
Lucretius c. 94B.C.-c. 49B.C. ...... **CMLC 48, 170; PC 143**
See also AW 2; CDWLB 1; DLB 211; EFS 1:2, 2:2; RGWL 2, 3; WLIT 8
Ludlam, Charles 1943-1987 ...... **CLC 46, 50**
See also CA 85-88; 122; CAD; CANR 72, 86; DLB 266
Ludlum, Robert 1927-2001 .... **CLC 22, 43**
See also AAYA 10, 59; BEST 89:1, 90:3; BPFB 2; CA 33-36R; 195; CANR 25, 41, 68, 105, 131; CMW 4; CPW; DA3; DAM NOV, POP; DLBY 1982; MSW; MTCW 1, 2; MTFW 2005
Ludwig, Ken 1950- .... **CLC 60**
See also CA 195; CAD; CD 6
Ludwig, Otto 1813-1865 .... **NCLC 4**
See also DLB 129
Lugones, Leopoldo 1874-1938 .... **HLCS 2; TCLC 15**
See also CA 116; 131; CANR 104; DLB 283; EWL 3; HW 1; LAW
Lu Hsun
See Lu Xun
Lu Hsun
See Shu-Jen, Chou
Lukacs, George
See Lukacs, Gyorgy
Lukacs, Gyorgy 1885-1971 .... **CLC 24**
See also CA 101; 29-32R; CANR 62; CDWLB 4; DLB 215, 242; EW 10; EWL 3; MTCW 1, 2
Lukacs, Gyorgy Szegeny von
See Lukacs, Gyorgy
Luke, Peter (Ambrose Cyprian)
1919-1995 .... **CLC 38**
See also CA 81-84; 147; CANR 72; CBD; CD 5, 6; DLB 13
Lumet, Sidney 1924-2011 .... **CLC 341**
Lunar, Dennis
See Mungo, Raymond
Luo Guanzhong 1315(?)-1385(?) .... **LC 12, 209**
Lurie, Alison 1926- ... **CLC 4, 5, 18, 39, 175**
See also BPFB 2; CA 1-4R; CANR 2, 17, 50, 88; CN 1, 2, 3, 4, 5, 6, 7; DLB 2, 350; MAL 5; MTCW 1; NFS 24; SATA 46, 112; TCLE 1:1
Lustig, Arnost 1926-2011 .... **CLC 56**
See also AAYA 3; CA 69-72; CANR 47, 102; CWW 2; DLB 232, 299; EWL 3; RGHL; SATA 56
Luther, Martin 1483-1546 ..... **LC 9, 37, 150**
See also CDWLB 2; DLB 179; EW 2; RGWL 2, 3
Luxemburg, Rosa 1870(?)-1919 .... **TCLC 63**
See also CA 118
Lu Xun 1881-1936 ... **SSC 158; TCLC 3, 289**
See also CA 243; DLB 328; RGSF 2; RGWL 2, 3
Luzi, Mario (Egidio Vincenzo)
1914-2005 .... **CLC 13**
See also CA 61-64; 236; CANR 9, 70; CWW 2; DLB 128; EWL 3
Levi-Strauss, Claude
1908-2008 .... **CLC 38, 302, 374**
See also CA 1-4R; CANR 6, 32, 57; DLB 242; EWL 3; GFL 1789 to the Present; MTCW 1, 2; TWA
L'vov, Arkady .... **CLC 59**
Lydgate, John c. 1370-1450(?) ... **LC 81, 175**
See also BRW 1; DLB 146; RGEL 2
Lyly, John 1554(?)-1606 .... **DC 7; LC 41, 187**
See also BRW 1; DAM DRAM; DLB 62, 167; RGEL 2
L'Ymagier
See Gourmont, Remy(-Marie-Charles) de
Lynch, B. Suarez
See Borges, Jorge Luis
Lynch, David 1946- .... **CLC 66, 162**
See also AAYA 55; CA 124; 129; CANR 111
Lynch, David Keith
See Lynch, David
Lynch, James
See Andreyev, Leonid
Lyndsay, Sir David 1485-1555 .... **LC 20**
See also RGEL 2
Lynn, Kenneth S(chuyler) 1923-2001 .. **CLC 50**
See also CA 1-4R; 196; CANR 3, 27, 65
Lynx
See West, Rebecca
Lyons, Marcus
See Blish, James
Lyotard, Jean-Francois 1924-1998 .. **TCLC 103**
See also DLB 242; EWL 3
Lyre, Pinchbeck
See Sassoon, Siegfried
Lytle, Andrew (Nelson) 1902-1995 .... **CLC 22**
See also CA 9-12R; 150; CANR 70; CN 1, 2, 3, 4, 5, 6; CSW; DLB 6; DLBY 1995; RGAL 4; RHW

Lyttelton, George 1709-1773 .... **LC 10**
See also RGEL 2

Lytton, Edward G.E.L. Bulwer-Lytton Baron
See Bulwer-Lytton, Edward

Lytton of Knebworth, Baron
See Bulwer-Lytton, Edward

M. E.
See Mangan, James Clarence

Maalouf, Amin 1949- .... **CLC 248**
See also CA 212; CANR 194; DLB 346

Maas, Peter 1929-2001 .... **CLC 29**
See also CA 93-96; 201; INT CA-93-96; MTCW 2; MTFW 2005

Mac A'Ghobhainn, Iain
See Smith, Iain Crichton

Macaulay, Catharine 1731-1791 ... **LC 64, 227**
See also BRWS 17; DLB 104, 336

Macaulay, (Emilie) Rose
1881(?)-1958 .... **TCLC 7, 44**
See also CA 104; DLB 36; EWL 3; RGEL 2; RHW

Macaulay, Thomas Babington
1800-1859 .... **NCLC 42, 231**
See also BRW 4; CDBLB 1832-1890; DLB 32, 55; RGEL 2

MacBeth, George (Mann)
1932-1992 .... **CLC 2, 5, 9**
See also CA 25-28R; 136; CANR 61, 66; CP 1, 2, 3, 4, 5; DLB 40; MTCW 1; PFS 8; SATA 4; SATA-Obit 70

MacCaig, Norman (Alexander)
1910-1996 .... **CLC 36**
See also BRWS 6; CA 9-12R; CANR 3, 34; CP 1, 2, 3, 4, 5, 6; DAB; DAM POET; DLB 27; EWL 3; RGEL 2

MacCarthy, Sir (Charles Otto) Desmond
1877-1952 .... **TCLC 36**
See also CA 167

MacDiarmid, Hugh
See Grieve, C. M.

MacDonald, Anson
See Heinlein, Robert A.

Macdonald, Cynthia 1928- .... **CLC 13, 19**
See also CA 49-52; CANR 4, 44, 146; DLB 105

MacDonald, George 1824-1905 ..... **TCLC 9, 113, 207**
See also AAYA 57; BYA 5; CA 106; 137; CANR 80; CLR 67; DLB 18, 163, 178; FANT; MAICYA 1, 2; RGEL 2; SATA 33, 100; SFW 4; SUFW; WCH

Macdonald, John
See Millar, Kenneth

MacDonald, John D.
1916-1986 .... **CLC 3, 27, 44**
See also BPFB 2; CA 1-4R; 121; CANR 1, 19, 60; CMW 4; CPW; DAM NOV, POP; DLB 8, 306; DLBY 1986; MSW; MTCW 1, 2; MTFW 2005; SFW 4

Macdonald, John Ross
See Millar, Kenneth

Macdonald, Ross
See Millar, Kenneth

MacDonald Fraser, George
See Fraser, George MacDonald

MacDougal, John
See Blish, James

MacDowell, John
See Parks, Tim

MacEwen, Gwendolyn (Margaret)
1941-1987 .... **CLC 13, 55**
See also CA 9-12R; 124; CANR 7, 22; CP 1, 2, 3, 4; DLB 53, 251; SATA 50; SATA-Obit 55

MacGreevy, Thomas 1893-1967 .... **PC 82**
See also CA 262

Macha, Karel Hynek
1810-1846 .... **NCLC 46**

Machado (y Ruiz), Antonio
1875-1939 .... **TCLC 3**
See also CA 104; 174; DLB 108; EW 9; EWL 3; HW 2; PFS 23; RGWL 2, 3

Machado de Assis, Joaquim Maria
1839-1908 .... **BLC 1:2; HLCS 2; SSC 24, 118; TCLC 10, 269**
See also CA 107; 153; CANR 91; DLB 307; LAW; RGSF 2; RGWL 2, 3; TWA; WLIT 1

Machaut, Guillaume de
c. 1300-1377 .... **CMLC 64**
See also DLB 208

Machen, Arthur
See Jones, Arthur Llewellyn

Machen, Arthur Llewelyn Jones
See Jones, Arthur Llewellyn

Machiavelli, Niccolo 1469-1527 .... **DC 16; LC 8, 36, 140; WLCS**
See also AAYA 58; DA; DAB; DAC; DAM MST; EW 2; LAIT 1; LMFS 1; NFS 9; RGWL 2, 3; TWA; WLIT 7

MacInnes, Colin 1914-1976 .... **CLC 4, 23**
See also CA 69-72; 65-68; CANR 21; CN 1, 2; DLB 14; MTCW 1, 2; RGEL 2; RHW

MacInnes, Helen (Clark)
1907-1985 .... **CLC 27, 39**
See also BPFB 2; CA 1-4R; 117; CANR 1, 28, 58; CMW 4; CN 1, 2; CPW; DAM POP; DLB 87; MSW; MTCW 1, 2; MTFW 2005; SATA 22; SATA-Obit 44

Mackay, Mary 1855-1924 .... **TCLC 51**
See also CA 118; 177; DLB 34, 156; FANT; RGEL 2; RHW; SUFW 1

Mackay, Shena 1944- .... **CLC 195**
See also CA 104; CANR 88, 139, 207; DLB 231, 319; MTFW 2005

Mackenzie, Compton (Edward Montague)
1883-1972 .... **CLC 18; TCLC 116**
See also CA 21-22; 37-40R; CAP 2; CN 1; DLB 34, 100; RGEL 2

Mackenzie, Henry 1745-1831 **NCLC 41, 284**
See also DLB 39; RGEL 2

Mackey, Nathaniel 1947- ... **BLC 2:3; PC 49**
See also CA 153; CANR 114; CP 6, 7; DLB 169

Mackey, Nathaniel Ernest
See Mackey, Nathaniel

MacKinnon, Catharine
See MacKinnon, Catharine A.

MacKinnon, Catharine A. 1946- ... **CLC 181**
See also CA 128; 132; CANR 73, 140, 189; FW; MTCW 2; MTFW 2005

Mackintosh, Elizabeth 1896(?)-1952 .. **TCLC 14**
See also CA 110; CMW 4; DLB 10, 77; MSW

Macklin, Charles 1699-1797 .... **LC 132**
See also DLB 89; RGEL 2

MacLaren, James
See Grieve, C. M.

MacLaverty, Bernard 1942- .... **CLC 31, 243**
See also CA 116; 118; CANR 43, 88, 168; CN 5, 6, 7; DLB 267; INT CA-118; RGSF 2

MacLean, Alistair 1922(?)-1987 .... **CLC 3, 13, 50, 63**
See also CA 57-60; 121; CANR 28, 61; CMW 4; CP 2, 3, 4, 5, 6, 7; CPW; DAM POP; DLB 276; MTCW 1; SATA 23; SATA-Obit 50; TCWW 2

MacLean, Alistair Stuart
See MacLean, Alistair

Maclean, Norman (Fitzroy)
1902-1990 .... **CLC 78; SSC 13, 136**
See also AMWS 14; CA 102; 132; CANR 49; CPW; DAM POP; DLB 206; TCWW 2

MacLeish, Archibald
1892-1982 .... **CLC 3, 8, 14, 68; DC 43; PC 47; TCLC 276**
See also AMW; CA 9-12R; 106; CAD; CANR 33, 63; CDALBS; CP 1, 2; DAM POET; DFS 15; DLB 4, 7, 45; DLBY 1982; EWL 3; EXPP; MAL 5; MTCW 1, 2; MTFW 2005; PAB; PFS 5; RGAL 4; TUS

MacLennan, (John) Hugh
1907-1990 .... **CLC 2, 14, 92**
See also CA 5-8R; 142; CANR 33; CN 1, 2, 3, 4; DAC; DAM MST; DLB 68; EWL 3; MTCW 1, 2; MTFW 2005; RGEL 2; TWA

MacLeod, Alistair 1936- .... **CLC 56, 165; SSC 90**
See also CA 123; CCA 1; DAC; DAM MST; DLB 60; MTCW 2; MTFW 2005; RGSF 2; TCLE 1:2

Macleod, Fiona
See Sharp, William

Mac Low, Jackson 1922-2004 .... **PC 138**
See also CA 81-84; 234; CAD; CANR 90; CD 5, 6; CP 1, 2, 3, 4, 5, 6, 7; DLB 193

MacNeice, (Frederick) Louis
1907-1963 ..... **CLC 1, 4, 10, 53; PC 61**
See also BRW 7; CA 85-88; CANR 61; DAB; DAM POET; DLB 10, 20; EWL 3; MTCW 1, 2; MTFW 2005; RGEL 2

MacNeill, Dand
See Fraser, George MacDonald

Macpherson, James 1736-1796 ... **CMLC 28; LC 29, 196; PC 97**
See also BRWS 8; DLB 109, 336; RGEL 2

Macpherson, (Jean) Jay 1931- .... **CLC 14**
See also CA 5-8R; CANR 90; CP 1, 2, 3, 4, 6, 7; CWP; DLB 53

Macrobius fl. 430 .... **CMLC 48, 153**

MacShane, Frank 1927-1999 .... **CLC 39**
See also CA 9-12R; 186; CANR 3, 33; DLB 111

Macumber, Mari
See Sandoz, Mari(e Susette)

Madach, Imre 1823-1864 .... **NCLC 19**

Madden, (Jerry) David 1933- ..... **CLC 5, 15**
See also CA 1-4R; CAAS 3; CANR 4, 45; CN 3, 4, 5, 6, 7; CSW; DLB 6; MTCW 1

Maddern, Al(an)
See Ellison, Harlan

Madhubuti, Haki R. 1942- .... **BLC 1:2; CLC 2; PC 5**
See also BW 2, 3; CA 73-76; CANR 24, 51, 73, 139; CP 2, 3, 4, 5, 6, 7; CSW; DAM MULT, POET; DLB 5, 41; DLBD 8; EWL 3; MAL 5; MTCW 2; MTFW 2005; RGAL 4

Madison, James 1751-1836 .... **NCLC 126**
See also DLB 37

Maepenn, Hugh
See Kuttner, Henry

Maepenn, K. H.
See Kuttner, Henry

Maeterlinck, Maurice 1862-1949 ...... **DC 32; TCLC 3, 251**
See also CA 104; 136; CANR 80; DAM DRAM; DLB 192, 331; EW 8; EWL 3; GFL 1789 to the Present; LMFS 2; RGWL 2, 3; SATA 66; TWA

Maginn, William 1794-1842 .... **NCLC 8**
See also DLB 110, 159

Magona, Sindiwe 1943- .... **CLC 377**
See also BW 3; CA 170; DLB 360; NFS 43

Mahapatra, Jayanta 1928- ...... **CLC 33, 348**
See also CA 73-76; CAAS 9; CANR 15, 33, 66, 87; CP 4, 5, 6, 7; DAM MULT; DLB 323

Mahfouz, Nagib
See Mahfouz, Naguib

Mahfouz, Naguib 1911(?)-2006 ...... **CLC 52, 55, 153; SSC 66**
See also AAYA 49; AFW; BEST 89:2; CA 128; 253; CANR 55, 101; DA3; DAM NOV; DLB 346; DLBY 1988; MTCW 1, 2; MTFW 2005; NFS 42; RGSF 2; RGWL 2, 3; SSFS 9, 33; WLIT 2

Mahfouz, Naguib Abdel Aziz Al-Sabilgi
See Mahfouz, Naguib

Mahfouz, Najib
See Mahfouz, Naguib
Mahfuz, Najib
See Mahfouz, Naguib
Mahon, Derek 1941- .... **CLC 27; PC 60**
See also BRWS 6; CA 113; 128; CANR 88; CP 1, 2, 3, 4, 5, 6, 7; DLB 40; EWL 3
Maiakovskii, Vladimir
See Mayakovski, Vladimir
Mailer, Norman 1923-2007 ..... **CLC 1, 2, 3, 4, 5, 8, 11, 14, 28, 39, 74, 111, 234, 345**
See also AAYA 31; AITN 2; AMW; AMWC 2; AMWR 2; BPFB 2; CA 9-12R; 266; CABS 1; CANR 28, 74, 77, 130, 196; CDALB 1968-1988; CN 1, 2, 3, 4, 5, 6, 7; CPW; DA; DA3; DAB; DAC; DAM MST, NOV, POP; DLB 2, 16, 28, 185, 278; DLBD 3; DLBY 1980, 1983; EWL 3; MAL 5; MTCW 1, 2; MTFW 2005; NFS 10; RGAL 4; TUS
Mailer, Norman Kingsley
See Mailer, Norman
Maillet, Antonine 1929- .... **CLC 54, 118**
See also CA 115; 120; CANR 46, 74, 77, 134; CCA 1; CWW 2; DAC; DLB 60; INT CA-120; MTCW 2; MTFW 2005
Maimonides, Moses 1135-1204 .... **CMLC 76**
See also DLB 115
Mais, Roger 1905-1955 .... **TCLC 8**
See also BW 1, 3; CA 105; 124; CANR 82; CDWLB 3; DLB 125; EWL 3; MTCW 1; RGEL 2
Maistre, Joseph 1753-1821 .... **NCLC 37**
See also GFL 1789 to the Present
Maitland, Frederic William
1850-1906 .... **TCLC 65**
Maitland, Sara 1950- .... **CLC 49**
See also BRWS 11; CA 69-72; CANR 13, 59, 221; DLB 271; FW
Maitland, Sara Louise
See Maitland, Sara
Major, Clarence 1936- .... **BLC 1:2; CLC 3, 19, 48**
See also AFAW 2; BW 2, 3; CA 21-24R; CAAS 6; CANR 13, 25, 53, 82; CN 3, 4, 5, 6, 7; CP 2, 3, 4, 5, 6, 7; CSW; DAM MULT; DLB 33; EWL 3; MAL 5; MSW
Major, Kevin (Gerald) 1949- .... **CLC 26**
See also AAYA 16; CA 97-100; CANR 21, 38, 112; CLR 11; DAC; DLB 60; INT CANR-21; JRDA; MAICYA 1, 2; MAICYAS 1; SATA 32, 82, 134; WYA; YAW
Makanin, Vladimir 1937- .... **CLC 380**
See also DLB 285
Maki, James
See Ozu, Yasujiro
Makin, Bathsua 1600-1675(?) .... **LC 137**
Makine, Andrei 1957- .... **CLC 198**
See also CA 176; CANR 103, 162; MTFW 2005
Makine, Andreï
See Makine, Andrei
Malabaila, Damiano
See Levi, Primo
Malamud, Bernard 1914-1986 ..... **CLC 1, 2, 3, 5, 8, 9, 11, 18, 27, 44, 78, 85; SSC 15, 147; TCLC 129, 184; WLC 4**
See also AAYA 16; AMWS 1; BPFB 2; BYA 15; CA 5-8R; 118; CABS 1; CANR 28, 62, 114; CDALB 1941-1968; CN 1, 2, 3, 4; CPW; DA; DA3; DAB; DAC; DAM MST, NOV, POP; DLB 2, 28, 152; DLBY 1980, 1986; EWL 3; EXPS; LAIT 4; LATS 1:1; MAL 5; MTCW 1, 2; MTFW 2005; NFS 27; RGAL 4; RGHL; RGSF 2; SSFS 8, 13, 16; TUS
Malan, Herman
See Bosman, Herman Charles; Bosman, Herman Charles
Malaparte, Curzio 1898-1957 .... **TCLC 52**
See also DLB 264
Malcolm, Dan
See Silverberg, Robert
Malcolm, Janet 1934- .... **CLC 201**
See also CA 123; CANR 89, 199; NCFS 1
Malcolm X 1925-1965 ... **BLC 1:2; CLC 82, 117; WLCS**
See also BW 1, 3; CA 125; 111; CANR 82; DA; DA3; DAB; DAC; DAM MST, MULT; LAIT 5; MTCW 1, 2; MTFW 2005; NCFS 3
Malebranche, Nicolas 1638-1715 ..... **LC 133**
See also GFL Beginnings to 1789
Malherbe, Francois de 1555-1628 .... **LC 5**
See also DLB 327; GFL Beginnings to 1789
Mallarme, Stephane 1842-1898 ..... **NCLC 4, 41, 210; PC 4, 102**
See also DAM POET; DLB 217; EW 7; GFL 1789 to the Present; LMFS 2; RGWL 2, 3; TWA
Mallet-Joris, Francoise 1930- .... **CLC 11**
See also CA 65-68; CANR 17; CWW 2; DLB 83; EWL 3; GFL 1789 to the Present
Malley, Ern
See McAuley, James Phillip
Mallon, Thomas 1951- .... **CLC 172**
See also CA 110; CANR 29, 57, 92, 196; DLB 350
Mallowan, Agatha Christie
See Christie, Agatha
Maloff, Saul 1922- .... **CLC 5**
See also CA 33-36R
Malone, Louis
See MacNeice, (Frederick) Louis
Malone, Michael 1942- .... **CLC 43**
See also CA 77-80; CANR 14, 32, 57, 114, 214
Malone, Michael Christopher
See Malone, Michael
Malory, Sir Thomas
1410(?)-1471(?) .... **LC 11, 88, 229; WLCS**
See also BRW 1; BRWR 2; CDBLB Before 1660; DA; DAB; DAC; DAM MST; DLB 146; EFS 1:2, 2:2; RGEL 2; SATA 59; SATA-Brief 33; TEA; WLIT 3
Malouf, David 1934- .... **CLC 28, 86, 245**
See also BRWS 12; CA 124; CANR 50, 76, 180, 224; CN 3, 4, 5, 6, 7; CP 1, 3, 4, 5, 6, 7; DLB 289; EWL 3; MTCW 2; MTFW 2005; SSFS 24
Malouf, George Joseph David
See Malouf, David
Malraux, Andre 1901-1976 ..... **CLC 1, 4, 9, 13, 15, 57; TCLC 209**
See also BPFB 2; CA 21-22; 69-72; CANR 34, 58; CAP 2; DA3; DAM NOV; DLB 72; EW 12; EWL 3; GFL 1789 to the Present; MTCW 1, 2; MTFW 2005; RGWL 2, 3; TWA
Malraux, Georges-Andre
See Malraux, Andre
Malthus, Thomas Robert
1766-1834 .... **NCLC 145**
See also DLB 107, 158; RGEL 2
Malzberg, Barry N(athaniel) 1939- ... **CLC 7**
See also CA 61-64; CAAS 4; CANR 16; CMW 4; DLB 8; SFW 4
Mamet, David 1947- .... **CLC 9, 15, 34, 46, 91, 166; DC 4, 24**
See also AAYA 3, 60; AMWS 14; CA 81-84; CABS 3; CAD; CANR 15, 41, 67, 72, 129, 172; CD 5, 6; DA3; DAM DRAM; DFS 2, 3, 6, 12, 15; DLB 7; EWL 3; IDFW 4; MAL 5; MTCW 1, 2; MTFW 2005; RGAL 4
Mamet, David Alan
See Mamet, David
Mamoulian, Rouben (Zachary)
1897-1987 .... **CLC 16**
See also CA 25-28R; 124; CANR 85
Man in the Cloak, The
See Mangan, James Clarence
Mandelshtam, Osip
See Mandelstam, Osip
Mandel'shtam, Osip Emil'evich
See Mandelstam, Osip
Mandelstam, Osip 1891(?)-1943(?) ... **PC 14; TCLC 2, 6, 225**
See also CA 104; 150; DLB 295; EW 10; EWL 3; MTCW 2; RGWL 2, 3; TWA
Mandelstam, Osip Emilievich
See Mandelstam, Osip
Mander, (Mary) Jane
1877-1949 .... **TCLC 31**
See also CA 162; RGEL 2
Mandeville, Bernard 1670-1733 .... **LC 82**
See also DLB 101
Mandeville, Sir John fl. 1350 ...... **CMLC 19**
See also DLB 146
Mandiargues, Andre Pieyre de
See Pieyre de Mandiargues, Andre
Mandrake, Ethel Belle
See Thurman, Wallace (Henry)
Mangan, James Clarence
1803-1849 .... **NCLC 27, 316**
See also BRWS 13; RGEL 2
Maniere, J. E.
See Giraudoux, Jean
Mankell, Henning 1948- .... **CLC 292**
See also CA 187; CANR 163, 200
Mankiewicz, Herman (Jacob)
1897-1953 .... **TCLC 85**
See also CA 120; 169; DLB 26; IDFW 3, 4
Manley, (Mary) Delariviere
1672(?)-1724 .... **LC 1, 42**
See also DLB 39, 80; RGEL 2
Mann, Abel
See Creasey, John
Mann, Emily 1952- .... **DC 7**
See also CA 130; CAD; CANR 55; CD 5, 6; CWD; DFS 28; DLB 266
Mann, Erica
See Jong, Erica
Mann, (Luiz) Heinrich
1871-1950 .... **TCLC 9, 279**
See also CA 106; 164, 181; DLB 66, 118; EW 8; EWL 3; RGWL 2, 3
Mann, Paul Thomas
See Mann, Thomas
Mann, Thomas 1875-1955 .... **SSC 5, 80, 82, 170, 172, 174; TCLC 2, 8, 14, 21, 35, 44, 60, 168, 236, 292, 293, 303, 312; WLC 4**
See also BPFB 2; CA 104; 128; CANR 133; CDWLB 2; DA; DA3; DAB; DAC; DAM MST, NOV; DLB 66, 331; EW 9; EWL 3; GLL 1; LATS 1:1; LMFS 1; MTCW 1, 2; MTFW 2005; NFS 17; RGSF 2; RGWL 2, 3; SSFS 4, 9; TWA
Mannheim, Karl 1893-1947 .... **TCLC 65**
See also CA 204
Manning, David
See Faust, Frederick
Manning, Frederic 1882-1935 .... **TCLC 25**
See also CA 124; 216; DLB 260
Manning, Olivia 1915-1980 .... **CLC 5, 19**
See also CA 5-8R; 101; CANR 29; CN 1, 2; EWL 3; FW; MTCW 1; RGEL 2
Mannyng, Robert c. 1264-c. 1340 **CMLC 83**
See also DLB 146
Mano, D. Keith 1942- .... **CLC 2, 10**
See also CA 25-28R; CAAS 6; CANR 26, 57; DLB 6
Mansfield, Katherine 1888-1923 .... **SSC 9, 23, 38, 81; TCLC 2, 8, 39, 164; WLC 4**
See also BPFB 2; BRW 7; CA 104; 134; DA; DA3; DAB; DAC; DAM MST; DLB 162; EWL 3; EXPS; FW; GLL 1; MTCW 2; RGEL 2; RGSF 2; SSFS 2, 8, 10, 11, 29; TEA; WWE 1

Mansfield, Kathleen
See Mansfield, Katherine
Manso, Peter 1940- .... **CLC 39**
See also CA 29-32R; CANR 44, 156
Mantecon, Juan Jimenez
See Jimenez, Juan Ramon
Mantel, Hilary 1952- ..... **CLC 144, 309, 354**
See also CA 125; CANR 54, 101, 161, 207; CN 5, 6, 7; DLB 271; RHW
Mantel, Hilary Mary
See Mantel, Hilary
Manto, Saadat Hasan 1912-1955 ... **SSC 208**
See also RGEL 2; SSFS 15
Manton, Peter
See Creasey, John
Man Without a Spleen, A
See Chekhov, Anton
Manzano, Juan Franciso
1797(?)-1854 .... **NCLC 155**
Manzoni, Alessandro
1785-1873 .... **NCLC 29, 98**
See also EW 5; RGWL 2, 3; TWA; WLIT 7
Mao Dun 1896-1981 .... **TCLC 299**
See also CA 103; DLB 328; EWL 3; RGSF 3
Mao Lin
See Shen Congwen
Mao Tun
See Mao Dun
Map, Walter 1140-1209 .... **CMLC 32, 147**
Mapu, Abraham (ben Jekutiel)
1808-1867 .... **NCLC 18**
Mara, Sally
See Queneau, Raymond
Maracle, Lee 1950- .... **NNAL**
See also CA 149
Marat, Jean Paul 1743-1793 .... **LC 10**
Marcabru fl. 1129-1150 .... **CMLC 172**
Marcel, Gabriel Honore 1889-1973 **CLC 15**
See also CA 102; 45-48; EWL 3; MTCW 1, 2
March, William 1893-1954 .... **TCLC 96**
See also CA 108; 216; DLB 9, 86, 316; MAL 5
Marchbanks, Samuel
See Davies, Robertson
Marchi, Giacomo
See Bassani, Giorgio
Marcus Aurelius
See Aurelius, Marcus
Marcuse, Herbert 1898-1979 ...... **TCLC 207**
See also CA 188; 89-92; DLB 242
Marguerite
See de Navarre, Marguerite
Marguerite d'Angouleme
See de Navarre, Marguerite
Marguerite de Navarre
See de Navarre, Marguerite
Margulies, Donald 1954- .... **CLC 76**
See also AAYA 57; CA 200; CD 6; DFS 13; DLB 228
Marias, Javier 1951- .... **CLC 239**
See also CA 167; CANR 109, 139, 232; DLB 322; HW 2; MTFW 2005
Marie de France c. 12th cent. .... **CMLC 8, 111; PC 22**
See also DLB 208; FW; RGWL 2, 3
Marie de l'Incarnation
1599-1672 .... **LC 10, 168**
Marier, Captain Victor
See Griffith, D.W.
Mariner, Scott
See Pohl, Frederik
Marinetti, Filippo Tommaso
1876-1944 .... **TCLC 10**
See also CA 107; DLB 114, 264; EW 9; EWL 3; WLIT 7
Marino, Giambattista 1569-1625 ..... **LC 181**
See also DLB 339; WLIT 7
Marivaux, Pierre Carlet de Chamblain de
1688-1763 .... **DC 7, 52; LC 4, 123**
See also DLB 314; GFL Beginnings to 1789; RGWL 2, 3; TWA
Markandaya, Kamala
1924-2004 .... **CLC 8, 38, 290**
See also BYA 13; CA 77-80; 227; CN 1, 2, 3, 4, 5, 6, 7; DLB 323; EWL 3; MTFW 2005; NFS 13
Markfield, Wallace (Arthur)
1926-2002 .... **CLC 8**
See also CA 69-72; 208; CAAS 3; CN 1, 2, 3, 4, 5, 6, 7; DLB 2, 28; DLBY 2002
Markham, Edwin 1852-1940 .... **TCLC 47**
See also CA 160; DLB 54, 186; MAL 5; RGAL 4
Markham, Robert
See Amis, Kingsley
Marks, J.
See Highwater, Jamake (Mamake)
Marks-Highwater, J.
See Highwater, Jamake (Mamake)
Markson, David M. 1927-2010 .... **CLC 67**
See also AMWS 17; CA 49-52; CANR 1, 91, 158; CN 5, 6
Markson, David Merrill
See Markson, David M.
Marlatt, Daphne (Buckle) 1942- ... **CLC 168**
See also CA 25-28R; CANR 17, 39; CN 6, 7; CP 4, 5, 6, 7; CWP; DLB 60; FW
Marley, Bob 1945-1981 .... **CLC 17**
See also CA 107; 103
Marley, Robert Nesta
See Marley, Bob
Marlowe, Christopher 1564-1593 .... **DC 1; LC 22, 47, 117, 201, 232; PC 57; WLC 4**
See also BRW 1; BRWR 1; CDBLB Before 1660; DA; DA3; DAB; DAC; DAM DRAM, MST; DFS 1, 5, 13, 21; DLB 62; EXPP; LMFS 1; PFS 22; RGEL 2; TEA; WLIT 3
Marlowe, Kit
See Marlowe, Christopher
Marlowe, Stephen 1928-2008 .... **CLC 70**
See also CA 13-16R; 269; CANR 6, 55; CMW 4; SFW 4
Marmion, Shakerley 1603-1639 .... **LC 89**
See also DLB 58; RGEL 2
Marmontel, Jean-Francois
1723-1799 .... **LC 2**
See also DLB 314
Maron, Monika 1941- .... **CLC 165**
See also CA 201
Marot, Clement c. 1496-1544 .... **LC 133**
See also DLB 327; GFL Beginnings to 1789
Marquand, John P(hillips)
1893-1960 .... **CLC 2, 10**
See also AMW; BPFB 2; CA 85-88; CANR 73; CMW 4; DLB 9, 102; EWL 3; MAL 5; MTCW 2; RGAL 4
Marquez, Gabriel Garcia
See Garcia Marquez, Gabriel
Marquis, Don(ald Robert Perry)
1878-1937 .... **TCLC 7**
See also CA 104; 166; DLB 11, 25; MAL 5; RGAL 4
Marquis de Sade
See Sade, Marquis de
Marques, Rene 1919-1979 ... **CLC 96; HLC 2**
See also CA 97-100; 85-88; CANR 78; DAM MULT; DLB 305; EWL 3; HW 1, 2; LAW; RGSF 2
Marra, Anthony 1984- .... **CLC 370**
See also CLC 350
Marric, J. J.
See Creasey, John
Marryat, Frederick 1792-1848 .... **NCLC 3**
See also DLB 21, 163; RGEL 2; WCH
Marryat, Florence 1833-1899 ..... **NCLC 297**
Marse, Juan 1933- .... **CLC 302**
See also CA 254; DLB 322
Marsden, James
See Creasey, John
Marsh, Edith Ngaio
See Marsh, Ngaio
Marsh, Edward 1872-1953 .... **TCLC 99**
Marsh, Ngaio 1895-1982 .... **CLC 7, 53**
See also CA 9-12R; CANR 6, 58; CMW 4; CN 1, 2, 3; CPW; DAM POP; DLB 77; MSW; MTCW 1, 2; RGEL 2; TEA
Marshall, Alan
See Westlake, Donald E.
Marshall, Allen
See Westlake, Donald E.
Marshall, Garry 1934- .... **CLC 17**
See also AAYA 3; CA 111; SATA 60
Marshall, Paule 1929- .... **BLC 1:3, 2:3; CLC 27, 72, 253; SSC 3**
See also AFAW 1, 2; AMWS 11; BPFB 2; BW 2, 3; CA 77-80; CANR 25, 73, 129, 209; CN 1, 2, 3, 4, 5, 6, 7; DA3; DAM MULT; DLB 33, 157, 227; EWL 3; LATS 1:2; MAL 5; MTCW 1, 2; MTFW 2005; NFS 36; RGAL 4; SSFS 15
Marshallik
See Zangwill, Israel
Marsilius of Inghen c. 1340-1396 .. **CMLC 106**
Marsten, Richard
See Hunter, Evan
Marston, John
1576-1634 .... **DC 37; LC 33, 172**
See also BRW 2; DAM DRAM; DLB 58, 172; RGEL 2
Martí, José 1853-1895 ... **HLC 2; NCLC 63, 313; PC 76**
See also DAM MULT; DLB 290; HW 2; LAW; RGWL 2, 3; WLIT 1
Martel, Yann 1963- .... **CLC 192, 315**
See also AAYA 67; CA 146; CANR 114, 226; DLB 326, 334; LNFS 2; MTFW 2005; NFS 27
Martens, Adolphe-Adhemar
See Ghelderode, Michel de
Martha, Henry
See Harris, Mark
Marti y Perez, Jose Julian
See Martí, José
Martial c. 40-c. 104 ... **CMLC 35, 169; PC 10**
See also AW 2; CDWLB 1; DLB 211; RGWL 2, 3
Martin, Ken
See Hubbard, L. Ron
Martin, Richard
See Creasey, John
Martin, Steve 1945- .... **CLC 30, 217**
See also AAYA 53; CA 97-100; CANR 30, 100, 140, 195, 227; DFS 19; MTCW 1; MTFW 2005
Martin, Valerie 1948- .... **CLC 89**
See also BEST 90:2; CA 85-88; CANR 49, 89, 165, 200
Martin, Violet Florence
1862-1915 .... **SSC 56; TCLC 51**
Martin, Webber
See Silverberg, Robert
Martindale, Patrick Victor
See White, Patrick
Martin du Gard, Roger
1881-1958 .... **TCLC 24**
See also CA 118; CANR 94; DLB 65, 331; EWL 3; GFL 1789 to the Present; RGWL 2, 3
Martineau, Harriet
1802-1876 .... **NCLC 26, 137**
See also BRWS 15; DLB 21, 55, 159, 163, 166, 190; FW; RGEL 2; YABC 2

Martines, Julia
See O'Faolain, Julia
Martinez, Enrique Gonzalez
See Gonzalez Martinez, Enrique
Martinez, Jacinto Benavente y
See Benavente, Jacinto
Martinez Ruiz, Jose 1873-1967 ...... **CLC 11**
See also CA 93-96; DLB 322; EW 3; EWL 3; HW 1
Martinez Sierra, Gregorio
1881-1947 .... **TCLC 6**
See also CA 115; EWL 3
Martinsen, Martin
See Follett, Ken
Martinson, Harry (Edmund)
1904-1978 .... **CLC 14**
See also CA 77-80; CANR 34, 130; DLB 259, 331; EWL 3
Martinez de la Rosa, Francisco de Paula
1787-1862 .... **NCLC 102**
See also TWA
Martinez Sierra, Gregorio
See Martinez Sierra, Maria
Martinez Sierra, Maria 1874-1974 ... **TCLC 6**
See also CA 250; 115; EWL 3
Martinez Sierra, Maria de la O'LeJarraga
See Martinez Sierra, Maria
Martyn, Edward 1859-1923 .... **TCLC 131**
See also CA 179; DLB 10; RGEL 2
Martyr, Peter 1457-1526 .... **LC 241**
Marut, Ret
See Traven, B.
Marut, Robert
See Traven, B.
Marvell, Andrew 1621-1678 .... **LC 4, 43, 179, 226; PC 10, 86, 144, 154; WLC 4**
See also BRW 2; BRWR 2; CDBLB 1660-1789; DA; DAB; DAC; DAM MST, POET; DLB 131; EXPP; PFS 5; RGEL 2; TEA; WP
Marx, Karl 1818-1883 .... **NCLC 17, 114**
See also DLB 129; LATS 1:1; TWA
Marx, Karl Heinrich
See Marx, Karl
Masaoka, Shiki -1902
See Masaoka, Tsunenori
Masaoka, Tsunenori 1867-1902 .... **TCLC 18**
See also CA 117; 191; EWL 3; RGWL 3; TWA
Masaoka Shiki
See Masaoka, Tsunenori
Masefield, John (Edward)
1878-1967 .... **CLC 11, 47; PC 78**
See also CA 19-20; 25-28R; CANR 33; CAP 2; CDBLB 1890-1914; CLR 164; DAM POET; DLB 10, 19, 153, 160; EWL 3; EXPP; FANT; MTCW 1, 2; PFS 5; RGEL 2; SATA 19
Maso, Carole 1955(?)- .... **CLC 44**
See also CA 170; CANR 148; CN 7; GLL 2; RGAL 4
Mason, Bobbie Ann 1940- .... **CLC 28, 43, 82, 154, 303; SSC 4, 101, 193**
See also AAYA 5, 42; AMWS 8; BPFB 2; CA 53-56; CANR 11, 31, 58, 83, 125, 169, 235; CDALBS; CN 5, 6, 7; CSW; DA3; DLB 173; DLBY 1987; EWL 3; EXPS; INT CANR-31; MAL 5; MTCW 1, 2; MTFW 2005; NFS 4; RGAL 4; RGSF 2; SSFS 3, 8, 20; TCLE 1:2; YAW
Mason, Ernst
See Pohl, Frederik
Mason, Hunni B.
See Sternheim, (William Adolf) Carl
Mason, Lee W.
See Malzberg, Barry N(athaniel)
Mason, Nick 1945- .... **CLC 35**
Mason, Tally
See Derleth, August (William)
Mass, Anna .... **CLC 59**
Mass, William
See Gibson, William
Massinger, Philip 1583-1640 .... **DC 39; LC 70**
See also BRWS 11; DLB 58; RGEL 2
Master Lao
See Lao Tzu
Masters, Edgar Lee 1868-1950 ..... **PC 1, 36; TCLC 2, 25; WLCS**
See also AMWS 1; CA 104; 133; CDALB 1865-1917; DA; DAC; DAM MST, POET; DLB 54; EWL 3; EXPP; MAL 5; MTCW 1, 2; MTFW 2005; PFS 37; RGAL 4; TUS; WP
Masters, Hilary 1928- .... **CLC 48**
See also CA 25-28R, 217; CAAE 217; CANR 13, 47, 97, 171, 221; CN 6, 7; DLB 244
Masters, Hilary Thomas
See Masters, Hilary
Mastrosimone, William 1947- .... **CLC 36**
See also CA 186; CAD; CD 5, 6
Mathe, Albert
See Camus, Albert
Mather, Cotton 1663-1728 .... **LC 38**
See also AMWS 2; CDALB 1640-1865; DLB 24, 30, 140; RGAL 4; TUS
Mather, Increase 1639-1723 .... **LC 38, 161**
See also DLB 24
Mathers, Marshall
See Eminem
Mathers, Marshall Bruce
See Eminem
Matheson, Richard 1926-2013 .. **CLC 37, 267**
See also AAYA 31; CA 97-100; CANR 88, 99, 236; DLB 8, 44; HGG; INT CA-97-100; SCFW 1, 2; SFW 4; SUFW 2
Matheson, Richard Burton
See Matheson, Richard
Mathews, Harry 1930- .... **CLC 6, 52**
See also CA 21-24R; CAAS 6; CANR 18, 40, 98, 160; CN 5, 6, 7
Mathews, John Joseph
1894-1979 .... **CLC 84; NNAL**
See also CA 19-20; 142; CANR 45; CAP 2; DAM MULT; DLB 175; TCWW 1, 2
Mathias, Roland 1915-2007 .... **CLC 45**
See also CA 97-100; 263; CANR 19, 41; CP 1, 2, 3, 4, 5, 6, 7; DLB 27
Mathias, Roland Glyn
See Mathias, Roland
Matshoba, Mtutuzeli 1950- .... **SSC 173**
See also CA 221
Matsuo Basho 1644(?)-1694 .... **LC 62; PC 3, 125**
See also DAM POET; PFS 2, 7, 18; RGWL 2, 3; WP
Mattheson, Rodney
See Creasey, John
Matthew, James
See Barrie, J. M.
Matthew of Vendome
c. 1130-c. 1200 .... **CMLC 99**
See also DLB 208
Matthew Paris
See Paris, Matthew
Matthews, (James) Brander
1852-1929 .... **TCLC 95**
See also CA 181; DLB 71, 78; DLBD 13
Matthews, Greg 1949- .... **CLC 45**
See also CA 135
Matthews, William (Procter III)
1942-1997 .... **CLC 40**
See also AMWS 9; CA 29-32R; 162; CAAS 18; CANR 12, 57; CP 2, 3, 4, 5, 6; DLB 5
Matthias, John (Edward) 1941- .... **CLC 9**
See also CA 33-36R; CANR 56; CP 4, 5, 6, 7
Matthiessen, F(rancis) O(tto)
1902-1950 .... **TCLC 100**
See also CA 185; DLB 63; MAL 5
Matthiessen, Francis Otto
See Matthiessen, F(rancis) O(tto)
Matthiessen, Peter 1927- .... **CLC 5, 7, 11, 32, 64, 245**
See also AAYA 6, 40; AMWS 5; ANW; BEST 90:4; BPFB 2; CA 9-12R; CANR 21, 50, 73, 100, 138; CN 1, 2, 3, 4, 5, 6, 7; DA3; DAM NOV; DLB 6, 173, 275; MAL 5; MTCW 1, 2; MTFW 2005; SATA 27
Maturin, Charles Robert
1780(?)-1824 .... **NCLC 6, 169**
See also BRWS 8; DLB 178; GL 3; HGG; LMFS 1; RGEL 2; SUFW
Matute (Ausejo), Ana Maria 1925- .. **CLC 11, 352**
See also CA 89-92; CANR 129; CWW 2; DLB 322; EWL 3; MTCW 1; RGSF 2
Maugham, W. S.
See Maugham, W. Somerset
Maugham, W. Somerset
1874-1965 .... **CLC 1, 11, 15, 67, 93; SSC 8, 94, 164; TCLC 208; WLC 4**
See also AAYA 55; BPFB 2; BRW 6; CA 5-8R; 25-28R; CANR 40, 127; CDBLB 1914-1945; CMW 4; DA; DA3; DAB; DAC; DAM DRAM, MST, NOV; DFS 22; DLB 10, 36, 77, 100, 162, 195; EWL 3; LAIT 3; MTCW 1, 2; MTFW 2005; NFS 23, 35; RGEL 2; RGSF 2; SATA 54; SSFS 17
Maugham, William S.
See Maugham, W. Somerset
Maugham, William Somerset
See Maugham, W. Somerset
Maupassant, Guy de 1850-1893 .... **NCLC 1, 42, 83, 234; SSC 1, 64, 132; WLC 4**
See also BYA 14; DA; DA3; DAB; DAC; DAM MST; DLB 123; EW 7; EXPS; GFL 1789 to the Present; LAIT 2; LMFS 1; RGSF 2; RGWL 2, 3; SSFS 4, 21, 28, 31; SUFW; TWA
Maupassant, Henri Rene Albert Guy de
See Maupassant, Guy de
Maupin, Armistead 1944- .... **CLC 95**
See also CA 125; 130; CANR 58, 101, 183; CPW; DA3; DAM POP; DLB 278; GLL 1; INT CA-130; MTCW 2; MTFW 2005
Maupin, Armistead Jones, Jr.
See Maupin, Armistead
Maurhut, Richard
See Traven, B.
Mauriac, Claude 1914-1996 .... **CLC 9**
See also CA 89-92; 152; CWW 2; DLB 83; EWL 3; GFL 1789 to the Present
Mauriac, Francois (Charles)
1885-1970 .... **CLC 4, 9, 56; SSC 24; TCLC 281**
See also CA 25-28; CAP 2; DLB 65, 331; EW 10; EWL 3; GFL 1789 to the Present; MTCW 1, 2; MTFW 2005; RGWL 2, 3; TWA
Mavor, Osborne Henry 1888-1951 ... **TCLC 3**
See also CA 104; DLB 10; EWL 3
Maxwell, Glyn 1962- .... **CLC 238**
See also CA 154; CANR 88, 183; CP 6, 7; PFS 23
Maxwell, William (Keepers, Jr.)
1908-2000 .... **CLC 19**
See also AMWS 8; CA 93-96; 189; CANR 54, 95; CN 1, 2, 3, 4, 5, 6, 7; DLB 218, 278; DLBY 1980; INT CA-93-96; MAL 5; SATA-Obit 128
May, Elaine 1932- .... **CLC 16**
See also CA 124; 142; CAD; CWD; DLB 44
Mayakovski, Vladimir
1893-1930 .... **TCLC 4, 18**

See also CA 104; 158; EW 11; EWL 3; IDTP; MTCW 2; MTFW 2005; RGWL 2, 3; SFW 4; TWA; WP
Mayakovski, Vladimir Vladimirovich
See Mayakovski, Vladimir
Mayakovsky, Vladimir
See Mayakovski, Vladimir
Mayhew, Henry 1812-1887 .... **NCLC 31**
See also BRWS 16; DLB 18, 55, 190
Mayle, Peter 1939(?)- .... **CLC 89**
See also CA 139; CANR 64, 109, 168, 218
Maynard, Joyce 1953- .... **CLC 23**
See also CA 111; 129; CANR 64, 169, 220
Mayne, William 1928-2010 .... **CLC 12**
See also AAYA 20; CA 9-12R; CANR 37, 80, 100; CLR 25, 123; FANT; JRDA; MAICYA 1, 2; MAICYAS 1; SAAS 11; SATA 6, 68, 122; SUFW 2; YAW
Mayne, William James Carter
See Mayne, William
Mayo, Jim
See L'Amour, Louis
Maysles, Albert 1926- .... **CLC 16**
See also CA 29-32R
Maysles, David 1932-1987 .... **CLC 16**
See also CA 191
Mazer, Norma Fox 1931-2009 .... **CLC 26**
See also AAYA 5, 36; BYA 1, 8; CA 69-72; 292; CANR 12, 32, 66, 129, 189; CLR 23; JRDA; MAICYA 1, 2; SAAS 1; SATA 24, 67, 105, 168, 198; WYA; YAW
Mažuranić, Ivan 1814-1890 .... **NCLC 259**
See also DLB 147
Mazzini, Guiseppe 1805-1872 .... **NCLC 34**
McAlmon, Robert (Menzies) 1895-1956 .... **TCLC 97**
See also CA 107; 168; DLB 4, 45; DLBD 15; GLL 1
McAuley, James Phillip 1917-1976 ... **CLC 45**
See also CA 97-100; CP 1, 2; DLB 260; RGEL 2
McBain, Ed
See Hunter, Evan
McBride, James 1957- .... **CLC 370**
See also BW 3; CA 153; CANR 113, 194, 266; CMTFW; MTFW
McBrien, William 1930- .... **CLC 44**
See also CA 107; CANR 90
McBrien, William Augustine
See McBrien, William
McCabe, Pat
See McCabe, Patrick
McCabe, Patrick 1955- .... **CLC 133**
See also BRWS 9; CA 130; CANR 50, 90, 168, 202; CN 6, 7; DLB 194
McCaffrey, Anne 1926-2011 .... **CLC 17**
See also AAYA 6, 34; AITN 2; BEST 89:2; BPFB 2; BYA 5; CA 25-28R, 227; CAAE 227; CANR 15, 35, 55, 96, 169, 234; CLR 49, 130; CPW; DA3; DAM NOV, POP; DLB 8; JRDA; MAICYA 1, 2; MTCW 1, 2; MTFW 2005; SAAS 11; SATA 8, 70, 116, 152; SATA-Essay 152; SFW 4; SUFW 2; WYA; YAW
McCaffrey, Anne Inez
See McCaffrey, Anne
McCall, Nathan 1955(?)- .... **CLC 86**
See also AAYA 59; BW 3; CA 146; CANR 88, 186
McCall Smith, Alexander
See Smith, Alexander McCall
McCann, Arthur
See Campbell, John W.
McCann, Colum 1965- ... **CLC 299; SSC 170**
See also CA 152; CANR 99, 149; DLB 267
McCann, Edson
See Pohl, Frederik
McCarthy, Charles
See McCarthy, Cormac
McCarthy, Charles, Jr.
See McCarthy, Cormac
McCarthy, Cormac 1933- .... **CLC 4, 57, 101, 204, 295, 310**
See also AAYA 41; AMWS 8; BPFB 2; CA 13-16R; CANR 10, 42, 69, 101, 161, 171; CN 6, 7; CPW; CSW; DA3; DAM POP; DLB 6, 143, 256; EWL 3; LATS 1:2; LNFS 3; MAL 5; MTCW 2; MTFW 2005; NFS 36, 40; TCLE 1:2; TCWW 2
McCarthy, Mary 1912-1989 .... **CLC 1, 3, 5, 14, 24, 39, 59; SSC 24**
See also AMW; BPFB 2; CA 5-8R; 129; CANR 16, 50, 64; CN 1, 2, 3, 4; DA3; DLB 2; DLBY 1981; EWL 3; FW; INT CANR-16; MAL 5; MBL; MTCW 1, 2; MTFW 2005; RGAL 4; TUS
McCarthy, Mary Therese
See McCarthy, Mary
McCartney, James Paul
See McCartney, Paul
McCartney, Paul 1942- .... **CLC 12, 35**
See also CA 146; CANR 111
McCauley, Stephen 1955- .... **CLC 50**
See also CA 141
McClaren, Peter .... **CLC 70**
McClure, Michael 1932- ... **CLC 6, 10; PC 136**
See also BG 1:3; CA 21-24R; CAD; CANR 17, 46, 77, 131, 231; CD 5, 6; CP 1, 2, 3, 4, 5, 6, 7; DLB 16; WP
McClure, Michael Thomas
See McClure, Michael
McCorkle, Jill 1958- .... **CLC 51**
See also CA 121; CANR 113, 218; CSW; DLB 234; DLBY 1987; SSFS 24
McCorkle, Jill Collins
See McCorkle, Jill
McCourt, Francis
See McCourt, Frank
McCourt, Frank 1930-2009 ... **CLC 109, 299**
See also AAYA 61; AMWS 12; CA 157; 288; CANR 97, 138; MTFW 2005; NCFS 1
McCourt, James 1941- .... **CLC 5**
See also CA 57-60; CANR 98, 152, 186
McCourt, Malachy 1931- .... **CLC 119**
See also SATA 126
McCoy, Edmund
See Gardner, John
McCoy, Horace (Stanley) 1897-1955 .... **TCLC 28**
See also AMWS 13; CA 108; 155; CMW 4; DLB 9
McCrae, John 1872-1918 .... **TCLC 12**
See also CA 109; DLB 92; PFS 5
McCreigh, James
See Pohl, Frederik
McCullers, Carson 1917-1967 ...... **CLC 1, 4, 10, 12, 48, 100; DC 35; SSC 9, 24, 99; TCLC 155; WLC 4**
See also AAYA 21; AMW; AMWC 2; BPFB 2; CA 5-8R; 25-28R; CABS 1, 3; CANR 18, 132; CDALB 1941-1968; DA; DA3; DAB; DAC; DAM MST, NOV; DFS 5, 18; DLB 2, 7, 173, 228; EWL 3; EXPS; FW; GLL 1; LAIT 3, 4; MAL 5; MBL; MTCW 1, 2; MTFW 2005; NFS 6, 13; RGAL 4; RGSF 2; SATA 27; SSFS 5, 32; TUS; YAW
McCullers, Lula Carson Smith
See McCullers, Carson
McCulloch, John Tyler
See Burroughs, Edgar Rice
McCullough, Colleen 1937- ..... **CLC 27, 107**
See also AAYA 36; BPFB 2; CA 81-84; CANR 17, 46, 67, 98, 139, 203; CPW; DA3; DAM NOV, POP; MTCW 1, 2; MTFW 2005; RHW
McCunn, Ruthanne Lum 1946- .... **AAL**
See also CA 119; CANR 43, 96; DLB 312; LAIT 2; SATA 63
McDermott, Alice 1953- .... **CLC 90**
See also AMWS 18; CA 109; CANR 40, 90, 126, 181; CN 7; DLB 292; MTFW 2005; NFS 23
McDonagh, Martin 1970(?)- .... **CLC 304**
See also AAYA 71; BRWS 12; CA 171; CANR 141; CD 6
McElroy, Joseph 1930- .... **CLC 5, 47**
See also CA 17-20R; CANR 149, 236; CN 3, 4, 5, 6, 7
McElroy, Joseph Prince
See McElroy, Joseph
McElroy, Lee
See Kelton, Elmer
McEwan, Ian 1948- .... **CLC 13, 66, 169, 269; SSC 106**
See also AAYA 84; BEST 90:4; BRWS 4; CA 61-64; CANR 14, 41, 69, 87, 132, 179, 232; CN 3, 4, 5, 6, 7; DAM NOV; DLB 14, 194, 319, 326; HGG; MTCW 1, 2; MTFW 2005; NFS 32; RGSF 2; SUFW 2; TEA
McEwan, Ian Russell
See McEwan, Ian
McFadden, David 1940- .... **CLC 48**
See also CA 104; CP 1, 2, 3, 4, 5, 6, 7; DLB 60; INT CA-104
McFarland, Dennis 1950- .... **CLC 65**
See also CA 165; CANR 110, 179
McGahern, John 1934-2006 .... **CLC 5, 9, 48, 156, 371; SSC 17, 181**
See also CA 17-20R; 249; CANR 29, 68, 113, 204; CN 1, 2, 3, 4, 5, 6, 7; DLB 14, 231, 319; MTCW 1
McGinley, Patrick (Anthony) 1937- ... **CLC 41**
See also CA 120; 127; CANR 56; INT CA-127
McGinley, Phyllis 1905-1978 .... **CLC 14**
See also CA 9-12R; 77-80; CANR 19; CP 1, 2; CWRI 5; DLB 11, 48; MAL 5; PFS 9, 13; SATA 2, 44; SATA-Obit 24
McGinniss, Joe 1942- .... **CLC 32**
See also AITN 2; BEST 89:2; CA 25-28R; CANR 26, 70, 152, 235; CPW; DLB 185; INT CANR-26
McGivern, Maureen Daly
See Daly, Maureen
McGivern, Maureen Patricia Daly
See Daly, Maureen
McGrath, Patrick 1950- .... **CLC 55**
See also CA 136; CANR 65, 148, 190; CN 5, 6, 7; DLB 231; HGG; SUFW 2
McGrath, Thomas (Matthew) 1916-1990 .... **CLC 28, 59**
See also AMWS 10; CA 9-12R; 132; CANR 6, 33, 95; CP 1, 2, 3, 4, 5; DAM POET; MAL 5; MTCW 1; SATA 41; SATA-Obit 66
McGuane, Thomas 1939- .... **CLC 3, 7, 18, 45, 127**
See also AITN 2; BPFB 2; CA 49-52; CANR 5, 24, 49, 94, 164, 229; CN 2, 3, 4, 5, 6, 7; DLB 2, 212; DLBY 1980; EWL 3; INT CANR-24; MAL 5; MTCW 1; MTFW 2005; TCWW 1, 2
McGuane, Thomas Francis III
See McGuane, Thomas
McGuckian, Medbh 1950- ...... **CLC 48, 174; PC 27**
See also BRWS 5; CA 143; CANR 206; CP 4, 5, 6, 7; CWP; DAM POET; DLB 40
McGuffin, P. V.
See Mangan, James Clarence
McHale, Tom 1942(?)-1982 .... **CLC 3, 5**
See also AITN 1; CA 77-80; 106; CN 1, 2, 3
McHugh, Heather 1948- .... **PC 61**
See also CA 69-72; CANR 11, 28, 55, 92; CP 4, 5, 6, 7; CWP; PFS 24

McIlvanney, William 1936- .... **CLC 42**
See also CA 25-28R; CANR 61; CMW 4; DLB 14, 207
McIlwraith, Maureen Mollie Hunter
See Hunter, Mollie
McInerney, Jay 1955- .... **CLC 34, 112**
See also AAYA 18; BPFB 2; CA 116; 123; CANR 45, 68, 116, 176, 219; CN 5, 6, 7; CPW; DA3; DAM POP; DLB 292; INT CA-123; MAL 5; MTCW 2; MTFW 2005
McIntyre, Vonda N. 1948- .... **CLC 18**
See also CA 81-84; CANR 17, 34, 69; MTCW 1; SFW 4; YAW
McIntyre, Vonda Neel
See McIntyre, Vonda N.
McKay, Claude 1889-1948 .... **BLC 1:3; HR 1:3; PC 2, 135; TCLC 7, 41; WLC 4**
See also AFAW 1, 2; AMWS 10; BW 1, 3; CA 104; 124; CANR 73; DA; DAB; DAC; DAM MST, MULT, NOV, POET; DLB 4, 45, 51, 117; EWL 3; EXPP; GLL 2; LAIT 3; LMFS 2; MAL 5; MTCW 1, 2; MTFW 2005; PAB; PFS 4, 44; RGAL 4; TUS; WP
McKay, Festus Claudius
See McKay, Claude
McKuen, Rod 1933- .... **CLC 1, 3**
See also AITN 1; CA 41-44R; CANR 40; CP 1
McLoughlin, R. B.
See Mencken, H. L.
McLuhan, (Herbert) Marshall 1911-1980 .... **CLC 37, 83**
See also CA 9-12R; 102; CANR 12, 34, 61; DLB 88; INT CANR-12; MTCW 1, 2; MTFW 2005
McMahon, Pat
See Hoch, Edward D.
McManus, Declan Patrick Aloysius
See Costello, Elvis
McMillan, Terry 1951- ...... **BLCS; CLC 50, 61, 112**
See also AAYA 21; AMWS 13; BPFB 2; BW 2, 3; CA 140; CANR 60, 104, 131, 230; CN 7; CPW; DA3; DAM MULT, NOV, POP; MAL 5; MTCW 2; MTFW 2005; RGAL 4; YAW
McMillan, Terry L.
See McMillan, Terry
McMurtry, Larry 1936- .... **CLC 2, 3, 7, 11, 27, 44, 127, 250**
See also AAYA 83; AITN 2; AMWS 5; BEST 89:2; BPFB 2; CA 5-8R; CANR 19, 43, 64, 103, 170, 206; CDALB 1968-1988; CN 2, 3, 4, 5, 6, 7; CPW; CSW; DA3; DAM NOV, POP; DLB 2, 143, 256; DLBY 1980, 1987; EWL 3; MAL 5; MTCW 1, 2; MTFW 2005; RGAL 4; TCWW 1, 2
McMurtry, Larry Jeff
See McMurtry, Larry
McNally, Terrence 1939- .... **CLC 4, 7, 41, 91, 252; DC 27**
See also AAYA 62; AMWS 13; CA 45-48; CAD; CANR 2, 56, 116; CD 5, 6; DA3; DAM DRAM; DFS 16, 19; DLB 7, 249; EWL 3; GLL 1; MTCW 2; MTFW 2005
McNally, Thomas Michael
See McNally, T.M.
McNally, T.M. 1961- .... **CLC 82**
See also CA 246
McNamer, Deirdre 1950- .... **CLC 70**
See also CA 188; CANR 163, 200
McNeal, Tom .... **CLC 119**
See also CA 252; CANR 185; SATA 194
McNeile, Herman Cyril 1888-1937 ... **TCLC 44**
See also CA 184; CMW 4; DLB 77
McNickle, D'Arcy 1904-1977 .... **CLC 89; NNAL**
See also CA 9-12R; 85-88; CANR 5, 45; DAM MULT; DLB 175, 212; RGAL 4; SATA-Obit 22; TCWW 1, 2
McNickle, William D'Arcy
See McNickle, D'Arcy
McPhee, John 1931- .... **CLC 36**
See also AAYA 61; AMWS 3; ANW; BEST 90:1; CA 65-68; CANR 20, 46, 64, 69, 121, 165; CPW; DLB 185, 275; MTCW 1, 2; MTFW 2005; TUS
McPhee, John Angus
See McPhee, John
McPherson, James Alan, Jr.
See McPherson, James Alan
McPherson, James Alan 1943- .... **BLCS; CLC 19, 77; SSC 95**
See also BW 1, 3; CA 25-28R, 273; CAAE 273; CAAS 17; CANR 24, 74, 140; CN 3, 4, 5, 6; CSW; DLB 38, 244; EWL 3; MTCW 1, 2; MTFW 2005; RGAL 4; RGSF 2; SSFS 23
McPherson, William (Alexander) 1933- .... **CLC 34**
See also CA 69-72; CANR 28; INT CANR-28
McTaggart, J. McT. Ellis
See McTaggart, John McTaggart Ellis
McTaggart, John McTaggart Ellis 1866-1925 .... **TCLC 105**
See also CA 120; DLB 262
Mda, Zakes 1948- .... **BLC 2:3; CLC 262**
See also BRWS 15; CA 205; CANR 151, 185; CD 5, 6; DLB 225
Mda, Zanemvula
See Mda, Zakes
Mda, Zanemvula Kizito Gatyeni
See Mda, Zakes
Mead, George Herbert 1863-1931 .... **TCLC 89**
See also CA 212; DLB 270
Mead, Margaret 1901-1978 .... **CLC 37**
See also AITN 1; CA 1-4R; 81-84; CANR 4; DA3; FW; MTCW 1, 2; SATA-Obit 20
Meaker, M. J.
See Meaker, Marijane
Meaker, Marijane 1927- .... **CLC 12, 35**
See also AAYA 2, 23, 82; BYA 1, 7, 8; CA 107; CANR 37, 63, 145, 180; CLR 29; GLL 2; INT CA-107; JRDA; MAICYA 1, 2; MAICYAS 1; MTCW 1; SAAS 1; SATA 20, 61, 99, 160; SATA-Essay 111; WYA; YAW
Meaker, Marijane Agnes
See Meaker, Marijane
Mechthild von Hackeborn 1240(?)-1298(?) .... **CMLC 150**
Mechthild von Magdeburg c. 1207-c. 1282 .... **CMLC 91**
See also DLB 138
Medoff, Mark (Howard) 1940- ... **CLC 6, 23**
See also AITN 1; CA 53-56; CAD; CANR 5; CD 5, 6; DAM DRAM; DFS 4; DLB 7; INT CANR-5
Medvedev, P. N.
See Bakhtin, Mikhail Mikhailovich
Meged, Aharon
See Megged, Aharon
Meged, Aron
See Megged, Aharon
Megged, Aharon 1920- .... **CLC 9**
See also CA 49-52; CAAS 13; CANR 1, 140; EWL 3; RGHL
Mehta, Deepa 1950- .... **CLC 208**
Mehta, Gita 1943- .... **CLC 179**
See also CA 225; CN 7; DNFS 2
Mehta, Ved 1934- .... **CLC 37**
See also CA 1-4R, 212; CAAE 212; CANR 2, 23, 69; DLB 323; MTCW 1; MTFW 2005
Melanchthon, Philipp 1497-1560 .... **LC 90**
See also DLB 179
Melanter
See Blackmore, R(ichard) D(oddridge)
Meleager c. 140B.C.-c. 70B.C. ..... **CMLC 53**
Meléndez Valdés, Juan 1754-1817 .... **NCLC 278**
Melies, Georges 1861-1938 .... **TCLC 81**
Melikow, Loris
See Hofmannsthal, Hugo von
Melmoth, Sebastian
See Wilde, Oscar
Melo Neto, Joao Cabral de
See Cabral de Melo Neto, Joao
Meltzer, Milton 1915-2009 .... **CLC 26**
See also AAYA 8, 45; BYA 2, 6; CA 13-16R; 290; CANR 38, 92, 107, 192; CLR 13; DLB 61; JRDA; MAICYA 1, 2; SAAS 1; SATA 1, 50, 80, 128, 201; SATA-Essay 124; WYA; YAW
Melville, Herman 1819-1891 .... **NCLC 3, 12, 29, 45, 49, 91, 93, 123, 157, 181, 193, 221, 234, 277, 304, 306; PC 82; SSC 1, 17, 46, 95, 141, 183; WLC, 4**
See also AAYA 25; AMW; AMWR 1; CDALB 1640-1865; DA; DA3; DAB; DAC; DAM MST, NOV; DLB 3, 74, 250, 254, 349, 366; EXPN; EXPS; GL 3; LAIT 1, 2; NFS 7, 9, 32, 41; RGAL 4; RGSF 2; SATA 59; SSFS 3; TUS
Members, Mark
See Powell, Anthony
Membreno, Alejandro .... **CLC 59**
Mena, Maria Cristina 1893-1965 ... **SSC 165**
See also DLB 209, 221
Menand, Louis 1952- .... **CLC 208**
See also CA 200
Menander c. 342B.C.-c. 293B.C. ... **CMLC 9, 51, 101; DC 3**
See also AW 1; CDWLB 1; DAM DRAM; DLB 176; LMFS 1; RGWL 2, 3
Menchu, Rigoberta 1959- ..... **CLC 160, 332; HLCS 2**
See also CA 175; CANR 135; DNFS 1; WLIT 1
Mencken, H. L. 1880-1956 ..... **TCLC 13, 18**
See also AAYA 85; AMW; CA 105; 125; CDALB 1917-1929; DLB 11, 29, 63, 137, 222; EWL 3; MAL 5; MTCW 1, 2; MTFW 2005; NCFS 4; RGAL 4; TUS
Mencken, Henry Louis
See Mencken, H. L.
Mendelsohn, Jane 1965- .... **CLC 99**
See also CA 154; CANR 94, 225
Mendelssohn, Moses 1729-1786 .... **LC 142**
See also DLB 97
Mendoza, Eduardo 1943- .... **CLC 366**
See also DLB 322
Mendoza, Inigo Lopez de
See Santillana, Inigo Lopez de Mendoza, Marques de
Menken, Adah Isaacs 1835-1868 .... **NCLC 270**
Menton, Francisco de
See Chin, Frank
Mercer, David 1928-1980 .... **CLC 5**
See also CA 9-12R; 102; CANR 23; CBD; DAM DRAM; DLB 13, 310; MTCW 1; RGEL 2
Merchant, Paul
See Ellison, Harlan
Mercier, Louis-Sébastien 1740-1814 .... **NCLC 255**
See also DLB 314
Meredith, George 1828-1909 .... **PC 60; TCLC 17, 43**
See also CA 117; 153; CANR 80; CDBLB 1832-1890; DAM POET; DLB 18, 35, 57, 159; RGEL 2; TEA
Meredith, William 1919-2007 .... **CLC 4, 13, 22, 55; PC 28**

Author Index

See also CA 9-12R; 260; CAAS 14; CANR 6, 40, 129; CP 1, 2, 3, 4, 5, 6, 7; DAM POET; DLB 5; MAL 5

Meredith, William Morris
See Meredith, William

Merezhkovsky, Dmitrii Sergeevich
See Merezhkovsky, Dmitry Sergeyevich

Merezhkovsky, Dmitry Sergeevich
See Merezhkovsky, Dmitry Sergeyevich

Merezhkovsky, Dmitry Sergeyevich 1865-1941 .... **TCLC 29**
See also CA 169; DLB 295; EWL 3

Merezhkovsky, Zinaida
See Gippius, Zinaida

Merkin, Daphne 1954- .... **CLC 44**
See also CA 123

Merleau-Ponty, Maurice 1908-1961 .... **TCLC 156**
See also CA 114; 89-92; DLB 296; GFL 1789 to the Present

Merlin, Arthur
See Blish, James

Mernissi, Fatima 1940- .... **CLC 171**
See also CA 152; DLB 346; FW

Merrill, James 1926-1995 .... **CLC 2, 3, 6, 8, 13, 18, 34, 91; PC 28; TCLC 173**
See also AMWS 3; CA 13-16R; 147; CANR 10, 49, 63, 108; CP 1, 2, 3, 4; DA3; DAM POET; DLB 5, 165; DLBY 1985; EWL 3; INT CANR-10; MAL 5; MTCW 1, 2; MTFW 2005; PAB; PFS 23; RGAL 4

Merrill, James Ingram
See Merrill, James

Merriman, Alex
See Silverberg, Robert

Merriman, Brian 1747-1805 .... **NCLC 70**

Merritt, E. B.
See Waddington, Miriam

Merton, Thomas 1915-1968 ... **CLC 1, 3, 11, 34, 83; PC 10**
See also AAYA 61; AMWS 8; CA 5-8R; 25-28R; CANR 22, 53, 111, 131; DA3; DLB 48; DLBY 1981; MAL 5; MTCW 1, 2; MTFW 2005

Merton, Thomas James
See Merton, Thomas

Merwin, W. S. 1927- .... **CLC 1, 2, 3, 5, 8, 13, 18, 45, 88; PC 45**
See also AMWS 3; CA 13-16R; CANR 15, 51, 112, 140, 209; CP 1, 2, 3, 4, 5, 6, 7; DA3; DAM POET; DLB 5, 169, 342; EWL 3; INT CANR-15; MAL 5; MTCW 1, 2; MTFW 2005; PAB; PFS 5, 15; RGAL 4

Merwin, William Stanley
See Merwin, W. S.

Metastasio, Pietro 1698-1782 .... **LC 115**
See also RGWL 2, 3

Metcalf, John 1938- .... **CLC 37; SSC 43**
See also CA 113; CN 4, 5, 6, 7; DLB 60; RGSF 2; TWA

Metcalf, Suzanne
See Baum, L. Frank

Mew, Charlotte (Mary) 1870-1928 .... **PC 107; TCLC 8**
See also CA 105; 189; DLB 19, 135; RGEL 2

Mewshaw, Michael 1943- .... **CLC 9**
See also CA 53-56; CANR 7, 47, 147, 213; DLBY 1980

Meyer, Conrad Ferdinand 1825-1898 .... **NCLC 81, 249; SSC 30**
See also DLB 129; EW; RGWL 2, 3

Meyer, Gustav 1868-1932 .... **TCLC 21**
See also CA 117; 190; DLB 81; EWL 3

Meyer, June
See Jordan, June

Meyer, Lynn
See Slavitt, David R.

Meyer, Stephenie 1973- .... **CLC 280**
See also AAYA 77; CA 253; CANR 192; CLR 142, 180; SATA 193

Meyer-Meyrink, Gustav
See Meyer, Gustav

Meyers, Jeffrey 1939- .... **CLC 39**
See also CA 73-76, 186; CAAE 186; CANR 54, 102, 159; DLB 111

Meynell, Alice (Christina Gertrude Thompson) 1847-1922 .... **PC 112; TCLC 6**
See also CA 104; 177; DLB 19, 98; RGEL 2

Meyrink, Gustav
See Meyer, Gustav

Mhlophe, Gcina 1960- .... **BLC 2:3**

Michaels, Leonard 1933-2003 .... **CLC 6, 25; SSC 16**
See also AMWS 16; CA 61-64; 216; CANR 21, 62, 119, 179; CN 3, 45, 6, 7; DLB 130; MTCW 1; TCLE 1:2

Michaux, Henri 1899-1984 .... **CLC 8, 19**
See also CA 85-88; 114; DLB 258; EWL 3; GFL 1789 to the Present; RGWL 2, 3

Micheaux, Oscar (Devereaux) 1884-1951 .... **TCLC 76**
See also BW 3; CA 174; DLB 50; TCWW 2

Michelangelo 1475-1564 .... **LC 12**
See also AAYA 43

Michelet, Jules 1798-1874 .... **NCLC 31, 218**
See also EW 5; GFL 1789 to the Present

Michels, Robert 1876-1936 .... **TCLC 88**
See also CA 212

Michener, James A. 1907(?)-1997 ... **CLC 1, 5, 11, 29, 60, 109**
See also AAYA 27; AITN 1; BEST 90:1; BPFB 2; CA 5-8R; 161; CANR 21, 45, 68; CN 1, 2, 3, 4, 5, 6; CPW; DA3; DAM NOV, POP; DLB 6; MAL 5; MTCW 1, 2; MTFW 2005; RHW; TCWW 1, 2

Michener, James Albert
See Michener, James A.

Mickiewicz, Adam 1798-1855 .... **NCLC 3, 101, 265; PC 38**
See also EW 5; RGWL 2, 3

Middleton, (John) Christopher 1926- .... **CLC 13**
See also CA 13-16R; CANR 29, 54, 117; CP 1, 2, 3, 4, 5, 6, 7; DLB 40

Middleton, Richard (Barham) 1882-1911 .... **TCLC 56**
See also CA 187; DLB 156; HGG

Middleton, Stanley 1919-2009 ..... **CLC 7, 38**
See also CA 25-28R; 288; CAAS 23; CANR 21, 46, 81, 157; CN 1, 2, 3, 4, 5, 6, 7; DLB 14, 326

Middleton, Thomas 1580-1627 .... **DC 5, 40; LC 33, 123**
See also BRW 2; DAM DRAM, MST; DFS 18, 22; DLB 58; RGEL 2

Migueis, Jose Rodrigues 1901-1980 .... **CLC 10**
See also DLB 287

Mihura, Miguel 1905-1977 .... **DC 34**
See also CA 214

Mikszath, Kalman 1847-1910 .... **TCLC 31**
See also CA 170

Miles, Jack .... **CLC 100**
See also CA 200

Miles, John Russiano
See Miles, Jack

Miles, Josephine (Louise) 1911-1985 .... **CLC 1, 2, 14, 34, 39**
See also CA 1-4R; 116; CANR 2, 55; CP 1, 2, 3, 4; DAM POET; DLB 48; MAL 5; TCLE 1:2

Militant
See Sandburg, Carl

Mill, Harriet (Hardy) Taylor 1807-1858 .... **NCLC 102**
See also FW

Mill, John Stuart 1806-1873 .... **NCLC 11, 58, 179, 223**
See also CDBLB 1832-1890; DLB 55, 190, 262, 366; FW 1; RGEL 2; TEA

Millar, Kenneth 1915-1983 ...... **CLC 1, 2, 3, 14, 34, 41**
See also AAYA 81; AMWS 4; BPFB 2; CA 9-12R; 110; CANR 16, 63, 107; CMW 4; CN 1, 2, 3; CPW; DA3; DAM POP; DLB 2, 226; DLBD 6; DLBY 1983; MAL 5; MSW; MTCW 1, 2; MTFW 2005; RGAL 4

Millay, E. Vincent
See Millay, Edna St. Vincent

Millay, Edna St. Vincent 1892-1950 ... **PC 6, 61; TCLC 4, 49, 169; WLCS**
See also AMW; CA 104; 130; CDALB 1917-1929; DA; DA3; DAB; DAC; DAM MST, POET; DFS 27; DLB 45, 249; EWL 3; EXPP; FL 1:6; GLL 1; MAL 5; MBL; MTCW 1, 2; MTFW 2005; PAB; PFS 3, 17, 31, 34, 41; RGAL 4; TUS; WP

Miller, Arthur 1915-2005 .... **CLC 1, 2, 6, 10, 15, 26, 47, 78, 179; DC 1, 31; WLC 4**
See also AAYA 15; AITN 1; AMW; AMWC 1; CA 1-4R; 236; CABS 3; CAD; CANR 2, 30, 54, 76, 132; CD 5, 6; CDALB 1941-1968; CLR 195; DA; DA3; DAB; DAC; DAM DRAM, MST; DFS 1, 3, 8, 27; DLB 7, 266; EWL 3; LAIT 1, 4; LATS 1:2; MAL 5; MTCW 1, 2; MTFW 2005; RGAL 4; RGHL; TUS; WYAS 1

Miller, Frank 1957- .... **CLC 278**
See also AAYA 45; CA 224

Miller, Henry (Valentine) 1891-1980 .... **CLC 1, 2, 4, 9, 14, 43, 84; TCLC 213; WLC 4**
See also AMW; BPFB 2; CA 9-12R; 97-100; CANR 33, 64; CDALB 1929-1941; CN 1, 2; DA; DA3; DAB; DAC; DAM MST, NOV; DLB 4, 9; DLBY 1980; EWL 3; MAL 5; MTCW 1, 2; MTFW 2005; RGAL 4; TUS

Miller, Hugh 1802-1856 .... **NCLC 143**
See also DLB 190

Miller, Jason 1939(?)-2001 .... **CLC 2**
See also AITN 1; CA 73-76; 197; CAD; CANR 130; DFS 12; DLB 7

Miller, Sue 1943- .... **CLC 44**
See also AMWS 12; BEST 90:3; CA 139; CANR 59, 91, 128, 194, 231; DA3; DAM POP; DLB 143

Miller, Walter M(ichael, Jr.) 1923-1996 .... **CLC 4, 30**
See also BPFB 2; CA 85-88; CANR 108; DLB 8; SCFW 1, 2; SFW 4

Millett, Kate 1934- .... **CLC 67**
See also AITN 1; CA 73-76; CANR 32, 53, 76, 110; DA3; DLB 246; FW; GLL 1; MTCW 1, 2; MTFW 2005

Millhauser, Steven 1943- .... **CLC 21, 54, 109, 300; SSC 57**
See also AAYA 76; CA 110; 111; CANR 63, 114, 133, 189; CN 6, 7; DA3; DLB 2, 350; FANT; INT CA-111; MAL 5; MTCW 2; MTFW 2005

Millhauser, Steven Lewis
See Millhauser, Steven

Millin, Sarah Gertrude 1889-1968 ... **CLC 49**
See also CA 102; 93-96; DLB 225; EWL 3

Milne, A. A. 1882-1956 .... **TCLC 6, 88**
See also BRWS 5; CA 104; 133; CLR 1, 26, 108; CMW 4; CWRI 5; DA3; DAB; DAC; DAM MST; DLB 10, 77, 100, 160, 352; FANT; MAICYA 1, 2; MTCW 1, 2; MTFW 2005; RGEL 2; SATA 100; WCH; YABC 1

Milne, Alan Alexander
See Milne, A. A.

Milner, Ron(ald) 1938-2004 .... **BLC 1:3; CLC 56**
See also AITN 1; BW 1; CA 73-76; 230; CAD; CANR 24, 81; CD 5, 6; DAM MULT; DLB 38; MAL 5; MTCW 1
Milnes, Richard Monckton 1809-1885 .... **NCLC 61**
See also DLB 32, 184
Milosz, Czeslaw 1911-2004 .... **CLC 5, 11, 22, 31, 56, 82, 253; PC 8, 136; WLCS**
See also AAYA 62; CA 81-84; 230; CANR 23, 51, 91, 126; CDWLB 4; CWW 2; DA3; DAM MST, POET; DLB 215, 331; EW 13; EWL 3; MTCW 1, 2; MTFW 2005; PFS 16, 29, 35; RGHL; RGWL 2, 3
Milton, John 1608-1674 .... **LC 9, 43, 92, 205, 225; PC 19, 29, 141; WLC 4**
See also AAYA 65; BRW 2; BRWR 2; CDBLB 1660-1789; DA; DA3; DAB; DAC; DAM MST, POET; DLB 131, 151, 281; EFS 1:1, 2:2; EXPP; LAIT 1; PAB; PFS 3, 17, 37, 44; RGEL 2; TEA; WLIT 3; WP
Min, Anchee 1957- .... **CLC 86, 291**
See also CA 146; CANR 94, 137, 222; MTFW 2005
Minehaha, Cornelius
See Wedekind, Frank
Miner, Valerie 1947- .... **CLC 40**
See also CA 97-100; CANR 59, 177; FW; GLL 2
Minimo, Duca
See D'Annunzio, Gabriele
Minot, Susan (Anderson) 1956- .... **CLC 44, 159**
See also AMWS 6; CA 134; CANR 118; CN 6, 7
Minus, Ed 1938- .... **CLC 39**
See also CA 185
Mirabai 1498(?)-1550(?) .... **LC 143; PC 48**
See also PFS 24
Miranda, Javier
See Bioy Casares, Adolfo
Mirbeau, Octave 1848-1917 .... **TCLC 55**
See also CA 216; DLB 123, 192; GFL 1789 to the Present
Mirikitani, Janice 1942- .... **AAL**
See also CA 211; DLB 312; RGAL 4
Mirk, John (?)-c. 1414 .... **LC 105**
See also DLB 146
Miro (Ferrer), Gabriel (Francisco Victor) 1879-1930 .... **TCLC 5**
See also CA 104; 185; DLB 322; EWL 3
Misharin, Alexandr .... **CLC 59**
Mishima, Yukio
See Hiraoka, Kimitake
See also NFS 43
Mishima Yukio
See Hiraoka, Kimitake
Miss C. L. F.
See Grimke, Charlotte L. Forten
Mister X
See Hoch, Edward D.
Mistral, Frederic 1830-1914 .... **TCLC 51**
See also CA 122; 213; DLB 331; GFL 1789 to the Present
Mistral, Gabriela 1899-1957 .... **HLC 2; PC 32; TCLC 2, 277**
See also BW 2; CA 104; 131; CANR 81; DAM MULT; DLB 283, 331; DNFS; EWL 3; HW 1, 2; LAW; MTCW 1, 2; MTFW 2005; PFS 37, 42; RGWL 2, 3; WP
Mistry, Rohinton 1952- .... **CLC 71, 196, 281; SSC 73**
See also BRWS 10; CA 141; CANR 86, 114; CCA 1; CN 6, 7; DAC; DLB 334; NFS 43; SSFS 6
Mitchell, Clyde
See Ellison, Harlan; Silverberg, Robert
Mitchell, David 1969- .... **CLC 311**
See also BRWS 14; CA 210; CANR 159, 224
Mitchell, Emerson Blackhorse Barney 1945- .... **NNAL**
See also CA 45-48
Mitchell, James Leslie 1901-1935 .... **TCLC 4**
See also BRWS 14; CA 104; 188; DLB 15; RGEL 2
Mitchell, Joni 1943- .... **CLC 12**
See also CA 112; CCA 1
Mitchell, Joseph (Quincy) 1908-1996 .... **CLC 98**
See also CA 77-80; 152; CANR 69; CN 1, 2, 3, 4, 5, 6; CSW; DLB 185; DLBY 1996
Mitchell, Margaret 1900-1949 .... **TCLC 11, 170**
See also AAYA 23; BPFB 2; BYA 1; CA 109; 125; CANR 55, 94; CDALBS; CLR 190; DA3; DAM NOV, POP; DLB 9; LAIT 2; MAL 5; MTCW 1, 2; MTFW 2005; NFS 9, 38; RGAL 4; RHW; TUS; WYAS 1; YAW
Mitchell, Margaret Munnerlyn
See Mitchell, Margaret
Mitchell, Peggy
See Mitchell, Margaret
Mitchell, S(ilas) Weir 1829-1914 .... **TCLC 36**
See also CA 165; DLB 202; RGAL 4
Mitchell, W(illiam) O(rmond) 1914-1998 .... **CLC 25**
See also CA 77-80; 165; CANR 15, 43; CN 1, 2, 3, 4, 5, 6; DAC; DAM MST; DLB 88; TCLE 1:2
Mitchell, William (Lendrum) 1879-1936 .... **TCLC 81**
See also CA 213
Mitford, Mary Russell 1787-1855 .... **NCLC 4**
See also DLB 110, 116; RGEL 2
Mitford, Nancy 1904-1973 .... **CLC 44**
See also BRWS 10; CA 9-12R; CN 1; DLB 191; RGEL 2
Mieville, China 1972- .... **CLC 235**
See also AAYA 52; CA 196; CANR 138, 214, 239; MTFW 2005
Miyamoto, (Chujo) Yuriko 1899-1951 .... **TCLC 37**
See also CA 170, 174; DLB 180
Miyamoto Yuriko
See Miyamoto, (Chujo) Yuriko
Miyazawa, Kenji 1896-1933 .... **TCLC 76**
See also CA 157; EWL 3; RGWL 3
Miyazawa Kenji
See Miyazawa, Kenji
Mizoguchi, Kenji 1898-1956 .... **TCLC 72**
See also CA 167
Mkha, NoViolet
See Bulawayo, Noviolet
Mo, Timothy (Peter) 1950- .... **CLC 46, 134**
See also CA 117; CANR 128; CN 5, 6, 7; DLB 194; MTCW 1; WLIT 4; WWE 1
Mo, Yan
See Yan, Mo
Moberg, Carl Arthur
See Moberg, Vilhelm
Moberg, Vilhelm 1898-1973 .... **TCLC 224**
See also CA 97-100; 45-48; CANR 135; DLB 259; EW 11; EWL 3
Modarressi, Taghi (M.) 1931-1997 .... **CLC 44**
See also CA 121; 134; INT CA-134
Modiano, Patrick (Jean) 1945- .... **CLC 18, 218, 389**
See also CA 85-88; CANR 17, 40, 115; CWW 2; DLB 83, 299; EWL 3; RGHL
Mofolo, Thomas 1875(?)-1948 .... **BLC 1:3; TCLC 22**
See also AFW; CA 121; 153; CANR 83; DAM MULT; DLB 225; EWL 3; MTCW 2; MTFW 2005; WLIT 2
Mofolo, Thomas Mokopu
See Mofolo, Thomas
Moggach, Lottie 1977- .... **CLC 370**
See also CA 351
Mohr, Nicholasa 1938- .... **CLC 12; HLC 2**
See also AAYA 8, 46; CA 49-52; CANR 1, 32, 64; CLR 22; DAM MULT; DLB 145; HW 1, 2; JRDA; LAIT 5; LLW; MAICYA 2; MAICYAS 1; RGAL 4; SAAS 8; SATA 8, 97; SATA-Essay 113; WYA; YAW
Moi, Toril 1953- .... **CLC 172**
See also CA 154; CANR 102; FW
Mojtabai, A.G. 1938- .... **CLC 5, 9, 15, 29**
See also CA 85-88; CANR 88, 238
Mojtabai, Ann Grace
See Mojtabai, A.G.
Mokeddem, Malika 1949- .... **CLC 357**
See also CA 271
Molin, Charles
See Mayne, William
Molina, Antonio Munoz 1956- .... **CLC 289**
See also DLB 322
Moliere 1622-1673 .... **DC 13; LC 10, 28, 64, 125, 127, 200; WLC 4**
See also DA; DA3; DAB; DAC; DAM DRAM, MST; DFS 13, 18, 20; DLB 268; EW 3; GFL Beginnings to 1789; LATS 1:1; RGWL 2, 3; TWA
Molnar, Ferenc 1878-1952 .... **TCLC 20**
See also CA 109; 153; CANR 83; CDWLB 4; DAM DRAM; DLB 215; EWL 3; RGWL 2, 3
Momaday, N. Scott 1934- .... **CLC 2, 19, 85, 95, 160, 330; NNAL; PC 25; WLCS**
See also AAYA 11, 64; AMWS 4; ANW; BPFB 2; BYA 12; CA 25-28R; CANR 14, 34, 68, 134; CDALBS; CN 2, 3, 4, 5, 6, 7; CPW; DA; DA3; DAB; DAC; DAM MST, MULT, NOV, POP; DLB 143, 175, 256; EWL 3; EXPP; INT CANR-14; LAIT 4; LATS 1:2; MAL 5; MTCW 1, 2; MTFW 2005; NFS 10; PFS 2, 11, 37, 41; RGAL 4; SATA 48; SATA-Brief 30; TCWW 1, 2; WP; YAW
Momaday, Navarre Scott
See Momaday, N. Scott
Momala, Ville i
See Moberg, Vilhelm
Monette, Paul 1945-1995 .... **CLC 82**
See also AMWS 10; CA 139; 147; CN 6; DLB 350; GLL 1
Monroe, Harriet 1860-1936 .... **TCLC 12**
See also CA 109; 204; DLB 54, 91
Monroe, Lyle
See Heinlein, Robert A.
Montagu, Elizabeth 1720-1800 .... **NCLC 7, 117**
See also DLB 356; FW
Montagu, Lady Mary Wortley 1689-1762 .... **LC 9, 57, 204; PC 16**
See also DLB 95, 101, 366; FL 1:1; RGEL 2
Montagu, W. H.
See Coleridge, Samuel Taylor
Montague, John (Patrick) 1929- .... **CLC 13, 46; PC 106**
See also BRWS 15; CA 9-12R; CANR 9, 69, 121; CP 1, 2, 3, 4, 5, 6, 7; DLB 40; EWL 3; MTCW 1; PFS 12; RGEL 2; TCLE 1:2
Montaigne, Michel de 1533-1592 .... **LC 8, 105, 194; WLC 4**
See also DA; DAB; DAC; DAM MST; DLB 327; EW 2; GFL Beginnings to 1789; LMFS 1; RGWL 2, 3; TWA
Montaigne, Michel Eyquem de
See Montaigne, Michel de
Montale, Eugenio 1896-1981 .... **CLC 7, 9, 18; PC 13**

See also CA 17-20R; 104; CANR 30; DLB 114, 331; EW 11; EWL 3; MTCW 1; PFS 22; RGWL 2, 3; TWA; WLIT 7

Montemayor, Jorge de 1521(?)-1561(?) .... **LC 185**
See also DLB 318

Montero, Rosa 1951- .... **CLC 353**
See also CA 254; DLB 322

Montesquieu, Charles-Louis de Secondat 1689-1755 .... **LC 7, 69, 189**
See also DLB 314; EW 3; GFL Beginnings to 1789; TWA

Montessori, Maria 1870-1952 ..... **TCLC 103**
See also CA 115; 147

Montgomery, Bruce 1921(?)-1978 ... **CLC 22**
See also CA 179; 104; CMW 4; DLB 87; MSW

Montgomery, L. M. 1874-1942 .... **TCLC 51, 140**
See also AAYA 12; BYA 1; CA 108; 137; CLR 8, 91, 145; DA3; DAC; DAM MST; DLB 92, 362; DLBD 14; JRDA; MAICYA 1, 2; MTCW 2; MTFW 2005; RGEL 2; SATA 100; TWA; WCH; WYA; YABC 1

Montgomery, Lucy Maud
See Montgomery, L. M.

Montgomery, Marion, Jr. 1925- .... **CLC 7**
See also AITN 1; CA 1-4R; CANR 3, 48, 162; CSW; DLB 6

Montgomery, Marion H. 1925-
See Montgomery, Marion, Jr.

Montgomery, Max
See Davenport, Guy (Mattison, Jr.)

Montgomery, Robert Bruce
See Montgomery, Bruce

Montherlant, Henry de 1896-1972 .... **CLC 8, 19**
See also CA 85-88; 37-40R; DAM DRAM; DLB 72, 321; EW 11; EWL 3; GFL 1789 to the Present; MTCW 1

Montherlant, Henry Milon de
See Montherlant, Henry de

Monty Python
See Chapman, Graham; Cleese, John (Marwood); Gilliam, Terry; Idle, Eric; Jones, Terence Graham Parry; Palin, Michael

Moodie, Susanna (Strickland) 1803-1885 .... **NCLC 14, 113**
See also DLB 99

Moody, Hiram
See Moody, Rick

Moody, Hiram F. III
See Moody, Rick

Moody, Minerva
See Alcott, Louisa May

Moody, Rick 1961- .... **CLC 147**
See also CA 138; CANR 64, 112, 179; MTFW 2005

Moody, William Vaughan 1869-1910 .... **TCLC 105**
See also CA 110; 178; DLB 7, 54; MAL 5; RGAL 4

Mooney, Edward
See Mooney, Ted

Mooney, Ted 1951- .... **CLC 25**
See also CA 130; CANR 229

Moorcock, Michael 1939- .... **CLC 5, 27, 58, 236**
See also AAYA 26; CA 45-48; CAAS 5; CANR 2, 17, 38, 64, 122, 203; CN 5, 6, 7; DLB 14, 231, 261, 319; FANT; MTCW 1, 2; MTFW 2005; SATA 93, 166; SCFW 1, 2; SFW 4; SUFW 1, 2

Moorcock, Michael John
See Moorcock, Michael

Moorcock, Michael John
See Moorcock, Michael

Moore, Al
See Moore, Alan

Moore, Alan 1953- .... **CLC 230**
See also AAYA 51; CA 204; CANR 138, 184; DLB 261; MTFW 2005; SFW 4

Moore, Alice Ruth
See Nelson, Alice Ruth Moore Dunbar

Moore, Brian 1921-1999 ...... **CLC 1, 3, 5, 7, 8, 19, 32, 90**
See also BRWS 9; CA 1-4R; 174; CANR 1, 25, 42, 63; CCA 1; CN 1, 2, 3, 4, 5, 6; DAB; DAC; DAM MST; DLB 251; EWL 3; FANT; MTCW 1, 2; MTFW 2005; RGEL 2

Moore, Edward
See Muir, Edwin

Moore, G. E. 1873-1958 .... **TCLC 89**
See also DLB 262

Moore, George Augustus 1852-1933 .... **SSC 19, 134; TCLC 7, 265**
See also BRW 6; CA 104; 177; DLB 10, 18, 57, 135; EWL 3; RGEL 2; RGSF 2

Moore, Lorrie 1957- .... **CLC 39, 45, 68, 165, 315; SSC 147**
See also AMWS 10; CA 116; CANR 39, 83, 139, 221; CN 5, 6, 7; DLB 234; MTFW 2005; SSFS 19

Moore, Marianne 1887-1972 .... **CLC 1, 2, 4, 8, 10, 13, 19, 47; PC 4, 49; WLCS**
See also AMW; CA 1-4R; 33-36R; CANR 3, 61; CDALB 1929-1941; CP 1; DA; DA3; DAB; DAC; DAM MST, POET; DLB 45; DLBD 7; EWL 3; EXPP; FL 1:6; MAL 5; MBL; MTCW 1, 2; MTFW 2005; PAB; PFS 14, 17, 38; RGAL 4; SATA 20; TUS; WP

Moore, Marianne Craig
See Moore, Marianne

Moore, Marie Lorena
See Moore, Lorrie

Moore, Michael 1954- .... **CLC 218**
See also AAYA 53; CA 166; CANR 150, 235

Moore, Thomas 1779-1852 .... **NCLC 6, 110, 283**
See also BRWS 17; DLB 96, 144; RGEL 2

Moorhouse, Frank 1938- .... **SSC 40**
See also CA 118; CANR 92; CN 3, 4, 5, 6, 7; DLB 289; RGSF 2

Mootoo, Shani 1958(?)- .... **CLC 294**
See also CA 174; CANR 156

Mora, Pat 1942- .... **HLC 2**
See also AMWS 13; CA 129; CANR 57, 81, 112, 171; CLR 58; DAM MULT; DLB 209; HW 1, 2; LLW; MAICYA 2; MTFW 2005; PFS 33, 35, 40; SATA 92, 134, 186, 232

Moraga, Cherrie 1952- .... **CLC 126, 250, 345; DC 22**
See also AMWS 23; CA 131; CANR 66, 154; DAM MULT; DLB 82, 249; FW; GLL 1; HW 1, 2; LLW

Moran, J.L.
See Whitaker, Rod

Morand, Paul 1888-1976 ... **CLC 41; SSC 22**
See also CA 184; 69-72; DLB 65; EWL 3

Morante, Elsa 1918-1985 .... **CLC 8, 47**
See also CA 85-88; 117; CANR 35; DLB 177; EWL 3; MTCW 1, 2; MTFW 2005; RGHL; RGWL 2, 3; WLIT 7

Moratín, Leandro Fernández de 1760-1828 .... **NCLC 280**

Moreas, Jean
See Papadiamantopoulos, Johannes

Moravia, Alberto
See Pincherle, Alberto

More, Hannah 1745-1833 ..... **NCLC 27, 141**
See also DLB 107, 109, 116, 158; RGEL 2

More, Henry 1614-1687 .... **LC 9**
See also DLB 126, 252

More, Sir Thomas 1478-1535 .... **LC 10, 32, 140, 246**
See also BRWC 1; BRWS 7; DLB 136, 281; LMFS 1; NFS 29; RGEL 2; TEA

Moreto y Cabaña, Agustín 1618-1669 ... **LC 231**

Moreton, Andrew Esq.
See Defoe, Daniel

Moreton, Lee
See Boucicault, Dion

Morgan, Berry 1919-2002 .... **CLC 6**
See also CA 49-52; 208; DLB 6

Morgan, Claire
See Highsmith, Patricia

Morgan, Edwin 1920-2010 .... **CLC 31**
See also BRWS 9; CA 5-8R; CANR 3, 43, 90; CP 1, 2, 3, 4, 5, 6, 7; DLB 27

Morgan, Edwin George
See Morgan, Edwin

Morgan, (George) Frederick 1922-2004 .... **CLC 23**
See also CA 17-20R; 224; CANR 21, 144; CP 2, 3, 4, 5, 6, 7

Morgan, Harriet
See Mencken, H. L.

Morgan, Jane
See Cooper, James Fenimore

Morgan, Janet 1945- .... **CLC 39**
See also CA 65-68

Morgan, Lady 1776(?)-1859 .... **NCLC 29, 275**
See also DLB 116, 158; RGEL 2

Morgan, Robert 1944- .... **CLC 339**
See also CA 33-36R, 201; CAAE 201; CAAS 20; CANR 21, 89, 144, 186; CP 7; CSW; DLB 120, 292

Morgan, Robin (Evonne) 1941- .... **CLC 2**
See also CA 69-72; CANR 29, 68; FW; GLL 2; MTCW 1; SATA 80

Morgan, Scott
See Kuttner, Henry

Morgan, Seth 1949(?)-1990 .... **CLC 65**
See also CA 185; 132

Morgenstern, Christian (Otto Josef Wolfgang) 1871-1914 .... **TCLC 8**
See also CA 105; 191; EWL 3

Morgenstern, S.
See Goldman, William

Mori, Rintaro
See Mori Ogai

Mori, Toshio 1910-1980 ... **AAL; SSC 83, 123**
See also CA 116; 244; DLB 312; RGSF 2

Moricz, Zsigmond 1879-1942 .... **TCLC 33**
See also CA 165; DLB 215; EWL 3

Morin, Jean-Paul
See Whitaker, Rod

Mori Ogai 1862-1922 .... **TCLC 14**
See also CA 110; 164; DLB 180; EWL 3; MJW; RGWL 3; TWA

Moritz, Karl Philipp 1756-1793 ... **LC 2, 162**
See also DLB 94

Morland, Peter Henry
See Faust, Frederick

Morley, Christopher (Darlington) 1890-1957 .... **TCLC 87**
See also CA 112; 213; DLB 9; MAL 5; RGAL 4

Morren, Theophil
See Hofmannsthal, Hugo von

Morris, Bill 1952- .... **CLC 76**
See also CA 225

Morris, Julian
See West, Morris L(anglo)

Morris, Steveland Judkins (?)-
See Wonder, Stevie

Morris, William 1834-1896 .... **NCLC 4, 233; PC 55**

See also BRW 5; CDBLB 1832-1890; DLB 18, 35, 57, 156, 178, 184; FANT; RGEL 2; SFW 4; SUFW
Morris, Wright (Marion) 1910-1998 .... **CLC 1, 3, 7, 18, 37; TCLC 107**
See also AMW; CA 9-12R; 167; CANR 21, 81; CN 1, 2, 3, 4, 5, 6; DLB 2, 206, 218; DLBY 1981; EWL 3; MAL 5; MTCW 1, 2; MTFW 2005; RGAL 4; TCWW 1, 2
Morrison, Arthur 1863-1945 .... **SSC 40; TCLC 72**
See also CA 120; 157; CMW 4; DLB 70, 135, 197; RGEL 2
Morrison, Chloe Anthony Wofford
See Morrison, Toni
Morrison, James Douglas
See Morrison, Jim
Morrison, Jim 1943-1971 .... **CLC 17**
See also CA 73-76; CANR 40
Morrison, John Gordon 1904-1998 .... **SSC 93**
See also CA 103; CANR 92; DLB 260
Morrison, Toni 1931- .... **BLC 1:3, 2:3; CLC 4, 10, 22, 55, 81, 87, 173, 194, 344, 363, 366; SSC 126; WLC 4**
See also AAYA 1, 22, 61; AFAW 1, 2; AMWC 1; AMWS 3; BPFB 2; BW 2, 3; CA 29-32R; CANR 27, 42, 67, 113, 124, 204; CDALB 1968-1988; CLR 99, 190; CN 3, 4, 5, 6, 7; CPW; DA; DA3; DAB; DAC; DAM MST, MULT, NOV, POP; DLB 6, 33, 143, 331; DLBY 1981; EWL 3; EXPN; FL 1:6; FW; GL 3; LAIT 2, 4; LATS 1:2; LMFS 2; MAL 5; MBL; MTCW 1, 2; MTFW 2005; NFS 1, 6, 8, 14, 37, 40; RGAL 4; RHW; SATA 57, 144, 235; SSFS 5; TCLE 1:2; TUS; YAW
Morrison, Van 1945- .... **CLC 21**
See also CA 116; 168
Morrissy, Mary 1957- .... **CLC 99**
See also CA 205; DLB 267
Mortimer, John 1923-2009 .... **CLC 28, 43**
See Morton, Kate
See also CA 13-16R; 282; CANR 21, 69, 109, 172; CBD; CD 5, 6; CDBLB 1960 to Present; CMW 4; CN 5, 6, 7; CPW; DA3; DAM DRAM, POP; DLB 13, 245, 271; INT CANR-21; MSW; MTCW 1, 2; MTFW 2005; RGEL 2
Mortimer, John C.
See Mortimer, John
Mortimer, John Clifford
See Mortimer, John
Mortimer, Penelope (Ruth) 1918-1999 .... **CLC 5**
See also CA 57-60; 187; CANR 45, 88; CN 1, 2, 3, 4, 5, 6
Mortimer, Sir John
See Mortimer, John
Morton, Anthony
See Creasey, John
Morton, Thomas 1579(?)-1647(?) ...... **LC 72**
See also DLB 24; RGEL 2
Mosca, Gaetano 1858-1941 .... **TCLC 75**
Moses, Daniel David 1952- .... **NNAL**
See also CA 186; CANR 160; DLB 334
Mosher, Howard Frank 1943- .... **CLC 62**
See also CA 139; CANR 65, 115, 181
Mosley, Nicholas 1923- .... **CLC 43, 70**
See also CA 69-72; CANR 41, 60, 108, 158; CN 1, 2, 3, 4, 5, 6, 7; DLB 14, 207
Mosley, Walter 1952- .... **BLCS; CLC 97, 184, 278**
See also AAYA 57; AMWS 13; BPFB 2; BW 2; CA 142; CANR 57, 92, 136, 172, 201, 239; CMW 4; CN 7; CPW; DA3; DAM MULT, POP; DLB 306; MSW; MTCW 2; MTFW 2005
Moss, Howard 1922-1987 .... **CLC 7, 14, 45, 50**
See also CA 1-4R; 123; CANR 1, 44; CP 1, 2, 3, 4; DAM POET; DLB 5
Mossgiel, Rab
See Burns, Robert
Motion, Andrew 1952- .... **CLC 47**
See also BRWS 7; CA 146; CANR 90, 142; CP 4, 5, 6, 7; DLB 40; MTFW 2005
Motion, Andrew Peter
See Motion, Andrew
Motley, Willard (Francis) 1909-1965 .. **CLC 18**
See also AMWS 17; BW 1; CA 117; 106; CANR 88; DLB 76, 143
Motoori, Norinaga 1730-1801 .... **NCLC 45**
Mott, Michael (Charles Alston) 1930- .... **CLC 15, 34**
See also CA 5-8R; CAAS 7; CANR 7, 29
Moulsworth, Martha 1577-1646 ...... **LC 168**
Mountain Wolf Woman 1884-1960 .... **CLC 92; NNAL**
See also CA 144; CANR 90
Moure, Erin 1955- .... **CLC 88**
See also CA 113; CP 5, 6, 7; CWP; DLB 60
Mourning Dove 1888-1936 .... **NNAL; TCLC 304**
See also CA 144; CANR 90; DAM MULT; DLB 175, 221
Mowat, Farley 1921- .... **CLC 26**
See also AAYA 1, 50; BYA 2; CA 1-4R; CANR 4, 24, 42, 68, 108; CLR 20; CPW; DAC; DAM MST; DLB 68; INT CANR-24; JRDA; MAICYA 1, 2; MTCW 1, 2; MTFW 2005; SATA 3, 55; YAW
Mowat, Farley McGill
See Mowat, Farley
Mowatt, Anna Cora 1819-1870 .... **NCLC 74**
See also RGAL 4
Moye, Guan
See Yan, Mo
Mo Yen
See Yan, Mo
Moyers, Bill 1934- .... **CLC 74**
See also AITN 2; CA 61-64; CANR 31, 52, 148
Mphahlele, Es'kia 1919-2008 .... **BLC 1:3; CLC 25, 133, 280**
See also AFW; BW 2, 3; CA 81-84; 278; CANR 26, 76; CDWLB 3; CN 4, 5, 6; DA3; DAM MULT; DLB 125, 225; EWL 3; MTCW 2; MTFW 2005; RGSF 2; SATA 119; SATA-Obit 198; SSFS 11
Mphahlele, Ezekiel
See Mphahlele, Es'kia
Mphahlele, Zeke
See Mphahlele, Es'kia
Mpe, Phaswane 1970-2004 .... **CLC 338**
Mqhayi, S(amuel) E(dward) K(rune Loliwe) 1875-1945 .... **BLC 1:3; TCLC 25**
See also CA 153; CANR 87; DAM MULT
Morck, Paul
See Rolvaag, O.E.
Morike, Eduard (Friedrich) 1804-1875 .... **NCLC 10, 201**
See also DLB 133; RGWL 2, 3
Merimee, Prosper 1803-1870 .... **DC 33; NCLC 6, 65; SSC 7, 77**
See also DLB 119, 192; EW 6; EXPS; GFL 1789 to the Present; RGSF 2; RGWL 2, 3; SSFS 8; SUFW
Mrozek, Slawomir 1930- .... **CLC 3, 13**
See also CA 13-16R; CAAS 10; CANR 29; CDWLB 4; CWW 2; DLB 232; EWL 3; MTCW 1
Marquez, Gabriel Garcia
See Garcia Marquez, Gabriel
Mrs. Belloc-Lowndes
See Lowndes, Marie Adelaide (Belloc)
Mrs. Fairstar
See Horne, Richard Henry Hengist
M'Taggart, John M'Taggart Ellis
See McTaggart, John McTaggart Ellis
Mtwa, Percy (?)- .... **CLC 47**
See also CD 6
Mueenuddin, Daniyal 1963- .... **CLC 299**
See also CA 292
Mueller, Lisel 1924- ...... **CLC 13, 51; PC 33**
See also CA 93-96; CP 6, 7; DLB 105; PFS 9, 13
Muggeridge, Malcolm (Thomas) 1903-1990 .... **TCLC 120**
See also AITN 1; CA 101; CANR 33, 63; MTCW 1, 2
Muggins
See Twain, Mark
Muhammad 570-632 .... **WLCS**
See also DA; DAB; DAC; DAM MST; DLB 311
Muir, Edwin 1887-1959 .... **PC 49; TCLC 2, 87**
See also BRWS 6; CA 104; 193; DLB 20, 100, 191; EWL 3; RGEL 2
Muir, John 1838-1914 .... **TCLC 28**
See also AMWS 9; ANW; CA 165; DLB 186, 275
Mujica Lainez, Manuel 1910-1984 .. **CLC 31**
See also CA 81-84; 112; CANR 32; EWL 3; HW 1
Mukherjee, Bharati 1940- ... **AAL; CLC 53, 115, 235; SSC 38, 173**
See also AAYA 46; BEST 89:2; CA 107, 232; CAAE 232; CANR 45, 72, 128, 231; CN 5, 6, 7; DAM NOV; DLB 60, 218, 323; DNFS 1, 2; EWL 3; FW; MAL 5; MTCW 1, 2; MTFW 2005; NFS 37; RGAL 4; RGSF 2; SSFS 7, 24, 32; TUS; WWE 1
Muldoon, Paul 1951- .... **CLC 32, 72, 166, 324; PC 143**
See also BRWS 4; CA 113; 129; CANR 52, 91, 176; CP 2, 3, 4, 5, 6, 7; DAM POET; DLB 40; INT CA-129; PFS 7, 22; TCLE 1:2
Mulisch, Harry 1927-2010 ...... **CLC 42, 270**
See also CA 9-12R; CANR 6, 26, 56, 110; CWW 2; DLB 299; EWL 3
Mulisch, Harry Kurt Victor
See Mulisch, Harry
Mull, Martin 1943- .... **CLC 17**
See also CA 105
Mullen, Harryette 1953- .... **CLC 321**
See also CA 218; CP 7
Mullen, Harryette Romell
See Mullen, Harryette
Muller, Heiner 1929-1995 .... **DC 47**
See also CA 193; CWW 2; EWL 3
Müller, Herta 1953- .... **CLC 299**
Muller, Wilhelm .... **NCLC 73**
Mulock, Dinah Maria
See Craik, Dinah Maria (Mulock)
Multatuli 1820-1881 .... **NCLC 165**
See also RGWL 2, 3
Munday, Anthony 1560-1633 .... **LC 87**
See also DLB 62, 172; RGEL 2
Munford, Robert 1737(?)-1783 .... **LC 5**
See also DLB 31
Mungo, Raymond 1946- .... **CLC 72**
See also CA 49-52; CANR 2
Munnings, Clare
See Conway, Jill K.
Munro, Alice 1931- .... **CLC 6, 10, 19, 50, 95, 222, 370; SSC 3, 95, 208; WLCS**
See also AAYA 82; AITN 2; BPFB 2; CA 33-36R; CANR 33, 53, 75, 114, 177; CCA 1; CN 1, 2, 3, 4, 5, 6, 7; DA3; DAC; DAM MST, NOV; DLB 53; EWL 3; LNFS 3; MTCW 1, 2; MTFW 2005; NFS 27; RGEL

Author Index

2; RGSF 2; SATA 29; SSFS 5, 13, 19, 28; TCLE 1:2; WWE 1
Munro, Alice Anne
See Munro, Alice
Munro, H. H.
See Saki
Munro, Hector H.
See Saki
Munro, Hector Hugh
See Saki
Murakami, Haruki 1949- ..... **CLC 150, 274; SSC 204**
See also CA 165; CANR 102, 146, 212; CWW 2; DLB 182; EWL 3; LNFS 2; MJW; RGWL 3; SFW 4; SSFS 23, 36
Murakami Haruki
See Murakami, Haruki
Murasaki, Lady
See Murasaki Shikibu
Murasaki Shikibu 978(?)-1014(?) .... **CMLC 1, 79, 160**
See also EFS 1:2, 2:2; LATS 1:1; RGWL 2, 3
Murdoch, Iris 1919-1999 ..... **CLC 1, 2, 3, 4, 6, 8, 11, 15, 22, 31, 51; TCLC 171**
See also BRWS 1; CA 13-16R; 179; CANR 8, 43, 68, 103, 142; CBD; CDBLB 1960 to Present; CN 1, 2, 3, 4, 5, 6; CWD; DA3; DAB; DAC; DAM MST, NOV; DLB 14, 194, 233, 326; EWL 3; INT CANR-8; MTCW 1, 2; MTFW 2005; NFS 18; RGEL 2; TCLE 1:2; TEA; WLIT 4
Murdoch, Jean Iris
See Murdoch, Iris
Murfree, Mary Noailles 1850-1922 .... **SSC 22; TCLC 135**
See also CA 122; 176; DLB 12, 74; RGAL 4
Murglie
See Murnau, F.W.
Murnane, Gerald 1939- .... **CLC 362**
See also CA 164; CN 5, 6, 7; DLB 289; SFW 4
Murnau, Friedrich Wilhelm
See Murnau, F.W.
Murnau, F.W. 1888-1931 .... **TCLC 53**
See also CA 112
Murphy, Arthur 1727-1805 .... **NCLC 229**
See also DLB 89, 142; RGEL 2
Murphy, Richard 1927- .... **CLC 41**
See also BRWS 5; CA 29-32R; CP 1, 2, 3, 4, 5, 6, 7; DLB 40; EWL 3
Murphy, Sylvia 1937- .... **CLC 34**
See also CA 121
Murphy, Thomas 1935- .... **CLC 51**
See also CA 101; DLB 310
Murphy, Thomas Bernard
See Murphy, Thomas
Murphy, Tom
See Murphy, Thomas
Murray, Albert 1916- .... **BLC 2:3; CLC 73**
See also BW 2; CA 49-52; CANR 26, 52, 78, 160; CN 7; CSW; DLB 38; MTFW 2005
Murray, Albert L.
See Murray, Albert
Murray, Diane Lain Johnson
See Johnson, Diane
Murray, James Augustus Henry 1837-1915 .... **TCLC 117**
Murray, Judith Sargent 1751-1820 .... **NCLC 63, 243**
See also DLB 37, 200
Murray, Les 1938- ... **CLC 40, 326; PC 153**
See also BRWS 7; CA 21-24R; CANR 11, 27, 56, 103, 199, 236; CP 1, 2, 3, 4, 5, 6, 7; DAM POET; DLB 289; DLBY 2001; EWL 3; RGEL 2
Murray, Leslie Allan
See Murray, Les
Murry, J. Middleton
See Murry, John Middleton
Murry, John Middleton 1889-1957 .... **TCLC 16**
See also CA 118; 217; DLB 149
Musgrave, Susan 1951- .... **CLC 13, 54**
See also CA 69-72; CANR 45, 84, 181; CCA 1; CP 2, 3, 4, 5, 6, 7; CWP
Musil, Robert (Edler von) 1880-1942 ... **SSC 18; TCLC 12, 68, 213, 291**
See also CA 109; CANR 55, 84; CDWLB 2; DLB 81, 124; EW 9; EWL 3; MTCW 2; RGSF 2; RGWL 2, 3
Muske, Carol
See Muske-Dukes, Carol
Muske, Carol Anne
See Muske-Dukes, Carol
Muske-Dukes, Carol 1945- .... **CLC 90**
See also CA 65-68, 203; CAAE 203; CANR 32, 70, 181; CWP; PFS 24
Muske-Dukes, Carol Ann
See Muske-Dukes, Carol
Muske-Dukes, Carol Anne
See Muske-Dukes, Carol
Musset, Alfred de 1810-1857 .... **DC 27; NCLC 7, 150**
See also DLB 192, 217; EW 6; GFL 1789 to the Present; RGWL 2, 3; TWA
Musset, Louis Charles Alfred de
See Musset, Alfred de
Mussolini, Benito (Amilcare Andrea) 1883-1945 .... **TCLC 96**
See also CA 116
Mutanabbi, Al-
See al-Mutanabbi, Ahmad ibn al-Husayn Abu al-Tayyib al-Jufi al-Kindi
Mutis, Alvaro 1923-2013 .... **CLC 283**
See also CA 149; CANR 118; DLB 283; EWL 3; HW 1; LAWS 1
My Brother's Brother
See Chekhov, Anton
Myers, L(eopold) H(amilton) 1881-1944 .... **TCLC 59**
See also CA 157; DLB 15; EWL 3; RGEL 2
Myers, Walter Dean 1937- .... **BLC 1:3, 2:3; CLC 35**
See also AAYA 4, 23, 88; BW 2; BYA 6, 8, 11; CA 33-36R; CANR 20, 42, 67, 108, 184; CLR 4, 16, 35, 110; DAM MULT, NOV; DLB 33; INT CANR-20; JRDA; LAIT 5; LNFS 1; MAICYA 1, 2; MAICYAS 1; MTCW 2; MTFW 2005; NFS 30, 33, 40; SAAS 2; SATA 41, 71, 109, 157, 193, 229; SATA-Brief 27; SSFS 31; WYA; YAW
Myers, Walter M.
See Myers, Walter Dean
Myles, Symon
See Follett, Ken
Nabokov, Vladimir 1899-1977 .... **CLC 1, 2, 3, 6, 8, 11, 15, 23, 44, 46, 64; PC 167; SSC 11, 86, 163; TCLC 108, 189; WLC 4**
See also AAYA 45; AMW; AMWC 1; AMWR 1; BPFB 2; CA 5-8R; 69-72; CANR 20, 102; CDALB 1941-1968; CN 1, 2; CP 2; DA; DA3; DAB; DAC; DAM MST, NOV; DLB 2, 244, 278, 317; DLBD 3; DLBY 1980, 1991; EWL 3; EXPS; LATS 1:2; MAL 5; MTCW 1, 2; MTFW 2005; NCFS 4; NFS 9; RGAL 4; RGSF 2; SSFS 6, 15; TUS
Nabokov, Vladimir Vladimirovich
See Nabokov, Vladimir
Naden, Constance 1858-1889 ...... **NCLC 313**
See also DLB 199
Naevius c. 265B.C.-201B.C. .... **CMLC 37**
See also DLB 211
Nafisi, Azar 1955- .... **CLC 313, 358**
See also CA 222; CANR 203; DLB 366; LNFS 2
Nagai, Kafu 1879-1959 .... **TCLC 51**
See also CA 117; 276; DLB 180; EWL 3; MJW
Nagai, Sokichi
See Nagai, Kafu
Nagai Kafu
See Nagai, Kafu
na gCopaleen, Myles
See O Nuallain, Brian
na Gopaleen, Myles
See O Nuallain, Brian
Nagy, Laszlo 1925-1978 .... **CLC 7**
See also CA 129; 112
Naidu, Sarojini 1879-1949 .... **TCLC 80**
See also EWL 3; RGEL 2
Naipaul, Shiva 1945-1985 .... **CLC 32, 39; TCLC 153**
See also CA 110; 112; 116; CANR 33; CN 2, 3; DA3; DAM NOV; DLB 157; DLBY 1985; EWL 3; MTCW 1, 2; MTFW 2005
Naipaul, Shivadhar Srinivasa
See Naipaul, Shiva
Naipaul, Vidiahar Surajprasad
See Naipaul, V. S.
Naipaul, V. S. 1932- .... **CLC 4, 7, 9, 13, 18, 37, 105, 199; SSC 38, 121**
See also BPFB 2; BRWS 1; CA 1-4R; CANR 1, 33, 51, 91, 126, 191; CDBLB 1960 to Present; CDWLB 3; CN 1, 2, 3, 4, 5, 6, 7; DA3; DAB; DAC; DAM MST, NOV; DLB 125, 204, 207, 326, 331; DLBY 1985, 2001; EWL 3; LATS 1:2; MTCW 1, 2; MTFW 2005; NFS 37; RGEL 2; RGSF 2; SSFS 29; TWA; WLIT 4; WWE 1
Nair, Kamala
See Das, Kamala
Nakos, Lilika 1903-1989 .... **CLC 29**
See also CA 217
Nalapat, Kamala
See Das, Kamala
Napoleon
See Yamamoto, Hisaye
Narayan, R. K. 1906-2001 .... **CLC 7, 28, 47, 121, 211; SSC 25, 154**
See also BPFB 2; CA 81-84; 196; CANR 33, 61, 112; CN 1, 2, 3, 4, 5, 6, 7; DA3; DAM NOV; DLB 323; DNFS 1; EWL 3; MTCW 1, 2; MTFW 2005; NFS 41; RGEL 2; RGSF 2; SATA 62; SSFS 5, 29; WWE 1
Narayan, Rasipuram Krishnaswami
See Narayan, R. K.
Nash, Fredric Ogden
See Nash, Ogden
Nash, Ogden 1902-1971 .... **CLC 23; PC 21; TCLC 109**
See also CA 13-14; 29-32R; CANR 34, 61, 185; CAP 1; CP 1; DAM POET; DLB 11; MAICYA 1, 2; MAL 5; MTCW 1, 2; PFS 31; RGAL 4; SATA 2, 46; WP
Nashe, Thomas 1567-1601(?) ...... **LC 41, 89, 184, 248; PC 82**
See also DLB 167; RGEL 2
Nathan, Daniel
See Dannay, Frederic
Nathan, George Jean 1882-1958 ... **TCLC 18**
See also CA 114; 169; DLB 137; MAL 5
Natsume Kinnosuke
See Soseki Natsume
Natsume Soseki
See Soseki Natsume
Natti, Lee 1919- .... **CLC 17**
See also CA 5-8R; CANR 2; CWRI 5; SAAS 3; SATA 1, 67
Natti, Mary Lee
See Natti, Lee
Navarre, Marguerite de
See de Navarre, Marguerite

Naylor, Gloria 1950- ..... **BLC 1:3; CLC 28, 52, 156, 261, 375, 383; WLCS**
See also AAYA 6, 39; AFAW 1, 2; AMWS 8; BW 2, 3; CA 107; CANR 27, 51, 74, 130; CLR 202; CN 4, 5, 6, 7; CPW; DA; DA3; DAC; DAM MST, MULT, NOV, POP; DLB 173; EWL 3; FW; MAL 5; MTCW 1, 2; MTFW 2005; NFS 4, 7; RGAL 4; TCLE 1:2; TUS

Ni Chuilleanain, Eilean 1942- .... **PC 34**
See also CA 126; CANR 53, 83, 241; CP 5, 6, 7; CWP; DLB 40

Ndebele, Njabulo (Simakahle) 1948- .... **SSC 135**
See also CA 184; DLB 157, 225; EWL 3

Neal, John 1793-1876 .... **NCLC 161**
See also DLB 1, 59, 243; FW; RGAL 4

Neff, Debra .... **CLC 59**

Negri, Antonio 1933- .... **CLC 368**
See also CA 235

Neidhart von Reuental c. 1185-c. 1240 .... **CMLC 145**
See also DLB 138

Neihardt, John Gneisenau 1881-1973 .... **CLC 32**
See also CA 13-14; CANR 65; CAP 1; DLB 9, 54, 256; LAIT 2; TCWW 1, 2

Nekrasov, Nikolai Alekseevich 1821-1878 .... **NCLC 11, 294**
See also DLB 277

Nelligan, Emile 1879-1941 .... **TCLC 14**
See also CA 114; 204; DLB 92; EWL 3

Nelson, Alice Ruth Moore Dunbar 1875-1935 .... **HR 1:2; SSC 132**
See also BW 1, 3; CA 122; 124; CANR 82; DLB 50; FW; MTCW 1

Nelson, Willie 1933- .... **CLC 17**
See also CA 107; CANR 114, 178

Nemerov, Howard 1920-1991 .... **CLC 2, 6, 9, 36; PC 24; TCLC 124**
See also AMW; CA 1-4R; 134; CABS 2; CANR 1, 27, 53; CN 1, 2, 3; CP 1, 2, 3, 4, 5; DAM POET; DLB 5, 6; DLBY 1983; EWL 3; INT CANR-27; MAL 5; MTCW 1, 2; MTFW 2005; PFS 10, 14; RGAL 4

Nemerov, Howard Stanley
See Nemerov, Howard

Nepos, Cornelius c. 99B.C.-c. 24B.C. .... **CMLC 89**
See also DLB 211

Neruda, Pablo 1904-1973 .... **CLC 1, 2, 5, 7, 9, 28, 62; HLC 2; PC 4, 64; WLC 4**
See also CA 19-20; 45-48; CANR 131; CAP 2; DA; DA3; DAB; DAC; DAM MST, MULT, POET; DLB 283, 331; DNFS 2; EWL 3; HW 1; LAW; MTCW 1, 2; MTFW 2005; PFS 11, 28, 33, 35, 41; RGWL 2, 3; TWA; WLIT 1; WP

Nerval, Gerard de 1808-1855 .... **NCLC 1, 67, 250; PC 13; SSC 18**
See also DLB 217, 366; EW 6; GFL 1789 to the Present; RGSF 2; RGWL 2, 3

Nervo, (Jose) Amado (Ruiz de) 1870-1919 .... **HLCS 2; TCLC 11**
See also CA 109; 131; DLB 290; EWL 3; HW 1; LAW

Nesbit, Malcolm
See Chester, Alfred

Nessi, Pio Baroja y
See Baroja, Pio

Nestroy, Johann 1801-1862 .... **DC 46; NCLC 42**
See also DLB 133; RGWL 2, 3

Nethersole, Lady Olga
See Harwood, Gwen

Netterville, Luke
See O'Grady, Standish (James)

Neufeld, John (Arthur) 1938- .... **CLC 17**
See also AAYA 11; CA 25-28R; CANR 11, 37, 56; CLR 52; MAICYA 1, 2; SAAS 3; SATA 6, 81, 131; SATA-Essay 131; YAW

Neumann, Alfred 1895-1952 .... **TCLC 100**
See also CA 183; DLB 56

Neumann, Ferenc
See Molnar, Ferenc

Neville, Emily Cheney 1919- .... **CLC 12**
See also BYA 2; CA 5-8R; CANR 3, 37, 85; JRDA; MAICYA 1, 2; SAAS 2; SATA 1; YAW

Neville, Henry 1619-1694 .... **LC 244**

Newbound, Bernard Slade 1930- .. **CLC 11, 46**
See also CA 81-84; CAAS 9; CANR 49; CCA 1; CD 5, 6; DAM DRAM; DLB 53

Newby, P(ercy) H(oward) 1918-1997 .... **CLC 2, 13**
See also CA 5-8R; 161; CANR 32, 67; CN 1, 2, 3, 4, 5, 6; DAM NOV; DLB 15, 326; MTCW 1; RGEL 2

Newcastle
See Cavendish, Margaret

Newlove, Donald 1928- .... **CLC 6**
See also CA 29-32R; CANR 25

Newlove, John (Herbert) 1938- ...... **CLC 14**
See also CA 21-24R; CANR 9, 25; CP 1, 2, 3, 4, 5, 6, 7

Newman, Charles 1938-2006 .... **CLC 2, 8**
See also CA 21-24R; 249; CANR 84; CN 3, 4, 5, 6

Newman, Charles Hamilton
See Newman, Charles

Newman, Edwin 1919-2010 .... **CLC 14**
See also AITN 1; CA 69-72; CANR 5

Newman, Edwin Harold
See Newman, Edwin

Newman, John Henry 1801-1890 .... **NCLC 38, 99**
See also BRWS 7; DLB 18, 32, 55; RGEL 2

Newton, (Sir) Isaac 1642-1727 ..... **LC 35, 53**
See also DLB 252

Newton, Suzanne 1936- .... **CLC 35**
See also BYA 7; CA 41-44R; CANR 14; JRDA; SATA 5, 77

New York Dept. of Ed. .... **CLC 70**

Nexo, Martin Andersen 1869-1954 .... **TCLC 43**
See also CA 202; DLB 214; EWL 3; NFS 34

Nezval, Vitezslav 1900-1958 .... **TCLC 44**
See also CA 123; CDWLB 4; DLB 215; EWL 3

Ng, Fae Myenne 1956- .... **CLC 81, 379**
See also BYA 11; CA 146; CANR 191; NFS 37

Ngcobo, Lauretta 1931- .... **BLC 2:3**
See also CA 165

Ngema, Mbongeni 1955- .... **CLC 57**
See also BW 2; CA 143; CANR 84; CD 5, 6

Ngugi, James T.
See Ngugi wa Thiong'o

Ngugi, James Thiong'o
See Ngugi wa Thiong'o

Ngugi wa Thiong'o 1938- .... **BLC 1:3, 2:3; CLC 3, 7, 13, 36, 182, 275**
See also AFW; BRWS 8; BW 2; CA 81-84; CANR 27, 58, 164, 213; CD 3, 4, 5, 6, 7; CDWLB 3; CN 1, 2; DAM MULT, NOV; DLB 125; DNFS 2; EWL 3; MTCW 1, 2; MTFW 2005; RGEL 2; WWE 1

Niatum, Duane 1938- .... NNAL
See also CA 41-44R; CANR 21, 45, 83; DLB 175

Nichol, B(arrie) P(hillip) 1944-1988 .... **CLC 18; PC 165**
See also CA 53-56; CP 1, 2, 3, 4; DLB 53; SATA 66

Nicholas of Autrecourt c. 1298-1369 .... **CMLC 108**

Nicholas of Cusa 1401-1464 .... **LC 80**
See also DLB 115

Nichols, John 1940- .... **CLC 38**
See also AMWS 13; CA 9-12R, 190; CAAE 190; CAAS 2; CANR 6, 70, 121, 185; DLBY 1982; LATS 1:2; MTFW 2005; TCWW 1, 2

Nichols, Leigh
See Koontz, Dean

Nichols, Peter (Richard) 1927- ... **CLC 5, 36, 65**
See also CA 104; CANR 33, 86; CBD; CD 5, 6; DLB 13, 245; MTCW 1

Nicholson, Linda .... **CLC 65**

Nicolas, F. R. E.
See Freeling, Nicolas

Ni Dhomhnaill, Nuala 1952- .... **PC 128**
See also CA 190; CWP

Niedecker, Lorine 1903-1970 .... **CLC 10, 42; PC 42, 163**
See also CA 25-28; CAP 2; DAM POET; DLB 48

Niekerk, Marlene van
See van Niekerk, Marlene

Nietzsche, Friedrich 1844-1900 ... **TCLC 10, 18, 55, 289, 290**
See also CA 107; 121; CDWLB 2; DLB 129; EW 7; RGWL 2, 3; TWA

Nietzsche, Friedrich Wilhelm
See Nietzsche, Friedrich

Nievo, Ippolito 1831-1861 .... **NCLC 22**

Nightingale, Anne Redmon 1943- .... **CLC 22**
See also CA 103; DLBY 1986

Nightingale, Florence 1820-1910 ... **TCLC 85**
See also CA 188; DLB 166

Nijo Yoshimoto 1320-1388 .... **CMLC 49**
See also DLB 203

Nik. T. O.
See Annensky, Innokenty (Fyodorovich)

Nin, Anais 1903-1977 .... **CLC 1, 4, 8, 11, 14, 60, 127; SSC 10; TCLC 224**
See also AITN 2; AMWS 10; BPFB 2; CA 13-16R; 69-72; CANR 22, 53; CN 1, 2; DAM NOV, POP; DLB 2, 4, 152; EWL 3; GLL 2; MAL 5; MBL; MTCW 1, 2; MTFW 2005; RGAL 4; RGSF 2

Nisbet, Robert A(lexander) 1913-1996 .... **TCLC 117**
See also CA 25-28R; 153; CANR 17; INT CANR-17

Nishida, Kitaro 1870-1945 .... **TCLC 83**

Nishiwaki, Junzaburo 1894-1982 .... **PC 15**
See also CA 194; 107; EWL 3; MJW; RGWL 3

Nissenson, Hugh 1933- .... **CLC 4, 9**
See also CA 17-20R; CANR 27, 108, 151; CN 5, 6; DLB 28, 335

Nister, Der
See Der Nister

Niven, Larry 1938- .... **CLC 8**
See also AAYA 27; BPFB 2; BYA 10; CA 21-24R, 207; CAAE 207; CAAS 12; CANR 14, 44, 66, 113, 155, 206; CPW; DAM POP; DLB 8; MTCW 1, 2; SATA 95, 171; SCFW 1, 2; SFW 4

Niven, Laurence Van Cott
See Niven, Larry

Niven, Laurence VanCott
See Niven, Larry

Nixon, Agnes Eckhardt 1927- .... **CLC 21**
See also CA 110

Nizāmī Ganjavī c. 1141-c. 1209 .... **PC 165**

Nizan, Paul 1905-1940 .... **TCLC 40**
See also CA 161; DLB 72; EWL 3; GFL 1789 to the Present

Nkosi, Lewis 1936-2010 .... **BLC 1:3; CLC 45, 377**
See also BW 1, 3; CA 65-68; CANR 27, 81; CBD; CD 5, 6; DAM MULT; DLB 157, 225; WWE 1

Nodier, (Jean) Charles (Emmanuel) 1780-1844 ... **NCLC 19**
See also DLB 119; GFL 1789 to the Present
Noguchi, Yone 1875-1947 ... **TCLC 80**
Nolan, Brian
See O Nuallain, Brian
Nolan, Christopher 1965-2009 ... **CLC 58**
See also CA 111; 283; CANR 88
Nolan, Christopher John
See Nolan, Christopher
Noon, Jeff 1957- ... **CLC 91**
See also CA 148; CANR 83; DLB 267; SFW 4
Nooteboom, Cees 1933- ... **CLC 323**
See also CA 124; 130; CANR 120, 177; EWL 3; RGWL 3
Nordan, Lewis 1939-2012 ... **CLC 304**
See also CA 117; CANR 40, 72, 121; CSW; DLB 234, 350
Norden, Charles
See Durrell, Lawrence
Nordhoff, Charles Bernard 1887-1947 ... **TCLC 23**
See also CA 108; 211; DLB 9; LAIT 1; RHW 1; SATA 23
Norfolk, Lawrence 1963- ... **CLC 76**
See also CA 144; CANR 85; CN 6, 7; DLB 267
Norman, Marsha (Williams) 1947- ... **CLC 28, 186; DC 8**
See also CA 105; CABS 3; CAD; CANR 41, 131; CD 5, 6; CSW; CWD; DAM DRAM; DFS 2; DLB 266; DLBY 1984; FW; MAL 5
Normyx
See Douglas, (George) Norman
Norris, Benjamin Franklin, Jr.
See Norris, Frank
Norris, Frank 1870-1902 ... **SSC 28; TCLC 24, 155, 211**
See also AAYA 57; AMW; AMWC 2; BPFB 2; CA 110; 160; CDALB 1865-1917; DLB 12, 71, 186; LMFS 2; MAL 5; NFS 12; RGAL 4; TCWW 1, 2; TUS
Norris, Kathleen 1947- ... **CLC 248**
See also CA 160; CANR 113, 199
Norris, Leslie 1921-2006 ... **CLC 14, 351**
See also CA 11-12; 251; CANR 14, 117; CAP 1; CP 1, 2, 3, 4, 5, 6, 7; DLB 27, 256
North, Andrew
See Norton, Andre
North, Anthony
See Koontz, Dean
North, Captain George
See Stevenson, Robert Louis
North, Captain George
See Stevenson, Robert Louis
North, Milou
See Erdrich, Louise
Northrup, B. A.
See Hubbard, L. Ron
North Staffs
See Hulme, T(homas) E(rnest)
Northup, Solomon 1808-1863 ... **NCLC 105**
Norton, Alice Mary
See Norton, Andre
Norton, Andre 1912-2005 ... **CLC 12**
See also AAYA 83; BPFB 2; BYA 4, 10, 12; CA 1-4R; 237; CANR 2, 31, 68, 108, 149; CLR 50, 184; DLB 8, 52; JRDA; MAICYA 1, 2; MTCW 1; SATA 1, 43, 91; SUFW 1, 2; YAW
Norton, Caroline 1808-1877 ... **NCLC 47, 205**
See also DLB 21, 159, 199
Norway, Nevil Shute
See Shute, Nevil
Norwid, Cyprian Kamil 1821-1883 .. **NCLC 17**
See also RGWL 3
Nosille, Nabrah
See Ellison, Harlan
Nossack, Hans Erich 1901-1977 ... **CLC 6**
See also CA 93-96; 85-88; CANR 156; DLB 69; EWL 3
Nostradamus 1503-1566 ... **LC 27**
Nosu, Chuji
See Ozu, Yasujiro
Notenburg, Eleanora (Genrikhovna) von
See Guro, Elena (Genrikhovna)
Nothomb, Amélie 1967- ... **CLC 344**
See also CA 205; CANR 154, 205
Nova, Craig 1945- ... **CLC 7, 31**
See also CA 45-48; CANR 2, 53, 127, 223
Novak, Joseph
See Kosinski, Jerzy
Novalis 1772-1801 ... **NCLC 13, 178; PC 120**
See also CDWLB 2; DLB 90; EW 5; RGWL 2, 3
Novick, Peter 1934-2012 ... **CLC 164**
See also CA 188
Novis, Emile
See Weil, Simone
Nowlan, Alden (Albert) 1933-1983 ... **CLC 15**
See also CA 9-12R; CANR 5; CP 1, 2, 3; DAC; DAM MST; DLB 53; PFS 12
Nowra, Louis 1950- ... **CLC 372**
See also CA 195; CD 5, 6; DLB 325; IDTP
Noyes, Alfred 1880-1958 ... **PC 27; TCLC 7**
See also CA 104; 188; DLB 20; EXPP; FANT; PFS 4; RGEL 2
Nugent, Richard Bruce 1906(?)-1987 ... **HR 1:3**
See also BW 1; CA 125; CANR 198; DLB 51; GLL 2
Nunez, Elizabeth 1944- ... **BLC 2:3**
See also CA 223; CANR 220
Nunn, Kem ... **CLC 34**
See also CA 159; CANR 204
Nussbaum, Martha 1947- ... **CLC 203**
See also CA 134; CANR 102, 176, 213, 241
Nussbaum, Martha Craven
See Nussbaum, Martha
Nwapa, Flora (Nwanzuruaha) 1931-1993 ... **BLCS; CLC 133**
See also BW 2; CA 143; CANR 83; CDWLB 3; CLR 162; CWRI 5; DLB 125; EWL 3; WLIT 2
Nye, Robert 1939- ... **CLC 13, 42**
See also BRWS 10; CA 33-36R; CANR 29, 67, 107; CN 1, 2, 3, 4, 5, 6, 7; CP 1, 2, 3, 4, 5, 6, 7; CWRI 5; DAM NOV; DLB 14, 271; FANT; HGG; MTCW 1; RHW; SATA 6
Nyro, Laura 1947-1997 ... **CLC 17**
See also CA 194
O. Henry
See Henry, O.
Oates, Joyce Carol 1938- ... **CLC 1, 2, 3, 6, 9, 11, 15, 19, 33, 52, 108, 134, 228; SSC 6, 70, 121; WLC 4**
See also AAYA 15, 52; AITN 1; AMWS 2; BEST 89:2; BPFB 2; BYA 11; CA 5-8R; CANR 25, 45, 74, 113, 129, 165; CDALB 1968-1988; CN 1, 2, 3, 4, 5, 6, 7; CP 5, 6, 7; CPW; CWP; DA; DA3; DAB; DAC; DAM MST, NOV, POP; DLB 2, 5, 130; DLBY 1981; EWL 3; EXPS; FL 1:6; FW; GL 3; HGG; INT CANR-25; LAIT 4; MAL 5; MBL; MTCW 1, 2; MTFW 2005; NFS 8, 24; RGAL 4; RGSF 2; SATA 159; SSFS 1, 8, 17, 32; SUFW 2; TUS
Obradovic, Dositej 1740(?)-1811 .. **NCLC 254**
See also DLB 147
O'Brian, E.G.
See Clarke, Arthur C.
O'Brian, Patrick 1914-2000 ... **CLC 152**
See also AAYA 55; BRWS 12; CA 144; 187; CANR 74, 201; CPW; MTCW 2; MTFW 2005; RHW
O'Brien, Darcy 1939-1998 ... **CLC 11**
See also CA 21-24R; 167; CANR 8, 59
O'Brien, Edna 1930- ... **CLC 3, 5, 8, 13, 36, 65, 116, 237; SSC 10, 77, 192**
See also BRWS 5; CA 1-4R; CANR 6, 41, 65, 102, 169, 213; CDBLB 1960 to Present; CN 1, 2, 3, 4, 5, 6, 7; DA3; DAM NOV; DLB 14, 231, 319; EWL 3; FW; MTCW 1, 2; MTFW 2005; RGSF 2; WLIT 4
O'Brien, E.G.
See Clarke, Arthur C.
O'Brien, Fitz-James 1828-1862 ... **NCLC 21**
See also DLB 74; RGAL 4; SUFW
O'Brien, Flann
See O Nuallain, Brian
Ono no Komachi fl. c. 850- ... **CMLC 134**
O'Brien, Richard 1942- ... **CLC 17**
See also CA 124
O'Brien, Tim 1946- ... **CLC 7, 19, 40, 103, 211, 305; SSC 74, 123**
See also AAYA 16; AMWS 5; CA 85-88; CANR 40, 58, 133; CDALBS; CN 5, 6, 7; CPW; DA3; DAM POP; DLB 152; DLBD 9; DLBY 1980; LATS 1:2; MAL 5; MTCW 2; MTFW 2005; NFS 37; RGAL 4; SSFS 5, 15, 29, 32; TCLE 1:2
O'Brien, William Timothy
See O'Brien, Tim
Obstfelder, Sigbjorn 1866-1900 ... **TCLC 23**
See also CA 123; DLB 354
Ocampo, Silvina 1906-1993 ... **SSC 175**
See also CA 131; CANR 87, CWW 2, HW 1, RGSF 2
O'Casey, Brenda
See Haycraft, Anna
O'Casey, Sean 1880-1964 ... **CLC 1, 5, 9, 11, 15, 88; DC 12; WLCS**
See also BRW 7; CA 89-92; CANR 62; CBD; CDBLB 1914-1945; DA3; DAB; DAC; DAM DRAM, MST; DFS 19; DLB 10; EWL 3; MTCW 1, 2; MTFW 2005; RGEL 2; TEA; WLIT 4
O'Cathasaigh, Sean
See O'Casey, Sean
Occom, Samson 1723-1792 ... **LC 60; NNAL**
See also DLB 175
Occomy, Marita (Odette) Bonner 1899(?)-1971 ... **HR 1:2; PC 72; TCLC 179**
See also BW 2; CA 142; DFS 13; DLB 51, 228
Ochs, Phil(ip David) 1940-1976 ... **CLC 17**
See also CA 185; 65-68
O'Connor, Edwin (Greene) 1918-1968 ... **CLC 14**
See also CA 93-96; 25-28R; MAL 5
O'Connor, Flannery 1925-1964 ... **CLC 1, 2, 3, 6, 10, 13, 15, 21, 66, 104; SSC 1, 23, 61, 82, 111, 168, 173, 190, 195, 196, 199; TCLC 132, 305; WLC 4**
See also AAYA 7; AMW; AMWR 2; BPFB 3; BYA 16; CA 1-4R; CANR 3, 41; CDALB 1941-1968; DA; DA3; DAB; DAC; DAM MST, NOV; DLB 2, 152; DLBD 12; DLBY 1980; EWL 3; EXPS; LAIT 5; MAL 5; MBL; MTCW 1, 2; MTFW 2005; NFS 3, 21; RGAL 4; RGSF 2; SSFS 2, 7, 10, 19, 34; TUS
O'Connor, Frank 1903-1966 ... **CLC 14, 23; SSC 5, 109, 177**
See also BRWS 14; CA 93-96; CANR 84; DLB 162; EWL 3; RGSF 2; SSFS 5, 34
O'Connor, Mary Flannery
See O'Connor, Flannery
O'Dell, Scott 1898-1989 ... **CLC 30**
See also AAYA 3, 44; BPFB 3; BYA 1, 2, 3, 5; CA 61-64; 129; CANR 12, 30, 112; CLR 1, 16, 126; DLB 52; JRDA; MAICYA 1, 2; SATA 12, 60, 134; WYA; YAW
Odets, Clifford 1906-1963 ... **CLC 2, 28, 98; DC 6; TCLC 244**

See also AMWS 2; CA 85-88; CAD; CANR 62; DAM DRAM; DFS 3, 17, 20; DLB 7, 26, 341; EWL 3; MAL 5; MTCW 1, 2; MTFW 2005; RGAL 4; TUS
O'Doherty, Brian 1928- .... **CLC 76**
See also CA 105; CANR 108
O'Donnell, K. M.
See Malzberg, Barry N(athaniel)
O'Donnell, Lawrence
See Kuttner, Henry
O'Donovan, Michael Francis
See O'Connor, Frank
Oe, Kenzaburo 1935- .... **CLC 10, 36, 86, 187, 303; SSC 20, 176**
See also CA 97-100; CANR 36, 50, 74, 126; CWW 2; DA3; DAM NOV; DLB 182, 331; DLBY 1994; EWL 3; LATS 1:2; MJW; MTCW 1, 2; MTFW 2005; RGSF 2; RGWL 2, 3
Oe Kenzaburo
See Oe, Kenzaburo
O'Faolain, Julia 1932- ... **CLC 6, 19, 47, 108**
See also CA 81-84; CAAS 2; CANR 12, 61; CN 2, 3, 4, 5, 6, 7; DLB 14, 231, 319; FW; MTCW 1; RHW
O'Faolain, Sean 1900-1991 ... **CLC 1, 7, 14, 32, 70; SSC 13, 194; TCLC 143**
See also CA 61-64; 134; CANR 12, 66; CN 1, 2, 3, 4; DLB 15, 162; MTCW 1, 2; MTFW 2005; RGEL 2; RGSF 2
O'Flaherty, Liam 1896-1984 ...... **CLC 5, 34; SSC 6, 116**
See also CA 101; 113; CANR 35; CN 1, 2, 3; DLB 36, 162; DLBY 1984; MTCW 1, 2; MTFW 2005; RGEL 2; RGSF 2; SSFS 5, 20
Ogai
See Mori Ogai
Ogilvy, Gavin
See Barrie, J. M.
O'Grady, Standish (James) 1846-1928 .... **TCLC 5**
See also CA 104; 157
O'Grady, Timothy 1951- .... **CLC 59**
See also CA 138
O'Hara, Frank 1926-1966 ..... **CLC 2, 5, 13, 78; PC 45**
See also AMWS 23; CA 9-12R; 25-28R; CANR 33; DA3; DAM POET; DLB 5, 16, 193; EWL 3; MAL 5; MTCW 1, 2; MTFW 2005; PFS 8, 12, 34, 38; RGAL 4; WP
O'Hara, John 1905-1970 ..... **CLC 1, 2, 3, 6, 11, 42; SSC 15**
See also AMW; BPFB 3; CA 5-8R; 25-28R; CANR 31, 60; CDALB 1929-1941; DAM NOV; DLB 9, 86, 324; DLBD 2; EWL 3; MAL 5; MTCW 1, 2; MTFW 2005; NFS 11; RGAL 4; RGSF 2
O'Hara, John Henry
See O'Hara, John
O'Hehir, Diana 1929- .... **CLC 41**
See also CA 245; CANR 177
O'Hehir, Diana F.
See O'Hehir, Diana
Ohiyesa
See Eastman, Charles A(lexander)
Okada, John 1923-1971 .... **AAL**
See also BYA 14; CA 212; DLB 312; NFS 25
O'Kelly, Seamus 1881(?)-1918 .... **SSC 136**
Okigbo, Christopher 1930-1967 ... **BLC 1:3; CLC 25, 84; PC 7, 128; TCLC 171**
See also AFW; BW 1, 3; CA 77-80; CANR 74; CDWLB 3; DAM MULT, POET; DLB 125; EWL 3; MTCW 1, 2; MTFW 2005; RGEL 2
Okigbo, Christopher Ifenayichukwu
See Okigbo, Christopher
Okri, Ben 1959- .... **BLC 2:3; CLC 87, 223, 337; SSC 127**
See also AFW; BRWS 5; BW 2, 3; CA 130; 138; CANR 65, 128; CN 5, 6, 7; DLB 157, 231, 319, 326; EWL 3; INT CA-138; MTCW 2; MTFW 2005; RGSF 2; SSFS 20; WLIT 2; WWE 1
Old Boy
See Hughes, Thomas
Olds, Sharon 1942- .... **CLC 32, 39, 85, 361; PC 22**
See also AMWS 10; CA 101; CANR 18, 41, 66, 98, 135, 211; CP 5, 6, 7; CPW; CWP; DAM POET; DLB 120; MAL 5; MTCW 2; MTFW 2005; PFS 17
Oldstyle, Jonathan
See Irving, Washington
Olesha, Iurii
See Olesha, Yuri (Karlovich)
Olesha, Iurii Karlovich
See Olesha, Yuri (Karlovich)
Olesha, Yuri (Karlovich) 1899-1960 ... **CLC 8; SSC 69; TCLC 136**
See also CA 85-88; DLB 272; EW 11; EWL 3; RGWL 2, 3
Olesha, Yury Karlovich
See Olesha, Yuri (Karlovich)
Oliphant, Mrs.
See Oliphant, Margaret (Oliphant Wilson)
Oliphant, Laurence 1829(?)-1888 .. **NCLC 47**
See also DLB 18, 166
Oliphant, Margaret (Oliphant Wilson) 1828-1897 ... **NCLC 11, 61, 221; SSC 25**
See also BRWS 10; DLB 18, 159, 190; HGG; RGEL 2; RGSF 2; SUFW
Oliver, Mary 1935- .... **CLC 19, 34, 98, 364; PC 75**
See also AMWS 7; CA 21-24R; CANR 9, 43, 84, 92, 138, 217; CP 4, 5, 6, 7; CWP; DLB 5, 193, 342; EWL 3; MTFW 2005; PFS 15, 31, 40
Olivi, Peter 1248-1298 .... **CMLC 114**
Olivier, Laurence (Kerr) 1907-1989 ... **CLC 20**
See also CA 111; 150; 129
O.L.S.
See Russell, George William
Olsen, Tillie 1912-2007 ...... **CLC 4, 13, 114; SSC 11, 103**
See also AAYA 51; AMWS 13; BYA 11; CA 1-4R; 256; CANR 1, 43, 74, 132; CDALBS; CN 2, 3, 4, 5, 6, 7; DA; DA3; DAB; DAC; DAM MST; DLB 28, 206; DLBY 1980; EWL 3; EXPS; FW; MAL 5; MTCW 1, 2; MTFW 2005; RGAL 4; RGSF 2; SSFS 1, 32; TCLE 1:2; TCWW 2; TUS
Olson, Charles 1910-1970 .... **CLC 1, 2, 5, 6, 9, 11, 29; PC 19**
See also AMWS 2; CA 13-16; 25-28R; CABS 2; CANR 35, 61; CAP 1; CP 1; DAM POET; DLB 5, 16, 193; EWL 3; MAL 5; MTCW 1, 2; RGAL 4; WP
Olson, Charles John
See Olson, Charles
Olson, Merle Theodore
See Olson, Toby
Olson, Toby 1937- .... **CLC 28**
See also CA 65-68; CAAS 11; CANR 9, 31, 84, 175; CP 3, 4, 5, 6, 7
Olyesha, Yuri
See Olesha, Yuri (Karlovich)
Olympiodorus of Thebes c. 375-c. 430 .... **CMLC 59**
Omar Khayyam
See Khayyam, Omar
Ondaatje, Michael 1943- .... **CLC 14, 29, 51, 76, 180, 258, 322; PC 28**
See also AAYA 66; CA 77-80; CANR 42, 74, 109, 133, 172; CN 5, 6, 7; CP 1, 2, 3, 4, 5, 6, 7; DA3; DAB; DAC; DAM MST; DLB 60, 323, 326; EWL 3; LATS 1:2; LMFS 2; MTCW 2; MTFW 2005; NFS 23; PFS 8, 19; TCLE 1:2; TWA; WWE 1
Ondaatje, Philip Michael
See Ondaatje, Michael
Oneal, Elizabeth 1934- .... **CLC 30**
See also AAYA 5, 41; BYA 13; CA 106; CANR 28, 84; CLR 13, 169; JRDA; MAICYA 1, 2; SATA 30, 82; WYA; YAW
Oneal, Zibby
See Oneal, Elizabeth
O'Neill, Eugene 1888-1953 .... **DC 20; TCLC 1, 6, 27, 49, 225; WLC 4**
See also AAYA 54; AITN 1; AMW; AMWC 1; CA 110; 132; CAD; CANR 131; CDALB 1929-1941; DA; DA3; DAB; DAC; DAM DRAM, MST; DFS 2, 4, 5, 6, 9, 11, 12, 16, 20, 26, 27; DLB 7, 331; EWL 3; LAIT 3; LMFS 2; MAL 5; MTCW 1, 2; MTFW 2005; RGAL 4; TUS
O'Neill, Eugene Gladstone
See O'Neill, Eugene
Onetti, Juan Carlos 1909-1994 ... **CLC 7, 10; HLCS 2; SSC 23; TCLC 131**
See also CA 85-88; 145; CANR 32, 63; CDWLB 3; CWW 2; DAM MULT, NOV; DLB 113; EWL 3; HW 1, 2; LAW; MTCW 1, 2; MTFW 2005; RGSF 2
Lonnrot, Elias 1802-1884 .... **NCLC 53**
See also EFS 1:1, 2:1
O'Nolan, Brian
See O Nuallain, Brian
O Nuallain, Brian 1911-1966 .... **CLC 1, 4, 5, 7, 10, 47**
See also BRWS 2; CA 21-22; 25-28R; CAP 2; DLB 231; EWL 3; FANT; RGEL 2; TEA
Ophuls, Max 1902-1957 .... **TCLC 79**
See also CA 113
Opie, Amelia 1769-1853 .... **NCLC 65**
See also DLB 116, 159; RGEL 2
Opitz, Martin 1597-1639 .... **LC 207**
See also DLB 164
Oppen, George 1908-1984 ... **CLC 7, 13, 34; PC 35; TCLC 107**
See also CA 13-16R; 113; CANR 8, 82; CP 1, 2, 3; DLB 5, 165
Oppenheim, E(dward) Phillips 1866-1946 .... **TCLC 45**
See also CA 111; 202; CMW 4; DLB 70
Oppenheimer, Max
See Ophuls, Max
Opuls, Max
See Ophuls, Max
Ophuls, Max
See Ophuls, Max
Orage, A(lfred) R(ichard) 1873-1934 .... **TCLC 157**
See also CA 122
Oresme, Nicole 1320/1325?-1382 ..... **CMLC 163**
Origen c. 185-c. 254 .... **CMLC 19**
Orlovitz, Gil 1918-1973 .... **CLC 22**
See also CA 77-80; 45-48; CN 1; CP 1, 2; DLB 2, 5
Orosius c. 385-c. 420 .... **CMLC 100**
O'Rourke, P. J. 1947- .... **CLC 209**
See also CA 77-80; CANR 13, 41, 67, 111, 155, 217; CPW; DAM POP; DLB 185
O'Rourke, Patrick Jake
See O'Rourke, P.J.
Orrery
See Boyle, Roger
Orris
See Ingelow, Jean
Ortega y Gasset, Jose 1883-1955 .... **HLC 2; TCLC 9**
See also CA 106; 130; DAM MULT; EW 9; EWL 3; HW 1, 2; MTCW 1, 2; MTFW 2005

Ortese, Anna Maria 1914-1998 ...... **CLC 89**
See also DLB 177; EWL 3

Ortiz, Simon
See Ortiz, Simon J.

Ortiz, Simon J. 1941- .... **CLC 45, 208; NNAL; PC 17; SSC 213**
See also AMWS 4; CA 134; CANR 69, 118, 164; CP 3, 4, 5, 6, 7; DAM MULT, POET; DLB 120, 175, 256, 342; EXPP; MAL 5; PFS 4, 16; RGAL 4; SSFS 22; TCWW 2

Ortiz, Simon Joseph
See Ortiz, Simon J.

Orton, Joe
See Orton, John Kingsley

Orton, John Kingsley 1933-1967 ..... **CLC 4, 13, 43; DC 3; TCLC 157**
See also BRWS 5; CA 85-88; CANR 35, 66; CBD; CDBLB 1960 to Present; DAM DRAM; DFS 3, 6; DLB 13, 310; GLL 1; MTCW 1, 2; MTFW 2005; RGEL 2; TEA; WLIT 4

Orwell, George 1903-1950 .... **SSC 68; TCLC 2, 6, 15, 31, 51, 123, 128, 129, 276; WLC 4**
See also BPFB 3; BRW 7; BYA 5; CA 104; 132; CDBLB 1945-1960; CLR 68, 171, 196; DA; DA3; DAB; DAC; DAM MST, NOV; DLB 15, 98, 195, 255; EWL 3; EXPN; LAIT 4, 5; LATS 1:1; MTCW 1, 2; MTFW 2005; NFS 3, 7; RGEL 2; SATA 29; SCFW 1, 2; SFW 4; SSFS 4; TEA; WLIT 4; YAW X

Osborne, David
See Silverberg, Robert

Osborne, Dorothy 1627-1695 .... **LC 141**

Osborne, George
See Silverberg, Robert

Osborne, John 1929-1994 .... **CLC 1, 2, 5, 11, 45; DC 38; TCLC 153; WLC 4**
See also BRWS 1; CA 13-16R; 147; CANR 21, 56; CBD; CDBLB 1945-1960; DA; DAB; DAC; DAM DRAM, MST; DFS 4, 19, 24; DLB 13; EWL 3; MTCW 1, 2; MTFW 2005; RGEL 2

Osborne, Lawrence 1958- .... **CLC 50**
See also CA 189; CANR 152

Osbourne, Lloyd 1868-1947 .... **TCLC 93**

Osceola
See Blixen, Karen

Osgood, Frances Sargent 1811-1850 .... **NCLC 141**
See also DLB 250

Oshima, Nagisa 1932- .... **CLC 20**
See also CA 116; 121; CANR 78

Oskison, John Milton 1874-1947 ...... **NNAL; TCLC 35**
See also CA 144; CANR 84; DAM MULT; DLB 175

Osofisan, Femi 1946- .... **CLC 307; DC 52**
See also AFW; BW 2; CA 142; CANR 84; CD 5, 6; CDWLB 3; DLB 125; EWL 3

Ossian c. 3rd cent.
See Macpherson, James

Ossoli, Sarah Margaret
See Fuller, Margaret

Ossoli, Sarah Margaret Fuller
See Fuller, Margaret

Ostriker, Alicia 1937- .... **CLC 132**
See also CA 25-28R; CAAS 24; CANR 10, 30, 62, 99, 167; CWP; DLB 120; EXPP; PFS 19, 26

Ostriker, Alicia Suskin
See Ostriker, Alicia

Ostrovsky, Aleksandr Nikolaevich
See Ostrovsky, Alexander

Ostrovsky, Alexander 1823-1886 .... **NCLC 30, 57**
See also DLB 277

Osundare, Niyi 1947- .... **BLC 2:3**
See also AFW; BW 3; CA 176; CDWLB 3; CP 7; DLB 157

Oswald von Wolkenstein 1377(?)-1455 .... **LC 208**

Otero, Blas de 1916-1979 .... **CLC 11**
See also CA 89-92; DLB 134; EWL 3

O'Trigger, Sir Lucius
See Horne, Richard Henry Hengist

Otto, Rudolf 1869-1937 .... **TCLC 85**

Otto, Whitney 1955- .... **CLC 70**
See also CA 140; CANR 120

Otway, Thomas 1652-1685 .... **DC 24; LC 106, 170**
See also DAM DRAM; DLB 80; RGEL 2

Ouida
See De La Ramee, Marie Louise

Ouologuem, Yambo 1940- ..... **CLC 146, 293**
See also CA 111; 176

Ousmane, Sembene 1923-2007 ..... **BLC 1:3, 2:3; CLC 66**
See also AFW; BW 1, 3; CA 117; 125; 261; CANR 81; CWW 2; DLB 360; EWL 3; MTCW 1; WLIT 2

Out and Outer, An
See Mangan, James Clarence

Ovid 43B.C.-17 .... **CMLC 7, 108; PC 2, 135**
See also AW 2; CDWLB 1; DA3; DAM POET; DLB 211; PFS 22; RGWL 2, 3; WLIT 8; WP

Owen, Hugh
See Faust, Frederick

Owen, Wilfred (Edward Salter) 1893-1918 .... **PC 19, 102; TCLC 5, 27; WLC 4**
See also BRW 6; CA 104; 141; CDBLB 1914-1945; DA; DAB; DAC; DAM MST, POET; DLB 20; EWL 3; EXPP; MTCW 2; MTFW 2005; PFS 10, 37; RGEL 2; WLIT 4

Owens, Louis (Dean) 1948-2002 .... **CLC 321; NNAL**
See also CA 137, 179; 207; CAAE 179; CAAS 24; CANR 71

Owens, Rochelle 1936- .... **CLC 8**
See also CA 17-20R; CAAS 2; CAD; CANR 39; CD 5, 6; CP 1, 2, 3, 4, 5, 6, 7; CWD; CWP

Owenson, Sydney
See Morgan, Lady

Oz, Amos 1939- .... **CLC 5, 8, 11, 27, 33, 54; SSC 66**
See also AAYA 84; CA 53-56; CANR 27, 47, 65, 113, 138, 175, 219; CWW 2; DAM NOV; EWL 3; MTCW 1, 2; MTFW 2005; RGHL; RGSF 2; RGWL 3; WLIT 6

Ozeki, Ruth L. 1956- .... **CLC 307**
See also CA 181

Ozick, Cynthia 1928- .... **CLC 3, 7, 28, 62, 155, 262; SSC 15, 60, 123**
See also AMWS 5; BEST 90:1; CA 17-20R; CANR 23, 58, 116, 160, 187; CN 3, 4, 5, 6, 7; CPW; DA3; DAM NOV, POP; DLB 28, 152, 299; DLBY 1982; EWL 3; EXPS; INT CANR-23; MAL 5; MTCW 1, 2; MTFW 2005; RGAL 4; RGHL; RGSF 2; SSFS 3, 12, 22

Ozu, Yasujiro 1903-1963 .... **CLC 16**
See also CA 112

Pabst, G. W. 1885-1967 .... **TCLC 127**

Pacheco, C.
See Pessoa, Fernando

Pacheco, José Emilio 1939- .... **CLC 376; HLC 2**
See also CA 111; 131; CANR 65; CWW 2; DAM MULT; DLB 290; EWL 3; HW 1, 2; RGSF 2

Pa Chin
See Jin, Ba

Pack, Robert 1929- .... **CLC 13**
See also CA 1-4R; CANR 3, 44, 82; CP 1, 2, 3, 4, 5, 6, 7; DLB 5; SATA 118

Packard, Mrs. Clarissa
See Caroline Gilman

Packer, Vin
See Meaker, Marijane

Padgett, Lewis
See Kuttner, Henry

Padilla (Lorenzo), Heberto 1932-2000 .... **CLC 38**
See also AITN 1; CA 123; 131; 189; CWW 2; EWL 3; HW 1

Padura, Leonardo 1955- .... **CLC 365**
See also CA 256; CANR 218

Paerdurabo, Frater
See Crowley, Edward Alexander

Page, James Patrick 1944- .... **CLC 12**
See also CA 204

Page, Jimmy 1944-
See Page, James Patrick

Page, Louise 1955- .... **CLC 40**
See also CA 140; CANR 76; CBD; CD 5, 6; CWD; DLB 233

Page, Patricia Kathleen
See Page, P.K.

Page, P.K. 1916-2010 ..... **CLC 7, 18; PC 12**
See also CA 53-56; CANR 4, 22, 65; CCA 1; CP 1, 2, 3, 4, 5, 6, 7; DAC; DAM MST; DLB 68; MTCW 1; RGEL 2

Page, Stanton
See Fuller, Henry Blake

Page, Thomas Nelson 1853-1922 ...... **SSC 23**
See also CA 118; 177; DLB 12, 78; DLBD 13; RGAL 4

Pagels, Elaine
See Pagels, Elaine Hiesey

Pagels, Elaine Hiesey 1943- .... **CLC 104**
See also CA 45-48; CANR 2, 24, 51, 151; FW; NCFS 4

Paget, Violet 1856-1935 .... **SSC 33, 98, 216; TCLC 5**
See also CA 104; 166; DLB 57, 153, 156, 174, 178; GLL 1; HGG; SUFW 1

Paget-Lowe, Henry
See Lovecraft, H. P.

Paglia, Camille 1947- .... **CLC 68**
See also CA 140; CANR 72, 139; CPW; FW; GLL 2; MTCW 2; MTFW 2005

Pagnol, Marcel (Paul) 1895-1974 ... **TCLC 208**
See also CA 128; 49-52; DLB 321; EWL 3; GFL 1789 to the Present; MTCW 1; RGWL 2, 3

Paige, Richard
See Koontz, Dean

Paine, Thomas 1737-1809 ..... **NCLC 62, 248**
See also AMWS 1; CDALB 1640-1865; DLB 31, 43, 73, 158; LAIT 1; RGAL 4; RGEL 2; TUS

Pakenham, Antonia
See Fraser, Antonia

Palahniuk, Chuck 1962- .... **CLC 359**
See also AAYA 59; CA 198; CANR 140, 171, 223; CEAL; CMTFW; MTFW

Palamas, Costis
See Palamas, Kostes

Palamas, Kostes 1859-1943 .... **TCLC 5**
See also CA 105; 190; EWL 3; RGWL 2, 3

Palamas, Kostis
See Palamas, Kostes

Palazzeschi, Aldo 1885-1974 .... **CLC 11; TCLC 316**
See also CA 89-92; 53-56; DLB 114, 264; EWL 3

Pales Matos, Luis 1898-1959 .... **HLCS 2**
See Pales Matos, Luis
See also DLB 290; HW 1; LAW

Paley, Grace 1922-2007 .... **CLC 4, 6, 37, 140, 272; SSC 8, 165**

See also AMWS 6; CA 25-28R; 263; CANR 13, 46, 74, 118; CN 2, 3, 4, 5, 6, 7; CPW; DA3; DAM POP; DLB 28, 218; EWL 3; EXPS; FW; INT CANR-13; MAL 5; MBL; MTCW 1, 2; MTFW 2005; RGAL 4; RGSF 2; SSFS 3, 20, 27
Paley, Grace Goodside
See Paley, Grace
Palin, Michael 1943- .... **CLC 21**
See also CA 107; CANR 35, 109, 179, 229; DLB 352; SATA 67
Palin, Michael Edward
See Palin, Michael
Palliser, Charles 1947- .... **CLC 65**
See also CA 136; CANR 76; CN 5, 6, 7
Palma, Ricardo 1833-1919 .... **SSC 175; TCLC 29**
See also CA 168; LAW
Palmer, Michael 1943- .... **PC 172**
See also CA 114; CANR 35, 150, 238; CP 3, 4, 5, 6, 7; CPW; DLB 169; DAM POET
Pamuk, Orhan 1952- .... **CLC 185, 288, 377**
See also AAYA 82; CA 142; CANR 75, 127, 172, 208; CWW 2; NFS 27; WLIT 6
Panbury, Theophilus
See Harwood, Gwen
Pancake, Breece Dexter
1952-1979 .... **CLC 29; SSC 61**
See also CA 123; 109; DLB 130
Pancake, Breece D'J
See Pancake, Breece Dexter
Panchenko, Nikolai .... **CLC 59**
Pankhurst, Emmeline (Goulden)
1858-1928 .... **TCLC 100**
See also CA 116; FW
Panko, Rudy
See Gogol, Nikolai
Papadiamantis, Alexandros
1851-1911 .... **TCLC 29**
See also CA 168; EWL 3
Papadiamantopoulos, Johannes
1856-1910 .... **TCLC 18**
See also CA 117; 242; GFL 1789 to the Present
Papadiamantopoulos, Yannis
See Papadiamantopoulos, Johannes
Papini, Giovanni 1881-1956 .... **TCLC 22**
See also CA 121; 180; DLB 264
Paracelsus 1493-1541 .... **LC 14, 228**
See also DLB 179
Parasol, Peter
See Stevens, Wallace
Pardo Bazan, Emilia 1851-1921 ...... **SSC 30, 158; TCLC 189**
See also EWL 3; FW; RGSF 2; RGWL 2, 3; SSFS 36
Paredes, Americo 1915-1999 .... **PC 83**
See also CA 37-40R; 179; DLB 209; EXPP; HW 1
Pareto, Vilfredo 1848-1923 .... **TCLC 69**
See also CA 175
Paretsky, Sara 1947- .... **CLC 135**
See also AAYA 30; BEST 90:3; CA 125; 129; CANR 59, 95, 184, 218; CMW 4; CPW; DA3; DAM POP; DLB 306; INT CA-129; MSW; RGAL 4
Paretsky, Sara N.
See Paretsky, Sara
Parfenie, Maria
See Codrescu, Andrei
Parini, Jay 1948- .... **CLC 54, 133**
See also CA 97-100, 229; CAAE 229; CAAS 16; CANR 32, 87, 198, 230
Parini, Jay Lee
See Parini, Jay
Paris, Matthew c. 1200-1259 ..... **CMLC 152**
Park, Jordan
See Kornbluth, C(yril) M.; Pohl, Frederik
Park, Robert E(zra) 1864-1944 .... **TCLC 73**
See also CA 122; 165
Parker, Bert
See Ellison, Harlan
Parker, Dorothy 1893-1967 ...... **CLC 15,68; DC 40; PC 28; SSC 2, 101; TCLC 143**
See also AMWS 9; CA 19-20; 25-28R; CAP 2; DA3; DAM POET; DLB 11, 45, 86; EXPP; FW; MAL 5; MBL; MTCW 1, 2; MTFW 2005; PFS 18, 43; RGAL 4; RGSF 2; TUS
Parker, Dorothy Rothschild
See Parker, Dorothy
Parker, Robert B. 1932-2010 ... **CLC 27, 283**
See also AAYA 28; BEST 89:4; BPFB 3; CA 49-52; CANR 1, 26, 52, 89, 128, 165, 200; CMW 4; CPW; DAM NOV, POP; DLB 306; INT CANR-26; MSW; MTCW 1; MTFW 2005
Parker, Robert Brown
See Parker, Robert B.
Parker, Theodore 1810-1860 .... **NCLC 186**
See also DLB 1, 235
Parkes, Lucas
See Harris, John (Wyndham Parkes Lucas) Beynon
Parkin, Frank 1940-2011 .... **CLC 43**
See also CA 147
Parkman, Francis, Jr. 1823-1893 ... **NCLC 12**
See also AMWS 2; DLB 1, 30, 183, 186, 235; RGAL 4
Parks, Gordon 1912-2006 .... **BLC 1:3; CLC 1, 16**
See also AAYA 36; AITN 2; BW 2, 3; CA 41-44R; 249; CANR 26, 66, 145; DA3; DAM MULT; DLB 33; MTCW 2; MTFW 2005; NFS 32; SATA 8, 108; SATA-Obit 175
Parks, Gordon Roger Alexander
See Parks, Gordon
Parks, Suzan-Lori 1964(?)- .... **BLC 2:3; CLC 309; DC 23**
See also AAYA 55; CA 201; CAD; CD 5, 6; CWD; DFS 22; DLB 341; RGAL 4
Parks, Tim 1954- .... **CLC 147**
See also CA 126; 131; CANR 77, 144, 202; CN 7; DLB 231; INT CA-131
Parks, Timothy Harold
See Parks, Tim
Parmenides c. 515B.C.-c. 450B.C. ... **CMLC 22**
See also DLB 176
Parnell, Thomas 1679-1718 .... **LC 3**
See also DLB 95; RGEL 2
Parr, Catherine c. 1513(?)-1548 .... **LC 86**
See also DLB 136
Parra, Nicanor 1914- .... **CLC 2, 102; HLC 2; PC 39**
See also CA 85-88; CANR 32; CWW 2; DAM MULT; DLB 283; EWL 3; HW 1; LAW; MTCW 1
Parra Sanojo, Ana Teresa de la 1890-1936
See de la Parra, Teresa
Parrish, Mary Frances
See Fisher, M. F. K.
Parshchikov, Aleksei 1954- .... **CLC 59**
See also DLB 285
Parshchikov, Aleksei Maksimovich
See Parshchikov, Aleksei
Parson, Professor
See Coleridge, Samuel Taylor
Parson Lot
See Kingsley, Charles
Parton, Sara Payson Willis
1811-1872 .... **NCLC 86, 257**
See also DLB 43, 74, 239
Partridge, Anthony
See Oppenheim, E(dward) Phillips
Pascal, Blaise 1623-1662 .... **LC 35**
See also DLB 268; EW 3; GFL Beginnings to 1789; RGWL 2, 3; TWA
Pascoli, Giovanni 1855-1912 .... **TCLC 45**
See also CA 170; EW 7; EWL 3
Pasolini, Pier Paolo 1922-1975 ...... **CLC 20, 37, 106; PC 17**
See also CA 93-96; 61-64; CANR 63; DLB 128, 177; EWL 3; MTCW 1; RGWL 2, 3
Pasquil
See Nashe, Thomas
Pasquini
See Silone, Ignazio
Pastan, Linda 1932- .... **CLC 27**
See also CA 61-64; CANR 18, 40, 61, 113, 233; CP 3, 4, 5, 6, 7; CSW; CWP; DAM POET; DLB 5; PFS 8, 25, 32, 40
Pastan, Linda Olenik
See Pastan, Linda
Pasternak, Boris 1890-1960 ... **CLC 7, 10, 18, 63; PC 6; SSC 31; TCLC 188; WLC 4**
See also BPFB 3; CA 127; 116; DA; DA3; DAB; DAC; DAM MST, NOV, POET; DLB 302, 331; EW 10; MTCW 1, 2; MTFW 2005; NFS 26; RGSF 2; RGWL 2, 3; TWA; WP
Pasternak, Boris Leonidovich
See Pasternak, Boris
Patchen, Kenneth 1911-1972 ... **CLC 1, 2, 18**
See also BG 1:3; CA 1-4R; 33-36R; CANR 3, 35; CN 1; CP 1; DAM POET; DLB 16, 48; EWL 3; MAL 5; MTCW 1; RGAL 4
Patchett, Ann 1963- .... **CLC 244**
See also AAYA 69; AMWS 12; CA 139; CANR 64, 110, 167, 200, 235; DLB 350; MTFW 2005; NFS 30
Pater, Walter (Horatio)
1839-1894 .... **NCLC 7, 90, 159**
See also BRW 5; CDBLB 1832-1890; DLB 57, 156; RGEL 2; TEA
Paterson, A(ndrew) B(arton)
1864-1941 .... **TCLC 32**
See also CA 155; DLB 230; RGEL 2; SATA 97
Paterson, Banjo
See Paterson, A(ndrew) B(arton)
Paterson, Katherine 1932- .... **CLC 12, 30**
See also AAYA 1, 31; BYA 1, 2, 7; CA 21-24R; CANR 28, 59, 111, 173, 196; CLR 7, 50, 127; CWRI 5; DLB 52; JRDA; LAIT 4; MAICYA 1, 2; MAICYAS 1; MTCW 1; SATA 13, 53, 92, 133, 204; WYA; YAW
Paterson, Katherine Womeldorf
See Paterson, Katherine
Patmore, Coventry Kersey Dighton
1823-1896 .... **NCLC 9; PC 59**
See also DLB 35, 98; RGEL 2; TEA
Paton, Alan 1903-1988 .... **CLC 4, 10, 25, 55, 106; TCLC 165; WLC 4**
See also AAYA 26; AFW; BPFB 3; BRWS 2; BYA 1; CA 13-16; 125; CANR 22; CAP 1; CN 1, 2, 3, 4; DA; DA3; DAB; DAC; DAM MST, NOV; DLB 225; DLBD 17; EWL 3; EXPN; LAIT 4; MTCW 1, 2; MTFW 2005; NFS 3, 12; RGEL 2; SATA 11; SATA-Obit 56; SSFS 29; TWA; WLIT 2; WWE 1
Paton, Alan Stewart
See Paton, Alan
Paton Walsh, Gillian
See Paton Walsh, Jill
Paton Walsh, Jill 1937- .... **CLC 35**
See also AAYA 11, 47; BYA 1, 8; CA 262; CAAE 262; CANR 38, 83, 158, 229; CLR 2, 6, 128; DLB 161; JRDA; MAICYA 1, 2; SAAS 3; SATA 4, 72, 109, 190; SATA-Essay 190; WYA; YAW
Patsauq, Markoosie 1942- .... **NNAL**
See also CA 101; CLR 23; CWRI 5; DAM MULT
Patterson, (Horace) Orlando (Lloyd)
1940- .... **BLCS**
See also BW 1; CA 65-68; CANR 27, 84; CN 1, 2, 3, 4, 5, 6

Patton, George S(mith), Jr. 1885-1945 .... **TCLC 79**
See also CA 189
Paulding, James Kirke 1778-1860 ... **NCLC 2**
See also DLB 3, 59, 74, 250; RGAL 4
Paulhan, Jean 1884-1968 .... **TCLC 313**
See also CA 25-28R, 249; EWL 3
Paulin, Thomas Neilson
See Paulin, Tom
Paulin, Tom 1949- .... **CLC 37, 177**
See also CA 123; 128; CANR 98; CP 3, 4, 5, 6, 7; DLB 40
Paulinus of Nola 353?-431 .... **CMLC 156**
Pausanias c. 1st cent. .... **CMLC 36**
Paustovsky, Konstantin (Georgievich) 1892-1968 .... **CLC 40**
See also CA 93-96; 25-28R; DLB 272; EWL 3
Pavese, Cesare 1908-1950 .... **PC 13; SSC 19; TCLC 3, 240**
See also CA 104; 169; DLB 128, 177; EW 12; EWL 3; PFS 20; RGSF 2; RGWL 2, 3; TWA; WLIT 7
Pavic, Milorad 1929-2009 .... **CLC 60**
See also CA 136; CDWLB 4; CWW 2; DLB 181; EWL 3; RGWL 3
Pavlov, Ivan Petrovich 1849-1936 ... **TCLC 91**
See also CA 118; 180
Pavlova, Karolina Karlovna 1807-1893 .... **NCLC 138**
See also DLB 205
Payne, Alan
See Jakes, John
Payne, John Howard 1791-1852 ... **NCLC 241**
See also DLB 37; RGAL 4
Payne, Rachel Ann
See Jakes, John
Paz, Gil
See Lugones, Leopoldo
Paz, Octavio 1914-1998 ..... **CLC 3, 4, 6, 10, 19, 51, 65, 119; HLC 2; PC 1, 48; TCLC 211; WLC 4**
See also AAYA 50; CA 73-76; 165; CANR 32, 65, 104; CWW 2; DA; DA3; DAB; DAC; DAM MST, MULT, POET; DLB 290, 331; DLBY 1990, 1998; DNFS 1; EWL 3; HW 1, 2; LAW; LAWS 1; MTCW 1, 2; MTFW 2005; PFS 18, 30, 38; RGWL 2, 3; SSFS 13; TWA; WLIT 1
p'Bitek, Okot 1931-1982 .... **BLC 1:3; CLC 96; TCLC 149**
See also AFW; BW 2, 3; CA 124; 107; CANR 82; CP 1, 2, 3; DAM MULT; DLB 125; EWL 3; MTCW 1, 2; MTFW 2005; RGEL 2; WLIT 2
Peabody, Elizabeth Palmer 1804-1894 .... **NCLC 169**
See also DLB 1, 223
Peacham, Henry 1578-1644(?) .... **LC 119**
See also DLB 151
Peacock, Molly 1947- .... **CLC 60**
See also CA 103, 262; CAAE 262; CAAS 21; CANR 52, 84, 235; CP 5, 6, 7; CWP; DLB 120, 282
Peacock, Thomas Love 1785-1866 .... **NCLC 22; PC 87**
See also BRW 4; DLB 96, 116; RGEL 2; RGSF 2
Peake, Mervyn 1911-1968 .... **CLC 7, 54**
See also CA 5-8R; 25-28R; CANR 3; DLB 15, 160, 255; FANT; MTCW 1; RGEL 2; SATA 23; SFW 4
Pearce, Ann Philippa
See Pearce, Philippa
Pearce, Philippa 1920-2006 .... **CLC 21**
See also BRWS 19; BYA 5; CA 5-8R; 255; CANR 4, 109; CLR 9; CWRI 5; DLB 161; FANT; MAICYA 1; SATA 1, 67, 129; SATA-Obit 179
Pearl, Eric
See Elman, Richard (Martin)
Pearson, Jean Mary
See Gardam, Jane
Pearson, Thomas Reid
See Pearson, T.R.
Pearson, T.R. 1956- .... **CLC 39**
See also CA 120; 130; CANR 97, 147, 185; CSW; INT CA-130
Peck, Dale 1967- .... **CLC 81**
See also CA 146; CANR 72, 127, 180; GLL 2
Peck, John (Frederick) 1941- .... **CLC 3**
See also CA 49-52; CANR 3, 100; CP 4, 5, 6, 7
Peck, Richard 1934- .... **CLC 21**
See also AAYA 1, 24; BYA 1, 6, 8, 11; CA 85-88; CANR 19, 38, 129, 178; CLR 15, 142; INT CANR-19; JRDA; MAICYA 1, 2; SAAS 2; SATA 18, 55, 97, 110, 158, 190, 228; SATA-Essay 110; WYA; YAW
Peck, Richard Wayne
See Peck, Richard
Peck, Robert Newton 1928- .... **CLC 17**
See also AAYA 3, 43; BYA 1, 6; CA 81-84, 182; CAAE 182; CANR 31, 63, 127; CLR 45, 163; DA; DAC; DAM MST; JRDA; LAIT 3; MAICYA 1, 2; NFS 29; SAAS 1; SATA 21, 62, 111, 156; SATA-Essay 108; WYA; YAW
Peckinpah, David Samuel
See Peckinpah, Sam
Peckinpah, Sam 1925-1984 .... **CLC 20**
See also CA 109; 114; CANR 82
Pedersen, Knut 1859-1952 .... **TCLC 2, 14, 49, 151, 203**
See also AAYA 79; CA 104; 119; CANR 63; DLB 297, 330; EW 8; EWL 8; MTCW 1, 2; RGWL 2, 3
Peele, George 1556-1596 ..... **DC 27; LC 115**
See also BRW 1; DLB 62, 167; RGEL 2
Peeslake, Gaffer
See Durrell, Lawrence
Peguy, Charles (Pierre) 1873-1914 .... **TCLC 10**
See also CA 107; 193; DLB 258; EWL 3; GFL 1789 to the Present
Penninc fl. 13th cent. .... **CMLC 173**
Peirce, Charles Sanders 1839-1914 .... **TCLC 81**
See also CA 194; DLB 270
Pelagius c. 350-c. 418 .... **CMLC 118**
Pelecanos, George P. 1957- .... **CLC 236**
See also CA 138; CANR 122, 165, 194, 243; DLB 306
Pelevin, Victor 1962- .... **CLC 238**
See also CA 154; CANR 88, 159, 197; DLB 285
Pelevin, Viktor Olegovich
See Pelevin, Victor
Pellicer, Carlos 1897(?)-1977 .... **HLCS 2**
See also CA 153; 69-72; DLB 290; EWL 3; HW 1
Pena, Ramon del Valle y
See Valle-Inclan, Ramon del
Pendennis, Arthur Esquir
See Thackeray, William Makepeace
Penn, Arthur
See Matthews, (James) Brander
Penn, William 1644-1718 .... **LC 25**
See also DLB 24
Penny, Carolyn
See Chute, Carolyn
PEPECE
See Prado (Calvo), Pedro
Pepys, Samuel 1633-1703 .... **LC 11, 58; WLC 4**
See also BRW 2; CDBLB 1660-1789; DA; DA3; DAB; DAC; DAM MST; DLB 101, 213; NCFS 4; RGEL 2; TEA; WLIT 3
Percy, Thomas 1729-1811 .... **NCLC 95**
See also DLB 104
Percy, Walker 1916-1990 ..... **CLC 2, 3, 6, 8, 14, 18, 47, 65**
See also AMWS 3; BPFB 3; CA 1-4R; 131; CANR 1, 23, 64; CN 1, 2, 3, 4; CPW; CSW; DA3; DAM NOV, POP; DLB 2; DLBY 1980, 1990; EWL 3; MAL 5; MTCW 1, 2; MTFW 2005; RGAL 4; TUS
Percy, William Alexander 1885-1942 .... **TCLC 84**
See also CA 163; MTCW 2
Perdurabo, Frater
See Crowley, Edward Alexander
Pereda (y Sanchez de Porrua), Jose Maria de 1833-1906 .... **TCLC 16**
See also CA 117
Pereda y Porrua, Jose Maria de
See Pereda (y Sanchez de Porrua), Jose Maria de
Peregoy, George Weems
See Mencken, H. L.
Perelman, Bob 1947- .... **PC 132**
See also CA 154; CANR 85, 160; CP 5, 6, 7; DLB 193; RGAL 4
Perelman, Robert
See Perelman, Bob
Perelman, S(idney) J(oseph) 1904-1979 ...... **CLC 3, 5, 9, 15, 23, 44, 49; SSC 32**
See also AAYA 79; AITN 1, 2; BPFB 3; CA 73-76; 89-92; CANR 18; DAM DRAM; DLB 11, 44; MTCW 1, 2; MTFW 2005; RGAL 4
Perets, Yitskhok Leybush
See Peretz, Isaac Loeb
Peretz, Isaac Leib (?)-
See Peretz, Isaac Loeb
Peretz, Isaac Loeb 1851-1915 .... **SSC 26; TCLC 16**
See Peretz, Isaac Leib
See also CA 109; 201; DLB 333
Peretz, Yitzkhok Leibush
See Peretz, Isaac Loeb
Peri Rossi, Cristina 1941- .... **CLC 156; HLCS 2**
See also CA 131; CANR 59, 81; CWW 2; DLB 145, 290; EWL 3; HW 1, 2
Perkins, W. Epaminondas Adrastus
See Twain, Mark
Perlata
See Peret, Benjamin
Perloff, Marjorie G(abrielle) 1931- .... **CLC 137**
See also CA 57-60; CANR 7, 22, 49, 104
Perrault, Charles 1628-1703 .... **LC 2, 56; SSC 144**
See also BYA 4; CLR 79, 134; DLB 268; GFL Beginnings to 1789; MAICYA 1, 2; RGWL 2, 3; SATA 25; WCH
Perrotta, Tom 1961- .... **CLC 266**
See also CA 162; CANR 99, 155, 197
Perry, Anne 1938- .... **CLC 126**
See also CA 101; CANR 22, 50, 84, 150, 177, 238; CMW 4; CN 6, 7; CPW; DLB 276
Perry, Brighton
See Sherwood, Robert E(mmet)
Perse, St.-John
See Leger, Alexis Saint-Leger
Perse, Saint-John
See Leger, Alexis Saint-Leger
Persius 34-62 .... **CMLC 74**
See also AW 2; DLB 211; RGWL 2, 3
Perutz, Leo(pold) 1882-1957 .... **TCLC 60**
See also CA 147; DLB 81
Peseenz, Tulio F.
See Lopez y Fuentes, Gregorio
Pesetsky, Bette 1932- .... **CLC 28**
See also CA 133; DLB 130

Peshkov, Alexei Maximovich
See Gorky, Maxim
Pessoa, Fernando 1888-1935 .... **HLC 2; PC 20, 165; TCLC 27, 257**
See also CA 125; 183; CANR 182; DAM MULT; DLB 287; EW 10; EWL 3; RGWL 2, 3; WP
Pessoa, Fernando António Nogueira
See Pessoa, Fernando
Peterkin, Julia Mood 1880-1961 .... **CLC 31**
See also CA 102; DLB 9
Peter of Blois c. 1135-c. 1212 .... **CMLC 127**
Peters, Joan K(aren) 1945- .... **CLC 39**
See also CA 158; CANR 109
Peters, Robert L(ouis) 1924- .... **CLC 7**
See also CA 13-16R; CAAS 8; CP 1, 5, 6, 7; DLB 105
Peters, S. H.
See Henry, O.
Petofi, Sandor 1823-1849 ...... **NCLC 21, 264**
See also RGWL 2, 3
Petrakis, Harry Mark 1923- .... **CLC 3**
See also CA 9-12R; CANR 4, 30, 85, 155; CN 1, 2, 3, 4, 5, 6, 7
Petrarch 1304-1374 .... **CMLC 20; PC 8**
See also DA3; DAM POET; EW 2; LMFS 1; PFS 42; RGWL 2, 3; WLIT 7
Petrarch, Francesco
See Petrarch
Petronius c. 20-66 .... **CMLC 34, 170**
See also AW 2; CDWLB 1; DLB 211; RGWL 2, 3; WLIT 8
Petrov, Eugene
See Kataev, Evgeny Petrovich
Petrov, Evgenii
See Kataev, Evgeny Petrovich
Petrov, Evgeny
See Kataev, Evgeny Petrovich
Petrovsky, Boris
See Mansfield, Katherine
Petrushevskaia, Liudmila
1938- .... **CLC 387**
See also CWW 2; DLB 285; EWL 3
Petry, Ann 1908-1997 .... **CLC 1, 7, 18; SSC 161; TCLC 112**
See also AFAW 1, 2; BPFB 3; BW 1, 3; BYA 2; CA 5-8R; 157; CAAS 6; CANR 4, 46; CLR 12; CN 1, 2, 3, 4, 5, 6; DLB 76; EWL 3; JRDA; LAIT 1; MAICYA 1, 2; MAICYAS 1; MTCW 1; NFS 33; RGAL 4; SATA 5; SATA-Obit 94; TUS
Petry, Ann Lane
See Petry, Ann
Petursson, Halligrimur 1614-1674 .... **LC 8**
Peychinovich
See Vazov, Ivan (Minchov)
Phaedrus c. 15B.C.-c. 50 ..... **CMLC 25, 171**
See also DLB 211
Phelge, Nanker
See Richards, Keith
Phelps (Ward), Elizabeth Stuart
See Phelps, Elizabeth Stuart
Phelps, Elizabeth Stuart
1844-1911 .... **TCLC 113, 296**
See also CA 242; DLB 74; FW
Pheradausi
See Ferdowsi, Abu'l Qasem
Philip, M(arlene) Nourbese 1947- ... **CLC 307, 360**
See also BW 3; CA 163; CWP; DLB 157, 334
Philippe de Remi
c. 1247-1296 .... **CMLC 102**
Philips, Katherine
1632-1664 .... **LC 30, 145; PC 40**
See also DLB 131; RGEL 2
Philipson, Ilene J. 1950- .... **CLC 65**
See also CA 219
Philipson, Morris H. 1926-2011 ..... **CLC 53**
See also CA 1-4R; CANR 4
Phillips, Caryl 1958- ... **BLCS; CLC 96, 224**
See also BRWS 5; BW 2; CA 141; CANR 63, 104, 140, 195; CBD; CD 5, 6; CN 5, 6, 7; DA3; DAM MULT; DLB 157; EWL 3; MTCW 2; MTFW 2005; WLIT 4; WWE 1
Phillips, David Graham 1867-1911 **TCLC 44**
See also CA 108; 176; DLB 9, 12, 303; RGAL 4
Phillips, Jack
See Sandburg, Carl
Phillips, Jayne Anne 1952- ...... **CLC 15, 33, 139, 296; SSC 16**
See also AAYA 57; BPFB 3; CA 101; CANR 24, 50, 96, 200; CN 4, 5, 6, 7; CSW; DLBY 1980; INT CANR-24; MTCW 1, 2; MTFW 2005; RGAL 4; RGSF 2; SSFS 4
Phillips, Richard
See Dick, Philip K.
Phillips, Robert (Schaeffer) 1938- ... **CLC 28**
See also CA 17-20R; CAAS 13; CANR 8; DLB 105
Phillips, Ward
See Lovecraft, H. P.
Philo c. 20B.C.-c. 50 .... **CMLC 100**
See also DLB 176
Philostratus, Flavius
c. 179-c. 244 .... **CMLC 62, 171**
Phiradausi
See Ferdowsi, Abu'l Qasem
Piccolo, Lucio 1901-1969 .... **CLC 13**
See also CA 97-100; DLB 114; EWL 3
Pickthall, Marjorie L(owry) C(hristie)
1883-1922 .... **TCLC 21**
See also CA 107; DLB 92
Pico della Mirandola, Giovanni
1463-1494 .... **LC 15**
See also LMFS 1
Piercy, Marge 1936- .... **CLC 3, 6, 14, 18, 27, 62, 128, 347; PC 29**
See also BPFB 3; CA 21-24R, 187; CAAE 187; CAAS 1; CANR 13, 43, 66, 111; CN 3, 4, 5, 6, 7; CP 1, 2, 3, 4, 5, 6, 7; CWP; DLB 120, 227; EXPP; FW; MAL 5; MTCW 1, 2; MTFW 2005; PFS 9, 22, 32, 40; SFW 4
Pinero, Miguel (Antonio Gomez)
1946-1988 .... **CLC 4, 55**
See also CA 61-64; 125; CAD; CANR 29, 90; DLB 266; HW 1; LLW
Piers, Robert
See Anthony, Piers
Pieyre de Mandiargues, Andre
1909-1991 .... **CLC 41**
See also CA 103; 136; CANR 22, 82; DLB 83; EWL 3; GFL 1789 to the Present
Pilkington, Laetitia 1709?-1750 .... **LC 211**
Pil'niak, Boris
See Vogau, Boris Andreyevich
Pil'niak, Boris Andreevich
See Vogau, Boris Andreyevich
Pilnyak, Boris 1894-1938
See Vogau, Boris Andreyevich
Pinchback, Eugene
See Toomer, Jean
Pincherle, Alberto 1907-1990 .... **CLC 2, 7, 11, 27, 46; SSC 26**
See also CA 25-28R; 132; CANR 33, 63, 142; DAM NOV; DLB 127; EW 12; EWL 3; MTCW 2; MTFW 2005; RGSF 2; RGWL 2, 3; WLIT 7
Pinckney, Darryl 1953- .... **CLC 76**
See also BW 2, 3; CA 143; CANR 79
Pindar 518(?)B.C.-438(?)B.C. ...... **CMLC 12, 130; PC 19**
See also AW 1; CDWLB 1; DLB 176; RGWL 2
Pineda, Cecile 1942- .... **CLC 39**
See also CA 118; DLB 209
Pinero, Arthur Wing 1855-1934 ... **TCLC 32**
See also CA 110; 153; DAM DRAM; DLB 10, 344; RGEL 2
Pinget, Robert 1919-1997 ..... **CLC 7, 13, 37**
See also CA 85-88; 160; CWW 2; DLB 83; EWL 3; GFL 1789 to the Present
Pink Floyd
See Barrett, Syd; Gilmour, David; Mason, Nick; Waters, Roger; Wright, Rick
Pinkney, Edward 1802-1828 .... **NCLC 31**
See also DLB 248
Pinkwater, D. Manus
See Pinkwater, Daniel
Pinkwater, Daniel 1941- .... **CLC 35**
See also AAYA 1, 46; BYA 9; CA 29-32R; CANR 12, 38, 89, 143; CLR 4, 175; CSW; FANT; JRDA; MAICYA 1, 2; SAAS 3; SATA 8, 46, 76, 114, 158, 210, 243; SFW 4; YAW
Pinkwater, Daniel M.
See Pinkwater, Daniel
Pinkwater, Daniel Manus
See Pinkwater, Daniel
Pinkwater, Manus
See Pinkwater, Daniel
Pinsky, Robert 1940- ...... **CLC 9, 19, 38, 94, 121, 216; PC 27**
See also AMWS 6; CA 29-32R; CAAS 4; CANR 58, 97, 138, 177; CP 3, 4, 5, 6, 7; DA3; DAM POET; DLBY 1982, 1998; MAL 5; MTCW 2; MTFW 2005; PFS 18, 44; RGAL 4; TCLE 1:2
Pinta, Harold
See Pinter, Harold
Pinter, Harold 1930-2008 .... **CLC 1, 3, 6, 9, 11, 15, 27, 58, 73, 199; DC 15; WLC 4**
See also BRWR 1; BRWS 1; CA 5-8R; 280; CANR 33, 65, 112, 145; CBD; CD 5, 6; CDBLB 1960 to Present; CP 1; DA; DA3; DAB; DAC; DAM DRAM, MST; DFS 3, 5, 7, 14, 25; DLB 13, 310, 331; EWL 3; IDFW 3, 4; LMFS 2; MTCW 1, 2; MTFW 2005; RGEL 2; RGHL; TEA
Piozzi, Hester Lynch (Thrale)
1741-1821 .... **NCLC 57, 294**
See also DLB 104, 142
Pirandello, Luigi 1867-1936 .... **DC 5; SSC 22, 148; TCLC 4, 29, 172; WLC 4**
See also CA 104; 153; CANR 103; DA; DA3; DAB; DAC; DAM DRAM, MST; DFS 4, 9; DLB 264, 331; EW 8; EWL 3; MTCW 2; MTFW 2005; RGSF 2; RGWL 2, 3; SSFS 30, 33; WLIT 7
Pirdousi
See Ferdowsi, Abu'l Qasem
Pirdousi, Abu-l-Qasim
See Ferdowsi, Abu'l Qasem
Pirsig, Robert M(aynard)
1928- .... **CLC 4, 6, 73**
See also CA 53-56; CANR 42, 74; CPW 1; DA3; DAM POP; MTCW 1, 2; MTFW 2005; NFS 31; SATA 39
Pisan, Christine de
See Christine de Pizan
Pisarev, Dmitrii Ivanovich
See Pisarev, Dmitry Ivanovich
Pisarev, Dmitry Ivanovich
1840-1868 .... **NCLC 25**
See also DLB 277
Pix, Mary (Griffith) 1666-1709 .... **LC 8, 149, 226**
See also DLB 80
Pixerecourt, (Rene Charles) Guilbert de
1773-1844 .... **NCLC 39**
See also DLB 192; GFL 1789 to the Present
Pizarnik, Alejandra
1936-1972 .... **TCLC 318**
See also DLB 283

Plaatje, Sol(omon) T(shekisho) 1878-1932 .... **BLCS; TCLC 73**
See also BW 2, 3; CA 141; CANR 79; DLB 125, 225

Plaidy, Jean
See Hibbert, Eleanor Alice Burford

Planche, James Robinson 1796-1880 .... **NCLC 42**
See also RGEL 2

Plant, Robert 1948- .... **CLC 12**

Plante, David 1940- .... **CLC 7, 23, 38**
See also CA 37-40R; CANR 12, 36, 58, 82, 152, 191, 230; CN 2, 3, 4, 5, 6, 7; DAM NOV; DLBY 1983; INT CANR-12; MTCW 1

Plante, David Robert
See Plante, David

Plath, Sylvia 1932-1963 .... **CLC 1, 2, 3, 5, 9, 11, 14, 17, 50, 51, 62, 111; PC 1, 37, 153; TCLC 252; WLC 4**
See also AAYA 13; AMWR 2; AMWS 1; BPFB 3; CA 19-20; CANR 34, 101; CAP 2; CDALB 1941-1968; DA; DA3; DAB; DAC; DAM MST, POET; DLB 5, 6, 152; EWL 3; EXPN; EXPP; FL 1:6; FW; LAIT 4; MAL 5; MBL; MTCW 1, 2; MTFW 2005; NFS 1; PAB; PFS 1, 15, 28, 33; RGAL 4; SATA 96; TUS; WP; YAW

Plato c. 428B.C.-347B.C. .... **CMLC 8, 75, 98; WLCS**
See also AW 1; CDWLB 1; DA; DA3; DAB; DAC; DAM MST; DLB 176; LAIT 1; LATS 1:1; RGWL 2, 3; WLIT 8

Platonov, Andrei
See Klimentov, Andrei Platonovich

Platonov, Andrei Platonovich
See Klimentov, Andrei Platonovich

Platonov, Andrey Platonovich
See Klimentov, Andrei Platonovich

Platt, Kin 1911- .... **CLC 26**
See also AAYA 11; CA 17-20R; CANR 11; JRDA; SAAS 17; SATA 21, 86; WYA

Plautus c. 254B.C.-c. 184B.C. ..... **CMLC 24, 92; DC 6**
See also AW 1; CDWLB 1; DLB 211; RGWL 2, 3; WLIT 8

Plick et Plock
See Simenon, Georges

Plieksans, Janis
See Rainis, Janis

Plimpton, George 1927-2003 .... **CLC 36**
See also AITN 1; AMWS 16; CA 21-24R; 224; CANR 32, 70, 103, 133; DLB 185, 241; MTCW 1, 2; MTFW 2005; SATA 10; SATA-Obit 150

Plimpton, George Ames
See Plimpton, George

Pliny the Elder c. 23-79 .... **CMLC 23**
See also DLB 211

Pliny the Younger c. 61-c. 112 .... **CMLC 62**
See also AW 2; DLB 211

Plomer, William Charles Franklin 1903-1973 .... **CLC 4, 8**
See also AFW; BRWS 11; CA 21-22; CANR 34; CAP 2; CN 1; CP 1, 2; DLB 20, 162, 191, 225; EWL 3; MTCW 1; RGEL 2; RGSF 2; SATA 24

Plotinus 204-270 .... **CMLC 46, 163**
See also CDWLB 1; DLB 176

Plowman, Piers
See Kavanagh, Patrick (Joseph)

Plum, J.
See Wodehouse, P. G.

Plumly, Stanley 1939- .... **CLC 33**
See also CA 108; 110; CANR 97, 185; CP 3, 4, 5, 6, 7; DLB 5, 193; INT CA-110

Plumly, Stanley Ross
See Plumly, Stanley

Plumpe, Friedrich Wilhelm
See Murnau, F.W.

Plunkett, Edward John Moreton Drax
See Lord Dunsany

Plutarch c. 46-c. 120 .... **CMLC 60, 146**
See also AW 2; CDWLB 1; DLB 176; RGWL 2, 3; TWA; WLIT 8

Po Chu-i 772-846 .... **CMLC 24**

Podhoretz, Norman 1930- .... **CLC 189**
See also AMWS 8; CA 9-12R; CANR 7, 78, 135, 179

Poe, Edgar Allan 1809-1849 ... **NCLC 1, 16, 55, 78, 94, 97, 117, 211; PC 1, 54; SSC 1, 22, 34, 35, 54, 88, 111, 156, 188, 192, 198, 199, 202; WLC 4**
See also AAYA 14; AMW; AMWC 1; AMWR 2; BPFB 3; BYA 5, 11; CDALB 1640-1865; CMW 4; DA; DA3; DAB; DAC; DAM MST, POET; DLB 3, 59, 73, 74, 248, 254; EXPP; EXPS; GL 3; HGG; LAIT 2; LATS 1:1; LMFS 1; MSW; PAB; PFS 1, 3, 9, 42; RGAL 4; RGSF 2; SATA 23; SCFW 1, 2; SFW 4; SSFS 2, 4, 7, 8, 16, 26, 29, 34; SUFW; TUS; WP; WYA

Poet of Titchfield Street, The
See Pound, Ezra

Poggio Bracciolini, Gian Francesco 1380-1459 .... **LC 125**

Pohl, Frederik 1919-2013 ... **CLC 18; SSC 25**
See also AAYA 24; CA 61-64, 188; CAAE 188; CAAS 1; CANR 11, 37, 81, 140, 234; CN 1, 2, 3, 4, 5, 6; DLB 8; INT CANR-11; MTCW 1, 2; MTFW 2005; SATA 24; SCFW 1, 2; SFW 4

Poirier, Louis
See Gracq, Julien

Poitier, Sidney 1927- .... **CLC 26**
See also AAYA 60; BW 1; CA 117; CANR 94

Pokagon, Simon 1830-1899 .... **NNAL**
See also DAM MULT

Polanski, Roman 1933- .... **CLC 16, 178**
See also CA 77-80

Poliakoff, Stephen 1952- .... **CLC 38**
See also CA 106; CANR 116; CBD; CD 5, 6; DLB 13

Police, The
See Copeland, Stewart; Sting; Summers, Andy

Polidori, John William 1795-1821 .... **NCLC 51; SSC 97**
See also DLB 116; HGG

Poliziano, Angelo 1454-1494 .... **LC 120**
See also WLIT 7

Pollard, Velma 1937- .... **SSC 180**

Pollitt, Katha 1949- .... **CLC 28, 122**
See also CA 120; 122; CANR 66, 108, 164, 200, 229; MTCW 1, 2; MTFW 2005

Pollock, (Mary) Sharon 1936- .... **CLC 50**
See also CA 141; CANR 132; CD 5; CWD; DAC; DAM DRAM, MST; DFS 3; DLB 60; FW

Pollock, Sharon 1936- .... **DC 20**
See also CD 6

Polo, Marco 1254-1324 .... **CMLC 15, 144**
See also WLIT 7

Polonsky, Abraham (Lincoln) 1910-1999 .... **CLC 92**
See also CA 104; 187; DLB 26; INT CA-104

Polybius c. 200B.C.-c. 118B.C. .... **CMLC 17**
See also AW 1; DLB 176; RGWL 2, 3

Pomerance, Bernard 1940- .... **CLC 13**
See also CA 101; CAD; CANR 49, 134; CD 5, 6; DAM DRAM; DFS 9; LAIT 2

Ponge, Francis 1899-1988 .... **CLC 6, 18; PC 107; TCLC 320**
See also CA 85-88; 126; CANR 40, 86; DAM POET; DLBY 2002; EWL 3; GFL 1789 to the Present; RGWL 2, 3

Poniatowska, Elena 1932- .... **CLC 140, 343; HLC 2**
See also CA 101; CANR 32, 66, 107, 156; CDWLB 3; CWW 2; DAM MULT; DLB 113; EWL 3; HW 1, 2; LAWS 1; WLIT 1

Pontoppidan, Henrik 1857-1943 ... **TCLC 29**
See also CA 170; DLB 300, 331

Ponty, Maurice Merleau
See Merleau-Ponty, Maurice

Poole, (Jane Penelope) Josephine
See Helyar, Jane Penelope Josephine

Poole, Josephine
See Helyar, Jane Penelope Josephine

Popa, Vasko 1922-1991 .... **CLC 19; TCLC 167**
See also CA 112; 148; CDWLB 4; DLB 181; EWL 3; RGWL 2, 3

Pope, Alexander 1688-1744 .... **LC 3, 58, 60, 64, 164; PC 26, 167; WLC 5**
See also BRW 3; BRWC 1; BRWR 1; CDBLB 1660-1789; DA; DA3; DAB; DAC; DAM MST, POET; DLB 95, 101, 213; EXPP; PAB; PFS 12; RGEL 2; WLIT 3; WP

Popov, Evgenii Anatol'evich
See Popov, Yevgeny

Popov, Yevgeny .... **CLC 59**
See also DLB 285

Poquelin, Jean-Baptiste
See Moliere

Porete, Marguerite (?)-1310 ... **CMLC 73, 156**
See also DLB 208

Porphyry c. 233-c. 305 .... **CMLC 71**

Porter, Connie (Rose) 1959(?)- .... **CLC 70**
See also AAYA 65; BW 2, 3; CA 142; CANR 90, 109; SATA 81, 129

Porter, Gene Stratton
See Stratton-Porter, Gene

Porter, Geneva Grace
See Stratton-Porter, Gene

Porter, Jane 1776-1850 .... **NCLC 267**
See also DLB 116, 159

Porter, Katherine Anne 1890-1980 ... **CLC 1, 3, 7, 10, 13, 15, 27, 101; SSC 4, 31, 43, 108; TCLC 233**
See also AAYA 42; AITN 2; AMW; BPFB 3; CA 1-4R; 101; CANR 1, 65; CDALBS; CN 1, 2; DA; DA3; DAB; DAC; DAM MST, NOV; DLB 4, 9, 102; DLBD 12; DLBY 1980; EWL 3; EXPS; LAIT 3; MAL 5; MBL; MTCW 1, 2; MTFW 2005; NFS 14; RGAL 4; RGSF 2; SATA 39; SATA-Obit 23; SSFS 1, 8, 11, 16, 23; TCWW 2; TUS

Porter, Peter 1929-2010 .... **CLC 5, 13, 33**
See also CA 85-88; CP 1, 2, 3, 4, 5, 6, 7; DLB 40, 289; WWE 1

Porter, Peter Neville Frederick
See Porter, Peter

Porter, R. E.
See Hoch, Edward D.

Porter, William Sydney
See Henry, O.

Portillo (y Pacheco), Jose Lopez
See Lopez Portillo (y Pacheco), Jose

Portillo Trambley, Estela 1927-1998 ... **HLC 2; SSC 180; TCLC 163**
See also CA 77-80; CANR 32; DAM MULT; DLB 209; HW 1; RGAL 4

Posey, Alexander (Lawrence) 1873-1908 .... **NNAL**
See also CA 144; CANR 80; DAM MULT; DLB 175

Posse, Abel .... **CLC 70, 273**
See also CA 252

Post, Melville Davisson 1869-1930 **TCLC 39**
See also CA 110; 202; CMW 4

Postl, Carl
See Sealsfield, Charles

Postman, Neil 1931(?)-2003 .... **CLC 244**
See also CA 102; 221
Potocki, Jan 1761-1815 .... **NCLC 229**
Potok, Chaim 1929-2002 .... **CLC 2, 7, 14, 26, 112, 325**
See also AAYA 15, 50; AITN 1, 2; BPFB 3; BYA 1; CA 17-20R; 208; CANR 19, 35, 64, 98; CLR 92; CN 4, 5, 6; DA3; DAM NOV; DLB 28, 152; EXPN; INT CANR-19; LAIT 4; MTCW 1, 2; MTFW 2005; NFS 4, 34, 38; RGHL; SATA 33, 106; SATA-Obit 134; TUS; YAW
Potok, Herbert Harold
See Potok, Chaim
Potok, Herman Harold
See Potok, Chaim
Potter, Dennis (Christopher George) 1935-1994 .... **CLC 58, 86, 123**
See also BRWS 10; CA 107; 145; CANR 33, 61; CBD; DLB 233; MTCW 1
Pound, Ezra 1885-1972 .... **CLC 1, 2, 3, 4, 5, 7, 10, 13, 18, 34, 48, 50, 112; PC 4, 95, 160; WLC 5**
See also AAYA 47; AMW; AMWR 1; CA 5-8R; 37-40R; CANR 40; CDALB 1917-1929; CP 1; DA; DA3; DAB; DAC; DAM MST, POET; DLB 4, 45, 63; DLBD 15; EFS 1:2, 2:1; EWL 3; EXPP; LMFS 2; MAL 5; MTCW 1, 2; MTFW 2005; PAB; PFS 2, 8, 16, 44; RGAL 4; TUS; WP
Pound, Ezra Weston Loomis
See Pound, Ezra
Povod, Reinaldo 1959-1994 .... **CLC 44**
See also CA 136; 146; CANR 83
Powell, Adam Clayton, Jr. 1908-1972 .... **BLC 1:3; CLC 89**
See also BW 1, 3; CA 102; 33-36R; CANR 86; DAM MULT; DLB 345
Powell, Anthony 1905-2000 ..... **CLC 1, 3, 7, 9, 10, 31**
See also BRW 7; CA 1-4R; 189; CANR 1, 32, 62, 107; CDBLB 1945-1960; CN 1, 2, 3, 4, 5, 6; DLB 15; EWL 3; MTCW 1, 2; MTFW 2005; RGEL 2; TEA
Powell, Dawn 1896(?)-1965 .... **CLC 66**
See also CA 5-8R; CANR 121; DLBY 1997
Powell, Padgett 1952- .... **CLC 34**
See also CA 126; CANR 63, 101, 215; CSW; DLB 234; DLBY 01; SSFS 25
Power, Susan 1961- .... **CLC 91**
See also BYA 14; CA 160; CANR 135; NFS 11
Powers, J(ames) F(arl) 1917-1999 ... **CLC 1, 4, 8, 57; SSC 4**
See also CA 1-4R; 181; CANR 2, 61; CN 1, 2, 3, 4, 5, 6; DLB 130; MTCW 1; RGAL 4; RGSF 2
Powers, John
See Powers, John R.
Powers, John R. 1945- .... **CLC 66**
See also CA 69-72
Powers, Kevin 1980- .... **CLC 354**
Powers, Richard 1957- .... **CLC 93, 292**
See also AMWS 9; BPFB 3; CA 148; CANR 80, 180, 221; CN 6, 7; DLB 350; MTFW 2005; TCLE 1:2
Powers, Richard S.
See Powers, Richard
Pownall, David 1938- .... **CLC 10**
See also CA 89-92, 180; CAAS 18; CANR 49, 101; CBD; CD 5, 6; CN 4, 5, 6, 7; DLB 14
Powys, John Cowper 1872-1963 ..... **CLC 7, 9, 15, 46, 125**
See also CA 85-88; CANR 106; DLB 15, 255; EWL 3; FANT; MTCW 1, 2; MTFW 2005; RGEL 2; SUFW
Powys, T(heodore) F(rancis) 1875-1953 .... **TCLC 9**
See also BRWS 8; CA 106; 189; DLB 36, 162; EWL 3; FANT; RGEL 2; SUFW
Pozzo, Modesta
See Fonte, Moderata
Prado (Calvo), Pedro 1886-1952 ... **TCLC 75**
See also CA 131; DLB 283; HW 1; LAW
Praed, Rosa 1851-1935 .... **TCLC 319**
See also DLB 230; HGG
Prager, Emily 1952- .... **CLC 56**
See also CA 204
Pratchett, Terence David John
See Pratchett, Terry
Pratchett, Terry 1948- .... **CLC 197**
See also AAYA 19, 54; BPFB 3; CA 143; CANR 87, 126, 170; CLR 64; CN 6, 7; CPW; CWRI 5; FANT; MTFW 2005; SATA 82, 139, 185; SFW 4; SUFW 2
Pratolini, Vasco 1913-1991 .... **TCLC 124**
See also CA 211; DLB 177; EWL 3; RGWL 2, 3
Pratt, E(dwin) J(ohn) 1883(?)-1964 ... **CLC 19**
See also CA 141; 93-96; CANR 77; DAC; DAM POET; DLB 92; EWL 3; RGEL 2; TWA
Perec, Georges 1936-1982 .... **CLC 56, 116**
See also CA 141; DLB 83, 299; EWL 3; GFL 1789 to the Present; RGHL; RGWL 3
Premacanda
See Srivastava, Dhanpat Rai
Premchand
See Srivastava, Dhanpat Rai
Prem Chand, Munshi
See Srivastava, Dhanpat Rai
Premchand, Munshi
See Srivastava, Dhanpat Rai
Prescott, William Hickling 1796-1859 .... **NCLC 163**
See also DLB 1, 30, 59, 235
Preseren, France 1800-1849 .... **NCLC 127**
See also CDWLB 4; DLB 147
Preston, Thomas 1537-1598 .... **LC 189**
See also DLB 62
Peret, Benjamin 1899-1959 .. **PC 33; TCLC 20**
See also CA 117; 186; GFL 1789 to the Present
Preussler, Otfried 1923- .... **CLC 17**
See also CA 77-80; SATA 24
Perez Galdos, Benito 1843-1920 .... **HLCS 2; TCLC 27**
See also CA 125; 153; EW 7; EWL 3; HW 1; RGWL 2, 3
Price, Edward Reynolds
See Price, Reynolds
Price, Reynolds 1933-2011 .... **CLC 3, 6, 13, 43, 50, 63, 212, 341; SSC 22**
See also AMWS 6; CA 1-4R; CANR 1, 37, 57, 87, 128, 177, 217; CN 1, 2, 3, 4, 5, 6, 7; CSW; DAM NOV; DLB 2, 218, 278; EWL 3; INT CANR-37; MAL 5; MTFW 2005; NFS 18
Price, Richard 1949- .... **CLC 6, 12, 299**
See also CA 49-52; CANR 3, 147, 190; CN 7; DLBY 1981
Prichard, Katharine Susannah 1883-1969 .... **CLC 46**
See also CA 11-12; CANR 33; CAP 1; DLB 260; MTCW 1; RGEL 2; RGSF 2; SATA 66
Priestley, J(ohn) B(oynton) 1894-1984 .... **CLC 2, 5, 9, 34**
See also BRW 7; CA 9-12R; 113; CANR 33; CDBLB 1914-1945; CN 1, 2, 3; DA3; DAM DRAM, NOV; DLB 10, 34, 77, 100, 139; DLBY 1984; EWL 3; MTCW 1, 2; MTFW 2005; RGEL 2; SFW 4
Prince 1958- .... **CLC 35**
See also CA 213
Prince, F(rank) T(empleton) 1912-2003 .... **CLC 22, PC 122**
See also CA 101; 219; CANR 43, 79; CP 1, 2, 3, 4, 5, 6, 7; DLB 20
Prince Kropotkin
See Kropotkin, Peter
Prince, Mary c. 1788-1833? .... **NCLC 282**
See also AAYA 71
Prior, Matthew 1664-1721 .... **LC 4; PC 102**
See also DLB 95; RGEL 2
Prior, Capt. Samuel
See Galt, John
Prishvin, Mikhail 1873-1954 .... **TCLC 75**
See also DLB 272; EWL 3
Prishvin, Mikhail Mikhailovich
See Prishvin, Mikhail
Pritchard, William H(arrison) 1932- .... **CLC 34**
See also CA 65-68; CANR 23, 95; DLB 111
Pritchett, V(ictor) S(awdon) 1900-1997 .. **CLC 5, 13, 15, 41; SSC 14, 126**
See also BPFB 3; BRWS 3; CA 61-64; 157; CANR 31, 63; CN 1, 2, 3, 4, 5, 6; DA3; DAM NOV; DLB 15, 139; EWL 3; MTCW 1, 2; MTFW 2005; RGEL 2; RGSF 2; TEA
Private 19022
See Manning, Frederic
Probst, Mark 1925- .... **CLC 59**
See also CA 130
Procaccino, Michael
See Cristofer, Michael
Proclus c. 412-c. 485 .... **CMLC 81**
Procopius of Caesarea 500?-560? .... **CMLC 161**
Procter, Adelaide Anne 1825-1864 .... **NCLC 305**
See also DLB 32, 199
Prokosch, Frederic 1908-1989 .... **CLC 4, 48**
See also CA 73-76; 128; CANR 82; CN 1, 2, 3, 4; CP 1, 2, 3, 4; DLB 48; MTCW 2
Propertius, Sextus c. 50B.C.-c. 16B.C. ...... **CMLC 32, 140**
See also AW 2; CDWLB 1; DLB 211; RGWL 2, 3; WLIT 8
Prophet, The
See Dreiser, Theodore
Prose, Francine 1947- .... **CLC 45, 231**
See also AMWS 16; CA 109; 112; CANR 46, 95, 132, 175, 218; DLB 234; MTFW 2005; SATA 101, 149, 198
Protagoras c. 490B.C.-420B.C. ..... **CMLC 85**
See also DLB 176
Proudhon
See Cunha, Euclides (Rodrigues Pimenta) da
Proulx, Annie 1935- .... **CLC 81, 158, 250, 331; SSC 128, 168**
See also AAYA 81; AMWS 7; BPFB 3; CA 145; CANR 65, 110, 206; CN 6, 7; CPW 1; DA3; DAM POP; DLB 335, 350; MAL 5; MTCW 2; MTFW 2005; NFS 38; SSFS 18, 23
Proulx, E. Annie
See Proulx, Annie
Proulx, Edna Annie
See Proulx, Annie
Proust, Marcel 1871-1922 .... **SSC 75; TCLC 7, 13, 33, 220; WLC 5**
See also AAYA 58; BPFB 3; CA 104; 120; CANR 110; DA; DA3; DAB; DAC; DAM MST, NOV; DLB 65; EW 8; EWL 3; GFL 1789 to the Present; MTCW 1, 2; MTFW 2005; RGWL 2, 3; TWA
Proust, Valentin-Louis-George-Eugene Marcel
See Proust, Marcel
Prowler, Harley
See Masters, Edgar Lee
Prudentius, Aurelius Clemens 348-c. 405 .... **CMLC 78**
See also EW 1; RGWL 2, 3
Prudhomme, Rene Francois Armand
See Sully Prudhomme, Rene-Francois-Armand

Prus, Boleslaw 1845-1912 .... **TCLC 48**
See also RGWL 2, 3
Prevert, Jacques 1900-1977 .... **CLC 15**
See also CA 77-80; 69-72; CANR 29, 61, 207; DLB 258; EWL 3; GFL 1789 to the Present; IDFW 3, 4; MTCW 1; RGWL 2, 3; SATA-Obit 30
Prevert, Jacques Henri Marie
See Prevert, Jacques
Prevost, (Antoine Francois)
1697-1763 .... **LC 1, 174**
See also DLB 314; EW 4; GFL Beginnings to 1789; RGWL 2, 3
Prynne, William 1600-1669 .... **LC 148**
Prynne, Xavier
See Hardwick, Elizabeth
Pryor, Aaron Richard
See Pryor, Richard
Pryor, Richard 1940-2005 .... **CLC 26**
See also CA 122; 152; 246
Pryor, Richard Franklin Lenox Thomas
See Pryor, Richard
Przybyszewski, Stanislaw
1868-1927 .... **TCLC 36**
See also CA 160; DLB 66; EWL 3
Pseudo-Dionysius the Areopagite
fl. c. 5th cent. .... **CMLC 89**
See also DLB 115
Pteleon
See Grieve, C. M.
Puckett, Lute
See Masters, Edgar Lee
Puff, Peter, Secundus
See Mangan, James Clarence
Puig, Manuel 1932-1990 ... **CLC 3, 5, 10, 28, 65, 133; HLC 2; TCLC 227**
See also BPFB 3; CA 45-48; CANR 2, 32, 63; CDWLB 3; DA3; DAM MULT; DLB 113; DNFS 1; EWL 3; GLL 1; HW 1, 2; LAW; MTCW 1, 2; MTFW 2005; RGWL 2, 3; TWA; WLIT 1
Pulci, Luigi 1432-1484 .... **LC 246**
Pulitzer, Joseph 1847-1911 .... **TCLC 76**
See also CA 114; DLB 23
Pullman, Philip 1946- .... **CLC 245**
See also AAYA 15, 41; BRWS 13; BYA 8, 13; CA 127; CANR 50, 77, 105, 134, 190; CLR 20, 62, 84, 202; JRDA; MAICYA 1, 2; MAICYAS 1; MTFW 2005; SAAS 17; SATA 65, 103, 150, 198; SUFW 2; WYAS 1; YAW
Purchas, Samuel 1577(?)-1626 .... **LC 70**
See also DLB 151
Purdy, A(lfred) W(ellington)
1918-2000 ... **CLC 3, 6, 14, 50; PC 171**
See also CA 81-84; 189; CAAS 17; CANR 42, 66; CP 1, 2, 3, 4, 5, 6, 7; DAC; DAM MST, POET; DLB 88; PFS 5; RGEL 2
Purdy, James 1914-2009 .... **CLC 2, 4, 10, 28, 52, 286**
See also AMWS 7; CA 33-36R; 284; CAAS 1; CANR 19, 51, 132; CN 1, 2, 3, 4, 5, 6, 7; DLB 2, 218; EWL 3; INT CANR-19; MAL 5; MTCW 1; RGAL 4
Purdy, James Amos
See Purdy, James
Purdy, James Otis
See Purdy, James
Pure, Simon
See Swinnerton, Frank Arthur
Pushkin, Aleksandr Sergeevich
See Pushkin, Alexander
Pushkin, Alexander 1799-1837 ...... **NCLC 3, 27, 83, 278; PC 10; SSC 27, 55, 99, 189; WLC 5**
See also DA; DA3; DAB; DAC; DAM DRAM, MST, POET; DLB 205; EW 5; EXPS; PFS 28, 34; RGSF 2; RGWL 2, 3; SATA 61; SSFS 9; TWA
Pushkin, Alexander Sergeyevich
See Pushkin, Alexander
P'u Sung-ling 1640-1715 .... **LC 49; SSC 31**
Putnam, Arthur Lee
See Alger, Horatio, Jr.
Puttenham, George 1529(?)-1590 .... **LC 116**
See also DLB 281
Puzo, Mario 1920-1999 .... **CLC 1, 2, 6, 36, 107**
See also BPFB 3; CA 65-68; 185; CANR 4, 42, 65, 99, 131; CN 1, 2, 3, 4, 5, 6; CPW; DA3; DAM NOV, POP; DLB 6; MTCW 1, 2; MTFW 2005; NFS 16; RGAL 4
Pygge, Edward
See Barnes, Julian
Pyle, Ernest Taylor
See Pyle, Ernie
Pyle, Ernie
1900-1945 .... **TCLC 75**
See also CA 115; 160; DLB 29, 364; MTCW 2
Pyle, Howard 1853-1911 .... **TCLC 81**
See also AAYA 57; BYA 2, 4; CA 109; 137; CLR 22, 117; DLB 42, 188; DLBD 13; LAIT 1; MAICYA 1, 2; SATA 16, 100; WCH; YAW
Pym, Barbara (Mary Crampton)
1913-1980 .... **CLC 13, 19, 37, 111; TCLC 279**
See also BPFB 3; BRWS 2; CA 13-14; 97-100; CANR 13, 34; CAP 1; DLB 14, 207; DLBY 1987; EWL 3; MTCW 1, 2; MTFW 2005; RGEL 2; TEA
Pynchon, Thomas 1937- ...... **CLC 2, 3, 6, 9, 11, 18, 33, 62, 72, 123, 192, 213; SSC 14, 84; WLC 5**
See also AMWS 2; BEST 90:2; BPFB 3; CA 17-20R; CANR 22, 46, 73, 142, 198; CN 1, 2, 3, 4, 5, 6, 7; CPW 1; DA; DA3; DAB; DAC; DAM MST, NOV, POP; DLB 2, 173; EWL 3; MAL 5; MTCW 1, 2; MTFW 2005; NFS 23, 36; RGAL 4; SFW 4; TCLE 1:2; TUS
Pynchon, Thomas Ruggels, Jr.
See Pynchon, Thomas
Pynchon, Thomas Ruggles
See Pynchon, Thomas
Pythagoras c. 582B.C.-c. 507B.C. ... **CMLC 22**
See also DLB 176
Q
See Quiller-Couch, Sir Arthur (Thomas)
Qian, Chongzhu
See Qian, Zhongshu
Qian, Sima
See Sima Qian
Qian, Zhongshu 1910-1998 .... **CLC 22**
See also CA 130; CANR 73, 216; CWW 2; DLB 328; MTCW 1, 2
Qroll
See Dagerman, Stig (Halvard)
Quarles, Francis 1592-1644 .... **LC 117**
See also DLB 126; RGEL 2
Quarrington, Paul 1953-2010 .... **CLC 65**
See also CA 129; CANR 62, 95, 228
Quarrington, Paul Lewis
See Quarrington, Paul
Quasimodo, Salvatore
1901-1968 .... **CLC 10; PC 47**
See also CA 13-16; 25-28R; CAP 1; DLB 114, 332; EW 12; EWL 3; MTCW 1; RGWL 2, 3
Quatermass, Martin
See Carpenter, John
Quay, Stephen 1947- .... **CLC 95**
See also CA 189
Quay, Timothy 1947- .... **CLC 95**
See also CA 189
Queen, Ellery
See Dannay, Frederic; Hoch, Edward D.; Lee, Manfred B.; Marlowe, Stephen; Sturgeon, Theodore (Hamilton); Vance, Jack
Queneau, Raymond 1903-1976 .... **CLC 2, 5, 10, 42; TCLC 233**
See also CA 77-80; 69-72; CANR 32; DLB 72, 258; EW 12; EWL 3; GFL 1789 to the Present; MTCW 1, 2; RGWL 2, 3
Quevedo, Francisco de 1580-1645 ... **LC 23, 160**
Quiller-Couch, Sir Arthur (Thomas)
1863-1944 .... **TCLC 53**
See also CA 118; 166; DLB 135, 153, 190; HGG; RGEL 2; SUFW 1
Quin, Ann 1936-1973 .... **CLC 6**
See also CA 9-12R; 45-48; CANR 148; CN 1; DLB 14, 231
Quin, Ann Marie
See Quin, Ann
Quinault, Philippe 1635-1688 .... **LC 229**
See also DLB 268; IDTP
Quincey, Thomas de
See De Quincey, Thomas
Quindlen, Anna 1953- .... **CLC 191**
See also AAYA 35; AMWS 17; CA 138; CANR 73, 126; DA3; DLB 292; MTCW 2; MTFW 2005
Quinn, Martin
See Smith, Martin Cruz
Quinn, Peter 1947- .... **CLC 91**
See also CA 197; CANR 147, 239
Quinn, Peter A.
See Quinn, Peter
Quinn, Simon
See Smith, Martin Cruz
Quintana, Leroy V. 1944- .... **HLC 2; PC 36**
See also CA 131; CANR 65, 139; DAM MULT; DLB 82; HW 1, 2
Quintasket, Christal
See Mourning Dove
Quintasket, Christine
See Mourning Dove
Quintilian c. 40-c. 100 .... **CMLC 77**
See also AW 2; DLB 211; RGWL 2, 3
Quiroga, Horacio (Sylvestre)
1878-1937 .... **HLC 2; SSC 89; TCLC 20**
See also CA 117; 131; DAM MULT; EWL 3; HW 1; LAW; MTCW 1; RGSF 2; SSFS 37; WLIT 1
Quoirez, Francoise
See Sagan, Francoise
Raabe, Wilhelm (Karl)
1831-1910 .... **TCLC 45**
See also CA 167; DLB 129
Rabe, David 1940- .... **CLC 4, 8, 33, 200; DC 16**
See also CA 85-88; CABS 3; CAD; CANR 59, 129, 218; CD 5, 6; DAM DRAM; DFS 3, 8, 13; DLB 7, 228; EWL 3; MAL 5
Rabe, David William
See Rabe, David
Rabelais, Francois 1494-1553 .... **LC 5, 60, 186; WLC 5**
See also DA; DAB; DAC; DAM MST; DLB 327; EW 2; GFL Beginnings to 1789; LMFS 1; RGWL 2, 3; TWA
Rabi`a al-`Adawiyya
c. 717-c. 801 .... **CMLC 83, 145**
See also DLB 311
Rabinovitch, Sholem
See Aleichem, Sholom
Rabinovitsh, Sholem Yankev
See Aleichem, Sholom
Rabinowitz, Sholem Yakov
See Rabinovitch, Sholem
Rabinyan, Dorit 1972- .... **CLC 119**
See also CA 170; CANR 147

Rachilde
See Vallette, Marguerite Eymery; Vallette, Marguerite Eymery
Racine, Jean 1639-1699 .... **DC 32; LC 28, 113**
See also DA3; DAB; DAM MST; DFS 28; DLB 268; EW 3; GFL Beginnings to 1789; LMFS 1; RGWL 2, 3; TWA
Radcliffe, Ann 1764-1823 .... **NCLC 6, 55, 106, 223**
See also BRWR 3; DLB 39, 178; GL 3; HGG; LMFS 1; RGEL 2; SUFW; WLIT 3
Radclyffe-Hall, Marguerite
See Hall, Radclyffe
Radiguet, Raymond 1903-1923 ..... **TCLC 29**
See also CA 162; DLB 65; EWL 3; GFL 1789 to the Present; RGWL 2, 3
Radishchev, Aleksandr Nikolaevich 1749-1802 .... **NCLC 190**
See also DLB 150
Radishchev, Alexander
See Radishchev, Aleksandr Nikolaevich
Radnoti, Miklos 1909-1944 .... **TCLC 16**
See also CA 118; 212; CDWLB 4; DLB 215; EWL 3; RGHL; RGWL 2, 3
Rado, James 1939- .... **CLC 17**
See also CA 105
Radvanyi, Netty 1900-1983 .... **CLC 7**
See also CA 85-88; 110; CANR 82; CDWLB 2; DLB 69; EWL 3
Rae, Ben
See Griffiths, Trevor
Raeburn, John (Hay) 1941- .... **CLC 34**
See also CA 57-60
Ragni, Gerome 1942-1991 .... **CLC 17**
See also CA 105; 134
Rahv, Philip
See Greenberg, Ivan
Rai, Navab
See Srivastava, Dhanpat Rai
Raimund, Ferdinand Jakob 1790-1836 .... **NCLC 69**
See also DLB 90
Raine, Craig 1944- .... **CLC 32, 103**
See also BRWS 13; CA 108; CANR 29, 51, 103, 171; CP 3, 4, 5, 6, 7; DLB 40; PFS 7
Raine, Craig Anthony
See Raine, Craig
Raine, Kathleen (Jessie) 1908-2003 .... **CLC 7, 45**
See also CA 85-88; 218; CANR 46, 109; CP 1, 2, 3, 4, 5, 6, 7; DLB 20; EWL 3; MTCW 1; RGEL 2
Rainis, Janis 1865-1929 .... **TCLC 29**
See also CA 170; CDWLB 4; DLB 220; EWL 3
Rakosi, Carl
See Rawley, Callman
Ralegh, Sir Walter
See Raleigh, Sir Walter
Raleigh, Richard
See Lovecraft, H. P.
Raleigh, Sir Walter 1554(?)-1618 ..... **LC 31, 39; PC 31**
See also BRW 1; CDBLB Before 1660; DLB 172; EXPP; PFS 14; RGEL 2; TEA; WP
Rallentando, H. P.
See Sayers, Dorothy L(eigh)
Ramal, Walter
See de la Mare, Walter (John)
Ramana Maharshi 1879-1950 .... **TCLC 84**
Ramon, Juan
See Jimenez, Juan Ramon
Ramoacn y Cajal, Santiago 1852-1934 .... **TCLC 93**
Ramos, Graciliano 1892-1953 .... **TCLC 32**
See also CA 167; DLB 307; EWL 3; HW 2; LAW; WLIT 1
Rampersad, Arnold 1941- .... **CLC 44**
See also BW 2, 3; CA 127; 133; CANR 81; DLB 111; INT CA-133
Rampling, Anne
See Rice, Anne
Ramsay, Allan 1686(?)-1758 .... **LC 29**
See also DLB 95; RGEL 2
Ramsay, Jay
See Campbell, Ramsey
Ramus, Peter
See La Ramee, Pierre de
Ramus, Petrus
See La Ramee, Pierre de
Ramuz, Charles-Ferdinand 1878-1947 .... **TCLC 33**
See also CA 165; EWL 3
Rand, Ayn 1905-1982 .... **CLC 3, 30, 44, 79; SSC 116; TCLC 261; WLC 5**
See also AAYA 10; AMWS 4; BPFB 3; BYA 12; CA 13-16R; 105; CANR 27, 73; CDALBS; CN 1, 2, 3; CPW; DA; DA3; DAC; DAM MST, NOV, POP; DLB 227, 279; MTCW 1, 2; MTFW 2005; NFS 10, 16, 29; RGAL 4; SFW 4; TUS; YAW
Randall, Dudley 1914-2000 .... **BLC 1:3; CLC 1, 135; PC 86**
See also BW 1, 3; CA 25-28R; 189; CANR 23, 82; CP 1, 2, 3, 4, 5; DAM MULT; DLB 41; PFS 5
Randall, Dudley Felker
See Randall, Dudley
Randall, Robert
See Silverberg, Robert
Randolph, Thomas 1605-1635 .... **LC 195**
See also DLB 58, 126; RGEL 2
Ranger, Ken
See Creasey, John
Rank, Otto 1884-1939 .... **TCLC 115**
Rankin, Ian 1960- .... **CLC 257**
See also BRWS 10; CA 148; CANR 81, 137, 171, 210; DLB 267; MTFW 2005
Rankin, Ian James
See Rankin, Ian
Ransom, John Crowe 1888-1974 ..... **CLC 2, 4, 5, 11, 24; PC 61**
See also AMW; CA 5-8R; 49-52; CANR 6, 34; CDALBS; CP 1, 2; DA3; DAM POET; DLB 45, 63; EWL 3; EXPP; MAL 5; MTCW 1, 2; MTFW 2005; RGAL 4; TUS
Rao, Raja 1908-2006 .... **CLC 25, 56, 255; SSC 99**
See also CA 73-76; 252; CANR 51; CN 1, 2, 3, 4, 5, 6; DAM NOV; DLB 323; EWL 3; MTCW 1, 2; MTFW 2005; RGEL 2; RGSF 2
Raphael, Frederic 1931- .... **CLC 2, 14**
See also CA 1-4R; CANR 1, 86, 223; CN 1, 2, 3, 4, 5, 6, 7; DLB 14, 319; TCLE 1:2
Raphael, Frederic Michael
See Raphael, Frederic
Raphael, Lev 1954- .... **CLC 232**
See also CA 134; CANR 72, 145, 217; GLL 1
Rastell, John c. 1475(?)-1536(?) .... **LC 183**
See also DLB 136, 170; RGEL 2
Ratcliffe, James P.
See Mencken, H. L.
Rathbone, Julian 1935-2008 .... **CLC 41**
See also CA 101; 269; CANR 34, 73, 152, 221
Rathbone, Julian Christopher
See Rathbone, Julian
Rattigan, Terence 1911-1977 .... **CLC 7; DC 18**
See also BRWS 7; CA 85-88; 73-76; CBD; CDBLB 1945-1960; DAM DRAM; DFS 8; DLB 13; IDFW 3, 4; MTCW 1, 2; MTFW 2005; RGEL 2
Rattigan, Terence Mervyn
See Rattigan, Terence
Ratushinskaya, Irina 1954- .... **CLC 54**
See also CA 129; CANR 68; CWW 2
Raven, Simon (Arthur Noel) 1927-2001 .... **CLC 14**
See also CA 81-84; 197; CANR 86; CN 1, 2, 3, 4, 5, 6; DLB 271
Ravenna, Michael
See Welty, Eudora
Rawley, Callman 1903-2004 .... **CLC 47; PC 126**
See also CA 21-24R; 228; CAAS 5; CANR 12, 32, 91; CP 1, 2, 3, 4, 5, 6, 7; DLB 193
Rawlings, Marjorie Kinnan 1896-1953 .... **TCLC 4, 248**
See also AAYA 20; AMWS 10; ANW; BPFB 3; BYA 3; CA 104; 137; CANR 74; CLR 63; DLB 9, 22, 102; DLBD 17; JRDA; MAICYA 1, 2; MAL 5; MTCW 2; MTFW 2005; RGAL 4; SATA 100; WCH; YABC 1; YAW
Raworth, Thomas Moore 1938- .... **PC 107**
See also CA 29-32R; CAAS 11; CANR 46; CP 1, 2, 3, 4, 5, 7; DLB 40
Raworth, Tom
See Raworth, Thomas Moore
Ray, Satyajit 1921-1992 .... **CLC 16, 76**
See also CA 114; 137; DAM MULT
Read, Herbert Edward 1893-1968 ... **CLC 4**
See also BRW 6; CA 85-88; 25-28R; DLB 20, 149; EWL 3; PAB; RGEL 2
Read, Piers Paul 1941- .... **CLC 4, 10, 25**
See also CA 21-24R; CANR 38, 86, 150; CN 2, 3, 4, 5, 6, 7; DLB 14; SATA 21
Reade, Charles 1814-1884 ... **NCLC 2, 74, 275**
See also DLB 21; RGEL 2
Reade, Hamish
See Gray, Simon
Reading, Peter 1946-2011 .... **CLC 47**
See also BRWS 8; CA 103; CANR 46, 96; CP 5, 6, 7; DLB 40
Reaney, James 1926-2008 .... **CLC 13**
See also CA 41-44R; CAAS 15; CANR 42; CD 5, 6; CP 1, 2, 3, 4, 5, 6, 7; DAC; DAM MST; DLB 68; RGEL 2; SATA 43
Reaney, James Crerar
See Reaney, James
Rebreanu, Liviu 1885-1944 .... **TCLC 28**
See also CA 165; DLB 220; EWL 3
Rechy, John 1934- .... **CLC 1, 7, 14, 18, 107; HLC 2**
See also CA 5-8R, 195; CAAE 195; CAAS 4; CANR 6, 32, 64, 152, 188; CN 1, 2, 3, 4, 5, 6, 7; DAM MULT; DLB 122, 278; DLBY 1982; HW 1, 2; INT CANR-6; LLW; MAL 5; RGAL 4
Rechy, John Francisco
See Rechy, John
Redcam, Tom 1870-1933 .... **TCLC 25**
Reddin, Keith 1956- .... **CLC 67**
See also CAD; CD 6
Redgrove, Peter (William) 1932-2003 .... **CLC 6, 41**
See also BRWS 6; CA 1-4R; 217; CANR 3, 39, 77; CP 1, 2, 3, 4, 5, 6, 7; DLB 40; TCLE 1:2
Redmon, Anne
See Nightingale, Anne Redmon
Reed, Eliot
See Ambler, Eric
Reed, Ishmael 1938- .... **BLC 1:3; CLC 2, 3, 5, 6, 13, 32, 60, 174; PC 68**
See also AFAW 1, 2; AMWS 10; BPFB 3; BW 2, 3; CA 21-24R; CANR 25, 48, 74, 128, 195; CN 1, 2, 3, 4, 5, 6, 7; CP 1, 2, 3, 4, 5, 6, 7; CSW; DA3; DAM MULT; DLB 2, 5, 33, 169, 227; DLBD 8; EWL 3; LMFS 2; MAL 5; MSW; MTCW 1, 2; MTFW 2005; PFS 6; RGAL 4; TCWW 2

Reed, Ishmael Scott
See Reed, Ishmael
Reed, John (Silas) 1887-1920 .... **TCLC 9**
See also CA 106; 195; MAL 5; TUS
Reed, Lou 1942- .... **CLC 21**
See also CA 117
Reese, Lizette Woodworth
1856-1935 .... **PC 29; TCLC 181**
See also CA 180; DLB 54
Reeve, Clara 1729-1807 .... **NCLC 19**
See also DLB 39; RGEL 2
Reich, Wilhelm 1897-1957 .... **TCLC 57**
See also CA 199
Reid, Christopher 1949- .... **CLC 33**
See also CA 140; CANR 89, 241; CP 4, 5, 6, 7; DLB 40; EWL 3
Reid, Christopher John
See Reid, Christopher
Reid, Desmond
See Moorcock, Michael
Reid, Thomas 1710-1796 .... **LC 201**
See also DLB 31, 252
Reid Banks, Lynne 1929- .... **CLC 23**
See also AAYA 6; BYA 7; CA 1-4R; CANR 6, 22, 38, 87; CLR 24, 86; CN 4, 5, 6; JRDA; MAICYA 1, 2; SATA 22, 75, 111, 165; YAW
Reilly, William K.
See Creasey, John
Reiner, Max
See Caldwell, (Janet Miriam) Taylor (Holland)
Reis, Ricardo
See Pessoa, Fernando
Reizenstein, Elmer Leopold
See Rice, Elmer (Leopold)
Remark, Erich Paul
See Remarque, Erich Maria
Remarque, Erich Maria
1898-1970 .... **CLC 21**
See also AAYA 27; BPFB 3; CA 77-80; 29-32R; CDWLB 2; CLR 159; DA; DA3; DAB; DAC; DAM MST, NOV; DLB 56; EWL 3; EXPN; LAIT 3; MTCW 1, 2; MTFW 2005; NFS 4, 36; RGHL; RGWL 2, 3
Remington, Frederic S(ackrider)
1861-1909 .... **TCLC 89**
See also CA 108; 169; DLB 12, 186, 188; SATA 41; TCWW 2
Remizov, A.
See Remizov, Aleksei (Mikhailovich)
Remizov, A. M.
See Remizov, Aleksei (Mikhailovich)
Remizov, Aleksei (Mikhailovich)
1877-1957 .... **TCLC 27**
See also CA 125; 133; DLB 295; EWL 3
Remizov, Alexey Mikhaylovich
See Remizov, Aleksei (Mikhailovich)
Renan, Joseph Ernest
1823-1892 .... **NCLC 26, 145**
See also GFL 1789 to the Present
Renard, Jules(-Pierre) 1864-1910 ... **TCLC 17**
See also CA 117; 202; GFL 1789 to the Present
Renart, Jean fl. 13th cent. .... **CMLC 83**
Renault, Mary 1905-1983 ..... **CLC 3, 11, 17**
See also BPFB 3; BYA 2; CA 81-84; 111; CANR 74; CN 1, 2, 3; DA3; DLBY 1983; EWL 3; GLL 1; LAIT 1; MTCW 2; MTFW 2005; RGEL 2; RHW; SATA 23; SATA-Obit 36; TEA
Rendell, Ruth
See Rendell, Ruth
Rendell, Ruth
1930- .... **CLC 28, 48, 50, 295**
See also BEST 90:4; BPFB 3; BRWS 9; CA 109; CANR 32, 52, 74, 127, 162, 190, 227; CN 5, 6, 7; CPW; DAM POP; DLB 87, 276; INT CANR-32; MSW; MTCW 1, 2; MTFW 2005
Rendell, Ruth Barbara
See Rendell, Ruth
Renoir, Jean 1894-1979 .... **CLC 20**
See also CA 129; 85-88
Rensie, Willis
See Eisner, Will
Resnais, Alain 1922- .... **CLC 16**
Restif de la Bretonne, Nicolas-Anne-Edme
1734-1806 .... **NCLC 257**
See also DLB 314; GFL Beginnings to 1789
Reuental, Niedhart von
See Neidhart von Ruental
Rev. D Blair
See Fenwick, Eliza
Revard, Carter 1931- .... **NNAL**
See also CA 144; CANR 81, 153; PFS 5
Reverdy, Pierre 1889-1960 .... **CLC 53**
See also CA 97-100; 89-92; DLB 258; EWL 3; GFL 1789 to the Present
Reverend Mandju
See Su, Chien
Rexroth, Kenneth 1905-1982 .... **CLC 1, 2, 6, 11, 22, 49, 112; PC 20, 95**
See also BG 1:3; CA 5-8R; 107; CANR 14, 34, 63; CDALB 1941-1968; CP 1, 2, 3; DAM POET; DLB 16, 48, 165, 212; DLBY 1982; EWL 3; INT CANR-14; MAL 5; MTCW 1, 2; MTFW 2005; RGAL 4
Reyes, Alfonso 1889-1959 .... **HLCS 2; TCLC 33**
See also CA 131; EWL 3; HW 1; LAW
Reyes y Basoalto, Ricardo Eliecer Neftali
See Neruda, Pablo
Reymont, Wladyslaw (Stanislaw)
1868(?)-1925 .... **TCLC 5**
See also CA 104; DLB 332; EWL 3
Reynolds, John Hamilton
1794-1852 .... **NCLC 146**
See also DLB 96
Reynolds, Jonathan 1942- .... **CLC 6, 38**
See also CA 65-68; CANR 28, 176
Reynolds, Joshua 1723-1792 .... **LC 15**
See also DLB 104
Reynolds, Michael S(hane)
1937-2000 .... **CLC 44**
See also CA 65-68; 189; CANR 9, 89, 97
Reza, Yasmina 1959- .... **CLC 299; DC 34**
See also AAYA 69; CA 171; CANR 145; DFS 19; DLB 321
Reznikoff, Charles 1894-1976 .... **CLC 9; PC 124**
See also AMWS 14; CA 33-36; 61-64; CAP 2; CP 1, 2; DLB 28, 45; RGHL; WP
Rezzori, Gregor von
See Rezzori d'Arezzo, Gregor von
Rezzori d'Arezzo, Gregor von
1914-1998 .... **CLC 25**
See also CA 122; 136; 167
Rhine, Richard
See Silverstein, Alvin; Silverstein, Virginia B.
Rhodes, Eugene Manlove
1869-1934 .... **TCLC 53**
See also CA 198; DLB 256; TCWW 1, 2
R'hoone, Lord
See Balzac, Honore de
Rhys, Jean 1890-1979 .... **CLC 2, 4, 6, 14, 19, 51, 124; SSC 21, 76**
See also BRWS 2; CA 25-28R; 85-88; CANR 35, 62; CDBLB 1945-1960; CDWLB 3; CN 1, 2; DA3; DAM NOV; DLB 36, 117, 162; DNFS 2; EWL 3; LATS 1:1; MTCW 1, 2; MTFW 2005; NFS 19; RGEL 2; RGSF 2; RHW; TEA; WWE 1
Ribeiro, Darcy 1922-1997 .... **CLC 34**
See also CA 33-36R; 156; EWL 3
Ribeiro, Joao Ubaldo (Osorio Pimentel)
1941- .... **CLC 10, 67**
See also CA 81-84; CWW 2; EWL 3
Ribeyro, Julio Ramón 1929-1994 ... **SSC 204**
See also CA 180, 181; DLB 145; EWL 3
Ribman, Ronald (Burt) 1932- .... **CLC 7**
See also CA 21-24R; CAD; CANR 46, 80; CD 5, 6
Ricci, Nino 1959- .... **CLC 70**
See also CA 137; CANR 130; CCA 1
Ricci, Nino Pio
See Ricci, Nino
Rice, Anne 1941- .... **CLC 41, 128, 349**
See also AAYA 9, 53; AMWS 7; BEST 89:2; BPFB 3; CA 65-68; CANR 12, 36, 53, 74, 100, 133, 190; CN 6, 7; CPW; CSW; DA3; DAM POP; DLB 292; GL 3; GLL 2; HGG; MTCW 2; MTFW 2005; SUFW 2; YAW
Rice, Elmer (Leopold) 1892-1967 .... **CLC 7, 49; DC 44; TCLC 221**
See also CA 21-22; 25-28R; CAP 2; DAM DRAM; DFS 12; DLB 4, 7; EWL 3; IDTP; MAL 5; MTCW 1, 2; RGAL 4
Rice, Tim 1944- .... **CLC 21**
See also CA 103; CANR 46; DFS 7
Rice, Timothy Miles Bindon
See Rice, Tim
Rich, Adrienne 1929-2012 .... **CLC 3, 6, 7, 11, 18, 36, 73, 76, 125, 328, 354; PC 5, 129**
See also AAYA 69; AMWR 2; AMWS 1; CA 9-12R; CANR 20, 53, 74, 128, 199, 233; CDALBS; CP 1, 2, 3, 4, 5, 6, 7; CSW; CWP; DA3; DAM POET; DLB 5, 67; EWL 3; EXPP; FL 1:6; FW; MAL 5; MBL; MTCW 1, 2; MTFW 2005; PAB; PFS 15, 29, 39; RGAL 4; RGHL; WP
Rich, Adrienne Cecile
See Rich, Adrienne
Rich, Barbara
See Graves, Robert
Rich, Robert
See Trumbo, Dalton
Richard, Keith
See Richards, Keith
Richards, David Adams 1950- .... **CLC 59**
See also CA 93-96; CANR 60, 110, 156; CN 7; DAC; DLB 53; TCLE 1:2
Richards, I(vor) A(rmstrong)
1893-1979 .... **CLC 14, 24**
See also BRWS 2; CA 41-44R; 89-92; CANR 34, 74; CP 1, 2; DLB 27; EWL 3; MTCW 2; RGEL 2
Richards, Keith 1943- .... **CLC 17**
See also CA 107; CANR 77
Richards, Scott
See Card, Orson Scott
Richardson, Anne
See Roiphe, Anne
Richardson, Dorothy Miller
1873-1957 .... **TCLC 3, 203**
See also BRWS 13; CA 104; 192; DLB 36; EWL 3; FW; RGEL 2
Richardson, Ethel Florence Lindesay
1870-1946 .... **TCLC 4**
See also CA 105; 190; DLB 197, 230; EWL 3; RGEL 2; RGSF 2; RHW
Richardson, Henrietta
See Richardson, Ethel Florence Lindesay
Richardson, Henry Handel
See Richardson, Ethel Florence Lindesay
Richardson, John 1796-1852 .... **NCLC 55**
See also CCA 1; DAC; DLB 99
Richardson, Samuel 1689-1761 ..... **LC 1, 44, 138, 204; WLC 5**
See also BRW 3; CDBLB 1660-1789; DA; DAB; DAC; DAM MST, NOV; DLB 154; RGEL 2; TEA; WLIT 3
Richardson, Willis 1889-1977 .... **HR 1:3**
See also BW 1; CA 124; DLB 51; SATA 60

Richardson Robertson, Ethel Florence Lindesay
See Richardson, Ethel Florence Lindesay
Richler, Mordecai 1931-2001 .... **CLC 3, 5, 9, 13, 18, 46, 70, 185, 271**
See also AITN 1; CA 65-68; 201; CANR 31, 62, 111; CCA 1; CLR 17; CN 1, 2, 3, 4, 5, 7; CWRI 5; DAC; DAM MST, NOV; DLB 53; EWL 3; MAICYA 1, 2; MTCW 1, 2; MTFW 2005; RGEL 2; RGHL; SATA 44, 98; SATA-Brief 27; TWA
Richter, Conrad (Michael) 1890-1968 .... **CLC 30**
See also AAYA 21; AMWS 18; BYA 2; CA 5-8R; 25-28R; CANR 23; DLB 9, 212; LAIT 1; MAL 5; MTCW 1, 2; MTFW 2005; NFS 43; RGAL 4; SATA 3; TCWW 1, 2; TUS; YAW
Ricostranza, Tom
See Ellis, Trey
Riddell, Charlotte 1832-1906 .... **TCLC 40**
See also CA 165; DLB 156; HGG; SUFW
Riddell, Mrs. J. H.
See Riddell, Charlotte
Ridge, John Rollin 1827-1867 .... **NCLC 82; NNAL**
See also CA 144; DAM MULT; DLB 175
Ridgeway, Jason
See Marlowe, Stephen
Ridgway, Keith 1965- .... **CLC 119**
See also CA 172; CANR 144
Riding, Laura
See Jackson, Laura
Riefenstahl, Berta Helene Amalia
See Riefenstahl, Leni
Riefenstahl, Leni 1902-2003 .... **CLC 16, 190**
See also CA 108; 220
Riefenstahl, Leni
See Riefenstahl, Berta Helene Amalia
Riera, Carme 1948- .... **CLC 368; SSC 177**
See also CA 254, DLB 322, EWL 3
Riffaterre, Michael 1924-2006
See also CA 183, 250; DLB 67
Riffe, Ernest
See Bergman, Ingmar
Riffe, Ernest Ingmar
See Bergman, Ingmar
Riggs, (Rolla) Lynn 1899-1954 .... **NNAL; TCLC 56**
See also CA 144; DAM MULT; DLB 175
Riis, Jacob A(ugust) 1849-1914 .... **TCLC 80**
See also CA 113; 168; DLB 23
Rikki
See Ducornet, Erica
Riley, James Whitcomb 1849-1916 ... **PC 48; TCLC 51**
See also CA 118; 137; DAM POET; MAICYA 1, 2; RGAL 4; SATA 17
Riley, Tex
See Creasey, John
Rilke, Rainer Maria 1875-1926 .. **PC 2, 140; TCLC 1, 6, 19, 195, 310**
See also CA 104; 132; CANR 62, 99; CDWLB 2; DA3; DAM POET; DLB 81; EW 9; EWL 3; MTCW 1, 2; MTFW 2005; PFS 19, 27; RGWL 2, 3; TWA; WP
Rimbaud, Arthur 1854-1891 ... **NCLC 4, 35, 82, 227; PC 3, 57; WLC 5**
See also DA; DA3; DAB; DAC; DAM MST, POET; DLB 217; EW 7; GFL 1789 to the Present; LMFS 2; PFS 28; RGWL 2, 3; TWA; WP
Rimbaud, Jean Nicholas Arthur
See Rimbaud, Arthur
Rinehart, Mary Roberts 1876-1958 .. **TCLC 52**
See also BPFB 3; CA 108; 166; RGAL 4; RHW
Ringmaster, The
See Mencken, H. L.
Ringwood, Gwen(dolyn Margaret) Pharis 1910-1984 .... **CLC 48**
See also CA 148; 112; DLB 88
Rio, Michel 1945(?)- .... **CLC 43**
See also CA 201
Ritchie, Anne Thackeray 1837-1919 .... **TCLC 297**
See also CA 180; DLB 18
Ritsos, Giannes
See Ritsos, Yannis
Ritsos, Yannis 1909-1990 ...... **CLC 6, 13, 31**
See also CA 77-80; 133; CANR 39, 61; EW 12; EWL 3; MTCW 1; RGWL 2, 3
Ritter, Erika 1948- .... **CLC 52**
See also CA 318; CD 5, 6; CWD; DLB 362
Rivera, Jose Eustasio 1889-1928 ... **TCLC 35**
See also CA 162; EWL 3; HW 1, 2; LAW
Rivera, Tomas 1935-1984 .... **HLCS 2; SSC 160**
See also CA 49-52; CANR 32; DLB 82; HW 1; LLW; RGAL 4; SSFS 15; TCWW 2; WLIT 1
Rivers, Conrad Kent 1933-1968 .... **CLC 1**
See also BW 1; CA 85-88; DLB 41
Rivers, Elfrida
See Bradley, Marion Zimmer
Riverside, John
See Heinlein, Robert A.
Rizal, Jose 1861-1896 .... **NCLC 27**
See also DLB 348
Rolaag, Ole Edvart
See Rolvaag, O.E.
Rolvaag, O.E.
See Rolvaag, O.E.
Rolvaag, O.E. 1876-1931 ...... **TCLC 17, 207**
See also AAYA 75; CA 117; 171; DLB 9, 212; MAL 5; NFS 5; RGAL 4; TCWW 1, 2
Roa Bastos, Augusto 1917-2005 .... **CLC 45, 316, 355; HLC 2; SSC 174**
See also CA 131; 238; CWW 2; DAM MULT; DLB 113; EWL 3; HW 1; LAW; RGSF 2; WLIT 1
Roa Bastos, Augusto Jose Antonio
See Roa Bastos, Augusto
Robbe-Grillet, Alain 1922-2008 .... **CLC 1, 2, 4, 6, 8, 10, 14, 43, 128, 287**
See also BPFB 3; CA 9-12R; 269; CANR 33, 65, 115; CWW 2; DLB 83; EW 13; EWL 3; GFL 1789 to the Present; IDFW 3, 4; MTCW 1, 2; MTFW 2005; RGWL 2, 3; SSFS 15
Robbins, Harold 1916-1997 .... **CLC 5**
See also BPFB 3; CA 73-76; 162; CANR 26, 54, 112, 156; DA3; DAM NOV; MTCW 1, 2
Robbins, Thomas Eugene
See Robbins, Tom
Robbins, Tom 1936- ...... **CLC 9, 32, 64, 362**
See also AAYA 32; AMWS 10; BEST 90:3; BPFB 3; CA 81-84; CANR 29, 59, 95, 139; CN 3, 4, 5, 6, 7; CPW; CSW; DA3; DAM NOV, POP; DLBY 1980; MTCW 1, 2; MTFW 2005
Robbins, Trina 1938- .... **CLC 21**
See also AAYA 61; CA 128; CANR 152
Robert de Boron fl. 12th cent. ..... **CMLC 94**
Roberts, Charles G(eorge) D(ouglas) 1860-1943 .... **SSC 91; TCLC 8**
See also CA 105; 188; CLR 33; CWRI 5; DLB 92; RGEL 2; RGSF 2; SATA 88; SATA-Brief 29
Roberts, Elizabeth Madox 1886-1941 .... **TCLC 68**
See also CA 111; 166; CLR 100; CWRI 5; DLB 9, 54, 102; RGAL 4; RHW; SATA 33; SATA-Brief 27; TCWW 2; WCH
Roberts, Kate 1891-1985 .... **CLC 15**
See also CA 107; 116; DLB 319
Roberts, Keith (John Kingston) 1935-2000 .... **CLC 14**
See also BRWS 10; CA 25-28R; CANR 46; DLB 261; SFW 4
Roberts, Kenneth (Lewis) 1885-1957 .... **TCLC 23**
See also CA 109; 199; DLB 9; MAL 5; RGAL 4; RHW
Roberts, Michele 1949- .... **CLC 48, 178**
See also BRWS 15; CA 115; CANR 58, 120, 164, 200; CN 6, 7; DLB 231; FW
Roberts, Michele Brigitte
See Roberts, Michele
Robertson, Ellis
See Ellison, Harlan; Silverberg, Robert
Robertson, Thomas William 1829-1871 .... **NCLC 35**
See also DAM DRAM; DLB 344; RGEL 2
Robertson, Tom
See Robertson, Thomas William
Robeson, Kenneth
See Dent, Lester
Robinson, Eden 1968- .... **CLC 301**
See also CA 171
Robinson, Edwin Arlington 1869-1935 .... **PC 1, 35; TCLC 5, 101**
See also AAYA 72; AMW; CA 104; 133; CDALB 1865-1917; DA; DAC; DAM MST, POET; DLB 54; EWL 3; EXPP; MAL 5; MTCW 1, 2; MTFW 2005; PAB; PFS 4, 35; RGAL 4; WP
Robinson, Henry Crabb 1775-1867 .... **NCLC 15, 239**
See also DLB 107
Robinson, Jill 1936- .... **CLC 10**
See also CA 102; CANR 120; INT CA-102
Robinson, Kim Stanley 1952- .... **CLC 34, 248**
See also AAYA 26; CA 126; CANR 113, 139, 173; CN 6, 7; MTFW 2005; SATA 109; SCFW 2; SFW 4
Robinson, Lloyd
See Silverberg, Robert
Robinson, Marilynne 1943- .... **CLC 25, 180, 276**
See also AAYA 69; AMWS 21; CA 116; CANR 80, 140, 192, 240; CN 4, 5, 6, 7; DLB 206, 350; MTFW 2005; NFS 24, 39
Robinson, Mary 1758-1800 .... **NCLC 142**
See also BRWS 13; DLB 158; FW
Robinson, Smokey 1940- .... **CLC 21**
See also CA 116
Robinson, William, Jr.
See Robinson, Smokey
Robison, Christopher
See Burroughs, Augusten
Robison, Mary 1949- .... **CLC 42, 98**
See also CA 113; 116; CANR 87, 206; CN 4, 5, 6, 7; DLB 130; INT CA-116; RGSF 2; SSFS 33
Roche, Regina Maria 1764-1845 ... **NCLC 308**
Rochester
See Wilmot, John
Rod, Edouard 1857-1910 .... **TCLC 52**
Rodo, Jose Enrique 1871(?)-1917 ... **HLCS 2**
See also CA 178; EWL 3; HW 2; LAW
Roddenberry, Eugene Wesley
See Roddenberry, Gene
Roddenberry, Gene 1921-1991 .... **CLC 17**
See also AAYA 5; CA 110; 135; CANR 37; SATA 45; SATA-Obit 69
Rodgers, Mary 1931- .... **CLC 12**
See also BYA 5; CA 49-52; CANR 8, 55, 90; CLR 20; CWRI 5; DFS 28; INT CANR-8; JRDA; MAICYA 1, 2; SATA 8, 130
Rodgers, W(illiam) R(obert) 1909-1969 .... **CLC 7**
See also CA 85-88; DLB 20; RGEL 2

Rodman, Eric
See Silverberg, Robert
Rodman, Howard 1920(?)-1985 ...... **CLC 65**
See also CA 118
Rodman, Maia
See Wojciechowska, Maia (Teresa)
Rodolph, Utto
See Ouologuem, Yambo
Rodoreda, Mercè 1908-1983 .... **SSC 221**
See also CA 243; DLB 322; EWL 3; RGSF 2
Rodriguez, Claudio 1934-1999 .... **CLC 10**
See also CA 188; DLB 134
Rodriguez, Richard 1944- .... **CLC 155, 321; HLC 2**
See also AMWS 14; CA 110; CANR 66, 116; DAM MULT; DLB 82, 256; HW 1, 2; LAIT 5; LLW; MTFW 2005; NCFS 3; WLIT 1
Roethke, Theodore 1908-1963 ..... **CLC 1, 3, 8, 11, 19, 46, 101; PC 15, 137**
See also AMW; CA 81-84; CABS 2; CDALB 1941-1968; DA3; DAM POET; DLB 5, 206; EWL 3; EXPP; MAL 5; MTCW 1, 2; PAB; PFS 3, 34, 40; RGAL 4; WP
Roethke, Theodore Huebner
See Roethke, Theodore
Rogers, Carl R(ansom)
1902-1987 .... **TCLC 125**
See also CA 1-4R; 121; CANR 1, 18; MTCW 1
Rogers, Samuel 1763-1855 .... **NCLC 69**
See also DLB 93; RGEL 2
Rogers, Thomas 1927-2007 .... **CLC 57**
See also CA 89-92; 259; CANR 163; INT CA-89-92
Rogers, Thomas Hunton
See Rogers, Thomas
Rogers, Will(iam Penn Adair)
1879-1935 .... **NNAL; TCLC 8, 71**
See also CA 105; 144; DA3; DAM MULT; DLB 11; MTCW 2
Rogin, Gilbert 1929- .... **CLC 18**
See also CA 65-68; CANR 15
Rohan, Koda
See Koda Shigeyuki
Rohlfs, Anna Katharine Green
See Green, Anna Katharine
Rohmer, Eric 1920-2010 .... **CLC 16**
See also CA 110
Rohmer, Sax
See Ward, Arthur Henry Sarsfield
Roiphe, Anne 1935- .... **CLC 3, 9**
See also CA 89-92; CANR 45, 73, 138, 170, 230; DLBY 1980; INT CA-89-92
Roiphe, Anne Richardson
See Roiphe, Anne
Rojas, Fernando de 1475-1541 ...... **HLCS 1, 2; LC 23, 169**
See also DLB 286; RGWL 2, 3
Rojas, Gonzalo 1917-2011 .... **HLCS 2**
See also CA 178; HW 2; LAWS 1
Rojas Zorrilla, Francisco de
1607-1648 .... **LC 204**
Roland (de la Platiere), Marie-Jeanne
1754-1793 .... **LC 98**
See also DLB 314
Rolfe, Frederick (William Serafino Austin Lewis Mary) 1860-1913 .... **TCLC 12**
See also CA 107; 210; DLB 34, 156; GLL 1; RGEL 2
Rolland, Romain 1866-1944 .... **TCLC 23**
See also CA 118; 197; DLB 65, 284, 332; EWL 3; GFL 1789 to the Present; RGWL 2, 3
Rolle, Richard
c. 1300-c. 1349 .... **CMLC 21, 165**
See also DLB 146; LMFS 1; RGEL 2
Rolvaag, O.E.
See Rolvaag, O.E.
Romain Arnaud, Saint
See Aragon, Louis
Romains, Jules 1885-1972 .... **CLC 7**
See also CA 85-88; CANR 34; DLB 65, 321; EWL 3; GFL 1789 to the Present; MTCW 1
Romero, Jose Ruben 1890-1952 ... **TCLC 14**
See also CA 114; 131; EWL 3; HW 1; LAW
Ronsard, Pierre de 1524-1585 ..... **LC 6, 54; PC 11, 105**
See also DLB 327; EW 2; GFL Beginnings to 1789; RGWL 2, 3; TWA
Rooke, Leon 1934- .... **CLC 25, 34**
See also CA 25-28R; CANR 23, 53; CCA 1; CPW; DAM POP
Roosevelt, Franklin Delano
1882-1945 .... **TCLC 93**
See also CA 116; 173; LAIT 3
Roosevelt, Theodore 1858-1919 .... **TCLC 69**
See also CA 115; 170; DLB 47, 186, 275
Roper, Margaret c. 1505-1544 .... **LC 147**
Roper, William 1498-1578 .... **LC 10**
Roquelaure, A. N.
See Rice, Anne
Rios, Alberto 1952- .... **PC 57**
See also AAYA 66; AMWS 4; CA 113; CANR 34, 79, 137; CP 6, 7; DLB 122; HW 2; MTFW 2005; PFS 11
Rios, Alberto Alvaro
See Rios, Alberto
Rosa, Joao Guimaraes
See Guimaraes Rosa, Joao
Rose, Wendy 1948- .... **CLC 85; NNAL; PC 13**
See also CA 53-56; CANR 5, 51; CWP; DAM MULT; DLB 175; PFS 13; RGAL 4; SATA 12
Rosen, R.D. 1949- .... **CLC 39**
See also CA 77-80; CANR 62, 120, 175; CMW 4; INT CANR-30
Rosen, Richard
See Rosen, R.D.
Rosen, Richard Dean
See Rosen, R.D.
Rosenberg, Isaac 1890-1918 .... **PC 146; TCLC 12; 314**
See also BRW 6; CA 107; 188; DLB 20, 216; EWL 3; PAB; RGEL 2
Rosenblatt, Joe
See Rosenblatt, Joseph
Rosenblatt, Joseph 1933- .... **CLC 15**
See also CA 89-92; CP 3, 4, 5, 6, 7; INT CA-89-92
Rosenfeld, Samuel
See Tzara, Tristan
Rosenstock, Sami
See Tzara, Tristan
Rosenstock, Samuel
See Tzara, Tristan
Rosenthal, M(acha) L(ouis)
1917-1996 .... **CLC 28**
See also CA 1-4R; 152; CAAS 6; CANR 4, 51; CP 1, 2, 3, 4, 5, 6; DLB 5; SATA 59
Ross, Barnaby
See Dannay, Frederic; Lee, Manfred B.
Ross, Bernard L.
See Follett, Ken
Ross, J. H.
See Lawrence, T. E.
Ross, John Hume
See Lawrence, T. E.
Ross, Martin 1862-1915
See Martin, Violet Florence
See also DLB 135; GLL 2; RGEL 2; RGSF 2
Ross, (James) Sinclair 1908-1996 ... **CLC 13; SSC 24**
See also CA 73-76; CANR 81; CN 1, 2, 3, 4, 5, 6; DAC; DAM MST; DLB 88; RGEL 2; RGSF 2; TCWW 1, 2
Rossetti, Christina 1830-1894 .... **NCLC 2, 50, 66, 186; PC 7, 119; WLC 5**
See also AAYA 51; BRW 5; BRWR 3; BYA 4; CLR 115; DA; DA3; DAB; DAC; DAM MST, POET; DLB 35, 163, 240; EXPP; FL 1:3; LATS 1:1; MAICYA 1, 2; PFS 10, 14, 27, 34; RGEL 2; SATA 20; TEA; WCH
Rossetti, Christina Georgina
See Rossetti, Christina
Rossetti, Dante Gabriel
1828-1882 .... **NCLC 4, 77; PC 44; WLC 5**
See also AAYA 51; BRW 5; CDBLB 1832-1890; DA; DAB; DAC; DAM MST, POET; DLB 35; EXPP; RGEL 2; TEA
Rossi, Cristina Peri
See Peri Rossi, Cristina
Rossi, Jean-Baptiste 1931-2003 .... **CLC 90**
See also CA 201; 215; CMW 4; NFS 18
Rossner, Judith 1935-2005 ..... **CLC 6, 9, 29**
See also AITN 2; BEST 90:3; BPFB 3; CA 17-20R; 242; CANR 18, 51, 73; CN 4, 5, 6, 7; DLB 6; INT CANR-18; MAL 5; MTCW 1, 2; MTFW 2005
Rossner, Judith Perelman
See Rossner, Judith
Rostand, Edmond 1868-1918 .... **DC 10; TCLC 6, 37**
See also CA 104; 126; DA; DA3; DAB; DAC; DAM DRAM, MST; DFS 1; DLB 192; LAIT 1; MTCW 1; RGWL 2, 3; TWA
Rostand, Edmond Eugene Alexis
See Rostand, Edmond
Rostopchine, Sophie, Comtesse de Ségur
See Ségur, Sophie Rostopchine, Comtesse de
Roth, Henry 1906-1995 .... **CLC 2, 6, 11, 104; SSC 134**
See also AMWS 9; CA 11-12; 149; CANR 38, 63; CAP 1; CN 1, 2, 3, 4, 5, 6; DA3; DLB 28; EWL 3; MAL 5; MTCW 1, 2; MTFW 2005; RGAL 4
Roth, (Moses) Joseph
1894-1939 .... **TCLC 33, 277**
See also CA 160; DLB 85; EWL 3; RGWL 2, 3
Roth, Philip 1933- ...... **CLC 1, 2, 3, 4, 6, 9, 15, 22, 31, 47, 66, 86, 119, 201, 336; SSC 26, 102, 176; WLC 5**
See also AAYA 67; AMWR 2; AMWS 3; BEST 90:3; BPFB 3; CA 1-4R; CANR 1, 22, 36, 55, 89, 132, 170, 241; CDALB 1968-1988; CN 3, 4, 5, 6, 7; CPW 1; DA; DA3; DAB; DAC; DAM MST, NOV, POP; DLB 2, 28, 173; DLBY 1982; EWL 3; MAL 5; MTCW 1, 2; MTFW 2005; NFS 25; RGAL 4; RGHL; RGSF 2; SSFS 12, 18; TUS
Roth, Philip Milton
See Roth, Philip
Rothenberg, Jerome 1931- .... **CLC 6, 57; PC 129**
See also CA 45-48; CANR 1, 106; CP 1, 2, 3, 4, 5, 6, 7; DLB 5, 193
Rotrou, Jean 1609-1650 .... **LC 241**
See also DLB 268; GFL
Rotter, Pat .... **CLC 65**
Roubaud, Jacques 1932- .... **CLC 358**
See also CA 249
Roumain, Jacques 1907-1944 .... **BLC 1:3; TCLC 19**
See also BW 1; CA 117; 125; DAM MULT; EWL 3
Roumain, Jacques Jean Baptiste
See Roumain, Jacques
Rourke, Constance Mayfield
1885-1941 .... **TCLC 12**
See also CA 107; 200; MAL 5; YABC 1

Rousseau, Jean-Baptiste 1671-1741 ..... **LC 9**
Rousseau, Jean-Jacques 1712-1778 ... **LC 14, 36, 122, 198; WLC 5**
See also DA; DA3; DAB; DAC; DAM MST; DLB 314; EW 4; GFL Beginnings to 1789; LMFS 1; RGWL 2, 3; TWA
Roussel, Raymond 1877-1933 .... **TCLC 20**
See also CA 117; 201; EWL 3; GFL 1789 to the Present
Rovit, Earl (Herbert) 1927- .... **CLC 7**
See also CA 5-8R; CANR 12
Rowe, Elizabeth Singer 1674-1737 ... **LC 44, 234**
See also DLB 39, 95
Rowe, Nicholas 1674-1718 .... **LC 8**
See also DLB 84; RGEL 2
Rowlandson, Mary 1637(?)-1678 .... **LC 66**
See also DLB 24, 200; RGAL 4
Rowley, Ames Dorrance
See Lovecraft, H. P.
Rowley, William
1585(?)-1626 .... **DC 43; LC 100, 123**
See also DFS 22; DLB 58; RGEL 2
Rowling, J.K. 1965- .... **CLC 137, 217**
See also AAYA 34, 82; BRWS 16; BYA 11, 13, 14; CA 173; CANR 128, 157; CLR 66, 80, 112, 183; LNFS 1, 2, 3; MAICYA 2; MTFW 2005; SATA 109, 174; SUFW 2
Rowling, Joanne Kathleen
See Rowling, J.K.
Rowson, Susanna Haswell
1762(?)-1824 .... **NCLC 5, 69, 182**
See also AMWS 15; DLB 37, 200; RGAL 4
Roy, Arundhati 1961- ... **CLC 109, 210, 364**
See also CA 163; CANR 90, 126, 217; CN 7; DLB 323, 326; DLBY 1997; EWL 3; LATS 1:2; MTFW 2005; NFS 22; WWE 1
Roy, Gabrielle 1909-1983 .... **CLC 10, 14; TCLC 256**
See also CA 53-56; 110; CANR 5, 61; CCA 1; DAB; DAC; DAM MST; DLB 68; EWL 3; MTCW 1; RGWL 2, 3; SATA 104; TCLE 1:2
Roy, Suzanna Arundhati
See Roy, Arundhati
Royko, Mike 1932-1997 .... **CLC 109**
See also CA 89-92; 157; CANR 26, 111; CPW
Rozanov, Vasilii Vasil'evich
See Rozanov, Vassili
Rozanov, Vasily Vasilyevich
See Rozanov, Vassili
Rozanov, Vassili 1856-1919 .... **TCLC 104**
See also DLB 295; EWL 3
Rozewicz, Tadeusz 1921- .... **CLC 9, 23, 139**
See also CA 108; CANR 36, 66; CWW 2; DA3; DAM POET; DLB 232; EWL 3; MTCW 1, 2; MTFW 2005; RGHL; RGWL 3
Ruark, Gibbons 1941- .... **CLC 3**
See also CA 33-36R; CAAS 23; CANR 14, 31, 57; DLB 120
Rubens, Bernice (Ruth)
1923-2004 .... **CLC 19, 31**
See also CA 25-28R; 232; CANR 33, 65, 128; CN 1, 2, 3, 4, 5, 6, 7; DLB 14, 207, 326; MTCW 1
Rubin, Harold
See Robbins, Harold
Rudkin, (James) David 1936- .... **CLC 14**
See also CA 89-92; CBD; CD 5, 6; DLB 13
Rudnik, Raphael 1933- .... **CLC 7**
See also CA 29-32R
Ruffian, M.
See Hasek, Jaroslav
Rufinus c. 345-410 .... **CMLC 111**
Ruiz, Jose Martinez
See Martinez Ruiz, Jose
Ruiz, Juan c. 1283-c. 1350 ... **CMLC 66, 143**
Rukeyser, Muriel 1913-1980 ...... **CLC 6, 10, 15, 27; PC 12, 137**
See also AMWS 6; CA 5-8R; 93-96; CANR 26, 60; CP 1, 2, 3; DA3; DAM POET; DLB 48; EWL 3; FW; GLL 2; MAL 5; MTCW 1, 2; PFS 10, 29; RGAL 4; SATA-Obit 22
Rule, Jane 1931-2007 .... **CLC 27, 265**
See also CA 25-28R; 266; CAAS 18; CANR 12, 87; CN 4, 5, 6, 7; DLB 60; FW
Rule, Jane Vance
See Rule, Jane
Rulfo, Juan 1918-1986 .... **CLC 8, 80; HLC 2; SSC 25**
See also CA 85-88; 118; CANR 26; CDWLB 3; DAM MULT; DLB 113; EWL 3; HW 1, 2; LAW; MTCW 1, 2; RGSF 2; RGWL 2, 3; WLIT 1
Rumi
See Rumi, Jalal al-Din
Rumi, Jalal al-Din 1207-1273 .... **CMLC 20; PC 45, 123**
See also AAYA 64; RGWL 2, 3; WLIT 6; WP
Runeberg, Johan 1804-1877 .... **NCLC 41**
Runyon, (Alfred) Damon 1884 (?)-1946 .... **TCLC 10**
See also CA 107; 165; DLB 11, 86, 171; MAL 5; MTCW 2; RGAL 4
Rush, Benjamin 1746-1813 .... **NCLC 251**
See also DLB 37
Rush, Norman 1933- .... **CLC 44, 306**
See also CA 121; 126; CANR 130; INT CA-126
Rushdie, Ahmed Salman
See Rushdie, Salman
Rushdie, Salman 1947- ...... **CLC 23, 31, 55, 100, 191, 272, 382; SSC 83, 183; WLCS**
See also AAYA 65; BEST 89:3; BPFB 3; BRWS 4; CA 108; 111; CANR 33, 56, 108, 133, 192; CLR 125; CN 4, 5, 6, 7; CPW 1; DA3; DAB; DAC; DAM MST, NOV, POP; DLB 194, 323, 326; EWL 3; FANT; INT CA-111; LATS 1:2; LMFS 2; MTCW 1, 2; MTFW 2005; NFS 22, 23, 41; RGEL 2; RGSF 2; TEA; WLIT 4
Rushforth, Peter 1945-2005 .... **CLC 19**
See also CA 101; 243
Rushforth, Peter Scott
See Rushforth, Peter
Ruskin, John 1819-1900 .... **TCLC 63**
See also BRW 5; BYA 5; CA 114; 129; CDBLB 1832-1890; DLB 55, 163, 190; RGEL 2; SATA 24; TEA; WCH
Russ, Joanna 1937-2011 .... **CLC 15**
See also BPFB 3; CA 25-28; CANR 11, 31, 65; CN 4, 5, 6, 7; DLB 8; FW; GLL 1; MTCW 1; SCFW 1, 2; SFW 4
Russ, Richard Patrick
See O'Brian, Patrick
Russell, Bertrand (Arthur William)
1872-1970 .... **TCLC 273**
See also CA 13-16; 25-28R; CANR 44; CAP 1; DLB 100, 262, 332; MTCW 1, 2; TEA
Russell, George William
1867-1935 .... **PC 133; TCLC 3, 10**
See also BRWS 8; CA 104; 153; CDBLB 1890-1914; DAM POET; DLB 19; EWL 3; RGEL 2
Russell, Henry Kenneth Alfred
See Russell, Ken
Russell, Jeffrey Burton 1934- .... **CLC 70**
See also CA 25-28R; CANR 11, 28, 52, 179
Russell, Karen 1981- .... **CLC 334**
See also CA 255
Russell, Ken 1927-2011 .... **CLC 16**
See also CA 105
Russell, William Martin 1947- .... **CLC 60**
See also CA 164; CANR 107; CBD; CD 5, 6; DLB 233
Russell, Willy
See Russell, William Martin
Russo, Richard 1949- .... **CLC 181**
See also AMWS 12; CA 127; 133; CANR 87, 114, 194; NFS 25
Rutebeuf fl. c. 1249-1277 .... **CMLC 104**
See also DLB 208
Rutherford, Mark
See White, William Hale
Ruysbroeck, Jan van 1293-1381 ... **CMLC 85**
Ruyslinck, Ward
See Belser, Reimond Karel Maria de
Ryan, Cornelius (John) 1920-1974 ... **CLC 7**
See also CA 69-72; 53-56; CANR 38
Ryan, Donal 1976- .... **CLC 370**
Ryan, Michael 1946- .... **CLC 65**
See also CA 49-52; CANR 109, 203; DLBY 1982
Ryan, Tim
See Dent, Lester
Rybakov, Anatoli (Naumovich)
1911-1998 .... **CLC 23, 53**
See also CA 126; 135; 172; DLB 302; RGHL; SATA 79; SATA-Obit 108
Rybakov, Anatolii (Naumovich)
See Rybakov, Anatoli (Naumovich)
Ryder, Jonathan
See Ludlum, Robert
Ryga, George 1932-1987 .... **CLC 14**
See also CA 101; 124; CANR 43, 90; CCA 1; DAC; DAM MST; DLB 60
Rymer, Thomas 1643(?)-1713 .... **LC 132**
See also DLB 101, 336
S. H.
See Hartmann, Sadakichi
S. L. C.
See Twain, Mark
S. S.
See Sassoon, Siegfried
Sa'adawi, al- Nawal
See El Saadawi, Nawal
Saadawi, Nawal El
See El Saadawi, Nawal
Saadiah Gaon 882-942 .... **CMLC 97**
Saavedra, Angel de 1791-1865 ... **NCLC 295**
Saba, Umberto 1883-1957 .... **TCLC 33**
See also CA 144; CANR 79; DLB 114; EWL 3; RGWL 2, 3
Sabatini, Rafael 1875-1950 .... **TCLC 47**
See also BPFB 3; CA 162; RHW
Sabato, Ernesto 1911-2011 **CLC 10, 23, 334; HLC 2**
See also CA 97-100; CANR 32, 65; CDWLB 3; CWW 2; DAM MULT; DLB 145; EWL 3; HW 1, 2; LAW; MTCW 1, 2; MTFW 2005
Sacastru, Martin
See Bioy Casares, Adolfo
Sacher-Masoch, Leopold von
1836(?)-1895 .... **NCLC 31**
Sachs, Hans 1494-1576 .... **LC 95**
See also CDWLB 2; DLB 179; RGWL 2, 3
Sachs, Marilyn 1927- .... **CLC 35**
See also AAYA 2; BYA 6; CA 17-20R; CANR 13, 47, 150; CLR 2; JRDA; MAICYA 1, 2; SAAS 2; SATA 3, 68, 164; SATA-Essay 110; WYA; YAW
Sachs, Marilyn Stickle
See Sachs, Marilyn
Sachs, Nelly 1891-1970 .... **CLC 14, 98; PC 78**
See also CA 17-18; 25-28R; CANR 87; CAP 2; DLB 332; EWL 3; MTCW 2; MTFW 2005; PFS 20; RGHL; RGWL 2, 3
Sackler, Howard (Oliver)
1929-1982 .... **CLC 14**
See also CA 61-64; 108; CAD; CANR 30; DFS 15; DLB 7

Sacks, Oliver 1933- .... **CLC 67, 202**
See also CA 53-56; CANR 28, 50, 76, 146, 187, 230; CPW; DA3; INT CANR-28; MTCW 1, 2; MTFW 2005
Sacks, Oliver Wolf
See Sacks, Oliver
Sackville, Thomas 1536-1608 .... **LC 98**
See also DAM DRAM; DLB 62, 132; RGEL 2
Sadakichi
See Hartmann, Sadakichi
Sa'dawi, Nawal al-
See El Saadawi, Nawal
Sade, Donatien Alphonse François
See Sade, Marquis de
Sade, Marquis de
1740-1814 .... **NCLC 3, 47, 263, 271**
See also DLB 314; EW 4; GFL Beginnings to 1789; RGWL 2, 3
Sadoff, Ira 1945- .... **CLC 9**
See also CA 53-56; CANR 5, 21, 109; DLB 120
Saetone
See Camus, Albert
Safire, William 1929-2009 .... **CLC 10**
See also CA 17-20R; 290; CANR 31, 54, 91, 148
Safire, William L.
See Safire, William
Safire, William Lewis
See Safire, William
Sagan, Carl 1934-1996 .... **CLC 30, 112**
See also AAYA 2, 62; CA 25-28R; 155; CANR 11, 36, 74; CPW; DA3; MTCW 1, 2; MTFW 2005; SATA 58; SATA-Obit 94
Sagan, Francoise 1935-2004 .... **CLC 3, 6, 9, 17, 36**
See also CA 49-52; 231; CANR 6, 39, 73, 216; CWW 2; DLB 83; EWL 3; GFL 1789 to the Present; MTCW 1, 2; MTFW 2005; TWA
Sahgal, Nayantara (Pandit)
1927- .... **CLC 41**
See also CA 9-12R; CANR 11, 88; CN 1, 2, 3, 4, 5, 6, 7; DLB 323
Said, Edward W. 1935-2003 .... **CLC 123**
See also CA 21-24R; 220; CANR 45, 74, 107, 131; DLB 67, 346; MTCW 2; MTFW 2005
Saikaku, Ihara 1642-1693 .... **LC 141**
See also RGWL 3
Saikaku Ihara
See Saikaku, Ihara
Saint, H(arry) F. 1941- .... **CLC 50**
See also CA 127
St. Aubin de Teran, Lisa 1953- ...... **CLC 36**
See also CA 118; 126; CANR 215; CN 6, 7; INT CA-126
Saint Birgitta of Sweden
c. 1303-1373 .... **CMLC 24, 146**
St. E. A. of M. and S
See Crowley, Edward Alexander
Sainte-Beuve, Charles Augustin
1804-1869 .... **NCLC 5; PC 110**
See also DLB 217; EW 6; GFL 1789 to the Present
Saint-Exupery, Antoine Jean Baptiste Marie Roger de
See Saint-Exupery, Antoine de
Saint-Exupery, Antoine de
1900-1944 ...... **TCLC 2, 56, 169; WLC**
See also AAYA 63; BPFB 3; BYA 3; CA 108; 132; CLR 10, 142; DA3; DAM NOV; DLB 72; EW 12; EWL 3; GFL 1789 to the Present; LAIT 3; MAICYA 1, 2; MTCW 1, 2; MTFW 2005; NFS 30; RGWL 2, 3; SATA 20; TWA
St. John, David
See Hunt, E. Howard
St. John, Henry
1678-1751 .... **LC 178**
See also DLB 101, 336
St. John, J. Hector
See Crevecoeur, J. Hector St. John de
Saint-John Perse
See Leger, Alexis Saint-Leger
Saintsbury, George (Edward Bateman)
1845-1933 .... **TCLC 31**
See also CA 160; DLB 57, 149
Sait Faik
See Abasiyanik, Sait Faik
Saki 1870-1916 .... **SSC 12, 115; TCLC 3; WLC 5**
See also AAYA 56; BRWS 6; BYA 11; CA 104; 130; CANR 104; CDBLB 1890-1914; DA; DA3; DAB; DAC; DAM MST, NOV; DLB 34, 162; EXPS; LAIT 2; MTCW 1, 2; MTFW 2005; RGEL 2; SSFS 1, 15, 36; SUFW
Sala, George Augustus
1828-1895 .... **NCLC 46**
Saladin 1138-1193 .... **CMLC 38**
Salama, Hannu 1936- .... **CLC 18**
See also CA 244; EWL 3
Salamanca, J(ack) R(ichard)
1922- .... **CLC 4, 15**
See also CA 25-28R, 193; CAAE 193
Salas, Floyd Francis 1931- .... **HLC 2**
See also CA 119; CAAS 27; CANR 44, 75, 93; DAM MULT; DLB 82; HW 1, 2; MTCW 2; MTFW 2005
Sale, J. Kirkpatrick
See Sale, Kirkpatrick
Sale, John Kirkpatrick
See Sale, Kirkpatrick
Sale, Kirkpatrick 1937- .... **CLC 68**
See also CA 13-16R; CANR 10, 147
Salernitano, Masuccio
c. 1420-c. 1475 .... **SSC 152**
Salinas, Luis Omar
1937- .... **CLC 90; HLC 2**
See also AMWS 13; CA 131; CANR 81, 153; DAM MULT; DLB 82; HW 1, 2
Salinas (y Serrano), Pedro 1891 (?)-1951 .... **TCLC 17, 212**
See also CA 117; DLB 134; EWL 3
Salinger, J. D. 1919-2010 .... **CLC 1, 3, 8, 12, 55, 56, 138, 243, 318, 378; CLR 18, 181; SSC 2, 28, 65, 146; WLC 5**
See also AAYA 2, 36; AMW; AMWC 1; BPFB 3; CA 5-8R; CANR 39, 129; CDALB 1941-1968; CLR 18, 181; CN 1, 2, 3, 4, 5, 6, 7; CPW 1; DA; DA3; DAB; DAC; DAM MST, NOV, POP; DLB 2, 102, 173; EWL 3; EXPN; LAIT 4; MAICYA 1, 2; MAL 5; MTCW 1, 2; MTFW 2005; NFS 1, 30; RGAL 4; RGSF 2; SATA 67; SSFS 17; TUS; WYA; YAW
Salinger, Jerome David
See Salinger, J. D.
Salisbury, John
See Caute, (John) David
Sallust c. 86B.C.-35B.C. .... **CMLC 68**
See also AW 2; CDWLB 1; DLB 211; RGWL 2, 3
Salter, James 1925- ..... **CLC 7, 52, 59, 275; SSC 58**
See also AMWS 9; CA 73-76; CANR 107, 160; DLB 130; SSFS 25
Saltus, Edgar (Everton) 1855-1921 ... **TCLC 8**
See also CA 105; DLB 202; RGAL 4
Saltykov, Mikhail Evgrafovich 1826-1889 .... **NCLC 16**
See also DLB 238:
Saltykov-Shchedrin, N.
See Saltykov, Mikhail Evgrafovich
Samarakis, Andonis
See Samarakis, Antonis
Samarakis, Antonis 1919-2003 .... **CLC 5**
See also CA 25-28R; 224; CAAS 16; CANR 36; EWL 3
Samigli, E.
See Schmitz, Aron Hector
San Pedro, Diego de c. 1437-1498 .. **LC 247**
See also DLB 286
Sanchez, Federico
See Semprun, Jorge
Sanchez, Sonia 1934- .... **BLC 1:3, 2:3; CLC 5, 116, 215; PC 9**
See also BW 2, 3; CA 33-36R; CANR 24, 49, 74, 115; CLR 18; CP 2, 3, 4, 5, 6, 7; CSW; CWP; DA3; DAM MULT; DLB 41; DLBD 8; EWL 3; MAICYA 1, 2; MAL 5; MTCW 1, 2; MTFW 2005; PFS 26; SATA 22, 136; WP
Sancho, Ignatius 1729-1780 .... **LC 84**
Sand, George 1804-1876 **DC 29; NCLC 2, 42, 57, 174, 234; WLC 5**
See also DA; DA3; DAB; DAC; DAM MST, NOV; DLB 119, 192; EW 6; FL 1:3; FW; GFL 1789 to the Present; RGWL 2, 3; TWA
Sandburg, Carl 1878-1967 .... **CLC 1, 4, 10, 15, 35; PC 2, 41; WLC 5**
See also AAYA 24; AMW; BYA 1, 3; CA 5-8R; 25-28R; CANR 35; CDALB 1865-1917; CLR 67; DA; DA3; DAB; DAC; DAM MST, POET; DLB 17, 54, 284; EWL 3; EXPP; LAIT 2; MAICYA 1, 2; MAL 5; MTCW 1, 2; MTFW 2005; PAB; PFS 3, 6, 12, 33, 36; RGAL 4; SATA 8; TUS; WCH; WP; WYA
Sandburg, Carl August
See Sandburg, Carl
Sandburg, Charles
See Sandburg, Carl
Sandburg, Charles A.
See Sandburg, Carl
Sanders, Ed 1939- .... **CLC 53**
See also BG 1:3; CA 13-16R; CAAS 21; CANR 13, 44, 78; CP 1, 2, 3, 4, 5, 6, 7; DAM POET; DLB 16, 244
Sanders, Edward
See Sanders, Ed
Sanders, James Edward
See Sanders, Ed
Sanders, Lawrence 1920-1998 .... **CLC 41**
See also BEST 89:4; BPFB 3; CA 81-84; 165; CANR 33, 62; CMW 4; CPW; DA3; DAM POP; MTCW 1
Sanders, Noah
See Blount, Roy, Jr.
Sanders, Winston P.
See Anderson, Poul
Sandoz, Mari(e Susette) 1900-1966 .... **CLC 28**
See also CA 1-4R; 25-28R; CANR 17, 64; DLB 9, 212; LAIT 2; MTCW 1, 2; SATA 5; TCWW 1, 2
Sandys, George 1578-1644 .... **LC 80**
See also DLB 24, 121
Saner, Reg(inald Anthony) 1931- ..... **CLC 9**
See also CA 65-68; CP 3, 4, 5, 6, 7
Sankara 788-820 .... **CMLC 32, 149**
Sannazaro, Jacopo 1456(?)-1530 .... **LC 8**
See also RGWL 2, 3; WLIT 7
Sansom, William 1912-1976 .... **CLC 2, 6; SSC 21**
See also CA 5-8R; 65-68; CANR 42; CN 1, 2; DAM NOV; DLB 139; EWL 3; MTCW 1; RGEL 2; RGSF 2
Santayana, George
1863-1952 .... **TCLC 40**
See also AMW; CA 115; 194; DLB 54, 71, 246, 270; DLBD 13; EWL 3; MAL 5; RGAL 4; TUS
Santiago, Danny
See James, Daniel (Lewis)

Santiago, Esmeralda 1948- .... **CLC 363**
See also AAYA 43; BYA 12; CA 179; CANR 130, 235; LLW; SATA 129
Santillana, Inigo Lopez de Mendoza, Marques de 1398-1458 .... **LC 111**
See also DLB 286
Santmyer, Helen Hooven 1895-1986 .... **CLC 33; TCLC 133**
See also CA 1-4R; 118; CANR 15, 33; DLBY 1984; MTCW 1; RHW
Santoka, Taneda 1882-1940 .... **TCLC 72**
Santos, Bienvenido N(uqui) 1911-1996 .... **AAL; CLC 22; TCLC 156**
See also CA 101; 151; CANR 19, 46; CP 1; DAM MULT; DLB 312, 348; EWL; RGAL 4; SSFS 19
Santos, Miguel
See Mihura, Miguel
Sapir, Edward 1884-1939 .... **TCLC 108**
See also CA 211; DLB 92
Sapper
See McNeile, Herman Cyril
Sapphire 1950- .... **CLC 99**
See also CA 262
Sapphire, Brenda
See Sapphire
Sappho c. 630 B.C.-c. 570 B.C. .... **CMLC 3, 67, 160; PC 5, 117**
See also CDWLB 1; DA3; DAM POET; DLB 176; FL 1:1; PFS 20, 31, 38, 44; RGWL 2, 3; WLIT 8; WP
Saramago, Jose 1922-2010 ... **CLC 119, 275; HLCS 1**
See also CA 153; CANR 96, 164, 210, 242; CWW 2; DLB 287, 332; EWL 3; LATS 1:2; NFS 27; SSFS 23
Sarduy, Severo 1937-1993 .... **CLC 6, 97; HLCS 2; TCLC 167**
See also CA 89-92; 142; CANR 58, 81; CWW 2; DLB 113; EWL 3; HW 1, 2; LAW
Sargeson, Frank 1903-1982 .... **CLC 31; SSC 99**
See also CA 25-28R; 106; CANR 38, 79; CN 1, 2, 3; EWL 3; GLL 2; RGEL 2; RGSF 2; SSFS 20
Sarmiento, Domingo Faustino 1811-1888 .... **HLCS 2; NCLC 123**
See also LAW; WLIT 1
Sarmiento, Felix Ruben Garcia
See Dario, Ruben
Saro-Wiwa, Ken(ule Beeson) 1941-1995 .... **CLC 114; TCLC 200**
See also BW 2; CA 142; 150; CANR 60; DLB 157, 360
Saroyan, William 1908-1981 .... **CLC 1, 8, 10, 29, 34, 56; DC 28; SSC 21; TCLC 137; WLC 5**
See also AAYA 66; CA 5-8R; 103; CAD; CANR 30; CDALBS; CN 1, 2; DA; DA3; DAB; DAC; DAM DRAM, MST, NOV; DFS 17; DLB 7, 9, 86; DLBY 1981; EWL 3; LAIT 4; MAL 5; MTCW 1, 2; MTFW 2005; NFS 39; RGAL 4; RGSF 2; SATA 23; SATA-Obit 24; SSFS 14; TUS
Sarraute, Nathalie 1900-1999 ...... **CLC 1, 2, 4, 8, 10, 31, 80; TCLC 145**
See also BPFB 3; CA 9-12R; 187; CANR 23, 66, 134; CWW 2; DLB 83, 321; EW 12; EWL 3; GFL 1789 to the Present; MTCW 1, 2; MTFW 2005; RGWL 2, 3
Sarton, May 1912-1995 .... **CLC 4, 14, 49, 91; PC 39; TCLC 120**
See also AMWS 8; CA 1-4R; 149; CANR 1, 34, 55, 116; CN 1, 2, 3, 4, 5, 6; CP 1, 2, 3, 4, 5, 6; DAM POET; DLB 48; DLBY 1981; EWL 3; FW; INT CANR-34; MAL 5; MTCW 1, 2; MTFW 2005; RGAL 4; SATA 36; SATA-Obit 86; TUS
Sartre, Jean-Paul 1905-1980 ... **CLC 1, 4, 7, 9, 13, 18, 24, 44, 50, 52; DC 3; SSC 32; WLC 5**
See also AAYA 62; CA 9-12R; 97-100; CANR 21; DA; DA3; DAB; DAC; DAM DRAM, MST, NOV; DFS 5, 26; DLB 72, 296, 321, 332; EW 12; EWL 3; GFL 1789 to the Present; LMFS 2; MTCW 1, 2; MTFW 2005; NFS 21; RGHL; RGSF 2; RGWL 2, 3; SSFS 9; TWA
Sassoon, Siegfried 1886-1967 .... **CLC 36, 130; PC 12**
See also BRW 6; CA 104; 25-28R; CANR 36; DAB; DAM MST, NOV, POET; DLB 20, 191; DLBD 18; EWL 3; MTCW 1, 2; MTFW 2005; PAB; PFS 28; RGEL 2; TEA
Sassoon, Siegfried Lorraine
See Sassoon, Siegfried
Satrapi, Marjane 1969- .... **CLC 332**
See also AAYA 55; CA 246
Satterfield, Charles
See Pohl, Frederik
Satyremont
See Peret, Benjamin
Saul, John 1942- .... **CLC 46**
See also AAYA 10, 62; BEST 90:4; CA 81-84; CANR 16, 40, 81, 176, 221; CPW; DAM NOV, POP; HGG; SATA 98
Saul, John W.
See Saul, John
Saul, John Woodruff III
See Saul, John
Saunders, Abel
See Pound, Ezra
Saunders, Caleb
See Heinlein, Robert A.
Saunders, George 1958- .... **CLC 325**
See also CA 164; CANR 98, 157, 197; DLB 335
Saunders, George W.
See Saunders, George
Saura (Atares), Carlos 1932-1998 ... **CLC 20**
See also CA 114; 131; CANR 79; HW 1
Sauser, Frederic Louis
See Sauser-Hall, Frederic
Sauser-Hall, Frederic 1887-1961 .... **CLC 18, 106**
See also CA 102; 93-96; CANR 36, 62; DLB 258; EWL 3; GFL 1789 to the Present; MTCW 1; WP
Saussure, Ferdinand de 1857-1913 .... **TCLC 49**
See also DLB 242
Savage, Catharine
See Brosman, Catharine Savage
Savage, Richard 1697(?)-1743 .... **LC 96**
See also DLB 95; RGEL 2
Savage, Thomas 1915-2003 .... **CLC 40**
See also CA 126; 132; 218; CAAS 15; CN 6, 7; INT CA-132; SATA-Obit 147; TCWW 2
Savan, Glenn 1953-2003 .... **CLC 50**
See also CA 225
Savonarola, Girolamo 1452-1498 .... **LC 152**
See also LMFS 1
Sax, Robert
See Johnson, Robert
Saxo Grammaticus c. 1150-c. 1222 .... **CMLC 58, 141**
Saxton, Robert
See Johnson, Robert
Sayers, Dorothy L(eigh) 1893-1957 ... **SSC 71; TCLC 2, 15, 237**
See also BPFB 3; BRWS 3; CA 104; 119; CANR 60; CDBLB 1914-1945; CMW 4; DAM POP; DLB 10, 36, 77, 100; MSW; MTCW 1, 2; MTFW 2005; RGEL 2; SSFS 12; TEA
Sayers, Valerie 1952- .... **CLC 50, 122**
See also CA 134; CANR 61; CSW
Sayles, John 1950- .... **CLC 7, 10, 14, 198**
See also CA 57-60; CANR 41, 84; DLB 44
Sayles, John Thomas
See Sayles, John
Scalapino, Leslie 1947-2010 .... **PC 114**
See also CA 123; CANR 67, 103; CP 5, 6, 7; CWP; DLB 193
Scamander, Newt
See Rowling, J.K.
Scammell, Michael 1935- .... **CLC 34**
See also CA 156; CANR 222
Scannel, John Vernon
See Scannell, Vernon
Scannell, Vernon 1922-2007 .... **CLC 49**
See also CA 5-8R; 266; CANR 8, 24, 57, 143; CN 1, 2; CP 1, 2, 3, 4, 5, 6, 7; CWRI 5; DLB 27; SATA 59; SATA-Obit 188
Scarlett, Susan
See Streatfeild, Noel
Sa-Carneiro, Mario de 1890-1916 .... **TCLC 83**
See also DLB 287; EWL 3
Scarron 1847-1910
See Mikszath, Kalman
Scarron, Paul 1610-1660 .... **LC 116**
See also GFL Beginnings to 1789; RGWL 2, 3
Schaeffer, Susan Fromberg 1940-2011 .... **CLC 6, 11, 22**
See also CA 49-52; CANR 18, 65, 160; CN 4, 5, 6, 7; DLB 28, 299; MTCW 1, 2; MTFW 2005; SATA 22
Schama, Simon 1945- .... **CLC 150**
See also BEST 89:4; CA 105; CANR 39, 91, 168, 207, 237
Schama, Simon Michael
See Schama, Simon
Schary, Jill
See Robinson, Jill
Schell, Jonathan 1943- .... **CLC 35**
See also CA 73-76; CANR 12, 117, 187
Schelling, Friedrich Wilhelm Joseph von 1775-1854 .... **NCLC 30, 261**
See also DLB 90, 366
Scherer, Jean-Marie Maurice
See Rohmer, Eric
Schevill, James (Erwin) 1920- .... **CLC 7**
See also CA 5-8R; CAAS 12; CAD; CD 5, 6; CP 1, 2, 3, 4, 5
Schiller, Friedrich von 1759-1805 .... **DC 12; NCLC 39, 69, 166**
See also CDWLB 2; DAM DRAM; DLB 94; EW 5; RGWL 2, 3; TWA
Schisgal, Murray (Joseph) 1926- ..... **CLC 6**
See also CA 21-24R; CAD; CANR 48, 86; CD 5, 6; MAL 5
Schlee, Ann 1934- .... **CLC 35**
See also CA 101; CANR 29, 88; SATA 44; SATA-Brief 36
Schlegel, August Wilhelm von 1767-1845 .... **NCLC 15, 142, 262**
See also DLB 94; RGWL 2, 3
Schlegel, Dorothea 1764-1839 ..... **NCLC 296**
See also DLB 90
Schlegel, Friedrich 1772-1829 .... **NCLC 45, 226**
See also DLB 90; EW 5; RGWL 2, 3; TWA
Schlegel, Johann Elias (von) 1719 (?)-1749 .... **LC 5**
Schleiermacher, Friedrich 1768-1834 .... **NCLC 107**
See also DLB 90

Author Index

Schlesinger, Arthur M., Jr. 1917-2007 .... **CLC 84**
See Schlesinger, Arthur Meier
See also AITN 1; CA 1-4R; 257; CANR 1, 28, 58, 105, 187; DLB 17; INT CANR-28; MTCW 1, 2; SATA 61; SATA-Obit 181

Schlink, Bernhard 1944- .... **CLC 174, 347**
See also CA 163; CANR 116, 175, 217; RGHL

Schmidt, Arno (Otto) 1914-1979 .... **CLC 56**
See also CA 128; 109; DLB 69; EWL 3

Schmitz, Aron Hector 1861-1928 ... **SSC 25; TCLC 2, 35, 244**
See also CA 104; 122; DLB 264; EW 8; EWL 3; MTCW 1; RGWL 2, 3; WLIT 7

Schnackenberg, Gjertrud 1953- .... **CLC 40; PC 45**
See also AMWS 15; CA 116; CANR 100; CP 5, 6, 7; CWP; DLB 120, 282; PFS 13, 25

Schnackenberg, Gjertrud Cecelia
See Schnackenberg, Gjertrud

Schneider, Leonard Alfred
See Bruce, Lenny

Schnitzler, Arthur 1862-1931 .... **DC 17; SSC 15, 61, 198; TCLC 4, 275**
See also CA 104; CDWLB 2; DLB 81, 118; EW 8; EWL 3; RGSF 2; RGWL 2, 3

Schoenberg, Arnold Franz Walter 1874-1951 .... **TCLC 75**
See also CA 109; 188

Schonberg, Arnold
See Schoenberg, Arnold Franz Walter

Schopenhauer, Arthur 1788-1860 .... **NCLC 51, 157**
See also DLB 90; EW 5

Schor, Sandra (M.) 1932(?)-1990 ... **CLC 65**
See also CA 132

Schorer, Mark 1908-1977 .... **CLC 9**
See also CA 5-8R; 73-76; CANR 7; CN 1, 2; DLB 103

Schrader, Paul (Joseph) 1946- .... **CLC 26, 212**
See also CA 37-40R; CANR 41; DLB 44

Schreber, Daniel 1842-1911 .... **TCLC 123**

Schreiner, Olive 1855-1920 .... **TCLC 9, 235, 309**
See also AFW; BRWS 2; CA 105; 154; DLB 18, 156, 190, 225; EWL 3; FW; RGEL 2; TWA; WLIT 2; WWE 1

Schreiner, Olive Emilie Albertina
See Schreiner, Olive

Schulberg, Budd 1914-2009 .... **CLC 7, 48**
See also AMWS 18; BPFB 3; CA 25-28R; 289; CANR 19, 87, 178; CN 1, 2, 3, 4, 5, 6, 7; DLB 6, 26, 28; DLBY 1981, 2001; MAL 5

Schulberg, Budd Wilson
See Schulberg, Budd

Schulberg, Seymour Wilson
See Schulberg, Budd

Schulman, Arnold
See Trumbo, Dalton

Schulz, Bruno 1892-1942 ... **SSC 13; TCLC 5, 51, 273**
See also CA 115; 123; CANR 86; CDWLB 4; DLB 215; EWL 3; MTCW 2; MTFW 2005; RGSF 2; RGWL 2, 3

Schulz, Charles M. 1922-2000 .... **CLC 12**
See also AAYA 39; CA 9-12R; 187; CANR 6, 132; CLR 188; INT CANR-6; MTFW 2005; SATA 10; SATA-Obit 118

Schulz, Charles Monroe
See Schulz, Charles M.

Schumacher, E(rnst) F(riedrich) 1911-1977 .... **CLC 80**
See also CA 81-84; 73-76; CANR 34, 85

Schumann, Robert 1810-1856 ..... **NCLC 143**

Schuyler, George Samuel 1895-1977 **HR 1:3**
See also BW 2; CA 81-84; 73-76; CANR 42; DLB 29, 51

Schuyler, James Marcus 1923-1991 .... **CLC 5, 23; PC 88**
See also CA 101; 134; CP 1, 2, 3, 4, 5; DAM POET; DLB 5, 169; EWL 3; INT CA-101; MAL 5; WP

Schwartz, Delmore (David) 1913-1966 .... **CLC 2, 4, 10, 45, 87; PC 8; SSC 105**
See also AMWS 2; CA 17-18; 25-28R; CANR 35; CAP 2; DLB 28, 48; EWL 3; MAL 5; MTCW 1, 2; MTFW 2005; PAB; RGAL 4; TUS

Schwartz, Ernst
See Ozu, Yasujiro

Schwartz, John Burnham 1965- ..... **CLC 59**
See also CA 132; CANR 116, 188

Schwartz, Lynne Sharon 1939- ...... **CLC 31**
See also CA 103; CANR 44, 89, 160, 214; DLB 218; MTCW 2; MTFW 2005

Schwartz, Muriel A.
See Eliot, T. S.

Schwartzman, Adam 1973- .... **CLC 318**
See also CA 307

Schwarz-Bart, Andre 1928-2006 ... **CLC 2, 4**
See also CA 89-92; 253; CANR 109; DLB 299; RGHL

Schwarz-Bart, Simone 1938- .... **BLCS; CLC 7**
See also BW 2; CA 97-100; CANR 117; EWL 3

Schwerner, Armand 1927-1999 .... **PC 42**
See also CA 9-12R; 179; CANR 50, 85; CP 2, 3, 4, 5, 6; DLB 165

Schwitters, Kurt (Hermann Edward Karl Julius) 1887-1948 .... **TCLC 95**
See also CA 158

Schwob, Marcel (Mayer Andre) 1867-1905 .... **TCLC 20**
See also CA 117; 168; DLB 123; GFL 1789 to the Present

Sciascia, Leonardo 1921-1989 .... **CLC 8, 9, 41**
See also CA 85-88; 130; CANR 35; DLB 177; EWL 3; MTCW 1; RGWL 2, 3

Scoppettone, Sandra 1936- .... **CLC 26**
See also AAYA 11, 65; BYA 8; CA 5-8R; CANR 41, 73, 157; GLL 1; MAICYA 2; MAICYAS 1; SATA 9, 92; WYA; YAW

Scorsese, Martin 1942- ..... **CLC 20, 89, 207**
See also AAYA 38; CA 110; 114; CANR 46, 85

Scotland, Jay
See Jakes, John

Scott, Duncan Campbell 1862-1947 .... **TCLC 6**
See also CA 104; 153; DAC; DLB 92; RGEL 2

Scott, Evelyn 1893-1963 .... **CLC 43**
See also CA 104; 112; CANR 64; DLB 9, 48; RHW

Scott, F(rancis) R(eginald) 1899-1985 .... **CLC 22**
See also CA 101; 114; CANR 87; CP 1, 2, 3, 4; DLB 88; INT CA-101; RGEL 2

Scott, Frank
See Scott, F(rancis) R(eginald)

Scott, Joan
See Scott, Joan Wallach

Scott, Joan W.
See Scott, Joan Wallach

Scott, Joan Wallach 1941- .... **CLC 65**
See also CA 293

Scott, Joanna 1960- .... **CLC 50**
See also AMWS 17; CA 126; CANR 53, 92, 168, 219

Scott, Joanna Jeanne
See Scott, Joanna

Scott, Paul (Mark) 1920-1978 ..... **CLC 9, 60**
See also BRWS 1; CA 81-84; 77-80; CANR 33; CN 1, 2; DLB 14, 207, 326; EWL 3; MTCW 1; RGEL 2; RHW; WWE 1

Scott, Ridley 1937- .... **CLC 183**
See also AAYA 13, 43

Scott, Sarah 1723-1795 .... **LC 44, 233**
See also DLB 39

Scott, Sir Walter 1771-1832 .... **NCLC 15, 69, 110, 209, 241, 270; PC 13; SSC 32; WLC 5**
See also AAYA 22; BRW 4; BYA 2; CDBLB 1789-1832; CLR 154; DA; DAB; DAC; DAM MST, NOV, POET; DLB 93, 107, 116, 144, 159, 366; GL 3; HGG; LAIT 1; NFS 31; RGEL 2; RGSF 2; SSFS 10; SUFW 1; TEA; WLIT 3; YABC 2

Scotus, John Duns 1266(?)-1308 .... **CMLC 59, 138**
See also DLB 115

Scribe, Augustin Eugene
See Scribe, (Augustin) Eugene

Scribe, (Augustin) Eugene 1791-1861 .... **DC 5; NCLC 16**
See also DAM DRAM; DLB 192; GFL 1789 to the Present; RGWL 2, 3

Scrum, R.
See Crumb, R.

Scudery, Georges de 1601-1667 .... **LC 75**
See also GFL Beginnings to 1789

Scudery, Madeleine de 1607-1701 .. **LC 2, 58**
See also DLB 268; GFL Beginnings to 1789

Scum
See Crumb, R.

Scumbag, Little Bobby
See Crumb, R.

Sceve, Maurice c. 1500-c. 1564 ...... **LC 180; PC 111**
See also DLB 327; GFL Beginnings to 1789

Schüler, Elisabeth
See Lasker-Schueler, Else

Seabrook, John
See Hubbard, L. Ron

Seacole, Mary Jane Grant 1805-1881 .... **NCLC 147, 305**
See also DLB 166

Sealsfield, Charles 1793-1864 ..... **NCLC 233**
See also DLB 133, 186

Sealy, I(rwin) Allan 1951- .... **CLC 55**
See also CA 136; CN 6, 7

Search, Alexander
See Pessoa, Fernando

Seare, Nicholas
See Whitaker, Rod

Sears, Djanet 1959- .... **DC 46**
See also CA 259

Sears, Janet
See Sears, Djanet

Sebald, W(infried) G(eorg) 1944-2001 .... **CLC 194, 296**
See also BRWS 8; CA 159; 202; CANR 98; MTFW 2005; RGHL

Sebastian, Lee
See Silverberg, Robert

Sebastian Owl
See Thompson, Hunter S.

Sebbar, Leïla 1941- .... **CLC 365**
See also CA 199; CANR 177; EWL 3

Sebestyen, Igen
See Sebestyen, Ouida

Sebestyen, Ouida 1924- .... **CLC 30**
See also AAYA 8; BYA 7; CA 107; CANR 40, 114; CLR 17; JRDA; MAICYA 1, 2; SAAS 10; SATA 39, 140; WYA; YAW

Sebold, Alice 1963- .... **CLC 193**
See also AAYA 56; CA 203; CANR 181; LNFS 1; MTFW 2005
Second Duke of Buckingham
See Villiers, George
Secundus, H. Scriblerus
See Fielding, Henry
Sedges, John
See Buck, Pearl S.
Sedgwick, Eve Kosofsky 1950-2009 ... **CLC 363**
See also CA 145, 285; CANR 90; DLB 246
Sedgwick, Catharine Maria 1789-1867 .... **NCLC 19, 98, 238**
See also DLB 1, 74, 183, 239, 243, 254; FL 1:3; RGAL 4
Sedley, Sir Charles 1639-1701 .... **LC 168**
See also BRW 2; DLB 131; RGEL 2
Sedulius Scottus 9th cent. -c. 874 .... **CMLC 86**
Seebohm, Victoria
See Glendinning, Victoria
Seelye, John (Douglas) 1931- .... **CLC 7**
See also CA 97-100; CANR 70; INT CA-97-100; TCWW 1, 2
Seferiades, Giorgos Stylianou
See Seferis, George
Seferis, George 1900-1971 .... **CLC 5, 11; TCLC 213**
See also CA 5-8R; 33-36R; CANR 5, 36; DLB 332; EW 12; EWL 3; MTCW 1; RGWL 2, 3
Segal, Erich 1937-2010 .... **CLC 3, 10**
See also BEST 89:1; BPFB 3; CA 25-28R; CANR 20, 36, 65, 113; CPW; DAM POP; DLBY 1986; INT CANR-20; MTCW 1
Segal, Erich Wolf
See Segal, Erich
Segal, Francesca 1980- .... **CLC 354**
Seger, Bob 1945- .... **CLC 35**
Seghers
See Radvanyi, Netty
Seghers, Anna
See Radvanyi, Netty
Ségur, Sophie Rostopchine, Comtesse de 1799-1874 .... **NCLC 312**
Seidel, Frederick 1936- .... **CLC 18**
See also CA 13-16R; CANR 8, 99, 180; CP 1, 2, 3, 4, 5, 6, 7; DLBY 1984
Seidel, Frederick Lewis
See Seidel, Frederick
Seifert, Jaroslav 1901-1986 ...... **CLC 34, 44, 93; PC 47**
See also CA 127; CDWLB 4; DLB 215, 332; EWL 3; MTCW 1, 2
Sei Shonagon c. 966-1017(?) ... **CMLC 6, 89**
Sejour, Victor 1817-1874 .... **DC 10**
See also DLB 50
Sejour Marcou et Ferrand, Juan Victor
See Sejour, Victor
Selber
See Mangan, James Clarence
Selby, Hubert, Jr. 1928-2004 ... **CLC 1, 2, 4, 8; SSC 20**
See also CA 13-16R; 226; CANR 33, 85; CN 1, 2, 3, 4, 5, 6, 7; DLB 2, 227; MAL 5
Self, Will 1961- .... **CLC 282**
See also BRWS 5; CA 143; CANR 83, 126, 171, 201; CN 6, 7; DLB 207
Self, William
See Self, Will
Selvon, Samuel 1923-1994 .... **SSC 181**
See also BW 2; CDWLB 3; CA 117, 128, 147; CN 5; DLB 125, 362; EWL 3; MTCW 1; RGEL 2
Self, William Woodward
See Self, Will
Selvadurai, Shyam 1965- .... **CLC 348**
See also CA 167; CANR 88; CN 7; SATA 171
Selvon, Samuel 1923-1994 .... **SSC 181**
See also BW 2; CDWLB; CA 117, 128, 146; CN 5; DLB 125, 362; EWL 3; MTCW 1; RGEL 2
Selzer, Richard 1928- .... **CLC 74**
See also CA 65-68; CANR 14, 106, 204
Sembene, Ousmane
See Ousmane, Sembene
Semprun, Jorge 1923-2011 .... **CLC 334**
See also CA 111; 158; CANR 87; IDFW 4; RGHL
Senancour, Etienne Pivert de 1770-1846 .... **NCLC 16**
See also DLB 119; GFL 1789 to the Present
Sender, Ramon (Jose) 1902-1982 .... **CLC 8; HLC 2; TCLC 136**
See also CA 5-8R; 105; CANR 8; DAM MULT; DLB 322; EWL 3; HW 1; MTCW 1; RGWL 2, 3
Seneca, Lucius Annaeus c. 4B.C.-c. 65 ...... **CMLC 6, 107; DC 5**
See also AW 2; CDWLB 1; DAM DRAM; DLB 211; RGWL 2, 3; TWA; WLIT 8
Seneca the Younger
See Seneca, Lucius Annaeus
Senghor, Leopold Sedar 1906-2001 .... **BLC 1:3; CLC 54, 130; PC 25**
See also AFW; BW 2; CA 116; 125; 203; CANR 47, 74, 134; CWW 2; DAM MULT, POET; DNFS 2; EWL 3; GFL 1789 to the Present; MTCW 1, 2; MTFW 2005; PFS 36; TWA
Senior, Olive (Marjorie) 1941- .... **SSC 78**
See also BW 3; CA 154; CANR 86, 126; CN 6; CP 6, 7; CWP; DLB 157; EWL 3; RGSF 2
Senna, Danzy 1970- .... **CLC 119**
See also CA 169; CANR 130, 184, 235
Sepheriades, Georgios
See Seferis, George
Serling, (Edward) Rod(man) 1924-1975 .... **CLC 30**
See also AAYA 14; AITN 1; CA 162; 57-60; DLB 26; SFW 4
Serna, Ramon Gomez de la
See Gomez de la Serna, Ramon
Serote, Mongane Wally 1944- .... **PC 113**
See also BW 2, 3; CA 142; CANR 81; CP 5, 6, 7; DLB 125, 225
Serpieres
See Guillevic, (Eugene)
Service, Robert
See Service, Robert W.
Service, Robert W. 1874(?)-1958 ...... **PC 70; TCLC 15; WLC 5**
See also BYA 4; CA 115; 140; CANR 84; DA; DAB; DAC; DAM MST, POET; DLB 92; PFS 10; RGEL 2; SATA 20
Service, Robert William
See Service, Robert W.
Servius c. 370-c. 431 .... **CMLC 120**
Seth, Vikram 1952- .... **CLC 43, 90, 277; PC 118**
See also BRWS 10; CA 121; 127; CANR 50, 74, 131; CN 6, 7; CP 5, 6, 7; DA3; DAM MULT; DLB 120, 271, 282, 323; EWL 3; INT CA-127; MTCW 2; MTFW 2005; WWE 1
Setien, Miguel Delibes
See Delibes Setien, Miguel
Seton, Cynthia Propper 1926-1982 .... **CLC 27**
See also CA 5-8R; 108; CANR 7
Seton, Ernest (Evan) Thompson 1860-1946 .... **TCLC 31**
See also ANW; BYA 3; CA 109; 204; CLR 59; DLB 92; DLBD 13; JRDA; SATA 18
Seton-Thompson, Ernest
See Seton, Ernest (Evan) Thompson
Settle, Mary Lee 1918-2005 .... **CLC 19, 61, 273**
See also BPFB 3; CA 89-92; 243; CAAS 1; CANR 44, 87, 126, 182; CN 6, 7; CSW; DLB 6; INT CA-89-92
Seuphor, Michel
See Arp, Jean
Seventeenth Earl of Oxford
See de Vere, Edward
Sewall, Samuel 1652-1730 .... **LC 38**
See also DLB 24; RGAL 4
Seward, Anna 1742-1809 .... **NCLC 265**
See also BRWS 17; RGEL 2
Sexton, Anne 1928-1974 .... **CLC 2, 4, 6, 8, 10, 15, 53, 123; PC 2, 79; TCLC 252; WLC 5**
See also AMWS 2; CA 1-4R; 53-56; CABS 2; CANR 3, 36; CDALB 1941-1968; CP 1, 2; DA; DA3; DAB; DAC; DAM MST, POET; DLB 5, 169; EWL 3; EXPP; FL 1:6; FW; MAL 5; MBL; MTCW 1, 2; MTFW 2005; PAB; PFS 4, 14, 30, 36, 40; RGAL 4; RGHL; SATA 10; TUS
Sexton, Anne Harvey
See Sexton, Anne
Shaara, Jeff 1952- .... **CLC 119**
See also AAYA 70; CA 163; CANR 109, 172; CN 7; MTFW 2005
Shaara, Michael 1929-1988 .... **CLC 15**
See also AAYA 71; AITN 1; BPFB 3; CA 102; 125; CANR 52, 85; DAM POP; DLBY 1983; MTFW 2005; NFS 26
Shackleton, C.C.
See Aldiss, Brian W.
Shacochis, Bob
See Shacochis, Robert G.
Shacochis, Robert G. 1951- .... **CLC 39**
See also CA 119; 124; CANR 100; INT CA-124
Shadwell, Thomas 1641(?)-1692 ...... **LC 114**
See also DLB 80; IDTP; RGEL 2
Shaffer, Anthony 1926-2001 .... **CLC 19**
See also CA 110; 116; 200; CBD; CD 5, 6; DAM DRAM; DFS 13; DLB 13
Shaffer, Anthony Joshua
See Shaffer, Anthony
Shaffer, Peter 1926- .... **CLC 5, 14, 18, 37, 60, 291; DC 7**
See also BRWS 1; CA 25-28R; CANR 25, 47, 74, 118; CBD; CD 5, 6; CDBLB 1960 to Present; DA3; DAB; DAM DRAM, MST; DFS 5, 13; DLB 13, 233; EWL 3; MTCW 1, 2; MTFW 2005; RGEL 2; TEA
Shakespeare, William 1564-1616 .... **PC 84, 89, 98, 101, 128; WLC 5**
See also AAYA 35; BRW 1; BRWR 3; CDBLB Before 1660; DA; DA3; DAB; DAC; DAM DRAM, MST, POET; DFS 20, 21; DLB 62, 172, 263; EXPP; LAIT 1; LATS 1:1; LMFS 1; PAB; PFS 1, 2, 3, 4, 5, 8, 9, 35; RGEL 2; TEA; WLIT 3; WP; WS; WYA
Shakey, Bernard
See Young, Neil
Shalamov, Varlam (Tikhonovich) 1907-1982 .... **CLC 18; SSC 205**
See also CA 129; 105; DLB 302; RGSF 2
Shamloo, Ahmad
See Shamlu, Ahmad
Shamlou, Ahmad
See Shamlu, Ahmad
Shamlu, Ahmad 1925-2000 .... **CLC 10**
See also CA 216; CWW 2
Shammas, Anton 1951- .... **CLC 55**
See also CA 199; DLB 346
Shandling, Arline
See Berriault, Gina

Shange, Ntozake 1948- .... **BLC 1:3, 2:3; CLC 8, 25, 38, 74, 126; DC 3**
See also AAYA 9, 66; AFAW 1, 2; BW 2; CA 85-88; CABS 3; CAD; CANR 27, 48, 74, 131, 208; CD 5, 6; CP 5, 6, 7; CWD; CWP; DA3; DAM DRAM, MULT; DFS 2, 11; DLB 38, 249; FW; LAIT 4, 5; MAL 5; MTCW 1, 2; MTFW 2005; NFS 11; RGAL 4; SATA 157; YAW
Shanley, John Patrick 1950- .... **CLC 75**
See also AAYA 74; AMWS 14; CA 128; 133; CAD; CANR 83, 154; CD 5, 6; DFS 23, 28
Shapcott, Thomas W(illiam) 1935- .... **CLC 38**
See also CA 69-72; CANR 49, 83, 103; CP 1, 2, 3, 4, 5, 6, 7; DLB 289
Shapiro, Jane 1942- .... **CLC 76**
See also CA 196
Shapiro, Karl 1913-2000 .... **CLC 4, 8, 15, 53; PC 25**
See also AMWS 2; CA 1-4R; 188; CAAS 6; CANR 1, 36, 66; CP 1, 2, 3, 4, 5, 6; DLB 48; EWL 3; EXPP; MAL 5; MTCW 1, 2; MTFW 2005; PFS 3; RGAL 4
Sharp, William 1855-1905 .... **TCLC 39**
See also CA 160; DLB 156; RGEL 2; SUFW
Sharpe, Thomas Ridley 1928- .... **CLC 36**
See also CA 114; 122; CANR 85; CN 4, 5, 6, 7; DLB 14, 231; INT CA-122
Sharpe, Tom
See Sharpe, Thomas Ridley
Shatrov, Mikhail .... **CLC 59**
Shaw, Bernard
See Shaw, George Bernard
Shaw, G. Bernard
See Shaw, George Bernard
Shaw, George Bernard 1856-1950 ... **DC 23; TCLC 3, 9, 21, 45, 205, 293; WLC 5**
See also AAYA 61; BRW 6; BRWC 1; BRWR 2; CA 104; 128; CDBLB 1914-1945; DA; DA3; DAB; DAC; DAM DRAM, MST; DFS 1, 3, 6, 11, 19, 22, 30; DLB 10, 57, 190, 332; EWL 3; LAIT 3; LATS 1:1; MTCW 1, 2; MTFW 2005; RGEL 2; TEA; WLIT 4
Shaw, Henry Wheeler
1818-1885 .... **NCLC 15**
See also DLB 11; RGAL 4
Shaw, Irwin 1913-1984 .... **CLC 7, 23, 34**
See also AITN 1; BPFB 3; CA 13-16R; 112; CANR 21; CDALB 1941-1968; CN 1, 2, 3; CPW; DAM DRAM, POP; DLB 6, 102; DLBY 1984; MAL 5; MTCW 1, 21; MTFW 2005
Shaw, Robert (Archibald) 1927-1978 ... **CLC 5**
See also AITN 1; CA 1-4R; 81-84; CANR 4; CN 1, 2; DLB 13, 14
Shaw, T. E.
See Lawrence, T. E.
Shawn, Wallace 1943- .... **CLC 41**
See also CA 112; CAD; CANR 215; CD 5, 6; DLB 266
Shaykh, Hanan al- 1945- .... **CLC 218**
See also CA 135; CANR 111, 220; CWW 2; DLB 346; EWL 3; WLIT 6
Shchedrin, N.
See Saltykov, Mikhail Evgrafovich
Shea, Lisa 1953- .... **CLC 86**
See also CA 147
Sheed, Wilfrid 1930-2011 .... **CLC 2, 4, 10, 53**
See also CA 65-68; CANR 30, 66, 181; CN 1, 2, 3, 4, 5, 6, 7; DLB 6; MAL 5; MTCW 1, 2; MTFW 2005
Sheed, Wilfrid John Joseph
See Sheed, Wilfrid
Sheehy, Gail 1937- .... **CLC 171**
See also CA 49-52; CANR 1, 33, 55, 92; CPW; MTCW 1
Sheldon, Alice Hastings Bradley
1915(?)-1987 .... **CLC 48, 50**
See also CA 108; 122; CANR 34; DLB 8; INT CA-108; MTCW 1; SCFW 1, 2; SFW 4
Sheldon, John
See Bloch, Robert (Albert)
Sheldon, Raccoona
See Sheldon, Alice Hastings Bradley
Shelley, Mary
See Shelley, Mary Wollstonecraft
Shelley, Mary Wollstonecraft
1797-1851 ...... **NCLC 14, 59, 103, 170; SSC 92; WLC 5**
See also AAYA 20; BPFB 3; BRW 3; BRWC 2; BRWR 3; BRWS 3; BYA 5; CDBLB 1789-1832; CLR 133; DA; DA3; DAB; DAC; DAM MST, NOV; DLB 110, 116, 159, 178; EXPN; FL 1:3; GL 3; HGG; LAIT 1; LMFS 1, 2; NFS 1, 37; RGEL 2; SATA 29; SCFW 1, 2; SFW 4; TEA; WLIT 3
Shelley, Percy Bysshe
1792-1822 ...... **NCLC 18, 93, 143, 175; PC 14, 67, 158, 161; WLC 5**
See also AAYA 61; BRW 4; BRWR 1; CDBLB 1789-1832; DA; DA3; DAB; DAC; DAM MST, POET; DLB 96, 110, 158; EXPP; LMFS 1; PAB; PFS 2, 27, 32, 36; RGEL 2; TEA; WLIT 3; WP
Shen Cong Wen
See Shen Congwen
Shen Congwen 1902-1988 .... **TCLC 301**
See also CA 125, 303; DLB 328; RGSF 2
Shen Ts'ung-Wen
See Shen Congwen
Shepard, James R.
See Shepard, Jim
Shepard, Jim 1956- .... **CLC 36**
See also AAYA 73; CA 137; CANR 59, 104, 160, 199, 231; SATA 90, 164
Shepard, Lucius 1947- .... **CLC 34**
See also CA 128; 141; CANR 81, 124, 178; HGG; SCFW 2; SFW 4; SUFW 2
Shepard, Sam 1943- .... **CLC 4, 6, 17, 34, 41, 44, 169; DC 5**
See also AAYA 1, 58; AMWS 3; CA 69-72; CABS 3; CAD; CANR 22, 120, 140, 223; CD 5, 6; DA3; DAM DRAM; DFS 3, 6, 7, 14; DLB 7, 212, 341; EWL 3; IDFW 3, 4; MAL 5; MTCW 1, 2; MTFW 2005; RGAL 4
Shepherd, Jean (Parker)
1921-1999 .... **TCLC 177**
See also AAYA 69; AITN 2; CA 77-80; 187
Shepherd, Michael
See Ludlum, Robert
Sherburne, Zoa (Lillian Morin)
1912-1995 .... **CLC 30**
See also AAYA 13; CA 1-4R; 176; CANR 3, 37; MAICYA 1, 2; SAAS 18; SATA 3; YAW
Sheridan, Frances 1724-1766 .... **LC 7**
See also DLB 39, 84
Sheridan, Richard Brinsley
1751-1816 .... **DC 1; NCLC 5, 91; WLC 5**
See also BRW 3; CDBLB 1660-1789; DA; DAB; DAC; DAM DRAM, MST; DFS 15; DLB 89; WLIT 3
Sherman, Jonathan Marc 1968- ..... **CLC 55**
See also CA 230
Sherman, Martin 1941(?)- .... **CLC 19**
See also CA 116; 123; CAD; CANR 86; CD 5, 6; DFS 20; DLB 228; GLL 1; IDTP; RGHL
Sherwin, Judith Johnson
See Johnson, Judith
Sherwood, Frances 1940- .... **CLC 81**
See also CA 146, 220; CAAE 220; CANR 158
Sherwood, Mary Martha
1775-1851 .... **NCLC 301**
See also DLB 163
Sherwood, Robert E(mmet)
1896-1955 .... **DC 36; TCLC 3**
See also CA 104; 153; CANR 86; DAM DRAM; DFS 11, 15, 17; DLB 7, 26, 249; IDFW 3, 4; MAL 5; RGAL 4
Shestov, Lev 1866-1938 .... **TCLC 56**
Shevchenko, Taras 1814-1861 .... **NCLC 54, 281**
Shiel, M. P. 1865-1947 .... **TCLC 8**
See also CA 106; 160; DLB 153; HGG; MTCW 2; MTFW 2005; SCFW 1, 2; SFW 4; SUFW
Shiel, Matthew Phipps
See Shiel, M. P.
Shields, Carol 1935-2003 .... **CLC 91, 113, 193, 298; SSC 126**
See also AMWS 7; CA 81-84; 218; CANR 51, 74, 98, 133; CCA 1; CN 6, 7; CPW; DA3; DAC; DLB 334, 350; MTCW 2; MTFW 2005; NFS 23
Shields, David 1956- .... **CLC 97**
See also CA 124; CANR 48, 99, 112, 157
Shields, David Jonathan
See Shields, David
Shiga, Naoya 1883-1971 .... **CLC 33; SSC 23; TCLC 172**
See also CA 101; 33-36R; DLB 180; EWL 3; MJW; RGWL 3
Shiga Naoya
See Shiga, Naoya
Shilts, Randy 1951-1994 .... **CLC 85**
See also AAYA 19; CA 115; 127; 144; CANR 45; DA3; GLL 1; INT CA-127; MTCW 2; MTFW 2005
Shimazaki, Haruki 1872-1943 .... **TCLC 5**
See also CA 105; 134; CANR 84; DLB 180; EWL 3; MJW; RGWL 3
Shimazaki Toson
See Shimazaki, Haruki
Shi Mo
See Bei Dao
Shirley, James 1596-1666 ..... **DC 25; LC 96**
See also DLB 58; RGEL 2
Shklovsky, Viktor 1893-1984 ..... **TCLC 295**
See also CA 114, 144
Sholokhov, Mikhail 1905-1984 .... **CLC 7, 15**
See also CA 101; 112; DLB 272, 332; EWL 3; MTCW 1, 2; MTFW 2005; RGWL 2, 3; SATA-Obit 36
Sholokhov, Mikhail Aleksandrovich
See Sholokhov, Mikhail
Shone, Patric
See Hanley, James
Showalter, Elaine 1941- .... **CLC 169**
See also CA 57-60; CANR 58, 106, 208; DLB 67; FW; GLL 2
Shreve, Susan
See Shreve, Susan Richards
Shreve, Susan Richards 1939- .... **CLC 23**
See also CA 49-52; CAAS 5; CANR 5, 38, 69, 100, 159, 199; MAICYA 1, 2; SATA 46, 95, 152; SATA-Brief 41
Shteyngart, Gary 1972- .... **CLC 319**
See also AAYA 68; CA 217; CANR 175
Shteyngart, Igor
See Shteyngart, Gary
Shue, Larry 1946-1985 .... **CLC 52**
See also CA 145; 117; DAM DRAM; DFS 7
Shu-Jen, Chou 1881-1936 .. **SSC 20; TCLC 3**
See also CA 104; EWL 3
Shukshin, Vasily 1929-1974 .... **SSC 203**
See also CA 135; CANR 87; DLB 302; EWL 3
Shulman, Alix Kates 1932- .... **CLC 2, 10**
See also CA 29-32R; CANR 43, 199; FW; SATA 7
Shuster, Joe 1914-1992 .... **CLC 21**
See also AAYA 50

Shute, Nevil 1899-1960 .... **CLC 30**
See also BPFB 3; CA 102; 93-96; CANR 85; DLB 255; MTCW 2; NFS 9, 38; RHW 4; SFW 4

Shuttle, Penelope (Diane) 1947- .... **CLC 7**
See also CA 93-96; CANR 39, 84, 92, 108; CP 3, 4, 5, 6, 7; CWP; DLB 14, 40

Shvarts, Elena 1948-2010 .... **PC 50**
See also CA 147

Sībawayhi 750?-796? .... **CMLC 161**
See also DLB 311

Sidhwa, Bapsi 1939-
See Sidhwa, Bapsy (N.)

Sidhwa, Bapsy (N.) 1938- .... **CLC 168**
See also CA 108; CANR 25, 57; CN 6, 7; DLB 323; FW

Sidney, Mary 1561-1621 ...... **LC 19, 39, 182**
See also DLB 167

Sidney, Sir Philip 1554-1586 .... **LC 19, 39, 131, 197, 240, 241; PC 32**
See also BRW 1; BRWR 2; CDBLB Before 1660; DA; DA3; DAB; DAC; DAM MST, POET; DLB 167; EXPP; PAB; PFS 30; RGEL 2; TEA; WP

Sidney Herbert, Mary
See Sidney, Mary

Siegel, Jerome 1914-1996 .... **CLC 21**
See also AAYA 50; CA 116; 169; 151

Siegel, Jerry
See Siegel, Jerome

Sienkiewicz, Henryk (Adam Alexander Pius) 1846-1916 .... **TCLC 3**
See also CA 104; 134; CANR 84; DLB 332; EWL 3; RGSF 2; RGWL 2, 3

Sierra, Gregorio Martinez
See Martinez Sierra, Gregorio

Sierra, Maria de la O'LeJarraga Martinez
See Martinez Sierra, Maria

Sigal, Clancy 1926- .... **CLC 7**
See also CA 1-4R; CANR 85, 184; CN 1, 2, 3, 4, 5, 6, 7

Siguenza y Gongora, Carlos de 1645-1700 .... **HLCS 2; LC 8**
See also LAW

Siger of Brabant 1240(?)-1284(?) ... **CMLC 69**
See also DLB 115

Sigourney, Lydia H.
See Sigourney, Lydia Howard

Sigourney, Lydia Howard 1791-1865 .... **NCLC 21, 87**
See also DLB 1, 42, 73, 183, 239, 243

Sigourney, Lydia Howard Huntley
See Sigourney, Lydia Howard

Sigourney, Lydia Huntley
See Sigourney, Lydia Howard

Sigurjonsson, Johann
See Sigurjonsson, Johann

Sigurjonsson, Johann 1880-1919 ... **TCLC 27**
See also CA 170; DLB 293; EWL 3

Sikelianos, Angelos 1884-1951 .... **PC 29; TCLC 39**
See also EWL 3; RGWL 2, 3

Silkin, Jon 1930-1997 .... **CLC 2, 6, 43**
See also CA 5-8R; CAAS 5; CANR 89; CP 1, 2, 3, 4, 5, 6; DLB 27

Silko, Leslie 1948- .... **CLC 23, 74, 114, 211, 302; NNAL; SSC 37, 66, 151; WLCS**
See also AAYA 14; AMWS 4; ANW; BYA 12; CA 115; 122; CANR 45, 65, 118, 226; CN 4, 5, 6, 7; CP 4, 5, 6, 7; CPW 1; CWP; DA; DA3; DAC; DAM MST, MULT, POP; DLB 143, 175, 256, 275; EWL 3; EXPP; EXPS; LAIT 4; MAL 5; MTCW 2; MTFW 2005; NFS 4; PFS 9, 16; RGAL 4; RGSF 2; SSFS 4, 8, 10, 11; TCWW 1, 2

Silko, Leslie Marmon
See Silko, Leslie

Sillanpaa, Frans Eemil 1888-1964 .. **CLC 19**
See also CA 129; 93-96; DLB 332; EWL 3; MTCW 1

Sillitoe, Alan 1928-2010 .... **CLC 1, 3, 6, 10, 19, 57, 148, 318**
See also AITN 1; BRWS 5; CA 9-12R, 191; CAAE 191; CAAS 2; CANR 8, 26, 55, 139, 213; CDBLB 1960 to Present; CN 1, 2, 3, 4, 5, 6; CP 1, 2, 3, 4, 5; DLB 14, 139; EWL 3; MTCW 1, 2; MTFW 2005; RGEL 2; RGSF 2; SATA 61

Silone, Ignazio 1900-1978 .... **CLC 4**
See also CA 25-28; 81-84; CANR 34; CAP 2; DLB 264; EW 12; EWL 3; MTCW 1; RGSF 2; RGWL 2, 3

Silone, Ignazione
See Silone, Ignazio

Siluriensis, Leolinus
See Jones, Arthur Llewellyn

Silva, José Asunción 1865-1896 .... **NCLC 114, 280**
See also DLB 283; LAW

Silver, Joan Micklin 1935- .... **CLC 20**
See also CA 114; 121; INT CA-121

Silver, Nicholas
See Faust, Frederick

Silverberg, Robert 1935- .... **CLC 7, 140**
See also AAYA 24; BPFB 3; BYA 7, 9; CA 1-4R, 186; CAAE 186; CAAS 3; CANR 1, 20, 36, 85, 140, 175, 236; CLR 59; CN 6, 7; CPW; DAM POP; DLB 8; INT CANR-20; MAICYA 1, 2; MTCW 1, 2; MTFW 2005; SATA 13, 91; SATA-Essay 104; SCFW 1, 2; SFW 4; SUFW 2

Silverstein, Alvin 1933- .... **CLC 17**
See also CA 49-52; CANR 2; CLR 25; JRDA; MAICYA 1, 2; SATA 8, 69, 124

Silverstein, Shel 1932-1999 .... **PC 49**
See also AAYA 40; BW 3; CA 107; 179; CANR 47, 74, 81; CLR 5, 96; CWRI 5; JRDA; MAICYA 1, 2; MTCW 2; MTFW 2005; SATA 33, 92; SATA-Brief 27; SATA-Obit 116

Silverstein, Sheldon Allan
See Silverstein, Shel

Silverstein, Virginia B. 1937- .... **CLC 17**
See also CA 49-52; CANR 2; CLR 25; JRDA; MAICYA 1, 2; SATA 8, 69, 124

Silverstein, Virginia Barbara Opshelor
See Silverstein, Virginia B.

Sim, Georges
See Simenon, Georges

Sima Qian 145B.C.-c. 89B.C. .. **CMLC 72, 146**
See also DLB 358

Simak, Clifford D(onald) 1904-1988 .... **CLC 1, 55**
See also CA 1-4R; 125; CANR 1, 35; DLB 8; MTCW 1; SATA-Obit 56; SCFW 1, 2; SFW 4

Simenon, Georges 1903-1989 .... **CLC 1, 2, 3, 8, 18, 47**
See also BPFB 3; CA 85-88; 129; CANR 35; CMW 4; DA3; DAM POP; DLB 72; DLBY 1989; EW 12; EWL 3; GFL 1789 to the Present; MSW; MTCW 1, 2; MTFW 2005; RGWL 2, 3

Simenon, Georges Jacques Christian
See Simenon, Georges

Simic, Charles 1938- .... **CLC 6, 9, 22, 49, 68, 130, 256; PC 69**
See also AAYA 78; AMWS 8; CA 29-32R; CAAS 4; CANR 12, 33, 52, 61, 96, 140, 210, 240; CP 2, 3, 4, 5, 6, 7; DA3; DAM POET; DLB 105; MAL 5; MTCW 2; MTFW 2005; PFS 7, 33, 36; RGAL 4; WP

Simmel, Georg 1858-1918 .... **TCLC 64**
See also CA 157; DLB 296

Simmons, Charles (Paul) 1924- ...... **CLC 57**
See also CA 89-92; INT CA-89-92

Simmons, Dan 1948- .... **CLC 44**
See also AAYA 16, 54; CA 138; CANR 53, 81, 126, 174, 204, 241; CPW; DAM POP; HGG; SUFW 2

Simmons, James (Stewart Alexander) 1933- .... **CLC 43**
See also CA 105; CAAS 21; CP 1, 2, 3, 4, 5, 6, 7; DLB 40

Simmons, Richard
See Simmons, Dan

Simms, William Gilmore 1806-1870 .... **NCLC 3, 241**
See also DLB 3, 30, 59, 73, 248, 254; RGAL 4

Simon, Carly 1945- .... **CLC 26**
See also CA 105

Simon, Claude 1913-2005 .... **CLC 4, 9, 15, 39**
See also CA 89-92; 241; CANR 33, 117; CWW 2; DAM NOV; DLB 83, 332; EW 13; EWL 3; GFL 1789 to the Present; MTCW 1

Simon, Claude Eugene Henri
See Simon, Claude

Simon, Claude Henri Eugene
See Simon, Claude

Simon, Marvin Neil
See Simon, Neil

Simon, Myles
See Follett, Ken

Simon, Neil 1927- .... **CLC 6, 11, 31, 39, 70, 233; DC 14**
See also AAYA 32; AITN 1; AMWS 4; CA 21-24R; CAD; CANR 26, 54, 87, 126; CD 5, 6; DA3; DAM DRAM; DFS 2, 6, 12, 18, 24, 27; DLB 7, 266; LAIT 4; MAL 5; MTCW 1, 2; MTFW 2005; RGAL 4; TUS

Simon, Paul 1941(?)- .... **CLC 17**
See also CA 116; 153; CANR 152

Simon, Paul Frederick
See Simon, Paul

Simonon, Paul 1956(?)- .... **CLC 30**

Simonson, Helen 1963- .... **CLC 318**
See also CA 307

Simonson, Rick .... **CLC 70**

Simpson, Harriette
See Arnow, Harriette (Louisa) Simpson

Simpson, Louis 1923- ... **CLC 4, 7, 9, 32, 149**
See also AMWS 9; CA 1-4R; CAAS 4; CANR 1, 61, 140; CP 1, 2, 3, 4, 5, 6, 7; DAM POET; DLB 5; MAL 5; MTCW 1, 2; MTFW 2005; PFS 7, 11, 14; RGAL 4

Simpson, Mona 1957- .... **CLC 44, 146**
See also CA 122; 135; CANR 68, 103, 227; CN 6, 7; EWL 3

Simpson, Mona Elizabeth
See Simpson, Mona

Simpson, N. F. 1919-2011 .... **CLC 29**
See also CA 13-16R; CBD; DLB 13; RGEL 2

Simpson, Norman Frederick
See Simpson, N. F.

Sinclair, Andrew (Annandale) 1935- .... **CLC 2, 14**
See also CA 9-12R; CAAS 5; CANR 14, 38, 91; CN 1, 2, 3, 4, 5, 6, 7; DLB 14; FANT; MTCW 1

Sinclair, Emil
See Hesse, Hermann

Sinclair, Iain 1943- .... **CLC 76**
See also BRWS 14; CA 132; CANR 81, 157; CP 5, 6, 7; HGG

Sinclair, Iain MacGregor
See Sinclair, Iain

Sinclair, Irene
See Griffith, D.W.

Sinclair, Julian
See Sinclair, May

Sinclair, Mary Amelia St. Clair (?)-
See Sinclair, May

Sinclair, May 1865-1946 .... **TCLC 3, 11**
See also CA 104; 166; DLB 36, 135; EWL 3; HGG; RGEL 2; RHW; SUFW

Sinclair, Roy
See Griffith, D.W.

Sinclair, Upton 1878-1968 .... **CLC 1, 11, 15, 63; TCLC 160; WLC 5**
See also AAYA 63; AMWS 5; BPFB 3; BYA 2; CA 5-8R; 25-28R; CANR 7; CDALB 1929-1941; DA; DA3; DAB; DAC; DAM MST, NOV; DLB 9; EWL 3; INT CANR-7; LAIT 3; MAL 5; MTCW 1, 2; MTFW 2005; NFS 6; RGAL 4; SATA 9; TUS; YAW

Sinclair, Upton Beall
See Sinclair, Upton

Singe, (Edmund) J(ohn) M(illington) 1871-1909 .... **WLC**

Singer, Isaac
See Singer, Isaac Bashevis

Singer, Isaac Bashevis 1904-1991 .... **CLC 1, 3, 6, 9, 11, 15, 23, 38, 69, 111; SSC 3, 53, 80, 154; WLC 5**
See also AAYA 32; AITN 1, 2; AMW; AMWR 2; BPFB 3; BYA 1, 4; CA 1-4R; 134; CANR 1, 39, 106; CDALB 1941-1968; CLR 1; CN 1, 2, 3, 4; CWRI 5; DA; DA3; DAB; DAC; DAM MST, NOV; DLB 6, 28, 52, 278, 332, 333; DLBY 1991; EWL 3; EXPS; HGG; JRDA; LAIT 3; MAICYA 1, 2; MAL 5; MTCW 1, 2; MTFW 2005; RGAL 4; RGHL; RGSF 2; SATA 3, 27; SATA-Obit 68; SSFS 2, 12, 16, 27, 30; TUS; TWA

Singer, Israel Joshua 1893-1944 ... **TCLC 33**
See also CA 169; DLB 333; EWL 3

Singer, Peter 1946- .... **CLC 330**
See also CA 57-60; CANR 8, 51, 85, 102, 202

Singer, Peter Albert David
See Singer, Peter

Singh, Khushwant 1915- .... **CLC 11**
See also CA 9-12R; CAAS 9; CANR 6, 84; CN 1, 2, 3, 4, 5, 6, 7; DLB 323; EWL 3; RGEL 2

Singleton, Ann
See Benedict, Ruth

Singleton, John 1968(?)- .... **CLC 156**
See also AAYA 50; BW 2, 3; CA 138; CANR 67, 82; DAM MULT

Siniavskii, Andrei
See Sinyavsky, Andrei (Donatevich)

Sinibaldi, Fosco
See Kacew, Romain

Sinjohn, John
See Galsworthy, John

Sinyavsky, Andrei (Donatevich) 1925-1997 .... **CLC 8**
See also CA 85-88; 159; CWW 2; EWL 3; RGSF 2

Sinyavsky, Andrey Donatovich
See Sinyavsky, Andrei (Donatevich)

Sirin, V.
See Nabokov, Vladimir

Sissman, L(ouis) E(dward) 1928-1976 .... **CLC 9, 18**
See also CA 21-24R; 65-68; CANR 13; CP 2; DLB 5

Sisson, C(harles) H(ubert) 1914-2003 ... **CLC 8**
See also BRWS 11; CA 1-4R; 220; CAAS 3; CANR 3, 48, 84; CP 1, 2, 3, 4, 5, 6, 7; DLB 27

Sitting Bull 1831(?)-1890 .... **NNAL**
See also DA3; DAM MULT

Sitwell, Dame Edith 1887-1964 .... **CLC 2, 9, 67; PC 3**
See also BRW 7; CA 9-12R; CANR 35; CDBLB 1945-1960; DAM POET; DLB 20; EWL 3; MTCW 1, 2; MTFW 2005; RGEL 2; TEA

Siwaarmill, H. P.
See Sharp, William

Sjoewall, Maj 1935- .... **CLC 7**
See also BPFB 3; CA 65-68; CANR 73; CMW 4; MSW

Sjowall, Maj
See Sjoewall, Maj

Skármeta, Antonio 1940- .... **CLC 386**
See also CA 131; CANR 80, 189, 270; CDWLB; CWW 2; DLB 145; EWL 3; HW 1, 2; LAWS 1; RGWL 3; SATA 57

Skelton, John 1460(?)-1529 .... **LC 71, 244; PC 25**
See also BRW 1; DLB 136; RGEL 2

Skelton, Robin 1925-1997 .... **CLC 13**
See also AITN 2; CA 5-8R; 160; CAAS 5; CANR 28, 89; CCA 1; CP 1, 2, 3, 4, 5, 6; DLB 27, 53

Skolimowski, Jerzy 1938- .... **CLC 20**
See also CA 128

Skovoroda, Hryhorii 1722-1794 ...... **LC 249**

Skram, Amalie (Bertha) 1846-1905 .... **TCLC 25**
See also CA 165; DLB 354

Skvorecky, Josef 1924-2012 ...... **CLC 15, 39, 69, 152, 354**
See also CA 61-64; CAAS 1; CANR 10, 34, 63, 108; CDWLB 4; CWW 2; DA3; DAC; DAM NOV; DLB 232; EWL 3; MTCW 1, 2; MTFW 2005

Skvorecky, Josef Vaclav
See Skvorecky, Josef

Slade, Bernard 1930-
See Newbound, Bernard Slade

Slaughter, Carolyn 1946- .... **CLC 56**
See also CA 85-88; CANR 85, 169; CN 5, 6, 7

Slaughter, Frank G(ill) 1908-2001 ..... **CLC 29**
See also AITN 2; CA 5-8R; 197; CANR 5, 85; INT CANR-5; RHW

Slavitt, David R. 1935- .... **CLC 5, 14**
See also CA 21-24R; CAAS 3; CANR 41, 83, 166, 219; CN 1, 2; CP 1, 2, 3, 4, 5, 6, 7; DLB 5, 6

Slavitt, David Rytman
See Slavitt, David R.

Slavutych, Yar 1918-2011 .... **PC 163**
See also CA 45-48; CANR 2, 17, 38

Slesinger, Tess 1905-1945 .... **TCLC 10**
See also CA 107; 199; DLB 102

Slessor, Kenneth 1901-1971 .... **CLC 14**
See also CA 102; 89-92; DLB 260; RGEL 2

Slick, Jonathan, Esq.
See Stephens, Ann Sophia

Slowacki, Juliusz 1809-1849 .... **NCLC 15**
See also RGWL 3

Small, David 1945- .... **CLC 299**
See also CLR 53; MAICYA 2; SATA 50, 95, 126, 183, 216; SATA-Brief 46

Smart, Christopher 1722-1771 ... **LC 3, 134; PC 13**
See also DAM POET; DLB 109; RGEL 2

Smart, Elizabeth 1913-1986 .... **CLC 54; TCLC 231**
See also CA 81-84; 118; CN 4; DLB 88

Smiley, Jane 1949- .... **CLC 53, 76, 144, 236**
See also AAYA 66; AMWS 6; BPFB 3; CA 104; CANR 30, 50, 74, 96, 158, 196, 231; CN 6, 7; CPW 1; DA3; DAM POP; DLB 227, 234; EWL 3; INT CANR-30; MAL 5; MTFW 2005; NFS 32; SSFS 19

Smiley, Jane Graves
See Smiley, Jane

Smith, A(rthur) J(ames) M(arshall) 1902-1980 .... **CLC 15**
See also CA 1-4R; 102; CANR 4; CP 1, 2, 3; DAC; DLB 88; RGEL 2

Smith, Adam 1723(?)-1790 .... **LC 36**
See also DLB 104, 252, 336; RGEL 2

Smith, Alexander 1829-1867 .... **NCLC 59**
See also DLB 32, 55

Smith, Alexander McCall 1948- ... **CLC 268**
See also CA 215; CANR 154, 196; SATA 73, 179

Smith, Anna Deavere 1950- .... **CLC 86, 241**
See also CA 133; CANR 103; CD 5, 6; DFS 2, 22; DLB 341

Smith, Betty 1904-1972 .... **CLC 19**
See also AAYA 72; AMWS 23; BPFB 3; BYA 3; CA 5-8R; 33-36R; CLR 202; DLBY 1982; LAIT 3; NFS 31; RGAL 4; SATA 6

Smith, Charlotte Turner 1749-1806 .... **NCLC 23, 115; PC 104**
See also BRWS 19; DLB 39, 109; RGEL 2; TEA

Smith, Clark Ashton 1893-1961 ..... **CLC 43**
See also AAYA 76; CA 143; CANR 81; FANT; HGG; MTCW 2; SCFW 1, 2; SFW 4; SUFW

Smith, Dave
See Smith, David (Jeddie)

Smith, David (Jeddie) 1942- ..... **CLC 22, 42**
See also CA 49-52; CAAS 7; CANR 1, 59, 120; CP 3, 4, 5, 6, 7; CSW; DAM POET; DLB 5

Smith, Iain Crichton 1928-1998 ..... **CLC 64**
See also BRWS 9; CA 21-24R; 171; CN 1, 2, 3, 4, 5, 6; CP 1, 2, 3, 4, 5, 6; DLB 40, 139, 319, 352; RGSF 2

Smith, John 1580(?)-1631 .... **LC 9**
See also DLB 24, 30; TUS

Smith, Johnston
See Crane, Stephen

Smith, Joseph, Jr. 1805-1844 .... **NCLC 53**

Smith, Kevin 1970- .... **CLC 223**
See also AAYA 37; CA 166; CANR 131, 201

Smith, Lee 1944- .... **CLC 25, 73, 258; SSC 142**
See also CA 114; 119; CANR 46, 118, 173, 225; CN 7; CSW; DLB 143; DLBY 1983; EWL 3; INT CA-119; RGAL 4

Smith, Martin
See Smith, Martin Cruz

Smith, Martin Cruz 1942- ... **CLC 25; NNAL**
See Smith, Martin Cruz
See also BEST 89:4; BPFB 3; CA 85-88; CANR 6, 23, 43, 65, 119, 184; CMW 4; CPW; DAM MULT, POP; HGG; INT CANR-23; MTCW 2; MTFW 2005; RGAL 4

Smith, Patti 1946- .... **CLC 12, 318**
See also CA 93-96; CANR 63, 168, 232

Smith, Pauline (Urmson) 1882-1959 .... **TCLC 25**
See also DLB 225; EWL 3

Smith, R. Alexander McCall
See Smith, Alexander McCall

Smith, Rosamond
See Oates, Joyce Carol

Smith, Seba 1792-1868 .... **NCLC 187**
See also DLB 1, 11, 243

Smith, Sheila Kaye
See Kaye-Smith, Sheila

Smith, Stevie 1902-1971 .... **CLC 3, 8, 25, 44; PC 12, 172**
See also BRWR 3; BRWS 2; CA 17-18; 29-32R; CANR 35; CAP 2; CP 1; DAM POET; DLB 20; EWL 3; MTCW 1, 2; PAB; PFS 3; RGEL 2; TEA

Smith, Wilbur 1933- .... **CLC 33**
See also CA 13-16R; CANR 7, 46, 66, 134, 180, 236; CPW; MTCW 1, 2; MTFW 2005

Smith, Wilbur Addison
See Smith, Wilbur

Smith, William Jay 1918- .... **CLC 6**
See also AMWS 13; CA 5-8R; CANR 44, 106, 211; CP 1, 2, 3, 4, 5, 6, 7; CSW; CWRI 5; DLB 5; MAICYA 1, 2; SAAS 22; SATA 2, 68, 154; SATA-Essay 154; TCLE 1:2

Smith, Woodrow Wilson
See Kuttner, Henry
Smith, Zadie 1975- .... **CLC 158, 306**
See also AAYA 50; CA 193; CANR 204; DLB 347; MTFW 2005; NFS 40
Smolenskin, Peretz 1842-1885 .... **NCLC 30**
Smollett, Tobias (George)
1721-1771 .... **LC 2, 46, 188, 247, 248**
See also BRW 3; CDBLB 1660-1789; DLB 39, 104; RGEL 2; TEA
Sanchez, Florencio 1875-1910 .... **TCLC 37**
See also CA 153; DLB 305; EWL 3; HW 1; LAW
Sanchez, Luis Rafael 1936- .... **CLC 23**
See also CA 128; DLB 305; EWL 3; HW 1; WLIT 1
Snodgrass, Quentin Curtius
See Twain, Mark
Snodgrass, Thomas Jefferson
See Twain, Mark
Snodgrass, W. D. 1926-2009 .... **CLC 2, 6, 10, 18, 68; PC 74**
See also AMWS 6; CA 1-4R; 282; CANR 6, 36, 65, 85, 185; CP 1, 2, 3, 4, 5, 6, 7; DAM POET; DLB 5; MAL 5; MTCW 1, 2; MTFW 2005; PFS 29; RGAL 4; TCLE 1:2
Snodgrass, W. de Witt
See Snodgrass, W. D.
Snodgrass, William de Witt
See Snodgrass, W. D.
Snodgrass, William De Witt
See Snodgrass, W. D.
Snorri Sturluson 1179-1241 **CMLC 56, 134**
See also RGWL 2, 3
Snow, C(harles) P(ercy)
1905-1980 .... **CLC 1, 4, 6, 9, 13, 19**
See also BRW 7; CA 5-8R; 101; CANR 28; CDBLB 1945-1960; CN 1, 2; DAM NOV; DLB 15, 77; DLBD 17; EWL 3; MTCW 1, 2; MTFW 2005; RGEL 2; TEA
Snow, Frances Compton
See Adams, Henry
Snyder, Gary 1930- .... **CLC 1, 2, 5, 9, 32, 120; PC 21**
See also AAYA 72; AMWS 8; ANW; BG 1:3; CA 17-20R; CANR 30, 60, 125; CP 1, 2, 3, 4, 5, 6, 7; DA3; DAM POET; DLB 5, 16, 165, 212, 237, 275, 342; EWL 3; MAL 5; MTCW 2; MTFW 2005; PFS 9, 19; RGAL 4; WP
Snyder, Gary Sherman
See Snyder, Gary
Snyder, Zilpha Keatley 1927- .... **CLC 17**
See also AAYA 15; BYA 1; CA 9-12R, 252; CAAE 252; CANR 38, 202; CLR 31, 121; JRDA; MAICYA 1, 2; SAAS 2; SATA 1, 28, 75, 110, 163, 226; SATA-Essay 112, 163; YAW
Soares, Bernardo
See Pessoa, Fernando
Sobh, A.
See Shamlu, Ahmad
Sobh, Alef
See Shamlu, Ahmad
Sobol, Joshua 1939- .... **CLC 60**
See also CA 200; CWW 2; RGHL
Sobol, Yehoshua 1939-
See Sobol, Joshua
Socrates 470B.C.-399B.C. .... **CMLC 27**
Soderberg, Hjalmar 1869-1941 ..... **TCLC 39**
See also DLB 259; EWL 3; RGSF 2
Soderbergh, Steven 1963- .... **CLC 154**
See also AAYA 43; CA 243
Soderbergh, Steven Andrew
See Soderbergh, Steven
Sodergran, Edith 1892-1923 .... **TCLC 31**
See also CA 202; DLB 259; EW 11; EWL 3; RGWL 2, 3
Soedergran, Edith Irene
See Sodergran, Edith
Softly, Edgar
See Lovecraft, H. P.
Softly, Edward
See Lovecraft, H. P.
Sokolov, Alexander V. 1943- .... **CLC 59**
See also CA 73-76; CWW 2; DLB 285; EWL 3; RGWL 2, 3
Sokolov, Alexander Vsevolodovich
See Sokolov, Alexander V.
Sokolov, Raymond 1941- .... **CLC 7**
See also CA 85-88
Sokolov, Sasha
See Sokolov, Alexander V.
Soleather
See Twain, Mark
Soli, Tatjana .... **CLC 318**
See also CA 307
Solo, Jay
See Ellison, Harlan
Sologub, Fedor
See Teternikov, Fyodor Kuzmich
Sologub, Feodor
See Teternikov, Fyodor Kuzmich
Sologub, Fyodor
See Teternikov, Fyodor Kuzmich
Solomons, Ikey Esquir
See Thackeray, William Makepeace
Solomos, Dionysios 1798-1857 ...... **NCLC 15**
Solon c. 630-c. 560 BC .... **CMLC 175**
Solwoska, Mara
See French, Marilyn
Solzhenitsyn, Aleksandr 1918-2008 ... **CLC 1, 2, 4, 7, 9, 10, 18, 26, 34, 78, 134, 235; SSC 32, 105; WLC 5**
See also AAYA 49; AITN 1; BPFB 3; CA 69-72; CANR 40, 65, 116; CWW 2; DA; DA3; DAB; DAC; DAM MST, NOV; DLB 302, 332; EW 13; EWL 3; EXPS; LAIT 4; MTCW 1, 2; MTFW 2005; NFS 6; PFS 38; RGSF 2; RGWL 2, 3; SSFS 9; TWA
Solzhenitsyn, Aleksandr I.
See Solzhenitsyn, Aleksandr
Solzhenitsyn, Aleksandr Isayevich
See Solzhenitsyn, Aleksandr
Somers, Jane
See Lessing, Doris
Somerville, Edith Oenone
1858-1949 .... **SSC 56; TCLC 51**
See also CA 196; DLB 135; RGEL 2; RGSF 2
Somerville & Ross
See Martin, Violet Florence; Somerville, Edith Oenone
Sommer, Scott 1951- .... **CLC 25**
See also CA 106
Sommers, Christina Hoff 1950- .... **CLC 197**
See also CA 153; CANR 95
Sondheim, Stephen 1930- .... **CLC 30, 39, 147; DC 22**
See also AAYA 11, 66; CA 103; CANR 47, 67, 125; DAM DRAM; DFS 25, 27, 28; LAIT 4
Sondheim, Stephen Joshua
See Sondheim, Stephen
Sone, Monica 1919- .... **AAL**
See also DLB 312
Song, Cathy 1955- .... **AAL; PC 21**
See also CA 154; CANR 118; CWP; DLB 169, 312; EXPP; FW; PFS 5, 43
Sontag, Susan 1933-2004 .... **CLC 1, 2, 10, 13, 31, 105, 195, 277**
See also AMWS 3; CA 17-20R; 234; CANR 25, 51, 74, 97, 184; CN 1, 2, 3, 4, 5, 6, 7; CPW; DA3; DAM POP; DLB 2, 67; EWL 3; MAL 5; MBL; MTCW 1, 2; MTFW 2005; RGAL 4; RHW; SSFS 10
Sophocles 496(?)B.C.-406(?)B.C. ... **CMLC 2, 47, 51, 86; DC 1; WLCS**
See also AW 1; CDWLB 1; DA; DA3; DAB; DAC; DAM DRAM, MST; DFS 1, 4, 8, 24; DLB 176; LAIT 1; LATS 1:1; LMFS 1; RGWL 2, 3; TWA; WLIT 8
Sor Juana
See Juana Inés de la Cruz, Sor
Sordello 1189-1269 .... **CMLC 15**
Sorel, Georges 1847-1922 .... **TCLC 91**
See also CA 118; 188
Sorel, Julia
See Drexler, Rosalyn
Sorokin, Vladimir 1955- .... **CLC 59, 374**
See also CA 258; CANR 233; DLB 285
Sorokin, Vladimir Georgievich
See Sorokin, Vladimir
Sorrentino, Gilbert 1929-2006 ..... **CLC 3, 7, 14, 22, 40, 247**
See also AMWS 21; CA 77-80; 250; CANR 14, 33, 115, 157; CN 3, 4, 5, 6, 7; CP 1, 2, 3, 4, 5, 6, 7; DLB 5, 173; DLBY 1980; INT CANR-14
Soto, Gary 1952- .... **CLC 32, 80; HLC 2; PC 28**
See also AAYA 10, 37; BYA 11; CA 119; 125; CANR 50, 74, 107, 157, 219; CLR 38; CP 4, 5, 6, 7; DAM MULT; DFS 26; DLB 82; EWL 3; EXPP; HW 1, 2; INT CA-125; JRDA; LLW; MAICYA 2; MAICYAS 1; MAL 5; MTCW 2; MTFW 2005; PFS 7, 30; RGAL 4; SATA 80, 120, 174; SSFS 33; WYA; YAW
Soupault, Philippe 1897-1990 .... **CLC 68**
See also CA 116; 147; 131; EWL 3; GFL 1789 to the Present; LMFS 2
Souster, (Holmes) Raymond
1921- .... **CLC 5, 14**
See also CA 13-16R; CAAS 14; CANR 13, 29, 53; CP 1, 2, 3, 4, 5, 6, 7; DA3; DAC; DAM POET; DLB 88; RGEL 2; SATA 63
Southern, Terry 1924(?)-1995 .... **CLC 7**
See also AMWS 11; BPFB 3; CA 1-4R; 150; CANR 1, 55, 107; CN 1, 2, 3, 4, 5, 6; DLB 2; IDFW 3, 4
Southerne, Thomas 1660-1746 .... **LC 99**
See also DLB 80; RGEL 2
Southey, Robert 1774-1843 ..... **NCLC 8, 97; PC 111**
See also BRW 4; DLB 93, 107, 142; RGEL 2; SATA 54
Southwell, Robert 1561(?)-1595 .... **LC 108**
See also DLB 167; RGEL 2; TEA
Southworth, Emma Dorothy Eliza Nevitte
1819-1899 .... **NCLC 26**
See also DLB 239
Souza, Ernest
See Scott, Evelyn
Soyinka, Wole 1934- .... **BLC 1:3, 2:3; CLC 3, 5, 14, 36, 44, 179, 331; DC 2; PC 118; WLC 5**
See also AFW; BW 2, 3; CA 13-16R; CANR 27, 39, 82, 136; CD 5, 6; CDWLB 3; CN 6, 7; CP 1, 2, 3, 4, 5, 6 ,7; DA; DA3; DAB; DAC; DAM DRAM, MST, MULT; DFS 10, 26; DLB 125, 332; EWL 3; MTCW 1, 2; MTFW 2005; PFS 27, 40; RGEL 2; TWA; WLIT 2; WWE 1
Spackman, W(illiam) M(ode)
1905-1990 .... **CLC 46**
See also CA 81-84; 132
Spacks, Barry (Bernard) 1931- ...... **CLC 14**
See also CA 154; CANR 33, 109; CP 3, 4, 5, 6, 7; DLB 105
Spanidou, Irini 1946- .... **CLC 44**
See also CA 185; CANR 179
Spark, Muriel 1918-2006 .... **CLC 2, 3, 5, 8, 13, 18, 40, 94, 242; PC 72; SSC 10, 115**
See also BRWS 1; CA 5-8R; 251; CANR 12, 36, 76, 89, 131; CDBLB 1945-1960; CN 1, 2, 3, 4, 5, 6, 7; CP 1, 2, 3, 4, 5, 6, 7; DA3;

DAB; DAC; DAM MST, NOV; DLB 15, 139; EWL 3; FW; INT CANR-12; LAIT 4; MTCW 1, 2; MTFW 2005; NFS 22; RGEL 2; SSFS 28; TEA; WLIT 4; YAW
Spark, Muriel Sarah
See Spark, Muriel
Spaulding, Douglas
See Bradbury, Ray
Spaulding, Leonard
See Bradbury, Ray
Speght, Rachel 1597-c. 1630 .... **LC 97**
See also DLB 126
Spence, J. A. D.
See Eliot, T. S.
Spencer, Anne 1882-1975 .... **HR 1:3; PC 77**
See also BW 2; CA 161; DLB 51, 54
Spencer, Elizabeth 1921- .... **CLC 22; SSC 57**
See also CA 13-16R; CANR 32, 65, 87; CN 1, 2, 3, 4, 5, 6, 7; CSW; DLB 6, 218; EWL 3; MTCW 1; RGAL 4; SATA 14
Spencer, Leonard G.
See Silverberg, Robert
Spencer, Scott 1945- .... **CLC 30**
See also CA 113; CANR 51, 148, 190; DLBY 1986
Spender, Stephen 1909-1995 .... **CLC 1, 2, 5, 10, 41, 91; PC 71**
See also BRWS 2; CA 9-12R; 149; CANR 31, 54; CDBLB 1945-1960; CP 1, 2, 3, 4, 5, 6; DA3; DAM POET; DLB 20; EWL 3; MTCW 1, 2; MTFW 2005; PAB; PFS 23, 36; RGEL 2; TEA
Spender, Stephen Harold
See Spender, Stephen
Spengler, Oswald (Arnold Gottfried) 1880-1936 .... **TCLC 25**
See also CA 118; 189
Spenser, Edmund c. 1552-1599 ..... **LC 5, 39, 117, 233; PC 8, 42, 170; WLC 5**
See also AAYA 60; BRW 1; CDBLB Before 1660; DA; DA3; DAB; DAC; DAM MST, POET; DLB 167; EFS 1:2, 2:1; EXPP; PAB; PFS 32; RGEL 2; TEA; WLIT 3; WP
Spicer, Jack 1925-1965 .... **CLC 8, 18, 72**
See also BG 1:3; CA 85-88; DAM POET; DLB 5, 16, 193; GLL 1; WP
Spiegelman, Art 1948- .... **CLC 76, 178**
See also AAYA 10, 46; CA 125; CANR 41, 55, 74, 124; DLB 299; MTCW 2; MTFW 2005; NFS 35; RGHL; SATA 109, 158; YAW
Spielberg, Peter 1929- .... **CLC 6**
See also CA 5-8R; CANR 4, 48; DLBY 1981
Spielberg, Steven 1947- .... **CLC 20, 188**
See also AAYA 8, 24; CA 77-80; CANR 32; SATA 32
Spillane, Frank Morrison
See Spillane, Mickey
Spillane, Mickey 1918-2006 .... **CLC 3, 13, 241**
See also BPFB 3; CA 25-28R; 252; CANR 28, 63, 125, 238; CMW 4; DA3; DLB 226; MSW; MTCW 1, 2; MTFW 2005; SATA 66; SATA-Obit 176
Spinoza, Benedictus de 1632-1677 .... **LC 9, 58, 177**
Spinrad, Norman (Richard) 1940- ... **CLC 46**
See also BPFB 3; CA 37-40R, 233; CAAE 233; CAAS 19; CANR 20, 91; DLB 8; INT CANR-20; SFW 4
Spiotta, Dana 1966- .... **CLC 328**
See also CA 246; CANR 238
Spitteler, Carl 1845-1924 .... **TCLC 12**
See also CA 109; DLB 129, 332; EWL 3
Spitteler, Karl Friedrich Georg
See Spitteler, Carl
Spivack, Kathleen (Romola Drucker) 1938- .... **CLC 6**
See also CA 49-52
Spivak, Gayatri Chakravorty 1942- .... **CLC 233**
See also CA 110; 154; CANR 91; FW; LMFS 2
Spofford, Harriet (Elizabeth) Prescott 1835-1921 .... **SSC 87**
See also CA 201; DLB 74, 221
Spoto, Donald 1941- .... **CLC 39**
See also CA 65-68; CANR 11, 57, 93, 173, 212
Springsteen, Bruce 1949- .... **CLC 17**
See also CA 111
Springsteen, Bruce F.
See Springsteen, Bruce
Spurling, Hilary 1940- .... **CLC 34**
See also CA 104; CANR 25, 52, 94, 157, 224
Spurling, Susan Hilary
See Spurling, Hilary
Spyker, John Howland
See Elman, Richard (Martin)
Squared, A.
See Abbott, Edwin A.
Squires, (James) Radcliffe 1917-1993 .... **CLC 51**
See also CA 1-4R; 140; CANR 6, 21; CP 1, 2, 3, 4, 5
Surdas c. 1478-c. 1583 .... **LC 163**
See also RGWL 2, 3
Srivastav, Dhanpat Ray
See Srivastava, Dhanpat Rai
Srivastav, Dheanpatrai
See Srivastava, Dhanpat Rai
Srivastava, Dhanpat Rai 1880(?)-1936 .... **TCLC 21**
See also CA 118; 197; EWL 3
Soseki Natsume 1867-1916 .... **TCLC 2, 10, 271**
See also CA 104; 195; DLB 180; EWL 3; MJW; RGWL 2, 3; TWA
Ssu-ma Ch'ien c. 145B.C.-c. 86B.C. .... **CMLC 96**
Ssu-ma T'an (?)-c. 110B.C. .... **CMLC 96**
Stacy, Donald
See Pohl, Frederik
Stafford, Jean 1915-1979 .... **CLC 4, 7, 19, 68; SSC 26, 86**
See also CA 1-4R; 85-88; CANR 3, 65; CN 1, 2; DLB 2, 173; MAL 5; MTCW 1, 2; MTFW 2005; RGAL 4; RGSF 2; SATA-Obit 22; SSFS 21; TCWW 1, 2; TUS
Stafford, William 1914-1993 .... **CLC 4, 7, 29; PC 71**
See also AMWS 11; CA 5-8R; 142; CAAS 3; CANR 5, 22; CP 1, 2, 3, 4, 5; DAM POET; DLB 5, 206; EXPP; INT CANR-22; MAL 5; PFS 2, 8, 16; RGAL 4; WP
Stafford, William Edgar
See Stafford, William
Stagnelius, Eric Johan 1793-1823 ... **NCLC 61**
Staines, Trevor
See Brunner, John (Kilian Houston)
Stairs, Gordon
See Austin, Mary Hunter
Stael
See Stael-Holstein, Anne Louise Germaine Necker
Stael, Germaine de
See Stael-Holstein, Anne Louise Germaine Necker
Stael-Holstein, Anne Louise Germaine Necker 1766-1817 .... **NCLC 3, 91**
See also DLB 119, 192; EW 5; FL 1:3; FW; GFL 1789 to the Present; RGWL 2, 3; TWA
Stalin, Joseph 1879-1953 .... **TCLC 92**
Stampa, Gaspara c. 1524-1554 .... **LC 114; PC 43**
See also RGWL 2, 3; WLIT 7
Stampflinger, K.A.
See Benjamin, Walter
Stancykowna
See Szymborska, Wislawa
Standing Bear, Luther 1868(?)-1939(?) .... **NNAL**
See also CA 113; 144; DAM MULT
Stanislavsky, Constantin 1863(?)-1938 .... **TCLC 167**
See also CA 118
Stanislavsky, Konstantin
See Stanislavsky, Constantin
Stanislavsky, Konstantin Sergeievich
See Stanislavsky, Constantin
Stanislavsky, Konstantin Sergeivich
See Stanislavsky, Constantin
Stanislavsky, Konstantin Sergeyevich
See Stanislavsky, Constantin
Stannard, Martin 1947- .... **CLC 44**
See also CA 142; CANR 229; DLB 155
Stanton, Elizabeth Cady 1815-1902 .... **TCLC 73**
See also CA 171; DLB 79; FL 1:3; FW
Stanton, Maura 1946- .... **CLC 9**
See also CA 89-92; CANR 15, 123; DLB 120
Stanton, Schuyler
See Baum, L. Frank
Stapledon, (William) Olaf 1886-1950 .... **TCLC 22**
See also CA 111; 162; DLB 15, 255; SCFW 1, 2; SFW 4
Starbuck, George (Edwin) 1931-1996 .... **CLC 53**
See also CA 21-24R; 153; CANR 23; CP 1, 2, 3, 4, 5, 6; DAM POET
Stark, Richard
See Westlake, Donald E.
Statius c. 45-c. 96 .... **CMLC 91**
See also AW 2; DLB 211
Staunton, Schuyler
See Baum, L. Frank
Stead, Christina (Ellen) 1902-1983 ..... **CLC 2, 5, 8, 32, 80; TCLC 244**
See also BRWS 4; CA 13-16R; 109; CANR 33, 40; CN 1, 2, 3; DLB 260; EWL 3; FW; MTCW 1, 2; MTFW 2005; NFS 27; RGEL 2; RGSF 2; WWE 1
Stead, Robert J(ames) C(ampbell) 1880-1959 .... **TCLC 225**
See also CA 186; DLB 92; TCWW 1, 2
Stead, William Thomas 1849-1912 .. **TCLC 48**
See also BRWS 13; CA 167
Stebnitsky, M.
See Leskov, Nikolai (Semyonovich)
Stedman, M. L. 19??- .... **CLC 354**
Steele, Richard 1672-1729 .... **LC 18, 156, 159**
See also BRW 3; CDBLB 1660-1789; DLB 84, 101; RGEL 2; WLIT 3
Steele, Timothy (Reid) 1948- .... **CLC 45**
See also CA 93-96; CANR 16, 50, 92; CP 5, 6, 7; DLB 120, 282
Steffens, (Joseph) Lincoln 1866-1936 .... **TCLC 20**
See also CA 117; 198; DLB 303; MAL 5
Stegner, Wallace 1909-1993 .... **CLC 9, 49, 81; SSC 27; TCLC 281**
See also AITN 1; AMWS 4; ANW; BEST 90:3; BPFB 3; CA 1-4R; 141; CAAS 9; CANR 1, 21, 46; CN 1, 2, 3, 4, 5; DAM NOV; DLB 9, 206, 275; DLBY 1993; EWL 3; MAL 5; MTCW 1, 2; MTFW 2005; RGAL 4; TCWW 1, 2; TUS
Stegner, Wallace Earle
See Stegner, Wallace
Stein, Gertrude 1874-1946 ... **DC 19; PC 18; SSC 42, 105; TCLC 1, 6, 28, 48, 276; WLC 5**

See also AAYA 64; AMW; AMWC 2; CA 104; 132; CANR 108; CDALB 1917-1929; DA; DA3; DAB; DAC; DAM MST, NOV, POET; DLB 4, 54, 86, 228; DLBD 15; EWL 3; EXPS; FL 1:6; GLL 1; MAL 5; MBL; MTCW 1, 2; MTFW 2005; NCFS 4; NFS 27; PFS 38; RGAL 4; RGSF 2; SSFS 5; TUS; WP

Steinbeck, John 1902-1968 ...... **CLC 1, 5, 9, 13, 21, 34, 45, 75, 124; DC 46; SSC 11, 37, 77, 135; TCLC 135; WLC 5**
See also AAYA 12; AMW; BPFB 3; BYA 2, 3, 13; CA 1-4R; 25-28R; CANR 1, 35; CDALB 1929-1941; CLR 172, 194, 195; DA; DA3; DAB; DAC; DAM DRAM, MST, NOV; DLB 7, 9, 212, 275, 309, 332, 364; DLBD 2; EWL 3; EXPS; LAIT 3; MAL 5; MTCW 1, 2; MTFW 2005; NFS 1, 5, 7, 17, 19, 28, 34, 37, 39; RGAL 4; RGSF 2; RHW; SATA 9; SSFS 3, 6, 22; TCWW 1, 2; TUS; WYA; YAW

Steinbeck, John Ernst
See Steinbeck, John

Steinem, Gloria 1934- .... **CLC 63**
See also CA 53-56; CANR 28, 51, 139; DLB 246; FL 1:1; FW; MTCW 1, 2; MTFW 2005

Steiner, George 1929- .... **CLC 24, 221**
See also CA 73-76; CANR 31, 67, 108, 212; DAM NOV; DLB 67, 299; EWL 3; MTCW 1, 2; MTFW 2005; RGHL; SATA 62

Steiner, K. Leslie
See Delany, Samuel R., Jr.

Steiner, Rudolf 1861-1925 .... **TCLC 13**
See also CA 107

Stendhal 1783-1842 .... **NCLC 23, 46, 178, 292; SSC 27; WLC 5**
See also DA; DA3; DAB; DAC; DAM MST, NOV; DLB 119; EW 5; GFL 1789 to the Present; RGWL 2, 3; TWA

Stephen, Adeline Virginia
See Woolf, Virginia

Stephen, Sir Leslie 1832-1904 .... **TCLC 23**
See also BRW 5; CA 123; DLB 57, 144, 190

Stephen, Sir Leslie
See Stephen, Sir Leslie

Stephen, Virginia
See Woolf, Virginia

Stephens, Ann Sophia 1810-1886 .. **NCLC 303**
See also DLB 3, 73, 250

Stephens, James 1882(?)-1950 .... **SSC 50; TCLC 4**
See also CA 104; 192; DLB 19, 153, 162; EWL 3; FANT; RGEL 2; SUFW

Stephens, Reed
See Donaldson, Stephen R.

Stephenson, Neal 1959- .... **CLC 220**
See also AAYA 38; CA 122; CANR 88, 138, 195; CN 7; MTFW 2005; SFW 4

Steptoe, Lydia
See Barnes, Djuna

Sterchi, Beat 1949- .... **CLC 65**
See also CA 203

Sterling, Brett
See Bradbury, Ray; Hamilton, Edmond

Sterling, Bruce 1954- .... **CLC 72**
See also AAYA 78; CA 119; CANR 44, 135, 184; CN 7; MTFW 2005; SCFW 2; SFW 4

Sterling, George 1869-1926 .... **TCLC 20**
See also CA 117; 165; DLB 54

Stern, Gerald 1925- ... **CLC 40, 100; PC 115**
See also AMWS 9; CA 81-84; CANR 28, 94, 206; CP 3, 4, 5, 6, 7; DLB 105; PFS 26; RGAL 4

Stern, Richard (Gustave) 1928- ... **CLC 4, 39**
See also CA 1-4R; CANR 1, 25, 52, 120; CN 1, 2, 3, 4, 5, 6, 7; DLB 218; DLBY 1987; INT CANR-25

Sternberg, Josef von 1894-1969 ..... **CLC 20**
See also CA 81-84

Sterne, Laurence 1713-1768 .... **LC 2, 48, 156; WLC 5**
See also BRW 3; BRWC 1; CDBLB 1660-1789; DA; DAB; DAC; DAM MST, NOV; DLB 39; RGEL 2; TEA

Sternheim, (William Adolf) Carl 1878-1942 .... **TCLC 8, 223**
See also CA 105; 193; DLB 56, 118; EWL 3; IDTP; RGWL 2, 3

Stesichorus 630?-555? BC .... **CMLC 167**

Stetson, Charlotte Perkins
See Gilman, Charlotte Perkins

Stevens, Margaret Dean
See Aldrich, Bess Streeter

Stevens, Mark 1951- .... **CLC 34**
See also CA 122

Stevens, R. L.
See Hoch, Edward D.

Stevens, Wallace 1879-1955 .... **PC 6, 110; TCLC 3, 12, 45; WLC 5**
See also AMW; AMWR 1; CA 104; 124; CANR 181; CDALB 1929-1941; DA; DA3; DAB; DAC; DAM MST, POET; DLB 54, 342; EWL 3; EXPP; MAL 5; MTCW 1, 2; PAB; PFS 13, 16, 35, 41; RGAL 4; TUS; WP

Stevenson, Anne (Katharine) 1933- .... **CLC 7, 33**
See also BRWS 6; CA 17-20R; CAAS 9; CANR 9, 33, 123; CP 3, 4, 5, 6, 7; CWP; DLB 40; MTCW 1; RHW

Stevenson, Robert Louis 1850-1894 ... **NCLC 5, 14, 63, 193, 274, 289, 292, 308; PC 84; SSC 11, 51, 126; WLC 5**
See also AAYA 24; BPFB 3; BRW 5; BRWC 1; BRWR 1; BYA 1, 2, 4, 13; CDBLB 1890-1914; CLR 10, 11, 107, 180; DA; DA3; DAB; DAC; DAM MST, NOV; DLB 18, 57, 141, 156, 174; DLBD 13; GL 3; HGG; JRDA; LAIT 1, 3; MAICYA 1, 2; NFS 11, 20, 33; RGEL 2; RGSF 2; SATA 100; SUFW; TEA; WCH; WLIT 4; WYA; YABC 2; YAW

Stevenson, Robert Louis Balfour
See Stevenson, Robert Louis

Stewart, Douglas 1913-1985 .... **TCLC 317**
See also CA 81-84; CP 1, 2, 3, 4; DLB 260; RGEL 2

Stewart, J(ohn) I(nnes) M(ackintosh) 1906-1994 .... **CLC 7, 14, 32**
See also CA 85-88; 147; CAAS 3; CANR 47; CMW 4; CN 1, 2, 3, 4, 5; DLB 276; MSW; MTCW 1, 2

Stewart, Mary (Florence Elinor) 1916- .... **CLC 7, 35, 117**
See also AAYA 29, 73; BPFB 3; CA 1-4R; CANR 1, 59, 130; CMW 4; CPW; DAB; FANT; RHW; SATA 12; YAW

Stewart, Mary Rainbow
See Stewart, Mary (Florence Elinor)

Stewart, Will
See Williamson, John Stewart

Stifle, June
See Campbell, Maria

Stifter, Adalbert 1805-1868 .... **NCLC 41, 198; SSC 28**
See also CDWLB 2; DLB 133; RGSF 2; RGWL 2, 3

Still, James 1906-2001 .... **CLC 49**
See also CA 65-68; 195; CAAS 17; CANR 10, 26; CSW; DLB 9; DLBY 01; SATA 29; SATA-Obit 127

Sting 1951- .... **CLC 26**
See also CA 167

Stirling, Arthur
See Sinclair, Upton

Stitt, Milan 1941-2009 .... **CLC 29**
See also CA 69-72; 284

Stitt, Milan William
See Stitt, Milan

Stockton, Francis Richard 1834-1902 .... **TCLC 47**
See also AAYA 68; BYA 4, 13; CA 108; 137; DLB 42, 74; DLBD 13; EXPS; MAICYA 1, 2; SATA 44; SATA-Brief 32; SFW 4; SSFS 3; SUFW; WCH

Stockton, Frank R.
See Stockton, Francis Richard

Stoddard, Charles
See Kuttner, Henry

Stoker, Abraham
See Stoker, Bram

Stoker, Bram 1847-1912 .... **SSC 62; TCLC 8, 144; WLC 6**
See also AAYA 23; BPFB 3; BRWS 3; BYA 5; CA 105; 150; CDBLB 1890-1914; CLR 178; DA; DA3; DAB; DAC; DAM MST, NOV; DLB 304; GL 3; HGG; LATS 1:1; MTFW 2005; NFS 18; RGEL 2; SATA 29; SUFW; TEA; WLIT 4

Stolz, Mary 1920-2006 .... **CLC 12**
See also AAYA 8, 73; AITN 1; CA 5-8R; 255; CANR 13, 41, 112; JRDA; MAICYA 1, 2; SAAS 3; SATA 10, 71, 133; SATA-Obit 180; YAW

Stolz, Mary Slattery
See Stolz, Mary

Stone, Irving 1903-1989 .... **CLC 7**
See also AITN 1; BPFB 3; CA 1-4R; 129; CAAS 3; CANR 1, 23; CN 1, 2, 3, 4; CPW; DA3; DAM POP; INT CANR-23; MTCW 1, 2; MTFW 2005; RHW; SATA 3; SATA-Obit 64

Stone, Lucy 1818-1893 .... **NCLC 250**
See also DLB 79, 239

Stone, Miriam
See Harwood, Gwen

Stone, Oliver 1946- .... **CLC 73**
See also AAYA 15, 64; CA 110; CANR 55, 125

Stone, Oliver William
See Stone, Oliver

Stone, Robert 1937- .... **CLC 5, 23, 42, 175, 331**
See also AMWS 5; BPFB 3; CA 85-88; CANR 23, 66, 95, 173; CN 4, 5, 6, 7; DLB 152; EWL 3; INT CANR-23; MAL 5; MTCW 1; MTFW 2005

Stone, Robert Anthony
See Stone, Robert

Stone, Ruth 1915-2011 .... **PC 53**
See also CA 45-48; CANR 2, 91, 209; CP 5, 6, 7; CSW; DLB 105; PFS 19, 40

Stone, Zachary
See Follett, Ken

Stoppard, Tom 1937- .... **CLC 1, 3, 4, 5, 8, 15, 29, 34, 63, 91, 328; DC 6, 30; WLC 6**
See also AAYA 63; BRWC 1; BRWR 2; BRWS 1; CA 81-84; CANR 39, 67, 125; CBD; CD 5, 6; CDBLB 1960 to Present; DA; DA3; DAB; DAC; DAM DRAM, MST; DFS 2, 5, 8, 11, 13, 16; DLB 13, 233; DLBY 1985; EWL 3; LATS 1:2; LNFS 3; MTCW 1, 2; MTFW 2005; RGEL 2; TEA; WLIT 4

Storey, David (Malcolm) 1933- .... **CLC 2, 4, 5, 8; DC 40**
See also BRWS 1; CA 81-84; CANR 36; CBD; CD 5, 6; CN 1, 2, 3, 4, 5, 6; DAM DRAM; DLB 13, 14, 207, 245, 326; EWL 3; MTCW 1; RGEL 2

Storm, Hyemeyohsts 1935- ... **CLC 3; NNAL**
See also CA 81-84; CANR 45; DAM MULT

Storm, (Hans) Theodor (Woldsen) 1817-1888 .... **NCLC 1, 195; SSC 27, 106**

Author Index

See also CDWLB 2; DLB 129; EW; RGSF 2; RGWL 2, 3

Storni, Alfonsina 1892-1938 .... **HLC 2; PC 33; TCLC 5, 281**
See also CA 104; 131; DAM MULT; DLB 283; HW 1; LAW

Stoughton, William 1631-1701 .... **LC 38**
See also DLB 24

Stout, Rex (Todhunter) 1886-1975 ... **CLC 3**
See also AAYA 79; AITN 2; BPFB 3; CA 61-64; CANR 71; CMW 4; CN 2; DLB 306; MSW; RGAL 4

Stow, John 1525-1605 .... **LC 186**
See also DLB 132; RGEL 2

Stow, (Julian) Randolph 1935- .... **CLC 23, 48**
See also CA 13-16R; CANR 33; CN 1, 2, 3, 4, 5, 6, 7; CP 1, 2, 3, 4; DLB 260; MTCW 1; RGEL 2

Stowe, Harriet Beecher 1811-1896 ... **NCLC 3, 50, 133, 195; SSC 159; WLC 6**
See also AAYA 53; AMWS 1; CDALB 1865-1917; CLR 131; DA; DA3; DAB; DAC; DAM MST, NOV; DLB 1, 12, 42, 74, 189, 239, 243; EXPN; FL 1:3; JRDA; LAIT 2; MAICYA 1, 2; NFS 6; RGAL 4; TUS; YABC 1

Stowe, Harriet Elizabeth Beecher
See Stowe, Harriet Beecher

Strabo c. 63B.C.-c. 21 .... **CMLC 37, 121**
See also DLB 176

Strachey, (Giles) Lytton 1880-1932 .. **TCLC 12**
See also BRWS 2; CA 110; 178; DLB 149; DLBD 10; EWL 3; MTCW 2; NCFS 4

Stramm, August 1874-1915 .... **PC 50**
See also CA 195; EWL 3

Strand, Mark 1934- .... **CLC 6, 18, 41, 71; PC 63**
See also AMWS 4; CA 21-24R; CANR 40, 65, 100; CP 1, 2, 3, 4, 5, 6, 7; DAM POET; DLB 5; EWL 3; MAL 5; PAB; PFS 9, 18; RGAL 4; SATA 41; TCLE 1:2

Stratton-Porter, Gene 1863-1924 ... **TCLC 21**
See also AMWS 20; ANW; BPFB 3; CA 112; 137; CLR 87; CWRI 5; DLB 221; DLBD 14; MAICYA 1, 2; RHW; SATA 15

Stratton-Porter, Geneva Grace
See Stratton-Porter, Gene

Straub, Peter 1943- .... **CLC 28, 107**
See also AAYA 82; BEST 89:1; BPFB 3; CA 85-88; CANR 28, 65, 109; CPW; DAM POP; DLBY 1984; HGG; MTCW 1, 2; MTFW 2005; SUFW 2

Straub, Peter Francis
See Straub, Peter

Strauss, Botho 1944- .... **CLC 22**
See also CA 157; CWW 2; DLB 124

Strauss, Leo 1899-1973 .... **TCLC 141**
See also CA 101; 45-48; CANR 122

Streatfeild, Mary Noel
See Streatfeild, Noel

Streatfeild, Noel 1897(?)-1986 .... **CLC 21**
See also CA 81-84; 120; CANR 31; CLR 17, 83; CWRI 5; DLB 160; MAICYA 1, 2; SATA 20; SATA-Obit 48

Stribling, T(homas) S(igismund) 1881-1965 .... **CLC 23**
See also CA 189; 107; CMW 4; DLB 9; RGAL 4

Strindberg, August 1849-1912 .... **DC 18; TCLC 1, 8, 21, 47, 231; WLC 6**
See also CA 104; 135; DA; DA3; DAB; DAC; DAM DRAM, MST; DFS 4, 9, 29; DLB 259; EW 7; EWL 3; IDTP; LMFS 2; MTCW 2; MTFW 2005; RGWL 2, 3; TWA

Strindberg, Johan August
See Strindberg, August

Stringer, Arthur 1874-1950 .... **TCLC 37**
See also CA 161; DLB 92

Stringer, David
See Roberts, Keith (John Kingston)

Stroheim, Erich von 1885-1957 .... **TCLC 71**

Strout, Elizabeth 1956- .... **CLC 299**
See also AMWS 23; CA 178; CANR 154, 190; NFS 39

Strugatskii, Arkadii 1925-1991 .... **CLC 27**
See also CA 106; 135; DLB 302; SFW 4

Strugatskii, Arkadii Natanovich
See Strugatskii, Arkadii

Strugatskii, Boris 1933-2012 .... **CLC 27**
See also CA 106; DLB 302; SFW 4

Strugatskii, Boris Natanovich
See Strugatskii, Boris

Strugatsky, Arkadii Natanovich
See Strugatskii, Arkadii

Strugatsky, Boris
See Strugatskii, Boris

Strugatsky, Boris Natanovich
See Strugatskii, Boris

Strummer, Joe 1952-2002 .... **CLC 30**

Strunk, William, Jr. 1869-1946 .... **TCLC 92**
See also CA 118; 164; NCFS 5

Stryk, Lucien 1924- .... **PC 27**
See also CA 13-16R; CANR 10, 28, 55, 110; CP 1, 2, 3, 4, 5, 6, 7

Stuart, Don A.
See Campbell, John W.

Stuart, Ian
See MacLean, Alistair

Stuart, Jesse (Hilton) 1906-1984 ..... **CLC 1, 8, 11, 14, 34; SSC 31**
See also CA 5-8R; 112; CANR 31; CN 1, 2, 3; DLB 9, 48, 102; DLBY 1984; SATA 2; SATA-Obit 36

Stubblefield, Sally
See Trumbo, Dalton

Sturgeon, Theodore (Hamilton) 1918-1985 .... **CLC 22, 39**
See also AAYA 51; BPFB 3; BYA 9, 10; CA 81-84; 116; CANR 32, 103; DLB 8; DLBY 1985; HGG; MTCW 1, 2; MTFW 2005; SCFW; SFW 4; SUFW

Sturges, Preston 1898-1959 .... **TCLC 48**
See also CA 114; 149; DLB 26

Styron, William 1925-2006 ...... **CLC 1, 3, 5, 11, 15, 60, 232, 244; SSC 25**
See also AMW; AMWC 2; BEST 90:4; BPFB 3; CA 5-8R; 255; CANR 6, 33, 74, 126, 191; CDALB 1968-1988; CN 1, 2, 3, 4, 5, 6, 7; CPW; CSW; DA3; DAM NOV, POP; DLB 2, 143, 299; DLBY 1980; EWL 3; INT CANR-6; LAIT 2; MAL 5; MTCW 1, 2; MTFW 2005; NCFS 1; NFS 22; RGAL 4; RGHL; RHW; TUS

Styron, William C.
See Styron, William

Styron, William Clark
See Styron, William

Su, Chien 1884-1918 .... **TCLC 24**
See also CA 123; EWL 3

Suarez Lynch, B.
See Bioy Casares, Adolfo; Borges, Jorge Luis

Suassuna, Ariano Vilar 1927- .... **HLCS 1**
See also CA 178; DLB 307; HW 2; LAW

Suckert, Kurt Erich
See Malaparte, Curzio

Suckling, Sir John 1609-1642 .... **LC 75; PC 30**
See also BRW 2; DAM POET; DLB 58, 126; EXPP; PAB; RGEL 2

Suckow, Ruth 1892-1960 .... **SSC 18; TCLC 257**
See also CA 193; 113; DLB 9, 102; RGAL 4; TCWW 2

Sudermann, Hermann 1857-1928 ... **TCLC 15**
See also CA 107; 201; DLB 118

Sue, Eugene 1804-1857 .... **NCLC 1**
See also DLB 119

Sueskind, Patrick
See Suskind, Patrick

Suetonius c. 70-c. 130 .... **CMLC 60**
See also AW 2; DLB 211; RGWL 2, 3; WLIT 8

Su Hsuan-ying
See Su, Chien

Su Hsuean-ying
See Su, Chien

Sui Sin Far
See Eaton, Edith Maude

Sukenick, Ronald 1932-2004 .... **CLC 3, 4, 6, 48**
See also CA 25-28R, 209; 229; CAAE 209; CAAS 8; CANR 32, 89; CN 3, 4, 5, 6, 7; DLB 173; DLBY 1981

Suknaski, Andrew 1942- .... **CLC 19**
See also CA 101; CP 3, 4, 5, 6, 7; DLB 53

Sullivan, Vernon
See Vian, Boris

Sully Prudhomme, Rene-Francois-Armand 1839-1907 .... **TCLC 31**
See also CA 170; DLB 332; GFL 1789 to the Present

Sulpicius Severus c. 363-c. 425 ... **CMLC 120**

Su Man-shu
See Su, Chien

Sumarokov, Aleksandr Petrovich 1717-1777 .... **LC 104**
See also DLB 150

Summerforest, Ivy B.
See Kirkup, James

Summers, Andrew James
See Summers, Andy

Summers, Andy 1942- .... **CLC 26**
See also CA 255

Summers, Hollis (Spurgeon, Jr.) 1916- .... **CLC 10**
See also CA 5-8R; CANR 3; CN 1, 2, 3; CP 1, 2, 3, 4; DLB 6; TCLE 1:2

Summers, (Alphonsus Joseph-Mary Augustus) Montague 1880-1948 .... **TCLC 16**
See also CA 118; 163

Sumner, Gordon Matthew
See Sting

Sun Tzu c. 400B.C.-c. 320B.C. .... **CMLC 56**

Surayya, Kamala
See Das, Kamala

Surayya Kamala
See Das, Kamala

Surrey, Henry Howard 1517-1574 .... **LC 121; PC 59, 167**
See also BRW 1; RGEL 2

Surtees, Robert Smith 1805-1864 .... **NCLC 14**
See also DLB 21; RGEL 2

Susann, Jacqueline 1921-1974 .... **CLC 3**
See also AITN 1; BPFB 3; CA 65-68; 53-56; MTCW 1, 2

Su Shi 1037-1101 .... **CMLC 15, 139**
See also RGWL 2, 3

Su Shih 1037-1101 .... **CMLC 15, 139**
See also RGWL 2, 3

Suskind, Patrick 1949- .... **CLC 44, 182, 339**
See also BPFB 3; CA 145; CWW 2

Suso, Heinrich c. 1295-1366 ... **CMLC 87, 150**

Sutcliff, Rosemary 1920-1992 .... **CLC 26**
See also AAYA 10; BRWS 16; BYA 1, 4; CA 5-8R; 139; CANR 37; CLR 1, 37, 138; CPW; DAB; DAC; DAM MST, POP; JRDA; LATS 1:1; MAICYA 1, 2; MAICYAS 1; RHW; SATA 6, 44, 78; SATA-Obit 73; WYA; YAW

Sutherland, Efua (Theodora Morgue) 1924-1996 .... **BLC 2:3**

See also AFW; BW 1; CA 105; CWD; DLB 117; EWL 3; IDTP; SATA 25
Sutro, Alfred 1863-1933 .... **TCLC 6**
See also CA 105; 185; DLB 10; RGEL 2
Sutton, Henry
See Slavitt, David R.
Su Yuan-ying
See Su, Chien
Su Yuean-ying
See Su, Chien
Suzuki, D. T.
See Suzuki, Daisetz Teitaro
Suzuki, Daisetz T.
See Suzuki, Daisetz Teitaro
Suzuki, Daisetz Teitaro
1870-1966 .... **TCLC 109**
See also CA 121; 111; MTCW 1, 2; MTFW 2005
Suzuki, Teitaro
See Suzuki, Daisetz Teitaro
Svareff, Count Vladimir
See Crowley, Edward Alexander
Svevo, Italo
See Schmitz, Aron Hector
Sevigne, Marie (de Rabutin-Chantal)
1626-1696 .... **LC 11, 144**
See also DLB 268; GFL Beginnings to 1789; TWA
Sevigne, Marie de Rabutin Chantal
See Sevigne, Marie (de Rabutin-Chantal)
Swados, Elizabeth 1951- .... **CLC 12**
See also CA 97-100; CANR 49, 163; INT CA-97-100
Swados, Elizabeth A.
See Swados, Elizabeth
Swados, Harvey 1920-1972 .... **CLC 5**
See also CA 5-8R; 37-40R; CANR 6; CN 1; DLB 2, 335; MAL 5
Swados, Liz
See Swados, Elizabeth
Swan, Gladys 1934- .... **CLC 69**
See also CA 101; CANR 17, 39; TCLE 1:2
Swanson, Logan
See Matheson, Richard
Swarthout, Glendon (Fred)
1918-1992 .... **CLC 35**
See also AAYA 55; CA 1-4R; 139; CANR 1, 47; CN 1, 2, 3, 4, 5; LAIT 5; NFS 29; SATA 26; TCWW 1, 2; YAW
Swedenborg, Emanuel 1688-1772 .... **LC 105**
Sweet, Sarah C.
See Jewett, Sarah Orne
Swenson, May 1919-1989 .... **CLC 4, 14, 61, 106; PC 14**
See also AMWS 4; CA 5-8R; 130; CANR 36, 61, 131; CP 1, 2, 3, 4; DA; DAB; DAC; DAM MST, POET; DLB 5; EXPP; GLL 2; MAL 5; MTCW 1, 2; MTFW 2005; PFS 16, 30, 38; SATA 15; WP
Swift, Augustus
See Lovecraft, H. P.
Swift, Graham 1949- .. **CLC 41, 88, 233, 353**
See also BRWC 2; BRWS 5; CA 117; 122; CANR 46, 71, 128, 181, 218; CN 4, 5, 6, 7; DLB 194, 326; MTCW 2; MTFW 2005; NFS 18; RGSF 2
Swift, Jonathan 1667-1745 .... **LC 1, 42, 101, 201; PC 9, 133; WLC 6**
See also AAYA 41; BRW 3; BRWC 1; BRWR 1; BYA 5, 14; CDBLB 1660-1789; CLR 53, 161; DA; DA3; DAB; DAC; DAM MST, NOV, POET; DLB 39, 95, 101; EXPN; LAIT 1; NFS 6; PFS 27, 37; RGEL 2; SATA 19; TEA; WCH; WLIT 3
Swinburne, Algernon Charles 1837-1909 ... **PC 24; TCLC 8, 36; WLC 6**
See also BRW 5; CA 105; 140; CDBLB 1832-1890; DA; DA3; DAB; DAC; DAM MST, POET; DLB 35, 57; PAB; RGEL 2; TEA
Swinfen, Ann .... **CLC 34**
See also CA 202
Swinnerton, Frank (Arthur)
1884-1982 .... **CLC 31**
See also CA 202; 108; CN 1, 2, 3; DLB 34
Swinnerton, Frank Arthur
1884-1982 .... **CLC 31**
See also CA 108; DLB 34
Swithen, John
See King, Stephen
Syjuco, Miguel 1976- .... **CLC 318**
See also CA 305
Sylvia
See Ashton-Warner, Sylvia (Constance)
Symmes, Robert Edward
See Duncan, Robert
Symonds, John Addington
1840-1893 .... **NCLC 34**
See also BRWS 14; DLB 57, 144
Symons, Arthur 1865-1945 .... **PC 119; TCLC 11, 243**
See also BRWS 14; CA 107; 189; DLB 19, 57, 149; RGEL 2
Symons, Julian (Gustave)
1912-1994 .... **CLC 2, 14, 32**
See also CA 49-52; 147; CAAS 3; CANR 3, 33, 59; CMW 4; CN 1, 2, 3, 4, 5; CP 1, 3, 4; DLB 87, 155; DLBY 1992; MSW; MTCW 1
Synge, Edmund John Millington
See Synge, John Millington
Synge, J. M.
See Synge, John Millington
Synge, John Millington 1871-1909 ..... **DC 2; TCLC 6, 37, 257**
See also BRW 6; BRWR 1; CA 104; 141; CDBLB 1890-1914; DAM DRAM; DFS 18; DLB 10, 19; EWL 3; RGEL 2; TEA; WLIT 4
Syruc, J.
See Milosz, Czeslaw
Szirtes, George 1948- .... **CLC 46; PC 51**
See also CA 109; CANR 27, 61, 117; CP 4, 5, 6, 7
Szymborska, Wislawa 1923-2012 .. **CLC 99, 190; PC 44**
See also AAYA 76; CA 154; CANR 91, 133, 181, 241; CDWLB 4; CWP; CWW 2; DA3; DLB 232, 332; DLBY 1996; EWL 3; MTCW 2; MTFW 2005; PFS 15, 27, 31, 34, 41; RGHL; RGWL 3
T. O., Nik
See Annensky, Innokenty (Fyodorovich)
Taban lo Liyong
See Liyong, Taban lo
Tabori, George 1914-2007 .... **CLC 19**
See also CA 49-52; 262; CANR 4, 69; CBD; CD 5, 6; DLB 245; RGHL
Tacitus c. 55-c. 117 .... **CMLC 56, 131**
See also AW 2; CDWLB 1; DLB 211; RGWL 2, 3; WLIT 8
Tadjo, Veronique 1955- .... **BLC 2:3**
See also DLB 360; EWL 3
Tagore, Rabindranath 1861-1941 .... **PC 8; SSC 48; TCLC 3, 53**
See also CA 104; 120; DA3; DAM DRAM, POET; DFS 26; DLB 323, 332; EWL 3; MTCW 1, 2; MTFW 2005; PFS 18; RGEL 2; RGSF 2; RGWL 2, 3; TWA
Taine, Hippolyte Adolphe
1828-1893 .... **NCLC 15**
See also EW 7; GFL 1789 to the Present
Talayesva, Don C. 1890-(?) .... **NNAL**
Talese, Gay 1932- .... **CLC 37, 232**
See also AITN 1; AMWS 17; CA 1-4R; CANR 9, 58, 137, 177; DLB 185; INT CANR-9; MTCW 1, 2; MTFW 2005
Tallent, Elizabeth 1954- .... **CLC 45**
See also CA 117; CANR 72; DLB 130
Tallmountain, Mary 1918-1997 .... **NNAL**
See also CA 146; 161; DLB 193
Tally, Ted 1952- .... **CLC 42**
See also CA 120; 124; CAD; CANR 125; CD 5, 6; INT CA-124
Talvik, Heiti 1904-1947 .... **TCLC 87**
See also EWL 3
Tamayo y Baus, Manuel
1829-1898 .... **NCLC 1**
Tammsaare, A(nton) H(ansen)
1878-1940 .... **TCLC 27**
See also CA 164; CDWLB 4; DLB 220; EWL 3
Tam'si, Tchicaya U
See Tchicaya, Gerald Felix
Tan, Amy 1952- .... **AAL; CLC 59, 120, 151, 257**
See also AAYA 9, 48; AMWS 10; BEST 89:3; BPFB 3; CA 136; CANR 54, 105, 132; CDALBS; CN 6, 7; CPW 1; DA3; DAM MULT, NOV, POP; DLB 173, 312; EXPN; FL 1:6; FW; LAIT 3, 5; MAL 5; MTCW 2; MTFW 2005; NFS 1, 13, 16, 31, 35; RGAL 4; SATA 75; SSFS 9; YAW
Tan, Amy Ruth
See Tan, Amy
Tandem, Carl Felix
See Spitteler, Carl
Tandem, Felix
See Spitteler, Carl
Tang Xianzu 1550-1616 .... **LC 227**
See also RGWL 3
Tania B.
See Blixen, Karen
Tanizaki, Jun'ichirō 1886-1965 .... **CLC 8, 14, 28; SSC 21, 197**
See also CA 93-96; 25-28R; DLB 180; EWL 3; MJW; MTCW 2; MTFW 2005; RGSF 2; RGWL 2
Tanizaki Jun'ichiro
See Tanizaki, Jun'ichiro
Tannen, Deborah 1945- .... **CLC 206**
See also CA 118; CANR 95
Tannen, Deborah Frances
See Tannen, Deborah
Tanner, William
See Amis, Kingsley
Tante, Dilly
See Kunitz, Stanley
Tao Lao
See Storni, Alfonsina
Tapahonso, Luci 1953- .... **NNAL; PC 65**
See also CA 145; CANR 72, 127, 214; DLB 175
Tarantino, Quentin 1963- ...... **CLC 125, 230**
See also AAYA 58; CA 171; CANR 125
Tarantino, Quentin Jerome
See Tarantino, Quentin
Tarassoff, Lev
See Troyat, Henri
Tarbell, Ida 1857-1944 .... **TCLC 40**
See also CA 122; 181; DLB 47
Tarbell, Ida Minerva
See Tarbell, Ida
Tarchetti, Ugo 1839(?)-1869 .... **SSC 119**
Tardieu d'Esclavelles, Louise-Florence-Petronille
See Epinay, Louise d'
Tarkington, (Newton) Booth
1869-1946 .... **TCLC 9**
See also BPFB 3; BYA 3; CA 110; 143; CWRI 5; DLB 9, 102; MAL 5; MTCW 2; NFS 34; RGAL 4; SATA 17
Tarkovskii, Andrei Arsen'evich
See Tarkovsky, Andrei (Arsenyevich)

Tarkovsky, Andrei (Arsenyevich) 1932-1986 .... **CLC 75**
See also CA 127
Tartt, Donna 1964(?)- .... **CLC 76, 389**
See also AAYA 56; CA 142; CANR 135; LNFS 2; MTFW 2005
Tasso, Torquato 1544-1595 .... **LC 5, 94; PC 170**
See also EFS 1:2, 2:1; EW 2; RGWL 2, 3; WLIT 7
Tate, (John Orley) Allen 1899-1979 .... **CLC 2, 4, 6, 9, 11, 14, 24; PC 50**
See also AMW; CA 5-8R; 85-88; CANR 32, 108; CN 1, 2; CP 1, 2; DLB 4, 45, 63; DLBD 17; EWL 3; MAL 5; MTCW 1, 2; MTFW 2005; RGAL 4; RHW
Tate, Ellalice
See Hibbert, Eleanor Alice Burford
Tate, James 1943- .... **CLC 2, 6, 25; PC 133**
See also CA 21-24R; CANR 29, 57, 114, 224; CP 1, 2, 3, 4, 5, 6, 7; DLB 5, 169; EWL 3; PFS 10, 15; RGAL 4; WP
Tate, James Vincent
See Tate, James
Tate, Nahum 1652(?)-1715 .... **LC 109**
See also DLB 80; RGEL 2
Tauler, Johannes c. 1300-1361 ..... **CMLC 37**
See also DLB 179; LMFS 1
Tavel, Ronald 1936-2009 .... **CLC 6**
See also CA 21-24R; 284; CAD; CANR 33; CD 5, 6
Taviani, Paolo 1931- .... **CLC 70**
See also CA 153
Tawada, Yoko 1960- .... **CLC 310**
See also CA 296
Taylor, Bayard 1825-1878 .... **NCLC 89**
See also DLB 3, 189, 250, 254, 366; RGAL 4
Taylor, C(ecil) P(hilip) 1929-1981 .. **CLC 27**
See also CA 25-28R; 105; CANR 47; CBD
Taylor, Charles 1931- .... **CLC 317**
See also CA 13-16R; CANR 11, 27, 164, 200, 241
Taylor, Charles Margrave
See Taylor, Charles
Taylor, Edward 1642(?)-1729 ... **LC 11, 163; PC 63**
See also AMW; DA; DAB; DAC; DAM MST, POET; DLB 24; EXPP; PFS 31; RGAL 4; TUS
Taylor, Eleanor Ross 1920-2011 .... **CLC 5**
See also CA 81-84; CANR 70
Taylor, Elizabeth 1912-1975 .... **CLC 2, 4, 29; SSC 100**
See also CA 13-16R; CANR 9, 70; CN 1, 2; DLB 139; MTCW 1; RGEL 2; SATA 13
Taylor, Frederick Winslow 1856-1915 .... **TCLC 76**
See also CA 188
Taylor, Henry 1942- .... **CLC 44**
See also CA 33-36R; CAAS 7; CANR 31, 178; CP 6, 7; DLB 5; PFS 10
Taylor, Henry Splawn
See Taylor, Henry
Taylor, Jane 1783-1824 .... **NCLC 279**
See also DLB 163; SATA 35, 41
Taylor, Kamala
See Markandaya, Kamala
Taylor, Mildred D. 1943- .... **CLC 21**
See also AAYA 10, 47; BW 1; BYA 3, 8; CA 85-88; CANR 25, 115, 136; CLR 9, 59, 90, 144; CSW; DLB 52; JRDA; LAIT 3; MAICYA 1, 2; MTFW 2005; SAAS 5; SATA 135; WYA; YAW
Taylor, Peter (Hillsman) 1917-1994 .... **CLC 1, 4, 18, 37, 44, 50, 71; SSC 10, 84**
See also AMWS 5; BPFB 3; CA 13-16R; 147; CANR 9, 50; CN 1, 2, 3, 4, 5; CSW; DLB 218, 278; DLBY 1981, 1994; EWL 3; EXPS; INT CANR-9; MAL 5; MTCW 1, 2; MTFW 2005; RGSF 2; SSFS 9; TUS
Taylor, Robert Lewis 1912-1998 .... **CLC 14**
See also CA 1-4R; 170; CANR 3, 64; CN 1, 2; SATA 10; TCWW 1, 2
Tchekhov, Anton
See Chekhov, Anton
Tchicaya, Gerald Felix 1931-1988 **CLC 101**
See also CA 129; 125; CANR 81; EWL 3
Tchicaya U Tam'si
See Tchicaya, Gerald Felix
Teasdale, Sara 1884-1933 ... **PC 31; TCLC 4**
See also CA 104; 163; DLB 45; GLL 1; PFS 14; RGAL 4; SATA 32; TUS
Tecumseh 1768-1813 .... **NNAL**
See also DAM MULT
Tegner, Esaias 1782-1846 .... **NCLC 2**
Teilhard de Chardin, (Marie Joseph) Pierre 1881-1955 .... **TCLC 9**
See also CA 105; 210; GFL 1789 to the Present
Temple, Ann
See Mortimer, Penelope (Ruth)
Tennant, Emma 1937- .... **CLC 13, 52**
See also BRWS 9; CA 65-68; CAAS 9; CANR 10, 38, 59, 88, 177; CN 3, 4, 5, 6, 7; DLB 14; EWL 3; SFW 4
Tenneshaw, S.M.
See Silverberg, Robert
Tenney, Tabitha Gilman 1762-1837 .... **NCLC 122, 248**
See also DLB 37, 200
Tennyson, Alfred 1809-1892 .... **NCLC 30, 65, 115, 202; PC 6, 101; WLC 6**
See also AAYA 50; BRW 4; BRWR 3; CDBLB 1832-1890; DA; DA3; DAB; DAC; DAM MST, POET; DLB 32; EXPP; PAB; PFS 1, 2, 4, 11, 15, 19, 44; RGEL 2; TEA; WLIT 4; WP
Teran, Lisa St. Aubin de
See St. Aubin de Teran, Lisa
Terence c. 184B.C.-c. 159B.C. ..... **CMLC 14, 132; DC 7**
See also AW 1; CDWLB 1; DLB 211; RGWL 2, 3; TWA; WLIT 8
Teresa de Jesus, St. 1515-1582 ... **LC 18, 149**
Teresa of Avila, St.
See Teresa de Jesus, St.
Terkel, Louis
See Terkel, Studs
Terkel, Studs 1912-2008 .... **CLC 38**
See also AAYA 32; AITN 1; CA 57-60; 278; CANR 18, 45, 67, 132, 195; DA3; MTCW 1, 2; MTFW 2005; TUS
Terkel, Studs Louis
See Terkel, Studs
Terry, C. V.
See Slaughter, Frank G(ill)
Terry, Megan 1932- .... **CLC 19; DC 13**
See also CA 77-80; CABS 3; CAD; CANR 43; CD 5, 6; CWD; DFS 18; DLB 7, 249; GLL 2
Tertullian c. 155-c. 245 .... **CMLC 29**
Tertz, Abram
See Sinyavsky, Andrei (Donatevich)
Tesich, Steve 1943(?)-1996 .... **CLC 40, 69**
See also CA 105; 152; CAD; DLBY 1983
Tesla, Nikola 1856-1943 .... **TCLC 88**
See also CA 157
Teternikov, Fyodor Kuzmich 1863-1927 .... **TCLC 9, 259**
See also CA 104; DLB 295; EWL 3
Tevis, Walter 1928-1984 .... **CLC 42**
See also CA 113; SFW 4
Tey, Josephine
See Mackintosh, Elizabeth
Thackeray, William Makepeace 1811-1863 .... **NCLC 5, 14, 22, 43, 169, 213, 294; WLC 6**
See also BRW 5; BRWC 2; CDBLB 1832-1890; DA; DA3; DAB; DAC; DAM MST, NOV; DLB 21, 55, 159, 163; NFS 13; RGEL 2; SATA 23; TEA; WLIT 3
Thakura, Ravindranatha
See Tagore, Rabindranath
Thames, C. H.
See Marlowe, Stephen
Tharoor, Shashi 1956- .... **CLC 70**
See also CA 141; CANR 91, 201; CN 6, 7
Thaxter, Celia 1835-1894 .... **NCLC 308**
See also ANW; DLB 239
The Coen Brothers
See Coen, Ethan; Coen, Joel
Thelwall, John 1764-1834 .... **NCLC 162**
See also DLB 93, 158
Thelwell, Michael Miles 1939- .... **CLC 22**
See also BW 2; CA 101
Theo, Ion
See Arghezi, Tudor
Theobald, Lewis, Jr.
See Lovecraft, H. P.
Theocritus c. 310B.C. .... **CMLC 45, 167**
See also AW 1; DLB 176; RGWL 2, 3
Theodorescu, Ion N.
See Arghezi, Tudor
Theodoret of Cyrrhus 393-457? .... **CMLC 165**
Therion, Master
See Crowley, Edward Alexander
Theroux, Alexander 1939- .... **CLC 2, 25**
See also CA 85-88; CANR 20, 63, 190; CN 4, 5, 6, 7
Theroux, Alexander Louis
See Theroux, Alexander
Theroux, Paul 1941- .... **CLC 5, 8, 11, 15, 28, 46, 159, 303**
See also AAYA 28; AMWS 8; BEST 89:4; BPFB 3; CA 33-36R; CANR 20, 45, 74, 133, 179, 233; CDALBS; CN 1, 2, 3, 4, 5, 6, 7; CP 1; CPW 1; DA3; DAM POP; DLB 2, 218; EWL 3; HGG; MAL 5; MTCW 1, 2; MTFW 2005; RGAL 4; SATA 44, 109; TUS
Theroux, Paul Edward
See Theroux, Paul
Thesen, Sharon 1946- .... **CLC 56**
See also CA 163; CANR 125; CP 5, 6, 7; CWP
Thespis fl. 6th cent. B.C. .... **CMLC 51**
See also LMFS 1
Thevenin, Denis
See Duhamel, Georges
Thibault, Jacques Anatole Francois
See France, Anatole
Thiele, Colin 1920-2006 .... **CLC 17**
See also CA 29-32R; CANR 12, 28, 53, 105; CLR 27; CP 1, 2; DLB 289; MAICYA 1, 2; SAAS 2; SATA 14, 72, 125; YAW
Thiong'o, Ngugi Wa
See Ngugi wa Thiong'o
Thistlethwaite, Bel
See Wetherald, Agnes Ethelwyn
Thomas, Audrey (Callahan) 1935- ... **CLC 7, 13, 37, 107, 289; SSC 20**
See also AITN 2; CA 21-24R, 237; CAAE 237; CAAS 19; CANR 36, 58; CN 2, 3, 4, 5, 6, 7; DLB 60; MTCW 1; RGSF 2
Thomas, Augustus 1857-1934 .... **TCLC 97**
See also MAL 5
Thomas, D.M. 1935- ... **CLC 13, 22, 31, 132**
See also BPFB 3; BRWS 4; CA 61-64, 303; CAAE 303; CAAS 11; CANR 17, 45, 75; CDBLB 1960 to Present; CN 4, 5, 6, 7; CP 1, 2, 3, 4, 5, 6, 7; DA3; DLB 40, 207, 299; HGG; INT CANR-17; MTCW 1, 2; MTFW 2005; RGHL; SFW 4

Thomas, Donald Michael
See Thomas, D.M.
Thomas, Dylan 1914-1953 .... **PC 2, 52; SSC 3, 44; TCLC 1, 8, 45, 105; WLC 6**
See also AAYA 45; BRWR 3; BRWS 1; CA 104; 120; CANR 65; CDBLB 1945-1960; DA; DA3; DAB; DAC; DAM DRAM, MST, POET; DLB 13, 20, 139; EWL 3; EXPP; LAIT 3; MTCW 1, 2; MTFW 2005; PAB; PFS 1, 3, 8; RGEL 2; RGSF 2; SATA 60; TEA; WLIT 4; WP
Thomas, Dylan Marlais
See Thomas, Dylan
Thomas, (Philip) Edward
1878-1917 .... **PC 53; TCLC 10**
See also BRW 6; BRWS 3; CA 106; 153; DAM POET; DLB 19, 98, 156, 216; EWL 3; PAB; RGEL 2
Thomas, J. F.
See Fleming, Thomas
Thomas, Joyce Carol 1938- .... **CLC 35**
See also AAYA 12, 54; BW 2, 3; CA 113; 116; CANR 48, 114, 135, 206; CLR 19; DLB 33; INT CA-116; JRDA; MAICYA 1, 2; MTCW 1, 2; MTFW 2005; SAAS 7; SATA 40, 78, 123, 137, 210; SATA-Essay 137; WYA; YAW
Thomas, Lewis 1913-1993 .... **CLC 35**
See also ANW; CA 85-88; 143; CANR 38, 60; DLB 275; MTCW 1, 2
Thomas, M. Carey 1857-1935 ...... **TCLC 89**
See also FW
Thomas, Paul
See Mann, Thomas
Thomas, Piri 1928-2011 .. **CLC 17; HLCS 2**
See also CA 73-76; HW 1; LLW; SSFS 28
Thomas, R(onald) S(tuart)
1913-2000 .... **CLC 6, 13, 48; PC 99**
See also BRWS 12; CA 89-92; 189; CAAS 4; CANR 30; CDBLB 1960 to Present; CP 1, 2, 3, 4, 5, 6, 7; DAB; DAM POET; DLB 27; EWL 3; MTCW 1; RGEL 2
Thomas, Ross (Elmore)
1926-1995 .... **CLC 39**
See also CA 33-36R; 150; CANR 22, 63; CMW 4
Thompson, Francis (Joseph)
1859-1907 .... **TCLC 4**
See also BRW 5; CA 104; 189; CDBLB 1890-1914; DLB 19; RGEL 2; TEA
Thompson, Francis Clegg
See Mencken, H. L.
Thompson, Hunter S.
1937(?)-2005 .... **CLC 9, 17, 40, 104, 229**
See also AAYA 45; BEST 89:1; BPFB 3; CA 17-20R; 236; CANR 23, 46, 74, 77, 111, 133; CPW; CSW; DA3; DAM POP; DLB 185; MTCW 1, 2; MTFW 2005; TUS
Thompson, Hunter Stockton
See Thompson, Hunter S.
Thompson, James Myers
See Thompson, Jim
Thompson, Jim 1906-1977 .... **CLC 69**
See also BPFB 3; CA 140; CMW 4; CPW; DLB 226; MSW
Thompson, Judith (Clare Francesca)
1954- .... **CLC 39**
See also CA 143; CD 5, 6; CWD; DFS 22; DLB 334
Thomson, James 1700-1748 ... **LC 16, 29, 40**
See also BRWS 3; DAM POET; DLB 95; RGEL 2
Thomson, James 1834-1882 .... **NCLC 18**
See also DAM POET; DLB 35; RGEL 2
Thoreau, Henry David
1817-1862 .... **NCLC 7, 21, 61, 138, 207; PC 30; WLC 6**
See also AAYA 42; AMW; ANW; BYA 3; CDALB 1640-1865; DA; DA3; DAB; DAC; DAM MST; DLB 1, 183, 223, 270, 298, 366; LAIT 2; LMFS 1; NCFS 3; RGAL 4; TUS
Thorndike, E. L.
See Thorndike, Edward L(ee)
Thorndike, Edward L(ee)
1874-1949 .... **TCLC 107**
See also CA 121
Thornton, Hall
See Silverberg, Robert
Thorpe, Adam 1956- .... **CLC 176**
See also CA 129; CANR 92, 160; DLB 231
Thorpe, Thomas Bangs
1815-1878 .... **NCLC 183**
See also DLB 3, 11, 248; RGAL 4
Theriault, Yves 1915-1983 .... **CLC 79**
See also CA 102; CANR 150; CCA 1; DAC; DAM MST; DLB 88; EWL 3
Thubron, Colin 1939- .... **CLC 163**
See also CA 25-28R; CANR 12, 29, 59, 95, 171, 232; CN 5, 6, 7; DLB 204, 231
Thubron, Colin Gerald Dryden
See Thubron, Colin
Thucydides
c. 455B.C.-c. 399B.C. .... **CMLC 17, 117**
See also AW 1; DLB 176; RGWL 2, 3; WLIT 8
Thumboo, Edwin Nadason
1933- .... **CLC 360; PC 30**
See also CA 194; CP 1
Thurber, James 1894-1961 .... **CLC 5, 11, 25, 125; SSC 1, 47, 137**
See also AAYA 56; AMWS 1; BPFB 3; BYA 5; CA 73-76; CANR 17, 39; CDALB 1929-1941; CWRI 5; DA; DA3; DAB; DAC; DAM DRAM, MST, NOV; DLB 4, 11, 22, 102; EWL 3; EXPS; FANT; LAIT 3; MAICYA 1, 2; MAL 5; MTCW 1, 2; MTFW 2005; RGAL 4; RGSF 2; SATA 13; SSFS 1, 10, 19, 37; SUFW; TUS
Thurber, James Grover
See Thurber, James
Thurman, Wallace (Henry)
1902-1934 .... **BLC 1:3; HR 1:3; TCLC 6**
See also BW 1, 3; CA 104; 124; CANR 81; DAM MULT; DLB 51
Toibin, Colm 1955- .... **CLC 162, 285**
See also CA 142; CANR 81, 149, 213; CN 7; DLB 271
Tibullus c. 54B.C.-c. 18B.C. .... **CMLC 36**
See also AW 2; DLB 211; RGWL 2, 3; WLIT 8
Ticheburn, Cheviot
See Ainsworth, William Harrison
Ticknor, George
1791-1871 .... **NCLC 255**
See also DLB 1, 59, 140, 235
Tieck, (Johann) Ludwig 1773-1853 ... **DC 53; NCLC 5, 46; SSC 31, 100**
See also CDWLB 2; DLB 90; EW 5; IDTP; RGSF 2; RGWL 2, 3; SUFW
Tiger, Derry
See Ellison, Harlan
Tilghman, Christopher 1946- .... **CLC 65**
See also CA 159; CANR 135, 151; CSW; DLB 244
Tillich, Paul (Johannes)
1886-1965 .... **CLC 131**
See also CA 5-8R; 25-28R; CANR 33; MTCW 1, 2
Tillinghast, Richard (Williford)
1940- .... **CLC 29**
See also CA 29-32R; CAAS 23; CANR 26, 51, 96; CP 2, 3, 4, 5, 6, 7; CSW
Tillman, Lynne (?)- .... **CLC 231, 312**
See also CA 173; CANR 144, 172, 238
Timrod, Henry 1828-1867 .... **NCLC 25**
See also DLB 3, 248; RGAL 4
Tindall, Gillian (Elizabeth) 1938- ..... **CLC 7**
See also CA 21-24R; CANR 11, 65, 107; CN 1, 2, 3, 4, 5, 6, 7
Ting Ling
See Chiang, Pin-chin
Tiny Tim
See Harwood, Gwen
Tiptree, James, Jr.
See Sheldon, Alice Hastings Bradley
Tirone Smith, Mary-Ann 1944- ...... **CLC 39**
See also CA 118; 136; CANR 113, 210; SATA 143
Tirso de Molina 1580(?)-1648 .... **DC 13; HLCS 2; LC 73**
See also RGWL 2, 3
Titmarsh, Michael Angelo
See Thackeray, William Makepeace
Tiutchev, Fedor
See Tyutchev, Fyodor
Tjutčev, Fedor
See Tyutchev, Fyodor
Tocqueville, Alexis (Charles Henri Maurice Clerel Comte) de
1805-1859 .... **NCLC 7, 63, 267**
See also EW 6; GFL 1789 to the Present; TWA
Toe, Tucker
See Westlake, Donald E.
Toer, Pramoedya Ananta
1925-2006 .... **CLC 186**
See also CA 197; 251; CANR 170; DLB 348; RGWL 3
Toffler, Alvin 1928- .... **CLC 168**
See also CA 13-16R; CANR 15, 46, 67, 183; CPW; DAM POP; MTCW 1, 2
Tolkien, J. R. R. 1892-1973 .... **CLC 1, 2, 3, 8, 12, 38; SSC 156; TCLC 137, 299; WLC 6**
See also AAYA 10; AITN 1; BPFB 3; BRWC 2; BRWS 2; CA 17-18; 45-48; CANR 36, 134; CAP 2; CDBLB 1914-1945; CLR 56, 152; CN 1; CPW 1; CWRI 5; DA; DA3; DAB; DAC; DAM MST, NOV, POP; DLB 15, 160, 255; EFS 1:2, 2:1; EWL 3; FANT; JRDA; LAIT 1; LATS 1:2; LMFS 2; MAICYA 1, 2; MTCW 1, 2; MTFW 2005; NFS 8, 26; RGEL 2; SATA 2, 32, 100; SATA-Obit 24; SFW 4; SUFW; TEA; WCH; WYA; YAW
Tolkien, John Ronald Reuel
See Tolkien, J. R. R.
Toller, Ernst 1893-1939 .... **TCLC 10, 235**
See also CA 107; 186; DLB 124; EWL 3; RGWL 2, 3
Tolson, M. B.
See Tolson, Melvin B(eaunorus)
Tolson, Melvin B(eaunorus)
1898(?)-1966 .... **BLC 1:3; CLC 36, 105; PC 88**
See also AFAW 1, 2; BW 1, 3; CA 124; 89-92; CANR 80; DAM MULT, POET; DLB 48, 76; MAL 5; RGAL 4
Tolstoi, Aleksei Nikolaevich
See Tolstoy, Alexey Nikolaevich
Tolstoi, Lev
See Tolstoy, Leo
Tolstoy, Aleksei Nikolaevich
See Tolstoy, Alexey Nikolaevich
Tolstoy, Alexey Nikolaevich
1882-1945 .... **TCLC 18**
See also CA 107; 158; DLB 272; EWL 3; SFW 4
Tolstoy, Leo 1828-1910 .... **SSC 9, 30, 45, 54, 131; TCLC 4, 11, 17, 28, 44, 79, 173, 260; WLC 6**
See also AAYA 56; CA 104; 123; DA; DA3; DAB; DAC; DAM MST, NOV; DLB 238;

Author Index

EFS 1:2, 2:2; EW 7; EXPS; IDTP; LAIT 2; LATS 1:1; LMFS 1; NFS 10, 28, 37; RGSF 2; RGWL 2, 3; SATA 26; SSFS 5, 28; TWA

Tolstoy, Count Leo
See Tolstoy, Leo

Tolstoy, Leo Nikolaevich
See Tolstoy, Leo

Tomalin, Claire 1933- .... **CLC 166**
See also CA 89-92; CANR 52, 88, 165; DLB 155

Tomasi di Lampedusa, Giuseppe
See Lampedusa, Giuseppe di

Tomlin, Lily 1939(?)- .... **CLC 17**
See also CA 117

Tomlin, Mary Jane
See Tomlin, Lily

Tomlin, Mary Jean
See Tomlin, Lily

Tomline, F. Latour
See Gilbert, W(illiam) S(chwenck)

Tomlinson, (Alfred) Charles
1927- .... **CLC 2, 4, 6, 13, 45; PC 17**
See also CA 5-8R; CANR 33; CP 1, 2, 3, 4, 5, 6, 7; DAM POET; DLB 40; TCLE 1:2

Tomlinson, H(enry) M(ajor)
1873-1958 .... **TCLC 71**
See also CA 118; 161; DLB 36, 100, 195

Tomlinson, Mary Jane
See Tomlin, Lily

Tomson, Graham R.
See Watson, Rosamund Marriott

Tonna, Charlotte Elizabeth
1790-1846 .... **NCLC 135**
See also DLB 163

Tonson, Jacob fl. 1655(?)-1736 .... **LC 86**
See also DLB 170

Toole, John Kennedy 1937-1969 ... **CLC 19, 64**
See also BPFB 3; CA 104; DLBY 1981; MTCW 2; MTFW 2005

Toomer, Eugene
See Toomer, Jean

Toomer, Eugene Pinchback
See Toomer, Jean

Toomer, Jean 1894-1967 .... **BLC 1:3; CLC 1, 4, 13, 22; HR 1:3; PC 7; SSC 1, 45, 138; TCLC 172, 288; WLCS**
See also AFAW 1, 2; AMWS 3, 9; BW 1; CA 85-88; CDALB 1917-1929; DA3; DAM MULT; DLB 45, 51; EWL 3; EXPP; EXPS; LMFS 2; MAL 5; MTCW 1, 2; MTFW 2005; NFS 11; PFS 31, 43; RGAL 4; RGSF 2; SSFS 5

Toomer, Nathan Jean
See Toomer, Jean

Toomer, Nathan Pinchback
See Toomer, Jean

Torley, Luke
See Blish, James

Tornimparte, Alessandra
See Ginzburg, Natalia

Torre, Raoul della
See Mencken, H. L.

Torrence, Ridgely 1874-1950 .... **TCLC 97**
See also DLB 54, 249; MAL 5

Torrey, E. Fuller 1937- .... **CLC 34**
See also CA 119; CANR 71, 158

Torrey, Edwin Fuller
See Torrey, E. Fuller

Torsvan, Ben Traven
See Traven, B.

Torsvan, Benno Traven
See Traven, B.

Torsvan, Berick Traven
See Traven, B.

Torsvan, Berwick Traven
See Traven, B.

Torsvan, Bruno Traven
See Traven, B.

Torsvan, Traven
See Traven, B.

Tourneur, Cyril 1575(?)-1626 ..... **LC 66, 181**
See also BRW 2; DAM DRAM; DLB 58; RGEL 2

Tournier, Michel 1924- .... **CLC 6, 23, 36, 95, 249; SSC 88**
See also CA 49-52; CANR 3, 36, 74, 149; CWW 2; DLB 83; EWL 3; GFL 1789 to the Present; MTCW 1, 2; SATA 23

Tournier, Michel Edouard
See Tournier, Michel

Tournimparte, Alessandra
See Ginzburg, Natalia

Towers, Ivar
See Kornbluth, C(yril) M.

Towne, Robert (Burton) 1936(?)- ... **CLC 87**
See also CA 108; DLB 44; IDFW 3, 4

Townsend, Sue 1946- .... **CLC 61**
See also AAYA 28; CA 119; 127; CANR 65, 107, 202; CBD; CD 5, 6; CPW; CWD; DAB; DAC; DAM MST; DLB 271, 352; INT CA-127; SATA 55, 93; SATA-Brief 48; YAW

Townsend, Susan Lilian
See Townsend, Sue

Townshend, Pete
See Townshend, Peter

Townshend, Peter 1945- .... **CLC 17, 42**
See also CA 107

Townshend, Peter Dennis Blandford
See Townshend, Peter

Tozzi, Federigo 1883-1920 .... **TCLC 31**
See also CA 160; CANR 110; DLB 264; EWL 3; WLIT 7

Trafford, F. G.
See Riddell, Charlotte

Traherne, Thomas
1637(?)-1674 .... **LC 99; PC 70**
See also BRW 2; BRWS 11; DLB 131; PAB; RGEL 2

Traill, Catharine Parr 1802-1899 ... **NCLC 31**
See also DLB 99

Trakl, Georg 1887-1914 .... **PC 20; TCLC 5, 239**
See also CA 104; 165; EW 10; EWL 3; LMFS 2; MTCW 2; RGWL 2, 3

Trambley, Estela Portillo
See Portillo Trambley, Estela

Tranquilli, Secondino
See Silone, Ignazio

Transtromer, Tomas 1931- .... **CLC 52, 65, 334**
See also CA 117; 129; CAAS 17; CANR 115, 172; CWW 2; DAM POET; DLB 257; EWL 3; PFS 21, 44

Transtromer, Tomas Goesta
See Transtromer, Tomas

Transtromer, Tomas Gosta
See Transtromer, Tomas

Transtromer, Tomas Gosta
See Transtromer, Tomas

Traven, B. 1882(?)-1969 .... **CLC 8, 11**
See also CA 19-20; 25-28R; CAP 2; DLB 9, 56; EWL 3; MTCW 1; RGAL 4

Trediakovsky, Vasilii Kirillovich
1703-1769 .... **LC 68**
See also DLB 150

Treitel, Jonathan 1959- .... **CLC 70**
See also CA 210; DLB 267

Trelawny, Edward John
1792-1881 .... **NCLC 85**
See also DLB 110, 116, 144

Tremain, Rose 1943- .... **CLC 42**
See also CA 97-100; CANR 44, 95, 186, 232; CN 4, 5, 6, 7; DLB 14, 271; RGSF 2; RHW

Tremblay, Michel 1942- ... **CLC 29, 102, 225**
See also CA 116; 128; CCA 1; CWW 2; DAC; DAM MST; DLB 60; EWL 3; GLL 1; MTCW 1, 2; MTFW 2005

Trethewey, Natasha 1966- .... **CLC 340**
See also AMWS 21; CA 203; PFS 29, 39

Trevanian
See Whitaker, Rod

Trevisa, John c. 1342-c. 1402 .... **LC 139**
See also BRWS 9; DLB 146

Trevor, Frances
See Teasdale, Sara

Trevor, Glen
See Hilton, James

Trevor, William 1928- ...... **CLC 7, 9, 14, 25, 71, 116, 266, 376; SSC 21, 58**
See also BRWS 4; CA 9-12R; CANR 4, 37, 55, 76, 102, 139, 195, 236; CBD; CD 5, 6; DAM NOV; DLB 14, 139; EWL 3; INT CANR-37; LATS 1:2; MTCW 1, 2; MTFW 2005; RGEL 2; RGSF 2; SSFS 10, 33; TCLE 1:2; TEA

Triana, Jose 1931(?)- .... **DC 39**
See also CA 131; DLB 305; EWL 3; HW 1; LAW

Trifonov, Iurii (Valentinovich)
See Trifonov, Yuri (Valentinovich)

Trifonov, Yuri (Valentinovich)
1925-1981 .... **CLC 45**
See also CA 126; 103; DLB 302; EWL 3; MTCW 1; RGWL 2, 3

Trifonov, Yury Valentinovich
See Trifonov, Yuri (Valentinovich)

Trilling, Diana (Rubin)
1905-1996 .... **CLC 129**
See also CA 5-8R; 154; CANR 10, 46; INT CANR-10; MTCW 1, 2

Trilling, Lionel 1905-1975 .... **CLC 9, 11, 24; SSC 75**
See also AMWS 3; CA 9-12R; 61-64; CANR 10, 105; CN 1, 2; DLB 28, 63; EWL 3; INT CANR-10; MAL 5; MTCW 1, 2; RGAL 4; TUS

Trimball, W. H.
See Mencken, H. L.

Tristan
See Gomez de la Serna, Ramon

Tristram
See Housman, A. E.

Trogdon, William
See Heat-Moon, William Least

Trogdon, William Lewis
See Heat-Moon, William Least

Trollope, Anthony 1815-1882 .... **NCLC 6, 33, 101, 215, 269, 274, 275; SSC 28, 133; WLC 6**
See also BRW 5; CDBLB 1832-1890; DA; DA3; DAB; DAC; DAM MST, NOV; DLB 21, 57, 159, 366; NFS 42; RGEL 2; RGSF 2; SATA 22

Trollope, Frances 1779-1863 .... **NCLC 30**
See also DLB 21, 166

Trollope, Joanna 1943- .... **CLC 186**
See also CA 101; CANR 58, 95, 149, 191; CN 7; CPW; DLB 207; RHW

Trotsky, Leon 1879-1940 .... **TCLC 22**
See also CA 118; 167

Trotter, Catharine 1679-1749 .... **LC 8, 165**
See also BRWS 16; DLB 84, 252

Trotter, Wilfred 1872-1939 .... **TCLC 97**

Troupe, Quincy 1943- .... **BLC 2:3**
See also BW 2; CA 113; 124; CANR 43, 90, 126, 213; DLB 41

Trout, Kilgore
See Farmer, Philip Jose

Trow, George William Swift
See Trow, George W.S.

Trow, George W.S. 1943-2006 .... **CLC 52**
See also CA 126; 255; CANR 91
Troyat, Henri
1911-2007 .... **CLC 23**
See also CA 45-48; 258; CANR 2, 33, 67, 117; GFL 1789 to the Present; MTCW 1
Trudeau, Garretson Beekman
See Trudeau, Garry
Trudeau, Garry 1948- .... **CLC 12**
See also AAYA 10, 60; AITN 2; CA 81-84; CANR 31; SATA 35, 168
Trudeau, Garry B.
See Trudeau, Garry
Trudeau, G.B. 1948- .... **CLC 12**
See also AAYA 10, 60; AITN 2; CA 81-84; CANR 31; SATA 35, 168
Truffaut, Francois
1932-1984 .... **CLC 20, 101**
See also AAYA 84; CA 81-84; 113; CANR 34
Trumbo, Dalton
1905-1976 .... **CLC 19**
See also CA 21-24R; 69-72; CANR 10; CN 1, 2; DLB 26; IDFW 3, 4; YAW
Trumbull, John
1750-1831 .... **NCLC 30**
See also DLB 31; RGAL 4
Trundlett, Helen B.
See Eliot, T. S.
Truth, Sojourner
1797(?)-1883 .... **NCLC 94**
See also DLB 239; FW; LAIT 2
Tryon, Thomas
1926-1991 .... **CLC 3, 11**
See also AITN 1; BPFB 3; CA 29-32R; 135; CANR 32, 77; CPW; DA3; DAM POP; HGG; MTCW 1
Tryon, Tom
See Tryon, Thomas
Ts'ao Hsueh-ch'in 1715(?)-1763 .... **LC 1**
Toson
See Shimazaki, Haruki
Tsurayuki Ed. fl. 10th cent. .... **PC 73**
Tsvetaeva, Marina 1892-1941 .... **PC 14; TCLC 7, 35**
See also CA 104; 128; CANR 73; DLB 295; EW 11; MTCW 1, 2; PFS 29; RGWL 2, 3
Tsvetaeva Efron, Marina Ivanovna
See Tsvetaeva, Marina
Tuck, Lily 1938- .... **CLC 70**
See also AAYA 74; CA 139; CANR 90, 192
Tuckerman, Frederick Goddard
1821-1873 .... **PC 85**
See also DLB 243; RGAL 4
Tu Fu 712-770 .... **PC 9**
See also DAM MULT; PFS 32; RGWL 2, 3; TWA; WP
Tulsidas, Gosvami 1532(?)-1623 ...... **LC 158**
See also RGWL 2, 3
Tunis, John R(oberts) 1889-1975 ... **CLC 12**
See also BYA 1; CA 61-64; CANR 62; DLB 22, 171; JRDA; MAICYA 1, 2; SATA 37; SATA-Brief 30; YAW
Tuohy, Frank
See Tuohy, John Francis
Tuohy, John Francis 1925- .... **CLC 37**
See also CA 5-8R; 178; CANR 3, 47; CN 1, 2, 3, 4, 5, 6, 7; DLB 14, 139
Turco, Lewis 1934- .... **CLC 11, 63**
See also CA 13-16R; CAAS 22; CANR 24, 51, 185; CP 1, 2, 3, 4, 5, 6, 7; DLBY 1984; TCLE 1:2
Turco, Lewis Putnam
See Turco, Lewis
Turgenev, Ivan 1818-1883 .... **DC 7; NCLC 21, 37, 122, 269; SSC 7, 57; WLC 6**
See also AAYA 58; DA; DAB; DAC; DAM MST, NOV; DFS 6; DLB 238, 284; EW 6; LATS 1:1; NFS 16; RGSF 2; RGWL 2, 3; TWA
Turgenev, Ivan Sergeevich
See Turgenev, Ivan
Turgot, Anne-Robert-Jacques
1727-1781 .... **LC 26**
See also DLB 314
Turlin, Heinrich von dem
See Heinrich von dem Tuerlin
Turner, Frederick 1943- .... **CLC 48**
See also CA 73-76, 227; CAAE 227; CAAS 10; CANR 12, 30, 56; DLB 40, 282
Turrini, Peter 1944- .... **DC 49**
See also CA 209; DLB 124
Turton, James
See Crace, Jim
Tutu, Desmond M. 1931- .... **BLC 1:3; CLC 80**
See also BW 1, 3; CA 125; CANR 67, 81, 242; DAM MULT
Tutu, Desmond Mpilo
See Tutu, Desmond M.
Tutuola, Amos 1920-1997 ...... **BLC 1:3, 2:3; CLC 5, 14, 29; TCLC 188**
See also AAYA 76; AFW; BW 2, 3; CA 9-12R; 159; CANR 27, 66; CDWLB 3; CN 1, 2, 3, 4, 5, 6; DA3; DAM MULT; DLB 125; DNFS 2; EWL 3; MTCW 1, 2; MTFW 2005; RGEL 2; WLIT 2
Twain, Mark 1835-1910 .... **SSC 6, 26, 34, 87, 119, 210; TCLC 6, 12, 19, 36, 48, 59, 161, 185, 260; WLC 6**
See also AAYA 20; AMW; AMWC 1; BPFB 3; BYA 2, 3, 11, 14; CA 104; 135; CDALB 1865-1917; CLR 58, 60, 66, 156, 187; DA; DA3; DAB; DAC; DAM MST, NOV; DLB 11, 12, 23, 64, 74, 186, 189, 11, 343; EXPN; EXPS; JRDA; LAIT 2; LMFS 1; MAICYA 1, 2; MAL 5; NCFS 4; NFS 1, 6; RGAL 4; RGSF 2; SATA 100; SFW 4; SSFS 1, 7, 16, 21, 27, 33; SUFW; TUS; WCH; WYA; YABC 2; YAW
Twohill, Maggie
See Angell, Judie
Tyard, Pontus de 1521?-1605 .... **LC 243**
See also DLB 327
Tyler, Anne 1941- .... **CLC 7, 11, 18, 28, 44, 59, 103, 205, 265**
See also AAYA 18, 60; AMWS 4; BEST 89:1; BPFB 3; BYA 12; CA 9-12R; CANR 11, 33, 53, 109, 132, 168; CDALBS; CN 1, 2, 3, 4, 5, 6, 7; CPW; CSW; DAM NOV, POP; DLB 6, 143; DLBY 1982; EWL 3; EXPN; LATS 1:2; MAL 5; MBL; MTCW 1, 2; MTFW 2005; NFS 2, 7, 10, 38; RGAL 4; SATA 7, 90, 173; SSFS 1, 31; TCLE 1:2; TUS; YAW
Tyler, Royall 1757-1826 .... **NCLC 3, 244**
See also DLB 37; RGAL 4
Tynan, Katharine
1861-1931 .... **PC 120; TCLC 3, 217**
See also CA 104; 167; DLB 153, 240; FW
Tyndale, William c. 1484-1536 .... **LC 103**
See also DLB 132
Tyutchev, Fyodor
1803-1873 .... **NCLC 34, 291**
Tzara, Tristan
1896-1963 .... **CLC 47; PC 27; TCLC 168**
See also CA 153; 89-92; DAM POET; EWL 3; MTCW 2
Uc de Saint Circ
c. 1190B.C.-13th cent. B.C. .... **CMLC 102**
Uchida, Yoshiko
1921-1992 .... **AAL**
See also AAYA 16; BYA 2, 3; CA 13-16R; 139; CANR 6, 22, 47, 61; CDALBS; CLR 6, 56; CWRI 5; DLB 312; JRDA; MAICYA 1, 2; MTCW 1, 2; MTFW 2005; NFS 26; SAAS 1; SATA 1, 53; SATA-Obit 72; SSFS 31
Udall, Nicholas 1504-1556 .... **LC 84**
See also DLB 62; RGEL 2
Ueda Akinari
1734-1809 .... **NCLC 131**
Ugrešić, Dubravka 1949- .... **CLC 375**
See also CA 136, CANR 90, 159, 198; CWW 2; DLC 181
Uhry, Alfred 1936- .... **CLC 55; DC 28**
See also CA 127; 133; CAD; CANR 112; CD 5, 6; CSW; DA3; DAM DRAM, POP; DFS 11, 15; INT CA-133; MTFW 2005
Ulf, Haerved
See Strindberg, August
Ulf, Harved
See Strindberg, August
Ulibarri, Sabine R(eyes)
1919-2003 .... **CLC 83; HLCS 2**
See also CA 131; 214; CANR 81; DAM MULT; DLB 82; HW 1, 2; RGSF 2
Ulyanov, V. I.
See Lenin, Vladimir
Ulyanov, Vladimir Ilyich
See Lenin, Vladimir
Ulyanov-Lenin
See Lenin, Vladimir
Unamuno, Miguel de
1864-1936 .... **DC 45; HLC 2; SSC 11, 69; TCLC 2, 9, 148, 237**
See also CA 104; 131; CANR 81; DAM MULT, NOV; DLB 108, 322; EW 8; EWL 3; HW 1, 2; MTCW 1, 2; MTFW 2005; RGSF 2; RGWL 2, 3; SSFS 20; TWA
Unamuno y Jugo, Miguel de
See Unamuno, Miguel de
Uncle Shelby
See Silverstein, Shel
Undercliffe, Errol
See Campbell, Ramsey
Underwood, Miles
See Glassco, John
Undset, Sigrid 1882-1949 ...... **TCLC 3, 197; WLC 6**
See also AAYA 77; CA 104; 129; DA; DA3; DAB; DAC; DAM MST, NOV; DLB 293, 332; EW 9; EWL 3; FW; MTCW 1, 2; MTFW 2005; RGWL 2, 3
Ungaretti, Giuseppe 1888-1970 .... **CLC 7, 11, 15; PC 57; TCLC 200**
See also CA 19-20; 25-28R; CAP 2; DLB 114; EW 10; EWL 3; PFS 20; RGWL 2, 3; WLIT 7
Unger, Douglas 1952- .... **CLC 34**
See also CA 130; CANR 94, 155
Unsworth, Barry 1930-2012 .... **CLC 76, 127**
See also BRWS 7; CA 25-28R; CANR 30, 54, 125, 171, 202; CN 6, 7; DLB 194, 326
Unsworth, Barry Forster
See Unsworth, Barry
Updike, John 1932-2009 ..... **CLC 1, 2, 3, 5, 7, 9, 13, 15, 23, 34, 43, 70, 139, 214, 278; PC 90; SSC 13, 27, 103; WLC 6**
See also AAYA 36; AMW; AMWC 1; AMWR 1; BPFB 3; BYA 12; CA 1-4R; 282; CABS 1; CANR 4, 33, 51, 94, 133, 197, 229; CDALB 1968-1988; CN 1, 2, 3, 4, 5, 6, 7; CP 1, 2, 3, 4, 5, 6, 7; CPW 1; DA; DA3; DAB; DAC; DAM MST, NOV, POET, POP; DLB 2, 5, 143, 218, 227; DLBD 3; DLBY 1980, 1982, 1997; EWL 3; EXPP; HGG; MAL 5; MTCW 1, 2; MTFW 2005; NFS 12, 24; RGAL 4; RGSF 2; SSFS 3, 19, 37; TUS
Updike, John Hoyer
See Updike, John
Upshaw, Margaret Mitchell
See Mitchell, Margaret

Upton, Mark
See Sanders, Lawrence
Upward, Allen
1863-1926 .... **TCLC 85**
See also CA 117; 187; DLB 36
Urdang, Constance (Henriette)
1922-1996 .... **CLC 47**
See also CA 21-24R; CANR 9, 24; CP 1, 2, 3, 4, 5, 6; CWP
Urfé, Honoré d'
1567(?)-1625 .... **LC 132, 232**
See also DLB 268; GFL Beginnings to 1789; RGWL 2, 3
Uriel, Henry
See Faust, Frederick
Uris, Leon
1924-2003 .... **CLC 7, 32**
See also AITN 1, 2; AMWS 20; BEST 89:2; BPFB 3; CA 1-4R; 217; CANR 1, 40, 65, 123; CN 1, 2, 3, 4, 5, 6; CPW 1; DA3; DAM NOV, POP; MTCW 1, 2; MTFW 2005; RGHL; SATA 49; SATA-Obit 146
Urista, Alberto
See Alurista
Urmuz
See Codrescu, Andrei
Urquhart, Guy
See McAlmon, Robert (Menzies)
Urquhart, Jane 1949- .... **CLC 90, 242**
See also CA 113; CANR 32, 68, 116, 157; CCA 1; DAC; DLB 334
Usigli, Rodolfo 1905-1979 .... **HLCS 1**
See also CA 131; DLB 305; EWL 3; HW 1; LAW
Usk, Thomas
(?)-1388 .... **CMLC 76**
See also DLB 146
Ustinov, Peter (Alexander)
1921-2004 .... **CLC 1**
See also AITN 1; CA 13-16R; 225; CANR 25, 51; CBD; CD 5, 6; DLB 13; MTCW 2
U Tam'si, Gerald Felix Tchicaya
See Tchicaya, Gerald Felix
U Tam'si, Tchicaya
See Tchicaya, Gerald Felix
Vachss, Andrew 1942- .... **CLC 106**
See also CA 118, 214; CAAE 214; CANR 44, 95, 153, 197, 238; CMW 4
Vachss, Andrew H.
See Vachss, Andrew
Vachss, Andrew Henry
See Vachss, Andrew
Vaculik, Ludvik
1926- .... **CLC 7**
See also CA 53-56; CANR 72; CWW 2; DLB 232; EWL 3
Vaihinger, Hans
1852-1933 .... **TCLC 71**
See also CA 116; 166
Valdez, Luis (Miguel) 1940- .... **CLC 84; DC 10; HLC 2**
See also CA 101; CAD; CANR 32, 81; CD 5, 6; DAM MULT; DFS 5, 29; DLB 122; EWL 3; HW 1; LAIT 4; LLW
Valenzuela, Luisa 1938- .... **CLC 31, 104; HLCS 2; SSC 14, 82**
See also CA 101; CANR 32, 65, 123; CDWLB 3; CWW 2; DAM MULT; DLB 113; EWL 3; FW; HW 1, 2; LAW; RGSF 2; RGWL 3; SSFS 29
Valera y Alcala-Galiano, Juan
1824-1905 .... **TCLC 10**
See also CA 106
Valerius Maximus .... **CMLC 64**
See also DLB 211
Valle-Inclan, Ramon del
1866-1936 .... **HLC 2; TCLC 5, 228**
See also CA 106; 153; CANR 80; DAM MULT; DLB 134, 322; EW 8; EWL 3; HW 2; RGSF 2; RGWL 2, 3
Valle-Inclan, Ramon Maria del
See Valle-Inclan, Ramon del
Vallejo, Antonio Buero
See Buero Vallejo, Antonio
Vallejo, Cesar 1892-1938 .... **HLC 2; TCLC 3, 56**
See also CA 105; 153; DAM MULT; DLB 290; EWL 3; HW 1; LAW; PFS 26; RGWL 2, 3
Vallejo, Cesar Abraham
See Vallejo, Cesar
Vallette, Marguerite Eymery
1860-1953 .... **TCLC 67**
See also CA 182; DLB 123, 192; EWL 3
Valle Y Pena, Ramon del
See Valle-Inclan, Ramon del
Valles, Jules
1832-1885 .... **NCLC 71**
See also DLB 123; GFL 1789 to the Present
Valery, Ambroise Paul Toussaint Jules
See Valery, Paul
Valery, Paul 1871-1945 .... **PC 9; TCLC 4, 15, 231**
See also CA 104; 122; DA3; DAM POET; DLB 258; EW 8; EWL 3; GFL 1789 to the Present; MTCW 1, 2; MTFW 2005; RGWL 2, 3; TWA
Van Ash, Cay 1918-1994 .... **CLC 34**
See also CA 220
Vanbrugh, Sir John 1664-1726 .... **DC 40; LC 21**
See also BRW 2; DAM DRAM; DLB 80; IDTP; RGEL 2
Van Campen, Karl
See Campbell, John W.
Vance, Gerald
See Silverberg, Robert
Vance, Jack 1916- .... **CLC 35**
See also CA 29-32R; CANR 17, 65, 154, 218; CMW 4; DLB 8; FANT; MTCW 1; SCFW 1, 2; SFW 4; SUFW 1, 2
Vance, John Holbrook
See Vance, Jack
Van Den Bogarde, Derek Jules Gaspard Ulric Niven
See Bogarde, Dirk
Vandenburgh, Jane .... **CLC 59**
See also CA 168; CANR 208
Vanderhaeghe, Guy 1951- .... **CLC 41**
See also BPFB 3; CA 113; CANR 72, 145; CN 7; DLB 334
van der Post, Laurens (Jan)
1906-1996 .... **CLC 5**
See also AFW; CA 5-8R; 155; CANR 35; CN 1, 2, 3, 4, 5, 6; DLB 204; RGEL 2
van de Wetering, Janwillem
1931-2008 .... **CLC 47**
See also CA 49-52; 274; CANR 4, 62, 90; CMW 4
Van Dine, S. S.
See Wright, Willard Huntington
Van Doren, Carl (Clinton)
1885-1950 .... **TCLC 18**
See also CA 111; 168
Van Doren, Mark 1894-1972 .... **CLC 6, 10**
See also CA 1-4R; 37-40R; CANR 3; CN 1; CP 1; DLB 45, 284, 335; MAL 5; MTCW 1, 2; RGAL 4
Van Druten, John (William)
1901-1957 .... **TCLC 2**
See also CA 104; 161; DFS 30; DLB 10; MAL 5; RGAL 4
Van Duyn, Mona 1921-2004 .... **CLC 3, 7, 63, 116**
See also CA 9-12R; 234; CANR 7, 38, 60, 116; CP 1, 2, 3, 4, 5, 6, 7; CWP; DAM POET; DLB 5; MAL 5; MTFW 2005; PFS 20
Van Dyne, Edith
See Baum, L. Frank
van Herk, Aritha
1954- .... **CLC 249**
See also CA 101; CANR 94; DLB 334
van Itallie, Jean-Claude
1936- .... **CLC 3**
See also CA 45-48, 311; CAAS 2, 311; CAD; CANR 1, 48; CD 5, 6; DLB 7
Van Loot, Cornelius Obenchain
See Roberts, Kenneth (Lewis)
van Niekerk, Marlene
1954- .... **CLC 324**
See also CA 229
van Ostaijen, Paul
1896-1928 .... **TCLC 33**
See also CA 163
Van Peebles, Melvin 1932- .... **CLC 2, 20**
See also BW 2, 3; CA 85-88; CANR 27, 67, 82; DAM MULT
van Schendel, Arthur(-Francois-Emile)
1874-1946 .... **TCLC 56**
See also EWL 3
van Schurman, Anna Maria
1607-1678 .... **LC 199**
Van See, John
See Vance, Jack
Vansittart, Peter
1920-2008 .... **CLC 42**
See also CA 1-4R; 278; CANR 3, 49, 90; CN 4, 5, 6, 7; RHW
Van Vechten, Carl
1880-1964 .... **CLC 33; HR 1:3**
See also AMWS 2; CA 183; 89-92; DLB 4, 9, 51; RGAL 4
van Vogt, A(lfred) E(lton)
1912-2000 .... **CLC 1**
See also BPFB 3; BYA 13, 14; CA 21-24R; 190; CANR 28; DLB 8, 251; SATA 14; SATA-Obit 124; SCFW 1, 2; SFW 4
Vara, Madeleine
See Jackson, Laura
Varda, Agnes 1928- .... **CLC 16**
See also CA 116; 122
Vargas Llosa, Jorge Mario Pedro
See Vargas Llosa, Mario
Vargas Llosa, Mario 1936- .... **CLC 3, 6, 9, 10, 15, 31, 42, 85, 181, 318; HLC 2**
See also BPFB 3; CA 73-76; CANR 18, 32, 42, 67, 116, 140, 173, 213; CDWLB 3; CWW 2; DA; DA3; DAB; DAC; DAM MST, MULT, NOV; DLB 145; DNFS 2; EWL 3; HW 1, 2; LAIT 5; LATS 1:2; LAW; LAWS 1; MTCW 1, 2; MTFW 2005; RGWL 2, 3; SSFS 14; TWA; WLIT 1
Varnhagen von Ense, Rahel
1771-1833 .... **NCLC 130**
See also DLB 90
Vasari, Giorgio
1511-1574 .... **LC 114**
Vasilikos, Vasiles
See Vassilikos, Vassilis
Vasiliu, Gheorghe
See Bacovia, George
Vassa, Gustavus
See Equiano, Olaudah
Vassanji, M.G. 1950- .... **CLC 326**
See also CA 136; CANR 186; CN 6, 7; DLB 334; EWL 3
Vassanji, Moyez G.
See Vassanji, M.G.
Vassilikos, Vassilis 1933- .... **CLC 4, 8**
See also CA 81-84; CANR 75, 149; EWL 3
Vaughan, Henry
1621-1695 .... **LC 27; PC 81**
See also BRW 2; DLB 131; PAB; RGEL 2

Vaughn, Stephanie .... **CLC 62**
Vazov, Ivan (Minchov)
1850-1921 .... **TCLC 25**
See also CA 121; 167; CDWLB 4; DLB 147
Vázquez, Joseph
See Cadalso y Vázquez, José de
Vázquez, Don Joseph
See Cadalso y Vázquez, José de
Veblen, Thorstein B(unde)
1857-1929 .... **TCLC 31**
See also AMWS 1; CA 115; 165; DLB 246; MAL 5
Vega, Ana Lydia 1946- .... **SSC 150**
See also CA 193; CWW 2; EWL 3
Vega, Lope de 1562-1635 .... **DC 44; HLCS 2; LC 23, 119**
See also EW 2; RGWL 2, 3
Veldeke, Heinrich von
c. 1145-c. 1190 .... **CMLC 85**
Vendler, Helen 1933- .... **CLC 138**
See also CA 41-44R; CANR 25, 72, 136, 190; MTCW 1, 2; MTFW 2005
Vendler, Helen Hennessy
See Vendler, Helen
Venison, Alfred
See Pound, Ezra
Ventsel, Elena Sergeevna
1907-2002 .... **CLC 59**
See also CA 154; CWW 2; DLB 302
Venttsel', Elena Sergeevna
See Ventsel, Elena Sergeevna
Verdi, Marie de
See Mencken, H. L.
Verdu, Matilde
See Cela, Camilo Jose
Verga, Giovanni (Carmelo)
1840-1922 ... **SSC 21, 87; TCLC 3, 227**
See also CA 104; 123; CANR 101; EW 7; EWL 3; RGSF 2; RGWL 2, 3; WLIT 7
Vergil 70B.C.-19B.C. ...... **CMLC 9, 40, 101; PC 12; WLCS**
See also AW 2; CDWLB 1; DA; DA3; DAB; DAC; DAM MST, POET; DLB 211; EFS 1:1, 2:1; LAIT 1; LMFS 1; RGWL 2, 3; WLIT 8; WP
Vergil, Polydore c. 1470-1555 .... **LC 108**
See also DLB 132
Verhaeren, Emile (Adolphe Gustave)
1855-1916 .... **TCLC 12**
See also CA 109; EWL 3; GFL 1789 to the Present
Verlaine, Paul 1844-1896 .... **NCLC 2, 51, 230; PC 2, 32**
See also DAM POET; DLB 217; EW 7; GFL 1789 to the Present; LMFS 2; RGWL 2, 3; TWA
Verlaine, Paul Marie
See Verlaine, Paul
Verne, Jules 1828-1905 ..... **TCLC 6, 52, 245**
See also AAYA 16; BYA 4; CA 110; 131; CLR 88; DA3; DLB 123; GFL 1789 to the Present; JRDA; LAIT 2; LMFS 2; MAICYA 1, 2; MTFW 2005; NFS 30, 34; RGWL 2, 3; SATA 21; SCFW 1, 2; SFW 4; TWA; WCH
Verne, Jules Gabriel
See Verne, Jules
Verus, Marcus Annius
See Aurelius, Marcus
Very, Jones 1813-1880 .... **NCLC 9; PC 86**
See also DLB 1, 243; RGAL 4
Very, Rev. C.
See Crowley, Edward Alexander
Vesaas, Tarjei 1897-1970 .... **CLC 48**
See also CA 190; 29-32R; DLB 297; EW 11; EWL 3; RGWL 3
Vialis, Gaston
See Simenon, Georges
Vian, Boris 1920-1959(?) .... **TCLC 9, 283**
See also CA 106; 164; CANR 111; DLB 72, 321; EWL 3; GFL 1789 to the Present; MTCW 2; RGWL 2, 3
Viator, Vacuus
See Hughes, Thomas
Viaud, Julien 1850-1923 .... **TCLC 11, 239**
See also CA 107; DLB 123; GFL 1789 to the Present
Viaud, Louis Marie Julien
See Viaud, Julien
Vicar, Henry
See Felsen, Henry Gregor
Vicente, Gil 1465-c. 1536 .... **LC 99**
See also DLB 318; IDTP; RGWL 2, 3
Vicker, Angus
See Felsen, Henry Gregor
Vico, Giambattista
See Vico, Giovanni Battista
Vico, Giovanni Battista 1668-1744 .. **LC 138**
See also EW 3; WLIT 7
Vidal, Eugene Luther Gore
See Vidal, Gore
Vidal, Gore 1925-2012 .... **CLC 2, 4, 6, 8, 10, 22, 33, 72, 142, 289**
See also AAYA 64; AITN 1; AMWS 4; BEST 90:2; BPFB 3; CA 5-8R; CAD; CANR 13, 45, 65, 100, 132, 167; CD 5, 6; CDALBS; CN 1, 2, 3, 4, 5, 6, 7; CPW; DA3; DAM NOV, POP; DFS 2; DLB 6, 152; EWL 3; GLL 1; INT CANR-13; MAL 5; MTCW 1, 2; MTFW 2005; RGAL 4; RHW; TUS
Viereck, Peter 1916-2006 ...... **CLC 4; PC 27**
See also CA 1-4R; 250; CANR 1, 47; CP 1, 2, 3, 4, 5, 6, 7; DLB 5; MAL 5; PFS 9, 14
Viereck, Peter Robert Edwin
See Viereck, Peter
Vigny, Alfred de 1797-1863 .... **NCLC 7, 102, 278; PC 26**
See also DAM POET; DLB 119, 192, 217; EW 5; GFL 1789 to the Present; RGWL 2, 3
Vigny, Alfred Victor de
See Vigny, Alfred de
Vilakazi, Benedict Wallet
1906-1947 .... **TCLC 37**
See also CA 168
Vile, Curt
See Moore, Alan
Villa, Jose Garcia 1914-1997 .... **AAL; PC 22; TCLC 176**
See also CA 25-28R; CANR 12, 118; CP 1, 2, 3, 4; DLB 312; EWL 3; EXPP
Villard, Oswald Garrison
1872-1949 .... **TCLC 160**
See also CA 113; 162; DLB 25, 91
Villarreal, Jose Antonio 1924- .... **HLC 2**
See also CA 133; CANR 93; DAM MULT; DLB 82; HW 1; LAIT 4; RGAL 4
Villaurrutia, Xavier 1903-1950 ..... **TCLC 80**
See also CA 192; EWL 3; HW 1; LAW
Villaverde, Cirilo 1812-1894 .... **NCLC 121**
See also LAW
Villedieu, Madame de 1640?-1683 ... **LC 231**
See also DLB 268
Villehardouin, Geoffroi de
1150(?)-1218(?) .... **CMLC 38**
Villiers, George 1628-1687 .... **LC 107**
See also DLB 80; RGEL 2
Villiers de l'Isle Adam, Jean Marie Mathias Philippe Auguste
1838-1889 .... **NCLC 3, 237; SSC 14**
See also DLB 123, 192; GFL 1789 to the Present; RGSF 2
Villon, Francois 1431-1463(?) .... **LC 62, 166; PC 13**
See also DLB 208; EW 2; RGWL 2, 3; TWA
Vine, Barbara
See Rendell, Ruth
Vinge, Joan (Carol) D(ennison)
1948- .... **CLC 30; SSC 24**
See also AAYA 32; BPFB 3; CA 93-96; CANR 72; SATA 36, 113; SFW 4; YAW
Viola, Herman J(oseph) 1938- .... **CLC 70**
See also CA 61-64; CANR 8, 23, 48, 91; SATA 126
Violis, G.
See Simenon, Georges
Viramontes, Helena Maria
1954- .... **HLCS 2; SSC 149**
See also CA 159; CANR 182; CLR 285; DLB 122, 350; HW 2; LLW
Virgil
See Vergil
Virilio, Paul 1932- .... **CLC 358**
Visconti, Luchino 1906-1976 .... **CLC 16**
See also CA 81-84; 65-68; CANR 39
Vitry, Jacques de
See Jacques de Vitry
Vittorini, Elio 1908-1966 .... **CLC 6, 9, 14**
See also CA 133; 25-28R; DLB 264; EW 12; EWL 3; RGWL 2, 3
Vivekananda, Swami 1863-1902 ... **TCLC 88**
Vives, Juan Luis 1493-1540 .... **LC 170**
See also DLB 318
Vizenor, Gerald Robert 1934- ..... **CLC 103, 263; NNAL; SSC 179**
See also CA 13-16R, 205; CAAE 205; CAAS 22; CANR 5, 21, 44, 67, 233; DAM MULT; DLB 175, 227; MTCW 2; MTFW 2005; TCWW 2
Vizinczey, Stephen 1933- .... **CLC 40**
See also CA 128; CCA 1; INT CA-128
Vladislavic, Ivan 1957- .... **SSC 178**
See also CA 259
Vliet, R(ussell) G(ordon)
1929-1984 .... **CLC 22**
See also CA 37-40R; 112; CANR 18; CP 2, 3
Vogau, Boris Andreevich
See Vogau, Boris Andreyevich
Vogau, Boris Andreyevich 1894-1938 ... **SSC 48; TCLC 23**
See also CA 123; 218; DLB 272; EWL 3; RGSF 2; RGWL 2, 3
Vogel, Paula A. 1951- .... **CLC 76, 290; DC 19**
See also CA 108; CAD; CANR 119, 140; CD 5, 6; CWD; DFS 14; DLB 341; MTFW 2005; RGAL 4
Vogel, Paula Anne
See Vogel, Paula A.
Vogelweide, Walther von der
See Walther von der Vogelweide
Voigt, Cynthia 1942- .... **CLC 30**
See also AAYA 3, 30; BYA 1, 3, 6, 7, 8; CA 106; CANR 18, 37, 40, 94, 145; CLR 13, 48, 141; INT CANR-18; JRDA; LAIT 5; MAICYA 1, 2; MAICYAS 1; MTFW 2005; SATA 48, 79, 116, 160; SATA-Brief 33; WYA; YAW
Voigt, Ellen Bryant 1943- .... **CLC 54**
See also CA 69-72; CANR 11, 29, 55, 115, 171; CP 5, 6, 7; CSW; CWP; DLB 120; PFS 23, 33
Voinovich, Vladimir 1932- .... **CLC 10, 49, 147**
See also CA 81-84; CAAS 12; CANR 33, 67, 150; CWW 2; DLB 302; MTCW 1
Voinovich, Vladimir Nikolaevich
See Voinovich, Vladimir
Vollmann, William T. 1959- .... **CLC 89, 227**
See also AMWS 17; CA 134; CANR 67, 116, 185; CN 7; CPW; DA3; DAM NOV, POP; DLB 350; MTCW 2; MTFW 2005
Voloshinov, V. N.
See Bakhtin, Mikhail Mikhailovich

Author Index

Voltaire 1694-1778 .... **LC 14, 79, 110; SSC 12, 112, 167; WLC 6**
See also BYA 13; DA; DA3; DAB; DAC; DAM DRAM, MST; DLB 314; EW 4; GFL Beginnings to 1789; LATS 1:1; LMFS 1; NFS 7; RGWL 2, 3; TWA

von Aschendrof, Baron Ignatz
See Ford, Ford Madox

von Chamisso, Adelbert
See Chamisso, Adelbert von

von Daeniken, Erich 1935- .... **CLC 30**
See also AITN 1; CA 37-40R; CANR 17, 44

von Daniken, Erich
See von Daeniken, Erich

von dem Turlin, Heinrich
See Heinrich von dem Tuerlin

von der Vogelweide, Walther
See Walther von der Vogelweide

von Eschenbach, Wolfram
c. 1170-c. 1220 ..... **CMLC 5, 145, 153; PC 131**
See also CDWLB 2; DLB 138; EW 1; RGWL 2, 3

von Hartmann, Eduard
1842-1906 .... **TCLC 96**

von Hayek, Friedrich August
See Hayek, F(riedrich) A(ugust von)

von Heidenstam, (Carl Gustaf) Verner
See Heidenstam, (Carl Gustaf) Verner von

von Heyse, Paul (Johann Ludwig)
See Heyse, Paul (Johann Ludwig von)

von Hofmannsthal, Hugo
See Hofmannsthal, Hugo von

von Horvath, Oedoen
See Horvath, Odon von

von Horvath, Odon
See Horvath, Odon von

von Kleist, Heinrich
See Kleist, Heinrich von

von Reuental, Neidhart
See Neidhart von Reuental

Vonnegut, Kurt, Jr.
See Vonnegut, Kurt

Vonnegut, Kurt
1922-2007 .... **CLC 1, 2, 3, 4, 5, 8, 12, 22, 40, 60, 111, 212, 254, 387; SSC 8, 155; WLC 6**
See also AAYA 6, 44; AITN 1; AMWS 2; BEST 90:4; BPFB 3; BYA 3, 14; CA 1-4R; 259; CANR 1, 25, 49, 75, 92, 207; CDALB 1968-1988; CN 1, 2, 3, 4, 5, 6, 7; CPW 1; DA; DA3; DAB; DAC; DAM MST, NOV, POP; DLB 2, 8, 152; DLBD 3; DLBY 1980; EWL 3; EXPN; EXPS; LAIT 4; LMFS 2; MAL 5; MTCW 1, 2; MTFW 2005; NFS 3, 28; RGAL 4; SCFW; SFW 4; SSFS 5; TUS; YAW

Von Rachen, Kurt
See Hubbard, L. Ron

von Sternberg, Josef
See Sternberg, Josef von

Vorster, Gordon 1924- .... **CLC 34**
See also CA 133

Vosce, Trudie
See Ozick, Cynthia

Vostaert, Pieter fl. 13th cent. ...... **CMLC 173**

Voznesensky, Andrei 1933-2010 .... **CLC 1, 15, 57**
See also CA 89-92; CANR 37; CWW 2; DAM POET; DLB 359; EWL 3; MTCW 1

Voznesensky, Andrei Andreievich
See Voznesensky, Andrei

Voznesensky, Andrey
See Voznesensky, Andrei

Wace, Robert c. 1100-c. 1175 ...... **CMLC 55**
See also DLB 146

Waddington, Miriam 1917-2004 ..... **CLC 28**
See also CA 21-24R; 225; CANR 12, 30; CCA 1; CP 1, 2, 3, 4, 5, 6, 7; DLB 68

Wade, Alan
See Vance, Jack

Wagman, Fredrica 1937- .... **CLC 7**
See also CA 97-100; CANR 166; INT CA-97-100

Wagner, Linda W.
See Wagner-Martin, Linda (C.)

Wagner, Linda Welshimer
See Wagner-Martin, Linda (C.)

Wagner, Richard 1813-1883 .... **NCLC 9, 119, 258**
See also DLB 129; EW 6

Wagner-Martin, Linda (C.) 1936- ... **CLC 50**
See also CA 159; CANR 135

Wagoner, David (Russell) 1926- ...... **CLC 3, 5, 15; PC 33**
See also AMWS 9; CA 1-4R; CAAS 3; CANR 2, 71; CN 1, 2, 3, 4, 5, 6, 7; CP 1, 2, 3, 4, 5, 6, 7; DLB 5, 256; SATA 14; TCWW 1, 2

Wah, Fred(erick James)
1939- .... **CLC 44, 338; PC 172**
See also CA 107; 141; CP 1, 6, 7; DLB 60

Wahloo, Per 1926-1975 .... **CLC 7**
See also BPFB 3; CA 61-64; CANR 73; CMW 4; MSW

Wahloo, Peter
See Wahloo, Per

Wain, John 1925-1994 .... **CLC 2, 11, 15, 46**
See also BRWS 16; CA 5-8R; 145; CAAS 4; CANR 23, 54; CDBLB 1960 to Present; CN 1, 2, 3, 4, 5; CP 1, 2, 3, 4, 5; DLB 15, 27, 139, 155; EWL 3; MTCW 1, 2; MTFW 2005

Wajda, Andrzej 1926- .... **CLC 16, 219**
See also CA 102

Wakefield, Dan 1932- .... **CLC 7**
See also CA 21-24R, 211; CAAE 211; CAAS 7; CN 4, 5, 6, 7

Wakefield, Herbert Russell
1888-1965 .... **TCLC 120**
See also CA 5-8R; CANR 77; HGG; SUFW

Wakoski, Diane 1937- .... **CLC 2, 4, 7, 9, 11, 40; PC 15**
See also CA 13-16R, 216; CAAE 216; CAAS 1; CANR 9, 60, 106; CP 1, 2, 3, 4, 5, 6, 7; CWP; DAM POET; DLB 5; INT CANR-9; MAL 5; MTCW 2; MTFW 2005; PFS 43

Wakoski-Sherbell, Diane
See Wakoski, Diane

Walcott, Derek 1930- .... **BLC 1:3, 2:3; CLC 2, 4, 9, 14, 25, 42, 67, 76, 160, 282; DC 7; PC 46**
See also BW 2; CA 89-92; CANR 26, 47, 75, 80, 130, 230; CBD; CD 5, 6; CDWLB 3; CP 1, 2, 3, 4, 5, 6, 7; DA3; DAB; DAC; DAM MST, MULT, POET; DLB 117, 332; DLBY 1981; DNFS 1; EFS 1:1, 2:2; EWL 3; LMFS 2; MTCW 1, 2; MTFW 2005; PFS 6, 34, 39; RGEL 2; TWA; WWE 1

Walcott, Derek Alton
See Walcott, Derek

Waldman, Anne 1945- .... **CLC 7**
See also BG 1:3; CA 37-40R; CAAS 17; CANR 34, 69, 116, 219; CP 1, 2, 3, 4, 5, 6, 7; CWP; DLB 16

Waldman, Anne Lesley
See Waldman, Anne

Waldo, E. Hunter
See Sturgeon, Theodore (Hamilton)

Waldo, Edward Hamilton
See Sturgeon, Theodore (Hamilton)

Waldrop, Rosmarie
1935- .... **PC 109**
See also CA 101; CAAS 30; CANR 18, 39, 67; CP 6, 7; CWP; DLB 169

Walker, Alice 1944- ...... **BLC 1:3, 2:3; CLC 5, 6, 9, 19, 27, 46, 58, 103, 167, 319, 381; PC 30; SSC 5; WLCS**
See also AAYA 3, 33; AFAW 1, 2; AMWS 3; BEST 89:4; BPFB 3; BW 2, 3; CA 37-40R; CANR 9, 27, 49, 66, 82, 131, 191, 238; CDALB 1968-1988; CN 4, 5, 6, 7; CLR 198; CPW; CSW; DA; DA3; DAB; DAC; DAM MST, MULT, NOV, POET, POP; DLB 6, 33, 143; EWL 3; EXPN; EXPS; FL 1:6; FW; INT CANR-27; LAIT 3; MAL 5; MBL; MTCW 1, 2; MTFW 2005; NFS 5; PFS 30, 34; RGAL 4; RGSF 2; SATA 31; SSFS 2, 11; TUS; YAW

Walker, Alice Malsenior
See Walker, Alice

Walker, David Harry 1911-1992 .... **CLC 14**
See also CA 1-4R; 137; CANR 1; CN 1, 2; CWRI 5; SATA 8; SATA-Obit 71

Walker, Edward Joseph
1934-2004 .... **CLC 13**
See also CA 21-24R; 226; CANR 12, 28, 53; CP 1, 2, 3, 4, 5, 6, 7; DLB 40

Walker, George F(rederick)
1947- .... **CLC 44, 61**
See also CA 103; CANR 21, 43, 59; CD 5, 6; DAB; DAC; DAM MST; DLB 60

Walker, Joseph A. 1935-2003 .... **CLC 19**
See also BW 1, 3; CA 89-92; CAD; CANR 26, 143; CD 5, 6; DAM DRAM, MST; DFS 12; DLB 38

Walker, Margaret 1915-1998 .... **BLC 1:3; CLC 1, 6; PC 20; TCLC 129**
See also AFAW 1, 2; BW 2, 3; CA 73-76; 172; CANR 26, 54, 76, 136; CN 1, 2, 3, 4, 5, 6; CP 1, 2, 3, 4, 5, 6; CSW; DAM MULT; DLB 76, 152; EXPP; FW; MAL 5; MTCW 1, 2; MTFW 2005; PFS 31; RGAL 4; RHW

Walker, Ted
See Walker, Edward Joseph

Wallace, David Foster 1962-2008 ... **CLC 50, 114, 271, 281; SSC 68**
See also AAYA 50; AMWS 10; CA 132; 277; CANR 59, 133, 190, 237; CN 7; DA3; DLB 350; MTCW 2; MTFW 2005

Wallace, Dexter
See Masters, Edgar Lee

Wallace, (Richard Horatio) Edgar
1875-1932 .... **TCLC 57**
See also CA 115; 218; CMW 4; DLB 70; MSW; RGEL 2

Wallace, Irving 1916-1990 .... **CLC 7, 13**
See also AITN 1; BPFB 3; CA 1-4R; 132; CAAS 1; CANR 1, 27; CPW; DAM NOV, POP; INT CANR-27; MTCW 1, 2

Wallant, Edward Lewis
1926-1962 .... **CLC 5, 10**
See also CA 1-4R; CANR 22; DLB 2, 28, 143, 299; EWL 3; MAL 5; MTCW 1, 2; RGAL 4; RGHL

Wallas, Graham 1858-1932 .... **TCLC 91**

Waller, Edmund 1606-1687 ... **LC 86; PC 72**
See also BRW 2; DAM POET; DLB 126; PAB; RGEL 2

Walley, Byron
See Card, Orson Scott

Walls, Jeannette 1960(?)- .... **CLC 299**
See also CA 242; CANR 220

Walpole, Horace 1717-1797 ... **LC 2, 49, 152**
See also BRW 3; DLB 39, 104, 213; GL 3; HGG; LMFS 1; RGEL 2; SUFW 1; TEA

Walpole, Hugh 1884-1941 .... **TCLC 5**
See also CA 104; 165; DLB 34; HGG; MTCW 2; RGEL 2; RHW

Walpole, Hugh Seymour
See Walpole, Hugh

Walrond, Eric (Derwent)
1898-1966 .... **HR 1:3**
See also BW 1; CA 125; DLB 51

Walser, Martin 1927- .... **CLC 27, 183**
See also CA 57-60; CANR 8, 46, 145; CWW 2; DLB 75, 124; EWL 3
Walser, Robert 1878-1956 .... **SSC 20; TCLC 18, 267**
See also CA 118; 165; CANR 100, 194; DLB 66; EWL 3
Walsh, Gillian Paton
See Paton Walsh, Jill
Walsh, Jill Paton
See Paton Walsh, Jill
Walter, Villiam Christian
See Andersen, Hans Christian
Walter of Chatillon
c. 1135-c. 1202 .... **CMLC 111**
Walters, Anna L(ee) 1946- .... **NNAL**
See also CA 73-76
Walther von der Vogelweide
c. 1170-1228 .... **CMLC 56**
Walther von der Vogelweide c. 1170-c. 1230 .... **CMLC 147**
See also DLB 138; EW 1; RGWL 2, 3
Walton, Izaak 1593-1683 .... **LC 72**
See also BRW 2; CDBLB Before 1660; DLB 151, 213; RGEL 2
Walzer, Michael 1935- .... **CLC 238**
See also CA 37-40R; CANR 15, 48, 127, 190
Walzer, Michael Laban
See Walzer, Michael
Wambaugh, Joseph, Jr. 1937- .... **CLC 3, 18**
See also AITN 1; BEST 89:3; BPFB 3; CA 33-36R; CANR 42, 65, 115, 167, 217; CMW 4; CPW 1; DA3; DAM NOV, POP; DLB 6; DLBY 1983; MSW; MTCW 1, 2
Wambaugh, Joseph Aloysius
See Wambaugh, Joseph, Jr.
Wang Wei 699(?)-761(?) .... **CMLC 100; PC 18**
See also TWA
Warburton, William 1698-1779 .... **LC 97**
See also DLB 104
Ward, Arthur Henry Sarsfield
1883-1959 .... **TCLC 28**
See also AAYA 80; CA 108; 173; CMW 4; DLB 70; HGG; MSW; SUFW
Ward, Douglas Turner 1930- .... **CLC 19**
See also BW 1; CA 81-84; CAD; CANR 27; CD 5, 6; DLB 7, 38
Ward, E. D.
See Lucas, E(dward) V(errall)
Ward, Mrs. Humphry 1851-1920
See Ward, Mary Augusta
See also RGEL 2
Ward, Mary Augusta
1851-1920 .... **TCLC 55**
See Ward, Mrs. Humphry
See also DLB 18
Ward, Nathaniel 1578(?)-1652 .... **LC 114**
See also DLB 24
Ward, Peter
See Faust, Frederick
Warhol, Andy 1928(?)-1987 .... **CLC 20**
See also AAYA 12; BEST 89:4; CA 89-92; 121; CANR 34
Warner, Francis (Robert Le Plastrier)
1937- .... **CLC 14**
See also CA 53-56; CANR 11; CP 1, 2, 3, 4
Warner, Marina 1946- .... **CLC 59, 231**
See also CA 65-68; CANR 21, 55, 118; CN 5, 6, 7; DLB 194; MTFW 2005
Warner, Rex (Ernest)
1905-1986 .... **CLC 45**
See also CA 89-92; 119; CN 1, 2, 3, 4; CP 1, 2, 3, 4; DLB 15; RGEL 2; RHW
Warner, Susan (Bogert)
1819-1885 .... **NCLC 31, 146**
See also AMWS 18; CLR 179; DLB 3, 42, 239, 250, 254
Warner, Sylvia (Constance) Ashton
See Ashton-Warner, Sylvia (Constance)
Warner, Sylvia Townsend
1893-1978 .... **CLC 7, 19; SSC 23; TCLC 131**
See also BRWS 7; CA 61-64; 77-80; CANR 16, 60, 104; CN 1, 2; DLB 34, 139; EWL 3; FANT; FW; MTCW 1, 2; RGEL 2; RGSF 2; RHW
Warren, Mercy Otis
1728-1814 .... **NCLC 13, 226**
See also DLB 31, 200; RGAL 4; TUS
Warren, Robert Penn 1905-1989 ..... **CLC 1, 4, 6, 8, 10, 13, 18, 39, 53, 59; PC 37; SSC 4, 58, 126; WLC 6**
See also AITN 1; AMW; AMWC 2; BPFB 3; BYA 1; CA 13-16R; 129; CANR 10, 47; CDALB 1968-1988; CN 1, 2, 3, 4; CP 1, 2, 3, 4; DA; DA3; DAB; DAC; DAM MST, NOV, POET; DLB 2, 48, 152, 320; DLBY 1980, 1989; EWL 3; INT CANR-10; MAL 5; MTCW 1, 2; MTFW 2005; NFS 13; RGAL 4; RGSF 2; RHW; SATA 46; SATA-Obit 63; SSFS 8; TUS
Warrigal, Jack
See Furphy, Joseph
Warshofsky, Isaac
See Singer, Isaac Bashevis
Warton, Joseph 1722-1800 .... **LC 128; NCLC 118**
See also DLB 104, 109; RGEL 2
Warton, Thomas
1728-1790 .... **LC 15, 82**
See also DAM POET; DLB 104, 109, 336; RGEL 2
Waruk, Kona
See Harris, (Theodore) Wilson
Warung, Price
See Astley, William
Warwick, Jarvis
See Garner, Hugh
Washington, Alex
See Harris, Mark
Washington, Booker T.
1856-1915 .... **BLC 1:3; TCLC 10**
See also BW 1; CA 114; 125; DA3; DAM MULT; DLB 345; LAIT 2; RGAL 4; SATA 28
Washington, Booker Taliaferro
See Washington, Booker T.
Washington, George 1732-1799 .... **LC 25**
See also DLB 31
Wassermann, (Karl) Jakob
1873-1934 .... **TCLC 6**
See also CA 104; 163; DLB 66; EWL 3
Wasserstein, Wendy 1950-2006 ...... **CLC 32, 59, 90, 183; DC 4**
See also AAYA 73; AMWS 15; CA 121; 129; 247; CABS 3; CAD; CANR 53, 75, 128; CD 5, 6; CWD; DA3; DAM DRAM; DFS 5, 17, 29; DLB 228; EWL 3; FW; INT CA-129; MAL 5; MTCW 2; MTFW 2005; SATA 94; SATA-Obit 174
Waterhouse, Keith 1929-2009 .... **CLC 47**
See also BRWS 13; CA 5-8R; 290; CANR 38, 67, 109; CBD; CD 6; CN 1, 2, 3, 4, 5, 6, 7; DLB 13, 15; MTCW 1, 2; MTFW 2005
Waterhouse, Keith Spencer
See Waterhouse, Keith
Waters, Frank (Joseph)
1902-1995 .... **CLC 88**
See also CA 5-8R; 149; CAAS 13; CANR 3, 18, 63, 121; DLB 212; DLBY 1986; RGAL 4; TCWW 1, 2
Waters, Mary C. .... **CLC 70**
Waters, Roger 1944- .... **CLC 35**
Watkins, Frances Ellen
See Harper, Frances Ellen Watkins
Watkins, Gerrold
See Malzberg, Barry N(athaniel)
Watkins, Gloria Jean
See hooks, bell
Watkins, Paul 1964- .... **CLC 55**
See also CA 132; CANR 62, 98, 231
Watkins, Vernon Phillips
1906-1967 .... **CLC 43**
See also CA 9-10; 25-28R; CAP 1; DLB 20; EWL 3; RGEL 2
Watson, Irving S.
See Mencken, H. L.
Watson, John H.
See Farmer, Philip Jose
Watson, Richard F.
See Silverberg, Robert
Watson, Rosamund Marriott
1860-1911 .... **PC 117**
See also CA 207; DLB 240
Watson, Sheila 1909-1998 .... **SSC 128**
See also AITN 2; CA 155; CCA 1; DAC; DLB 60
Watts, Ephraim
See Horne, Richard Henry Hengist
Watts, Isaac 1674-1748 .... **LC 98**
See also DLB 95; RGEL 2; SATA 52
Waugh, Auberon (Alexander)
1939-2001 .... **CLC 7**
See also CA 45-48; 192; CANR 6, 22, 92; CN 1, 2, 3; DLB 14, 194
Waugh, Evelyn 1903-1966 .... **CLC 1, 3, 8, 13, 19, 27, 107; SSC 41; TCLC 229, 318; WLC 6**
See also AAYA 78; BPFB 3; BRW 7; CA 85-88; 25-28R; CANR 22; CDBLB 1914-1945; DA; DA3; DAB; DAC; DAM MST, NOV, POP; DLB 15, 162, 195, 352; EWL 3; MTCW 1, 2; MTFW 2005; NFS 13, 17, 34; RGEL 2; RGSF 2; TEA; WLIT 4
Waugh, Evelyn Arthur St. John
See Waugh, Evelyn
Waugh, Harriet 1944- .... **CLC 6**
See also CA 85-88; CANR 22
Ways, C.R.
See Blount, Roy, Jr.
Waystaff, Simon
See Swift, Jonathan
Webb, Beatrice 1858-1943 .... **TCLC 22**
See also CA 117; 162; DLB 190; FW
Webb, Beatrice Martha Potter
See Webb, Beatrice
Webb, Charles 1939- .... **CLC 7**
See also CA 25-28R; CANR 114, 188
Webb, Charles Richard
See Webb, Charles
Webb, Frank J. .... **NCLC 143**
See also DLB 50
Webb, James, Jr.
See Webb, James
Webb, James 1946- .... **CLC 22**
See also CA 81-84; CANR 156
Webb, James H.
See Webb, James
Webb, James Henry
See Webb, James
Webb, Mary Gladys (Meredith)
1881-1927 .... **TCLC 24**
See also CA 182; 123; DLB 34; FW; RGEL 2
Webb, Mrs. Sidney
See Webb, Beatrice
Webb, Phyllis 1927- .... **CLC 18; PC 124**
See also CA 104; CANR 23; CCA 1; CP 1, 2, 3, 4, 5, 6, 7; CWP; DLB 53

Webb, Sidney 1859-1947 .... **TCLC 22**
See also CA 117; 163; DLB 190
Webb, Sidney James
See Webb, Sidney
Webber, Andrew Lloyd
See Lloyd Webber, Andrew
Weber, Lenora Mattingly
1895-1971 .... **CLC 12**
See also CA 19-20; 29-32R; CAP 1; SATA 2; SATA-Obit 26
Weber, Max 1864-1920 .... **TCLC 69**
See also CA 109; 189; DLB 296
Webster, Augusta 1837-1894 .... **NCLC 230**
See also DLB 35, 240
Webster, John 1580(?)-1634(?) .... **DC 2; LC 33, 84, 124; WLC 6**
See also BRW 2; CDBLB Before 1660; DA; DAB; DAC; DAM DRAM, MST; DFS 17, 19; DLB 58; IDTP; RGEL 2; WLIT 3
Webster, Noah 1758-1843 ..... **NCLC 30, 253**
See also DLB 1, 37, 42, 43, 73, 243
Wecker, Helene 1975- .... **CLC 370**
Wedekind, Benjamin Franklin
See Wedekind, Frank
Wedekind, Frank 1864-1918 ... **TCLC 7, 241**
See also CA 104; 153; CANR 121, 122; CDWLB 2; DAM DRAM; DLB 118; EW 8; EWL 3; LMFS 2; RGWL 2, 3
Weems, Mason Locke 1759-1825 ... **NCLC 245**
See also DLB 30, 37, 42
Wehr, Demaris .... **CLC 65**
Weidman, Jerome 1913-1998 .... **CLC 7**
See also AITN 2; CA 1-4R; 171; CAD; CANR 1; CD 1, 2, 3, 4, 5; DLB 28
Weil, Simone 1909-1943 .... **TCLC 23, 280**
See also CA 117; 159; EW 12; EWL 3; FW; GFL 1789 to the Present; MTCW 2
Weil, Simone Adolphine
See Weil, Simone
Weininger, Otto 1880-1903 .... **TCLC 84**
Weinstein, Nathan
See West, Nathanael
Weinstein, Nathan von Wallenstein
See West, Nathanael
Weir, Peter 1944- .... **CLC 20**
See also CA 113; 123
Weir, Peter Lindsay
See Weir, Peter
Weiss, Peter (Ulrich) 1916-1982 ...... **CLC 3, 15, 51; DC 36; TCLC 152**
See also CA 45-48; 106; CANR 3; DAM DRAM; DFS 3; DLB 69, 124; EWL 3; RGHL; RGWL 2, 3
Weiss, Theodore (Russell)
1916-2003 .... **CLC 3, 8, 14**
See also CA 9-12R, 189; 216; CAAE 189; CAAS 2; CANR 46, 94; CP 1, 2, 3, 4, 5, 6, 7; DLB 5; TCLE 1:2
Welch, (Maurice) Denton
1915-1948 .... **TCLC 22**
See also BRWS 8; CA 121; 148; RGEL 2
Welch, James 1940-2003 ...... **CLC 6, 14, 52, 249; NNAL; PC 62**
See also CA 85-88; 219; CANR 42, 66, 107; CN 5, 6, 7; CP 2, 3, 4, 5, 6, 7; CPW; DAM MULT, POP; DLB 175, 256; LATS 1:1; NFS 23; RGAL 4; TCWW 1, 2
Welch, James Phillip
See Welch, James
Weld, Angelina Grimke
See Grimke, Angelina Weld
Weldon, Fay 1931- .... **CLC 6, 9, 11, 19, 36, 59, 122**
See also BRWS 4; CA 21-24R; CANR 16, 46, 63, 97, 137, 227; CDBLB 1960 to Present; CN 3, 4, 5, 6, 7; CPW; DAM POP; DLB 14, 194, 319; EWL 3; FW; HGG; INT CANR-16; MTCW 1, 2; MTFW 2005; RGEL 2; RGSF 2
Wellek, Rene 1903-1995 .... **CLC 28**
See also CA 5-8R; 150; CAAS 7; CANR 8; DLB 63; EWL 3; INT CANR-8
Weller, Michael 1942- .... **CLC 10, 53**
See also CA 85-88; CAD; CD 5, 6
Weller, Paul 1958- .... **CLC 26**
Wellershoff, Dieter 1925- .... **CLC 46**
See also CA 89-92; CANR 16, 37
Welles, (George) Orson
1915-1985 .... **CLC 20, 80**
See also AAYA 40; CA 93-96; 117
Wellman, John McDowell 1945- .... **CLC 65**
See also CA 166; CAD; CD 5, 6; RGAL 4
Wellman, Mac
See Wellman, John McDowell; Wellman, John McDowell
Wellman, Manly Wade 1903-1986 .. **CLC 49**
See also CA 1-4R; 118; CANR 6, 16, 44; FANT; SATA 6; SATA-Obit 47; SFW 4; SUFW
Wells, Carolyn 1869(?)-1942 .... **TCLC 35**
See also CA 113; 185; CMW 4; DLB 11
Wells, H. G. 1866-1946 .... **SSC 6, 70, 151; TCLC 6, 12, 19, 133, 317; WLC 6**
See also AAYA 18; BPFB 3; BRW 6; CA 110; 121; CDBLB 1914-1945; CLR 64, 133, 200; DA; DA3; DAB; DAC; DAM MST, NOV; DLB 34, 70, 156, 178; EWL 3; EXPS; HGG; LAIT 3; LMFS 2; MTCW 1, 2; MTFW 2005; NFS 17, 20, 36; RGEL 2; RGSF 2; SATA 20; SCFW 1, 2; SFW 4; SSFS 3, 34; SUFW; TEA; WCH; WLIT 4; YAW
Wells, Herbert George
See Wells, H. G.
Wells, Rosemary 1943- .... **CLC 12**
See also AAYA 13; BYA 7, 8; CA 85-88; CANR 48, 120, 179; CLR 16, 69; CWRI 5; MAICYA 1, 2; SAAS 1; SATA 18, 69, 114, 156, 207, 237; YAW
Wells-Barnett, Ida B(ell)
1862-1931 .... **TCLC 125**
See also CA 182; DLB 23, 221
Welsh, Irvine 1958- .... **CLC 144, 276**
See also BRWS 17; CA 173; CANR 146, 196; CN 7; DLB 271
Welty, Eudora 1909-2001 .... **CLC 319; SSC 1, 27, 51, 111; WLC 6**
See also AAYA 48; AMW; AMWR 1; BPFB 3; CA 9-12R; 199; CABS 1; CANR 32, 65, 128; CDALB 1941-1968; CN 1, 2, 3, 4, 5, 6, 7; CSW; DA; DA3; DAB; DAC; DAM MST, NOV; DFS 26; DLB 2, 102, 143; DLBD 12; DLBY 1987, 2001; EWL 3; EXPS; HGG; LAIT 3; MAL 5; MBL; MTCW 1, 2; MTFW 2005; NFS 13, 15, 42; RGAL 4; RGSF 2; RHW; SSFS 2, 10, 26; TUS
Welty, Eudora Alice
See Welty, Eudora
Wendt, Albert 1939- .... **CLC 317**
See also CA 57-60; CN 3, 4, 5, 6, 7; CP 5, 6, 7; EWL 3; RGSF 2
Wen I-to 1899-1946 .... **TCLC 28**
See also EWL 3
Wentworth, Robert
See Hamilton, Edmond
Werfel, Franz (Viktor)
1890-1945 .... **PC 101; TCLC 8, 248**
See also CA 104; 161; DLB 81, 124; EWL 3; RGWL 2, 3
Wergeland, Henrik Arnold
1808-1845 .... **NCLC 5**
See also DLB 354
Werner, Friedrich Ludwig Zacharias
1768-1823 .... **NCLC 189**
See also DLB 94
Werner, Zacharias
See Werner, Friedrich Ludwig Zacharias
Wersba, Barbara 1932- .... **CLC 30**
See also AAYA 2, 30; BYA 6, 12, 13; CA 29-32R, 182; CAAE 182; CANR 16, 38; CLR 3, 78; DLB 52; JRDA; MAICYA 1, 2; SAAS 2; SATA 1, 58; SATA-Essay 103; WYA; YAW
Wertmueller, Lina 1928- .... **CLC 16**
See also CA 97-100; CANR 39, 78
Wescott, Glenway 1901-1987 .... **CLC 13; SSC 35; TCLC 265**
See also CA 13-16R; 121; CANR 23, 70; CN 1, 2, 3, 4; DLB 4, 9, 102; MAL 5; RGAL 4
Wesker, Arnold 1932- .... **CLC 3, 5, 42**
See also CA 1-4R; CAAS 7; CANR 1, 33; CBD; CD 5, 6; CDBLB 1960 to Present; DAB; DAM DRAM; DLB 13, 310, 319; EWL 3; MTCW 1; RGEL 2; TEA
Wesley, Charles 1707-1788 .... **LC 128**
See also DLB 95; RGEL 2
Wesley, John 1703-1791 .... **LC 88**
See also DLB 104
Wesley, Richard (Errol) 1945- .... **CLC 7**
See also BW 1; CA 57-60; CAD; CANR 27; CD 5, 6; DLB 38
Wessel, Johan Herman 1742-1785 ...... **LC 7**
See also DLB 300
West, Anthony (Panther)
1914-1987 .... **CLC 50**
See also CA 45-48; 124; CANR 3, 19; CN 1, 2, 3, 4; DLB 15
West, C. P.
See Wodehouse, P. G.
West, Cornel 1953- .... **BLCS; CLC 134**
See also CA 144; CANR 91, 159; DLB 246
West, Cornel Ronald
See West, Cornel
West, Delno C(loyde), Jr. 1936- ..... **CLC 70**
See also CA 57-60
West, Dorothy 1907-1998 .... **HR 1:3; TCLC 108**
See also AMWS 18; BW 2; CA 143; 169; DLB 76
West, Edwin
See Westlake, Donald E.
West, (Mary) Jessamyn
1902-1984 .... **CLC 7, 17**
See also CA 9-12R; 112; CANR 27; CN 1, 2, 3; DLB 6; DLBY 1984; MTCW 1, 2; RGAL 4; RHW; SATA-Obit 37; TCWW 2; TUS; YAW
West, Morris L(anglo) 1916-1999 ... **CLC 6, 33**
See also BPFB 3; CA 5-8R; 187; CANR 24, 49, 64; CN 1, 2, 3, 4, 5, 6; CPW; DLB 289; MTCW 1, 2; MTFW 2005
West, Nathanael 1903-1940 ..... **SSC 16, 116; TCLC 1, 14, 44, 235**
See also AAYA 77; AMW; AMWR 2; BPFB 3; CA 104; 125; CDALB 1929-1941; DA3; DLB 4, 9, 28; EWL 3; MAL 5; MTCW 1, 2; MTFW 2005; NFS 16; RGAL 4; TUS
West, Owen
See Koontz, Dean
West, Paul 1930- .... **CLC 7, 14, 96, 226**
See also CA 13-16R; CAAS 7; CANR 22, 53, 76, 89, 136, 205; CN 1, 2, 3, 4, 5, 6, 7; DLB 14; INT CANR-22; MTCW 2; MTFW 2005
West, Rebecca 1892-1983 .... **CLC 7, 9, 31, 50**
See also BPFB 3; BRWS 3; CA 5-8R; 109; CANR 19; CN 1, 2, 3; DLB 36; DLBY 1983; EWL 3; FW; MTCW 1, 2; MTFW 2005; NCFS 4; RGEL 2; TEA
Westall, Robert (Atkinson)
1929-1993 .... **CLC 17**
See also AAYA 12; BYA 2, 6, 7, 8, 9, 15; CA 69-72; 141; CANR 18, 68; CLR 13,

177; FANT; JRDA; MAICYA 1, 2; MAICYAS 1; SAAS 2; SATA 23, 69; SATA-Obit 75; WYA; YAW
Westermarck, Edward 1862-1939 ... **TCLC 87**
Westlake, Donald E. 1933-2008 ... **CLC 7, 33**
See also BPFB 3; CA 17-20R; 280; CAAS 13; CANR 16, 44, 65, 94, 137, 192; CMW 4; CPW; DAM POP; INT CANR-16; MSW; MTCW 2; MTFW 2005
Westlake, Donald E. Edmund
See Westlake, Donald E.
Westlake, Donald Edwin
See Westlake, Donald E.
Westlake, Donald Edwin Edmund
See Westlake, Donald E.
Westmacott, Mary
See Christie, Agatha
Weston, Allen
See Norton, Andre
Wetcheek, J. L.
See Feuchtwanger, Lion
Wetering, Janwillem van de
See van de Wetering, Janwillem
Wetherald, Agnes Ethelwyn
1857-1940 .... **TCLC 81**
See also CA 202; DLB 99
Wetherell, Elizabeth
See Warner, Susan (Bogert)
Whale, James 1889-1957 .... **TCLC 63**
See also AAYA 75
Whalen, Philip (Glenn) 1923-2002 .. **CLC 6, 29**
See also BG 1:3; CA 9-12R; 209; CANR 5, 39; CP 1, 2, 3, 4, 5, 6, 7; DLB 16; WP
Wharton, Edith 1862-1937 ... **SSC 6, 84, 120; TCLC 3, 9, 27, 53, 129, 149; WLC 6**
See also AAYA 25; AMW; AMWC 2; AMWR 1; BPFB 3; CA 104; 132; CDALB 1865-1917; CLR 136; DA; DA3; DAB; DAC; DAM MST, NOV; DLB 4, 9, 12, 78, 189; DLBD 13; EWL 3; EXPS; FL 1:6; GL 3; HGG; LAIT 2, 3; LATS 1:1; MAL 5; MBL; MTCW 1, 2; MTFW 2005; NFS 5, 11, 15, 20, 37; RGAL 4; RGSF 2; RHW; SSFS 6, 7; SUFW; TUS
Wharton, Edith Newbold Jones
See Wharton, Edith
Wharton, James
See Mencken, H. L.
Wharton, William 1925-2008 .... **CLC 18, 37**
See also CA 93-96; 278; CN 4, 5, 6, 7; DLBY 1980; INT CA-93-96
Whately, Richard 1787-1863 .... **NCLC 299**
See also DLB 190
Wheatley, Phillis 1753(?)-1784 ...... **BLC 1:3; LC 3, 50, 183; PC 3, 142; WLC 6**
See also AFAW 1, 2; AMWS 20; CDALB 1640-1865; DA; DA3; DAC; DAM MST, MULT, POET; DLB 31, 50; EXPP; FL 1:1; PFS 13, 29, 36; RGAL 4
Wheatley Peters, Phillis
See Wheatley, Phillis
Wheelock, John Hall 1886-1978 ..... **CLC 14**
See also CA 13-16R; 77-80; CANR 14; CP 1, 2; DLB 45; MAL 5
Whim-Wham
See Curnow, (Thomas) Allen (Monro)
Whisp, Kennilworthy
See Rowling, J.K.
Whitaker, Rod 1931-2005 .... **CLC 29**
See also CA 29-32R; 246; CANR 45, 153; CMW 4
Whitaker, Rodney
See Whitaker, Rod
Whitaker, Rodney William
See Whitaker, Rod
White, Babington
See Braddon, Mary Elizabeth
White, E. B. 1899-1985 ...... **CLC 10, 34, 39**
See also AAYA 62; AITN 2; AMWS 1; CA 13-16R; 116; CANR 16, 37; CDALBS; CLR 1, 21, 107; CPW; DA3; DAM POP; DLB 11, 22; EWL 3; FANT; MAICYA 1, 2; MAL 5; MTCW 1, 2; MTFW 2005; NCFS 5; RGAL 4; SATA 2, 29, 100; SATA-Obit 44; TUS
White, Edmund 1940- .... **CLC 27, 110**
See also AAYA 7; CA 45-48; CANR 3, 19, 36, 62, 107, 133, 172, 212; CN 5, 6, 7; DA3; DAM POP; DLB 227; MTCW 1, 2; MTFW 2005
White, Edmund Valentine III
See White, Edmund
White, Elwyn Brooks
See White, E. B.
White, Hayden V. 1928- .... **CLC 148**
See also CA 128; CANR 135; DLB 246
White, Patrick 1912-1990 .... **CLC 3, 4, 5, 7, 9, 18, 65, 69; SSC 39; TCLC 176**
See also BRWS 1; CA 81-84; 132; CANR 43; CN 1, 2, 3, 4; DLB 260, 332; EWL 3; MTCW 1; RGEL 2; RGSF 2; RHW; TWA; WWE 1
White, Patrick Victor Martindale
See White, Patrick
White, Phyllis Dorothy James
See James, P. D.
White, T(erence) H(anbury)
1906-1964 .... **CLC 30**
See also AAYA 22; BPFB 3; BYA 4, 5; CA 73-76; CANR 37; CLR 139; DLB 160; FANT; JRDA; LAIT 1; MAICYA 1, 2; NFS 30; RGEL 2; SATA 12; SUFW 1; YAW
White, Terence de Vere 1912-1994 .... **CLC 49**
See also CA 49-52; 145; CANR 3
White, Walter
See White, Walter F(rancis)
White, Walter F(rancis)
1893-1955 .... **BLC 1:3; HR 1:3; TCLC 15**
See also BW 1; CA 115; 124; DAM MULT; DLB 51
White, William Hale 1831-1913 ... **TCLC 25**
See also CA 121; 189; DLB 18; RGEL 2
Whitehead, Alfred North
1861-1947 .... **TCLC 97**
See also CA 117; 165; DLB 100, 262
Whitehead, Colson
1969- .... **BLC 2:3; CLC 232, 348**
See also CA 202; CANR 162, 211
Whitehead, E(dward) A(nthony)
1933- .... **CLC 5**
See also CA 65-68; CANR 58, 118; CBD; CD 5, 6; DLB 310
Whitehead, Ted
See Whitehead, E(dward) A(nthony)
Whiteman, Roberta J. Hill 1947- ...... **NNAL**
See also CA 146
Whitemore, Hugh (John)
1936- .... **CLC 37**
See also CA 132; CANR 77; CBD; CD 5, 6; INT CA-132
Whitman, Sarah Helen (Power)
1803-1878 .... **NCLC 19**
See also DLB 1, 243
Whitman, Walt 1819-1892 .... **NCLC 4, 31, 81, 205, 268; PC 3, 91; WLC 6**
See also AAYA 42; AMW; AMWR 1; CDALB 1640-1865; DA; DA3; DAB; DAC; DAM MST, POET; DLB 3, 64, 224, 250; EXPP; LAIT 2; LMFS 1; PAB; PFS 2, 3, 13, 22, 31, 39; RGAL 4; SATA 20; TUS; WP; WYAS 1
Whitman, Walter
See Whitman, Walt
Whitney, Isabella
fl. 1565-fl. 1575 .... **LC 130; PC 116**
See also DLB 136
Whitney, Phyllis A. 1903-2008 .... **CLC 42**
See also AAYA 36; AITN 2; BEST 90:3; CA 1-4R; 269; CANR 3, 25, 38, 60; CLR 59; CMW 4; CPW; DA3; DAM POP; JRDA; MAICYA 1, 2; MTCW 2; RHW; SATA 1, 30; SATA-Obit 189; YAW
Whitney, Phyllis Ayame
See Whitney, Phyllis A.
Whittemore, Edward Reed
See Whittemore, Reed, Jr.
Whittemore, Reed, Jr.
1919-2012 .... **CLC 4**
See also CA 9-12R, 219; CAAE 219; CAAS 8; CANR 4, 119; CP 1, 2, 3, 4, 5, 6, 7; DLB 5; MAL 5
Whittier, John Greenleaf
1807-1892 .... **NCLC 8, 59; PC 93**
See also AMWS 1; DLB 1, 243; PFS 36; RGAL 4
Whittlebot, Hernia
See Coward, Noel
Wicker, Thomas Grey
See Wicker, Tom
Wicker, Tom 1926-2011 .... **CLC 7**
See also CA 65-68; CANR 21, 46, 141, 179
Wickham, Anna 1883-1947 .... **PC 110**
See also DLB 240
Wicomb, Zoe 1948- .... **BLC 2:3**
See also CA 127; CANR 106, 167; DLB 225
Wideman, John Edgar 1941- .... **BLC 1:3, 2:3; CLC 5, 34, 36, 67, 122, 316; SSC 62**
See also AFAW 1, 2; AMWS 10; BPFB 4; BW 2, 3; CA 85-88; CANR 14, 42, 67, 109, 140, 187; CN 4, 5, 6, 7; DAM MULT; DLB 33, 143; MAL 5; MTCW 2; MTFW 2005; RGAL 4; RGSF 2; SSFS 6, 12, 24; TCLE 1:2
Wiebe, Rudy 1934- .... **CLC 6, 11, 14, 138, 263**
See also CA 37-40R; CANR 42, 67, 123, 202; CN 1, 2, 3, 4, 5, 6, 7; DAC; DAM MST; DLB 60; RHW; SATA 156
Wiebe, Rudy Henry
See Wiebe, Rudy
Wieland, Christoph Martin
1733-1813 .... **NCLC 17, 177**
See also DLB 97; EW 4; LMFS 1; RGWL 2, 3
Wiene, Robert 1881-1938 .... **TCLC 56**
Wieners, John 1934- .... **CLC 7; PC 131**
See also BG 1:3; CA 13-16R; CP 1, 2, 3, 4, 5, 6, 7; DLB 16; WP
Wiesel, Elie 1928- .... **CLC 3, 5, 11, 37, 165; WLCS**
See also AAYA 7, 54; AITN 1; CA 5-8R; CAAS 4; CANR 8, 40, 65, 125, 207; CDALBS; CLR 192; CWW 2; DA; DA3; DAB; DAC; DAM MST, NOV; DLB 83, 299; DLBY 1987; EWL 3; INT CANR-8; LAIT 4; MTCW 1, 2; MTFW 2005; NCFS 4; NFS 4; RGHL; RGWL 3; SATA 56; YAW
Wiesel, Eliezer
See Wiesel, Elie
Wiggins, Marianne 1947- .... **CLC 57**
See also AAYA 70; BEST 89:3; CA 130; CANR 60, 139, 180; CN 7; DLB 335
Wigglesworth, Michael 1631-1705 ... **LC 106**
See also DLB 24; RGAL 4
Wiggs, Susan .... **CLC 70**
See also CA 201; CANR 173, 217
Wight, James Alfred
See Herriot, James
Wilbur, Richard 1921- .... **CLC 3, 6, 9, 14, 53, 110; PC 51**
See also AAYA 72; AMWS 3; CA 1-4R; CABS 2; CANR 2, 29, 76, 93, 139, 237; CDALBS; CP 1, 2, 3, 4, 5, 6, 7; DA; DAB; DAC; DAM MST, POET; DLB 5, 169; EWL 3; EXPP; INT CANR-29; MAL 5;

MTCW 1, 2; MTFW 2005; PAB; PFS 11, 12, 16, 29; RGAL 4; SATA 9, 108; WP

Wilbur, Richard Purdy
See Wilbur, Richard

Wild, Peter 1940- .... **CLC 14**
See also CA 37-40R; CP 1, 2, 3, 4, 5, 6, 7; DLB 5

Wilde, Oscar 1854(?)-1900 .... **DC 17; PC 111; SSC 11, 77, 208; TCLC 1, 8, 23, 41, 175, 272; WLC 6**
See also AAYA 49; BRW 5; BRWC 1, 2; BRWR 2; BYA 15; CA 104; 119; CANR 112; CDBLB 1890-1914; CLR 114; DA; DA3; DAB; DAC; DAM DRAM, MST, NOV; DFS 4, 8, 9, 21; DLB 10, 19, 34, 57, 141, 156, 190, 344; EXPS; FANT; GL 3; LATS 1:1; NFS 20; RGEL 2; RGSF 2; SATA 24; SSFS 7; SUFW; TEA; WCH; WLIT 4

Wilde, Oscar Fingal O'Flahertie Willis
See Wilde, Oscar

Wilder, Billy 1906-2002 .... **CLC 20**
See also AAYA 66; CA 89-92; 205; DLB 26

Wilder, Samuel
See Wilder, Billy

Wilder, Samuel 1906-2002 .... **CLC 20**
See also AAYA 66; CA 89-92; 205; DLB 26

Wilder, Stephen
See Marlowe, Stephen

Wilder, Thornton 1897-1975 .... **CLC 1, 5, 6, 10, 15, 35, 82; DC 1, 24; TCLC 284; WLC 6**
See also AAYA 29; AITN 2; AMW; CA 13-16R; 61-64; CAD; CANR 40, 132; CDALBS; CN 1, 2; DA; DA3; DAB; DAC; DAM DRAM, MST, NOV; DFS 1, 4, 16; DLB 4, 7, 9, 228; DLBY 1997; EWL 3; LAIT 3; MAL 5; MTCW 1, 2; MTFW 2005; NFS 24; RGAL 4; RHW; WYAS 1

Wilder, Thornton Niven
See Wilder, Thornton

Wilding, Michael 1942- .... **CLC 73; SSC 50**
See also CA 104; CANR 24, 49, 106; CN 4, 5, 6, 7; DLB 325; RGSF 2

Wiley, Richard 1944- .... **CLC 44**
See also CA 121; 129; CANR 71

Wilhelm, Kate
See Wilhelm, Katie

Wilhelm, Katie 1928- .... **CLC 7**
See also AAYA 83; BYA 16; CA 37-40R; CAAS 5; CANR 17, 36, 60, 94; DLB 8; INT CANR-17; MTCW 1; SCFW 2; SFW 4

Wilhelm, Katie Gertrude
See Wilhelm, Katie

Wilkins, Mary
See Freeman, Mary E(leanor) Wilkins

Willard, Nancy 1936- .... **CLC 7, 37**
See also BYA 5; CA 89-92; CANR 10, 39, 68, 107, 152, 186; CLR 5; CP 2, 3, 4, 5; CWP; CWRI 5; DLB 5, 52; FANT; MAICYA 1, 2; MTCW 1; SATA 37, 71, 127, 191; SATA-Brief 30; SUFW 2; TCLE 1:2

William of Malmesbury
c. 1090B.C.-c. 1140B.C. .. **CMLC 57, 140**

William of Moerbeke
c. 1215-c. 1286 .... **CMLC 91**

William of Ockham
1290-1349 .... **CMLC 32, 129**

Williams, Ben Ames 1889-1953 .... **TCLC 89**
See also CA 183; DLB 102

Williams, Charles
See Collier, James Lincoln

Williams, Charles 1886-1945 ... **TCLC 1, 11**
See also BRWS 9; CA 104; 163; DLB 100, 153, 255; FANT; RGEL 2; SUFW 1

Williams, Charles Walter Stansby
See Williams, Charles

Williams, C.K. 1936- ... **CLC 33, 56, 148, 306**
See also CA 37-40R; CAAS 26; CANR 57, 106, 225; CP 1, 2, 3, 4, 5, 6, 7; DAM POET; DLB 5; MAL 5

Williams, Ella Gwendolen Rees
See Rhys, Jean

Williams, Emlyn 1905-1987 .... **CLC 15**
See also CA 104; 123; CANR 36; DAM DRAM; DLB 10, 77; IDTP; MTCW 1

Williams, George Emlyn
See Williams, Emlyn

Williams, Hank 1923-1953 .... **TCLC 81**
See Williams, Hiram King
See also CA 188

Williams, Helen Maria
1761-1827 .... **NCLC 135**
See also DLB 158

Williams, Hiram King 1923-1953
See Williams, Hank

Williams, Hugo (Mordaunt)
1942- .... **CLC 42**
See also CA 17-20R; CANR 45, 119; CP 1, 2, 3, 4, 5, 6, 7; DLB 40

Williams, J. Walker
See Wodehouse, P. G.

Williams, John A(lfred) 1925- ...... **BLC 1:3; CLC 5, 13, 347**
See also AFAW 2; BW 2, 3; CA 53-56, 195; CAAE 195; CAAS 3; CANR 6, 26, 51, 118; CN 1, 2, 3, 4, 5, 6, 7; CSW; DAM MULT; DLB 2, 33; EWL 3; INT CANR-6; MAL 5; RGAL 4; SFW 4

Williams, Jonathan 1929-2008 .... **CLC 13**
See also CA 9-12R; 270; CAAS 12; CANR 8, 108; CP 1, 2, 3, 4, 5, 6, 7; DLB 5

Williams, Jonathan Chamberlain
See Williams, Jonathan

Williams, Joy 1944- .... **CLC 31**
See also CA 41-44R; CANR 22, 48, 97, 168; DLB 335; SSFS 25

Williams, Norman 1952- .... **CLC 39**
See also CA 118

Williams, Paulette Linda
See Shange, Ntozake

Williams, Roger 1603(?)-1683 .... **LC 129**
See also DLB 24

Williams, Sherley Anne
1944-1999 .... **BLC 1:3; CLC 89**
See also AFAW 2; BW 2, 3; CA 73-76; 185; CANR 25, 82; DAM MULT, POET; DLB 41; INT CANR-25; SATA 78; SATA-Obit 116

Williams, Shirley
See Williams, Sherley Anne

Williams, Terry Tempest 1955- .... **CLC 362**
See also ANW; CA 153; CANR 106, 197, 253; DLB 206, 275

Williams, Tennessee 1911-1983 .... **CLC 1, 2, 5, 7, 8, 11, 15, 19, 30, 39, 45, 71, 111; DC 4; SSC 81; WLC 6**
See also AAYA 31; AITN 1, 2; AMW; AMWC 1; CA 5-8R; 108; CABS 3; CAD; CANR 31, 132, 174; CDALB 1941-1968; CN 1, 2, 3; DA; DA3; DAB; DAC; DAM DRAM, MST; DFS 17; DLB 7, 341; DLBD 4; DLBY 1983; EWL 3; GLL 1; LAIT 4; LATS 1:2; MAL 5; MTCW 1, 2; MTFW 2005; RGAL 4; TUS

Williams, Thomas (Alonzo)
1926-1990 .... **CLC 14**
See also CA 1-4R; 132; CANR 2

Williams, Thomas Lanier
See Williams, Tennessee

Williams, William C.
See Williams, William Carlos

Williams, William Carlos 1883-1963 .. **CLC 1, 2, 5, 9, 13, 22, 42, 67; PC 7, 109; SSC 31; TCLC 272; WLC 6**
See also AAYA 46; AMW; AMWR 1; CA 89-92; CANR 34; CDALB 1917-1929; DA; DA3; DAB; DAC; DAM MST, POET; DLB 4, 16, 54, 86; EWL 3; EXPP; MAL 5; MTCW 1, 2; MTFW 2005; NCFS 4; PAB; PFS 1, 6, 11, 34, 43; RGAL 4; RGSF 2; SSFS 27; TUS; WP

Williamson, David (Keith) 1942- ... **CLC 56; DC 47**
See also CA 103; CANR 41; CD 5, 6; DLB 289

Williamson, Jack
See Williamson, John Stewart

Williamson, John Stewart
1908-2006 .... **CLC 29**
See also AAYA 76; CA 17-20R; 255; CAAS 8; CANR 23, 70, 153; DLB 8; SCFW 1, 2; SFW 4

Willie, Frederick
See Lovecraft, H. P.

Willingham, Calder (Baynard, Jr.)
1922-1995 .... **CLC 5, 51**
See also CA 5-8R; 147; CANR 3; CN 1, 2, 3, 4, 5; CSW; DLB 2, 44; IDFW 3, 4; MTCW 1

Willis, Charles
See Clarke, Arthur C.

Willis, Nathaniel Parker
1806-1867 .... **NCLC 194**
See also DLB 3, 59, 73, 74, 183, 250; DLBD 13; RGAL 4

Willy
See Colette

Willy, Colette
See Colette

Wilmot, John 1647-1680 .... **LC 75; PC 66**
See also BRW 2; DLB 131; PAB; RGEL 2

Wilson, A. N. 1950- .... **CLC 33**
See also BRWS 6; CA 112; 122; CANR 156, 199; CN 4, 5, 6, 7; DLB 14, 155, 194; MTCW 2

Wilson, Andrew Norman
See Wilson, A. N.

Wilson, Angus 1913-1991 .... **CLC 2, 3, 5, 25, 34; SSC 21**
See also BRWS 1; CA 5-8R; 134; CANR 21; CN 1, 2, 3, 4; DLB 15, 139, 155; EWL 3; MTCW 1, 2; MTFW 2005; RGEL 2; RGSF 2

Wilson, Angus Frank Johnstone
See Wilson, Angus

Wilson, August 1945-2005 .... **BLC 1:3, 2:3; CLC 39, 50, 63, 118, 222; DC 2, 31; WLCS**
See also AAYA 16; AFAW 2; AMWS 8; BW 2, 3; CA 115; 122; 244; CAD; CANR 42, 54, 76, 128; CD 5, 6; DA; DA3; DAB; DAC; DAM DRAM, MST, MULT; DFS 3, 7, 15, 17, 24, 30; DLB 228; EWL 3; LAIT 4; LATS 1:2; MAL 5; MTCW 1, 2; MTFW 2005; RGAL 4

Wilson, Brian 1942- .... **CLC 12**

Wilson, Colin 1931- .... **CLC 3, 14**
See also CA 1-4R, 315; CAAE 315; CAAS 5; CANR 1, 22, 33, 77; CMW 4; CN 1, 2, 3, 4, 5, 6; DLB 14, 194; HGG; MTCW 1; SFW 4

Wilson, Colin Henry
See Wilson, Colin

Wilson, Dirk
See Pohl, Frederik

Wilson, Edmund 1895-1972 .... **CLC 1, 2, 3, 8, 24**
See also AMW; CA 1-4R; 37-40R; CANR 1, 46, 110; CN 1; DLB 63; EWL 3; MAL 5; MTCW 1, 2; MTFW 2005; RGAL 4; TUS

Wilson, Ethel Davis (Bryant)
1888(?)-1980 .... **CLC 13**
See also CA 102; CN 1, 2; DAC; DAM POET; DLB 68; MTCW 1; RGEL 2

Wilson, G. Willow 1982- .... **CLC 354**
See also CA 302

Wilson, Harriet
See Wilson, Harriet E. Adams

Wilson, Harriet E.
See Wilson, Harriet E. Adams
Wilson, Harriet E. Adams 1827(?)-1863(?) .... **BLC 1:3; NCLC 78, 219**
See also DAM MULT; DLB 50, 239, 243
Wilson, John 1785-1854 .... **NCLC 5**
See also DLB 110
Wilson, John Anthony Burgess
See Burgess, Anthony
Wilson, John Burgess
See Burgess, Anthony
Wilson, Katharina .... **CLC 65**
Wilson, Kevin 1978- .... **CLC 334**
See also CA 295; CANR 236
Wilson, Lanford 1937-2011 .... **CLC 7, 14, 36, 197; DC 19**
See also CA 17-20R; CABS 3; CAD; CANR 45, 96; CD 5, 6; DAM DRAM; DFS 4, 9, 12, 16, 20; DLB 7, 341; EWL 3; MAL 5; TUS
Wilson, Robert M. 1941- .... **CLC 7, 9**
See also CA 49-52; CAD; CANR 2, 41; CD 5, 6; MTCW 1
Wilson, Robert McLiam 1964- .... **CLC 59**
See also CA 132; DLB 267
Wilson, Sloan 1920-2003 .... **CLC 32**
See also CA 1-4R; 216; CANR 1, 44; CN 1, 2, 3, 4, 5, 6
Wilson, Snoo 1948- .... **CLC 33**
See also CA 69-72; CBD; CD 5, 6
Wilson, Thomas 1523(?)-1581 .... **LC 184**
See also DLB 132, 236
Wilson, William S(mith) 1932- .... **CLC 49**
See also CA 81-84
Wilson, (Thomas) Woodrow 1856-1924 .... **TCLC 79**
See also CA 166; DLB 47
Winchelsea
See Finch, Anne
Winchester, Simon 1944- .... **CLC 257**
See also AAYA 66; CA 107; CANR 90, 130, 194, 228
Winchilsea, Anne (Kingsmill) Finch 1661-1720
See Finch, Anne
See also RGEL 2
Winckelmann, Johann Joachim 1717-1768 .... **LC 129, 242**
See also DLB 97
Windham, Basil
See Wodehouse, P. G.
Wingrove, David 1954- .... **CLC 68**
See also CA 133; SFW 4
Winnemucca, Sarah 1844-1891 ... **NCLC 79; NNAL**
See also DAM MULT; DLB 175; RGAL 4
Winstanley, Gerrard 1609-1676 .... **LC 52**
Wintergreen, Jane
See Duncan, Sara Jeannette
Winters, Arthur Yvor
See Winters, Yvor
Winters, Janet Lewis
See Lewis, Janet
Winters, Yvor 1900-1968 ...... **CLC 4, 8, 32; PC 82**
See also AMWS 2; CA 11-12; 25-28R; CAP 1; DLB 48; EWL 3; MAL 5; MTCW 1; RGAL 4
Winterson, Jeanette 1959- **CLC 64, 158, 307; SSC 144**
See also BRWS 4; CA 136; CANR 58, 116, 181; CN 5, 6, 7; CPW; DA3; DAM POP; DLB 207, 261; FANT; FW; GLL 1; MTCW 2; MTFW 2005; RHW; SATA 190
Winthrop, John 1588-1649 .... **LC 31, 107**
See also DLB 24, 30
Winthrop, Theodore 1828-1861 ... **NCLC 210**
See also DLB 202
Winton, Tim 1960- .... **CLC 251; SSC 119**
See also AAYA 34; CA 152; CANR 118, 194; CN 6, 7; DLB 325; SATA 98
Wirth, Louis 1897-1952 .... **TCLC 92**
See also CA 210
Wiseman, Frederick 1930- .... **CLC 20**
See also CA 159
Wister, Owen 1860-1938 .... **SSC 100; TCLC 21**
See also BPFB 3; CA 108; 162; DLB 9, 78, 186; RGAL 4; SATA 62; TCWW 1, 2
Wither, George 1588-1667 .... **LC 96**
See also DLB 121; RGEL 2
Witkacy
See Witkiewicz, Stanislaw Ignacy
Witkiewicz, Stanislaw Ignacy 1885-1939 .... **TCLC 8, 237**
See also CA 105; 162; CDWLB 4; DLB 215; EW 10; EWL 3; RGWL 2, 3; SFW 4
Wittgenstein, Ludwig (Josef Johann) 1889-1951 .... **TCLC 59**
See also CA 113; 164; DLB 262; MTCW 2
Wittig, Monique 1935-2003 .... **CLC 22**
See also CA 116; 135; 212; CANR 143; CWW 2; DLB 83; EWL 3; FW; GLL 1
Wittlin, Jozef 1896-1976 .... **CLC 25**
See also CA 49-52; 65-68; CANR 3; EWL 3
Wodehouse, P. G. 1881-1975 ... **CLC 1, 2, 5, 10, 22; SSC 2, 115; TCLC 108**
See also AAYA 65; AITN 2; BRWS 3; CA 45-48; 57-60; CANR 3, 33; CDBLB 1914-1945; CN 1, 2; CPW 1; DA3; DAB; DAC; DAM NOV; DLB 34, 162, 352; EWL 3; MTCW 1, 2; MTFW 2005; RGEL 2; RGSF 2; SATA 22; SSFS 10
Wodehouse, Pelham Grenville
See Wodehouse, P. G.
Woiwode, L.
See Woiwode, Larry
Woiwode, Larry 1941- .... **CLC 6, 10**
See also CA 73-76; CANR 16, 94, 192; CN 3, 4, 5, 6, 7; DLB 6; INT CANR-16
Woiwode, Larry Alfred
See Woiwode, Larry
Wojciechowska, Maia (Teresa) 1927-2002 .... **CLC 26**
See also AAYA 8, 46; BYA 3; CA 9-12R, 183; 209; CAAE 183; CANR 4, 41; CLR 1; JRDA; MAICYA 1, 2; SAAS 1; SATA 1, 28, 83; SATA-Essay 104; SATA-Obit 134; YAW
Wojtyla, Karol (Jozef)
See John Paul II, Pope
Wojtyla, Karol (Josef)
See John Paul II, Pope
Wolf, Christa 1929-2011 ... **CLC 14, 29, 58, 150, 261, 334**
See also CA 85-88; CANR 45, 123; CDWLB 2; CWW 2; DLB 75; EWL 3; FW; MTCW 1; RGWL 2, 3; SSFS 14
Wolf, Naomi 1962- .... **CLC 157**
See also CA 141; CANR 110; FW; MTFW 2005
Wolfe, Gene 1931- .... **CLC 25**
See also AAYA 35; CA 57-60; CAAS 9; CANR 6, 32, 60, 152, 197; CPW; DAM POP; DLB 8; FANT; MTCW 2; MTFW 2005; SATA 118, 165; SCFW 2; SFW 4; SUFW 2
Wolfe, Gene Rodman
See Wolfe, Gene
Wolfe, George C. 1954- ...... **BLCS; CLC 49**
See also CA 149; CAD; CD 5, 6
Wolfe, Thomas 1900-1938 .... **SSC 33, 113; TCLC 4, 13, 29, 61, 279; WLC 6**
See also AMW; BPFB 3; CA 104; 132; CANR 102; CDALB 1929-1941; DA; DA3; DAB; DAC; DAM MST, NOV; DLB 9, 102, 229; DLBD 2, 16; DLBY 1985, 1997; EWL 3; MAL 5; MTCW 1, 2; NFS 18; RGAL 4; SSFS 18; TUS
Wolfe, Thomas Clayton
See Wolfe, Thomas
Wolfe, Thomas Kennerly
See Wolfe, Tom, Jr.
Wolfe, Tom, Jr. 1931- .... **CLC 1, 2, 9, 15, 35, 51, 147**
See also AAYA 8, 67; AITN 2; AMWS 3; BEST 89:1; BPFB 3; CA 13-16R; CANR 9, 33, 70, 104; CN 5, 6, 7; CPW; CSW; DA3; DAM POP; DLB 152, 185 185; EWL 3; INT CANR-9; LAIT 5; MTCW 1, 2; MTFW 2005; RGAL 4; TUS
Wolff, Geoffrey 1937- .... **CLC 41**
See also CA 29-32R; CANR 29, 43, 78, 154, 233
Wolff, Geoffrey Ansell
See Wolff, Geoffrey
Wolff, Sonia
See Levitin, Sonia
Wolff, Tobias 1945- .... **CLC 39, 64, 172; SSC 63, 136**
See also AAYA 16; AMWS 7; BEST 90:2; BYA 12; CA 114; 117; CAAS 22; CANR 54, 76, 96, 192; CN 5, 6, 7; CSW; DA3; DLB 130; EWL 3; INT CA-117; MTCW 2; MTFW 2005; RGAL 4; RGSF 2; SSFS 4, 11, 35
Wolff, Tobias Jonathan Ansell
See Wolff, Tobias
Wolfram von Eschenbach
See von Eschenbach, Wolfram
Wolitzer, Hilma 1930- .... **CLC 17**
See also CA 65-68; CANR 18, 40, 172; INT CANR-18; SATA 31; YAW
Wolkenstein, Oswald von 1376/1377-1445 .... **LC 208**
See also DLB 179
Wollstonecraft, Mary 1759-1797 .... **LC 5, 50, 90, 147**
See also BRWS 3; CDBLB 1789-1832; DLB 39, 104, 158, 252; FL 1:1; FW; LAIT 1; RGEL 2; TEA; WLIT 3
Wonder, Stevie 1950- .... **CLC 12**
See also CA 111
Wong, Jade Snow 1922-2006 .... **CLC 17**
See also CA 109; 249; CANR 91; SATA 112; SATA-Obit 175
Wood, Ellen Price
See Wood, Mrs. Henry
Wood, Mrs. Henry 1814-1887 .... **NCLC 178**
See also CMW 4; DLB 18; SUFW
Wood, James 1965- .... **CLC 238**
See also CA 235; CANR 214
Woodberry, George Edward 1855-1930 .... **TCLC 73**
See also CA 165; DLB 71, 103
Woodcott, Keith
See Brunner, John (Kilian Houston)
Woodruff, Robert W.
See Mencken, H. L.
Woodward, Bob 1943- .... **CLC 240**
See also CA 69-72; CANR 31, 67, 107, 176; MTCW 1
Woodward, Robert Upshur
See Woodward, Bob
Woolf, Adeline Virginia
See Woolf, Virginia
Woolf, Virginia 1882-1941 .... **SSC 7, 79, 161; TCLC 1, 5, 20, 43, 56, 101, 123, 128, 268; WLC 6**
See also AAYA 44; BPFB 3; BRW 7; BRWC 2; BRWR 1; CA 104; 130; CANR 64, 132; CDBLB 1914-1945; DA; DA3; DAB; DAC; DAM MST, NOV; DLB 36, 100, 162; DLBD 10; EWL 3; EXPS; FL 1:6; FW; LAIT 3; LATS 1:1; LMFS 2; MTCW

1, 2; MTFW 2005; NCFS 2; NFS 8, 12, 28, 42; RGEL 2; RGSF 2; SSFS 4, 12, 34; TEA; WLIT 4
Woollcott, Alexander (Humphreys) 1887-1943 .... **TCLC 5**
See also CA 105; 161; DLB 29
Woolman, John 1720-1772 .... **LC 155**
See also DLB 31
Woolrich, Cornell
See Hopley-Woolrich, Cornell George
Woolson, Constance Fenimore 1840-1894 .... **NCLC 82, 293; SSC 90**
See also DLB 12, 74, 189, 221; RGAL 4
Wordsworth, Dorothy 1771-1855 .... **NCLC 25, 138**
See also DLB 107
Wordsworth, William 1770-1850 .... **NCLC 12, 38, 111, 166, 206; PC 4, 67; WLC 6**
See also AAYA 70; BRW 4; BRWC 1; CDBLB 1789-1832; DA; DA3; DAB; DAC; DAM MST, POET; DLB 93, 107; EXPP; LATS 1:1; LMFS 1; PAB; PFS 2, 33, 38; RGEL 2; TEA; WLIT 3; WP
Wotton, Sir Henry 1568-1639 .... **LC 68**
See also DLB 121; RGEL 2
Wouk, Herman 1915- .... **CLC 1, 9, 38**
See also BPFB 2, 3; CA 5-8R; CANR 6, 33, 67, 146, 225; CDALBS; CN 1, 2, 3, 4, 5, 6; CPW; DA3; DAM NOV, POP; DLBY 1982; INT CANR-6; LAIT 4; MAL 5; MTCW 1, 2; MTFW 2005; NFS 7; TUS
Wright, Charles 1932-2008 .... **BLC 1:3; CLC 49**
See also BW 1; CA 9-12R; 278; CANR 26; CN 1, 2, 3, 4, 5, 6, 7; DAM MULT, POET; DLB 33
Wright, Charles 1935- .... **CLC 6, 13, 28, 119, 146; PC 142**
See also AMWS 5; CA 29-32R; CAAS 7; CANR 23, 36, 62, 88, 135, 180; CP 3, 4, 5, 6, 7; DLB 165; DLBY 1982; EWL 3; MTCW 1, 2; MTFW 2005; PFS 10, 35
Wright, Charles Penzel, Jr.
See Wright, Charles
Wright, Charles Stevenson
See Wright, Charles
Wright, Frances 1795-1852 .... **NCLC 74**
See also DLB 73
Wright, Frank Lloyd 1867-1959 .... **TCLC 95**
See also AAYA 33; CA 174
Wright, Harold Bell 1872-1944 .. **TCLC 183**
See also BPFB 3; CA 110; DLB 9; TCWW 2
Wright, Jack R.
See Harris, Mark
Wright, James (Arlington) 1927-1980 ..... **CLC 3, 5, 10, 28; PC 36**
See also AITN 2; AMWS 3; CA 49-52; 97-100; CANR 4, 34, 64; CDALBS; CP 1, 2; DAM POET; DLB 5, 169, 342; EWL 3; EXPP; MAL 5; MTCW 1, 2; MTFW 2005; PFS 7, 8; RGAL 4; TUS; WP
Wright, Judith 1915-2000 .... **CLC 11, 53, 327; PC 14**
See also CA 13-16R; 188; CANR 31, 76, 93; CP 1, 2, 3, 4, 5, 6, 7; CWP; DLB 260; EWL 3; MTCW 1, 2; MTFW 2005; PFS 8; RGEL 2; SATA 14; SATA-Obit 121
Wright, Judith Arundell
See Wright, Judith
Wright, L(aurali) R. 1939- .... **CLC 44**
See also CA 138; CMW 4
Wright, Richard 1908-1960 .... **BLC 1:3; CLC 1, 3, 4, 9, 14, 21, 48, 74; SSC 2, 109; TCLC 136, 180; WLC 6**
See also AAYA 5, 42; AFAW 1, 2; AMW; BPFB 3; BW 1; BYA 2; CA 108; CANR 64; CDALB 1929-1941; DA; DA3; DAB; DAC; DAM MST, MULT, NOV; DLB 76, 102; DLBD 2; EWL 3; EXPN; LAIT 3, 4; MAL 5; MTCW 1, 2; MTFW 2005; NCFS 1; NFS 1, 7; RGAL 4; RGSF 2; SSFS 3, 9, 15, 20; TUS; YAW
Wright, Richard B. 1937- .... **CLC 6**
See also CA 85-88; CANR 120; DLB 53
Wright, Richard Bruce
See Wright, Richard B.
Wright, Richard Nathaniel
See Wright, Richard
Wright, Rick 1945- .... **CLC 35**
Wright, Rowland
See Wells, Carolyn
Wright, Stephen 1946- .... **CLC 33**
See also CA 237; DLB 350
Wright, Willard Huntington 1888-1939 .... **TCLC 23**
See also CA 115; 189; CMW 4; DLB 306; DLBD 16; MSW
Wright, William 1930- .... **CLC 44**
See also CA 53-56; CANR 7, 23, 154
Wroblewski, David 1959- .... **CLC 280**
See also CA 283
Wroth, Lady Mary 1587-1653(?) ..... **LC 30, 139; PC 38**
See also DLB 121
Wu Ch'eng-en 1500(?)-1582(?) .... **LC 7, 213**
Wu Ching-tzu 1701-1754 .... **LC 2**
Wulfstan c. 10th cent. -1023 ... **CMLC 59, 135**
Wurlitzer, Rudolph 1938(?)- ..... **CLC 2, 4, 15**
See also CA 85-88; CN 4, 5, 6, 7; DLB 173
Wyatt, Sir Thomas c. 1503-1542 ...... **LC 70; PC 27, 169**
See also BRW 1; DLB 132; EXPP; PFS 25; RGEL 2; TEA
Wycherley, William 1640-1716 .... **DC 41; LC 8, 21, 102, 136**
See also BRW 2; CDBLB 1660-1789; DAM DRAM; DLB 80; RGEL 2
Wyclif, John c. 1330-1384 ... **CMLC 70, 143**
See also DLB 146
Wyld, Evie 1980- .... **CLC 334**
See also CA 299
Wylie, Elinor (Morton Hoyt) 1885-1928 .... **PC 23; TCLC 8**
See also AMWS 1; CA 105; 162; DLB 9, 45; EXPP; MAL 5; RGAL 4
Wylie, Philip (Gordon) 1902-1971 .... **CLC 43**
See also CA 21-22; 33-36R; CAP 2; CN 1; DLB 9; SFW 4
Wyndham, John
See Harris, John (Wyndham Parkes Lucas) Beynon
Wyss, Johann David Von 1743-1818 .... **NCLC 10**
See also CLR 92; JRDA; MAICYA 1, 2; SATA 29; SATA-Brief 27
X, Malcolm
See Malcolm X
Xenophon c. 430B.C.-c. 354B.C. .... **CMLC 17, 137**
See also AW 1; DLB 176; RGWL 2, 3; WLIT 8
Xingjian, Gao 1940- .... **CLC 167, 315**
See also CA 193; DFS 21; DLB 330; MTFW 2005; RGWL 3
Xuan Zhu
See Mao Dun
Yakamochi 718-785 .... **CMLC 45; PC 48**
Yakumo Koizumi
See Hearn, Lafcadio
Yamada, Mitsuye (May) 1923- .... **PC 44**
See also CA 77-80
Yamamoto, Hisaye 1921-2011 ..... **AAL; CLC 343; SSC 34**
See also CA 214; DAM MULT; DLB 312; LAIT 4; SSFS 14
Yamashita, Karen Tei 1951- .... **AAL; CLC 382**
See also CA 166; CANR 129, 223; DLB 312
Yamauchi, Wakako 1924- .... **AAL**
See also CA 214; DLB 312
Yan, Mo 1956(?)- .... **CLC 257, 354**
See also CA 201; CANR 192; EWL 3; RGWL 3
Yanez, Jose Donoso
See Donoso, Jose
Yanovsky, Basile S.
See Yanovsky, V(assily) S(emenovich)
Yanovsky, V(assily) S(emenovich) 1906-1989 .... **CLC 2, 18**
See also CA 97-100; 129
Yates, Richard 1926-1992 .... **CLC 7, 8, 23**
See also AMWS 11; CA 5-8R; 139; CANR 10, 43; CN 1, 2, 3, 4, 5; DLB 2, 234; DLBY 1981, 1992; INT CANR-10; SSFS 24
Yau, John 1950- .... **PC 61**
See also CA 154; CANR 89; CP 4, 5, 6, 7; DLB 234, 312; PFS 26
Yearsley, Ann 1753-1806 .. **NCLC 174; PC 149**
See also DLB 109
Yeats, W. B.
See Yeats, William Butler
Yeats, William Butler 1865-1939 ...... **DC 33; PC 20, 51, 129; TCLC 1, 11, 18, 31, 93, 116; WLC 6**
See also AAYA 48; BRW 6; BRWR 1; CA 104; 127; CANR 45; CDBLB 1890-1914; DA; DA3; DAB; DAC; DAM DRAM, MST, POET; DLB 10, 19, 98, 156, 332; EWL 3; EXPP; MTCW 1, 2; MTFW 2005; NCFS 3; PAB; PFS 1, 2, 5, 7, 13, 15, 34, 42; RGEL 2; TEA; WLIT 4; WP
Yehoshua, A. B. 1936- ...... **CLC 13, 31, 243**
See also CA 33-36R; CANR 43, 90, 145, 202; CWW 2; EWL 3; RGHL; RGSF 2; RGWL 3; WLIT 6
Yehoshua, Abraham B.
See Yehoshua, A. B.
Yellow Bird
See Ridge, John Rollin
Yep, Laurence 1948- .... **CLC 35**
See also AAYA 5, 31; BYA 7; CA 49-52; CANR 1, 46, 92, 161; CLR 3, 17, 54, 132; DLB 52, 312; FANT; JRDA; MAICYA 1, 2; MAICYAS 1; SATA 7, 69, 123, 176, 213, 242; WYA; YAW
Yep, Laurence Michael
See Yep, Laurence
Yerby, Frank G(arvin) 1916-1991 .... **BLC 1:3; CLC 1, 7, 22**
See also BPFB 3; BW 1, 3; CA 9-12R; 136; CANR 16, 52; CN 1, 2, 3, 4, 5; DAM MULT; DLB 76; INT CANR-16; MTCW 1; RGAL 4; RHW
Yesenin, Sergei Aleksandrovich
See Esenin, Sergei
Yevtushenko, Yevgeny Alexandrovich
See Yevtushenko, Yevgenyn
Yevtushenko, Yevgenyn 1933- ...... **CLC 1, 3, 13, 26, 51, 126; PC 40**
See also CA 81-84; CANR 33, 54; CWW 2; DAM POET; DLB 359; EWL 3; MTCW 1; PFS 29; RGHL; RGWL 2, 3
Yezierska, Anzia 1885(?)-1970 .... **CLC 46; SSC 144; TCLC 205**
See also CA 126; 89-92; DLB 28, 221; FW; MTCW 1; NFS 29; RGAL 4; SSFS 15
Yglesias, Helen 1915-2008 .... **CLC 7, 22**
See also CA 37-40R; 272; CAAS 20; CANR 15, 65, 95; CN 4, 5, 6, 7; INT CANR-15; MTCW 1
Y.O.
See Russell, George William

Yokomitsu, Riichi 1898-1947 .... **TCLC 47**
See also CA 170; EWL 3
Yolen, Jane 1939- .... **CLC 256**
See also AAYA 4, 22, 85; BPFB 3; BYA 9, 10, 11, 14, 16; CA 13-16R; CANR 11, 29, 56, 91, 126, 185; CLR 4, 44, 149; CWRI 5; DLB 52; FANT; INT CANR-29; JRDA; MAICYA 1, 2; MTFW 2005; NFS 30; SAAS 1; SATA 4, 40, 75, 112, 158, 194, 230; SATA-Essay 111; SFW 4; SSFS 29; SUFW 2; WYA; YAW
Yolen, Jane Hyatt
See Yolen, Jane
Yonge, Charlotte 1823-1901 ... **TCLC 48, 245**
See also BRWS 17; CA 109; 163; DLB 18, 163; RGEL 2; SATA 17; WCH
Yonge, Charlotte Mary
See Yonge, Charlotte
York, Jeremy
See Creasey, John
York, Simon
See Heinlein, Robert A.
Yorke, Henry Vincent
1905-1974 .... **CLC 2, 13, 97**
See also BRWS 2; CA 85-88, 175; 49-52; DLB 15; EWL 3; RGEL 2
Yosano, Akiko 1878-1942 .... **PC 11; TCLC 59**
See also CA 161; EWL 3; RGWL 3
Yoshimoto, Banana
See Yoshimoto, Mahoko
Yoshimoto, Mahoko 1964- .... **CLC 84**
See also AAYA 50; CA 144; CANR 98, 160, 235; NFS 7; SSFS 16
Young, Al(bert James) 1939- .... **BLC 1:3; CLC 19**
See also BW 2, 3; CA 29-32R; CANR 26, 65, 109; CN 2, 3, 4, 5, 6, 7; CP 1, 2, 3, 4, 5, 6, 7; DAM MULT; DLB 33
Young, Andrew (John) 1885-1971 .... **CLC 5**
See also CA 5-8R; CANR 7, 29; CP 1; RGEL 2
Young, Collier
See Bloch, Robert (Albert)
Young, Edward 1683-1765 .... **LC 3, 40**
See also DLB 95; RGEL 2
Young, Marguerite (Vivian)
1909-1995 .... **CLC 82**
See also CA 13-16; 150; CAP 1; CN 1, 2, 3, 4, 5, 6
Young, Neil 1945- .... **CLC 17**
See also CA 110; CCA 1
Young Bear, Ray A. 1950- .... **CLC 94; NNAL**
See also CA 146; DAM MULT; DLB 175; MAL 5
Yourcenar, Marguerite
1903-1987 .... **CLC 19, 38, 50, 87; TCLC 193**
See also BPFB 3; CA 69-72; CANR 23, 60, 93; DAM NOV; DLB 72; DLBY 1988; EW 12; EWL 3; GFL 1789 to the Present; GLL 1; MTCW 1, 2; MTFW 2005; RGWL 2, 3
Yuan, Chu
340(?)B.C.-278(?)B.C. .... **CMLC 36**
Yu Dafu 1896-1945 .... **SSC 122**
See also DLB 328; RGSF 2
Yurick, Sol 1925- .... **CLC 6**
See also CA 13-16R; CANR 25; CN 1, 2, 3, 4, 5, 6, 7; MAL 5
Zabolotsky, Nikolai
See Zabolotsky, Nikolai Alekseevich
Zabolotsky, Nikolai Alekseevich
1903-1958 .... **TCLC 52**
See also CA 116; 164; DLB 359; EWL 3
Zabolotsky, Nikolay Alekseevich
See Zabolotsky, Nikolai Alekseevich
Zagajewski, Adam 1945- .... **PC 27**
See also CA 186; DLB 232; EWL 3; PFS 25, 44
Zakaria, Fareed 1964- .... **CLC 269**
See also CA 171; CANR 151, 189
Zalygin, Sergei -2000 .... **CLC 59**
Zalygin, Sergei (Pavlovich)
1913-2000 .... **CLC 59**
See also DLB 302
Zamiatin, Evgenii
See Zamyatin, Evgeny Ivanovich
Zamiatin, Evgenii Ivanovich
See Zamyatin, Evgeny Ivanovich
Zamiatin, Yevgenii
See Zamyatin, Evgeny Ivanovich
Zamora, Bernice (B. Ortiz)
1938- .... **CLC 89; HLC 2**
See also CA 151; CANR 80; DAM MULT; DLB 82; HW 1, 2
Zamyatin, Evgeny Ivanovich
1884-1937 ... **SSC 89; TCLC 8, 37, 302**
See also CA 105; 166; DLB 272; EW 10; EWL 3; RGSF 2; RGWL 2, 3; SFW 4
Zamyatin, Yevgeny
See Zamyatin, Evgeny Ivanovich
Zamyatin, Yevgeny Ivanovich
See Zamyatin, Evgeny Ivanovich
Zangwill, Israel 1864-1926 .... **SSC 44; TCLC 16**
See also CA 109; 167; CMW 4; DLB 10, 135, 197; RGEL 2
Zanzotto, Andrea 1921- .... **PC 65**
See also CA 208; CWW 2; DLB 128; EWL 3
Zappa, Francis Vincent, Jr.
See Zappa, Frank
Zappa, Frank 1940-1993 .... **CLC 17**
See also CA 108; 143; CANR 57
Zaturenska, Marya 1902-1982 .... **CLC 6, 11**
See also CA 13-16R; 105; CANR 22; CP 1, 2, 3
Zayas y Sotomayor, Maria de
1590-c. 1661 ...... **LC 102, 238; SSC 94**
See also RGSF 2
Zeami 1363-1443 .... **DC 7; LC 86, 243**
See also DLB 203; RGWL 2, 3
Zelazny, Roger 1937-1995 .... **CLC 21**
See also AAYA 7, 68; BPFB 3; CA 21-24R; 148; CANR 26, 60, 219; CN 6; DLB 8; FANT; MTCW 1, 2; MTFW 2005; SATA 57; SATA-Brief 39; SCFW 1, 2; SFW 4; SUFW 1, 2
Zelazny, Roger Joseph
See Zelazny, Roger
Zephaniah, Benjamin 1958- .... **BLC 2:3**
See also CA 147; CANR 103, 156, 177; CP 5, 6, 7; DLB 347; SATA 86, 140, 189
Azevedo, Angela de
fl. 17th cent. - .... **LC 218**
Zhang Ailing
See Chang, Eileen
Zhdanov, Andrei Alexandrovich
1896-1948 .... **TCLC 18**
See also CA 117; 167
Zhenkai, Zhao
See Bei Dao
Zhou Shuren
See Lu Xun
Zhukovsky, Vasilii Andreevich
See Zhukovsky, Vasily (Andreevich)
Zhukovsky, Vasily (Andreevich)
1783-1852 .... **NCLC 35, 292**
See also DLB 205
Ziegenhagen, Eric .... **CLC 55**
Zimmer, Jill Schary
See Robinson, Jill
Zimmerman, Robert
See Dylan, Bob
Zindel, Paul 1936-2003 .... **CLC 6, 26; DC 5**
See also AAYA 2, 37; BYA 2, 3, 8, 11, 14; CA 73-76; 213; CAD; CANR 31, 65, 108; CD 5, 6; CDALBS; CLR 3, 45, 85, 186; DA; DA3; DAB; DAC; DAM DRAM, MST, NOV; DFS 12; DLB 7, 52; JRDA; LAIT 5; MAICYA 1, 2; MTCW 1, 2; MTFW 2005; NFS 14; SATA 16, 58, 102; SATA-Obit 142; WYA; YAW
Zinger, Yisroel-Yehoyshue
See Singer, Israel Joshua
Zinger, Yitskhok
See Singer, Isaac Bashevis
Zinn, Howard 1922-2010 .... **CLC 199**
See also CA 1-4R; CANR 2, 33, 90, 159
Zinov'Ev, A.A.
See Zinoviev, Alexander
Zinov'ev, Aleksandr
See Zinoviev, Alexander
Zinoviev, Alexander 1922-2006 .... **CLC 19**
See also CA 116; 133; 250; CAAS 10; DLB 302
Zinoviev, Alexander Aleksandrovich
See Zinoviev, Alexander
Zizek, Slavoj 1949- .... **CLC 188**
See also CA 201; CANR 171; MTFW 2005
Zobel, Joseph 1915-2006 .... **BLC 2:3; CLC 373**
Zoilus
See Lovecraft, H. P.
Zola, Émile Edouard Charles Antione
See Zola, Émile
Zola, Émile 1840-1902 .... **SSC 109; TCLC 1, 6, 21, 41, 219; WLC 6**
See also CA 104; 138; DA; DA3; DAB; DAC; DAM MST, NOV; DLB 123; EW 7; GFL 1789 to the Present; IDTP; LMFS 1, 2; RGWL 2; TWA
Zoline, Pamela 1941- .... **CLC 62**
See also CA 161; SFW 4
Zoroaster date unknown .... **CMLC 40, 154**
Zorrilla y Moral, Jose
1817-1893 .... **NCLC 6, 298**
Zoshchenko, Mikhail
1895-1958 .... **SSC 15; TCLC 15**
See also CA 115; 160; EWL 3; RGSF 2; RGWL 3
Zoshchenko, Mikhail Mikhailovich
See Zoshchenko, Mikhail
Zuckmayer, Carl 1896-1977 .... **CLC 18; TCLC 191**
See also CA 69-72; DLB 56, 124; EWL 3; RGWL 2, 3
Zuk, Georges
See Skelton, Robin
Zukofsky, Louis 1904-1978 .... **CLC 1, 2, 4, 7, 11, 18; PC 11, 121**
See also AMWS 3; CA 9-12R; 77-80; CANR 39; CP 1, 2; DAM POET; DLB 5, 165; EWL 3; MAL 5; MTCW 1; RGAL 4
Zweig, Arnold 1887-1968 .... **TCLC 199**
See also CA 189; 115; DLB 66; EWL 3
Zweig, Paul 1935-1984 .... **CLC 34, 42**
See also CA 85-88; 113
Zweig, Stefan 1881-1942 .... **TCLC 17, 290**
See also CA 112; 170; DLB 81, 118; EWL 3; RGHL
Zwingli, Huldreich 1484-1531 .... **LC 37**
See also DLB 179

Literary Criticism Series Cumulative Topic Index

This index lists all topic entries in Gale's *Children's Literature Review* (CLR), *Classical and Medieval Literature Criticism* (CMLC), *Contemporary Literary Criticism* (CLC), *Drama Criticism* (DC), *Literature Criticism from 1400 to 1800* (LC), *Nineteenth-Century Literature Criticism* (NCLC), *Poetry Criticism* (PC), *Short Story Criticism* (SSC), and *Twentieth-Century Literary Criticism* (TCLC). The index also lists topic entries in the Gale Critical Companion Collection, which includes the following publications: *The Beat Generation* (BG), *Feminism in Literature* (FL), *Gothic Literature* (GL), and *Harlem Renaissance* (HR).

Abbey Theatre TCLC 258: 1-123
overview and history, 2-71
major figures, 71-109
plays and productions, 109-123

Abbey Theatre in the Irish Literary Renaissance TCLC 154: 1-114
origins and development, 2-14
major figures, 14-30
plays and controversies, 30-59
artistic vision and significance, 59-114

Abolitionist Literature of Cuba and Brazil, Nineteenth-Century NCLC 132: 1-94
overviews, 2-11
origins and development, 11-23
sociopolitical concerns, 23-39
poetry, 39-47
prose, 47-93

The Aborigine in Nineteenth-Century Australian Literature NCLC 120: 1-88
overviews, 2-27
representations of the Aborigine in Australian literature, 27-58
Aboriginal myth, literature, and oral tradition, 58-88

Acting on the Restoration and Eighteenth-Century English Stage LC 148: 1-116
overviews 2-23
acting styles 23-43
influential actors 43-70
introduction of actresses 70-86
influence of the actress 86-115

Adultery in 19th-Century Literature NCLC 220:1-102
background: transgression and moral rhetoric, 2-6
adultery and censure, 6-38
major authors and significant works, 38-101

Adventure Literature TCLC 202: 1-89
overviews and general studies 2-32
juvenile adventure narratives 32-8
adventure literature and imperialism 38-57
war and adventure 57-88

The Aesopic Fable LC 51: 1-100
the British Aesopic Fable, 1-54
the Aesopic tradition in non-English-speaking cultures, 55-66
political uses of the Aesopic fable, 67-88
the evolution of the Aesopic fable, 89-99

Aesop's Fables CLR 115: 1-55
overviews and general studies, 4-29
morality in Aesop's fables, 29-39
historical editions of Aesop's fables, 39-53
reviews of contemporary editions of Aesop's fables, 53-55

African-American Folklore and Literature TCLC 126: 1-67
African-American folk tradition, 1-16
representative writers, 16-34
hallmark works, 35-48
the study of African-American literature and folklore, 48-64

Age of al-Andalus CMLC 81: 1-174
overviews, 1-48
history, society, and culture, 48-127
Andalusī poetry, 127-73

Age of Eleanor of Aquitaine CMLC 125: 1-72
overview, 4-21
courtly love, 21-53
medieval verse romances, 53-71

Age of Johnson LC 15: 1-87
Johnson's London, 3-15
aesthetics of neoclassicism, 15-36
"age of prose and reason," 36-45
clubmen and bluestockings, 45-56
printing technology, 56-62
periodicals: "a map of busy life," 62-74
transition, 74-86

The Age of King Alfred the Great CMLC 79: 1-141
overviews and historical background, 4-17
the Alfredian translations, 17-43
King Alfred's prefaces, 43-84
Alfred and Boethius, 84-140

Age of Spenser LC 39: 1-70
overviews and general studies, 2-21
literary style, 22-34
poets and the crown, 34-70

AIDS in Literature CLC 81: 365-416

Alchemy in Seventeenth-Century England LC 148: 117-241
overviews 118-47
the last alchemists 147-69
Ben Jonson and *The Alchemist* 169-88
alchemy and poetry 188-239

Alcohol and Literature TCLC 70: 1-58
overview, 2-8
fiction, 8-48
poetry and drama, 48-58

Alexander the Great in Literature CMLC 112: 1-255
overviews and major works, 2-57
Alexander according to Greek and Roman historians, 57-178
the Medieval Alexander, 178-255

The Algonquin Round Table TCLC 242: 1-46
overviews, 2-15
political and social pressures, 15-45

American Abolitionism NCLC 44: 1-73
overviews and general studies, 2-26
abolitionist ideals, 26-46
the literature of abolitionism, 46-72

American Autobiography TCLC 86: 1-115
overviews and general studies, 3-36
American authors and autobiography, 36-82
African-American autobiography, 82-114

American Black Humor Fiction TCLC 54: 1-85
characteristics of black humor, 2-13
origins and development, 13-38
black humor distinguished from related literary trends, 38-60
black humor and society, 60-75
black humor reconsidered, 75-83

American Civil War Era Memoirs and Autobiographies NCLC 272: 1-133
memoirs by generals and officers, 3-21
memoirs by common soldiers, 21-110
memoirs by civilians, 110-130

American Civil War in Literature NCLC 32: 1-109
overviews and general studies, 2-20
regional perspectives, 20-54
fiction popular during the war, 54-79
the historical novel, 79-108
NCLC 212: 1-148

overviews, 4-32
gender roles, 32-70
race and slavery, 70-104
physicality and mortality, 104-47

The American Dream in Literature TCLC 210: 1-105
overviews, 2-11
the American Dream and popular culture, 11-27
the immigrant experience and the American Dream, 27-40
American authors and the American Dream, 40-105

American Frontier in Literature NCLC 28: 1-103
definitions, 2-12
development, 12-17
nonfiction writing about the frontier, 17-30
frontier fiction, 30-45
frontier protagonists, 45-66
portrayals of Native Americans, 66-86
feminist readings, 86-98
twentieth-century reaction against frontier literature, 98-100

American Frontier Literature TCLC 194: 1-125
overviews and general studies, 2-26
the frontier thesis and frontier literature, 26-51
major authors and frontier literature, 51-125

American Humor Writing NCLC 52: 1-59
overviews and general studies, 2-12
the Old Southwest, 12-42
broader impacts, 42-5
women humorists, 45-58
NCLC 232: 1-95
race, 2-49
Southwestern writers, 49-62
women writers, 62-95

American Immigrant Literature TCLC 206: 1-131
overviews and general studies, 2-33
cultural displacement, 33-78
stereotypes, identity, representation, 78-104
literary technique and use of language, 104-31

American Literary Naturalism TCLC 182: 1-95
overviews, 2-20
major authors, 20-77
themes and literary techniques, 77-94

The American Literary Renaissance NCLC 184: 1-107
overviews, 3-22
race and revolution, 22-40
gender, 41-106

***American Mercury,* The** TCLC 74: 1-80

American Naturalism in Short Fiction SSC 77: 1-103
overviews and general studies, 2-30
major authors of American literary Naturalism, 30-102
Ambrose Bierce, 30
Stephen Crane, 30-53
Theodore Dreiser, 53-65
Jack London, 65-80
Frank Norris, 80-9
Edith Wharton, 89-102

American Novel of Manners TCLC 130: 1-42
history of the Novel of Manners in America, 4-10
representative writers, 10-18
relevancy of the Novel of Manners, 18-24
hallmark works in the Novel of Manners, 24-36
Novel of Manners and other media, 36-40

American Poetry of the Vietnam War PC 143: 1-87
overviews and general studies, 5-44
civilian poetry, 44-61
veteran poetry, 61-78
writing from the margins, 78-85

American Political Drama TCLC 242: 47-168
political drama and the Communist Movement, 49-83
political drama in the Cold War years, 83-140
political drama and the Civil Rights Movement: the late 1950s and '60s, 140-61
political drama and Women's Movement: the late 1960s through the '80s, 161-67

American Popular Song, Golden Age of TCLC 42: 1-49
background and major figures, 2-34
the lyrics of popular songs, 34-47

American Proletarian Literature TCLC 54: 86-175
overviews and general studies, 87-95
American proletarian literature and the American Communist Party, 95-111
ideology and literary merit, 111-17
novels, 117-36
Gastonia, 136-48
drama, 148-54
journalism, 154-9
proletarian literature in the United States, 159-74

American Realism NCLC 120: 89-246
overviews, 91-112
background and sources, 112-72
social issues, 172-223
women and realism, 223-45

American Reform Writers TCLC 266: 1-124
urban reform, 2-10
social reformers, 10-50
women reformers, 50-124

American Renaissance SSC 64: 46-193
overviews and general studies, 47-103
major authors of short fiction, 103-92

American Romanticism NCLC 44: 74-138
overviews and general studies, 74-84
sociopolitical influences, 84-104
romanticism and the American frontier, 104-15
thematic concerns, 115-37

American Short Fiction since World War II TCLC 282: 1-110
overview, 2-18
major authors, 18-46
women authors, 46-72
multiculturalism in the short story, 72-90
regionalism and "place," 90-110

American Transcendentalism NCLC 224: 1-116
overviews, 3-26
religion and spirituality, 27-57
women authors, 57-115

American Western Literature TCLC 46: 1-100
definition and development of American Western literature, 2-7
characteristics of the Western novel, 8-23
Westerns as history and fiction, 23-34
critical reception of American Western literature, 34-41
the Western hero, 41-73
women in Western fiction, 73-91
later Western fiction, 91-9

American Westerns, Contemporary See Westerns, Contemporary American

American Writers in Paris TCLC 98: 1-156
overviews and general studies, 2-155

Anarchism NCLC 84: 1-97
overviews and general studies, 2-23
the French anarchist tradition, 23-56
Anglo-American anarchism, 56-68
anarchism: incidents and issues, 68-97

Angry Young Men TCLC 166: 1-80
overviews, 2-18
major figures, 18-58
themes and style, 58-79

Animal Stories CLR 132: 1-37
overviews and general studies, 5-7
animal fantasies in children's literature, 7-25
realistic children's animal stories, 25-36

Animals in Literature TCLC 106: 1-120
overviews and general studies, 2-8
animals in American literature, 8-45
animals in Canadian literature, 45-57
animals in European literature, 57-100
animals in Latin American literature, 100-06
animals in women's literature, 106-20

Antebellum South, Literature of the NCLC 112:1-188
overviews, 4-55
culture of the Old South, 55-68
antebellum fiction: pastoral and heroic romance, 68-120
role of women: a subdued rebellion, 120-59
slavery and the slave narrative, 159-85

Anti-Americanism TCLC 158: 1-98
overviews and general studies, 3-18
literary and intellectual perspectives, 18-36
social and political reactions, 36-98

Anti-Apartheid TCLC 162: 1-121
overviews, 3-45
major authors, 45-74
anti-apartheid literature and the liberal tradition, 74-101
writing under apartheid: historical views, 101-20

Antitheatrical Writing of the Renaissance LC 164: 1-140
overviews, 2-37
Stephen Gosson and Philip Stubbes, 37-65
antitheatrical drama, 65-104
antitheatrical rhetoric and religion, 104-39

The Apocalypse Theme in Twentieth-Century Literature TCLC 218: 1-113
overviews and general studies, 2-36
the theme of apocalypse in fiction, 36-77
the theme of apocalypse in poetry, 77-112

The Apocalyptic Movement TCLC 106: 121-69

Apollo Myth in Classical and Medieval Literature CMLC 113: 1-106
Apollo and the Greeks, 3-55
Apollo and the Romans, 55-65
The Myth of Apollo in the Middle Ages, 65-106

Argentine Literature TCLC 210: 106-209
overviews, 108-31
dictatorship and its aftermath, 131-48
Borges and Cortázar, 148-81
women and minorities in argentine literature, 181-209

The Aristotelian Arts Masters Controversy CMLC 136: 1-142

overview, 4-11
major figures, 11-52
the condemnation of 1277, 52-78
philosophical legacy of the condemnation, 78-140

Aristotle CMLC 31: 1-397
philosophy, 3-100
poetics, 101-219
rhetoric, 220-301
science, 302-397

Ars moriendi LC 172
overviews, 3-49
ars moriendi and the reformation, 49-86
ars moriendi and literature, 86-126
ars moriendi and women, 126-35

Art and Literature TCLC 54: 176-248
overviews and general studies, 176-93
definitions, 193-219
influence of visual arts on literature, 219-31
spatial form in literature, 231-47

Arthurian Legends for Children CLR 155: 1-75
overviews and general studies, 6-31
Howard Pyle and the Arthurian legend, 32-44
Sir Gawain stories for children, 44-60
contemporary Arthur stories for children, 60-75

Arthurian Literature CMLC 10: 1-127
historical context and literary beginnings, 2-27
development of the legend through Malory, 27-64
development of the legend from Malory to the Victorian Age, 65-81
themes and motifs, 81-95
principal characters, 95-125

Arthurian Revival NCLC 36: 1-77
overviews and general studies, 2-12
Tennyson and his influence, 12-43
other leading figures, 43-73
the Arthurian legend in the visual arts, 73-6

Asian American Literature CLC 340: 1-163
theorizing Asian American literature, 4-59
themes of transnationalism, 59-109
themes of sexuality and sexual identity, 109-38
the role of food in identity formation, 138-52
Asian American spirituality, 152-62

Astronomy in Nineteenth-Century Literature NCLC 228: 1-59
Herman Melville, 2-19
poetry, 19-47
women writers, 47-59

The Audience and Nineteenth-Century Literature NCLC 160: 1-158
overviews, 3-35
race, class, gender, 35-89
America, 89-102
Britain and Europe, 102-30
genre and audience, 130-57

Australian Children's Literature CLR 148: 1-58
overviews and general studies, 4-24
nineteenth-century Australian children's literature, 24-36
multiculturalism in Australian children's literature, 36-58

Australian Cultural Identity in Nineteenth-Century Literature NCLC 124: 1-164
overviews and general studies, 4-22
poetry, 22-67
fiction, 67-135
role of women writers, 135-64

Australian Literature TCLC 50: 1-94
origins and development, 2-21
characteristics of Australian literature, 21-33
historical and critical perspectives, 33-41
poetry, 41-58
fiction, 58-76
drama, 76-82
Aboriginal literature, 82-91

Australian Literature TCLC 278: 1-152
background: white settler nationalism, 4-32
national identity and themes of place, 33-65
the Aboriginal response, 65-92
postcolonial perspectives, 92-118
major authors, 118-50

Autobiographical Writing TCLC 214: 1-134
overviews and general studies, 3-34
significant autobiographical works, 34-66
African American autobiographical writing, 66-87
immigrant autobiographies, 87-134

Aztec Myths and Literature LC 122: 1-182
overviews and general studies, 3-68
cosmology, 68-136
language and literature, 136-81

Baseball in Contemporary Literature CLC 333: 1-83
introduction to baseball in contemporary literature, 1-6
major themes, 6-32
a gendered fiction, 32-67
the many genres of baseball literature, 67-83

The Beat Generation BG 1:1-562
the Beat Generation: an overview, 1-137
primary sources, 3-32
overviews and general studies, 32-47
Beat Generation as a social phenomenon, 47-65
drugs, inspiration, and the Beat Generation, 65-92
religion and the Beat Generation, 92-124
women of the Beat Generation, 124-36
Beat "scene": East and West, 139-259
primary sources, 141-77
Beat scene in the East, 177-218
Beat scene in the West, 218-59
Beat Generation publishing: periodicals, small presses, and censorship, 261-349
primary sources, 263-74
overview, 274-88
Beat periodicals: "little magazines," 288-311
Beat publishing: small presses, 311-24
Beat battles with censorship, 324-49
performing arts and the Beat Generation, 351-417
primary sources, 353-58
Beats and film, 358-81
Beats and music, 381-415
visual arts and the Beat Generation, 419-91
primary sources, 421-24
critical commentary, 424-90

The Beat Generation TCLC 222: 1-129
overviews, 2-59
major authors of the Beat Generation, 60-110
Beat poetry, 110-28

Beat Generation, Literature of the TCLC 42: 50-102
overviews and general studies, 51-9
the Beat generation as a social phenomenon, 59-62
development, 62-5
Beat literature, 66-96
influence, 97-100

The Bell Curve Controversy CLC 91: 281-330

Bereavement in Nineteenth-Century Literature NCLC 216: 1-103
overview, 3-13
psychological interpretations, 13-60
elegies, 60-102
major authors, 62-115
technique and narrative, 115-127

Betrayal in Short Fiction SSC 194: 1-116
betrayal in short stories about love, 4-7
betrayal in short stories about good and evil, 7-35
betrayal, order, and disorder, 35-58
the betrayal of ideals, 58-64
betrayal and cultural difference, 64-115

The Bible and Children's Literature CLR 145: 1-72
overviews and general studies, 3-24
biblical influence on children's literature, 24-67
responses to the Bible in children's literature, 67-72

***Bildungsroman* in Nineteenth-Century Literature** NCLC 20: 92-168
surveys, 93-113
in Germany, 113-40
in England, 140-56
female *Bildungsromane,* 156-67
NCLC 152: 1-129
overview, 3-16
definition and issues, 16-52
female *Bildungsromane*, 52-83
ideology and nationhood, 83-128
NCLC 240: 1-110
overviews, 1-39
female *Bildungsromane,* 39-80
national and cultural identity, 80-109

Black Humor, Contemporary CLC 196: 1-128
overviews and general studies, 2-18
black humor in American fiction, 18-28
development and history, 29-62
major authors, 62-115
technique and narrative, 115-127

Black Humor in Children's Literature CLR 104: 76-145
overviews and general studies, 79-96
examples of black humor in Victorian children's literature, 96-110
examples of black humor in twentieth-century children's literature, 110-28
black humor in the works of Roald Dahl, 128-44

Black Mountain Poets TCLC 230: 1-86
overviews, 2-23
Olson and Creeley, 23-68
other figures, 68-86

The Bloomsbury Group TCLC 34: 1-73
history and major figures, 2-13
definitions, 13-7
influences, 17-27
thought, 27-40
prose, 40-52
and literary criticism, 52-4
political ideals, 54-61
response to, 61-71
TCLC 138: 1-59
representative members of the Bloomsbury Group, 9-24
literary relevance of the Bloomsbury Group, 24-36
Bloomsbury's hallmark works, 36-48
other modernists studied with the Bloomsbury Group, 48-54
TCLC 266: 126-216

major figures, 126-73
legacy and themes, 173-216

The Blues in Literature TCLC 82: 1-71

The Bluestockings LC 189: 1-153
overviews, 3-22
the learned ladies, 22-74
Bluestocking ideas and ideals, 74-153

Bly, Robert, *Iron John: A Book about Men and Men's Work* CLC 70: 414-62

Book Clubs, Contemporary and Historic CLC 235: 1-94
the book club phenomenon, 1-72
Oprah Winfrey's book club, 72-90
reviews of books about book clubs, 90-94

The Book of Common Prayer LC 118: 1-76
overviews, 2-43
translation and diffusion, 44-63
influence of the Prayer Book, 63-76

The Book of J CLC 65: 289-311

Brazilian Literature TCLC 134: 1-126
overviews and general studies, 3-33
Brazilian poetry, 33-48
contemporary Brazilian writing, 48-76
culture, politics, and race in Brazilian writing, 76-100
modernism and postmodernism in Brazil, 100-25

Brazilian Literature, Contemporary CLC 311: 94-190
race relations and national identity in Brazil, 96-113
background trends in poetry, 113-23
surveys: fiction and poetry, 123-68
major authors, 168-89

British Ephemeral Literature LC 59: 1-70
overviews and general studies, 1-9
broadside ballads, 10-40
chapbooks, jestbooks, pamphlets, and newspapers, 40-69

British Laboring-Class Women's Poetry of the Eighteenth Century PC 145: 1-132
general and thematic studies, 3-24
Mary Collier, 25-43
Mary Barber, 43-65
Mary Leapor, 65-81
Ann Yearsley, 81-93
Janet Little, 93-8
Mary Scott, 98-108
Anne Wilson, 108-19
Elizabeth Hands, 119-30

British Women Poets of World War I PC 162: 165-254
overviews and general studies, 167-80
recovering women's voices, 180-94
comparative studies, 194-225
poetry and women's experiences of war, 225-53

British Working-Class Literature NCLC 246: 1-162
literary depictions by the working class, 4-54
Chartist literature, 54-95
literary depictions of the working class, 95-135
relationship between class and gender, 135-60

Buddhism and Literature TCLC 70: 59-164
eastern literature, 60-113
western literature, 113-63

Buddhism in the Nineteenth-Century Western World NCLC 164: 1-88
overviews, 3-47
Buddhism and Western Philosophers, 47-74
Buddhism in Western Literature, 74-88

The *Bulletin* and the Rise of Australian Literary Nationalism NCLC 116: 1-121
overviews, 3-32
legend of the nineties, 32-55
Bulletin style, 55-71
Australian literary nationalism, 71-98
myth of the bush, 98-120

Businessman in American Literature TCLC 26: 1-48
portrayal of the businessman, 1-32
themes and techniques in business fiction, 32-47

The Calendar LC 55: 1-92
overviews and general studies, 2-19
measuring time, 19-28
calendars and culture, 28-60
calendar reform, 60-92

Calvinism in Nineteenth-Century Literature NCLC 192: 1-90
challenges to Calvinism, 2-13
literary expressions of Calvinist doctrine, 13-89

Canadian Literature TCLC 206: 132-233
overviews, 133-60
personal identity and national identity, 160-74
Native Canadian authors, 174-93
other major authors, 193-232

Canadian Poetry in English, Contemporary CLC 298: 1-105
overviews, 4-20
major Canadian poets, 20-51
diasporic voices, 51-67
experimental voices, 67-105

Canadian Short Fiction, Contemporary CLC 314: 175-265
two solitudes: Canadian short fiction in English and French, 178-193
women's and gender issues in Canadian short fiction, 193-228
identity and cultural crossings in Canadian short fiction, 228-250
history and memory: the past versus the present in Canadian short fiction, 250-264

Canadian Short Fiction SSC 157: 70-237
overviews, 71-95
major authors, 95-158
race, nationality, ethnicity, and identity in Canadian short fiction, 159-205
female authors and gender issues, 205-236

Canadian Women Writers TCLC 238: 1-141
overviews, 3-34
major authors, 34-80
feminism and gender, 80-114
ethnicity and race, 114-41

Captivity Narratives LC 82: 71-172
overviews, 72-107
captivity narratives and Puritanism, 108-34
captivity narratives and Native Americans, 134-49
influence on American literature, 149-72

Captivity Narratives, Nineteenth-Century NCLC 80:131-218
overview, 132-37
the political significance of captivity narratives, 137-67
images of gender, 167-96
moral instruction, 197-217

Caribbean Literature TCLC 138: 60-135
overviews and general studies, 61-9
ethnic and national identity, 69-107
expatriate Caribbean literature, 107-23
literary histoiography, 123-35

The Carolingian Renaissance CMLC 127: 1-114
overviews and major themes, 3-53
Charlemagne and the Church, 53-93
major figures, 93-113

Catholicism in Nineteenth-Century American Literature NCLC 64: 1-58
overviews, 3-14
polemical literature, 14-46
Catholicism in literature, 47-57

Cavalier Poetry and Drama LC 107: 1-71
overviews, 2-36
Cavalier drama, 36-48
major figures, 48-70

Celtic Mythology CMLC 26: 1-111
overviews and general studies, 2-22
Celtic myth as literature and history, 22-48
Celtic religion: Druids and divinities, 48-80
Fionn MacCuhaill and the Fenian cycle, 80-111

Celtic Twilight See Irish Literary Renaissance

Censorship and Contemporary World Literature CLC 194: 1-80
overviews and general studies, 2-19
notorious cases, 19-59
censorship in the global context, 59-79

Censorship in Children's Literature CLR 118: 29-87
overviews and general studies, 33-49
regional examples of children's literature censorship, 49-67
censorship in the juvenile fantasy and pulp novel genres, 67-78
author responses to the censorship of children's literature, 78-87

Censorship of the Press in the Nineteenth Century NCLC 156: 1-133
overviews, 3-29
censorship in Austria, Germany, and Russia, 29-87
censorship in France and Spain, 87-120
censorship in England and America, 120-33

Censorship in Twentieth-Century Literature TCLC 154: 115-238
overviews and general studies, 117-25
censorship and obscenity trials, 125-61
censorship and sexual politics, 161-81
censorship and war, 181-207
political censorship and the state, 207-28
censorship and the writer, 228-38

The Chartist Movement and Literature NCLC 60: 1-84
overview: nineteenth-century working-class fiction, 2-19
Chartist fiction and poetry, 19-73
the Chartist press, 73-84

The Chicago Renaissance TCLC 154: 239-341
overviews and general studies, 240-60
definitions and growth, 260-82
the language debate, 282-318
major authors, 318-40

Chicano/a Literature, Contemporary CLC 205: 82-181
overviews, 84-124
Chicana studies, 124-40
some representative works, 140-80

Chicano/a Short Fiction SSC 162: 1-102
overviews, 3-14
the search for identity, 14-67
crossing borders and boundaries, 67-84
reading and marketing strategies, 84-102

Chick-Lit and Lad-Lit CLC 210: 115-64
overviews, 117-25
the debate over Chick Lit, 125-46
representative authors, 146-64

Child Labor in Nineteenth-Century Literature NCLC 108: 1-133
overviews, 3-10
climbing boys and chimney sweeps, 10-16
the international traffic in children, 16-45
critics and reformers, 45-82
fictional representations of child laborers, 83-132

Childhood in Nineteenth-Century Literature NCLC 172: 1-140
overviews, 2-20
romanticism and childhood, 20-46
childhood in the works of William Wordsworth, 46-72
childhood in the works of Charles Dickens, 72-106
childhood in the works of Leo Tolstoy, 106-29
childhood in the works of Emily Dickinson, 129-39

Children's Biography CLR 129: 69-132
overviews and general studies, 69-93
critical approaches to children's biographies, 93-106
children's biographies on ethnic and minority figures, 106-32

Children's Diaries CLR 141: 18-94
overviews of Holocaust diaries, 20-41
critical evaluations of Anne Frank's "The Diary of a Young Girl," 41-57
critical evaluations of other Holocaust diaries, 57-62
critical evaluations of Victorian children's diaries, 62-76
critical evaluations of contemporary children's diaries, 76-94

Children's Fantasy CLR 150: 21-117
some representative works, 23-4
nineteenth century children's fantasy 24-55
children's fantasy, 1960-1989, 55-95
children's fantasy, 1990-2009, 95-117

Children's Literature Awards CLR 139: 1-52
overviews and general studies, 4-13
multicultural children's literature awards, 13-23
themes and trends in children's literature award winners, 23-52

Children's Literature Illustration CLR 144: 44-112
overviews and general studies, 47-84
history of children's book illustration, 84-88
communicative relationship between text and illustration in children's texts, 88-102
analyses of illustrative arts used in books: topographic, nonfiction, and nursery rhymes, 102-11

Children's Literature, Nineteenth-Century NCLC 52: 60-135
overviews and general studies, 61-72
moral tales, 72-89
fairy tales and fantasy, 90-119
making men/making women, 119-34

Children's Periodicals CLR 138: 25-125
overviews and general studies, 27-65
early children's periodicals, 65-70
St. Nicholas Magazine, 70-104
children's periodicals and war, 104-24

Children's Poetry CLR 120: 15-100
overviews and general studies, 19-48
defining children's poetry, 48-68
teaching children's poetry, 68-71
poetry for children in the nineteenth, twentieth, and twenty-first centuries, 71-99

Chilean Literature TCLC 206: 234-366
overviews, 235-53
major chilean authors, 253-313
chilean literature and politics, 313-65

Chilean Short-Fiction Writers SSC 215: 69-131
overview and general study, 73-75
early-twentieth-century fiction of oppression, 75-95
themes of identity and exile in boom and post-boom fiction, 95-111
depictions of women's lives, 112-129

Christian Saints and Mystics of the Early Modern Era LC 153: 1-128
overviews, 3-18
the great mystic saints, 18-44
lesser-known mystics, 44-89
mystic poets, 89-127

Christianity in Nineteenth-Century Literature NCLC 180: 1-111
overviews, 4-32
women writers, 32-66
social and political discourse, 66-77
Russian literature, 77-110

Christianity in Twentieth-Century Literature TCLC 110: 1-79
overviews and general studies, 2-31
Christianity in twentieth-century fiction, 31-78

Chronicle Plays LC 89: 1-106
development of the genre, 2-33
historiography and literature, 33-56
genre and performance, 56-88
politics and ideology, 88-106

Cinderella in Children's Literature CLR 149: 40-131
overviews and general studies, 43-68
origins of the Cinderella story, 68-76
studies of international variants of the Cinderella story, 76-120
contemporized versions of the Cinderella story, 120-131

The City and Literature TCLC 90: 1-124
overviews and general studies, 2-9
the city in American literature, 9-86
the city in European literature, 86-124

The City in Short Fiction SSC 153: 80-214
the city in short fiction—U.S., Canada, and South America, 81-133
short fiction and the European city, 133-65
short fiction—the African and Asian city, 165-213

City Comedy LC 118: 77-211
origins and development, 79-113
economic issues, 113-32
women and city comedy, 132-82
the plays of Thomas Middleton, 182-211

Civic Critics, Russian NCLC 20: 402-46
principal figures and background, 402-9
and Russian Nihilism, 410-6
aesthetic and critical views, 416-45

Civic Pageants LC 154: 1-123
overview and history, 2-16
pageants in text and performance, 16-69
pageantry and politics, 69-111
Restoration pageantry, 111-22

Civil Rights Literature TCLC 210: 210-354
major authors and voices, 212-96
memoirs and autobiographies, 296-320
rhetoric and strategy, 320-53

The Cockney School NCLC 68: 1-64
overview, 2-7
Blackwood's Magazine and the contemporary critical response, 7-24
the political and social import of the Cockneys and their critics, 24-63

Cold War Literature TCLC 186: 1-136
overviews 2-52
novels and the cold war 52-102
social, political, and cultural response 102-36

Colonial America: The Intellectual Background LC 25: 1-98
overviews and general studies, 2-17
philosophy and politics, 17-31
early religious influences in Colonial America, 31-60
consequences of the Revolution, 60-78
religious influences in post-revolutionary America, 78-87
colonial literary genres, 87-97

Colonialism in Victorian English Literature NCLC 56: 1-77
overviews and general studies, 2-34
colonialism and gender, 34-51
monsters and the occult, 51-76

Colombian Literature TCLC 254: 1-99
colonialism and national identity, 2-16
film and theater, 16-33
major authors, 33-72
major themes, 73-99

Columbus, Christopher, Books on the Quincentennial of His Arrival in the New World CLC 70: 329-60

Comic Books TCLC 66: 1-139
historical and critical perspectives, 2-48
superheroes, 48-67
underground comix, 67-88
comic books and society, 88-122
adult comics and graphic novels, 122-36

Comedy of Manners LC 92: 1-75
overviews, 2-21
comedy of manners and society, 21-47
comedy of manners and women, 47-74

Coming-of-Age Story SSC 130: 29-146
aspects of the initiation narrative, 32-61
themes of sexual awakening, 61-77
gender-specific rites of passage, 77-103
culturally-driven rites of passage, 103-131
variations on the Bildungsroman archetype, 131-45

Commedia dell'Arte LC 83: 1-147
overviews, 2-7
origins and development, 7-23
characters and actors, 23-45
performance, 45-62
texts and authors, 62-100
influence in Europe, 100-46

Commonwealth Literature TCLC 198: 1-137
overviews and general studies, 2-14
perceptions and definitions, 14-23
merging cultures, 23-73
commonwealth literature and post-colonial theory, 73-113
language and power113-36

Conduct Books in Nineteenth-Century Literature NCLC 152: 130-229
women's education, 131-68
feminist revisions, 168-82
American behavioral literature: cultivating national identity, 182-209

Topic Index

English behavioral literature: defining a middle class, 209-27

Confessional School of Poetry, The TCLC 258: 124-204
overviews and background, 126-54
major authors, 154-203

Connecticut Wits NCLC 48: 1-95
overviews and general studies, 2-40
major works, 40-76
intellectual context, 76-95

Contemporary Brazilian Literature See Brazilian Literature, Contemporary

Contemporary Scottish Novelists CLC 388: 1-274
political and social issues, 5-58
literary elements and context, 58-176
genre novelists, 176-233
gender and sexuality, 233-71

Counter-Reformation Literature See Literature of the Counter-Reformation

Country House Literature TCLC 190: 1-117
overviews 2-20
major works 20-58
gender and country house literature 58-77
the big house motif in Irish literature 77-117

Courtesans in Nineteenth-Century French Literature NCLC 247: 77-106
background studies, 80-110
major authors and significant works, 111-33
La Dame aux Camélias, 133-51
Nana, 151-69
the courtesan as novelist and memoirist, 169-205

Creation Myths CMLC 110: 203-380
overviews 204-18
Themes and Motifs 218-81
Creation Myths in the Americas 281-332
Genesis 332-380

Crime, Criminals, and Nineteenth-Century Literature NCLC 243: 1-140
overviews, 6-28
the aesthetics of crime writing, 28-61
sociology and psychology, 61-92
true crime and fiction, 92-111
fictionalizations of true crimes, 111-38

Crime Fiction, Contemporary CLC 209: 34-192
overviews, 37-61
ethnicity and race in crime fiction, 61-105
literary traditions and crime fiction, 105-43
themes, 143-81
representative authors, 181-92

Crime in Literature TCLC 54: 249-307
evolution of the criminal figure in literature, 250-61
crime and society, 261-77
literary perspectives on crime and punishment, 277-88
writings by criminals, 288-306

Crime-Mystery-Detective Stories SSC 59:89-226
overviews and general studies, 90-140
origins and early masters of the crime-mystery-detective story, 140-73
hard-boiled crime-mystery-detective fiction, 173-209
diversity in the crime-mystery-detective story, 210-25

Critical Pluralism TCLC 298: 253-340
overviews and surveys of Critical Pluralism, 254-271
specific applications of Critical Pluralism, 271-320
endorsements of Critical Pluralism, 320-338

The Crusades CMLC 38: 1-144
history of the Crusades, 3-60
literature of the Crusades, 60-116
the Crusades and the people: attitudes and influences, 116-44

Cuban Exile Literature, Contemporary CLC 207: 1-100
overviews, 2-20
Cubana writers and exile, 20-48
some representative works, 48-100

Cubism in Literature TCLC 274:1-305
contemporaries of Cubism, 2-52
Cubism: intersections between image and word, 52-63
Cubism and later twentieth-century writers, 63-85

Cyberpunk TCLC 106: 170-366
overviews and general studies, 171-88
feminism and cyberpunk, 188-230
history and cyberpunk, 230-70
sexuality and cyberpunk, 270-98
social issues and cyberpunk, 299-366

Cyberpunk Short Fiction SSC 60: 44-108
overviews and general studies, 46-78
major writers of cyberpunk fiction, 78-81
sexuality and cyberpunk fiction, 81-97
additional pieces, 97-108

Czechoslovakian Literature of the Twentieth Century TCLC 42:103-96
through World War II, 104-35
de-Stalinization, the Prague Spring, and contemporary literature, 135-72
Slovak literature, 172-85
Czech science fiction, 185-93

Dadaism TCLC 46: 101-71
background and major figures, 102-16
definitions, 116-26
manifestos and commentary by Dadaists, 126-40
theater and film, 140-58
nature and characteristics of Dadaist writing, 158-70

Dance in Nineteenth-Century Literature NCLC 204: 1-96
French literature, 2-40
Jane Austen, 40-61
danse macabre, 61-95

Dandyism in Nineteenth-Century Literature NCLC 240: 111-208
overviews, 113-45
identity and cultural commentary, 145-81
Charles Baudelaire and Barbey d'Aurevilly, 181-99
Oscar Wilde, 199-208

Danish Literature See Twentieth-Century Danish Literature

Darwinism NCLC 224: 117-215
gender and race, 118-74
literary representations of Darwinism, 174-214

Darwinism and Literature NCLC 32: 110-206
background, 110-31
direct responses to Darwin, 131-71
collateral effects of Darwinism, 171-205

The Dead Sea Scrolls CMLC 113: 107-269
Literary, Religious, and Historical Themes, 108-136
The Scrolls and the Old Testament, 136-155
The Scrolls and the New Testament, 155-210
Jesus and the Dead Sea Scrolls, 210-267

Death in American Literature NCLC 92: 1-170
overviews and general studies, 2-32
death in the works of Emily Dickinson, 32-72
death in the works of Herman Melville, 72-101
death in the works of Edgar Allan Poe, 101-43
death in the works of Walt Whitman, 143-70

Death in Nineteenth-Century British Literature NCLC 68: 65-142
overviews and general studies, 66-92
responses to death, 92-102
feminist perspectives, 103-17
striving for immortality, 117-41

Death in Literature TCLC 78: 1-183
fiction, 2-115
poetry, 115-46
drama, 146-81

Death in the Short Story SSC 141: 1-152
the death motif in American fiction, 4-61
the death motif in British and European short fiction, 61-118
death in Latino short stories, 118-51

Decadence in Nineteenth-Century Literature NCLC 164: 90-191
overviews, 90-132
Decadent literary subjects, 132-44
Decadence in British literature, 144-57
Decadence in French literature, 158-79
women writers and Decadence, 179-90

Deconstruction TCLC 138: 136-256
overviews and general studies, 137-83
deconstruction and literature, 183-221
deconstruction in philosophy and history, 221-56

Defense of Women Pamphlets in Early Modern England LC 191: 102-222
overviews, 103-38
the women pamphleteers, 138-222

Deism LC 157: 81-156
overviews, 83-110
European deism, 111-39
American deism, 139-54

de Man, Paul, Wartime Journalism of CLC 55: 382-424

Democracy in Nineteenth-Century Literature NCLC 180: 112-245
overviews, 113-27
anti-democratic sentiment, 127-68
Walt Whitman, 168-84
romanticism, 184-211
Henry James and American women, 211-44

Depictions of Islam in Modern Literature TCLC 166: 81-198
overviews, 82-115
literature in the Muslim world, 115-56
Western interpretations, 156-82
women, Islam, and literature, 182-97

Detective Fiction, Nineteenth-Century NCLC 36: 78-148
origins of the genre, 79-100
history of nineteenth-century detective fiction, 101-33
significance of nineteenth-century detective fiction, 133-46
NCLC 148: 1-161
overviews, 3-26
origins and influences, 26-63
major authors, 63-134
Freud and detective fiction, 134-59

Detective Fiction, Twentieth-Century TCLC 38: 1-96
genesis and history of the detective story, 3-22

defining detective fiction, 22-32
evolution and varieties, 32-77
the appeal of detective fiction, 77-90

Detective Story See Crime-Mystery-Detective Stories

Dime Novels NCLC 84: 98-168
overviews and general studies, 99-123
popular characters, 123-39
major figures and influences, 139-52
socio-political concerns, 152-167

Disabilities in Children's Literature CLR 126: 34-106
overviews and general studies, 37-60
presentation of mental disabilities in children's literature, 60-72
presentation of physical disabilities in children's literature, 72-84
presentation of cognitive and emotional disabilities in children's literature, 84-106

Disease and Literature
TCLC 66: 140-283
overviews and general studies, 141-65
disease in nineteenth-century literature, 165-81
tuberculosis and literature, 181-94
women and disease in literature, 194-221
plague literature, 221-53
AIDS in literature, 253-82

Domesticity in Nineteenth-Century Literature
NCLC 240: 209-310
overview, 211-25
female identity and individualism, 225-61
race and nationalism, 261-309

El Dorado, The Legend of See The Legend of El Dorado

The Double in Nineteenth-Century Literature
NCLC 40: 1-95
genesis and development of the theme, 2-15
the double and romanticism, 16-27
sociological views, 27-52
psychological interpretations, 52-87
philosophical considerations, 87-95
NCLC 192: 91-217
overviews and general studies, 93-151
psychology and the double, 151-93
race, gender, and the double, 193-216

The Double in Short Fiction SSC 149: 68-159
the symbolic significance of the double, 69-127
major short fiction works featuring the motif of the double, 127-58

Dramatic Realism NCLC 44: 139-202
overviews and general studies, 140-50
origins and definitions, 150-66
impact and influence, 166-93
realist drama and tragedy, 193-201

Drugs and Literature TCLC 78: 184-282
overviews and general studies, 185-201
pre-twentieth-century literature, 201-42
twentieth-century literature, 242-82

Dystopias in Contemporary Literature
CLC 168: 1-91
overviews and general studies, 2-52
dystopian views in Margaret Atwood's *The Handmaid's Tale* (1985), 52-71
feminist readings of dystopias, 71-90

Early Modern English Science Fiction
LC 205: 1-136
overviews, 2-49
authors and their works, 49-136

Early Modern Folk Literature LC 171: 123-288
overviews, 125-45
popular themes and figures, 145-69
folk literature in Britain, 169-240
folk literature in Europe, 240-88

Early Twentieth-Century Children's Literature TCLC 246: 1-110
overviews and general studies, 2-40
early twentieth-century children's fantasists, 40-70
early twentieth-century girls' books, 70-99
early twentieth-century nursery books, 99-109

Early Twentieth-Century Drama TCLC 246: 111-97
American realism, 114-47
realism and the Moscow Art Theatre, 147-82
the Irish literary renaissance and the Abbey Theatre, 182-96

East Asian Literature TCLC 254: 100-77
overviews and major themes, 102-12
China and Taiwan, 112-36
Japan and Korea, 136-76

Eastern Mythology CMLC 26: 112-92
heroes and kings, 113-51
cross-cultural perspective, 151-69
relations to history and society, 169-92

Ecocriticism and Nineteenth-Century Literature NCLC 140: 1-168
overviews, 3-20
American literature: Romantics and Realists, 20-76
American explorers and naturalists, 76-123
English literature: Romantics and Victorians, 123-67

Ecofeminism and Nineteenth-Century Literature NCLC 136: 1-110
overviews, 2-24
the local landscape, 24-72
travel writing, 72-109

Ecofeminism in Literature TCLC 278: 153-218
overviews and history, 154-79
representative studies, 179-216

The Ecological Short Story SSC 163: 59-195
overviews, 60-70
Faulkner and Ecological Short Fiction, 70-94
Short Ecofiction: Topics, Themes, Styles, 94-161
Latin American Ecological Short Fiction, 162-77
Ecofeminist Short Fiction, 177-94

Edwardian Literature TCLC 186: 137-282
overviews 138-74
culture and society in the edwardian age 174-203
nation and empire 203-34
images of money 234-52
Edwardians and Modernists 252-71
Edwardian novels 271-81

Eighteenth-Century British Periodicals
LC 63: 1-123
rise of periodicals, 2-31
impact and influence of periodicals, 31-64
periodicals and society, 64-122

Eighteenth Century Children's Books
CLR 152: 111-86
overviews and general studies, 114-29
eighteenth-century criticism of period children's books, 129-44
eighteenth-century British children's books, 144-66
eighteenth-century American children's books, 166-86

Eighteenth-Century Travel Narratives LC 77: 252-355
overviews and general studies, 254-79
eighteenth-century European travel narratives, 279-334
non-European eighteenth-century travel narratives, 334-55

Electronic "Books": Hypertext and Hyperfiction CLC 86: 367-404
books vs. CD-ROMS, 367-76
hypertext and hyperfiction, 376-95
implications for publishing, libraries, and the public, 395-403

Eliot, T. S., Centenary of Birth CLC 55: 345-75

Elizabethan Drama LC 22: 140-240
origins and influences, 142-67
characteristics and conventions, 167-83
theatrical production, 184-200
histories, 200-12
comedy, 213-20
tragedy, 220-30

Elizabethan Prose Fiction LC 41: 1-70
overviews and general studies, 1-15
origins and influences, 15-43
style and structure, 43-69

The Emergence of the Short Story in the Nineteenth Century NCLC 140: 169-279
overviews, 171-74
the American short story, 174-214
the short story in Great Britain and Ireland, 214-235
stories by women in English, 235-45
the short story in France and Russia, 245-66
the Latin American short story, 266-77

Enclosure of the English Common NCLC 88: 1-57
overviews and general studies, 1-12
early reaction to enclosure, 12-23
nineteenth-century reaction to enclosure, 23-56

The Encyclopedists LC 26: 172-253
overviews and general studies, 173-210
intellectual background, 210-32
views on esthetics, 232-41
views on women, 241-52

English Abolitionist Literature of the Nineteenth Century NCLC 136: 111-235
overview, 112-35
origins and development, 135-42
poetry, 142-58
prose, 158-80
sociopolitical concerns, 180-95
English abolitionist literature and feminism, 195-233

English Caroline Literature LC 13: 221-307
background, 222-41
evolution and varieties, 241-62
the Cavalier mode, 262-75
court and society, 275-91
politics and religion, 291-306

English Decadent Literature of the 1890s
NCLC 28: 104-200
fin de siècle: the Decadent period, 105-19
definitions, 120-37
major figures: "the tragic generation," 137-50
French literature and English literary Decadence, 150-7
themes, 157-61
poetry, 161-82
periodicals, 182-96

Topic Index

English Emblem Books LC 125: 1-99
overviews, 2-27
background and contexts, 27-63
major emblem writers, 63-83
religion and emblem books, 83-99

English Essay, Rise of the LC 18: 238-308
definitions and origins, 236-54
influence on the essay, 254-69
historical background, 269-78
the essay in the seventeenth century, 279-93
the essay in the eighteenth century, 293-307

English-Irish Relations from Spenser to Swift LC 160: 1-172
historical and political background, 3-38
Spenser and Ireland, 39-71
Ireland and English drama, 71-117
Ireland in the age of Swift, 117-72

English Literary Criticism in the Later Seventeenth and Eighteenth Centuries LC 203: 1-121
overviews, 3-58
the critics, 58-121

English Mystery Cycle Dramas LC 34: 1-88
overviews and general studies, 1-27
the nature of dramatic performances, 27-42
the medieval worldview and the mystery cycles, 43-67
the doctrine of repentance and the mystery cycles, 67-76
the fall from grace in the mystery cycles, 76-88

The English Realist Novel, 1740-1771 LC 51: 102-98
overviews and general studies, 103-22
from romanticism to realism, 123-58
women and the novel, 159-175
the novel and other literary forms, 176-197

English Renaissance Literary Criticism LC 201: 1-178
overviews, 3-123
the critics, 123-78

English Revolution, Literature of the LC 43: 1-58
overviews and general studies, 2-24
pamphlets of the English Revolution, 24-38
political sermons of the English Revolution, 38-48
poetry of the English Revolution, 48-57

English Romantic Hellenism NCLC 68: 143-250
overviews and general studies, 144-69
historical development of English Romantic Hellenism, 169-91
influence of Greek mythology on the Romantics, 191-229
influence of Greek literature, art, and culture on the Romantics, 229-50

English Romantic Poetry NCLC 28: 201-327
overviews and reputation, 202-37
major subjects and themes, 237-67
forms of Romantic poetry, 267-78
politics, society, and Romantic poetry, 278-99
philosophy, religion, and Romantic poetry, 299-324

Epistolary Fiction TCLC 230: 87-208
overviews, 88-105
major authors, 105-46
the epistolatory novel in Hispanic literature, 146-77
other epistolary genres, 177-207

The Epistolary Novel LC 59: 71-170
overviews and general studies, 72-96
women and the Epistolary novel, 96-138
principal figures: Britain, 138-53
principal figures: France, 153-69

Epithalamia: Poems Celebrating Marriages PC 171: 77-200
epithalamia of the classical period, 80-8
epithalamia of the English Renaissance, 88-167
epithalamia of the nineteenth and twentieth centuries, 167-98

Espionage Literature TCLC 50: 95-159
overviews and general studies, 96-113
espionage fiction/formula fiction, 113-26
spies in fact and fiction, 126-38
the female spy, 138-44
social and psychological perspectives, 144-58

Euro-American Literary Representations of Native Americans, Nineteenth-Century NCLC 104: 132-264
overviews and general studies, 134-53
Native American history, 153-72
the Indians of the Northeast, 172-93
the Indians of the Southeast, 193-212
the Indians of the West, 212-27
Indian-hater fiction, 227-43
the Indian as exhibit, 243-63

European Debates on the Conquest of the Americas LC 67: 1-129
overviews and general studies, 3-56
major Spanish figures, 56-98
English perceptions of Native Americans, 98-129

European Romanticism NCLC 36: 149-284
definitions, 149-77
origins of the movement, 177-82
Romantic theory, 182-200
themes and techniques, 200-23
romanticism in Germany, 223-39
romanticism in France, 240-61
romanticism in Italy, 261-4
romanticism in Spain, 264-8
impact and legacy, 268-82

Evolution of Fairy Tales CLR 106: 89-164
overviews and general studies, 93-102
the value of fairy tales for children, 102-19
contemporary adaptations of classic fairy tales, 119-45
characteristics of twentieth-century fairy tales, 145-63

Exile in Literature TCLC 122: 1-129
overviews and general studies, 2-33
exile in fiction, 33-92
German literature in exile, 92-129

Exile in Nineteenth-Century European and American Literature NCLC 172: 141-248
overview, 143-51
exile in French literature, 151-81
exile in British literature, 181-202
exile in American literature, 202-27
women and exile, 227-47

Exile in Short Fiction SSC 145: 1-138
Metaphorical/Internal Exile, 4-51
Exile in Slavic/Eastern European Culture, 51-78
Exile to and from Africa, 78-97
Exile in Hispanic Short Fiction, 97-137

Existentialism and Literature TCLC 42: 197-268
overviews and definitions, 198-209
history and influences, 209-19
Existentialism critiqued and defended, 220-35
philosophical and religious perspectives, 235-41
Existentialist fiction and drama, 241-67

Ezra Pound Controversy TCLC 150: 1-132
politics of Ezra Pound, 3-42
anti-semitism of Ezra Pound, 42-57
the Bollingen Award controversy, 57-76
Pound's later writing, 76-104
criticism of *The Pisan Cantos,* 104-32

Fabian Literature TCLC 190: 118-217
overviews 119-143
Shaw and Fabianism 143-69
other major figures 169-216

Fables SSC 124: 173-360
overviews 174-282
major authors and works 282-358

Fairy Tales and Nineteenth-Century Literature NCLC 212: 149-268
overview, 151-65
The Brothers Grimm, 165-86
Charles Dickens, 186-217
Oscar Wilde, 217-45
women authors, 245-67

Familiar Essay NCLC 48: 96-211
definitions and origins, 97-130
overview of the genre, 130-43
elements of form and style, 143-59
elements of content, 159-73
the Cockneys: Hazlitt, Lamb, and Hunt, 173-91
status of the genre, 191-210

Fantasy in Contemporary Literature CLC 193: 137-250
overviews and general studies, 139-57
language, form, and theory, 157-91
major writers, 191-230
women writers and fantasy, 230-50

Fashion in Nineteenth-Century Literature NCLC 128: 104-93
overviews and general studies, 105-38
fashion and American literature, 138-46
fashion and English literature, 146-74
fashion and French literature, 174-92

The Faust Legend LC 47: 1-117

The Faust Legend in Twentieth-Century Literature TCLC 182: 96-238
overviews, 97-121
Faust in the modern world, 121-74
major works, 174-208
comparative studies, 208-38

Fear in Literature TCLC 74: 81-258
overviews and general studies, 81
pre-twentieth-century literature, 123
twentieth-century literature, 182

Female Dramatists of the Restoration and Eighteenth Century LC 163: 1-137
overviews, 4-55
The Female Wits (1696), 55-80
major plawrights, 80-113
transforming gender, 113-121
minor playwrights, 121-37

Feminism in the 1990s: Commentary on Works by Naomi Wolf, Susan Faludi, and Camille Paglia CLC 76: 377-415

Feminism in Children's Literature CLR 146: 18-111
overviews and general studies, 21-38
feminism in classic girls' stories, 38-61
feminism in series fiction, 61-89
feminism in young adult poetry, 89-111

Feminist Criticism, Contemporary CLC 180: 1-103
overviews and general studies, 2-59
modern French feminist theory, 59-102

Feminist Criticism in 1990 CLC 65: 312-60

Feminism in Literature FL 1: 1-279; 2: 1-295; 4: 1-626
women and women's writings from antiquity through the middle ages, 1:1-99
primary sources, 1:4-12
women in the ancient world, 1:12-34
women in the medieval world, 1:34-56
women in classical art and literature, 1:56-74
classical and medieval women writers, 1:74-96
women in the 16th, 17th, and 18th centuries: an overview, 1:101-91
primary sources, 1:104-11
overviews, 1:112-32
society, 1:132-64
politics, 1:164-77
women in literature, 1:177-90
women's literature in the 16th, 17th, and 18th centuries 1:193-279
primary sources, 1:195-201
overviews, 1:202-39
women's literature in the 16th, 17th, and 18th centuries, 1:239-78
women in the 19th century: an overview, 2:1-88
primary sources, 2:3-15
overviews, 2:15-50
early feminists, 2:50-67
representations of women in literature and art in the 19th century, 2:67-86
women's literature in the 19th century, 2:89-206
primary sources, 2:91-9
overviews, 2:99-140
American women writers, 2:141-77
British women writers, 2:177-204
United States suffrage movement in the 19th century, 2:207-95
primary sources, 2:209-29
overviews, 2:229-39
the civil war and its effect on suffrage, 2:239-53
suffrage: issues and individuals, 2:253-94
women in the early to mid-20th century (1900-1960): an overview, 4:1-126
primary sources, 4:1-14
overviews, 4:14-48
social and economic conditions, 4:48-67
women and the arts, 4:67-125
suffrage in the 20th century, 4:127-234
primary sources, 4:129-36
overviews, 4:136-77
major figures and organizations, 4:177-214
women and law, 4:214-32
women's literature from 1900 to 1960, 4:235-344
primary sources, 4:238-41
overviews, 4:241-61
impact of the world wars, 4:261-304
women and the dramatic tradition, 4:304-39
Asian American influences, 4:339-42
the feminist movement in the 20th century, 4:345-443
primary sources, 4:347-58
overviews, 4:358-403
feminist legal battles, 4:403-34
third-wave feminism, 4:434-42
women's literature from 1960 to the present, 4:445-536
primary sources, 4:448-60
overviews, 4:460-83
women authors of color, 4:483-97
feminist literary theory, 4:497-511
modern lesbian literature, 4:511-534

Feminism in Nineteenth-Century Literature NCLC 236: 1-104
overview, 3-6
feminist readings of fiction by women, 6-44
women author activists, 44-78
male authors, 78-103

Fifteenth-Century Spanish Poetry LC 100:82-173
overviews and general studies, 83-101
the Cancioneros, 101-57
major figures, 157-72

The Figure of La Malinche in Mexican Literature LC 127: 91-172
overview, 92-108
the historical Malinche, 108-33
Malinche reinvented, 133-72

Film and Literature TCLC 38: 97-226
overviews and general studies, 97-119
film and theater, 119-34
film and the novel, 134-45
the art of the screenplay, 145-66
genre literature/genre film, 167-79
the writer and the film industry, 179-90
authors on film adaptations of their works, 190-200
fiction into film: comparative essays, 200-23

***Fin de siècle* Literature** TCLC 250: 1-107
overviews, 2-24
fin de siècle poetry, 24-57
fin de siècle fiction and drama, 57-91
fin de siècle writers, 91-107

Finance and Money as Represented in Nineteenth-Century Literature NCLC 76: 1-69
historical perspectives, 2-20
the image of money, 20-37
the dangers of money, 37-50
women and money, 50-69

Folk Literature See Early Modern Folk Literature

Folklore and Literature TCLC 86: 116-293
overviews and general studies, 118-144
Native American literature, 144-67
African-American literature, 167-238
folklore and the American West, 238-57
modern and postmodern literature, 257-91

Food in Literature TCLC 114: 1-133
food and children's literature, 2-14
food as a literary device, 14-32
rituals invloving food, 33-45
food and social and ethnic identity, 45-90
women's relationship with food, 91-132

Food in Nineteenth-Century Literature NCLC 108: 134-288
overviews, 136-74
food and social class, 174-85
food and gender, 185-219
food and love, 219-31
food and sex, 231-48
eating disorders, 248-70
vegetarians, carnivores, and cannibals, 270-87

Food in Short Fiction SSC 154: 1-122
food in the short fiction of Europe, 2-42
food in the short fiction of Asia, 42-78
food in the short fiction of the Americas, 78-122

French Drama in the Age of Louis XIV LC 28: 94-185
overview, 95-127
tragedy, 127-46
comedy, 146-66
tragicomedy, 166-84

French Enlightenment LC 14: 81-145
the question of definition, 82-9
le siècle des lumières, 89-94
women and the salons, 94-105
censorship, 105-15
the philosophy of reason, 115-31
influence and legacy, 131-44

French Literature TCLC 262: 1-94
major works of French literature, 3-93

French New Novel TCLC 98: 158-234
overviews and general studies, 158-92
influences, 192-213
themes, 213-33

French Realism NCLC 52: 136-216
origins and definitions, 137-70
issues and influence, 170-98
realism and representation, 198-215

French Revolution and English Literature NCLC 40: 96-195
history and theory, 96-123
romantic poetry, 123-50
the novel, 150-81
drama, 181-92
children's literature, 192-5

French Symbolist Poetry NCLC 144: 1-107
overviews, 2-14
Symbolist aesthetics, 14-47
the Symbolist lyric, 47-60
history and influence, 60-105

Friendship in Nineteenth-Century Literature NCLC 196: 1-97
spiritual and personal fulfillment, 3-31
friendships between men, 31-64
friendships between women, 64-96

The Fronde LC 200:124-230
background and history, 125-49
mazarinades, 149-72
memoirs, 172-229

Frontiersmen in American Literature NCLC 208: 1-102
overview, 3-31
masculinity and the frontiersman, 31-54
frontier heroines, 54-101

The Fugitives and Their Poetry TCLC 290: 1-114
overviews and general studies, 3-67
Donald Davidson, 67-73
John Crowe Ransom, 73-90
Allen Tate, 90-8
Robert Penn Warren, 98-112

Futurism TCLC 166: 199-338
overviews, 200-10
poetry, 210-23
theater, 223-32
music, 232-46
Futurism and Fascism, 246-312
women Futurist writers, 312-37

Futurism, Italian TCLC 42: 269-354
principles and formative influences, 271-9
manifestos, 279-88
literature, 288-303
theater, 303-19
art, 320-30
music, 330-6
architecture, 336-9
and politics, 339-46
reputation and significance, 346-51

Gaelic Revival See Irish Literary Renaissance

Gates, Henry Louis, Jr., and African-American Literary Criticism CLC 65: 361-405

Gaucho Literature TCLC 158: 99-195
overviews and general studies, 101-43
major works, 143-95

Gambling in Nineteenth-Century Literature NCLC 168: 1-84
overview, 2-7
gambling in American literature, 7-39
gambling in British literature, 39-57
gambling in Russian literature, 57-84

Gangsta Fiction See Street Lit

Gay and Lesbian Literature CLC 76: 416-39

Gay and Lesbian Literature, Contemporary CLC 171: 1-130
overviews and general studies, 2-43
contemporary gay literature, 44-95
lesbianism in contemporary literature, 95-129

Gay and Lesbian Literature in the Twentieth Century TCLC 218: 114-59
overviews and general studies, 115-38
major authors and works, 138-60
homosexuality and race, 161-93
lesbian literature, 193-258

Gender and Sexuality in Early Seventeenth-Century English Literature LC 149: 1-159
overview, 3-7
crossdressing, 7-70
sexual practices, 70-92
sexual difference, 92-114
homoerotic desire, 114-58

Gender and Sexuality in Eighteenth-Century British Literature LC 155: 85-224
desire and the body, 87-115
sexual difference, 115-75
societal norms, 175-203
gender and politics, 203-23

Gender and Sexuality in Eighteenth-Century European Literature LC 175: 142-242
representations of sexuality, 144-76
notions of gender, 176-200
erotic and pornographic works, 200-23
sexuality and non-Europeans, 223-42

Gender and Sexuality in Fifteenth-Century Literature LC 145: 1-147
gender and sexuality in English literature, 3-83
gender and sexuality in European literature, 83-119
the sexuality of the "other" 119-46

Gender and Sexuality in Seventeenth-Century European Literature LC 153: 219-362
overviews, 221-30
cross-dressing, 230-71
gender identification and difference, 271-337
sexual liberation, 337-61

Gender and Sexuality in Sixteenth-Century Literature LC 147: 90-248
overviews, 92-123
gender conformation and construction, 123-53
visions and constructions of sexuality, 153-72
sex, gender, and power, 172-205
female representation and self-representation, 205-47

Gender in Nineteenth-Century Literature NCLC 168: 192-352
overviews, 195-256
gender and race, 256-83
gender and men, 283-309
gender and class, 309-20
gender and the text, 320-51

The Generation of 1898 TCLC 198: 138-235
overviews and general studies, 139-71
formation and history, 171-201
literary criticism and the generation of 1898, 201-18
the generation of 1898 and the development of the novel, 218-34

Generation of 1898 Short Fiction SSC 75: 182-287
overviews and general studies, 182-210
major short story writers of the Generation of 1898, 210-86
Azorín, 210-16
Emilia Pardo Bazán, 216-34
Vicente Blasco Ibáñez, 234-36
Gabriel Miró, 236-43
Miguel de Unamuno, 243-68
Ramon del Valle-Inclán, 268-86

The Generation of 1927 TCLC 178: 1-109
overviews 2-17
literary and thematic assessments 17-59
major authors 59-108

The Genteel Tradition NCLC 188: 1-89
overviews, 3-43
women and the Genteel Tradition, 43-61
works in the Genteel Tradition, 61-89

Georgian Poetry TCLC 174:1-103
overviews, 2-28
cultural and literary context, 28-74
World War I and Georgian poetry, 74-103

German Baroque Novelists LC 225: 1-184
Anton Ulrich, Duke of Brunswick-Lüneberg (later Brunswick-Wolfenbüttel), 25-9
Johann Beer, 29-52
August Bohse, 53-79
Johann Christoph Ettner, 79-87
Johann Jakob Christoffel von Grimmelshausen, 87-122
Eberhard Werner Happel, 122-31
Johann Kuhnau, 132-42
Daniel Casper von Lohenstein, 142-60
Wolfgang Caspar Printz, 160-64
Christian Weise, 164-82

German Courtly Epic CMLC 132: 1-156
sources and influences, 4-21
historical context, 21-45
conventions of the courtly epic, 45-101
analyses of central texts and authors, 101-27
love and gender in the courtly epic, 128-55

German Exile Literature TCLC 30: 1-58
the writer and the Nazi state, 1-10
definition of, 10-4
life in exile, 14-32
surveys, 32-50
Austrian literature in exile, 50-2
German publishing in the United States, 52-7

German Expressionism TCLC 34: 74-160
history and major figures, 76-85
aesthetic theories, 85-109
drama, 109-26
poetry, 126-38
film, 138-42
painting, 142-7
music, 147-53
and politics, 153-8

German Humanists LC 234: 71-210
Desiderius Erasmus, 74-126
Martin Luther, 126-157
the humanistic tradition: Fischart, Wyle, and others, 157-208

German Images of America in the Nineteenth Century NCLC 254: 71-241
theory and context, 74-90
America and the German imagination, 90-147
race: German portrayals of Black and Native Americans, 147-194
German women and America, 194-201
regional perspectives, 201-239

German Naturalism TCLC 302: 1-111
literary context of German Naturalism, 3-41
sociohistorical context of German Naturalism, 41-64
specific themes and motifs in German Naturalist literature, 64-95
German Naturalism and other literary modes, 95-109

Ghetto Fiction See Street Lit

The Ghost Story SSC 58: 1-142
overviews and general studies, 1-21
the ghost story in American literature, 21-49
the ghost story in Asian literature, 49-53
the ghost story in European and English literature, 54-89
major figures, 89-141

The Gilded Age NCLC 84: 169-271
popular themes, 170-90
realism, 190-208
Aestheticism, 208-26
socio-political concerns, 226-70

***Glasnost* and Contemporary Soviet Literature** CLC 59: 355-97

Golden Age of Children's Illustrated Books CLR 113: 93-156
overviews and general studies, 96-114
Victorian masters of the Golden Age, 115-34
the Brandywine School of children's illustration, 134-56

***Gone with the Wind* as Cultural Phenomenon** TCLC 170: 1-103
overviews, 2-60
race, gender, and class in *Gone with the Wind,* 60-102

Gothic Drama NCLC 132: 95-198
overviews, 97-125
sociopolitical contexts, 125-58
Gothic playwrights, 158-97

Gothic Literature GL 1: 1-577
Gothic Literature: an overview, 1-106
primary sources, 4-16
overviews, 16-40
origins of the Gothic, 40-57
American Gothic, 57-74
European Gothic, 74-104
society, culture, and the Gothic, 107-229
primary sources, 110-27
overviews, 127-80
race and the Gothic, 180-210
women and the Gothic, 210-28
gothic themes, settings, and figures, 231-387
primary sources, 236-49
overviews, 249-64
haunted dwellings and the supernatural, 264-301
psychology and the Gothic, 301-42
vampires, 342-85
performing arts and the Gothic, 389-474
primary sources, 394-401
drama, 401-15
film, 415-52
television, 452-60
music, 461-73
visual arts and the Gothic, 475-526
primary sources, 477-80
overviews, 480-86
architecture, 486-506
art, 506-525

Gothic Literature TCLC 202: 90-220
overviews and general studies 91-111
evolution of Gothic style 111-33
gender and the Gothic imagination 133-74
literary and thematic connections 174-95
race, society, and politics 195-219

Gothic Novel NCLC 28: 328-402
development and major works, 328-34
definitions, 334-50
themes and techniques, 350-78
in America, 378-85
in Scotland, 385-91
influence and legacy, 391-400

The Governess in Nineteenth-Century Literature NCLC 104: 1-131
overviews and general studies, 3-28
social roles and economic conditions, 28-86
fictional governesses, 86-131

The Grail Theme in Twentieth-Century Literature TCLC 142: 1-89
overviews and general studies, 2-20
major works, 20-89

Graphic Narratives CLC 86: 405-32
history and overviews, 406-21
the "Classics Illustrated" series, 421-2
reviews of recent works, 422-32

Graphic Novels CLC 177: 163-299
overviews and general studies, 165-198
critical readings of major works, 198-286
reviews of recent graphic novels, 286-299

Graphic Novels CLR 165: 1-79
overviews and general studies, 4-10
literary elements in graphic novels, 10-42
coming-of-age and immigrant perspectives in graphic novels, 42-59
Jewish graphic novels, 59-79

Graveyard Poets LC 67: 131-212
origins and development, 131-52
major figures, 152-75
major works, 175-212

The Great War, Literature of the See Literature of the Great War

Greek Historiography CMLC 17: 1-49

Greek Lyric Poetry, The Rise of CMLC 77: 226-329
overviews, 229-46
literary history, 246-72
themes and style, 272-302
representative authors, 302-28

Greek Mythology CMLC 26: 193-320
overviews and general studies, 194-209
origins and development of Greek mythology, 209-29
cosmogonies and divinities in Greek mythology, 229-54
heroes and heroines in Greek mythology, 254-80
women in Greek mythology, 280-320

Greek Theater CMLC 51: 1-58
criticism, 2-58

Hard-Boiled Crime Novels TCLC 317: 1-199
overviews and general studies, 5-41
what is hard-boiled fiction?, 41-87
feminism and hard-boiled crime novels, 87-176
the African American perspective in hard-boiled fiction, 176-94
the lasting influence of the hard-boiled tradition, 194-98

Hard-Boiled Detective Stories SSC 212: 93-230
overview and general study, 95-108
pulp magazines, 108-46
hard-boiled short fiction, 146-228

Hard-Boiled Fiction TCLC 118: 1-109
overviews and general studies, 2-39
major authors, 39-76
women and hard-boiled fiction, 76-109

The Harlem Renaissance HR 1: 1-563
overviews and general studies of the Harlem Renaissance, 1-137
primary sources, 3-12
overviews, 12-38
background and sources of the Harlem Renaissance, 38-56
the New Negro aesthetic, 56-91
patrons, promoters, and the New York Public Library, 91-121
women of the Harlem Renaissance, 121-37
social, economic, and political factors that influenced the Harlem Renaissance, 139-240
primary sources, 141-53
overviews, 153-87
social and economic factors, 187-213
Black intellectual and political thought, 213-40
publishing and periodicals during the Harlem Renaissance, 243-339
primary sources, 246-52
overviews, 252-68
African American writers and mainstream publishers, 268-91
anthologies: *The New Negro* and others, 291-309
African American periodicals and the Harlem Renaissance, 309-39
performing arts during the Harlem Renaissance, 341-465
primary sources, 343-48
overviews, 348-64
drama of the Harlem Renaissance, 364-92
influence of music on Harlem Renaissance writing, 437-65
visual arts during the Harlem Renaissance, 467-563
primary sources, 470-71
overviews, 471-517
painters, 517-36
sculptors, 536-58
photographers, 558-63

The Harlem Renaissance TCLC 26: 49-125
principal issues and figures, 50-67
the literature and its audience, 67-74
theme and technique in poetry, fiction, and drama, 74-115
and American society, 115-21
achievement and influence, 121-2

The Harlem Renaissance See Literature of the Harlem Renaissance

Havel, Václav, Playwright and President CLC 65: 406-63

Hawaiian Children's Literature CLR 125: 40-85
overviews and general studies, 43-9
depictions of Hawaiians in children's literature, 49-70
fantasy and myth in Hawaiian children's literature, 70-85

Hellenistic Age, The CMLC 87: 98-267
overviews, 101-48
library at Alexandria, 148-67
Hellenistic literature, 167-241
Hellenistic science and culture, 242-65

Heroic Drama LC 91: 249-373
definitions and overviews, 251-78
politics and heroic drama, 278-303
early plays: Dryden and Orrery, 303-51
later plays: Lee and Otway, 351-73

Hero's Journey in the Ancient Epic, The CMLC 148: 171-340
the journeys: incidents and themes, 173-217
the hero and the journey, 217-253
mythic elements of the journeys, 253-299
katabasis and *nostos* in the epics, 299-338

Hillarian Circle, The LC 223: 227-340
overviews, 230-69
Eliza Haywood, 269-310
Aaron Hill, 310-16
Martha Fowke Sansom, 316-39

Hip-hop Fiction See Street Lit

Historical Fiction in Children's Literature CLR 124: 121-92
overviews and general studies, 124-48
race, war, and genocide in historical fiction for children, 148-68
critical issues in historical fiction for children, 168-77
individual works of juvenile historical fiction, 177-91

Historical Fiction, Nineteenth-Century NCLC 48: 212-307
definitions and characteristics, 213-36
Victorian historical fiction, 236-65
American historical fiction, 265-88
realism in historical fiction, 288-306

Hollywood and Literature TCLC 118: 110-251
overviews and general studies, 111-20
adaptations, 120-65
socio-historical and cultural impact, 165-206
theater and hollywood, 206-51

Holocaust and the Atomic Bomb: Fifty Years Later CLC 91: 331-82
the Holocaust remembered, 333-52
Anne Frank revisited, 352-62
the atomic bomb and American memory, 362-81

Holocaust, Contemporary Literature of the CLC 252: 60-217
general overviews, 63-106
literary models of Holocaust representation, 106-36
the generation after, 136-201
post-Holocaust philosophy, theology, and ethics, 201-06
the Binjamin Wilkomirski affair, 206-16

Holocaust Denial Literature TCLC 58: 1-110
overviews and general studies, 1-30
Robert Faurisson and Noam Chomsky, 30-52
Holocaust denial literature in America, 52-71
library access to Holocaust denial literature, 72-5
the authenticity of Anne Frank's diary, 76-90
David Irving and the "normalization" of Hitler, 90-109

Holocaust in Children's Literature, Representations of the CLR 110: 104-75
overviews and general studies, 107-36
fictional accounts of the Holocaust for children, 136-68
Holocaust diaries written by children and young adults, 168-74

Holocaust, Literature of the TCLC 42: 355-450
historical overview, 357-61
critical overview, 361-70
diaries and memoirs, 370-95
novels and short stories, 395-425
poetry, 425-41
drama, 441-8

Homosexuality in Children's Literature CLR 119: 101-69
overviews and general studies, 104-12
portrayals of gay and lesbian adolescence, 112-53
presentations of gay and lesbian families in children's literature, 153-68

Homosexuality in Nineteenth-Century Literature NCLC 56: 78-182
defining homosexuality, 80-111
Greek love, 111-44
trial and danger, 144-81
NCLC 180: 246-358
defining homosexuality, 249-84
treatment by women writers, 284-327
treatment in works by Henry James, Nathaniel Hawthorne, and Fitz-Greene Halleck, 327-58

Humanism NCLC 228: 60-145
criticism, 61-145

Humor in Children's Literature CLR 147: 65-133
overviews and general studies, 68-78
analyses of humor in individual and series works for children, 78-109
authorial perspectives on writing humor for children, 109-18
cultural humor in children's literature, 118-32

Humors Comedy LC 85: 194-324
overviews, 195-251
major figures: Ben Jonson, 251-93
major figures: William Shakespeare, 293-324

Hungarian Literature of the Twentieth Century TCLC 26: 126-88
surveys of, 126-47
Nyugat and early twentieth-century literature, 147-56
mid-century literature, 156-68
and politics, 168-78
since the 1956 revolt, 178-87

Hysteria in Nineteenth-Century Literature NCLC 64: 59-184
the history of hysteria, 60-75
the gender of hysteria, 75-103
hysteria and women's narratives, 103-57
hysteria in nineteenth-century poetry, 157-83

Image of the Noble Savage in Literature LC 79: 136-252
overviews and development, 136-76
the Noble Savage in the New World, 176-221
Rousseau and the French Enlightenment's view of the noble savage, 221-51

Imagism TCLC 74: 259-454
history and development, 260
major figures, 288
sources and influences, 352
Imagism and other movements, 397
influence and legacy, 431

Immigrants in Nineteenth-Century Literature, Representation of NCLC 112: 188-298
overview, 189-99
immigrants in America, 199-223
immigrants and labor, 223-60
immigrants in England, 260-97

Imperialism NCLC 208: 103-277
overview, 106-31
British Imperialism in Africa, 131-43
Imperialism in juvenile literature, 143-203
British Imperialism in India, 203-39
Imperialism and adventure literature, 240-62
British Imperialism in Scotland, 262-75

Imperialism in Short Fiction SSC 216: 1-121
Imperialism as a social force, 4-50
Imperialism, violence, and corruption, 50-91
lasting effects of Imperialism, 92-119

Incest in Nineteenth-Century American Literature NCLC 76: 70-141
overview, 71-88
the concern for social order, 88-117
authority and authorship, 117-40

Incest in Victorian Literature NCLC 92: 172-318
overviews and general studies, 173-85
novels, 185-276
plays, 276-84
poetry, 284-318

India, Representations of, in Early Modern Literature See Representations of India in Early Modern Literature

Indian Literature, Contemporary CLC 247: 218-90
overviews, 221-36
Indian writing in English, 236-63
trends and themes, 263-90

Indian Literature in English TCLC 54: 308-406
overview, 309-13
origins and major figures, 313-25
the Indo-English novel, 325-55
Indo-English poetry, 355-67
Indo-English drama, 367-72
critical perspectives on Indo-English literature, 372-80
modern Indo-English literature, 380-9
Indo-English authors on their work, 389-404

Indian Literature in English TCLC 226: 1-164
overviews, 2-24
major authors, 24-81
female Indian authors writing in English, 81-97
postcolonialism and disapora, 97-117
Indian poetry written in English, 117-163

The Industrial Revolution in Literature NCLC 56: 183-273
historical and cultural perspectives, 184-201
contemporary reactions to the machine, 201-21
themes and symbols in literature, 221-73

The Influence of Disney on Children's Literature CLR 143: 20-102
overviews and general studies, 24-39
Disney's adaptation of A. A. Milne's *Winnie-the-Pooh,* 39-52
other adaptations of children's literature by Disney, 52-72
approaches to feminist themes in Disney films, 72-86
depictions of colonialism and animal rights in Disney films, 86-101

The Influence of Ernest Hemingway TCLC 162: 122-259
overviews, 123-43
writers on Hemingway, 143-58
Hemingway's evocation of place, 158-84
gender and identity, 184-229
Hemingway and the quest for meaning, 229-58

The Influence of William Faulkner TCLC 170: 104-255
overviews, 105-16
Faulkner and narrative, 116-60
Faulkner and psychology, 160-80
Faulkner and race, 180-219
impact on contemporary culture, 219-43
Faulkner and women, 243-54

The Inklings TCLC 258: 205-313
overview, 207-14
group dynamics, 214-65
major authors, 266-313

International Children's Literature CLR 114: 55-120
overviews and general studies, 57-64
cultural and political influences on international children's literature, 64-105
examinations of regional and national children's literature, 105-120

Interregnum Literature See Literature of the Interregnum

Iranian Diaspora, Writers of See Writers of the Iranian Diaspora

Iraq War Literature CLC 346: 118-201
politics and media in the Iraq War, 120-50
combat trauma, 150-56
gendering the Iraq War, 156-71
writing the enemy, 171-200

Irish Children's Literature CLR 123: 77-127
overviews and general studies, 81-93
mythology in Irish children's literature, 93-100
history in Irish children's literature, 100-119
studies of children's works by Irish authors, 119-127

The Irish Famine as Represented in Nineteenth-Century Literature NCLC 64: 185-261
overviews and general studies, 187-98
historical background, 198-212
famine novels, 212-34
famine poetry, 234-44
famine letters and eye-witness accounts, 245-61

Irish Literary Renaissance TCLC 46: 172-287
overview, 173-83
development and major figures, 184-202
influence of Irish folklore and mythology, 202-22
Irish poetry, 222-34
Irish drama and the Abbey Theatre, 234-56
Irish fiction, 256-86

The Irish Literary Renaissance TCLC 222: 130-245
overviews, 131-88
influences, 188-218
genres and styles, 218-44

Irish Nationalism and Literature NCLC 44: 203-73
the Celtic element in literature, 203-19
anti-Irish sentiment and the Celtic response, 219-34
literary ideals in Ireland, 234-45
literary expressions, 245-73

The Irish Novel NCLC 80: 1-130
overviews and general studies, 3-9
principal figures, 9-22
peasant and middle class Irish novelists, 22-76
aristocratic Irish and Anglo-Irish novelists, 76-129

Irony in Renaissance Love Poetry LC 247: 1-66
origins of irony in Renaissance love poetry, 3-23
irony in early-Renaissance sonnets and sonnet sequences, 23-35
irony in mid- to late-Renaissance love poetry, 35-64

Islam in Contemporary Literature CLC 301: 107-235
Islam in Anglophone Literature or English Translation, 109-149
Islam in Francophone Literature, 149-182
Islam in African Literature, 182-202
Women and Islam, 202-234

Islam in Western Nineteenth-Century Life and Literature NCLC 188: 90-173
Islam in European literature and thought, 92-154
Islam in Russian life and literature, 154-73

Islamic Literature in English TCLC 238: 142-255
overviews and general studies, 143-78
major authors, 178-213
africa and Islam, 213-24
women and Islamic literature, 225-54

Israeli Literature TCLC 94: 1-137
overviews and general studies, 2-18
Israeli fiction, 18-33
Israeli poetry, 33-62
Israeli drama, 62-91
women and Israeli literature, 91-112
Arab characters in Israeli literature, 112-36

Israeli Literature, Contemporary CLC 240: 152-278
overviews and general studies, 156-86
major authors and representative works, 186-268
poets, 268-77

Italian Futurism See Futurism, Italian

Italian Humanism LC 12: 205-77
origins and early development, 206-18
revival of classical letters, 218-23
humanism and other philosophies, 224-39
humanism and humanists, 239-46
the plastic arts, 246-57
achievement and significance, 258-76

The Italian Novella SSC 164: 230-318
overviews and general studies, 231-272
major authors in the Italian novella tradition, 272-318

Italian Romanticism NCLC 60: 85-145
origins and overviews, 86-101
Italian Romantic theory, 101-25
the language of romanticism, 125-45

Jacobean Drama LC 33: 1-37
the Jacobean worldview: an era of transition, 2-14
the moral vision of Jacobean drama, 14-22
Jacobean tragedy, 22-3
the Jacobean masque, 23-36

Jamaican Literature TCLC 246: 198-309
overviews and general studies, 201-34
major Jamaican writers, 234-62
Jamaican fiction, 262-74
Jamaican poetry, 274-308

Japanese Women Short-Fiction Writers SSC 221: 55-143
challenges to the Japanese literary tradition 60-67
gender discourse 67-89
bodies, sexuality, and pregnancy 89-141

Jazz and Literature TCLC 102: 3-124

Jewish American Fiction TCLC 62: 1-181
overviews and general studies, 2-24
major figures, 24-48
Jewish writers and American life, 48-78
Jewish characters in American fiction, 78-108
themes in Jewish-American fiction, 108-43
Jewish-American women writers, 143-59
the Holocaust and Jewish-American fiction, 159-81

Jewish American Literature TCLC 250: 108-240
the immigrant experience, 131-75
major authors, 175-200
Holocaust literature, 200-39

Jewish American Poetry CLC 323: 151-250
the identity of the Jewish American poet, 153-87
major themes, 187-227
a voice for women, 227-35
major poets, 235-50

Jewish Children's Literature CLR 154: 1-49
Jewish characters in children's literature, 19-40
Jewish culture in children's literature, 40-5
reviews of Jewish children's literature, 45-9

Jews in Literature TCLC 118: 252-417
overviews and general studies, 253-97
representing the Jew in literature, 297-351
the Holocaust in literature, 351-416

The Journals of Lewis and Clark NCLC 100: 1-88
overviews and general studies, 4-30
journal-keeping methods, 30-46
Fort Mandan, 46-51
the Clark journal, 51-65
the journals as literary texts, 65-87

Judaism in Nineteenth-Century Literature NCLC 176: 1-89
contemporary commentary, 3-7
Judaism in German theory and culture, 7-63
treatment of Zionism, 63-88

Juvenile and Young Adult Science Fiction CLR 116: 135-89
overviews and general studies, 139-61
appeal of science fiction to young readers, 161-68
futurism in young adult science fiction, 168-89

Juvenile Detective Fiction CLR 158: 62-130
overviews and general studies, 65-78
cultural and national juvenile detective literatures, 78-107
juvenile detective series fiction, 107-30

Kabuki DC 42: 217-312
overviews and general studies, 219-36
significant works, 236-64
Kabuki conventions and techniques, 264-311

Kabuki LC 73: 118-232
overviews and general studies, 120-40
the development of Kabuki, 140-65
major works, 165-95
Kabuki and society, 195-231

King Alfred the Great, The Age of See The Age of King Alfred the Great

The Kit-Kat Club LC 71: 66-112
overviews and general studies, 67-88
major figures, 88-107
attacks on the Kit-Kat Club, 107-12

The Knickerbocker Group NCLC 56: 274-341
overviews and general studies, 276-314
Knickerbocker periodicals, 314-26
writers and artists, 326-40

Künstlerroman TCLC 150: 133-260
overviews and general studies, 135-51
major works, 151-212
feminism in the *Künstlerroman,* 212-49
minority *Künstlerroman,* 249-59

The Lake Poets NCLC 52: 217-304
characteristics of the Lake Poets and their works, 218-27
literary influences and collaborations, 227-66
defining and developing Romantic ideals, 266-84
embracing Conservatism, 284-303

Language Poets TCLC 126: 66-172
overviews and general studies, 67-122
selected major figures in language poetry, 122-72

Larkin, Philip, Controversy CLC 81: 417-64

Latin American Literature, Twentieth-Century TCLC 58: 111-98
historical and critical perspectives, 112-36
the novel, 136-45
the short story, 145-9
drama, 149-60
poetry, 160-7
the writer and society, 167-86
Native Americans in Latin American literature, 186-97

Law and Literature TCLC 126: 173-347
overviews and general studies, 174-253
fiction critiquing the law, 253-88
literary responses to the law, 289-346

The Legend of El Dorado LC 74: 248-350
overviews, 249-308
major explorations for El Dorado, 308-50

The Legend of Pope Joan LC 123: 1-88
overviews and general studies, 3-87

Lesbian Literature, Contemporary CLC 320: 215-328
groundbreaking books and authors: the pulps and beyond, 217-29
patriarchal cultures: reclaiming female history and identity, 229-58
genre fiction, 258-89
more margins: the immigrant lesbian experience, 289-94
the publishing and marketing of lesbian literature, 294-327

The Levellers LC 51: 200-312
overviews and general studies, 201-29
principal figures, 230-86
religion, political philosophy, and pamphleteering, 287-311

The Lilith Legend in Modern Literature TCLC 170: 256-319
overviews, 257-67
historical and literary background, 267-89
the Lilith legend in twentieth-century literature, 289-319

Literary Criticism in the Nineteenth Century, American NCLC 128: 1-103
overviews and general studies, 2-44
the transcendentalists, 44-65
"young America," 65-71
James Russell Lowell, 71-9
Edgar Allan Poe, 79-97
Walt Whitman, 97-102

Literary Darwinism CLC 385: 131-323
overviews and general studies, 133-252
Literary Darwinism's critique of post-structuralism, 252-79
criticism of Literary Darwinism, 279-82
Darwinian analysis of literature, 282-322

Literary Expressionism TCLC 142: 90-185
overviews and general studies, 91-138
themes in literary expressionism, 138-61
expressionism in Germany, 161-84

The Literary Marketplace Nineteenth-Century NCLC 128: 194-368
overviews and general studies, 197-228
British literary marketplace, 228-66
French literary marketplace, 266-82
American literary marketplace, 282-323
women in the literary marketplace, 323-67

Literary Patronage in the Elizabethan Age LC 60-147
overviews 61-80
the patrons 80-92
the poets 92-130
theatrical patronage 130-145

Literary Prizes TCLC 122: 130-203
overviews and general studies, 131-34
the Nobel Prize in Literature, 135-83
the Pulitzer Prize, 183-203

Literature and Millenial Lists CLC 119: 431-67
the Modern Library list, 433
the Waterstone list, 438-439

Literature in Response to the September 11 Attacks CLC 174: 1-46
major works about September 11, 2001, 2-22
critical, artistic, and journalistic responses, 22-45

Literature of the American Cowboy NCLC 96: 1-60
overview, 3-20
cowboy fiction, 20-36
cowboy poetry and songs, 36-59

Literature of the California Gold Rush NCLC 92: 320-85
overviews and general studies, 322-24
early California Gold Rush fiction, 324-44
Gold Rush folklore and legend, 344-51
the rise of Western local color, 351-60
social relations and social change, 360-385

Literature of the Counter-Reformation LC 109: 213-56
overviews and general studies, 214-33
influential figures, 233-56

Literature of the Great War TCLC 226: 165-273
overviews, 165-95
the great war's impact on writers, 195-244
poetry of the great war, 244-73

Literature of the Great War TCLC 230: 209-380
women writers and the great war, 211-68
World War I and modernism, 268-330
propaganda and World War I literature, 330-79

Literature of the Harlem Renaissance TCLC 218: 260-376
overviews and general studies, 261-78
major figures, 279-318
poetry of the Harlem Renaissance, 318-47
women of the Harlem Renaissance, 347-75

Literature of the Interregnum LC 159: 219-301
Interregnum views on theater, 221-39
poetry of the Interregnum, 239-59
prose of the Interregnum, 259-301

Little Magazines TCLC 194: 126-240
overviews, 127-46
little magazines and African American literature, 146-84
little magazines and literary trends, 184-227
little magazines and poetry, 227-39

The Living Theatre DC 16: 154-214

The Lost Generation See Writers of the Lost Generation

Luddism in Nineteenth-Century Literature NCLC 140: 280-365
overviews, 281-322
the literary response, 322-65

Lynching in Nineteenth-Century Literature NCLC 148: 162-247
lynching in literature and music, 163-92
Ida B. Wells-Barnett and the anti-lynching movement, 192-221
resistance to lynching in society and the press, 221-46

Machiavellism LC 167: 160-259
overview, 161-73
Machiavellism in literature, 173-212
Machiavellism in philosophy, politics, and religion, 212-58

MAD Magazine CLR 109: 156-208
overviews and general studies, 158-74
Harvey Kurtzman and the founding of MAD Magazine, 174-84
critical commentary on MAD Magazine, 184-203
the evolving role of MAD Magazine in modern society, 203-07

Madness in Nineteenth-Century Literature NCLC 76: 142-284
overview, 143-54
autobiography, 154-68
poetry, 168-215
fiction, 215-83
NCLC 228: 146-310
British fiction writers: Stevenson, Dickens, Collins, and Hardy, 148-83
English poets: Shelley, Byron, Hopkins, and Tennyson, 183-220
French writers, 220-48
Herman Melville, 248-58
women writers, 258-309

Madness in Twentieth-Century Literature TCLC 50: 160-225
overviews and general studies, 161-71
madness and the creative process, 171-86
suicide, 186-91
madness in American literature, 191-207
madness in German literature, 207-13
madness and feminist artists, 213-24

Magic Realism TCLC 110: 80-327
overviews and general studies, 81-94
magic realism in African literature, 95-110
magic realism in American literature, 110-32
magic realism in Canadian literature, 132-46
magic realism in European literature, 146-66
magic realism in Asian literature, 166-79
magic realism in Latin-American literature, 179-223
magic realism in Israeli literature and the novels of Salman Rushdie, 223-38
magic realism in literature written by women, 239-326

Magical Realism in Short Fiction SSC 148: 106-205
magical realism in Hispanic short fiction, 108-65
magical realism in North American short fiction, 165-84
magical realism as protest, 184-205

Major Cities in Nineteenth-Century Literature NCLC 176: 90-233
London and Paris in poetry, 93-99
London, 99-122
New York City, 122-65
Paris, 165-94
Rome, 194-217
St. Petersburg, 217-32

Marriage in Nineteenth-Century Life and Literature NCLC 232: 96-221
overview, 98-110
divorce, 110-32
social and literary conventions, 132-77
women writers, 177-220

Marriage in the Short Story SSC 139: 204-332
international perspectives on marriage in the short story, 206-66
feminist perspectives on marriage in the short story, 266-318
the depiction of infidelity in the short story, 318-332

The Martin Marprelate Tracts LC 101: 165-240
criticism, 166-240

Marxist Criticism TCLC 134: 127-57
overviews and general studies, 128-67
Marxist interpretations, 167-209
cultural and literary Marxist theory, 209-49
Marxism and feminist critical theory, 250-56

Masculinity in the Short Story SSC 138: 90-128
masculinity in gothic short fiction 93-128
masculinity and sexual orientation 128-76
masculinity from a feminist perspective 176-205
masculinity in modern society 205-34

The Masque LC 63: 124-265
development of the masque, 125-62
sources and structure, 162-220
race and gender in the masque, 221-64

McCarthyism and Literature TCLC 190: 218-383
overviews 220-58
poetry and fiction in the McCarthy era 258-316
theater in the McCarthy era 316-50
film and television in the McCarthy era 351-83

Medical Writing LC 55: 93-195
colonial America, 94-110
enlightenment, 110-24
medieval writing, 124-40
sexuality, 140-83
vernacular, 185-95

Memoirs of Trauma CLC 109: 419-466
overview, 420
criticism, 429

Memoirs, Truth in CLC 226: 253-88
arguments for and against fictionalization, 254-69
reaction to James Frey's *A Million Little Pieces,* 269-80
other suspected and proven memoir hoaxes, 280-88

Mental Illness in Short Fiction SSC 146: 74-232
depictions of mental illness in European and Russian short fiction, 75-127
depictions of mental illness in American short fiction, 127-75
women and mental illness in short fiction, 175-232

Mesmerism in Nineteenth-Century Literature NCLC 216: 104-264
overviews, 106-24
women authors, 125-49
Nathaniel Hawthorne, 149-204
other authors, 205-64

Metafiction TCLC 130: 43-228
overviews and general studies, 44-85
Spanish metafiction, 85-117
studies of metafictional authors and works, 118-228

Metaphysical Poets LC 24: 356-439
early definitions, 358-67
surveys and overviews, 367-92
cultural and social influences, 392-406
stylistic and thematic variations, 407-38

Metrical Psalms LC 129: 85-180
overviews, 87-180

Mexican Literature, Nineteenth-Century NCLC 200: 1-159
overviews, 2-49
national identity, 49-95
politics and reform, 96-136
race and culture, 136-59

Middle Eastern Literature TCLC 262: 95-200
overviews and general studies, 96-113
major Middle Eastern authors and works, 113-69
the role of women writers in Middle Eastern literature, 169-99

Missionaries in the Nineteenth-Century, Literature of NCLC 112: 299-392
history and development, 300-16
uses of ethnography, 316-31
sociopolitical concerns, 331-82
David Livingstone, 382-91

Modern Arabic Literature TCLC 282: 111-220
the historical context, 113-37
major authors, 137-47
women authors and gender issues, 147-89
the Arab Jew, 189-219

The Modern Essay TCLC 58: 199-273
overview, 200-7
the essay in the early twentieth century, 207-19
characteristics of the modern essay, 219-32
modern essayists, 232-45
the essay as a literary genre, 245-73

Modern French Literature TCLC 122: 205-359
overviews and general studies, 207-43
French theater, 243-77
gender issues and French women writers, 277-315
ideology and politics, 315-24
modern French poetry, 324-41
resistance literature, 341-58

Modern Irish Literature TCLC 102: 125-321
overview, 129-44
dramas, 144-70
fiction, 170-247
poetry, 247-321

Modern Japanese Literature TCLC 66: 284-389
poetry, 285-305
drama, 305-29
fiction, 329-61
western influences, 361-87

Modernism TCLC 70: 165-275
definitions, 166-84
Modernism and earlier influences, 184-200
stylistic and thematic traits, 200-29
poetry and drama, 229-42
redefining Modernism, 242-75

Modernist Lyric Poetry TCLC 270: 1-105
overviews, 2-21
major poets, 21-104

Monasticism and Literature CMLC 74: 88-294
major figures, 89-132
secular influences, 132-54
monastic principles and literary practices, 154-232
women and monasticism, 232-93

Monster Literature, Contemporary CLC 330: 193-319
introduction: monsters and their meanings, 195-217
surveys of the literature, 217-51
major authors and works, 251-300
the vampire in popular culture, 300-18

Money in Nineteenth-Century Literature NCLC 236: 105-97
ethics, morality, and civilization, 106-66
women authors, 166-96

Mother Goose CLR 117: 35-123
overviews and general studies, 38-50
historical and literary origins of Mother Goose, 50-84
gender, race, and pedagogy in Mother Goose, 84-120
contemporary editions of Mother Goose nursery rhymes, 120-22

Motherhood in Nineteenth-Century Literature NCLC 176: 234-338
overviews, 236-60
maternal archetypes: good, bad, and absent, 260-89
motherhood, patriarchy, and the social order, 289-316
motherhood and oppression, 316-338

Mothers in Short Fiction SSC 150: 108-237
the role of the mother in society, 111-50
major themes, 150-96
mothers and daughters, 196-216
mothers and sons, 216-36

Motivational Literature CLC 269: 244-373
the early positive psychology movement, 245-48
religious and spiritual inspiration, 248-80
the "Chicken Soup" phenomenon, 280-99
new age messages, 299-330
the modern motivational industry, 330-45

Mozambican Short-Fiction Writers SSC 216: 241-320
themes of political oppression, 243-253
effects of colonialism, 253-288
depictions of Mozambican life, 288-318

Muckraking Movement in American Journalism TCLC 34: 161-242
development, principles, and major figures, 162-70
publications, 170-9
social and political ideas, 179-86
targets, 186-208
fiction, 208-19
decline, 219-29
impact and accomplishments, 229-40

Multiculturalism CLC 189: 167-254
overviews and general studies, 168-93
the effects of multiculturalism on global literature, 193-213
multicultural themes in specific contemporary works, 213-53

Multiculturalism in Literature and Education CLC 70: 361-413

Music and Modern Literature TCLC 62: 182-329
overviews and general studies, 182-211
musical form/literary form, 211-32
music in literature, 232-50
the influence of music on literature, 250-73
literature and popular music, 273-303
jazz and poetry, 303-28

The Musical DC 34: 147-360
overviews and general studies, 149-78
race and the musical, 178-256
women and the musical, 256-84
Rodgers and Hammerstein, 284-319
Stephen Sondheim, 319-44
other major figures, 344-58

Mystery Story See Crime-Mystery-Detective Stories

Native American Autobiography, Nineteenth-Century NCLC 64: 262-389
overview, 263-8
problems of authorship, 268-81
the evolution of Native American autobiography, 281-304
political issues, 304-15
gender and autobiography, 316-62
autobiographical works during the turn of the century, 362-88

Native American Children's Literature CLR 130: 123-87
overviews and general studies, 127-48
critically evaluating Native American children's literature, 148-74
native versus non-native authorship of Native American children's literature, 174-87

Native American Literature CLC 76: 440-76

Native American Short Stories SSC 140: 171-340
overviews, 174-87
oral tales: literary renderings, transcriptions, and translations, 187-211
major authors and their works, 211-44
women and native american short stories, 244-338

Native North American Literature, Contemporary CLC 265: 87-209
themes of identity in Native North American Literature, 89-157
representative poetry, prose, and drama, 157-185
women and Native North American Literature, 185-208

Natural School, Russian NCLC 24: 205-40
history and characteristics, 205-25
contemporary criticism, 225-40

Naturalism NCLC 36: 285-382
definitions and theories, 286-305
critical debates on Naturalism, 305-16
Naturalism in theater, 316-32
European Naturalism, 332-61
American Naturalism, 361-72
the legacy of Naturalism, 372-81

Negritude TCLC 50: 226-361
origins and evolution, 227-56
definitions, 256-91
Negritude in literature, 291-343
Negritude reconsidered, 343-58

Negritude TCLC 158: 196-280
overviews and general studies, 197-208
major figures, 208-25
Negritude and humanism, 225-29
poetry of Negritude, 229-47
politics of Negritude, 247-68
the Negritude debate, 268-79

The New Criticism TCLC 34: 243-318
development and ideas, 244-70
debate and defense, 270-99
influence and legacy, 299-315
TCLC 146: 1-108
overviews and general studies, 3-19
defining New Criticism, 19-28
place in history, 28-51
poetry and New Criticism, 51-78
major authors, 78-108
TCLC 266: 217-308
themes and applications, 218-81
the critics, 281-308

The New Humanists TCLC 162: 260-341
overviews, 261-92

major figures, 292-310
New Humanism in education and literature, 310-41

New South, Literature of the NCLC 116: 122-240
overviews, 124-66
the novel in the New South, 166-209
myth of the Old South in the New, 209-39

The New Woman in Nineteenth-Century Literature NCLC 156: 134-281
overview, 136-39
historical and social context, 139-57
contemporary descriptions of the new woman, 157-65
the new woman and popular fiction, 165-86
the new woman and the decadents, 187-207
the new woman and the theater, 207-48
Henry James, Bram Stoker, and Others, 248-80

The New World in Renaissance Literature LC 31: 1-51
overview, 1-18
utopia vs. terror, 18-31
explorers and Native Americans, 31-51

New York Intellectuals and *Partisan Review* TCLC 30: 117-98
development and major figures, 118-28
influence of Judaism, 128-39
Partisan Review, 139-57
literary philosophy and practice, 157-75
political philosophy, 175-87
achievement and significance, 187-97

The New Yorker TCLC 58: 274-357
overviews and general studies, 274-95
major figures, 295-304
New Yorker style, 304-33
fiction, journalism, and humor at *The New Yorker,* 333-48
the new *New Yorker,* 348-56

Newgate Novel NCLC 24: 166-204
development of Newgate literature, 166-73
Newgate Calendar, 173-7
Newgate fiction, 177-95
Newgate drama, 195-204

New Orleans in Nineteenth-Century Literature NCLC 216: 265-356
overview, 266-80
Kate Chopin, 280-301
Creole authors, 301-30
drama, 330-56

New Zealand Literature TCLC 134: 258-368
overviews and general studies, 260-300
Maori literature, 300-22
New Zealand drama, 322-32
New Zealand fiction, 332-51
New Zealand poetry, 351-67

Nigerian Fiction, Contemporary CLC 343: 106-205
Chinua Achebe: the progenitor of contemporary African literature, 108-31
post-independence disillusionment, 131-50
the new Nigerian novel, 150-86
market literature: the popular Romance, 186-204

Nigerian Literature of the Twentieth Century TCLC 30: 199-265
surveys of, 199-227
English language and African life, 227-45
politics and the Nigerian writer, 245-54
Nigerian writers and society, 255-62

Nihilism and Literature TCLC 110: 328-93
overviews and general studies, 328-44
European and Russian nihilism, 344-73
nihilism in the works of Albert Camus, Franz Kafka, and John Barth, 373-92

Nineteenth-Century American Women Social Activists: Emancipation NCLC 300: 1-164
overviews and general studies, 4-33
views from white writers, 33-67
views from black writers, 67-143
black oratory, 143-62

Nineteenth-Century American Women Social Activists: Indian Rights NCLC 300: 165-324
white women writers and Indian reform, 168-226
Indian rights and feminism, 226-76
Native American women writers, 276-91
tropes of Indianness in nineteenth-century American literature, 291-322

Nineteenth-Century American Women Social Activists: Labor NCLC 310: 1-76
perspectives on Lowell, 3-20
work and the "cult of true womanhood", 20-30
women's labor movements and race, 30-51
poverty and pollution, 51-75

Nineteenth-Century American Women Social Activists: Temperance NCLC 310: 77-168
temperance activism, 81-110
temperance literature, 110-131
temperance and women's rights, 131-166

Nineteenth-Century American Women Social Activists: Woman's Rights NCLC 310: 169-322
overviews and general studies, 173-270
rights for African American women, 270-300
rights in marriage and divorce, 300-304
right to vote, 304-320

Nineteenth-Century Spanish *Costumbrista* Writers NCLC 304: 239-323
Madrilenian *Costumbrista* writers, 241-77
Andalusian *Costumbrista* writers, 277-322

Noh Drama LC 103: 189-270
overviews, 190-94
origins and development, 194-214
structure, 214-28
types of plays, 228-45
masks in Noh drama, 245-57
Noh drama and the audience, 257-69

Noh Theater CMLC 109: 119-207
overviews and general studies, 120-35
history and development of Noh, 135-71
staging, characters, and themes in Noh theater, 171-207

Noh Theater DC 46: 76-200
overviews and general studies, 79-101
origins and development, 101-18
characters and conventions, 118-36
Noh in performance, 136-81
Noh and society, 182-99

Nonsense Verse CLR 140: 76-126
overviews and general studies, 79-90
Victorian nonsense verse, 90-112
contemporary nonsense verse, 112-25

Norse Mythology CMLC 26: 321-85
history and mythological tradition, 322-44
Eddic poetry, 344-74
Norse mythology and other traditions, 374-85

Norse Mythology CMLC 158: 219-340
general studies: the *Poetic Edda,* 221-45
general studies: the *Prose Edda,* 245-67
the *Eddas*: myths and themes, 267-301
Christian influences on the *Eddas,* 301-03
cross-disciplinary studies of the *Eddas,* 303-39

Northern Humanism LC 16: 281-356
background, 282-305
precursor of the Reformation, 305-14
the Brethren of the Common Life, the Devotio Moderna, and education, 314-40
the impact of printing, 340-56

The Novel of Manners NCLC 56: 342-96
social and political order, 343-53
domestic order, 353-73
depictions of gender, 373-83
the American novel of manners, 383-95

Novels of the Ming and Early Ch'ing Dynasties LC 76: 213-356
overviews and historical development, 214-45
major works—overview, 245-85
genre studies, 285-325
cultural and social themes, 325-55

Nuclear Literature: Writings and Criticism in the Nuclear Age TCLC 46: 288-390
overviews and general studies, 290-301
fiction, 301-35
poetry, 335-8
nuclear war in Russo-Japanese literature, 338-55
nuclear war and women writers, 355-67
the nuclear referent and literary criticism, 367-88

Occultism in Modern Literature TCLC 50: 362-406
influence of occultism on literature, 363-72
occultism, literature, and society, 372-87
fiction, 387-96
drama, 396-405

Opium and the Nineteenth-Century Literary Imagination NCLC 20:250-301
original sources, 250-62
historical background, 262-71
and literary society, 271-9
and literary creativity, 279-300

Orientalism NCLC 96: 149-364
overviews and general studies, 150-98
Orientalism and imperialism, 198-229
Orientalism and gender, 229-59
Orientalism and the nineteenth-century novel, 259-321
Orientalism in nineteenth-century poetry, 321-63

Orphan Stories CLR 137: 90-167
overviews and general studies, 93-123
Dickensian orphan stories, 123-41
moral, colonialist, and naturalist themes in orphan stories, 141-67

Overpopulation in Nineteenth-Century Literature NCLC 184: 108-246
overviews, 110-34
literary representations of social and economic theories, 134-205
regulation of the body, 205-46

The Oxford Movement NCLC 72: 1-197
overviews and general studies, 2-24
background, 24-59
and education, 59-69
religious responses, 69-128
literary aspects, 128-178
political implications, 178-196

The Parnassian Movement NCLC 72: 198-241
overviews and general studies, 199-231
and epic form, 231-38
and positivism, 238-41

Pastoral Literature of the English Renaissance LC 59: 171-282
overviews and general studies, 172-214
principal figures of the Elizabethan period, 214-33

principal figures of the later Renaissance, 233-50
pastoral drama, 250-81

Penny Dreadfuls CLR 105: 123-93
overviews and general studies, 125-63
critical reviews of penny dreadfuls featuring Jack Sheppard, 163-80
penny dreadful authors and publishers, 180-93

Periodicals, Nineteenth-Century American NCLC 132: 199-374
overviews, chronology, and development, 200-41
literary periodicals, 241-83
regional periodicals, 283-317
women's magazines and gender issues, 317-47
minority periodicals, 347-72

Periodicals, Nineteenth-Century British NCLC 24: 100-65
overviews and general studies, 100-30
in the Romantic Age, 130-41
in the Victorian era, 142-54
and the reviewer, 154-64

Physiognomy in Nineteenth-Century Literature NCLC 212: 269-361
overviews, 271-329
women authors, 329-40
theater, 340-60

Picaresque Literature of the Sixteenth and Seventeenth Centuries LC 78: 223-355
context and development, 224-71
genre, 271-98
the picaro, 299-326
the picara, 326-53

Picture Books CLR 142: 65-147
overviews and general studies, 68-116
multicultural picture books, 116-40
literary aspects of picture books, 140-47

Pilgrimage Literature CMLC 115: 233-393
overviews and themes, 234-300
major authors and works, 300-72
pilgrimage in travel writing, 372-91

Plath, Sylvia, and the Nature of Biography CLC 86: 433-62
the nature of biography, 433-52
reviews of *The Silent Woman,* 452-61

Poetomachia LC 193: 239-338
the quarrel, 240-55
the plays, 255-338

The Political Novel TCLC 234: 1-127
overviews, 3-30
major authors and works, 30-63
African American political novels, 64-92
the political novel abroad, 92-126

Political Theory from the 15th to the 18th Century LC 36: 1-55
overview, 1-26
natural law, 26-42
empiricism, 42-55

Polish Romanticism NCLC 52: 305-71
overviews and general studies, 306-26
major figures, 326-40
Polish Romantic drama, 340-62
influences, 362-71

Politics and Literature TCLC 94: 138-61
overviews and general studies, 139-96
Europe, 196-226
Latin America, 226-48
Africa and the Caribbean, 248-60

Pornography, Nineteenth-Century NCLC 144: 108-202
nineteenth-century pornographers, 110-64
pornography and literature, 164-91
pornography and censorship, 191-201

The Portrayal of Mormonism NCLC 96: 61-148
overview, 63-72
early Mormon literature, 72-100
Mormon periodicals and journals, 100-10
women writers, 110-22
Mormonism and nineteenth-century literature, 122-42
Mormon poetry, 142-47

Post-apartheid Literature CLC 187: 284-382
overviews and general studies, 286-318
the post-apartheid novel, 318-65
post-apartheid drama, 365-81

Postcolonial African Literature TCLC 146: 110-239
overviews and general studies, 111-45
ideology and theory, 145-62
postcolonial testimonial literature, 162-99
major authors, 199-239

Postcolonialism TCLC 114: 134-239
overviews and general studies, 135-153
African postcolonial writing, 153-72
Asian/Pacific literature, 172-78
postcolonial literary theory, 178-213
postcolonial women's writing, 213-38
TCLC 254: 178-302
overviews and postcolonial literary theory, 180-99
major postcolonial authors, 199-279
themes and regions in postcolonial literature, 279-302

Postcolonial Literature: Asia and Africa CLC 336: 186-271
postcolonial literary theory, 188-223
the postcolonial novel in Africa, 223-49
the postcolonial novel in Asia, 249-71

Postmodernism TCLC 90:125-307
overview, 126-166
criticism, 166-224
fiction, 224-282
poetry, 282-300
drama, 300-307

Poverty and Wealth in Eighteenth-Century English Literature LC 131:192-291
overview, 193-99
Defoe and the Augustans, 199-239
the novel and sensibility, 239-67
poetry and Pre-romanticism, 267-90

Pragmatism in Nineteenth-Century Literature NCLC 168: 85-209
overviews, 86-133
pragmatism and literature, 133-52
Charles Sanders Peirce, 152-65
William James, 165-208

Pre-Raphaelite Movement NCLC 20: 302-401
overview, 302-4
genesis, 304-12
Germ and *Oxford and Cambridge Magazine,* 312-20
Robert Buchanan and the "Fleshly School of Poetry," 320-31
satires and parodies, 331-4
surveys, 334-51
aesthetics, 351-75
sister arts of poetry and painting, 375-94
influence, 394-9

The Pre-Raphaelites NCLC 196: 98-239
overview, 100-24
sources of inspiration, 124-55
women and sexuality, 156-223
impact on individual works, 223-39

Pre-romanticism LC 40: 1-56
overviews and general studies, 2-14
defining the period, 14-23
new directions in poetry and prose, 23-45
the focus on the self, 45-56

The Presentation of Literature in the Nineteenth Century NCLC 160: 159-226
book design, 160-71
gift books, 172-91
serial novels, 191-214
dime novels, 214-226

Presidential Memoirs, Contemporary CLC 272
general commentary, 177-79
Presidents' memoirs, 179-208
First Ladies' memoirs, 208-17
candidates' memoirs, 217-44

Pre-Socratic Philosophy CMLC 22: 1-56
overviews and general studies, 3-24
the Ionians and the Pythagoreans, 25-35
Heraclitus, the Eleatics, and the Atomists, 36-47
the Sophists, 47-55

The Prison in Nineteenth-Century Literature NCLC 116: 241-357
overview, 242-60
romantic prison, 260-78
domestic prison, 278-316
America as prison, 316-24
physical prisons and prison authors, 324-56

Prophesy in Nineteenth-Century Literature NCLC 204: 97-165
American literature, 98-119
English Romantic poetry, 119-65

Prostitution in Nineteenth-Century Literature NCLC 192: 218-338
overview, 220-32
prostitution and women's identity, 232-79
prostitution as a moral and social concern, 279-306
prostitutes as "other," 306-37

Protestant Hagiography and Martyrology LC 84: 106-217
overview, 106-37
John Foxe's *Book of Martyrs,* 137-97
martyrology and the feminine perspective, 198-216

Protestant Reformation, Literature of the LC 37: 1-83
overviews and general studies, 1-49
humanism and scholasticism, 49-69
the reformation and literature, 69-82

Psychoanalysis and Literature TCLC 38: 227-338
overviews and general studies, 227-46
Freud on literature, 246-51
psychoanalytic views of the literary process, 251-61
psychoanalytic theories of response to literature, 261-88
psychoanalysis and literary criticism, 288-312
psychoanalysis as literature/literature as psychoanalysis, 313-34

Pulp Fiction TCLC 214: 135-260
overviews and general studies, 136-61
pulp magazines, 161-93
gender and pulp fiction, 193-219
science fiction and pulp, 219-40
detective pulp fiction, 240-59

Pulp Fiction, Contemporary CLC 264: 241-367
overviews and general studies, 242-71
new pulp fiction, 271-98
pulp from overseas, 298-330
women's pulp fiction, 330-67

The Quarrel between the Ancients and the Moderns LC 63: 266-381
overviews and general studies, 267-301
Renaissance origins, 301-32
Quarrel between the Ancients and the Moderns in France, 332-58
Battle of the Books in England, 358-80

Racism in Literature TCLC 138: 257-373
overviews and general studies, 257-326
racism and literature by and about African Americans, 292-326
theme of racism in literature, 326-773

The Railroad in Nineteenth-Century Literature NCLC 184: 247-372
overviews, 249-80
symbolism, 280-314
La Bête humaine and *Anna Karenina*, 314-44
realism, sensationalism, and the railroad, 344-71

Rap Music CLC 76: 477-50

Reader-Response Criticism TCLC 146: 240-357
overviews and general studies, 241-88
critical approaches to reader response, 288-342
reader-response interpretation, 342-57

Reader Response Theory TCLC 270:106-73
theories of reader response: a review of the literature, 108-24
the emotional response of the reader, 124-45
reading strategy, 145-52
empirical studies of reader response, 152-73

Realism in Children's Literature CLR 136: 45-98
overviews and general studies, 48-57
narrative voice in realistic fiction for children, 57-75
realism and historical fiction for children, 75-98

Realism in Short Fiction SSC 63: 128-57
overviews and general studies, 129-37
realist short fiction in France, 137-62
realist short fiction in Russia, 162-215
realist short fiction in England, 215-31
realist short fiction in the United States, 231-56

Regionalism and Local Color in Short Fiction SSC 65: 160-289
overviews and general studies, 163-205
regionalism/local color fiction of the west, 205-42
regionalism/local color fiction of the midwest, 242-57
regionalism/local color fiction of the south, 257-88

Regionalism and Local Color in Nineteenth-Century Literature NCLC 188: 174-339
women, regionalism, and local color, 177-225
Midwestern literature, 225-48
New England literature, 248-89
Southern literature, 289-339

Religion in Children's Literature CLR 121: 66-153
overviews and general studies, 69-103
religious values and didacticism in children's literature, 103-23
presentation of spirituality in children's literature, 123-33
religious themes in specific works of children's literature, 133-53

Renaissance Depictions of Islam LC 137: 256-362
overview, 258-70
travelers and captives, 270-85
religious contrasts, 286-342
English Renaissance views, 342-61

Renaissance Natural Philosophy LC 27: 201-87
cosmology, 201-28
astrology, 228-54
magic, 254-86

Renaissance Neoplatonism LC 181: 110-222
overview, 112-122
Neoplatonism in literature, 122-95
the Cambridge Platonists, 195-222

Renaissance Numerology PC 169: 79-166
overviews and general studies, 82-94
numerology in Edmund Spenser, 94-139
numerology in William Shakespeare, 139-148
numerology in George Herbert, 148-152
numerology in John Milton, 152-164

Renaissance Tragicomedy LC 169: 130-238
overviews, 132-50
sociopolitical context, 150-88
English tragicomedy, 188-214
European tragicomedy, 214-37

Renaissance Views of Kingship LC 133: 270-369
philosophical and historical views 272-305
literary views 305-68

Representations of Africa in Nineteenth-Century Literature NCLC 148: 248-351
overview, 251-66
Northeast and Central Africa, 266-76
South Africa, 276-301
West Africa, 301-49

Representations of India in Early Modern Literature LC 195: 193-301
overviews, 195-244
ideology and the view of India, 244-73
images of and by Women, 273-301

Representations of the Devil in Nineteenth-Century Literature NCLC 100: 89-223
overviews and general studies, 90-115
the Devil in American fiction, 116-43
English romanticism: the satanic school, 143-89
Luciferian discourse in European literature, 189-222

Republican Era Chinese Fiction TCLC 270: 174-298
overview and general studies, 175-91
major authors and works of Chinese fiction, 191-236
women Chinese fiction writers, 236-97

Restoration Drama LC 21: 184-275
general overviews and general studies, 185-230
Jeremy Collier stage controversy, 230-9
other critical interpretations, 240-75

The Restoration Rake LC 140: 240-352
overviews 241-77
the philosophical and political rake 277-309
Rochester: the model rake 309-31
variations on the rake 331-51

Revenge Tragedy LC 71: 113-242
overviews and general studies, 113-51
Elizabethan attitudes toward revenge, 151-88
the morality of revenge, 188-216
reminders and remembrance, 217-41

Revising the Literary Canon CLC 81: 465-509

Revising the Literary Canon TCLC 114: 240-84
overviews and general studies, 241-85
canon change in American literature, 285-339
gender and the literary canon, 339-59
minority and third-world literature and the canon, 359-84

Revolutionary Astronomers LC 51: 314-65
overviews and general studies, 316-25
principal figures, 325-51
Revolutionary astronomical models, 352-64

Robin Hood, Legend of LC 19: 205-58
origins and development of the Robin Hood legend, 206-20
representations of Robin Hood, 220-44
Robin Hood as hero, 244-56

Roman Drama CMLC 92: 252-374
overviews, 254-85
style and characteristics, 286-310
Roman comedy, 310-44
Roman drama, 344-73

Roman Historiography CMLC 106: 189-383
overviews, 190-239
major historians, 239-340
the place of history in Rome, 340-83

Romance Fiction, Contemporary CLC 206: 178-271
overviews, 180-93
literary conventions, 193-215
opposing viewpoints, 215-20
reader response to Romance literature, 220-37
Romance literature in the world, 237-70

Romance Fiction in the Twentieth Century TCLC 198: 236-341
overviews and general studies, 237-57
literary conventions, 257-72
reading and interpretation, 272-99
social and cultural response, 299-323
"scorned literature," 323-40

Romantic Literary Criticism NCLC 144: 203-357
background and overviews, 205-30
literary reviews, 230-38
the German Romantics, 238-81
Wordsworth and Coleridge, 281-326
variations on Romantic critical theory, 326-56

Romanticism: German and British Crosscurrents NCLC 295: 1-174
two Romanticisms: a general comparison, 6-96
William Wordsworth: a case study, 96-101
Romanticism in art, science, and music, 101-17
stylistic and thematic parallels, 117-60
German reception of British works, 160-72

Rushdie, Salman, *Satanic Verses* Controversy CLC 55: 214-63; 59:404-56

Russian Émigré Literature TCLC 242: 169-331
overviews and general studies, 171-93
the first wave of Russian émigré literature, 193-215
the second and third waves of Russian émigre literature, 215-34
representative figures, 234-75
representative themes, 275-330

Russian Nihilism NCLC 28: 403-47
definitions and overviews, 404-17
women and Nihilism, 417-27
literature as reform: the Civic Critics, 427-33
Nihilism and the Russian novel: Turgenev and Dostoevsky, 433-47

Russian Poets of the Soviet Era TCLC 282: 221-345
overviews, 222-42
major authors, 242-300
women and gender, 300-44

Russian Thaw TCLC 26: 189-247
literary history of the period, 190-206
theoretical debate of socialist realism, 206-11
Novy Mir, 211-7
Literary Moscow, 217-24
Pasternak, *Zhivago,* and the Nobel prize, 224-7
poetry of liberation, 228-31
Brodsky trial and the end of the Thaw, 231-6
achievement and influence, 236-46

Saladin in Middle Eastern and European Literature and Film CMLC 157: 243-342
life of Saladin, 245-273
Saladin in Middle Eastern literature and film, 273-314
Saladin in western literature and film, 315-41

Salem Witch Trials LC 38: 1-145
overviews and general studies, 2-30
historical background, 30-65
judicial background, 65-78
the search for causes, 78-115
the role of women in the trials, 115-44

Salinger, J. D., Controversy Surrounding *In Search of J. D. Salinger* CLC 55: 325-44

Samizdat Literature TCLC 150: 261-342
overviews and general studies, 262-64
history and development, 264-309
politics and Samizdat, 309-22
voices of Samizdat, 322-42

San Francisco Renaissance Poetry TCLC 250: 241-323
overviews, 242-72
primary poets of the San Francisco Renaissance, 272-322

Sanitation Reform, Nineteenth-Century NCLC 124: 165-257
overviews and general studies, 166
primary texts, 186-89
social context, 189-221
public health in literature, 221-56

School Stories CLR 128: 111-73
overviews and general studies, 114-23
boys' school stories, 123-46
girls' school stories, 146-73

Science and Modern Literature TCLC 90: 308-419
overviews and general studies, 295-333
fiction, 333-95
poetry, 395-405
drama, 405-19

Science in Nineteenth-Century Literature NCLC 100: 224-366
overviews and general studies, 225-65
major figures, 265-336
sociopolitical concerns, 336-65

Science Fiction Film Adaptations TCLC 202: 221-339
overviews and general studies 223-81
major science fiction films 281-315
text and representation 315-38

Science Fiction, Nineteenth-Century NCLC 24: 241-306
background, 242-50
definitions of the genre, 251-56
representative works and writers, 256-75
themes and conventions, 276-305
NCLC 200: 160-224
creators and creation, 162-78
responses to scientific advances, 178-224

Science Fiction Short Stories SSC 127: 125-387
roots in the nineteenth century, 129-164
overviews and major themes, 164-217
major authors and works, 217-88
the magazines, 288-336
science fiction and gender, 336-86

Scottish Chaucerians LC 20: 363-412

The Scottish Enlightenment LC 179: 197-314
overview, 199-214
major figures, 214-49
theories and ideas, 249-88
influence on literature, 288-313

Scottish Novelists, Contemporary See Contemporary Scottish Novelists

Scottish Poetry, Eighteenth-Century LC 29: 95-167
overviews and general studies, 96-114
the Scottish Augustans, 114-28
the Scots Vernacular Revival, 132-63
Scottish poetry after Burns, 163-66

Scottish Renaissance TCLC 234: 128-210
overviews, 129-76
major figures, 176-210

The Sea in Literature TCLC 82: 72-191
drama, 73-9
poetry, 79-119
fiction, 119-91

The Sea in Nineteenth-Century English and American Literature NCLC 104: 265-362
overviews and general studies, 267-306
major figures in American sea fiction—Cooper and Melville, 306-29
American sea poetry and short stories, 329-45
English sea literature, 345-61

The Sensation Novel NCLC 80: 219-330
overviews and general studies, 221-46
principal figures, 246-62
nineteenth-century reaction, 262-91
feminist criticism, 291-329

Sentimental Comedy LC 192: 214-328
overviews, 215-38
theories of sentimental comedy, 238-60
early sentimental comedies, 260-99
The Conscious Lovers and later plays, 299-327

The Sentimental Novel NCLC 60: 146-245
overviews and general studies, 147-58
the politics of domestic fiction, 158-79
a literature of resistance and repression, 179-212
the reception of sentimental fiction, 213-44

September 11 Attacks See Literature in Response to the September 11 Attacks

Sex and Literature TCLC 82: 192-434
overviews and general studies, 193-216
drama, 216-63
poetry, 263-87
fiction, 287-431

Sexuality in Short Fiction SSC 152: 180-312
performing sexual identity, 181-211
male romantic relationships, 211-39
female sexual freedom, 239-76
sexuality and the national cultural ideal, 276-97
sexuality and the Victorian cultural ideal, 297-311

Sherlock Holmes Centenary TCLC 26: 248-310
Doyle's life and the composition of the Holmes stories, 248-59
life and character of Holmes, 259-78
method, 278-79
Holmes and the Victorian world, 279-92
Sherlockian scholarship, 292-301
Doyle and the development of the detective story, 301-07
Holmes's continuing popularity, 307-09

Short Fiction of World War II SSC 147: 207-325
overviews, 208-31
major authors, 231-80
themes and symbolism, 280-325

Short Science Fiction, Golden Age of, 1938-1950 SSC 73: 1-145
overviews and general studies, 3-48
publishing history of Golden Age Short Science Fiction, 48-65
major Golden Age Short Science Fiction authors and editors
Isaac Asimov, 65-77
Ray Bradbury, 77-92
John W. Campbell, 92-106
Arthur C. Clarke, 106-15
Robert A. Heinlein, 115-29
Damon Knight, 129-40
Frederik Pohl, 141-43

Short-Short Fiction SSC 61: 311-36
overviews and general studies, 312-19
major short-short fiction writers, 319-35

Short Story Cycles SSC 166: 176-343
short story cycles in American literature, 178-227
short story cycles in English literature, 227-44
Asian American and Asian Canadian short story cycles, 244-69
short story cycles in Canadian Literature, 269-304
short story cycles in South African Litterature, 304-21
short story cycles and identity, 321-42

Silver Age of Russian Poetry TCLC 302: 113-224
overview and general study, 118-27
symbolism, 127-49
acmeism, 149-70
futurism, 170-222

The Silver Fork Novel NCLC 88: 58-140
criticism, 59-139

Sixteenth-Century Spanish Poetry LC 194: 183-302
overview, 184-94
classical and humanist influences, 194-227
poetry and Spanish imperialism, 227-73
poetry and mysticism, 273-301

Skaldic Poetry PC 147: 257-340
form and style in Skaldic verse, 260-88
old Norse poetic and religious culture, 288-306
issues in modern Skaldic studies, 306-38

Slave Narratives, American NCLC 20: 1-91
background, 2-9
overviews and general studies, 9-24
contemporary responses, 24-7
language, theme, and technique, 27-70
historical authenticity, 70-5
antecedents, 75-83
role in development of Black American literature, 83-8

The Slave Trade in British and American Literature LC 59: 283-369
overviews and general studies, 284-91
depictions by white writers, 291-331
depictions by former slaves, 331-67

Social Conduct Literature LC 55: 196-298
overviews and general studies, 196-223

prescriptive ideology in other literary forms, 223-38
role of the press, 238-63
impact of conduct literature, 263-87
conduct literature and the perception of women, 287-96
women writing for women, 296-98

Social Protest Literature of Victorian England NCLC 160: 227-359
overviews: protest in Victorian literature, 229-62
woman question, 262-304
condition-of-England novel, 304-58

Social Protest Literature Outside England, Nineteenth-Century NCLC 124: 258-350
overviews and general studies, 259-72
oppression revealed, 272-306
literature to incite or prevent reform, 306-50

Social Realism TCLC 174: 104-229
overviews, 105-43
representative authors, 143-229

Socialism NCLC 88: 141-237
origins, 142-54
French socialism, 154-83
Anglo-American socialism, 183-205
Socialist-Feminism, 205-36

Southern Gothic Literature TCLC 142: 186-270
overviews and general studies, 187-97
major authors in southern Gothic literature, 197-230
structure and technique in southern Gothic literature, 230-50
themes in southern Gothic literature, 250-70

Southern Literature, Contemporary CLC 167: 1-132
criticism, 2-131

Southern Literature of the Reconstruction NCLC 108: 289-369
overview, 290-91
reconstruction literature: the consequences of war, 291-321
old south to new: continuities in southern culture, 321-68

Southwestern Humor SSC 81: 105-248
overviews, 106-83
Mark Twain, 183-97
George Washington Harris, 197-208
other major figures, 208-46

The Spanish Civil War in Literature TCLC 174: 230-374
overviews, 231-47
major authors, 247-73
poetry of the Spanish Civil War, 273-302
the literary context of the Spanish Civil War, 302-43
literature and politics in the Spanish Civil War, 343-74

Spanish Civil War Literature TCLC 26: 311-85
topics in, 312-33
British and American literature, 333-59
French literature, 359-62
Spanish literature, 362-73
German literature, 373-75
political idealism and war literature, 375-83

Spanish Golden Age Literature LC 23: 262-332
overviews and general studies, 263-81
verse drama, 281-304
prose fiction, 304-19
lyric poetry, 319-31

Spanish Poetry, Fifteenth-Century See Fifteenth-Century Spanish Poetry

Spanish Poetry, Sixteenth Century See Sixteenth-Century Spanish Poetry

Spanish Romanticism NCLC 232: 222-306
overviews, 223-87
drama, 287-305

Sparta in Literature CMLC 70: 145-271
overviews, 147-61
Spartan poetry, 161-72
the Spartan myth, 172-200
historical background, 200-27
Spartan society and culture, 227-69

Spasmodic School of Poetry NCLC 24: 307-52
history and major figures, 307-21
the Spasmodics on poetry, 321-7
Firmilian and critical disfavor, 327-39
theme and technique, 339-47
influence, 347-51

Speculative Fiction in North America, Contemporary CLC 327: 185-259
surveys of the literature, 187-8
major authors, 188-213
imagining an alternative female identity, 213-230
speculative fiction and technocapitalism, 230-51
the debate: "popular" fiction or "literary" fiction, 251-8

Sports in Literature TCLC 86: 294-445
overviews and general studies, 295-324
major writers and works, 324-402
sports, literature, and social issues, 402-45

Spy Novels in the Twentieth Century TCLC 182: 239-353
overviews, 240-53
major authors and themes, 253-96
spy novels and history, 296-326
literary techniques, 326-52

Steinbeck, John, Fiftieth Anniversary of *The Grapes of Wrath* CLC 59: 311-54

The Stream-of-Consciousness Novel TCLC 178: 110-95
style and development 111-43
representative authors 134-95

Street Lit CLC 267: 258-348
overviews, 260-88
the roots of street lit: Donald Goines and Iceberg Slim, 288-324
the emergence of contemporary street lit: Sister Souljah, 324-47

Sturm und Drang NCLC 40: 196-276
definitions, 197-238
poetry and poetics, 238-58
drama, 258-75

Struwwelpeter CLR 122: 124-90
overviews and general studies, 128-45
impact of "Der Struwwelpeter" on children's literature, 145-71
alternate versions of "Der Struwwelpeter," 171-90

Suffrage Literature TCLC 214: 261-360
overviews and general studies, 262-82
major figures, 282-323
suffrage on stage, 323-59

Supernatural Fiction in the Nineteenth Century NCLC 32: 207-87
major figures and influences, 208-35
the Victorian ghost story, 236-54
the influence of science and occultism, 254-66
supernatural fiction and society, 266-86

Supernatural Fiction, Modern TCLC 30: 59-116
evolution and varieties, 60-74
"decline" of the ghost story, 74-86
as a literary genre, 86-92
technique, 92-101
nature and appeal, 101-15

Surrealism TCLC 30: 334-406
history and formative influences, 335-43
manifestos, 343-54
philosophic, aesthetic, and political principles, 354-75
poetry, 375-81
novel, 381-6
drama, 386-92
film, 392-8
painting and sculpture, 398-403
achievement, 403-5

Surrealism in Children's Literature CLR 103: 127-200
overviews and general studies, 130-52
critical analysis of surrealist children's authors and works, 152-99

Sylvia Beach and Company TCLC 158: 281-370
overviews and general studies, 282-97
Shakespeare and Company, 297-314
the business of publishing, 315-40
Sylvia Beach and James Joyce, 341-70

Symbolism, Russian TCLC 30: 266-333
doctrines and major figures, 267-92
theories, 293-8
and French Symbolism, 298-310
themes in poetry, 310-4
theater, 314-20
and the fine arts, 320-32

Symbolist Movement, French NCLC 20: 169-249
background and characteristics, 170-86
principles, 186-91
attacked and defended, 191-7
influences and predecessors, 197-211
and Decadence, 211-6
theater, 216-26
prose, 226-33
decline and influence, 233-47

Syphilis See Writings on Syphilis in the Early Modern Period

Television and Literature TCLC 78: 283-426
television and literacy, 283-98
reading vs. watching, 298-341
adaptations, 341-62
literary genres and television, 362-90
television genres and literature, 390-410
children's literature/children's television, 410-25

Temperance in Nineteenth-Century Literature NCLC 196: 240-345
influences on major literary figures, 242-304
drama, 304-22
women's issues, 322-44

Theater of the Absurd TCLC 38: 339-415
"The Theater of the Absurd," 340-7
major plays and playwrights, 347-58
and the concept of the absurd, 358-86
theatrical techniques, 386-94
predecessors of, 394-402
influence of, 402-13

Theater of the Absurd TCLC 226: 274-356
overviews and major themes, 275-308
major figures, 308-55

Theater of Cruelty DC 41: 146-248
Antonin Artaud's Works and Theories, 147-200

Other Significant Authors and Works, 200-48

Time-Slip Novels CLR 151: 155-93
overviews and general studies, 158-66
Canadian and Antipodean time-slip novels, 166-80
the time-slip novels of E. Nesbit and Rudyard Kipling, 180-92

Time Travel in Literature and Film TCLC 234: 211-358
overviews, 215-44
major authors and works, 244-97
H.G. Wells's *Time Machine,* 297-323
time travel in film, 323-57

Tin Pan Alley See American Popular Song, Golden Age of

Tobacco Culture LC 55: 299-366
social and economic attitudes toward tobacco, 299-344
tobacco trade between the old world and the new world, 344-55
tobacco smuggling in Great Britain, 355-66

Transcendentalism, American NCLC 24: 1-99
overviews and general studies, 3-23
contemporary documents, 23-41
theological aspects of, 42-52
and social issues, 52-74
literature of, 74-96

Translation in Children's Literature CLR 135: 112-89
overviews and general studies, 116-40
ethics, challenges, and strategies for translating children's works, 140-65
cultural factors in the translation of children's books, 165-88

Travel Narratives in Contemporary Literature CLC 204: 260-351
overviews, 261-76
major authors, 276-311
modern travel writing, 311-31
women writers and travel, 331-51

Travel Writing in the Nineteenth Century NCLC 44: 274-392
the European grand tour, 275-303
the Orient, 303-47
North America, 347-91
NCLC 168: 210-347
overviews, 212-43
women's travel writing, 243-311
other notable travel writers and their works, 312-47

Travel Writing in the Twentieth Century TCLC 30: 407-56
conventions and traditions, 407-27
and fiction writing, 427-43
comparative essays on travel writers, 443-54

Treatment of Death in Children's Literature CLR 101: 152-201
overviews and general studies, 155-80
analytical and bibliographical reviews of death in children's literature, 180-97
death of animals in children's literature, 197-200

Tristan and Isolde Legend CMLC 42: 311-404

Troubadours CMLC 66: 244-383
overviews, 245-91
politics, economics, history, and the troubadours, 291-344
troubadours and women, 344-82

True-Crime Literature CLC 99: 333-433
history and analysis, 334-407
reviews of true-crime publications, 407-23
writing instruction, 424-29
author profiles, 429-33

Turkish Literature TCLC 274: 86-217
historical background: the literature of nation formation, 88-107
women authors and gender issues, 107-23
major authors, 123-63
the East-West divide, 163-90
rewriting the national history, 190-216

Twentieth-Century Danish Literature TCLC 142: 271-344
major works, 272-84
major authors, 284-344

***Ulysses* and the Process of Textual Reconstruction** TCLC 26:386-416
evaluations of the new *Ulysses,* 386-94
editorial principles and procedures, 394-401
theoretical issues, 401-16

Unconventional Family in Children's Literature CLR 102: 146-213
overviews and general studies, 149-79
analytical and bibliographical reviews, 179-97
types of unconventional families: foster, adopted, homosexual, 197-212

University Wits LC 161: 291-351
overviews, 293-311
the dramatists and their works, 311-350

Urban Fantasy CLC 308: 251-320
general overviews, 253-255
Political, economic, and historical perspectives reflected in urban fantasy fiction, 256-284
geographical themes and the importance of place in urban fantasy, 284-320

Urban Fiction See Street Lit

Urban Life in Nineteenth-Century Literature NCLC 172: 249-334
overviews, 250-77
urban poetry, 277-304
urban life and individual identity, 304-34

Utilitarianism NCLC 84: 272-340
J. S. Mill's Utilitarianism: liberty, equality, justice, 273-313
Jeremy Bentham's Utilitarianism: the science of happiness, 313-39

Ut pictura poesis LC 176: 264-384
background and overview, 266-85
ut pictura poesis in the Renaissance, 285-336
ut pictura poesis in the eighteenth century, 336-61
Lessing and his contemporaries, 361-82

Utopianism NCLC 88: 238-346
overviews: Utopian literature, 239-59
Utopianism in American literature, 259-99
Utopianism in British literature, 299-311
Utopianism and feminism, 311-45

Utopian Children's Literature CLR 153: 110-211
overviews and general studies, 113-64
critical theory and utopian children's books, 164-87
queer utopianism in young adult fiction, 187-211

Utopian Communities NCLC 208: 278-350
Icaria, 280-90
transcendental utopias: Brook Farm, Fruitlands, and Walden, 290-331
Pantisocracy, 331-49

Utopian Literature, Nineteenth-Century NCLC 24: 353-473
definitions, 354-74
overviews and general studies, 374-88
theory, 388-408
communities, 409-26
fiction, 426-53
women and fiction, 454-71

Utopian Literature, Renaissance LC 32: 1-63
overviews and general studies, 2-25
classical background, 25-33
utopia and the social contract, 33-9
origins in mythology, 39-48
utopia and the Renaissance country house, 48-52
influence of millenarianism, 52-62

Vampire in Literature TCLC 46: 391-454
origins and evolution, 392-412
social and psychological perspectives, 413-44
vampire fiction and science fiction, 445-53

The Vampire in Literature and Film TCLC 238: 256-337
overviews and general studies, 258-76
major thematic trends, 276-307
women writers and vampires, 307-29
vampires in film, 329-36

Vernacular Bibles LC 67: 214-388
overviews and general studies, 215-59
the English Bible, 259-355
the German Bible, 355-88

Victorian Autobiography NCLC 40: 277-363
development and major characteristics, 278-88
themes and techniques, 289-313
the autobiographical tendency in Victorian prose and poetry, 313-47
Victorian women's autobiographies, 347-62
NCLC 152: 230-365
overviews and general studies, 232-61
autobiography and the self, 261-93
autobiography and gender, 293-307
autobiography and class, 307-36
autobiography and fiction, 336-64

Victorian Critical Theory NCLC 136: 236-379
overviews and general studies, 237-86
Matthew Arnold, 286-324
Walter Pater and aestheticism, 324-36
other Victorian critics, 336-78

Victorian Fantasy Literature NCLC 60: 246-384
overviews and general studies, 247-91
major figures, 292-366
women in Victorian fantasy literature, 366-83

Victorian Ghost Stories NCLC 220: 103-86
overviews, 105-25
background: ghost stories of the early nineteenth century, 125-41
major authors and significant works, 141-85

Victorian Hellenism NCLC 68: 251-376
overviews and general studies, 252-78
the meanings of Hellenism, 278-335
the literary influence, 335-75

Victorian Illustrated Fiction NCLC 120: 247-356
overviews and development, 128-76
technical and material aspects of book illustration, 276-84
Charles Dickens and his illustrators, 284-320
William Makepeace Thackeray, 320-31
George Eliot and Frederic Leighton, 331-51
Lewis Carroll and John Tenniel, 351-56

Victorian Novel NCLC 32: 288-454
development and major characteristics, 290-310
themes and techniques, 310-58
social criticism in the Victorian novel, 359-97
urban and rural life in the Victorian novel, 397-406
women in the Victorian novel, 406-25
Mudie's Circulating Library, 425-34
the late-Victorian novel, 434-51

Vietnamese Literature TCLC 102: 322-386

Vietnam War in Literature and Film CLC 91: 383-437
overview, 384-8
prose, 388-412
film and drama, 412-24
poetry, 424-35

Vietnam War, Contemporary Literature Arising from the CLC 254: 172-286
overviews, 173-202
representative authors, 202-50
Vietnam war poetry, 250-62
women in Vietnam war literature, 262-86

The Vietnam War in Short Fiction SSC 79: 83-177
overviews and general studies, 84-93
women authors of Vietnam War short fiction, 93-116
Robert Olen Butler: *A Good Scent from a Strange Mountain* (1992), 116-31
Barry Hannah: *Airships* (1978), 131-50
Tim O'Brien: *The Things They Carried* (1990), 150-65
Tobias Wolff: *Back in the World* (1985), 165-69
other authors and works, 169-76

Violence in Literature TCLC 98: 235-358
overviews and general studies, 236-74
violence in the works of modern authors, 274-358

Violence in Nineteenth-Century Literature NCLC 236: 198-326
civilization and law, 200-24
gender and sexuality, 224-53
race and ethnicity, 253-88
violence against women, 288-326

Virtue and Vice in the Middle Ages CMLC 159: 141-340
theology and philosophy of virtue and vice, 145-87
pastoral and instructional literature, 187-297
virtue and vice in poetry and romance, 297-320
medieval drama: miracle, mystery, and morality plays, 321-37

Vorticism TCLC 62: 330-426
Wyndham Lewis and Vorticism, 330-8
characteristics and principles of Vorticism, 338-65
Lewis and Pound, 365-82
Vorticist writing, 382-416
Vorticist painting, 416-26

War in Children's Literature CLR 127: 149-97
overviews and general studies, 152-70
World Wars I and II in children's literature, 170-86
other presentations of war in children's literature, 186-97

The War Novel TCLC 278: 218-330
overview, 219-28
the World War I novel, 228-64
the World War II novel, 264-324
the Vietnam War novel, 324-29

Warfare and Chivalry in the Medieval Epic CMLC 154: 127-284
overviews and general studies, 130-245
medieval epic as a record of chivalric warfare, 245-64
influence of the medieval epic on the practice of chivalry, 265-83

Watergate and Journalism TCLC 186: 283-334
overviews 284-304
anonymous sources 304-22
lessons learned 322-33

The Well-Made Play NCLC 80: 331-370
overviews and general studies, 332-45
Scribe's style, 345-56
the influence of the well-made play, 356-69

Welsh Literature TCLC 262: 201-302
overviews, 203-38
major authors, 238-301

West African Literature, Contemporary CLC 317: 234-356
contemporary West African literature: an Introduction
magical realism and the oral tradition
West African women: gender issues and female resistance in literature
themes and motifs in contemporary West African literature

Westerns, Contemporary American CLC 260: 260-382
New Westerns/Anti-Westerns, 263-309
traditional Westerns, 309-17
Native American voices, 317-64
film and television, 364-70
depictions of women in literature of the American West, 370-81

Western Literature in Japan, Nineteenth-Century NCLC 156: 282-352
overviews, 283-305
European literature in Japan, 305-28
American literature in Japan, 328-52

William Shakespeare and His Works in Nineteenth-Century Literature and Culture NCLC 204: 166-340
overviews, 168-92
English poetry, 192-231
Emily Dickinson, 231-59
Herman Melville, 259-72
Charles Dickens, 273-300
Alexander Pushkin, 300-40

Witchcraft NCLC 224: 216-304
overviews, 217-51
society and literature, 251-68
women, 268-304

Women and Medicine NCLC 220: 187-328
overviews, 190-250
the "Doctress," 251-80
major authors and significant works, 280-327

Women in Modern Literature TCLC 94: 262-425
overviews and general studies, 263-86
American literature, 286-304
other national literatures, 304-33
fiction, 333-94
poetry, 394-407
drama, 407-24

Women in Old Norse Sagas CMLC 139: 275-347
overview, 278-95
women and the transmission of saga literature, 295-302
women and christianity in the sagas, 302-28
the vengeful woman in the sagas, 328-32
the characterization of women in the sagas, 332-45

Women Philosophers of the Eighteenth Century LC 187: 184-308
the philosophers, 186-267
critiques of male thinkers, 267-308

Women Philosophers of the Seventeenth Century LC 185: 226-329
overviews, 228-42
the philosophers, 242-97
relationships with male contemporaries, 297-314
gender, philosophy, and science, 314-28

Women Playwrights, Nineteenth-Century NCLC 200: 225-334
European authors, 227-65
North American authors, 265-334

Women Writers, Seventeenth-Century LC 30: 2-58
overview, 2-15
women and education, 15-9
women and autobiography, 19-31
women's diaries, 31-9
early feminists, 39-58

Women's Autobiographical Writing TCLC 222: 246-393
overviews, 247-86
individual authors and works, 287-332
the mother in women's autobiography, 332-55
foreign autobiographies, 355-92

Women's Autobiography, Nineteenth Century NCLC 76: 285-368
overviews and general studies, 287-300
autobiographies concerned with religious and political issues, 300-15
autobiographies by women of color, 315-38
autobiographies by women pioneers, 338-51
autobiographies by women of letters, 351-68

Women's Diaries, Nineteenth-Century NCLC 48: 308-54
overview, 308-13
diary as history, 314-25
sociology of diaries, 325-34
diaries as psychological scholarship, 334-43
diary as autobiography, 343-8
diary as literature, 348-53

Women's Periodicals LC 134: 292-382
English women's periodicals: overviews, 293-307
French women's periodicals: overviews, 307-19
early imitators of Addison and Steele, 320-42
The Female Spectator, 342-70
Journal des dames, 370-80

World War I Literature See Literature of the Great War

World War I Literature TCLC 34: 392-486
overview, 393-403
English, 403-27
German, 427-50
American, 450-66
French, 466-74
and modern history, 474-82

World War I Short Fiction SSC 71: 187-347
overviews and general studies, 187-206

female short fiction writers of World War I, 206-36
Central Powers
Czechoslovakian writers of short fiction, 236-44
German writers of short fiction, 244-61
Entente/Allied Alliance
Australian writers of short fiction, 261-73
English writers of short fiction, 273-305
French writers of short fiction, 305-11
Associated Power: American writers of short fiction, 311-46

World War II Literature TCLC 194: 241-397
overviews, 242-99
the literary response to war and violence, 299-329
wartime propaganda, 329-45
writing from exile, 345-59
World War II drama, 359-97

World War II Women's Writing TCLC 274: 218-305
autobiographical writings, 219-53
World War II women's fiction, 253-79
women and World War II: roles and responses, 279-305

Writers of the Iranian Diaspora CLC 386: 157-322
overviews and general studies, 160-72
literary, political, and cultural context, 172-208
national and transnational identity, 208-41
Iranian diaspora in performance, 241-74
mass media and digital technology, 274-321

Writers of the Lost Generation TCLC 178: 196-369
overviews 197-225
major figures 225-98
women of the Lost Generation 298-341
expatriate writers and Paris 341-68

Writings on Syphilis in the Early Modern Period LC 144: 245-350
overview 247-56
William Clowes' *Short and Profitable Treatise* 256-57
Fracastoro's *Syphilis* 257-89
Medieval and Renaissance Literary Representations of Syphilis 289-333
Eighteenth-Century Literary Representations of Syphilis 333-48

Yellow Journalism NCLC 36: 383-456
overviews and general studies, 384-96
major figures, 396-413

Yiddish Literature TCLC 130: 229-364
overviews and general studies, 230-54
major authors, 254-305
Yiddish literature in America, 305-34
Yiddish and Judaism, 334-64

Young Adult Literature, Contemporary CLC 234: 267-341
general overviews, representative authors, and reviews, 270-83
feminism and young adult literature for young women, 283-305
interviews with YA authors, 305-14
using YA fiction in the classroom, 314-26
religious issues, sexual orientation, and alternative communities in YA lit, 326-41

Young Playwrights Festival
1988 CLC 55: 376-81
1989 CLC 59: 398-403
1990 CLC 65: 444-8

NCLC Cumulative Nationality Index

AMERICAN

Adams, John **106**
Adams, John Quincy **175**
Alcott, Amos Bronson **1, 167**
Alcott, Louisa May **6, 58, 83, 218**
Alger, Horatio Jr. **8, 83, 260**
Allston, Washington **2**
Apess, William **73**
Audubon, John James **47**
Bacon, Delia **315**
Barlow, Joel **23, 223**
Bartram, William **145**
Beecher, Catharine Esther **30**
Bellamy, Edward **4, 86, 147**
Bird, Robert Montgomery **1, 197**
Boker, George Henry **125**
Boucicault, Dion **41, 306**
Boyesen, Hjalmar Hjorth **135**
Brackenridge, Hugh Henry **7, 227**
Brentano, Clemens (Maria) **1, 191**
Brown, Charles Brockden **22, 74, 122, 246**
Brown, William Wells **2, 89, 247**
Brownson, Orestes Augustus **50**
Bryant, William Cullen **6, 46, 284**
Calhoun, John Caldwell **15**
Callahan, S. Alice **315**
Channing, William Ellery **17**
Chesnut, Mary Boykin **250**
Child, Francis James **173**
Child, Lydia Maria **6, 73, 289**
Chivers, Thomas Holley **49**
Cooke, John Esten **5**
Cooke, Rose Terry **110**
Cooper, James Fenimore **1, 27, 54, 203, 279, 312**
Cooper, Susan Fenimore **129**
Cranch, Christopher Pearse **115**
Crèvecoeur, Michel Guillaume Jean de **105**
Crockett, David **8**
Cummins, Maria Susanna **139**
Dana, Richard Henry Sr. **53**
Delany, Martin Robinson **93**
Dennie, Joseph **249**
Dickinson, Emily (Elizabeth) **21, 77, 171**
Douglass, Frederick **7, 55, 141**
Dunlap, William **2, 244**
Dwight, Timothy **13, 245**
Emerson, Mary Moody **66**
Emerson, Ralph Waldo **1, 38, 98, 252**
Field, Eugene **3**
Field, Kate **307**
Foster, Hannah Webster **99, 252**
Foster, Stephen Collins **26**
Fuller, Margaret **5, 50, 211**
Frederic, Harold **10, 175**
Freneau, Philip Morin **1, 111, 253**
Garrison, William Lloyd **149**
Gilman, Caroline **302**
Hale, Sarah Josepha (Buell) **75**
Halleck, Fitz-Greene **47**
Hamilton, Alexander **49**
Hammon, Jupiter **5**
Harris, George Washington **23, 165**
Hawthorne, Nathaniel **2, 10, 17, 23, 39, 79, 95, 158, 171, 191, 226**
Hawthorne, Sophia Peabody **150**
Hayne, Paul Hamilton **94**
Hentz, Caroline Lee **281**
Holmes, Oliver Wendell **14, 81**
Hooper, Johnson Jones **177**
Horton, George Moses **87**
Irving, Washington **2, 19, 95**
Jackson, Helen Hunt **90, 256**
Jacobs, Harriet A(nn) **67, 162**
James, Alice **206**
James, Henry Sr. **53**
Jefferson, Thomas **11, 103**
Kennedy, John Pendleton **2**
Kirkland, Caroline M. **85, 309**
Lanier, Sidney **6, 118**
Larcom, Lucy **179**
Lazarus, Emma **8, 109**
Lincoln, Abraham **18, 201**
Lippard, George **198**
Longfellow, Henry Wadsworth **2, 45, 101, 103**
Longstreet, Augustus Baldwin **159**
Lowell, James Russell **2, 90**
Madison, James **126**
Melville, Herman **3, 12, 29, 45, 49, 91, 93, 123, 157, 181, 193, 221, 234, 277, 304, 306**
Menken, Adah Isaacs **270**
Mowatt, Anna Cora **74**
Murray, Judith Sargent **63, 243**
Neal, John **161**
Osgood, Frances Sargent **141**
Parker, Theodore **186**
Parkman, Francis Jr. **12**
Parton, Sara Payson Willis **86, 257**
Paulding, James Kirke **2**
Peabody, Elizabeth Palmer **169**
Pinkney, Edward **31**
Poe, Edgar Allan **1, 16, 55, 78, 94, 97, 117, 211**
Prescott, William Hickling **163**
Rowson, Susanna Haswell **5, 69, 182**
Rush, Benjamin **251**
Sealsfield, Charles **233**
Sedgwick, Catharine Maria **19, 98**
Shaw, Henry Wheeler **15**
Sigourney, Lydia Howard (Huntley) **21, 87**
Simms, William Gilmore **3**
Smith, Joseph Jr. **53**
Smith, Seba **187**
Solomon, Northup **105**
Southworth, Emma Dorothy Eliza Nevitte **26**
Stephens, Ann Sophia **303**
Stone, Lucy **250**
Stowe, Harriet (Elizabeth) Beecher **3, 50, 133, 195**
Taylor, Bayard **89**
Tenney, Tabitha Gilman **122, 248**
Thaxter, Celia **308**
Thoreau, Henry David **7, 21, 61, 138, 207**
Thorpe, Thomas Bangs **183**
Ticknor, George **255**
Timrod, Henry **25**
Trumbull, John **30**
Truth, Sojourner **94**
Tyler, Royall **3, 244**
Very, Jones **9**
Warner, Susan (Bogert) **31, 146**
Warren, Mercy Otis **13, 226**
Webster, Noah **30, 253**
Webb, Frank J. **143**
Weems, Mason Locke **245**
Whitman, Sarah Helen (Power) **19**
Whitman, Walt(er) **4, 31, 81, 205, 268**
Whittier, John Greenleaf **8, 59**
Willis, Nathaniel Parker **194**
Wilson, Harriet E. Adams **78, 219**
Winnemucca, Sarah **79**
Winthrop, Theodore **210**
Woolson, Constance Fenimore **82, 293**

ARGENTINEAN

Echeverría, (Jose) Esteban (Antonino) **18, 309**
Gorriti, Juana Manuela **298**
Hernández, José **17, 269**
Sarmiento, Domingo Faustino **123**

AUSTRALIAN

Adams, Francis **33**
Clarke, Marcus (Andrew Hislop) **19, 258**
Gordon, Adam Lindsay **21**
Harpur, Charles **114**
Kendall, Henry **12**

AUSTRIAN

Grillparzer, Franz **1, 102, 245**
Lenau, Nikolaus **16**
Nestroy, Johann **42**
Raimund, Ferdinand Jakob **69**
Sacher-Masoch, Leopold von **31**
Stifter, Adalbert **41, 198**

BERMUDIAN

Prince, Mary **282**

BRAZILIAN

Alencar, Jose de **157**
Alves, Antônio de Castro **205**

CANADIAN

Crawford, Isabella Valancy **12, 127**
De Mille, James **123**
Haliburton, Thomas Chandler **15, 149**
Lampman, Archibald **25, 194**
Moodie, Susanna (Strickland) **14, 113**

Richardson, John **55, 290**
Traill, Catharine Parr **31**

CHINESE

Li Ju-chen **137**

COLOMBIAN

Isaacs, Jorge Ricardo **70**
Silva, José Asunción **114, 280**

CROATIAN

Mažuranić, Ivan **259**

CUBAN

Casal, Julián del **131**
Gómez de Avellaneda, Gertrudis **111, 264**
Heredia, José Maráa **209**
Manzano, Juan Francisco **155**
Martí (y Pérez), José (Julian) **63, 313**
Villaverde, Cirilo **121**

CZECH

Macha, Karel Hynek **46**

DANISH

Andersen, Hans Christian **7, 79, 214**
Grundtvig, Nicolai Frederik Severin **1, 158**
Jacobsen, Jens Peter **34**
Kierkegaard, Søren **34, 78, 125, 265**

DUTCH

Charrière, Isabelle de **66, 314**
Multatuli (Eduard Douwes Dekker) **165**

ENGLISH

Ainsworth, William Harrison **13**
Arnold, Matthew **6, 29, 89, 126, 218**
Arnold, Thomas **18**
Austen, Jane **1, 13, 19, 33, 51, 81, 95, 119, 150, 207, 210, 222, 242, 271, 314, 316**
Bage, Robert **182**
Bagehot, Walter **10**
Barbauld, Anna Laetitia **50, 185**
Barham, Richard Harris **77**
Barnes, William **75, 283**
Beardsley, Aubrey **6**
Beckford, William **16, 214, 291**
Beddoes, Thomas Lovell **3, 154**
Bentham, Jeremy **38**
Blake, William **13, 37, 57, 127, 173, 190, 201**
Blessington, Marguerite, Countess of **297**
Blind, Mathilde **202**
Bloomfield, Robert **145**
Borrow, George (Henry) **9**
Bowles, William Lisle **103**
Brontë, Anne **4, 71, 102**
Brontë, Charlotte **3, 8, 33, 58, 105, 155, 217, 229, 280**
Brontë, Emily (Jane) **16, 35, 165, 244**
Brontë, (Patrick) Branwell **109**
Browning, Elizabeth Barrett **1, 16, 61, 66, 170**
Browning, Robert **19, 79**
Bulwer-Lytton, Edward (George Earle Lytton) **1, 45**
Burney, Fanny **12, 54, 107, 251, 299, 306**
Burton, Richard F(rancis) **42**
Byron, George Gordon (Noel) **2, 12, 109, 149, 256**
Carlyle, Jane Welsh **181**
Carlyle, Thomas **22, 70, 248**
Carroll, Lewis **2, 53, 139, 258, 308**
Carter, Elizabeth **277**
Clare, John **9, 86, 259**
Clough, Arthur Hugh **27, 163**
Cobbett, William **49, 288**
Coleridge, Hartley **90, 283**
Coleridge, Samuel Taylor **9, 54, 99, 111, 177, 197, 231**
Coleridge, Sara **31**
Collier, John Payne **286**
Collins, (William) Wilkie **1, 18, 93, 255, 272**
Colman, George, the Younger **302**
Cowper, William **8, 94**
Crabbe, George **26, 121**
Craik, Dinah Maria (Mulock) **38, 286**
Cumberland, Richard **167**
Dacre, Charlotte **151**
Darwin, Charles **57**
Darwin, Erasmus **106**
De Quincey, Thomas **4, 87, 198**
Dickens, Charles (John Huffam) **3, 8, 18, 26, 37, 50, 86, 105, 113, 161, 187, 203, 206, 211, 217, 219, 230, 231, 285, 307**
Disraeli, Benjamin **2, 39, 79, 272**
D'Israeli, Isaac **217**
Dobell, Sydney Thompson **43**
Duff Gordon, Lucie **262**
Du Maurier, George **86**
Dyer, George **129**
Eden, Emily **10**
Eliot, George **4, 13, 23, 41, 49, 89, 118, 183, 199, 209, 233**
Fenwick, Eliza **301**
FitzGerald, Edward **9, 153**
Forster, John **11**
Froude, James Anthony **43, 311**
Gaskell, Elizabeth Cleghorn **5, 70, 97, 137, 214, 264**
Gilpin, William **30**
Gladstone, William Ewart **213**
Godwin, William **14, 130, 287**
Gore, Catherine **65**
Hallam, Arthur Henry **110**
Haydon, Benjamin Robert **146**
Hayley, William **286**
Hays, Mary **114**
Hazlitt, William **29, 82**
Hemans, Felicia **29, 71, 291**
Holcroft, Thomas **85**
Hood, Thomas **16**
Hopkins, Gerard Manley **17, 189**
Horne, Richard Hengist **127**
Horne Tooke, John **195**
Hughes, Thomas **207**
Hunt, (James Henry) Leigh **1, 70**
Huxley, T(homas) H(enry) **67**
Inchbald, Elizabeth **62, 276**
Ingelow, Jean **39, 107**
Jameson, Anna **43, 282**
Jefferies, (John) Richard **47**
Jerrold, Douglas William **2**
Jewsbury, Geraldine (Endsor) **22**
Jones, Ernest Charles **222**
Keats, John **8, 73, 121, 225**
Keble, John **87**
Kemble, Fanny **18**
Kingsley, Charles **35**
Kingsley, Henry **107**
Lamb, Charles **10, 113, 298**
Lamb, Lady Caroline **38, 261**
Lamb, Mary **125, 285**
Landon, Letitia Elizabeth **15, 266**
Landor, Walter Savage **14, 290**
Lear, Edward **3**
Lee, Sophia **191**
Lennox, Charlotte **23, 134, 263**
Levy, Amy **59, 203**
Lewes, George Henry **25, 215**
Lewis, Matthew Gregory **11, 62**
Linton, Eliza Lynn **41**
Macaulay, Thomas Babington **42, 231**
Malthus, Thomas Robert **145**
Marryat, Frederick **3**
Marryat, Florence **297**
Martineau, Harriet **26, 137**
Mayhew, Henry **31**
Mill, Harriet (Hardy) Taylor **102**
Mill, John Stuart **11, 58, 179, 223**
Mitford, Mary Russell **4**
Montagu, Elizabeth **117**
More, Hannah **27, 141**
Morris, William **4, 233**
Murphy, Arthur **229**
Naden, Constance **313**
Newman, John Henry **38, 99**
Norton, Caroline **47, 205**
Oliphant, Laurence **47**
Opie, Amelia **65**
Paine, Thomas **62, 248**
Pater, Walter (Horatio) **7, 90, 159**
Patmore, Coventry Kersey Dighton **9**
Peacock, Thomas Love **22**
Percy, Thomas **95**
Piozzi, Hester Lynch (Thrale) **57, 294**
Planché, James Robinson **42**
Polidori, John William **51**
Porter, Jane **267**
Procter, Adelaide Anne **305**
Radcliffe, Ann (Ward) **6, 55, 106, 223**
Reade, Charles **2, 74, 275**
Reeve, Clara **19**
Reynolds, John Hamilton **146**
Robertson, Thomas William **35**
Robinson, Henry Crabb **15**
Robinson, Mary **142**
Rogers, Samuel **69**
Rossetti, Christina (Georgina) **2, 50, 66, 186**
Rossetti, Dante Gabriel **4, 77**
Sala, George Augustus **46**
Seward, Anna **265**
Shelley, Mary Wollstonecraft (Godwin) **14, 59, 103, 170**
Shelley, Percy Bysshe **18, 93, 143, 175**
Sherwood, Mary Martha **301**
Smith, Charlotte (Turner) **23, 115**
Southey, Robert **8, 97**
Surtees, Robert Smith **14**
Symonds, John Addington **34**
Taylor, Jane **279**
Tennyson, Alfred **30, 65, 115, 202**
Thackeray, William Makepeace **5, 14, 22, 43, 169, 213, 294**
Thelwall, John **162**
Tonna, Charlotte Elizabeth **135**
Trelawny, Edward John **85**
Trollope, Anthony **6, 33, 101, 215, 269, 274, 275**
Trollope, Frances **30**
Warton, Joseph **118**
Webster, Augusta **230**
Whately, Richard **299**
Williams, Helen Maria **135**
Wood, Mrs. Henry **178**
Wordsworth, Dorothy **25, 138**
Wordsworth, William **12, 38, 111, 166, 206**
Yearsley, Ann **174**

FILIPINO

Rizal, José **27**

FINNISH

Kivi, Aleksis **30**
Lonnrot, Elias **53**
Runeberg, Johan **41**

FRENCH

Augier, Emile **31**
Balzac, Honoré de **5, 35, 53, 153, 273, 311**
Banville, Théodore (Faullain) de **9**
Barbey d'Aurevilly, Jules-Amédée **1, 213**

Baudelaire, Charles **6, 29, 55, 155, 303**
Becque, Henri **3**
Beranger, Pierre Jean de **34**
Bernardin de Saint-Pierre, Jacques-Henri **297**
Bertrand, Aloysius **31**
Borel, Pétrus **41**
Chamisso, Adelbert von **82**
Chateaubriand, François René de **3, 134**
Comte, Auguste **54**
Constant (de Rebecque), (Henri) Benjamin **6, 182**
Corbière, Tristan **43**
Crèvecoeur, Michel Guillaume Jean de **105**
Daudet, (Louis Marie) Alphonse **1, 312**
Delacroix, Eugene **133**
Desbordes-Valmore, Marceline **97, 293**
Dumas, Alexandre (fils) **9**
Dumas, Alexandre (pere) **11, 71, 271**
Duras, Claire de **154, 304**
Feuillet, Octave **45**
Flaubert, Gustave **2, 10, 19, 62, 66, 135, 179, 185, 251**
Fourier, Charles **51**
Fromentin, Eugène (Samuel Auguste) **10, 125**
Gaboriau, Émile **14**
Gautier, Théophile **1, 59, 243, 267**
Genlis, Stéphanie-Félicité de **166**
Girardin, Delphine Gay de **290**
Gobineau, Joseph-Arthur **17, 259**
Goncourt, Edmond (Louis Antoine Huot) de **7**
Goncourt, Jules (Alfred Huot) de **7**
Hugo, Victor (Marie) **3, 10, 21, 161, 189, 303**
Joubert, Joseph **9**
Kock, Charles Paul de **16**
Laclos, Pierre Ambroise François **4, 87**
Laforgue, Jules **5, 53, 221**
Lamartine, Alphonse (Marie Louis Prat) de **11, 190**
Lautréamont **12, 194**
Leconte de Lisle, Charles-Marie-René **29**
Maistre, Joseph **37**
Mallarmé, Stéphane **4, 41, 210**
Maupassant, (Henri René Albert) Guy de **1, 42, 83**
Mercier, Louis-Sébastien **255**
Mérimée, Prosper **6, 65**
Michelet, Jules **31, 218**
Musset, (Louis Charles) Alfred de **7, 150**
Nerval, Gérard de **1, 67, 250**
Nodier, (Jean) Charles (Emmanuel) **19**
Pixérécourt, (René Charles) Guilbert de **39**
Renan, Joseph Ernest **26, 145**
Restif de la Bretonne, Nicolas-Edme **257**
Rimbaud, (Jean Nicolas) Arthur **4, 35, 82, 227**
Sade, Donatien Alphonse François **3, 47, 263, 271**
Sainte-Beuve, Charles Augustin **5**
Sand, George **2, 42, 57, 174**
Scribe, (Augustin) Eugène **16**
Ségur, Sophie Rostopchine, Comtesse de **312**
Senancour, Etienne Pivert de **16**
Staël-Holstein, Anne Louise Germaine Necker **3**
Stendhal **23, 46, 178, 292**
Sue, Eugene **1**
Taine, Hippolyte Adolphe **15**
Tocqueville, Alexis (Charles Henri Maurice Clérel Comte) de **7, 63, 267**
Vallès, Jules **71**
Verlaine, Paul (Marie) **2, 51, 230**
Vigny, Alfred (Victor) de **7, 102, 278**
Villiers de l'Isle Adam, Jean Marie Mathias Philippe Auguste **3**

GERMAN

Arnim, Achim von (Ludwig Joachim von Arnim) **5, 159**
Arnim, Bettina von **38, 123**
Auerbach, Berthold **171**
Beethoven, Ludwig van **227**
Bonaventura **35, 252**
Börne, Ludwig **193**
Büchner, (Karl) Georg **26, 146**
Chamisso, Adelbert von **82**
Claudius, Matthias **75**
Clausewitz, Carl von **296**
Droste-Hülshoff, Annette Freiin von **3, 133, 273**
Eichendorff, Joseph **8, 225, 246**
Engels, Friedrich **85, 114**
Feuerbach, Ludwig **139**
Fichte, Johann Gottlieb **62, 261**
Fontane, Theodor **26, 163**
Fouqué, Caroline de la Motte **307**
Fouqué, Friedrich (Heinrich Karl) de la Motte **2**
Freytag, Gustav **109**
Goethe, Johann Wolfgang von **4, 22, 34, 90, 154, 247, 266, 270, 284, 287**
Grabbe, Christian Dietrich **2**
Grimm, Jacob Ludwig Karl **3, 77, 288**
Grimm, Wilhelm Karl **3, 77, 288**
Hauff, Wilhelm **185**
Hebbel, Friedrich **43, 287**
Hegel, Georg Wilhelm Friedrich **46, 151**
Heine, Heinrich **4, 54, 147, 249**
Heinse, Wilhelm **289**
Herder, Johann Gottfried von **8, 186**
Hoffmann, E(rnst) T(heodor) A(madeus) **2, 183**
Hölderlin, (Johann Christian) Friedrich **16, 187, 263**
Humboldt, Alexander von **170**
Humboldt, Wilhelm von **134, 256**
Immermann, Karl (Lebrecht) **4, 49**
Jean Paul **7, 268**
Kant, Immanuel **27, 67, 253**
Kleist, Heinrich von **2, 37, 222, 293, 313**
Klinger, Friedrich Maximilian von **1**
Klopstock, Friedrich Gottlieb **11, 225**
Kotzebue, August (Friedrich Ferdinand) von **25, 260**
La Roche, Sophie von **121, 262**
Lewald, Fanny **275**
Ludwig, Otto **4**
Marx, Karl (Heinrich) **17, 114**
Mörike, Eduard (Friedrich) **10, 201**
Novalis **13, 178**
Schelling, Friedrich Wilhelm Joseph von **30, 261**
Schiller, Friedrich von **39, 69, 166**
Schlegel, August Wilhelm von **15, 142, 262**
Schlegel, Dorothea **296**
Schlegel, Friedrich **45, 226**
Schleiermacher, Friedrich **107**
Schopenhauer, Arthur **51, 157**
Schumann, Robert **143**
Storm, (Hans) Theodor (Woldsen) **1, 195**
Tieck, (Johann) Ludwig **5, 46**
Varnhagen, Rahel **130**
Wagner, Richard **9, 119, 258**
Werner, Friedrich Ludwig Zacharias **189**
Wieland, Christoph Martin **17, 177**

GREEK

Foscolo, Ugo **8, 97, 274**
Solomos, Dionysios **15**

HUNGARIAN

Arany, Janos **34**
Liszt, Franz **199**
Madach, Imre **19**
Petőfi, Sándor **21, 264**

INDIAN

Chatterji, Bankim Chandra **19**
Dutt, Michael Madhusudan **118**
Dutt, Toru **29**

IRISH

Allingham, William **25**
Banim, John **13**
Banim, Michael **13**
Blanco White, Joseph **305**
Boucicault, Dion **41, 306**
Carleton, William **3, 199**
Croker, John Wilson **10**
Darley, George **2**
Edgeworth, Maria **1, 51, 158, 279**
Ferguson, Samuel **33**
Griffin, Gerald **7**
Jameson, Anna **43, 282**
Le Fanu, Joseph Sheridan **9, 58, 282**
Lever, Charles (James) **23**
Maginn, William **8**
Mangan, James Clarence **27, 316**
Maturin, Charles Robert **6, 169**
Merriman, Brian **70**
Moore, Thomas **6, 110, 283**
Morgan, Lady **29, 276**
O'Brien, Fitz-James **21**
Roche, Regina Maria **308**
Sheridan, Richard Brinsley **5, 91**

ITALIAN

Alfieri, Vittorio **101**
Collodi, Carlo **54, 299**
Da Ponte, Lorenzo **50**
Foscolo, Ugo **8, 97, 274**
Gozzi, (Conte) Carlo **23**
Leopardi, Giacomo **22, 129**
Manzoni, Alessandro **29, 98**
Mazzini, Guiseppe **34**
Nievo, Ippolito **22**

JAMAICAN

Seacole, Mary Jane Grant **147, 305**

JAPANESE

Akinari, Ueda **131**
Ichiyō, Higuchi **49**
Motoori, Norinaga **45**

LITHUANIAN

Mapu, Abraham (ben Jekutiel) **18**

MEXICAN

Lizardi, Jose Joaquin Fernandez de **30**
Najera, Manuel Gutierrez **133**

NORWEGIAN

Collett, (Jacobine) Camilla (Wergeland) **22**
Wergeland, Henrik Arnold **5**

POLISH

Fredro, Aleksander **8**
Krasicki, Ignacy **8**
Krasiński, Zygmunt **4**
Mickiewicz, Adam **3, 101, 265**
Norwid, Cyprian Kamil **17**
Potocki, Jan **229**
Slowacki, Juliusz **15**

PORTUGUESE

Garrett, Almeida **316**

ROMANIAN

Eminescu, Mihail **33, 131**

RUSSIAN

Aksakov, Sergei Timofeevich **2, 181**
Bakunin, Mikhail (Alexandrovich) **25, 58**
Baratynsky, Evgenii Abramovich **103**
Bashkirtseff, Marie **27**

Batiushkov, Konstantin Nikolaevich **254**
Belinski, Vissarion Grigoryevich **5**
Bestuzhev, Aleksandr Aleksandrovich **131**
Chaadaev, Petr Iakovlevich **197**
Chernyshevsky, Nikolay Gavrilovich **1**
Derzhavin, Gavriil Romanovich **215**
Dobrolyubov, Nikolai Alexandrovich **5**
Dostoevsky, Fyodor Mikhailovich **2, 7, 21, 33, 43, 119, 167, 202, 268, 273**
Garshin, Vsevolod Mikhailovich **257**
Gogol, Nikolai (Vasilyevich) **5, 15, 31, 162, 281, 315**
Goncharov, Ivan Alexandrovich **1, 63**
Granovsky, Timofei Nikolaevich **75**
Griboedov, Aleksandr Sergeevich **129**
Herzen, Aleksandr Ivanovich **10, 61**
Karamzin, Nikolai Mikhailovich **3, 173**
Krylov, Ivan Andreevich **1**
Lermontov, Mikhail Yuryevich **5, 47, 126, 288**
Leskov, Nikolai (Semyonovich) **25, 174**
Nekrasov, Nikolai Alekseevich **11, 294**
Ostrovsky, Alexander **30, 57**
Pavlova, Karolina Karlovna **138**
Pisarev, Dmitry Ivanovich **25**
Pushkin, Alexander (Sergeyevich) **3, 27, 83, 278**
Radishchev, Alexander **190**
Saltykov, Mikhail Evgrafovich **16**
Ségur, Sophie Rostopchine, Comtesse de **312**
Smolenskin, Peretz **30**
Turgenev, Ivan **21, 37, 122, 269**
Tyutchev, Fyodor **34, 291**
Zhukovsky, Vasily (Andreevich) **35, 292**

SCOTTISH

Baillie, Joanna **2, 151**
Ballantyne, R. M. **301**
Beattie, James **25**
Blair, Hugh **75**
Campbell, Thomas **19, 314**
Carlyle, Thomas **22, 70**
Ferrier, Susan (Edmonstone) **8**
Galt, John **1, 110, 296**
Grant, Anne MacVicar **302**
Hamilton, Elizabeth **153, 309**
Hogg, James **4, 109, 260**
Jeffrey, Francis **33**
Lockhart, John Gibson **6**
Mackenzie, Henry **41, 284**
Miller, Hugh **143**
Oliphant, Margaret (Oliphant Wilson) **11, 61, 221**
Pringle, Thomas **290**
Scott, Walter **15, 69, 110, 209, 270**
Smith, Alexander **59**
Stevenson, Robert Louis **5, 14, 63, 193, 274, 289, 292, 308**
Thomson, James **18**
Wilson, John **5**
Wright, Frances **74**

SERBIAN

Karadžić, Vuk Stefanović **115**
Obradović, Dositej **254**

SLOVENIAN

Kopitar, Jernej **117**
Prešeren, Francè **127**

SOUTH AFRICAN

Pringle, Thomas **290**

SPANISH

Alarcón, Pedro Antonio de **1, 219**
Bécquer, Gustavo Adolfo **106, 285**
Blanco White, Joseph **305**
Caballero, Fernan **10, 262**
Castro, Rosalia de **3, 78**
Espronceda, José de **39, 276**
Larra (y Sanchez de Castro), Mariano Jose de **17, 130**
Martínez de la Rosa, Francisco de Paula **102**
Meléndez Valdés, Juan **278**
Moratín, Leandro Fernández de **280**
Saavedra, Angel de **295**
Tamayo y Baus, Manuel **1**
Zorrilla y Moral, Jose **6, 298**

SWEDISH

Almqvist, Carl Jonas Love **42**
Bremer, Fredrika **11**
Stagnelius, Eric Johan **61**
Tegner, Esaias **2**

SWISS

Amiel, Henri Frederic **4**
Burckhardt, Jacob (Christoph) **49**
Charrière, Isabelle de **66, 314**
Gotthelf, Jeremias **117**
Keller, Gottfried **2, 277**
Lavater, Johann Kaspar **142**
Meyer, Conrad Ferdinand **81, 249**
Wyss, Johann David Von **10**

UKRAINIAN

Shevchenko, Taras **54, 281**

VENEZUELAN

Bello, Andrés **131**
Simón Bolívar **266**

NCLC-316 Title Index

"A Délia" (Garrett) **316**:171-72
"A Domingo Sequeira" (Garrett) **316**:172
"A Julia" (Garrett) **316**:171, 175
"A um amigo" (Garrett) **316**:174
"A um joven poeta" (Garrett) **316**:175
"A uma viajante" (Garrett) **316**:174
"Adeus" (Garrett) **316**:171-72, 174-75
"Adeus mãe" (Garrett) **316**:172
"Advice (from the Ottoman)" (Mangan) **316**:254
"Ah, Helen" (Garrett)
See "Ai, Helena"
"Ai, Helena" (Garrett) **316**:172
"Alexander and the Tree" (Mangan) **316**:254
"O amor paternal" (Garrett) **316**:173
"O Ananaz" (Garrett) **316**:174
"And Then No More" (Mangan) **316**:230
"O anjo cahido" (Garrett) **316**:171
"Anjo és" (Garrett) **316**:171
"Anniversario da Revolução de 24 de Agosto" (Garrett) **316**:172, 175
"Anniversary of the Revolution of August 24th" (Garrett)
See "Anniversario da Revolução de 24 de Agosto"
"O anno novo" (Garrett) **316**:172, 174
"O anno velho" (Garrett) **316**:173
Anthologia Germanica = German Anthology: A Series of Translations from the Most Popular of the German Poets (Mangan) **316**:198, 202-03, 222, 226, 236, 253, 303, 311
"Anthologia Germanica, VII" (Mangan) **316**:279
"Anthologia Hibernica" (Mangan) **316**:213
"Anthologia Hibernica 1" (Mangan) **316**:268
"Ao corpo academico" (Garrett) **316**:172-73
"Ao rei" (Garrett) **316**:172
"Aquella noite" (Garrett) **316**:175
Autobiografia (Garrett) **316**:166
Autobiography (Mangan) **316**:227-30, 247-49, 256, 258-59, 269, 273-80, 286, 288-90, 292, 295, 303-05
"Ave Maria" (Garrett) **316**:173
"Barca bella" (Garrett) **316**:175
"Bare Branch" (Garrett)
See "Ramo secco"
"Bare Trunk" (Garrett)
See "Tronco despido"
"Bear Up" (Mangan) **316**:295
"Beautiful Boat" (Garrett)
See "Barca bella"
"O beijo" (Garrett) **316**:175
"Bella d'amor" (Garrett) **316**:171
"The Belle of Love" (Garrett)
See "Bella d'amor"
"The Birth of Christ" (Garrett)
See "O natal de Christo"
"Bodach an Chota-Lachtna; or, The Clown with the Grey Coat" (Mangan) **316**:212
"Book of Life" (Garrett)
See "Livro da vida"
"O Brasil liberto" (Garrett) **316**:173
"Brazil Freed" (Garrett)
See "O Brasil liberto"
"The Bride" (Garrett)
See "A noiva"
"The Brightest of the Bright" (Mangan)
See "The Vision of Egan O'Reilly"
"A Broken-Hearted Lay" (Mangan) **316**:262
Camões (Garrett) **316**:167-68
"O campo de Sant'Anna" (Garrett) **316**:173-74
"Canto I" (Garrett) **316**:167
"Canto IV" (Garrett) **316**:167
"Canto V" (Garrett) **316**:167
"Canto VII" (Garrett) **316**:168
"Canto VIII" (Garrett) **316**:168
"Canto IX" (Garrett) **316**:168
"Canto X" (Garrett) **316**:168-69
"The Caramanian Exile" (Mangan) **316**:201, 318
"O carcere" (Garrett) **316**:175
"Cascaes" (Garrett)
See "Cascais"
"Cascais" (Garrett) **316**:174, 176
Catão (Garrett) **316**:181
Catharine; or, The Bower (Austen) **316**:62, 64
"The Cavern of Viriathus" (Garrett)
See "A caverna de Viriatho"
"A caverna de Viriatho" (Garrett) **316**:172-73, 175
"Chapters on Ghostcraft" (Mangan) **316**:227, 304-08
"Childhood" (Garrett)
See "A infancia"
"Os cinco sentidos" (Garrett) **316**:174
"The Civil War" (Garrett)
See "A Guerra Civil"
"The Clan Daly" (Mangan) **316**:218
The Collected Works of James Clarence Mangan: Poems (Mangan) **316**:312-13
The Collected Works of James Clarence Mangan: Prose (Mangan) **316**:311-19
The Collected Works of James Clarence Mangan: Prose, 1832-1839 (Mangan) **316**:276-80, 304-05, 307-09
The Collected Works of James Clarence Mangan: Prose, 1840-1882 (Mangan) **316**:273-80, 287, 290-92, 306-08
"The Color of the Rose" (Garrett)
See "A côr da rosa"
"The Coming Event" (Mangan) **316**:201
"The Coming Time" (Mangan) **316**:236
"Consolações a um namorado" (Garrett) **316**:171-72
"Consolation to a Lover" (Garrett)
See "Consolações a um namorado"
"Coquette dos prados" (Garrett) **316**:171, 174
"A côr da rosa" (Garrett) **316**:171
"A corôa" (Garrett) **316**:171
"Correspondence" (Mangan) **316**:267-72
"The Crown" (Garrett)
See "A corôa"
"A Cry for Ireland" (Mangan) **316**:205, 207, 298
"The Dame of the Slender Wattle" (Mangan) **316**:207
"Dark Rosaleen" (Mangan) **316**:205, 207, 213, 245, 247, 265, 270, 300, 311
"The Daunishmend's Lamentation" (Mangan) **316**:313
"Dawn" (Garrett)
See "Madrugada"
"Death" (Garrett)
See "A morte"
"The Death of Riego" (Garrett)
See "A morte de Riego"
"Despedidas do Campo" (Garrett) **316**:173
"Destiny" (Garrett)
See "Sina"
"A Dialogue in the Shades" (Mangan) **316**:211
"Disaster" (Mangan) **316**:262
"The Diver" (Mangan) **316**:254
"The Domiciliary Visit" (Mangan) **316**:207
"Double Trouble" (Mangan) **316**:261
"The Dream of John McDonnell" (Mangan)
See "The Dream of Mac Donnell Claragh"
"The Dream of Mac Donnell Claragh" (Mangan) **316**:205, 210, 213
"The Dying Enthusiast to His Friend" (Mangan) **316**:210, 262, 317
"E dos olhos gentis da minha amada" (Garrett) **316**:173
Echoes of Foreign Song (Mangan) **316**:203
"Eighteen-Hundred Fifty" (Mangan) **316**:254
"Elegiac Verses on the Early Death of a Beloved Friend" (Mangan) **316**:211, 260
"Elegy on the Death of Sultan Suleimaun the Magnificent" (Mangan) **316**:318
"An Elegy on the Tyronian and Tyrconnellian Princes, Buried at Rome" (Mangan) **316**:212, 235, 244-45, 296
"Ella" (Garrett) **316**:172, 175
Emma: A Novel (Austen) **316**:13, 21-2, 27, 29, 46, 66-8, 87, 97, 118-20, 123-24, 131
"O emprazado" (Garrett) **316**:175
"The Erl-King" (Mangan) **316**:305
Essays in Prose and Verse (Mangan) **316**:288
"Este inferno de amar" (Garrett) **316**:172
"Estes sitios" (Garrett) **316**:174
"A estrella" (Garrett) **316**:171, 175
"Evelyn" (Austen) **316**:139
"Exile" (Garrett)
See "O exilio"
"O exilio" (Garrett) **316**:171, 174
"An Extraordinary Adventure in the Shades" (Mangan) **316**:277, 288-89, 304
"The Fair Hills of Erin" (Mangan) **316**:207
"The Fallen Angel" (Garrett)
See "O anjo cahido"
Fallen Leaves (Garrett)
See *Folhas caídas*
"The Famine" (Mangan) **316**:272, 318

"Farewell" (Garrett)
See "Adeus"
"Farewell, Mother" (Garrett)
See "Adeus mãe"
"Farewell to the Country" (Garrett)
See "Despedidas do dampo"
"Farewell to the Maig" (Mangan) **316**:298
"Fatherly Love" (Garrett)
See "O amor paternal"
"*Faust* and the Minor Poems of Goethe" (Mangan) **316**:311
"Faz hoje um anno" (Garrett) **316**:172, 175
"As férias" (Garrett) **316**:171, 173
"Filinto" (Garrett) **316**:172, 174
"The Five Senses" (Garrett)
See "Os cinco sentidos"
"Flirt of the Fields" (Garrett)
See "Coquette dos prados"
"Flor de ventura" (Garrett) **316**:172
"Flor singela" (Garrett) **316**:173
Flores sem fructo (Garrett) **316**:170-75
"The Flower of All Maidens" (Mangan) **316**:214
"Flower of Good Luck" (Garrett)
See "Flor de ventura"
Flowers without Fruit (Garrett)
See *Flores sem fructo*
Folhas caídas (Garrett) **316**:170-76
"For Soul and Country" (Mangan) **316**:267, 295
Frederic and Elfrida: A Novel (Austen) **316**:52
"The Freedom of the Press" (Garrett)
See "A liberdade da imprensa"
Frei Luís de Sousa (Garrett) **316**:180-82, 184-87
"From My Lady's Gentle Eyes" (Garrett)
See "E dos olhos gentis da minha amada"
"The Funerals" (Mangan) **316**:269
"Genius" (Mangan) **316**:249, 263
"Ghazel" (Mangan) **316**:317, 260
"Gone in the Wind" (Mangan) **316**:198, 264
"The Good People (Not the Fairies) of Ara" (Mangan) **316**:218
"The Groans of Despair" (Mangan) **316**:262-63
"A Guerra Civil" (Garrett) **316**:174-75
"Henry and Eliza" (Austen) **316**:81
The History of England (Austen) **316**:52
"The Holidays" (Garrett)
See "As férias"
"The Homeland" (Garrett)
See "A patria"
"The Howling Song of Al Mohara" (Mangan) **316**:254, 264
"I Am No Longer a Poet" (Garrett)
See "Já não sou poeta"
"I Do Not Love" (Garrett)
See "Não te amo"
"Ichabod! Thy Glory Has Departed" (Mangan) **316**:264
"In a Friend's Album" (Garrett)
See "No album de um amigo"
"A infancia" (Garrett) **316**:171, 173-74
"Irish National Hymn" (Mangan) **316**:236, 269
"It Is Not You" (Garrett)
See "Não és tu"
"Já não sou poeta" (Garrett) **316**:174
"Jack and Alice" (Austen) **316**:81
Jane Austen's Letters (Austen) **316**:10, 30, 39, 45, 55, 128
"Jealousy" (Mangan) **316**:260
"O juramento" (Garrett) **316**:172
Juvenilia (Austen) **316**:138, 140
"Kathaleen Ny-Houlahan" (Mangan) **316**:212-13, 235, 246-47
"Khidder" (Mangan) **316**:254
"The Kiss" (Garrett)
See "O beijo"
Lady Susan (Austen) **316**:11
"The Lament" (Mangan) **316**:264
"Lament for Kilcash" (Mangan) **316**:298
"A Lament for Sir Maurice Fitzgerald" (Mangan) **316**:205, 298
"The Lament of Leeah Rewaan" (Mangan) **316**:313
"Lament over the Ruins of the Abbey of Teach Molaga" (Mangan) **316**:264, 296, 298-99
"Lamentation for Maurice FitzGerald" (Mangan)
See "A Lament for Sir Maurice Fitzgerald"
"The Lamentation of Mac Liag for Kincora" (Mangan) **316**:212, 263, 296
"Lamii's Apology for His Nonsense (from the Ottoman)" (Mangan) **316**:243
"Leaflets from the German Oak" (Mangan) **316**:202
"Lenore" (Mangan) **316**:305
"Letter the 13th" (Austen) **316**:52
"A liberdade da imprensa" (Garrett) **316**:172
"Life, Death, and Eternity" (Mangan) **316**:247
"Life Is the Desert and the Solitude" (Mangan) **316**:229, 262
"The Lighthouse and the Vessel" (Garrett)
See "O pharol e o baixel"
"Lines on the Death of ***" (Mangan)
See "Elegiac Verses on the Early Death of a Beloved Friend"
"Lines on the Death of a Beloved Friend" (Mangan)
See "Elegiac Verses on the Early Death of a Beloved Friend"
"Lines on the Launching of the Bashtardah" (Mangan) **316**:315
Lírica de João Mínimo (Garrett) **316**:170-76
"Literæ Orientales" (Mangan) **316**:198, 230, 291, 311-17, 319
"Livro da vida" (Garrett) **316**:173
"Lonely from Home I Come" (Mangan) **316**:260
"Long Sea-Voyage" (Garrett)
See "Longa viagem de mar"
"Longa viagem de mar" (Garrett) **316**:174-75
"Longing" (Garrett)
See "A saudade"
"Longings" (Garrett)
See "Saudades"
"Love" (Mangan) **316**:260
Love and Friendship (Austen) **316**:11, 52, 139
"Love, Mystery and Murder: A Tale (Foundered on Facts)" (Mangan) **316**:274, 276-77, 304-05, 307
"The Lover's Farewell" (Mangan) **316**:260
"Love's Quarrel" (Garrett)
See "Porfia de amor"
"Lucinda" (Garrett) **316**:171, 175
Lucrécia (Garrett) **316**:181
"A lyra do proscripto" (Garrett) **316**:172
"The Lyre of the Exile" (Garrett)
See "A lyra do proscripto"
Lyrica de João Minimo (Garrett)
See *Lírica de João Mínimo*
Lyrics of John the Least (Garrett)
See *Lyrica de João Minimo*
"Madrugada" (Garrett) **316**:173-75
"The Man in the Cloak (A Very German Story)" (Mangan) **316**:257-58, 274, 277-80, 308-09
Mansfield Park: A Novel (Austen) **316**:3-159
"O mar" (Garrett) **316**:172-73, 175
"Mares' Nests" (Mangan) **316**:203
"Melancholia" (Garrett) **316**:173, 175-76
"Melancholy" (Garrett)
See "Melancholia"
"Memória ao Conservatório Real" (Garrett) **316**:180-82
"Os meus desejos" (Garrett) **316**:174
"The Miller's Daughter" (Mangan) **316**:260
"A minha Rosa" (Garrett) **316**:171, 175
"As minhas azas" (Garrett) **316**:172, 175
Minor Works (Austen) **316**:52, 81-2, 86
"The Monument" (Garrett)
See "O Monumento"
"O Monumento" (Garrett) **316**:174
"A morte" (Garrett) **316**:171-75
"A morte de Riego" (Garrett) **316**:173-74
Mérope (Garrett) **316**:181
"My Adieu to the Muse" (Mangan) **316**:297-98
"My Bugle, and How I Blow It" (Mangan) **316**:198, 253, 258, 280
"My Dark Rosaleen" (Mangan)
See "Dark Rosaleen"
"My Desires" (Garrett)
See "Os meus desejos"
"My Three Plagues" (Mangan) **316**:217
"My Rose" (Garrett)
See "A minha rosa"
"My Transformation: A Wonderful Tale" (Mangan) **316**:259, 277
"My Wings" (Garrett)
See "As minhas azas"
"The Nameless One" (Mangan) **316**:199, 262, 276, 290, 295, 297
"Não és tu" (Garrett) **316**:171
"Não te amo" (Garrett) **316**:171
"The Nap" (Garrett)
See "A sesta"
"Nas froixas, debeis azas da saudade" (Garrett) **316**:173-74
"O natal de Christo" (Garrett) **316**:173-74
"The *Nation*'s First Number" (Mangan) **316**:198
"Neither One Thing nor t'Other" (Mangan) **316**:290
"Nevermore" (Garrett)
See "Nunca mais"
"The New Year" (Garrett)
See "O anno novo"
"The Nightingale" (Garrett)
See "O rouxinol"
"No album de um amigo" (Garrett) **316**:173
"No lumiar" (Garrett) **316**:172-74
"A noiva" (Garrett) **316**:175
Northanger Abbey (Austen) **316**:8-9, 11, 15, 21-2, 87, 101
"Nunca mais" (Garrett) **316**:171-73, 175
"The Oath" (Garrett)
See "O juramento"
"Oath of Fealty" (Garrett)
See "Preito"
Obras completas de Almeida Garrett (Garrett) **316**:167
"An Ode of Hafiz" (Mangan) **316**:312
"Of the Nightmare" (Mangan) **316**:203-04
"Oh Strew the Way with Rosy Flowers" (Mangan) **316**:264
"O'Hussey's Ode to the Maguire" (Mangan) **316**:213, 243-44, 263, 296, 298
"The Old Year" (Garrett)
See "O anno velho"
"On the Feeble Wings of Longing" (Garrett)
See "Nas froixas, debeis azas da saudade"
"On the Threshold" (Garrett)
See "No lumiar"
"The One Mystery" (Mangan) **316**:262
"Opinions of *Emma*" (Austen) **316**:101
"Opinions of *Mansfield Park*" (Austen) **316**:45, 101
"Opinions of *Mansfield Park* and *Emma*" (Austen) **316**:81
"Oriental Nights" (Mangan) **316**:202
"Pale One" (Garrett)
See "Pallida"
"Pallida" (Garrett) **316**:171
"Paraphrase of Katheleen [*sic*] ny Houlahan" (Mangan)
See "Kathaleen Ny-Houlahan"
"Pathetic Hypathetics" (Mangan) **316**:201
"A patria" (Garrett) **316**:172-73

"The Peal of Another Trumpet" (Mangan) **316**:204, 269
"Perfume da rosa" (Garrett) **316**:171
"The Perfume of the Rose" (Garrett)
See "Perfume da rosa"
Persuasion (Austen) **316**:8, 13, 21-2, 29, 42, 61-2, 64, 66-70, 87
"O pharol e o baixel" (Garrett) **316**:172, 175
"The Pineapple Tree" (Garrett)
See "O ananaz"
Poems (Mangan) **316**:222, 243, 288, 313, 315-18
Poems of James Clarence Mangan (Many Hitherto Uncollected) (Mangan) **316**:222, 243, 288
The Poets and Poetry of Munster: A Selection of Irish Songs by the Poets of the Last Century (Mangan) **316**:207, 214, 217-18, 220-21
"A Polyglott Anthology" (Mangan) **316**:211
"Pompeii" (Mangan) **316**:299
"Porfia de amor" (Garrett) **316**:171-72
"Preito" (Garrett) **316**:171
Pride and Prejudice: A Novel (Austen) **316**:8-13, 15-16, 21-2, 29, 45, 49, 61, 80-3, 87, 90-1, 95, 98, 106, 120, 128, 131, 157
"A primavera" (Garrett) **316**:172-74
"The Prison" (Garrett)
See "O carcere"
"Prophetic Dream" (Garrett)
See "Sonho prophetico"
"Pulse of the Bards" (Mangan) **316**:298
"Ramo secco" (Garrett) **316**:173-74
"The Redeemer" (Garrett)
See "O redemptor"
"O redemptor" (Garrett) **316**:173-74
O retrato de Vénus (Garrett) **316**:167
"A rosa" (Garrett) **316**:171-72, 175
"Rosa e Lirio" (Garrett) **316**:171
"Rosa sem espinhos" (Garrett) **316**:171, 174
"The Rose" (Garrett)
See "A rosa"
"Rose and Lily" (Garrett)
See "Rosa e Lirio"
"Rose without Thorns" (Garrett)
See "Rosa sem espinhos"
"O rouxinol" (Garrett) **316**:172, 174
"Ruins of Donegal Castle" (Mangan) **316**:213
"The Rye Mill" (Mangan) **316**:205
"Saint Anne's Field" (Garrett)
See "O campo de Sant'Anna"
Sanditon (Austen) **316**:67, 70
"Sapho" (Garrett) **316**:173-74
"Sappho" (Garrett)
See "Sapho"
"A saudade" (Garrett) **316**:171
"Saudades" (Garrett) **316**:173
"The Saw Mill" (Mangan)
See "The Rye Mill"
"The Sea" (Garrett)
See "O mar"
Selected Poems of James Clarence Mangan (Mangan) **316**:243, 246
Sense and Sensibility: A Novel (Austen) **316**:9, 11, 13, 15, 21-2, 25, 45, 61, 80, 82, 84-5, 87, 89-90, 152, 157
"A sesta" (Garrett) **316**:174-75
"Shane Bwee; or, The Captivity of the Gaels" (Mangan) **316**:205, 298
"She" (Garrett)
See "Ella"
"Siberia" (Mangan) **316**:205, 263-65, 298
"Simple Flower" (Garrett)
See "Flor singela"
"Sina" (Garrett) **316**:172
"A Sixty-Drop Dose of Laudanum" (Mangan) **316**:252-53, 256
"Sketches and Reminiscences of Irish Writers" (Mangan) **316**:274
"Sketches of Modern Irish Writers. James Clarence Mangan" (Mangan) **316**:312
"A soledade" (Garrett) **316**:173
"Solidão" (Garrett) **316**:173-74
"Solitude" (Garrett)
See "A soledade"
"Solitude" (Garrett)
See "Solidão"
Sonetos (Garrett) **316**:170
"The Song of the Albanian" (Mangan) **316**:299
"Sonho prophetico" (Garrett) **316**:172, 175
"Sonnet 1" (Garrett)
See "Porfia de amor"
"Sonnet 4" (Garrett)
See "Suffoque as iras, cale e sinta e gema"
"Sonnet 5" (Garrett)
See "E dos olhos gentis da minha amada"
"Sonnet 6" (Garrett)
See "Nas froixas, debeis azas da saudade"
"Sonnet 7" (Garrett)
See "O campo de Sant'Anna"
"Sonnet 8" (Garrett)
See "Virtude sem prazer não é virtude"
Sonnets (Garrett)
See *Sonetos*
"The Spectre-Caravan" (Mangan) **316**:254
"Spring" (Garrett)
See "A primavera"
"The Star" (Garrett)
See "A estrella"
"Stifle Your Anger, Be Still and Suffer and Groan" (Garrett)
See "Suffoque as iras, cale e sinta e gema"
"The Storm" (Garrett)
See "A tempestade"
"Suffoque as iras, cale e sinta e gema" (Garrett) **316**:172
"The Summoned One" (Garrett)
See "O emprazado"
"A tempestade" (Garrett) **316**:175
"Testament of Cathaeir Mor" (Mangan) **316**:296
"That Night" (Garrett)
See "Aquella noite"
"These Places" (Garrett)
See "Estes sitios"
"The Thirty Flasks" (Mangan) **316**:257, 277, 279, 304-05
"This Hell of Loving" (Garrett)
See "Este inferno de amar"
"The Three Half-Crowns" (Mangan) **316**:199
"The Three Plagues" (Mangan) **316**:213
"The Threefold Prediction: A Psychological Narrative" (Mangan) **316**:277, 304
"The Thugs' Ditty" (Mangan) **316**:317
"Tim Sullivan's Plea" (Mangan) **316**:211
"The Time of the Barmecides" (Mangan) **316**:235, 313, 315, 318
"Timid Love" (Mangan) **316**:209-10
"To a Friend" (Garrett)
See "A um amigo"
"To a Traveler" (Garrett)
See "A uma viajante"
"To a Young Poet" (Garrett)
See "A um joven poeta"
"To Délia" (Garrett)
See "A Délia"
"To Domingo Sequeira" (Garrett)
See "A Domingo Sequeira"
"To Julia" (Garrett)
See "A Julia"
"To Laura" (Mangan) **316**:260
"To Mihri" (Mangan) **316**:260
"To the Ingleezee Khafir, Calling Himself Djaun Bool Djenkinzun" (Mangan) **316**:317
"To the King" (Garrett)
See "Ao rei"
"To the Members of the Academy" (Garrett)
See "Ao corpo academico"
"To the Pens of *The Nation*" (Mangan) **316**:318
"Treacherous Black Guards" (Mangan) **316**:315
"A Treatise on a Pair of Tongs" (Mangan) **316**:288
The Tribes of Ireland: A Satire. With Poetical Translation by the Late James Clarence Mangan; together with an Historical Account of the Family of O'Daly; and an Introduction to the History of Satire in Ireland by John O'Donovan (Mangan) **316**:214-15, 217, 219-21
"Tronco despido" (Garrett) **316**:174
"Twenty Golden Years Ago" (Mangan) **316**:260, 262, 289, 297, 313
"The Twenty-Fourth of February, 1837" (Mangan) **316**:304
"The Two Envoys" (Mangan) **316**:269
"The Two Flats: Our Quackstitution" (Mangan) **316**:288
"The Unrealities" (Mangan) **316**:227, 229
"A Verye Splendidde and Ryghte Conceited Dittie of ande Concernyinge the Newe Yeare" (Mangan) **316**:254
Viagens na minha terra (Garrett) **316**:169, 176-79, 188
"Vibora" (Garrett) **316**:172, 174
"A victoria na praia" (Garrett) **316**:172, 174-75
"Victory on the Beach" (Garrett)
See "A victoria na praia"
"Viper" (Garrett)
See "Vibora"
"Virtude sem prazer não é virtude" (Garrett) **316**:173
"Virtue without Pleasure Is Not Virtue" (Garrett)
See "Virtude sem prazer não é virtude"
"A Vision: A.D. 1848" (Mangan) **316**:270
"A Vision of Connaught in the Thirteenth Century" (Mangan) **316**:205, 254, 263, 269, 296, 318
"The Vision of Egan O'Reilly" (Mangan) **316**:296, 270
"A Voice of Encouragement: A New Year's Lay" (Mangan) **316**:235, 266-67, 269-70, 295
Volume the First: Now First Printed from the Manuscript in the Bodleian Library (Austen) **316**:45
"The Wail and Warning of the Three Khalendeers" (Mangan) **316**:201, 254
"The Wandering Jew" (Mangan) **316**:305
"The Warning Voice" (Mangan) **316**:204-06, 235, 267, 269
"What Is Love?" (Mangan) **316**:261
"Where's My Money?" (Mangan) **316**:200
"Woman of the Piercing Wail" (Mangan)
See "An Elegy on the Tyronian and Tyrconnellian Princes, Buried at Rome"
"The Woman of Three Cows" (Mangan) **316**:212
"The World's Changes" (Mangan) **316**:254
"A Year Ago Today" (Garrett)
See "Faz hoje um anno"
"You Are an Angel" (Garrett)
See "Anjo és"